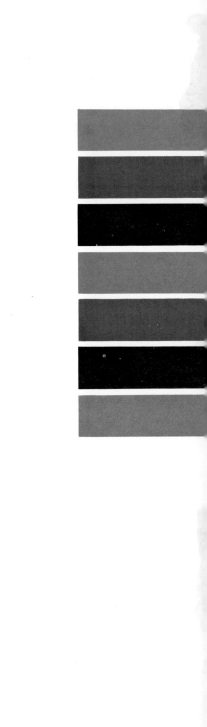

POPULATION AND SOCIETY

A Textbook of Readings

EDITED BY Charles B. Nam, THE FLORIDA STATE UNIVERSITY

HOUGHTON MIFFLIN COMPANY · BOSTON

NEW YORK ATLANTA GENEVA, ILL. DALLAS PALO ALTO

Printed in the U.S.A.

TO

Rupert B. Vance

PIONEER IN AMERICAN SOCIAL DEMOGRAPHY

PREFACE

Population as a subject of national and international interest is of recent vintage. For decades, scholars in universities, specialists in government census and vital statistic work, city planners, market researchers, and others have devoted time to measuring population trends and studying their consequences for societies and communities. It is only recently, however, that the general public has recognized population development as a crucial matter for the welfare of nations, and still more recently that governments have acted to try to bring about a more harmonious relationship between population and social and economic progress.

Knowledge about population matters is still rather sketchy in the public mind. Popular conceptions of population trends and what factors have been responsible for them are as much based on myths as on facts. Demography, the science of population, is growing rapidly, and we are now acquiring a reliable body of knowledge about the status, causes, and consequences of population trends.

This book is designed to present some of the information now existing about population within a framework which stresses the social importance of demographic developments. While the volume is essentially a reader in population, introductory remarks to each part and chapter of the book, study exercises and discussion questions, and suggested additional readings make the volume useful as either a self-contained textbook or as a reader to be used in conjunction with another textbook. A correlation chart in the back of the book shows the relationship between chapters in this book and those in standard textbooks on population.

Readings for the book have been selected mainly for their relevance but also on the basis of their readability and freedom from technical discussion. The content of the book and its organization are somewhat different from those found in standard population textbooks, in that Part I is concerned with the elements of population analysis and Part II deals with the interrelationships between population and selected areas of social life. In this way, it is hoped that the place of demography in the study of society is established.

The intent of this volume is not only to acquaint a large audience with a full and accurate understanding of population matters, but also to stimulate many to study the questions about population which the book examines but leaves unanswered.

A number of persons have directly or indirectly contributed to the preparation of this volume. I would particularly like to acknowledge the late Meyer F. Nimkoff, former colleague and editor of the Houghton Mifflin series in sociology, for his encouragement in the development of the book at the outset; Robert C. Rooney, Houghton Mifflin editor, for his advice and patience as the book proceeded through several stags of preparation; Nancy G. Bergman, of the Houghton Mifflin editorial staff, for her careful editing of the manuscript; Susan Orr, a most valuable graduate assistant, who reviewed some of the introductory text material, prepared many of the study exercises and discussion questions, and helped put the manuscript together; and the several authors of selections included in the reader whose scholarly efforts and writing skills have enabled me to assemble a broad picture of population research and thought.

CHARLES B. NAM

CONTENTS

PART I

Elements of Population Analysis

Part I is concerned with an examination of the principles of population structure and change. Since demographic analysis is so much dependent on empirical data, Chapter 1 reviews the sources of population data, how these sources are generally used, and some of the difficulties involved in collecting and analyzing these data. Chapter 2 traces the development of population thought from early times to the present, looks at the state of present-day population theory, and provides a factual basis for understanding world, regional, and national demographic trends.

The basic components of population change are mortality (deaths), fertility (births), and migration (geographic mobility). Populations vary in size over time as a result of the balance of these factors. In Chapter 3, the nature of mortality trends and differentials are studied, with some attention to health conditions of people as these conditions relate to mortality. Fertility trends and differentials are examined in Chapters 4 and 5. The first of these chapters views the world situation in fertility, the latter examines patterns in the United States. The greater attention given to this subject here is based on the recognition that most persons now see fertility as the main variable in population change. Moreover, a disproportionate amount of current research on population has dealt with the study of fertility.

Geographic mobility of population is the topic for Chapters 6 and 7. The first deals with international migration, the latter with movements of people within countries, or internal migration. Chapters 8 and 9 cover population composition and population distribution, respectively. The characteristics of individuals who make up the population and where these individuals are located are important for analysis of population structure and change, and vital to appreciation of the ways in which demographic factors interrelate with other factors which produce changes in societies.

Once the student of demography has grasped these fundamentals of population dynamics, he is prepared to consider the ways in which a broad range of social factors influence population change and, in turn, how population factors help shape the institutions of society and the social behavior of individuals. These topics are the subject matter of Part II.

CHAPTER 1

The Nature of Population Data

Demography, like other sciences, employs a rigorous body of methods for the collection and analysis of data. Some persons have pointed out that demography is one of the empirical sciences whose data are produced by the observation and recording of events occurring naturally in the external world, as contrasted to those whose data are generated by experiments conducted in the laboratory under conditions controlled to a greater or lesser degree by the experimenter. Like sociology generally, within which field it is most often included, demography is concerned with observing people, recording information about human events, and seeking explanations about human behavior. Thus, whether demography is considered a part of or separate from sociology, their general methods are the same and many of their data sources are identical.

Among the social sciences, demography has the reputation for being one of the most exact sciences. The principal variables of population analysis can be measured in relatively clear-cut fashion, and demography has a long history of data-collection systems and of methodological refinements which make the science today quite precise in its measurement and analysis. This does not mean that all demographic variables are amenable to quantification; many subjects of interest to population specialists and variables relevant to demographic analysis cannot easily be quantified, yet are amenable to classification and interpretation. Such nominal classifications as sex and race are examples, as are descriptions of various social and economic characteristics. But information on all topics of interest can be collected through one or more of the data sources on which demographers have become dependent, and this information can be arranged in a way that is useful for analysis.

Generally speaking, the main sources of demographic data are population censuses, vital registration systems, population registers, sample household surveys, and other governmental and private administrative records. Some kinds of population information can be obtained from only one source; other kinds require a combination of two sources. Thus, a birth rate or death rate, common measures of sources of population change, are based on a combination of a vital record statistic (the number of births or deaths in a population) and a census or household survey statistic (the population denominator of the rate). While censuses and vital registration are the mainstays of a demographic data system, other sources, especially the sample survey, are increasingly being used to supplement them. In addition, particularly for areas where traditional sources of population data are lacking or of poor quality, demographers often "create" data through estimation techniques.

Census-taking has a long history. The Bible mentions enumerations of the population for taxation and to determine the availability of military resources. There are some accounts of population enumerations as far back as 3,800 B.C. in Babylonia and 3,000 B.C. in China, but the nature of these early censuses is not known and they were probably quite crude in comparison with contemporary censuses. When and where the first modern census was taken is debatable, but some place it in Quebec in 1666. Regular censuses became a function of government in the United States in 1790, in England and Wales in 1801, and in India about 1881. By 1960, approximately 80 per cent of the world's population was covered by a census, but censuses have not yet been taken in a substantial part of the world.

As the first selection from the United Nations indicates, a *census of population* may be defined as the total process of collecting, compiling, and publishing demographic, economic, and social data pertaining, at a specified time or times, to all persons in a country or other delimited territory. Censuses are costly operations and require much advance planning and preparation and much painstaking work leading to the summarization of the results for some time after the census is taken. Any reliable census of population must clearly specify in advance the area and population to be covered, the time periods to which questions will refer, and the procedures by which the census is to be taken. It is advisable that procedures be tried on a small scale, in what are called pretests, before the full canvass takes place. During the enumeration, decisions must be made about who is to be considered a resident of a particular place and how persons are to be grouped into family units. Additional questions to be decided include: Shall every person be asked every question on the census schedule, or shall some questions be asked on a sample basis only? Shall information be obtained by trained interviewers, or shall questionnaires be left for, or sent to, individuals, to be filled out by the persons themselves and returned to the census office? What items of information should be obtained? Shall persons be required to answer all questions or shall the answering of some of them be optional?

The census returns must be carefully edited and further inquiry made of the respondents where necessary. Those responses which do not lend themselves to quantification must be coded to provide a meaningful way of classifying them. Finally, the data must be tabulated according to the requirements of the data users, who may include governments, business organizations, other private organizations, and individual researchers. How these steps are carried out in a modern census is described in the report by the U.S. Bureau of the Census.

Vital registration is concerned with the registration of vital events — births, deaths, stillbirths, marriages, divorces, adoptions, annulments, and separations. As indicated in the second United Nations article, these events have to do with an individual's entrance into or departure from life, together with the changes in civil status which may occur to him during his lifetime. Vital statistics provide the means for measuring changes in population between censuses, as well as serving many other purposes.

The collection of vital data is not as firmly rooted in history as is census-taking, but it does have its origins at least as far back as the Middle Ages. At that time, some vital statistics were gathered for certain classes of the population. It has only been in the past few decades that countries have set out to develop complete systems of vital registration, and as yet few countries have accomplished the task. In the United States, the collection of birth and death certificates, a function of state and local governments, was not universal until 1933, and systematic collection and reporting of marriages and divorces is not yet complete.

The principal source of vital data has been the registration systems maintained by local authorities who report the vital statistics at periodic intervals to a central agency. Vital data are sometimes collected through other means, as through a census of population or through a sample household survey. This usually involves asking people for information about vital events occurring to residents of the household during the year preceding the time of the census or survey. A census which is taken as infrequently as every five or ten years cannot obtain a continuous recording of vital events, although it does provide some basis for gauging population change in the absence of a registration system.

Population data are also obtained in some countries through a *population register*. The register is kept by local authorities who record in it every birth, death, marriage, divorce, and movement into and out of the area. In this way, the population register serves both as a source of vital statistics and as a census of the population in the area as of a point of time; however, countries which have population registers usually have censuses and vital registration as well. At present, such registers are maintained principally in European countries, particularly in Scandinavia and the Netherlands. No official population register has ever existed in the United States, although the registration system adopted during World War II for rationing of food and other scarce materials approximated a population register.

Because censuses are expensive and are usually taken only once every five or ten years, and because vital registration only identifies that part of the population which is changing, the *sample household survey* has increasingly become a valuable source of demographic information. In the United States and some other countries, such a survey for a small but representative sample of the population is conducted monthly to obtain statistics on population size, composition, and distribution, and on the labor force, with frequent supplements covering other characteristics of the population. The subject matter of the survey is essentially the subject matter of a census but, as mentioned, the sample survey is sometimes used to collect vital data, and some types of information are gathered in a survey which are difficult to obtain from either of the other two sources.

Other government and private administrative records are used to supplement the population sources already mentioned. Among these are *immigration and naturalization records, social security records, unemployment insurance records, hospital and other health agency records, life insurance records, and armed forces and military conscription records.*

In many parts of the world, censuses have never been taken, vital statistics have also been lacking or are of extremely poor quality, and other sources of population information are not available. In such cases, where data about the population are needed, demographers have estimated the size, composition, distribution, and characteristics of the population using various estimation techniques. These techniques involve making use of what little demographic data may be available, along with knowledge about trends of, and relationships among, population variables as they exist in other countries, particularly countries of a similar type. While these estimates are sometimes subject to errors of considerable magnitude, they are usually reasonable enough to provide the data user with sufficient information, in the absence of collected data, to make judicious interpretations and decisions.

Census-taking and vital registration are not without their difficulties. On the one hand, there are several possible hazards in acquiring census information. Geographic obstacles to travel, adverse weather conditions, threats posed by animals (ranging from snakes and tigers in jungle country to domesticated dogs in modernized areas), and expenditures of time and energy are all relevant here. On the other hand, there is the problem of locating all persons for whom information should be obtained and the unwillingness or inability of some respondents to provide the necessary data. In some developing societies, inhabitants view censuses and vital registration with suspicion. These suspicions are deeply rooted in the traditional beliefs of the people. The selection by You Poh Seng deals with a different kind of problem, that of the validity and reliability of demographic information. Each culture has its own peculiar system of age-reckoning, he points out, and one must consider age responses in the light of the way a question about age is asked. Data for the Chinese population of Singapore are used for illustration. The same caution should be applied to any question asked in any census, since within a country there are different ethnic groups and persons with different amounts of education, and questions may well be interpreted differently by these groups on the basis of the knowledge they possess about the subject and their traditional way of viewing things.

*The Utility and Modern Conception of a Population Census**

STATISTICAL OFFICE OF THE UNITED NATIONS

A. GENERAL VALUE OF CENSUSES

The principal original objectives of censuses were to determine the military, tax and labour obligations of individuals and to ascertain changes in their legal status. With the spread of suffrage, the fixing of electoral representation came to depend on official census results. Since the early nineteenth century, however, the scope of censuses has changed and expanded and the sphere of their utility has been enlarged. Through the years, questionnaires have reflected the increasing interest in such factors as migration, economic characteristics, fertility and social security which has accompanied the economic and social development of many modern countries. The inclusion of such topics in censuses has provided factual data about important characteristics of the population which meet the need for information on the part of governments, business, industry, labour, educational and research bodies and the general public.

Today, in most countries, any connexion between the census inquiry into personal characteristics and the use of such information for purposes of taxation or military enlistment is specifically avoided. The possibility that personal information would be used for either of these purposes has been known to arouse strong and often insuperable resistance to the census as a whole. For this reason, the use of personal information contained in the census returns for other than strictly statistical purposes is positively prohibited in most countries, with severe penalties often laid down for census officials who reveal such information.

The United Nations document *Principles and Recommendations for National Population Censuses* (ST/STAT/SER.M/27) includes the following statement on the value of population censuses:

The population census is a statistical operation of great value to every country. It is the primary source of basic national population data for administration and for many aspects of economic and social planning. The census provides a base or reference point for current statistics and a statistical frame for sampling surveys and studies. Population censuses were among the first forms of national statistical activity and some form of "counting of people" has been conducted from very ancient times. The tradition of taking periodic and scientifically designed censuses extends back for more than 150 years in many modern countries. No country denies the importance of knowing the essential demographic, social and economic facts about its people. Numerous international recommendations have stressed the basic importance of population censuses and have suggested methods for increasing their scope and validity and for improving their national value and international comparability.

In the decade from 1945 to 1954, at least 150 countries or areas took population censuses collecting individual data on more than 2,000,000,000 people. The extent of census activity, past and present, is a manifestation of the appreciation by countries that census-type data are essential for good national administration and development.

Although the economic and social development of a country requires the strengthening of the entire range of statistics, it is recognized that the population census is one of the important methods of collecting basic data required for many national purposes. The original and perhaps fundamental purpose of the census is to provide the facts essential as a basis for governmental policy and administration. National electoral distribution and certain aspects of the legal or administrative status of provinces or cities are often dependent upon population counts. Legislative consideration of questions of economic and social development, employment, migration, housing, public health and welfare,

* Reprinted with permission from Statistical Office of the United Nations, *Handbook of Population Census Methods,* Vol. I. New York: United Nations, 1958, pp. 3-8.

and numerous other governmental activities are facilitated if accurate facts about the population and the conditions of living are known. Without a census to be used in conjunction with current vital statistics, reliable estimates cannot be made of the future financial requirements for the payment of old age pensions or of the needed educational facilities for the rising generation. The various plans of social insurance and security depend for their actuarial calculations upon census material. Knowledge of census facts, even where not directly contributing to the solution of the problems of State policy, nevertheless form a background for the study and evaluation of such policies.

In addition to specific administrative uses, the population census provides indispensable data for scientific analysis and appraisal of the composition, distribution and growth of the population. The changing patterns of urban-rural concentration, the development of urbanized areas, the geographic distribution of the population according to different variables such as occupation or education, the evolution of the age structure of the population, and the mortality and natality differentials for various population groups are questions of scientific interest and research, the importance of which extends beyond the academic to practical problems of industrial and commercial growth and management. The census has many important uses for individuals and private institutions in business and industrial planning.

Quite apart from its direct applications, the census is becoming increasingly important as a frame for the development of other data-collecting procedures: There are various possibilities of combining, interrelating and checking the census data with those from other sources. Census data can be used in initiating statistical series and checking the accuracy or improving the quality and comparability of existing series. The rapid increase of the use of sampling procedures for surveys in various subject fields is facilitated if a population census is available to provide the data for scientific sample design. Census questionnaires may in themselves form a universe for random sampling. In certain instances, the census collection machinery can also be used to obtain listings of areas, dwellings, or establishments which are needed for the subsequent collection of data on other social or economic subjects.

B. The Modern Conception of a Population Census

The United Nations document *Principles and Recommendations for National Population Censuses* (ST/STAT/SER.M/27) states:

A census of population may be defined as the total process of collecting, compiling and publishing demographic, economic and social data pertaining, at a specified time or times, to all persons in a country or delimited territory.

Essential features of the census

Some of the essential features of an official national census are:

A. *Sponsorship.* An official national census is sponsored and carried out by the national government, sometimes with the co-operation of provincial and local governments.

B. *Defined territory.* The coverage of a census operation should relate to a precisely defined territory.

C. *Universality.* The enumeration should include every member of the community within the scope of the census without omission or duplication.

D. *Simultaneity.* The total population enumerated should refer to one well-defined point of time. Similarly, the data collected should refer to a well-defined point or period of time.

E. *Individual units.* A census implies that separate data are recorded for each individual by direct enumeration and not by registration, although the mechanics of collection may make it possible to record information common to all members of a household or family for the group as a whole. A procedure by which "totalled" or summarized data are collected for groups of individuals is not a census in the strict sense of the term because the various characteristics of an individual cannot then be interrelated. It should be noted, however, that group enumeration can be considered to be a census if the way in which the information is collected and recorded is so devised that cross-tabulations can be made in the same way as in a census of individuals.

F. *Compilation and publication.* The compilation and publication of data by geographic areas and by basic demographic variables is an integral part of a census.

The above description of a census does not preclude the simultaneous use of sampling techniques for obtaining data on supplementary topics. Basic information which is to be tabulated for small geographic areas or for which detailed cross-tabulations are required should, however, be collected for every person.

Each of the features mentioned above is of considerable importance to the successful execution of a census.

1. Sponsorship

Censuses are undertakings requiring a vast organization and involving considerable expenditure. For a proper census, an extensive administrative machinery has to be mobilized and supported with adequate legislative and legal authority. Only national governments can provide the necessary resources and enact suitable legislation. In certain cases, national governments enlist the co-operation of provincial and local governments, each of which receives some measure of responsibility for the carrying out of the census.

2. Defined Territory

Population figures have no meaning unless they refer to a precisely defined territory. The territory covered, along with any changes in its area in successive censuses, should be clearly and explicitly stated.

3. Universality

Inclusion of each person within the scope of the census is a requisite for accuracy and completeness. If, in certain cases, a country is not interested in enumerating certain specific groups of its population, such as aborigines, the concept of universality is still applicable to those groups of the community whose enumeration is intended.

4. Simultaneity

This feature is essential both to an accurate count of the total population and the relationship of the facts about that population to a specific point or period of time. As a general rule, a day is fixed for the census, and almost always also an hour and a particular moment which is *the census moment.* This moment is often fixed at midnight. It becomes the chronological line which separates persons born or dying before or after that time and determines which of these persons should be included in the census. It is, of course, obvious that persons born after the census moment are not included in the census. Persons who died before that time must also be omitted.

In those censuses in which persons are counted at the place at which they were at the time of the census (*de facto*), the time reference is usually extended to the entire night of the census, so that persons are counted at the place where they spent most of the night.

Some of the particulars, such as age and marital status, relating to the persons enumerated must also refer to the exact census date. Others, such as occupation and status (as employer, employee, etc.) generally refer to a period of time. To insure simultaneity, these periods must be carefully delimited.

The setting of a definite census date and time becomes particularly important if the actual enumeration extends over more than a day or two, so that persons may have moved about to some extent during the period. In fact, although it may appear simple in theory to say that the census was taken on a certain day, and that the particulars relating to the persons enumerated refer to a certain hour of that day, yet in practice this ideal cannot be completely attained. It can, however, be more nearly approached if the choice of date of enumeration is so made that the displacement and movement of population is at a minimum and there is an absence of other unusual temporary changes in the population structure.

5. Individual Units

Census data must be collected separately for each individual enumerated so that detailed classifications may be provided in all the required combinations. Information which applies to all the members of a household or family, such as geographic items or the language spoken in the home, need not be entered separately for each person appearing on the questionnaire but all individual information must be entered separately. It is because of this requirement of individual information that group enumeration generally cannot be considered a census in the strict sense of the term. In group enumeration, only "totalled" or summarized information for a group of persons is usually shown on the questionnaire. Hence, although a classification by age and one by marital status might appear on the questionnaire, it is not possible to determine the marital status of each person according to his age. This system of entering summarized information for a group should not be confused with the special practice sometimes followed of assembling all the inhabitants of a small area for enumeration at one central point, rather than having the canvasser visit each dwelling. In the latter instance, data may well be collected for each individual.

6. Compilation and Publication

A census is not complete unless the data collected are compiled and published by geographic areas and by basic demographic variables. There have been instances in which information collected during the enumeration has gone to waste because of failure to make adequate provisions for the processing, tabulation and publication of these data. Since unpublished data are of no value to the greatest number of potential users of the census results, a census limited to the investigation of a few important characteristics, the results of which are published as soon as possible after the enumeration, is better than a very detailed census whose too ambitious coverage in terms of characteristics investigated jeopardizes the timely processing and publication of the data collected.

C. Periodicity and International Simultaneity

The United Nations document *Principles and Recommendations for National Population Censuses* (ST/STAT/SER.M/27) states:

Census periodicity

Census data are of greater value if censuses are taken at regular intervals. A series of periodic censuses is of great importance in assessing trends — the past can be appraised, the present accurately described, and the future estimated.

It is recommended that every country develop a census programme which will provide that a population census be taken every ten years. Since regular population censuses involve complex and costly statistical operations, if, between decennial censuses, data are needed for those characteristics which change more rapidly, simplified censuses or sampling inquiries might be undertaken, preferably midway beween the regular censuses.

International simultaneity

The census of any country is of greater value nationally, regionally and internationally if it can be compared with censuses of other countries which were taken at approximately the same time.

It is obvious that legal, administrative, financial and other considerations often make it inadvisable for a country to adhere to a standard pattern in the timing of its population censuses. In fixing a census date, such national factors, or a long-established tradition for a definite census year, should be given greater weight than the desirability for international simultaneity.

It is, however, recommended that whenever possible, each country undertake a population census in the years ending in "0" or as near to those years as feasible.

The census, as now conceived, has two main objects. First, it provides an instantaneous photograph of a community, which is valid for a particular moment of time. This may be called the static aspect of a census. Secondly, each census should be regarded as an item in a consecutive series — the dynamic aspect, comparable to a motion picture of the population. Only from a succession of censuses of a community is it possible to assess the magnitude and direction of the various trends.

Consecutive censuses are essential in studying the growth, decline, or other important changes that take place in the population of a country. Information referring to dates separated by equal intervals of time provides data which lend themselves to convenient comparisons. Further, a regular schedule of census-taking, if adopted by all countries, would greatly facilitate international comparisons. To make comparisons more accurate, individual countries try to fix a census date and time to which they can adhere as far as possible in all censuses, but the choice of the day and month is generally determined by criteria based on the situation of the population, the climatic factors, transport facilities, etc., as also on the facilities for the census organization and other resources available on a particular date.

Censuses should be taken as frequently as is practicable, especially if they are not supplemented by current data from surveys or other sources. With relatively short intervals between censuses, interpolation of population estimates for the intercensal periods can become more accurate, and an extensive series of past censuses facilitates the calculation of accurate post-censal estimates. The changes in population distribution, brought about by industrial conditions and new inventions, by improved transport and communication, and by other factors, are now far more rapid than formerly. There is, therefore, considerable justification for more frequent censuses. Some other advantages of more frequent censuses are perhaps that the people enumerated come to regard the census as of routine occurrence and learn to appreciate its utility and importance for the common good.

TABLE 1

Population Censuses Taken in Selected Countries During the Period 1855-1957

Continent and country	Population census decades 1855–1864	1865–1874	1875–1884	1885–1894	1895–1904
AFRICA					
Egypt	----------	----------	-------A--	----------	--A-------
Libya	----------	----------	----------	----------	----------
Sudan	----------	----------	----------	----------	----------
Tunisia	----------	----------	----------	----------	----------
Union of South Africa	----------	----------	----------	----------	---------A
AMERICA					
Argentina	----------	----A-----	----------	----------	A---------
Bolivia	----------	----------	-------F--	----------	-----A----
Brazil	----------	-------A--	----------	-----A----	-----A----
Canada	------A---	------A---	------A---	------A---	------A---
Chile	----------	A---------	A---------	A---------	A---------
Colombia	---------F	-----F----	----------	----------	----------
Costa Rica	---------A	----------	A-------A-	---A---A--	----------
Cuba	------F---	----------	--F-------	--F-------	----F-----
Dominican Republic	----------	----------	----------	----------	----------
Ecuador	----------	----------	----------	----------	----------
El Salvador	----------	----------	---F---F--	--------F-	------S---
Guatemala	----------	----------	-----A----	--------A-	----------
Haiti	----------	----------	----------	----------	----------
Honduras	----------	----------	------F---	--F-------	------S---
Mexico	----------	----------	----------	----------	A----A----
Nicaragua	----------	----------	----------	----------	----------
Panama	----------	----------	----------	----------	----------
Paraguay	----------	----------	----------	-F--------	----A-----
Peru	-------A--	----------	-A--------	----------	----------
United States	-----A----	-----A----	-----A----	-----A----	-----A----
Uruguay	-----F----	----------	----------	----------	-----S----
Venezuela	----------	--------F-	------A---	------A---	----------
ASIA					
Burma	----------	-------F--	------A---	------A---	------A---
Ceylon	----------	------A---	------A---	------A---	------A---
China, Mainland	----------	----------	----------	----------	----------
China, Taiwan	----------	----------	----------	----------	----------
Malaya, Federation of	----------	----------	----------	------A---	------A---
India	----------	----------	------A---	------A---	------A---
Indonesia	----------	----------	-----F----	-----F----	-----F----
Iran	----------	----------	----------	----------	----------
Iraq	----------	----------	----------	----------	----------
Israel	----------	----------	----------	----------	----------

Japan	----------	-------A--	----------	----------	---A----A-
Lebanon	----------	----------	----------	----------	----------
Nepal	----------	----------	----------	----------	----------
Pakistan	----------	----------	------A---	------A---	------A---
Philippines	----------	----------	--A-------	--A-------	---------A
Syria	----------	----------	----------	----------	----------
Thailand	----------	----------	----------	----------	----------
Turkey	----------	----------	----------	----------	----------
EUROPE					
Albania	----------	----------	----------	----------	----------
Austria	--A-------	----A-----	-----A----	-----A----	-----A----
Belgium	-A--------	-A--------	-A---A----	-----A----	-----A----
Bulgaria	----------	----------	-----A----	--A----A--	-----A----
Czechoslovakia	----------	----------	-----F----	-----F----	-----F----
Denmark	A----A----	-----A----	-----A----	-----A----	------A---
Finland	A----A----	A----A----	A----A----	-----A----	-----A----
France	-A----A---	-A-----A--	-A----A---	-A----A---	-A----A---
Germany (Democratic Republic)	----------	------A---	A----A----	A----A----	A----A----
Germany (Federal Republic)	----------	------A---	A----A----	A----A----	A----A----
Greece	-A----A---	-----A----	----A-----	----A-----	-A--------
Hungary	----------	----A-----	-----A----	-----A----	-----A----
Iceland	A----A----	-----A----	-----A----	-----A----	------A---
Ireland	------A---	------A---	------A---	------A---	------A---
Italy	------A---	------A---	------A---	------F---	------A---
Liechtenstein	----------	-------A--	-----A----	------A---	------A---
Luxembourg	A-----A--A	--A---A---	A----A----	A----A----	A----A----
Monaco	---------A	----A---A-	---A---A--	---A----A-	--F-----A-
Netherlands	----A-----	----A-----	----A-----	----A-----	----A-----
Norway	A---------	A---------	A---------	-----A----	-----A----
Poland	----------	----------	----------	----------	----------
Portugal	---A--A--A	----------	---A------	-----A----	-----A----
Romania	----A-----	----------	----------	----------	----A-----
Spain	--A--A----	----------	--A-------	--A-------	--A--A----
Sweden	A----A----	-----A----	-----A----	-----A----	-----A----
Switzerland	-----A----	-----A----	-----A----	--A-------	-----A----
United Kingdom	------A---	------A---	------A---	------A---	------A---
USSR	----------	----------	----------	----------	--A-------
Yugoslavia	----A---A-	-A-------A	---------A	-----A----	A----A----
OCEANIA					
Australia	----------	----------	------A---	------A---	------A---
New Zealand	---A--A--A	--A---A--A	---A--A---	-A----A---	-A----A---

TABLE 1

Population Censuses Taken in Selected Countries During the Period 1855-1957 (Continued)

Continent and country	Population census decades					
	1905–1914	1915–1924	1925–1934	1935–1944	1945–1954	1955–1957
AFRICA						
Egypt	--A-------	--A-------	--A-------	--A-------	--F-------	---
Libya	----------	----------	------F---	-F--------	---------F	---
Sudan	----------	----------	----------	----------	----------	-F-
Tunisia	------F---	------F---	-F----F---	-F-------F	----------	-F-
Union of South Africa	------A---	---A--A---	-A----A---	-A----S---	-F----F---	---
AMERICA						
Argentina	----------	A---------	----------	----------	--F-------	---
Bolivia	----------	----------	----------	----------	-----F----	---
Brazil	----------	-----A----	----------	-----S----	-----F----	---
Canada	------A---	------A---	------A---	------S---	------F---	-F-
Chile	--A-------	-----A----	-----A----	-----S----	-------F--	---
Colombia	A------A--	---A------	---A------	---S------	------F---	---
Costa Rica	----------	----------	--A-------	----------	-----F----	---
Cuba	--A-------	----A-----	------A---	---------S	--------F-	---
Dominican Republic	----------	-----A----	----------	A---------	-----F----	---
Ecuador	----------	----------	----------	----------	-----F----	---
El Salvador	----------	----------	-----A----	----------	-----F----	---
Guatemala	----------	------A---	----------	-----S----	-----F----	---
Haiti	----------	---A------	----------	----------	-----F----	---
Honduras	S----S----	-A--------	-A---A----	S----S----	S----F----	---
Mexico	-----A----	------A---	-----A----	-----S----	-----F----	---
Nicaragua	-F--------	-----A----	----------	-----S----	-----F----	---
Panama	------A---	-----A----	-----A----	-----S----	-----F----	---
Paraguay	----------	----------	----------	-S--------	-----F----	---
Peru	----------	----------	----------	-----S----	----------	---
United States	-----A----	-----A----	-----A----	-----S----	-----F----	---
Uruguay	---A------	----------	----------	----------	----------	---
Venezuela	----------	-----A----	-A--------	-A----S---	-----F----	---
ASIA						
Burma	------A---	------A---	------A---	------S---	--------F-	---
Ceylon	------A---	------A---	------A---	----------	-F------F-	---
China, Mainland	-F--F-FF--	----------	---F------	----------	--------F-	---
China, Taiwan	----------	-----F----	F----F----	-----F----	----------	-F-
Malaya, Federation of	------A---	------A---	------A---	----------	--F-------	--F
India	------A---	------A---	------A---	------S---	------F---	---
Indonesia	F---------	----F-----	-----F----	----------	----------	---
Iran	----------	----------	----------	----F-----	----------	-F-
Iraq	----------	-----A----	---------A	----------	--F-------	--F
Israel	----------	-------F--	------F---	----------	---F------	---

Japan	---A----A-	---A-A----	A----A----	A----S---S	SSF--F----	F--
Lebanon	----------	------A---	-A----A---	A------F--	----------	---
Nepal	----------	----------	----------	----------	---------F	---
Pakistan	------A---	------A---	------A---	------S---	------F---	---
Philippines	----------	---A------	----------	----F-----	---F------	---
Syria	----------	------A---	-A----A---	A--F------	--F-------	---
Thailand	------F---	----A-----	----A-----	--A-------	--F-------	---
Turkey	----------	----------	--A-------	A----F----	F----F----	F--
EUROPE						
Albania	----------	----------	-----A----	----------	F---------	F--
Austria	-----A----	-----A--A-	---------A	----S-----	------F---	---
Belgium	-----A----	-----A----	-----A----	----------	--F-------	---
Bulgaria	A----A----	-----A----	-A-------A	----------	-F--------	-F-
Czechoslovakia	-----F----	------A---	-----A----	----------	--F--F----	---
Denmark	-A----A---	-A----A---	A----A----	A----S----	S----F----	F--
Finland	-----A----	-----A----	-----A----	-----S----	-----F----	---
France	-A----A---	------A---	-A----A---	-A--------	-S-------F	---
Germany (Democratic Republic)	A----A----	----------	A-------A-	----S-----	-S---F----	---
Germany (Federal Republic)	A----A----	----------	A-------A-	----S-----	-S---F----	---
Greece	--A-------	-----A----	---A------	-----S----	------F---	---
Hungary	-----A----	-----A----	-----A----	----S-S---	----F-----	---
Iceland	-----A----	-----A----	-----A----	-----S----	-----F----	---
Ireland	------A---	----------	-A--------	-A----F---	-F----F---	-F-
Italy	------A---	------A---	------A---	-A--------	------F---	---
Liechtenstein	------A---	----------	-----A----	------F---	-----F----	---
Luxembourg	A----A----	-A-----A--	--A--A----	A-----F-F-	F-F-------	---
Monaco	----------	------A-A-	---A----A-	----------	-F----F---	-F-
Netherlands	----A-----	-----A----	-----A----	----------	--F-------	---
Norway	-----A----	-----A----	-----A----	----------	-F---F----	---
Poland	----------	------A---	------A---	----------	-S---F----	---
Portugal	------A---	-----A----	-----A----	-----S----	-----F----	---
Romania	-------A--	----------	-----A----	------S---	---F------	-F-
Spain	-----A----	-----A----	-----A----	-----S----	-----F----	---
Sweden	-----A----	-----A----	-----A----	A----S----	S----F----	---
Switzerland	-----A----	-----A----	-----A----	------S---	-----F----	---
United Kingdom	------A---	------A---	------A---	----------	------F---	---
USSR	----------	-----A----	-A--------	--F-S-----	------F---	---
Yugoslavia	A----A----	------A---	------A---	----------	---F----F-	---
OCEANIA						
Australia	------A---	------A---	--------A-	----------	--F------F	---
New Zealand	-A----A---	-A----A---	-A--------	-A--------	S-----F---	-F-

SOURCES: A: Institut international de statistique. *Aperçu de la démographie des divers pays du monde, 1929-1936.* Le Haye, 1939.
F: Files of the Statistical Office of the United Nations.
S: United States. National Office of Vital Statistics. *Summary of International Vital Statistics, 1937-1944. Washington, D. C.*, 1947.

On the other hand, the intervals at which censuses are taken should not be too short because, first, major demographic changes in population do not take place in very short periods, and secondly, frequent repetition of the effort of organization and the considerable expense required to take a census of population would not be justified.

Table 1 shows the years between 1855 and 1957 in which population censuses were taken in selected countries. The information in the table is based on the most reliable sources. In cases of doubt about the year in which a particular census was taken, the census year shown in the table is the one which is supported by the greatest volume of evidence. Neither the completeness of the enumeration nor the accuracy of the returns has been taken into account. Therefore, some censuses conducted in China (1907, 1909, 1911-12, 1928), Haiti (1918-19) and Paraguay (1936) are included even though they were regarded as incomplete. Some censuses which were officially invalidated, such as those taken in Columbia in 1928 and in the Soviet Union in 1937, are also included in the table since, in any event, they were actually held. Censuses based on population counts derived from continuous population registers as well as on *ad hoc* registrations of population are shown when regarded as "censuses" in the sources consulted. Countries are shown as they were constituted at the end of 1957, without regard to changes in area or political status since 1855. As a result, what was actually a single census is shown twice in a few instances.

The table covers 76 countries, of which 5 are in Africa, 22 in the Americas, 18 in Asia, 29 in Europe and 2 in Oceania.

An examination of the dates of the population censuses taken in the various countries on the table shows that censuses have most usually been held at ten-year intervals since the turn of the century.

Table 2 summarizes the number of population censuses taken by the countries listed in table 1, according to the final digit of each year in each census decade from 1855 to 1954. Except for a slight decline in the decade 1935-1944 because of World War II, the total number of censuses taken in each decade has been increasing constantly since 1885. Only in the last decade under review, however, is there an average of one population census for each of the 76 countries during the 10-year period.

The two tables also reveal a traditional preference for holding population censuses in years

TABLE 2

Number of National Population Censuses Taken in Each Year of Each Census Decade, 1855 to 1954

Last digit of census year	Population census decades										Total censuses for each digit
	1855-64	1865-74	1875-84	1885-94	1895-1904	1905-14	1915-24	1925-34	1935-44	1945-54	
5	6	3	7	4	7	8	1	5	9	8	58
6	3	3	3	3	3	5	4	11	9	11	55
7	2	2	3	5	4	4	1	4	3	12	40
8	2	0	4	3	1	2	5	4	2	4	27
9	3	5	2	2	4	2	2	1	7	1	29
0	8	8	17	17	21	18	25	25	19	30	188
1	10	9	13	14	17	20	22	18	12	12	147
2	1	5	3	3	0	3	2	0	1	1	19
3	1	2	2	2	3	1	2	4	2	5	24
4	6	2	1	0	1	0	0	3	2	4	19
Total censuses in each decade	42	39	55	53	61	63	64	75	66	88	606

ending in "0" or "1" and a decidedly secondary preference for years ending in "5" or "6". In fact, of a total of 606 censuses taken in the hundred-year period covered in table 2, 335, or 55 per cent, were held in years ending in "0" or "1". This percentage would probably be even greater if not for the noticeable reduction in census taking in 1940 and 1941, during the war, as compared with the years ending in "0" and "1" in the two previous decades, and the comparatively large number of censuses taken immediately after the war, in 1947. In addition, there appears to be a trend in favour of years ending in "0" rather than those ending in "1".

*Fact Finder for the Nation**

U. S. BUREAU OF THE CENSUS

HOW THE CENSUS BUREAU DEVELOPED

Factfinding is one of the country's oldest activities. In the early 1600's a census was taken in Virginia, and censuses were taken in nearly all of the Northern colonies before the Revolutionary War.

Need for a Nationwide Census

The need for a census of the entire country arose soon after the colonies broke their ties with Great Britain. The costs of war had been high and the country had to find ways to pay the debt. Under the Articles of Confederation, each State was to contribute to the common defense and general welfare in proportion to the value of its land; but under the Constitution, each State was to pay according to the number of people living there. The Constitution also provided that Representatives in the Congress should be apportioned to the States according to the number of their inhabitants. Out of these provisions came the need for a count of the people in each State and the beginning of our national censuses.

The Constitution, adopted in 1787, provided: "Representatives and direct taxes shall be apportioned among the several States which may be included within this Union, according to their respective numbers, . . . The actual enumeration shall be made within three years after the first meeting of the Congress of the United States, and within every subsequent term of ten years, in such manner as they shall by law direct."

Taking the Early Censuses

Within a year after George Washington became President, the first census was taken. Compared with modern censuses, it was a crude operation. The law required that the returns be made in a specified form; but the Government did not provide printed forms, and the enumerators furnished their own stationery, using all sorts of books and sheets to record the information.

After the returns were completed, the enumerator was required to post them "at two of the most public places . . . to remain for the inspection of all concerned." This practice is in striking contrast to modern procedures. Today, if an enumerator tells any unauthorized person what is in the returns, he is liable to fine or imprisonment.

In taking the 1790 census, enumerators encountered many obstacles. The Nation had only 4 million people — about half the 1960 population of New York City — but they were scattered from Maine to Georgia and westward to the Mississippi River. The enumerators had to cover much of this territory on horseback, but in thinly settled areas roads were few and bridges were all but unknown. Hostile bands of Indians menaced them in the border country. The boundaries of

* Reprinted from U.S. Bureau of the Census, *Bureau of the Census — Fact Finder for the Nation.* Washington, D.C.: U.S. Government Printing Office, 1965, pp. 2-3, 6-7, 10-21, 24-25.

towns, other minor civil divisions, and some counties were poorly defined; and often an enumerator could not enter a specific location for a family. Moreover, many people did not know why the enumerator was taking the census, and they were suspicious and uncooperative. It is no wonder that it took 18 months to collect the data.

The U.S. marshals supervised the enumeration of the first nine censuses. Census work, however, was only a small part of their regular duties, and they could not give it adequate time and attention. For the 1880 census, the Congress provided supervisors of the census to be appointed by the President and confirmed by the Senate. The number permitted was 150, which was more than twice the number of marshals. Each supervisor was to select enumerators solely with reference to their fitness for the job and without reference to their political or party affiliations. This change in supervision improved public relations and accelerated the collection process.

Until 1902, the census organization was temporary. It was built up before each decennial census and disbanded after the work was finished. In 1902, the Congress set up a permanent office to take the census and to collect other statistics. At first, this office was in the Department of Interior; but in 1903 it was transferred to the new Department of Commerce and Labor. When that Department was split in 1913, the Bureau of the Census was placed in the Department of Commerce.

Questions Asked in the Census

The content of the first census was simple. Under the Constitution, the Government had to determine only the number of free and slave persons in each State. James Madison, however, recognized that the Congress needed information to enact laws and that the census was a convenient means of getting it. He "observed that they had now an opportunity of obtaining the most useful information for those who should hereafter be called upon to legislate for their country, if this bill was extended to embrace some other objects besides the bare enumeration of the inhabitants; it would enable them to adapt the public measures to the particular circumstances of the community." He suggested that white persons be classified by sex and white males by age and that a count be made of people employed in each occupation. The Congress rejected his last proposal but accepted his other suggestions.

Down through the years, the content of the decennial census changed as the Nation's needs and interests shifted. For example, the first inquiry on manufactures was made in 1810; questions on agriculture, mining, and fisheries were added in 1840; and in 1850 the census included inquiries on "social statistics" — taxation, churches, pauperism, and crime. The question on slaves was dropped from the 1870 and subsequent censuses.

Inquiries were greatly increased, both in number and type, in the censuses of 1880 and 1890. Five regular questionnaires covered population, agriculture, manufactures, social statistics, and mortality; while supplemental questionnaires called for special information on the insane, idiots, deaf-mutes, blind, homeless children, prisoners, and paupers. Almost a full decade was needed to complete each of these censuses, and it was evident that, although the census furnished large quantities of information, it was failing to provide that information when it was most needed.

Accordingly, the Congress limited the 1900 census to questions on population, manufactures, agriculture, and mortality. Several changes made it feasible to collect other information at later dates. The census office was scheduled to be in continuous operation after the 1900 census. Furthermore, information could be collected several times during the decade without undue hardship or excessive cost, because the country was more thickly settled and more generally accessible. The introduction of punchcard equipment to process the data also played a part in spacing the censuses. This equipment could be utilized more economically if inquiries were carried out at different times.

The Congress has added new censuses as more facts were needed. The Secretary of Commerce is now directed by law to take censuses of population, housing, agriculture, irrigation, drainage, manufactures, mineral industries, business (wholesale, retail, and service trades), governments, and transportation; he is also authorized to take a census of religious bodies and to collect decennial statistics on crime and on defective, dependent, and delinquent classes.

Collection of Current Data

As the Nation grew and its industry developed, changes in the economy became more frequent and far-reaching. Since Government officials and businessmen had to adjust their plans as these changes occurred, they needed more frequent reports on them. The Congress responded to this need by authorizing current surveys on the subjects covered by the censuses.

An effective way to provide current statistics is to collect data from samples of people and businesses. Using experts in sampling and survey techniques to plan the surveys, an efficient field organization to collect the data, and modern machinery to process the results, the Bureau can publish some reports as promptly as 5 days after the nationwide collection of the data. It makes weekly, monthly, quarterly, or annual reports on population, housing, manufactures, business, construction, and governments. Since 1941, it has had responsibility for compiling current statistics on foreign trade, and it publishes reports on exports, imports, and shipping.

The Bureau not only publishes current statistics itself, but it enables other Government agencies, businessmen, and others to do so. They use the censuses as benchmarks for sample surveys, projections, and other devices for obtaining current statistics. The usefulness of censuses for this purpose was pointed out by the Joint Economic Committee of the Congress, which said, "The census data are the foundation of an adequate program of economic statistics. Economists and statisticians recognize that current economic data based on sample and spot studies must be corrected periodically by the use of censuses if they are to maintain their accuracy." Someone has said that the census benchmarks are as useful to businessmen as the compass is to a mariner.

If a Government agency needs data but lacks facilities for collecting or tabulating them, it may contract with the Bureau to do this work. The other agency can then concentrate its efforts on analyzing the data according to the needs of its own program. Both agencies gain from this specialization.

The Census Bureau as Fact Finder

Many decades of collecting data have brought experience to the Bureau of the Census, and for several reasons it is especially qualified to be the Nation's major fact finder. First, it has established a reputation for trustworthiness, and people are generally willing to give it accurate and confidential information. Second, the Bureau collects data throughout the country and from one generation to the next; consequently, its statistics for different areas or different periods are more comparable than statistics collected by different unrelated agencies. Third, the Census Bureau statistics are available to almost anyone who needs them; they are deposited in libraries throughout the country and they can be purchased at relatively low cost. Finally, the Bureau has developed a staff that not only keeps abreast of the latest methods and machinery for collecting and processing data, but also devises new procedures and invents new machines for its statistical work. Among its recent achievements are advances in scientific sampling methods, extension of the use of data from administrative records of other Government agencies, and development of new kinds of electronic devices.

Finding the Facts

The Census Bureau gets facts by taking surveys, and every survey differs a little from the others. In some, the information is collected by mail, or it is partially obtained from the administrative records of other Government agencies; in others, it is collected by direct interview. Some surveys are taken only once; others are taken every month, year, or decade. Some require only a few hundred copies of a questionnaire; others require millions. Some cost little, others cost a great deal. Some can be reported in a leaflet a few weeks after the data are collected; others run into several volumes and take 3 or more years to complete.

Despite these variations, the Bureau follows the same general procedure for all surveys. It plans the survey, it collects the data, it processes them and presents the results, and it evaluates the operation.

The oldest and largest survey is the census of population. In the years ending in "0," the Bureau collects information from every home in the country — houses, apartments, tents, trailers, railroad cars, shacks, lighthouses. More than that, it hunts out the homeless people and counts them too. Every effort is made to account for every person. Because this census involves everyone in the United States, the 1960 Census of Population will be used in this chapter to show how the Census Bureau collects statistics.

In Planning, the Bureau

1. Checks the legal authority for the survey
2. Estimates the cost and obtains funds
3. Chooses the questions to be asked
4. Selects the sampling plans
5. Tests the questionnaires
6. Defines geographic areas
7. Prepares training materials
8. Plans publications, tabulations, and personnel needs
9. Informs the people

1. Checking Legal Authority. The Congress gives authority to take a survey when it sees the need for statistics. Usually, this authority is rather specific, requiring information in a certain subject field at specified times; but sometimes it is general, authorizing the Secretary of Commerce to make necessary investigations.

The Constitution authorizes the census of population, but it provides that "the actual enumeration shall be made . . . in such a manner as they [the Congress] shall by law direct." In 1929, the Congress, which previously had authorized each decennial census separately, passed a permanent census law, which has been subsequently amended in some details. Before the 1960 census was taken, the Congress amended it to give the Bureau specific authority to develop electronic equipment, use sampling, purchase maps and other materials, and reimburse enumerators for the use of unusual types of transportation (such as mules in the hills of Kentucky, pirogues in the Louisiana marshlands, and dog or motorized sleds in Alaska).

2. Estimating Costs and Obtaining Funds. The Bureau has to estimate the cost of a survey before it can get the money to take it. That money usually is appropriated to the Bureau by the Congress, but sometimes another Government agency or a private group will ask the Bureau to take a survey and will pay for it.

The census of population has always been considered essential to the public interest, and the Congress directly appropriates the funds needed to take it. Estimating costs for this census presents special problems because the census work runs for several years, and many changes may occur during that period. The Congress wants to know the total cost of the project before it launches it with a first-year appropriation. At the outset, therefore, the Bureau estimates the total cost and the amount to be spent in each year.

3. Choosing the Questions. The Bureau is not free to ask any questions it chooses. Each question must be within the authority granted by the Congress, it must fill an important need for information, and it must be one for which people can readily provide accurate answers. The amount of money available from the Congress must also be considered because each question adds to the cost of the census.

In choosing the questions, the Census Bureau decides which ones are most important by consulting people who need the statistics. The needs of Government agencies take top priority, but those of businessmen, labor groups, research workers, and others are also considered — often through the use of advisory committees.

In all these operations, the Bureau works closely with the Bureau of the Budget, which must approve the questionnaire before funds can be used to collect the information. Attention is also given to recommendations of the United Nations, both because they may be intrinsically helpful and because adoption of them will make the U.S. statistics more comparable with those of other nations.

4. Selecting the Sampling Plan. In the population census, a count of all the people is necessary to satisfy the requirements of the Constitution with respect to congressional apportionment, but the needs for some information can be satisfied by collecting it from only a sample, such as every fourth person or household. When such persons or households are selected according to scientific sampling principles, and when the number is large, the sample provides results that are close to those from a complete count.

Whether to use sampling in the census and what sampling plan to use depend on the funds available, the time allowed, the amount of detail needed, and the accuracy required. Sampling is cheaper than complete enumeration and it provides results more quickly; but it cannot be used for a question if very detailed information on that subject is required for small areas or for subclasses containing a small part of the total population.

In the 1960 census, all questions except those on age, sex, color or race, marital status, and household relationship were put in the sample. This sample included every fourth housing unit on the enumerators' lists. In group quarters, such as lodginghouses and institutions, every fourth person was selected.

5. Testing the Questions and the Questionnaire. After the questions are chosen, they must be worded so that the respondents will understand them and the answers will be definite.

The Bureau first makes informal tests of the census questions and questionnaires, sometimes with some of its employees acting as respondents. Then, it may try the questions in a neighborhood near its offices. The next step may be to add some questions to the Current Population Survey, which covers a nationwide sample of 35,000 households and permits a test in all parts of the country. Finally, the Bureau conducts pretest or dress rehearsal censuses in selected areas. These pretests enable the Bureau to test operating procedures as well as questionnaires and to estimate costs. Some of these pretests are followed by postenumeration surveys, in which the information is obtained in a different way and compared with the results in the original enumeration.

6. Defining Geographic Areas. The information collected must be related to particular geographic areas. No one of the thousands of areas that make up the Nation can be overlooked, and all must fit together like a giant jigsaw puzzle.

Within the limits set by law, the Bureau must select the areas for which statistics will be published; and sometimes it sets up special kinds of areas to make the census statistics more useful. For example, in the 1950 census, it introduced the urbanized area, which includes not only the city but also the adjacent built-up area beyond the city limits. Other special areas that the Bureau helps to delineate are: Standard metropolitan statistical areas (an area containing a city of 50,000 inhabitants or more with its surrounding county or counties) and census tracts (neighborhoods of about 3,000 to 6,000 persons into which large cities or entire standard metropolitan statistical areas are divided).

In the census of population, figures are needed for States, counties, cities, and other political subdivisions of the country, and also for the special areas. The Bureau gets up-to-date maps and locates the boundaries of each area for which statistics are to be published. After it knows the boundaries, it can mark them on its own maps, and the enumerator can collect information from all the people living in the designated area. Frequently, however, the population of a political or special area is so large that one enumerator cannot canvass it in the time that the law allows him. The Bureau then divides the area into enumeration districts, each of which is small enough for one enumerator to cover.

The boundaries of some enumeration districts can be kept the same from one census to another. In 10 years, however, many changes occur. Population increases, people move, new communities spring up, and cities change their boundary lines. Before each census, the Bureau finds out what changes have taken place; where necessary, it changes the boundaries of the enumeration districts; then it prepares a map for each district.

7. Preparing Instructions. To be precise and meaningful, data must be collected in the same way in every place. Accordingly, the Bureau issues precise instructions.

Fieldworkers especially need instructions, because nearly all of them are new employees, and they are scattered throughout the country. The Bureau prepares separate manuals — some for training and some for reference purposes — for enumerators, crew leaders, technical officers, and district supervisors. In addition, the Bureau issues instructions for specific functions, such as training and office procedures; and, as problems arise in the enumeration, it sends out memoranda that supplement or modify the original instructions.

8. Planning the Workload. For many purposes, statistics get out of date very soon; accordingly, the Bureau treats them as a perishable commodity that must be marketed quickly. Because timing is important, workers and facilities must be available at scheduled times to complete each part of the job.

The census of population creates a great surge of activity. The Bureau makes a timetable showing when each part of the work should be started and completed. It calculates the number of enumerators needed from estimates of the number of persons to be counted and of the days allowed for enumeration. For processing and publication of the collected data, "how many workers?" and "when?" have to be worked out in detail. First, with the help of extensive advice, the Bureau decides exactly what tables it will publish. Then, it outlines the operations that are needed to provide those tables — preparing computer programs, coding the information on the questionnaires (if necessary), microfilming the questionnaires, transferring the data on the microfilm to magnetic tape, editing and tabulating the data with the computer, printing out the resulting tables, reviewing the tables, and reproducing the tables for publication. As the Bureau shapes these plans, it can estimate the number of workers and the length of time each kind of work will take. Related activities, such as recruiting and training new employees and locating new office space, can be planned from the timetable for primary operations.

9. Informing the People. People give information to the Census Bureau more readily if they understand the need for the statistics. Time, trouble, and expense are saved by informing them. The Bureau, moreover, recognizes the right of the people to be informed of important governmental activities. It therefore tries to explain each census and major survey in newspapers and magazines, over the radio and television, and in other ways that will reach the respondents and prepare them for its request.

The census of population reaches every home in the country, and its information program is necessarily extensive. Several months before enumeration starts, national magazines carry stories about the census, and national organizations ask their members to help publicize and promote the census as a public service.

As the census date draws near, the Bureau gets the cooperation of nationwide press, radio, and television facilities. In the cities and towns, the local supervisory staff members of the Bureau make speeches, organize committees to spread the word, and interest local newspapers and broadcasting stations in the census. In the schools, teachers explain the census to the children.

As a result of this publicity, nearly every family knows that it will receive a census form in the mail.

Collecting the Information

Collecting the information for a census or survey is, in some respects, like erecting the walls for a building. It is a basic operation on which other operations depend; it is done relatively quickly; and the results — the stacks of questionnaires — are readily apparent.

Most of the information for the population census is collected within a few weeks. A job so big, completed in so short a time, requires a vast expansion of Bureau employment. (About 170,000 fieldworkers were hired in 1960 to take the population and housing censuses.) Most of the activity takes place in the field offices in four operations:

1. Hiring and training the field staff
2. Enumerating the population
3. Reviewing the enumerators' work
4. Making preliminary counts

1. Hiring and Training the Field Staff. The Bureau looks for capable civicminded persons to take the decennial census. Wherever possible, workers in the regular field offices are temporarily transferred to census work. Candidates for crew leader and enumerator jobs have to take a test to show that they can understand detailed written instructions, read maps, and make computations. After the Bureau has selected the workers, it trains them for the jobs they are to do.

Training in enumeration starts at Bureau headquarters, where Bureau staff members train about 40 chief instructors. The chief instructors fan out to the Bureau's regional offices where they train about 400 technical officers and 70 program technicians. Thereafter, each technical officer goes to a district office and trains the crew leaders who in turn train the enumerators.

The new enumerator learns how to find all the places in his district where people might live, how

DATA PROCESSING PROCEDURES. *The procedures illustrated are as nearly standard as procedures can be at this stage in the development of high-speed equipment. The illustration shows the processing of data from large censuses where the use of FOSDIC is justified. An alternate procedure is used for smaller jobs where the transfer of data to computer tape is accomplished faster or more economically by other means.*

A simplified diagram like this is a little misleading in suggesting these processes are entirely mechanized. Actually, documents must be handled individually in the microfilming process and to accomplish certain codings. Also, the movement is a series of steps at various locations rather than a continuous flow.

For smaller censuses and surveys, some questionnaires are of the mark-sense type, and when put through a specially designed machine, produce punchcards automatically. Other questionnaires are in plain language, and operators must punch cards manually.

In either case, the cards are converted to magnetic tape. This process transfers the information from the cards to magnetic tape, which is then fed into the computer. From that point, processing continues as in the basic procedure.

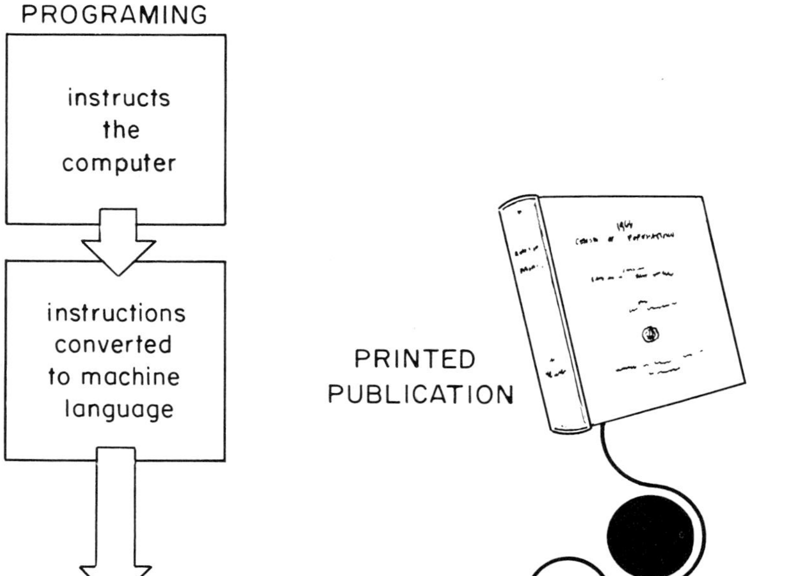

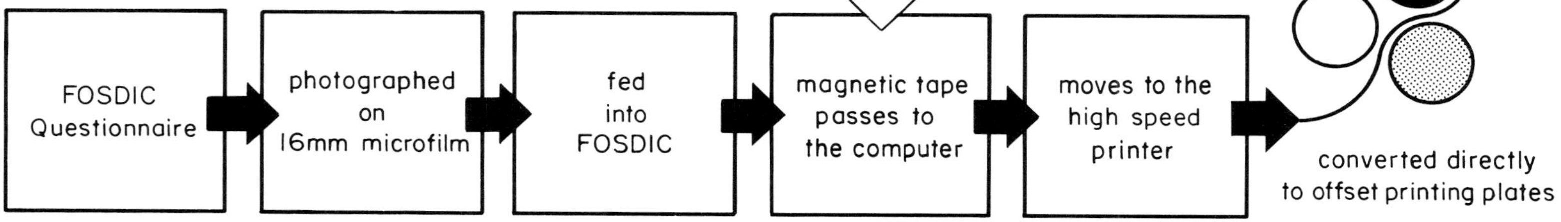

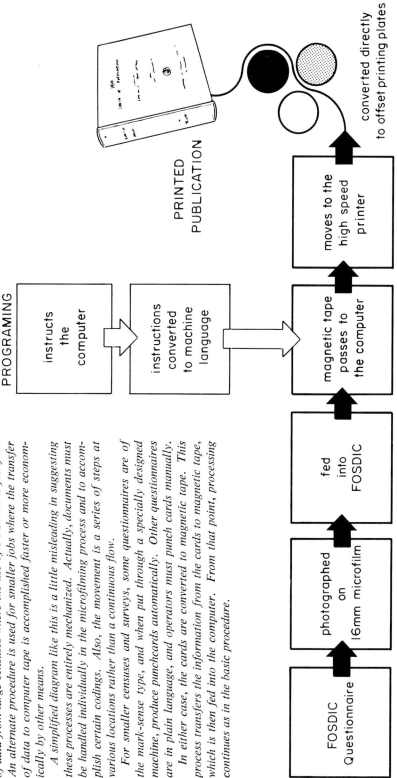

to list those places systematically, how to interview householders and enter the census information on the enumeration forms, and how to designate the sample.

2. Enumerating the Population. In 1960, the Bureau introduced new methods of enumerating the population. Late in March every household in the United States received through the mail an advance census report. On this form, the householder was requested to enter information for each member of the household — age, sex, color or race, marital status, and relationship to household head. These were the 100-percent questions, the ones asked for every person in the country.

On the 1st of April, or soon thereafter, the enumerator visited each dwelling. He checked the information supplied by the householder and entered it on a Fosdic form, a form especially designed to be read by an electronic machine called Film Optical Sensing Device for Input to Computers. This form had a series of circles for each piece of information, and the enumerator darkened some circles with his pencil to show the correct answer; thus, if he was enumerating a man, he would darken the circle marked "male" and leave blank the circle marked "female."

In the areas where the enumeration was done in two stages — including about four-fifths of the population — the enumerator left a new form for the one household in every four that fell in the sample. This form carried the questions on the sample items — birthplace, parents' birthplace, mother tongue, mobility, education, school enrollment, number of times married, number of children, employment status, occupation, industry, place of work, income, and veteran status. The householder filled this second form and mailed it to the district office.

When the sample forms were received in the district office, enumerators checked them to see if the information was consistent and complete. If it was not, or if a form was not received, they called the householder and obtained the information. After that, they transcribed the sample information to Fosdic forms, on which the 100-percent information for that household had been marked.

In the sparsely settled areas where the enumeration was done in a single stage in order to reduce traveling, the enumerator collected information on the sample items at the same time that he obtained the answers to the 100-percent questions.

As the enumerator visited the housing units in his district, he recorded each one in a listing book.

Special arrangements were made to collect information from persons overseas and from persons living in certain types of living quarters, such as military installations, Indian reservations, vessels, institutions, and hospitals.

In 1960 all persons who were staying in large hotels, tourist camps, or similar transient accommodations were enumerated on one night, "T-Night"; the reports of these transients were checked with reports made at their homes, and duplicates were eliminated. Another night was set aside for the enumeration in missions, flophouses, all-night movie houses, city parks, hobo jungles, and the like.

When the enumeration of a city or county was about completed, a "Were you counted?" form was printed in the local newspapers. This form asked any person who believed he was not enumerated to enter his name and address on the form and send it to the district office. There the forms were checked against the records, and a person whose name was not found was visited and enumerated.

3. Reviewing the Enumerator's Work. In 1960, the Bureau used several procedures to insure reasonable accuracy in enumeration. One was to have the crew leader list some of the addresses in each enumeration district and then check to see if the enumerator included them in his canvass. Another was to have the crew leader accompany the enumerator on his first few household visits to make sure that he understood the procedures. Still another was to have the crew leader check regularly on the enumerator's work and to take prescribed measures if it was not satisfactory. The technical officer in turn checked the work of the crew leader.

When the enumerator completed his district, his materials were examined first by the crew leader and then by a quality control clerk in the district office. Unacceptable work was sent back to the crew leader for correction.

Under this program, high standards of accomplishment could be maintained, and many errors could be corrected before the field organization was disbanded.

4. Making Preliminary Counts of the People. As soon as the enumerators' work had been checked, the district office counted the people enumerated in each county and city in the district and announced the results. This count was preliminary because it did not include the people who were enumerated away from home and who would later be allocated to the places where they usually live.

The announcement of the preliminary count gave the city a chance to see about what its population would be and to question the figure if it appeared to be inaccurate. If a city believed the reported figure was too low, the Bureau encouraged it to submit names of persons believed to have been missed by the enumerators. Any names submitted were then checked by the district office. Such use of the preliminary count increased the completeness of the enumeration.

Compiling and Presenting the Results

The individual records collected in the census were translated into statistical tables with assembly-line methods and modern machines.

Speed was emphasized in the population census because the law requires that the final count of inhabitants for each State be completed by December 1 of the census year, and "reported by the Director of the Census to the Secretary of Commerce and by him to the President of the United States." On the basis of this report, the apportionment of Representatives among the States is made, as required by the Constitution.

Preparing Preliminary Reports. The enumeration books poured into the central processing office (Jeffersonville, Ind.), where workers checked the materials, recorded receipt of them, and stored them systematically.

The first operation was to prepare the preliminary reports from the counts made in the field offices. Population totals from the enumeration books were transferred to work sheets, from which tables were typed. Less than 6 months after the start of the 1960 enumeration, the Bureau published a preliminary report for each State showing the population of counties and of incorporated places with 1,000 inhabitants or more.

Preparing Data for Editing and Tabulation. Since the 100-percent information required no coding, it could be sent immediately to the microfilm cameras. There — in half a second — the Fosdic form was photographed, each 14- by 16-inch sheet requiring about 1 square inch of space on the filmstrip.

The film was sent to Washington, where it was developed and fed into the Fosdic machine. Fosdic scanned the microfilm, noted in each section the position of the darkened circle, and put magnetic spots on tape according to the instructions given to it. The tape then carried the 100-percent information in a form that could be read and tabulated by the electronic computer.

For sample information, the 1960 procedure was similar, but one additional operation — coding — was needed. Coding was required because there were often a great many possible answers to some of the sample questions. For example, in the question on birthplace of the foreign born, more than a hundred answers were possible and there was not room for all of them on the questionnaire. Accordingly, the enumerator wrote in the answer, such as "Netherlands."

Fosdic cannot read the enumerator's handwriting, but it can read darkened circles. Consequently, a coder assigned a code for each entry made by the enumerator — such as "18" for Netherlands — and then darkened the appropriate circles — circle 1 in the first column of 10 circles and circle 8 in the second column. When all the sample information was in the form of darkened circles, the sample sheets were ready to be microfilmed.

By the time the sample information was collected and coded, much of the 100-percent information had been put on magnetic tape. The Fosdic equipment was therefore available for processing the sample data.

Editing and Tabulating the Data. Adding the results in all the different questionnaires and making them into tables was only one of the jobs done by the electronic computer. It also checked the questionnaires to see if answers were missing or if one answer was inconsistent with another. Instructions for all these operations were given in the program prepared for each tabulation. Like the data, this program was put on magnetic tape. It was fed into the computer ahead of the data from the questionnaires. After the computer had the program, it worked automatically, carrying out the instructions for storing the data from the questionnaires in its memory, checking them, and compiling the tables.

Because the computer is fast and can keep immense quantities of data readily available, it was especially useful in editing. For example, if wage or salary income was not reported for a nonwhite male farm laborer, aged 39, who worked 25 weeks in 1959, the computer assigned to him the income of the last person in the same area answering that description. Then it reported on a diary tape that it allocated income for that person. The total number of allocations for each item on the questionnaire was recorded on the diary tape for each enumeration district. This diary tape was reviewed to see if allocations were excessive and if corrective action — such as hand editing and reprocessing — was needed for that district.

The computer also checked the reasonableness of some figures. For example, when it calculated the total number of World War II veterans in an area, it compared that total with the number of adult males; then, it checked to see if the ratio was within the limits of acceptability stored in the computer. If it was not — e.g., if the number of veterans was only 5 percent of the number of adult males — the computer printed out the result, which could be checked further.

After the computer refined the data, it added up the items by groups. For example, it looked at the race entry for each person in Roundup, Mont., and tallied it in the white, Negro, or other races group. After it completed its tally, it put the totals for each group on magnetic tape. The computer also calculated percentages and averages as the program directed.

When the computer worked with sample data, it had to do one more thing — weight the data. Generally, this meant counting each person as four instead of one, because the sample covered one household in four, but sometimes a slightly different weight had to be given to make the sample total exactly equal the 100-percent total.

The final step in processing was translating the results (which appeared as magnetized spots on tape) into a printed document. This was done by the electronically controlled high-speed printer, acting on the instructions fed into the computer. It printed the results on sheets of paper at a rate of 400 to 600 lines per minute and the tables were ready for review.

Reviewing the Tables. Despite the Bureau's efforts to prevent errors, some appeared in the tables that came from the high-speed printer. This is not surprising, because these tables are the end result of many operations (enumerating, coding, transferring to tape, editing, tabulating, and printing) in which errors can occur. To detect these errors, a Bureau staff member who was familiar with the subject reviewed the tables. He examined them to see if they showed the usual relationships, and he compared the figures with those of the previous census and with other data.

Publishing the Results. Publication — the last of the census operations — put the statistical tables into books or pamphlets. These tables had to be produced as quickly as possible to meet the needs of government officials and businessmen. The Bureau used several devices to make simple counts available quickly and to make more detailed classifications available at an early date. It published the preliminary counts that were made in the field offices, it selected figures from the final publications and issued them as advance reports, and it published parts of some books before the entire volume was ready.

To help users understand the statistics, the Bureau defined and explained the terms in the publications. Some of these terms, like urbanized areas, were coined by the Bureau. Others, like household, were given specific meanings. If the 1960 definition of the term differed from the 1950 definition, the Bureau explained the change and showed the effect on the figures. It also described other changes which affected the comparability of the 1960 figures with those for previous censuses.

Finally, the Bureau discussed the quality of the data. It explained factors affecting their accuracy, showed the amount of nonresponse for certain figures and the extent to which the computer allocated replies; and, where the data were based on a sample, it gave the amount of the sampling error. These "tips on the market," as they were called by an early Superintendent of the Census, aid readers in using the statistics properly.

Evaluating the Operation

After the census was completed, the Bureau reviewed the operation, methodically and in detail, from planning to publication. The formal evaluation program included resurveys and other checks on the adequacy of the enumeration (both on coverage of the population and on correctness of the information supplied) and on the accuracy of the field transcription, the coding, and the processing. In addition, for items which could be matched with other records, the Bureau compared samples of the information it collected with that collected by other agencies.

In reviewing the census operation, the Bureau tried to see where things were done well and where they went badly. For the benefit of the next generation of census takers, it recorded its failures and successes, thus laying the groundwork for a more effective operation in the next decade.

What Facts the Bureau Collects

The Bureau of the Census issues periodic reports to show where the country stands in population, housing, agriculture, manufacturers, mineral industries, business (retail, wholesale, and service trades), foreign trade, government finances and employment, construction, and transportation. In addition to giving an overall view of the status of the Nation, these reports present a multitude of facts that can be used singly or in combination for a variety of purposes.

Population

Oldest of the fact collections is the census of population, which was described in the preceding section. That census provides a vast amount of detailed information, which is especially valuable in showing the characteristics of counties, cities, and towns, and in analyzing specific subjects, such as marital status or education. The population census is taken, however, only once in 10 years, and between times information is needed on changes in employment, school enrollment, income, family status and other matters. To get such information, the Bureau takes monthly, quarterly, and annual sample surveys, which indicate trends for the country as a whole.

The Current Population Survey, which the Bureau takes every month, is a quick operation. In the middle of the month, enumerators visit some 35,000 households scattered throughout the country. These households are selected by scientific sampling methods so that, taken together, they give a good cross section of all the people. The hills of Kentucky, the farms of Iowa, and the crowded sections of Chicago are all represented. When the questionnaires reach Washington, the data are transferred to magnetic tape and tabulated on electronic computers.

This survey enables the Bureau to report between censuses on the characteristics of the population. Changes in income, education, marital status, size of families, number of children, and migration are reported annually. Changes in intentions of householders to purchase large consumer durable goods are reported quarterly. Data on employment and unemployment are collected and tabulated each month and transmitted to the Department of Labor where they are analyzed and released. Other subjects appear at various intervals or on a one-time basis.

The Bureau takes special censuses of localities that request them and pay the cost of the operation. The city or town making such a request is usually a growing one that wishes to prove that it is entitled to wider civic powers or a greater share of State tax receipts. More than 1,500 of these censuses were taken between the 1950 and 1960 national censuses.

The Bureau also makes monthly estimates of the population of the United States. To do this, it takes the number counted in the last census, adds the number born since then, subtracts the number who died, adds the number who moved in, and subtracts the number who moved out. In April 1964, the Bureau estimated that the population in this country was 191 million, compared with 179 million recorded 4 years earlier in the 1960 census.

Visitors to Washington, D.C., often go to the lobby of the Department of Commerce building to look at the "census clock." This clock ticks off the results of the Bureau's population estimates, currently showing a birth every 7½ seconds, a death every 17 seconds, an immigrant every 90 seconds, and an emigrant every 23 minutes. Every 12 seconds, one more person is added to the total population.

The results of the decennial census are always eagerly received, but the 1960 results created more than the usual amount of interest. People were amazed, not at the growth of the population between 1950 and 1960 because that had been anticipated from the population estimates, but at the places where the growth occurred or failed to occur. Officials of many of the large cities, in particular, were taken by surprise. Beset by traffic problems and other evidences of congestion, they had assumed that their populations increased between 1950 and 1960; but the census showed that their populations had declined, while the population in the nearby suburbs had increased at a great rate. Nearly one-third of the central cities in the standard metropolitan statistical areas lost population during the decade, although nearly every standard metropolitan statistical area (which includes the suburbs as well as the city) gained population. In the rural areas, population generally declined.

People also moved from one region of the country to another. The historic trek to the West continued, and California bid to overtake New York for the position as the most populous State. (Current estimates indicate it has now done so.) But a State in the Southeast — Florida — had the highest rate of increase. Of the 19 States with the greatest rates of increase, 16 are on the borders of the country — the Mexican border, the Great Lakes, and the Atlantic and Pacific Oceans. Negroes continued to move from the rural areas of the South to the large industrial cities of the North and West.

Largely because of the high birth rates before 1900 and since World War II, the oldest and youngest groups in the population increased between 1950 and 1960. Lower death rates also contributed to these changes. In 1960, only 52 percent of the population was between 20 and 65, compared with 58 percent in 1950.

*Evolution and Present Status of Vital Records and Statistics**

STATISTICAL OFFICE OF THE UNITED NATIONS

To place vital-statistics methods in their proper perspective, it is necessary first to have an understanding of the history of vital records and statistics. Knowledge of the origin of vital records, the various methods by which vital statistics may be obtained, the present status of vital-statistics systems, and the efforts of international organizations, past and present, to remedy deficiences, provides the background against which current methods, procedures, and recommendations can be evaluated.

A. Definitions and History

Vital records may be defined as those concerned with live births, deaths, foetal deaths, (stillbirths), marriages, divorces, adoptions, legitimations, recognitions, annulments, and separations, in short all the events which have to do with an individual's entrance into or departure from life, together with the changes in civil status which may occur to him during his lifetime. It follows that vital statistics are those statistics which, for a designated population group, provide a description of the number and characteristics of the vital events which are taking place therein. These events are the "statistical units" with which this *Handbook* will be concerned.

Vital statistics have to do with people rather than with things and, consequently, this branch of statistics has perhaps the second oldest history in the world, surpassed in antiquity only by the closely related population enrolment or census.

* Reprinted with permission from Statistical Office of the United Nations, *Handbook of Vital Statistics Methods*. New York: United Nations, 1955, pp. 3-9, 12-18.

The population census or human inventory, which is the most fundamental and far-reaching statistical inquiry that can be undertaken, provides a picture of the population and its characteristics at one moment of time; vital statistics provide the tools for measuring the dynamics of, or the changes which continuously occur in, this instantaneous picture.

The fundamental character of the events with which vital statistics are concerned and their basic importance in the culture of a people are the reasons why the recording of births, deaths, marriages, and divorces has been an established procedure in all civilized nations for many years. However, the vital events which are now identified as the "units" of vital statistics were not always so recognized. A glance into the origins of the registration system and its transition from an ecclesiastical to a secular undertaking will show why this was so.

1. Origin — Ecclesiastical Rolls

Except for fragmentary vital registration during the pre-Christian era, which in Egypt, Greece, and Rome for example appears to have been carried out by civil authorities for revenue or military purposes, the recording of vital events was originally the unco-ordinated concern of the individual ecclesiastical authorities. The "vital events" for which ecclesiastical authorities, then as now, had a responsibility were baptisms, burials, and weddings rather than births, deaths, and marriages. In the church of the Middle Ages, baptism of every child was compulsory; likewise, in order to receive the sanction of the church, burials and weddings also came within the purview of the clergy. The participation of the clergy in ceremonies associated with any of these three acts was usually rewarded by a payment of some sort, and the recording of these payments, or the lack thereof, produced a limited register of baptisms, burials, and weddings.

It is easy to see why registers so produced would be limited in coverage and quality. The fundamental deficiency, of course, stems from the fact that the ecclesiastical registers recorded payment for ceremonies rather than the occurrence of events. Secondly, such registers were restricted to religious rites among a specified denomination of one parish, and they were maintained solely at the discretion of the priest in charge. Because of this factor, they could not fail to be of limited coverage with respect to members of other religious faiths (non-conformists) as well as to be unsystematic and non-uniform from parish to parish. Finally, the records themselves were designed not to attest to civil or biological facts, but to record the payment of a fee for a service. Hence, they would tend to include those data deemed relevant, such as the date of the ceremony involved, rather than the date of the occurrence of the event in question, which was not considered pertinent. These defects in ecclesiastical rolls as registers of vital events persisted in spite of statutes and ordinances promulgated by the church authorities in an effort to make church registers furnish proof of kinship as well as a means of enforcing the rules of ecclesiastical law which forbade the marriage of relatives.

2. Systematic Ecclesiastical Registration

As early as A.D. 720, there appears to have been a system of registration for births, deaths, and marriages in some parts of Japan. It is not known whether this system was religious or secular, but it is known that Buddhist temple registers were established in that country in 1635.

In Europe, the beginning of systematic vital registration may be traced back to Spain in the fifteenth century when Cardinal Ximenes, Archbishop of Toledo, provided for the introduction of registers which were to be maintained regularly by the parish priests. In 1538, by order of Thomas Cromwell, Vicar General under Henry VIII, the clergy of England were required to record baptisms, marriages, and burials. France, by the Ordinance of Villers-Cotterets in 1539, required the curates to keep registers of baptisms and burials, a measure which by the Council of Trent in 1563 was extended to marriages. By 1608, the first systematic parish register was established in Sweden, followed by similar registers in Canada (Quebec, 1610), Finland (1628) and in Denmark (1646).

3. Civil Registration

But all of these developments were still in the church, still governed by religious orders, and still related essentially to the ceremonies of baptisms, burials, or weddings. It remained for the New World of the Western Hemisphere to introduce civil registration — the first such system being the registers of births and deaths established by the Incas in Peru,[1] and the second, the civil legislation introduced in the Colonies of Massachusetts Bay and New Plymouth in the early seventeenth century (1639).[2] In England and on the Continent, as noted above, the *ecclesiastical* authorities were in charge of registration; but in Peru and in these two British colonies, government clerks were made the record keepers and, still more important, births, deaths, and marriages were recorded rather than baptisms, burials, and weddings. Thus, Massachusetts became the first state in the Christian world to record the actual events and the dates thereof, rather than the occurrence and date of the subsequent ecclesiastical ceremonies, and the first to place this registration function under the civil authorities rather than under the clergy.

The secularization of vital registration continued with the adoption of the Napoleonic Code in the France of 1804. The civil section of this Code, which was destined to influence strongly the development of vital-registration systems throughout Western Europe, Latin America, and the parts of the Middle East which came under French influence, placed the responsibility for recording births, deaths, and marriages on the state. It set forth exact provisions for determining who should report the event, who should record it, and what the record should include. All of the provisions of the civil code were concerned with the legal or civil rights of an individual, because civil rights could be granted only by the state and proof of one's claim to such rights was dependent on official registration. Thus, the "legal" purpose for which civil registration of vital events was designed began to assume an importance which was to increase in subsequent years. Moreover, the "individual" as the unit of the vital registration system was established firmly by these codes.

4. Vital Statistics

Although registration of births, deaths, and marriages was an established fact in England in 1538 and in most countries of the rest of Europe by the early seventeenth century, vital records were not used for other than legal purposes until John Graunt in 1662 saw the possibilities of using the "bills of mortality" for another purpose. Using these rudimentary lists, Graunt derived and published a series of inductive observations under the title *Natural and Political Observations Mentioned in a following Index, and made upon the Bills of Mortality*,[3] which constituted the first modern use of the registration method for obtaining statistical information. It is true that counts of births and deaths had been maintained for military and fiscal purposes in Egypt, Rome, Greece, and in Peru, but the systematic analysis of registration statistics as we know it began with John Graunt.

Possibly influenced by John Graunt's work, several cities in Germany, notably Brandenburg in 1684, began an annual accounting of births, deaths, and marriages from registration records. In France, the statistical utilization of the registers of the parishes became possible with the declaration of 9 April 1736 which required the curates, vicars, parish priests, and other church officers, to deposit with the bailiwick every year a duplicate of their registers of baptisms, burials, and weddings and provided that records of deaths

[1] According to Garcilasso de la Vega (born 1539 in Cuzco of an Incan mother and a Spanish father), the Incas, who had no written characters for simple sounds, used intertwining of coloured strings and knots to record facts. These record-keeping mechanisms known as *quipus* were in charge of *Quipucamayus* who "noted, by means of the knots, all of the tribute that was given to the Inca every year, specifying each household and its peculiar mode of service. They also recorded the number of men who went to the wars, those who died in them, those who were born and those who died in each month". (*Royal Commentaries* by Garcilasso de la Vega. Reprinted in *The Ancient Quipu or Peruvian Knot Record,* by Leslie Leland Locke. The American Museum of Natural History, 1923, p. 41.)

According to William H. Prescott, information on the resources of the country and on the character of the inhabitants of the different provinces "was obtained by an admirable regulation, which has scarcely a counterpart in the annals of a semi-civilized people. A register was kept of all the births and deaths throughout the country, and exact returns of the actual population were made to government every year, by means of the *quipus* . . ." (*History of the conquest of Peru, with a preliminary view of the civilization of the Incas* by William H. Prescott, 2nd ed. In two volumes. London, Richard Bentley, 1847. Vol. 1, p. 50.)

[2] "The Registration Laws in the Colonies of Massachusetts Bay and New Plymouth" by Robert R. Kuczynski. *Publications of the American Statistical Association,* Vol. 7 (New Series), No. 7. Boston, September 1900. p. 1-9.

[3] *Natural and Political Observations Mentioned in a following Index, and made upon the Bills of Mortality,* by John Graunt. 4th ed. Oxford, printed by William Hall, for John Martyn and James Allestry, Printers to the Royal Society, 1665.

of persons not accorded ecclesiastical burial be kept by the police officers.[4] This was augmented in 1772 by a circular addressed by the Abbé Terray to the *intendants* requesting them to prepare from the register each year beginning 1770 a resumé of births, deaths, and marriages which had occurred in their districts. Thus, to Terray goes the credit for initiating the permanent and regular counting of *actes de l'état-civil* in France — a system which was maintained up to the beginning of the twentieth century.

In spite of these examples of the use of registration records for statistical purposes, the subject received only fragmentary and desultory treatment until 1839 when Dr. William Farr became "Compiler of Abstracts" in the newly created General Register Office of England and Wales. The impact of this great vital statistician has been described[5] as follows:

> Dr. Farr was appointed to the General Register Office on 10 July 1839. . . . The next 40 years of his life were almost exclusively devoted to the, to him, congenial task of creating and developing a national system of vital statistics, which has not only popularized sanitary questions in England in such a manner as to render rapid health progress an accomplished fact, but which has, practically, been adopted in all the civilized countries of the world.

There is no question but that this is an altogther valid evaluation of Dr. Farr's influence. His penetrating analyses of the deficiencies in, and the methods of improving vital statistics, as well as his conclusions as to the implications to be drawn from them, are still models for workers in the fields of public health and demography.

B. Methods of Obtaining Vital Statistics Systematically

1. The Registration Method

Because, historically, vital statistics have been either wholly or partially derived from information obtained at the time when the occurrence of a vital event and its characteristics were inscribed in a register for legal purposes, they have come to be known also as "registration statistics," that is, statistics obtained by the registration method. The term "registration method" describes the procedure employed in gathering the basic observations upon which vital statistics are based, and is used in contradistinction to the "enumeration method" which produces population and other census or survey statistics, or the "administrative method" which produces statistics as a by-product of management controls as, for example, statistics of foreign trade from ships' manifests or customs declarations.

The registration method may be defined as the continuous and permanent, compulsory recording of the occurrence and the characteristics of vital events, primarily for their value as legal documents and secondarily for their usefulness as a source of statistics. An examination of the component parts of this definition will clarify the basic differences between this method of making observations for a statistical inquiry and other methods which have been used.

Consider first the "continuous" aspect. Vital statistics are not prevalence but *incidence* statistics — statistics which provide a measure of the occurrences of certain events during or within a specified period of time and, moreover, provide this measure currently. Experience has shown that the only successful method of obtaining a continuous and current record of events which occur throughout a period is the registration method. In order to ensure the current nature of the statistics and their accuracy with respect to dates and characteristics, the registration record should be drawn up as soon after the occurrence of the event as possible. It is apparent that the simplest and quickest way of accomplishing this end is to require the informant to provide the information as soon as the event occurs.

The continous aspect of registration implies also the permanence of the procedure. Registration maintained for short periods and then allowed to lapse will not produce vital statistics which are useful as current incidence statistics.

Continuous, permanent recording of vital events can best be ensured by means of legislation which makes registration compulsory. Such legislation should also provide sanctions for the enforcement of the obligation. Thus, it will be

[4] "The Development and Progress of Statistics in France" by Fernand Faure. *The History of Statistics — Their Development and Progress in Many Countries,* collected and edited by John Koren. Published for the American Statistical Association by The Macmillan Co. of New York, 1918. p. 262-265.

[5] *Vital Statistics: A Memorial Volume of Selections from the Reports and Writings of William Farr, M.D.* Edited for The Sanitary Institute of Great Britain by Noel A. Humphreys. London, 1885. p. xii-xiii.

seen that the registration method is characterized not only by the continuous character of the observations, but also by the compulsory nature of the method. Both provisions are fundamental.

It may be noted that the definition of the registration method given above is applicable equally to ecclesiastical and to civil registration. Determination of the means by which the continuous, permanent, and compulsory provisions are implemented is not requisite to the method. Ecclesiastical registers are set up under religious law, while civil registers operate under civil law. The registration method of obtaining vital statistics is possible under either.

2. The Enumeration Method

(a) *Census Enumeration.* Because of the fact that registration of vital events for legal purposes is an almost universal requirement, statistical processing of registration records has become the accepted or conventional method of producing vital statistics. Nevertheless, alternative methods have been in use from time to time, notably in those countries of the North American continent in which vital registration is considered solely within the competence of each state or provincial government. The attempts made by Canada and the United States to obtain national vital statistics from the population-census enumeration may be of interest. The two histories are very similar.

Canada. In Canada, interest in public health began to emerge in the early eighteen eighties, and naturally this interest focused attention on mortality statistics. However, as R. H. Coats noted,[6] the recording of births and deaths up until 1883 had been the "unchecked and unrewarded" responsibility of clergymen, coroners, clerks of townships, clerks of peace, and so forth, with the result that registration was far from complete. Obviously, some other method of producing mortality statistics seemed required.

In addition to unsystematic registration, the number of births and the number of deaths together with their causes had, from an early year, been collected on the population census schedule. It was thought that once every ten years this enumeration of births and deaths would provide an over-all check on the registration, but results were so poor that in 1911 the method was discontinued. From that time forward, every effort was devoted to establishing the registration method by improving and standardizing the provincial legislation with the aim of securing uniform registration laws and procedures throughout the provinces.

United States. A similar history obtains in the United States. In recognition of the importance of mortality statistics, the Act of 23 May 1850 required the return, by the canvassers of population, of all deaths occurring during the census year.[7] But despite the good intent, statistics of mortality obtained through the census were always defective as shown by the absurdly low ratios of deaths to population which resulted from this method. It was not possible, however, to know how defective the record was until some basis for comparison existed. Such a basis became available when the registration area for deaths was established in 1880 — an area comprising at that time the two States of Massachusetts and New Jersey, the District of Columbia, and 19 cities, the combined population of which was 8,538,366 — 17 per cent of the United States total. In 1880, a death rate of 19.8 was obtained for this area by the registration method, while in the remaining States and cities, which in effect constituted the "non-registration area," a rate of only 13.5 was computed from the census returns. In 1890, the comparative rates for the two areas were 19.6 and 10.6; for 1900, 17.8 against 11.2. It was abundantly clear that the census method would not give results comparable in accuracy with the method of continuous registration, and the mortality census schedule was abandoned after the census of 1900. From that time onward, efforts were concentrated on developing vital statistics by the registration method.

The fundamental deficiency of the census method for collecting vital statistics is that it can, at best, produce returns for the census year and no other. Census years are usually ten

[6] "Beginnings in Canadian Statistics" by R. H. Coats. *The Canadian Historical Review,* Vol. XXVII, No. 2, Toronto, June 1946. p. 120.

[7] *The Federal Registration Service of the United States: Its Development, Problems, and Defects,* by Cressy L. Wilbur. Department of Commerce. Bureau of the Census. Gov. Print. Off., Washington, 1916. p. 8

years apart. For the intercensal years, current vital statistics are not produced by the census method and, thus, that method fails in the first and minimum requisite for vital statistics, i.e., the production of data on a current basis.

Not only does the census method fail to provide intercensal data but, as seen above, it fails also to record completely the occurrence of births and deaths even for the census year. In some cases, the census enumerator may fail to ask the question or, if he asks it, he may misunderstand the answer or record it incorrectly. The answer of the respondent, on the other hand, is affected by the factor of memory. Because of the long retrospective period involved — a year ending with the date of enumeration — the informant may fail to recall the *fact* of the event, but more especially, he may fail to recall correctly the *date* of its occurrence, with the result that the birth or death, if reported, may be allocated to the incorrect time period. In the reporting of the birth and death of infants who are born alive and die within the same calendar year, the effect of the memory factor may be extremely important. It is well known that infants are generally underenumerated. Moreover, in a small-scale investigation[8] of the problems involved in the enumeration procedure as a means of collecting information about deaths, memory was found to be a significant factor especially in connexion with infants who had been born and died in a hospital. Apparently, such infants were never consciously recognized as members of the household.

With respect to deaths of adults, the event itself may have removed the last member of a family, with the result that the death would go unreported at the time of a subsequent enumeration. A somewhat similar result would occur when a death breaks up a family and scatters the surviving members. Since the enumeration of population and hence the filling of a census mortality schedule is on a family basis, the likelihood of such a death being reported at the time of the enumeration is diminished by the disruption of the family. This particular effect is intensified in the case of deaths in boarding houses or hotels, the members of which households are so loosely associated that the chances of deaths being remembered and reported at the census are slight.

Quite aside from the underenumeration and the consequent deficiencies of coverage in terms of recording all vital events which occurred in the specified period, there is the problem of the adequacy of the information about each event which can conveniently be obtained by the census method. Only a limited amount of information can be requested at a census if the cost of the procedure is not to be prohibitive and if the returns are to be manageable. Therefore, except for the most general inquiries, many details of medical or public-health interest most likely could not be included on a census schedule.

The recognized decrease in trustworthiness of data with the passage of time must also be borne in mind in evaluating the enumeration method. Details recorded immediately, or within a short interval after the occurrence of the event, naturally tend to be more accurate than those dependent on memory.

(b) *The Survey*. The census method of securing vital statistics is one example, and the most extensive, of the retrospective type of survey by enumeration. The census method, which takes advantage of the census organization, usually requires reports on the experience of one calendar year preceding the date of the enumeration. Since faults of memory are an important factor in the success or failure of this type of procedure, there is reason to believe that results might be improved if a shorter period of experience were investigated. However, because of seasonal variations, vital statistics are required for time periods which together can produce an unbroken series of data for an annual period. To produce annual data by the survey method using shorter retrospective time periods would, therefore, require a number of contiguous surveys distributed throughout the year.

In meeting these requirements, the basic advantage provided by the census, that is, the advantage of an existing nation-wide organization manned by trained personnel, would of course disappear, and the ultimate cost of replacing the registration method by continuous surveying would be prohibitive. If sampling is resorted to, as it usually must be in surveys for reasons of

[8] Conducted in the District of Columbia by the United States National Office of Vital Statistics in 1949.

economy, there is the problem of designing the sample in such a way that due consideration is given to population differentials and mobility and so as to provide data for the small geographic units which are the necessary basis of public-health work. Because of such factors, the survey method appears to be ill-suited to the collection of vital statistics on a routine and permanent basis.

Periodic surveys have been employed, however, to secure *ad hoc* information on births and deaths in areas where the registration method has not yet been established or where it is very defective. In such situations, surveys have the distinct advantage of making available some vital statistics not otherwise obtainable and of securing at the same time the corresponding population.

A very good example of the application of the survey method in an under-developed area is found in the experience of Southern Rhodesia. The impossibility of conducting a complete enumeration of the widely scattered, illiterate population of this largely unmapped territory, and of establishing a registration system which could produce vital statistics in the near future, led to the application of sampling survey methods. Beginning in August 1948, enumeration of sample villages was carried out by trained field staff, aided by interpreters. The information collected included (1) the total number of persons who had died during the twelve months preceding the field officer's visit, and (2) from each female over puberty (*a*) the number of live births she had had during the previous twelve months and (*b*) the number of children under 1 year of age who had died during the previous twelve months. The natality rates which were derived appeared to be somewhat overstated, while the general and infant mortality rates varied widely from district to district. At the time of the reports quoted, the results of the survey awaited more intensive study and the returns from the next survey.[9]

The use of sample surveys to obtain demographic information for India has been described by P. C. Mahalanobis and Agit Das Gupta of the Indian Statistical Institute, in a paper (United Nations document E/CONF.13/294) prepared for the World Population Conference held in Rome, 31 August-10 September 1954.

3. *Analytical Method — Estimation of Vital Rates Using Census Data*

If it is assumed that the derivation of birth, death, and marriage rates is the object of collecting vital statistics, then there is still another method which could be employed to yield these bare facts. This method is a mathematical one, based on an analysis of the returns of two consecutive censuses of population. The census returns employed must of necessity be the result of very accurate and dependable enumerations, which have produced reliable age and marital-status distributions of the population. If certain assumptions are made regarding migration and the reliability of the enumeration is assured, data from censuses of population can be used to derive information on the approximate number of births, deaths, and marriages which have occurred in this population over the intercensal period. This indirect method yields aggregates only and these solely for the year of the census. It does not, therefore, justify its consideration as a method of developing vital statistics which by definition must be current and continuous. However, it is a method which has been developed for estimating vital statistics in Brazil[10] for example and, as such, should be mentioned for its applicability to the relatively rare areas which have non-existent or deficient registration statistics but a reliable census of population.

4. *The Vital Statistics System Defined*

It will be clear from the above discussion that to meet the criterion of providing reliable annual, national and local vital statistics on a continuous basis and with the least expense, the registration method has no peer. When in addition,

[9] "Sampling Surveys in Central Africa" by J. R. H. Shaul. *Journal of the American Statistical Association*, Vol. 47, No. 258, June 1952. p. 239-254. "Sample Census of the Indigenous African Population 1948". *Economic and Statistical Bulletin of Southern Rhodesia.* Central African Statistical Office, Vol. XVII. No. 8, 21 July 1949. p. 7.

[10] *Methods of Using Census Statistics for the Calculation of Life Tables and Other Demographic Measures (with Applications to the Population of Brazil)*, by Giorgio Mortara. United Nations. Department of Social Affairs. Document ST/SOA/Series A/7, November 1949. 60 p. Sales No. 1950.XIII.3)

the need for vital records for their legal value is recognized, the development and maintenance of registers for both legal and statistical purposes emerges as the method best adapted to producing vital statistics. Surveys in connexion with the census enumeration of population or on an *ad hoc* basis can be used as interim arrangements to secure current estimates of vital rates or for evaluating the efficiency of the registration system but, in the last analysis, the firm and permanent basis for vital statistics must be registration records.

The merits of the registration method set forth above scarcely take into consideration the fundamental fact which is the compelling need for vital records themselves. Even if equally adequate vital statistics could be obtained as efficiently by the enumeration method mentioned above, the indispensable nature of the original record of birth, death, marriage and divorce would remain.

Once the premise is accepted that the registration method is the cornerstone of vital statistics, one may procced to a consideration of the vital-statistics system itself. The word "system" usually implies the interaction of component parts to fulfil a common purpose. This is precisely the meaning it is meant to convey in connexion with vital statistics.

Functionally, according to the concept, a vital-statistics system begins with the legal registration of vital events and culminates with the distribution of vital statistics to the potential users. In between, there is found (1) statistical recording and reporting which is the procedure of transcribing registered data for statistical purposes and of transmitting them to the statistical authorities, (2) the collection process, which brings together and controls the receipt of the statistical reports on vital events, (3) the compilation procedure which embraces the classifying and tabulating of the observations, (4) the presentation of the statistics in tabular or graphic form, and (5) the analysis of these data in terms of the problems to be studied. . . .

The vital-statistics system defined above in terms of functions still requires definition in terms of "events". It will be recalled that, in the beginning, vital statistics were concerned with baptisms, burials, and weddings. Although, with the coming of civil registration, marriages were often included in the original registration acts, the public-health concept which dominated the growth of vital statistics in Europe and the Americas tended to limit the fields to statistics of deaths and to a lesser degree to statistics of births. Statistics of marriages were considered somewhat secondary in importance, while those of divorce did not even exist in many cases. This restrictive influence of public-health dominance on vital statistics is set forth in *Measures Relating to Vital Records and Vital Statistics,*[11] in which it is said that:

> To consider vital statistics as entirely a concern of public health not only overlooks historical precedents from colonial days, but fails to meet present-day necessities for stressing the 'competent evidence' character of vital records. At the same time, this concept tends to limit the subject matter of vital statistics to birth and death registration, since marriage and divorce registration can be considered only remotely as a public-health measure.
>
> But just as public-health needs for vital statistics aided the substitution of "deaths" for "burials" and "births" for "baptisms," the need for statistics to meet the requirements of demographers — whose interest was and is primarily population movement and analysis — has tended to broaden the field beyond the confines of public health. In response to all of these needs . . . "vital statistics" has come to mean statistics of live birth, death, foetal death (stillbirth), marriage, divorce, adoption, legitimation, recognition, annulment and legal separation.

In summary then, it may be said that the vital-statistics system includes the legal registration, the statistical recording and reporting of the occurrence of, and the collection, compilation, presentation, analysis, and distribution of statistics pertaining to "vital events," i.e., live births, deaths, foetal deaths, marriages, divorces, adoptions, legitimations, recognitions, annulments and legal separations. From time to time, events other than those mentioned here may be recorded and processed in the vital-statistics system of a country, or priority may be given to the registration of only certain events of those mentioned. Nevertheless, statistics on all of the

[11] *Message from The President of the United States Transmitting Report of the Bureau of the Budget.* House Document No. 242, 78th Congress, 1st Session. Gov. Print. Off., Washington, 1943. p. 98.

events mentioned should represent the goal of the vital-statistics system. This concept of the vital-statistics system has been given international approval in Principle 101 of the United Nations *Principles for a Vital Statistics System.*[12]

C. Present Status of Vital Statistics

It is clear from the history of vital statistics that the establishment of vital registration, civil or ecclesiastical, does not always guarantee that vital statistics will be forthcoming. It will be recalled that over 100 years elapsed from the initiation of registration in England in 1537 to the first use of vital records for statistical purposes by John Graunt in 1662. Moreover, the establishment of a vital-statistics system does not guarantee the production of reliable or useful vital statistics. In some cases, vital statistics are produced currently with no regard for the fact that they are inadequate to meet many national needs and unreliable for international comparison. These defects may be classified into three general types as follows:

1. Complete Absence of Data

In order to gain some rough conception of the past availability of vital statistics, we may quote the estimates made by Walter F. Willcox.[13] According to Willcox, by 1833, births and deaths were being registered for less than 100 million people, or about one tenth of the world's population. During the ensuing 100 years, that is, by 1933, nearly 1,000 million, or one half of the world's population, were part of a "world-registration area" and were required to register births and deaths. Although it by no means follows that vital statistics are available whenever vital events are registered, by inference, vital statistics could also have been available for one half the world. Mr. Willcox' estimates terminate here, but if one analyzes the coverage of the United Nations *Demographic Yearbook* which publishes essentially all available vital statistics, it is found that the tables on total births and deaths for the period 1935-1950 include data for 132 areas, representing 55 per cent of the world's population in 1951. These data, substantiating Mr. Willcox' estimates, would indicate that some 300 years of experience have resulted in the establishment of vital-statistics systems which can produce minimum results for only a little over one half of the world's population. The need for developmental measures is obvious.

2. Fragmentary Data

Fragmentary data may be the result of one or more of at least three major causes. The first of these may be described as incomplete geographic coverage at the national level, that is, exclusion from final tabulations of reports from certain parts of the country, in an attempt to improve the quality of the tabulations by limiting them to areas of known reliability, or by restricting registration to selected areas. The unsystematic and sporadic collection of reports from subnational areas may also be a factor in incomplete geographic coverage.

Incomplete ethnic coverage, which is usually due to the exclusion of certain racial or ethnic groups from the provisions of the registration law or to failure to enforce registration and reporting for such groups, constitutes a second cause of fragmentary data.

Finally, and perhaps the most fundamental though often unrecognized cause of fragmentary information, is a general deficiency or incompleteness of registration and a consequent shortage in the number of events tabulated.

3. Non-Comparable Data

Lack of international comparability in the matter of definitions and concepts is a third major defect of vital statistics, and this may extend through the definition of the events to the definition of informational items as simple as "age" and as complex as "cause of death". Variation in the number and types of items on which data are collected and the manner in which these items are coded, classified, and tabulated, add to the potential lack of comparability.

Lack of internal (national) comparability may be due to the same factors of dissimilar definitions, concepts, codes, classification schemes, and tabulating procedures as are operative at the in-

[12] *Principles for a Vital Statistics System; Recommendations for the Improvement and Standardization of Vital Statistics.* United Nations. Statistical Office. Document ST/STAT/SER. M/19, 26 August 1953. p. 4. (Sales No. 1953.XVII.8)

[13] *Studies in American Demography* by Walter F. Willcox. Ithaca, Cornell University Press, 1940. p. 200.

ternational level. Statistics produced by a decentralized national system are particularly subject to this type of defect, although even in a centralized system the changing of concepts and definitions over time introduces lack of comparability into a time series for the same area.

The present status of vital statistics throughout the world may, therefore, be summarized as follows. For a large segment of the world's population, vital statistics are non-existent; for another, they are fragmentary for one reason or another; for the third group of countries, vital statistics are obtainable, but the accuracy or quality of the fundamental information varies over a wide range and the definitions, concepts, and classifications employed are not always comparable from country to country or even from one part of a country to another. . . . Irrespective of the cause involved, the fact remains that vital statistics for a large proportion of the world's population are deficient and measures designed to improve these data are desirable. . . .

The establishment or improvement of a system of vital statistics depends on demonstration of the need for such a system. The need for the vital-statistics system will, in turn, be based on a demand for the products which the system will yield. Since registration of vital events is the initial and fundamental component of the system, there should be first a demonstrated use for the product of this function, namely a need for the vital records of live birth, death, foetal death, marriage, divorce, and such other events as may be registrable. Secondly, there should be a well justified need for statistics based on these records. These uses for both records and statistics must be important enough to justify governmental action to meet the needs.

It has been demonstrated that the development of vital-statistics systems in the various countries came about not by chance but in response to needs for records and statistics. The demands for vital records stem from their value as legal documents. The need for legal documents with evidentiary value arose as society became more complex and man began to be required to prove his right to his name, his citizenship, and his place in society, especially with respect to the privileges and duties of a member. The more complex the society, the more uses were found for records to prove facts which in previous years may not have required any type of proof or at the most a verbal certification. It need hardly be pointed out that needs for vital records change with the times.

Recognition of the value of vital records as a source of statistics was slower in developing than was their value as vital records. Vital statistics, like all statistics and unlike vital records, are not ends in themselves but tools for the study and understanding of other phenomena. The utilization of vital statistics as administrative and research tools stimulated both demographic research and public-health planning, with the consequent reciprocal effect on statistics of births and deaths, and to a lesser degree, on those of marriage. Without incentives in the form of important uses which, in their turn, create demands, there would be little reason for governments to establish and maintain expensive vital statistics systems.

Since the vital-statistics programme in any country requires constant revision and augmentation to adjust it to changing demands, an attempt has been made below to set forth many of the known needs for and uses of the products of the system. This comprehensive discussion is designed to be a check-list or guide for administrators who are seeking the fullest utilization of the vital-statistics system. The discussion is divided into two main sections, the first of which deals with the need for vital records and the second with the uses of vital statistics.

A. Uses of Vital records

1. Use to the Individual

Records of birth, death, marriage, and divorce, as well as those of legitimation, recognition, adoption, and so forth, are of paramount use to the individual. The basic registration document or a certified copy thereof has legal significance to the person concerned, which is equalled by few of the other documents a man may acquire in his lifetime. A review of the principal uses which the individual makes of records of live birth, death, foetal death, marriage and divorce, namely their use as proof of the *fact*, the *date*, and the *place* of occurrence of the event, will show why this is so. For convenience, the discussion is restricted to the five vital events noted above, but it should be pointed out that records of other vital events such as adoptions, legitimations, recognitions, and so forth, are used in much the same way.

(a) *Live-birth Record.* The establishment of the identity of an individual, that is, the proof of the facts of his birth, is probably the most important of the uses to which a birth record can be placed. The birth-registration record is especially adaptable to this role, because it is a legal record and it will normally include the individual's name and that of his father and of his mother, together with certain other identifying information. Legal proof of birth is required primarily for establishing family relationships such as parentage, legitimacy, dependency, ancestry or lineage — any of which might be necessary for settling inheritance or insurance claims or for arranging the transfer of property.

The establishment of rights contingent upon attainment of a certain age is often dependent on the proof of age or, in other words, the *date* of birth. Privileges such as being allowed to enter school or to obtain permission to work — especially in certain industries or in government civil service — are often contingent upon proof of age; as is the obligation to serve in, or the right to be excused from service in, the armed forces; the right to apply for a license such as that required to operate a motor vehicle or to carry firearms; to enter certain professions; to marry without parental consent; to exercise voting rights; to qualify for social-security pensions payable only at a specified age; to enter into legal contracts; and to establish inheritance rights contingent upon age.

The birth-registration record is also the legal document which will establish nationality or, more correctly, citizenship by birth. It may be necessary to establish such facts in order to obtain passports for foreign travel; to qualify for voting privileges; to be employed in government service or in restricted industries; to own property; to obtain exemption from alien restrictions, or conversely, if an alien, to obtain exemption from taxes or military service in the country of residence.

(b) *Death Record.* The primary use of proof of death registration is, of course, its role in the issuance of a burial permit, for which it is a prerequisite in almost every country of the world. There are, however, other important uses of the proof of death. Settlement of inheritance or insurance claims, for example, requires proof of the death of the decedent, as well as proof of inheritance rights on the part of the beneficiaries. Claims for family allowances of various types may be dependent on proof of the death of the family wage-earner.

The date of death of the testator, in conjunction with the date of birth of a legatee, may be required to prove rights of inheritance contingent upon age. It also may be valuable in avoiding inheritance taxes enforced as of a certain date, in disproving paternity, and for other uses, primarily legal in character.

The use of death records to certify to the exact location at which the death occurred may be useful in connexion with accident cases in which some claim is to be made contingent upon place of occurrence. On a geographic basis, proof of place of death in terms of political units might be of importance in connexion with the levying of inheritance taxes or the establishing of inheritance rights in the absence of a will. In some countries, the exact place of death may be significant in establishing the right to be buried or cremated in a specially designated place.

(c) *Foetal-death Record.* The record of a foetal death, which proves the *fact,* the *date,* and the *place* of delivery, is of limited use in a legal sense. One possible role which can be visualized is its use in establishing certain legal questions contingent upon family composition and birth order — questions which may deal with rights to inheritance and such.

(d) *Marriage Record.* The *fact* of the occurrence of a marriage must be proven to ensure legal responsibility for family support, to establish rights to inheritance or pensions, to confer legitimacy, and to help prove ancestry and lineage. The *date* of marriage, in conjunction with the birth date of offspring, is essential for proving legitimacy and, by itself, to qualify for certain pensions or social-security payments. The date of marriage may also provide indirect or supplementary evidence for the registration of a birth after the expiration of the normal registration period. The *place* of marriage may be a factor in establishing the legality of the ceremony.

(e) *Divorce Record.* The *fact* of divorce is required to establish the right to remarry. This is perhaps the principal use of the divorce registration, as it is of the record of annulment, although either may be a factor in inheritance litigation or in obtaining release from financial obligations incurred by the other party. Like that on the marriage records, some information on the divorce records may also be of value as evidence to support a request for a delayed registration of a birth.

The *date* when a divorce became effective is of importance in establishing paternity or the legality of a subsequent marriage. It also may be required to establish rights contingent upon marital status and age and to prove absence of responsibility of a financial nature.

The *place* where the divorce was granted is especially important from the standpoint of establishing the legality of the divorce in other jurisdictions.

2. Use to Operating Agencies

Records of births, deaths, and marriages are useful to governmental agencies for a variety of administrative purposes. The most common of these will be presented below in terms of each event.

(a) *Birth Record.* Public-health programmes of post-natal care for the mother and the child usually have their starting point in the birth register and the corresponding birth indexes. Next to their legal role, this is perhaps the most important use to which birth records can be placed — a use which has been described in terms of the City of New York as follows:[14]

Because it is required that births be reported within two days, it is possible to place sufficient information from birth records in the hands of the visiting nurse so that she can arrange to make a home visit to any mother and child, not attended by a private physician, immediately after their return from the hospital. Every day the Statistical Division of the Bureau of Vital Records sends to each district health center a list of the births to mothers residing in that district as reported the previous day. These lists are prepared from index tabulating cards and give the name, home address, place of birth, color, and sex of each infant born alive, together with information regarding the number of this child in the family, its birth weight, and whether the case was that of a private practitioner or a general service (ward) case. From a study of these lists the visiting nurse in each district determines just which mothers and babies should be called upon and, should selection be necessary, preference is given to those whose records show that they are either first-born or were underweight at birth.

Vaccination and immunization programmes, as well as those for the physically handicapped or premature babies, also can make use of the birth register for their more effective implementation.

(b) *Death Record.* Control programmes for infectious diseases within the family and within the community often depend on the death-registration report for their initiation. For example, measures to find cases of tuberculosis within a family may be undertaken upon the registration of the death of a member from that disease. In areas where major epidemic diseases such as smallpox or plague have been eradicated, the appearance of a death from one of these causes will set in motion a chain of actions designed to uncover all possible contacts which the decedent may have had during the time he had had the disease.

Public-safety, accident-prevention, and crime-eradication programmes make use of the death-registration records in somewhat the same way as does the public-health programme.

The death-registration record also finds a use in clearing social-security files, morbidity-case registers, electoral lists, military-service and tax registers, and in completing records for medical study of disease processes. Police checks for missing persons and curtailment of rationing or benefit programmes which should terminate at death are also partially dependent on the use of death registers.

(c) *Birth, Death, Marriage, Divorce.* The two essential elements of the system of popula-

[14] "The Use of Vital Records in the Reduction of Fetal, Infant, and Maternal Mortality" by Thomas J. Duffield and Louis Weiner. *American Journal of Public Health*, Vol. 32, No. 8, August 1942. p. 803-810.

tion registers are the universal, simultaneous registration of all residents of a country and the continuous maintenance of individual or family records to show each change in physical, civil, or geographic status, such as change of address or of name, loss or addition to family, and change in marital status. The first element is provided either by the census enumeration of population or by a special registration. The second component of the system is supplied in part by the officially authenticated records of birth, death, marriage, divorce, annulment, and so forth. The role of vital records in maintaining population registers is, therefore, one of their important uses wherever such systems exist.

B. National Uses of Vital Statistics

The multiple uses of the legal record of birth, death, marriage, and divorce in the life of the individual, as well as in the activities of governmental and private agencies which carry out public-health, welfare, and other programmes, have been described above. The legal significance of the records for proving the *fact,* the *time,* or the *place* of the occurrence of an event cannot be disputed. But this important function of providing evidentiary records is not the ultimate aim of the system from the point of view of statistics. Unless the information on the records is used also for statistical purposes, much of its value will be neglected.

For the individual himself, whose needs were met on so many fronts by the record of the vital event, vital statistics hold relatively little interest, except in so far as they may be used as tools in planning, operating, and evaluating programmes. On the other hand, the activities of official governmental agencies, of commercial interests, and of the workers in the public-health field are dependent in a multitude of ways on the statistics derived from vital records. This role of vital statistics in national affairs may be discussed under two principal headings, namely (1) the use of vital statistics as basic elements in research — both demographic and medical; and (2) their role as indispensable elements in public administration and as determinants of administrative action. Much has been written about the dominant needs and priorities of one of these "consumers" with respect to another. But, as will be seen below, there is great need in each field of activity — needs which can be met by no other branch of statistics. Hence, in the development of the vital-statistics system, no single use should be allowed to obscure the others.

1. Vital Statistics as Elements in Research

(a) *Demographic Research.* One of the most important uses of vital statistics is their role in the demographic analysis of population for economic and social purposes. The study of population movement and of the interrelationships of demographic with economic and social factors is of fundamental importance to society and will become increasingly more so as the advances in technology and public health focus attention on demographic problems. The three directions which such an analysis may take are (1) population estimation, (2) population projection, and (3) analytical studies.

Population Estimation. From the most elementary viewpoint, knowledge of the number of persons inhabiting the earth and their distribution thereon is fundamental. Planning of transportation facilities, agricultural production, production and distribution of economic commodities, employment, housing, and public-health programmes are impossible in the absence of a population base figure. This basic population figure has its origin in the almost universal national censuses of population but, since complete censuses are costly, they are usually carried out only at intervals of ten years. During the intercensal periods, population figures must be estimated with the help of vital statistics. The census figure, increased by births and, if available, immigrants, and decreased by deaths and emigrants, gives an estimate of the population of the area. For this crucial segment of information which makes popluation estimation possible, the demographer must depend primarily on "human book-keeping" [15] — the accounting of births and deaths which is vital statistics.

To know the size of a population at any chosen moment is desirable and useful for many pur-

[15] *Vital Statistics and Public Health Work in the Tropics Including Supplement on the Genealogy of Vital Statistics* by P. Granville Edge. Baillière, Tindall and Cox, London, 1947. p. 4.

poses. But to know also its composition in terms of age, sex, and marital status, for example, is even more desirable in view of the requirements for economic and social research. Vital statistics provide the basis for an annual adjustment of the census enumeration, considering the current mortality, nuptiality, and natality patterns, and producing thereby estimates of population by age, sex and marital status.

The estimation of population by using data on natural increase is recognized as the most reliable method, provided that the registration statistics are reasonably accurate. The exact techniques and assumptions involved in the method will be found elsewhere,[16] but it should be pointed out that the degree to which application of vital statistics may provide estimates of population distributed by such factors as race, nationality, and so forth, is limited primarily by the amount of detail which is recorded at the original registration, the definitions employed at that time, and the types of tabulations made. For purposes of population estimation, the value of vital statistics, based on complete registration, accurate and prompt statistical reporting, and a broad tabulation programme, cannot be questioned.

Population Projections. Important as is the knowledge of the present status of the population, the knowledge of its probable size, geographic distribution, and composition at a future date is even more important for purposes of economic and social planning. Planning in these fields has focused attention on the need for trustworthy projections of population, in turn based on projections of vital-statistics data. The analysis of the effect of the trends of natality, mortality, nuptiality, and divorce on the size and distribution of population and on the formation of families provides the material from which future population estimates may be computed.

Analytical Studies. Closely linked with the projecting of population is the use of vital statistics in analysing demographic situations and in predicting future developments. There is also great scientific interest in analysing the size and the course of the birth, death, marriage, and divorce rates to elucidate their influence on various social and political problems within and between geographic areas. Marriage statistics are not of interest solely in relation to the birth rate and to population increase, but also as indicators of national economic trends and of local *mores*. Statistics of births are primarily factors in a study of population size and characteristics, but they also have a bearing on social problems as revealed in studies of legitimacy and fertility by social differentials. Mortality statistics are not only the most complex but also the most interesting indices from the viewpoint of their reflection of public-health and sanitary conditions. The calculation and study of indices such as these as well as life-table functions, reproduction rates, cohort analyses, and so forth, are all techniques for demographic analysis.

All of these analytical techniques demand detailed and consistent series of vital statistics, complete and accurate within and among themselves. The interrelationship of all the demographic factors and, in turn, their individual and combined relationship with economic and social factors, forms the basis of demographic research from which population policy is derived.

(b) *Medical Research.* Very closely allied to the role of vital statistics in demographic research are their uses by the medical profession engaged in research. Medical and pharmaceutical research, like demographic research, requires a certain number of guideposts. This guidance may be found in part at least in mortality and natality statistics.

Investigations into such causes of death as pneumonia, cancer, and cardiovascular-renal disease, to name only a few, have been initiated by concern over the loss of human life from these causes, as revealed by the death rates. New remedies have been sought and found to decrease the loss of life from diabetes, for example, while appendicitis as a cause of death has been largely eliminated as a result of the research initiated on the strength of the once-high death rate. Statistics of occupational diseases, such as lead poisoning, have led to the establishment of industrial-hygiene measures. The levels of

[16] *Methods of Estimating Total Population for Current Dates,* Manual I of Manuals on Methods of Estimating Population. United Nations. Department of Social Affairs, Population Division. Document ST/SOA/Series A/10, 1952. 45 p. (Sales No. 1952.XIII.5)

maternal and infant mortality rates have influenced the medical profession profoundly in its approach to problems of pregnancy and post-natal care.

It may truthfully be said that virtually every large-scale problem in preventive medicine has been brought to light — in part at least — by statistics of death, and further that the adequacy of remedial or curative action is, in the last analysis, reflected in these same statistics. The trend of the tuberculosis death rate in response to streptomycin, that of malaria in response to DDT, and that of the maternal mortality rate in response to the antibiotics clearly delineate the second stage of this process.

2. Vital Statistics in Administration — Public and Private

Statistics in general and vital statistics in particular are fundamental elements in public and private administration, which is the machinery and methods underlying all official programmes of economic and social development in either "developed" or "under-developed" areas. According to a study of the standards and techniques of public administration made by a special committee of the United Nations Technical Assistance Administration,[17] "little can be done [in government planning, which may be the most determining influence in any programme of economic and social development or administrative reform] without at least a reasonable minimum of basic data and reliable statistics. . . . Basic statistics will have to be made available in the . . . demographic and social [field] showing birth, deaths, [and] morbidity. . . ." The Committee goes on to say that "the most pointed statistics which might help weigh the extent to which progress has been made are the . . . infant mortality and average life span. . . ." No more explicit or far-reaching use could be set forth for vital statistics.

The role of vital statistics in over-all planning and evaluation of economic and social development is the most important use to which this body of data may be placed. However, there are other less far-reaching uses in connexion with specific aspects of a nation's life which are also of major importance. The first of these is the use of vital statistics in the field of public health.

(a) *As Used by Public-Health Organizations.* Nationally and internationally, statistics of births, deaths, and foetal deaths are required for planning, operating, and evaluating programmes in the field of public health. Public health has, in the past, relied almost entirely upon statistics of mortality by cause of death and personal characteristics to determine the direction and scope of its programmes. Both progress and regression in the programme are subject to measurement by vital indices. The problem of infant and maternal mortality is reflected in the birth rate, in the infant mortality rate, and in the maternal mortality rate. Other rates are relevant to other aspects of the public-health programme.

Infant Mortality. The infant mortality rate is recognized as perhaps the most sensitive index of the effectiveness of health and sanitation programmes, since it measures the loss of life during the first year when environment and personal care are the most influential factors in its maintenance. The infant mortality rate reflects also the effectiveness of public-health nursing programmes and, indirectly, the adequacy of prenatal care. It is the one rate which can and does serve the local health officer as his programme guide, at least until it is brought within the range where factors other than sanitation and environmental care begin to be prominent.

The magnitude of the pregnancy-wastage problem, involving all foetal, neo-natal, and infant deaths, is one engaging much attention at the present time, and one which is related to the statistics of live birth, stillbirth, and infant death. The definition of "prematurity" at birth, the criteria to be employed, the chances of life under such conditions — all are derived from an analysis of vital statistics tabulated by such characteristics as duration of pregnancy, weight at birth, duration of life, and the like. Correlation of the infant-death reports with the birth record will reveal, in addition, the characteristics of the mother such as age, marital status, race, socio-

[17] *Standards and Techniques of Public Administration with special reference to Technical Assistance for Under-developed Countries.* Report by the Special Committee on Public Administration Problems. United Nations. Technical Assistance Administration. Document ST/TAA/M/1, 20 November 1951. 65 p. (Sales No. 1951.II.B.7)

economic status, and so forth, which may have a bearing on the outcome of the pregnancy.

Foetal Mortality. Although true measures of foetal mortality are not yet available, due to problems of definitions and of difficulties in attaining moderately complete registration . . . it still remains that such data as are available on "late foetal mortality" have been influential in determining public-health programmes. In countries where infant mortality has been reduced to a minimum, it is obvious that the attention of the medical and public-health profession might well begin to focus on foetal mortality. The foreward to a report on *Major Problems in Fetal Mortality*[18] notes that there is little statistical information available on the subject and that there are many difficulties in obtaining complete statistics on foetal deaths, but it goes on to say:

> Rough estimates indicate that fetal mortality today represents a medical and social problem of equal or greater magnitude than that of infant mortality at the turn of the century. Because of the progress made in the reduction of infant mortality, the health interests are now in a position to turn their attention to the problems of pregnancy wastage.

Maternity Mortality. Excessively high maternal mortality rates suggest a need for further study, not only of the causes of maternal mortality, which is a medical research problem, but of the circumstances under which these deaths take place. In this connexion, tabulations of maternal deaths by type of attendant may reveal that the incidence of maternal deaths among home deliveries is excessive and would, therefore, justify increased appropriations for hospital facilities or other preventive measures. It will be noted that both the infant mortality rate and the maternal mortality rate, which are of such fundamental importance to the health authorities, are based on births. This means that they are independent of population estimates (or lack of them) which in so many instances, especially for small areas, limits the compilation of public-health indices to census years. In the case of infant and maternal mortality, the health authorities have in the vital-statistics compilations the elements for significant studies. Analyses may be made of the geographic distribution of births; the exact place of occurrence, i.e., in hospitals or clinics, or at home; attended or unattended by a physician or midwife; the socio-economic status of the parents; the age of the parents; and the question of legitimacy. Important statistical elements required for the intelligent planning of programmes for maternal and infant care can be found in the statistics of births and deaths.

Cause of Death. In the absence of adequate morbidity statistics, the problems of tuberculosis, cancer, and malaria control, for example, are first delineated in terms of the cause-specific death rates.

Hospitals for the care of tuberculosis patients are usually established as a result of concern for the high incidence of the disease as expressed by the death rate. Private organizations for the control of tuberculosis, for example, utilize the specific death rates to establish the urgency of their programmes and also to evaluate their success or failure. Tuberculosis death rates by age, sex, and race have been useful not only in determining the allocation of funds for research and treatment, but also in directing public-health education through the schools and through the family.

Cancer mortality rates have highlighted the need for adequate medical care and also for research into the causes of the disease and possible new types of therapy. Cancer death rates specific for certain factors such as occupation, race, and age have been used to direct the programmes toward the most effective utilization of resources. They have also been used, as has the tuberculosis death rate, to bring the problem to the attention of the public and to delineate the field in which health education may be most effective.

Statistics on deaths from injurious drugs or from poisoning have been instrumental in obtaining passage of legislation designed to protect the individual. The elimination of lead from a formula for paint used on children's toys and

[18] *Major Problems in Fetal Mortality,* by J. Yerushalmy and Jessie M. Bierman. Federal Security Agency, Public Health Service, National Office of Vital Statistics. Vital Statistics — Special Reports. Selected Studies, Vol. 33, No. 13, Washington, 22 May 1952. p. 215.

furniture was a direct result of the tracing of deaths from lead poisoning (which showed up in death rates) to the chewing of articles painted with a specific paint.

Communicable diseases, such as malaria and typhoid fever, constitute major public-health problems but they are, fortunately, subject to direct control by public-health methods. The draining of swamps, the screening of houses, the installation of sanitary water supplies and sewers together with provision for their maintenance, the eradication of the vector — all these require first an evaluation of the problem and its geographic distribution.

It may be said that practically every public-health problem — be it environmental sanitation, communicable-disease control, or nutrition — has been revealed more clearly through analysis of vital statistics data. P. Granville Edge has said, *"Vital records are the intelligence services of public health* provided an organized system ensures (*a*) the prompt assembly of reliable facts, (*b*) the intelligent interpretation of data, and (*c*) that information thus made available is acted upon with promptitude."[19] Delineation of public-health problems is thus only a first step. With the initation of programmes to ameliorate conditions comes the need for additional statistics to measure both the progress achieved and the concomitant administrative costs involved. Finally, the evaluation of results and the reassessment of the programme complete the circle.

(b) *As Used by Government Agencies Other Than Public Health.* Vital statistics are also utilized extensively in the programmes of governmental agencies other than those concerned with public health.

Birth, death, and marriage rates — both current and projected — as well as data on family size and structure, are essential to intelligent and financially wise planning in the field of public housing. No other indices provide current guides to the size and distribution of population segments necessary for the location of new housing.

Provision of the physical facilities for education, as well as training of teachers, must be coordinated with the need expressed in the trend of the birth and marriage rates and their geographic differentials. Public insurance enterprises, as well as social-security systems, are directly dependent on life tables which, in turn, are computed from population and death rates. Unless the basic vital statistics are both reliable and adequate, the computed values will be in error and the systems of insurance unsound financially, or the public itself will suffer through payment of excessive premiums. In addition to the role of the life tables in insurance enterprises, the incidence of widowhood, remarriage, and orphanhood also plays a large part in determining types of insurance coverage.

Provision of food supplies in areas where they are government-controlled or rationed is usually planned in accordance with the probable need as reflected in the birth and death rates. Likewise, in long-range planning for economic development, it may sometimes be necessary to rely on the birth and death rates to provide some idea of the potential supply of labour in various geographic and occupational sectors.

In many of these questions, not only birth and death statistics are involved; statistics of marriage and divorce are also of great importance. In instance after instance, various types of vital statistics have been major factors in initiating programmes in the field of education, housing, welfare, and so forth, or in affecting the course of programmes already underway.

(c) *As Used by Commercial Interests.* Perhaps the most important consumer of vital statistics in the commercial field is the insurance agency. Actuarial science is rooted in vital statistics, and the success or failure of the enterprise may rest on the reliability of the statistics and the estimates made upon them.

The problem of gauging the requirements of the public in terms of consumer goods such as medicine, food, clothing, furniture, etc., is one which depends to a large extent on vital statistics for its solution. If the birth rate remains high over a long period, it may safely be assumed that the demand for maternity clothing will remain high, that medicine, food, clothing, equipment and furniture for infants will remain in demand, that housing and house furnishings will be at a premium. Projecting high birth rates ahead, commercial enterprises may safely plan

[19] *Vital Statistics and Public Health Work in the Tropics . . . op. cit.* p. 3.

for enlarged stocks of clothing for growing children, for larger houses, for an increase in the demand for toys and other play equipment, for automobiles, and so forth. Mention may also be made of the market-analysis function of advertising agencies, an analysis in which they employ vital statistics, especially marriage and birth rates.

In addition to its over-all effect on population growth, the current death rate and its geographic distribution is important to the business planning of various commercial interests — from the drug manufacturer and the hospital administrator to the undertaker and the casket maker.

The number of marriages has importance for the building industry, and the trend of the marriage rate influences the business prospects of jewellers and of clothing and furniture manufacturers.

The range of business enterprises which are interested to some extent in vital statistics is very wide. The examples given above are set forth to suggest the extent of the commercial uses which may be found for these products of the vital-statistics system.

C. International Uses of Vital Statistics

The above discussion of the needs and uses of vital records and statistics is largely in terms of the individual and the state or national government. Little if anything has been said with respect to the uses of vital statistics from the international viewpoint — the larger aim which G. H. Knibbs pointed out in the Appendix to the Statistician's Report on the 1911 *Census of the Commonwealth of Australia.*[20] More than forty years ago, Knibbs realized the need for a systematic world-wide study of population statistics when he said:

> Only by a sufficiently wide survey of human facts can the required *norms* of all sorts be established, norms which represent the characters of the great unit constituted by the aggregation of all the nations. It is only in the comparatively slow secular changes of these norms, that the drift of mankind in the gross can be unequivocally revealed; when that drift is ascertained, the quicker and the more marked variations of individual nations and populations can then be forced to disclose the real significance of their differentiating tendencies.

[20] Vol. I, issued under the Authority of the Minister of State for Home and Territories, Melbourne, 1917. 504 p.

He went on to set forth the uses he saw for statistics of population, and his statement stands even today as a classic. It reads as follows:

> In earlier days monarchs utilized statistics as a basis for judging the probability of success in operations of war and plunder. That use has not disappeared, but the plexus of relations, which, through the fructifying power of science, the modern world has seen established, particularly in the realms of industry and commerce, has shewn a growing measure of economic solidarity in the affairs of mankind. The modern world responds to everything that profoundly touches any one nation. By the conditions of modern life mankind tends to be welded into a unit. By the magic of invention, humanity has been quickened; distance — if not annihilated — has been immensely shortened; life has been enriched in the potentialities of material and physical enjoyment, and be it said also in the plane of its possible intellectual and moral effort. The destiny of mankind will therefore be the supreme problem of those statisticians of the future, who have an adequate outlook on that science and art with which it is their privilege to concern themselves. For the craftsman with acute and microscopic vision there are a multitude of analyses to be made; for one with the capacity for reaching wide generalisations there is no end of larger work, while for him who is happily able to see both the trees *and* the forest of the statistical landscape, there is the most far-reaching task of all, the creation of a statistical world-picture, which shall reveal the secrets of man's place in the many-sided world of social-economics, using that word in its fullest and most ideal sense.

To assist in the creation of the "statistical world-picture, which shall reveal the secrets of man's place in the many-sided world of social-economics," the Statistical Office of the United Nations has been given the task — among others — of assembling and publishing international vital statistics. The accomplishment of this function demands first a large and carefully integrated network of relationships with individual governments in order that statistics, produced on a national basis, may be presented for international study.

Presentation of data takes various forms, but for vital statistics, the most important is the *Demographic Yearbook.* This compendium of national data on population and vital statistics was published first in 1948, and it has continued to be issued each year since that date. The data included are not strictly comparable yet, but their deviations are clearly marked and the tabulations can serve admirably for the "multitude of analyses" that Knibbs foresaw so long ago. They bring to the general public in every country the experience of every other country and provide the basis not only for national "stock-taking" but for international planning in the realm of public health and socio-economic development.

*Errors in Age Reporting in Statistically Underdeveloped Countries (With Special Reference to the Chinese Population of Singapore)**

YOU POH SENG

One of the main problems in the demographic analysis of the population of an underdeveloped country is the inaccuracy of age statements. This inaccuracy is caused by two groups of factors, one group giving rise to deliberate mis-statements of age and the other giving rise to involuntary mis-statements.

The first group of factors are in some cases general to most populations; in some other cases they are dependent on circumstances in any one particular country. An example of the former is the overstatement of age by older persons, and as examples of the latter we have the circumstances giving rise to under-enumeration of infants and of males in the age group liable to compulsory military service.

The second group of factors are those which are largely beyond the control of the respondents. The most important example is the tendency to forget ages, especially in the case of older persons. Closely allied to this is the unwillingness on the part of the respondents to recalculate their ages according to the officially required system of age reckoning.

Quite generally the error resulting from most of these factors is one of digital preference, while the error that is likely to arise from circumstances peculiar to a particular country is one of under-enumeration of persons of certain ages, with corresponding over-enumeration of those of neighbouring ages.[1] Some study has been made into these errors, into their nature, their measurement and their reduction. This has been mainly due to the efforts of the Population Division of the United Nations Secretariat,[2] but the recent paper by Carrier and Farrag[3] is a major contribution in that it is the first attempt at a systematic presentation of the problems and a general methodology for their solution.

However, most of the studies have started with demographic data already collected and tabulated, and considered the solution of the problems caused by age mis-statements by adjusting the population at individual ages or age-groups by more or less mathematical techniques. In general these techniques involve some form of smoothing or graduation making use of

* Reprinted with permission from *Population Studies,* Vol. 13, Part 2 (November 1959), pp. 164-171.

[1] In this connection it ought to be noted that the complete non-enumeration of persons in the ages affected, without corresponding compensation in the neighbouring ages, is a distinct and serious possibility.

[2] See, for example, *Age and Sex Patterns of Mortality,* ST/SOA/Series A, Population Studies, No. 22, United Nations, New York 1955, and *Methods for Population Projections by Sex and Age,* ST/SOA/Series A, Population Studies, No. 25, United Nations, New York, 1956.

[3] N. H. Carrier and A. M. Farrag, "The Reduction of Errors in Census Populations for Statistically Underdeveloped Countries", *Population Studies,* Vol. XII, No. 3, March 1959, pp. 240-285.

mathematical models that "at best, . . . can be but a rough approximation to reality . . .".[4]

In this paper we propose to approach the problem one stage earlier, at the point before the data are collected. We face up to this question: Do we have to accept the implied fact that age statements in statistically underdeveloped countries are necessarily inaccurate, or in any case as inaccurate as the analysis of the collected data make them out to be? If the answer to this question is in the affirmative, then we have no alternative but be satisfied with the indirect methods of obtaining a "rough approximation to reality". But what if the answer is in the negative? In that case we have the possibility of getting at the truth directly and without approximation.

At first consideration there does not appear to be any doubt as to the answer to the question. For have not all the data collected in statistically underdeveloped countries shown obvious tendencies to undercount at certain ages, overcount at certain other ages, digital preferences, and so on? Have not the responsible superintendents of censuses and other officials stated that they have been as careful as possible in their collection of the age data, but that inaccuracies still arose because of many reasons beyond their control?

However, there is one major weakness in the collection of age data in statistically underdeveloped countries generally, and we suggest that this weakness, where it applies, underlies most of the inaccuracies found in their age distributions. The weakness is this: that in many cases the statisticians ask for ages according to Western reckoning. The question in the census or any other survey questionnaire relating to age generally takes the following form: "What is your age?" or "Age at last birthday" or "Age according to Western (or English) reckoning". In the case of the last two forms of the question, the nature of the age statement required is clear. In the first form the informant is free to state his age according to any system of reckoning to which he is accustomed or which he prefers. The age distributions based on these statements are then presented and used for analysis and international comparison as if they were reckoned on the Western method of age-reckoning.

The point we are making is that in many of the statistically underdeveloped countries the reckoning of ages used generally by the population may not be that of the Western countries. Their local culture or tradition or custom may give rise to a different method of age reckoning to that employed in the Western countries. If this is the case, the effect on the age statements and therefore on the age data of the population can be significant.

If the people are asked to state their ages according to Western reckoning they would, if they are conscientious, have to convert their ages which they know, to ages by Western reckoning. This conversion may not be at all easy to carry out, especially for the illiterate sections of the population. It is then a natural step to simply and conveniently ignore the half-hearted request for Western reckoning and to state their ages as they know them in their everyday life. The introduction of the phrase 'according to Western reckoning' therefore does not solve the problem, although its use shows that the statisticians are aware of the existence of other methods of age reckoning.

In effect therefore, the age statements supplied by the local population are based on their method of age counting, while the age distributions derived from such age statements are published, used and analysed as if these were based on the Western method. The effect on the age distributions depends then on the difference between the methods of age reckoning. However, a general point may be mentioned here. Where a traditional method of age counting exists, it is possible that the majority of the population may have forgotten this through lack of usage. If they are simply asked what their ages are, although they should be able to work out their correct ages from some supplementary information which they possess, the procedure may be so laborious as to discourage them from making the effort. They would then state some approximate age. From this there arises the problem of digital preference.

We propose in this paper to illustrate the points above by means of data collected in an actual survey carried out in Singapore in connection with 1957 Population Census.

[4] Carrier and Farrag, *op. cit.*, p. 264.

Age Reporting and Census Age Data in Singapore

The age distribution of the population of Singapore has, before 1957, always shown an anomaly for the first few years of life. Before the Second World War the population had grown mainly as a result of large-scale immigration, so that the bulk of the people was concentrated in the young adult age groups. After the war migration no longer played a significant part in the growth of the population, and indeed from the late thirties the growth has been dependent largely on natural factors. This growth has been, and continues to be, very rapid. With such a rapidly increasing population the age structure should have a broad base gradually tapering away as we proceed towards the older ages. However, if we look at Table 1, this expectation does not seem to be confirmed. In all the censuses held in the period 1881–1947, the proportion of persons in the 0–4 age group is consistently lower than that of the 5–9 group. The distributions before 1947 clearly show the influence of migration on population growth, and that for 1947 brings out the relatively greater importance of natural factors. In all cases the pattern of the population from age ten onwards conforms very much to expectation, bearing in mind the major growth factors. For the two age groups before age ten, the systematic excess of the 5–9 group over the 0–4 group suggests that there must be some factor or factors tending to cause an underenumeration in the latter group with a compensating overenumeration in the former group.[5]

The difficulty is not connected with any major imperfection in the vital registration system. In the National Statement on the demographic situation of Singapore submitted as a background document to the Asia and the Far East Seminar on Population organised by the United Nations and held in Bandung in 1955, it was stated that: "A sound system of vital registration has been developed in this territory. It is now claimed that vital registration (in Singapore) is virtually complete".[6] In other words, there is a means, for the

[5] This systematic nature also serves to rule out the possibility that the 5-9 group was affected by the in-movement of migrants' children. It can hardly be argued that immigrants' children of that age group always tend to preponderate over those of the younger age group.

[6] The summary of the discussions and the conclusions of the Seminar are published in the United Nations publication ST/TAA/SER.C/26, 1957. The various National Statements and other background documents are not contained in this publication, but are listed in Annex 11, the National Statement for Singapore being listed under the symbols W.P./A.6.

TABLE 1

Singapore—Census Population at Various Censuses 1881–1947, Showing the Per Cent. Distribution of Each Population by Broad Age-groups

<table>
<tr><th>Age group</th><th>1881</th><th>1891</th><th>1901</th><th>1911*</th><th>1921</th><th>1931</th><th>1947</th></tr>
<tr><td>0—</td><td>5.4</td><td>4.8</td><td>5.8</td><td>5.5</td><td>6.6</td><td>8.8</td><td>12.2</td></tr>
<tr><td>5—</td><td>6.2</td><td>5.2</td><td>6.1</td><td>6.5</td><td>7.5</td><td>9.4</td><td>12.6</td></tr>
<tr><td>10—</td><td>5.3</td><td>4.6</td><td>5.7</td><td>5.7</td><td>6.8</td><td>8.0</td><td>11.2</td></tr>
<tr><td>15—</td><td>7.3</td><td>7.8</td><td>11.3</td><td>7.7</td><td>7.8</td><td>8.8</td><td>9.4</td></tr>
<tr><td>20—</td><td rowspan="8">75.8</td><td rowspan="8">77.7</td><td rowspan="8">71.1</td><td rowspan="8">74.5</td><td>11.5</td><td>11.6</td><td>8.6</td></tr>
<tr><td>25—</td><td>15.0</td><td>12.4</td><td>8.2</td></tr>
<tr><td>30—</td><td>12.7</td><td>11.3</td><td>8.1</td></tr>
<tr><td>35—</td><td>9.6</td><td>8.6</td><td>8.1</td></tr>
<tr><td>40—</td><td>7.8</td><td>7.5</td><td>6.6</td></tr>
<tr><td>45—</td><td>4.9</td><td>4.7</td><td>5.1</td></tr>
<tr><td>50—</td><td>4.0</td><td>4.5</td><td>3.8</td></tr>
<tr><td>55—</td><td>5.7</td><td>4.3</td><td>6.1</td></tr>
<tr><td>Total</td><td>100.0</td><td>100.0</td><td>100.0</td><td>100.0</td><td>100.0</td><td>100.0</td><td>100.0</td></tr>
</table>

* The distribution for this year is based on the population of the three major ethnic groups, the Chinese, the Malaysians and the Indians. These accounted for over 95% of the total population of the island at that date.

majority of the infants, to have their ages stated by their parents correctly by reference to their birth registration documents. The real difficulty is that a large number of parents do not go to the trouble to refer to these documents, but have their own traditional way of calculating and reporting their children's ages and their own ages. This is particularly so in the case of the Chinese, and the object of this paper is to show that this is true without prejudicing the possibility that it may be so for the other ethnic groups comprising the remainder of the population of the island.

The Chinese have always been numerically the most important section of the population of Singapore, making up about 70% or more of the total population, and in 1947 reaching nearly 78%. The influence of the Chinese age distribution on that of the total population is therefore important, as can be seen from Table 2. This table shows for the three censuses up to 1947, the single-year age distribution up to age five, and thereafter the two very broad groups 5–9 and 10 and over.

This table brings to light one further point. The underenumeration of the group aged under 5, is seen to be concentrated in the first two years of life, and particularly at ages 1–2. This will be shown later to be consistent with the Chinese method of reckoning age, but in the meantime it is interesting to cite some more examples from areas with a fair number of Chinese. This will serve to show that the underenumeration in Singapore is not due to any factor peculiar to the island, but to the Chinese themselves. Table 3 presents the percentage age distribution for the Chinese in several surrounding areas as obtained from the most recent census for each area.

The Chinese Traditional Method of Age Counting

According to the traditional method of age counting, a Chinese is one year old at birth, and thereafter becomes a year older at every Chinese New Year.[7] Since the Chinese New Year is based on a form of lunar calendar, New Year's Day varies from year to year, but usually it falls round about February. An extreme case would be the following: A child is born, say a week before the Chinese New Year. He is one year old at birth, and one week later, on the occasion of the New Year, he becomes two years old, whereas strictly he is only one week old.

The effect of this traditional method of age counting on the age distribution of the population can be visualised from the following extreme example. If *all* the Chinese in a country were to count their ages and the ages of their children by

[7] T. E. Smith in his *Population Growth in Malaya* (London and New York, Royal Institute of International Affairs, 1952) refers to this Chinese method of age counting (p. 69). He says, however, that instead of the Chinese New Year, ". . . often the Christian New Year is used as a base for computation". There is no reason why a traditional Chinese should do this, and in any case there is no evidence of this tendency.

TABLE 2

Singapore—Census Population for 1921, 1931 and 1947, Showing for Each Census (a) the Percentage Distribution for the Total Population, and (b) the Percentage Distribution for the Chinese

	1921		1931		1947	
Age	Total	Chinese	Total	Chinese	Total	Chinese
Under 1	6.6 (ages under 1 to 4—)	0.6	1.1	1.0	2.9	2.6
1—		0.6	0.9	0.7	2.1	2.0
2—		1.6	2.2	2.2	2.5	2.7
3—		1.8	2.3	2.4	2.3	2.4
4—		1.6	2.3	2.4	2.4	2.5
5—	7.5	7.6	9.4	9.6	12.6	13.3
10 and over	85.9	86.1	81.7	81.8	75.2	74.4
	100.0	100.0	100.0	100.0	100.0	100.0

TABLE 3

Chinese—Percentage Age Distribution of Chinese in the Federation of Malaya, Sarawak and Brunei, and North Borneo at Latest Census

Age Group	Federation of Malaya at 1947 Census	Sarawak and Brunei at 1947 Census	North Borneo at 1951 Census
Under 1	1.7	2.6	2.6
1 —	1.7	2.3	2.0
2 —	2.9	3.4	3.5
3 —	2.7	3.3	3.7
4 —	2.9	3.4	3.4
5 —	15.1	16.7	12.3
10 —	12.7	12.7	13.8
15 —	9.4	9.3	9.3
20 and over	50.9	46.3	49.5
	100.0	100.0	100.0

the traditional method, and if there is no provision in the census procedures to take care of this tendency, then for the Chinese population in that country there will be *no* children under 1 year. The effect on the numbers of persons in the succeeding ages can best be shown by considering a situation such as this: the census was carried out on June 1st in year C, and the Chinese New Year in that year was February 1st. Of the children who were born between June 1st of year C-1 and May 31st of year C and who were therefore strictly under 1 year of age at census date, those born between February 1st and May 31st of year C would be reported as 1 year old, while those born between June 1st of year C-1 and February 1st of year C could be reported as 2 years old. Continuing in this fashion, and assuming for convenience's sake evenness of vital events in any one year, we obtain the following picture: —[8]

[8] Strictly of course we should have, not 'persons born', but 'persons born and survived'. This, however, does not affect the picture.

Thus apart from the effect that no children under 1 year of age will be reported, the number of children 1 year old will be deficient to an extent dependent on the date of the census.[9] For children over 1 year and the rest of the population this very method of age counting seems to provide the compensation for any underenumeration at any one age. However, even on the basis

[9] It would thus appear a wise policy to carry out the census at a date immediately preceding the Chinese New Year, for then there will be no under-enumeration of the 1 year old. What would happen then is that *all* under 1 will be reported as 1, all aged 1 will be reported as 2, etc. This would seem to have an advantage in that the reported age distribution could be converted to the true age distribution by simply shifting all the reported ages back 1 year.

There are, however, two snags to make this possibility a purely academic one. First, the large movement of the population at about the time of a new year celebration makes census taking impracticable. Second, the situation postulated here is a very simplified one. In actual fact many problems arise to complicate the picture. These problems are discussed later in the text.

Persons Born	*Actual Age*	*Reported Age*
Between 1.6 (C–1) and 31.5 (C)	Under 1	One-third age 1 Two-thirds age 2
Between 1.6 (C–2) and 31.5 (C–1)	1	One-third age 2 Two-thirds age 3
Between 1.6 (C–3) and 31.5 (C–2)	2	One-third age 3 Two-thirds age 4
etc.	etc.	etc.

of this simplified illustration it is clear that the compensation will be satisfactory only if (*a*) the rates of survival of persons at least two years apart are not too different, and (*b*) there has been no sharp trend over time in the occurrence of vital events. Otherwise biases will arise which can be corrected.

However, any theoretical consideration of the situation is in practice vitiated to a large extent by several complications, at least as far as Singapore is concerned. First, not all the Chinese use the traditional age counting method. Education and the steady improvement in the level of literacy are main factors in the tendency to break the hold of tradition.[10] But education is not yet universal, nor has literacy reached a high level; and, in any case, among people where large families are a common feature, tradition takes a long time to die. The situation is one where a certain unknown section of the population is adopting the modern method of age counting and a certain unknown section is continuing to use the traditional method of age counting.

Second, in past censuses, census superintendents were only partly aware of the problems posed by the Chinese traditional method of age counting and only went some way towards solving them. One such attempt was to ask enumerators to take particular account of the age of babies and to make the entry in months for children under one. The difficulty here is that respondents would, in the first instance, have to report children under one before the enumerators would ask for the age in months, so that in the section of the population who did not use the Western method, this provision would not bring in many children, and those that were brought in could reduce the number enumerated at age 1.

Where census superintendents have instructed their enumerators, for example to "enter the age in years at the last birthday *according to the English reckoning*",[11] the results have been variable depending on the degree of conscientiousness on the part of the enumerators, the pressure under which enumerators worked, and the effort required of the respondents to convert their ages from the traditional method to the 'English' method of reckoning. The degree of non-uniformity in response is not known.

Under these circumstances there would appear to be little that can be done to collect age data free of the effects of the Chinese method of reckoning. A closer study of the Chinese tradition, however, shows a way out of this difficulty.

Traditionally the Chinese have several ways of designating individual years. The most important for our purpose is one in which there are recurrent cycles of 12 years each. Any individual year within a cycle 'belongs' to one of 12 animals, namely, the rat, the ox, the tiger, the rabbit, the dragon, the snake, the horse, the goat, the monkey, the cockerel, the dog, and the pig. Thus the Chinese year which fell mainly in 1957 was the year of the cockerel; so were the years which fell mainly in 1945, 1933, 1921, 1909, etc.; so will the years which fall mainly in 1969, 1981, etc.

The relevance of this method of designating individual years to the problem of age counting is that traditional Chinese reckon themselves and their children as 'belonging' to the animal in whose year they happen to be born. Thus persons born in the Chinese years falling mainly in 1909, 1921, 1933, 1945, 1957, 1969, 1981, etc., all 'belong' to the 'cockerel', while persons born in the Chinese years falling mainly in 1908, 1920, 1932, 1944, 1956, 1968, 1980, etc. all 'belong' to the 'monkey', and so on. Conversely, there is a series of possible ages at intervals of 12 years corresponding to each animal. Thus if a person stated that he 'belongs' to the monkey, and if this statement was made in 1957, he could be approximately 1, 13, 25, 37, 49 years old. If he gave his age in 1957 as 14 we may estimate him more accurately to be 13 years old.

The ages in the above example, as would be the case for all ages, are, of course, only approximate since the exact birthday of the person was not known. We can now attempt to pinpoint his age more accurately, and see what additional information is needed. If the person stated in 1957 that he belonged to the monkey and if his age was known to be between 10 and 15, we can say at once that he must have been born some time during the Chinese year which fell mainly

[10] The provision of the facilities to register birth and to issue birth documents, and the incentives offered in the possession of such documents are not by themselves sufficient to break the tradition. People will use these documents as and when required, but will continue to remember their children's ages according to the traditional method.

[11] M. V. del Tufo, *Malaya — A Report of the 1947 Census of Population,* London: Crown Agents for the Colonies, 1947, p. 49.

in 1944. Now by the Chinese method of age reckoning he would be 14, but if we wish to convert his age to 'age at last birthday' we can say that he would be 13 or 12 depending on whether he was born in 1944 before or after the date corresponding to the 1957 census day. If the 1957 census fell on June 1st, and if he was born before June 1st, 1944, he would be aged 13; but if he was born after June 1st, 1944, he would be aged 12. Thus to obtain his age accurately we would require to know his birthday. But it has already been pointed out that information of such detailed nature is not readily available or obtainable from the population in general, although it is possible that most people would know their birthday by the month and perhaps day of the Chinese year. Further there is a strong probability that the majority of the people would know whether they have passed their birthday at the time of the census.[12]

Possibility of Obtaining Improved Age Data Tested at the 1956 Trial Census of Singapore

The means for getting at the ages of the Chinese much more accurately are thus indicated in the foregoing discussion. It is also obvious that the conversion of individual ages involves a rather elaborate procedure which is best carried out at the census office from supplementary data.

However, before this procedure could be undertaken in a full census, it had to be tested in a smaller scale survey for general validity and applicability. Accordingly the Technical Committee responsible for the planning of the 1957 Census of Singapore recommended in 1956 that a trial census be carried out to test this matter among others. This trial census was taken towards the end of September 1956, and covered several areas of the island, both urban and rural, comprising a total survey population of just over 10,000. The Chinese numbered 8,047 and it is from a detailed study of the age data and statements of these 8,000 odd Chinese that the analyses and discussion in this section are derived.[13]

In respect of age statements of the Chinese, the trial census required the following items of information to be obtained: —

(1) Stated age in years. The instructions asked for the age to be entered in years; but if an age was given in months, then it was to be entered as a fraction of 12 months. This information was required to facilitate pinpointing a person's age at the stage when the conversion to his correct age was carried out later on in the office.

The instruction also specified that once an age had been entered as stated, it should under no circumstances be corrected. The purpose of this was to prevent the respondent, on being asked for supplementary information, from making his own conversion and correcting the age. The idea was that the converted age should later be compared with the stated age as the latter had generally been obtained in the past, without prompting by means of supplementary information.[14] Another reason was, of course, to prevent the enumerators making on-the-spot conversions and corrections in the field. The conversion is a rather elaborate procedure and could be done accurately and uniformly only in the office.

[12] There is a slight problem here connected with the difference of a month between the Western New Year's Day and the Chinese New Year's Day. In the case of the person exemplified here, he might have been born towards the end of the year of the monkey around 1944/5, that is he might in fact have been born early in 1945 just before the Chinese New Year Day of that year. On being asked on census day if he has passed his birthday he would reply yes or no according to whether he thinks in terms of the Western year or the Chinese year respectively. It is easy to see that the negative answer yields the correct converted age, namely 12. However, the problem is only slight since traditional Chinese would think, in terms of the Chinese year in general.

It is to be mentioned that Chinese born before the Chinese New Year in 1944 and after the Chinese New Year in 1945 present no problem at all for the animal to which they 'belong' would be different and the conversion of their age follows the procedure as outlined in the text.

[13] From the 1957 Census the total population of Singapore was found to be just about 1,450,000, with the Chinese forming about 75% of the total.

[14] Even where in the past the stated age had been obtained with the rider 'according to English reckoning', this latter really did not constitute supplementary information.

Reference is made to the discussion later on in this section on this point.

(2) English date of birth (day/month/year). The instruction also asked for a check whether the respondents were in possession of birth certificates or other relevant documents. All respondents were to be asked for this information, and where a particular question could not be answered, a dash was to be put in the space for the answers. This was to provide for cases where, for example, the respondent knew the month and year of birth but not the day, and other similar situations. In other words the aim was to get at minimum conditions for conversion to ages which are more accurate than stated ages.

(3) Chinese date of birth (day/month/year). The same comments apply here except that the day, month and year, of course, refer to Chinese reckoning. For the sake of comparative analysis, the instruction required that all Chinese should be asked for this information, even though they had already supplied their English date of birth.

It may be mentioned that no specific instruction was given on how to report the year, and that the name of the animal of the year in which a person was born was mentioned as one of the ways in which this could be reported. This was necessary because there are several other ways in which a Chinese year may be reported, such as the year of the reign of one of the emperors, or up to the Second World War, the year of the Republic, and there is even a 60-year cycle of designating years. All these are convertible to the year according to the Western calendar, and some of the old Chinese may still be using them for counting their year of birth. It is generally believed, however, that these ways of designating years are not popular, but the trial census was designed to prove this and to explore every possibility.

The procedure for converting ages in the office followed the procedure outlined, but individual conversion of ages would have been too costly in time and labour. However, conversion tables for most of the Chinese systems of year-designation to years according to the Western calendar have been published locally and in surrounding areas,[15] and these can be used with a little adaptation to construct tables for immediate conversion from the different systems of year-designation. Thus for the animal conversion, for example, two tables would be compiled, one for conversion in respect of those persons whose birthday fell on or before the date of the census and one in respect of those whose birthday fell after the date of the census.[16] In each table the 12 animals are set down with the various possible ages against each animal. There was no necessity to extend the table much beyond 100 years. The converted age for any person could now be determined by referring to his stated age and his birthday and consulting the tables.[17]

The remainder of this section will be devoted to a discussion of the trial census results with regard to the age conversion procedures used.

A total of 8,047 Chinese were covered in the trial census. For all these the information on stated age was obtained. Apart from this the table below [4] shows the other items of information obtained for the purpose of age conversion.

In the above table, wherever the term 'date of birth' appears, it means that at least the year of birth according to the relevant system of

[15] See, e.g., *100 Years Chinese-English, Calendar, 1864-1963,* 2nd Edition, Singapore, 1951.

[16] This was in fact the procedure used for the 1957 full census. In the trial census itself only one table was used, and no use was made of the information whether a person had passed his birthday on trial census day. The effect of this is to cause a bias against children who were under one since these children included only those infants who were born between the Chinese New Year in 1956 and the trial census day (i.e., between February and the end of September, 1956). Persons 'belonging' to the other animals would be fairly well covered since there were complete years corresponding to these animals; the only element of bias being due to the fact that the general population from one onwards was consistently counted as being about five months older.

[17] The single table mentioned in the previous footnote as used in the 1956 trial census corresponds to the 'birthday passed' table. That is, according to this procedure every person was assumed to have passed his birthday on trial census day; hence the bias of about five months between that day (September 23rd) and the following Chinese New Year Day. However, the use of this single table required only reference to the stated age. The experience of the trial census indicated that reference to whether birthday had or had not been passed could be added in the conversion without excessive difficulty, and in any case the bias in the case of children under one warranted the use of the full conversion technique including the birthday. The bias is discussed later on in the present section.

TABLE 4

Trial Census of Singapore, 1956—Showing Availability of Data for Age Conversion for Chinese

Type of data available	Number of persons
a. English date of birth only	1,601
b. 'Animal' date of birth only	2,580
c. Other Chinese date of birth only	112
d. English date of birth plus 'animal' year of birth	1,838
e. English date of birth plus other Chinese date of birth	57
f. 'Animal' year of birth plus other Chinese date of birth	34
g. English date, 'animal' year, and other Chinese date of birth	14
Total persons with some birth date available for conversion	6,236
Persons with no birth date available for conversion	1,811
All persons	8,047

reckoning was given, in most cases the month and day of birth were available also. In some cases the day and month of birth were only available by one system of reckoning. As a matter of fact, of the 6,236 persons who supplied birth data, only a handful failed to give month and day of birth apart from year of birth. Even for the 2,580 persons who could only supply their 'animal' year of birth nearly all knew their Chinese month and day of birth. We conclude that practically all persons who could supply information about birth, could supply sufficient information to make precise conversion to the Western calendar possible.

There are two further points to be mentioned in connection with the above table. First, it shows the very small number of persons who use any of the Chinese systems of year-designation other than the 'animal' year system. In view of the effort and expense involved in collecting and processing answers to questions, even where the majority of the replies may be negative, it was not difficult to reach the decision that no question on 'other Chinese date of birth' should be included in the main census.

The second matter concerns the number of persons who could not supply any birth data. They amounted to just about one-quarter of the Chinese included in the trial census. For these persons stated ages would have to be used in default of converted ages, and we must consider whether this would cause any difficulty in an age tabulation using mainly converted ages. Two points are relevant here. The trial census was entirely voluntary. There was no known instance of refusal, but there was also no authority behind the request for detailed information from respondents. As a result any item which entailed some effort on the part of the interviewers could not be expected to be met with whole-hearted response. The main census in 1957 had the authority of legislation behind it, and in addition it was supported by an intensive publicity campaign. No study has yet been made of the effect of the various procedures adopted in the main census and it is therefore not known to what extent the response to the request for supplementary birth data has improved.

Secondly, of the 1,811 persons who did not supply any birth data most were middle-aged or old, and only a very small proportion were children.[18] We shall show below that the main effort of converted-age tabulation is an improvement in the age distribution of young children; the influence of lack of response on birth date is therefore less important than its size would indicate.

[18] To be exact the percentages for the various broad age-groups of the 1,811 persons are as follows, the figures in brackets being the percentages referring to the Chinese population according to the subsequent 1957 Census: — Under 1, 0.7 (3.9); age 1, 0.7 (3.6); 2-4, 5.6 (10.6); 5-14, 17.3 (25.7); 15-44, 48.9 (40.5); 45 and over, 26.7 (15.7).

In studying the effect of age conversion on the age distribution of the population and in comparing the converted age distribution with the staged age distribution, the categories a, b and c of Table 4 are straightforward, representing only one particular type of available data in each case. The other four categories (d, e, f and g) are cases where two or more types of birth data are available. Since the English system and any of the Chinese systems are completely independent systems of year designation, Categories d and e could logically be regarded as providing two useful items of information for each person. Categories f and g are different in that the Chinese systems of year designation are not independent. All the 14 cases of Category g can be used for the analysis of the English birth date conversion, and these same 14 cases together with the 34 cases of Category f were finally examined individually, and after comparing birth date with the stated age in each case, a decision was reached to make use of the most consistent Chinese system in that case.

In the actual analysis, therefore, the following main categories were distinguished: 3,510 English birth data available, 4,429 'animal' birth data available, and 209 other Chinese birth data available.

Table 5 shows for each of these three categories, the comparison between the converted and the stated age. It sets out for each converted age or age-range the number of persons whose stated age coincides with the converted age, and where the stated age differs from the converted age, the distribution of persons by direction and the magnitude of the difference. This analysis enables us to see immediately whether and to what extent stated age differs from converted age.

The result of this analysis is to bear out clearly and convincingly all the points that have been suggested so far. A very large proportion of Chinese do still use their traditional method of age reckoning which tends to make their stated age exceed their converted age by one or two years, and the two main methods of age conversion, that using the English birth data and that using the 'animal' birth data, are without doubt useful in enabling us to obtain a better and much more accurate age distribution of the Chinese population.

Table 5 (c) includes too few persons for any clearcut analysis, though the overall evidence points in the same direction. Table 5 (b) is most interesting from many points of view. It shows first of all the extent to which stated ages differ from converted ages; nearly 70% of the trial census Chinese who provided their 'animal' birth data stated their age as one year older than their true converted age and only just over 20% had their stated age coincide with their converted age.

What appears at first sight to be inconsistent with the Chinese method of age reckoning is the small number of persons whose stated age is two years more than their converted age. The explanation for this apparent inconsistency is that in the trial census months and days of birth were not taken into consideration when converting ages of those whose 'animal' and other birth data were available. This procedure, as was shown above, is biased against the number of infants under one.[19] Such infants only included those born between the Chinese New Year of 1956 and the trial census day (September 23rd, 1956). This undercount of the infants under one can be seen in the last column of Table 5 (b).[20]

Another effect of the trial census age conversion procedure was the small number of persons whose stated age exceeded their converted age by two years. To explain this, let us take a concrete illustration. Let us take the case of persons born between Chinese New Year 1955 and Chinese New Year 1956. All or most of these would state their age as two by Chinese reckoning and their converted age would be one; if their English birth data were given the conversion procedure was different (see later on in the discussion of Table 5 (a)). It is quite obvious therefore that in all or most cases the stated age should exceed the converted age by one year, and cases where the stated age exceeded the converted age by two or more were fortuitous.

Now if the months and days of birth of these persons had been considered, we should have obtained the following results. Children born between September 23rd, 1955, and trial census

[19] See footnote 16.

[20] This bias was avoided in the main census in 1957. See footnote 17 and also the next section.

TABLE 5

Trial Census of Singapore, 1956—Showing for Each Main Category of Birth Data Availability the Comparison of Converted Age and Stated Age

Converted age or age-group	Stated age = Converted age +							Total
	− 3 +	− 2	− 1	0	1	2	3 +	
(a) *English Birth Data Available*								
Under 1				146	80	45	1	272
1			1	72	141	50	1	265
2				70	131	50	3	254
3				64	128	40	1	233
4			1	56	132	41	1	231
5– 9	1	1	16	249	491	187	7	952
10–14	1	1	6	152	233	87	6	486
15–19		1	8	139	155	48	4	355
20–24		3	9	81	47	15	4	159
25–29	3		8	36	29	6	1	83
30–34	2		3	30	16	2	3	56
35–44	4		6	52	17	7	1	87
45–54	1		5	26	9	2		43
55–64			5	15	1	1		22
65–			3	7	2			12
Total	12	6	71	1,195	1,612	581	33	3,510
Per Cent	0.5		2.0	34.0	45.9	16.6	0.9	100.0
(b) *'Animal' Birth Data Available*								
Under 1				67	35	2	3	107
1			10	40	126	2	2	180
2			1	35	134		1	169
3			4	39	116	1		160
4	1	4	8	36	124	3	3	179
5– 9	15	3	17	180	457	12	5	689
10–14	14	2	18	122	326	8	5	495
15–19	1	5	29	135	315	6	5	496
20–24	4	4	13	80	249	11	3	364
25–29	1	1	7	52	239	4	1	305
30–34	2	2	3	38	190	7	3	245
35–44	9	4	11	62	282	13	9	390
45–54	12	3	10	49	244	17	11	346
55–64	7	1	4	24	152	8	6	202
65–	3		2	9	76	8	4	102
Total	69	29	137	996	3,065	102	61	4,429
Per Cent	2.2		3.1	21.8	69.2	2.3	1.4	100.0
(c) *Other Chinese Birth Data Available*								
Under 1					4			4
1			3		3			6
2			2	1	1			4
3				1	3		1	5
4				3	3			6
5– 9			1	8	13			22
10–14			2	1	6	1	1	11
15–19	1			1	2	1		5
20–24			1	5	9	1	1	17
25–29	1		2		3	1	1	8
30–34			3	4	6		1	14
35–44	1	1	6	13	18	2	2	43
45–54		1	1	10	13	1	2	28
55–64	2	1	2	3	11			19
65–	2		1	5	9		1	17
Total	7	3	24	55	103	7	10	209
Per Cent	4.5		11.5	26.3	49.3	3.3	4.8	100.0

day 1956 would have a converted age of less than one. This would remedy the undercount of infants, but apart from this, those infants born between September 23rd, 1955, and Chinese New Year, 1956, whose converted age is now less than one were stated as being two years old by the Chinese method of reckoning. They would therefore appear in the category: stated age = converted age + 2. Proceeding in this way the persons whose stated age exceeded their converted age by two years would have been put into their correct category, and this reallocation would have been at the expense of the category stated age = converted age + 1. The converted age distribution would have remained almost the same.[21]

We come now to Table 5 (a). This table is interesting in showing the strong hold of tradition in the matter of age reckoning. Persons for whom English birth data are available might be expected to reckon their age also by the English method. Yet Table 5 (a) shows how far this is from being the case. Although as a whole there were relatively more persons whose stated age coincided with their converted age, the proportions of persons whose stated age exceeded their converted age by one or two years amounted to over 60%. In other words, notwithstanding their knowledge of their English birth date, nearly all these persons still use the Chinese method of age reckoning. Incidentally, the trial census procedure of age conversion for persons with English birth data took into account the month and day of birth; hence the large proportion of persons whose stated age exceeded their converted age by two years indicates what the proportion would be in the same category in Table 5 (b) if a similar procedure of conversion were used.

One more point in Table 5 (a) is worthy of mention. The proportions of persons whose stated age exceeded their converted age by one or two years are very large up to the age of 20 and particularly so up to age 10. From age 20 onwards the proportions fall appreciably. It is possible that children's ages may be returned by other people, who are more influenced by tradition. These latter would in most cases not appear in Table 5 (a). On the other hand, of those adults who knew their English birth dates and probably returned their age themselves a higher proportion tended to reckon their ages by the Western method.

Finally there remain those persons whose stated age either fell short of their converted age or exceeded it by more than two years. Strictly there should have been no case in any of these categories, and the fact that an appreciable number was found illustrates the point that, particularly among the illiterate section of the population, there is at all times a tendency to wild mis-statements of age. That there is a tendency to provide wildly incorrect birth data cannot, of course, be overlooked. However, for several reasons mis-statement of age is more likely. There is no reason why people should remember their ages, except in a very vague and approximate way, and when asked to return them they are unlikely to make the mental effort to work them out; any age that is fairly approximate would do. On the other hand they will have known the animal to which they 'belong' since childhood; some parents even use the animals to which their children 'belong' as nicknames. Moreover, there is a close connection between the animal year of birth and a person's horoscope, in foretelling his fortune, in determining in association with other factors the propitiousness or otherwise of an action which he is contemplating to undertake or which is being planned for him, such as a marriage.[22]

We next take the comparison of stated age and converted age one stage further. In Table 6 we present the stated age distribution and the converted age distribution for the 6,236 persons for whom birth data were available, each person's age being converted once only. Where the English birth data were available, these were preferred for use in the conversion, and where these were not available the choice of either the

[21] It would in fact have been improved by the reallocation of some of the age one to age under one and also by the avoidance of the slight bias mentioned in the last part of footnote 16.

[22] It is sometimes possible that horoscopically the occurrence of an 'animal' at a particular year in a particular cycle was regarded as a bad omen, and persons born in that year tend to avoid mentioning the fact that they 'belong' to that animal. Where this happens, it could easily be detected in a systematic undercount both in the stated age and in the converted age. As it happened no such bias was apparent in Singapore.

'animal' birth data or other Chinese birth data was made on the basis of internal consistency. That the English birth data should be preferred is perfectly justifiable and this was also the procedure used in the main Census. In the case of the Chinese birth data the number of persons with 'animal' birth data as well as other Chinese birth data was too small (there were only 34 of them) to affect the distribution whatever choice was made in individual cases.

A comparison of the stated age distribution of Table 6 with past census age distributions (Tables 1 to 3) shows that if the age distribution of the Chinese population were based on the stated ages, the number in the first two years of life would continue to be underestimated. On the other hand the converted age distribution proves that the problem can be solved, and that the procedure may be applied in the full census with gratifying results as shown below.

The trial census still shows a slight undercount for persons aged less than one, but this is closely

TABLE 6

Trial Census of Singapore, 1956—Showing the Comparison of the Stated Age and the Converted Age Distributions

Age or Age Group	Converted Age Distribution Persons	Converted Age Distribution Per Cent	Stated Age Distribution Persons	Stated Age Distribution Per Cent
Under 1	295	4.7	157	2.5
1	312	5.0	174	2.8
2	299	4.8	298	4.8
3	271	4.3	294	4.7
4	269	4.3	277	4.4
0–4	1,446	23.2	1,200	19.2
5	233	3.7	263	4.2
6	228	3.7	243	3.9
7	234	3.8	235	3.8
8	223	3.6	235	3.8
9	199	3.2	209	3.4
5–9	1,117	17.9	1,185	19.0
10–14	674	10.8	750	12.0
15–19	644	10.3	670	10.7
20–24	460	7.4	481	7.7
25–29	363	5.8	366	5.9
30–34	299	4.8	305	4.9
35–39	233	3.7	240	3.8
40–44	250	4.0	251	4.0
45–49	196	3.1	213	3.4
50–54	197	3.2	179	2.9
55–59	136	2.2	157	2.5
60–64	100	1.6	98	1.6
65–69	65	1.0	77	1.2
70–74	35	0.6	38	0.6
75–79	14	0.2	18	0.3
88–	7	0.1	8	0.1
Total	6,236	100.0	6,236	100.0

NOTE: The two sets of percentages do not add up to 100 owing to rounding.

connected with the age conversion procedure used. We shall now turn our attention to the 1957 full census and examine the results of the full conversion procedure.

The 1957 Census of Singapore

In the full census the procedure for obtaining the birth data of the Chinese was somewhat simplified, while at the same time the age conversion procedure was tightened so as to avoid the biases encountered in the previous section.

As it was too expensive to ask respondents to return alternative birth data in the main census, enumerators were asked to ascertain the date of birth (month, day and year) by English reckoning and only to ask those who could not supply this information for their age in years, their 'animal' year of birth, and whether or not they had passed their birthday on census date. In some cases, of course, only stated age could be obtained.

It is clear that these questions were the minimum necessary to enable ages to be converted and that they did not involve duplication of information. Age conversion was carried out as in the trial census but the additional information on whether the birthday had been passed on census day made for greater accuracy.

The census analysis did not provide figures on the number of people answering these different questions. In the meantime the age tabulations have been completed. The age analysis is now given in single years of age, which is itself an improvement compared with previous censuses which gave ages in quinary groups except for the first few years of life.

Table 7 is a summary for the Chinese population for the same ages and age groups as used in Table 6 to facilitate comparison.

TABLE 7

1957 Census of Singapore—Distribution of the Chinese by Single Years of Age up to Age 10 and by Five-year Age Groups

Age or Age Group	Persons	Per Cent
Under 1	42,469	3.9
1	39,342	3.6
2	39,713	3.6
3	39,041	3.6
4	37,193	3.4
0–4	197,758	18.1
5	35,493	3.3
6	34,167	3.1
7	34,673	3.2
8	33,574	3.1
9	32,267	3.0
5– 9	170,174	15.6
10–14	109,703	10.1
15–19	107,156	9.8
20–24	85,913	7.9
25–29	76,611	7.0
30–34	59,344	5.4
35–39	55,917	5.1
40–44	57,277	5.3
45–49	51,888	4.8
50–54	41,617	3.8
55–59	30,509	2.8
60–64	20,461	1.9
65–69	13,264	1.2
70–74	7,414	0.7
75–79	3,640	0.3
80–	1,950	0.2
Total	1,090,596	100.0

Source: 1957 *Census of Population, Singapore — Preliminary Release No. 5,* Singapore, Government Printing Office, 1959.

In comparing the full census with the trial census results, it should be mentioned that the latter was planned to test the applicability and efficacy of a variety of census techniques and procedures, and not for age reporting alone. Among the more important practical problems were those connected with census reticulation, numbering of households as against the old method of numbering houses, the procedure to be used for household numbering within reticulated units, a much improved procedure of two-stage enumeration, and many others. The primary considerations in the selection of areas for the trial census were geographical to ensure adequate urban and rural representation; appropriate representation of congested and surburban areas; and, in rural areas of various types of farming areas and other rural communities. Since the testing of the census schedules with many complicated definitions and instructions formed another important aspect of the trial census, adequate representation of the various ethnic groups and sub-groups imposed a further restraint. With all these conditions and with the additional difficulty that the necessary data for the planning of a fully representative sample were not available, it could not be expected that the trial census would be a 'miniature' census apart from largely practical details.

As it happened, a comparison of Table 7 with Table 6 showed that the trial census comprised a population which was very young, with about two-fifths of the persons under 10 years of age as compared to just over one-third for the whole population. However, the full census proved conclusively that the new procedures for obtaining age data and of age conversion were not only applicable, but also produced unbiased results. As a matter of fact even the slight bias against infants under one year of age resulting from the very simple but incomplete conversion procedure of the trial census has disappeared, as was anticipated.

The 1957 age distribution of the Chinese as well as of the whole population in Singapore shows the broad base characteristic of a fast-growing population. There are some very slight unevennesses which can mostly be explained. Thus the slight bulge at two was most probably caused by those children for whom no birth data were supplied by their parents or guardians and for whom stated age had to be used. It would be useful, if later on the census machinery could be used for some more detailed analysis of the census returns in the interests of research, aimed at, among other things, the improvement of the collection of vital data. For example, the comparison of stated age and converted age where applicable might enable us to adjust the bulge of the children aged two and perhaps also the bulge of those aged seven. As for the small excess in the 40–44 group, that was largely the remainder of the immigrants of the thirties who were able-bodied enough to withstand the privations of the Japanese occupation. Space does not permit the full representation of the population by single years of age, but a reference to the census publication shows that, by and large, there were no irregularities apart from those noted above as well as at the ages 12 to 15 corresponding to children born during the Japanese occupation, which quite naturally brought about a disruption in the vital trends of the population as a whole.

Conclusion

The 1956 trial census in Singapore has thus proved, and the full census in 1957 has confirmed, that for the Chinese population the infants in the first two years of life have always been undercounted in the past, and that this undercount was caused by the Chinese method of age-reckoning which tends to exaggerate real age by one or two years. The undercount is therefore not one in which children are left out of the census altogether,[23] but that there is a corresponding overcount in the older children. An examination of Tables 6 and 7 shows that this overcount is not restricted to a few years but extends to age 10 and perhaps slightly over. The solution to the problem is to be found in obtaining supplementary birth data which need not be confined to the birth data by Western calendar, but is again based on the Chinese traditional method of year-designation which is very closely connected with their system of age-reckoning.

In countries where vital registration is comprehensive and reliable it is arguable that the solution might be sought more simply by building on birth and death data for the past 10 years or so and comparing the results with the census data. This argument is subject to three objections. First, in very few statistically underdeveloped countries is vital registration comprehensive; in most of these it is either non-existent or quite incomplete. Second, where population movement is important, migration data would have to be used as well, and these data are notoriously inadequate in nearly all countries. Third, and perhaps most important of all, the vital data themselves are affected by the system of age-reckoning; specifically, the age statements relating to deceased persons would be biased in the same way that age statements are biased in the census.

[23] This problem is itself not the subject of this discussion. It is in fact not proven conclusively whether physical under-enumeration is prevalent among the Chinese children, and this is one of the topics that could probably be studied in connection with the 1957 census, by comparing the census data with the vital registration data. In this comparison the difficulty that will be raised later on in this section should be borne in mind. Reference is also made to a similar study made in connection with the 1947 Census, see M. V. del Tufo, *op. cit.*, pp. 50 *et seq.*

Another consideration is the strong likelihood that the data obtained by age-conversion would yield a much better age distribution than the stated age distribution for all ages, particularly in countering other biases such as digital preference. In Singapore past censuses have never provided the age distribution of the population by single years of age so that it cannot be shown whether or not digital preferences are prevalent among the Chinese, and a careful study of this factor will have to be made when the 1957 census data in respect of age are analysed in detail, for a comparison of stated age against converted age where both are available. From the discussion above, it seems probable that should there be digital preferences in the stated age, the conversion procedure should show this.

Finally some general conclusions from the discussion. First, it is very probable that in all areas where the number of Chinese is substantial, the same kind of biases can be detected and the same solution may be applied. The age data of the population of such areas can thus be improved on the basis of the findings in Singapore. Second, it is not unreasonable to surmise that the age statements among other ethnic groups may be biased in some way or ways peculiar to their systems of age counting, and it is possible that these ethnic groups may possess their own supplementary birth data, based on their traditional system of year designation. If so, the means would exist of improving their age distribution by pre-census preparation rather than by post-census adjustment. In any case it is important to remember that even post-census adjustment should be carried out by reference to the factors underlying the various biases rather than by cut-and-dried mathematical formulae.

STUDY AND DISCUSSION QUESTIONS

1. What are the sociological implications of establishing a population register in the United States? What are the advantages and disadvantages of such a register?
2. Using vital statistics reports in your library, find out how many people were born and how many died in the United States during the past year.
3. Using the U.S. Census volumes in your library, look up the number of persons in your home city who are your age, and who have at least four years of high school. How many persons in your home county have an income of $10,000 or more? How many are laborers by occupation?
4. How many persons in your class have ever been interviewed by a U.S. Census worker or filled out a U.S. Census questionnaire? Why do you think some of the class members may never have had this experience if the census counts everyone?
5. Find out what kind of vital records your state keeps. Do they maintain a central file of marriages, divorces, births, and deaths?
6. What kinds of questions which the census asks would you feel hesitant to answer? What steps might the government take to insure that information provided will remain confidential?
7. If you were going to take a census of your campus population, what kinds of steps would such a census include? What kinds of information would be most pertinent for a census of this kind?

SUGGESTED ADDITIONAL READING

Hauser, Philip M. and Otis Dudley Duncan, eds. *The Study of Population; an Inventory and Appraisal.* Chicago: University of Chicago Press, 1959.
A general survey of the state of demography as a field of scientific study, Part I of which examines the theory, data, methods, knowledge, and professional status of the field.

U. S. Bureau of the Census. *1960 Censuses of Population and Housing: Procedural History.* Washington: U.S. Government Printing Office, 1966.
A step-by-step review of a census from the planning stages through publication, which reveals how massive an undertaking a census can be.

Spiegelman, Mortimer. *Introduction to Demography.* Chicago: The Society of Actuaries, 1955.

Barclay, George W. *Techniques of Population Analysis.* New York: John Wiley and Sons, 1958.

Jaffe, A. J. *Handbook of Statistical Methods for Demographers.* Washington: Government Printing Office, 1951.
Standard treatments of the methodology of population analysis.

Demography. Chicago: The Population Association of America. Semiannual.

Eugenics Quarterly. New York: American Eugenics Society, Inc. Quarterly.

The Milbank Memorial Fund Quarterly. New York: The Milbank Fund. Quarterly.

Population. Paris: Institut National d'Etudes Demographiques. Six yearly.

Population Bulletin. Washington: Population Reference Bureau. Six yearly.

Population Index. Princeton: Office of Population Research, Princeton University and Population Association of America. Quarterly.

Population Studies. London: The Population Investigating Committee. Three yearly.

Statistical Bulletin. New York: Metropolitan Life Insurance Company. Monthly.
A selection of outstanding periodicals focusing on population matters.

CHAPTER 2

Population Growth: Theory and Fact

Theory in a science should serve two purposes: it should provide a basis for integrating the knowledge that already exists about a subject, and it should enable scientists to locate gaps in the body of knowledge which need to be filled in order to improve explanation and prediction of behavior and events peculiar to the subject area.

Theoretical development leads to accumulation of a systematic body of knowledge in a given subject area in two ways: first, through a conceptual framework, in which the meaningful concepts or terms of the science are identified, and a hypothetical structure, in which the nature of relationships among these concepts or terms are indicated; and second, through amassing of data which fit parts of the hypothetical structure and allow for testing of the hypotheses.

It has been said of demography that it is rich in data and poor in theory. A great many statistics about population have been compiled over the years but relatively little attention has been given to the extent to which these statistics are providing a systematic body of knowledge about population behavior. Part of the reason for this theoretical deficiency lies in the very empirical advances made by demographers. Population specialists have largely occupied themselves with improving methods of data-collection and analysis and with summarizing the rich body of data which pours forth from censuses, surveys, and vital statistics reports. But part of the theoretical deficiency may also stem from the interdisciplinary nature of the subject matter. While demography has been principally the province of sociology, it is generally viewed as drawing its orientation from a number of disciplines. Whether demography should borrow the theoretical framework of sociology, economics, social psychology, biology, some other discipline, or adopt a framework of its own has been a concern to scientists in the field and has probably served to retard theoretical development in the study of population.

Demography has not been devoid of theory. Like other social sciences, the early development of the field included much speculative thought about important issues, and later development focussed more and more on the kind of theory outlined above. Some discussion of the implications of population growth and decline can be found in antiquity: in the Old Testament and the Talmud, in the later works of Confucius in China, in the writings of Plato and Aristotle in Greece, and in those of Cicero in the Roman Empire. These early writings were concerned primarily with questions of public policy relevant to population. Medieval Christian writings considered population especially from a moral and ethical standpoint. In the seventeenth and early eighteenth centuries, the views of the mercantilists and cameralists of Europe stressed the political and social advantages of population increase. At this time, economic thought occupied a strategic position in social philosophy and economists were well aware of the importance of population to the economy and to the welfare of individuals, as indicated in the United Nations selection.

During this period Thomas Robert Malthus

wrote his classic essay on population. His main thesis was that (a) population was necessarily limited by the means of subsistence, and (b) population invariably increases where the means of subsistence increase, unless prevented by some very powerful and obvious checks. These checks, which keep population on a level with subsistence, he said, were all resolvable into moral restraint, vice, and misery. Included among these checks were delayed marriage, promiscuity, wars, unwholesome occupations, extreme poverty, diseases and epidemics, and excesses of all kinds. Malthus did not foresee the widespread adoption of a variety of methods of family limitation, nor did he envision the great advances that were to be made in agriculture and manufacturing. But perhaps his arguments fall short of theory principally in the confusion of moral evaluation with scientific analysis. For all the weaknesses of his thesis, Malthus' name has gone down in history primarily because he set the challenge for those who followed him to refute or refine his arguments. In one sense, every population theorist since that time has taken Malthus' thesis as a point of reference; in fact, however, as Robinson notes, demography has shifted away from Malthusian thinking.

Post-Malthusian theories of population are sometimes classified into "naturalistic" and "social" theories. In the first group are those theories which have posited biological bases for population change or which have described population growth in terms of a mathematical growth curve. The second group of theories has related population movements to social and cultural change or to economic factors. Most of these theories have lacked the rigor of present-day formulations.

As Robinson indicates, contemporary theorizing in population focuses on variations in the basic components of population change over time and the factors accounting for these variations. The theory of the demographic transition, currently popular among students of the field, deals with historic changes in birth and death rates as a function of underlying social, economic, and psychological forces. Demographers are turning their attention more and more to the way in which the basic components of population change — fertility, mortality, and migration — are modified. Future advances in demographic theory are likely to depend on the testing and verification of propositions which relate basic demographic components to individual, group, and societal factors. Later chapters will examine some of these propositions in more detail.

However weak our theories of population change might be, our knowledge of population trends in the world is reasonably thorough. It has been estimated that nearly 80 billion people have ever lived on earth. Today's world population of about 3-1/3 billion is roughly 4 per cent of that total. Considering that man probably appeared on earth 600,000 years ago, 4 per cent might be regarded as a large proportion. World population size was relatively stable over a long period of history and a precipitous increase in population size has occurred only during the last few centuries.

The rapid rise in world population can best be analyzed by examining population trends in various parts of the world. Estimates shown in the article by Durand indicate that the modern rise in numbers of people was not peculiar to any part of the globe; population growth increased in all world areas. The rate of growth was steepest in Northern America in the nineteenth century and in Latin America, Asia, and Africa in the twentieth century. This picture of world demographic growth is somewhat at variance with that often presented, in which Europe is identified as the area which initiated the rapid expansion of population.

Between 1958 and 1963, the average annual percentage increase in population was generally highest in Latin America, Asia, and Africa, but the percentage increase varied from country to country within continents. Within Europe, the change ranged from decreases of 0.2 and 0.1 per cent in East Germany and Ireland, respectively, to an increase of 3.2 per cent in Albania. The rate of increase for most countries of Europe was in the neighborhood of 0.5 to 1.0 per cent. The rate in northern America, as in the U.S.S.R., was in the area of 1.5 to 2.0 per cent. The average annual growth rate ranged from 1.2 in Uruguay to 4.5 in Costa Rica within Latin America, and from 1.4 in Liberia and Nigeria to an estimated 4.3 in Burundi within Africa. The variation in growth rates in Asia was from 0.9 for Japan to 10.7 for Kuwait. For Africa as a whole, it was about 2.3 per cent, as compared with 1.8 per cent in Asia and 2.7 per cent in Latin America.

The 3-1/3 billion people in the world today are very unevenly distributed over the face of the earth. Over one-fifth of the world's population is in mainland China alone. About one-seventh is in India. Over half the people in the world are in Asia as a whole. Given recent growth rates, the Asian population will exceed half of the world population for at least several decades, with Africa and Latin America each having roughly one-tenth of the world's population. Northern America and the U.S.S.R. combined have only slightly over 10 per cent of world population. The world growth rate of about 2.0 per cent per year means that the population of the world will double in thirty-five years if that growth rate is maintained. A possibility is that the growth rate may actually increase slightly during the next few decades and the population of the world may approach 7 billion by the year 2000.

Logic alone indicates that the present rate of world population growth cannot continue indefinitely. For example, Ansley Coale has pointed out that continuation of the world's present growth rate would mean that in 6500 years people would be accumulating so rapidly on earth that human bodies would not only cover the sphere but would be piling up away from the earth at a speed exceeding the velocity of light! Fantastic? Yes, but the illustration demonstrates that population growth rates must ultimately come down. How will this come about? Demographers often talk of the *population equation*. The equation indicates that population growth of an area is equal to the number of births minus the number of deaths in the area plus the number of people moving into the area minus the number of people moving out of the area. Population change, no matter what its source or cause, must come about through the components of this equation.

For the world as a whole, barring an invasion from Mars or the colonization of astronauts on other planets, the course of future population will depend on the balance of births and deaths. If the birth rate exceeds the death rate, the population will continue to increase. For population growth to be slowed down, either the birth rate must decrease or the death rate increase, or both. In specific countries, the net result of movement in and out of the country will help determine the course of population. The slight decline in the growth rates of East Germany and Ireland has been due to the fact that natural increase (an excess of births over deaths) was more than offset by net emigration from those countries.

The future population prospects for the world or for any country within it are based on the way in which these component factors — fertility, mortality, immigration, and emigration — behave in the years to come. In the next few chapters, particular attention will be paid to these factors, what may cause them to change, and the impact their change has on population growth.

*History of Population Theories**

Population Division, United Nations

A. Introduction

Questions of population have occupied the attention of statesmen and philosophers since ancient times, but it is only recently that scholars have attempted to investigate systematically the factors of population growth or decline and the specific ways in which population changes may influence social institutions and human welfare. The early writers in this field were concerned primarily with questions of public policy relevant to population; the policies which they recommended or attempted to justify were predicated,

* Reprinted with permission from *The Determinants and Consequences of Population Trends*. New York: United Nations, 1953, pp. 21-44.

of course, on certain assumptions as to the causes and consequences of population changes, but the assumptions were not always explicitly stated and there was generally little effort to test them by factual investigations. It is hardly surprising that this is so, since few of the statistical records that are necessary for such investigations were in existence more than two centuries ago, and the pertinent methods of analysis were only crudely developed before that time.[1] Consequently, the thought of early writers on these subjects was influenced more than that of modern scholars by their preconceptions and relatively superficial observations. Their works do not contain many useful ideas that cannot be found better developed in more recent literature on population theory. Nevertheless, some of the early writings are briefly reviewed in this chapter, in order to show how much of modern thought concerning the causes and consequences of population changes has been inherited from the past, and how much men's thinking on this subject has been influenced, in all ages, by the conditions of the times.

The publication of Malthus' Essay at the end of the eighteenth century brought the question of population for the first time into a prominent position in the literature on economics and related subjects. The works on population theory published since that time are far more numerous and weightier than the earlier writings in the field, and more relevant to the problems of the present day. An effort has therefore been made in the present summary to indicate their contents in greater detail. Even with reference to the writings of the nineteenth and twentieth centuries, however, the summary is inevitably highly selective and compressed. In selecting the material to be included, the aim has been not only to indicate the trends in the development of modern thought on population questions, but also to present an epitome of the theories of certain representative writers. Some of the details of works briefly summarized here will be found in the reviews of findings on specific aspects of interrelationships of demographic, economic, and social factors contained in subsequent chapters.

[1] On the careless use of statistics by early writers, see Delbruck, *Numbers in history* (1913); Delbruck, *Geschichte der Kriegskunst in Rahmen der politische Geschichte,* (1908), Vol. I, pp. 20-24.

B. Ancient and Medieval Writings on Population

Germs of certain ideas which have figured prominently in recent theoretical works on population can be found in very ancient writings. The thesis that excessive growth of population may reduce output per worker, depress the level of living of the masses, and engender strife is of great antiquity. It appears in the works of Confucius and his school, as well as in the works of other schools of ancient Chinese philosophers. In fact, these writers had the concept of optimum numbers, so far as the population engaged in agriculture is concerned. They postulated an ideal proportion between land and population, any major deviation from which would create poverty. They held the government primarily responsible for maintaining such a proportion by moving people from over-populated to under-populated areas, though they noted that governmental action was reinforced at times by spontaneous migration.

These ancient Chinese writers also paid some attention to another topic which has occupied much space in subsequent literature on population theory — namely, the checks to population growth. They observed that mortality increases when the food supply is insufficient; that premature marriage makes for high infant mortality rates; that war checks population growth; and that costly marriage ceremonies reduce the marriage rate. They did not attempt to show how the variations of mortality, fertility, and nuptiality, as well as migration, might affect the balance between population and resources.[2]

[2] Huan-Chang, *The economic principles of Confucius and his school* (1911), Vol. I, pp. 180, 186-187, 249-250, 297-309, 322-323, 328-330, 338-339, 345-346, 355-356, 361-362; Chi Chao, *History of Chinese political thought during the early Tain period* (1930), pp. 65-66, 128-129, 187-188; Lee, *The economic history of China with special reference to agriculture* (1921), pp. 144-146, 155-156, 159, 201, 229, 292, 416-417, 419, 436-437; Weber, *Gesammelte Aufsätze zur Religionssoziologie* (1920), pp. 276-536. That little attention was paid to the manner in which numbers are adjusted to resources is implied, for example, by the treatment of population and migration in Swann, *Food and money in ancient China* (1950), pp. 61, 126-127, 302, and Wittfogal and Chia-Sheng, *History of Chinese society: Liao, 907-1125* (1949), pp. 41-112.

Plato and Aristotle[3] considered the question of optimum size of population in their discussions of the ideal conditions of a city-state in which man's potentialities could be fully developed and his "highest good" realized. Their treatment of this question was by no means limited to its economic aspects. The "good life" could be attained, they believed, only if the population was large enough to be economically self-sufficient and capable of defending itself, but not too large for constitutional government. Self-sufficiency required the possession of enough territory to supply the needs of the people and to make possible a moderate level of living.[4] However, neither Plato nor Aristotle inquired explicitly into the relation between population density and *per capita* output or the connexion between the size of the population and the opportunities for division of labour. Plato specified 5,040 as the number of citizens "most likely to be useful to all cities", because it has "fifty-nine divisors" and "will furnish numbers for war and peace, and for all contracts and dealings, including taxes and divisions of the land." [5] Aristotle was less specific with regard to the optimum number, but he held that unless the size of the population was appropriately limited, poverty would be the result, for land and property could not be increased as rapidly as population would grow; civil discord would ensue, and it would be impossible for the government to function effectively.[6]

The views of Plato and Aristotle regarding the means of controlling the size of population are noteworthy. Plato proposed to restrict births, if necessary, by restraining the reproduction of those "in whom generation is affluent"; if a higher birth rate were required, he would achieve it by means of rewards, stigmas, advice and rebuke to the young men from their elders. Should the population grow too large in spite of these precautions, it could be reduced by colonization, and immigration could be used if absolutely necessary to replenish a population greatly diminished by wars or epidemics.[7] Aristotle mentioned child-exposure and abortion as suitable means of preventing an excessive number of children, and in this connection paid some attention to eugenics.[8]

[3] The theories of Plato and Aristotle were treated by Moreau in "Les théories démographiques dans l'antiquité grecque" (1949). Other ancient Greek writers had little to say about questions of population. Xenophon described certain population policies of the Lacedaemonians and Persians in his *Constitution of the Lacedaemonians* (ca. 370 B.C.), and in his *The Oeconomicus* (ca. 370 B.C.). For a brief account see Trever, *A history of Greek economic thought* (1916), Chapter 4; also Michell, *The economics of ancient Greece* (1940), paras. 40, 224, 352. Herodotus in his *History* (ca. 440 B.C.; 1921 edit.), Bk. I. paras. 58, 66, 136; Bk. II, paras. 44, 60, 87, 103-104; Bk. III, paras. 65, 108-109, 159; Bk. IV, paras. 13, 147, 150, occasionally referred to population growth and migration, but did not discuss the causes and consequences of these phenomena. Thucydides in *History* (ca. 145 B.C.; 1919 edit.), Bk. I, paras. 1-3, made passing references to migrations caused by population pressure. See also Bilabel, *Die ionische Kolonisation* (1920), pp. 2-5.

[4] Plato, *Laws* (ca. 340 B.C.; 1926 edit.), Bk. V, para. 737; Aristotle, *Politica* (ca. 354 B.C.; 1932 edit.), Bk. I, para. 1; Bk. VII, para. 4. These two authors did not share the opposition of the Greek primitivists to the concentration of population in cities. Lovejoy and others (eds.), *A documentary history of primitivism and related ideas* (1935).

[5] Plato, *Laws* (ca. 340 B.C.; 1926 edit.), Bk. V, paras. 737-738. See also Plato, *Republic* (ca. 370-380 B.C.; 1930 edit.), Bk. II, para. 372; Bk. IV, para. 423; Bk. V, paras. 459-461. A state with 5,040 citizens would have a total population of about 60,000 and, given the various amounts of territory assigned to ideal city-states, a population density of 75 to 300 per square mile. Welles, "The economic background of Plato's communism" (1948). In Plato's time the density of population in Attica was about 200 per square mile, and did not permit a comfortable level of living. Glotz, "La cité grecque" (1928), pp. 29-31.

[6] Aristotle, *Politica* (ca. 354 B.C.; 1932 edit.), Bk. VII, paras. 4-5; Bk. II, paras. 6-9. In the latter place Aristotle declared that failure to limit population was "a never-failing cause of poverty," and that poverty was "the parent of revolution and crime." However, in his criticism of Plato's proposed community of women and property, he did not include the later Malthusian argument that such arrangements would stimulate excessive population growth. *Ibid.*, Bk. II, paras. 1-5; von Bortkiewicz did not consider Aristotle a fore-runner of Malthus; see von Bortkiewicz, "War Aristoteles Malthusianer?" (1906). But see Moissides, "Le Malthusianisme dans l'antiquité grecque" (1932), and Himes, *Medical history of contraception* (1936), Chapter 4.

[7] Plato, *Laws* (ca. 340 B.C.; 1926 edit.), Bk. V, paras. 739-741, and on colonization Bk. IV, paras. 707-709; Bk. V, para. 736; Bk. VI, para. 754. Colonization was a traditional Greek remedy for over-population. See Michell, *The economics of . . .* (1940), pp. 217-224; Isocrates, *Panegyricus* (ca. 80 B.C.; 1928 edit.), paras. 34-36.

[8] See Aristotle, *Politica* (ca. 354 B.C.; 1932 edit.), Bk. VII, para. 16, where exposure of deformed children is advocated. Aristotle mentioned homosexuality as a means of population control used by the Cretans; *ibid.*, Bk. II, para. 10. For his views on colonization, see *ibid.*, Bk. II, para. 11; Bk. VI, para. 5.

The Romans, like the Chinese, viewed population questions in the perspective of a great empire rather than a small city-state. They were less conscious than the Greeks of possible limits to population growth and more alert to its advantages for military and related purposes. Perhaps partly because of this difference in outlook, Roman writers paid less attention than the Greeks to population theory, but were much concerned with the practical problem of stimulating population increase. Their attitude was indicated by their disapproval of celibacy, their writings in defence of marriage and procreation, and by their legislation aimed at raising the marriage and birth rates.[9] Cicero, touching upon this subject, rejected Plato's communism in wives and children and held that the State's population must be kept up by monogamous marriage.[10] He listed various checks to population growth — floods, epidemics, famines, wild animals, war, revolution — but did not attempt to state a general theory of the determinants of population increase or decrease.[11]

Medieval Christian writers considered questions of population almost entirely from a moral and ethical standpoint. Since they were concerned more with the next world than with the present, they did not stress material values. Their doctrines were mainly populationist, but they placed less emphasis than earlier Hebrew and other religious writers on maxims adjuring men to multiply and people the earth.[12] On the one hand, they condemned abortion, infanticide, child-exposure, divorce, and polygamy; on the other hand, they glorified virginity and continence, considered celibacy superior to marriage though suited only to certain persons, and frowned on second marriage.[13] Unlike the Greeks and Romans, early

[9] Stangeland, *Pre-Malthusian doctrines of population* (1904), Chapter 1; Gonnard, *Histoire des doctrines de la population* (1923), Chapters 2-3; Ferlet, *L'abaissement de la natalité à Rome et la dépopulation des campagnes, les réformes d'Auguste* (1902), Chapters 1-4; Frank, *An economic survey of Ancient Rome* (1933), Vol. I, pp. 40-42; Vol. III, pp. 313-322; Vol. V, p. 130; Simkovitch, *Towards the understanding of Jesus* (1937), pp. 128 ff; Ciccotti, "Considerazioni sulle leggi matrimoniali di Augusto" (1938); Cochrane, *Christianity and classical culture* (1944), pp. 198-201, 219-220. For examples of references to Roman population laws in the works of contemporary writers, see Suetonius, *Octavius Augustus* (ca. A.D. 123; 1914 edit.), pp. 123-287; Tacitus, *Annals* (ca. A.D. 104-109; 1931 edit.), Bk. III, paras. 25-28; and *ibid.,* (ca. A.D. 104-109; 1937 edit.), Bk. XV, para. 19; Plutarch, *De amore prolis* (ca. A.D. 100; 1939 edit.), pp. 331-497. See also citations in Lovejoy and others (eds.), *A documentary history . . .* (1935), pp. 408-411.

[10] Cicero, *De re publica* (ca. 44 B.C.; 1928 edit.), Bk. IV, para. 5.

[11] Cicero, *De officis* (ca. 44 B.C.; 1913 edit.), Bk. II, para. 5. The list of checks is from a non-extant work. "The destruction of human life" by Dicaerchus, a pupil of Aristotle and a primitivist. Diodorus Siculus in his *Library of history* (ca. 60 B.C.; 1933 edit.), Bk. I, para. 80, attributed the large population of Egypt to the ease and cheapness of rearing children there. Pliny's works contain almost nothing about population, although they did imply that immigration might check population and that cities grew through immigration. Pliny, *Historia naturalis* (ca. A.D. 75; 1942 edit.), Bk. IV, paras. 21 and 24.

[12] With the exception of certain Brahmins and Buddhists the spokesmen for the Oriental religions appear to have favoured fertility and multiplication. See Stangeland, *Pre-Malthusian doctrines . . .* (1904), Chapter 2. For the earlier Hebrew view see *Genesis,* Chapter i, verse 28; Chapter ix, verse 1; Chapter xiii, verse 6; *Leviticus,* Chapter xxvi, verse 9; *Deuteronomy,* Chapter xiv, verse 28; Chapter xvii, verse 6. Apparently, upon Palestine's becoming fully peopled, it was the preservation of the race rather than its increase that was emphasized. See Himes, *Medical history . . .* (1936), pp. 69 ff.

[13] See, among the ante-Nicene writers: St. Paul, *I Corinthians* (ca. A.D. 60) Chapter vii, verses 1-40; St. Paul, *I Timothy* (ca. A.D. 66), Chapter v, verses 3, 11-14; Ignatius, "Epistle to the Philadelphians" (ca. A.D. 80; 1947 edit.); Origen, "Commentaries on Matthew" (ca. A.D. 246-248; 1903 edit.); Cyprian, "Of the discipline and advantages of chastity" (ca. A.D. 240; 1880 edit.) and Cyprian, "On works and alms" (ca. A.D. 240; 1880 edit.); Clement of Alexandria, "The miscellanies: on marriage" (ca. A.D. 170; 1869 edit.). See among the post-Nicene writers: Athemasius, "Letter 48" (ca. A.D. 354; 1892 edit.); Chrysostom, "Homilies on the gospel of St. John" (ca. A.D. 390; 1890 edit.); Cyril, "Lecture 12" (ca. A.D. 340; 1894 edit.); Basil, "Letter to a fallen virgin" (ca. A.D. 350; 1895 edit); Ambrose, "Concerning virgins" (ca. A.D. 377; 1896 edit.); Nazianzen, "On the death of his father" (ca. A.D. 374; 1894 edit.); St. Augustine, "City of God" (ca. A.D. 413-426; 1887 edit.); and St. Augustine, "Good of marriage" (ca. A.D. 400; 1887 edit.); Gregory the Great, "Book of pastoral rule: on the life of the pastor" (ca. A.D. 580; 1895 edit.); Tertullian, "Against Marcion" (ca. A.D. 200; 1868 edit.); Tertullian, "To his wife" (ca. A.D. 200; 1869 edit.); Tertullian, "On monogamy" (ca. A.D. 200; 1870 edit.); Irenaeus, *Against heresies* (ca. A.D. 182-188; 1868 edit.). These writings may be found in Schopp, *The Fathers of the Church* (1946); Roberts and Donaldson (eds.), *Ante-Nicene Christian Library* (1867-1880); Schaff, *A select library of the Nicene and post-Nicene Fathers of the Christian Church* (First series, 1886; second series, 1890). See also Stangeland, *Pre-Malthusian doctrines . . .* (1904), pp. 55-82;

medieval authors did not attach great importance to population growth as a source of strength for the State, but in time, with the reappearance of Aristotle's influence, this point was again emphasized.[14] Some medieval defenders of ecclesiastical celibacy resorted to economic arguments of a vaguely proto-Malthusian character, noting the extent to which the population of the world had grown, attributing observed poverty and want to this cause, and citing pestilence, famine, war etc., as nature's means of pruning excess population.[15] The prevailing tendency, however, was to favour population increase, as it had been in earlier times. The high rates of mortality which were found throughout the world, and the constant threat of sudden depopulation through famines, epidemics and wars predisposed ancient and medieval writers alike to favour maintenance of a high birth rate.[16]

Arguments in favor of population increase predominated in the writings of European authors on population during the early modern, as well as the medieval, period. The discovery of the New World, the increase of commerce between Europe and Asia, the rise of national states, and the Protestant Reformation[17] brought some revision of the terms of discussion of population questions, but until the latter part of the eighteenth century there was no widespread change of attitude with regard to the desirability of a large and increasing population.[18]

Two writers of the period now under consideration require special mention. One is Ibn Khaldun, a fourteenth-century Muslim author, who expounded in detail a theory of cyclical variations of population and their relation to economic, political, and social-psychological conditions.[19] Khaldun's writings, though perceptive, apparently had little influence in the East and remained unknown in the West until the nineteenth

Riquet, "Christianisme et population" (1949). Some of these views are reflected in the instructions for the clergy incorporated in the medieval handbooks of penance. McNeil and Gamer, *Medieval handbooks of penance* (1938), see for example p. 294; also Russell, *British medieval population* (1948), pp. 159-164. The social arrangements in effect often made for the postponement of marriage, the ideal in medieval England being, according to Russell, "that a living must precede marriage." *Ibid.*, p. 164.

[14] Gonnard, *Histoire des doctrines èconomiques* (1930), p. 41; Mombert, *Geschichte der Nationalökonomie* (1927), p. 81; Thomas Aquinas, "De regemine principum" (ca. A.D. 1260; 1939 edit.); Thomas Aquinas, "Summa theologica" (ca. A.D. 1265-1272; 1935 edit.), Question 186, Art. 4, Sec. 3.

[15] Theophilus, "Theophilus to Antolychus" (ca. A.D. 170; 1867 edit.), Bk. II, para. 32; Bk. III, para. 6; Methodius, "The banquet of the ten virgins; or concerning chastity," (ca. A.D. 270; 1869 edit.); Jerome, "Letter 22" (ca. A.D. 384; 1893 edit.); Dionysius Exiguus, "Libri de creatione hominis" (ca. A.D. 520; 1848 edit.); Tertullian, "De anima" (ca. A.D. 200; 1870 edit.); Eusebius, "Oration in praise of Constantine" (ca. A.D. 300; 1890 edit.). Raoul des Presles argued in a like manner in the fourteenth century; see Brants, *L'èconomie politique au moyen-age* (1895), pp. 238-240.

[16] With regard to the bearing of mortality experience on both custom and collective policy concerning marriage and child-bearing, see Korherr, "Die Bevölkerungspolitik der alten Kulturvölker" (1938).

[17] Luther and other leaders of the Reformation condemned celibacy, but otherwise their teachings on matters relevant to population did not greatly differ from the medieval Christian doctrines.

[18] An exception should be noted in the case of England, where most writers until near the middle of the seventeenth century believed the country to be over-populated and in need of colonies to draw off the excess. For summaries of the many works relevant to population during the fifteenth and sixteenth centuries, too numerous to list here, see Knorr, *British colonial theories* (1944), pp. 41-47, 68-81; Stangeland, *Pre-Malthusian doctrines . . .* (1904), Chapter 3; also Gonnard, *Histoire des doctrines . . .* (1923), pp. 89-129; Spengler, *French predecessors of Malthus* (1942), Chapter 1; Beer, *The origins of the British colonial system* (1908), Chapters 1-2.

[19] Khaldun held that a densely settled population was conducive to high *per capita* income, since it permitted a greater division of labour, a greater variety of occupations, more military and political security, and more effective use of resources than could be achieved by a sparse population. Population growth was affected by what men believed the future held in store; favourable expectations made for fertility and growth while unfavourable expectations made for decline. Good economic conditions and political order stimulated population growth by increasing natality and checking mortality. The populations of states tended to undergo cyclical change. With the establishment of domination, came political order, population growth, division of labour, and rising income; in their wake came luxury, rising taxes and other changes which in several generations produced political decay, economic decline, and depopulation. Representative selections from Khaldun's "Prolegomena" are available in Issawi, *An Arab philosophy of history* (1950), Chapter 5, which is based on the Quatremère and Beirut-Cairo editions. A French translation by de Slane, *Notices et extraits de la bibliothèque imperiale et autres bibliothèques,* Vols. 19-21, appeared in 1862-68. See also Qadir, "The economic ideas of Ibn Khaldun" (1942).

century. The other writer worthy of special note is Botero, an Italian of the sixteenth century, who set forth ably some of the arguments later developed by Malthus. Botero held that man's generative powers operate with undiminished vigor irrespective of his numbers, whereas man's capacity to produce subsistence is subject to limits. The limitation of subsistence limits population through war, strife and various secondary checks to which the struggle for a limited subsistence gives rise. Presumably, Botero believed that the limits of subsistence had been reached, and that a further increase in population could not in general augment the flow of the means of support, since he declared that the population and the supply of food had remained constant for three thousand years or longer.[20]

C. Mercantilist and Related Theories

The mercantilist and cameralist schools of political economy, which flourished in Europe during much of the seventeenth and eighteenth centuries, emphasized the economic, political and military advantages of a large and growing population,[21] and favoured various measures to stimulate population growth.[22] Writers in these traditions were concerned primarily with the ways and means of increasing the wealth and power of the state, and in particular its supplies of precious metals. Their aim was not to raise *per capita* income but to increase either the aggregate national income or the excess of national income over the wage-cost of production, which excess was viewed as a source of tax revenues for the state. Population growth would augment national income and at the same time depress the hourly wage rate, giving the workers an incentive to work longer hours and widening the margin between national income and wage costs. The benefit to the state would be especially great if the additional labour supply were used to develop manufactures, for manufactured goods could be exchanged abroad for gold and silver. Many writers thought that manufacturing yielded increasing returns, presumably because of the greater possibilities of division of labour in a larger population; some held that agriculture was subject to diminishing returns and that there were limits to its expansion.[23] It was generally recognized that a large labour supply was useful only if it could be employed, and certain writers stated the thesis that population was determined by the amount of employment that could be made available.

The mercantilists paid special attention to the relation between population and foreign trade. Cantillon suggested that, if the agriculture of a country could not be expanded in proportion to the population, or if such an expansion would involve diminishing returns, additional agricultural products could be obtained abroad in exchange for manufactured goods.[24] Steuart put it that "work" should be exported and "matter" imported so long as satisfactory terms of trade could be obtained; otherwise, population would have to be contained within the limits of home-

[20] Botero, *Delle cause della grandezza delle città* (1558), pp. 220-224, 376-381.

[21] The views of individual writers in these schools are summarized in dictionaries and encyclopedias of political economy. Mercantilist and cameralist views on population are summarized in Stangeland, *Pre-Malthusian doctrines . . .* (1904), Chapters 4-6, and parts of 7-9; Gonnard, *Histoire des doctrines . . .* (1923), Part 2; Reynaud, *La théorie de la population en Italie du xvi*e *au xviii*e *siècle* (1904), Part I; Furniss, *The position of the laborer in a system of nationalism* (1920), pp. 5, 31, 59, 62; Small, *The Cameralists; the pioneers of German social policy* (1909); Viner, *Studies in the theory of international trade* (1937), Chapters 1-2; Johnson, *Predecessors of Adam Smith; the growth of British economic thought* (1937), especially Part 2; Heckscher, *Merkantilismen* (1931), Vol. 2, pp. 139-145; Spengler, *French predecessors . . .* (1942), Chapters 2-3, 9; Cole, *French mercantilist doctrines before Colbert* (1931), especially Chapters 1 and 4; Cole *Colbert and a century of French mercantilism* (1939), Vol. I, pp. 19-26, 45; Cole, *French mercantilism (1683-1700)* (1943), pp. 3-6, 229-272, 284-286; Beer, *Early British economics* (1938), pp. 41, 62, 78, 183-184; Silberner, "La guerre dans la pensée économique du xvie au xviiie siècle" (1939); Wermel, *The evolution of the classical wage theory* (1939).

[22] These measures included the imposition of disabilities on celibates; the employment of penalities, favours, and monetary rewards to encourage marriage and production of large families; the removal of disabilities on illegitimate children; checks to emigration and stimuli to immigration; and improvements in medicine and public health.

[23] Such was the view of Serra, as stated in his "Breve trattato delle cause che possono far abbondare li regni d'oro e d'argento dove non sono miniere con applicazione al Regno di Napoli" (1613; 1913 edit.).

[24] Cantillon, *Essai sur la nature du commerce en général* (1755; 1952 edit.), Chapters 15-16.

produced subsistence.[25] Several writers remarked that the size of a country's population was determined by the amount of subsistence that could be produced at home or obtained abroad. Few mercantilist or cameralist writers attempted a systematic explanation of population changes, but they did discuss a variety of checks to population growth: plagues, wars, accidents, uncongenial climate, infecundity due to urbanization and other causes, vice, abortion, deferment of marriage, celibacy, monopoly, luxurious living, emigration, etc.[26]

The period in which mercantilism flourished saw the beginning of scientific analysis and measurement of population trends.[27] The first of the writers to discern an underlying order in vital statistics was Graunt, who observed "the numerical regularity of deaths and births, of the ratios of the sexes at death and birth, and of the proportions of deaths from certain causes to all deaths in successive years and in different areas; in general terms, the uniformity and predictability of many important biological phenomena in the mass." [28] Petty, more speculative than Graunt, stressed the advantages of a large population on fiscal, administrative, and economic grounds. He noted that, should the population double every 360 years, there would in 2,000 years be one person for every two acres of habitable land, and, in consequence, "wars and great slaughter." [29]

Süssmilch, author of the first complete treatise on population, was influenced by the work of both Graunt and Petty.[30] Birth and death rates were regular, he observed, and numbers normally increased, although urban mortality sometimes exceeded urban natality. Süssmilch thought that population normally tended to double every century, but that the period required for doubling would lengthen as population grew. Fixing the population capacity of the world at 4,000 to 5,000 million and the present world population around 1,000 million, he inferred that population could grow without causing difficulties for at least two centuries and probably much longer if the rate of increase fell and agriculture were greatly improved. Population growth, he said, was restrained by celibacy and deferred marriage and, above all, by pestilence, war, earthquakes,

[25] Steuart, *An enquiry into the principles of political economy* (1767), Bk. 2, Chapters 24-25. See also Johnson, *Predecessors of . . .* (1937), Chapters 11-12, 15.

[26] In England, before the mid-seventeenth century, emigration to colonies was approved on the ground that it relieved population pressure at home; during the century that followed it was sometimes condemned on the ground that it reduced the size of the domestic population. This latter view was usually rejected, however, on the ground that colonies were complementary to the mother country and that emigrants to colonies brought into being supplies and markets which operated in time to increase the population capacity of the mother country. See Knorr, *British colonial . . .* (1944), pp. 41-48, 68-81. Franklin developed the argument that the American population was complementary to the British, and hence its expansion would augment the population of Britain. See Spengler, "Malthusianism in late eighteenth century America" (1935).

[27] For a concise summary of the views of British writers on fecundity and factors affecting fertility, see Kuczynski, "British demographers' opinions on fertility, 1660 to 1760" (1938).

[28] Willcox in his introduction to Graunt's *Natural and political observations made upon the Bills of Mortality* (1662; 1939 edit.), p. xii of introductory chapter.

[29] Here Petty was under the influence of Hale's *Primitive origination of mankind* (1677), Section II, Chapter 9. Hale, observing that population increased geometrically and could double in as few as 35 years, and that the available means of subsistence could not long sustain such a rate of growth, concluded that the growth of population was restrained by war, famine, floods, pestilence, and earthquakes. Petty's main writings are included in Hull, *The economic writings of Sir William Petty* (1899), especially Vol. II, pp. 537-548. For Halley's life table, which was much more complete than Graunt's skeleton table, see Halley's "An estimate of the degree of the mortality of mankind" (1693). On these writers and their relation to the originators of actuarial science see Bonar, *Theories of population from Raleigh to Arthur Young* (1931), Chapters 3-5, 7.

[30] Süssmilch was influenced also by others who had noted that population grew in geometric progression, among them Nichols, Scheucher, Wideburg, Euler, Whiston, Hume, Wallace, Gregory King, and Charles Davenant. Süssmilch knew Derham's *Physicotheology* (1723), p. 208, in which it was asserted that Divine Providence had established a balance in the world of living creatures to which man's numbers were made to conform, sometimes apparently through plagues and war. See Bonar, *Theories of population . . .* (1931), Chapter 5. Süssmilch's contemporary, Gottfried Achenwall, and his predecessor, Herman Conring, have sometimes been honoured as the founders of statistics, though their works bear no resemblance to modern statistical studies. Conring, who stressed the military value of large populations, discussed the checks to population operating in Spain; he included emigration and celibacy among the checks. See Conring, "Examen rerum publicarum potiorum totius orbis" (1677; 1926 edit.).

floods and starvation. Because he expected only advantages from population growth, and because he set no store by a rising standard of living, Süssmilch favoured measures which would accelerate growth.[31]

D. The Theories of Malthus and His Immediate Predecessors

During the last half of the eighteenth century, more and more writers on economic and social questions rejected mercantilist doctrine and, with it, the long-established idea that population growth was advantageous and should be actively encouraged by the State.[32] Particularly in England, France, and Italy, there was increasing emphasis on the dependence of population upon subsistence and increasing appreciation of the complex manner in which checks on population growth operated. Certain writers, including Cantillon and his followers, developed the thesis that population growth was dependent upon the scale of living and upon how much of the subsistence produced was available for the support of the people.[33] Few writers asserted that population was *determined* by the means of subsistence; most tended to say that, since the standard of living varied, numbers were merely *affected* by the means of subsistence. Among the checks to further growth of population mentioned were dangerous occupations, poor sanitary conditions, contraceptive practices, divorce, urbanization and hindrances to production. It was noted that with the advance of civilization, physical checks gave way somewhat to psychological checks and that the operation of checks became more complex.

The opponents of mercantilist doctrine tended, as a rule, to minimize the possible achievements of the state in augmenting subsistence and improving the lot of the people, and to favour a policy of *laissez-faire*. In this connexion, it was pointed out that, if population adjusted itself to the food supply or to the demand for labour, legislation designed to influence natural increase or migration could have little effect. Some authors, especially in England and France, opposed arrangements for poor relief on the ground that they might undermine frugality, make for labour immobility and misuse of resources, and thus increase the pressure of numbers on subsistence. These arguments were turned against such ad-

[31] Süssmilch, *Die Göttliche Ordnung in den Veränderungen des menschlichen Geschlechte aus der Geburt, dem Tode und der Fortpflanzung desselben erwiesen* (1775), Vol. I, pp. 17 ff.

[32] For summaries of late eighteenth century writings on population see Stangeland, *Pre-Malthusian doctrines* . . . (1904), pp. 224-356; Gonnard, *Histoire des doctrines* . . . (1923), pp. 160-258; Spengler, *French predecessors* . . . (1942), especially Chapters 4-9; Reynaud, *La théorie de la population en Italie* . . . (1904), Part 2; Bonar, *Theories of population* . . . (1931), Chapters 6-8; Wermel, *The evolution of* . . . (1939), Chapters 2-6; Knorr, *British colonial* . . . (1944), pp. 219-228. See also Vincent, "French demography in the eighteenth century" (1947). A number of writers touched upon factors affecting the location of cities, but these views are not considered here. For example, see Maunier, "Théories sur la fonction des villes" (1910).

[33] In Cantillon's view the amount of subsistence produced would depend upon the uses to which proprietors put their land; while the number of people a given amount of subsistence could support would depend upon how poorly people were "content to live." See Cantillon, *Essai sur la nature* . . . (1775; 1952 edit.), Part I, Chapter 15. The full implication of this theory and its development have been treated by Landry in "Une théorie négligée. De l'influence de la direction de la demande sur la productivité du travail, les salaries et la population" (1910). Landry examined the Physiocratic argument, usually denied by the contemporaries of Physiocrats, that, under certain conditions, an increase in food consumption per head or in grain exports could stimulate domestic prosperity and population growth. See Landry, "Les idées de Quesnay sur la population" (1909). Condillac pointed out that the population of a country would not exceed that number which it could nourish. The population would be less if *per capita* consumption increased; it would decrease further if land were used for production which did not increase consumption. Condillac, *Le commerce et le gouvernement* (1776), p. 252. Ferguson argued, "men will crowd where the situation is tempting, and in a few generations will people every country to the measure of its subsistence"; but he added that, other conditions being given, numbers would vary inversely with the "standard" according to which men wished to live, and that this standard tended to rise with civilization. Ferguson, *An essay on the history of civil society* (1767), pp. 216-218; Chalmers, *An estimate of the strength of Great Britain during the present and four preceding reigns* (1794), pp. 1-2. For other works during this period concerned with the balance of population and subsistence and its consequences for population growth, see Reynaud, *La théorie de la population en Italie* . . . (1904), pp. 109, 131; Spengler, *French predecessors* . . . (1942), pp. 230-241; Stangeland, *Pre-Malthusian doctrines* . . . (1904), pp. 227, 237-238, 266, 275 ff, 347; Smith, *An enquiry into the nature and causes of the wealth of nations* (1776; 1937 edit.), Book I, Chapter 8.

vocates of social reform as Godwin and Condorcet, in an effort to show that any benefits from reform would be cancelled by a consequent increase of population.[34]

It was in this period of reaction against mercantilist doctrine that Malthus wrote the first edition of his essay on the "principle of population."[35] The first edition was essentially a polemic directed primarily against Condorcet's conjectures regarding the perfectibility of man, against Godwin's system of equality and his allegation that the vices of mankind originated in human institutions, and against Wallace's contention that over-population would develop only in the distant future. Malthus asserted "the absolute impossibility from the fixed laws of our nature, that the pressure of want can ever be completely removed from the lower classes of society"; and that schemes for social reform such as Condorcet and Godwin had proposed would only increase the number of the poor by removing existing barriers to marriage and multiplication.

Malthus' argument rested upon the supposition that man's capacity to increase his means of subsistence was much less than his capacity to multiply; he asserted that man could increase his subsistence only in arithmetical progression, whereas his numbers tended to increase in geometrical progression. The history of mankind demonstrated, he said, that population always tended toward the limit set by subsistence and was contained within that limit by the operation of positive and preventive checks. The checks (e.g., want, famine, pestilence, premature mortality) were all resolvable into terms of "misery" and "vice," he declared, though he did describe as a check deferment of marriage "from a foresight of the difficulties attending a family." It followed, he believed, that existing institutional and psychological barriers to marriage and population growth should not be relaxed, since such relaxation would make matters even worse; but it did not follow that salutary population pressure should be eliminated were that possible.[36]

In the second and later editions of his *Essay,* Malthus examined at greater length what he regarded as the principal cause of mass poverty, namely, population pressure and the diversion of too large an amount of productive resources to population growth. While still maintaining that "population is necessarily limited by the means of subsistence" and "population invariably increases where the means of subsistence increase, unless prevented by some very powerful and obvious checks", he introduced a new check, "moral restraint", or the deferment of marriage by prospective spouses until they were in a position to support a family.

In opposition to the assertion that an indefinite increase of population could be supported, since in agriculture returns were at least in proportion to the labour bestowed upon the land, Malthus suggested the law of diminishing returns in agriculture.[37] He argued that fertile land was limited in amount and not capable of continuous and sufficient improvement.[38] Therefore, the practice of "moral restraint," together with frugal conduct, appeared as the only practicable and morally satisfactory alternative to unrestrained population growth. Since this practice was most likely

[34] See Wallace, *Various prospects of mankind, nature, and providence* (1761), p. 114. Godwin denied that such could be the final outcome, while Condorcet considered the possibility only to indicate that man could cope with it. Godwin, *Political justice* (1793), Bk. 8, Chapter 7. On Condorcet see Spengler, *French predecessors . . .* (1942), pp. 259-263, Chapters 7-8; Stangeland, *Pre-Malthusian doctrines . . .* (1904), pp. 228, 273, 283, 344. See also Griffith, *Population problems of the age of Malthus* (1925), Chapter VI.

[35] Malthus, *An essay on the principle of population* (1798). See also Griffith, *Population problems of . . .* (1925), Chapter IV. On the condition giving rise to Malthus's *Essay,* see Nitti and Buer, "The historical setting of the Malthusian controversy" (1927).

[36] Malthus, *An essay . . .* (1798), Chapters 2, 4, 7. In Chapters 18-19 population pressure was described as part of the scheme of life, as compatible with Providential design, and as essential to man's development.

[37] Malthus, *Observations on the effects of the Corn Laws, and of a rise or fall in the price of corn on the agriculture and general wealth of the country* (1814), pp. 40-41. Better formulations were expressed by West and Ricardo. See Cannan, *A history of the theories of production and distribution in English political economy* (1903), especially pp. 147-182. The law had been suggested earlier but had not been incorporated into the body of population theory. See Byé, *Les lois des rendements non proportionnels* (1928), Chapter 4. Turgot had formulated the law but had not explicitly used it in his treatment of population.

[38] Malthus, *An essay on the principle of population; or a view of its past and present effects on human happiness; with an inquiry into our prospects respecting the removal or mitigation of the evils which it occasions* (1803), pp. 7 and 473.

to prevail in a society founded upon individual responsibility, Malthus advocated the abolition of poor laws and other arrangements which freed the individual of responsibility for the results of his behaviour.[39]

Malthus anticipated no significant change in the structure and the class composition of society, but asserted that "the principal and most permanent cause of poverty has little or no *direct* relation to forms of government, or the unequal division of property". Poverty had its origin in the pressure of population upon subsistence, and were this truth to become generally known, prudence might increase. In fact, with the progress of society and civilization and under the impact of man's desire to better his condition, the "prudential check to marriage" had increased in Europe, and the "evils resulting from the principle of population" had diminished. Britain's population, "in the course of some centuries, might double or treble" and yet every man in the kingdom be much better fed and clothed than he is at present.[40]

Malthus' contribution to the development of population theory was far greater than his writings reveal. His essay aroused a storm of controversy which long outlived Malthus himself and which made both his followers and his opponents conscious of the need for adequate information about population trends and for painstaking investigation of their relations with social and economic conditions. Thus Malthus was indirectly responsible for a large measure of the progress which has been made since his time, in developing population censuses and vital statistics, improving the techniques of demographic analysis, and formulating better grounded population theories.

[39] He advocated public works in times of cyclical unemployment, in part because the unemployed were not responsible for the occurrence of such unemployment.

[40] See Malthus, *An essay* . . . (1803), Bk. 3, Chapter 14; Bk. 4, Chapters 4, 13-14. The checks are treated in Bks. 1-2; past expedients for coping with population pressure and poverty are appraised in Bk. 3, while the role of moral restraint and man's future prospects are discussed in Bk. 4. For a summary of Malthus' views as set forth in the various editions of Malthus, *An essay* . . . (1803); and Malthus, *Principles of political economy considered with a view to their practical application* (1836), see Spengler, "Malthus's total population theory: a restatement and reappraisal" (1945). Malthus's sources are indicated. See also Bonar, *Malthus and his work* (1924), especially Bk. I, Chapter III, pp. 319 ff. The critical literature is discussed below.

E. Writings of the Nineteenth Century "Classical School" of Economists

The development of population theory from the early part of the nineteenth century up to about 1870 was largely dominated by two distinct schools of thought: first, the "classical school" of political economy in England and its counterparts on the European continent and in America, and second, the writers in the socialist and Marxian traditions.

The theorists of the "classical school"[41] were concerned with the causes and consequences of population changes in their efforts to discover the "laws" governing the levels and trends of production, wages, interest, rents and profits. From their theories flowed arguments, far more sophisticated than Malthus' ratios, to support the thesis that population growth tended to depress wages and create poverty.

One such argument was derived from the "laws" of diminishing or increasing returns in various branches of economic activity, which had been advanced by earlier writers, such as Serra, Adam Smith, and his contemporaries,[42] as well as by certain mercantilist writers. It was generally believed that the cost of production of agricultural commodities tended to rise as a result of increases in population and consequent increases in demand and output, while the cost of producing manufactured goods tended to fall. Decreasing costs (i.e., "increasing returns") in manufacturing presumably occurred because of the possibilities of increasing division of labour and continuing technical improvements. Increas-

[41] See Cannan, *A review of economic theory* (1929), especially Chapters 1 and 4; Gide and Rist, *Histoire des doctrines économiques* (1947), Vol. I, Bk. I, Chapters 2-3; Bk. II, Chapter 1. Adam Smith, Jeremy Bentham, James Mill, David Ricardo, T. R. Malthus and others contributed to the formation of the classical system.

[42] Smith, *An enquiry into* . . . (1776; 1937 edit.), Bk. I, Chapter 11; Malthus, *The nature and progress of rent* (1815), p. 45; West, *Essay on the application of capital to land, with observations shewing the impolicy of any great restriction of the importation of corn, and that the bounty of 1688 did not lower the price of it* (1815), p. 7; Serra, "Breve trattato . . ." (1613; 1913 edit.).

ing costs in agriculture[43] were expected, at least in the long run, since it was thought that (*a*) land was nearly fixed in quantity and quality, and an increase in the volume of production, with given techniques, involved the use of poorer lands or a less efficient combination of labour and capital with lands already in use; and (*b*) within agriculture there was little opportunity for the extension of division of labour and the application of invention.[44] It followed that, as population increased and more labour was employed, in agriculture and manufactures, the increase in agricultural output would be less than proportional.[45] Thus, depending on the relative strength of the opposing tendencies in manufacturing and in agriculture, population growth would be accompanied either by an increase or by a decrease in output *per capita.*

Economists of this period varied in the emphasis placed on diminishing returns in agriculture; also some did not agree that manufacturing was characterized by increasing returns. Mill held that the tendency of returns in agriculture to fall as population increased could not be indefinitely offset by capital accumulation or by extension of division of labour and the introduction of technological improvements in non-agricultural industries. Since manufacturing was dependent upon the land for raw materials, "the general law of production from the land, the law of diminishing return, must in the last resort be applicable to manufacturing as well as to agricultural history." Without improvements in techniques, therefore, "the average condition of the people" must deteriorate if population continued to increase. "After a degree of density has been attained, sufficient to allow the principal benefits of combination of labour, all further increase tends in itself to mischief, so far as regards the average condition of the people; but the progress of improvement has a counteracting operation, and allows of increased numbers without any deterioration, and even consistently with a higher average of comfort." However, Mill apparently doubted whether improvements in the techniques of production would be made rapidly enough to offset the depressing effect of undue population growth on *per capita* income.[46]

Certain writers noted that the operation of the laws of returns in any particular country engaged in international trade might differ from that which would be expected in a closed economy or in the world as a whole. A nation might avoid diminishing returns in agriculture by exchanging manufactured products for agricultural commodities; and it might maintain satisfactory terms of trade by sending emigrants and capital to other parts of the world.[47] This view was criticized by those who believed the amount of accessible land to be limited and continuous, large-scale emigration to be impractical.[48]

[43] Some writers denied this, suggesting that agriculture too was subject to increasing returns. Carey, *Principles of social science* (1858), Vol. I, p. 267; Kaplan, *Henry Charles Carey. A study in American economic thought* (1931), Chapters 2-3. While Carey believed agriculture and manufacturing to be subject to increasing returns only within limits, he did not suggest that these would soon be attained.

[44] Ricardo observed that mineral production too was subject to increasing cost, but this point was not immediately stressed by writers on population, since minerals did not bulk as large in living budgets as agricultural produce did. Ricardo, *Principles of political economy and taxation* (1821), Chapters 2-3.

[45] For example, see Senior, "An outline of the science of political economy" (1850); Bowley, *Nassau Senior and classical economics* (1937), pp. 122-126; Cairnes, *Some leading principles of political economy newly expounded* (1874), pp. 130-135; Bailey, *A critical dissertation on the nature, measures, and causes of value* (1825), pp. 125 ff; Mill, *Principles of political economy* (1848; 1936 edit.), Bk. IV, Chapter 2; McCulloch, *Principles of political economy* (1864), Part III, Chapter 6; Cannan, *A history of the theories . . .* (1903), Chapter 5. See also Say, *Traité d'économie politique* (1826), Bk. I, Chapter 8; Courcelle-Seneuil, *Traité d'économie politique* (1857; 1891 edit.), Bk. I, Chapter 7.

[46] Mill, *Principles of political . . .* (1848; 1936 edit.), Bk. I, Chapters 10-13.

[47] See Fawcett, *Manual of political econmy* (1863), pp. 159-160, 249-250. Fawcett, though a disciple of Mill, put the advent of world over-population in the remote future, since Australia alone could "maintain in comfort a population of 100,000,000." Presumably, so long as unoccupied fertile land existed, emigrants could move there and provide the mother country with "cheap food." *Ibid.*, p. 160; von Storch, *Cours d'économie politique* (1823), Vol. III, pp. 318-322.

[48] Mill, *Principles of political . . .* (1848; 1936 edit.), Bk. I, Chapter 13. Say stressed, as had Malthus, the risks involved in a nation's becoming dependent in part upon foreign produce. Say, *Traité d'économie . . .* (1826), Bk. II, Chapter 11. Presumably Cairnes did not take much stock in the trade and emigration arguments, though he failed to treat them specifically. Cairnes, *The character and logical method of political economy* (1875), pp. 149-181, 207-313; see also Garnier, *Du principe de population* (1857; 1885 edit.), pp. 71-75, 149-156.

Classical economists of this period also developed theories of distribution of the product among the factors of production, which were relevant to population theory. That the level of wages depended largely on the ratio of population to capital was a commonly held view, the inference being that wages would rise if capital increased more rapidly than population.[49] The rate of population increase was regarded as a function of the level of wages and the standard of living of the workers, since in the long run, wages must cover the cost of production of labour. Thus, while an increase in capital and hence in wage levels stimulated population growth, population increase would be greater if the standard of living remained relatively low, or rose only temporarily, than if it rose permanently. Workers could therefore improve their position by insisting on higher standards of living and thus keeping the rate of increase in their numbers below the rate of capital formation.[50]

The relationships of population growth to wages and capital formation were incorporated into the classical theory of the "stationary state," a theory designed to explain how the forces making for economic growth became equilibrated.[51] According to this theory, continuing increases in capital and labour would eventually reduce the rate of returns on capital to a level where the stock of capital was constant, while the level of wages would reach a point exactly commensurate with the standard of living. The growth of both capital and population would then cease, and the stationary state would be at hand. This equilibrium would be compatible either with a relatively small population and high wages or a larger population and lower wages. It could be modified by new changes in the stock of capital, by changes in population due to a rise or fall of living standards, by improvements in the methods of production, or by extension of the known and accessible stock of land.

A different theory of wages, to the effect that the remuneration of workers depended largely on the value of their services, was expounded by von Thünen, Longfield, Senior, Say, and most of the orthodox theorists following Say.[52] Von Thünen attributed the low wages of workers to their low marginal productivity and to their exposure to exploitation by employers, both conditions which were largely traceable to the rapidity (about 1 per cent per year, he said) with which population increased. The remedy consisted in reducing the ratio of workers to capital and to the entrepreneurial and bureaucratic classes. Other German economists observed that the level of wages was affected both by the productivity and the standard of life of the workers, and that with an increase in the number of workers, there was often a diminution in the welfare of the working population.[53]

The French liberal economists of this period, including Say, Destutt de Tracy, Courcelle-Seneuil, Liesse, and others, called attention to the importance of the distribution of income as a factor affecting population growth. They contended, in general, that the size of a country's population varies inversely with the *per capita* consumption, which in turn varies directly with the degree of inequality of incomes.[54] A similar view was put forward by von Storch, founder of the Germano-Russian school of economics.[55]

[49] See Cannan, *A history of the theories* . . . (1903), Chapter 17; von Storch, *Cours d'économie* . . . (1823), Vol. I, pp. 309-321.

[50] Taussig, *Wages and capital* (1896), p. 224; Bowley, *Nassau Senior and* . . . (1937), Chapters 3 and 5.

[51] Schumpeter, *Epochen der Methoden- und Dogmengeschichte* (1914), pp. 53 ff.; Baumol, *Economic dynamics, an introduction* (1951), Chapter 2; Robbins, "On a certain ambiguity in the conception of stationary equilibrium" (1930).

[52] Bowley, *Nassau Senior and* . . . (1937), pp. 75-81, 179-200. One of the best of the early statements of a marginal productivity theory of wages is Longfield's *Lectures on political economy* (1834), Lecture X. See von Thünen, *Der isolierte Staat* (1850; 1921 edit.), Bk. II, Part I, pp. 43-51, 140-148, 185-193, 206-212; Part II, pp. 140-145.

[53] Von Mohl, *Geschichte und Literatur der Staatswissenschaften* (1856), pp. 462-517; von Mangoldt, "Bevölkerung" (1857); Elster, "Bevölkerungswesen" (1909).

[54] Such a proposition had been stated in a different form by Cantillon. Ortes had reasoned similarly. Courcelle-Seneuil stated this view in his *Traité d'économie* . . . (1857) but later rejected it. *Ibid.*, (1891, 3rd edit.), p. 151. See Liesse, *Leçons d'économie politique* (1892), pp. 44-52, 70-74; also Block's criticism in *Les progrés de la science économique* (1890), Vol. I, pp. 540-541.

[55] Von Storch, *Cours d'économie* . . . (1823), Vol. 3, Part II, Bk. ii, Chapter 2. The Italian, Scialoja, reasoned that population varied inversely with the number and intensity of man's wants and directly with the means of existence available. Scialoja, *I principi della economia sociale* (1846), pp. 153-160.

The relation of the size and growth of population to unemployment was also given some consideration during this period. The Venetian economist Ortes had stated earlier that, as a rule, the demand for labour was not sufficient to afford employment for more than half the population,[56] and a similar view was held by certain nineteenth-century French economists.[57] To refute the argument that an increase of population and labour supply would increase unemployment, Say developed his "law of markets", that an increment in supply tends to generate its own demand.[58]

Various views regarding the need for controlling population growth were held during this period. Mill believed that population growth must be effectively controlled, since there were limits in the extent to which the flow of goods and services in any particular country could be increased and since international trade and emigration could afford little relief from population pressure should numbers continue to grow.[59] Mill believed that in the most populous countries a desirable density had been achieved, and he hoped that the people of these countries would be content to keep their numbers constant, lest by necessity they be compelled to do so. Regarding man's capacity to control numbers, Mill was more optimistic than Malthus; he observed that checks always operated to contain population growth within the limits set by man's resources and his productive efforts. In primitive societies the increase was checked largely by misery and premature mortality; in more advanced societies by man's "fear of want" and his indisposition to give "existence to beings born only to misery and premature death". Circumstances such as peasant ownership, the independence of women, national education, and progress in civilization, restricted population growth. Most effective were changes such as an increase in the scale of comfort, sufficiently great and lasting to produce a permanent alteration of a people's habits. Mill declared it quite possible that socialism would prove the most suitable form of society to deal with the population problem.[60]

In America, where the works of Smith, Say, and later Mill were popular, Malthus's inferences had been anticipated in part by Franklin and Madison. Perhaps the most outstanding of the American disciples of Malthus was Tucker, who discovered that the rate of natural increase was falling and predicted that it would continue to fall; who indicated that the terms of trade would turn against manufacturing countries where population continued to increase; and who supposed that increasing population pressure might depress the wages of free labour to the point where it would displace slave labour. Several defenders of the slave economy contended that this type of economy was relatively immune to such population pressure as tended to develop in free-labour economies. In general the American writers distinguished between old countries, where population pressure was manifesting itself, and new countries like America, where it would develop eventually should the rate of increase not gradually fall to an insignificant level as some anticipated it might.[61]

[56] Ortes, *Riflessioni sulla popolazione delle nazioni per rapporto all'economia nazionale* (1790), Chapter 7. See also Reynaud, *La théorie de la population* (1904), Part 2, Chapter 1; Marsigli, *Il problema demografico nelle dottrine politiche ed economiche Italiani* (1934), Chapter 5.

[57] See for example Destutt de Tracy, *Traité d'économie politique* (1823), pp. 185-197, 226.

[58] Courcelle-Seneuil, *Traité d'économie* . . . (1857; 1891 edit.), Bk. I, Chapter 7.

[59] According to Mill, the supply of food actually and potentially available from exporting countries was quite limited, for their accessible territory was restricted, their population was growing, and their productive efforts were subject to diminishing returns and capital shortage. Mill, *Principles of political* . . . (1848; 1936 edit.), Bk. I, Chapter 13.

[60] *Ibid.*, Bk. I, Chapters 10 and 13; Bk. II, Chapters 6 and 11; Bk. III, Chapters 2-3, 6-7; also Mill, "Chapters in socialism" (1879). On Mill's connexion with the early birth control movement see Himes, "John Stuart Mill's attitude toward Neo-Malthusianism" (1929), and Himes, *Medical history* . . . (1936). Mill's views concerning the influence of peasant ownership were inspired by Sismondi. See also Fawcett, *Manual of* . . . (1863), Bk. II, Chapters 4, 6, 8. Keynes, in *The scope and method of political economy* (1890; 1904 edit.), Chapter 9, Section 2, found in the permanent rise of wages after the Black Death an illustration of Mill's theory that large improvements are most likely to have permanent effects.

[61] Dorfman, *The economic mind in American civilization* (1946), pp. 178-195, 365; Cady, "The early American reaction to the theory of Malthus" (1931); Spengler, "Population doctrines in the United States" (1933); Spengler, "Population theory in the ante-bellum South" (1936); Spengler, "Evolutionism in American economics 1800-1850" (1950).

Although Say did not emphasize the need for moral restraint as did Malthus, presumably because he believed increments in population to be desirable as long as they could produce enough to live comfortably,[62] certain other French writers [63] supported Malthus more vigorously. Garnier, after formulating Malthus' main findings and their implications for man's welfare, proceeded to refute various criticisms which had been directed against Malthus' *Essay* and to question the adequacy of the various palliatives which had been proposed for the relief of poverty attributable, in Garnier's opinion, to population pressure. Garnier was, however, more optimistic than Malthus, since he believed men could escape poverty through the practice of prudence, through capital formation, through the regulation of family size, and through work and effort.[64] De Molinari, proceeding upon the hypothesis that population has a supply price and that man seeks pleasure and avoids pain, believed that credit and related institutions could be established which would assure something like the appropriate number of births.[65]

Reactions to Malthus elsewhere on the European continent were various. Roscher, in Germany, gave qualified support to Malthus, stressing the need for a "morally rational check on the sexual impulse" and noting that with the advance of civilization and technology, people became more free of Malthusian poverty and became more concerned with the future and with wants other than "subsistence".[66] In the Netherlands, Malthus had a supporter in Mees,[67] and in Geneva, Sismondi, though believing that the food supply would prove adequate, asserted that the prevailing distribution of property checked production and undermined prudence. He recommended that workers regulate their numbers and that institutional arrangements conducive to such regulation (e.g., peasant ownership) be promoted. Perhaps his most important contribution consisted in the observation that industrial capitalism had undermined the institutional and psychological checks to population growth which the precapitalist system provided, and as yet no suitable substitutes had appeared.[68] Rossi, although advocating moral restraint and thrift, believed that with advances in civilization changes in man's wants and productive capacity would establish a satisfactory equilibrium between numbers and resources.[69] Francesco Ferrara, somewhat influenced by Carey's views on rent and cost, supported Malthus's position in part although he placed a more optimistic interpretation upon the working of the principle of population and upon the population prospect.[70] Messedaglia criticized Malthus' progressions on the ground that they were not independent of one another as Malthus implied, since man was both a producer and a being disposed to increase in response to improvements in the opportunity to produce. The progression of population, being dependent on that of subsistence, was also neces-

[62] Say, *Cours complet d'économie politique* (1840), Part 6; Say, *Traité d'économie . . .* (1826), Bk. II; Bowley, *Nassau Senior and . . .* (1937), pp. 74-81.

[63] The views of French writers on population have been summarized by Gonnard in *Histoire des doctrines . . .* (1923), Part III; Gide and Rist, *Histoire des . . .* (1947), Vol. I, Bk. I, Chapter 2; Kretschmann, *Storia delle dottrine economiche* (1949), Chapter 31. See also Spengler, "French population theory since 1800" (1936) and Spengler, *France faces depopulation* (1938). French as well as Italian, German and English views are summarized in Nitti, *La popolazione e il sistema sociale* (1894).

[64] Garnier, *Du principe . . .* (1857; 1885 edit.), Chapters 1, 4-11. De Molinari, *La viriculture* (1897), pp. 118-119, 228-230; De Molinari's introduction to Garnier's *Du principe . . .* (1857; 1885 edit.).

[65] De Molinari, *Cours d'économie politique* (1855), Leçon 8-10; De Molinari, *La viriculture* (1897), pp. 118-119, 228-230; De Molinari's introduction to Garnier's *Du principe . . .* (1857; 1885 edit.).

[66] Roscher, "Grundlagen der Nationalökonomie" (1880); see also Rumelin, *Reden und Aufsätze* (1881), pp. 305-332.

[67] Mees, *Overzicht van enige Hoofdstukken der Staathuishoudekunde* (1866), pp. 26 ff.

[68] Sismondi, *Le nouveaux principes d'économie politique ou de la richesse dans ses rapports avec la population* (1819; 1827 edit.), Vol. II, Bk. 7. See also Amonn, *Simonde de Sismondi als Nationalökonom* (1949), Bk. II, pp. 324-378.

[69] Rossi, *Cours d'économie politique* (1840), Bk. I, pp. 200-256. His contemporary, Romagnosi, was a critic of Malthus. On the Italian theories see Marsigli, *Il problema demografico . . .* (1934); Kretschmann, *Storia delle . . .* (1949), especially Chapter 24; and Cossa, *Il principio di popolazione de Tomaso Roberto Malthus* (1895).

[70] Ferrara, *Œuvres économiques choisies* (1938), pp. 28-29, 146-147; Volta, "Francisco Ferrara et son œuvre économique" (1902); Virgilii, "Il problema della popolazione negli scritti di F. Ferrara" (1895).

sarily arithmetical, but was double the progression of subsistence.[71]

Certain early nineteenth-century authors fundamentally disagreed both with Malthus and with the writers in the tradition of the "classical school", so far as population questions were concerned. Apart from the socialists and Marxists, whose views will be taken up in a later section of this chapter, there were some writers who contended either that an increase in population density made for an increase in productivity, or that, irrespective of the rate of population growth, there was a tendency for productivity to increase, thus insuring a steady rise in *per capita* income. Such writers have either denied the law of diminishing returns altogether, or admitting its existence at least in agriculture, have asserted that its action was more than counterbalanced by a law of increasing return outside agriculture, by technical progress, or by a combination of increasing non-agricultural returns and technical progress.[72] As a rule, the argument of Malthus's early critics rested upon the supposition that division of labour increased as population became more dense,[73] though some were content to note that technical progress would be more than sufficient to counterbalance population growth, or to infer from past trends that output per head would continue to increase.[74]

One of those subscribing to the idea that with population increase there was further division of labour was Everett, who contended in addition that population did not tend to grow so rapidly as Malthus supposed and, further, that any nation could import raw produce. Everett declared "that an increase of population on a given territory necessarily and naturally produced a division of labour, and a consequent increase of skill in its application". The natural result, he said, was an extension of manufacturing and trade, with a rise in wages due to the increasing productivity of labour.[75]

Carey stressed what he called "the power of association", which grew as population grew and thereby made possible greater diversity of employments, greater development of the human faculties, and increasing *per capita* output.[76] In Carey's opinion, this tendency was not checked, as some of Malthus's other critics as-

[71] Messedaglia, *Della teoria della popolazione, principalmente sotto l'aspetto del metodo* (1858). For appraisals of Messedaglia's treatment of Malthus's two progressions, see Benini, *Principi di demografia* (1901), pp. 229-233; Pareto, *Cours d'économie politique* (1896), Vol. I, para. 192. See also Virgilii, "Il problema della popolazione negli . . . " (1895) for treatment of the amendments to Malthus's progressions suggested by Messedaglia, Pareto, Quetelet, and others.

[72] Some writers stressed rather the argument that returns in agriculture long tended to be constant. For example, see Alison, *The principles of population and their connection with human happiness* (1840), Bk. I, pp. 35-36, 55, 62, 217-220. Alison admitted that there were limits to food production, but he expected that population growth would cease before these limits were reached. *Ibid.*, pp. 42-46, 84-85. See also Kropotkin's *The conquest of bread* (1907), especially Chapter 17; Kropotkin, *Fields, factories and workshops* (1899), especially Chapters 3-5.

[73] For summaries of such arguments, see Smith, *The Malthusian controversy* (1951), pp. 58, 118-119, 147, 191, 229; Cady, "The early American reaction . . . " (1931); Spengler, "Population doctrines . . . " (1933); Bowley, *Nassau Senior and* . . . (1937), pp. 123-126; Mohl, *Geschichte* . . . (1856), pp. 462-467, 490-517. George reasoned in *Progress and poverty* (1879), Bk. 2, Chapter 4, that the economies arising out of increasing division of labour would in the long run more than compensate for the resort to poorer soils which accompanied population growth; and that so long as this was the case, but presumably not longer, population would grow.

[74] Critics of Malthus who subscribed to the "theory of increasing misery" had to build their argument on the premise that prevailing institutional conditions were making for increasing inequality. For one of the earliest critiques of Malthus's *Essay*, see Hall's *The effects of civilization on the people in European states* (1805), in which the growth of inequality was stressed. Hall said that since 0.5-0.7 acre would support a person, overpopulation would not develop in England for more than a century. By contrast Godwin indicated that 2.75 acres were required per person. See Smith, *The Malthusian* . . . (1951), pp. 54, 129. On the sources and the development of the doctrine of increasing misery see Michels, *La teoria di C. Marx sulla miseria crecente e le sue origini* (1922).

[75] Everett, *New ideas on population* (1823), Chapters 4-5, and especially pp. 28, 38-42, 111, 120-121. See also Spengler, "Alexander Hill Everett, early American opponent of Malthus" (1936).

[76] Carey's doctrine of association resembles somewhat Spencer's doctrine of increasing heterogeneity. Spencer indicated that population growth made for increasing specialization and skill. "In all ways increase of population by its actions and reactions develops a social organism which becomes more heterogeneous as it grows larger." Spencer, *Principles of sociology* (1896), Vol. III, Part VIII, Chapters 2-3. Spencer subscribed in essence to Mill's doctrine of the "stationary state". Spencer, *First principles* (1898), Part II, Chapter 22.

serted,[77] by diminishing returns in agriculture, since, contrary to Ricardo's assumption, cultivation proceeded from inferior to superior soils,[78] with the result that *per capita* output in agriculture tended to increase as population grew and settlement spread.[79] Carey believed that population growth would long continue to be conducive to increasing output *per capita,* though he admitted the existence of limits to production.[80] He did not anticipate population pressure, for he supposed that man would so develop mentally, morally, and physiologically that a suitable balance would be established between natality and mortality, on the one hand, and the resources at man's disposal, on the other.[81]

Rogers was one of the writers who did not specifically argue that population growth was a source of abundance, as did Everett and Carey, but noted that, historically, *per capita* output had tended to increase, in part because of technical progress and the fact that the better lands were sometimes the last to be brought under cultivation.[82]

Late nineteenth century opponents of Malthus seem to have placed more importance upon technical progress as such and less emphasis upon increasing specialization and division of labour than did the earlier writers. For example, Leroy-Beaulieu stated that technical progress, together with capital accumulation and the development of international division of labour, would continue to increase output per man.[83] In the view of Oppenheimer, the continuing improvement in the welfare of the masses indicated that any tendency to diminishing returns in agriculture was more than compensated for by an improved facility in manufacturing, and that an increasing productivity of labour was associated with an increasing population.[84] Much later, Wagemann stated that in the long run the law of diminishing returns was more than counterbalanced by technical progress. A condition of over-population might be replaced by one of under-population due to improved methods of social organization and production, capital formation, and other adjustments to the initial condition of over-population. But in time this condition of under-population would be again replaced by one of over-population to which further adjustments must be made. Thus Wagemann viewed demographic history as a sequence of alternating under- and overpopulation, with population growth both responding to and helping to generate economic change.[85]

The writers who drew conclusions contrary to those of Malthus from arguments relating to the "preventive checks" to population growth can be divided into three main groups. One group maintained that preventive checks would become more and more effective in slowing down population growth, though they offered little rationale to support this belief. Representatives of this group during the early part of the nineteenth century include Hazlitt, who supposed that moral restraint would prove adequate; Hamilton, who held the opinion that the rate of increase would

[77] Bowley, *Nassau Senior and . . .* (1937), pp. 123-126.

[78] Certain earlier writers, as Chalmers, attributed increases in agricultural yields to improvements in agricultural techniques. Later writers, including Mill and Hearn, argued that Ricardo's assumption of progression from superior to inferior soils did not necessarily hold for new countries. Mill, *Principles of political . . .* (1848; 1936 edit.), Bk. I, Chapter 12, Section 2; Hearn, *Plutology* (1863), pp. 13-14; Chalmers, *On political economy, in connexion with the moral state and moral prospects of society* (1832), Section 2, pp. 10-14.

[79] Carey, *Principles of social sciences* (1858), Vol. I, Chapters VII-X; Kaplan, *Henry Charles Carey* (1931), Chapters 3-4.

[80] Carey, *Principles . . .* (1859), Vol. III, Chapter XLVI, Section 1. Bastiat and his disciples, some of whom were influenced by Carey, were less optimistic concerning the possibility of increasing output; but they supposed that man's growth would be brought under voluntary control. The French writers were not hostile to Malthus as was Carey. See Spengler, "French population theory . . . " (1936).

[81] Carey, *Principles . . .* (1859), Vol. III, Chapters XLVI-XLIX. Carey employed Spencer's physiological theory.

[82] Rogers, *A manual of political economy* (1869), pp. 14, 69, 154-159.

[83] Leroy-Beaulieu, *Traité théorique et pratique d'économie politique* (1900), Bk. I, pp. 740-776; Bk. III, p. 314. Not even agriculture was an exception to the law of falling price or falling labour input per unit of output.

[84] Oppenheimer, *Das Bevölkerungsgesetz des T. R. Malthus unter der neuen Nationalökonomie* (1900), Chapters 2 and 4. Oppenheimer's views have been severely criticized. Wolf, "Une nouvelle loi de la population" (1902); Dietzel, "Der Streit um Malthus' Lehre" (1905).

[85] Wagemann, *Menschenzahl und Völkerschicksal* (1948), pp. 30 ff., 48-98, 135 ff., 210 ff., 269 ff., 308 ff., He suggested also that the earth could support in comfort 30,000 million inhabitants, given sufficient improvement. *Ibid.,* p. 229.

fall as civilization advanced; Moreton, who inferred that the failure of the "higher orders" to replace themselves and the consequent opportunity for ascent in social scale generated a tendency for a lower rate of reproduction to spread through the ranks of society; Weyland, who thought that population would cease to grow when a sufficiently high proportion of the people had located in cities, where birth rates tended to be below death rates; and many French, American, and other writers who presumed that the standard of living would continue to rise and check undue population growth.[86]

The second group of writers, not content to say that preventive checks would probably come more and more into play, attempted to demonstrate that such checks were the inevitable result of social and economic progress, and the guarantee of continuing progress. In the early part of the nineteenth century, such critics of Malthus as Senior,[87] Rickards,[88] and Alison[89] argued that as the real income of workers rose, they tended to adjust their standards of life accordingly, and that the higher standards, once attained, would not willingly be relinquished. As they became more self-respecting, workers would protect their position the more zealously by postponing marriage and limiting their families, as well as in other ways.[90] Later, as the practice of contraception became more general, anti-Malthusian writers placed increasing emphasis on arguments in this vein.[91]

The third group of anti-Malthusian writers dealing with preventive checks emphasized the reduction of natural fecundity which, they believed, would necessarily occur in the course of economic development, as a result of social selection and changes in the milieu. Many writers believed that man's fecundity would decline in response to increases in mental exertion and inbreeding and to modifications of diet,[92] and Spencer attempted to infer a self-adjusting biological principle of population growth. Spencer supposed that there existed an antagonism between the power to maintain life and the power to propagate; he considered that fertility varied inversely, while the power to maintain life varied directly, with the development of the nervous system. Where the power to maintain life was low, survival of the population required high fertility, and this in turn made the struggle for existence severe. The high fertility under such conditions tended, Spencer reasoned, to produce population pressure; and this pressure was conducive to improvements in the methods of production; intensified the need for skill, intelligence, self-control, and education; and made difficult the survival of the mentally sluggish. In consequence, man's nervous centres became enlarged, with the result that his power to maintain life increased while his power to reproduce diminished. The evolutionary tendency initially set in motion by excess fertility would tend to persist until both fertility and mortality had declined to a low level where they would balance one another.[93]

[86] Hazlitt, *A reply to the essay on population by the Rev. T. R. Malthus* (1807), Letter 4; Hamilton, *The progress of society* (1830), Chapter 18; Moreton, *Civilization, or a brief analysis of the natural laws that regulate the numbers and condition of mankind* (1836), Chapter 9; Weyland, *Principles of population and production as they are affected by the progress of society, with a view to moral and political consequences* (1816), Bk. 1, Chapters 2, 7; Bk. 3, Chapter 11; Spengler, "Population doctrines in . . . " (1933); Spengler, "French population theory . . . " (1936); Smith, *The Malthusian . . .* (1951), especially Bk. 4.

[87] Senior, *Two lectures on population, delivered before the University of Oxford in Easter term, 1828, to which is added, a correspondence between the author and the Rev. T. R. Malthus* (1829), pp. 27, 34-35; also Bowley, *Nassau Senior and . . .* (1937), Chapter 3.

[88] Rickards, *Population and capital* (1854), p. 251.

[89] Alison, *The principles of population . . .* (1840), p. 105.

[90] Sadler, in *The law of population* (1830), Bk. IV, went so far as to propose as a law that the prolificness of men varied inversely with population density.

[91] Even in the early part of the nineteenth century, some writers, including Francis Place and Robert Owen, indicated that more than moral restraint was required. See Himes, *Medical history . . .* (1936), Chapter 11.

[92] For example, on diet see Doubleday, *The true law of population, shown to be connected with the food of the people* (1841); Purves [Simon Gray], *Gray versus Malthus* (1818), Bk. 2. On mental exertion see Jarrold, *Dissertations on man, philosophical, physiological, and political; in answer to Mr. Malthus's "Essay on the Principle of Population"* (1806), pp. 245-274, 306-313. On diet and inbreeding, see Hickson, "Laws on population" (1850). Recently protein deficiency has been described as favourable to fertility by de Castro in *The geography of hunger* (1952), pp. 70-72.

[93] See Spencer, *The principles of biology* (1867), Bk. II, pp. 406-410, 479-508. Spencer's theory, first announced in 1852, was adopted by Henry Carey and other American writers, as well as by a number of continental writers.

F. Socialist and Marxist Writings

Socialist and Marxist writers since the early part of the nineteenth century have, for the most part, either denied the existence of a population problem or maintained that it would be solved through reorganization of society. They have generally attributed human misery, not to excessive population growth, but to the maldistribution of income and other supposed defects in the existing social order. They have held that under the new form of society which they advocate adequate preventive checks on population growth would operate, and that the productive forces of the people would increase more rapidly than their numbers.[94]

Among the pre-Marxian socialists of the nineteenth century, such views were not so consistently and fully developed as they were later by Marx and his followers.

Pre-Marxian socialists, concerned in one way or another with matters of population, included the English Ricardian socialists and various socialist groups in France, Germany and Italy. Considerable differences in thought on matters of population are evident from the writings of these various groups. English Ricardian socialists in general tended to reject Malthus's views. Thompson believed that population growth could be controlled in his envisioned co-operative society. Gray criticized Malthus's ratios and implied that numbers would be brought under control. Gray indicated that, since labour produced all wealth, production would keep pace with population as long as raw materials were available; hence there would be no population problem for centuries. Hodgskin, after initially accepting Malthus's views, in part rejected them, since he believed that population growth was desirable insofar as it generated a division of labour and stimulated invention.[95]

Most early French socialists opposed Malthus's views, but for different reasons than the English Ricardian socialists. Malthus's views were opposed because of their ascetic implications, their denial of the bounty of nature, their opposition to social reform and reorganization, and also because of their denial that maldistribution was a major source of misery.[96] Fourier, while believing that France was over-populated and that the world's population capacity probably did not exceed 5,000 millions, advocated emigration and control of conception for the time being instead of moral restraint as recommended by Malthus. However, Fourier and certain of his followers believed that, with the establishment of the "societary state", physiological, dietary, and other changes would bring numbers under effective control. Malthus's solution was rejected by the Saint-Simonians for the reason, among others, that it denied happiness to the worker. Louis Blanc and Pierre Leroux were critical of Malthus's views and asserted that imprudence itself was the product of misery. If misery were removed through reorganization of society, numbers would be brought under control with the more productive system which would be introduced. Proudhon, too, argued that under a system of social organization that insured justice, the population problem would disappear, since numbers would increase no more than was desirable in view of the new arrangements for production.[97] Ferdinand Lassalle believed that the reason why average wages of workers did not rise

[94] For general accounts of socialism and the theory of population, see Dumas, *Le socialisme et le principe de population* (1908); Sonolet, *Principe de population et socialisme* (1907); Soetbeer, *Die Stellung der Sozialisten zur Malthusischen Bevölkerungslehre* (1886); Martello, *L'economia politica antimalthusiana e il socialismo* (1894); Mombert, *Geschichte der Nationalökonomie* (1927), pp. 410-416; Mombert, *Bevölkerungslehre* (1929), pp. 214-235; Lowenthal, "The Ricardian socialists" (1911). For later representative statements that collectivism made for imprudence in matters of population, see Naquet, *Socialisme collectiviste, et socialisme liberal* (1890), Chapter IV; Hadley, *Economics* (1896), pp. 45-51; Budge, *Das Malthusische Bevölkerungsgesetz und die theoretische Nationalökonomie der letzten Jahrzehnte* (1912), p. 218. Lloyd early questioned this thesis on the ground that since the gain from restricting family size is largely diffused to others, the individual under capitalism has little incentive to restrict family size. See Lloyd, *Two lectures on the checks to population* (1833), p. 22.

[95] See Lowenthal, "The Ricardian . . . " (1911); Smith, *The Malthusian* . . . . (1951), Bk. II, Chapter IV; Bk. IV, Chapter III.

[96] Gonnard, *Histoire des doctrines de la population* (1923), pp. 317 ff.

[97] For detailed reference to the works of Fourier, the Saint-Simonians. Blanc, Leroux, and Proudhon, see Dumas, *Le socialisme* . . . (1908); Nitti, *La popo!azione* . . . (1894), Bk. I; Spengler, "French population theory . . . " (1936), pp. 747-753. See also Bergues, "La population vue par les utopiste" (1951).

above the level necessary to provide subsistence and to permit the maintenance of the population, was the exploitation of workers by consolidated capital. He indicated, however, that with an increase in the wage bill the population tended to increase. His solution for this dilemma was the organization of workers' productive associations.[98] Rodbertus too believed that workers normally received only a subsistence wage, but held that population increases tended to intensify the exploitation of workers. He denied that productivity tended to fall in agriculture and declared that, as a result of the development of chemistry and mechanics, "the increase in productiveness is incalculable". The solution for depressed wages and rapid population growth was to be found initially in reform and eventually in social reorganization.[99]

Achilla Loria and others developed the thesis that population pressure is characteristic only of certain stages of economic development.[100] According to Loria, an excess of population in his day — by which he meant an excess with respect to capital rather than to food — had its origin in the prevailing capitalistic wage system which operated, on the one hand, to restrict production, capital formation, and the productive employment of capital and, on the other hand, to compel the masses to work for miserable wages, thereby undermining their continence and exciting them to excessive procreation. Given sufficient capital formation and the productive use of capital, wage-depressing unemployment would be removed, wages would rise, and the living conditions and aspirations of the workers would improve, with the result that they would procreate less without resorting to contraceptive practices. Population growth itself, being the primary cause of economic evolution and of the historical succession of social forms, would directly and indirectly bring into being a form of organization free of excess population and attendant evils. This growth had long ago eliminated free land and caused the more productive system of forced association of labour, which was typical of capitalism, to replace the previous system of isolated labour. It would eventually cause the capitalistic system in turn to give place to a system of freely associated labour, since only under this latter system could agricultural workers produce enough to maintain themselves under conditions of high population density.[101]

Nitti also attributed the level of the birth rate to economic factors. Birth rates were high where poor economic conditions restricted the pleasures of the "popular classes". Each improvement in their economic condition operated to bring about a lowering of the birth rate.[102] Nitti did not consider the solution of the population problem as inevitable, but believed that it would gradually be realized by establishing a strong social organization with opportunity for the development of individuality.[103]

Marx's characterization of the population problem differed considerably from that of earlier socialist writers concerned with the Mal-

[98] See Lassalle, *Kapital und Arbeit* (1864), Chapter 4, pp. 237-239.

[99] See Rodbertus, "Zweiter Brief" (1899), pp. 5 ff., 35 ff., 71-74, 78-80; Gonner, *The social philosophy of Rodbertus* (1899), especially the introduction, Part II, Chapters 2-3, 5. On Lassalle and Rodbertus, see Dawson, *German socialism and Ferdinand Lassalle* (1888), especially Chapters 3, 6, 12-13.

[100] In a sense, this was Schäffle's opinion also, but he believed that enforced birth-limitation and relative labour scarcity would so modify economic organization as to remove the existing pressure of numbers upon subsistence. See Schäffle, *Bau und Leben des sozialen Körpers* (1878), Zweiter Band; also Marlo, *Untersuchungen über die Organisation der Arbeit, oder System der Weltökonomie* (1885) Bk. I, pp. 238-239; Bk. III, Chapter 12.

[101] Loria, *La legge di popolazione ed il sistema sociale* (1882). Loria, *Analisi della proprietá capitalista* (1889).

[102] Nitti, *La popolazione . . .* (1894), p. 162. This book is dedicated to Loria. Nitti emphasized the importance of social capillarity, as defined by Dumont, and of "civilisation" which made for "human individuality" (i.e., "an increase of functions, either in number or in density") and was antagonistic to "individualism" (i.e., "egotistical sentiment"). See Nitti, *La popolazione . . .* (1894), pp. 86-88, 126-140, 149-170, 182. Spencer's theory too, received his qualified approval. *Ibid., pp.* 66-71, 175-178, 182-184.

[103] According to Nitti: "In every society where individuality will be strongly developed, but where progress of socialisation will not extinguish individual activity; in every society where wealth will be largely sub-divided and where the social cause of inequality will be eliminated by an elevated form of co-operation, the birth-rate will tend to become equal with the means of subsistence, and the regular variations of demographic evolution will not have, as in the past, an element of fear and terror." *Ibid.*, p. 191.

thusian question.[104] He held that there could be no universal law of population, and that the source of existing "over-population" was not to be found in man's supposed biological proclivities but in the prevailing capitalist mode of production. This "over-population" arose from the fact that, because of capital accumulation, "variable capital", the source of demand for labour, increased less rapidly than did the labouring population.[105] The capitalistic mode of production thus created its own "relative surplus-population" or army of unemployed, independently of the actual rate of population increase. This Marx took to be the "law of population" under capitalism, and he held that every mode of production had its peculiar laws of population. Surplus population was not only a necessary consequence of capitalistic accumulation, but also a necessary condition to the existence and continuation of the capitalistic form of economic organization, for that mode of production required "the readily exploitable manpower".[106] Only when this reserve was sufficiently great could the pretensions of the employed workers be held in check and the rates of surplus value and profit be maintained.[107]

Marx identified three forms of "relative surplus population", or unemployment: "the floating, the latent, the stagnant". The *floating* category was recruited in large part from those displaced by machinery. The *latent* category was made up of that part of the agricultural population which was on the verge of migrating to the cities, and the *stagnant* form comprised workers with highly irregular employment. Natural increase alone could not supply enough recruits for the industrial reserve army, partly because death and morbidity rates were high and because youthful workers were preferred in many employments.[108] Therefore, according to Marx, it was essential to the capitalist system that capital of the sort that displaced labour be accumulated in sufficient volume to generate unemployment.[109] Surplus population could be created also through expropriation of land and the movement of dispossessed peasants out of agriculture.[110]

Marx's explanation implied that relative over-population of the sort associated with the capitalist mode of production would disappear when capitalism was superseded by a collective mode of production. He had little to say explicitly about the manner in which population would grow thereafter. His analysis of reproductive behaviour under capitalism suggested, however, that the increase of income, the reduction of inequalities in income distribution, and the improvements in the living conditions of the masses, which he expected to result from the reorganization of society, would bring about a decline of the death rate. The birth rate also would presumably decline because of the rise in living

[104] For accounts see Sweezy, *The theory of capitalist development. Principles of Marxian political economy* (1942), pp. 86-92, 222-226; Levin, "Marx versus Malthus" (1936); Robinson, *An essay on Marxian economics* (1949); and Robinson, "Marx on unemployment" (1941); Dobb, *Political economy and capitalism* (1937), pp. 85-89, 98-103, 124, 207; Dobb, *Studies in the development of capitalism* (1947), especially Chapters 6-8; Bukarin and others, *Marxism and modern thought* (1938), pp. 193-195, 216-217.

[105] Marx, *Das Kapital. Kritik der politischen Oekonomie* (1867); (1903 edit.), Erster Band, p. 594.

[106] *Ibid.*, pp. 596-597. See also Marx, *Letters to Dr. Kugelmann* (1934), p. 111; Engels, *Dialectics of nature* (1940), pp. 208-209, 235.

[107] Marx, *Das Kapital* . . . (1867; 1903 edit.), Erster Band, pp. 598, 602-604; *Ibid.* (1894; 1904 edit.), Dritter Band, p. 217.

[108] *Ibid.*, Erster Band, pp. 606-608. Marx indicated that when the industrial reserve army was large and wages were kept down natural increase was greater. Birth rates, death rates, and the size of families, he held, varied in inverse proportion to the level of wages and the amount of means of subsistence at the disposal of various groups of workers. *Ibid.* (1867; 1903 edit.), Erster Band, pp. 608, 476-477; *Ibid.* (1894; 1904 edit.), Dritter Band, pp. 198-199.

[109] Crises and depressions also increased the number unemployed. For Marx's explanation of the manner in which capital accumulation generated unemployment, see *ibid.* (1867; 1903 edit.), Erster Band, pp. 372, 577-585, 594-596, 603, 610-611; *ibid.* (1894; 1904 edit.), Dritter Band, pp. 202-204. He recognized that at times the needs for accumulating capital were such that the demand for labour rose more rapidly than its supply, with the result that wages advanced. *Ibid.* (1867; 1903 edit.), Erster Band, pp. 577, 584-585. For Marx's views on emigration and urbanization, see *ibid.* (1867; 1903 edit.), Erster Band, pp. 470, 536-539. For his comment on the difficulties attending the formation of an industrial reserve army in colonies and newly settled lands, see *ibid.* (1867; 1903 edit.), Erster Band, pp. 729-739; also Pappe, "Wakefield and Marx" (1951).

[110] Marx, *Das Kapital* . . . (1867; 1903 edit.), Erster Band, pp. 682-714.

standards and the ending of the exploitation of children.[111]

Marx apparently placed no value upon moral restraint as a remedy to over-population. He stated, but did not elaborate, that a decline in the rate of population growth [112] might accentuate the tendency toward under-consumption and reduced profits, and thus expedite the breakdown of capitalism.[113]

The followers of Marx were not always in agreement in their views regarding the population problem, although in general they supported Marx. Bebel pointed, on the one hand, to the possibility of greatly augmenting the food supply, and on the other, to the presumption that, with improved economic conditions, human fertility would fall. He held that population was likely to increase more slowly in a socialistic society than in a bourgeois society, mainly because of the superior position of women under socialism.[114] Kautsky, unlike most socialists, initially attached considerable importance to the population question, suggesting among other things the possibility of both Marxian relative over-population and Malthusian absolute over-population.[115] Following Marx more closely in his later writings, he explained over-population as a result of the "variable constituent" of capital increasing less rapidly than both total capital and the labouring population. There might ensue an excess of population relative to variable capital and a deficiency of numbers relative to the means of life, with the result that wages would be depressed and profits would rise. This situation would disappear upon the collectivization of the economy.[116] He believed that under socialism conditions more conducive both to the appropriate regulation of numbers and to the increase of production would develop.[117]

Lenin, like Marx, rejected the Malthusian principle of population. He denied, also, that the law of diminishing returns applied under conditions of technological progress and changing methods of production, and maintained that it was applicable only where techniques remained unchanged.[118] By way of evidence, he pointed to the decline, or negligible increase, in the agricultural population of advanced countries, which had occurred simultaneously with the expansion of agricultural production.[119]

Although certain socialist writers in the 1920's and 1930's showed Malthusian leanings, the emphasis of contemporary socialist writings has been strongly anti-Malthusian.[120] The later writers have continued to assert that relative over-population, though characteristic of the capitalist mode of production, is avoided under socialism; and they have given much attention to the problem of converting rural population into the kind

[111] *Ibid.*, pp. 606-608, 621-624, 629. Elsewhere Marx indicated that, in the capitalistic society, a temporary excess of "surplus capital" over the working population would raise wages and thus reduce mortality and raise the marriage rate, so that the working population would increase. The relative over-population would be augmented also by the technological unemployment due to this capital surplus. *Ibid.* (1894; 1904 edit.), Dritter Band, pp. 198-199.

[112] *Ibid.* (1867; 1903 edit.), Erster Band, pp. 584-585. Engels pointed out to Bebel in a letter (March, 1875) that Marx had refuted the Malthusian basis for Lassalle's iron law of wages. See Marx and Engels, *Correspondence*, 1846-1895 (1934), p. 335.

[113] Sweezy, *The theory of . . .* (1942), pp. 222-226. Dobb pointed out, however, that a high correlation did not exist between the volume of employment and the rate of population growth in various countries.

[114] See Bebel, *Die Frau und der Sozialismus* (1894), pp. 441-463.

[115] See Kautsky, *Der Einfluss der Volksvermehrung auf den Fortschritt der Gesellschaft* (1880), especially Chapter 5 on the control of population growth. See also Schippel, *Das moderne Elend und die moderne Ubervölkerung* (1883), p. 242, and conclusion.

[116] See Kautsky, *The economic doctrines of Karl Marx* (1925), Part III, Chapter 5.

[117] See Kautsky, *Vermehrung und Entwicklung in Natur und Gesellschaft* (1920), especially Chapter 16.

[118] Lenin, *Theory of the agrarian question* (1938 trans.), pp. 52-54, 314-321; Lenin, *Marx-Engels Marxism* (1935 trans.), p. 23.

[119] Lenin, *Theory of the . . .* (1938 trans.), pp. 58-63. On the movement of migrants, imperialism, and the state of development of economies, see Lenin's *Imperializm* (1917), Chapter 8. Lenin used Marx's conception of "capitalist over-population" and the industrial reserve army, and made reply to those who misinterpreted Marx's views on population and related matters. See Lenin, *Marx-Engels Marxism* (1935 trans.), pp. 19-20, 24.

[120] Smulevich, *Burzhuaznye teorii narodonaseleniya v svete marksistskoleninskoy kritiki* (1936). Smulevich severely criticized Malthusian, racist, organic, Sombartian, fascist, and Nazi population theories; appraised bourgeois analyses of the decline in natality in capitalist countries; and attempted to account for this decline. See also Sauvy, "Doctrine soviétique en matiére de population" (1948).

of manpower needed for a modern economy.[121] They have also given considerable attention to the actual and prospective trends of natural increase, noting that in capitalistic countries, particularly mature ones, relative over-population and other conditions were slowing down population growth and might eventually bring about depopulation. In socialist countries, on the contrary, they have held that a healthy growth of population was assured, since the philosophy of family limitation was there disapproved,[122] and socialism did not necessitate family limitation as did capitalism.[123]

Stalin has looked with favour upon population growth, but in view of the teaching of dialectical and historical materialism, has said that the growth of population was not an important determinant of the character of the social system. Population growth facilitates or retards the development of society, but it does not determine its development. For example, population growth does not, in itself, explain why the primitive communal system has given way to the slave system, the slave system to the feudal system, and the feudal system to the bourgeois system, instead of to other forms of social and economic organization. Stalin has also pointed out that, were social development determined by the growth of population, "a higher density of population would be bound to give rise to a correspondingly higher type of social system". He has noted, however, that types of social systems are not correlated with the degree of population density. The chief force determining the character of the social system has not been population growth but "the *method of procuring the means of life* necessary for human existence, the *mode of production of material values* . . . which are indispensable for the life and development of society".[124]

While present day Russian writers are opposed to concern with matters of over-population because they believe that such a problem is non-existent under socialism, the subject has not been completely ignored by certain post-revolutionary writers.[125] The possibility has been noted

[121] For example, see Trubnikov, "Gosudarstvennye trudovye reservy: SSSR" (1940); Sonin, *Voprosy balansa rabochei sily* (1949); Mastikov, "Po vuprosa za dvizhenieto na selskoto rabotno naselenie v Bulgariâ" (1949). See also Granovskiy, "Sotsialisticheskaya i kapitalisticheskaya industrializatsiya" (1947). Latsis in his *Agrarnoye perenaseleniye i perspektivy borby s nim* (1929), noting that "agrarian over-population" was a result of existing but modifiable conditions, indicated that it could be eliminated but only through efforts spread over some years. See also Leontiev, *Political economy* (1935), pp. 122-125, 210-211; Dutt, *The problem of India* (1943), Part II. Dutt attributed the agricultural over-population of India to what he called "de-industrialization".

[122] For Lenin's views on neomalthusianism and the working class see Lenin, *Sochineniya* (1930), Vol. 16, pp. 497-499,

[123] For example, see Sulkevich, *Territoriya i naseleniye SSSR* (1940), pp. 8-9; Bosin and Dubrowitzki, "Perviye Itogi Vsesoyuznoi Perepisi Naseleniya 1939 g" (1939), p. 23; Besher attributed the decline of fertility in workers' families in capitalist countries to the recruitment of women for industry, and Smulevich to the hard conditions under which women worked. Besher, *Problemy naseleniya v narodnokhozyaystvennom planirovanii* (1937), p. 10; Smulevich, *Materinstvo pri kapitalizme i sotsializme* (1935), Chapter I. In an earlier study Smulevich observed that the entry of women into industry, assisted by the practice of contraception, was reducing fertility in capitalistic countries, and that even in socialist countries, in the transitional stage before socialistic organization could counteract individualism, motives resembling those characteristic of capitalist countries operated to produce family limitation. In time, however, under socialism these motives would disappear and the population would be under pressure to conform to the pattern of fertility established in the socialist society. Under socialism, therefore, population growth of desirable proportions would take place. But under capitalism the circumstances making for the limitation of numbers would gain in strength and perhaps finally make for depopulation. It was to be expected, therefore, that the demographic futures of capitalist and socialist countries would differ. See Smulevich, *Zabolevayemost i smertnost naseleniya gorodov i mestechek BSSR* (1928), especially Chapter 3. Smulevich stated that the rate of population increase depended upon the type of social organization, each type having its own law of population. Under capitalism natality tended to fall below mortality, and capitalist policies could not greatly modify this tendency. Under capitalism the wealthy restricted their families because they did not wish to subdivide their property holdings unduly; the petty bourgeois did so because they wanted to educate their children and prevent their becoming proletarians. The proletarians were less fertile than they had been formerly when they married early and did not seek to limit family size; for now, with child-labour and compulsory education laws, children could not begin to earn at so early an age, and more women were entering arduous employment outside the home. Under capitalism mortality was higher among the poor than existing medical knowledge warranted.

[124] See Stalin, *Voprosy leninizma* (1934), pp. 535-563.

[125] Peshchanskiy, for example, suggested that the observed decline in fertility might be considered as a posi-

of at least temporary relative over-population under socialism until the achievement of a desirable level of productivity and development.[126] While over-population, defined in terms of unused time,[127] has existed in various parts of the U.S.S.R., it has generally been believed that in the long-run Malthusian fears were unwarranted.[128]

G. Recent Development of Non-Socialist Theories Relevant to Population

During the period since about 1870, non-socialist writings on population have generally departed much more from Malthus' views than did those during the earlier part of the nineteenth century, with the result that the cleavage between socialist and non-socialist doctrine on this subject is no longer as distinct as it formerly was. The developments in non-socialist, like those in socialist theories, have been affected by several important changes in circumstances. First, statistical information relevant to population has been greatly extended and the methods of analysing demographic statistics have been much improved. Second, after about 1870 the birth rate and the rate of natural increase began to decline in certain of the economically most advanced countries. Third, significant improvements continued to be made in both manufacturing and the extractive industries, with the result that living conditions improved. Fourth, writers devoted to the developing science of sociology and the study of social evolution have taken an increasing part in the study of population questions. Meanwhile, new emphases have been introduced in economics. The marginalist school of economics, though not greatly concerned with population problems,[129] developed explanations of the principles governing production and the shares of labour and capital in the total product, which had evident bearings upon population theory.[130]

In England, Germany, Holland, the United States, and, to a lesser degree, in France and elsewhere a significant number of writers in the late nineteenth century and in the twentieth continued to emphasize that, unless population growth slowed down, the economic condition of the people would be adversely affected.[131] In England, perhaps more than elsewhere, the sup-

tive achievement of the October revolution. Peshchanskiy, "Osnovnye pokazateli yestestvennogo dvizheniya naseleniya Evropeyskoy chasti RSFSR v 1927 godu" (1928).

[126] Lubny-Gertsyk stated that a condition of over-population existed when the actual population exceeded the number that could attain a desirable level of productivity and development with the existing resources and technical conditions. Over-population might exist because natural resources were insufficient, because consumers' needs could not be satisfied, or because for various reasons production had fallen relative to population. Of the alternative remedies, a decrease in numbers or an increase in productivity, the latter was preferable. If, however, this was not easily accomplished, a regulation of fertility was indicated. Lubny-Gertsyk, *Chto takoye perenaseleniye* (1923), pp. 46, 56, 98, 100.

[127] Mints, *Agrarnoye perenaseleniye i rynok truda v SSSR* (1929).

[128] See, for example, Prasolov, "Kratkiy obzor geografii pochv vsey sushi" (1945).

[129] For example, Jevons said that the doctrine of population, though valid and important, "forms no part of the direct problem of economy" which had to do with maximizing the return from a given stock of productive agents. Jevons, *The theory of political economy* (1871), pp. 254-255. See also the treatment of population by Pantaleoni in his *Principii di economia pura* (1889), especially Chapter 1.

[130] See Douglas, "Elasticity of supply as a determinant of distribution" (1929); also Douglas, *The theory of wages* (1934), Part I. See also Davenport, *The economics of enterprise* (1913), pp. 180-181, 425-426.

[131] Representative of the views of the British economists are those of Marshall, *Principles of economics* (1898), especially the preface and Bk. IV, Chapter 4; Bk. VI, Chapter 2; Cunningham, "On the statement of the Malthusian principle" (1883); Price, *Chapters on political economy* (1878), pp. 185, 191-196; Huxley, *Methods and results* (1896), p. 315; Campbell, *The unseen foundations of society* (1893), pp. 452-503; Smart, *Studies in economics* (1895), p. 38; Hobson, *Problems of poverty: an enquiry into the industrial condition of the poor* (1896), p. 133; Bonar, "The centenary of Malthus" (1898); Nicholson, *Principles of political economy* (1893), pp. 187 ff. On the American and French writers, see Spengler, "Population doctrines . . ." (1933); Spengler, "Population theory . . ." (1936); Spengler, "French population theory . . ." (1936). On the German writers see Elster, "Bevölkerungswesen" (1909). On the Dutch writers see Pierson, *Leerboek der Staathuishondkunde* (1902), Vol. II, Part 3; deJong, *Inleiding tot het Bevolkingsvraagstuk* (1946), especially Chapter 6. On the Italian writers see Marsigli, *Il problema demografico . . .* (1934); and Cossa, *Introduzione allo studio dell'economia politica* (1892). Cossa subscribed to the substance of Malthus's doctrine. The Dutch, Italian, and other schools of economists are discussed in Palgrave's *Dictionary of political economy* (1915), Vol. I, especially pp. 656-660; Vol. II pp. 460-470.

posed benefits of emigration were stressed,[132] while in the United States and France the alleged disadvantages of immigration were expounded.

(1) Development of Theory Concerning the "Laws of Returns"

While earlier nineteenth-century writers had commonly believed that manufacturers were subject to constant or increasing returns and that the augmentation of production in the extractive industries involved increasing difficulties and rising costs in spite of technical progress, it came to be accepted before the close of the century that, other things being equal, average output per worker would fall in non-extractive as well as in extractive industries after the ratio of workers to the resources with which they work past a certain point.[133] It was recognized, however, that other things were not equal, and that the effects of population growth upon wages and *per capita* income depended upon accompanying changes in social organization, technological skill and productive wealth. The latter factors might change as a result of population growth, or for independent reasons, in such a way as to counterbalance the tendency toward diminishing returns.[134]

Out of consideration of these ideas came the modern notion of a dynamic variable optimum population advanced by Cannan and other writers.[135] Cannan defined optimum as a population that was moving in the right direction with respect to the increase of output *per capita*. "The right movement is that which will give the largest returns to industry in the long run, the interests

[132] See Carrothers, *Emigration from the British Isles* (1929), Chapter 3, 13-15; Erickson, "The encouragement of emigration by British trade unions, 1850-1900" (1949); Fawcett, *Manual of . . .* (1863), pp. 249 ff; Hobson, *Problems of poverty . . .* (1896), p. 133; Farr, *Vital statistics* (1885), pp. 59-62; Godard, *Poverty: its genesis and exodus* (1892), p. 141.

[133] Stigler, *Production and distribution theories* (1941), pp. 49 ff, 258, 265 ff, 358. Among the first to stress the universal character of the law of diminishing incremental returns under static conditions were Commons, in *The distribution of wealth* (1893), Chapters 3-4, and the Australian economist, Hearn, in *Plutology* (1863), pp. 117-119. Hearn pointed out that "in the absence of any increase of skill or improved machinery", diminishing returns must characterize manufacturing as well as agriculture, fishing, and other activities based upon the exploitation of "natural agents"; and that output per worker had not fallen with the growth of population only because of increases in the knowledge and skill of workers and in the equipment put at their disposal. Hearn was not apprehensive concerning the population prospect, however, even though he noted man's great capacity for natural increase and the limits to which augmentation of production was subject. He thought that growth of population, if accompanied by complex industrial reorganization, makes for "more complete control over nature" and for economies of the sort associated with extension of the division of labour. He believed that the effectiveness of the prudential check to population growth increased as a community advanced in civilization and wealth, though never enough, apparently, to stop population growth and remove the pressure of numbers upon wealth. *Ibid.*, pp. 389-395.

[134] Some writers paid little attention to the laws of returns. See Cassel, *Theoretische Sozialökonomie* (1918), Bk. I, Kap. III, para. 13; Bk. II, Kap. VI, para. 24; Bk. II, Kap. VIII, para. 35; von Wieser, "Theorie der gesellschaftlichen Wirtschaft" (1924); Clark, *Essentials of economic theory* (1907), Chapter 23. The opinions expressed in these works were formed around the turn of the century. Cassel, in *Theoretische Solzialökonomie* (1918), p. 306, agreed with Marshall that the "iron law of wages" held in most of the world. Von Wieser noted that the "law of population always exerts the most oppressive influence on the lowest strata of the workers". Von Wieser, "Theorie der . . ." (1924), p. 370. Pierson supported Malthus' views and emphasized the limits to production in Pierson, *Leerboek . . .* (1902), Vol. II, Part III, Chapter 3. Clark stated that population growth tended to depress average output. Clark, *Essentials of . . .* (1907), p. 317.

[135] See Cannan, *Elementary political economy* (1888), Part 1, para. 7; Cannan, *A history of the theories of production and distribution in English political economy from 1776-1848* (1894), Chapter 5; Cannan, *Wealth* (1928), Chapter 4. Historical accounts of the development of the optimum concept are given in Cohn, *Die Theorie des Bevölkerungs optimums* (1934), Part 3, Kap. 2; and Fua, *La conception économique de l'optimum du peuplement; population et bien-etre* (1940), Part I, div. 2. For shorter accounts see Wolfe, "The population problem since the World War: a survey of literature and research" (1928); Robbins, "The optimum theory . . ." (1927); Mombert, *Bevölkerungslehre* (1929); Mombert, "L'optimum de population" (1935); deJong, *Inleiding . . .* (1946), Chapter 6. On the more recent history of the optimum see Gottlieb, "The theory of optimum population for a closed economy" (1945); Gottlieb, "Optimum population, foreign trade and world economy" (1949). See also Ferenczi, *The synthetic optimum of population; an outline of an international demographic policy* (1938); Wright, *Population and peace; a survey of international opinion on claims for relief from population pressure* (1939). For further discussion of optimum population, see Chapter XIII, Section G. 1.

of the people of all the generations being taken into account." Cannan envisioned a "point of maximum return to all industries taken together," that is, a population, given which the productivity of labour would be at a maximum.[136] He indicated that the optimum magnitude changed as circumstances changed, usually faster than the actual population; generally, it tended to increase.[137]

Sidgwick, a late nineteenth-century economist, considered that the density of population in Great Britain had reached such a point that, without an adequate volume of foreign trade at satisfactory terms of exchange, no known improvements in the industrial arts could prevent further increases of population from depressing output per worker. He apparently anticipated no other change that would cause an increase in population density in Britain to augment average output.[138] Marshall, on the other hand, held that an increase of labour and capital generally led to improved organization and efficiency, thus offsetting the tendency toward diminishing returns which was inherent in "the part which nature plays in production". This proposition he called the "law of increasing return". He declared that an increase of population "accompanied by an equal increase in the material sources of enjoyment and aids to production" was likely to result in an economic benefit to the people, provided adequate supplies of raw materials could be obtained without too great difficulty and overcrowding did not impair health and opportunities for recreation. He believed that the growth of population in England and other "civilized countries" was, on the whole, advantageous. Should circumstances change, however, for instance, should foreign supplies be cut off, this growth might have disadvantageous effect.[139] But elsewhere in the world Marshall believed that the population situation was less favourable; only if numbers were effectively regulated could the "iron" law of wages be escaped and the comforts of western Europe be spread throughout the world.[140]

The fear that food imports might cease to be available to European countries was shared by Crookes and Giffen. From statistical evidence they inferred that the volume of food exports of export countries wtih a continuing growth of population would decline and, consequently, that the importing countries would be more dependent upon domestic production, that emigration to the new world would diminish, and that the condition of European workers would be adversely affected.[141] In Germany, which had become more dependent upon grain imports as industrialization proceeded,[142] Adolf

[136] See Cannan, *Wealth* (1928), Chapter 3. Wicksell, like Cannan, located the optimum at the point where the gains from division of labour, co-operation, industrial organization, etc., just balanced the productivity-decreasing effect of the diminution in land and natural resources *per capita* occasioned by population growth. This point was not fixed, but shifted with the introduction of new inventions and technical knowledge. For Wicksell's views see Cohn, *Die Theorie des . . .* (1934), pp. 81-83.

[137] Cannan was not apprehensive concerning overpopulation since upon analysis of trends he expected the English rate of growth to descend to a trifling level by 1950 and to zero by the close of the century. Cannan, "The probability of a cessation of the growth of population in England and Wales during the next century" (1895).

[138] Sidgwick, *Principles of political economy* (1887), Chapter 6, paras. 3-5. Robbins in "The optimum theory . . ." (1927), noted that "with a little judicious editing" a strong case "could be made out for the claim of Sidgwick to be the real parent" of the modern optimum theory. See Sidgwick, *The methods of ethics* (1890), p. 413; Sidgwick, *The elements of politics* (1897), pp. 317-318.

[139] See Marshall, *Elements of economics of industry* (1899), Bk. IV, Chapter 13; Marshall, *Principles of economics* (1898), Bk. IV, Chapter 13. In the same chapter, however, Marshall said that perhaps output per head would rise faster in advanced countries if population grew less rapidly. See also Wolf, "Ein neuer Gegner des Malthus" (1901); Wolf, *Nationalökonomie als exakte Wissenschaft* (1908), pp. 13, 191, 197. In his 1901 paper Wolf observed that within limits, increases in population density increased *per capita* output. In his 1908 work he regularly employed the term "optimum", indicating there was an optimum for each industry, and one for the whole population where labour input per unit of output was at a minimum. Also see Cohn, *Die Theorie des . . .* (1934), pp. 89-92.

[140] Marshall, *Principles of economics* (1898), pp. 180 and 531.

[141] See Davis, "The spectre of the dearth of food: history's answer to Sir William Crookes" (1932); Giffen, *Economic enquiries and studies* (1904), Vol. I, pp. 382 ff; Vol. II, pp. 14-27, 35-38, 46, 230, 340-344.

[142] List, critic of Malthus, advocate of German industrialization, and proponent of temporary protectionism for under-industrialized countries, had implied that Germany's population would be larger and of better quality, given industrialization. See List, *Das Nationale System der Politischen Oekonomie* (1841), pp. 573-586.

Wagner and others were apprehensive lest the population became too dependent upon foreign food supplies and thereby purchase numbers at the expense of security. Brentano and others challenged this view and the protectionist policies based on it. Brentano denied that diminishing returns and other circumstances would make it impossible for Germany's suppliers to provide agricultural commodities on terms satisfactory to Germany.[143]

Following World War I, Keynes pointed to the supposedly unfavourable trend in the terms of trade as evidence of over-population.[144] In his view, with Europe already dependent upon the agriculture of the new world and with agriculture there already subject to diminishing returns, the position of the population of Europe was precarious and the terms on which agricultural imports were to be had would turn increasingly against her.[145] The issue was discussed occasionally in the 1920's and 1930's[146] and received more attention after World War II as a result of the difficulties encountered by countries greatly dependent upon foreign trade.[147]

Some writers also expected that exhaustion or deterioration of natural resources would make it difficult for European industry to continue expanding more rapidly than population would grow. Jevons predicted that, with the exhaustion of Britain's richer veins of coal, the cost of extracting coal would steadily rise and check Britain's industrial progress. If changes in other countries did not bring Britain to "a stationary condition," it "must come when our mines have reached a certain depth".[148] While Jevons' view received relatively little favourable attention in France,[149] it did command interest in England and eventually elsewhere.[150]

[143] Wagner, *Agrar-und Industriestaat* (1902), pp. 23-38, 143, 152-160; Brentano, *Die Schrecken des überwiegenden Industriestaats* (1902), pp. 5-52. Dietzel, in *Weltwirtschaft und Volkswirtschaft* (1900), pp. 112-120, estimated that the world wheat supply would be adequate. On the controversy and the relevant literature see Haberler, "Der internationale Handel. Theorie der weltwirtschaftlichen Zusammenhänge sowie Darstellung und Analyse der Aussenhandelspolitik" (1933). See also Pierson's account of the inability of foreign trade to supply a growing and adequate volume of raw produce. Pierson, *Leerboek* . . . (1902), Vol. II, pp. 152-156.

[144] Keynes' argument was criticized by Beveridge, who sought to show that Keynes had misinterpreted the data. For a later comment by Beveridge, see his "Mr. Keynes' evidence for over-population" (1924). Concerning the difficulties attendant upon using the terms of trade as an index of population maladjustment, see Rostow, "The terms of trade in theory and practice" (1950); Rostow, "The historical analysis of the terms of trade" (1951). See also Clark, *The conditions of economic progress* (1940), Chapter 14. Recently Clark predicted that, in part because of the growth of population, the terms of trade would turn increasingly in favour of exporters of food and raw materials. Clark, "The future of the terms of trade" (1951).

[145] Keynes, *The economic consequences of the peace* (1920), Chapter 2. Keynes' inferences, together with a number of studies that purported to show the rate of natural increase to remain high, led to "the rediscovery of the geometrical ratio" and fear of eventual over-population. See Wolfe, "The population problem . . ." (1928).

[146] See Mombert, in *Bevölkerungslehre* (1929), pp. 373-419.

[147] It was suggested in an Australian study that "the advantage of protection is in the maintenance of a larger population than could have been expected at the same standard of living without the protective tariff. It is not an advantage to every part of the population, nor has it produced the maximum of income per head." See Brigden and others, *The Australian tariff* (1929), p. 140. Haberler pointed out that, if protection results in a net increase in population, it is at the expense of a diminution of social product per head. Haberler, "Der internationale Handel . . ." (1933). Clark stated, however, that industrial protectionism was restricting Australia's population capacity by preventing agricultural expansion. Clark, "Australian over-industrialisation" (1952).

[148] See Jevons, *The coal question; an inquiry concerning the progress of the nation, and the probable exhaustion of our coalmines* (1865), Chapter 10. Already in the early 1860's Jevons, concerned with the growth of the demand for coal, thought he detected the approach of the British population toward a stationary condition. Bobbage, as early as 1832, indicated that the world's coal mines might ultimately be exhausted. Bobbage, *On the economy of machinery and manufacturers* (1932), p. 317.

[149] Kerrilis stated that by the time the coal supplies of the world had been exhausted, men would be using the energy of the sun. Kerrilis, "Les ressources houillères du globe" (1876). Leroy-Beaulieu suggested, following Berthelot, that man would probably develop synthetic food and learn to harness the energy of the sun and of the interior of the earth. Leroy-Beaulieu, *Traité théorique et* . . . (1900), Vol. I, pp. 767-778; Vol. II, pp. 40-42, 283, 546; Vol. IV, pp. 537-540. Leroy-Beaulieu's optimism was shared by Jevons, who said solar energy would take the place of coal. See Jevons, *The British coal trade* (1915), p. 798. Charles Gide noted that manufacturing, while exempt from the working of the "law of decreasing returns", was subject to limits, but he did not include among them the decline in the

A number of writers took exception to the so-called law of increasing returns as formulated by Marshall and others, on the ground that it minimized the problems of realizing the potential increase in efficiency and output that growth of capital and labour supply might seem to make possible.[151] Wicksell pointed out that the validity of Marshall's "law" depended on the assumption, which he considered unacceptable, "that the raw materials required are to be found in practically unlimited quantities at an unchanged, or almost unchanged, price". Although increasing returns might well prevail for a time, Wicksell thought that diminishing returns would prevail in the long run.[152] Wolfe pointed out that natural resources always set a limit to production, though the limit was in all cases at least somewhat elastic and in some cases might be far in the future. Continuing population growth would therefore eventually bring the law of diminishing returns into operation, so that changed economic, social and political policies would be necessary to ensure continued progress in the material well-being of the people.[153]

Budge held that the limitations to human progress were to be found in nature rather than in man's institutions, and that population was tending to increase beyond the means of subsistence. He denied that diminishing returns in agriculture would be offset indefinitely by improvements in agricultural technique or counterbalanced by increasing returns in manufactures and transportation, or that population increases caused *per capita* product to rise.[154] Wolf drew attention to the various limitations to which technical progress itself is subject, thereby in effect denying the way of escape which many sought from the Malthusian problem.[155] Mombert, while admitting the operation of diminishing returns in agriculture and the limitations on technical progress, described by Wolf, believed that there existed many ways by which these tendencies could be counterbalanced; thus, he anticipated improving living conditions rather than increasing population pressure for some time to come.[156]

---

coal supply to which he drew attention. He doubted whether synthetic food would ever be available for the support of a dense population. See Gide, *Principes d'économie politique* (1889).

[150] Giffen, *Economic inquiries . . .* (1904), Vol. 2, p. 276, described metals as "presenting as much, or even more, difficulty than food". For subsequent developments see Wolfe, "The population . . . " (1928). For later treatments of the mineral exhaustion problem, see Tryon and Mann, "Mineral resources for future populations" (1926), Chapter 8; and Mitchell (ed.), *Recent social trends in the United States* (1933), Bk. I, Chapter 2.

[151] On the manner in which some of these laws of returns were formulated, see Stigler, *Production and . . .* (1941), pp. 48 ff., 350. An increase in average returns occasioned by fuller use of large, relatively indivisible, factors is of much less import for population theory than for cost theory and so is ignored here. But see Chamberlin, "Proportionality, divisibility, and economies of scale" (1948).

[152] See Wicksell, *Föreläsningar i nationalekonomi* (1928), Bk. I, p. 112. Wicksell wrote extensively on the mechanics of population growth and was one of the formulators of the concept of optimum population. See Kock, "Nymalthusianismens genombrott i Sverige" (1945), pp. 73-88.

[153] Wolfe, *Readings in social problems* (1916), p. 1. Wolfe emphasized the value of optimum population theory in focusing attention upon the problem of achieving a satisfactory adjustment of numbers to resources. Wolfe, "The population problem . . . " (1928); Wolfe, "The optimum size of population" (1926); Wolfe, "The theory of optimum population" (1936); Wolfe, "The rationalisation of production and of reproduction" (1935).

[154] Budge, *Das Malthus'sche Bevölkerungsgesetz . . .* (1912), especially Chapter 2. Budge attributed the decline in the birth rate to the fact that men wanted to maintain or elevate their standard of living; consequently, a falling death rate entailed a falling birth rate, since if more children survived the standard of living could be preserved only if fewer were born. He believed that socialism might weaken the tendency to restrict family size and that populations which did not regulate their numbers might over-run those which did. See *ibid.*, pp. 156, 184-185, 217-220.

[155] Wolf identified four factors limiting economic progress and accordingly formulated four "laws of retardation of progress". One of these "laws" was that "every technical improvement . . . bars the way to further progress" by reducing the number and the range of possibilities still open in a field until finally all possibilities have been exhausted and technical development has ceased. Wolf, *Die Volkswirtschaft der Gegenwart und Zukunft* (1912), pp. 335 ff.; Wolf, *Nahrungsspielraum und Menschenzahl* (1917), pp. 19-27.

[156] Mombert, *Bevölkerungslehre* (1929), pp. 356-372. Mombert indicated that a country might attempt to expand its capacity to support a population at a given level by augmenting domestic production for domestic consumption, or by exchanging products that embodied much labour for raw materials in foreign markets. He indicated, however, that the countries whence these raw materials came would in time require most of them for domestic use, and that consequently, both the terms of trade and the rate of capital formation in countries short

In recent literature less emphasis has been devoted to "laws of returns" [157] as such than to the sum total of the factors which affect the trends of aggregate income and *per capita* income, population being considered one of the more important of these factors.[158]

(2) DEVELOPMENT OF THEORIES CONCERNING THE DETERMINANTS OF POPULATION GROWTH

Writers in the eighteenth and the early nineteenth centuries generally thought that the increase of the food supply regulated the growth of population.[159] In more recent literature the idea has been developed that certain requirements other than food, which cannot readily be replaced by substitutes, may become population-limiting factors.[160] More and more the growth of population has been treated as a function of increasing income; thus the pertinence of Malthusian theory regarding the increase of "subsistence" and its relation to population growth has diminished.[161] There has, moreover, been an increasing recognition of the complexity of the factors affecting the rate of population growth. Bagehot, for example, stated that "the causes which determine the increases of mankind are little less than all the causes, outward and inward, which determine human action." [162] Pareto held a similar view, although he emphasized the importance of the economic factor in the slowing down of population growth in Europe.[163]

The reasons for the declining birth rates and natural increase rates in various European countries were a subject of considerable conjecture among writers of the late nineteenth and early twentieth centuries. A number of writers believed that similar development could be expected to occur elsewhere. Certain writers sought to demonstrate that a decline in the birth rate was inevitable in view of the natural processes of social change and the limits of economic expansion. Benini held that, when the earth had been peopled, natality and mortality would be brought into balance by the natural development of new customs relating to age at marriage and other factors.[164] Clark believed that in advanced countries the progress toward ever higher standards of living and wages was

of raw materials would be affected adversely. *Ibid.*, pp. 373-406. Some of the issues discussed in the text at this point are reviewed by Cohn in *Die Theorie . . .* (1934), Part 3.

[157] For representative recent accounts of the operation of "laws of returns" see Young, "Increasing returns and economic progress" (1928); Wolfe, "Arten und Erscheinungsformen von Kosten und Erträgen" (1934); Jones, *Increasing return* (1933), Parts 3-6; Kuznets, *Secular movements in production and prices* (1930), especially Chapter 4; Burns, *Production trends in the United States since 1870* (1934), especially Chapters 3-4, 6; Stigler, "The division of labour is limited by the extent of the market" (1951).

[158] Kuznets (ed.), *Problems in the study of economic growth* (1949), Parts 3-4; Kuznets, *Economic growth* (1952).

[159] Chalmers, under the influence of Smith and perhaps Cantillon, declared that "the market cannot permanently be overladen with corn" since, every increase of food being "followed up by an increase of population", a temporary surplus of corn "creates a market for itself" by stimulating population growth. "It is not so with any other manufactured goods, save in as far as they may work an increase of food." See Chalmers, *On political economy in . . .* (1832), pp. 56-57. Smith, *An enquiry . . .* (1776; 1937 edit.), Bk. I, Chapter 11, Parts 1 and 3. Malthus, as Budge did in *Das Malthus'-sche Bevölkerungsgesetz . . .* (1912), pp. 27 ff., conceived of the standard of living in elastic terms.

[160] On the development of consumption theory see Zimmerman, *Consumption and standards of living* (1936), especially Chapter 3.

[161] However, the diminishing pertinence of Malthus's notions was only slowly recognized. For example, Virgilii, who justified Malthus's use of the two progressions as a first approximation, supposed, following Berthelot, that the development of synthetic food would solve the population problem thereby ignoring the fact that the standard of living included many scare elements besides food. Virgilii denied that technical progress in agriculture alone would make sufficient food available. See Virgilii, *Il problema della popolazione* (1924), pp. 177, 513, 547, 551, 577; Nitti, *La popolazione . . .* (1894), pp. 109-123.

[162] See Morgan (ed.), *The works of Walter Bagehot* (1889), Vol. IV, pp. 570-574; Vol. V. pp. 332-338. Bagehot rejected Mill's thesis that a great change in income is most likely to elevate living standards, saying that the response of a people to changes, large or small, depends on what today are called values and aspirations.

[163] See Pareto, *Manuel d'économie politique* (1909), translated from the Italian, especially Chapter 7; also Spengler, "Pareto on population" (1945). In fact, a number of writers, both critics and supporters, indicated that, since societies are made up of different classes, the impact of any given changes upon population growth may vary by class.

[164] Benini, *Principi di . . .* (1901), p. 286.

self-perpetuating, and that it could be stopped only by "perversion of the system" through monopoly, war, bad government, or class struggle.[165] Pigou drew the conclusion that almost certainly population growth would not be allowed to absorb all the fruits of economic development.[166] However, some writers, like Pierson,[167] were not so sure that the birth rate would decline with advancing civilization and the Malthusian problem would be solved in this way.

Certain French theorists, while noting that economic changes affected population growth by diminishing the value of children as assets, stressed changes in the underlying pattern of values which were associated only indirectly with economic development. Most of all they stressed "arrivisme" and social capillarity, the tendency for modern civilization to value the development of the individual more than that of the group, and hence a more rationalistic attitude toward procreation.[168] Not only did these tendencies remove the threat of undue population growth; in France they had brought the birth rate below the death rate and they would have this effect elsewhere as civilization developed. Some of the exponents of this theory advocated state intervention for the purpose of stimulating population growth.[169]

Brentano argued that advances in income produced various cultural effects which in turn made for family limitation.[170] This interpretation was compatible with the theory of civilization developed by Patten, who wrote: "As civilization is the principle antagonistic to the law of diminishing returns, so productive power is the principle antagonistic to the law of increasing population. . . . Every stage in the advancing civilization, accompanied by an increase in the number of industrial qualities, will open up new sources of pleasure and create new social forces through which the strength of the primitive appetites and passions will be reduced." [171]

The influence of biological factors on fertility has been emphasized by some writers. For example, Hankins observed that in highly civilized societies the energies of the people tend to be diverted from reproduction to the demands of mental and physical activities. Group differences in fertility reflected in some degree differences in the pressure of these demands, and Hankins therefore attributed the decline in natality partly to an increase in these pressures.[172]

Gini assembled statistical data which he interpreted as indicating that the rate of reproduction of a population tended to describe a parabola reflecting, not variation in the amount of subsistence or in the environment, but changes in the quality of the "germinal cells". According

[165] Clark, *Essentials of . . .* (1907), Chapter 19.

[166] Pigou, *The economics of welfare* (1932), Part I, Chapter 9.

[167] Pierson, *Leerboek . . .* (1902), Vol. 2, pp. 172-188. He implied that moral restraint was inadequate, and pointed to the high fertility of the working classes as evidence that birth rates did not necessarily decline as civilization advanced.

[168] Concerning the rationalization of procreation, see Monheim, *Rationalisierung der Menschenvermehrung* (1928), especially part B; also Rost, "Der Wille zum Kinde bei den Kulturvölkern der Erde" (1941).

[169] See Dumont, *Dépopulation et civilisation. Étude démographique* (1890), Chapter 9; Leroy-Beaulieu, *La question de la population* (1913), Bk. 5, Chapter 11. For summaries see Gonnard, *Histoire des doctrines . . .* (1923), Part III, especially 341-350; Spengler, *France faces . . .* (1938), especially Chapter 7. On the development of state intervention, see Glass, *Population policies and movements in Europe* (1940), especially pp. 86-99. For the application of a kind of social-capillarity approach to the study of differential fertility, see Fisher, *The social selection of human fertility* (1932); Fisher, *The genetical theory of natural selection* (1930), Chapters 8-12.

[170] For the development of this argument early in the twentieth century, see Brentano, *Konkrete Grundbedingungen der Volkswirtschaft* (1924), Chapters 2-3; Brentano, "Die Malthussche Lehre und die Bevölkerungsbewegung der letzten Dezennien" (1909). See also Beatrice and Sidney Webb, *Industrial democracy* (1902), p. 636. That fertility had declined in spite of, and not because of, increases in income was inferred by many students who emphasized the relatively autonomous role of tastes and values. For an early study of this kind, see Wieth-Knudsen, *Natalité et progrès* (1908), Chapters 3 and 8. See also Meerdink, *De achteruitgang der geboorten* (1937), pp. 123-146, for development of the argument that the decline in natality was attributable immediately to changes in human mentality.

[171] Patten, *Essays in economic theory* (1895; 1924 edit.), pp. 199-201.

[172] See Hankins, "Does advancing civilization involve a decline in natural fertility?" (1930). For an analogous sociological explanation, see Spengler, *France faces . . .* (1938), pp. 280-288. For an account of the hereditary aspect of fertility as affected by social selection, see Wagner-Manslau, "Human fertility" (1932).

to his theory, a population cycle is initiated as a result of crossbreeding between groups that have become appropriately differentiated. Fecundity increases and the rate of growth rises for a time because fecundity is somewhat hereditary and each generation is largely the product of the relatively more fecund components of the preceding generation. In time, however, the forces making for an increase in fecundity are more than counterbalanced by the forces of "physical exhaustion" — principally a deterioration in the germinal cells which is accentuated by the movement of a relatively large fraction of the population into social classes which have characteristically low fecundity. In consequence, the rise in the rate of natural increase gives place to a decline which may continue to the zero level or below unless the population is reinvigorated through further crossbreeding (for example, with immigrants).[173] Gini's thesis has been criticized on the logical ground that it is impossible "to attribute any specific part of [an individual's] neuromuscular patterns or other characteristics to inherent qualities of the germ plasm and others to cultural or other environmental factors".[174]

In general, the majority of writers toward the end of the nineteenth century and early in the twentieth were more optimistic than the earlier nineteenth-century writers in their estimates of man's ability to control his numbers. Their optimism had its origin in the spread of contraceptive practices and the decline of birth rates in economically advanced countries,[175] and was reinforced by the thesis that the birth rate tends to decline with the advance of civilization.[176] This view has been considerably modified in the more recent literature. Many writers now hold that the decline of the birth rate in Europe and in certain countries populated by European stock overseas was associated with industrialization, urbanization, and accompanying changes in modes of living and attitudes of the various classes within these societies. Many agree in general with earlier writers that population growth will eventually be brought under control. They emphasize that as some of the changes characteristic of countries experiencing declines in the birth rate are spread to areas where the birth rate is still high, it is to be expected that birth and death rates will decline, thus resulting in less rapid population increase and less pressure upon resources.[177]

[173] See Gini, "The cyclical rise and fall of population" (1930), and the extensive bibliography included. See also Gini, *Le basi scientifiche della politica della popolazione* (1931); Gini, *Saggi di demografia* (1934), pp. 281 ff.; Gini, "Real and apparent exceptions to the uniformity of a lower natural increase of the upper classes" (1936); Gini, "Les facteurs de la décroissance de la natalité à l'époque contemporaine" (1940). See also Camavitto, *La decadenza delle popolazione messicane al tempo della Conquista* (1935), pp. 304-310; Snell, "Hybrids and history. The role of race and ethnic crossing in individual and national achievement" (1951); Vida, "La teoria della circolazione delle aristocrazie del Pareto e la teoria del ricambio sociale del Gini. Studio comparativo" (1936).

[174] See Lundberg, "The biology of population cycles" (1931).

[175] See Himes, *Medical history* . . . (1936), Part 6; Newsholme and Stevenson, "The decline of human fertility in the United Kingdom and other countries as shown by corrected birth rates" (1906); Newsholme, *The declining birth-rate* (1911), pp. 33 ff., Chapter 7; Grotjahn, *Geburten-rückgang und Geburten-regelung im Lichte der individuellen und der sozialen Hygiene* (1914), pp. 21-31; Budge, *Das Malthus'sche Bevölkerungsgesetz* . . . (1912). Landry, *Traité de démographie* (1945), p. 566. However, Virgilii attributed the decline in Australian natality to moral restraint rather than to contraception. See Virgilii, *Il problema* . . . (1924), p. 468. On the impact of contraception on natality, see Monheim, *Rationalisierung* . . . (1928), pp. 42-48. See also Wolfe, "The population problem . . . " (1928).

[176] Perhaps the most vigorous exponent of this view was Leroy-Beaulieu. See his *La question* . . . (1913), Bk. III, Chapter 1. Landry believed that the changes which had taken place could be summarized much as follows: Eighteenth-century writers had considered two population types: (*a*) the type conceived of by Townsend, in which it was assumed that man was governed by sex and hunger, that his standard of life was fixed, and that his numbers were *determined* by subsistence and kept adjusted thereto by variations in mortality; (*b*) the type conceived of by Cantillon, in which it was assumed that the standard of life was variable, and that numbers were *conditioned* by subsistence and adjusted thereto by variations in nuptiality. The late nineteenth-century writers, such as Dumont and Mombert, had pointed to a third type of population in which natality and growth were governed largely by psychological and sociological circumstances. Where this type was found — in advanced countries — it was possible to stimulate natality by governmental action. See Landry, *La révolution démographique* (1934), pp. 169-192.

[177] See Notestein (ed.), *Demographic studies of selected areas of rapid growth* (1944); Davis, *The population of India and Pakistan* (1951), Chapter 23, especially pp. 229 ff.

(3) Logistic and Related "Laws" of Population Growth

Attempts to formulate mathematical "laws" of population growth have been encouraged by the increasing availability of statistics relating to population trends, as well as by the development of mathematical techniques for analysing such data. One of the first attempts at such a statement of population growth was that advanced by Quetelet in 1835. He asserted that "the resistance or the sum of the obstacles opposed to the unlimited growth of population, increases in proportion *to the square of the velocity with which the population tends to increase*". Accordingly, in the absence of a change in "social state", a population tends to grow more and more slowly." [178] At Quetelet's request Verhulst submitted this principle to examination. In 1838 Verhulst suggested that a symmetrical theoretical curve which he named the "logistic" was suitable to describe the course of population growth. A few years later he made use of it to estimate the population of Belgium, to which he assigned maxima of 6.6-9.4 millions. Initially he supposed that the obstacles increase *"exactly in the same proportion* as the superabundant population" but he replaced this supposition with the hypothesis that the obstacles *"increase in proportion to the ratio of the superabundant population to the total population"*.[179]

For a long time the logistic curve was little used, in part because census data were lacking.[180] As a result Verhulst's work was generally forgotten until after 1920, when the logistic curve was independently rediscovered by Pearl and Reed.[181]

Certain assumptions underlie the theory of growth implicit in the simple logistic curve of population growth.[182] First, the physical environment or the area which the population under analysis utilizes for its support is constant. Second, the population N increases from a lower asymptotic limit of zero toward an upper asymptotic limit K, which represents the maximum population that can exist in the stipulated environment under the given cultural conditions and methods of production. Third, the proportional rate of population growth R steadily declines,[183] because of the damping effect produced

[178] See Quetelet, *Sur l'homme et le développement de ses facultés* (1835), Bk. I, pp. 277-278. On Quetelet's other contributions to population statistics see Hankins, *Adolphe Quetelet as statistician* (1908), Chapters 3-5.

[179] Verhulst, "Notice sur la loi que la population suit dans son accroissement", (1838); Verhulst, "Recherches mathématiques sur la loi d'accroissement de la population" (1845); Verhulst, "Deuxième mémoire sur la loi d'accroissement de la population" (1847). See also Miner, "Pierre-François Verhulst, the discoverer of the logistic curve" (1933), pp. 684-685; Yule, "The growth of population and the factors which control it" (1925).

[180] Miner, Pierre-François Verhulst . . . " (1933), p. 674, found but one modern reference to Verhulst's work, that of du Pasquier, "Esquisse d'une nouvelle théorie de la population" (1918).

[181] See Pearl and Reed, "On the rate of growth of the population of the United States since 1790 and its mathematical representation", (1920). Following the rediscovery of the logistic, it was discussed at great length. For example, see Pearl, *Medical biometry and statistics* (1940), especially Chapter 18; Pearl, *The biology of population growth* (1925), pp. 4, 17, 119, 125-130, 157; Lotka, *Elements of physical biology* (1925), pp. 66-76; Lotka, *Théorie analytique des associations biologiques* (1939), pp. 48-62; Allee and others, *Principles of animal ecology* (1949); Davis, *The analysis of economic time series* (1941), pp. 524-529; Rhodes, "Population mathematics" (1940); Kendall, "Stochastic processes and population growth" (1949); Corblau "La fonction logistique et la description des phénomènes de développement économiques et sociaux" (1947); Dor, "Analyse des phénomènes logistiques à l'aide de la courbe normale intégrale" (1948); Afzalipour, *Contribution à l'étude de la théorie mathématique de la démographie* (1936), Chapter VII; Glenday, *The economic consequences of progress* (1934), especially Part II.

[182] On the asymetrical generalized logistic, see Pearl, *Medical biometry* . . . (1940), p. 460; Vianelli, "A general dynamic demographic scheme and its application to Italy and the United States" (1936), pp. 271 ff.; Vianelli, "Evoluzione economica e demografica negli schemi delle curve logistiche" (1935), pp. 407 ff. See also Will, "On a general solution for the parameters of any function with application to the theory of organic growth" (1936); Hotelling, "Differential equations subject to error, and population estimates" (1927); Kostitzin, *Biologie mathématique* (1937), Chapter IV; Lotka, *Elements* of . . . (1925), Chapters 7-10.

[183] Let b represent the biotic potential, or maximum rate of increase per time period of which a population is capable in the absence of that environmental resistance to population growth which increases as N approaches the maximum K. Lotka, in *Théorie* . . . (1939), p. 12, put the value of b at .03—.04; Vincent and Henry in "Rhythm maximum d'accroissement d'une population stable" (1947), pp. 668 ff., put the value b at nearly .045 today and about .03 in Malthus's time. Let $(K - N)/K$ represent the fraction of the maximum

by the increase of population density.[184] The absolute increase per year or other time period generates a symmetrical bell-shaped curve which rises to a peak at the point where $N = K/2$ — that is, where the actual population is one-half the maximum — and then moves downward toward zero. Thus, the population follows an S-shaped curve as it moves from a very low value toward the maximum K.[185]

The logistic "law", and the modified logarithmic equation employed by Pearl and Reed to express it, commanded much attention in the 1920's,[186] and fairly distinctive types of criticism of the logistic were developed. First, it was noted that the logistic was not always the type of curve that best described the past population growth of a given country or region. Second, even where a logistic described the past growth more precisely than other curves, it did not follow that the population would continue to follow the curve.[187] Third, it had not been established that, because of the inherent nature of the growth process, a population must pursue the path of a logistic even when there were strong grounds for supposing that an S-shaped curve would be traced.[188] Fourth, and most important, it was asserted that the logistic law did not effectively take account of the changes in culture which permit a population to exploit its resources more effectively and to alter its relations with other populations, nor did it anticipate changes in aspirations, in tastes, and hence in reproductive behaviour. Yet, the magnitude of K, the trend of R, and the progress of population in general was largely dependent upon such changes.[189] Accordingly, until such changes could be foreseen, and their relation to population growth determined, population forecasting by means of the

population that remains to be brought into being before the population becomes stationary. The absolute increment per time period is $b\,N\,(K - N)/K$. The value of R is $b(K - N)/K$; it declines as N increases. See Gause, *The struggle for existence* (1934), Chapter 3, for an outline account.

[184] While Volterra noted that the damping effect could be traced to a steady decline, as population grows, in the ratio of births to matings between males and females, the damping effect is usually attributed to the diminution in the ratio of physical resources to population as N grows. The decline in this ratio is accompanied, in animal populations, by an increase in mortality and a decrease in natality, and in human populations, by a decrease in natality and sometimes by an increase in mortality. Volterra, "Population growth, equilibria, and extinctions under specified breeding conditions: a development and extension of the theory of the logistic curve" (1938), pp. 1-4; Allee and others, *Principles of . . .* (1949), pp. 346 ff.; Lotka, *Théorie . . .* (1939), pp. 48-63.

[185] Concerning the conditions under which the logistic is superior to other growth curves, see Winsor, "A comparison of certain symmetrical growth curves" (1932); Winsor, "The Grompertz curve as a growth curve" (1932).

[186] Concerning the early reactions to this "law", see Wolfe, "The population problem . . . " (1928). The favourable reaction was prompted in part by the fact that, though social scientists were postulating declining rates of growth, no mode of increase which seemed appropriate for the more distant future had been discovered by writers who had fitted curves to past population growth. This problem, moreover, had not received attention in the nineteenth and early twentieth century works on vital statistics. For example, see Farr, *Vital statistics* (1885); Newsholme, *The elements of vital statistics* (1899); Mayo-Smith, *Statistics and sociology* (1895); Whipple, *Vital statistics* (1919).

[187] It has been shown that the probable error of a future population estimate derived from a logistic increases continuously with time. See Hotelling, "Differential equation . . . " (1927), p. 311; Schultz, "The standard error of a forecast from a curve" (1930).

[188] Such a basis was not provided by the physiological theories of fertility change developed by Pell, Rutgers, Brownlee, Carli, Gini, Stieve and others, some of which continued the Spencer tradition. Wolfe, "The population problem . . . " (1928). It was essential to show that, as population density increased, fertility and/or mortality had to respond in such a way as to yield the appropriate slackening of the rate of increase. Pearl attempted to show that as the density of the relevant populations increased, egg production per hen, fertility of the fruit fly, and the human birth rate fell in an appropriate manner. Pearl, *The biology . . .* (1925), Chapter 6. It is generally accepted, however, that even though a rationale can be established for expecting a non-human population to grow in a certain predetermined manner, not even the empirical descriptions of growth of such populations are applicable to human populations. See Volterra and d'Ancona, *Les associations biologiques au point de vue mathématique* (1935); also, Rashevsky, *Advances and applications of mathematical biology* (1940); Rashevsky, *Mathematical theory of human relations; an approach to a mathematical biology of social phenomena* (1947). See also Pearl, *The natural history of population* (1939), Chapter I.

[189] Adherents to the logistic theory, when confronted by the possibilities of major cultural changes, looked upon the results as new logistic cycles of growth. For example, see Wolfe, "Is there a biological law of human population growth?" (1927); Vianelli, "A general dynamic demographic scheme . . . " (1936); Hart, "Technological acceleration and the atomic bomb" (1946).

logistic curve would be attended with considerable hazard. Critics of the logistic "law" therefore looked upon it primarily as an empirical formula which sometimes described the past course of population growth and might well represent the future tendency under certain conditions.[190]

The influence of immigration upon the domestic rate of natural increase as interpreted by certain nineteenth-century students of population has not been found to be incompatible with logistic theory. For example, Walker concluded, as Franklin had already said in the eighteenth century, that net immigration into the United States had not augmented the population of the United States but had reduced natural increase in the native population by an amount equal to the net immigration.[191] Logistic theory implies that Walker's thesis is essentially valid, at least in countries with relatively large populations, so long as immigration produces no cultural change,[192] however, given such change, immigration may increase or decrease a country's population in the long run.

Several theorists have tried to formulate a general law of population development which would not be based upon oversimplified hypotheses and predominantly biological analogies, and which would take account of various influences, particularly those within the economic sphere. In the opinion of these writers, hypotheses such as Verhulst's about the rate of growth, or Delevsky's about acceleration,[193] are not adequate.[194] They have argued that what is needed is a dynamic scheme of analysis of population growth.

An attempt at such a scheme was made by Amoroso [195] when he introduced the concept of "demographic elasticity" to represent the relation "between the logarithmic derivative of the population, considered as a function of time, and the corresponding logarithmic derivative of an index of economic activity".[196] This concept, in turn, was used by Vinci to obtain a "so-called generalized logistic curve". According to Vinci's formulation, (*a*) "demographic elasticity, consistently with an unknown function of time, becomes smaller and smaller as the population in its absolute value becomes greater and greater"; and (*b*) the "relative increase of real incomes is a function, also unknown, of time and of the relative magnitude of population".[197] Vianelli, on the basis of Vinci's scheme, undertook to discover, not the secular trend of population growth as Pearl had attempted, but the manner in which economic and demographic evolution, as represented by suitable indices, had mutually influenced one another in Italy and the United States. He found that demographic elasticity and the response of output to population growth varied in time and by country. He concluded, therefore, that demographic evolution was not a natural biological phenomenon, and that, given knowledge of the future behaviour of the functions which he employed, rational forecasts of population trends were possible.[198]

[190] On these matters see Wolfe, "Is there a biological . . . " (1927), pp. 557 ff; Knibbs, "The growth of human populations and the laws of their increase" (1925); Dor, "Analyse des phénomènes logistiques . . . " (1948), pp. 327 ff; Wilson and Puffer, "Least squares and population growth" (1933); Lotka, *Elements of . . .* (1925), p. 67; Hogben, *Genetic principles in medicine and social science* (1931), Chapter 7; Douglas, *The theory of . . .* (1934), especially Chapter 13; MacLean and Turner, "The logistic curve applied to Canada's population" (1937).

[191] Walker, *Discussions in economics and statistics* (1899), Vol. II, pp. 43, 121, 206, 419-425, 441; Franklin, *Observations concerning the increase of mankind, peopling of countries, etc.* (1755; 1918 edit.), pp. 8-10; Smyth, *The writings of Benjamin Franklin* (1907), Vol. III, pp. 43-44, 63-73.

[192] Pearl concluded that "the sole effect of the *net* immigration has been somewhat to steepen the general upward slope of the United States logistic curve, without either altering its fundamental shape or putting irregular waves in its course." Pearl, *The biology . . .* (1925), p. 13.

[193] Delevsky indicated that the rate of growth might sometimes increase and that a population might describe a sinusoidal curve. Delevsky, "Une formulation mathématique de la loi de la population" (1928).

[194] See Vianelli, "A general dynamic demographic scheme . . . " (1936), p. 270.

[195] Amoroso, "L'equazione differenziale del movimento della popolazione" (1929).

[196] See Vianelli, "A general dynamic demographic scheme . . . " (1936), p. 270.

[197] Vinci, "La logica della curva logistica" (1929), pp. 386-392; Vinci, "Ancora sulla curva logistica" (1930), pp. 105-106; and Vinci, *Manuale di statistica* (1934), Vol. II.

[198] See Vianelli, "A general dynamic demographic scheme . . . " (1936), and Vianelli, "Evoluzione economica e demografica . . . " (1935). Demographic elasticity apparently was influenced by variation in

A summary of the thinking of Amoroso, Vinci, and Vianelli can perhaps be presented in the following simplified terms: Let it be assumed that the population of a community increases in a small proportion, x, and its net income in a small proportion, y. Further, let it be assumed that the increment of income is composed of two parts, one of which (y_1) is due to population growth and the other (y_2) to other factors such as the advance of technology and discovery of new resources. Then the demographic elasticity, e, is represented by the ratio x/y and the elasticity of productivity of population, E, by the ratio y_1/x. If the demographic elasticity, e, is 0.5 per cent and the elasticity of productivity, E, is zero, and if the independent increase of income, y_2, is 2 per cent per annum, the population increases at the rate of 1 per cent per annum. But if E rises to, say 0.5 per cent, the rate of population growth becomes approximately 1.33 per cent per annum; that is, the contribution of population growth to the increase of income raises the rate of population growth by about one-third.

Should the values of e and E change, as population grows, these changes would be reflected in the rate of increase of population, as well as of income. The elasticity of productivity of population, E, may rise or fall, depending, *inter alia,* on the size of the population, the resources available and the techniques of production.[199] The demographic elasticity, e, depends on the trends of mortality, fertility, and migration, which respond differently to changes of income under various conditions; and these responses may change as the population increases. Also, the increment to income which comes from sources other than population changes, y_2, may be indirectly influenced by the growth of population. For example, the rate of population increase may affect the development of technology and the rate of capital formation. Thus, on the basis of present information, it is not possible to construct precise formulations of the relationships among these variables.

the rate of saving, since this variation produced changes in the rate of growth of consumption. Vianelli's scheme has since been applied with some modification by Figueroa, who has considered a variety of social and economic factors. Figueroa, "Un modelo dinámico general de desarrollo demográfico y sus aplicaciones" (1947).

[199] Changes in the rate of population growth entail changes in the age distribution of the population, which affect the ratio of the number of workers to the total population, and thus influence the trend of E.

(4) Population "Types" and "Stages" of Demographic Evolution

If population always grew logistically or in accordance with any standard pattern of development, it would be possible always to describe precisely what point of demographic evolution any given population had attained. Certain demographers who have rejected the logistic "law" have sought other means of making such a description. They have assumed that populations tend to evolve through certain stages, having characteristic tendencies of growth, and have subsequently classified given populations according to their position in this sequence of stages.

Blacker has identified five stages in demographic growth: (1) *the high stationary,* marked by high natality and mortality; (2) *the early expanding,* with high natality and high but declining mortality; (3) *the late expanding,* with declining natality but with mortality declining more rapidly; (4) *the low stationary,* with low natality balanced by equally low mortality; and (5) *the declining,* with low mortality, lower natality, and an excess of deaths over births.[200]

Thompson and others have reduced Blacker's stages or types to three: (1) that in which neither mortality nor natality is under reasonably secure control and where the potential growth is large despite a possible current low rate of increase; (2) that in which, while both natality and mortality are declining, natality decreases at first less rapidly and then more rapidly than mortality, and the population grows until it finally reaches the third stage: (3) that in which natality and mortality are low and under secure control, and the population is stationary or in a state of incipient decline.[201]

[200] See Blacker, "Stages in population growth" (1947).

[201] Thompson, "Population" (1929); Thompson, *Plenty of people* (1948), Chapter 6; and Thompson, *Population and peace in the Pacific* (1946), especially Chapter 2. For a different approach in terms of diverse assumptions, see United Nations, "The past and future growth of world populations: a long range view" (1951).

It has been suggested that another stage of growth or type of population should be added to those included in Blacker's and Thompson's classifications; namely, one in which natality, while relatively low and stable, remains above mortality and permits a significant rate of increase,[202] or one in which natality periodically rises above a low-level mortality, yielding alternately a stationary and a growing population.[203]

Another such classification has been presented by Landry, who has identified three "demographic régimes" based in large part upon the observations of Cantillon on the relation between production and consumers' preferences in determining population growth.[204] The three régimes are as follows: (1) A *primitive régime* exists during the period when population growth is controlled by the means of subsistence; a maximum population is reached when mortality, rising as the increase of population lowers the conditions of living, fluctuates around the level of fertility. The maximum population may rise or fall with changes in the conditions of production. (2) An *intermediate demographic régime* continues for the period in which the interests of individuals and of societies in the maintenance of a standard of living affects the growth of population by influencing marriage. Economic production tends to determine the size of population, but only indirectly and in relation to certain standards of living. (3) A *modern epoch,* introduced by the "demographic revolution", is characterized by general decline in fertility. Population changes no longer conform to any "population law" and economic influences no longer determine the trend of population. This period is characterized by "limited procreation" as contrasted with "unlimited procreation". Under the first two demographic régimes, technological advances are the prime source of increase of population. In the modern society technology progresses at an accelerated rate but ceases to have the same direct relationship with population changes.

[202] See Davis, "Population and resources" (1950), pp. 346 ff.

[203] See the "future" type of growth pattern described by Cowgill and distinguished from the "primitive" type in which mortality periodically falls below a high-level natality, and the "modern" type in which natality, though moving downward with mortality towards equilibrium at a low level, long exceeds mortality and permits considerable population growth. Cowgill, "The theory of population growth cycles" (1949).

[204] Landry, *Traité de . . .* (1945), Chapter IX; Cantillon, *Essai sur la nature . . .* (1755; 1952 edit.), Part I, Chapter XV.

*The Development of Modern Population Theory**

WARREN C. ROBINSON

I. INTRODUCTION

Recent discussions of the population "explosion" have focused public and scholarly attention on the question of population change to a greater degree than at any time since the high point of the Victorian controversies over birth control propaganda culminating in the Besant-Bradlaugh trials. Contemporary interest stems from the postwar upsurge in the birth rate in this country as well as the population problems of the emerging areas of Asia and Africa.

The best-known theory of population growth is that which was first expounded in 1798 by T. R. Malthus, and it still provides the starting place for most popular discussions of the subject of population change.[1] The Malthusian

* Reprinted with permission from *The American Journal of Economics and Sociology,* Vol. 23, No. 4 (October 1964), pp. 375-392.

[1] Thomas Robert Malthus, *An Essay on the Principle of Population* (London: 1798). A total of seven revised editions were issued between 1803 and 1834.

formula pictures a grim life cycle. The birth rate remains high, at the biological limit or close to it, and the death rate is the regulator of the size and rate of increase of the population, the rate rising as population becomes too numerous relative to resources, and falling as population is thinned out by disease and starvation and resources are freed from the press of excess people. Population changes consist, for the most part of fluctuations around an upper limit.[2]

Malthus' neat, almost syllogistic formulation, coupled with the strong plausibility of his basic premises, has combined to make his theory extremely popular and persistent. Indeed, it seems a common belief that modern population experts, who call themselves demographers, are still merely engaged in refining and validating the work of the master.

Nothing could be farther from the truth. Malthus is, and has been for a good, long time, in poor repute as a demographer among professional demographers. The whole focus of demographic research has shifted since his time, away from theory and toward empirical research. Kingsley Davis was speaking for the last several generations of demographers when he noted:

> It is difficult to avoid the conclusion that the major advances in the science of population have come from improvements in the sources of information and in the techniques of analysis, rather than from the broad interpretations. Ironically, the interpretive literature on population probably exceeds by many times (if not in pages, certainly in readers and attention) the amount of empirical publication. The discrepancy was already clear with Malthus. He did not fully understand the progress in systematic demography that had been made by this time, yet it was his work that captured most attention, and it is his work that is still debated today in general population theory. Despite the outpouring of books, pamphlets, and articles on population theory — Bevoelkerungslehre — it is hard to cite a single scientific advance since Malthus' day that this literature has contributed to the subject.[3]

Notestein puts it equally bluntly:

> . . . there is considerable warrant for the view that much of the progress made during the past two or three decades is due to the fact that demographers at long last managed to rid themselves of preoccupation with the over-arching theories which dominated so much of the nineteenth century work in the field. It seems likely that for the foreseeable future any such intellectual construct will have more the character of an ideology than a means of submitting reason to the test of experience.[4]

In spite of this emphasis on empirical research, theoretical innovations have also occurred.[5] Modern, non-Malthusian theory is much more firmly rested in empirical and historical research than were the propositions of Malthus or his predecessors; in turn, hypothesis and low-level theory are necessary forerunners to empirical research.

This relative disinterest in theorizing has had an unfortunate result: the lineage and development of modern theories have remained obscure and undocumented. This essay makes at least a beginning toward supplying such a documentation.

[2] For modern formal presentations of the Malthusian system, see Harvey Leibenstein, *A Theory of Economic-Demographic Development* (Princeton: Princeton University Press, 1954); D. V. Glass., *Introduction to Malthus* (London: 1952).

[3] "The Sociology of Demographic Behavior," *Sociology Today*. ed. by Robert K. Merton, Leonard Broom, and Leonard S. Cattrell, Jr. (New York: Basic Books, 1959), pp. 313-4.

[4] Comment by Notestein on "Population Theory" essay in *Survey of Contemporary Economics*, Vol. II, ed. by B. F. Haley (Homewood, Ill.: Irwin, 1952), p. 129.

[5] By a "theory of population" is understood an attempt to elucidate the major factor or factors determining population growth. (*Cf.* Sydney Coontz, *Population Theories and the Economic Interpretation* [London: Routledge and Kegan Paul, 1957], p. 13.) We use this definition since it follows "ordinary" usage and in spite of obvious shortcomings. Hauser and Duncan (*The Study of Population: An Inventory and Appraisal* [Chicago: Chicago University Press, 1959], p. 13) offer a more precise definition as follows: "What may be properly called a 'theory' of population consists of a body of interrelated principles which has at least some degree of empirical support, which affords an explanation or prediction of observed and observable relationships and which has heuristic implications in suggesting hypotheses for investigation." These authors make clear that their definition is framed purposely to "exclude from consideration both the purely speculative exposition of laws of population growth and the construction of minuscule models of relationships, whether hypothetical or empirical, without systematic relevance to other sets of hypotheses" (p. 13). They also refer to "empirical regularities" (for example, "the volume and rate of internal migration tends to fall off with increasing distance") which they do not consider theories.

II. The Backgrounds to Modern Theories

Throughout the nineteenth century Malthusianism dominated population theorizing. Fertility was high and virtually constant, while fluctuations in mortality occurred, thus leading alternately to periods of population growth and decline. Mortality rates were falling in Europe in the late nineteenth century, but this was seen as only a temporary phenomenon which would inevitably reverse itself when population grew so large as to press against resources again. It was against this intellectual background that the birth control movement in England was launched.

Around the turn of the century, however, population analysts discovered that birth rates in most Western European nations were declining. Fertility was not as constant as had been assumed and, indeed, for many nations could not even be described as high.[6]

Kuczynski observed:

> With a fertility and mortality as they prevailed in Western and Northern Europe forty or fifty years ago, the population would have doubled in three generations. With a fertility and a mortality as they have prevailed for some years, the population of Western and Northern Europe is bound to die out . . . The process . . . can be stopped by an essential change in mortality and fertility. But the future reduction of mortality in those ages which are the only decisive ones, that is, those under fifty years, cannot be very great after all that has already been accomplished. The future then depends mainly on the trend of fertility.[7]

These trends were simply not compatible with the Malthusian system. New theories capable of explaining the new facts were required, and several quite distinct new schools of thought took shape. Many of these had their roots in much earlier theories by contemporaries and even predecessors of Malthus. Most, however, continued the Malthusian methodological tradition of explaining population change in terms of a relatively small number of variables, related one to another in rigid, nearly mechanical fashion, operating as general if not universal principles. These theories were, in the meanings suggested by Warren Thompson, "natural" rather than "social" in content.

> The former [natural theories] are based on the belief that there is something inherent in the nature of man, or of the world in which he lives, that determines his growth at a rate and in a direction largely or wholly beyond his control . . . It is not surprising that wherever and whenever men have thought about population, many have been eager to find the natural law of its growth for this would give them a sure basis for reasoning on many related social problems. In the social theories of population growth, on the other hand, the underlying assumption is that population growth is not subject to any immutable natural law but is rather the resultant of the social conditions (social here is used to include economic) in which a people finds itself. To one who accepts this view it would appear to be folly to search for a simple natural law of population growth; what should receive attention is rather the factors which determine its growth in a particular community at a particular time.[8]

As we shall see, the evolution of post-Malthusian population theory has been from the "natural" toward the "social." The rigidly deterministic relationships originally postulated in order to explain the declines in the birth rate have gradually taken on almost purely social and economic colorations.

III. Natural Theories

Cyclical Theory

One of the first and most important of the modern "natural" theories to receive clear formulation was the cyclical theory, propounded by Corrado Gini beginning in the early Nineteen Twenties and still associated with his name.

> . . . the cyclical theory, which goes by our name, is often opposed to that of Malthus. This theory holds that independently of external circumstances,

[6] The economist Cannan was one of the first to notice and comment on this development. See "The Probability of the Cessation of the Growth of Population in England during the Next Century," *Economic Journal,* Vol. V (December, 1895), pp. 505-15.

[7] R. R. Kuczynski, *The Balance of Births and Deaths* (New York: Macmillan, 1928), Vol. I, p. 62. Kuczynski goes on to point out that, while increases in the birth rate had occurred before, they had always reversed themselves after a decade or so. The downturn in the birth rate which started in the last quarter of the nineteenth century had, he maintained, continued.

[8] Warren S. Thompson, *Population Problems,* 4th ed. (New York: McGraw-Hill, 1953), p. 45.

and as the result of internal factors, populations tend to follow a course analogous, from many points of view, to that of the life course of individual organisms, passing through successively the stages of development, maturity, and involution.[9]

Gini's emphasis is on the fecundity of the populations; "demographic metabolism" is the key variable in his theory, and it is changes in this biological, inherent quality which explain changes in total population and in growth rates.[10]

At times in his argument Gini seems to suggest that the biological decay of nations may also involve an increase in the susceptibility of nations or peoples to diseases of various sorts. But this is not elaborated upon. In the main, he dwells on the change in fecundity and, consequently, fertility as the cause of the cylical movements in total population which he argues takes place.

The cyclical theory has not gained too many adherents. Gini's biology is speculative and on some especially crucial points his theory is wholly non-quantitative, The theory is at least as philosophical as it is scientific and entails almost a whole theory of history as well as a theory of population change.

A few quotations will suffice to illustrate these aspects of his work.

> We must therefore conclude that the primary cause of the evolution of nations must be sought in biological factors.
>
> The biological theory of the evolution of nations also explains why the rise, the arrest, and the fall of populations are either accompanied or followed, at no great distance, by the expansion, the stoppage, or the decline of other national manifestations in the military, economic, political and scientific fields. The fact is that those same genetic forces which determine a rapid growth of the population cause at the same time a notable flowering of robust and daring individuals of keen, prompt, and adaptable intelligence.
>
> All these circumstances contribute to determine the golden age of a nation. It is no mere chance, therefore, that in periods of rapidly expanding population the nations find the great captains who lead them to victory, the industrial geniuses who provide them with the arms required for the needs of war and peace, the great poets who idealize their aspirations and electrify their enthusiasm, the great thinkers who systematize their conceptions of life and of the universe, and the great historians who transmit their deeds to posterity.
>
> As far as metabolism is concerned, there is no doubt that its intensification, more especially when marked differentiation reduces the fertility of those who rise or who hope to rise, hastens the demographic exhaustion of the nation. It is also certain that when the social metabolism becomes too rapid and intense, the individuals who rise to the upper classes are often lacking in that intellectual and moral preparation for occupying positions of responsibility which can only be supplied by a long family tradition.[11]

The introduction to this same volume discusses the "slow exhaustion of the reproductive powers of human population and of animal species, that is to say, of their germinal cells . . ." [12]

The Periodic

A variation of the cylical theory has come to be called the periodic. It differs from cyclical in that it explains movements in population by reference to an exogenous variable, the growth of some other population which "devours" the population in question. This is the cats-and-mice theory applied to humans and the growth, perhaps, of bacteria which slay humans, with the human population bearing an inverse relationship to the bacteria population, rising as the latter falls, and falling when it rises. Here the key factor for the human population is the death rate, which is, in turn, dependent on the growth rate in the bacteria population. The periodic theory, in other words, assumes levels of fertility and then makes the changes in death rates the dynamic factor.[13]

The Logistic

Perhaps almost as well known as the Malthusian theory itself is the proposition that popu-

[9] Corrado Gini, "A Coordination of the Different Population Theories," *Revue de l'Institut International de Statistique,* Vol. 11, Nos. 1-2 (1943), pp. 37-8.

[10] See the above-cited 1943 article and "The Cyclical Rise and Fall of Population," *Population,* Harris Foundation Lectures for 1929 (Chicago: Chicago University Press, 1930), pp. 1-140. Gini has written extensively, but these sources contain good summaries of his theory as well as references to his other writings.

[11] *Ibid.,* pp. 26, 28, 28-9, and 31, respectively.

[12] *Ibid.,* p. 9.

[13] This approach has been traced to Darwin. More recently, see V. Volterra, "Fluctuations dans la lutte pour la vie. Leur leis fondamentales et des réciprocité," *Réunion Internationale de Mathématiciens* (Paris, 1937-38). See also Gini's previously cited 1943 article, and Coontz, *op. cit.,* Chap. II.

lation growth curves follow a logistic function, gradually but asymptotically approaching an upper limit. Credit for the modern formulation must go to the biologist Raymond Pearl, although the roots of the theory are much older.[14]

> Almost half a century later than that of Malthus, and now a popular one in scientific circles, is the theory . . . that while population tends indeed to increase in geometrical progression with a constant coefficient, it is, from a certain point onwards, increasingly hindered by obstacles which lower that coefficient in a degree proportionate to the increase already realized, from that point onwards, in the size of the population. The combined effects of the force of growth and of the obstacles in its way give rise to the so-called "logistic" curve of growth, which tends asymptotically to attain a maximum . . . or rather a condition of stationary equilibrium.[15]

Pearl at first offered evidence to support his contention that populations tended to level off as they approached some upper limit without offering any logical scheme for explaining why this should be the case. He compared his results to Kepler's Law of the motion of planets or Boyle's Law before they had been reinforced with Newtonian and Maxwellian theory, respectively.[16] However, he did argue that, since his "law" seemed to hold for the non-human population too, the logical, or theoretical, explanation must not be couched in terms of social or economic institutions. He said:

> . . . these causes are not peculiar to human beings, such as the economic or social structure or organization of human society . . . This means that the search must be thrown back to more fundamental natural causes, biological, physical or chemical.[17]

Very early, Pearl made at least a beginning in presenting these fundamental causes, and not all of them were biological, physical or chemical.

> Fourth, that rate of reproduction or fertility is negatively correlated with density of population . . . This evidence indicates that in the direct and indirect biological effects of density of population upon reproduction exists one *vera causa* for the damping off of the growth of population as the upper limit of the logistic curve is approached . . . Fifth, that birth rate is negatively correlated with wealth (or positively correlated with poverty) . . . Sixth, that the indirect psychological and social effects of relative poverty as contrasted with relative wealth express themselves . . . in the sexual activity of human beings, and through sexual activity to birth rates.[18]

In later works, Pearl moved even farther away from his earlier biological determinism.

> This chart of factors affecting population increase, in common with most succinct classifications of complex human phenomena and relationships, falls short of logical perfection or completeness. But, perhaps it will in some degree serve two purposes: first, help to clarify and unite in a single view some of the more significant elements in an extremely complex matter; and, second, to get into the record, as the legal phrase has it, a formal statement of the fact that the writer is not unaware of the great importance of the influence of social and economic variables upon human fertility. Perhaps this chart will be permitted to take the place of tiresome reiteration of this awareness every time specifically biological aspects of fertility are discussed in the remainder of the book.[19]

And he then listed economic circumstances as being an indirect factor of the same sort as density of population.

Pearl allowed for the chance that his theory might be very wrong in times of great upheaval. The growth of the population as described by the curves always assumed that "no fundamentally new factor or forces influencing the rate of population growth different from those which have come into play."[20] And the forces he listed include great changes in the culture of nations, wars, famines, mass emigration and other catastrophes. Thus, Pearl perhaps would have argued that in normal times it is changes in fertility (because of changes in density) which are the dy-

[14] Raymond Pearl, *The Biology of Population Growth* (New York: Alfred Knopf, 1925). See also United Nations, *The Determinants and Consequences of Population Trends,* pp. 41*ff.*

[15] Corrado Gini, "A Coordination of Different Population Theories," *loc. cit.,* pp. 37-8.

[16] Raymond Pearl, *Studies in Human Biology* (Baltimore: Williams and Wilkins Co., 1924), p. 585.

[17] *Ibid.,* p. 585.

[18] Raymond Pearl, *The Biology of Population Growth,* op. cit., p. 209. The entire last half of this book, from p. 126 on, is devoted to discussing these causes.

[19] Raymond Pearl, *The Natural History of Population* (London: Oxford University Press, 1939), p. 95.

[20] *Ibid.,* p. 587.

namic factors, although he does not seem to have attempted to supply his own counterpart of Newtonian or Maxwellian theory to go with his empirical law.

Yule attempted to interpret the logistic theory in terms of the vital rates. Insofar as the modern period is concerned, he said:

> . . . all the facts seem consonant with the view that in recent historical times and in civilized States, it is the birth rate that must be regarded as the regulating factor in population; no other view seems possible.[21]

If Pearl had stuck to his original contention that the cause of the empirical law was not to be found in human institutions or habits, and accepted also Yule's contention, which indeed seems impossible not to accept, he would have been led to something very like Gini's notion of a decline in ability to reproduce as an explanation for the upper asymptote of his curve, and, in fact, in his early work he seemed to be moving in this direction.

The logistic gained wide currency in this country and abroad. Many of its advocates, however, have been even farther from purely biological in their interpretation of the factors underlying the curve — that is, in explaining what causes the changes in births and deaths which are observed in the population. Knibbs, for example, while accepting the validity of the law of growth, listed seven factors which affect population growth, including such things as social tradition, political and economic security and customary age at marriage.[22]

Reed likewise seems to have been willing to admit that social and economic factors may be important and suggested that such things be considered as parameters of the curve; he suggested fitting population growth curves to as many populations as possible and then seeing to what extent divergencies of the actual from the expected could be correlated with differences in these parameters.[23]

[21] G. Yule, "The Growth of Population and the factors which Control It," *Journal of the Royal Statistical Society,* Vol. 86, (1925), p. 33. Pearl quoted from this article by Yule at length and with obvious approval in the *Biology of Population Growth.*

[22] Sir George H. Knibbs, *Shadows of the World's Future* (London: 1928), p. 36*ff.*

[23] Lowell J. Reed, *op. cit.,* p. 166.

Thus, in its modified statements the logistic had nearly become a "social" rather than a "natural" theory.[24]

IV. Optimum Population Theory

Another important part of the gradual shift toward economic and social causation was the body of ideas and propositions which rose to popularity in the late Nineteen Twenties and early Thirties under the name "optimum population" theory.

Robbins had described the optimum population

> as a point at which population is neither too great nor too small, but is just such as to secure a maximum return per head, under the given conditions of production.[25]

Generally speaking, the factors determining the optimum population were: (a) natural resources available, (b) the skill, endowment, knowledge and habits of the population, (c) the opportunities for economic activity.[26] Given these factors, then, there would exist one "right" population to maximize per capita output and income. In essence, this is a variation on the economist's problem of factor proportions. The optimum population was that population which when combined with the given social capital stock yielded the highest marginal product per capita.[27]

[24] Criticisms of the logistic have been numerous, mostly on the count of its early biological formulations. See A. B. Wolfe, "The Population Problem Since the War: A Survey of Literature and Results," in Hauser and Duncan, *op. cit.,* p. 65; D. O. Cowgill, "The Theory of Population Growth Cycles," *The American Journal of Sociology,* Vol. 55, No. 2 (September, 1949), pp. 163-77; T. D. Hiller, "A Cultural Theory of Population Trends," *Journal of Political Economy,* Vol. 38 (October, 1930), pp. 523-50; and G. A. Lundberg, "The Biology of Population Cycles," *Social Forces,* Vol. 9, No. 3 (March, 1931), pp. 401-8.

[25] Lionel Robbins, "The Optimum Theory of Population," *London Essays in Economics in Honor of Edwin Cannan* (London: Routledge, 1927), p. 114.

[26] Sir A. M. Carr-Saunders, *World Population: Past Growth and Present Trends* (Oxford: Clarendon Press, 1936), p. 330.

[27] For a development of this point, see A. B. Wolfe, "The Theory of Optimum Population," *Annals of the American Academy of Political and Social Science,* Vol. 188 (October, 1936), p. 243. See also A. B. Wolfe,

Now, strictly speaking, this is not a theory at all. It is nothing but a description of what most people would view as a desirable situation for a society.

The entire question of population optimums was in great vogue in the decade of the Thirties, a time when falling growth rates seemed to presage stationary or even declining populations for most of the countries of the West. The optimum could, of course, be deliberately pursued for society by social engineers. It provided a target. Indeed, from its very inception this approach was policy-oriented. But even as a policy directive it is static in nature. That is, only given a certain capital stock can population be thought of as approaching an optimum. And once one admits the difficulties of imagining a constant stock of social capital, including human knowledge, then the meaning of the optimum as a real goal of policy becomes less and less clear.[28]

In order truly to be a theory of how population actually behaves, this approach would also have to describe some social or biological mechanisms whereby the birth rate and/or the death rate were affected so as to lead population to the optimum. Few writers argued that any such mechanism or tendency existed.

In retrospect, much of the discussion of population optimums which consumed so much time strikes one as an interesting, often ingenious, but altogether sterile exercise.[29]

V. The Social Theory of Population Change

The Background to the Theory

As the decline in the birth rate in the Western countries continued into the Thirties, more and more attention was given to the factors underlying the decline.[30]

Increasingly, the weight of evidence suggested that the decline in the birth rate was due to human volition; that is, it was the result of conscious and deliberate efforts by married couples to limit the size of their families.

Pearl, writing as a biologist rather than theorist, stated:

> All the evidence that has been accumulated by the work of the last quarter of a century on the subject agrees with cumulative force in showing that among civilized populations of the western world the main factors leading to group or class differential fertility are (non-genetic) in nature and that any group differences in innate biological (genetic) fertility, if they exist at all in such populations, play a small role in producing group differences in expressed fertility.[31]

And Carr-Saunders observed:

> So far as we have taken the matter, birth-control can be held to explain sufficiently the facts of the decline of the birth-rate within the sphere of European civilization.[32]

Thus, a "social" theory rather than a "natural" theory seemed to be required. As seen above, the logistic in its later variations was very close to a social theory. The last step toward a completely social theory capable of explaining the observed histories of Western populations and

"On the Criterion of Optimum Population," *American Journal of Sociology,* Vol. 39, No. 5 (March, 1934), pp. 585-99.

[28] Among the variants to this theory was the "optimum of welfare" theory, authored by Penrose and described as follows: "The per capita welfare optimum population for any area is that population in which per capita income stands at a maximum when it is spent in the consumption of the composite commodity that, in the light of existing scientific knowledge, makes a greater contribution to welfare than, in the existing state of the arts, can be made by any alternative composite commodity." E. F. Penrose, *Population Theories and Their Application* (Stanford: Food Research Institute, 1934), p. 84.

[29] Osborn writes of the optimum: "We conclude then that the concept of optimum size is hard for the scientist to handle, impractical for the politician or statesman, and does not interest the people who make the actual decisions as to size of family. The concept is likely to remain . . . a rather vague and theoretical objective." Frederick Osborn, "Optimum Rates of Population Growth," in *The Population Ahead,* ed. by Roy G. Francis (Minneapolis: University of Minnesota Press, 1958), p. 43. Osborn likens optimum population to the ideal of feminine beauty — a thing which continues to fascinate men but which is incapable of precise definition.

[30] See Roderich von Ungern-Sternberg, *The Causes of the Decline in Birth-Rate within the European Sphere of Civilization,* Eugenics Research Association Monograph No. 4 (Cold Spring Harbor, L. I., N. Y., 1931), Parts IV and V.

[31] Raymond Pearl, *The Natural History of Population* (Oxford University Press, 1939), p. 24.

[32] Sir A. M. Carr-Saunders, *World Population* (Oxford: Oxford University Press, 1936), p. 105.

capable also of being applied to other populations was taken with the development of what has come to be called Theory of the Demographic Transition, or, more simply, Transition Theory.

Instead of focusing on one or a few variables, such as demographic metabolism, rate of growth of agricultural output, or population density, as an explanation of population change, it takes into account a great many social and economic factors. It says that changes occur in fertility and mortality because of complicated processes not to be explained easily or neatly by any system.

The Theory Stated

Coale and Hoover write:

> In barest outline the sequence of events, according to the theory of the demographic transition, can be summarized as follows: The agrarian low-income economy is characterized by high birth and death rates — the birth rates relatively stable, and the death rates fluctuating in response to varying fortunes. Then as the economy changes its form to a more interdependent and specialized market-dominated economy, the average death rate declines. It continues to decline under the impact of better organization and improving medical knowledge and care. Somewhat later the birth rate begins to fall.
>
> The two rates pursue a more or less parallel downward course with the decline of the birth rate lagging behind. Finally, as further reduction of the death rate becomes harder to attain, the birth rate again approaches equality with death rate and a more gradual rate of growth is re-established, with, however, low risks of mortality and small families as the typical pattern. Mortality rates are now relatively stable from year to year and birth rates — now responsive to voluntary decisions rather than to deeply imbedded customs — may fluctuate from year to year. This short description fits the experience of most countries whose economies have undergone the kind of reorganization we have been calling economic development.[33]

The essence of the theory, then, is that the "transition" in fertility is from control by environment to control by calculated individual choice. Changes in mortality continue to be the result of social decisions and habits, but the "transition" implies an increasingly effective control.[34]

First Statements of the Theory

The transition approach is derived from the actual experience of the countries of the European sphere of civilization. It is a description of what has happened to these nations during the course of their economic and demographic development in approximately the last century.

Warren Thompson made one of the earliest attempts to generalize the demographic experience of Europe into a theoretical frame of reference which could apply to other areas as well. He grouped the nations of the world into three categories according to the level of their birth and death rates.

> Briefly stated, the characteristics of these groups from the standpoint of their vital statistics are: Group A: Very rapidly declining birth-rate and death-rate with the former declining more rapidly than the latter so that the rate of natural increase is also declining. Group B: Evidence that decline in both birth-rate and death-rates is under way in certain classes, but that the death-rate is declining as rapidly or even more rapidly than the birth-rate with the result that the rate of natural increase will probably remain for some time as great as now, or even become larger in the near future. Group C: Both birth-rates and death-rates are less controlled than in either A or B. But, in some of these countries . . . there is some indication that death rates are coming under control faster than birth rates . . .

[33] A. J. Coale, and E. M. Hoover, *Population Growth and Economic Development in Low Income Countries* (Princeton: Princeton University Press, 1958), pp. 12-3. See also N. Ryder, "The Conceptualization of the Transition in Fertility," Cold Spring Harbor Symposia on Quantitative Biology, Vol. XXII, *Population Studies: Animal Ecology and Demography,* 1957.

[34] For other statements of the theory, see F. W. Notestein, "The Population of the World in the Year 2000," *Journal of the American Statistical Association,* Vol. 45 (September, 1950), pp. 335-45; "Population Theory," in *A Survey of Contemporary Economics,* Vol. II, *op. cit.,* p. 95. See also Joe S. Davis, "Population and Resources," *Journal of the American Statistical Association,* Vol. XLV, No. 251 (September, 1950); C. P. Blacker, "Stages in Population Growth," *The Eugenics Review,* Vol. 39 (October, 1947), pp. 81-101, D. O. Cowgill, "Transition Theory as General Population Theory," *Social Forces,* Vol. 41, No. 3 (March, 1963), pp. 270-74.

there is likely to be a very rapid increase in numbers during the next few decades.[35]

A decade or so later, Wilcox noted the fundamental differences in the age structures of the "occidental-type" and "oriental-type" (*i.e.*, the larger percentage of the total made up of infants and children in the latter) populations and marked those populations in between as "transitional." [36] This seems to have been the first use of the word "transitional" in this connection. At about the same time the term "vital revolution," now often used as a synonym for "demographic transition," was coined by Himes. He defines it as "stabilization of population at a more economical level, *i.e.*, with low birth and death rates instead of high birth and death rates." [37]

Causes of Fertility Declines

Within the general framework of Transition Theory some debate occurred over the causes of the fertility declines which the theory described. All agreed that the causation was "social" rather than "natural," but the agreement ended there.

Carr-Saunders, Fairchild and others believed that modern contraceptive methods were responsible for a large part of the decline in the birth rate. They argued that only after the invention and mass availability of "appliance" techniques of contraception did widespread interest in family limitation arise and did effective human control over the birth rate become possible.[38]

This view was, however, disputed by Notestein and Stix, who pointed out that some form of birth limitation seems to have always existed in society and that sometimes relatively crude, non-appliance methods (notably coitus interruptus) proved quite effective.[39] They also pointed out that the decline in most Western nations began well before modern contraceptive techniques and appliances were widely known or used. They concluded that "the rapid decline in birth rates may be attributed in part to a rapid extension in the use of folkway contraception . . . New patterns of living and new values brought growing interest in family limitation that spread the use of known methods and stimulated the development of new ones. In a real sense, modern birth control is as much the result of new interest in family limitation as its cause." [40]

The Stix-Notestein position was supported by the findings of the Royal Commission on Population published in 1949. The commission reported that, in marriages occurring in England prior to 1910, 80 per cent of all contraception practiced was of the "non-appliance" type; moreover, it also reported that only in marriages occurring in the middle Thirties or later was "appliance" contraception more widespread than "non-appliance" methods. This lent strong support to the contention that the decline in the birth rate was caused by a rise in the desire of couples to limit family size with whatever techniques were available — in the earlier period of the late nineteenth century and early twentieth century with coitus interruptus, and in the more contemporary period with mechanical or chemical means.[41]

Other studies have also supported this approach, and the socio-economic interpretation put on "transition" by Notestein and Stix has gained general acceptance. Davis, for example, writes:

> . . . some of the most important developments (in the European transition) were doubtless intangible — the growth of democratic institutions, scientific ideals, humanitarian sentiments.[42]

And this is the interpretation of the transition taken in the numerous writings on the subject

[35] "Population," *American Journal of Sociology,* Vol. 34 (March, 1929) pp. 961-2.

[36] "The length of Life in the Early Roman Empire." *Démographie Historique,* Vol. II of the proceedings of Congrès International de la Population (Paris, 1937), pp. 20-2. A revised version of this paper appears as Chapter III of Wilcox's *Studies in American Demography* (Ithaca: Cornell University Press, 1940).

[37] Norman E. Himes, *Medical History of Contraception* (Baltimore: Williams and Wilkins Co., 1936), p. 391.

[38] Henry P. Fairchild, *People* (New York: Holt & Co., 1939), Chap. VII. See also A. M. Carr-Saunders, *World Population, op. cit.,* pp. 105ff.

[39] Frank W. Notestein and Regine K. Stix, *Controlled Fertility* (Baltimore: Williams and Wilkins Co., 1940), Chap. XV and especially pp. 148*ff.*

[40] *Ibid.,* pp. 149-50.

[41] E. Lewis-Faning, *Report on an Enquiry into Family Limitation and Its Influence on Human Fertility During the Past Fifty Years,* Papers of the Royal Commission on Population, Col. I (London: H.M.S.O., 1949).

[42] Kingsley Davis, "The World Demographic Transition," *World Population in Transition,* The Annals of the American Academy of Political and Social Science, Vol. 237 (January, 1945), pp. 4-5.

in the last two decades by Thompson, Notestein, Davis, Landry, Kirk and many others.[43]

The Transition Theory has gained wide acceptance in the last two decades. It would scarcely be an exaggeration to call it "The" modern population theory. As has been seen, it is based on the actual history of Europe and America and is a purely social theory. It is at the same time a very general theory, lacking in rigorous formulations or neat, precise answers to complex questions on population change. Seen in context, it is also a logical outgrowth and modification of the earlier work of such post-Malthusian determinists as Pearl and Gini.

The Present Status of the Theory

So much for the nature and development of Transition Theory. Dominant though it has been, this theory has by no means settled all questions of population growth. In the last decade, several developments have called into question the validity of the theory and led to renewed theoretical speculations. These developments have been: first, the postwar fertility upsurge in the United States; and second, the rapid growth of population in the lesser-developed areas of the world.

(a) Population Growth in Lesser-Developed Areas. The emerging Asian, African and Latin American countries are experiencing what Europe experienced a century or two ago — a period of falling death rates coupled with fairly constant birth rates, resulting inevitably in rapid growth. To be sure, the time scale of these changes is different in these areas than it was in Europe. Death rates have been halved in a matter of years, not centuries or decades, and that is why the growth in these areas has been an explosion. But the basic course of the growth — a growing social control over death rates — is the same in both cases. And the other stage of "transition" — control over birth rates — may ultimately be achieved in these areas too. The exact mechanisms of this control are far from clear to us today, but that is hardly surprising. The precise manner in which the "transition" to controlled fertility was to occur in Europe eluded Malthus and most other demographers even while this transition was taking place.[44] But the fact of this growth is not at all incompatible with Transition Theory.

(b) The Postwar Resurgence of Fertility in the United States. Some critics have interpreted the postwar upsurge in birth rates in the United States as disproof of Transition Theory. The failure of virtually all forecasts of postwar United States population is attributed to the widespread belief among demographers that the United States had reached the final evolutionary "stage" of growth characterized by a near equality between low death rates and low birth rates.[45]

To the extent that the completed "transition" does imply a forecast of ultimate stability in total population, then the postwar upsurge in United States and other Western populations would constitute a disproof of the theory. It seems clear that no balance of birth rates with death rates

[43] Warren S. Thompson, *Population and Peace in the Pacific* (Chicago: University of Chicago Press, 1945), Chap. II; *Plenty of People,* rev. ed. (New York: Ronald Press, 1948), Chap. VI; *Population Problems,* various editions (New York: McGraw-Hill), pp. 267-72 of the 4th ed. (Notestein, *op. cit.,* p. 335, and Paul K. Hatt, Nellie L. Farr and E. Weinstein, "Types of Population Balance," *American Sociological Review,* Vol. 20 (February, 1955), pp. 14-21, agree in crediting the 1929 Thompson article with being the first generalized statement of Transition Theory.) Notestein, "Economic Problems of Population Change," *Proceedings of the Eighth International Conference of Agricultural Economists* (London: Oxford University Press, 1953), pp. 13-31; *The Future Population of Europe and the Soviet Union* (New York: League of Nations, 1944), Chap. II. Adolphe Landry, *Traite de démographie* (Paris: 1945), Chap. IX. (Landry refers to the stages as "regimes," but they are substantially the same as those outlined by Thompson and Notestein.) Dudley Kirk, *Europe's Population in the Interwar Years* (Princeton: League of Nations, 1946), pp. 36*ff*.

[44] For a penetrating discussion of the applicability of Transition Theory to the lesser-developed areas, see Irene B. Taeuber, "The Future of the Transitional Areas," in *World Population and Future Resources,* ed. by Paul Hatt (New York: American Book Co., 1952). There has also been a renewal of interest in the Malthusian model. See, for example, R. R. Nelson, "A Theory of the Low-Level Equilibrium Trap in Underdeveloped Countries," *American Economic Review,* Vol. 46 (December, 1956), pp. 894-908; E. E. Hagen, "Population and Economic Growth," *American Economic Review,* Vol. 49, No. 3 (June, 1959), pp. 310-27.

[45] Kurt Mayer, "Fertility Changes and Population Forecasts in the United States," *Social Research,* Vol. 26, No. 3 (Autumn, 1959), pp. 347*ff*.

in this country is in the offing for the foreseeable future.

On the other hand, Notestein has answered this criticism of Transition Theory as follows:

> I have not been able to see that the current resurgence in the birth rates of the United States, Canada, Australia and New Zealand, for example, has any real bearing on the transitional argument. To repeat somewhat we may view the heart of transition theory as being based on two propositions:
> 1. The reduction of mortality can be rather quickly achieved because the necessary techniques can be borrowed and their application involves only slight adjustment in the existing value structures.
> 2. The reduction in fertility in modern times has come as the controls of fertility have been shifted from factors that were mainly institutional to factors that were mainly individual and rational.
>
> Nothing in the above gives us clues to the rate of population growth after the transition has taken place. At least nothing suggests that the rate of growth is necessarily slow. At the heart of the theory is the presumption that individually and rationally controlled fertility will be much lower than the high rates of the peasant societies, but with low death rates even moderate fertility rates can give high rates of population growth. I see no reason to suppose that fertility in the United States is not mainly under individual and rational control, and yet no reason to suppose that within the framework of the 2 to 4 child family, rational choice may not yield a distribution which continues to give us high rates of population increase.[46]

Crucial to this argument is what is meant by equilibrium. Ordinary usage defines the word as absence of change, but it is not clear whether this means stability in total numbers of population, stability of the growth rate over time, stability in the underlying vital rates, or something different from any of these. In any case, it seems clear that equilibrium does not necessarily and in all cases mean stability of total numbers. The pretransitional equilibria in the Western nations almost certainly did not involve any long-term stability in total numbers. But there was a stability in the social, economic and psychological environment which acted upon the vital rates. There was, in short, an equilibrium of the forces governing population change, and the breakdown of this equilibrium launched the "transitional" era. Now it is possible that a new equilibrium has been reached in the United States, one in which there is again an underlying stability in the social and psychological forces governing the vital rates but one which implies continued growth in total population.[47]

Thus, if one ignores total numbers and concentrates instead on the processes of movement from one equilibrium to another, in the above sense, then the postwar developments in Western fertility are quite compatible with the theory of the demographic transition. Admittedly, this interpretation marks a change of emphasis from some of the earlier formulations of the theory (including some of those cited earlier in this paper), but no useful, empirically based theory is ever a finished body of doctrine allowing no changes or amendments.[48]

VI. Summary and Conclusions

This paper has presented some of the highlights of population theorizing in the last half century. This has not been a thorough survey of all writings on the subject and, indeed, has not even covered all the major schools of thought. Most notable among the omissions are the whole body of Catholic Church writings on the subject,[49] as well as Marxist and neo-Marxist thought.[50]

[46] Letter from Frank W. Notestein to the author, December 8, 1958.

[47] Mayer, *loc. cit.,* argues that fairly accurate forecasts are again possible by focusing on completed generation fertility and that there exists a long-term stability in the average size of family. This same assumption is made by the population forecasts made in the recent Scripps Foundation-Survey Research Center Study. See Ronald Freedman, Pascal K. Whelpton, and Arthur A. Campbell, *Family Planning, Sterility and Population Growth,* (New York: McGraw-Hill, 1959), pp. 376*ff*.

[48] Some recent authors have stressed the more purely economic factors affecting fertility changes and variations. See Robert A. Easterlin, "The Baby Boom in Perspective," *American Economic Review,* Vol. 51, No. 5 (December, 1961), pp. 869-911. See also Gary S. Becker, "Economic Aspects of Fertility," in *Demographic and Economic Change in Developed Countries,* Universities-National Bureau of Economic Research Conference (Princeton, 1960). These works would still appear to be operating within the general structure of Transition Theory.

[49] John A. Ryan, "Population," *The Catholic Encyclopedia,* Vol. 12, pp. 276-80.

[50] Coontz, *op. cit.,* argues a neo-Marxist position and

The presently dominant theory is that commonly called the Theory of Demographic Transition. This body of general propositions, which explains population change in terms of a battery of complex social, economic and psychological factors, continues to provide what theoretical foundations exist for the diverse empirical researches under way into demographic behavior. As a frame of reference for understanding the major population changes occurring abroad and also in this country, Transition Theory is useful and important.

On the other hand, population theory is once again being discussed. Transition Theory is ultimately subject to the test of its ability to explain observed events and facts. Considering the fate of many other theories, there seems little room to doubt that ultimately it too may be replaced by some presently totally unsuspected view of why population growth occurs.

explains population growth in terms of the response of the supply of labor function to changes in real wages. He also reviews and summarizes Marxist population literature since Marx, almost none of which is in English.

*The Modern Expansion of World Population**

JOHN D. DURAND

The extraordinary proliferation of the human species which is going on in the world at present is part of a trend which began about two centuries ago and which has been gathering momentum since the beginning of the present century. This cannot fail to be recognized as one of the principal features of modern world history.[1] In historical perspective, it appears as a unique episode in the growth of the species since its origin; it has no parallel in previous history or prehistory for the speed and magnitude of expansion of numbers, and it seems highly unlikely that a comparable expansion would occur again in the future after the present trend has run its course.

The purposes of this paper are to portray the dimensions of the modern growth of world population against the background of previous long-range trends, to show how the trend has evolved during the last two centuries in the world as a whole and its major areas, and to consider some possibilities with regard to its continuation in the future.

MAGNITUDE OF WORLD POPULATION GROWTH DURING THE LAST TWO CENTURIES

Population estimates for the world and major areas since 1750 are shown in tables 1 and 2 along with projections to the year 2000. The figures in table 1 are "medium" estimates, intended to represent the center of a range of plausible figures for each area and date. The "low" and "high" variants given in table 2 are not intended to define absolute limits but to indicate the width of estimated ranges of relative plausibility without excluding the possibility that the true numbers might have been outside these ranges. No variants are shown where it seems possible to rely on the "medium" estimate for accuracy within relatively narrow margins of

* Reprinted with permission from *Proceedings of the American Philosophical Society,* June 1967. The original article includes an appendix, omitted here, which provides the bases for certain estimates cited.

[1] The importance of this feature has not escaped the attention of historians. Witness, for instance, the inclusion of a chapter on "World Population, 1800-1950", by D. V. Glass and E. Grebenik, in a prominent place in *The Cambridge Economic History, Volume VI. The Industrial Revolution and After* (H. J. Habakkuk and M. M. Postan, editors, Cambridge, 1965), Part I, chapter 2.

TABLE 1

"Medium" Estimates of Population of the World and Major Areas, 1750–1950, and Projections to 2000

Areas	Population (millions)						Annual rate of increase (percent)				
	1750	1800	1850	1900	1950	2000	1750–1800	1800–1850	1850–1900	1900–1950	1950–2000
World total	*791*	*978*	*1,262*	*1,650*	2,515	*6,130*	*0.4*	*0.5*	*0.5*	*0.8*	*1.8*
Asia (exc. U.S.S.R.)	*498*	*630*	*801*	*925*	1,381	*3,458*	*0.5*	*0.5*	*0.3*	*0.8*	*1.9*
China (Mainland)	*200*	*323*	*430*	*436*	560	*1,034*	*1.0*	*0.6*	*0.0*	*0.5*	*1.2*
India and Pakistan	*190*	*196*	233	285	434	*1,269*	*0.1*	*0.3*	0.4	0.8	*2.2*
Japan	30	30	31	44	83	*122*	0.0	0.1	0.7	1.3	*0.8*
Indonesia	*12*	*13*	*23*	42	77[a]	*250*	*0.2*	*1.2*	*1.2*	1.2	*2.4*
Remainder of Asia (exc. U.S.S.R.)	*67*	*69*	*87*	*118*	227	*783*	*0.1*	*0.5*	*0.7*	*1.3*	*2.5*
Africa	*106*	*107*	*111*	*133*	222	*768*	*0.0*	*0.1*	*0.4*	*1.0*	*2.5*
North Africa	*10*	*11*	*15*	27	53	*192*	*0.2*	*0.5*	*1.2*	1.4	*2.8*
Remainder of Africa	*96*	*96*	*96*	*106*	169	*576*	*0.0*	*0.0*	*0.2*	*0.9*	*2.5*
Europe (exc. U.S.S.R.)	*125*	152	208	296	392	*527*	*0.4*	0.6	0.7	0.6	*0.6*
U.S.S.R.	*42*	56	76	134	180	*353*	*0.6*	0.6	1.1	0.6	*1.4*
America	*18*	*31*	64	156	328	*992*	*1.1*	*1.5*	1.8	1.5	*2.2*
Northern America	*2*	7	26	82	166	354	...	2.7	2.3	1.4	*1.5*
Middle and South America	*16*	*24*	38	74	162	*638*	*0.8*	*0.9*	1.3	1.6	*2.8*
Oceania	*2*	*2*	2	6	13	*32*	...	...	...	1.6	*1.8*

[a] Calculated by assuming that Indonesia's share of the projected total for South-East Asia would be the same in 2000 as in 1980.

error. Estimates which lack a firm foundation are shown in italics. For the period 1750 to 1900, the estimates are the author's; their basis is stated briefly in the appendix. In the "medium" series, they differ from the well-known estimates by Willcox and Carr-Saunders,[2] slightly at some points and more considerably at others, mainly because they take account of new information which has become available since Willcox's and Carr-Saunders' works were published. The 1950 estimates (except the "low" and "high" variants shown for certain areas) and the projections to 2000 are United Nations figures.[3]

In round numbers, the world population in the middle of the eighteenth century is estimated at about 800 million, plus or minus about 150 million. Compared with the United Nations estimate of 3,281 million for 1965 (which also has margins of error, possibly exceeding 100 million in either direction[4]), the "low" estimate for 1750 indicates a five-fold increase and the "high" estimate an increase of more than three-

[2] See Table A in the Appendix and the sources cited there.

[3] United Nations, *World Population Prospects as Assessed in 1963* (New York, 1966). The population estimates for various dates since 1920, quoted hereinafter, are also from this source.

[4] The possibility of an error of about 100 million in the estimate of world population as of 1959 was indicated by calculations presented in the United Nations *Demographic Yearbook* (1960), pp. 1-9. The error margins about the 1965 estimate are likely to have been wider because of increasing uncertainty as to the amount of increase of China's population since the 1953 census. An error of 100 million in the 1965 population estimate for China alone is not out of the question.

TABLE 2

Range of "Low" and "High" Variants of Estimates of Population of the World and Major Areas, 1750–1950, and Projections to 2000

Areas	Population (millions)					
	1750	1800	1850	1900	1950	2000
World total	629–961	813–1,125	1,128–1,402	1,550–1,762	2,479–2,599	5,449–6,994
Asia (exc. U.S.S.R.)	408–595	524–721	711–893	853–1,006	1,353–1,453	3,103–4,067
China (Mainland)	180–234	290–360	390–480	385–494	540–620	882–1,333
India and Pakistan	160–214	160–214	215–242	285	434	1,163–1,464
Japan	30	30	31	44	83	115–139
Indonesia	7–17	9–17	19–27	40–45	77	227–267
Remainder of Asia (exc. U.S.S.R.)	31–100	35–100	56–113	99–138	219–239[a]	716–864
Africa	60–153	69–142	81–145	115–154	213–233	684–864
North Africa	6–18	8–18	12–21	26–30	53	166–205
Remainder of Africa	54–135	61–124	69–124	89–124	160–180	518–659
Europe (exc. U.S.S.R.)	115–135	147–157	208	296	392	491–563
U.S.S.R.	31–52	46–66	66–85	127–140	180	316–403
America	14–23	26–36	60–68	153–160	328	826–1,062
Northern America	2–3	6–7	26	82	166	294–376
Middle and South America	12–20	20–29	34–42	71–78	162	532–686
Oceania	1–3	1–3	2–3	6	13	28–35

[a] Calculated by assuming that Indonesia's share in the "low" and "high" projected totals for South-East Asia in 2000 would be the same as in the 1980 projections shown on page 140 of the United Nations report, *World Population Prospects as Assessed in 1963*.

fold during the last two centuries. By either measure, the growth during this period has been mammoth compared with that of earlier periods of history and prehistory.

Comparison with Population Growth in Earlier Periods

If we wish to trace the trend of world population back to ancient and prehistoric times, of course we have to be content with gross orders of magnitude, but these are sufficient to define the general form of the long-range growth curve. Over the last ten thousand years, the curve has taken approximately the form shown in figure 1. This has been charted with reference to the "medium" estimates in table 1 for dates since 1750 and the following "medium" estimates of world population at the birth of Christ and about 8000 B.C., prior to the appearance of the earliest known farming communities:

	A.D. 1	8000 B.C.
"Medium" estimates (millions)	300	5
Range of "low" and "high" variants (millions)	200–400	2–10

The estimate as of 8000 B.C. is based on what is known about the population densities of primitive non-agricultural societies.[5] For the estimate as of A.D. 1, the principal bases are the records of the ancient Chinese censuses, Beloch's pains-

[5] The estimate of 5 million implies an average density of about 15 persons per 100 square miles of land in regions of favorable climate for habitation by primitive nonagricultural peoples. This corresponds approximately to estimates of average density of the aboriginal population at times of early European contacts, in the non-desert regions of Australia and temperate zones of North America where agriculture was not practiced (with the exception of the very populous northwestern coastal region). Several writers have made similar estimates of the order of magnitude of world population just before the beginnings of agricultural economies.

taking estimate of the population of the Roman Empire at the death of Augustus, and Pran Nath's calculations with regard to the possible number of India's inhabitants in Acoka's time.[6] Substitution of different estimates within the ranges of the "low" and "high" variants for each date would make little difference in the shape of the long-range growth curve.

For example, see Julian Huxley, "Population and Human Destiny", *World Review* (January 1950) and *Harper's Magazine* (September 1950); Edward S. Deevey, Jr., "The Human Crop", *Scientific American* (September 1960).

[6] John D. Durand, "The Population Statistics of China, A.D. 2-1953", *Population Studies* 13 (1960); pp. 209-256; Julius Beloch, *Die Bevölkerung der Griechisch-Römischen Welt* (Leipzig, 1886), and "Die Bevölkerung im Altertum", *Zeitschrift für Socialwissenschaft,* II. Jahrgang (1899), pp. 505-514, 600-621; Pranatha Vidyalamkara, *A Study in the Economic Condition of Ancient India* (London, 1929), Chapter V. On the basis of these indications, the combined population of China, the Roman Empire, and India at the beginning of the Christian Era would seem to have been in excess of 150 million by a conservative assessment, and and it might have been twice that number. Information on the contemporary population in other parts of the world is poor, but in view of what is known about the forms and levels of development of economy, it is safe to presume that the total for China, the Roman Empire and India represented a substantial majority of the earth's inhabitants at the beginning of the Christian Era. A range of 200 to 300 million for the world population at that time was suggested in United Nations, *The Determinants and Consequences of Population Trends* (New York, 1953), p. 8. Estimates below 200 million, which have been proposed by some writers, are more difficult to reconcile with the indications given in the works cited above.

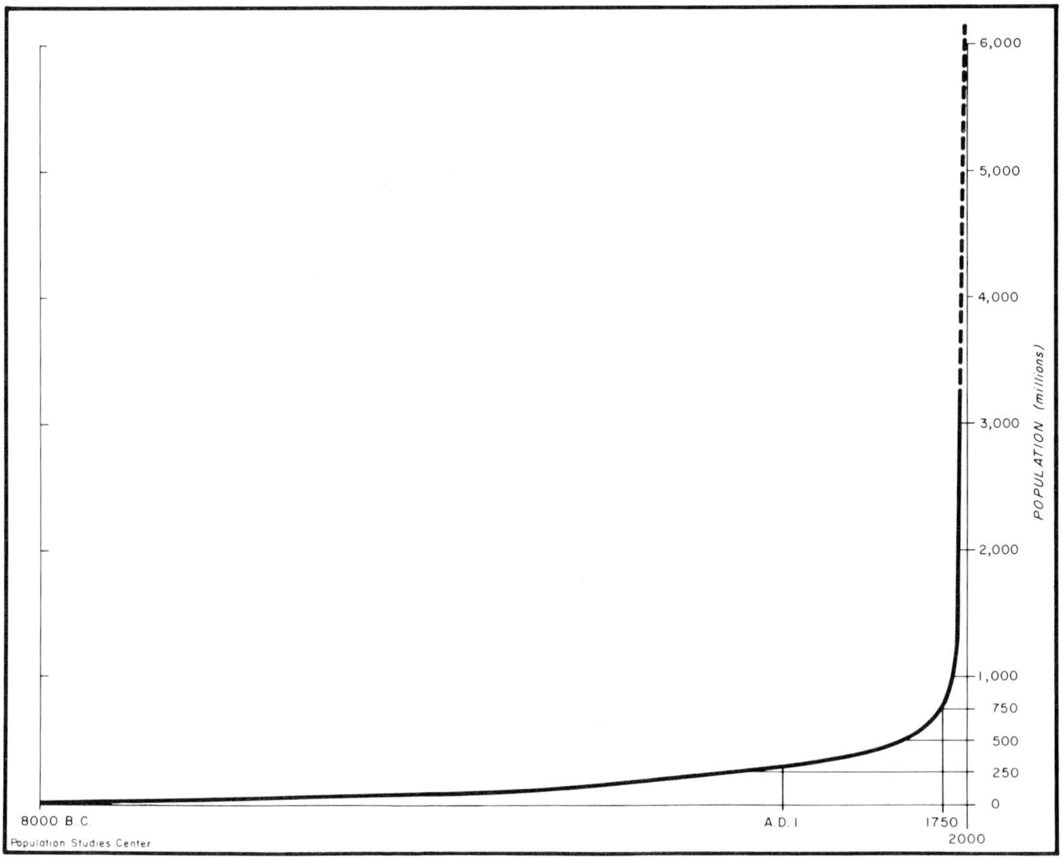

FIGURE 1

Long-range trend of world population growth.

It is interesting to calculate what share of the total increase of the human species since its origin is represented by the growth during the modern epoch. If we define the total increase as a net figure, disregarding whatever gains were cancelled out by subsequent losses, of course the measure of it is the present number of the population, estimated at 3,281 million in 1965. Approximately three-fourths of this increase has taken place since 1750 according to the "medium" estimates (or 70 percent if the "high" estimate of the 1750 population is taken as a basis). In speed as well as magnitude, the modern growth contrasts strongly with that of earlier times. Between 8000 B.C. and A.D. 1, according to the "medium" estimates, the population doubled not quite six times (multiplication of sixty-fold, whereas six doublings would multiply by sixty-four); in other words, the average doubling time was more than a thousand years. Again for the interval between A.D. 1 and 1750, the growth rate indicated by the "medium" estimates corresponds to a doubling time of more than a thousand years. This is the pace of a horse and buggy compared with the racing-car speed of the modern growth — doubling in approximately 150 years after 1750 and again in about 65 years after 1900, according to the "medium" estimates.[7]

It should be noted that the trend in past epochs was far from steady. If reliable measures of the world population could be obtained century by century since the birth of Christ and before, they would show some periods of growth at rates considerably exceeding the long-term average and other periods of relatively stationary or decreasing numbers. It is highly unlikely, though, that the speed of the modern growth was matched, in the world as a whole, during any previous period of considerable length.

[7] The contrast remains strong when the calculations are made with combinations of the "low" and "high" variants which minimize the doubling time for the earlier periods and maximize it for the period since 1750. Taking the "low" variant for 8000 B.C. with the "high" for A.D. 1, one obtains an average doubling time slightly in excess of 1,000 years, and a like calculation for the interval from A.D. 1 to 1750 yields a doubling time of slightly less than 800 years. The combination of the "high" variant for 1750 with a "low" estimate of 3,150 million for 1965 gives a doubling time of 122 years.

It is not possible to fix exactly the date when the extraordinary growth of the modern epoch began: i.e., the date since when the rate of population growth in the world as a whole has been distinctly and consistently above the average of previous centuries. Willcox and Carr-Saunders carried their estimates back to 1650 and both estimated a considerable increase in world population between 1650 and 1750, but the basis of estimates for that period is very weak. The author has refrained from attempting to extend the estimates in tables 1 and 2 back beyond 1750 in view of the poverty of information about earlier trends in almost every part of the world. Available data do suggest, though, that accelerated growth probably began somewhat before 1750 in parts of Europe, Russia, and America and possibly before 1700 in China.

Phases of World Population Growth Since 1750

When the growth of world population during the modern epoch is analyzed in terms of the trend of the growth rate over time and the variations in different areas, it is important to pay attention to the basis of estimates and their margins of error. Unguarded use of Willcox's and Carr-Saunders' estimates for such purposes has led many writers to dubious conclusions. With regard to the annual growth rates shown in table 1, which refer to the "medium" estimates, it should be emphasized that at many points they merely reflect assumptions adopted in making these estimates and that many of the rates would be changed considerably by selecting different, plausible combinations of population estimates for successive dates, within the ranges of the variants.

With due regard for these cautions, two phases of the world population trend since the eighteenth century can be distinguished: from 1750 to 1900, a phase of growth at relatively moderate speed (though much more rapid than that of earlier epochs), and since 1900, a phase of sharply accelerated growth. In the earlier phase, the "medium" estimates show steady growth of the world total at the rate of about ½ of 1 percent per annum during each fifty-year period. The estimated growth between 1900 and 1950 was at almost twice this rate, and United Nations estimates indicate a marked acceleration since 1920 with an impressive jump of the growth rate in the 1950's. (See table 3.)

TABLE 3

Estimates of World Population Growth, 1900–1960

Date	Population (millions)	Annual rate of increase since preceding date (percent)
1900	1,650	. . .
1920	1,860	0.6
1930	2,069	1.1
1940	2,295	1.0
1950	2,515	1.0
1960	2,998	1.8

It is commonly asserted that the rate of world population growth has been accelerating steadily during the last two or three centuries (and during all previous history as well, according to some writers). The present estimates do not bear out this idea; but neither do they disprove it, as there is ample room within the limits of the variants for either a rising or a falling trend of the growth rate between 1750 and 1900. Some acceleration of growth during that period is indicated by available data or else has been assumed in constructing the estimates for a majority of the areas, but this is counteracted by an opposite trend in the estimates for China's large population.

TRENDS IN MAJOR AREAS DURING THE INITIAL PHASE (1750-1900)

Variations of the population trend in different parts of the world are depicted in figure 2, where the "medium" estimates for each major area are charted on a logarithmic scale, so that the geometric rates of growth are reflected by the slopes of the curves. Where the estimates have a relatively weak basis, the curves are drawn with broken lines, and it will be noted that these occupy a large share of the chart, especially for the period before 1900. The picture for that period may be badly distorted, yet some of its broad outlines are probably representative of historical reality.

It seems to be commonly taken for granted that the European nations, as leaders in the Industrial Revolution, also took the lead in the modern population expansion and that they were responsible for most of the increase of the world total during the initial phase; but this is not apparent in the present estimates. Either in the chart or in the tabulation of estimated annual growth rates (table 1), Europe does not stand out among the major areas for speed of population growth at any time in the last two centuries. Europe's growth appears more remarkable for steadiness than for speed. It is true that the expansion of the European peoples is reflected partly in the figures for America and other areas to which tens of millions of Europeans emigrated during the last two centuries. In table 4, the estimates for America, Oceania, and the Soviet Union are added to those for Europe to make a total for the principal areas of European settlement and culture, and the growth rate of this total is found to have been appreciably higher than the rate for Europe alone in each period. By this measure, the European peoples appear to have had more than their proportionate share in the expansion of world population during the nineteenth century (though it is doubtfully warranted to say that their growth dominated the trend of the world total at that time). Between 1750 and 1800, on the other hand, it is not clear that the Europeans outpaced the rest of the world in population growth, and their increase since 1900 appears to have been nearly parallel with the trend of the world total.

There is some question whether it is appropriate to include in these totals the whole population of Middle and South America, much of which was of non-European or mixed stock. (This applies with less force to Northern America, the U.S.S.R., and Oceania.) If Middle and South America are excluded, the share of the European peoples in the growth of world population appears more modest, as shown by the figures in the lower panel of table 4.

In the case of western Europe, it may be true as postulated in the theory of the "demographic transition", that the cause of the population expansion in the initial phase was an improvement of economic conditions thanks to industrializa-

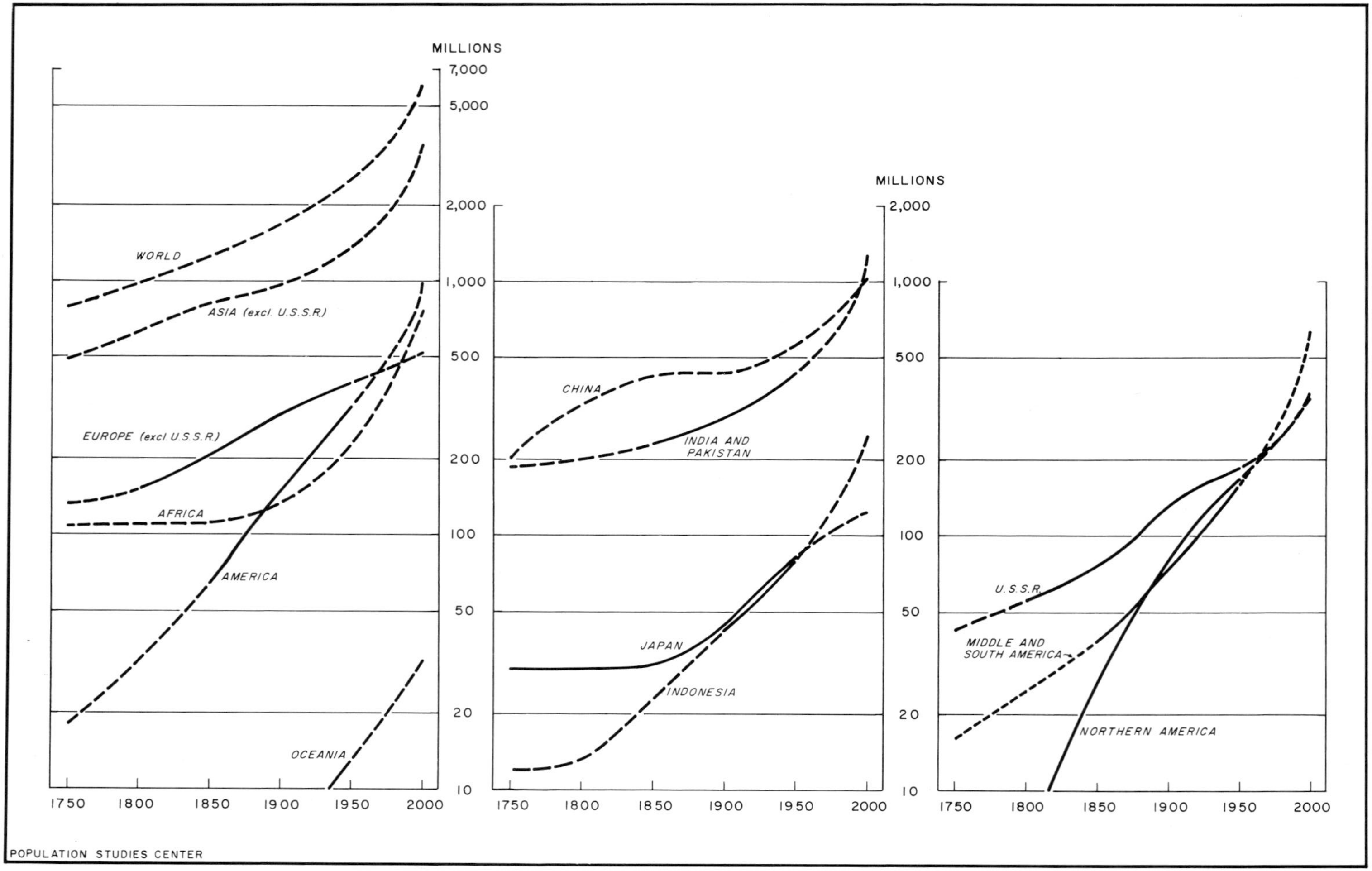

FIGURE 2

Growth of population in the world and major areas, "medium" estimates, 1750–1950, and projections to 2000.

TABLE 4

Growth of Population in Principal Areas of European Settlement: "Medium" Estimates, 1750–1950, and Projections to 2000

Date	Population (millions)	Share of world total (percent)	Increase since preceding date: Annual rate (percent)	Increase since preceding date: Share of world increase (percent)
A. Including Middle and South America				
1750	187	23.6	—	—
1800	241	24.6	0.5	28.9
1850	350	27.7	0.7	38.4
1900	592	35.9	1.1	62.4
1950	913	36.3	0.9	37.1
2000	1,904	31.1	1.5	27.4
B. Excluding Middle and South America				
1750	171	21.6	—	—
1800	217	22.2	0.5	24.6
1850	312	24.7	0.7	33.5
1900	518	31.4	1.0	53.1
1950	751	29.9	0.7	26.9
2000	1,266	20.7	1.1	14.2

tion, which made for a reduction of death rates.[8] This explanation does not apply so well to eastern Europe or to the area of the present Soviet Union, where there was little industrialization and economic conditions remained relatively poor until a much later time, yet population grew as much or more than it did in the West from the middle of the eighteenth century onward. The case of China, which appears as one of the areas of greatest expansion of population in the eighteenth century, again calls for a different explanation. In the world-wide picture as represented by the present estimates, little consistent relationship can be seen between the developments connected with the Industrial Revolution and the expansion of population in the initial phase.

What is the explanation, then, for the apparent, approximately simultaneous up-turn of the population trend during the eighteenth and early nineteenth century, in widely separated regions of the earth where economic conditions and developments were so diverse? It is hardly likely to be entirely a figment of errors in the estimates, and it is hardly credible that this rough parallel of trends in different areas could have been merely a coincidence of chance. The operation of some common causal factor or factors is strongly suggested, but the identification of the common causes is a puzzle which research in demographic history has yet to solve. Until a key to this puzzle is found, there cannot be much assurance in explanations for the trend in any area which only fit the history of that particular area.

This question calls for some new directions of research, and one direction which can be suggested is the study of world-wide epidemiological

[8] Historians are not agreed, however, either on the causal relationship between economic developments and accelerated population growth in western Europe during the eighteenth and the early nineteenth century, or on the question, whether the growth of population accelerated primarily through falling death rates or rising birth rates.

as well as economic repercussions of the European voyages of discovery and conquest from the fifteenth century onward. On the economic side, it is apparent that one of the most important early consequences was strengthening of agriculture, both in the Old and the New World, by the exchange of food plants, which made both for expansion of productive capacity and stabilization of agricultural output. The positive relation of this factor to the growth of population in the eighteenth century and later has been demonstrated, particularly as regards the introduction of the Irish potato in Europe and of maize and the sweet potato in China.[9] On the epidemiological side, the effects of the intrusion of Europeans into far regions of the globe have been considered mainly with regard to the epidemics and depopulation which ensued in some of the areas where they intruded, particularly in America and Oceania. In parts of America, depopulation seems to have continued for nearly two centuries after Columbus's voyages, before the indigenous peoples gained enough power of resistance through exposure to new diseases, to begin recouping their losses. But the exchange of diseases, like the exchange of food plants, was surely not only a one-way traffic. Rather little attention seems to have been given to the study of possible repercussions on health and mortality in Europe and other areas, such as China, with which the Europeans were in contact. The hypothesis suggested for study is that the potential stimulus to population growth resulting from the strengthening of agriculture was counteracted during the sixteenth and seventeenth centuries, in varying degrees in different areas, by the transmission of diseases around the globe; and that in the eighteenth century, growing natural resistance to the new diseases opened the way for an up-turn of the population trend in several areas.

To be sure, no single formula is likely to be found which would account for all the varieties of the trend in different parts of the world. For instance, the hypothesis just suggested does not very well fit the case of India, where population is thought to have been increasing in the sixteenth and seventeenth centuries and to have made little gain in the eighteenth. But for the sake of orderly historical interpretation of the initial phase of the world population expansion, it would be enough to find a formula which (modified as necessary to suit the circumstances of each area) would explain the curious parallel of apparent trends in Europe, the U.S.S.R., China, and America. With this object, it would be useful to formulate other hypotheses as well, for testing by historical studies in each area.

Divergent Trends in the Second Phase (Since 1900)

Since the beginning of the present century, the former ambiguous relationship between economic development and population in different areas has been transformed into a strong inverse relationship. This is shown by the comparison in table 5, where the "medium" estimates for Europe, the U.S.S.R., Northern America, Japan, and Oceania are combined to form a total for the areas which are relatively well developed economically at present, while the figures for the remainder of the world are taken to represent the trend in less developed areas.[10] It can be seen that since 1900, the less developed areas have forged far ahead in population growth; in fact, they have borne almost the whole responsibility for speeding up the expansion of world popula-

[9] B. H. Slicher van Bath, *The Agrarian History of Western Europe, A.D. 500-1850* (translated from Dutch by Olive Ordish, New York, 1963); Ho Ping-ti, *Studies on the Population of China, 1368-1953* (Cambridge, Mass., 1953) and "The Introduction of American Food Plants into China", *American Anthropologist* 57 (1955): No. 2, Part 1.

[10] This division between less developed and more developed areas is a crude one. Within Middle and South America, for instance, Argentina and Uruguay should be placed in the category of more developed areas, while the minority of Oceania's population outside Australia and New Zealand belongs in the less developed category. Such refinements require a more detailed areal classification of historical estimates than the author has attempted. In the United Nations estimates, the totals given for more developed and less developed regions are 1,032 and 2,249 million, respectively, as of 1965.

It should also be noted that the low estimated growth rate in less developed areas during 1850-1900 is much influenced by the estimates for China, which show almost no net increase of population during this period. Without China, the annual growth rate during 1850-1900 derived from the "medium" estimates for the less developed areas is 0.6 percent.

TABLE 5

Growth of Population in More Developed and Less Developed Areas of the World, 1850–2000

	"Medium" Estimates				Projections to 2000	
	1850	1900	1950	1965	"Low"	"High"
Population (millions)						
More developed areas	343	562	834	999	1,245	1,516
Less developed areas	919	1,088	1,682	2,281	4,204	5,478
Annual rate of increase since preceding date (percent)						
More developed areas	—	1.0	0.8	1.2	0.6	1.2
Less developed areas	—	0.3	0.9	2.1	1.8	2.5
Share of world total increase since preceding date (percent)						
More developed areas	—	56	31	22	11	14
Less developed areas	—	44	69	78	89	86

tion in the second phase, while the growth in more developed areas has proceeded at a relatively steady if not slackening pace.

The cause of this divergence of trends is well known. Great progress has been made since the beginning of the present century and especially since World War II, in developing knowledge of the causes, cure, and prevention of diseases and means of applying such knowledge for the prevention of premature death. While all the world has shared the benefit in the form of decreasing mortality, the main beneficiaries in the recent phase have been the peoples of the less developed areas, whose mortality rates were relatively high before. With increasing efficiency of life-saving techniques, the relative disadvantage in mortality of the economically handicapped nations has diminished, although they are still more or less far from equality with the wealthier nations in this respect. While death rates have decreased, the birth rates in less developed countries have generally shown little change, with the result that their rates of population growth have accelerated progressively. In more developed areas, on the other hand, the decrease of mortality in the second phase has been counteracted, by tightening control of births.

In some of the more developed areas, the death rate has decreased rather more than the birth rate since the end of the nineteenth century so that the rate of natural increase has risen to some extent in spite of the restriction of births. In other cases, the natural increase rate has been lowered considerably; but an equilibrium of births and deaths has not become established in any country of considerable population size (except temporarily in some European countries during the economic depression of the 1930's.) [11] On the average for the group of more developed areas, the population growth rate during 1900-1950 dropped slightly below the estimated level of 1850-1900, but it rose again slightly above that level during 1950-1965, as shown in table 5.

[11] In the comparison of crude birth and death rates, the balance between the forces of mortality and fertility is obscured by effects of variations in age structure of the population. A better measure of this balance is provided by the net reproduction rate, which represents the numerical ratio between successive female generations which would obtain if current age-specific rates of mortality and fertility should continue. Among more developed countries at present, net reproduction rates range from slightly less than unity in Hungary and Japan to approximately 1.8 in Canada (1962) and New Zealand (1964). The net rate for the United States in 1963 was 1.56; i.e., such as to increase numbers by slightly more than one-half in a generation. A compilation of these rates will be found in *Population Index,* April issue of each year.

TABLE 6

Percentages of Population Increase in Successive Decades, 1960–2000, According to Variants of the United Nations Projections.

	World Total			Less Developed Areas[a]			More Developed Areas[a]		
	Medium	*Low*	*High*	*Medium*	*Low*	*High*	*Medium*	*Low*	*High*
1960–1970.......	19.8	18.2	22.0	24.1	22.4	26.5	10.8	9.6	12.9
1970–1980.......	20.6	17.0	24.4	25.0	21.0	29.3	10.3	7.8	12.9
1980–1990.......	19.8	15.3	25.0	23.4	18.6	29.7	10.4	7.0	12.6
1990–2000.......	18.2	13.9	22.9	21.2	17.1	26.4	9.3	4.8	12.3

[a] Calculated from the totals for more developed and less developed areas shown in tables A3.2, A3.3, and A3.4 of the United Nations report, *World Population Prospects as Assessed* in 1963. The definition of the two groups of areas differ slightly from those used for table 5.

Prospect for Continuing Population Expansion

Evidently the modern expansion of population in the world as a whole is far from having run its course as yet. While it may soon reach its climax so far as the geometric rate of growth is concerned, in all likelihood it is not yet near the half-way mark of absolute numerical increase. If the assumptions of the latest United Nations projections are borne out, world population will rise into the range of approximately 5,500 to 7,000 million by the year 2000 and will still be growing vigorously at that time. Decade by decade, the rates of growth would follow the trends shown in table 6, according to the variants of the projections.

Both the "medium" and the "low" projections imply that the second phase of the modern population expansion — the phase of growth at an accelerating rate in the world as a whole — is now terminating and a third phase is about to begin: a phase in which the rate of growth will diminish, gradually at first and more rapidly later on. By the "medium" projection, the peak rate of growth would occur in the 1970's but the subsequent drop of the rate would be slow, so that the population would still be increasing in the 1990's almost as rapidly as it did in the 1950's. According to the "low projection, the growth rate in the 1990's would be well below the present level but still far above the average for the first half of the present century. If the future trend should follow the "high" projection, on the other hand, the world growth rate would go on rising until the 1980's and would not drop below the present level before the close of the century.

Even the "high" projection may be regarded from a certain point of view as a rather conservative one so far as the less developed areas are concerned, since it incorporates an assumption that considerable decreases of fertility will take place during the next few decades in a majority of those areas, although there are only a few areas where such a trend appears already to have set in. Earlier and more widespread fertility reductions in less developed areas are assumed for the "medium" and "low" projections. The growth which might be expected in the absence of any such change in fertility, but with continuing reductions of mortality rates, is represented by another variant of the projections, designated "constant fertility, no migration". According to this, the rate of growth in the world as a whole would speed up progressively throughout the projection period and the population in the year 2000 would reach a figure of approximately 7,500 million.

What of the farther future? It is idle to calculate how many human beings the earth would hold at some far future date if growth should continue at any specified rate, and it is not a much more useful occupation to try to estimate how many could be supported on the planet if all its resources (and perhaps those of the moon and more distant heavenly bodies as well) were fully exploited with the unknown technologies of the future. Without wandering away into those trackless fields, it may be of some value to consider the prospect for continuation and possible termination of the population expansion in the twenty-first century, supposing that the trend would go on evolving along the general lines assumed in the United Nations "medium" projection.

Of course, the main question relates to what may happen in the presently less developed areas. The United Nations projections are founded on the expectation that the population in these areas will undergo a process of demographic transition, associated with future economic and social developments and helped along by population policy measures, such that they would eventually arrive at a demographic position comparable to that of the more developed areas at present. Upon completion of the transition, it is assumed that they would have expectation of life at birth approximating 75 years and fertility rates at about half the present levels in the various less developed areas. The transition would begin sooner and proceed faster in some areas than in others; some would be far along in the process by the year 2000 whereas others would scarcely have entered it by that time, so far as the decreasing fertility trend is concerned. In the group of less developed areas as a whole, according to the "medium" projection (table 6), the per decade rate of population would reach a peak of 25 percent in the 1970's and subside by the 1990's to 21 percent. One may suppose that upon completion of the transition in all areas, the per decade growth rate for the group as a whole would be somewhere around 10 percent, corresponding roughly to the current level in the more developed group. Supposing further that the decreasing trend of the growth rate would speed up to some extent after 2000, one may imagine the 10 percent rate being reached perhaps about the year 2040. If so, the total population in the group of less developed areas would increase from the figure of 4,742 million projected for 2000 to something over 8,500 million by 2040, and the world total would then easily have reached the range of 10,000 million — well over ten times the number with which the modern expansion began two centuries ago.

If the third phase is regarded as completed when the world growth rate comes down to the present average for more developed areas, one still has to reckon with the question of a fourth phase. This would be the phase of transition to the worldwide equilibrium of births and deaths which must ultimately be achieved if the end is not to be a catastrophe. Experience up to the present time affords little basis for estimating how long this final achievement might take and how many more thousands of millions might be added in the process. Enough may have been said, though, to illustrate the point that the expansion of world population is not likely to spend its momentum very shortly. It is apparent that the twenty-first century might well surpass the twentieth for magnitude of its addition to the number of the earth's inhabitants, unless so great an increase should exceed possibilities of expanding production of the necessities of healthy life.

STUDY AND DISCUSSION QUESTIONS

1. Given the two purposes theory is supposed to serve (see introduction to chapter), discuss how the notion of the "demographic transition" fulfills or falls short of meeting these criteria.
2. Which of the two purposes of theory would you say Malthus' theory was most successful in accomplishing? Why?
3. Urbanization, industrialization, and rapid population growth as described by the demographic transition all occurred at about the same time in the Western world. Discuss how these three phenomena may affect one another. Which do you suppose came first?
4. What are the sociological implications of a sudden and severe drop in the death rate of an underdeveloped country today? If you were hired as a consultant in such a country, what recommendations would you make?
5. Have the librarian help you find some figures on population growth in at least one country from each continent during the past five years. What sources did you use? Compare these rates of growth.
6. Compare the development of sociological theory with the development of population theory. Which is more advanced? What kinds of questions does each try to answer? How are the two related?

SUGGESTED ADDITIONAL READING

Spengler, Joseph J., and Otis Dudley Duncan, eds. *Population Theory and Policy*. Glencoe: The Free Press, 1956.
A collection of readings on the title subject with a heavy economic orientation.

Glass, D. V. *Introduction to Malthus*. London: Watts, 1951.
Report and examination of the views of the man who provided much impetus for the scientific investigation of population.

Vance, Rupert B. "Is Theory for Demographers?," *Social Forces*, 31 (October, 1952), 9–13.
Presidential address read before the Population Association of America, which rekindled interest and renewed controversy in population theory.

Gutman, Robert. "In Defense of Population Theory," *American Sociological Review*, 25 (June, 1960), 325–333.
An optimistic view of theoretical development in demography which tries to distinguish the different levels of generalization that may result from population research.

United Nations. Department of Economics and Social Affairs. *Demographic Yearbook*. New York: United Nations.
An annual report on the level, trends, and characteristics of population in the world.

United Nations. *Population and Vital Statistics Report*. New York: United Nations.
Quarterly report on available population and vital statistics for a wide range of countries.

CHAPTER 3

Mortality Trends and Differentials

The population equation described earlier — population change coming about through the addition of births and in-migrants and the subtraction of deaths and out-migrants — identifies the main elements of demographic change. The element of deaths (or mortality) is examined here first, principally because a country undergoing the typical demographic transition seems to be affected most and earliest by changes in mortality. As a matter of fact, a singularly important contribution of demography has been the revelation that in countries undergoing rapid population increase it is mainly a sharply-declining death rate rather than an increasing birth rate that brings about the "population explosion."

The selection by Stolnitz deals with some of the long-term trends in world and regional mortality and discusses some of the factors associated with these trends. In all parts of the world, significant declines in mortality have been observed; but these declines have occurred at different rates in different areas. In most Western nations mortality has completed the transition from high to low levels, beginning with gradual declines in the death rate in the early nineteenth century, acceleration of its downward course in the later nineteenth and early twentieth century, and tapering off of death rates at relatively low levels in the middle of the twentieth century. This mortality transition, which took about 150 years to transpire in the Western world, is being effected in the developing nations of the globe at a much more rapid rate. As Stolnitz points out, the role of international health agencies, the use of antibiotics, the development of efficient methods for combating malaria and other contagious diseases, and other benefits to health in these countries resulting from contacts with developed nations, are factors that were not operative during the mortality transitions of the earlier periods and are designed to bring about more rapid declines in the death rate in countries where mortality is still relatively high.

As of the mid-1960's the *crude death rate* (deaths per 1,000 population) stood at 16 for the world as a whole, but varied considerably from continent to continent and from country to country within continents. It averaged about 10 in North America, Europe, and Oceania, about 15 in Latin America, about 20 in Asia, and about 25 in Africa. Within continents there was great variability, as illustrated by death rates of 8 in Argentina and 20-25 in Bolivia within South America, and 5 in Hong Kong and 23-27 in Iran within Asia. But the association between level of mortality and stage of socioeconomic development, a rough indicator of stage in the demographic transition, is reasonably high. Associated with socioeconomic development are such factors as improvements in level of living, advances in sanitation and hygiene, more effective medical knowledge, and expanding public health programs, all of which contribute to reductions in mortality.

A characteristic feature of mortality data is the definable pattern of death rates by age. Whatever the level of mortality in an area, the death rates for each age group are likely to be in a fixed order. That is, the risks of survival during the first year of life are much greater than in subsequent years of childhood and young adulthood. The death rate of infants in the year after birth is not matched in level again until the age of normal retirement from work. A high proportion of deaths in the first year of life, of course, occurs immediately after birth or during the first month of life. In economically-advanced countries, the prospects for survival improve quickly with time, the most favorable mortality rates being for elementary school-age children who are not subject to many of the mortal risks of other ages. The probability of death increases gradually with age, first reaching relatively high levels in post-retirement years. The average expected lifetime at birth (called "life expectancy" in life table formulations) is now seventy years in the United States. The ultimate age to which a person might expect to survive under most favorable conditions (usually referred to as "life span") is possibly in the neighborhood of 120, although the accuracy of age reports for people that old is difficult to determine. Extremely few people are believed to survive beyond that age. An important distinction between life expectancy and life span is that, over time, the former can be assumed to increase as more and more people survive through infancy and the ages of middle life, whereas the latter appears to remain fixed.

Within countries, mortality rates vary from group to group. Several of these group differentials have been of analytical interest to demographers. In particular, it is important to know what these differentials are, which of them are persisting or widening, and which are narrowing. One might asume that, as the overall level of mortality declines in a country, the advantages of long life are extended to all groups in the population, resulting in narrower differentials. This is not entirely the case; while many differentials are narrowing, some are getting wider.

One way in which death rates vary within a country is by geographic area. The range of death rates from one region or province to another or from one state to another is often considerable. These geographic differentials in mortality are, in large measure, the result of area differences in the composition and characteristics of the population of the areas. For example, if two states have similar health conditions but one has a younger population, the state with the younger population might be expected to have a lower death rate because death rates tend to be lower at younger ages. Another type of geographic differential is between urban and rural areas. In the nineteenth century, death rates were usually higher in urban areas than in rural areas; living conditions in the cities were poor and the risks of mortality were quite high there. While the urban-rural differential persists in some areas, the spread of hospitals, first in urban areas and then in rural areas, the extension of urban culture to rural places, and the lessening of differences in the level of living between the two types of areas has brought the death rates for the two types very close to each other. In countries where the difference persists, it is apt to be due, in large part, to variations in age or other compositional factors.

Ethnic and racial differentials in mortality have been narrowing in recent years, presumably due to the more similar environmental conditions these groups experience. Variations in mortality among marital classes (the more favorable rate being for married persons), may be explained partly on the basis of the physical selection of married persons. It is doubtful that the state of marriage itself contributes much longer life; although stable marriages may be associated with less stress and strain than are broken marriages or bachelorhood, there is little reason to believe that a very high proportion of marriages can be classified as stable.

A well-publicized group differential in mortality is that between the sexes. In most parts of the world, not only do women outlive men but the sex differential is widening. The life advantage which females have over males is strongest at older adult ages but is found at all ages. It is most pronounced in developed countries. A question which has confounded demographers for some time is whether this differential is culturally or biologically caused. On the one hand, men are subject to greater risks and pressures of modern life, and this may have something to do with their lower life expectancy, but the widening gulf in mortality of the sexes is inconsistent with the increasing participation of women in the world of work. On the other hand, there are constitutional differences between the sexes and this may provide women with greater physical ability to resist disease and injury. It is certainly true that causes of death that are relatively increasing are those which in the past took a greater toll of men than women. In an ingenious study described in this chapter, Madigan sought an answer to the biology versus culture argument by comparing the mortality experience of religious orders of brothers and sisters, both of which groups led similar lives. Despite the greater similarity of cultural factors among the men and women in this study than in the general population, the sex differential in mortality was seen to persist. Biological factors would thus seem to be more important in explaining these differences. But can the diverging death rates of the sexes be accounted for by biological factors? Medical and biological science would not support that hypothesis; physiologically, men and women have not changed that much over the past few decades. The argument continues and only further research will give us the answer.

Another differential in mortality is that among the social classes. In both theory and fact, reductions in mortality take place first among the upper classes, later filtering down to the middle and lower classes. As a result, socioeconomic differentials in mortality may be expected to narrow as nations move through the demographic transition. Stockwell's article summarizes the research in this area and points out some of the methodological difficulties in reaching conclusions about the status of, and changes in, socioeconomic differentials. The traditional inverse relationship between social class and mortality has been accounted for partly by the greater risks in occupations held by the lower classes but largely by the level of living typical of each social class. Even where an inverse relationship of social class and the death rate exists in a population, however, the relationship may be quite different with regard to specific causes of death. For example, fatal diseases associated with the digestive organs take a heavier toll of the upper classes than of the lower classes.

Because causes of death are distributed differently for the various social classes, races, and sexes in the population, the state of health of the population is of considerable interest to population experts. *Morbidity*, referring to the state of illness, is a subject which has not been examined as thoroughly as has mortality; in fact, for many years, morbidity conditions were estimated on the basis of mortality statistics. Increasingly it has been recognized that death is the concluding episode of a morbid state of health, and separate bodies of statistics are now being accumulated from special surveys designed to collect information on illness in the population. The National Health Survey in the United States, a government survey taken periodically of a representative sample of the population, produces much-needed data on the incidence and prevalence of the ailments people have. Anderson and Lerner summarize some of our knowledge about the state of health of the American population based on such government and private studies.

The phenomenon of mortality may be viewed from a number of different perspectives. From a sociological perspective, mortality can be seen as a function of (a) the workings of social institutions, (b) the influences of group norms, and (c) decisions made by individuals and families. All these operate within the limits defined by biological and geographical factors.

For example, prospects of survival are partly determined by an individual's genetic make-up, his physiology, and his anatomy, and partly by conditions of the natural environment, such as climate and terrain. A poorly-formed baby, one born very small, and one with the RH factor in his blood, have much less chance of surviving infancy than a baby who is normal in these respects. Air pollution increases the risk of lung disease, and poor land will not be especially productive of agriculture to feed the people who depend on it.

Institutional changes in the society may effect the person's life expectancy, through such actions as improvements or declines in the economy, advances in medicine and technology, and governmental policies regarding public health, sanitation, support of medical education, and regulation of automobile safety standards.

The groups to which the person belongs or aspires provide him with sources of values about life and death and they inculcate in him the norms, or expected patterns of behavior, concerning ways of preserving life and avoiding death. Japanese kamikaze pilots in World War II were expected to sacrifice their lives when such action would probably lead to the deaths of many of the enemy or inflict extensive damage to their military equipment. American soldiers are expected to risk their lives in battle if necessary, whereas as civilians they are expected to remain alive and healthy under almost all circumstances.

While all these factors affect an individual's chances of survival, the decisions the individual or his family make, as to what advantage they take of the opportunities for prolonging life, also determine his chances of living or dying. There may be enough doctors in a community to care for all the residents, but some persons in the community, even though they may be able to afford it, may neglect to see the doctor when necessary. Some persons choose to drive dangerously on the highways; others do not. Mortality is affected by these kinds of decisions.

*A Century of International Mortality Trends: I**

GEORGE J. STOLNITZ

Among sophisticated tools of demographic measurement the life table is by far the oldest. The concept of a stationary population dates back several centuries, at the least to Halley's celebrated paper on Breslau (1693), while probabilities of dying, the fundamental measures of the life table, have an even older history. It is true that correct methods of deriving such measures from vital and census statistics were first developed at a much later period. Indeed, the assumption that the life table could be constructed solely by means of deaths classified by age, which Halley had cautiously applied to a special case, continued to be used until well into the nineteenth century. Long before then, howevery, the basic elements of the modern approach had come to be formulated, in studies by Deparcieux, Struyck, Kersseboom and somewhat later, by Wargentin. The last, for example, pointed out about 1760 that reliable measures of mortality risks could ordinarily be derived only if deaths at each age were related to the number living. By the end of the eighteenth century, the conversion of age-specific mortality rates into probabilities and the computation of expectations of life and probable life times had become widely recognized techniques. The works of Milne, published at the end of the Napoleonic Wars, have a remarkably modern ring even today, while Farr's extensive writings on the life table reflect the substantial enrichment of pure and applied theory that had taken place before 1850.

From a demographic viewpoint at least, it is no great exaggeration to say that all of the fundamental steps to the modern theory of life tables had been taken before that date. The last great surge of theoretical investigation, involving prominently the work of Knapp, Lexis, Zeuner and Becker, was largely a more rigorous restatement of procedures which had long been known and applied. In any event, this phase had come to an end by 1875. Since then, the main improvements in life table methodology have been in such derivative areas as interpolation and smoothing and in the normal growth of experience with the problems of treating inadequate raw data. In contrast to techniques centering

* Reprinted with permission from *Population Studies*, Vol. 9, Part 1 (July 1955), pp. 24-55.

about the net reproduction rate, whose earliest origins are in the 1880's, or about stable population models, which were first developed after 1900, recognition of the nature and uses of the life table has been essentially unchanged for over a century.

The history of extensive applications of the theory is much more recent. Only scattered life tables are available for national populations before 1840 and most of these cover such long periods that the comparisons which can be made over time or space are awkward, if not misleading. Beginning with the 1840's, however, there is evidence in every decade on appreciable clusters of areas.

The purpose of this and a following article is to summarize what seem to be the highlights of this century-long accumulation of recorded experience. The series of summary propositions developed below describe or introduce most of the major findings. Some of these are well known; others are less familiar, while still others appear to have been largely overlooked. That past mortality trends have been predominantly downward or that female longevity almost always exceeds the male are, of course, among the most widely recognized generalizations in the social sciences. There is also a tremendous, if scattered, comparative literature bearing on mortality trends and levels among restricted numbers of populations or over limited periods. But synoptic studies have been surprisingly few and in every case highly fragmentary in relation to the evidence at hand. To my knowledge, no attempt has ever been made to examine the existing documentation systematically, with a view to eliciting at least an appreciable number of the most interesting generalizations and orders of magnitude suggested by the data.

The present article deals with mortality trends and differentials, and some leading prospects for future change, over the broad regions of the world. Its successor will have the same general orientation, but will be directly concerned with the potential effects of mortality on reproductivity and size of labour force, with sex differentials and with the reliability of some prominent hypotheses in the literature on mortality patterns. To these ends use has been made of well over 250 life tables, including nearly all of the materials ever published for national populations. Data for non-national groups have been used only occasionally, e.g., for parts of China, when they provided supplementary evidence of special interest. In general, however, information on regional, urban-rural or other component populations as well as on "primitive" societies has been excluded.

As will be noted below in numerous connections, the question of inaccuracies in the data has been a consistently troubling one. Almost no attempts at adjustment have been made, though the reliability of both current and historical life tables is very nearly an unexplored area of research and merits a thorough-going critical review. Nor was it possible to follow any single consistent procedure for selecting or rejecting data, in view of the varied uses to which the data were to be put. Some life tables were simply rejected outright; for example all of the pre-1920 material for Japan was discarded on the ground that it completely distorts the trends in that country in the years surrounding the introduction of a modern system of vital registration. In other instances, where no decisive grounds for rejection were manifest but the data seemed highly suspect, the available measures were applied only for making gross ordinal comparisons. Account has been taken throughout of the special uncertainties of reporting at the upper ages of life; thus only minimal statements, and these qualitative, are made about life expectancy beyond age 60 and about age-specific characteristics beyond 65 or 70.[1]

Fortunately there is reason to believe that most of the major conclusions reached below would have been substantially unchanged if ideally accurate (as opposed to complete) data had been available. In part this impression derives from a consideration of the evidence on probable margins of error. But in addition it reflects the rather high level of generality attempted here. Questions of quality would have arisen much more centrally, had our concern been with individual details or differences in the small. It is probably too much to expect, however, that the

[1] Extrapolatory techniques, rather than direct observations, are likely to be used beyond age 70 in the life tables for Latin America, Africa and Asia. The beginning ages for extrapolation are generally much higher in Europe, often beyond 85 or 90.

precautions taken have been adequate to eliminate all major errors in interpretation.

Some explanation is needed concerning the three population groupings used below — "the West," "non-Western Europe" and "Latin America-Africa-Asia." No clear-cut basis for classification exists in the literature, the general practice being to treat marginal cases according to the particular purpose at hand. The present classification was counselled by a variety of considerations. Thus the West includes the United Kingdom and Ireland; Scandinavia; the Low Countries, France, Germany and Switzerland; the United States and Canada; Australia and New Zealand; and three populations on record in Africa and Asia which can be characterized as more or less European.[2] In the main, therefore, this group includes the populations of the world which are generally regarded as the most advanced in economic and demographic terms; comparative homogeneity in these respects rather than geographic contiguity has been the guiding rule in this instance. The remaining two blocs of populations are defined residually, following fairly conventional lines. Non-Western Europe refers to all of the continent not in the West; included here are the Baltic and Balkan countries, the Iberian Peninsula, Italy, Poland, Hungary, European Russia, Malta, Czechoslovakia, Austria and Finland.[3] Latin America-Africa-Asia covers the rest of the world, or all of the populations on the three continents other than the few classed with the West. It is very nearly coterminous, therefore, with the areas which appear most prominently in current discussions of the "underdeveloped world".

[2] These are the white populations of the Union of South Africa and Southern Rhodesia and the Jews in Israel. Life tables are available on the first since the 1920's, on the second for the 1930's and on the third since about 1940. In almost every respect all three populations fit comfortably within the range of contemporary experience encountered elsewhere in the West. To have included them with either of the other two blocs would have greatly extended the group range.

[3] The last three are perhaps the most marginal cases, judging from other classifications in use. But with respect to mortality at least, Czechoslovakia and Austria have been far more similar to the rest of non-Western Europe than to the West over the past century. Finland, although a borderline case in more than one way, often provides a convenient upper estimate of life chances in non-Western Europe over most of this period.

A more functional classification might well have combined some of the populations in the last two groups (though hardly in all three). Certainly Japan to-day is more similar to much of non-Western Europe than to most underdeveloped areas. Whether this was also true in the earlier years is uncertain, however. As late as the 1920's expectation of life in Japan was no higher than in Russia, although the latter was one of the high-mortality areas in its region. In any event, Japan's is the only major national experience on record which serves as a useful estimate of favourable life chances in Latin America-Africa-Asia.[4]

The West

The natural starting point for any survey of long-run international trends in mortality is the experience of the West. Including all of the nations with 100-year life table records, the region as a whole has been effectively documented for close to a half century. The populations of the West are also the ones in which the processes of economic modernization took hold earliest and advanced the most, and where levels of living are the highest and mortality the lowest to-day. Implicitly or explicitly, this experience has influenced the programmes of economic and social change under way or contemplated in the underdeveloped areas, chiefly in Latin America-Africa-Asia. In mortality, as in other fields, a major interest is whether such areas can achieve similar progress or even overtake the West. Thus alone among the three broad groupings considered here, the West provides an adequate historical perspective for viewing developments elsewhere.

The outstanding aspect of Western mortality trends during the last century is, of course, their magnitude. But in addition such trends have been remarkable for the way in which they have varied over time, for their effects on international differentials within the region and for the very changed prospects they imply for the future.

[4] This is not to say that any absolute limits are involved. In fact the very slight evidence at hand suggests that life chances in Argentina have been a good deal higher. On the other hand, there can be little question that Japanese survivorship since World War I has exceeded that of all but a minor fraction of the region's inhabitants.

The following discussion centres about these four themes.

1. The Rise in Western Life Chances over the Past Century has Probably Been More Far-reaching than the Gains of the Previous 2,000 Years.

World longevity, as measured by expectation of life at birth, can hardly have averaged much below 20 years over any considerable period since the Roman era. On the other hand the Western average of some 40 years about 1850 almost certainly represents the maximum attained by that date in any major region.[5] An increase of 20 years would therefore appear to be an outside estimate of secular changes in the two millennia before the Industrial Revolution was well under way. This is not, of course, to say that the actual trends followed anything like a sustained course; probably a more realistic view is that the processes of change over the world as a whole were more nearly the net result of highly irregular, long "cycles" in the regions of major population settlement. But if we think of rather lengthy intervals as time units, the likelihood is that the fluctuation between any two periods fell within a range of 20 years. Indeed a range of 10–15 seems more reasonable in some ways; longevity in the regions of major population settlement outside the West probably averaged below 30 years up to the twentieth century and a leeway as high as 20 years would require earlier levels as low as 10.

Compared to the world as a whole or most of its major parts, the rise in the West since the 1840's may well have been more than 50% above the variations of the previous 2,000 years. The seven nations on record over the last century show a median increase of more than 25 years,[6] and there are indications that the rise in the United States and Scotland was not very different from this average. In Germany and Switzerland the trend appears to have been steeper, if anything. Only the Netherlands stand out as a clearly divergent case, and here the rise was some 34 years.

A remarkable aspect of this century-long growth in longevity has been the way in which the changes have varied over the life cycle. The rise in expectation of life at birth has been not far from twice the rise at age 15, the beginning of the young adult period, while the latter increase has itself been about double the change at age 45. Between the beginning of the middle and advanced periods of life, or 45 and 60, the ratio has been only somewhat lower, about 1.7.

There would be little point in attempting to compare the changes at these later ages with earlier world trends. The relative dispersions of national trends within the West are larger in the adult years than at birth, while pre-modern estimates are harder to come by and are probably

[5] See L. Dublin, A. Lotka and M. Spiegelman, *Length of Life* (Revised edition; New York, Ronald Press, 1949), ch. 2; also, W. Willcox, "The length of life in the early Roman Empire," in Congrès International de la Population, *Proceedings,* 1937 (Paris, Hermann & Cie., 1938), II, pp. 14-22. The meagre evidence on ancient longevity appears to be based wholly on deaths reported by age in various sources or on estimated ages of skeletal remains. The strong likelihood is that most published figures are upward-biased and can be used only broadly for approximating lower bounds. Such estimates as exist for the mediaeval and renaissance periods are generally biased in the same direction, in part because of their reference to selected sub-populations of higher than average social status. Longevity in cities is sometimes recorded as below or not much above 20 years, but here the biases probably run strongly the other way, in relation to the rural population.

An indirect approach is to consider that an average lifetime of 20 years implies a crude death rate approximating 50 per 1,000. No doubt such rates were often exceeded in the short run. Higher values are occasionally found in Sweden and parts of China in the modern era and the rate in Europe during the first impact of the Black Death may have been above 250; some authorities believe Europe's population before 1350 was first exceeded several centuries later. But a death rate of 50 matches the highest sustained birth rates ever recorded among large populations. On the assumption that world population was growing except for a few unusual setbacks, death rates averaging over 50 for extended periods would have been rare.

[6] This is very nearly the magnitude indicated by the medians on record for the 1840's and 1940's, despite the very different scope of the data for the two decades. Both the median changes and the changes in medians are probably downward-biased. In part, this is because the materials at hand for the 1840's underrepresent the populations of relatively high mortality; in part, too, most of the available earlier measures appear likely to err on the high side.

The seven countries referred to in the text are the Netherlands, Sweden, Norway, England and Wales, France, Denmark and Belgium.

TABLE 1

*Mortality Characteristics in 5 Western Countries: By Sex, 1840's and 1940's**

Country†	1840's					1940's				
	l_1	l_{15}	Quartile ages of death			l_1	l_{60}	Quartile ages of death		
			1st	2nd	3rd			1st	2nd	3rd
					I. Males					
Netherlands	776	615	2.5	37.5	62.5	967	805	62.5	72.5	82.5
Sweden	835	710	7.5	47.5	67.5	966	759	62.5	72.5	82.5
England and Wales	836	673	2.5	42.5	67.5	952	722	57.5	72.5	77.5
France	822	659	2.5	42.5	67.5	943	684	52.5	67.5	77.5
Belgium	836	655	2.5	42.5	67.5	936	673	52.5	67.5	77.5
					II. Females					
Netherlands	814	644	2.5	37.5	67.5	973	839	67.5	77.5	82.5
Sweden	859	741	12.5	57.5	72.5	974	802	62.5	77.5	82.5
England and Wales	865	697	7.5	47.5	72.5	963	799	62.5	77.5	82.5
France	847	676	2.5	47.5	72.5	957	776	62.5	77.5	82.5
Belgium	864	670	2.5	42.5	67.5	951	772	62.5	72.5	82.5

* The symbol l_x denotes the number in a group of 1,000 live births surviving to age *x*. Quartile ages of death are the ages at which a group of live births has been reduced by a quarter, a half, and three quarters, respectively; the figures cited are the mid-points of the five-year intervals including the quartile ages of death.

† Early values for France cover the period 1840-59; those for England and Wales cover 1838-54. Information available on the early life tables for Norway and Denmark did not include the data used here. All figures for the 1940's except those for Sweden relate to post war years.

less reliable.[7] Little or no doubt, however, attaches to the conclusions that can be drawn about the comparative trends in related mortality characteristics. Under conditions existing as late as the middle of the nineteenth century, a newborn Western cohort could on the average expect to lose one-quarter of its members long before age 10 and half before 45 (Table 1). A century later the first of these ages had increased by well over 50 years and the second by something like a generation. The number that could expect to survive the childhood years a century ago was substantially smaller than the number reaching old age to-day.

Increasing life chances are almost always explained by reference to two broad categories of causes: rising levels of living on the one hand (income, nutrition, housing, literacy), and on the other technological advances (medical science, public health, sanitation). The usual approach has been to regard these sets of factors as more or less coordinate, with little attempt to assess their relative importance. At the same time there has been considerable emphasis on their interdependence, a common observation being that the development and application of disease-control techniques would have been very different in the absence of widespread social change.[8]

[7] India in the influenza decade of the 1910's may not be a too remote example of pre-modern conditions, even in relatively unfavourable periods. It may be indicative that adult life expectancy in that population was closer to Western levels about 1850 than the latter were to Western experience a century later.

[8] To attempt a fairly definitive demarcation between these categories would probably be futile; the theoretical framework needed to guide such an endeavour simply does not exist. For present purposes the most fruitful distinction appears to be between (1) the enhanced health opportunities confronting the individual, as his personal economic and educational circumstances improve, and (2) the opportunities which can only be exploited through organization by the community or government, independently of income per head. Thus government-sponsored research and health education belong to the second category since neither is appreciably dependent on income per head or even revenues per head. The same is true of foreign aid for health purposes, whether on a grant or loan basis. Private medical research and care, and government-operated hospital facilities might all be classed under the first category, to be on the safe side.

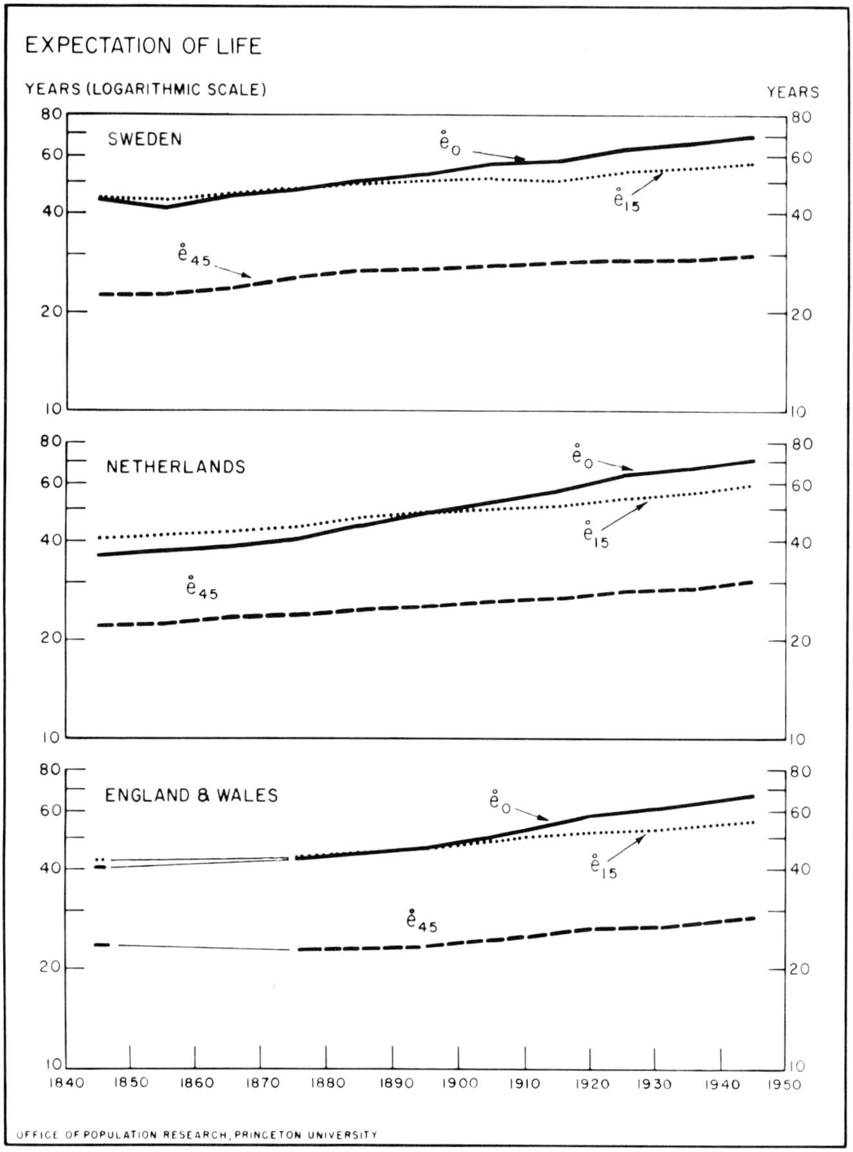

FIGURE 1

Expectation of life at ages 0, 15 and 45 in three Western countries, 1840's to 1940's. Averages of male and female values.

Both of these views, which evolved largely on the basis of Western mortality experience, have also been traditional explanations of the contrasting patterns found in other parts of the world. Only recently has their adequacy been seriously questioned, mainly as a result of developments in Latin America-Africa-Asia. The introduction of new disease-control methods in this region, usually unaccompanied by any important shifts in socio-economic conditions, has led to drastic mortality declines in the last few years.[9] It is worth noting, therefore, that a similar causal process may have been operative in the acceleration of Western survivorship a good deal earlier.

2. The Modern Rise in Western Life Chances First Became Marked Late in the Nineteenth Century. Very Probably, Most National Increases in Expectation of Life at Birth Since the 1890's Have Been More than Double the Gains Over the Preceding Half Century.

The middle decades of the last century were years of little or no change. The largest national gains in expectation of life at birth between the 1840's and 1860's appear to have been not far from 3 years, or a minor fraction of the 100-year increases noted previously (Figure 1). Correspondingly limited gains seem to have taken place in longevity at all stages of life and in survivorship at most ages. In particular, survival trends appear to have been minimal in the United Kingdom, France, Belgium and Germany.

Short-run declines in life chances, as measured by changes between the successive life tables on record for individual areas, were far more frequent in the third quarter of the century than subsequently. The relative frequency of such declines was over twice as large between the 1840's and 1870's as between the latter decade and World War I.[10] Conversely, almost all of the maximum changes on record between successive life tables occurred at the turn of the century or later. As can be seen from the entries for the first three areas in Table 2 (all neutrals in World War I), this is true even if we exclude the unusual variations between the influenza decade of the 1910's and the 1920's. With few exceptions, annual rates of change in life expectancy before the 1870's were only fractions of the maxima indicated in Table 2. Such changes also tended to be well below the movements which took place in the quarter century before World War I. Among the Western populations with reasonably long series of life tables before 1910, well over half of the maximum short-run trends on record occurred after 1890.

The 70 years ending in the first world war saw the West progress to a very nearly new range of survival experience. As the foregoing suggests, by far the largest part of the advance took place in the second half of the period. It is true that no simple comparison can properly be made between survival trends in the two generations following the 1840's; there were variations from age to age and the trends in life expectancy were generally in sharper contrast than those in age-specific survivorship. As a rule, however, the increases between the 1870's and 1900's were more than 50% higher than those in the preceding 30 years, and differences well above 100% were not uncommon.

So little attention has been devoted to the details of this remarkable acceleration that one can only speculate about its causes. It is tempting to adopt the eclectic view noted previously, and this may well be the wisest course in the present state of knowledge. The problem of establishing the relative importance of multiple causes is a difficult one at best while the data are no doubt a good deal short of adequate. Nevertheless, the question of the factors accounting for the above patterns is of considerable interest as well as current importance, and warrants far more investigation than it has received to date.[11] Without in any

[9] See p. 150.

[10] It is likely that year-to-year declines were more common in both periods. The changes under discussion, which are usually between the average experience of periods spanning a decade, are closer to the meaning of a short-run trend. Between the 1840's and 1900's, declines in life expectancy at the ages 0, 15, 45 and 60 occurred in about 1 of 10 changes on record. ("1900's" will be used throughout to designate the first decade of this century.) Most of the declines were at the last two ages, a suggestion that improving measurement may have biased the proportion upward. A similar count of age-specific survival measures, using the age intervals 0-1, 1-2.5, 2.5-7.5, . . . , 62.5-67.5, showed declines in 1 of 8 cases during the same period; many of these were in the infant and upper ages. Since 1900 the declines have been much less frequent, occurring in about 1 of 16 changes in the above life expectancies and in less than 1 of 25 age-specific variations.

Except for the males in France, no population on record in the West has shown repeated short-run declines over the past century. Interestingly, the two world wars had remarkably little effect on trends in longevity for either sex. Nearly all of the Western belligerent nations, including France, experienced increases in the 1910's-1920's or 1930's-1940's which compare favourably with the trends in the "more normal" 1920's-1930's.

[11] See, e.g., United Nations, *The Determinants and Consequences of Population Trends* (New York, 1953), p. 60, where a discussion of the factors affecting past mortality trends jumps from the situation before 1850 to the twentieth century. A recent treatment of the problem of multiple causation in mortality comparisons is by E. Buckatzsch, "The influence of social conditions on mortality rates," *Population Studies,* vol. 1 no. 3 (Dec., 1947), pp. 229-247.

TABLE 2

*Maximum Short-Run Increases in Expectation of Life; Magnitudes and Periods of Occurrence in 11 Western Countries: By Sex, 1840's–1940's**

Country	Expectation of life at			
	0	15	45	60
		I. Males		
Netherlands‡........	0.65 (1915–26) [0.48 (1895–05)]	0.30 (1915–26) [0.25 (1895–05)]	0.15 (1895–05)	0.10 (1936–48)
Sweden‡............	0.54 (1916–26) [0.44 (1936–43)]	0.36 (1916–26) [0.24 (1936–43)]	0.15 (1866–76)	0.11 (1866–76)
Norway‡...........	0.54 (1916–26) [0.44 (1896–06)]	0.34 (1916–26) [0.26 (1936–47)]	0.15 (1936–47)	0.11 (1936–47)
England and Wales‡.	0.54 (1906–11)	0.23 (1906–11)	0.13 (1911–21)	0.07 (1931–46)
France‡............	0.55 (1936–47)	0.44 (1936–47)	0.23 (1936–47)	0.14 (1936–47)
Germany‡..........	0.59 (1911–25)	0.23 (1911–25)	0.18 (1911–25)	0.10 (1911–25)
Switzerland‡........	0.50 (1911–26)	0.24 (1936–42)	0.16 (1936–42)	0.08 (1936–42)
Scotland‡...........	0.46 (1931–48)	†	†	0.08 (1931–48)
Denmark‡..........	0.49 (1898–03)	0.28 (1913–23)	0.16 (1913–23)	0.07 (1933–48)
Iceland§............	0.47 (1926–36)	†	†	0.16 (1896–06)
Australia§..........	0.41 (1896–06)	0.25 (1886–96)	0.10 (1886–96)	0.05 (1906–21)
		II. Females		
Netherlands‡........	0.61 (1915–26) [0.44 (1895–05)]	0.26 (1936–48)	0.18 (1936–48)	0.11 (1936–48)
Sweden‡............	0.48 (1936–43)	0.31 (1936–43)	0.16 (1936–43)	0.11 (1936–43)
Norway‡...........	0.51 (1916–26) [0.38 (1936–47)]	0.30 (1916–26) [0.30 (1936–47)]	0.18 (1936–47)	0.12 (1936–47)
England and Wales‡.	0.54 (1906–11)	0.25 (1931–46)	0.16 (1931–46)	0.11 (1931–46)
France‡............	0.55 (1936–47)	0.40 (1936–47)	0.23 (1936–47)	0.15 (1936–47)
Germany‡..........	0.56 (1911–25)	0.24 (1925–33)	0.12 (1911–25)	0.09 (1911–25)
Switzerland‡........	0.50 (1911–26)	0.30 (1936–42)	0.18 (1936–42)	0.13 (1936–42)
Scotland‡...........	0.48 (1931–48)	†	†	0.10 (1931–48)
Denmark‡..........	0.54 (1898–03)	0.25 (1933–48)	0.15 (1933–48)	0.10 (1933–48)
Iceland§............	0.49 (1906–16)	†	†	0.14 (1896–06)
Australia§..........	0.41 (1896–06)	0.24 (1886–96)	0.11 (1886–96)	0.06 (1906–21)

* All countries have life tables pertaining to at least six different decades between the 1840's and 1940's. Increases are the maximum average annual years of life gained between any pair of successive life tables. Figures in parentheses are the middle years of the life tables yielding the greatest increase. Figures in brackets are the magnitudes and periods of the second largest increases on record.

† Insufficient cases.

‡ Country has life tables covering at least four decades between the 1840's and 1900's and again between the 1900's and 1940's. No figures on expectation of life at 15 and 45 were available before the 1890's in Denmark and before the 1910's in Scotland.

§ Country has life tables covering less than four decades between the 1840's and 1900's.

way attempting to be definitive, the following outline seems to me to point to the most plausible explanation:

The main causes of the acceleration were of a rather narrowly technical kind, the influence of overall socio-economic conditions being comparatively secondary. Whatever may have been the earlier interrelations between income or productivity and the technological factors specifically affecting disease control, the latter had acquired sufficient momentum by 1870–1875 to have become in effect autonomous. Within a very broad range of variation in economic well-being, certainly extending well below Western levels about

1875, the strategic determinants of future survival trends were medical research skills, new discoveries in related fields, and the development of community responsibility and organization in public health. In brief, the suggested hypothesis is that the technical factors making for longer life by 1875 could be reinforced only to a secondary degree by rises in levels of living.

There are several reasons for advancing these views, at least before the fact. Intensive investigation would probably reveal that the late nineteenth-century upsurge in life chances occurred in the face of very substantial variations in economic levels and trends among the populations of the West. The upsurge also coincided closely with the momentous discoveries of Pasteur and Koch, the first substantial spread of environmental sanitation, and the transition from fact-finding to effective implementation of public health programming. It also seems likely that urban-rural mortality differentials since 1875 have changed in a way which cannot be significantly explained by reference to new conditions in the general environment.[12]

An interesting analogy to this line of argument can be drawn from the present. Most students would probably agree that even optimal diffusion of current skills in combating the diseases of old age would have only limited effects, whether or not the economies of the West continue to be highly expansive. And conversely, the discovery of methods for controlling cancer which are as effective as existing techniques against smallpox or malaria, would lead to unprecedented results, independently of economic trends. Put in other words, the above hypothesis is that Western prospects in 1875 for reducing mortality from infectious causes were not unlike the situation to-day with respect to the diseases of old age. If this interpretation is substantially correct, it would cast new light on recent events in many of the world's underdeveloped areas.

The predominance of technological factors as against more general socio-economic conditions may also underlie the phenomena to be considered next. Whatever their causes, however, the facts are clear enough.

3. Along With the Sharp Average Rise in Western Life Chances Since the Beginning of this Century, There Has Been a Remarkable Decline in International Differences Within the Region.

There is little basis for generalizing about the trends in international survival differences within the West before World War I. The gaps in the data are too large and such indications as can be had from the materials at hand are mixed. Thus, among the countries on record between the 1880's and 1900's, the differences in age-specific survivorship tended to diminish at the infant and childhood ages and again beyond the middle adult years. On the other hand, the differences often increased in the young adult ages, while in life expectancy the trends varied by sex as well as by age.

In contrast, the nearly complete information available since the beginning of this century reveal trends which are both consistent and pronounced.[13] Table 3 depicts some of the evidence for a substantial number of life table measures. It should be pointed out that the consistency of downward movements is somewhat overstated; in particular, the interquartile differences for females in the 1930's were no lower or somewhat higher than in the 1920's. On the other hand, the 1940's witnessed unprecedentedly low differences in female survival levels at all ages and the main exceptions to sustained downward movements are the increases shown between the 1920's

[12] *Cf.* Dublin and others, *op. cit.*, ch. 8; United Nations, *op. cit.*, ch. 4; C.-E. A. Winslow, "Public health," in *Encyclopedia of the Social Sciences,* vol. 12; W. Thompson, *Population Problems* (4th ed., New York, McGraw-Hill Co., 1953), chs. 5, 11, and *Plenty of People* (Rev. ed., New York, Ronald Press, 1948), ch. 4; R. Shryock, *The Development of Modern Medicine* (New York, Alfred A. Knopf, 1947), especially chs. 3-5, 12-14; B. Stern, *Society and Medical Progress* (Princeton University Press, 1941), especially chs. 3-8; M. Buer, *Health, Wealth and Population in the Early Days of the Industrial Revolution* (London, Routledge, 1926).

[13] The major gaps in the post-1900 data are the lack of life tables for Belgium before the 1930's, Canada before the 1920's and total Germany since the end of World War II. There is good reason to believe that more complete information for the first two areas would have had little or no effect on any of the conclusions reached in this section. The indications for Germany are similarly reassuring. By the end of the 1940's, the Federal Republic, which included the large majority of the population of former total Germany, was well within the range of contemporary Western experience. See also footnote 1, p. 126.

TABLE 3

*Interquartile Variations in National Life Expectancy and Survivorship in the West: By Sex, 1900's—1940's.**

Life table measure	Males			Females		
	1900's	1920's	1940's	1900's	1920's	1940's
Expectation of life at:						
0	6.3	5.0	4.4	5.6	4.7	2.5
15	3.6	2.8	3.2	3.4	2.1	1.3
45	3.0	2.5	2.8	2.4	2.2	0.8
60	1.9	1.4	1.7	1.6	1.6	0.8
Proportion surviving from:						
0 to 1	0.047	0.029	0.021	0.041	0.023	0.017
1 to 2.5	0.018	0.010	0.003	0.017	0.011	0.003
2.5 to 7.5	0.013	0.006	0.003	0.013	0.008	0.003
7.5 to 12.5	0.006	0.002	0.001	0.006	0.003	0.002
12.5 to 17.5	0.006	0.003	0.002	0.008	0.005	0.002
17.5 to 22.5	0.009	0.006	0.003	0.010	0.009	0.004
22.5 to 27.5	0.009	0.007	0.006	0.011	0.009	0.005
27.5 to 32.5	0.011	0.007	0.006	0.008	0.006	0.004
32.5 to 37.5	0.009	0.007	0.006	0.007	0.007	0.003
37.5 to 42.5	0.011	0.008	0.007	0.004	0.007	0.002
42.5 to 47.5	0.018	0.011	0.010	0.007	0.006	0.003
47.5 to 52.5	0.022	0.016	0.018	0.013	0.010	0.003
52.5 to 57.5	0.029	0.022	0.024	0.018	0.012	0.006
57.5 to 62.5	0.037	0.027	0.032	0.031	0.023	0.009
62.5 to 67.5	0.047	0.034	0.042	0.034	0.032	0.014

* Differences in each decade are between the upper and lower quartile national values, using all the nations on record. Differences in life expectancy are rounded to the nearest tenth of a year, those in age-specific survivorship to nearest thousandth.

and 1940's in male survivorship at the upper adult ages. With few exceptions for males and females alike, the interquartile differences in each of the last three decades have been substantially lower than in either the 1900's and 1910's.

The aggregate effects of the declines in the younger ages can be further seen from the trends in the dispersion of first quartile ages of death. The difference between the highest and lowest of such ages in the West declined from over 40 years in the 1900's to about 10 in the 1940's for males and from 35 to 15 for females.

As a rule, therefore, the increases in survival levels since the beginning of this century have been greatest in those parts of the West where the earlier levels were comparatively low. It is true that there are some conspicuous exceptions, such as the unusually steep trends in the Netherlands. Moreover, no simple inverse relation exists between early-century levels and subsequent movements, if all of the populations of the region are compared with one another. There has, however, been a striking relation in a more restricted sense. For each of the age-specific measures listed in Table 3 and for either sex, the populations with the three lowest values on record in the 1900's all experienced larger increases to the 1940's than did any of the populations with the three highest values.[14]

[14] Since the increases discussed here are absolute changes, greater rises in survivorship are equivalent to greater declines in mortality. Percentagewise, the situation is more complicated. A population with an initial mortality and trend which were both comparatively high might have had a smaller relative decline in mortality, though it obviously would have had a larger relative rise in survivorship.

With very few exceptions the same comparisons hold with respect to the life expectancies in Table 3.

These patterns are the more impressive when we consider that they are not merely a repetition of comparisons between two fixed groups of populations. The countries which can be identified as having had relatively high or low survival chances at the turn of the century often shifted from age to age. For example, England and Wales ranked with the "lows" in the early ages of life and with the "highs" from about age 10 to 30, while approximately the opposite was true of Norway. Thus the more appropriate interpretation of the above patterns is that they represent something like a "compression effect" at each age, operating more or less independently of the specific populations involved at other ages.[15] The result has been that the West to-day may more correctly be described as homogeneous than at any time in the last half century.

Barring a widespread return to higher mortality, it seems almost certain that national survival levels within the West will differ even less in the future than they do at present. As will be discussed shortly, the possibilities for further mortality declines between birth and the upper adult years are small by historical standards. It is, of course, conceivable that major innovations in the treatment of old-age and degenerative diseases could lead to a widening of differences at later ages. But if the last 75 years are any indication, such a development would prove highly transitory.

4. Many of the Trends in Western Life Chances Over the Last Century Are Unrepeatable Phenomena. The Main Developments of the Future Will Have To Come in the Old Ages, Beyond 60.

Between the 1840's and 1900 and again in the following half century, the West passed over to very nearly new ranges of survival experience. In each instance only minor fractions of the region's population had less favourable survival chances at the end of the period than the highest national levels existing at the beginning. The transitions were especially marked in life expectancy and age-specific survivorship before the late adult years. To-day expectation of life at birth is not far from the biblical three score and ten for the West as a whole and in most of its parts.[16]

Assuming a continuing movement to higher life chances, future trends are likely to be very different from those of the past. In many respects this will have to be the case. Thus the maximum increases still possible in age-specific survivorship before upper adult life are almost everywhere well below the changes that have actually taken place since the 1840's. In turn, the rises in life expectancy at birth that would result from such maximum increases are quite unexceptional by historical standards. It should be kept in mind that the hypothetical gains shown for the 1940's in Table 4 overstate the situation to-day. Even so, the increases cited assuming no mortality under age 15 are in almost every case only a half to two-thirds of those registered since as recent a period as the 1920's. Similarly, elimination of all mortality before 45 would result in gains which are nearly always no more than half of the rises since the beginning of this century. For the large majority of female populations in the West, such gains can also be described as far below the increases since the 1920's. The only conspicuous exception to all of these observations is Ireland; here past movements have been relatively small while the possibilities for future gains are unusually large.

Analogous limitations hold with respect to future mortality declines between the early adult and advanced ages. By the 1940's the average number of years lived between 15 and 60 had passed 40 in all of the populations of the West. Even with mortality eliminated, the rise from

[15] An interesting and perhaps more significant question is whether a similar "effect" can be established for actual cohorts in the West. This has apparently never been investigated, though the data for such a study are quite adequate.

The phenomenon of narrowing differences among English-speaking nations has been investigated by W. Taylor, "Changing mortality from 1841 to 1947 measured by the life table," *British Journal of Social Medicine*, vol. v, no. 3 (July, 1951). See also the sources cited in United Nations, *op. cit.*, ch. 4 section E, on mortality differentials within nations; J. Daric, "Mortalité, profession et situation sociale," *Population*, vol. IV, no. 4 (Oct.-Dec., 1949), pp. 671-694.

[16] I.e., for combined sexes; the difference between female and male life expectancy in the 1940's was the highest ever recorded in well over half the populations of the region.

TABLE 4

*Gains in Western Expectation of Life at Birth with Elimination of All Deaths Under the Ages 15 and 45; By Sex, 1940's.**

Country†	Males: Years of life gained with no deaths under 15	Males: Years of life gained with no deaths under 45	Females: Years of life gained with no deaths under 15	Females: Years of life gained with no deaths under 45
Netherlands	3.5	5.6	2.8	4.6
Sweden	3.7	7.2	2.9	5.8
Norway	4.1	7.9	3.2	5.8
England and Wales	4.4	7.4	3.6	6.3
France	5.7	9.4	4.5	7.6
Germany[a]	5.4	8.3	4.5	6.6
Switzerland	4.7	8.5	3.9	7.0
Scotland	4.6	7.8	3.6	7.2
Denmark	4.1	6.5	3.3	5.4
Belgium	5.6	9.4	4.7	7.5
Ireland[b]	6.7	11.0	5.8	10.5
Canada	5.3	8.4	4.5	7.3
U.S. (Whites)	3.8	6.9	3.1	5.5
Australia	3.2	5.8	2.6	4.8
New Zealand[c]	2.5	4.8	2.0	3.6
U. of So. Af. (Whites)	4.2	7.4	3.7	6.4

* Gains with no deaths under 15 were obtained by adding 15 to the reported expectation of life at that age in the 1940's and subtracting from the sum the reported expectation of life at birth; gains with no deaths under 45 were obtained in the same way.

† All figures except those for Sweden and Switzerland relate to post-war years.

[a] Federal Republic, 1949-51.

[b] Republic of Ireland.

[c] 1950-52.

current levels to the upper limit of 45 would almost always be less than the increases in the last 40 to 50 years. This would be true of all of the female populations on record and most of the male.

The ageing of the populations of the West and the near conquest of infectious causes of death have focused increasing attention on the prospects for future changes in the advanced years of life. A prominent speculation since the end of the war has been that revolutionary advances in the prevention and care of old-age diseases may not be far off, which could lead to unprecedented gains in the average lifetime of future generations. Obviously no one can foretell what will happen, but it is interesting to consider the sorts of developments that would be needed if the future were to begin to compare with Western trends in the last 75 to 100 years. If no one in the West died before 60 and all national life expectancies at that age rose by 50% over the 1940's, the increases in average lifetime would rarely exceed 20 years.[17] Thus, if the assumed national gains actually came to pass in the next 100 years, they would still be at least several years below the average changes in the region since the 1840's.

[17] Among the populations on record only three (Ireland, France and Belgium) would experience larger gains and none of these would be much above 22 years for either sex. The smallest increases would be between 15 and 16 years.

The above illustration does not, of course, deny the possibility of historically unique rises in the longevity of the aged. In fact no Western nation on record has even approximated a 50% rise in life expectancy at 60 over the last century.

Non-Western Europe

Classified by characteristic levels of mortality over the last century, the populations outside the West clearly fall into two distinct categories. For most of the period, it is doubtful that more than a small fraction of the inhabitants of Latin America-Africa-Asia has had higher survival levels than the lowest prevailing in non-Western Europe. Indeed, the chances are that these regions have generally been as far apart since 1850 as non-Western Europe from the West.

Separate consideration of the two groups of non-Western populations is further suggested by the contrasts in their statistical records. In non-Western Europe a sizeable proportion of national populations had been described by life tables before 1905, whereas the corresponding stage of statistical development in Latin America-Africa-Asia first came a generation later. Conversely, the 1940's, which witnessed an unprecedented increase in data for the latter region, saw a sharp decline in materials for the former. Thus the interesting things to be said concerning the populations of Latin America-Africa-Asia are mainly about the future. In non-Western Europe, to which we now turn, attention is of necessity directed to the past.

If appearances could be trusted, the transformation of survival characteristics in non-Western Europe over the last 50 years would have to be considered as outstanding in its way as the transitions in the West. Survival levels on record for females since 1930 have rarely been much below the highest anywhere in the region at the turn of the century. For males the changes have been generally similar at the infant and childhood years of life but, largely because of political disturbances, have been less marked at the adult ages. Almost certainly, the early-century maxima for either sex are currently matched — and much more often substantially exceeded — in all the non-Communist parts of the region (Finland, Austria, Italy, Spain, Portugal, Greece, Malta).

Whether anything like a corresponding transition has taken place in the rest of non-Western Europe cannot be judged with any confidence. There is sufficiently persuasive evidence that survival levels in Poland, Czechoslovakia and Hungary had come to exceed the region's early-century highs before the beginning of World War II. On the other hand, little can be said about pre-war conditions in Russia, Bulgaria, Roumania and Yugoslavia, where mortality had traditionally been among the highest in Europe; the latest official life tables for the first two areas relate to the 1920's, while none have apparently ever been published for the last two. If a comparison were to be ventured from the highly uncertain material at hand, it would be that, in general, pre-war life chances in these four areas were still below the levels attained in Finland and Italy about 1900.

What little can be gathered about the post-war situation is obscure at best. The numerous reports published in the West about declining consumption, large population displacements and forced labour practices might seem to make it clear that recent mortality must often have risen above pre-war levels. Against this, however, must be set the possibility that substantial progress has been achieved in public health, medical care and sanitation. If successful programmes have been carried out along these lines, their effect on the general population may have offset the experience of the sectors subject to special political or occupational discrimination. Such indirect clues as crude death rates would seem to place at least Poland, Czechoslovakia, Hungary and Yugoslavia within the current range of survival levels in the non-Communist areas of the region. It should be noted, however, that very little is known about the reliability or even the meaning of the published materials for these countries.[18] And in the case of Russia, Roumania

[18] Poland in 1948 is the one population under Communist rule for which a post-war life table exists and the data are such that post-war conditions are far from clear even here. Registration in civil offices rather than by the clergy was first instituted in 1946. The new system is reported to have encountered substantial early difficulties; death registration in 1947 was estimated to be 6% deficient, a figure which the Polish Central Statistical Office subsequently described as too low for the period. A further obstacle to an accurate life table for 1948 was the absence of reliable data on the age composition of the population. Presumably use was made of a sample "census" taken at the beginning of 1949; this was based on only 1% of the population, was admittedly deficient in sample design and, perhaps most important, was taken from population registers rather than by on-the-spot inquiry. That the registers could have been reliable in the face of the large population displacements which took place after the war

and Bulgaria, practically no published post-war evidence of any kind is as yet available.

Fortunately, these uncertainties can be largely ignored for the purpose of emphasizing the region's historical contrasts with the West. It seems clear that national survival levels in non-Western Europe between 1880 and World War II were rarely above those in Finland or Italy. Both countries have been consistently documented over this period and the indications they provide of regional maxima are more likely overestimates than the reverse, owing to errors in measurement. In addition, life tables are avail-

seems incredible. In situations of extensive migration such lists generally become padded by more complete reporting of in-movements than of out-movements. It is quite likely, therefore, that many of the 1948 death rates were downward-biased by excessive population counts as well as by defective registration. A further biasing factor may have been the exclusion of population sectors subject to special political or police supervision. F. Lorimer, "The nature of Soviet population and vital statistics," *The American Statistician,* vol. VII, no. 2 (April-May, 1953), pp. 13-18, points out that births and deaths within the "special populations" under control of police agencies were excluded from Russia's regional vital statistics during the late 1930's. Similar practices may have been adopted by other Communist states after the war.

See Poland, Central Statistical Office, *Contribution to vital statistics in Poland in 1946 and 1947,* Statistics of Poland, Series D, no. 10 (Warsaw, 1949), and *Statistical Yearbook of Poland 1948* (in English), vol. 12 (1949), p. 25; also United States, Bureau of the Census, *The Population of Poland,* by W. Mauldin and D. Akers (Washington, Government Printing Office, 1954), pp. 27, 38-40, Appendix A.

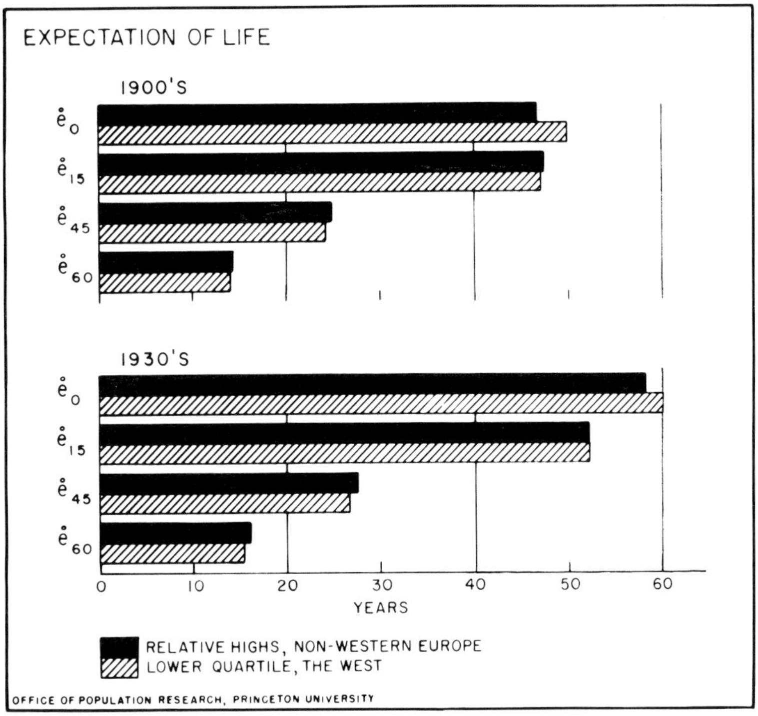

FIGURE 2

Relatively high expectation of life at 0, 15, 45 and 60 in non-Western Europe and relatively low expectations in the West, 1900's and 1930's. Averages of male and female values.

Note: At each age, the high value for non-Western Europe in the 1900's is the larger of the measures for Finland and Italy. The values for the 1930's are the highest on record anywhere in the region.

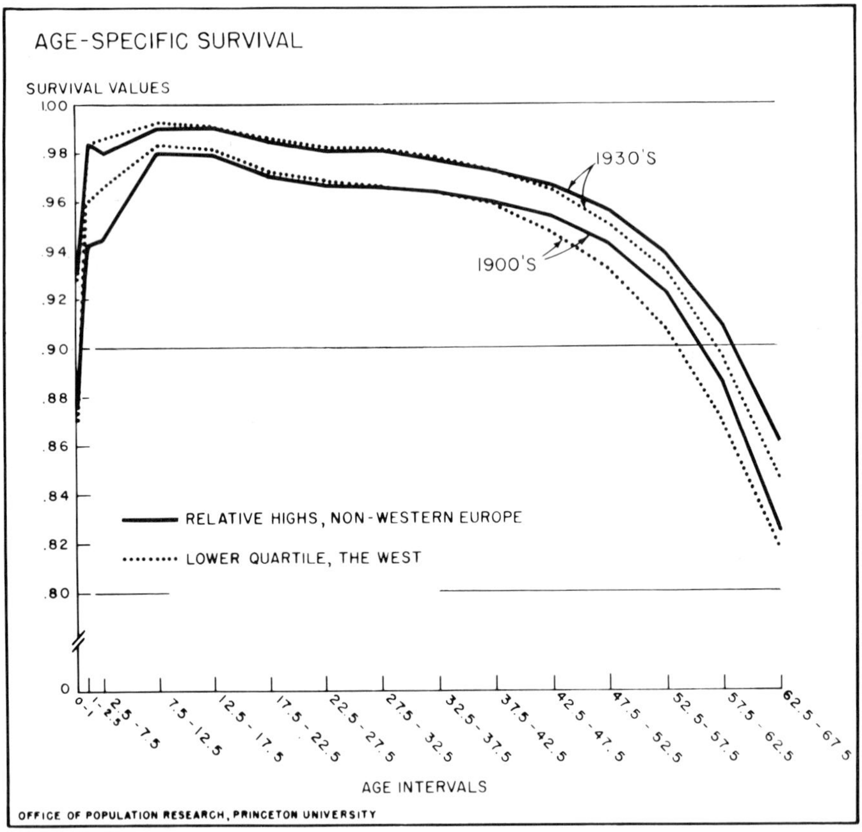

FIGURE 3

Relatively high age-specific survival chances in non-Western Europe and relatively low chances in the West, 1900's and 1930's. Averages of male and female values.

Note: The high values for non-Western Europe are as in Figure 2.

able for Latvia during the 1930's, or about the time it had in many respects overtaken these traditional leaders. There can be little doubt that the following generalization would be unchanged if it were based on information covering all the populations of the region.

5. Throughout the Last Century, the Highest Survival Levels in Non-Western Europe have Rarely Exceeded the Lower Ranges of Concurrent Experience in the West.

Up to 1900, pre-adult survival chances in non-Western Europe tended to be substantially lower than the ones characterizing the West about the middle of the nineteenth century. Whether the same was true at the adult ages is difficult to say; the data make it appear that conditions had generally improved over the earlier experience of most Western populations, but the accuracy of the available comparisons is open to considerable question.

During each of the first five decades of this century, the overlap in the contemporary experience of the two regions has been small to minimal. The 1900's and 1930's, described in Figures 2 and 3, are typical of the entire period. Before age 40, the highest age-specific survival chances in non-Western Europe have generally failed to reach even the lower quartile levels of the West. The main exception, in infant survivorship, is explained by the unusually high rate in Finland; with this country excluded, infant rates in non-Western Europe have consistently been close to or below the Western minima. As in the nineteenth century, the overlap in age-specific chances has been more substantial in the later adult years, though rarely extending beyond the Western medians.

These patterns are reflected in the corresponding comparisons of life expectancy. Even where relatively favourable, expectation of life at birth in the one region has generally fallen well within the lower range of values in the other. The disparities in later life have been less marked, owing to the smaller differences in age-specific survivorship at the upper adult years, but are still substantial. Almost certainly, an accurate series of consolidated life tables for the two regions would show the West to have had much the larger life chances at all ages in every decade since the 1840's.

The scope of these disparities makes it clear that survival levels in non-Western Europe have at any time in the last century been more nearly comparable with previous than with concurrent conditions in the West. This is further brought out by the "lags" presented in Table 5. The lag defined for each of the indicated measures in non-Western Europe is the interval between the period described by the measure and the approximate date at which the West had reached a comparable average experience. For example, the first entry for Italy in the 1900's indicates that expectation of life at birth in that country about 1905 was at the median level attained by the West a quarter of a century earlier.[19]

On the basis of the data at hand, it appears that the end of the inter-war period witnessed something of a turning point in the lag relationships for much of the region. Before 1930 survival levels were usually at least a quarter of a century removed from the time when the West was at a similar stage. In all likelihood the lags for most populations in non-Western Europe were actually between one and two generations;[20] indeed, lags approaching a century may not have been too uncommon before World War I. The situation since 1930 is more difficult to judge, for reasons already noted. Thus on the one hand it seems clear that the intervals between similar experiences in the two regions have often been lower than in earlier decades. In several instances — Austria, Finland and Italy being the most notable and reliable examples — lags of two decades or less have apparently become common.[21] On the other hand, it should be kept in mind that the available measures since the 1930's are probably not representative. In the first place, it is likely that many of the survival rates for the populations on record are over-estimates.[22] And secondly, the populations not on record have traditionally had the highest lags in the region.

Table 5 is also of interest in another connection. A traditional question in the literature on international demographic movements is whether the populations outside the West are "overtaking" that region. The usual approach is to compare trends during a given time interval; steeper trends (upward in survivorship, downward in fertility) in non-Western areas are interpreted as indicating an affirmative answer, since they imply smaller disparities at the end of the period under study. An alternative approach, which makes use of the above lags, is to consider whether demographic movements in non-Western areas have been occurring more or less rapidly than

[19] If anything the lags are conservative more often than not. Many of the entries shown as "<40's" undoubtedly involve much larger lags than the interval between the date of the given life table and 1840. Where the Western median fluctuated, as was often the case in the middle decades of the nineteenth century, the most recent period at which it reached the desired level was taken as the basis for computing the lag in question. This procedure compensates for the fact that the available medians before 1900 were often upward-biased.

Finally, the use of lags for females probably provides a closer view of "normal" patterns, particularly in recent decades.

[20] Scattered and highly uncertain estimates for Yugoslavia, Bulgaria and Roumania between 1900 and 1935 suggest lags of more than 4 decades in expectation of life at birth.

[21] Estimates of female expectation of life at birth in Italy about 1950 indicate a lag of one decade. For Austria and Finland see Table 5.

[22] As discussed previously, Poland seems to be a conspicuous case in point. The zero lags shown for adult life expectancy in Latvia and Estonia may or may not be reasonably indicative. Illiteracy in the 1930's was high among Latvian females aged 60 and over. On the other hand, it was reported as substantially lower in neighbouring Estonia, which had much the same recorded longevity at the upper adult ages.

TABLE 5

Lags behind Western Life Expectancy and Survivorship in Non-Western Europe: Females, 1880's to 1950.[1] (Lags are measured in decades)

Country	Expectation of life ($\mathring{e}_x$) at				Proportion surviving (${}_np_x$) from			
	0	15	45	60	0 to 1	7.5 to 12.5	17.5 to 22.5	37.5 to 42.5
				1880's				
Finland	0.5	0.5	0.5	2.5	0.0	2.5	0.5	0.0
Italy[2]	<40's	2.5	2.5	<40's	<40's	2.5	2.5	0.5
Austria[a]	<40's	<40's	<40's	<40's	<40's	<40's	<40's	<40's
Spain[a]	<40's	2.5	2.5	<40's	<40's	<40's	2.5	2.5
				1900's				
Finland	1.5	1.5	1.5	1.5	0.5	4.5	4.0	1.0
Italy	2.5	2.5	2.5	4.5	2.5	1.5	4.0	0.5
Austria[2]	4.5	4.5	4.5	<40's	<40's	2.5	4.5	2.0
Spain[2]	<40's	4.5	<40's	<40's	<40's	2.5	4.5	2.0
Czechoslovakia	4.0	2.0	4.0	<40's	<40's	2.0	4.0	1.0
Eur. Russia[b]	<40's	3.5†	3.5†	3.5†	<40's	<40's	3.5	3.5
				1920's				
Finland	1.5	2.5	0.5	2.5	0.5	2.5	4.5	2.0
Italy[2]	2.5	0.5	0.5	2.5	2.5	2.5	3.5	0.5
Spain[2]	4.5	3.5	4.5	6.5	3.5	3.0	4.5	2.5
Eur. Russia	4.5	3.5[f]	3.5[f]	4.5[f]	<40's	3.0	2.0	2.0
Hungary	*	*	*	*	<40's	4.5	6.5	2.5
				1930's				
Finland	1.5	1.5	1.5	0.5	1.5	1.5	3.0	1.5
Italy	1.5	0.5	0.5	1.5	2.5	1.5	1.0	0.5
Austria[c]	1.0	1.0	1.0	3.0	2.0	1.0	0.0	0.0
Czechoslovakia[c]	2.0	1.0	1.0	3.0	3.0	1.0	1.0	1.0
Hungary[2]	2.5	1.5	1.5	3.5	3.5	1.5	4.5	1.5
Poland[c]	3.0	3.0	3.0	4.0	5.0	1.5	4.0	2.5
Latvia	1.5	0.5	0.0	0.0	1.5	1.5	1.5	0.5
Estonia	1.5	0.5	0.0	0.0	1.5	2.0	1.5	0.5
				1940's				
Finland[d]	1.5	1.5	0.5	1.5	1.5	2.5	2.5	1.5
Hungary[d]	2.0	1.0	2.0	2.0	3.0	2.0	2.0	1.0
Poland[e]	2.0	1.0	1.0	1.0	4.0	1.5	1.0	1.0
Portugal[d]	4.0	2.0	1.0	2.0	4.0	2.0	2.0	2.0
Malta	3.0	2.0	3.0	1.0	7.0	1.5	1.0	2.0
				Early 1950's				
Finland	0.0	1.0	1.0	1.0	0.0	0.0	0.0	0.0
Austria	1.0	1.0	1.0	1.0	2.0	0.0	0.0	0.0

[1] For each measure the lag was taken to be the number of decades, to the nearest half unit, between two dates: (1) the middle year of the life table for the indicated population, and (2) the end of the most recent decade showing a lower median value in the West. Where a given measure was equal to the Western median for a decade and below all later medians, the second date used was the middle year of that decade.

The symbol "<40's" means that the cited measure was below all of the corresponding Western medians on record since 1840.

[2] Using interpolated values for the decade.

* Not available.

† Probably too low by a substantial margin. Similar biases, though not determinable, undoubtedly exist in other instances.

[a] Only available figures are for both sexes. Comparison with Western medians for females may have exaggerated the lags shown under some measures.

[b] 1896-97.

[c] Using values for the early part of the 1930's. Lags were probably smaller for the decade as a whole.

[d] Using values for the early part of the 1940's. In Finland and Portugal the lags were probably smaller between 1945 and 1950.

[e] See footnote 18.

[f] Using adjusted values from F. Lorimer, *The Population of the Soviet Union* (Princeton University Press, 1946), Table 46. The unadjusted value is comparable to the Western median of the 1930's.

was true of the same movements in the West at an earlier period. For example, the estimated lag of 4.5 decades in Austria's expectation of life at birth during the 1900's means that the West had very nearly the same average experience about 1860; similarly, Austria in the early 1930's was close to the West about 1920. In this instance a rise in a generation matched the corresponding Western change over something like double the period. Had the lags been the same, it would have meant that both areas had experienced the given rise over an equal time span. Thus the lags for a country at two different periods can be used to determine the times at which the West had the same initial and terminal experience and thereby the time interval over which the same change took place in the two areas.

It would be futile to debate whether this approach is preferable to the more traditional one. Each has its distinctive purpose and qualities.[23] What does merit emphasis is that the question of comparative movements can be usefully approached in more than one way.

6. Where Documented, Long-Run Peacetime Trends of Life Chances in Non-Western Europe Have Very Generally Been Much More Rapid than the Movements in the West at a Comparable Stage in Its Vital History.

In Austria, most changes since the 1880's have exceeded what the West, starting from similar situations, achieved in over a century. Finland originally lost ground in the late nineteenth century, corresponding to the period when Western life chances were accelerating, while the effects of the two world wars are perhaps the major explanation for the irregularities in that country's comparative trends since 1900. At the same time, it will be observed that the declines in lags between the more or less "normal" 1920's and 1950 were notable in most respects. Spain, Italy and Czechoslovakia between 1900 and the early 1930's, and Hungary in the inter-war decades, generally compare with Western trends over much longer periods. One can only guess, but it is also probable that the lags for Russia at the turn of the century were a good deal higher than in the mid-1920's and were again higher in the latter period compared to the late 1930's. This was almost certainly the case in the Baltic States and quite possibly in some Balkan areas.

That the lags in much of non-Western Europe must have often been subject to abrupt upward movements can scarcely be doubted, considering the political history of the region.[24] It seems equally clear that such movements had been short-lived before 1940. Whether rapid recoveries have been widespread since the end of the last war is still an unsolved problem.

Investigations of the causal factors underlying the acceleration of Western life chances in the late nineteenth century might well be supplemented by an examination of the reasons for the above patterns of declining lags. In turn, such comparative studies might usefully be considered in relation to a third group of events — the phenomenal drop in lags behind the West encountered in recent years among the populations of Latin America-Africa-Asia.

7. Such Comparisons as Can Be Made Indicate that the Rise in Female Survival Levels in Non-Western Europe Since the 1880's Has Often Been Well Above the Concurrent Movements in the West. For Males, the Contrasts Have Been Less Striking and In Some Areas Not on Record the Trends for Both Sexes May Have Been Unusually Low By Western Standards.

[23] A "lags" approach would seem the more appropriate one if the object is to use the historical interrelations between social or economic change and vital trends in the West as a benchmark for examining past or prospective interrelations elsewhere. Actually, this view has often been implicit in discussions of fertility, though it has been much less common in the field of mortality. It should be noted, however, that the lags in Table 5 suffer from a number of ambiguities: (1) Average Western experience cannot be measured precisely; (2) Even if the average were known accurately for each decade, the time at which it reached a given level could only be approximated; (3) A change in the Western average is not the same as the average change in the various parts of the region. There is some reason to believe, however, that the two types of change were generally similar (see Table 6); (4) Where only scattered life tables are available for an area, the particular lags that can be established may be somewhat fortuitous.

[24] This is more evident from the lags pertaining to the male populations. In Finland, adult life expectancy for males was generally further behind the West about 1950 than in the 1920's; there are also indications of increasing lags in Russia between 1900 and the mid-1920's. These are, however, the only major exceptions to the patterns discussed above for females.

TABLE 6

Long-Run Trends in Life Expectancy and Survivorship, Non-Western Europe and the West: By Sex

Area	Years gained in expectation of life at				Increases* in proportion surviving from			
	0	15	45	60	0 to 1	0 to 15	15 to 45	45 to 60
	I. Males							
	1880's–1900's							
Finland	3.9	0.6	0.4	0.3	0.03	0.06	0.01	0.01
Italy[a]	7.4	2.7	1.3	0.3	0.03	0.10	0.04	0.05
Austria[ab]	7.1	3.1	1.3	0.7	0.02	0.10	0.07	0.04
The West:								
Change in Median Value†	6.1	2.7	1.4	0.9	0.04	0.07	0.04	0.04
Median Change‡	6.1	2.8	1.3	0.6	0.04	0.08	0.05	0.03
	1900's–1930's							
Finland	9.1	1.4	0.8	1.0	0.06	0.14	0.01	0.00
Italy[a]	11.2	4.0	2.2	1.7	0.06	0.13	0.05	0.04
Austria[a]	15.4	5.1	2.4	1.4	0.12	0.19	0.08	0.07
Spain[a]	14.5	5.5	2.2	1.6	0.09	0.19	0.09	0.05
Czechoslovakia[a]	13.0	5.6	2.8	1.5	0.10	0.15	0.09	0.07
Eur. Russia[c]	10.5	2.6	1.2	0.8	0.09	0.15	0.04	0.03
The West:								
Change in Median Value†	10.8	3.9	1.6	0.8	0.07	0.09	0.07	0.05
Median Change‡	10.2	4.7	2.2	1.0	0.07	0.11	0.07	0.06
	1900's–Recent Years							
Finland[d]	16.4	4.7	0.9	0.4	0.09	0.21	0.10	0.02
Austria[d]	22.8	8.9	4.1	2.3	0.16	0.26	0.14	0.10
The West:[e]								
Change in Median Value†	14.6	6.1	2.2	1.0	0.08	0.14	0.10	0.05
Median Change‡	14.9	6.7	3.5	2.0	0.09	0.13	0.10	0.08

* Absolute increases in indicated proportions, rounded to nearest hundredth.

† Change between the medians of the values on record for individual Western populations in the indicated end-decades.

‡ Median of the changes on record among individual Western populations over the indicated period.

[a] Changes are between the early parts of the indicated decades. Most Western changes are between periods centering on the middle years of the decades.

[b] Using values for both sexes in the 1880's, for separate sexes in the 1900's. Changes are generally understated for males, overstated for females.

[c] 1896-97 to 1926-27. Figures are probably subject to unusually wide margins of error.

[d] 1900's to early 1950's.

[e] 1900's to 1940's.

TABLE 6 (continued)

Area	Years gained in expectation of life at 0	15	45	60	Increases* in proportion surviving from 0 to 1	0 to 15	15 tp 45	45 tp 60
				II. Females				
				1880's–1900's				
Finland	3.9	1.0	1.1	0.8	0.02	0.05	0.01	0.02
Italy[a]	7.4	3.0	1.6	0.7	0.03	0.10	0.04	0.06
Austria[ab]	9.0	3.6	2.5	1.0	0.06	0.12	0.06	0.08
The West:								
Change in Median Value†	6.1	3.0	1.1	1.0	0.03	0.06	0.04	0.04
Median Change‡	6.9	3.4	1.4	0.9	0.04	0.07	0.06	0.03
				1900's–1930's				
Finland	11.4	3.8	1.8	1.3	0.05	0.13	0.06	0.03
Italy[a]	13.0	5.8	3.1	2.5	0.06	0.16	0.09	0.05
Austria[a]	17.4	7.5	3.5	2.3	0.10	0.19	0.12	0.07
Spain[a]	15.9	6.7	3.6	2.6	0.08	0.19	0.09	0.08
Czechoslovakia[a]	13.5	6.1	2.9	2.0	0.08	0.14	0.09	0.06
Eur. Russia[c]	13.4	6.6	4.6	3.0	0.09	0.16	0.08	0.10
The West:								
Change in Median Value†	11.2	4.2	1.6	0.8	0.06	0.10	0.06	0.02
Median Change‡	10.5	5.2	2.2	1.4	0.06	0.10	0.07	0.04
				1900's–Recent Years				
Finland[d]	20.3	8.7	3.2	1.7	0.08	0.20	0.14	0.08
Austria[d]	25.9	12.4	6.2	4.2	0.13	0.25	0.17	0.13
The West:[e]								
Change in Median Value†	15.2	7.2	3.5	2.2	0.07	0.13	0.09	0.05
Median Change‡	14.8	8.3	4.2	2.7	0.08	0.11	0.11	0.07

* Absolute increases in indicated proportions, rounded to nearest hundredth.

† Change between the medians of the values on record for individual Western populations in the indicated end-decades.

‡ Median of the changes on record among individual Western populations over the indicated period.

[a] Changes are between the early parts of the indicated decades. Most Western changes are between periods centering on the middle years of the decades.

[b] Using values for both sexes in the 1880's, for separate sexes in the 1900's. Changes are generally understated for males, overstated for females.

[c] 1896-97 to 1926-27. Figures are probably subject to unusually wide margins of error.

[d] 1900's to early 1950's.

[e] 1900's to 1940's.

Table 6 summarizes most of the information that exists on comparative trends in the two regions.[25] Almost always, where a survival trend for only one of the sexes has exceeded the corresponding Western change, it is the females who compare favourably. This is especially evident in the case of Finland and Russia, although errors in measurement in the latter area may have distorted the trends for both sexes. Finland is the only country showing generally lower comparative trends for females as well as for males. Between 1900 and 1930, the rise in female life expectancy at all ages in Austria, Spain, Italy, Czechoslovakia and Russia appears to have been at least close to the highest national trends on record in the West. On the other hand, none of the male populations of these countries show such comparisons.

With respect to age-specific survivorship, the recorded contrasts between the two regions have been especially striking in the pre-adult years. For males and females alike, the 1900–1930 increases in the chances of surviving from birth to age 15 in non-Western Europe have consistently been above the upper quartile national change in the West. In the adult years, however, it is again necessary to distinguish between the sexes. Among female populations, recorded survival trends in the age intervals 15–45 and 45–60 have almost always been close to or above the West's upper quartile movements; the one exception is Finland. For males, on the other hand, the trends fall within all parts of the range of the corresponding Western experience.

Unfortunately, there is no basis for generalizing from these patterns, either over space or time. Such clues as can be found suggest that the undocumented trends in non-Western Europe before World War II were generally on the low side for both sexes, compared to the West. The uncertainties about developments since the 1930's are not only greater, but extend to a much larger group of populations.

Latin America-Africa-Asia

The study of mortality in this region, the "underdeveloped world," has its ironies. Greater longevity is probably the most universally and readily accepted of major human values, and the success of statistical analysis as a means to this end very likely matches that achieved in any area of social measurement. Yet the fact is that our knowledge to-day serves us least where it is needed most. Life tables, at best the bare bones of the information required for a moderately sufficient grasp of mortality conditions, are lacking, fragmentary, or deficient for the more than half of the world's population in Latin America-Africa-Asia.[26] Probably only the data for Japan and pre-war Formosa are comparable in accuracy with Western material. Less than a handful of life tables exist for native or non-European populations in Africa, while in Asia none is to be found for any part of the Middle East, Indonesia, Indo-China, Burma, Malaya, the Philippines or any substantial part of China. Despite their marked increase since 1940, the material for Latin America is more nearly characterized as scattered than substantial. The best documented sections are the small populations in the Caribbean and the available information is probably a good deal short of reliable even here.

As for trends, the inferences that can be made border on the minute. Long-run movements beginning before World War I can be documented for not much more than a half dozen areas — mainly India and Ceylon in Asia and several Caribbean countries. For a number of reasons, including the colonial status of all these areas until World War II, the strong presumption is that the data are unrepresentative of trends in most of the other parts of the region. The additional areas for which there is any information at all on trends are few: essentially completing the list are Japan and Costa Rica since the 1920's, Formosa in the inter-war period,

[25] The additional trend materials for non-Western Europe are scattered and consist mainly of shortrun movements, i.e., in Finland beginning with the 1880's; Italy at varying intervals between the 1880's and 1930's; Spain between 1900 and 1940; Hungary in the inter-war period; and Poland in the years surrounding World War II. The quarter-century trends which can be obtained for Bulgaria between 1900 and 1925 have been omitted as more likely to be misleading than informative.

[26] It is interesting to note an analogous situation in the West. Here the least reliable information is about past trends or the current status of mortality in the upper adult and advanced years of life. Yet the major future gains in longevity will have to come from changes in these age spans. See p. 134.

Mexico and Chile between 1930 and 1940 and a segment of the non-white population in the Union of South Africa since the mid-1930's. For many of these areas, it can legitimately be questioned whether the available material is better ignored than considered.[27]

Not all of the gaps in the record are equally important, however. The future may show that this region's historical transitions in mortality, were they known, would be more revealing as outmoded benchmarks than as a basis for prediction. There are mounting signs that the middle of this century has marked a revolutionary turning point in the life chances of the world's impoverished nations. Unless recent indications are seriously misleading, mortality in most or all of Latin America-Africa-Asia can be reduced with a rapidity unmatched in this or any other region over the last century and a half. Moreover, where such reductions fail to occur in the next few decades, the major causal factors will be very different from the ones which have historically kept mortality in this region so far above average levels in the rest of the world. The sufficient conditions in such instances will very likely be the breakdown of internal political order and international cooperation, rather than low levels of living, undeveloped resources and the resistance of traditional social forces to innovation.

To be sure, it remains to be seen whether the unprecedented declines in mortality recently encountered in much of the underdeveloped world can be preserved in the face of rapidly rising populations. But then it is ironic to reflect that past experience would be a very unsatisfactory guide in this contingency as well. So far as the documented evidence goes, declines in survivorship have been very much the exception to the rule in the past. No instances are to be found of continuing declines in longevity and those that are encountered over short time spans have often been suspect. The fact is that less can be said about the underdeveloped world itself than about its historical and prospective contrasts with the West.

8. Up To the End of World War II, It Is Doubtful that As Much As 5 Per Cent of the Population of Latin America-Africa-Asia Had Survival Levels Comparing Favourably With the Average Experience of the West At the Beginning of this Century. By 1950 the Proportion Had Risen, But Only to Some 10 Per Cent.

Despite remarkable advances in many areas since World War II, life chances in Latin America-Africa-Asia are still enormously lower than in the West. The maximum expectation of life at birth in 1950 for all but a minute fraction of the region, some 58 years in Japan and Puerto Rico, was 4–5 years below the contemporary minimum in the West and 9–10 years below the Western median.[28] Even where relatively advanced, mid-century longevity in the underdeveloped world was no higher than the average experience of the industrialized nations at the time of World War I. For the large majority of the inhabitants of the region, as exemplified by India, Mauritius, Guatemala and parts of China, life expectancy was lower or hardly above the minimum levels on record in Western and Northern Europe a century earlier.

The recent differentials depicted in Figures 4 and 5 probably understate by substantial margins the contrasts that have usually prevailed between Western lows and relative highs in Latin America-Africa-Asia since World War I. For example, expectation of life at birth in Japan was close to 10 years below the Western minimum in the 1920's and again in the 1930's, or about twice the disparity of the following decade. The situation before World War I is impossible to judge; on the one hand, the data for Latin America-Africa-Asia at the turn of

[27] Thus two life tables, apparently constructed independently, exist for Chile about 1930 and again about 1940. The differences indicated by the two sources at either date are not great, at least for purposes of interregional comparisons; on the other hand, the trends are often in marked contrast. In the case of Ceylon, a life table for 1893-1901 (not used here) shows a lower infant mortality rate than is found in 1945-47, despite the phenomenal decrease known to have taken place in the latter period. For Japan, there is a series of pre-1920 life tables, but these are misleading for most purposes and particularly so for measuring trends.

[28] The largest value ever recorded for any population of Latin America-Africa-Asia is 66 years, in Cyprus during 1948-50; possibly both Argentina and Uruguay have comparable values. The figure for Cyprus is very close to the Western median for the 1940's and there is reason to believe it is too high by several years.

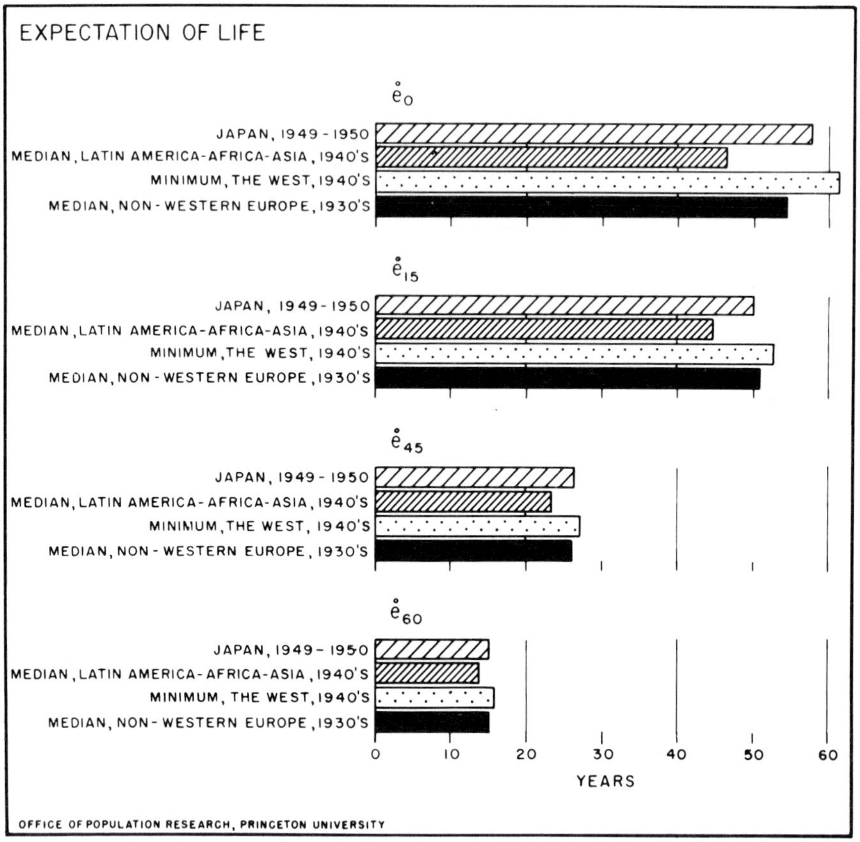

FIGURE 4

Expectation of life at 0, 15, 45 and 60 in Latin America-Africa-Asia and the West, 1940's, and in non-Western Europe, 1930's. Averages of male and female values.

the century are entirely inadequate, and on the other, the West itself experienced a very rapid rise in longevity between 1910 and the inter-war period.

With respect to average differences between the two regions, a conservative estimate would be that the disparity in expectation of life at birth has exceeded 20 and quite possibly 25 years during this century. The differences appear to have varied in roughly geometric fashion between birth and important stages of later life, amounting at a minimum to some 10, 5 and 2–3 years at ages 15, 45 and 60, respectively. These magnitudes are not far from the increases that the West has achieved in the last 100 years.

The traditional disparities between age-specific survival chances in these regions are suggested by the experience of the 1940's. According to the data for that decade, median chances of surviving the broad age intervals 0–15, 15–45 and 45–60 in the underdeveloped world were some 15–20% lower than in the West. If account is taken of omissions, errors and the weight of population sizes in individual areas, the differences between average levels were very probably well above 25%. Japanese survivorship in these age intervals at mid-century could scarcely have been exceeded by 5% of the contemporary population of Latin America-Africa-Asia, or by as much as 1–2% of the earlier inhabitants of the region. Yet the West had reached comparable average levels at the end of World War I. Japan in 1950

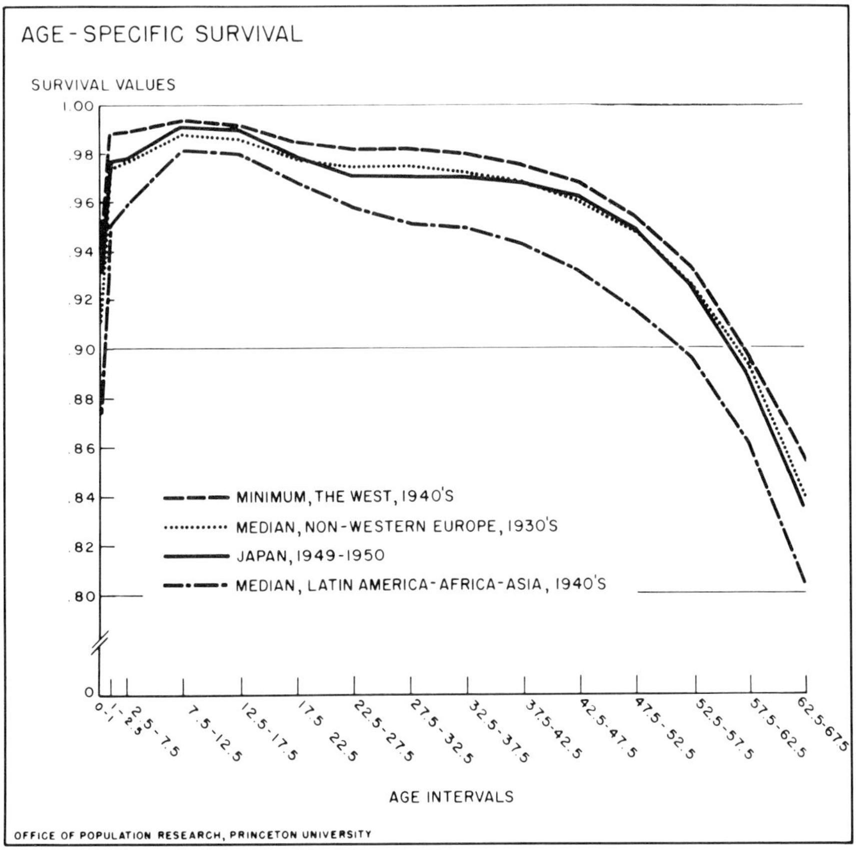

FIGURE 5

Age-specific survival chances in Latin America-Africa-Asia and the West, 1940's, and in non-Western Europe, 1930's. Averages of male and female values.

was almost identical to Australia in the 1900's.

Despite their probable downward biases, the above magnitudes may well turn out to be substantially above the differences that will emerge in the coming few decades.[29] The disparities between survival levels in the West and in Latin America-Africa-Asia have undoubtedly nar-

[29] The errors to which the above estimates may be subject can be brought out by the contrasts between the West and India. The difference in the 1940's between median life expectancy in the West and the Indian experience was 34 years at birth and 19, 10 and 6 years at the ages 15, 45 and 60, respectively; the corresponding figures for the 1900's were 29, 18, 9 and 5. Recent differences in the chances of surviving the broad age intervals 0-15, 15-45 and 45-60 have amounted to 30-35%. For Latin America-Africa-Asia as a whole, the true differences over the past half century have probably been between these values and the ones cited in the text.

The comparisons with non-Western Europe which are suggested by Figures 4 and 5 probably have only a formal interest. The differences in median longevity that can be reported between that region and Latin America-Africa-Asia since the 1930's seem generally to have been more than half the differences involving the West. These estimates are highly conjectural, however, and there is almost no basis for conclusions about earlier decades, other than that the disparities must have been substantial. The little that is known about post-war conditions in the two regions is of no help at all. If modern methods of disease control seem capable of offsetting the greater economic backwardness of the one, they may be as successful in adapting to the contrasting political circumstances of the other.

rowed significantly since the 1940's. Indeed, given world peace and in the absence of as yet unheralded gains in Western upper-age survivorship, it is not at all improbable that the traditional gaps between life chances in the two regions will have become dated within the next quarter of a century.

Much of the recent discussion on population prospects in Latin America-Africa-Asia has made use of what has come to be known as a "demographic transitions" frame of reference. To my knowledge, this approach has never been formalized as a logically structured chain of reasoning. Its basic propositions seem clear enough, however, at least for present purposes. These are: (1) Economic modernization or even selective technological advance, on the one hand, and social "Westernization" on the other, will reduce rather than raise fertility and mortality in today's underdeveloped areas. (2) The methods by which mortality may be lowered in these areas are more rapidly and efficiently introduced than the process making for reduced fertility. Moreover, longer survival is everywhere accepted in principle as a major positive value, while departures from traditional high-fertility patterns are often resisted as undesirable ends. (3) Accordingly, the expectation is that mortality will decline more rapidly than fertility, at least for some time to come, resulting in an accelerated population growth.

If this is an adequate summary, the essential aspects of the approach are that it is dynamic, it identifies the direction of change in vital movements and, more specifically, it stresses a lead-lag relationship between mortality and fertility trends. At the same time it will be apparent that nothing is said about magnitudes. The inception, timing, and degree of the anticipated vital transitions are left in question, as is the duration of the lead of mortality declines over those in fertility.[30] As a result, the approach accommodates any of a very large number of alternative paths of population change. For example, the population of pre-partition India would grow by only 7% between 1950 and 1980, if its birth rate in each of the three decades were to decline by the maximum percentage on record anywhere in Europe a hundred years earlier, and its death rate by the minimum on record. With the reverse assumptions about vital rates, the change in size would come to 110%. And if the European experience used for extrapolation were that of the 1800's–1830's, the implied rates of change would range from 40 to 80%.

It is true that the transitions approach, as developed to date, has never been proposed as a basis for quantitative projection. The tendency in practice, however, has been to illustrate possibilities by drawing on case histories in the West. Projections, whether illustrative or otherwise, are likely to be interpreted more literally than intended and a closer look at the data indicates the need for a very different approach to numerical possibilities.

9. Quantitative Application of the Concepts of Demographic Transitions, If Made By Analogy to Western Experience, Is Apt To Be Futile or Misleading As A Guide To the Mortality Pros-

[30] It is true that the late stages of demographic transitions have usually been represented as involving close to zero population growth, with birth and death rates approximately stabilized at "low" levels. Such situations, which were found in a number of European countries before the last war, have also been generally characterized as foreshadowing fairly early population declines, at least in the absence of strong countermeasures by governments. Either of these stages is, of course, largely irrelevant for the part of the world under present discussion. It is worth pointing out, however, that their relevance for much of the West as well has been increasingly questioned in the last few years.

A further point frequently made, that fertility declines are likely to come earlier or more rapidly in the urban sectors of societies beginning economic development, need not be considered here. The question of urban-rural differentials in mortality trends has received no comparable attention, but it may well be that the differentials found in the West in the latter nineteenth century will prove the reverse of the coming situation in today's underdeveloped areas.

A pervasive difficulty in putting the "transitions" theses to empirical test is the lack of any established position on what is meant by fertility and mortality or on how their respective changes are to be measured. In practice, the most common procedure has been to use crude birth and death rates, though it is questionable whether these are the most appropriate measures for many purposes. Similarly ambiguous are the kinds of changes that may be involved. Thus birth rates in many parts of the world are to-day more than twice as high as death rates. Declines in the birth rate which are 50% larger in absolute terms than the corresponding declines in the death rate would often represent a smaller relative change.

TABLE 7

*Lags behind Western Life Expectancy and Survivorship in Latin America-Africa-Asia: Females, 1900's to 1950.**

(Lags are measured in decades.)

Country	Expectation of life ($\mathring{e}_x$) at				Proportion surviving (${}_n p_x$) from			
	0	15	45	60	0 to 1	7.5 to 12.5	17.5 to 22.5	37.5 to 42.5
1900's								
Trinidad[a] [1]	<40's	<40's	<40's	<40's	2.5	4.5	<40's	<40's
India	<40's	<40's	<40's	<40's	<40's	<40's	<40's	<40's
1910 to World War I								
Trinidad[a]	5.0	<40's	<40's	<40's	3.0	4.0	<40's	<40's
Jamaica	5.0	5.0	3.0‡	1.0‡	<40's	4.0	<40's	<40's
Br. Guiana	<40's	<40's	<40's	<40's	<40's	4.5	<40's	<40's
Ceylon	<40's	<40's	<40's	<40's	<40's	<40's	<40's	<40's
1920's								
Trinidad[a] [1]	6.5	<40's	<40's	<40's	3.5	4.0	<40's	<40's
Jamaica[b]	<40's	<40's	<40's	6.0	<40's	6.0	<40's	<40's
Br. Guiana[1]	<40's	<40's	<40's	<40's	4.5	5.0	<40's	<40's
Ceylon[b]	<40's	<40's	<40's	<40's	<40's	<40's	<40's	<40's
India	<40's	<40's	<40's	<40's	<40's	<40's	<40's	<40's
Japan[1]	4.5	6.5	4.5	6.5	3.5	3.5	<40's	<4.5
Taiwan	7.0	7.0	7.0	7.0	5.0	3.0	6.5	7.0
1930's								
Trinidad[a] [1]	4.5	7.5	<40's	<40's	3.5	2.0	7.5	7.5
Br. Guiana[1]	5.5	<40's	<40's	<40's	3.5	3.5	<40's	<40's
Puerto Rico	5.5	7.5	5.5	†	3.5	5.0	8.0	†
Chile[1]	<40's	7.5	7.5	5.5‡	<40's	4.5	<40's	7.5
Mexico[1]	<40's	<40's	<40's	<40's	<40's	7.5	7.5	7.5
Egypt	8.0	4.0‡	2.0‡	2.0‡	<40's	4.0	2.5‡	4.5‡
U. of S. Af. (Col.)[c]	7.5	<40's	7.5	4.5‡	<40's	5.0	<40's	<40's
Japan	4.5	5.5	4.5	4.5	2.5	2.0	<40's	4.5
Taiwan[1]	5.5	5.5	7.5	7.5	4.5	3.5	5.5	7.5
1940's								
Trinidad[a]	2.5	5.5	6.5	4.5	2.5	2.5	5.5	4.5
Jamaica	3.5	5.5	4.5	2.5‡	3.0	2.5	6.0	4.5
Br. Guiana	4.5	8.5	8.5	8.5	2.5	2.5	7.0	6.5
Barbados	4.5	2.5‡	4.5	4.5	6.5	1.5‡	1.5‡	2.5‡
Venezuela[d]	5.0	6.0	6.0	4.0	4.0	5.0	7.5	8.0
Mauritius	<40's	<40's	<40's	<40's	<40's	7.5	<40's	<40's
U. of S. Af. (Col.)[c]	6.5	<40's	8.5	5.5	5.5	4.5	<40's	9.0
Ceylon	6.5	8.5	6.5	6.5	6.5	7.5	8.5	8.5
India	<40's	<40's	<40's	<40's	<40's	<40's	9.0	<40's
Japan[e]	3.5	5.5	4.5	4.5	2.5	2.5	8.0	4.5
Japan[f]	3.0	3.0	3.0	2.0	2.0	3.0	3.5	3.0
Thailand	5.0†	7.0	7.0	9.0	3.0‡	7.0	6.0	7.0
Chinese Area[g]	<40's	<40's	<40's	<40's	4.0‡	<40's	8.0	<40's

* See explanatory notes to Table 5.

† Not available.

‡ Probably too low by substantial margin, as suggested by several tests. Similar biases, though not determinable, undoubtedly exist in other instances.

[a] Including Tobago.

[b] Using values for 1920-22. In Jamaica the lags were probably smaller for the decade as a whole.

[c] "Coloured" population of the Union of South Africa.

[d] Early part of the 1940's. Lags were probably smaller at the end of World War II.

[e] 1947.

[f] 1949-50.

[g] Cheng Kung, Yunnan Province, 1942.

[1] Using interpolated values for the decade.

pects Confronting the Underdeveloped World To-day.[31]

The first and most obvious point to be made in this connection is the discrepancy in recordable starting points: The West at the beginning of its statistical era was further along in its mortality "transitions" than has been the case in most of Latin America-Africa-Asia. As can be seen from the lags shown in Table 7, most of the survival records that can be found for Latin America-Africa-Asia through the 1920's were below the Western averages of the 1840's. The same has been true in more recent periods of numerous other areas, some of which are shown and many more of which are as yet undocumented. Moreover, if the available survival data for Latin America-Africa-Asia have tended to be more upward-biased than the nineteenth-century records for the West, as seems likely, many of the lags in Table 7 are understated. In brief, the survival levels likely to be encountered in much of the underdeveloped world have no counterpart in any sizeable body of Western experience.

(It is interesting to note that the same difficulty arises with respect to fertility. Except perhaps for the United States, nineteenth-century birth rates recorded in the West are below the levels found to-day among the large majority of the populations in Latin America-Africa-Asia.)

Secondly, even where Western historical experience is useful for some ages, it may be highly unsatisfactory at others. Table 7 suggests a rough correlation among an area's lags at different ages during a single period and among the changes in lag between periods. At the same time it is obvious that the differences are often substantial; in particular, the lags at the infant and childhood ages are often smaller than those at later years. Very probably, the last is due in good part to relatively large upward biases in the survival measures available for early life. It should be noted, however, that similar patterns of bias have also been characteristic of the West in the past, which would tend to reduce the differences in lag from age to age. Moreover, relatively small lags at the young ages are encountered in Japan and Formosa, where there is reason to believe the data are reliable. Thus it seems likely that even when a particular segment of Western experience is an appropriate guide for projecting developments at some ages, it may also lead to substantial errors at others.

The third and most important consideration is the prospect that future changes in the world's high-mortality areas will occur at a far more rapid pace than was true of the comparable movements in the West at earlier periods. Thus survival trends in Trinidad, Jamaica and British Guiana between the 1920's and 1940's have generally been equal to what the West achieved in over a half century. Japan between 1920 and 1950 matched increases in the West which generally took 40 to 50 years or more in a period of accelerated change.[32]

Striking as they are, these comparisons seem highly conservative in the light of more recent developments. In Puerto Rico expectation of life at birth has increased by over 1 year per annum since 1940. This is at least twice and often three times higher than the maximum national rates ever recorded among the populations of the West (see Table 2). Yet the same value is less than a third of the annual rate in Ceylon between 1946 and 1949 and less than half the rate in Japan between 1947 and 1950.

It can hardly be doubted that similar comparisons could be made for numerous other areas, if direct evidence were available. To cite a few examples among many, the crude death rate in British Guiana, Chile and Malaya fell from approximately 20 per 1,000 about 1940 to 13–14 in the early 1950's. The same changes occurred between about 1850 and World War I

[31] Japan, the other area most often used by way of example, seems only slightly more appropriate at best and for the same reasons.

[32] It is safe to say that all three of the above difficulties would arise, if use were made of the experience of individual Western nations rather than the region's averages. Numerous lag-type comparisons were made between areas in Latin America-Africa-Asia and in Europe. For example, Japan was compared with Sweden, England and Wales, France, Switzerland and Germany, as well as with Italy in non-Western Europe; India, Ceylon and several Caribbean populations were considered in similar fashion. For each area in Latin America-Africa-Asia, both the size of the lags and their changes varied substantially according to the nation being used as a basis for comparison. Moreover, the variations in both respects often differed significantly from one span of ages to another. Occasionally, too, there were substantial variations by sex.

in Norway, Denmark and Sweden and between 1890 and 1920 in Switzerland and Belgium.

The causal factors underlying mortality trends in Latin America-Africa-Asia in the past decade have been widely discussed and need not be considered here in any detail. It is worth emphasizing, however, that the reasons for thinking future mortality developments in this region will be so different from Western history are all of recent origin. The primary rôle of international rather than national health agencies, the use of antibiotics, the development of cheap yet effective methods for combating malaria — each of these is very nearly a midcentury innovation.[33] Until the last few years most students would probably have estimated that the prospects were for slower uptrends in relation to the West, not more rapid ones.

One reason for this judgment has been the traditional emphasis on overall socio-economic conditions as determinants of survival levels, in the West as well as in Latin America-Africa-Asia. As suggested earlier, research into the justification or even the meaning of this emphasis has been negligible. A second reason has been the absence, for all practical purposes, of any adequate material on the ways in which increasing survivorship might affect productivity. It is fair to say that the relations between improving health or longevity and productive capacity are the least considered major aspect of the "population problem" to-day. Although there are indications that very substantial increases in output may accompany programmes of disease control, the available materials are perhaps better described as impressions than as evidence.[34] In contrast, the relations between consumer needs, declining mortality and rising population continue to receive far greater attention. Instances of this selective emphasis are readily cited. For example, the substantial literature on the capital needs of underdeveloped areas is almost exclusively concerned with the problem of absorbing population growth and at the same time attaining target levels of income per head. Practically none of this literature distinguishes between the fertility and mortality components of population growth and none between the effects of added capital resources, on the one hand, and heightened physical efficiency of the labour force, on the other.

It is, of course, much too soon to predict what will happen as the new factors affecting mortality in Latin America-Africa-Asia give rise to rapidly multiplying populations in already overcrowded areas. Nevertheless, there is already abundant evidence that the possibilities cannot be assessed in conventional terms, however events may turn out.

[33] The special significance of these factors is that they point to unusual departures from past patterns, not that they will be the only important determinants of future events in the underdeveloped areas. An adequate treatment of prospective survival trends in this part of the world would obviously have to include a much greater list of variables, such as climate, resources, agrarian density and productive organization.

[34] See, e.g., the materials reviewed by C.-E. A. Winslow, *The Cost of Sickness and the Price of Health,* World Health Organization Monograph Series, No. 7 (Geneva, 1951).

Are Sex Mortality Differentials Biologically Caused?[*1]

FRANCIS C. MADIGAN, S.J.

Several previous studies by demographers have drawn attention to the continuous divergence of male and female expectations of life in this country since 1900. Wiehl in 1938 pointed out the widening gap between the sexes, suggested the need for research into the causes, and called for medical specialization in care for men just as gynecologists have specialized in care of women.[2] Yerushalmy in a sex and age investigation of our population composition showed the striking increases which had occurred in the percentage of women among the older people of our country during the period from the census of 1920 to that of 1940.[3] More recently, Bowerman has produced new data which prove that the gap has continued to widen rather than to narrow.[4]

In 1900, the white women of this country enjoyed but a 2.85 year advantage over comparable males in expectation of life at birth. By 1950, this female advantage had doubled to 5.8 years, and the national abridged tables for 1954 show a difference of 6.2 years.

Why have men not profited from the better conditions of this century to the same extent as women? What are the chances that their days of life can be prolonged to equal those of the female sex?

Such questions raise further ones. Are these differentials in rates of dying chiefly reflections of the greater sociocultural pressures and strains which our culture lays upon male shoulders? Or are the differentials rather to be associated mainly with biological factors related to sex? If the former is the case, then probably little can be done to enable men to enjoy a life as long as women's. Short of a profound cultural revolution in our society, it appears that men must continue to experience greater stresses. However, if sex-linked biological factors principally underlie the differentials, the prognosis is more hopeful. It seems likely in this case that medical research can isolate the factors responsible for greater female viability, and use this knowledge to advantage in the treatment of middle-aged and old men, assuming of course that this can be done without disturbing psychological balance or causing observable physical reactions.

A quickening of interest in the problem of the diverging death trends of our men and women has occurred during the past few years and has resulted in a rather large amount of journal

* Reprinted with permission from *Milbank Memorial Fund Quarterly,* Vol. 35, No. 2 (April 1957), pp. 202-223.

[1] This project was financed by a grant from the National Institutes of Health for which help the writer is duly grateful. He is deeply indebted to Dr. Rupert B. Vance of the University of North Carolina who directed the dissertation upon which this paper reports. He also wishes to express gratitude to Dr. Daniel O. Price and Dr. Bernard G. Greenberg of the same University for assistance in the statistical analysis, as well as to Dr. Mortimer G. Spiegelman of the Metropolitan Life Insurance Company for valuable advice. Finally, he wishes to acknowledge his irreparable debt to the religious Communities who cooperated in this study, both by joining him in the collection of data and by making their files accessible to him: The Brothers of Christian Instruction, Alfred, Me.; The Franciscan Brothers of Cincinnati, O.; The Sisters of St. Joseph, Philadelphia, Pa.; The Sisters of the Holy Child, Rosemont, Pa.; The Ursuline Nuns of Cleveland, O.; The Ursuline Nuns of the Union, Eastern Province; and the many other Communities who wished to remain anonymous.

[2] Wiehl, Dorothy G.: Sex Differences in Mortality in the United States. *Milbank Memorial Fund Quarterly,* April, 1938, XVI, pp. 145-55.

[3] Yerushalmy, Jacob: The Age-Sex Composition of the Population Resulting from Natality and Mortality Conditions. *Milbank Memorial Fund Quarterly,* January, 1943, XXI, pp. 37-63.

[4] Bowerman, Walter G.: Annuity Mortality. *Actuarial Society of America: Transactions,* 1950, II, Part 2, pp. 76-102.

literature upon the question. However, most of this has been descriptive and speculative rather than analytic and research-oriented. The present article reports upon the results of a study which has attempted to shed some light upon the problem through the tools of demographic research.

Research Design

There seems to be no question that the differentials between the sexes in perinatal and infant mortality are due to biological rather than to sociocultural factors.[5] Accordingly, this study is concerned only with that part of the life from age fifteen onwards.

The design chosen was that of the "ex post facto experiment." Thus the problem was one of finding a male group and a female group in which cultural stresses and strains had been so standardized between sexes that one could observe the operation of biological factors in comparative isolation.

The subjects chosen for study were teachers and personnel of administrative staffs of Roman Catholic religious Brotherhoods and Sisterhoods engaged in educational work. Communities of these which operated hospitals were eliminated from the universe, and in communities actually studied the life records of Brothers and Sisters devoting their energies to household and manual duties were discarded as were those of infirmarians and nurses (who are in charge not of extern patients but of sick members).

Also eliminated from consideration were the records of those who had served in foreign missions, those who had been married before entrance into religious life, the foreign-born, the non-white, and those who had entered into the religious community on or after their twenty-seventh birthday. The reason for all these eliminations was the imposition of controls that would yield as homogeneous a group of subjects as possible.

While in the general public single men are more given to dissipation than single women, a life of dissipation is equally out of the question for both sexes in religious communities. Moreover, Brothers are not subject to military service after their entrance into religious life. Further, the daily regime of Brothers and Sisters is extremely similar as regards time for sleep, work, study, and recreation, and with respect to diet, housing, and medical care. (However, the life of the young Sisters seems to be slightly more stressful.)

It must be admitted that the Brothers are more likely to smoke and to take an occasional drink. Only recently have Sisters been permitted to smoke and only in a limited number of communities. An important factor that is not controlled because of the absence of relevant data is the relative incidence of obesity or of overeating within each sex group. However, it may be observed that Sisters do not have the same motives for slimness found among their sex in the general public.

Such control of sociocultural factors, it was assumed, would permit the desired operation of biological factors working in comparative isolation. Five highly significant sources of differential stress between the sexes had been eliminated: (1) male service in the armed forces; (2) greater male liberty to dissipate; (3) the dissimilar roles of husband and wife; (4) male employment in hazardous and life-shortening occupations; and (5) the employment of men and women in diverse occupations. Other sources of differential sociocultural stress also appear to have been eliminated or greatly curtailed. Maternal mortality, of course, had also been excluded by the very nature of the female group under observation.[6]

Health requirements suitable for the teaching

[5] The most pertinent and forceful of the many studies showing the existence of these differentials is that of Sam Shapiro: The Influence of Weight, Sex, and Plurality on Neonatal Loss in the United States. *American Journal of Public Health and the Nation's Health,* 1954, XLIV, pp. 1142-1153.

[6] A detailed discussion of the research design will be found in a previous article by Rupert B. Vance and Francis C. Madigan, S.J.: Differential Mortality and the "Style of Life" of Men and Women: Research Design. Trends and Differentials in Mortality. 1955 Annual Conference of the Milbank Memorial Fund. New York, Milbank Memorial Fund 1956, pp. 150-163. A later and more comprehensive treatment is also available in the writer's unpublished doctoral dissertation available in the University of North Carolina Library: The Differential Mortality of the Sexes, 1900-1954: Cultural and Biological Factors in the Diverging Life Chances of American Men and Women. University of North Carolina, Chapel Hill, 1956.

occupation were demanded of candidates for entrance into the religious life by both Brothers and Sisters during the entire period of observation. Such screening was based upon personal knowledge of the candidate's past health, his or her condition at time of entrance, and the person's health record during the one or more years of trial before the first vows are pronounced. It appears that Sisters required a medical examination by a physician earlier and more widely than the Brothers. This requirement seems to have become the common practice by about 1930.

Since stable death rates were desired, a large number of years of exposure to risk of dying was needed. Because the number of religious persons, especially of Brothers, was limited, the person-year of life was chosen as the unit of study, and the period of observation was extended from January 1, 1900 to December 31, 1954.

Sampling lists of all teaching communities of Brothers and Sisters in the United States were prepared from various editions of THE OFFICIAL CATHOLIC DIRECTORY.[7] A sample of twenty-two Brothers' communities and of fifty-three Sisters' communities was drawn by probability sampling from these lists. In terms of members living in 1927, which we treated as the mid-year of the study, the sample of Brothers comprised 100 per cent of the Brothers' universe, while that of the Sisters included 59.3 per cent of the Sisters' universe. The response from these communities was good with twenty communities of Brothers cooperating, representing more than 98 per cent of the Brothers' membership as measured in terms of 1927, and with forty-one communities of Sisters cooperating, representing 83.9 per cent of the membership in the Sisters' sample as measured, again, in terms of 1927.

In each of these communities life records were collected for the full membership of Brothers and Sisters since January 1, 1900, with the exception of persons who had not persevered for some part of three calendar years in the community. (The person-years in religious life of these latter were estimated on a sample basis.) All deaths were recorded, even if such death had occurred within the calendar year of entrance. When eliminations had been made according to the "experimental" controls described above, this left 9,813 life records of Brothers and 32,041 for Sisters.

In studying the literature, it had appeared to us that the greater weight of expert opinion lay on the side favoring biological factors as the principal causes for the sex differentials in the death rates. Accordingly, the research hypotheses were framed from this point of view and were expressed as follows:

1. Given two groups of American adults, one all male, the other all female, both drawn from the universe of healthy, native white persons in the United States who have reached age fifteen: if both groups are subjected to closely similar sociocultural stresses and strains over a long period of time, the female group will continue to show significantly more favorable death rates than the males.

2. The mortality differentials between the two experimental groups will not differ significantly from the patterns exhibited by the national population, or else will show increased female superiority.

While these hypotheses assume for testing purposes that biological factors linked with sex chiefly underlie women's pervasive advantage in length of life, and that the differing amounts of sociocultural stress borne by men and women have little relation to this female advantage, neither hypothesis should be misinterpreted to mean that social strains and pressures are believed to be unimportant in the chain of events which leads to an individual's death. In fact, evidence is strong that social strains may play a leading role in the deaths of both sexes. Rather, proper interpretation of these hypotheses understands them to mean that, other things being equal, the same objective stresses and strains upon equal numbers of men and women will lead to the deaths of more men than women during a given period of time.

METHODOLOGY

From the life records of these Sisters and Brothers age-specific death rates by ten year

[7] THE OFFICIAL CATHOLIC DIRECTORY. Milwaukee, Wiltzius and Company, 1900-1911. New York, Kenedy and Son, 1912-1955.

age groups were worked out for each decade, 1900–1950, and for the five years, 1950–1954, as well as for the entire period, 1900–1954. Ratios were formed by dividing the death rates of Brothers by those of American native white males, and the rates of Sisters by the corresponding females. Life tables were developed by the Reed-Merrell method for the same age groups and periods.[8]

Theoretical Model

On the assumption that the Brothers and Sisters studied constitute a group in which sociocultural stresses have been very greatly standardized between sexes, what results would indicate that such sociocultural factors are chiefly responsible for the differentials in mortality trends of American men and women? On the other hand, what results would point to biological factors as being the chief agents?

If the death rates of the Brothers should prove to have been lower than those of males of the general public, while Sisters exhibited death rates approximately equivalent to those of Brothers, the sociocultural hypothesis would be confirmed. For this should show that the variation in death rates of each sex is closely associated with variations in the amount of sociocultural stresses undergone.

On the other hand, this null hypothesis would be rejected and the biological hypothesis strengthened if the differences between the death rates of Brothers and Sisters should remain rather similar to the differentials found between death rates of men and women of the general public.

However, two points need emphasis here. The first concerns the Brothers. No matter which hypothesis is actually closer to the truth, Brothers should have experienced death rates somewhat lower than those of white males of the general public, at least at ages under forty-five. First, of all, they presumably suffer accident rates — especially motor vehicle accident rates — far below those of white males of the same age. Secondly, they would not have been exposed to the disabilities often resulting from military service (except Brothers who had been in service before entrance, none of whom would have been admitted to religious life if they had shown serious disability). Thirdly, their occupation, teaching, seems to be less stressful and dangerous than that of the average white male outside religious life. Finally, they have not carried on their shoulders the worries of a husband or a father about the security of his family.

The second point relates to the Sisters. Young Sisters at least (those up to about age 40) lead a life which appears more stressful than that of the average female in the general public. They teach long hours, and work on college and graduate degrees during their spare time. Most of them do not have a summer vacation but rather attend classes, teach catechism, take parish censuses, or participate in other activities.

Accordingly, even if sociocultural factors should be only of slight importance in relation to the observed sex mortality differentials of the general public, one would still not anticipate finding that young Sisters, at least, had experienced greater gains over females of the general public in mortality rates than Brothers had made over the corresponding males. Thus if Sisters have experienced significantly lower death rates than Brothers, and if at the same time the gains they made over females of the general public were not much smaller than those made by Brothers over the males, this would constitute strong evidence for rejecting the second null hypothesis. This hypothesis states that although biological factors may prove more important than sociocultural stresses, nevertheless sociocultural stresses still will be found to play an important part in the total effect of differential sex mortality.

Findings

Results confirm both research hypotheses and indicate (1) that biological factors are *more* important than sociocultural pressures and strains in relation to the different sex death rates; and (2) that the greater sociocultural stresses associated with the male role in our society play only a small and unimportant part in producing the differentials between male and female death rates.

[8] Quality checks were designed to keep error from all sources under control at two per cent or less. This error will be further reduced in forthcoming studies.

Analysis of Results by Expectation of Life [9]

In general, life expectations of Brothers at all ages but the oldest (where the frequencies were very small) proved to be considerably greater than those of white males of the general public.[10] Such a result was to have been anticipated under either biological or sociocultural hypotheses.

The important point, however, is that Sisters' expectations of life did not in general recede from the favored position of white females. Rather, they too usually made gains over these females. Table 1 shows that in thirty-eight cases Sisters had greater expectations of life than these white females, whereas the latter had greater expectations in only four cases.

Moreover, in these culturally standardized groups, Sisters' and Brothers' expectations of life did not tend to vary about the same means, but Sisters consistently exhibited greater expectations of life, and Brothers shorter expectations. Only seven times in the abridged life tables did Brothers enjoy longer expectations of life, while Sisters were favored in this manner thirty-three times. It is noteworthy that most of the Brothers' advantage came at ages 15–34 when they would be favored by accident rates, and in the years 1900–1919 when young Sisters appear to have had extremely high rates of tuberculosis.[11]

Comprehension of these results is aided by studying expectation of life at age 15, which summarizes results for the entire period of religious life from entrance until death; and expectation of life at age 45, which summarizes the experience for middle and old age only. This latter expectation is particularly important, in fact is crucial in this research design, because if social pressures were the main reason for the differentials in death rates of men and women in our general public, then at ages 45 and above in these standardized groups Brothers' and Sisters' death rates should show great convergence. For in the general public it is during the years from 45 to 65 that men seem to undergo greatest social strains and pressures. Accordingly, one would expect such pressures to exert an ever greater cumulative weight and to exact an increasing toll in the years following age 45. Therefore, on the hypothesis of sociocultural causation, standardization of such pressures ought to result in Brothers' and Sisters' death rates which vary about the same averages for each age group.

Figures 1 and 2 (which are based upon Table 1) make it abundantly clear that such convergence had not occurred at the middle and older ages, and they also show that even at age 15 the expectations have favored Sisters without exception from the third decade onwards. A comparison of the two figures also makes it evident that the Brothers' chief period of advantage was between ages 15 and 44.

The trends over time are important, too, for the consistency of the trend lines at age 15 minimizes the probability that Sisters' advantages after 1919 are due to chance factors, while the consistent upward secular trend of Sisters at age 45 and the fluctuation of Brothers' expectations around a mean of about 27.5 years of remaining life, appears even more cogent.

Are these differences between Brothers' and Sisters' expectations of life statistically significant? If so, the null hypothesis that sociocultural factors are the chief reasons for the differentials between male and female death rates may be rejected.

[9] The abridged life tables from which these expectations were drawn will be found in the writer's dissertation: The Differential Mortality of the Sexes, pp. 225-252. The fractions upon which the death rates were based will also be found in this place.

[10] When comparing Brothers' expectations with those of males of the general public, one must bear in mind that a small part of the Brothers' advantage is a statistical artifact. In the first four decades, for the age group 85 years and above, the central death rate used for the life tables of both Brothers and Sisters was the United States native white rate as common to both sexes. This device was employed because of the paucity of Brothers at these ages, and because of the desire to hold constant death rates of Brothers and Sisters at previous ages, while still finishing off the tables. A similar procedure was used in the first two decades for ages 75-84. Stable Brothers' rates — if they had been obtainable — would probably have been nearer those of native white males than the rates for both sexes taken together. On the other hand, Sisters' expectations were somewhat deflated, since in general at these ages the actual rates of Sisters were more favorable than the native white rates not specific for sex.

[11] *See* footnotes 13-18.

TABLE 1

Expectations of life in years at specified ages, Brothers and Sisters, and white males and females of the United States death registration states, with ratios of female to male expectancies, 1900–1954

Group	Ages							Period
	15	25	35	45	55	65	75	
E.G.M.[1]	49.72	41.98	35.13	27.35	21.96	14.97	7.18	1900–09[2]
E.G.F.	48.03	41.25	34.96	27.45	19.69	12.74	7.18	
Ratio	.97	.98	1.00	1.00	.90	.85	1.00	
U.S.M.	46.58	38.66	31.18	24.04	17.22	11.38	6.80	1900–11
U.S.F.	48.46	40.46	32.96	25.48	18.30	12.10	7.26	
Ratio	1.04	1.05	1.06	1.06	1.06	1.06	1.07	
E.G.M.	50.58	42.67	35.25	26.76	19.99	12.26	7.27	1910–19[2]
E.G.F.	49.80	42.46	35.65	27.81	20.15	12.69	7.27	
Ratio	.98	1.00	1.01	1.04	1.01	1.04	1.00	
U.S.M.	48.32	40.20	32.41	24.93	17.81	11.73	7.02	1909–21
U.S.F.	49.90	41.72	33.98	26.22	18.79	12.36	7.41	
Ratio	1.03	1.04	1.05	1.05	1.06	1.05	1.06	
E.G.M.	52.13	43.41	34.58	25.42	17.09	10.40	5.92	1920–29[2]
E.G.F.	53.83	45.11	37.01	28.97	20.75	13.55	8.32	
Ratio	1.03	1.04	1.07	1.14	1.21	1.30	1.41	
U.S.M.	50.06	41.69	33.54	25.64	18.28	11.99	7.16	1919–31
U.S.F.	51.84	43.40	35.30	27.18	19.50	12.78	7.59	
Ratio	1.04	1.04	1.05	1.06	1.07	1.07	1.06	
E.G.M.	53.85	44.17	34.58	25.96	18.52	12.20	6.83	1930–39
E.G.F.	56.78	47.31	38.32	29.74	21.65	14.28	8.48	
Ratio	1.05	1.07	1.11	1.15	1.17	1.17	1.24	
U.S.M.	51.36	42.53	33.84	25.58	18.16	11.92	7.10	1929–41
U.S.F.	54.54	45.52	36.72	28.14	20.16	13.18	7.74	
Ratio	1.06	1.07	1.09	1.10	1.11	1.11	1.09	
E.G.M.	56.32	46.60	36.99	27.95	19.80	13.24	7.81	1940–49
E.G.F.	60.18	50.39	40.77	31.47	22.81	14.74	8.71	
Ratio	1.07	1.08	1.10	1.13	1.15	1.11	1.12	
U.S.M.	53.26	44.10	35.02	26.37	18.72	12.41	7.47	1939–51
U.S.F.	57.73	48.28	38.99	30.01	21.66	14.28	8.40	
Ratio	1.08	1.09	1.11	1.14	1.16	1.15	1.12	
E.G.M.	57.14	47.37	37.61	28.27	20.21	12.85	7.75	1950–54
E.G.F.	62.97	52.97	43.25	33.83	24.87	16.55	9.62	
Ratio	1.10	1.12	1.15	1.20	1.23	1.29	1.24	
U.S.M.	54.4	45.2	35.9	27.1	19.3	13.0	8.0	1952
U.S.F.	59.9	50.3	40.8	31.6	23.0	15.3	9.1	
Ratio	1.10	1.11	1.14	1.17	1.19	1.18	1.14	

[1] E.G.M. and E.G.F. refer, respectively, to the Brothers and Sisters studied; U.S.M. and U.S.F. refer, respectively, to the white male and female populations of the expanding registration states. Decade expectations for the registration states' population were found by averaging the two values given for the triennium at each census date beginning and ending a decade, except the rates for 1952 which are the rates for this year.

[2] Because of the paucity of native Brothers at ages 75 and above in the decade 1900–1909, at ages above 85 in the 1910–1919, 1920–1929, and 1930–1939 decades, life tables for both Brothers and Sisters for these decades were finished off by using for both sexes the age-specific death rates of the United States native white population, as unsplit for sex. Interpolation between decades gave the decade value. This device permitted the finishing of the tables while keeping constant any differences Brothers and Sisters had manifested at younger ages.

SOURCES: For United States rates, 1900–1951: United States National Office of Vital Statistics: United States Life Tables, 1949–1951, VITAL STATISTICS, SPECIAL REPORTS, Vol. XLI, 1954, p. 30.

For United States rates, 1952: United States National Office of Vital Statistics, VITAL STATISTICS OF THE UNITED STATES, 1952, Vol. I. Washington, United States Government Printing Office, 1955, Table H, p. XXVI.

For Brothers and Sisters: Francis C. Madigan, S.J.: The Differential Mortality of the Sexes, 1900-1954. (Unpublished Doctoral Dissertation, University of North Carolina, Chapel Hill, 1956), pp. 118-120 and pp. 225-252. This source gives the abridged tables as well as the central death rates on which they were based.

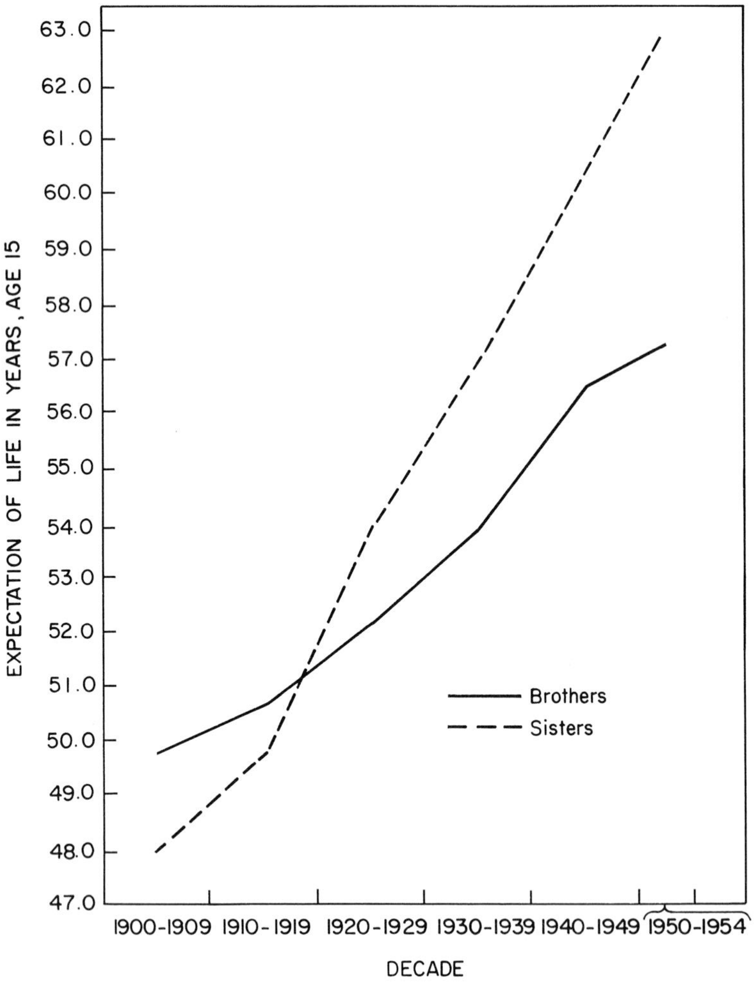

FIGURE 1

Expectations of life in years at age 15, Brothers and Sisters, 1900–1954. See Table 1.

In order to make this test, the data for the entire period of observation were pooled. Since the proportional age and decade distributions of Sisters resembled those of Brothers very closely, it was not necessary to weight Sisters' decade death rates to those of Brothers. However, the rates of United States native white males and females were weighted to those of Brothers and Sisters, respectively, in order to develop tables for comparison.

Such pooling gave more stable death rates; they were based on totals of 788 deaths and 130,863 person-years of life for Brothers, and of 6,144 deaths and 718,435 person-years of life for Sisters. The resulting expectations of life are set forth in Table 2.

When expectations of life at age 15 and at age 45 were tested, the advantages of Sisters in both cases proved significant at beyond the .001 level. Thus the first research hypothesis, that biological factors mainly underlie the differential death rates, was supported. It is interesting to

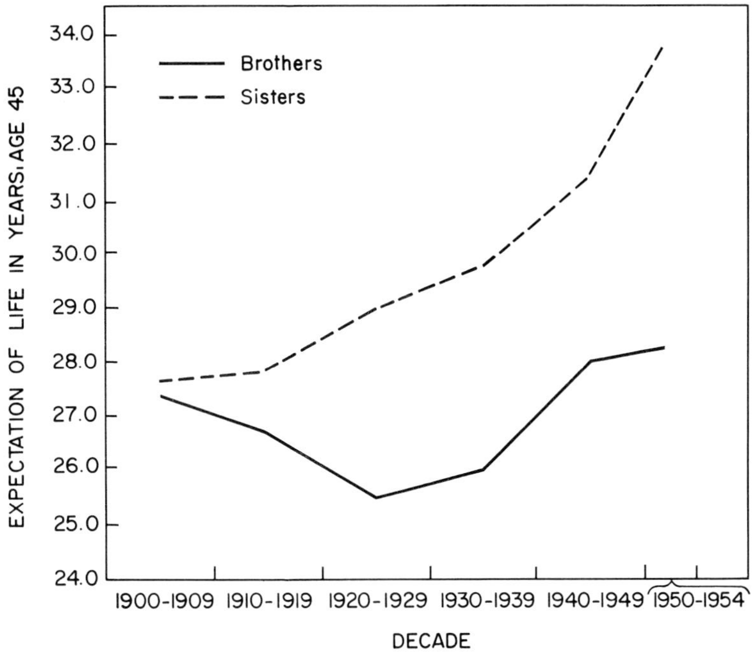

FIGURE 2

Expectations of life in years at age 45, Brothers and Sisters, 1900–1954. See Table 1.

note in this connection that in Table 2 the ratios showing Sisters' advantages became larger at each successive age interval — exactly the opposite of what would be expected under the sociocultural hypothesis. A somewhat similar trend appears in the ratios for the national population.

Analysis of Results by Age-Specific Death Rates [12]

We now turn our attention to the second research hypothesis, that not only are sociocultural pressures less important than biological factors in relation to the mortality differentials of the sexes, but they are of comparatively small importance in this respect. This hypothesis was examined by means of age-specific death rates.

[12] The fractions upon which these rates were based will be found in the writer's dissertation, The Differential Mortality, pp. 225-253.

A point of interest in regard to Table 3, which presents these death rates, is the spatial location of rates which favor Brothers over Sisters. If one imagines a rectangle enclosing the first three age groups, ages 15–44, and the first four decades, 1900–1939, he will discover that within this rectangle the rates of Sisters are higher than those of Brothers ten times out of twelve, 83 per cent. On the other hand, outside of this rectangle, he will discover that the Sisters are favored twenty-eight times out of a possible thirty-two, while Brothers' rates were lower only three times. In other words, 77 per cent of all rates unfavorable to Sisters are found within these early ages during the period 1900–1939. On the other hand, Sisters showed a clear advantage from age 45 upwards in all decades, and at all ages after 1939.

This finding supports the conclusion already reached in studying expectations of life that sociocultural pressures are not the main factors

TABLE 2

Expectations of life in years at specified ages, Brothers and Sisters, and native white males and females of the United States death registration states,[1] with ratios of female to male expectancies, for the period 1900–1954.

Group	Ages							Period
	15	25	35	45	55	65	75	
E.G.M.	54.00	44.80	35.62	26.71	19.09	12.27	7.14	1900–54
E.G.F.	56.58	47.75	39.35	30.75	22.45	14.78	8.92	
Ratio	1.05	1.07	1.10	1.15	1.18	1.20	1.25	
U.S.M.	51.80	43.09	34.41	26.08	18.57	12.23	7.47	1900–53
U.S.F.	55.12	46.34	37.82	29.34	21.27	14.07	8.41	
Ratio	1.06	1.08	1.10	1.13	1.15	1.15	1.13	

Standard error of $\mathring{e}_{15}$(E.G.M.) is .574. Standard error of $\mathring{e}_{15}$(E.G.F.) is .221.
Standard error of $\mathring{e}_{45}$(E.G.M.) is .569. Standard error of $\mathring{e}_{45}$(E.G.F.) is .202.
Standard error of difference between $\mathring{e}_{15}$(E.G.M.) and $\mathring{e}_{15}$(E.G.F.) is .615. Z is 4.20.
P is less than .001.
Standard error of difference between $\mathring{e}_{45}$(E.G.M.) and $\mathring{e}_{45}$(E.G.F.) is .605. Z is 6.61.
P is less than .001.

[1] United States rates for 1950–1953 are for white, not native white persons.
SOURCES: For Brothers and Sisters: The Differential Mortality of the Sexes, p. 126.
For United States population: Life tables developed from native white rates of United States population of Death Registration States as described in Table 3, weighted for each decade and age group, by sex, according to the proportion of the number of person-years lived by each experimental sex group in each decade and age group to the total person-years lived by that sex in that age group, 1900–1954. These tables are given in The Differential Mortality, pp. 249–252.

underlying sex differences in death rates, because it shows that Sisters enjoyed more favorable rates than Brothers at the crucial middle and older ages. It also indicates that Sisters' death rates at ages under 45 in the period 1900–1939 were anomalous. Analysis of the table for these ages and years makes it clear that Sisters' rates therein were at times exceptionally high. Since social pressures and degenerative diseases would hardly cause such high death rates between ages 15 and 24, and between ages 25 and 34, the conclusion seems warranted that some infectious or contagious disease or diseases plagued young Sisters in the early part of this century with unusually lethal effects.

A number of reasons suggest that this disease was tuberculosis. First, there was the greater difficulty of detecting incipient cases during the first quarter of the century in the medical examination required of candidates for admission, due to the less frequent use of X-ray pictures. Even in 1936, according to Dr. Frost, a large proportion of tubercular cases in the general public were not discovered until they had reached an advanced stage.[13] We may be fairly sure that the same would be true among Sisters in regard to those incipient cases of tuberculosis which had escaped detection at time of entrance. Secondly, the dangers of infection would be multiplied by the close life of the Sisters among themselves in the Convent, and the lack of general understanding then prevalent of prophylactic methods to prevent the spread of the germ. "Age and prior exposure bring no such immunity against tuberculosis as they establish against many of the acute infections." [14]

Again, the highest tuberculosis mortality of cohorts of birth appears to occur between ages 20–29.[15] Moreover, it has been a fairly common

[13] Frost, Wade Hampton: How Much Control of Tuberculosis. *In* PAPERS OF WADE HAMPTON FROST, M.D. Ed., Kenneth F. Maxcy, M.D. New York, Commonwealth Fund, 1941, p. 607.

[14] Frost, Wade Hampton: The Age Selection of Mortality from Tuberculosis in Successive Decades. *In* PAPERS OF WADE HAMPTON FROST, p. 594.

[15] *Ibid., American Journal of Hygiene,* 1939, XXX, Sec. A, p. 91, footnote (in letter of Dr. Frost to Dr. Sydenstricker, quoted.)

TABLE 3

Specific Death Rates per 1,000 Persons for Brothers and Sisters and Native White Males and Females of the United States Death Registration States,[1] *By Age Group and Sex, 1900–1954.*[2]

Period	Group	Ages 15–24	25–34	35–44	45–54	55–64	65–74	75–84	85 and Over
1900–09	E.G.M.	4.96	8.10	7.30	18.34	18.97	(0/44)	—	—
	E.G.F.	7.20	9.63	7.94	9.70	19.26	44.75	*126.32*[b]	—
1900–10	U.S.M.[a]	5.1	7.65	10.05	13.9	25.5	55.9	127.45	264.2
	U.S.F.	4.95	6.98	8.3	11.7	21.35	47.6	114.65	252.6
1910–19	E.G.M.	4.49	6.55	5.07	13.64	15.14	50.63	*216.22*	—
	E.G.F.	5.78	8.07	6.82	9.86	16.22	45.87	91.74[c]	*97.56*
1910–20	U.S.M.	4.9	7.56	9.4	13.54	24.9	54.55	123.95	253.4
	U.S.F.	4.4	6.4	7.52	10.9	21.1	48.0	113.8	244.45
1920–29	E.G.M.	2.68	3.00	2.93	8.31	24.87	65.83	165.61	—
	E.G.F.	2.63	4.64	5.92	7.38	16.93	43.24	94.43	256.88
1920–30	U.S.M.	3.3	4.3	6.64	11.45	24.0	54.15	120.1	242.45
	U.S.F.	3.2	4.4	5.94	9.7	19.95	46.45	109.6	233.3
1930–39	E.G.M.	0.66	1.11	4.73	11.72	24.19	48.55	132.04	(9/13.5)
	E.G.F.	1.03	2.39	4.23	7.58	15.14	37.25	90.94	222.22[d]
1930–40	U.S.M.	2.5	3.4	5.6	11.4	24.65	54.2	121.35	251.65
	U.S.F.	1.95	2.9	4.35	8.1	17.4	42.4	105.7	229.0
1940–49	E.G.M.	0.55	0.98	3.06	8.08	21.08	43.36	104.59	*255.81*
	E.G.F.	0.39	0.86	2.00	5.10	10.95	34.36	88.25	217.21[e]
1940–50	U.S.M.	1.75	2.35	4.4	10.45	23.65	50.3	113.05	243.4
	U.S.F.	1.05	1.65	2.95	6.25	14.0	35.0	92.75	211.85
1950–54	E.G.M.	0.44	0.60	2.16	8.18	16.74	47.06	106.48	*245.61*
	E.G.F.	0.01	0.60	1.56	3.67	8.54	24.56	74.92	191.89[f]
1950–53	U.S.M.	1.6	1.8	3.7	9.7	23.0	48.3	105.1	209.7
	U.S.F.	0.7	1.1	2.3	5.3	12.5	31.6	84.1	191.0
1900–54	E.G.M.	1.63	2.04	3.67	10.58	20.82	49.71	119.48	317.65
	E.G.F.	2.26	3.66	4.06	6.50	13.09	35.26	85.64	204.15
1900–53	U.S.M.	2.73	3.44	5.63	11.39	24.11	52.20	114.28	233.42
	U.S.F.	2.43	3.52	4.56	7.83	16.31	38.84	95.18	205.94

1 Rates for white, rather than native white persons were used for the years 1950–1953.

2 Rates for United States populations were computed by interpolating between rates for census years to secure a decade average. Results for ages 15-54 were corrected for the three decades 1900-1909, 1910-1919, and 1920-1929 by a factor obtained by forming a ratio between the average of yearly rates for the general white population for these years (in each decade) and the rates for the general white population after interpolation between census dates. Where interpolation had produced two decimal places, these places were both retained not to magnify the original rounding error.

a United States rates are for the expanding Death Registration States.

b *Italicized* rates are based on less than fifty person years.

c The Brothers' rate for this age group was based on deaths and person years for ages 75-79 only. Accordingly, in forming the ratio of Table 4, and in the life table for 1900-1954, the corresponding five-year rate of Sisters was used, viz. 73.56.

d For similar reasons, in forming the ratio of Table 4, and in the life table for 1900-1954, the five-year rate for ages 85-89 was used, viz. 204.35.

e For similar reasons, in forming the ratio of Table 4, and in the life tables for 1940-1949, and for 1900-1954, the Sisters' rate for ages 85-94 only was used, viz. 215.92.

f For similar reasons, in forming the ratio of Table 4, and in the life tables for 1950-1954, and for 1900-1954, the Sisters' rate for ages 85-99 only was used, viz. 190.77.

SOURCES: 1. For United States' rates, native white and white, respectively, 1900-1940: United States Bureau of the Census: VITAL STATISTICS RATES IN THE UNITED STATES, 1900-1940. Prepared by Forrest E. Linder and Robert D. Grove. Washington, United States Government Printing Office, 1943, Table 9, p. 186.

2. For United States' native white rates, 1950: United States National Office of Vital Statistics, Vital Statistics for Native White Males and Females (unpublished table, United States National Office of Vital Statistics, n.d.).

3. For United States' white rates, 1950-1953: United States National Office of Vital Statistics, VITAL STATISTICS OF THE UNITED STATES, 1953, Vol. I. Washington, United States Government Printing Office, 1956, Table AK, p. xlvi.

4. For United States' yearly white rates, 1900-1929, ages 15-54 (used in correction factors): United States National Office of Vital Statistics: Death Rates by Age, Race, and Sex: United States, 1900-1953: All Causes, VITAL STATISTICS, SPECIAL REPORTS, Vol. XLIII, 1956, pp. 14-15.

5. For United States' native white rates, 1900-1953: the decade rates, and the rates for 1950-1953 as shown in the table above. Each decade age-group death rate of males was weighted according to the proportion of the total person-years lived by Brothers in that decade age group. Females were similarly treated by weighting them to the distribution of Sisters' person-years.

6. For Brothers and Sisters' rates: The Differential Mortality of the Sexes, pp. 136-138, and p. 128.

observation that females between ages 10 and about 29 show higher susceptibility to tuberculosis than males of these ages, so much so, indeed, that in 1929 Sydenstricker called such women "relatively neglected groups" and found their death rates from tuberculosis were 59 per cent higher than the male rate at 10–14 years of age, 106 per cent higher at 15–19 years, and 43 per cent higher at 20–24 years.[16]

Finally, Fecher's work[17] as well as the British experience of 1930–1932[18] makes it evident that Catholic Sisters and nuns aged 15 to 34 years during the period 1900–1932 had rates of tuberculosis which were unusually high and which were far above the rates for single women. Single women at these ages generally showed rates higher than those of married women or of males. Dr. Taylor found similar results among Sisters in three American communities she studied from their foundation in the last century up through 1953.[19]

Ratios were formed from the values shown in Table 3 by dividing Brothers' death rates by those of native white males, and Sisters' death rates by those of native white females. In order not to bias the comparison, each ratio was weighted by the number of person-years out of the total that Brothers or Sisters had lived in the particular decade-age-group, and thus average weighted ratios were formed for ages 15–44, ages 15 and above, and ages 45 and above.

These average ratios show whether Brothers made greater gains over native white males than Sisters made over native white females and vice versa. Thus they permit comparison of the differences of patterns between sexes in death rates for the "experimental" groups and for the national population. Where the ratios are equal, this shows that the pattern between sexes of the national groups are perfectly reflected in the differential rates of Brothers and Sisters. However, where male ratios are lower, this indicates that Brothers have made greater gains, and that there has been convergence between death rates of Brothers and Sisters, when these are measured from the positions of male and female of the national population. On the other hand, where female ratios are lower, it indicates Sisters have made greater gains, and that there has been divergence.

We may again ask, what results would lead to the non-rejection of the second null hypothesis, that sociocultural factors are of more than small importance in effecting the sex differences in mortality rates? Taking into account the lower accident rates of younger Brothers, and the less hazardous and stressful occupation in which they are engaged in comparison with that of the average native white male, as well as the fact that young Sisters are probably under greater stresses than the average native white female, non-rejection of the null hypothesis would call for large divergences from the patterns of the general public which would (a) be particularly manifested during the crucial middle and old-age periods of life, and (b) which would be in the direction of convergence between Brothers and Sisters' death rates, rather than in the direction of greater divergence.

The results shown in Table 4 do not present a picture of convergence of Sisters' death rates towards Brothers nor divergence from the general public pattern of superior female death rates at the middle and the old ages. An examination of this table reveals that Sisters exhibited as much superiority over Brothers at these ages as females over males of the general public. Almost all comparative gains of Brothers occurred at ages 15–44, a period in which it is difficult to believe that the underlying causation could have been influenced much by social stress and strain. Rather the difference, particularly in the last fifteen years of observation, appears due to gains of Brothers over native white males in lower death rates from motor vehicle and other types of accidents, on the one hand, and on the other to high death rates from infectious disease such as tuberculosis among Sisters in the first quarter of this century.

[16] Sydenstricker, Edgar: Tuberculosis Among Relatively Neglected Groups. TRANSACTIONS OF THE NATIONAL TUBERCULOSIS ASSOCIATION, 1929, xxv, p. 268.

[17] Fecher, Constantine J.: THE LONGEVITY OF MEMBERS OF CATHOLIC RELIGIOUS SISTERHOODS. Washington: Catholic University of America, 1927, pp. 42-44. Fecher is at present bringing his interesting study up to date.

[18] Registrar General's Office, THE REGISTRAR GENERAL'S DECENNIAL SUPPLEMENT, ENGLAND AND WALES, 1931. Part IIa. Occupational Mortality. London, His Majesty's Stationery Office, 1938, Table 4c, p. 303.

[19] It is the writer's understanding that Dr. Ruth Taylor and Mr. Ben Carroll of the National Institutes of Health expect to publish these results in the near future.

Tests of significance were made by weighted analyses of variance upon each of the values shown in Table 4.[20] Brothers' ratios proved significantly lower than Sisters at ages 15–44 in the 1900, 1910, and 1950 decades, and for the period 1900–1954 (at .05 for each period, except 1910–1919 when the difference was significant at .001). In the decades 1920, 1930, and 1940 the differences were not significant.

At all ages, 15 and above, Brothers' ratios proved significantly lower in the 1910, and the 1930 decades, as well as in the period 1900–1954. (The level of significance was .01 except for 1930 when it stood at .05.)

At ages 45 and above, no differences were significant within decades, but the Sisters' lower ratio for the entire period 1900–1954 was significant at the .01 level.

Probably the Brothers' lower ratios at ages 15–44 would have been significant more often if more degrees of freedom had been available than the one and two present in each decade for sex differences, because the F scores were high. However, the number of degrees of freedom for ages 15 and above (all ages studied) ranged from one and five to one and seven.

Since there were no large departures among Brothers and Sisters at the middle and older ages from the patterns of female superiority observed in the general public and since, in fact, at these ages Sisters' ratios were generally somewhat lower, the null hypothesis was rejected and the research hypothesis, that sociocultural pressures made only small contributions to the differential mortality rates of the sexes, was supported. Because of the nature of the tests, it was not possible to set any precise level of probability for this rejection of the null hypothesis.

[20] The Method of Fitting Constants was used to obtain adjusted sums of squares for sex and for age. *Cf.* Snedecor, George W., STATISTICAL METHODS. Ames, Iowa, Collegiate Press, 1946, pp. 296-99.

EVALUATION OF RESULTS

The finding that biological factors played by far the chief part in differentiating the death rates of members of the universe studied is very important. Since these members were native white Americans of sufficient health to be admitted into religious communities engaged in the active occupation of teaching, the results point to the operation of similar biological factors as the chief agents in the differential death rates of the two sexes of the American general public.

An interesting lead for further research is the notable, even spectacular improvement of young Sisters under observation from the early to the late years of the study. From showing the poorest records of the four populations compared in the period 1900–1909, they improved rapidly to exhibit by far the best mortality records for the

TABLE 4

Average Weighted Ratios of Brothers' Death Rates to Death Rates of United States' Native White Males, and of Sisters' Death Rates to Death Rates of United States' White Native Females, For Ages 15–44, 15 and All Ages Over, and 45 and All Ages Over, 1900–1954.[1]

Group	1900–09	1910–19	1920–29	1930–39	1940–49	1950–54	1900–54	Ages
Brothers[2]	.94	.84	.73	.36	.44	.36	.61	15–44
Sisters	1.26	1.18	.97	.80	.55	.44	.96	
Brothers	.97	.85	.77	.45	.50	.44	.66	15 and
Sisters	1.18	1.09	.93	.83	.66	.56	.92	Over
Brothers	1.13	.87	.96	1.00	.83	.84	.92	45 and
Sisters	.85	.86	.82	.90	.85	.71	.84	Over

[1] The United States rates for 1950–1954 used were for the white rather than the native white population.
[2] "Brothers" was used here as a shorthand expression for the death rates of Brothers divided by the death rates of United States native white males and weighted according to the number of person years of exposure; similarly "Sisters."
SOURCE: The Differential Mortality of the Sexes, pp. 169–171, and p. 173.

years after 1939. This suggests the hypothesis that *under conditions of equal stress* women may be no more resistant to the *infectious* and *contagious* diseases than men — perhaps even less so — and that the gains which women have been making over men in this century may be chiefly bound up with a greater constitutional resistance to the *degenerative* diseases. This would account for the remarkable improvement of young Sisters vis-a-vis the other three populations, because of the spectacular advances made during this century in controlling the ravages of the infectious and contagious diseases. If this hypothesis is borne out by further research, one might then say that the growing advantage of American women over men is a function of the transition from conditions when infectious and contagious diseases were the main causes of death to conditions wherein the degenerative diseases play this role.

Of course, an alternative hypothesis is possible. There may have been some hidden selection of Sisters in the earlier quarter of the century which operated at a much reduced degree in the second quarter. What this selection would be is obscure. None of the convents took in girls to "let them die in the religious life." Nor was the ascetical life of the Sisters apparently more rigorous than that of the Brothers, although both regimes were more severe at the start of the century than they are now. Further, the physical examination of candidates for admission seems to have been more careful than that of the Brothers rather than less painstaking.[21]

The continuing phase of this study[22] should allow some test of these hypotheses, as well as the hypothesis that the chief reason for the poor showing of young Sisters during the first quarter century was tuberculosis. However, it is hoped that the results of the present study will stimulate further research by other interested parties, including both replications of the present study among other matched groups of men and women, and medical research, first, into causes of death which carry off more men than women when social stress differentials have been minimized, and, secondly, into specific biological factors which may be associated with the longer life of women. Such studies may advance the date when our men can enjoy an average lifetime as long as that of women.

[21] The writer learned these facts from a questionnaire which he circulated among the communities in his sample after the results had become available.

[22] In this further phase, causes of death will be analyzed for the Brothers and Sisters of the study. Dr. Rupert B. Vance of the University of North Carolina and Mr. William Haenszel and staff of the National Cancer Institute are collaborating with the writer in this extension of the study. Place of death is being secured from the communities in the sample, and the various state vital statistics offices will be searched for the death certificates.

*Socioeconomic Status and Mortality in the United States**

EDWARD G. STOCKWELL

The knowledge that differences in socioeconomic status are related to differences in mortality rates has long been of concern to persons seeking to improve levels of health and well-being. Ever since 1833, when Corbaux first called attention to their existence (*1*), the study of mortality in different socioeconomic groups has occupied the attention of many scholars in a variety of fields.

In view of this long concern, it is somewhat

* Reprinted by permission from *Public Health Reports,* Vol. 76, No. 12 (December 1961), pp. 1081-1086.

surprising that there exists a gap in our knowledge pertaining to the precise influence of socioeconomic factors on mortality rates compared with the influence of other more general demographic characteristics. In contrast to an abundance of fairly reliable published material showing the relationship of such characteristics as sex, age, and race to mortality rates, studies relating mortality to socioeconomic status are relatively rare. Although people have long been aware of the generalization that mortality is inversely related to socioeconomic status, very few empirical studies have been undertaken for the specific purpose of examining this relationship more thoroughly. Thus, this is clearly an area in which the need for additional research is especially acute.

OCCUPATION

The relative lack of studies pertaining to the relationship between socioeconomic status and mortality is due in part to the difficulty of obtaining the necessary data. Aside from occupation, no information is provided by the death certificate currently in use that would place the deceased directly in one or another socioeconomic class. However, a man's occupation is an extremely crucial factor in determining his socioeconomic status, and it has long been recognized that people in the higher social classes, as indicated by occupation, have an appreciably lower death rate than those at the other end of the social scale. As one group of authors (*2*) has noted, "The work a man does, the conditions under which his work is done, and the wages he receives for it determine in great measure the circumstances of his life, the house he lives in, the clothes he wears, the food he eats, and his recreation. A man's occupation is, therefore, one of the potent factors deciding the state of his health and fixing the length of his life."

For these reasons, several studies, both in this country and abroad, have been undertaken in an effort to understand more clearly the relationship between occupation and mortality. Daric (*3*) has made a comprehensive review of the literature on occupational differences in mortality up to 1950. The longest and most complete coverage of the relationship between occupation and mortality is found in the publications of the Registrar General's Office of England and Wales, dating back as far as 1851. Logan (*4*) has summarized the work of this office up to and including the census of 1951. In the United States, the studies of Dublin and his collaborators in the Metropolitan Life Insurance Company (*5*) date back as far as the period 1911–13.

Prior to 1911, the Bureau of the Census had published tables reporting mortality by occupation for the years 1890 (*6*) and 1900 (*7*). These early studies, which were oriented toward an examination of the mortality levels characteristic of particular occupations, did not, however, purport to provide any information pertaining to the existence of mortality differentials by occupational "classes." Although it was generally accepted that mortality rates were highest among persons in the more menial occupations, it was not until 1934, when the classic study by Whitney was published by the National Tuberculosis Association (*8*) that data concerning occupational class differences in mortality became available in this country. Using the Edwards classification scheme (*9*), Whitney compared death rates by occupation for those States where it was felt that occupational returns on the death certificate were sufficiently complete to justify relating them to census population data. Her findings indicated the existence of a pronounced inverse relationship between occupational class and mortality, the death rate of 13.1 per 1,000 for unskilled persons being nearly twice the rate of 7.0 per 1,000 for persons in professional occupations (*8*).

More recently, a preliminary report of a study carried out in connection with the 1950 census indicated that the inverse relationship between occupational class and mortality still prevails in the United States, and that the level of mortality among lower occupational classes is still approximately twice as high as that characterizing the professional and managerial group (*10*).

Although the studies of Whitney (*8*) and Moriyama and Guralnick (*10*) clearly point to the existence of a marked inverse gradient when mortality is related to occupational class in the United States, there are certain difficulties associated with the way in which occupation has been used as an index of socioeconomic status. These difficulties stem from several limitations inherent in the available data, and any person who either attempts research in this area or uses materials on occupational mortality should keep these limitations in mind.

The most outstanding difficulty in relating mortality to occupation is the computation of death rates. In order to compute death rates by occupation, two figures are needed: the number of persons in each occupation dying during a given period, and the total number of persons enumerated in each occupation during the same period. At first glance these figures would appear to be readily available from death certificates and from published census sources. However, for a variety of reasons, the comparability of these two sets of data may be questioned. In the first place, the two sources do not follow the same procedures in recording occupation. On the one hand, the death certificate currently in use asks for the usual occupation of the deceased, and further specifies the "kind of work done during most of life." The census, on the other hand, prior to 1960, recorded the occupation in which a person was engaged at the time of enumeration. Since a sizable proportion of the aged in the labor force work in occupations radically different from those in which they were engaged during the major part of their working lives (*11*), it is quite possible that the occupation reported in the census will differ from that which is subsequently recorded on the death certificate.

Comparability between death certificate and census data may also be affected by the fact that death certificates record an occupation for all deceased persons — whether employed at the time of death, unemployed, or retired. On the other hand, prior to 1960, the census presented occupational data which referred only to those persons who were active members of the labor force, either employed or seeking employment in a particular occupation, at the time of enumeration. This means that when death rates are computed for occupational classes, the population base does not include all persons who were "exposed to the risk of dying," and any differences between occupations concerning the number enumerated as opposed to the number who, although not working at the time, belonged to a particular occupational class could seriously bias the resulting occupational death rates.

Socioeconomic Status

Although the preceding discussion does not exhaust the ways in which comparability between data from death certificates and census reports might be affected (*12*), it clearly indicates the limitations of using occupational data from census and vital registration sources in the analysis of socioeconomic differentials in mortality. In view of these limitations, it is not surprising to find that several alternative approaches have been used to study the relationship between socioeconomic factors and levels of mortality. In these endeavors, the house-to-house canvass or sample survey has played a leading role.

Although not specifically concerned with mortality, Sydenstricker's early study of Hagerstown (*13*) may be regarded as the forerunner of surveys in this country designed to assess the influence of the socioeconomic environment on health. This study, which was based on a survey of 1,800 families in Hagerstown, Md., beginning in the autumn of 1921, showed that levels of health, as determined by the occurrence of illness, became noticeably poorer as family income decreased. Furthermore, it was found that the amount of medical care received decreased with income status; only 43 percent of the illnesses among the "very poor" were attended by a physician in contrast to 70 percent among the "well-to-do" families. Although some variations between income groups were observed when specific ages and causes were examined, Sydenstricker concluded: "Two facts remain fairly clear, however — one is that the illness rate as observed was higher for the poor than for those economically better off; the other is that, in general, those families which were definitely above the average of this community in economic condition had medical attention to a considerably greater extent than the remainder of the population."

The relationship between health and socioeconomic status was again examined a few years later in the spring of 1933. At this time, a house-to-house canvas, carried out in 10 localities that were particularly hard hit by the depression, showed that there was a marked increase in the incidence of disabling illness as per capita family income declined (*14*). Similarly, the National Health Survey conducted between November 1935 and March 1936 showed a very pronounced association between health and economic status. To illustrate, the case rate for acute and infectious illnesses, which was 160 per 1,000 among persons on relief, declined consistently as income rose so that the rate for the group with an annual income of $5,000 or more was only 107 per 1,000 population (*15*). Moreover, the National Health Survey found that socioeconomic status also bore a strong inverse association to the frequency of disabling accidents (*16*), accidental death (*17*), incidence of chronic impairments (*18*), and receipt of medical attention (*19*).

In more recent times, the adverse effect of a low socioeconomic status on levels of health is demonstrated by findings such as the existence of a direct relationship between family income and the proportion of illness and injury cases that receive medical attention (*20*), and an inverse relationship between income and the number of workdays lost per person per year as a result of disabling illnesses or injuries (*21*).

Another methodological approach which has been used to examine the relationship between socioeconomic status and health involves the use of census data to divide the country into broad socioeconomic areas. Pennell has shown, for example, that the existence and use of hospital facilities was inversely correlated with economic status when the 48 States and the District of Columbia were ranked according to average annual per capita income (*22*). Similarly, Dorn, using data from the 1930 census to group the rural counties of Ohio into two broad categories showed that the age-adjusted death rates in areas of "poor economic status," such as depressed agricultural and mining areas, were about 10 percent greater than the corresponding rates in the areas of "good economic status" (*23*). For males, the death rate in areas of good economic status was 8.3 per 1,000 as opposed to a rate of 9.3 in the poor areas; for females the corresponding rates were 7.9 and 8.7, respectively.

More recently, Altenderfer (*24*), using data on per capita income to rank 92 cities in the United States whose 1940 population exceeded 100,000, noted that the age-adjusted death rates showed a pronounced tendency to decline as the average income of a city rose. This inverse relationship was found to hold for all deaths from all causes, for infant deaths, for maternal deaths, and for deaths due to the major chronic diseases as well as to the infectious causes. A subsequent study (*25*) based on 973 cities of 10,000 or more population ranked according to infant mortality rates yielded similar findings: in cities having the lowest infant mortality rates the average annual per capita income was $722 as opposed to $595 among those cities in which infant mortality was greatest.

A third approach, which is being used more extensively as the data become increasingly available, also involves the use of census data. Using information on the death certificate pertaining to the usual place of residence of the deceased, mortality is examined in relation to certain social and economic characteristics of census tracts, the small, relatively homogeneous geographic areas into which many of the larger cities and their environs have been divided for statistical purposes (*26*). However, as when death certificate occupational entries are used to classify decedents into broad socioeconomic groups, use of census tracts as analytical units has many limitations. The pros and cons of the census tract approach have been discussed extensively elsewhere in the literature and therefore will not be taken up here. A brief review of the problems, as well as a pertinent bibliography, has been presented by Coulter and Guralnick (*27*).

Using the value of owned homes or monthly rental, as reported by the Federal census, Allen (*28–30*) has made a careful study of the relation between socioeconomic status and mortality in Cincinnati, Ohio. In 1930, 1940, and again in 1950 the adverse effect of a poor socioeconomic environment on levels of mortality was found to be very pronounced. In the most recent study, for example, the infant mortality of the white population was nearly three times as high in the lowest economic area as it was in the remainder of the city (*30*). Similar studies carried out in a number of other cities and using a variety of indices have also found mortality levels to vary inversely with socioeconomic status. In Chicago in 1920–40 the expectation of life at birth for both males and females increased markedly with socioeconomic status when the census tracts of that city were grouped according to median monthly rent (*31*). Similarly, a study made in New Haven, Conn., in 1930 demonstrated clearly that mortality rates tended to rise as socioeconomic status decreased (*32*), as did studies of Buffalo, N.Y., in 1940 (*33*) and Houston, Tex., in 1950 (*34*).

All of the studies mentioned so far have pointed out the existence of a pronounced inverse relationship between mortality and socioeconomic status. However, not all studies substantiate this conclusion. For example, a followup study of the participants in Sydenstricker's survey of Hagerstown showed an erratic pattern when the extent of illness was related to economic status (*35*). Similarly, a survey of Butler County, Pa., during the summer of 1954, which used the Edwards occupational classification as an index of socioeconomic status, concluded that there was no discernible difference in the incidence of illness among the several classes (*36*).

The existence of areas of disagreement becomes increasingly apparent when more specific cases are considered. To illustrate, in contrast to a very strong inverse relationship between socioeconomic status and infant mortality found in Houston, Tex., (*34*), the association appeared to be almost nonexistent in Syracuse, N.Y. (*37*), and in Providence, R.I. (*38*). Similarly, although some studies suggest that the relationship does not hold for the major chronic diseases (*4, 30*), still others would indicate that the inverse relationship is just as strong for deaths due to chronic ailments as it is for deaths resulting from infectious causes (*39*). Furthermore, even those studies that agree on the existence of a differential frequently disagree as to whether the differential is becoming smaller (*31*) or whether it is still the same or even more pronounced than it has been in the past (*30*). Such conflicting observations concerning the existence, nature, and extent of socioeconomic mortality differentials clearly indicate the need for additional research in this area.

Conclusion

The preceding review of the literature pertaining to socioeconomic mortality differentials in the United States indicates the type of research that has been done in this area and the nature of the results obtained. In the past, the general conclusion of all of these studies, many of which employed markedly different methodological approaches, demonstrated the existence of a definite inverse relationship between mortality rates and socioeconomic status. However, in the more recent period there seems to be some conflict as to whether or not such a differential exists, either for total mortality or for mortality from specific causes. Moreover, even when the existence of such a differential is agreed upon, there is disagreement as to whether or not it is narrowing. It may be that the existence of socioeconomic mortality differentials, and whether they are becoming smaller or larger, actually varies from one area to another. On the other hand, the presence and nature of a relationship may depend on the variables chosen to measure socioeconomic status, for example, income as opposed to rent or occupation, or the particular methodological procedures employed. One recent study has demonstrated that all of these factors may exert an influence on the nature of socioeconomic mortality differentials (*40*).

In order to clarify the present situation, and to determine validly whether or not the traditional socioeconomic differential still exists, whether it characterizes all or only a few aspects of total mortality or whether it is narrowing, a continuous series of comparative studies is needed. Moreover, the comparison of areas and the description of time trends must clearly indicate what is being compared and must include specific qualifications when different methodological procedures, different sources of data, and different universes are used in the comparison. Only when we have a continuous series of studies on the ways in which different status factors affect mortality will we have a sound basis for determining the effect of overall socioeconomic status on mortality.

A project of the 1960 census will be matching a sample of death certificates to census returns for the purpose of analyzing socioeconomic mortality differentials (*41*), and it is hoped that the completion of this work may provide a starting point for the much needed ongoing series of studies concerning the relationship between various aspects of mortality and the several components of socioeconomic status.

REFERENCES

1. Corbaux, F.: On the natural and mathematical laws concerning population, vitality, and mortality. Francis Corbaux, London, 1833.
2. Dublin, L. I., Lotka, A. J., and Spiegelman, M.: Length of life. Ronald Press Co., New York, 1949.
3. Daric, J.: Mortality, occupation, and socio-economic status. Vital Statistics — Special Reports, Selected Studies, vol. 33, No. 10, Sept. 21, 1951, pp. 175–187.

4. Logan, W. P. D.: Social class variations in mortality. Pub. Health Rep. 69: 1217–1223, December 1954.
5. Dublin, L. I.: Causes of death by occupation. U.S. Bureau of Labor Statistics Bulletin 207. U.S. Government Printing Office, Washington, D. C., 1917.
6. U.S. Bureau of the Census: Eleventh census of the United States, 1890. Vol. IV. Report on vital and social statistics in the United States, part 1. Analysis and rate tables. U.S. Government Printing Office, Washington, D. C., 1896.
7. U.S. Bureau of the Census: Twelfth census of the United States, 1900. Vol. III. Vital statistics, part 1. Analysis and ratio tables. U.S. Government Printing Office, Washington, D. C., 1902.
8. Whitney, J. S.: Death rates by occupation. National Tuberculosis Association, New York, 1934.
9. Edwards, A. M.: A social-economic grouping of the United States. J. Am. Statist. A. 28: 377–387, December 1933.
10. Moriyama, I. M., and Guralnick, L.: Occupational and social class differences in mortality. *In* Trends and differentials in mortality. Milbank Memorial Fund, New York, 1955, pp. 61–73.
11. Steiner, P. O., and Dorfman, R.: The economic status of the aged. University of California Press, Berkeley and Los Angeles, 1957, p. 34.
12. Kaplan, D. L., Parkhurst, E., and Whelpton, P. K.: The comparability of reports on occupation from vital records and the 1950 census. Vital Statistics — Special Reports, vol. 53, No. 1, June 1961, pp. 1–44.
13. Sydenstricker, E.: Economic status and the incidence of illness. Pub. Health Rep. 44: 1821–1833, July 26, 1929.
14. Collins, S. D., and Perrott, G. St.J.: The economic depression and sickness. J. Am. Statist. A. 29 (Supplement): 47–51, March 1934.
15. Britten, R. H., Collins, S. D., and Fitzgerald, J. S.: Some general findings as to disease, accidents, and impairments in urban areas. Pub. Health Rep. 55: 447–470, Mar. 15, 1940.
16. Britten, R. H., and Hailman, D.: Accidents in the urban environment as recorded in the National Health Survey. Pub. Health Rep. 55: 2061–2086, Nov. 8, 1940
17. Board, L. M.: The home environment and accidents. Pub. Health Rep. 64: 383–387, Mar. 25, 1949.
18. Britten, R. H.: Illness and accidents among persons living under different urban housing conditions. Pub. Health Rep. 56: 609–640, Mar. 28, 1941.
19. Britten, R. H.: The National Health Survey: Receipt of medical services in different urban population groups. Pub. Health Rep. 55: 2199–2224, Nov. 29, 1940.
20. U.S. National Health Survey: Persons injured by class of accident: United States, July 1957–June 1958. PHS Publication No. 584–B8. U.S. Government Printing Office, Washington, D. C., February 1959.
21. U.S. National Health Survey: Disability days; United States, July 1957–June 1958. PHS Publication No. 584–B10. U.S. Government Printing Office, Washington, D. C., May 1959.
22. Pennell, E. H.: Existence and use of hospital facilities among the several States in relation to wealth as expressed by per capita income. Pub. Health Rep. 55: 822–846, May 10, 1940.
23. Dorn, H. F.: Mortality rates and economic status in rural areas. Pub. Health Rep. 55: 3–12, Jan. 5, 1940.
24. Altenderfer, M. E.: Relationship between per capita income and mortality in the cities of 100,000 or more population. Pub. Health Rep. 62: 1681–1691, Nov. 28, 1947.
25. Altenderfer, M. E., and Crowther, B.: Relationship between infant mortality and socio-economic factors in urban areas. Pub. Health Rep. 64: 331–339, Mar. 18, 1949.
26. U.S. Bureau of the Census: Census tract manual. Ed. 4. U.S. Government Printing Office, Washington, D. C., 1959, p. 1.
27. Coulter, E. J., and Guralnick, L.: Analysis of vital statistics by census tract. J. Am. Statist. A. 54: 730–740, December 1959.
28. Allen, F. P.: A study of mortality in Cincinnati by census tracts for the period 1929–1931. Public Health Federation, Cincinnati, 1935.
29. Allen, F. P.: We pay with our lives. Public Health Federation, Cincinnati, 1948.
30. Allen, F. P.: People of the shadows. Public Health Federation, Cincinnati, 1954.
31. Mayer, A. J., and Hauser, P.: Class differentials in expectation of life at birth. *In* Class, status and power, edited by R. Bendix and S. M. Lipset. Free Press, Glencoe, Ill., 1953, pp. 281–284.
32. Sheps, C., and Watkins, J. H.: Mortality in the socioeconomic districts of New Haven. Yale J. Biol. & Med. 20: 51–80, October 1947.
33. Yeracaris, C. A.: Differential mortality, general and cause-specific in Buffalo, 1939–1941. J. Am. Statist. A. 50: 1235–1247, December 1955.
34. Ellis, J. M.: Mortality in Houston, Texas, 1949–1951; a study of socio-economic differentials. Ph.D. dissertation, University of Texas, Department of Sociology, Austin, 1956.
35. Lawrence, P. S.: Chronic illness and socio-economic status. Pub. Health Rep. 63: 1507–1521, Nov. 19, 1948.
36. Graham, S.: Socio-economic status, illness, and the use of medical services. Milbank Memorial Fund Quart. 35: 58–66, January 1957.

37. Willie, C. V.: A research note on the changing association between infant mortality and socio-economic status. Social Forces 37: 221–227, March 1959.
38. Stockwell, E. G.: Infant mortality and socio-economic status; a changing relationship. Milbank Memorial Fund Quart. To be published.
39. Ellis, J. M.: Socio-economic differentials in mortality from chronic diseases. Social Problems 5: 30–56, July 1957.
40. Stockwell, E. G.: Socio-economic mortality differentials in Hartford, Connecticut, and Providence, Rhode Island, 1949–1951; a methodological critique. Ph.D. dissertation, Brown University, Dept. of Sociology and Anthropology, Providence, R. I., 1960.
41. Hauser, P. M., and Kitagawa, E. M.: Social and economic mortality differentials in the United States, 1960; outline of a research project. *In* Proceedings of the Social Statistics Section, 1960. American Statistical Association, Washington, D. C., 1961, pp. 116–120.

*Measuring Health Levels in the United States, 1900–1958**

ODIN W. ANDERSON • MONROE LERNER

There have been dramatic improvements in the level of health since 1900 in the United States and throughout the Western world. A problem for research is to determine the causes of these improvements, their extent and distribution in the population, and their consequences for society. An additional and related problem is to find more precise ways of measuring the level of health.

The index of health levels most commonly used throughout medical history has been the mortality rate, but even with various refinements, this measure is no longer as suitable as formerly, particularly when it is employed as the only measure. Today mortality rates are best supplemented by morbidity (illness and disability) rates, and the result is a far more accurate picture of health levels.

Statistics on mortality and its causes, and changes in these measures over time, are available for many nations, and a large body of these data are published annually in the *United Nations Demographic Yearbook*. For the United States, extensive mortality data are available on an annual basis for a Death Registration Area since 1900 and for the entire nation since 1933, with many items tabulated by state and often by smaller administrative unit. Health Information Foundation has made extensive, systematic use of these data to interpret health trends, especially in its monthly publication *Progress in Health Services*.

In contrast to mortality, United States morbidity statistics, except for a few reportable communicable diseases accounting for only a small portion of the total amount of illness, have been collected only at irregular intervals and usually for populations representing somewhat less than the entire nation. However, illness and disability statistics were compiled from five separate household surveys between 1928 and 1943 and published in several Public Health Monographs.[1] Although not intended to represent a nationwide

* Reprinted with permission from *Health Information Foundation Research Series,* No. 11 (1960), pp. 3-8 and 32-37.

[1] S. D. Collins et al, *Public Health Monographs,* Nos. 25, 30, 31, 38 and 48, Washington, D. C., various dates. The surveys included were: Committee on the Costs of Medical Care, 1928-31, families observed a full year and families observed for part of a year (separate studies); Syracuse, New York, 1930-31; Cattaraugus County, New York, 1929-32; and Baltimore, Maryland, 1938-43.

sample, these data have been used to approximate the experience of the country as a whole for the 1930's. (A National Health Survey was conducted in 1935-36, but because of methodological differences its data are rarely used today for comparative purposes.) Similar data are currently being collected (beginning in 1957) from a national sample of the civilian non-institutional population of the United States by the National Health Survey of the U.S. Public Health Service. Also, Health Information Foundation has initiated a series of comparative analyses of these two sets of data to measure trends in illness over time, thus attempting to illuminate this additional dimension of health progress.

Because death is a clearly defined event and has important legal aspects, mortality registration has been fairly widespread and of long standing in many nations. The resulting statistical data have been very useful as one index of health levels. This is especially true where the numbers of deaths have been related to the size of population, so that mortality rates can be computed, and where the characteristics of deceased persons and the causes of death were known.

Among these characteristics, the more important have been age, sex, place of residence, color or ethnic group, and occupation. Use of specific death rates for age and for sex, for example, have made it possible to construct refined measures, e.g., adjusted death rates and life tables giving average life expectancy. Infant and maternal mortality rates have also been valuable, making it possible to contrast deaths associated with childbirth (for both mothers and infants) with the number of live births.

Mortality rates, however, were far more accurate indexes of health levels at earlier stages in the development of modern sanitation, public health and medical knowledge. At that time communicable diseases constituted the major causes of death and their impact was felt heavily among infants and the younger age groups. Case-fatality rates for most illnesses, especially the communicable, were far higher than today, so that illness and mortality patterns were more closely related. In other words, for some disease categories it was certain that the ill would die.

Today a far smaller proportion of illness results in death. Health is now thought of as more of a multi-dimensional concept,[2] and mortality rates — however refined, but representing nevertheless only the extreme termination of ill-health — have consequently sharp limitations as indicators of health levels. One of these is that changes in mortality rates and health levels (in multi-dimensional terms) are no longer as closely linked.

For example, it became relatively common during and after World War II to introduce simple public health measures to areas of poor sanitation in foreign countries — measures such as the spraying of insecticides, regulation of garbage disposal, and the establishment of community water resources. Mortality rates dropped sharply, in some areas by as much as 50 per cent. Yet the resulting level of health in these areas was by no means twice as high as before. Many diseases which usually cause severe disability or impairment but not death, remained endemic and widespread. An example of this in the Near East is trachoma, an illness which causes blindness but is not immeditately fatal.

Another discrepancy between changes in mortality and health levels has been found in the Western nations in recent years. Mortality rates in some instances have reached a plateau at very low levels and further decline has come very slowly or not at all. Some question exists as to whether overall mortality rates can drop much lower than they now are without a major breakthrough against heart disease or cancer. Yet there is little doubt that the health of Western populations is improving steadily. Advances are constantly made on many fronts, for example the polio vaccine, improvements in surgical techniques, a whole variety of new drugs and medications, fluoridation of water supplies, advances in radiological health and many others. Such advances, however, rarely have an appreciable impact on mortality rates.

Obviously, mortality rates alone are no longer sufficiently sensitive to indicate more than the grossest differences in health levels. This becomes more and more evident as increasingly larger proportions of all deaths take place at the older ages and are caused by the degenerative

[2] The World Health Organization defines health as follows: "Health is a state of complete physical, mental and social well-being and not merely the absence of disease or infirmity."

diseases, the diseases associated with the aging process. Nevertheless, the collection of mortality data must be continued and extended, especially because of their value for comparative purposes and as fundamental frames of reference, and because they can be further refined with the introduction of new variables such as body build and physical type, family history of mortality and illness, personal history of illness, income, occupation, marital history and many others. And they can be especially valuable if used in conjunction with data on illness and impairments.

Except for the reportable communicable diseases,[3] illness and impairment data are far more difficult and expensive to obtain. They pose complicated methodological problems, involving definitions of illness, disability and impairments, factors of memory and recall, and many others. In addition, even once obtained, they must be interpreted with special care because of at least these basic peculiarities:

(1) Decline of the death rate implies survival of greater numbers with illness and impairment. In this sense a higher reported frequency at least of some illnesses, or extended duration for some chronic disorders, may not mean a less healthy society;

(2) Illness has a social as well as a physiological component. Among some populations (e.g., the U.S. today) the level of health consciousness is high and individuals recognize and seek treatment more readily than in former years for minor conditions. At the same time, the penalties of illness and disability (loss of income, job, etc.) in such societies may not be as high as they once were, or the individual may be better protected against them. Under these circumstances, too, a higher frequency of reported illness than in former years may not necessarily mean a less healthy society.

[3] The most frequently reported communicable diseases in the United States today in their order of frequency are measles, scarlet fever and streptococcal sore throat, gonorrhea, syphilis, tuberculosis, whooping cough, infectious and serum hepatitis, bacillary dysentery, typhoid and paratyphoid fever, poliomyelitis, and amebiasis.

Among the many possible ways of collecting these statistics — through household surveys, physicians' records, hospital records, insurance claims, workmen's compensation records and others — all have advantages and drawbacks. For an overall national picture the current method of choice is the household survey technique, especially as employed by the National Health Survey of the U.S. Public Health Service.

This survey today is providing, for the first time in this country, nationwide data on illness, disability, impairments, hospital admissions, use of medical and dental services, and many other items as families and individuals report them. It gives a much clearer picture of many aspects of our national health than has ever been available in the past.

In addition, a recent study group of the World Health Organization suggested a search for new indicators of health in these fields: (a) morbidity, (b) nutrition, (c) mental health, (d) environmental sanitation, (e) health services, and (f) socio-economic conditions.[4] However, the group recognized that there were inherent difficulties in obtaining such data in those countries where statistics and research facilities are scarce.

FACTORS ASSOCIATED WITH CHANGES IN HEALTH

Levels of health, as expressed in patterns of mortality and morbidity, are roughly associated with the level of arts and sciences in a given society and with the habits and beliefs of its population. However, the correlation is by no means perfect, and specific diseases, especially the infectious and parasitic diseases, seem to behave erratically. They appear and disappear and rise and fall at different times and places. While much of this variation results from man's endeavor to control his environment, it also stems from reasons apparently unrelated to purposive human effort and having to do perhaps with the ecological balance of nature or in response to change in the biological environment.

Thus, leprosy appeared and disappeared in Europe in seeming independence of conscious

[4] World Health Organization, "Measurement of Levels of Health," *Technical Report Series,* No. 137, Geneva, 1957.

human efforts to control it. Typhus also appeared and disappeared, although its disappearance was probably related to a specific control measure which brought increased cleanliness and the extermination of body lice. The epidemic diseases prevalent in modern times — smallpox, diphtheria, measles, typhoid, tuberculosis, syphilis and others — were declining as causes of death before modern vaccination and environmental sanitation methods were perfected, possibly in response to slowly improving standards of living, but their decline was greatly accelerated after modern scientific methods were applied.

Research today seeks to determine direct cause-effect relations between changes in health levels and social and medical factors. But it is apparent that prior to the modern era of antibiotics and other life-saving drugs, this could be done only in rare and exceptional instances. Examples of these are the elimination in the late 18th and early 19th centuries of scurvy aboard ships by the use of lemon and lime juice (Vitamin C) and the reduction of smallpox following Jenner's discovery. Later examples are the elimination of pellagra in the southern region of the U.S. because of improved diet, the control of diabetes with insulin, diphtheria with antitoxin, and many others. Generally, however, the establishment of cause-effect relationships in these instances was possible only because of the gross nature of the changes involved.

Today research is attempting to define much more subtle instances of cause-effect relationships. In this area, primarily three methods are used. One of these — most suitable for studying changes of major magnitude — examines changes over time in mortality rates and in causes of death in specific populations (countries, states, cities, etc.) and also compares these indexes at a point in time in populations at varying stages of social, economic, and technological development. Such research finds, for example, that in Egypt the leading causes of death today are generally similar to those in the U.S. at the turn of the century. But also, upper-class Egyptians whose living conditions more nearly resemble those of the U.S., die of the same diseases as do most Americans, while lower-class Egyptians living under conditions possibly never seen in this country, die of diseases that are exceedingly rare here. These statements point up the relationship between health levels, as manifested in the patterns of disease and death, and the general level of development.

Another method, known as epidemiological research, consists of both extensive and intensive — long-term and short-term — studies of the distribution of specific diseases in a population. This method reveals most readily those changes in health that are perhaps less than global in scope and relates them to measurable modifications in the environment, including the introduction of specific control measures.

A third method uses laboratory and clinical techniques and tests both preventive and therapeutic measures in controlled situations. Each of these methods complements the others, and for a full understanding of the cause of changes in health levels all should be used.

Health Information Foundation, through its monthly bulletin *Progress in Health Services,* has conducted a large volume of research using the first two methods. But it has also surveyed extensively the results of the third — laboratory and clinical techniques — and incorporated these results in the analysis wherever they are relevant. Each bulletin, therefore, represents a synthesis of all three methods, a synthesis necessary for fullest understanding. In the following pages, changes in health levels in the United States are summarized, especially as these changes have been analyzed in *Progress in Health Services.*[5]

Shifting Patterns of Illness

While progress against the major communicable diseases as leading causes of death has been clearly evident, tremendous progress also has been made in reducing the amount of illness from some of the same communicable diseases and others that relatively seldom result in death. An additional change which has taken place is that the case-fatality rates from some of these diseases are today far lower than they once were.

Some of the most severe diseases have virtually disappeared today. For example, in the Collins surveys during the 1930's, 31 acute dis-

[5] Wherever more recent data were readily available, previously published statistics have been updated in this report.

abling cases of smallpox were recorded per 100,000 population. If this rate were in effect today, over 50,000 cases would occur annually. Actually, during the five-year period of 1954-58 only a total of 12 cases of this disease were reported in the entire U.S., and even these cases did not fulfill the generally accepted criteria for a diagnosis of smallpox.[6]

Similarly, for whooping cough (pertussis), once far more prevalent and serious than today, the rate in the Collins surveys, 893 per 100,000, would now result in 1,500,000 cases annually, but during 1958 only 32,150 cases were reported in the U.S. Other infectious-parasitic diseases for which similar statements hold true, and where comparative data are available, include at least these: typhoid fever, diphtheria, measles, scarlet fever, malaria, and undulant fever.

But also, many very serious disease entities today are far more amenable to treatment than formerly, and as a result, their case-fatality rates are far lower. Fatality rates in the U.S. from scarlet fever and streptococcal sore throat declined from 10 deaths per 1,000 reported cases in 1935 to one in 1957. For whooping cough the comparable decline was from 26 to 6.[7]

The dangers of venereal diseases, too, one of the world's major health problems for centuries, are now being greatly diminished, as a result of effective methods of treatment and the establishment of vigorous control and educational programs. The annual numbers of reported cases of syphilis and gonorrhea have been reduced sharply since the use of penicillin therapy. Thus, reported cases of syphilis dropped from 447 per 100,000 in fiscal 1943 to 69 in 1959.[8] The comparable figures for reported cases of gonorrhea

[6] U. S. National Office of Vital Statistics, *Morbidity and Mortality Annual Report,* Annual Supplement for 1958, Vol. 7, No. 54, Oct. 30, 1959.

[7] Computed from various reports by the U. S. Public Health Service.

[8] Health Information Foundation, "Control of Venereal Disease," *Progress in Health Services,* Vol. VIII, No. 9, November 1959.

TABLE 1

Maternal and Infant Except Early Neonatal Mortality Rates***
Five-year Averages of Annual Rates and Per cent Declines from Preceding Period
United States 1930–34 to 1955–58

	Mortality Rates		Per Cent Decline From Preceding Period	
Years	Maternal	Infant except early neonatal	Maternal	Infant except early neonatal
1930–34	63.6	33.9	—	—
1935–39	49.6	28.5	22.0	15.9
1940–44	28.5	21.3	42.5	25.3
1945–49	14.3	14.2	49.8	33.3
1950–54	7.4	10.8	48.3	23.9
1955–58†	4.6	9.7	37.8	10.2
1930–34 to 1955–58†			92.8	71.4

* "Infant except early neonatal" refers to the period of life extending from one week to one year.

** Maternal deaths per 10,000 live births and infant except early neonatal deaths per 1,000 live births. Maternal deaths since 1949 are adjusted to the Fifth Revision of the International List of Diseases and Causes of Death.

† Average of four-year period.

were 284 per 100,000 in 1947 and 137 in 1959.

Poliomyelitis in its epidemic form has been a late-comer on the morbidity scene in this country. In many ways it was a by-product of this century's higher living standards and progress in public health and sanitation. Until recently this disease was a widespread and constantly increasing danger, and little could be done to control it. But medical progress, culminating in the Salk vaccine, reduced this disease to its lowest levels in many years.[9] The rise in number of cases which took place in 1958 and 1959 has been generally attributed to the failure of many individuals to avail themselves of the benefits of the vaccine.

Even against the communicable diseases, where some of the greatest progress has been made, major efforts are still oriented toward control. Prevention of these diseases is still far from an accomplished fact. The recent Asian influenza epidemic and the rise in the incidence of respiratory conditions and other illnesses document this statement. To put it another way, even though many diseases have changed in character, they are more readily cured than formerly because of medical progress, new medications, etc., and the amount of disability they cause is therefore less. However, although some of the more severe illnesses have disappeared completely, others remain. Comparison of the National Health Survey data for 1957–58 with the Collins surveys suggests the possibility of an actual increase in the volume of acute disabling illness.[10]

The Effects on Society of Improved Health

Improvements in the level of health have resulted in many drastic changes in our society. Most of these are without doubt on the plus side, yet many also have created new and complex problems, difficult to solve. Nevertheless the major goal, improved health for the entire population, remains the same.

One striking change has been the substantial increase in life expectancy and survivorship. From 47 years in 1900 our average expectancy of life at birth increased to 69.5 years in 1958.[11] The increases in this country have parallelled those of other advanced (in the public health sense) nations.[12] Further sizable increases in life expectancy today depend on breakthroughs against the complex cardiovascular-renal diseases, cancer, and accidents.

As a corollary to increased life expectancy, the proportion of aged persons in our population has risen.[13] In turn, the problem of maintaining these individuals and of providing them with the requisite and necessary medical care looms as far more important than ever before.[14]

The American family has benefited greatly from improvements in health.[15] The decline in mortality, especially at the younger and middle ages, has increased average lifetime for the family unit as well as for each member. Thus, the dissolution of marriage by the death of one partner, especially at a young age, is less common than it once was. In 1900, 27.4 marriages in every 1,000 ended each year in the death of one spouse. By 1957 the rate had dropped to 16.6 per 1,000 or by about 40 per cent. Currently about 750,000 marriages are broken by the death of a husband or a wife each year. At 1900 rates an additional 400,000 would be dissolving annually.

Furthermore, marital dissolutions by death now occur at much older ages on the average, and after many more years of married life. The average individual today has a much greater chance of surviving to see his children past their dependency period. Widowhood has been largely

[9] Health Information Foundation, "The Changing Status of Polio," *Progress in Health Services,* Vol. VIII, No. 3, March 1959.

[10] Health Information Foundation, "Acute Illness in Two Surveys," *Progress in Health Services,* Vol. VIII, No. 10, December 1959.

[11] Health Information Foundation, "Increasing Life Expectancy at Birth," *Progress in Health Services,* Vol. V, No. 4, April 1956, and "Adding to Length of Life," *Progress in Health Services,* Vol. V, No. 5, May 1956.

[12] Health Information Foundation, "Health Levels in Four Advanced Nations," *Progress in Health Services,* Vol. VIII, No. 7, September 1959.

[13] Health Information Foundation, "Our Aging Population," *Progress in Health Services,* Vol. V, No. 6, June 1956.

[14] Health Information Foundation, "Voluntary Health Insurance Among the Aged," *Progress in Health Services,* Vol. VIII, No. 4, April 1959.

[15] Health Information Foundation, "Health and the Changing Family," *Progress in Health Services,* Vol. VII, No. 7, September 1958.

postponed to a period of life when responsibility for minor children is not as great. And even more striking, orphanhood is fast diminishing as a social problem even though these children, as all others, have a greatly improved chance of reaching adulthood.

By the same token, the person who begins his formal education (usually at ages 5 or 6 in this country) has a much better chance of surviving through the school years. Length of working life, too, has increased, so that the person entering the labor force has a far better chance than formerly to reach retirement age, and once retired, to enjoy many more years of leisure. The worklife expectancy for men increased from 32 years in 1900 to 42 in 1955.

Another consequence of increased survivorship, at least in part, is that many individuals who would formerly have died from severe illnesses, may today be living, although in somewhat less than perfect health. The load of illness, both acute disabling and chronic, may be somewhat larger than formerly. Partly in response to this, the use of physicians' services has increased.[16] Whereas 25 years ago the average individual may have made about 2.5 doctor visits annually, today the average is more likely to be about 5. Most of these visits are made to the family physician, still a key figure in medical practice.[17]

Similarly, hospital admissions and average annual days of use per person have also increased.[18] Admission rates to general hospitals in the United States increased from 56.7 per 1,000 population in 1928-43 (Collins' surveys) to 99.4 in 1956-58 (National Health Survey), or by 75 per cent. Hospital utilization increased from 712 to 851 annual patient-days per 1,000 population, or by 20 per cent. Much of the increase resulted from the growth in hospitalization for deliveries and related conditions, but even without that category the rise in admissions and utilization was impressive. Nearly all categories of diagnostic conditions shared in the increase, but again for nearly all diagnoses, the average duration of stay per admission declined. For all diagnoses combined, the average duration of stay dropped from 12.6 days per admission to 8.6, or by about one-third.

These changes in health levels and the resulting changes in hospital use have transformed the general hospital in this country.[19] Today each bed in general hospitals is used for the treatment of a larger number of patients annually. This is made possible by the decreased average length of stay per patient, but also by larger average occupancy ratios. Nevertheless, over the years our investment in hospitals in this country has grown considerably.[20] As a result, the number of beds in hospitals has increased by a substantial quantity,[21] and their distribution throughout the country has been altered radically.[22]

Since despite the improved levels of health in the United States there is likely to be an increased load of illness and disability, Americans use more health services than formerly and consequently spend more money on their health than they ever did.[23] Thus in 1929 Americans disbursed almost $3 billion as aggregate personal consumption expenditures for medical care, but by 1957 the total had reached $15 billion.

[16] Health Information Foundation, "The Increased Use of Medical Care," *Progress in Health Services,* Vol. VII, No. 8, October 1958.

[17] Health Information Foundation, "A View of Our Family Physicians," *Progress in Health Services,* Vol. VII, No. 6, June 1958.

[18] Health Information Foundation, "The Changing Pattern of Hospital Use," *Progress in Health Services,* Vol. VII, No. 5, May 1958, and "Trends in Use of General Hospitals," *Progress in Health Services,* Vol. VIII, No. 8, October 1959.

[19] Health Information Foundation, "The General Hospital in Transition," *Progress in Health Services,* Vol. VI, No. 7, September 1957.

[20] Health Information Foundation, "Our Growing Investment in Hospitals," *Progress in Health Services,* Vol. VII, No. 3, March 1958.

[21] Health Information Foundation, "The Growth of American Hospital Facilities," *Progress in Health Services,* Vol. V, No. 8, October 1956.

[22] Health Information Foundation, "The Distribution of American Hospital Facilities," *Progress in Health Services,* Vol. V, No. 10, December 1956.

[23] Health Information Foundation, "What Americans Spend for Personal Health Services," *Progress in Health Services,* Vol. V, No. 7, September 1956, and "Consumer Spending for Medical Care," *Progress in Health Services,* Vol. VII, No. 10, December 1958.

STUDY AND DISCUSSION QUESTIONS

1. Using vital statistics sources, compare the death rate in your community with the death rate in another community in your state without making any adjustments in the figures. From census reports, compare the age distributions of the two communities. How much do you think comparison of the death rates is affected by differences in the age distributions?
2. Using one of the books on population methods referred to at the end of Chapter 1, construct a current life table (abridged) for the United States population. What uses does such a life table have? What kinds of questions does it answer?
3. If you were to make a study of the sex differential in mortality, how would you design your study? What kinds of factors would you control? Can you think of ways to improve on Madigan's study?
4. Historically, the infant mortality rate has been a good index of socioeconomic levels and conditions in a nation. But recently this rate seems to be less sensitive to socioeconomic conditions in a country. What reasons for this change can you give?
5. As a special research project, look up what has happened to the mortality rate in Ceylon during the past fifty years. What are the sociological implications of the Ceylonese pattern? How would such a mortality pattern affect other population components?
6. What would you expect the United States death rate to be fifty years from now, barring nuclear holocaust? If the death rate comes down further, in what areas are improvements likely to be made?
7. We have discussed three types of factors (individual, group, and institutional) which affect a society's mortality rates. Construct a middle-range or small-scale theory of mortality incorporating these factors and fulfllling the two purposes of theory, at least to some extent, mentioned in the previous chapter.

SUGGESTED ADDITIONAL READING

Dublin, Louis I., Alfred J. Lotka, and Mortimer Spiegelman. *Length of Life: a Study of the Life Table*, rev. ed. New York: The Ronald Press Company, 1949.
A classic analysis and interpretation of the progress in health and mortality over time, with emphasis on the life table and on social and scientific influences that have brought about this progress.

Lerner, Monroe and Odin W. Anderson. *Health Progress in the United States, 1900–1960.* Chicago: University of Chicago Press, 1963.
Examines the causes of death and the state of health of the population, with implications for mortality trends and differentials.

United Nations. *Population Bulletin of the United Nations, No. 6.* New York: United Nations, 1962.
Surveys the situation and recent trends of mortality in the world.

U.S. National Center for Health Statistics. *Vital and Health Statistics.* Published irregularly.
Series 3 and 20 of these reports include data on mortality patterns, and Series 10, 11, and 12 discuss results of the National Health Survey.

CHAPTER 4

Fertility Trends and Differentials: The World Situation

It is perhaps ironic that the greatest part of the world's "population explosion" has resulted from the control societies have obtained over death. Yet the fact remains that large population increases in most nations have taken place during the decline of mortality while fertility remained relatively high. From a value standpoint, the downward trend in mortality is irreversible; the crux of the world population problem seems, therefore, to be the course of fertility. Unless the death rate is to take an upward turn, stabilization of the world population level must come about through a decline in fertility.

In Western societies, which have generally followed the model of the demographic transition, fertility declined significantly over a century or more. In most of the developing nations of the world, fertility has declined very little from its highest recorded level, but rapid social changes are taking place in some of these areas and the prospect of future fertility declines is problematic. As of the mid-1960's the *crude birth rate* (births per 1,000 population) was about 36 for the world as a whole. As in the case of the death rate, however, there was considerable variation between and within continents.

The United Nations report on fertility levels and trends describes the differing patterns of fertility around the world. Both the crude birth rate and a more refined index of fertility show similar continental and national differences in fertility. The crude birth rate, for example, is estimated at about 48 in Africa and about 41 in Asia and in Latin America, compared with 24 in North America and Oceania and 19 in Europe. Within continents, one finds a range from the mid-30's in Gabon to roughly 60 in Mali within Africa, and from 13 in Hungary to 38 in Albania within Europe.

Even within nations, as was observed about mortality, the level of fertility varies among different population subgroups. One of the more theoretically important differentials concerns social class, since demographic transition theory supposes that the eventual downward course of fertility comes about through the transmission of knowledge about fertility control from the upper to the lower classes. It is hypothesized that the upper classes first adopt and successfully use methods of family limitation and that later these methods filter down to the middle and lower classes. That social class differentials in fertility do exist and that they are found in developing as well as developed societies is shown in the article on class differences in fertility in Peru by Stycos.

The United Nations selection outlines some of the broad factors related to levels and trends of fertility. Mentioned are economic and social trends, density of population, and ecological, cultural, and legal factors. Davis and Blake have attempted to formalize some of these factors in a sociological framework. In trying to account for gross differences in fertility between the advanced and developing countries of the world, they outline the "intermediate variables" (factors affecting exposure to intercourse and to conception and those affecting gestation and successful parturition) through which other social forces influencing fertility levels must operate. Moreover, they indicate the way the particular type of social organization found in a society acts through the intermediate variables to change fertility. Their analysis points up the importance of social structure in helping to shape the fertility patterns of a society.

While Davis and Blake articulate the forms of fertility control and the broad institutional mechanisms which regulate these controls in different societies, they do not elaborate the cultural bases for these controls and mechanisms. Therefore the article by Freedman is a useful companion piece, in that it discusses the nature of cultural norms related to family size and how they support high fertility in developing areas. It is clearly brought out that controls on fertility are available in all societies and that it is primarily the cultural prescriptions and proscriptions regarding sexual practices and conception which are placed on individuals and couples by a society, or a segment of the society, that ultimately determine the course of the birth rate. In developing countries, these values and norms tend to center around two themes: the need to have many children to (a) affect the loss of some of them through death in early life, and (b) maintain strong kinship ties in community life. Thus, enough children must be born to insure that infant and other premature deaths will not deprive a family of the members it needs to survive and to carry out its desired functions.

The source of values related to fertility may be found in any of the several social institutional networks that structure the society. While fertility values are often considered in terms of their implications for the welfare of the family, their roots are generally found in traditional economic and religious institutions. The vast majority of the people in countries where fertility is high are economically deprived and their economic values sometimes dictate high fertility in order to produce more working hands. Their low social-class position also conditions them to a fatalistic attitude about ability to control family size. At the same time, values concerning fertility are imbedded in religious beliefs, and high fertility is in part a response to religious doctrine. This has been emphasized most in connection with the Roman Catholic religion, although high fertility is also found among people of other religions. Kirk concludes that the high birth rate in Moslem countries is due not only to religious doctrine but to "distinctive Islamic attitudes and practices in family life" as well.

Attempts to reduce the level of the birth rate in developing countries can be classified under two broad categories: those which emphasize the importance of developing the social and economic resources, thus changing the social class structure and thereby reducing family size, and those which stress the need for educating the people in the ways and means of family planning, thereby creating the desire for smaller families at the same time as the know-how to bring about change is introduced. This latter family-planning approach has been sustained by the knowledge obtained through surveys in many countries that most people in the underdeveloped countries want moderate-sized families rather than the large families typical of these areas. The fact remains, however, that several years of effort using one or the other or both approaches to reducing fertility in developing nations has brought about significant change in birth levels in only a few nations. Perhaps the time required to observe effects has been too short, or perhaps other approaches which get more directly at motivations for small families are required.

Like mortality, fertility can be viewed as the result of various types of behavior within a society. Although there are biological and geographical constraints on human reproduction, fertility too results from *decisions made by people*, as they are influenced by *group norms*, and from the *workings of social institutions*.

Several studies have shown that fecundity, or the physical ability to bear children, is impaired for some women, either through injury, disease, or genetic imbalance. Climate has been hypothesized by some researchers as affecting coital behavior and, hence, reproduction. Norms about ideal family size, relations between the sexes, and contraceptive behavior, which emanate from the groups to which one belongs or aspires, partly govern the fertility behavior of individuals and couples. The state of affluence in a society and governmental policies concerning birth control and abortion, on the one hand, and incentives to having many or few children, on the other, have had significant effects on fertility levels in different countries. Finally, the extent to which individuals and couples avail themselves of the knowledge of, and devices for, contraceptive behavior and plan the timing and spacing of childbearing have a profound effect on the birth rate. How fertility will change in any country will be determined by how these different types of behavior combine and how effective they are.

*Social Class and Differential Fertility in Peru**

J. MAYONE STYCOS

Theories concerning the dynamics of the fertility decline predicted in the demographic transition model are greatly handicapped by the dearth of data from countries in earlier stages of the population cycle. Previous field studies in the Caribbean by the author and his associates, while helping to furnish such data, have neglected an important theoretical component in fertility decline by focussing exclusively on lower class groups. Similar neglect of the class variable was seen in the Indianapolis study's narrow focus on a higher class group in the United States. Only recently have field studies in the Western Hemisphere been turning attention toward the full gamut of social class, and only two of these (Chile and Peru) have occurred outside the United States. The present paper is a preliminary report on certain aspects of class variation as revealed in a recent sample survey in Peru.

The sample, composed of 1995 cases from the capital city of Lima-Callao and 137 cases from a rural coastal village, is confined to currently mated Peruvian born women between the ages of 20 and 44. In the village the universe of women meeting these criteria was interviewed. In Lima 100 of the city's roughly 4500 blocks were chosen at random and a quota of 20 cases assigned to each block. Interviewers canvassed the selected blocks house to house in a systematic fashion until twenty eligible households were located. Because lower class blocks are more densely settled than upper class blocks, and because the rapidly growing slum areas were probably underrepresented in the mapping of blocks, the system probably resulted in an overrepresentation of upper class cases. Since comparisons among classes rather than description of the urban population as a whole is the major object of the study, this bias may not be serious in its consequences. Since a census has not been conducted in Peru for over two decades, no weighting, correction or evaluation of the sample is possible in any definitive fashion.

Interviews were conducted during November and December of 1960 by a staff of 40 third-year students of the Peruvian School of Social Work, under the supervision of the School's faculty.[1]

Class Groupings

In Lima, interviewers were asked to rate each household on a socio-economic scale ranging from one to four. A list of suggested criteria for distinguishing each class was given the interviewer, but emphasis was placed on her overall appraisal. The criteria were supplied by a

* Reprinted with permission from the *Proceedings of the International Population Conference, New York 1961,* Vol. II. London, 1963, pp. 123-128.

[1] The study was financed by grants from the Population Council and through the assistance of the Cornell Andean Research Program. The author expresses his appreciation to the Escuela de Servicio Social del Peru, to Dr. Cara Dobyns, the project's field director, and to Carlos Uriarte, who assisted in sampling procedures.

TABLE 1

Class Related Measures, According to Interviewers' Appraisal of Social Class

	Class I	Class II	Class III	Class IV	Class V
% of Husbands in White Collar Occupations	87	69	15	4	1
% of Wives with Less than Four Years Education	0	2	33	68	68
% of Households with Refrigerator	99	71	8	1	N.I.
% of Households with Television	85	59	9	1	N.I.
Number of Cases	(253)	(490)	(757)	(495)	(137)

Peruvian market research agency (Carlos Uriarte) which has utilized the system for a number of years in market surveys. While subsequent analyses may employ less subjective measures of class, the present paper will rely on the interviewers' evaluations.

In the urban area, 13 percent of the sample was placed in the highest class (I), 25 percent in class II, 38 percent in class III, and 25 percent in class IV. Despite some internal class differentiation, the small village sample will be treated as homogeneous and designated as class V. A notion of the makeup of the subjectively derived classes is provided in Table 1, which summarizes a number of social and economic characteristics.

A marked correlation between interviewers' evaluations and the objective measures is apparent. As regards occupation and household appliances, a very decided gap appears between classes II and III. Educational variation is more regular. Whereas 73 percent of the class I women have finished high school, for example, the median years of school for the other four classes is 9.0, 5.2, 2.9, and 2.7.

Differential Fertility

The most basic question to be answered by our survey was the extent to which differential fertility by class and residence exists. 1940 Census data revealed that rural-urban differentials (i.e., Lima-Callao compared to the rest of the nation) were minimal when measured by number of children ever born to mothers. Even assuming that a rural-urban differential exists in 1960, a more interesting question becomes the extent to which urban fertility declines are characteristic of the various social classes.

It is evident that there is an inverse relation between class and fertility, but, similar to the pattern in Table 1, differences between the two upper classes are small. Moreover, while the three highest classes are clearly limiting their fertility by some means, this may not be the case for classes IV and V. As a crude point of comparison, in 1940 the average mother aged 40-44 living outside of Lima-Callao had had only 6.1 live births according to the census. Thus in 1960 the average class IV urban wife was having one birth more than non-urban mothers had in 1940.

Perception of Differential Fertility

Presumably, an important factor in stimulating fertility control is the awareness that "others" are controlling fertility, or, at the very least, an awareness that differential fertility exists at all. In areas where fertility decline is beginning, it

TABLE 2

Live Births by Social Class

	I	II	III	IV	V
Age Standardized Mean	2.6	2.8	3.7	4.6	4.9
Class I = 100	100	108	142	177	189
Women 40–44	3.8	4.3	5.3	7.2	7.6
Class I = 100	100	113	139	189	200

TABLE 3

Perceptions of Generational Change in Fertility

	I %	II %	III %	IV %	V %
Women Had More Children Before	80	82	64	40	35
Women Have More Children Now	4	7	14	24	20
No Difference or Don't Know	16	11	22	36	45
Total	100	100	100	100	100

is possible for an individual to perceive the differential in various ways: e.g., as a *generational* phenomenon, as a *class* or *racial* phenomenon, or as a *residential* one. That is, one could perceive that contemporary couples do not have as many children as their parents, that the lower classes or the Indians have more children than the upper classes or *mestizos,* or that rural women have more children than urban.

Generational Differentiation

In response to the question "In your parents time, did women have more, less or the same number of births as now?" we see marked differences among the social classes. Eight out of every ten women in the two upper classes have observed a decline in fertility, but only a minority in the rural area and in the lowest social class have done so. If respondents are thinking largely in terms of their own social group, one could argue that the perceptions reflect the facts; i.e., that there has in fact been little decline in rural or lower class fertility. Astonishingly enough, however, one out of every four or five women in the latter groups claims to perceive an *increase* in fertility in the present generation, an assumption which is very likely erroneous.

That so few in the lower status groups see a decline in fertility is consistent with their view that average contemporary fertility is very high. When asked how many births the average woman has by age 55, the median numbers cited by the three lower classes were 10.3, 11.2, and 12.3. In the light of such a view of fertility, most women in the lower status groups would regard their own fertility as relatively low, or at the very least, not high.

Class, "Racial" and Residential Differentiation

Table 4 summarizes responses to questions asked about whether Indian, rich or country women generally have more, less or the same number of children as *mestizo,* poor and urban women. From these data it is clear that the average woman is indeed aware of contemporary differences in fertility. Economic class is the most discriminating characteristic, with nine out

TABLE 4

Perception of Differential Fertility Between "Racial," Residential, and Economic Groups

	I	II	III	IV	V
% Saying Indians have more than Mestizos	33	38	39	31	27
% Saying Poor have more than Rich	75	88	94	89	69
% Saying Rural have more than Urban	90	92	82	74	50

of every ten urban women maintaining that the poor have more children than the rich. The "racial" characteristic is the least discriminating, with 60 percent responding that there is no difference or that they do not know.

Interesting differences by status groups appear. Rich women (i.e., class I) are less likely to admit that rich women as a class have fewer children than the poor, and rural women (Class V as well as Class IV containing largely rural to urban migrants) are less likely to admit that they have more than urban women. Possibly there is a reluctance to admit that one's own group is different. This is more likely in the case of the rich women. In the case of rural women, ignorance due to lack of experience with the city is a plausible explanation.

Perception of Differential Mortality

The other side of the coin is the perception of change in mortality, since it is a popular hypothesis among demographers that awareness of infant mortality declines leads to downward revisions of desired numbers of births. To test the extent of awareness of mortality declines, we asked how many of every ten children died before reaching adulthood; and further whether in their parents' generation, more, less, or the same number of children died. The median number who die according to the village women is 3.0. City women cite higher mortality and the number varies inversely with class, rising from 3.3 among the top class to 3.8 among the bottom. Differences are more striking with respect to the question of generational difference.

The highest class generally believes a decline in mortality has occurred and the village women largely see no change; but within the city, as status declines, the belief that mortality has increased becomes dominant. In class IV, the number of women who believe that mortality has increased is 40 percent greater than the number who believe it has declined. Based on pre-test information, the most common explanation given for lower mortality a generation ago was that people lived healthier lives at that time — better food, more fresh air, lived closer to nature, etc.

Summary

A sample survey of 1995 currently mated women in the city of Lima, Peru, and 137 cases from a rural coastal village discloses marked differences in fertility by social class, ranging from completed fertility of 3.8 live births in the highest of four social classes to 7.2 in the lowest. While most women in the upper classes feel that fertility has declined in the past generation, most rural women and women of the lowest class feel that it has increased or remained the same. Further, most women have an exaggerated notion of average fertility. Differential fertility is perceived, however, more births being attributed to poor and rural women than to rich or urban women. A minority of lower class and rural women and only a small majority of upper class women believe that mortality has declined in the past generation, and a sizeable proportion feel it has increased. The belief that mortality and fertility are generally high, especially when one's own fertility tends to be lower than the presumed norm, would not seem to be the kind of psychological atmosphere conducive to controlled fertility. On the other hand, the facts of differential fertility indicate that at least three of the four urban social classes are curtailing fertility in some measure.

TABLE 5

Whether Mortality Has Declined Since Parents' Generation

	I %	II %	III %	IV %	V %
Mortality Higher Before	65	52	34	29	24
Mortality Lower Before	16	30	44	42	18
No Change or Don't Know	19	18	22	29	58
Total	100	100	100	100	100

*Conditions and Trends of Fertility in the World**

Statistical Office of the United Nations

A. Levels of Fertility

1. Scope of Data

There has been a considerable improvement during the last decade in information on fertility in the economically less developed regions of the world. Approximate values of crude birth rates and gross reproduction rates have been established for many countries, especially in Africa, where the level of fertility was previously a matter of conjecture. These new indications have been obtained in some cases by means of household sample-survey inquiries on births and deaths, while in other cases population censuses or demographic sample surveys have for the first time provided data on age structure of the population from which estimates of the fertility level could be derived. Thus it has become possible to chart previously unknown territories on the world map of fertility and to make a far more comprehensive study than was formerly possible on the variations of fertility and related factors in the less developed regions. Fertility levels in these regions are the principal concern of the present report, the United Nations having recently published a detailed analysis of fertility trends in industrialized countries.[1]

Data considered satisfactory at least as a basis for an approximate estimate of the level of the crude birth rate have been obtained for 123 countries (or other territorial units) having an estimated population of 250,000 or more in 1960. In nearly all cases it has been found possible also to estimate the gross reproduction rate (GRR). These countries contain approximately 70 per cent of the world population, including virtually all the population of Europe, the USSR, Northern America, Middle and South America and 87 per cent of that of Africa and Oceania, but only about 50 per cent of the population of Asia. The low figure for Asia is due mainly to the fact that satisfactory data are lacking for China (mainland). . . .

2. Average Levels of Fertility in Regions of the World

Fertility is about twice as high, on the average, in the developing as in the more developed regions of the world. This difference is brought out by the estimates of crude birth rates and gross reproduction rates for regions, presented in table 1. The average gross reproduction rate for the regions of Africa, Asia, Middle and South America is estimated to be about 2.7, while the average for Northern America, Europe, Oceania and the USSR is 1.4. These are weighted averages of recorded or estimated rates for countries within each region as of 1960 or the date of latest available information.[2] For the regions of Africa, Asia, and Middle and South America, there are some differences between the birth rate estimates shown in table 1 and those given in recent issues of the *Demographic Yearbook* and other United Nations publications prepared before the results of the present survey of fertility became available.

3. Distribution of Countries by Level of Fertility

The distribution of the 123 countries by estimated level of the crude birth rate is shown in table 2 for the world as a whole and each major region. The corresponding distribution by estimated level of the gross reproduction rate ap-

* Reprinted with permission from *Population Bulletin of the United Nations, No. 7-1963.* New York: United Nations, 1965, pp. 1-9.

[1] *Recent Trends in Fertility in Industrialized Countries,* United Nations publication, Sales No.: 57.XIII.2.

[2] In computing the estimate for East Asia, a range of values based on the best available information for China (mainland) was used.

TABLE 1

Estimated Crude Birth Rates and Gross Reproduction Rates for the Regions of the World

(Weighted averages of rates for 1960 or most recent dates of available data for countries within each region)

Region	Crude birth rate	Gross reproduction rate
World total	35–36[a]	2.25–2.31[a]
Developing regions	41–42[a]	2.6– 2.7[a]
Africa	48	3.0
North Africa	46	2.9
West Africa	54	3.4
South and East Africa	45	2.7
Asia (excluding USSR)	40–41[a]	2.5 –2.6[a]
South West Asia	45	3.0
South Central Asia	44	2.9
South East Asia	49	2.9
East Asia	35–37[a]	2.1 –2.3[a]
Middle and South America	41	2.8
Middle America	45	3.0
South America	40	2.7
More developed regions	22	1.4
Northern America	24	1.8
Europe	19	1.3
Northern and Western Europe	18	1.3
Central Europe	18	1.2
Southern Europe	21	1.3
Oceania	24	1.8
USSR	25	1.4

[a] Range of estimated values corresponding to alternative estimates for China (mainland).

pears in table 3 for the 122 countries for which this measure could be calculated.

The distributions for the world as a whole are strikingly bi-modal. Two groups of countries are clearly distinguished: a high-fertility group and a low-fertility group, with remarkably few countries on the borderline between them. The dividing line can be drawn at a crude birth rate of 30 per 1,000 population and a gross reproduction rate of 2.0.[3] As the two tables show, the division between the high-fertility and low-fertility groups of countries corresponds closely to the location of the countries in developing or more developed regions, respectively. The countries with birth rates above 30 and gross reproduction rates above 2.0 are found almost exclusively in Africa, Asia and Middle and South America, while countries with rates below these levels are located, with few exceptions, in the economically

[3] For countries with a GRR of 2.0 or higher, the unweighted mean rate is 2.94, while for countries with a GRR of less than 2.0 it is 1.41. The difference between the two means can be expressed as 1.53 $\pm$ 0.07, the latter value being the standard error. Since the difference between the means is more than 21 times its standard error, the two groups of countries are clearly distinct in a statistical sense, in respect of their fertility levels.

more advanced regions. The exceptions to this rule are generally countries which are not typical, in regard to their levels of economic and social development, of the regions in which they are located.

4. Differences in Fertility Levels Among Countries in Africa, Asia, Middle America and South America

The only exceptions to the rule of high fertility in Africa, Asia, Middle America and South

TABLE 2

Distribution of Countries by Level of Crude Birth Rate

(Excluding countries having fewer than 250,000 inhabitants in 1960 and those having no satisfactory data. Countries are classified according to levels of crude birth rates in 1960 or at the most recent dates of available data)

Crude Birth rate per 1,000 population	World total	Less developed regions	More developed regions	Africa	Asia (excluding USSR)	Middle and South America	Europe (excluding USSR)	Northern America	Oceania	USSR
Total.....	123	88	35	37	24	27	29	2	3	1
Under 15....	3	—	3	—	—	—	3	—	—	—
15.0-19.9....	18	1	17	—	1	—	17	—	—	—
20.0-24.9....	14	4	10	—	2	2	7	1	1	1
25.0-29.9....	4	1	3	—	1	—	1	1	1	—
30.0-34.9....	3	3	—	—	1	2	—	—	—	—
35.0-39.9....	11	11	—	3	4	4	—	—	—	—
40.0-44.9....	22	21	1	9	3	9	1	—	—	—
45.0-49.9....	29	28	1	13	7	8	—	—	1	—
50.0-54.9....	12	12	—	5	5	2	—	—	—	—
55.0-59.9....	5	5	—	5	—	—	—	—	—	—
60.0 and over	2	2	—	2	—	—	—	—	—	—

TABLE 3

Distribution of Countries by Level of Gross Reproduction rate (GRR)

(Excluding countries having fewer than 250,000 inhabitants in 1960 and those having no satisfactory data. Countries are classified according to levels of GRR in 1960 or at the most recent dates of available data)

Level of gross reproduction rate	World total	Less developed regions	More developed regions	Africa	Asia (excluding USSR)	Middle and South America	Europe (excluding USSR)	Northern America	Oceania	USSR
Total.....	122	87	35	37	24	26	29	2	3	1
Under 1.0...	1	—	1	—	—	—	1	—	—	—
1.0-1.2......	14	1	13	—	1	—	13	—	—	—
1.3-1.5......	13	2	11	—	—	2	10	—	—	1
1.6-1.9......	10	3	7	—	3	—	4	2	1	—
2.0-2.3......	7	6	1	3	—	3	—	—	1	—
2.4-2.6......	12	12	—	8	4	—	—	—	—	—
2.7-2.9......	24	24	—	9	6	9	—	—	—	—
3.0-3.2......	19	19	—	8	3	8	—	—	—	—
3.3-3.5......	20	18	2	8	7	3	1	—	1	—
3.6 and over.	2	2	—	1	—	1	—	—	—	—

America (i.e., estimated gross reproduction rates below 2.0 for countries considered in this study) are Argentina, Cyprus, Israel, Japan, the Ryukyu Islands, Uruguay and Zanzibar. Japan's gross reproduction rate in recent years has been at the level of 1.0 — one of the lowest in the world. The most recent estimated rates for Argentina, Cyprus, Israel, the Ryukyu Islands and Uruguay are in the range of 1.3 to 1.7, slightly above the average of the low-fertility group. Argentina, Israel, Japan and Uruguay are exceptions in their levels of development as well as fertility; their economic and social conditions contrast with those of their Latin American and Asian neighbours. Cyprus, the Ryukyu Islands and Zanzibar exhibit the rare combination of low fertility with a modest level of development. The influence of Greek culture doubtless has an important bearing on fertility in Cyprus, while Japanese influence is almost certainly the main factor responsible for the low present level of fertility in the Ryukyu Islands. Zanzibar, the one country in Africa with an estimated gross reproduction rate below 2.0 (1.9 for the Afro-Arab population in 1958), is a small, little-developed country with a predominantly urban population.

While all other African, Asian, Middle American and South American countries belong to the high-fertility group, the estimates show remarkable variations in degree of highness of their fertility levels.

In Africa, there seems to be a belt of exceedingly high fertility, composed of countries with gross reproduction rates estimated at 3.3 or higher, stretching across West Africa from Guinea and Mali to Niger and Nigeria. Some spots of equally high fertility appear in eastern and southern Africa, including Northern Rhodesia, Rwanda, possibly Kenya and the Sudan. As indicated [elsewhere], however, the basis for fertility estimates for some of these countries is weak. A zone of much lower fertility seems to centred in the Congo Basin; gross reproduction rates in the relatively moderate range of 2.1 to 2.4 are indicated for Congo (Leopoldville), Gabon, Cameroon and Central African Republic. Rates far below the African regional average are estimated also for Basutoland, Madagascar and Portuguese Guinea, as well as Zanzibar.

For certain countries in Asia, estimated fertility levels are considerably higher than the average for the region in which they are located. The Republic of Korea is outstanding in this respect in East Asia, while for a group of countries in the south-east, including the Philippines, North Borneo, Sarawak, Cambodia and Thailand, estimated gross reproduction rates of 3.2 and above are found. Singapore also belonged to this group in the early 1950's, but fertility in Singapore has dropped in the last few years to a more moderate level. Pakistan seems to have an exceptionally high fertility rate for the south central region. In the south-west, estimates for Iraq and Jordan are well above the regional average, and Iran also seems to be somewhat higher. A zone of more moderate fertility is located in South Central Asia, including India, Nepal, Burma and Ceylon, with estimated gross reproduction rates in the range of 2.5 to 2.7. If the estimate for China (mainland) is at all indicative, the average level of fertility in that country also is no more than moderately high. The dubious figure for the mainland, together with the much more reliable statistics of China (Taiwan), Hong Kong and now Singapore, suggest the definition of a Chinese cultural zone of relatively moderate fertility, gross reproduction rates not exceeding 2.8.

In Latin America, the area of generally highest fertility seems to be the Middle American mainland; gross reproduction rates at the exceedingly high level of 3.3 or more are estimated for Costa Rica, El Salvador, Guatemala and Honduras, and the rates for Mexico and Nicaragua appear only slightly lower. Panama is the only country in this area with an estimated rate below 3.0 for recent years. Brazil and the other principal countries of tropical South America make up a subregion of almost equally high fertility.

Countries of only moderately high fertility are found in two zones of Middle and South America: the Caribbean area and the temperate zone of South America. Gross reproduction rates in the relatively low range of 2.1 to 2.3 are estimated for Chile, Cuba and Puerto Rico — countries which stand near the borderline, in respect of economic and social conditions, between the developing and more developed groups. Rates in the range of 2.7 to 2.8 are estimated for the principal French and former British West Indies islands (Guadeloupe, Jamaica, Martinique and Trinidad) and for Haiti. In the Caribbean area, only the Dominican Republic appears to have exceptionally high fertility; the estimated gross reproduction rate of 3.2 for this country contrasts with the more moderate estimate of 2.8 for Haiti, sharing the same island; but the estimates for both these countries are based on weak statistics of population by age groups. Paraguay, the least developed country in temperate South America, also has the highest estimated gross reproduction rate in that area (2.9 for 1940–1945).

The differences in levels of fertility among developing countries have not received enough attention in demographic studies. The wide differences indicated by present information are highly significant for assessing future prospects for population growth and studying the determinants of fertility in countries where it is high. In general, little is yet known of the factors responsible for the differences of fertility among these countries. In some cases, they may be explained partly by errors of estimation or lack of up-to-date information. The present basis for estimates of the fertility level is weak in many cases, particularly for countries in Africa. It should be a priority task of demographic data-collection to fill the remaining gaps in data on the levels of fertility, to strengthen the basis for estimates where it is now weak, and to obtain necessary material for studying factors related to the fertility differences among the developing countries. Intensive field studies and analysis of existing data pertaining to such factors deserve high priority in programmes of research on the demography of these countries.

5. *Differences of Fertility Levels among Countries in Europe, Northern America, Oceania and the USSR*

The only country of high fertility in Europe at present is Albania, with a gross reproduction rate calculated at 3.4 for 1960. Albania is also an exception to the generally high position of the European countries on the world-wide scale of economic and social development. The remainder of Europe constitutes a relatively homogeneous region of quite low fertility, as 24 of the 29 European countries considered in the present study have gross reproduction rates of 1.5 or lower according to data for 1960. The Soviet Union, with an estimated gross reproduction rate of 1.4, can be considered as an eastward extension of this low-fertility region.

The principal countries of European settlement in Northern America and Oceania (Canada, the United States, Australia and New Zealand), and also Israel, belong to a group of not quite so low fertility, their gross reproduction rates being in the range from 1.7 to 2.0. The gross reproduction rate of the "white" population of South Africa is likewise at this level. The rate for Argentina is lower (1.4 according to the estimate for 1961).

Apart from Australia and New Zealand, the only country in Oceania represented in this study is the Fiji Islands. None of the other Pacific Islands meets the requirement of population size (250,000 or more inhabitants in 1960) except New Guinea and Papua, for which data are lacking. Like Fiji Islanders with their estimated gross reproduction rate of 3.5 for 1946–1951, the inhabitants of the lesser islands in the Pacific generally conform to the pattern of more or less high fertility and low level of development which is typical of Africa, Asia, Middle America and South America.

B. Trends of Fertility

1. *Scope of Data*

For nearly all countries where fertility is now low (in general, the more developed countries), series of birth registration statistics are available which provide a satisfactory basis for studying trends of fertility at least during the last three or four decades. In many cases, historical series of such statistics go back to the nineteenth century and in some cases to the eighteenth. One of the principal exceptions in this respect is the USSR, for which a continuing series of birth rates is on record only since 1950; but earlier data for the Soviet Union and the European part of the former Russian Empire make it possible to trace approximately the trend of fertility since the end of the nineteenth century.

On the past trends of fertility in countries where it is now high (in general, the developing countries), information is far less satisfactory. Of the 84 countries for which gross reproduction rates exceeding 2.0 have been estimated on the basis of the most recent data, only 15 have series of birth registration statistics reliable enough to serve as a basis for trend analysis over a period of two decades or longer. Estimates derived from census statistics provide indications of past levels and changes of fertility in some additional countries. In this study, series of such estimates relating to several time periods have been obtained for a number of countries of high fertility lacking reliable historical series of registration statistics. For the majority of high-fertility countries, however, no satisfactory data exist for the study of past trends. Almost all countries in Africa lack such data.

2. Trends in Low-Fertility Countries

The countries where fertility is low at present can be classified roughly into three groups with regard to the forms of fertility trends during the last three decades (disregarding some exceptions and variations in details of the trends).

The first group includes the majority of countries in northern, western and central Europe, together with Argentina, Australia, Canada, Israel, New Zealand and the United States — on the whole (though with some exceptions) a group of the world's most highly industrialized and economically developed countries, where fertility had been declining for a long time before 1930 and had reached the lowest levels recorded throughout the world at that time. Fertility in these countries dropped still lower in the 1930's, during the economic depression in the Western industrial countries, falling in many cases below the level required for permanent replacement of the population under the conditions of mortality existing at the time. The fertility trend turned upward during the middle or late 1930's in some countries of this group, and the early 1940's in others. Shortly after the Second World War, the group as a whole experienced an extraordinary rise of fertility — a "baby boom" linked with a "marriage boom" as well as with rising marital fertility rates — which brought the birth rates and gross reproduction rates to a peak in the late 1940's or early 1950's. From this high point, the rates dropped more or less sharply for a few years, then levelled off and appear to have become more or less stabilized, in general, at different levels in the last few years.

It seems that the long-term decline of fertility which began during the nineteenth or early twentieth century in the majority of this first group of countries may have run its course by the 1930's, and that the ups and downs of their fertility rates since that time might be considered as short-term fluctuations about a nearly constant level. In some countries of the group (notably Australia, Canada, New Zealand and the United States), the fertility rates of the late 1950's were considerably above the level reached in the early 1930's; the implication is that in these cases the long-term downward trend may have undershot its mark at that time. In other countries, including most of those in north-western Europe, the recent levels of fertility have been about the same as those of the early 1930's or slightly lower.

The second group consists of countries in southern and south-eastern Europe (except Spain). As a group, they were less advanced in industrialization and economic and social development generally than the first group of countries about the 1930's; their fertility rates had entered the long-term decline more recently, and their average fertility level was higher than the average of the first group. The general trend of fertility in countries of the second group continued downward through the 1930's, 1940's and early 1950's, though there were some variations in the tempo and minor interruptions of the trend, including notably some muted repercussions of the early post-war "baby boom" in the first group of countries. The average level of fertility of the second group in the late 1950's was much lower than it had been about 1930, and was nearly on a par with the average for the north-western and central European group.

In some countries of south-eastern and east-central Europe, fertility has not been stabilized recently, but has continued on a decidedly downward trend through the 1950's. This applies to Bulgaria and Hungary, which now have gross reproduction rates among the lowest in the world, and also to Czechoslovakia, Poland and Romania. Liberalization of abortion laws in these countries in the mid-1950's is clearly a factor of importance in the recent rapid declines of their birth rates.

The trend of fertility in the USSR since the 1920's, so far as it can be determined in view of the discontinuous statistical series prior to 1950, has been similar in some respects to that of the first group, and in other respects to that of the second group of countries now having low fertility. The level of Soviet fertility during the 1920's and earlier was quite high. It appears to have dipped sharply in the early 1930's, and to have partly recovered in the middle and later years of this decade, thus paralleling the trend of the first group. There is no indication, however, of any considerable rise of fertility in the Soviet Union following the end of the Second World War; this country seems to have come out of the war period with a distinctly lower fertility than it had in the 1930's and its fertility seems to have declined somewhat further during the early 1950's, to become stabilized at a level slightly higher than the north-western and central European average in the latter years of this decade.

The third group of low-fertility countries consists only of Japan and the Ryukyu Islands — the two countries in which fertility was high up to the end of the Second World War and dropped abruptly to a low level during the 1950's. The recent decline of fertility in these two countries is most impressive. Japan's gross reproduction rate was cut in half in eight years, falling from 2.1 in 1949 to 1.0 in 1957. The estimates for the Ryukyu Islands are much less reliable, but they show an almost equally large reduction, from a gross reproduction rate of 2.8 in 1950 to only 1.6 in 1960. In Japan, the reduction of the birth rate was encouraged by the Government, through legislation and other measures, including those aimed at promoting the use of contraceptives. In the Ryukyu Islands, on the other hand, the decisive decline of fertility has come about without any official encouragement or assistance.

3. *Trends in High-Fertility Countries*

Although data on past trends of fertility in countries where it is now high are far from sufficient for a general classification of types, they do furnish some indications which may be pertinent to the study of factors affecting fertility and prospects for its future changes in these parts of the world.

Few instances have been found, in this study, of long-continued upward or downward trends in high-fertility countries, resulting in large changes comparable to the past declines in countries where fertility is now low. In this sense, the data imply that the levels of fertility in high-fertility countries generally have probably been relatively stable during recent decades. On the other hand, it seems that rather large short-term variations and appreciable longer-term increases and decreases have not been uncommon. Some reservations should therefore be attached to the assumption often made in studies of the demography of high-fertility countries, that their fertility has generally remained nearly constant for long periods in the past.

Short-term variations more or less closely paralleling the ups and downs of fertility in industrialized, low-fertility countries during the last three decades appear to have been fairly common in high-fertility, developing countries. The dip of fertility rates during the early 1930's and the post-war "baby boom" with its sequel of diminishing fertility during the middle or late 1950's, have by no means been confined to parts of the world where the level of economic and social development is high and the level of fertility is low. In fact, one or both of these features appear in the trends for all the Asian high-fertility, developing countries for which pertinent records or estimates are available; also for Mauritius, Réunion, the United Arab Republic and some of the Middle American countries. The amplitude of these variations appears to have been generally smaller, however, in the countries of high fertility than in those of low fertility. The explanation of these parallels is not readily apparent.

Considerable decreases of birth rates have been recorded during the last few years in several Asian countries of high fertility. The most notable case is that of Singapore, where the registered crude birth rate dropped from 45.7 to 36.5 and the estimated gross reproduction rate from 3.3 to 2.7 between 1954 and 1961. Lesser decreases have been recorded recently in China (Taiwan) and the Federation of Malaya (now Malaysia) and also in Mauritius and Réunion. There is a suggestion that these countries might be following Japan and the Ryukyu Islands in a transition to a distinctly lower level of fertility. On the other hand, the previous ups and downs of their fertility rates during the last few decades are cause for hesitation in making any definite predictions of this kind.

The opposite tendency, of a persistent rise in recorded birth rates since the Second World War or the early 1950's, is observable in the statistics of several countries in the Caribbean and Middle American mainland areas. A real upward trend of fertility, however, is unequivocally established only for British Guiana, Jamaica, Trinidad and Tobago. For other countries in the areas mentioned, the rise of the recorded rates might be due merely to improving birth registration, although a real rise in fertility associated with better health and other conditions cannot be ruled out. In the countries of the former British West Indies, the recent rise appears to be the counterpart of a decline prior to the 1930's which had brought them to an appreciably lower level of fertility than prevailed in neighbouring Latin countries. Although certain hypotheses have been advanced with regard to causes of these variations, full and definite explanations have not yet been established.

In interpreting the trend of fertility in any country, whether the level be high or low and whether the country be advanced or retarded in development, it is pertinent not only to consider factors and conditions peculiar to the country concerned, but also to view the trend in its world-wide setting. While parallel trends in diverse circumstances may sometimes be attributed to coincidence, this is not, in numerous instances, a satisfactory explanation for similar patterns of trends.

C. Factors Related to Levels and Trends of Fertility

1. Economic and Social Factors

Relationships between levels of fertility and the degree of economic and social development of countries have been examined in this study by cross-classifying the estimates of gross reproduction rates for the most recent dates with selected economic and social indicators, and by comparing average gross reproduction rates for countries at different levels of these indicators, and average levels of the indicators for countries at different levels of gross reproduction rates. The indicators selected were income per head, energy consumption per head, proportion of labour force in nonagricultural industries, degree of urbanization, female literacy rate, number of hospital beds, newspaper circulation, cinema attendance, number of radio receivers per 1,000 population, expectation of life at birth, and infant mortality. The results bear out the generalization that a high level of fertility goes with a low degree of economic and social development, and *vice versa.* There are two distinct groups of countries, one standing high on the scale of fertility and generally low on the scales of economic and social indicators, and the other occupying the opposite position. Few countries exhibit the combination of high fertility with a very high value of any of the indicators, or low fertility with a very low value of any indicator. The typical country with a gross reproduction rate above 2.0 was characterized in the 1950's by, for example, an average annual income per head of about $170 (1957-1959 US dollars); about 40 per cent of the male labour force engaged in nonagricultural employment; about 17 per cent of the population residing in urban localities of 20,000 or more inhabitants; about 30 per cent of literates in the female population 15 years of age and over; and expectation of life at birth of about 50 years.

Coefficients of correlation have been calculated, which confirm the strong inverse association between the gross reproduction rate and each of the economic and social indicators when the data for all countries are considered. Yet *within* either group of countries — those with high fertility and a low degree of economic and social development, or those with low fertility and a high degree of development — there seems to be little association between the level of the gross reproduction rate and any of the economic and social indicators. Values of the coefficients of correlation are low and not statistically significant when they are calculated separately for countries having gross reproduction rates of 2.0 or higher, and those having rates below 2.0.

These observations are pertinent to the so-called theory of the demographic transition and its application to the problem of predicting future trends of fertility and population growth in developing countries. Although this theory has been stated in various forms, one of its central tenets is that the characteristically high fertility of pre-industrial societies is rooted in cultural determinants which are resistant to economic and social changes. As such societies undergo industrialization and related economic and social developments, their fertility is little affected, according to the theory, until a fairly high level of development is reached; then the factors maintaining high fertility give way and fertility drops to a much lower level. The findings summarized above are generally consistent with this hypothesis. The supposed resistance of factors of high fertility to social and economic changes is also borne out by the observation that the levels of fertility, in most high-fertility areas, do not appear to have changed very much during recent decades, in spite of considerable progress in health and education, and of accelerating urbanization.

Specific predictions of future fertility trends based on this theory are hazardous, however. One might be tempted to infer from the correlations mentioned above that a major decline of fertility in countries where it is now high would begin when (and not before) they reached a level of development corresponding to typical present values of the various indicators for the less developed countries of low fertility (i.e., something over $350 income per head, more than 60 per cent of male labour force in non-agricultural industries, etc.). But it is hardly necessary to point out that any such prediction depends on a highly unrealistic assumption, namely, that the reaction of fertility to changing economic and social conditions would be independent of all other factors — independent, for example, of the present level of fertility in each country, the characteristics of national culture and social institutions, the population policies adopted by the governments, and the progress of birth control technology.

It should also be noted that some of the ideas found in writings on the demographic transition theory appear artificial in the light of the findings of the present study — especially the characterization of the fertility of pre-industrial societies and those in early stages of industrial development simply as "high" without regard to the degree of highness. The starting-point of the supposed transition is often represented as a position of equilibrium between high fertility and high mortality rates, such an equilibrium being assumed to exist regardless of the levels of the rates. The subsequent course of population growth is then considered merely as a function of declining mortality and a supposed lag in decline of fertility under the impact of industrialization and connected social and economic changes. Such a representation is patently unrealistic as a general model and is quite inadequate to take account of the difference in growth potential which inheres in an initial gross reproduction rate of 3.5, for example, and one of 2.5. Moreover, variations in the actual course the demographic transition has taken in different countries point to the need for revision in such a model.[4] There is also little basis in present evidence for supposing, as has sometimes been suggested, that the transition would proceed continuously until, in all countries at advanced stages of industrial development, fertility would again be balanced with mortality on a uniform low plane.

2. Density of Population

Among low-fertility countries, some inverse association between fertility and crude measures of population density is apparent. This is shown, for example, by the following weighted averages of population density per square kilometre of land in three groups of low-fertility countries (GRR less than 2.0) classified according to estimated gross reproduction rate as of the latest date of available information:

Gross reproduction rate	*Average density*
Under 1.30	114
1.30-1.59	16
1.60-1.99	8

These figures reflect mainly the fact that fertility is higher in Canada, the United States, Australia, New Zealand and the Soviet Union than it is, on the average, in Europe and Japan, where the average density of population is comparatively high. But, an inverse relationship by no means holds for all countries. In fact, among the low-fertility countries as a whole, only a low negative correlation was found between population density and the gross reproduction rate. In any case, it does not follow that the lower density is necessarily a cause of higher fertility in the countries mentioned previously, though it is possible that

[4] Ronald Freedman, "The Sociology of Human Fertility: A Trend Report and Bibliography", *Current Sociology* (Oxford), vol. 10/11, No. 2, 1961-62, p. 53.

relatively ample space and plentiful natural resources might help to create an expansive national frame of mind more receptive to the formation of large families. Various other causal relationships between fertility and density of population have also been postulated in writings on population theory.[5]

Among the high-fertility countries, the association between fertility and density of population is less easy to establish, although it does appear that the countries with the highest gross reproduction rates are less densely populated on the average than those where fertility is more moderate. This is brought out by the following comparison of weighted average densities (persons per square kilometre of land area) for countries with gross reproduction rates of 2.0 and higher.

Gross reproduction rate	*Average density*
2.00-2.49[6]	47
2.50-3.09	29
3.10 and over	21

It should be emphasized that the relationship apparent in these averages is by no means consistent in comparisons of density and fertility levels between individual countries or groups of countries.

Some further analysis of the association between fertility and population density is needed. The findings are not conclusive; more detailed analyses would be required to establish whether there is any consistent pattern of relationships between these factors. It would be pertinent, for example, to use more refined measures of density, if possible relating agricultural population to cultivable land. In addition, information on the state of technology and the quality of land resources might give a better indication of the degree of population pressure. It would be appropriate also to extend the analysis to areas within both high- and low-fertility countries.

[5] A summary of various theories of this relationship will be found in: D. E. C. Eversley, *Social Theories of Fertility and the Malthusian Debate,* Oxford, Clarendon Press, 1959.

[6] Including China (mainland). If this country, for which estimates of fertility are not firmly established, were excluded, the inverse relationship would be less apparent.

3. *Ecological, Cultural and Legal Factors*

It is said in some current writings on population problems that the inhabitants of the developing countries generally are procreating with little restraint, at rates near the limits of their physiological capacity. Some writers go so far as to pretend that this was the general rule among human societies throughout the world in the past, before the beginning of the Industrial Revolution and the modern birth-control movement in the West, though those who have more regard for historical evidence make less sweeping generalizations in this respect. If it were true generally in the developing countries at present that free rein is given to the powers of procreation, then the differences in fertility levels among these countries would have to be explained mostly by differences in factors affecting physiological capacity to produce living offspring. Such factors include the general state of health and nutrition and the prevalence of diseases closely linked with pathological sterility, sub-fecundity, and foetal mortality: notably venereal diseases, malaria, and other debilitating illnesses. In some areas, especially in parts of Africa and in Mongolia, it has been suggested that the explanation of relatively low fertility might be found in factors of this sort. And a rise in fertility in several countries has been thought to be possibly related to the bringing under control of malaria and venereal diseases. In fact, present statistical and medical evidence is not sufficient for estimating the effects of health factors on fertility in Africa or any of the other developing regions, and this remains an important area for future research. On the basis of the information now available, it seems that while these factors may be quite relevant in certain instances, they are unlikely to furnish a general explanation for the wide differences of fertility among developing countries.

The absence of correlation between levels of fertility and levels of mortality in the developing countries is relevant to this question. While mortality rates are not precise measures of the state of health of a population, they nevertheless give some indication of health status, and it would not be unreasonable to expect to find a definite negative correlation between mortality and fertility levels if the differences in fertility levels were caused mainly by factors connected with the general state of health. But it has been found in this study that if any such correlation exists, it is of a low order. It is also relevant that the recent great improvements in health and reductions of mortality rates in many developing countries appear to have been accompanied at most by small increases of fertility, and no increase at all is apparent in the majority of cases where data to show the fertility trend are available. Although the prevalence of ailments most closely linked with sterility, sub-fecundity, and foetal mortality would not necessarily vary in direct proportion to the general level of mortality, these observations make it seem doubtful that such impairments of procreative capacity are mainly responsible for the differing levels of fertility in developing countries.

The alternative is that the powers of procreation are held in different degrees of restraint in these countries, voluntarily or involuntarily, by differences in behaviour pertaining to marriage, sexual relations, and birth of children. The evidence reviewed in the preceding section implies that such behavioural differences would not be related so much to differing economic and social circumstances as to differing cultural traditions. Among the cultural traits which may be important in this connexion are not only specific customs and behavioural norms (such as the moral disapproval of "artificial" birth-control in Roman Catholic societies or the traditional customs in many African societies of prolonging lactation and suspending sexual intercourse during rather long periods after child-birth), but also more general and more fundamental characteristics of culture, relating to such matters as the values attached to family life and children as opposed to competing interests and activities, the spirit of thrift, prudence, and self-discipline, rationality, and the disposition to attempt control of one's destiny. Differences in such characteristics of culture may find expression in patterns of behaviour that are more or less liberal or restrictive, so far as procreation is concerned. While it may be true that men and women in the less developed regions of the world are generally motivated to have numerous children, this does not mean that they necessarily desire to have as many as they are able to produce, nor that there are no important differences between countries in attitudes and aspirations in this respect.

The fertility level may be affected by social norms as to ideal family size, and less directly by norms regarding "intermediate variables",[7] such as age at marriage; forms of marital unions; extra-marital sexual relations; celibacy; divorce; re-marriage of widows and divorcees and the amount of time spent between unions; forms of coitus; frequency and spacing of coitus; inducement of abortion; pre-natal care; and contraceptive practices. Different combinations of these variables may produce the same fertility levels, or populations with different fertility levels may have similar values for some of the variables. Behaviour with respect to these variables may be affected both by socially recognized rules of approved and permissible conduct and by deliberate exercise of individual discretion.

Variations in kinship structure which affect the functional value of children may play a role in creating the existing differences in fertility levels among pre-industrial societies.[8] There is a theory that, in general, corporate kinship systems provide the greatest incentive for large numbers of children, joint-family systems somewhat less, and the nuclear family unit least of all.

Certain means of fertility control that have been prevalent in European societies — delayed marriage, celibacy, and in modern times the use of contraceptives — are known to have little currency in the less developed regions of the world. In fact it is the widespread practice of such forms of fertility control among the former and their virtual absence in the latter that accounts for the sharp existing division between high-fertility and low-fertility countries. But other means of control — notably inducement of abortions, *coitus interruptus,* and restraint in frequency of coitus — may be employed to an important extent and have an important effect on the level of fertility in many developing, as well as industrialized countries. Many demographers assume that deliberate control of fertility by any means is uncommon in the less developed parts of the world.

[7] For a classification of "intermediate variables" affecting fertility, *see* Kingsley Davis and Judith Blake, "Social Structure and Fertility: An Analytic Framework", *Economic Development and Cultural Change* (Chicago), vol. 4, April 1956, pp. 211-235.

[8] Ronald Freedman, "The Sociology of Human Fertility: A Trend Report and Bibliography", op. cit., pp. 50-51.

"Natural fertility" is assumed to prevail in these countries; i.e., behaviour of any kind tending to restrict births is held to be generally independent of such considerations as the economic means of the family or the community, the number of children desired, or the consequences of births for the welfare of the parents and of the children already born. This is not at all certain, however, as little investigation has yet been made of the relevant attitudes, motives, and patterns of behaviour in such countries.

In a recent study, the social and cultural factors relevant to fertility were examined for about 60 small population groups in non-industrial societies for which suitable anthropological and demographic data were available.[9] The conclusions were limited by the fact that the fertility estimates were in many cases not very reliable. Among the factors investigated for which a statistically significant association with the fertility level could not be established were age at marriage, polygamy, divorce, post-widowhood celibacy, contraception and abortion. The data on frequency of intercourse compiled in this study suggested that there were considerable group variations, but the data were inadequate to establish an association with the fertility level. On the other hand, a statistically significant negative association was found between the fertility level and post-partum abstinence. Intensification of research on such aspects of behaviour and customs is an indispensable prerequisite to understanding the determinants of fertility levels and their differences among the developing countries.

Legislation relating to the use, advertisement, and sale of contraceptive devices and to induced abortion may affect the fertility level in some countries, though it is difficult to determine empirically the extent of the influence of such legislation on the birth rate. Among countries of low fertility, there is some evidence of a negative association between the level of the birth rate and the extent of permissiveness of legislation relating to abortions. A causal relationship is not well defined, however, since, while fertility may have been lowered because of the laws, there is also the possibility that the laws were enacted as a response to prevailing practices.

[9] Moni Nag, *Factors Affecting Human Fertility in Nonindustrial Societies: A Cross-Cultural Study* (Yale University Publications in Anthropology, No. 66), New Haven, 1962.

*Social Structure and Fertility: An Analytic Framework**

KINGSLEY DAVIS • JUDITH BLAKE

A striking feature of underdeveloped areas is that virtually all of them exhibit a much higher fertility than do urban-industrial societies. This well-documented but insufficiently analyzed fact is known to be connected with profound differences in social organization as between the two types of society, and is therefore significant for the comparative sociology of reproduction. The clarity and importance of the contrast, however, should not be allowed to obscure the equally important fact that underdeveloped areas themselves differ markedly in social organization, and that these differences appear to bring about variations in fertility. Though the demographic statistics of backward regions have generally been so poor as to place in doubt the validity of reported differences, there are cases in which the evidence is reliable (e. g., as between Puerto Rico and Jamaica, or Arab Pales-

* Reprinted with permission from *Economic Development and Cultural Change,* Vol. 4 (April 1956), pp. 211-235.

tine and Ceylon). Of equal interest are the cases in which societies with differing social organization have the same level of fertility, for they may reach this common result by quite different institutional mechanisms. All told, ample opportunity exists for the comparative analysis of social structure as it affects fertility. In view of the bearing of future population trends on economic development, the pursuit of such analysis has a practical as well as a theoretical significance.

The present paper represents an attempt to set forth and utilize an analytical framework for the comparative sociology of fertility. It first presents a classification of the intermediate variables through which any social factors influencing the level of fertility must operate. It next tries to show, in broad outline, how some types and elements of social organization, acting through these variables, appear to enhance or depress societal fertility. Our hope is that as more sociological and demographic information becomes available, the theories advanced can be refined further and tested empirically.

THE INTERMEDIATE VARIABLES

The process of reproduction involves three necessary steps sufficiently obvious to be generally recognized in human culture: (1) intercourse, (2) conception, and (3) gestation and parturition.[1] In analyzing cultural influences on fertility, one may well start with the factors directly connected with these three steps. Such factors would be those through which, and only through which, cultural conditions *can* affect fertility. For this reason, by way of convenience, they can be called the "intermediate variables" and can be presented schematically as follows:

I. *Factors Affecting Exposure to Intercourse ("Intercourse Variables").*
   A. Those governing the formation and dissolution of unions in the reproductive period.[2]
      1. Age of entry into sexual unions.
      2. Permanent celibacy: proportion of women never entering sexual unions.
      3. Amount of reproductive period spent after or between unions.
         a. When unions are broken by divorce, separation, or desertion.
         b. When unions are broken by death of husband.
   B. Those governing the exposure to intercourse within unions.
      4. Voluntary abstinence.
      5. Involuntary abstinence (from impotence, illness, unavoidable but temporary separations).
      6. Coital frequency (excluding periods of abstinence).

II. *Factors Affecting Exposure to Conception ("Conception Variables").*
   7. Fecundity or infecundity, as affected by involuntary causes.
   8. Use or non-use of contraception.
      a. By mechanical and chemical means.
      b. By other means.[3]
   9. Fecundity or infecundity, as affected by voluntary causes (sterilization, subincision, medical treatment, etc.).

III. *Factors Affecting Gestation and Successful Parturition ("Gestation Variables").*
   10. Foetal mortality from involuntary causes.

[1] Although the physiologist sees more steps in the process, these can all be subsumed under the three headings given here. We are concerned only with the steps in reproduction as they may be socially recognized and utilized.

[2] Since sexual intercourse is not confined to wedlock, the term "sexual union" seems preferable to "marriage". A union is here defined as any heterosexual relationship in which either actual intercourse occurs or orgasm is produced for at least the male partner. Every society has a type of union (marriage) in which reproduction is expected, approved, and even enjoined. At the same time every society runs the risk of unions in which reproduction is condemned, either because they lack the legal form of marriage or because they violate one or more institutional taboos (adultery, incest, caste, or class endogamy, etc. — see K. Davis, "The Forms of Illegitimacy," *Social Forces,* Vol. 18, October 1939, pp. 77-89). Between the fully approved and the strongly proscribed unions, there may be other types which have a lesser grade than marriage but in which reproduction normally occurs. Such unions may be frequent, in some cases representing the majority of reproductive unions. Any satisfactory sociological analysis of reproduction must keep straight the different types of unions.

[3] Means of contraception other than mechanical and chemical include the "rhythm" method (which can also be classed as voluntary abstinence), withdrawal, simulated intercourse without penetration, various "perversions", etc.

11. Foetal mortality from voluntary causes.

It is clear that *any* cultural factor that affects fertility must do so in some way classifiable under one or another of our eleven intermediate variables.[4] Hence the latter provide a framework in terms of which the relevance of cultural factors to fertility can be judged. In fact, attempts to explain causal relationships between institutions and fertility without such a framework have led to inconclusive and confused writing on the subject.[5] The cultural factors, or "conditioning variables," are presumably many, and no effort is made here to classify them; but the "intermediate variables" offer a means of approach to selecting and analyzing these factors.

It is also clear that *each* of the eleven variables may have a negative (minus) or a positive (plus) effect on fertility. If by examining all societies we could find the range of influence of a given variable, any effect more negative than the midpoint of this range would be on the minus side, and any influence more positive would be on the plus side. If, for example, a society uses contraception successfully, it has a *minus* value with respect to variable number 8; if it uses *no* contraception, it has a plus value on this variable. The value of each variable refers to how it affects fertility in each case; so a positive use of something (e.g., contraception, abortion, abstinence) may mean that it has a "minus" fertility-value.

One cannot say, as is frequently implied in the literature, that some of these variables are affecting fertility in one society but not in another. *All* of the variables are present in *every* society. This is because, as mentioned before, each one *is* a variable — it can operate either to reduce or to enhance fertility. If abortion is *not* practiced, the fertility-value of variable number 11 is "plus." In other words, the absence of a specific practice does not imply "no influence" on fertility, because this very absence is a form of influence. It follows that the position of any society, if stated at all, must be stated on all eleven variables.

Societies differing in their social organization do not necessarily have different fertility-values with respect to all the variables. On some of the variables they may exhibit quite similar values. A nomadic tribe may have the same age at marriage as a settled agrarian village; a primitive group may practice the same rate of abortion as an industrial society. Two contrasting societies are not likely, however, to manifest similar values for all the variables; they are not likely to do this even when their general fertility level is practically the same. The actual birth rate depends on the net balance of the values of all the variables. Though societies which generate a high fertility tend to be predominantly on the plus side, no society has the highest plus value on all eleven variables; and societies with low fertility turn out to be amazingly positive on a number of them.

It should, of course, be mentioned that cultural influences affecting our eleven variables do not necessarily represent rational attempts to govern fertility. Many fertility consequences stemming from socio-cultural conditions (especially in underdeveloped regions) are by-products, being unanticipated and unrealized by members of the society. Surely by now social scientists know that they cannot confine their attention only to rational actions or treat non-rational actions as somehow defying systematic analysis. The requirements of a given society can be met just as well, and just as ill, by an unintentional level of fertility as by an intentional one.

Institutional Patterns and the Intermediate Variables: A Preliminary Analysis

From the standpoint of comparative sociology, an important question is how the fertility-values of our intermediate variables distribute themselves in different kinds of societies. A prelimi-

[4] The reader will note that our list of variables does not include infanticide or child care. The reason for this omission is that our analysis is focused on factors affecting fertility strictly defined. Infanticide does, of course, affect family size and natural increase and may serve as an alternative to factors affecting fertility. It is therefore discussed briefly at a later point.

[5] For instance, Frank Lorimer, *Culture and Human Fertility,* Paris, 1954, by failing to make clear the ways in which fertility *can* be affected, gives in some ways a confused picture of how it *is* affected. The reader may wish to compare our framework with a half-page outline of direct and indirect factors affecting fertility given by Raymond Pearl at the end of an article on "Biological Factors in Fertility", *Annals of the American Academy of Political and Social Science,* Vol. 188, November 1936, p. 24.

nary generalization is that underdeveloped societies tend to have high fertility-values for numbers 1, 2, 8, and 9 on the list; they *may* have high values for 3a, 3b, and 10; and they often have *low* values for 4 and 11. As for the remaining variables — 5, 6, and 7 — it is hard to prove that there are any consistent differences between pre-industrial and industrial societies. If this generalization is roughly accurate, then it becomes meaningful to re-group the eleven variables as follows:

The Intermediate Variables According to Their Values in Pre-Industrial Societies

Usually High Values

1. Age of entry into unions.
2. Permanent celibacy.
8. Contraception.
9. Sterilization, etc.

High or Low Values

3a. Time between unstable unions.
3b. Post-widowhood celibacy.
11. Foetal mortality — voluntary.

Usually Low Values

4. Voluntary abstinence.
10. Foetal mortality — involuntary

Indeterminate

5. Involuntary abstinence.
6. Frequency of coitus.
7. Involuntary sterility.

In attempting to analyze in a preliminary way how different institutional patterns affect the variables, we shall find it convenient to follow the order just given.

Number 1. Age of Entry into Unions

In beginning with age of entry into unions, we are dealing with one of the variables governing exposure to intercourse. It should be noted that these particular variables, however favorable they may be to fertility in themselves, may be counteracted in practice by other factors governing conception and gestation. For example, even though sexual unions begin early, pregnancy or childbirth may be prevented. This is often the case when the sexual union is not a marriage. Many societies, even though they permit premarital intercourse, strongly forbid illegitimate pregnancy.[6] With respect to marital unions, however, reproduction is specifically sanctioned, indeed expected. As already mentioned, there may be, in addition, non-marital unions in which reproduction also normally occurs. Consequently, in dealing with age of entry into unions, we shall separate those unions in which offspring normally appear (including both marital and non-marital types) from those in which reproduction is so strongly condemned that it is infrequent. We shall now deal with the first general class (paying attention mostly to marriage itself), leaving until later the discussion of non-reproductive sexual unions.

Since in pre-industrial societies the age of entry into reproductive unions is generally young, the question must be raised as to why the fertility-value of this variable is usually positive when on certain other variables it is often negative. From a broad functional standpoint, the explanation stems from high mortality. Not only does a high death rate normally prevail in underdeveloped societies from year to year, but there is always the danger of a sudden catastrophic rise in mortality. Early marriage therefore represents the maximum possible hedge against the threat of failure in population replacement. Entering a union at a young age does not commit one irretrievably to a large family, because all other means of reducing fertility come *after* this point. If a particular union is resulting in progeny that are too numerous under current circumstances, this eventuality can be obviated by abstinence, contraception, abortion, or infanticide. These means, precisely because they come later, can be utilized at a time closer to the actual impingement of new individuals on the resources of those responsible. If, on the other hand, the age of entry into unions is late, the potential fertility

[6] Among the 250 societies for which he had information, Murdock found that, apart from incest taboos, "premarital relations are fully permitted in 65 instances, and are conditionally approved in 43 and only mildly disapproved in 6, whereas they are forbidden in only 44. In other words, premarital license prevails in 70 per cent of our cases. In the rest, the taboo falls primarily upon females and appears to be largely a precaution against childbearing out of wedlock rather than a moral requirement." George P. Murdock, *Social Structure,* New York, 1949, p. 265. On p. 5 the author gives slightly different figures, but the majority of his societies still permit premarital sexual relations.

that is lost can never be recovered. The threat of mortality, from a societal standpoint, has reference not only to the potential offspring but also to the parents themselves. Early formation of unions helps to guarantee that the young adults will achieve at least some reproduction before they die.

This broad functional explanation does not, however, enlighten us concerning the specific institutional mechanisms by which early marriage is insured. These can best be understood in terms of family and kinship organization (involving rules of residence and rules of descent) and the control of property. Such mechanisms apply most clearly to formal marriage, although they may apply as well, though in lesser degree, to informal reproductive unions.

From the standpoint of kinship organization, an essential distinction is that between a joint household and/or clan system, on the one hand, and an independent nuclear family organization on the other. When the clan is the unit controlling the property (whether the latter consists in herds or land), the question of inheritance does not normally arise, because the clan is immortal. When the joint family is the controlling unit, the question arises only when the joint family divides; the joint family, however, does not divide when the offspring marry, but rather, at the earliest, when the father dies. Thus, in societies having a joint household (and *a fortiori* in those having a strong clan organization), marriage is in no way made contingent on the possession of separate property by the newly married pair.

Furthermore, with strong clan or joint-household control (or both), marriages are usually arranged by the elders, who are often motivated to make the arrangements early in the lifetime of the prospective mates, i.e., before puberty. Religious prescription may require this result, and the economic exchanges involved in betrothal may be structured in such a way as to yield an advantage to the parents who marry their daughter early. If the system is one of patrilocal residence, for example, a grown daughter remaining in her parental home is an anomaly. Not only does her presence run counter to the normal division of labor by sex, which assumes the complementarity of husband and wife, but she must adjust to the wives of her brothers coming into the household. Add to this fact that the daughter, as a prospective spouse, is most in demand by other families when she is young, first because she then has a greater potential fertility ahead of her, and, second, because she is more attractive sexually and fits more easily into a subordinate status in her husband's parental home. If, then, there is a substantial brideprice or groomprice at marriage, the girl's kin stand a better chance of a favorable bargain if they marry her off early. This may help them in procuring wives for their sons.

In societies having neither a strong clan nor a joint family, the forces leading to early marriage may be overbalanced by others. The Irish family, for instance, has long been organized in terms of neolocal residence and hence marital rather than filial solidarity. This being true, land had to be obtainable or marriage postponed. During the greater part of the eighteenth century land was scarce and could not be subdivided because the economy was predominantly pastoral. Consequently, an obstacle to early marriage "was the difficulty of acquiring a settlement *upon which a new family might depend*."[7] Later, during the sixty years before the Famine, when the potato became the staple food and the economy shifted from pastoralism to cultivation, couples could get property at marriage by subdivision of the land, thus removing temporarily the main obstacle to early marriage. But with the crisis of the Famine, the futility of progressive subdivision led to the Land Purchase Acts stipulating that the loans which transformed tenants into owners were granted only on condition that no subdivision would take place. Since the annuities ran for 35 years, this represented some restraint on subdivision.[8] A more powerful restraint was the fact that, once the tenants became owners, they grew unwilling to subdivide in behalf of their sons. The tendency was to retain only one son on the paternal land, the remainder of the children being dispersed, partly through migration abroad. The independent nuclear family was maintained, but the son who remained at home could not establish such a family until the father was willing to resign both authority and

[7] K. H. Connell, *The Population of Ireland, 1750-1845,* Oxford, 1950, p. 89 [italics ours].

[8] See Elizabeth R. Hooker, *Readjustments of Agricultural Tenure in Ireland,* Chapel Hill, 1938, esp. pp. 55-57, 106, 151, 208.

property. As a result the average age at marriage in Ireland became extremely advanced, reaching 29.1 for women by 1926.[9]

Lest our characterization of Irish family organization as neolocal appear surprising, it should be noted that although the Irish have been interpreted as having a joint household and patrilocal residence,[10] the opposite seems to be true. Even if one or two sons remain at home, the resulting menage is not what is ordinarily called a joint household; because in Ireland marriage implies the independence of the son. When the son brings a bride into what was the paternal homestead, he brings her into a home that has been redefined as his, no longer his father's. The father has relinquished both ownership of the farm and authority over the son. As long as the father continues to own the land, the son who remains at home cannot marry because the land is necessary for the "match." [11] If marriage occurs, therefore, the fact that the parents are still in the home is merely adventitious — they have entered "the age grade of the dying." [12] Significantly, if irreconcilable conflict develops in the shared household, it is the parents, not the son and his wife, who must leave. "The bond between them [husband and wife] is stronger than that between son and parent." [13] Thus in Ireland the fact of sharing a house with the parents is not a reflection of the joint family ideal but of the force of circumstances. The fact of a common menage is socially defined in such a way as to comply with the ideal of a neolocal and independent nuclear family.

This independent nuclear family organization is neither unique to Ireland nor modern in development. In Northwestern Europe the custom of impartible inheritance (e.g., by promigeniture or ultimogeniture) was found in many areas during the Middle Ages. In some sections it was apparently customary for the old people to give their land to the heir before they died. Surrendering their authority, they expected only their keep off the land. The heir's marriage was contingent on the land being turned over to him; if his sisters and brothers stayed on, they could claim their keep but not the privilege of marriage.[14] The principle of no holding, no marriage,[15] operated to advance the average age beyond what it otherwise would have been. Furthermore, the notion of the independence of the nuclear family also manifested itself in the master-apprentice relationship within the medieval guilds; for marriage often did not occur until an adequate guild status had been acquired by inheritance, purchase, or dower.[16] There is thus evidence that European society has long emphasized the marital rather than the filial bond as the basis of family organization, with a consequent tendency to delay marriage.[17]

The emphasis on marital rather than filial solidarity, on neolocal rather than patrilocal residence, which appears to have delayed marriage in Ireland and Northwestern Europe contrasts sharply with the forces operating to precipitate marriage in an extended family system. In a truly joint household the authority of the elders continues *after* marriage; the marital bond is therefore subordinate to the filial bond and does not require economic independence on the part of those getting married. Such a family pattern is well known as the ideal one in traditional China, India, Bantu Africa, and many other peasant or primitive cultures. In the Chinese case, the father maintains his tutelage over the married son and his control over the familial property until death. He consequently need not fear the marriage of his son as a threat to his authority, and therefore, unlike the Irish father,

[9] A. M. Carr-Saunders, *World Population,* Oxford, 1936, p. 91. Cf. James Meenan, "Some Causes and Consequences of the Low Irish Marriage Rate", *Journal of the Statistical and Social Inquiry Society of Ireland,* 86th session, 1932-33, pp. 19-27.

[10] E.g., Conrad M. Arensberg and Solon T. Kimball, *Family and Community in Ireland,* Cambridge, 1938, p. 80.

[11] Arensberg and Kimball, *op. cit.,* pp. 107-122.

[12] *Ibid.,* p. 123.

[13] *Ibid.,* p. 128.

[14] George C. Homans, *English Villagers of the Thirteenth Century,* Cambridge, 1942, Chs. 9-10.

[15] Josiah C. Russell, "Demographic Values in the Middle Ages", *Studies in Population,* George F. Mair, ed., Princeton, 1949, p. 104.

[16] Josiah C. Russell, *British Medieval Population,* Albuquerque, 1948, pp. 163-164.

[17] Of course, not every society with neolocal residence shows a retarded age at marriage. In a primitive economy with high mortality, where no formal training or other obstacles to adult status must be hurdled, and where scarcity of persons rather than scarcity of land is the felt need, independent nuclear families may be formed by early marriage, e.g., the Netsilik Eskimos, Fox Indians, Andaman Islanders, Ruthenians.

has no motive (at least in this regard) for postponing such marriage. On the contrary, to the extent that his son brings a wife into the house and has children, the old man's authority is extended. Indeed, it is only by the marriage of his son that the patriarch can fulfill *his* filial obligation to *his* father.[18]

Number 2. Extent of Permanent Celibacy

If late marriage can have a minus effect on fertility, so can permanent non-marriage. In both cases, if this effect is to be produced, there must be either continence outside of marriage, or the use of means to prevent intercourse from resulting in childbirth. In practice, non-marriage usually does produce a low rate of reproduction among the unmarried, because, as mentioned already, marriage in all societies is the preferred institutional arrangement for having children. It seems wise, therefore, to discuss "celibacy" primarily in terms of non-marriage, and to consider sexual continence only in so far as it illuminates that factor.

Although permanent non-marriage is obviously a more potent factor than mere postponement of marriage, it actually occurs less frequently and hence has less negative influence on fertility. Only rarely can a population be found where more than 20 per cent of the women complete the reproductive period without ever having married. Ireland is an extreme case, with 26.3% of its women aged 45–49 in 1946 still single.[19] If we assume that these women, had they married, would have had the same completed fertility as those who did, then their proportion represents an estimate of the loss of fertility due to non-marriage (excluding illegitimate births).[20] Thus the loss due to permanent non-marriage seems, even in the extreme case, scarcely to exceed one-fourth. Such a loss in fertility is greatly exceeded by that due to late age at marriage. For example, in Switzerland (where the data are readily available), if all women in 1941 who had ever married by ages 40–44, had married at ages 15–19 and had subsequently manifested the same age-specific fertility as those who had actually married then or did marry at some point prior to age 40, the reproduction would have been 75% greater than it actually was! [21] In other words, the gain in fertility if late marriage had been eliminated would have been approximately three times the gain (25%) if permanent non-marriage had been eliminated.

It is mainly in urban-industrial societies that the proportion of women never marrying by the end of the reproductive span exceeds 10%. In India in 1931 it was only 0.8%; in Ceylon in 1946, 3.4%; and in Malaya in 1947, 3.3%. Thus the underdeveloped areas generally show a very high plus value for fertility with respect both to variable number 1 (age at marriage) and variable number 2 (proportion ever married), whereas industrial societies often show rather low fertility-values on these.

We thus have to answer two questions: Why do all societies generally make less use of non-marriage than of late marriage in depressing fertility? Why do underdeveloped peoples make less use of *both* of these mechanisms than do industrial societies? Let us attempt to answer these two questions in order.

Given the low fecundity of the human species, no society can hope to replace itself unless either a majority of its women participate in reproduction or its mortality is rigorously controlled. Since most of man's history has occurred under conditions of heavy mortality — conditions

[18] Marion J. Levy, Jr., *The Family Revolution in Modern China,* Cambridge, 1949, pp. 168-170. When the family head dies there is the problem of one of the sons assuming authority over the others. It is precisely at this point that the joint household often dissolves; but if it survives this crisis, as it may, it does so because of the past institutionalization of relative age as a factor in authority.

[19] Other cases of high proportions never married are Sweden (1945) 20.9%, Switzerland (1941) 20.1%, England and Wales (1931) 16.8%, Belgium (1930) 13.3%.

[20] Differences in mortality and possible fecundity as between married and unmarried women may introduce a small but probably not serious error into this estimate.

[21] This calculation excludes non-marriage as a factor, because the women who had never married by age 40-44 were subtracted from the women under consideration in each age group. In other words, 21.4% of Swiss women at ages 40-44 had never married. But the remaining 78.6% had married at various ages. If this 78.6% had all married at ages 15-19 and had from that age experienced the same age-specific fertility as those ever married at each age, their total fertility would have been 76% greater. Stated in terms of the potential fertility lost by late marriage, the figure is approximately 64%. The calculation is rough, because the data refer to 1941 and thus do not represent a true cohort analysis; but a refined calculation on a cohort basis should yield rather similar results.

which still prevail for many of the world's peoples — all viable societies have evolved social mechanisms that lead the majority of women to participate in reproduction. Their participation is organized through the institution of marriage, which links sex and reproduction to the care and socialization of children. This institution is in turn supported by its articulation with the rest of the social order. The marital relation thus becomes a general norm in terms of which the hopes and expectations of virtually all individuals are channelized. If for some reason the pressure of mortality is relaxed, the norm still continues in effect. Not only do normative systems change slowly, but there still remains the necessity for a family organization in terms of which reproduction and child-rearing are provided for. Thus individuals continue to anticipate marriage as a normal and important part of life, an event more easily postponed than foregone altogether.

In any case, an increase in non-marriage would not reduce fertility unless either coitus outside of wedlock were successfully banned or contraception and abortion were freely used. If the latter were readily available, they could be used *within* marriage, and the consequent reduction in marital fertility would obviate the necessity of denying marriage to a substantial portion of the population. If contraception and abortion were not readily available, non-marriage would be an effective brake on fertility only at the price of permanent sexual celibacy. Everything we know about human society indicates that this price is so high that no population is willing to pay it.

Since no society has ever attempted to incorporate permanent celibacy as a widespread custom, we have no conclusive evidence as to what it would do to a social system. We can, however, obtain some clues by examining countries in which permanent celibacy has appeared to an unusual extent and by examining organizations which have enjoined it as a rule. We can also say something on purely theoretical grounds concerning what it might do if utilized as the chief means of reducing fertility to a modern level. Limitations of space prevent our giving a complete treatment along these lines, but something can be said about each of them.

Because Ireland has an unusually late age at marriage and a high proportion who never marry, together with a strong prejudice against coitus outside of marriage, it provides the main example of a rather extensive practice of celibacy.[22] Has this adjustment exacted a price? To answer such a question is difficult. A puritanical attitude toward sex cannot be listed as a consequence, because this is part of the celibacy itself. That the Irish avoid reproduction outside of marriage is shown by their low illegitimacy rate — 2.8% of all live births in 1921–1930 and 3.3% in 1931–1940.[23] However, such descriptions as we have suggest that a great amount of attention, community effort, and personality conflict go into controlling sexual expression. Having a social system that emphasized the marital bond and the nuclear family, the Irish cannot completely segregate unmarried females, as is done in Moslem countries. The young people must have some chance to participate in courtship and mate selection. But, given this system, the Irish seem to make an unusually strong effort to control sexual behavior. For a country not living under a dictatorship, the official censorship of literature and ideas is exceptionally rigid, and has as its main purpose the suppression of material pertaining to sex and reproduction.[24]

[22] David Glass, *Introduction to Malthus,* New York, 1953, pp. 27-54, shrewdly notes that Ireland is the only country which has come close to following Malthus' rules of conduct — "moral restraint" and no birth control. In other countries of Northwestern Europe, such as Sweden and Norway, a late age at marriage does not imply sexual abstinence, not only because illegitimacy is more tolerated but also because contraception is more freely practiced.

[23] *Ibid.,* p. 37.

[24] For attitudes toward sexual behavior see Arensberg and Kimball, *op. cit.,* Ch. 11; and also such literary and popular sources as Frank O'Connor, "Ireland", *Holiday,* Vol. 6, December 1949, p. 40; Seán O'Faoláin, "Love Among the Irish", *Life Magazine,* Vol. 34, March 16, 1953, pp. 140-157. Regarding censorship, the following passage from O'Faoláin is pertinent: " . . . Our censorship of books and publications, instigated by the clergy and submitted to, willy-nilly, by everybody, is a symbol of this fear of sex . . . In the 150 close-packed pages of the official register of books and periodicals banned by the Irish Censorship Board we find the names of almost every single Irish writer of note, some for one book, some for several. The banning is done in secret. There is no appeal to the courts of law . . . " See also an article, "Irish Challenge Censors' Methods", *The New York Times,* August 14, 1955, where it is pointed out that the Irish Censorship Board "has banned books by the most reputable Irish authors, including Sean O'Casey, Liam O'Flaherty, Sean O'Faolain, and Ireland's most brilliant short story writer, Frank O'Connor. Nobel

Furthermore, the data on mental illness, which show a high rate for Ireland, indicate a possible consequence of such repression.[25] There appear to be few features in Irish life that compensate for whatever is lost through celibacy. Ireland has, for example, the lowest level of living of any nation in Northwestern Europe. All told, there is some ground for the hypothesis that Ireland is paying a price for its unusual degree of celibacy.

Celibacy as an *organizational* rule has been almost solely applied to religious personnel. Among those few religions which have adopted such a rule for their clergy, our evidence is most readily available for the Roman Catholic priesthood. As is well known, the application of the rule in this case encountered great difficulties. It required nearly nine centuries before the edict of non-marriage itself could be enforced with relative success. Priests were first commanded to separate from their wives and remain continent in 385 A.D. After that date there were periods when the ban against marriage could be safely ignored by priests, followed by periods when the Church was militantly purging its married clergy. Pope Gregory (Hildebrand) encountered such obstacles in enforcing the rule of non-marriage that he ordered the laity to withdraw their obedience from all members of the clergy who disregarded the papal canons on simony and incontinence. By so doing, he undermined a basic principle of the Church — clerical immunity — and thus as early as 1074 directly laid one of the foundations of the Reformation. Only by placing the sacrament of marriage in a lower position than that of the religious vow (Lateran Council of 1123) did the Church finally settle the issue of clerical marriage, although in practice such marriages occurred with some frequency after that — as late as the nineteenth century in some parts of Latin America, for example. In periods when the ban against marriage was being enforced, the Church still had to deal with sexual incontinence among its priests and nuns. "Solicitation" (the seduction of female penitents), concubinage, and other violations were so common as to cause chronic public scandal. In some areas priestly concubinage became, for long periods, a customary practice, and the sons of priests received preferment.[26] We can thus see that the enforcement of celibacy even for that small fraction of the population represented by the clergy was anything but easy.

If we imagine a society in which celibacy is institutionalized and becomes a norm rivaling marriage, we can see that the result would be paradoxical and impossible. Should the celibate class be large enough to reduce the birth rate to a modern level without other means, it would have to contain at least half the population. For individuals on such a scale to be induced to make the sacrifice of celibacy, they would not only have to be firmly controlled (perhaps segregated from the rest of the community and thus divorced from the temptations of everyday life),

prize winners have even come under the interdict . . . many works of worth are condemned on a few isolated marked passages, while the general tenor of the book is ignored . . . Even the works of Roman Catholic authors approved by the church authorities in Britain have not escaped the five Irish Roman Catholic Censors."

[25] In 1949 the proportion of hospital beds devoted to mental cases was 57% in Ireland, whereas it was only 49% in the United States. The rate of mental patients per 100,000 population in 1948 was 603 in Ireland as contrasted to 382 in the United States. Adventitious circumstances seem not to account for this result. Though Ireland has a larger percentage of persons in the advanced ages than does the United States (24.7% at ages 50 and over as against 22.4% at these ages in the United States), she has a higher proportion under age 30. The fact that Irish medical services are less developed than in this country suggests that the comparison understates the difference in mental illness. In 1949 Ireland had only one hospital bed per 1,000 inhabitants, whereas the United States has 9.6, so that a higher proportion of mental cases in Ireland may never appear in the statistics.

[26] For the history of clerical celibacy in Europe, see Henry C. Lea, *History of Sacerdotal Celibacy in the Christian Church,* London, 1932, and *A History of the Inquisition of the Middle Ages,* Vol. 1, New York, 1888, pp. 31-32; Alexander C. Flick, *The Decline of the Medieval Church,* New York, 1930, Vols. 1-2, passim.; J. R. Tanner et al. (eds.), *Contest of Empire and Papacy,* Vol. 5 of *Cambridge Medieval History,* New York, 1926, esp. pp. 11-14, 40, 61-62, 73, 695; Eileen Power, *Medieval English Nunneries,* Cambridge, 1922, Ch. 11; Geoffrey Baskerville, *English Monks and the Suppression of the Monasteries,* New Haven, 1937, pp. 261-266; Joseph McSorley, *An Outline History of the Church by Centuries,* St. Louis, 1944, pp. 83, 154, 206-207, 237; H. J. Schroeder, *Disciplinary Decrees of the General Councils,* St. Louis, 1937, p. 193. For Latin America, see J. Lloyd Mecham, *Church and State in Latin America,* Chapel Hill, 1934, p. 48; Mary Watters, *A History of the Church in Venezuela, 1810-1930,* Chapel Hill, 1933, p. 211; Gilberto Freyre, *The Masters and the Slaves,* New York, 1946, pp. 446-452.

but would also have to be ideologically indoctrinated, and, above all, socially rewarded. If the rewards were great enough to recruit people for the numerous celibate portion of the population, this class would inevitably occupy the top of the social ladder. But the celibate class would be too big to be an elite. Furthermore, the sheer fact of celibacy would not represent in itself a contribution to the productive capacity of the society. If the celibate population were given useful tasks to perform, the variety of functions would necessarily be great; and if all these received an indiscriminately high reward, some celibates would be receiving this return not because of their productive contribution but because of their celibacy. In this way, seeking to give half or more of its population advantages that at best only a few can be given (and doing so regardless of productive merit), the society would suffer an intolerable economic and social burden.[27]

After this analysis of the relatively minor role of permanent celibacy in fertility limitation, we are now ready for our second question: Why are late marriage and non-marriage more frequent in industrial than in pre-industrial societies?

Perhaps non-marriage occurs more often in industrial societies because these societies depend less upon kinship and the family as bases of social organization. The fact of being or not being married affects less the individual's economic chances. In pre-industrial societies, where the family is a productive unit, marriage has a high value for the individual. Also, where the partners to marriage are self-selected by a competitive process of courtship, as in modern countries, there tends to be a substantial proportion who are not successful in attracting a suitable mate.

The greater postponement of marriage in urban-industrial nations can be similarly explained. The necessity of lengthy training for skilled positions in an industrial economy, the often lengthy trial-and-error process of courtship, the necessity of economic self-sufficiency on the part of the newly married couple — all are conducive to marital postponement.

But in neither type of society is non-marriage likely to be as important a depressant of fertility as late marriage, because marriage remains the institutional norm in both cases. Wedlock may be postponed with some equanimity, but individuals who actually never marry have, in most cases, hoped that this would not be their fate. In Ireland, for example, clerical celibacy is certainly valued, but not permanent celibacy among laymen.[28]

Once again let us note that neither the postponement nor the total abjuration of marriage necessarily implies sexual celibacy. Hence no industrial society today is required to use either method as a dominant means of controlling fertility, because other less drastic, less sacrificial, methods are available. It is clear that marital postponement, non-marriage, and abstinence within marriage, if they are effective in limiting fertility, all have a common feature — sexual denial; and all share the difficulties that this entails.

Number 8. Use or Non-Use of Contraception

Whereas the "intercourse variables" have a negative effect on fertility only through abstinence, neither the conception nor the gestation variables require this drastic behavior by the individual or the institutionalization necessary to insure such behavior. With the "conception variables" (of which the use or non-use of contraception is one), the pleasure of intercourse is not foregone. The individual, thus released from paying a heavy appetitive penalty for the decision not to have children, is much freer to decide this issue in terms of his economic and social interests alone.

With reference to contraception in particular, its apparent efficiency might lead one to expect a widespread use of it as a depressant of fertility. Yet we have already stated that this is one of the three variables which almost universally have a strong plus fertility-value in pre-industrial societies. Why, then, do these societies so widely exhibit the *non-use* of contraception? To answer

[27] Of course, a society could be imagined in which half or more of the women were forced to be celibate, the rest of the people living in polyandrous marriage. But such a speculation would evoke more paradoxes than that already sketched. A society capable of such deliberate organization could scarcely be expected to use celibacy alone as its means of controlling fertility. With other less drastic means available, the end would hardly justify the means.

[28] Arensberg and Kimball, *op. cit.*, p. 69.

this question, we must consider separately the two types of contraception.

8a. Contraception by chemical or mechanical means. In many primitive and peasant cultures the idea of chemical and mechanical contraception is known and attempts are made to apply it. Yet, even in situations motivating the individual to limit his fertility, this is *not* usually the means adopted, simply because the technology of underdeveloped societies cannot supply effective methods. In the absence of a knowledge of reproductive physiology, people in these societies have little sense of even the kind of instrumentalities to look for. Similarly, there is not enough knowledge of chemistry to give command over materials. The methods, therefore, tend to be hit or miss, with magic rather than science playing a prominent role. Lack of experimental technique leads one method to be valued as highly as another.[29] Even the methods that would actually accomplish the purpose of contraception are apt to be clumsy, sexually unsatisfactory, and unhealthful, e.g., insertion of an okra-like seed pod in the vagina (Bush Negroes of British Guiana); insertion of rags or finely chopped grass (Bapindas and Bambundas in Central Africa); insertion of dung (Egypt and other societies).[30] Furthermore, granted that a really satisfactory method is hit upon, such as possibly the use of a douche containing lemon juice or a decoction of the husks of mahogany nut (Martinique or Guiana),[31] the materials are likely to be available only in one locale or in certain seasons of the year. Thus the technology and economy of pre-industrial societies have not been equal to the task of providing a chemico-mechanical contraceptive that would be at once cheap, satisfactory, effective, and readily available.

8b. Contraception without chemical or mechanical means. Clearly such methods as withdrawal, intercourse without penetration, and various heterosexual "perversions" do not depend on scientific and technological progress. They are known and practiced in one form or another in nearly all societies.[32] Yet they seem to be insufficiently employed to represent a major control over fertility. They may be so employed in a few primitive societies, but apparently not in the civilizations such as that of China, India, and the Near East where huge population aggregates are found. For the most part, it seems, they are employed in extra-marital relations or in those cases where premarital intercourse is permitted but premarital pregnancy forbidden. But it is doubtful that such practices represent an important contribution to fertility control in whole societies. Numerous societies — some with a good share of the world's people — either do not permit the ordinary female to engage in premarital intercourse, or have such a young age at marriage that such intercourse would play a small role in any case. As for extra-marital relations, those societies which permit them under certain circumstances are not particularly concerned about the woman's becoming pregnant, because

[29] Norman E. Himes, *Medical History of Contraception,* Baltimore, 1936, pp. 53-54, 99. See also Clellan S. Ford, *A Comparative Study of Human Reproduction,* New Haven, 1945, pp. 40-42.

[30] Himes, *op. cit.,* pp. 10, 18-19, 63.

[31] *Ibid.,* p. 17. Also see M. Soors, "La denatalité chez les Mongo", *Zaïre,* Vol. 4, May 1950, pp. 525-532.

[32] Himes, speaking of Europe, says that "*coitus interruptus* is doubtless the most popular, widely diffused method of contraception . . . and has been for centuries . . . [It] is probably nearly as old as the group life of man." *Op. cit.,* pp. 183-184. He also cites numerous primitive tribes in which *coitus interruptus* is practiced. I. Schapera, writing of the Kgatla of Bechuanaland, says: "The commonest method of contraception locally practiced is *coitus interruptus* . . . It is widely employed not only by married people, but also by unmarried lovers." Sometimes the woman by moving her hips so as to extrude the penis just before ejaculation, accomplishes *coitus interruptus* without the male's cooperation. *Married Life in an African Tribe,* New York, 1941, pp. 222-223. *Coitus inter femora* is practiced in many societies, particularly by the Bantus in Africa. Girls may wear special girdles designed to avoid penetration. C. Daryll Forde, *Marriage and the Family among the Yakö of South-Eastern Nigeria,* London, 1941, p. 14. Bantu tribes, permitting sexual relations but not pregnancy before marriage, teach (or did teach) their young people how to have intercourse without penetration, the unbroken hymen in some tribes being regarded as an important index of virginity, insisted on at marriage.

Alfred C. Kinsey et al. found "petting to climax" to have been practiced by 24% of the male sample (blown up to represent the U.S. male population) by age 21, and by 50% of college-educated males. The cumulative incidence among females was less but still substantial, being 24% for the college-educated at age 20. *Sexual Behavior in the Human Male,* Philadelphia, 1948, pp. 531-542, and . . . *in the Human Female,* 1953, p. 270.

biological paternity is not stressed. Only those societies branding adulterous children as illegitimate would condemn the married woman's pregnancy by another man than the husband, and these would be societies which restrict extramarital intercourse. For these reasons, to have an independent and significant effect on fertility, non-mechanical contraceptive methods would have to be used *within* marriage. We are therefore forced to ask why such methods are not more widely used within wedlock in pre-industrial societies.

The reader should recall that any society with a high mortality must in general motivate its members to view legitimate reproduction favorably. Under this pressure the cultures in question, as already pointed out, are so organized as to maximize fertility values in the early stages of the reproductive process — e.g., by early marriage. Although intercourse is one step later, it is still so early as to involve a risk of inadequate fertility. If conditions subsequently make children undesirable, measures can still be taken after conception.

An additional consideration is that the physical burden and danger of childbearing, and the responsibility for nourishing and rearing the child, fall mainly on the mother. If therefore there is a wish to avoid childbirth, this wish is apt to be hers rather than her husband's. It happens, however, that the non-chemico-mechanical methods of contraception are the ones requiring the co-operation and partial frustration of the male. Since he is not under the pressures that affect his wife in this matter, he may be reluctant to aid her in avoiding pregnancy.

The social insulation of the two sexes is often carried so far that communication between them is difficult. This insulation is particularly observable in regard to sexual behavior, which tends to be surrounded by taboos and rituals. As between husband and wife, sexual intercourse, by virtue of being the special bond and therefore the focus of anxiety and conflict between them, may be the topic they discuss with least freedom. Thus the cooperation necessary for contraception is made difficult.

In such terms we can understand why the available methods of contraception receive scant use in underdeveloped societies. Which of the considerations mentioned plays the greatest role is hard to say, but the fact should be emphasized that not all the reasons for limiting births are predictable at the time of intercourse — particularly in simple societies that live close to the environment and are threatened by quick catastrophe. The individual couple may, therefore, as we shall see later, limit fertility *after* rather than *at* the time of intercourse.

Number 9. Voluntary Control over Fecundity

Like chemical and mechanical contraception, satisfactory control of fecundity is beyond the technical capacity of pre-industrial societies. Neither the reduction nor the enhancement of fecundity by harmless medical measures appears possible in such cultures. Operations on the male external genitalia can be performed, such as subincision and castration, but these are either too drastic to be harmless or have little effect on fecundity.[33]

We may conclude, then, that pre-industrial societies are plus on variable number 9. But so are industrial societies. The latter may have even more of a plus fertility-value on this variable than simple societies because they can, and usually do, forbid sterilization and, at the same time, foster medical treatment for sterility, thus *enhancing* the fecundity of partially sterile couples.

Although modern science makes harmless sterilization possible, it has not yet been used, except in Puerto Rico, as a popular method of avoiding children.[34] The Puerto Rican case suggests, however, that sterilization may in the future become more widely diffused in underdevel-

[33] Castration is so drastic that it is apparently never used with enough frequency to affect group fertility. Subincision, the splitting of the penis in such a way that the semen is expelled from the lower part rather than through the glans, seemingly has little effect on fecundity, depending in part on the position assumed during intercourse. Also the practice has a very limited distribution even in primitive society and seems unknown in more advanced pre-industrial societies. Among the Australian aborigines, where it is found, opinion differs as to its effects. German theorists, according to Himes, have generally held that the operation lowers fertility and is so intended. Modern anthropologists, on the other hand, have denied both these contentions. Himes himself believes it may have some negative effect of this kind. *Op. cit.*, pp. 41-51.

[34] See J. M. Stycos, "Female Sterilization in Puerto Rico," *Eugenics Quarterly*, Vol. 1, June 1954, pp. 3-9.

oped areas. If the operational technique were improved to the point where it could be easily reversed — so that it could be used for the spacing, as well as for limiting the total number, of children — it might become the principal means of reducing fertility in backward areas.

Number 3a. Time Between Unstable Unions

Any negative effect on fertility from variable 3a is a function of both the rate of dissolution of unions and the time lost between them. If unions are stable, or if they are unstable but no time is lost between them, fertility will not be affected adversely.

With reference to *marital* unions, pre-industrial societies seem generally to have a low rate of dissolution. True, there are certain exceptions to this rule. Some of the Islamic peoples show a tendency toward marital instability, and in some primitive societies the clan or joint household takes such precedence over the nuclear family that the latter tends to be somewhat unstable.[35] On the whole, however, the institutional structure of pre-industrial groups buttresses marriage in such ways as to give it considerable stability.

When a society has a significant proportion of informal unions which it regards as inferior to legal marriage but in which reproduction is neverthless expected (e.g., "consensual unions" in Latin America and "common law" unions in the British West Indies), one of the features of such unions is that they tend to be unstable. In such cases the woman may wait some time before entering a new union, and the fertility lost may be substantial. For a small sample of women in Jamaica (where around 70% of the births are illegitimate) the reduction in fertility due to the instability of unions was approximately 37%.[36] The informal type of union arises as an institutional form from various historical causes. In societies that have been disorganized by Western contact, they may appear abundantly, and legal marriage itself may become unstable.[37] In other instances where the social order has grown largely out of a former slave class, informal unions may be both more numerous and more unstable than legal marriages.[38]

With reference to premarital unions, there is every evidence that in the many societies where these are permitted they are, as a rule, highly unstable, amounting in many cases to adolescent promiscuity. However, there is ordinarily little time lost between such liaisons; few societies permit reproduction in them; and, given a young age at marriage, most such unions occur at an age when adolescent sterility seemingly reduces the number of conceptions.

It follows that pre-industrial societies generally have a plus fertility-value with respect to variable number 3a, but the exceptions are more numerous than was the case with the other variables so far considered.

Number 3b. Post-Widowhood Celibacy

What effect the high rate of widowhood found in pre-industrial societies has on fertility depends on the institutional position of the widow. In many such societies she loses little time from exposure to intercourse, because she soon marries again. In other pre-industrial cultures, however, the widow either must wait for a protracted period or is subject to a distinct prejudice against remarrying at all. An important problem in analyzing the institutional impingements on fer-

[35] See Ralph Linton, *Study of Man,* New York, 1936, Ch. 10. Murdock, *op. cit.,* p. 3, criticizes Linton for holding that in some societies organized on a "consanguine" basis the nuclear family plays an insignificant role, but the fact is that in such cultures marital instability may have little disorganizing effect. See K. Davis, "Children of Divorced Parents", *Law and Contemporary Problems,* Vol. 10, Summer 1944, pp. 700-710.

[36] Judith Blake, "Family Instability and Reproductive Behavior in Jamaica", *Current Research in Human Fertility,* Milbank Memorial Fund, New York, 1955, pp. 26-30.

[37] Margaret Mead, *Changing Culture of an Indian Tribe,* New York, 1932, pp. 14-15, Ch. 10. Schapera, *op. cit.,* Ch. 10; *Migrant Labour and Tribal Life,* London, 1947, pp. 183-189; and "Cultural Changes in Family Life", *The Bantu-Speaking Tribes of South Africa,* London, 1937, pp. 380-385. The literature covering the impact of Western culture on native peoples is so enormous that one could document indefinitely the tendency of such contact to produce illicit sexual unions and instability in such unions and in marriage.

[38] T. S. Simey, *Welfare and Planning in the West Indies,* Oxford, 1946, *passim.* F. M. Henriques, *Family and Colour in Jamaica,* London, 1953, *passim.* G. W. Roberts, "Some Aspects of Mating and Fertility in the West Indies", *Population Studies,* Vol. 8, March 1955, pp. 199-227. R. T. Smith, "Family Organization in British Guiana", *Social and Economic Studies,* Vol. I, February 1953, pp. 87-111.

tility is the discovery of why some societies take one course in this regard and others take the opposite course.

If we study those societies in which remarriage occurs universally and soon, we find that they are the ones requiring the widow to marry a kinsman of the deceased husband (levirate). Such societies are usually primitive, practicing a shifting cultivation, hunting, or pastoral pursuits, and are characterized by strong clan or lineage organization. Marriage involves substantial economic exchanges and, if the system is patrilineal and patrilocal, these are weighted in favor of the bride's lineage (brideprice). The woman brought into the clan or lineage as a wife is conceived as belonging to this clan, which has paid the brideprice; her children, who are automatically members of the husband's lineage, represent her contribution in return for the cost of procuring her. When the woman is widowed, the lineage retains control over her, not only because a price has been paid for her but also because her children must remain with the lineage. If she still is fecund, the lineage feels it would be losing potential children if she did not remarry. But remarriage to an outsider would be unsatisfactory, because the children of that union would belong to another lineage. Hence the remarriage must be within the clan. Since in the exchanges cementing the first marriage, the husband's nearest relatives bore the main cost, it is natural that his close kin (notably his brothers) should have first claim on the widow. If the deceased husband has no actual brothers, one of his "classificatory brothers" can be substituted. In anticipation of her possibly entering a leviratic union, a woman's relation with her husband's actual and classificatory brothers is often one of privileged familiarity. The term for "husband's brother" may be the same as that for "husband." The social structure clearly demonstrates that the clan is thinking of the widow in terms of her potential production of children. Among the Nuer, for instance, even if the widow should take as a lover a person outside the clan (she cannot legally marry outside), the children are viewed as the descendants of the dead husband and therefore as members of his, not the lover's clan.[39]

[39] E. E. Evans-Pritchard, *Kinship and Marriage among the Nuer,* Oxford, 1951, pp. 112-123.

In many societies, on the other hand, the widow is forbidden to marry a close relative of the deceased husband. These seem to be cases in which the clan, however important it may once have been, has receded in economic and political significance, seemingly as a result of technological advance and greater class stratification. The economy is that of a more stable agriculture in which the same land is intensively cultivated year in and year out. Under such circumstances the joint household acquires more independence and more significance as an economic unit than it seems to have in most primitive societies. The distinction between relatives in different households thus takes precedence over their solidarity as members of the same lineage or clan. To be sure, the woman marrying into the joint household may do so in terms of some form of economic exchange, but this exchange is between individual households rather than clans. The widow and her children accordingly belong to the deceased husband's household. Remarriage to one of her dead mate's brothers or other close male relatives, however, would be structurally inappropriate, because the joint household is always subject to dissolution and must be so organized as to minimize the complications of such dissolution. Unlike the clan or lineage, which is immortal and indefinitely expandable, the household is a residential economic unit which can easily grow too large for its immediate resources. With stable agriculture, the household must be near the land it works. If its memberships increases, it must ultimately break up because the land required for sustenance will be too distant. When the household does break up, usually at the death of the male head, it does so by the separation of its nuclear families.[40] Accordingly, even when the nuclear family forms part of a joint household, it is visualized not only as a separate unit but also as one that may in the future have its own independent residence. A widow's remarriage to one of her husband's relatives within the household would conflict with this idea of potential independence. It would inextricably merge two nuclear families. It would require polygyny and

[40] For mention of the joint household's vulnerability to change and its consequent fissive tendency, see Murdock, *op. cit.*, p. 36.

would emphasize the solidarity of the sibling relationship rather than the father-son relation so central to the independent joint household.

Stable agrarian societies not only forbid the widow to marry within the circle of her husband's kin but also often frown on her marrying anyone at all. This additional prejudice seems likewise to be explicable in structural terms. For the widow to marry outside would require that some agency make a match for her, because marriages in traditional agrarian societies are arranged by persons other than the parties to the union. However, her family of orientation is no longer responsible for her. The family of her deceased husband is restrained from taking the responsibility for several reasons. It would, in seeking a mate for the widow, have to treat her as a daughter, which might interfere with the rights of the actual daughters. Furthermore, since she is a widow and is older, she has become less valuable than upon her first marriage, so that it is difficult to get her married at a social level reflecting favorable on the family's prestige. If the widow has children, her marriage outside the immediate kin would require her separation from them. It is thus understandable why traditional agrarian societies, especially where the joint household is normally preferred, should exhibit a prejudice against widow remarriage. Such unions certainly do occur, particularly in the lower classes which cannot carry out the joint family ideal, but the prejudice may be strong enough to prevent a high proportion of widows in the upper classes from remarrying.[41] In India the caste controls reinforce those of the joint household in preventing widow remarriage. Since such unions are thought to lower the caste's prestige, and since marriage is endogamous within the caste, both parties to a remarriage are condemned. For this reason the reduction of fertility due to widow agamy is probably greater in India than in any other country, especially because of the early age at marriage and the high mortality there.

Number 11. Voluntary Control over Foetal Mortality

Underdeveloped societies have few means for *lessening* foetal mortality, but they do have readily available means, through abortion, for *increasing* such mortality. In fact, abortion is widely practiced in pre-industrial societies, being the individual's principal means of limiting fertility.[42] Since medical measures to avoid foetal mortality do not, at least as yet, have as much influence on fertility as voluntary abortion can and does, we can say that whether a society has a plus or minus fertility-value with respect to variable 11 depends primarily on the extent to which it practices abortion. Accordingly, some pre-industrial societies are on the "plus" side (forbidding abortion and practicing it little) but many other are on the "minus" side (practicing abortion to a considerable extent). If we grant that interference with conception is less hazardous to health than interference with pregnancy, an important question for us is why abortion is so much more frequently used in underdeveloped societies than contraception.

In answering this question, one can point to the following considerations: (a) as compared

[41] Levy, *op. cit.*, p. 46, points out that although the Chinese gentry have always frowned on widow remarriage, the peasants have usually practiced it. In fact, if a peasant widow was young and lacked grown sons, remarriage was inevitable. As the peasantry is said to comprise as much as 80% of the population (p. 44), widow celibacy is hardly characteristic of China as a whole, although gentry patterns set the ideals for the entire society. Olga Lang, without distinguishing between gentry and peasantry, says that remarriage is frowned on. *Chinese Family and Society,* New Haven, 1946, p. 53. She says (p. 126) that poor men often marry widows because they are easier to get than virgins. Any divorcee or widow can find a husband if she is willing to marry beneath her status. With regard to the absence of anything like the levirate in China, it is interesting to note that Miss Lang says (p. 21) that "early in the feudal period, under the Chou dynasty (ca. 1027-256 B.C.), the clan began to divide into economic families." Today, even in the South where clans are of some importance, they have no real authority in family matters. The strongest clans in Central and North China lack the essential of clan life, a fair amount of common property (pp. 177-178).

[42] Ford, *op. cit.*, pp. 50-51, found that most of his tribes took cognizance of abortion. In eleven it was specifically stated to be forbidden, and in eight it could be inferred to be forbidden; in 21 it was permitted to the young girl who finds herself pregnant, and in 4 this could be inferred to be the case; and in 12 a married woman was allowed to practice abortion if she believed that she had become pregnant through an adulterous intrigue. Himes regards abortion as widespread in primitive societies (*op. cit.*, p. 52). A recent study by George Devereaux, *Abortion in Primitive Society,* New York, 1955, pp. 25-26, cites cases of tribes where abortion is quite frequent.

to mechanical and chemical means of contraception, abortion is technically simple;[43] (b) In contrast to such non-chemico-mechanical methods as *coitus interruptus* or *coitus inter femora,* abortion is not applied at the time of intercourse and does not require cooperation between man and woman. It is a woman's method and can be practiced without the man's knowledge. (c) Unlike contraception, it is completely effective. (d) Once an undesired pregnancy has occurred, the need for abortion is certain, whereas at the time of intercourse there is always the chance that pregnancy will not eventuate anyway. (e) Although a child may be desired at the time of intercourse, subsequent events may alter this attitude, at which time abortion rather than contraception is a remedy.

A note on infanticide. Although infanticide is not dealt with as an integral part of our analysis because it does not affect fertility, one should note that it is virtually a functional equivalent of abortion in controlling family size, and that it too is practiced widely in pre-industrial societies, much more so than contraception. The rationale for its use is much the same as that for abortion, but it does differ from the latter in at least three respects. First, infanticide allows the progeny to be selected by sex, as shown by the custom of *female* infanticide. The logic of this practice is exemplified by the Netsilik Eskimos:

> The most glaring consequence of the struggle for existence is manifested in the way in which they try to breed the greatest possible number of boys and the fewest possible girls . . . girls are killed at birth, if they have not already been promised to a family where there is a son who some day is to have a wife . . . They hold the view that if a woman is to suckle a girl child it will be two or three years before she may expect her next confinement . . . A hunter must take into consideration that he can only subject himself and his constitution for comparatively few years to all the strain that hunting demands . . . Now if he has sons, they will as a rule be able to step in and help just when his own physique is beginning to fail. Thus it is life's own inexorability that has taught them the necessity of having as many sons as possible. Only by that means may they be certain that they will not need to put the rope around their own neck too early; for it is the common custom that old people who can no longer keep themselves, prefer to put an end to their life by hanging.[44]

Olga Lang discusses the persistence of the immemorial custom of female infanticide in China. The hospital records used for her study "contained matter-of-fact references to infanticide made by Chinese social and medical workers indicating that it was taken for granted. Much more often, however, infant daughters have not been killed outright. What happens is that the small amount of food available for the family is unequally distributed: the son gets the larger share and the daughters are practically starved. Hence the frequent epidemics have taken a heavier toll of girls than boys."[45] Much the same could be said of India.

Second, infanticide also allows the offspring to be selected according to physical status, weeding out those with deformities, bad health, or unacceptable physical or racial characteristics.[46] Third, it can be practiced when the circumstances of birth are considered to be abnormal and ritualistically taboo. Twins, children born with feet first or with teeth, infants whose mothers died at their birth,[47] and offspring born on unlucky days are typical victims.[48] Fourth, whereas abortion may injure the health of the mother, infanticide obviously does not.

A *disadvantage* of infanticide may seem to be that since a child has already been born, a living person is being killed. However, the newborn child is often not viewed as a member of society until he has passed through some sort of ceremony (*amphidromia* in ancient Greece, presenta-

[43] Premature labor can be induced by killing the foetus. This can be done by beating, pressing, or massaging the abdomen; by drinking poisons or strong emetics or laxatives; by piercing the foetus or amniotic sac with sharp reeds or instruments; or by wearing a tight belt. See Ford, *op. cit.*, p. 52; Devereaux, *op. cit.*, pp. 27-42.

[44] Knud Rasmussen, *The Netsilik Eskimos,* Copenhagen, 1931, pp. 139-140.

[45] Lang, *op. cit.*, p. 150.

[46] Hutton Webster, *Taboo: A Sociological Study,* Stanford, 1942, pp. 59-61.

[47] *Ibid.*, pp. 59-65.

[48] Linton, *Study of Man, op. cit.*, pp. 194-195, with reference to the Tanala of Madagascar. In a letter to W. Lloyd Warner quoted by Himes, *op. cit.*, p. 8, Linton says: "I do not think that there was any idea of limiting population in it [infanticide], but the losses were severe. In at least one tribe all children born on three days in each week were killed."

tion of the child to the father in China) which defines him as such. The destruction of the child is therefore viewed psychologically in much the same light as abortion.

Number 4. Voluntary Abstinence within Unions

Abstinence within unions is practiced much more, on the average, in pre-industrial than in industrial societies. The effect of such abstinence on fertility, however, depends on the circumstances; for there are at least four types of restriction — post-partum, occasional, gestational, and menstrual. The first two types tend to limit fertility, while the last two, if they have any effect at all, tend to increase it.

Post-partum abstinence occurs in nearly all societies, including our own. The amount of time involved, however, varies greatly — all the way from one to two weeks in some societies to two to three years in others. Many pre-industrial societies insist upon abstinence for an arbitrary period of time after birth, usually for several weeks or months. In a few instances the duration of abstinence is fixed by some developmental stage of the child — e. g., when the baby first crawls, sits up, walks, or cuts its teeth. In many cases the taboo on coitus extends through the lactation period, which may last two to three years.[49] Not all of the time involved, of course, represents a loss of fertility, because ovulation is often delayed or occurs sporadically for a time after parturition. It is only when the period of abstinence extends to two months or more that a loss of fertility can be assumed, although even then it may not be quite commensurate with the amount of time covered. These longer periods, though found frequently in primitive and peasant societies,[50] are not customary in industrial countries.

Long post-partum taboos on intercourse obviously help to space out children, but this is not the reason usually given in communities that practice such taboos. Instead, a violation of the taboo is viewed as being magically dangerous to the child or the parents.[51] Such notions probably lead to the observance of the abstinence rules. In addition, it should be noted that in many instances the male has access to another wife, (if he is polygynous) or to a concubine or other available woman. The social structure may encourage observance of the taboo in another way. When, as in India, the wife customarily goes to her parents' home to bear each of her first two or three children and stays there for a few months after the confinement, the taboo is enforced with ease. Thus the fact that 80% of Indian villagers in one study reported post-partum abstinence of six months or more indicates a significant loss of fertility from this cause.[52] Doubtless similar or greater losses occur in many other agrarian societies.

The "occasional" restrictions on sexual intercourse are those occurring in connection with regular holidays and special ceremonies, tabooed days of the week, and important communal tasks (war, economic undertakings, etc.).[53] The exact amount of time lost to reproduction in this way has seldom been calculated, but the Indian field study just cited found that the average number of days of avoidance for religious reasons was 24 per year in a rural village, while in a middle class housing project it was 19.[54] If these days occur sporadically, they hardly represent much loss of fertility, because they are practically comprised within the normal frequency of intercourse; but in many societies the abstentions extend over substantial periods. "The natives of the Mortlock Islands, a part of the Caroline group, proscribe any sexual intercourse in time of war; a man who violated the rule would die a sudden death. During the fishing season, which lasts for six to eight weeks, every Yap fisherman is subject to many restrictions . . . Women are very strictly tabooed to him . . ."[55]

In contrast to post-partum and "occasional" taboos on coitus, gestational abstinence obviously cannot diminish fertility. The only question is whether it may slightly *increase* fertility. Most societies proscribe intercourse during some part,

[49] Clellan S. Ford and Frank A. Beach, *Patterns of Sexual Behavior,* New York, 1951, p. 219.

[50] Webster, *op. cit.,* pp. 67-71.

[51] Ford and Beach, *op. cit.,* p. 219.

[52] C. Chandrasekaran, "Cultural Patterns in Relation to Family Planning in India", *Proceedings of the Third International Conference on Planned Parenthood, 1952,* Bombay, p. 78.

[53] Ford, *Comparative Study of Human Reproduction, op. cit.,* pp. 28-29. Webster, *op. cit.,* pp. 132-139.

[54] Chandrasekaran, *op. cit.,* p. 78.

[55] Webster, *op. cit.,* p. 134.

but seldom during all or even the major portion, of the gestation period. Only seven of the primitive groups in Ford's sample extended the taboo to the greater part of the period.[56] Usually it is toward the end of the pregnancy that the prohibition applies. If intercourse during the later stages occasionally induces miscarriage or causes puerperal infection, as is sometimes claimed,[57] then the taboo may enhance fertility, but only slightly.

Similarly, the almost universal prohibition of coitus during menstruation can have little or no negative effect on fertility. Such abstention, when fertilization is least likely, tends to concentrate sexual activity in the more fertile part of the menstrual cycle. In some pre-industrial cultures the taboo is extended for a few days after the menstrual flow has ceased (as among the ancient Hebrews), which has the effect of concentrating coital activity still more directly on the days when conception is most likely.

On the whole, primitive and peasant societies appear to have a greater fertility loss through intra-marital abstinence (variable number 4) than do industrial societies. They have considerably more post-partum and "occasional" abstinence, and the effect of these in inhibiting reproduction is not fully counterbalanced by the fact that underdeveloped societies also occasionally have longer menstrual and gestational taboos (which may slightly enhance fertility).

The Other Intermediate Variables

There remain four variables — number 10 (which usually has a low fertility-value in non-industrial societies) and numbers 5, 6, and 7 (which seem indeterminate in their values). All four of these variables appear not to be clearly determined by institutional patterns in different cultures. If there is any difference in their fertility-values as between one type of society and another, the difference seems to be more a function of the general level of living than of the specific institutional structures. Perhaps one clue to this circumstance lies in the fact that three of the four variables (10, 5, and 7) are defined as involuntary in the sense of not being under control and hence not amenable to motivational determination. The other variable (number 6, frequency of coitus), though subject to individual control, is possibly too private and too linked up with organic capacity to be culturally controlled.

With respect to number 10 — foetal mortality from involuntary causes — we have said that the fertility-value is generally low in pre-industrial societies; because the data available indicate that stillbirth rates are greater in such societies. However, the conclusion is tentative, because adequate comparative information does not exist for miscarriage rates.

Number 5 — involuntary abstinence — presumably varies according to several disparate factors. In so far as health or sickness may be involved, the non-industrial peoples would probably exhibit a higher degree of such abstinence. The same inference might be drawn with regard to impotency, except that this condition is often caused by psychological determinants which may be more prevalent in industrial cultures. Another cause of involuntary abstinence, the separation of couples due to migration, would seem to vary according to the particular historical circumstances of the society. Except under conditions of European contact, indigenous groups apparently have little individual mobility. Clearly, these divergent influences affecting involuntary abstinence can run counter to each other. It is therefore difficult to claim, for this variable, any consistent overall differences between societies. We are also handicapped by an almost total lack of data, for no comparative information has been collected with this issue in mind.

Variable number 6 — frequency of intercourse — possibly favors fertility more in underdeveloped than in industrial societies. But at best the evidence for this view is indirect, drawn solely from a few advanced societies where coital frequency appears greater among the manual than among the sedentary classes. Such direct evidence as we have supports no view at all. Average figures on "coital frequency" given in the literature, usually stated as so many times per week, are ambiguous, because it is unclear whether they mean *every* week or only those weeks when coitus is not impossible because of sickness, absence, menstrual, or other taboos, etc. Also, the comparative frequency figures cited in the literature are fantastic, showing variations from one society to another that are

[56] Ford, *op. cit.*, p. 48.
[57] *Ibid.*, p. 49.

wholly inexplicable.[58] We have found no reliable evidence that the average frequency of intercourse for comparable age groups varies significantly as between one society and another, and certainly none which indicates that this is a significant factor in inter-societal variations in fertility.

With respect to variable number 7 (involuntary sterility) we again have little evidence. The hard conditions of life in pre-industrial societies may give rise to a considerable amount of low fecundity or absolute sterility — particularly in the latter part of the woman's reproductive span; and in given instances, after contact with highly civilized peoples, venereal disease may have a pronounced effect of this sort. On the other hand, the nervous tension and artificial modes of life in urban-industrial populations may possibly tend to lower fecundity to some extent.

Patently, the comparative fertility-values of the four intermediate variables just discussed are unknown. Not only is evidence lacking, but there is no sound line of reasoning by which the behavior of these variables can be linked up with specific institutional patterns. At most, there may be some connection in each case with the general level of living. The evidence for this is best with respect to number 10, but the other three must be left for the time being as indeterminate.

Conclusion: The General Pattern

Any analysis of institutional factors in fertility must first explain the well known fact that underdeveloped societies in general have a higher rate of reproduction than industrial societies. The explanation, in brief, is that the pre-industrial peoples, in the face of high mortality, have had to develop an institutional organization which would give them sufficient reproduction to survive. However, analysis at this level does not carry us very far. In order to study the effects of institutional factors, one needs to break down the reproductive process itself so as to distinguish clearly the various mechanisms though which, and only through which, any social factor *can* influence fertility. In trying to do this, we have found eleven "intermediate variables". When analysis is made along those lines, it can be seen that the generally high fertility of underdeveloped areas does not mean that these areas encourage high fertility in every respect. As we have seen, they do not have high plus values on *all* the intermediate variables. Why, then, do they have low values in some respects and not in others?

It is possible to discern a systematic difference between underdeveloped and developed societies with reference to the eleven variables. In general, the pre-industrial societies have high fertility-value for those variables farthest removed from the actual moment of parturition and which, therefore, imply an overall outlook favorable to fertility. To a much greater degree than industrial societies, they tend to encourage early exposure to intercourse — exhibiting a far younger age at marriage and a higher proportion married. They thus lose little potential fertility by delaying or avoiding the formation of unions. After unions have been formed, these societies tend to enjoin more abstinence than industrial societies do (and therefore have lower values on variable number 4), but such "sexual fasting" arises from religious and magical motives rather than as a deliberate fertility control measure, and it does not appear to be great enough to have a substantial negative effect on fertility.

Underdeveloped societies also have high fertility-values for the conception variables. They practice little contraception and virtually no sterilization. Consequently, the tendency is to *postpone* the issue of controlling pregnancy until a later point in the reproductive process, which means that when a couple wishes to avoid children, those methods nearest the point of parturition — abortion and infanticide — are employed. These have the advantage, in societies living close to privation, of being nearer to the actual moment when the child must be supported.

[58] Thus Ford and Beach report as an apparent fact that "the Aranda of Australia have intercourse as often as three or five times nightly, sleeping between each sex act," and that for Chagga men "intercourse ten times in a single night is not unusual." Nothing is said about how these bizarre statistics are gathered, or about what age groups in the population are being considered. The authors say simply, "it is reported that," or "it is not unusual that," etc. Such reports are all the more questionable since societies apparently with a similar level of living are said to have extremely different figures — some at "once a week" or "once or twice a week" — without any explanation of why they should be so low and others fifteen or twenty times as high. *Op. cit.*, pp. 78-79.

Industrial societies, on the other hand, exhibit low fertility-values for those variables involving the early stages of the reproductive process, especially age at marriage, proportion married, and contraception; and they manifest high fertility-values for the variables in the later stages, especially infanticide. It follows that for many of the variables the two types of society exhibit opposite values. This is true for age of entry into unions, permanent celibacy, voluntary abstinence, contraception, and (if included as a variable) infanticide. It is not *necessarily* true of the time spent between or after unions, of sterilization, or of abortion; and it, of course, is not true of those variables characterized as "indeterminate" — involuntary abstinence, frequency of coitus, or involuntary infecundity. But the general contrast is sufficiently clear to require explanation.

A key to the position of the industrial societies lies in the fact that, as compared to pre-industrial cultures, they have achieved their lower reproduction, not by acquiring low fertility-values for *all* the intermediate variables, but by singling out particular ones as the means to that result. They took those means of reducing fertility which involved the least institutional organization and re-organization and which involved the least human cost. In the secular decline of the birth rate they relied more heavily on the mere postponement of marriage than on non-marriage. They relied less on abstinence, which makes heavy demands on the individual, and more on contraception and abortion, which do not. They dropped infanticide altogther and, in the later stages, tended to reduce abortion. In other words, they have undertaken to lower fertility, not primarily by extending further the negative effect on the variables by which fertility was lowered in the pre-industrial stage, but by using readily available institutional mechanisms with respect to marriage and by employing the possibilities of their advanced technology for conception control. Marital postponement was easily extended in the early and middle stages of industrialization because the basis for it already existed in Western society and because contraception and relatively safe abortion freed those who married late from the necessity of premarital celibacy. Gradually, in the late stages of industrial development, contraception has gained such predominance that it has made low fertility-values on the other variables (including abortion and late marriage) unnecessary.

*Norms for Family Size in Underdeveloped Areas**

RONALD FREEDMAN

It is a commonplace observation that fertility is high in the so-called underdeveloped societies. Sometimes this leads to the erroneous view that their fertility is limited only by what is biologically possible so that birth rates reach a mythologically high natural level. In this idealized view free and unrestrained sexual unions beginning at an early age produce very high fertility as an incidental result without deliberate intent and without much individual or social concern about family size.

A more plausible general proposition is that reproduction, whether at high or low levels, is so important to the family and to society everywhere that its level is more or less controlled by cultural norms about family size and such related matters as marriage, timing of intercourse, and abortion. In each society the cultural norms about these vital matters are consistent with social institutions in which they are deeply embedded. Changes in fertility are unlikely without prior or,

* Reprinted with permission from *Proceedings of the Royal Society,* Vol. 159 (1963), pp. 220-234.

at least, simultaneous changes in these institutions.

Before developing these ideas, it may be useful to consider briefly the variability in fertility among underdeveloped societies. A recent study of the Cocos Island population(1)* provides a unique example of exceptionally high fertility expected in the model of virtually unrestrained fertility. The Cocos Islanders, living between 1870 and 1947 under an exceptionally favourable paternalistic regime married early, and about two-thirds of their brides were pregnant at marriage. The birth rates between 1880 and 1947 averaged about 55 per thousand and reached 60 in several years. This may be contrasted with birth rates of about 35 per thousand in pre-industrial England. The gross reproduction rate for the Cocos Islands was about 4.2, perhaps the highest ever recorded with reliable data.

This is an exceptionally high fertility level. It is not characteristic of all underdeveloped areas, although it is not unlikely that there are many populations with a biological potential for a similar performance. Some African populations may reach similar levels.(2) In Appendix I estimated gross reproduction rates are listed for a number of high fertility populations, underdeveloped by most criteria. These reproduction rates are very high in comparison with the rates for the developed low-fertility countries shown for contrast. But, the rates generally are well below the Cocos rate or that for the American Hutterities. The rates do not conform to any uniform level.

The range of fertility rates currently found among underdeveloped areas is wide enough to include rates which characterized Western Europe before its modern fertility decline but long after social and economic development were under way. For example the gross reproduction rate of 2.4 for England in 1861, shortly before fertility began to decline, is lower than the rates for most but by no means all of the high fertility societies today. Married women born in England in 1841–45 had just under six children on the average,(3) if they survived to the end of the child-bearing period. This is about the same as the figure reported for India now,(4) although it is significantly less than the average of more than eight children born to the Cocos Island mothers and the average of more than ten to the American Hutterite mothers.(5)

These selected data are intended only to illustrate the idea that fertility, however measured, varies from moderately to very high levels in underdeveloped societies, even after allowing for inaccuracies of base data.

Genetic differentials in fecundity eventually may be shown to account for some of the existing variation between societies, but I think they are unlikely to explain the major variations in time or between societies. They are unlikely to explain why fertility is relatively high in underdeveloped societies and declines with development.

As a more plausible explanation, I begin with the thesis that societal levels of fertility are related to variations in cultural norms about reproduction, and these, in turn, are related to the nature of the society.

One of the fundamental principles of sociology is that when many members of a society face a recurrent common problem with important social consequences they tend to develop a normative solution for it. This solution, a set of rules for behaviour in a particular situation, becomes part of the culture, and the society indoctrinates its members to conform more or less closely to the norms by explicit or implicit rewards and punishments.

The problem of how many children a couple should have is so widely shared and has so many personal and social consequences that it would be a sociological anomaly if social norms regarding it did not develop. This is also true for such related problems as when to marry and when sexual intercourse is permitted. In view of the special importance attached to kinship ties in the underdeveloped societies, it would be particularly strange if the reproductive level of the familial unit were not a matter of normative concern.

Norms about family size are likely to be in terms of a range in numbers of children that are permissible or desirable. While specifying clearly that childlessness is an unspeakable tragedy and an only child very undesirable, the norm for a particular culture or group may be as vague as 'at least three or four children' or 'as many as

* The numbers in parentheses refer to the collected notes at the end of this paper.

possible'. But I know of no organized society, primitive or modern, in which the question of how many children are born is a matter of indifference either to the reproducing unit or to the community.

In various underdeveloped societies, a large number of sample interview surveys(6) have been made since the Second World War in which peasant populations have been asked such questions as how many children they want for themselves, how many are right for others, etc. In almost all of these studies only a small minority of the respondents found the questions ridiculous or meaningless or answered that such matters were up to fate or God, etc. Even where the answers invoke the Deity or fate, further inquiry frequently indicates that the respondent has rather firm ideas of what he desires that fate or divine providence should bring. In most such surveys the answers tend to be clustered about a moderate modal value rather than to be randomly distributed. Appendix II contains some illustrative frequency distributions of attitudes about family size and family growth from surveys in several different countries. Of special significance are data in a number of these studies indicating that a majority of those with three or four children want no more and many prefer a smaller number than they have. (Illustrations are found in Appendix II.)

There are a few studies in which it is reported that questions about the desired number of children are regarded by respondents as ludicrous. This is reported, for example, by Richards & Reining for the Bahaya of Africa.(7) But, the attitude expressed apparently does not result from the absence of a norm. The report is that, under existing conditions, most women do not have the four to six children in the household which they consider ideal and would approximate if they could. And even in this instance, the authors report that there are voluntary practices limiting reproduction during certain periods.

The exact meaning and accuracy of the answers obtained in such surveys is open to question, but there is little doubt that there is considerable consensus in such populations about desirable family size.

It must be admitted that much of the survey evidence is from societies that have been in touch with the West for many years, but some of the samples studied have been in village areas of India, the Near East and other places where illiteracy and immobility have isolated much of the population from modern ideas.

It is possible, but unlikely, that all of the populations studied through sample surveys have already been considerably influenced by modern Western values about reproduction. The same cannot be said for a large number of primitive societies whose ethnology with respect to sexual and reproductive behaviour was studied by Ford.(8) He concluded that childbirth is by no means universally accepted as either natural or inevitable. Many women are ambivalent about childbirth, so that considerable social pressure may be necessary to insure adequate reproduction.

Obviously, social norms encouraging reproduction at less than the physiological maximum can be implemented only if one or more practices for fertility reduction is fairly widespread in the population, so it is very relevant to ask what control practices are available. A variety of controls are possible and are used. In addition to such deliberate and obvious practices as contraception and abortion, there are a large number of others; for example, the age at first sexual union, timing and frequency of intercourse, voluntary or involuntary fecundity impairments, foetal mortality, etc.

Davis & Blake(9) have provided a useful classification of such control factors immediately determining the fertility level of a society. They call them 'intermediate variables' because they are the means of fertility control standing intermediate between the social institutions and norms on the one hand and actual fertility on the other. Any social influences on fertility can only operate by affecting one or more of these 'intermediate variables'. The Davis & Blake classification is shown in Appendix III. I will not duplicate the detailed discussion of these variables given in their excellent paper.

Different combinations of values for these intermediate variables may produce identical fertility levels. On the other hand, societies with very different fertility levels may have similar values on some though, of course, not all of the intermediate variables. It is unnecessary and often incorrect to assume that levels of these control variables always are manipulated deliberately to limit fertility. The limiting effect on fertility is often, probably usually, an unintended consequence of one or more cultural patterns that have no explicit connexion with fertility.

Contemporary data for high fertility societies make it evident that a combination of very different control variables may produce high fertility. Coale & Tye (10) have recently shown that high fertility in some Chinese populations results from late marriage followed by very high reproduction rates into the later child-bearing years. On the other hand, high fertility in India results from very early marriage and high reproduction rates in the early child-bearing years, with a sharp decline in the later years. While both types of controls may lead to similar average family size, the 'Chinese' pattern will result in a slower rate of population growth, other things being equal, because the length of a generation is greater.

Cultural norms controlling premarital intercourse and the age of marriage have been particularly important in reducing fertility levels in a number of pre-modern societies. Apparently, this explains the fact that fertility was only moderately high in pre-industrial Europe. Economic historians(11) have shown that property and labour arrangements in a number of West European areas encouraged celibacy or the postponement of marriage in order to maintain certain standards of what the economic unit should be, and of what a couple should have in order to marry and raise children. Together with controls on premarital intercourse such arrangements apparently kept fertility below the levels of other pre-industrial societies. The breakdown of these controls in the first stages of modern urban-industrial development apparently resulted in an increase in fertility in some places before the long-run decline in fertility set in. The fact that fertility was only moderately high in many areas of pre-industrial Europe is evidence that very high fertility is not a universal characteristic of such societies.

Davis & Blake point out that since having some children is very important in pre-industrial societies, a society with high and variable mortality often is likely to have built into its structure strong pressures for having children early in marriage before one or both of the parents die and also for having some 'extra' children as a safeguard against the catastrophic loss of the essential minimum number. If unfavourable economic conditions develop, this may result in 'too many' children. Therefore, there is likely to be a delicate balance of pressures toward higher fertility to insure at least a certain minimum number of children, and counterpressures to minimize an intolerable surplus of children under difficult subsistence conditions. Davis & Blake present the hypothesis that this necessary pressure in opposite directions accounts for the adoption in many pre-industrial societies of those control practices which insure a minimum fertility level but permit a reduction in the numbers of children late in the child-bearing process, principally abortion and infanticide. These counter-balancing pressures also may account for the failure to adopt contraception, which operates very early in the reproductive process.

It would be desirable to have a systematic classification of societies by the values of the intermediate variables. Then we could study how particular combinations of the control variables produce a particular fertility level, and how each pattern is related to social norms about family size and ultimately to the social structure. Unfortunately, the data for such systematic classifications are not available.

However, Carr-Saunders,(12) Himes,(13) Ford,(14) Devereaux(15) and others have assembled scattered evidence on the existence in many pre-industrial societies of a wide variety of fertility control measures including contraception, abstinence, abortion, infanticide and delayed marriage. In many cases the limiting practice is not perceived as having birth limitation as an objective. Most of the evidence demonstrates the existence of certain practices in a culture without specifying either the extent of use or the effect on fertility. Nevertheless, there is basis for the supposition that more or less effective methods of population control potentially were available in many pre-industrial societies and that this probably affected fertility levels in most of them. I venture the view that such practices might have had much wider use and greater effect were it not for the rewards derived from having children in such societies and the risk that these rewards would be lost because of unpredictably high mortality.

Contraception is not one of the potential control practices widely prevalent in any large underdeveloped society. An important unresolved question is whether this has been because adequate contraceptive technology was lacking or because normative pressures for high fertility precluded either the development of new methods or the adoption and dissemination of known methods beyond a small minority of the population.

Despite evidence that various types of contraception have been known and used by small numbers in many pre-industrial societies, there are very few examples of their adoption by sufficient numbers to affect the general fertility level. Coitus interruptus, requiring no mechanical or chemical materials, has been known in many societies for a long time. Potentially this practice might have diffused to a wider group from the small minority using it in pre-industrial societies with resultant impact on fertility levels. It is difficult to dismiss coitus interruptus as unsuitable for mass adoption, since this was the principal means by which the British and French drastically reduced their birth rates in the modern period.(16) Coitus interruptus is still one of the most important methods producing the relatively low birth rate in Britain.(17)

Many hypotheses have been advanced to explain why coitus interruptus and other possible methods were not adopted or why alternate methods were not developed before the modern period. Among various explanations two emphasize the internal structure of the family. The combination of male dominance and the lack of communication between husband and wife, especially on problems of family size and family planning, is said to retard the adoption of family planning. This might be especially true if, as has been suggested by some, the wife has the stronger interest in family limitation, while the husband is indifferent. Dominance of the husband combined with his indifference on the issue might be particularly important for such a male-dominated method as coitus interruptus. Hill, Stycos & Back(18) have provided some evidence from Puerto Rico that customary barriers to husband–wife communication may be related to failure to adopt family planning in Puerto Rico now.

Whether this type of explanation is valid is an open question. There is a *prima facie* case for the interest of the father, too, in limiting fertility in a subsistence economy, since children are consumers as well as producers. Some recent studies in underdeveloped areas indicate that the father's disinterest may have been exaggerated. Studies in India, Ceylon, Taiwan, Puerto Rico and elsewhere(19) indicate roughly similar attitudes on the part of husbands and wives on many issues about reproduction. If it is true that pre-industrial couples do not not discuss fertility control or family size, this may be because a long-standing consensus on high fertility leaves little to discuss.

Other explanations for lack of use of contraception in some cultures centre on the idea that modern contraceptives were not available and that coitus interruptus was not acceptable in many cultures. Whether it was simply the availability of contraceptive means which determined fertility levels historically is currently of great practical importance. If fertility levels were high in pre-industrial societies simply because of inadequate contraceptive technology, then current programmes for reducing fertility in such areas can concentrate on making modern contraceptives available. This very simple solution is no longer widely espoused, because programmes for making contraceptives available in underdeveloped areas have not been very successful to date. While it is true that no country as yet has mounted an efficient all-out campaign to disseminate contraceptive supplies and information the efforts made have been intensive enough in some places to indicate that the motivations to limit family size either are not yet very powerful or are restrained by powerful cultural counter-pressures.

While the issue is certainly very controversial, I take the position that a variety of control measures, including some forms of contraception, have been available potentially in underdeveloped areas and that past failure to use them more extensively has been a result of normative pressures for high fertility. On the individual psychological level this reduces to a simple statement that couples had many children because they wanted them, not because they were ignorant of how to avoid having them. This does not preclude the probability that ignorance about control methods was prevalent. Nor is it necessary to assume that the size of family achieved was deliberately planned. It does require an assumption that the the values about family size and limiting practices, deliberate or not, were in rough correspondence.

Obviously, at the proper time and place provision of suitable contraceptive supplies and information is indispensable for fertility decline. I am questioning only whether this necessary cause is also a sufficient cause for a fertility decline.

Up to this point, I have been concerned mainly with indicating that control measures were available potentially in the underdeveloped areas so that their absence is not the explanation for high fertility. But to support the position that high fertility was normative, it is also necessary to consider why there have been normative pressures for large numbers of births.

I believe that most demographers and sociologists would agree on two very general explanations. From either the individual or the social point of view, high fertility has been an adjustment both to high and variable mortality and to the central importance in community life of familial and kinship ties.

In most pre-industrial societies a wide range of activities involve interdependence with kinsmen and especially with children. These include production, consumption, leisure activity, assistance in illness and old age and many other activities covered by non-familial institutions in modern societies. To simplify greatly: large numbers of children are desired if the values considered worthwhile are obtained through familial ties rather than through other social institutions. If kinship ties are very important in a society where mortality is high and variable, the number of births desired and produced will be especially high in order to insure the survival to adulthood of the essential minimum number of children. Selective experience favours the development of beliefs and practices encouraging fertility high enough to minimize the grave risks of few or no surviving children.

Because mortality is such an important consideration in underdeveloped areas, it is necessary to distinguish between norms for large numbers of births and norms for large numbers of children. A considerable number of studies in contemporary underdeveloped areas have found that three or four children are reported as desired by the populations studied. This is contrasted with the six or more births women actually have had by the end of the child-bearing period. A frequent interpretation of these results is that the number of children desired has sharply declined from higher earlier levels, evidence of a trend to modern small-family values. But, it is quite possible that the number of living children desired really is not much lower now than it was 100 or more years ago. With high mortality, six or more births are required if three or four children are to survive.

For example, a United Nations study(20) in Mysore, India, in 1952 found that for a sample of living women about 45 years of age, only about 66% of the children they had ever born were still alive. This figure exaggerates somewhat the percentage of children surviving, since there is evidence of underreporting of children born alive but dead at the time of the survey. In the Mysore study, the average number of children considered ideal by respondents is fairly close to the average number surviving to women living to the end of the child-bearing period, although it is much lower than the number actually born.

In India and elsewhere the finding that three or four children are considered desirable frequently is considered paradoxical, since the populations surveyed make little use of family planning information and supplies when these are available. However, wanting three or four living children in a high mortality country is quite consistent with the much higher average number of births. Even if mortality is declining, the peasant who has learned from his culture to depend on his children for labour on the farm, for old-age security, and for other essentials cannot be expected to extrapolate declining mortality with the demographer and to calculate a long-range need for fewer children. Significantly, several studies indicate that favourable attitudes to the practice of family limitation are much more common among those who already have three or four living children. This is consistent with the view that the availability of means for birth control is largely irrelevant until what is regarded as the essential minimum number of children is secure.

This suggests that known low mortality is one of the necessary conditions for an effective social policy for reducing fertility. Historically developed normative pressures for large numbers of births may persist for a long time after mortality has fallen, since they are closely tied to many aspects of the social structure. Housing allocation and other social arrangements in high fertility countries are developed on the implicit assumption that many of the family members, and especially many infants, will die. When mortality declines, increasing pressure is exerted on many traditional social arrangements, thus creating a ferment for change. But this takes time, and historically there has been almost always a considerable lag between the fall of mortality and the fall of fertility. It is likely to be particularly difficult to counter the traditional pressures for high fertility when the mortality decline is only prospective. This is what is being attempted in many underdeveloped areas today.

Compensation for high mortality does not account alone for the differences in fertility between developed and underdeveloped areas. After taking into account the effects of mortality, the number of children desired probably is still somewhat larger, on the average, than in the more developed societies.

Why does the social norm prescribe a relatively large number of *living* children in underdeveloped countries? In seeking an answer, I begin with the premise that the norm depends on how having a particular number of children affects the ability of the familial unit to attain socially valued goals. This, in turn, depends on the division of labour between the family and other social institutions and on how much the performance of important functions by the family depends on the number of children produced in it. The assumption is that family size norms will tend to correspond to a number which maximizes the net utility to be derived from having children in that society. Obviously, different aspects of the society may exert opposing pressures on the norms, so a balance must be struck. Therefore, we must look for important aspects of the social organization which support the norms for family size by providing explicit or implicit social rewards or penalties depending on the number of children.

As already noted, the familial and kinship units are so important in underdeveloped societies that we may expect relatively high fertility in order to maintain them. This kind of global explanatory hypothesis lacks the precision to explain the existing and historical diversity ranging from moderately to very high fertility. But, if the general hypothesis is valid, then specific variations in kinship structure should help to explain the observed variations in fertility. Anthropological research reveals a rich diversity of kinship organization and functions in different societies. Unfortunately, systematic study of how these variations are related to variations in fertility, normative or actual, is not very advanced. Nevertheless, some broad speculative generalizations can be considered.

Corporate kinship systems involving an immortal clan with a patrilocal or matrilocal basis and affecting every aspect of life, even political organization and war, are seen by Lorimer(21) as greatly enhancing the valuation of children. Joint family systems combining several nuclear units but with periodic fission and reconstitution of the joint family make for somewhat lower fertility, since they encompass social relations less fully than the corporate system. Systems based on a nuclear, neolocal familial units make for still lower fertility, since fewer routine functions are carried out within the family unit.

These broad generalizations greatly oversimplify a complex subject. Both the theory and the evidence are in a rudimentary state. Lorimer has placed emphasis on kinship organization and especially on the role of corporate kinship systems in producing high fertility in African societies. But his work gives little attention to how the corporate kinship system affects the intermediate variables so as to produce the high fertility. Davis & Blake illustrate(22) how variations in the kinship structure operate through particular intermediate variables to affect fertility. For example, they analyze the probable functional significance of the joint family system in India in inhibiting widow remarriage and, thus, reducing fertility. The idea that neolocal nuclear family systems may lead to relatively lower fertility levels even in pre-industrial societies has been discussed mainly with reference to pre-industrial Europe. The discussion particularly has centred on various economic arrangements leading to late marriage or non-marriage, as already mentioned.

Studies in India about the comparative fertility of couples living in nuclear and joint family units yield contradictory results, with some studies indicating that couples living in nuclear units have fertility at least as high as the fertility of couples in joint households.(23) One possible explanation is that high fertility increases the likelihood that joint households will split up. But such comparisons within a society are unlikely to provide relevant evidence of how a dominant family system affects the society's reproduction level. For this purpose, the units of comparison must be whole societies or societies at different time periods.

Recent Japanese data provide a striking illustration of the close relation between norms about dependence on adult children and the course of fertility. Between 1950 and 1961 the Japanese birth rate fell spectacularly from 28 to 17 per 1000. In the same period the bienniel sample surveys by the Mainichi press(24) posed to a representative cross-section of the population the question: 'Do you expect to depend on your children in your old age?' In 1950 a majority, more than 55%, answered 'definitely yes'. The proportion giving this answer declined steadily in five succeeding surveys, reaching 27% by 1961. It is rare that public opinion on a matter this vital changes so steadily and rapidly and just as rare that we have statistical data with which to document the trend.

These are only illustrative of theories and data about how kinship is related to fertility. No one has yet been able to assemble more than illustrative evidence relating levels and determinants of fertility under varying kinship systems, but it is unlikely that significant general explanations will emerge which do not take into account the role of kinship in the society.

This is not to deny that social norms about family size may be affected by non-familial aspects of the social organization. For example, emphasis in the religious system on the importance of a male heir for ritual purposes probably produces pressures over time in a high mortality society for at least two sons to guarantee the survival of at least one. This means that on the average each family will want at least four children. Such values, based on long tradition and embedded in many aspects of the society, persist long after mortality has fallen.

Taiwan is an interesting case in point of the persistence of such traditional values after mortality has fallen and even after there is an apparent willingness to adopt family planning. Taiwan has a history of slowly but steadily declining mortality under Japanese rule, followed by very rapid mortality decline after the war. Average life expectancy is now more than 60 years. The probability has been high for some time that almost all children will survive to adulthood. Fertility has begun to fall according to statistics for the whole island. In several recent small-scale pilot surveys, both husbands and wives expressed strong approval of the idea of family planning; a significant minority had begun to practise it in some form and a large majority of those interviewed indicated a desire to do so in the future. But none of this seems to portend a disavowal of traditional Chinese values. True, there is a strong consensus on the desirability of three or four children and the undesirability of larger numbers. But the preference for a moderate number of children, the number formerly achieved with larger numbers of deaths, is qualified by a strong traditional preference that at least one and preferably two or more of the children should be sons. Couples seeking help under the Prepregnancy Health Program of the Taiwanese Provincial Health Department almost always are those with at least three or four children, but they also are almost always couples with at least two sons. Strong approval is expressed in the surveys for such traditional Chinese values as the joint family, the importance of a male heir, and responsibility of children for their older parents.

Under present mortality conditions in Taiwan a single son is very likely to survive to adulthood, so having additional sons as 'insurance' is probably an anachronism, but the traditional preference for several sons persists. The family size and sex composition being sought are approximately what a traditional Chinese family might have achieved with luck under high mortality and high fertility, but fewer births are needed now to achieve this goal. The present goal of many Taiwanese appears to be to maintain traditional values in the face of the pressures of higher survival rates by using family planning.

While a preference for sons is frequently embedded in religious institutions, it may have its origin in the value of sons for agricultural labour or for other purposes. The religious sanction may sanctify and insure what has been needed traditionally for other essential purposes.

Religious or other emphases on the importance of sons is only one of a large number of values that may affect the norms for family size, either indirectly or directly in relation to the role of the familial unit in the society. All of these must be taken into account in applying the general principle that the additional children are desired if they provide rewards greater than their costs under the particular familial arrangements of that society.

In seeking explanations for high fertility in supportive institutions and values, it would be grossly incorrect to suggest that the norms about the intermediate control variables are finely contrived in every society to produce results consistent with the norms about family size. On balance and in the long run a rough consistency is probable. But discrepancies between ends and means may develop and persist when aspects of the social structure not even recognized as related to fertility affect the reproductive level by their effect on the intermediate variables. For example, many religious systems prescribe periods of abstinence which usually (though not always) will have the effect of reducing fertility.

Illustrative of another 'unintended restraint' on fertility is the possible reduction in fecundity resulting from poor nutrition and poor health in the whole society or a stratum of it. For example, several recent Indian studies find relatively low fertility for the poorest social stratum. It is plausible that this may be a result of poor health and nutrition conditions in the lower status groups, although other explanations are possible.

A variety of such unintended effects of cultural factors in pre-industrial societies contribute to keeping fertility below its maximum biological potential. We really do not know, from systematic evidence, to what extent these operate selectively to keep fertility near the normative values. It is only a reasonable assumption that, if norms about family size are very important, the intermediate control variables will tend to reach a balance consistent with these norms. But, where social change is very rapid, such a long-run balance may not be struck exactly, and for short periods a large discrepancy between means and ends is probable.

Another approach to finding the variables that supported early high fertility is to study the correlates of the declines in fertility that have already occurred in developed societies. First of all, it is clear that in almost every case a substantial decline in mortality preceded fertility decline.(25) In Japan the period of lag was much shorter than in Western Europe. The lag may grow still shorter if social policy succeeds in accelerating fertility decline in such countries as Pakistan, India, Egypt and Korea. But, in all the countries that have such policies at present, mortality already has declined for several decades, with little evidence of fertility decline.

Apart from lower mortality, what social and economic variables are associated with fertility decline? Given the preceding analysis there is no surprise in the plausible hypothesis that a shift of functions from family to other specialized institutions is important. There is illustrative evidence that this shift has decreased the value and increased the costs of more than a small number of children for attaining the goals men seek in the more developed society. But the demonstrable changes in family functions are difficult to disentangle from the larger complex of social and economic changes in the course of social development. Broadly speaking, development is associated with many variables: e.g., urbanization, industrialization, more complex technology, greater capital investment per worker, higher living standards, and greater literacy. There is an increase in the mass media of communication and in transportation facilities which go with larger markets and the linkage of local populations in larger political, social, and economic units. In these larger units, a more complex division of labour exists not only with respect to economic life but also in almost every other aspect. Thus, the tasks of an urban society are divided among a much larger number of institutions. As the economic unit ceases to be the family, recruitment of workers is less closely linked to reproduction.

Because the development process is so complex, I have postponed any definition of development until this late point. At least with reference to fertility decline, I suggest that what is essential in the development process is the shift from major dependence on relatively self-contained local institutions, to dependence upon larger social, economic and political units. Such a shift implies a change in the division of labour from one in which the kinship unit is necessarily central to a larger complex in which such local units as family and village give up many functions to larger, non-familial specialized units. In such a shift, greater literacy and the development of effective communication networks are essential.

I have purposely avoided proposing industrialization and urbanization as the essential developmental changes for lower fertility, although they are usually part of the change process, and I do not minimize their importance. But I think that the essential change is the expansion of the unit within which most social and economic interchange occurs.

Some evidence that urbanization and industrialization alone may not provide the explanation for fertility decline appears in some unpublished work by Knodel & Tangoantiang at the Princeton Office of Population Research.

Tracing fertility declines from earlier times to the present, the Princeton group found that in all of the countries in Europe, with the exception of Albania, there has been a decline in fertility of 50% or more and that, with the further exception of France, the decline began some time between 1860 and 1920. The timing and steepness of the decline is not conspicuously associated with proportions of the labour force engaged in agriculture or changes in these proportions, nor is it associated consistently with urbanization. The only index examined whose movement seems almost universally to parallel that of fertility measures is illiteracy. The level of illiteracy varied widely between countries at the beginning of the decline, ranging from 24% reported in England to 79% for Russia. Yet, in each case, fertility and illiteracy declined together. A striking example of the unexpected lack of association between industrialization as normally visualized and declining fertility is that the decline began in the 1880's in Italy, Hungary and Finland, as well as in England and Wales. Literacy and mass education appear to deserve special attention in relation to changing fertility, along with the more frequently stressed urbanization and industrialization.

How can literacy and broad educational gains affect fertility? One indirect way is by helping to reduce mortality which will later reduce fertility in ways already indicated. Obviously, literacy also will facilitate the dissemination of information about the idea and means of family limitation. But I think the role of education and literacy is more basic. I suggest that with increased education and literacy the population becomes involved with the ideas and institutions of a larger modern culture. If the individual is, or believes he is, part of a larger non-familial system, he begins to find rewards in social relationships for which large numbers of children may be irrelevant. If this thesis is correct, major expenditures for education in a development programme are justified not only for developing worker skills but also for their potential effect on the fertility level, if lower fertility is a social objective.

It is pertinent that in every country for which we have empirical evidence the spread of family planning practices to attain a smaller family has been associated with a literate audience influenced by the mass media and by a person-to-person communication of their message that transcends local boundaries. In no case up to now has a government or private programme designed specifically to disseminate family planning or small family values been the principal agency for information and change.

In the pilot study in Taiwan, referred to earlier, education and contacts with the mass media were more closely related to the actual practice of family planning than were occupation, income, or rural background (see Appendix IV). It is relevant that Taiwan, a high fertility country in which a significant fertility decline has begun and where just now the probability of fertility decline seems great, has a relatively high literacy rate and also has had a rapid expansion in the circulation of the mass media and in the use of the mails for personal and business correspondence. Indicative of the possible importance of wider communication, is the symbolic, if humorous, fact that long-distance calls per capita are one of the best predictors of the 1961 fertility level for the 22 local administrative units in Taiwan.

I do not believe that education about fertility and family planning alone, completely in advance of other changes in the society, can be very effective for changing fertility norms and behaviour. Such a single specialized educational programme alone does not affect the linkage of the local population to the larger units in the broad and continuing way which can lead to the essential growing dependence on non-local and non-familial institutions. General education and literacy probably are required to do this.

High fertility norms and behaviour are too deeply embedded in traditional, emotionally-supported institutions — especially the familial — to be affected much by education or informational programmes centred on fertility alone. This is not to deny the potential importance of such programmes, once development is under way. Probably, reduced mortality sets the stage, providing the minimal threshold level required before fertility will drop. But, in addition, there must be at least minimal changes in the institutions which motivate high fertility by rewarding parents of relatively large numbers of children. There must be reason to believe that those who have smaller families can meet their needs in ways differing from the traditional patterns.

As Professor Glass has aptly put this matter: (26) 'The establishment of new demographic patterns involves the development of new incentives which press upon reproductive behavior. Such incentives need to be embedded in a social framework. They can be encouraged by persuasion but can hardly be created by an apparatus of symbols. Symbols are important. . . . But in countries with low levels of living, perhaps even more than elsewhere, it is necessary to have something material to be symbolic about.'

This view does not preclude the possibility that broad gains in literacy and education can facilitate lower fertility levels in advance of some other changes in the society. The extent to which this is possible and what associated changes are required is still an open question. Significant studies with careful controls are possible in some of the countries introducing family planning to test whether particular levels of literacy or of other development indices are a necessary threshold to a fertility decline.

The existence of the mass media and of postal networks already involves, to some extent, the larger interaction system of which I am speaking. If the literate regard themselves as members of a larger and less parochial society, the adoption of behaviours appropriate to that society may be accelerated, if at least minimal threshold changes in society make their new self-image plausible.

Obviously, changes in literacy, education and communication networks are related to many other aspects of development. Changes in all of them probably are related in interaction to fertility decline. But it is unnecessary to assume that all aspects of development must move together. We know that there have been uneven rates of movement in the past. From a policy point of view it is desirable to look for some elements subject to social control which might lead the development process and decrease the time-gap between mortality and fertility decline. I have emphasized education because it might be such a leading variable and it is given less attention usually than economic variables or urbanization.

To recapitulate, I have reviewed briefly the evidence that social norms support the moderately to very high fertility found in the so-called underdeveloped societies. I have suggested that high fertility and high fertility norms are not a result of unrestrained maximum fecundity but rather are an adjustment mainly to the high mortality and to dependence on kinship-based local institutions. Variations in the kinship structure were seen as a major possible explanation of variations from moderate to very high fertility. The net effect of a large number of possible control variables determines the extent to which the social norms about fertility are approximated in behaviour. Finally, I have suggested that the complex continuum from underdeveloped to developed societies is best represented for our purpose by a continuum from major dependence on relatively small local units to increasing interdependence in larger social units in which kinship plays a decreasing part. In this shift to larger units of interdependence, education and literacy not only have an important part to play but may lead other elements in their effect on fertility.

Appendix I. Estimated Gross Reproduction Rates for Selected Populations and Periods

1. Gross Reproduction Rates in Selected High Fertility Populations

(Statistical resources are usually poor in the high-fertility areas so data are often unavailable or of questionable reliability. Those presented below are for areas where special fertility investigations, adjustment by competent investigators or unusually good official statistics makes the data appear reasonably reliable. Nevertheless, these rates are less reliable than those for the low-fertility countries. They are cited to indicate the probable diversity in reproduction levels rather than as accurate measures in each individual case.)

Africa:(27)	
Centre-Oubangui (1959)	2.0
Dahomey (1961)	3.2
Guinea (1954–55)	2.9
Ivory Coast (1958)	2.4
Mali (1957–61)	3.3
Upper Volta (1960)	3.2
North Cameroons	2.3
Asia:	
Ceylon(28) (1952)	2.2
Cocos Islands(29)	4.2
India(30) (1956)	2.6
Malaysian population of Malaya(31) (1946–48)	2.7
Taiwan(32)	2.7
West Indies:(33)	
Jamaica (1943)	1.8
Barbados (1946)	1.9
British Guiana (1946)	2.4
Trinidad (1946)	2.4
American Hutterites(34) (1952)	4.0

2. Gross Reproduction Rates in Selected Low Fertility Areas (35)

England and Wales:	1861	2.4
	1901	1.7
	1940	0.8
	1958	1.2
Austria:	1931–32	0.9
	1959	1.3
Belgium:	1928–32	1.0
	1959	1.3
Norway:	1932–35	0.9
	1958	1.4
United States:	1930–35	1.1
	1959	1.8

Appendix II. Some Illustrative Results from Sample Surveys Dealing with Number of Children Wanted or Considered Ideal in Underdeveloped Societies

1. Puerto Rico(36)

A. Answers to question 'Suppose you were to get married again for the first time, how many children would you want to have?':

number of children wanted	sample of clinic out-patients (%)	general field sample (%)
0 or 1	16	8
2	40	43
3	18	26
4 or more	10	18
all God sends	16	5
total	100	100

2. India

A. Number of children considered ideal in Mysore area: (37)

	mean no. considered ideal by	
	wife	husband
Bangalore city	3.6	4.1
rural plains sample	4.7	4.6

B. Proportion of parents who say they want no more children, by present number of children: (37)

	percentage of parents who want no more			
	Bangalore city		rural plains	
number of living children	wife	husband	wife	husband
0	5	10	2	2
1–3	25	42	14	26
4–6	56	72	48	59

C. Number of children desired (from the point of view of finances) in several districts near Poona: (38)

	Nasik		Kalaba	
number of children desired	rural (%)	urban (%)	rural (%)	urban (%)
less than 3	20	27	9	18
4-5	38	46	35	34
6 or more	17	19	11	14
until a son comes	2	2	2	3

until 2 or 3 sons come	17	4	12	10
as many as are born	5	1	19	6
could not state a number	1	1	12	15
total	100	100	100	100

3. Jamaica: (39)

A. Answers to question 'If you could live your life over, how many children would you like to have?':

number of children	% of women wanting this number
3 or less	50
4	29
5 or more	18
up to God, fate	3
total	100

B. Percentage of women wanting more children, by number of children they have now:

number of living children	% wanting more children
0	92
1	64
2	44
3	32
4 or 5	20
6 or more	16

4. Taichung, Taiwan: (40)

A. Answers to question, 'How many children would you like if you could (start over) and have just the number you want?':

number of children wanted	% wanting this number	
	wife	husband
less than 2	0	0
2	9	7
3	33	32
4	56	50
5	12	12
6 or more	4	6
up to God, fate	1	*
cannot say	2	4
total	100	100

* Less than 1%

B. Number of children of each sex considered ideal for Taiwanese couples by wife:

number of children	% choosing each number for	
	sons	daughters
0	0	0
1	2	28
2	71	63
3	20	3
4	1	0
either sex satisfactory	2	2
up to God, fate	1	1
not ascertained	3	3
total	100	100

C. Percentage of wives and husbands who have more children than they want, by present number of children:

present number of children	% who would prefer fewer children than they have	
	wife	husband
1	0	0
2	0	2
3	2	4
4	12	12
5 or more	61	55

Appendix III. Classification of the 'Intermediate' Variables Affecting Fertility

Taken from K. Davis & J. Blake, 'Social structure and fertility: an analytic framework', *Economic Development and Cultural Change,* 4, No. 3 (April 1956), pp. 211–235.

I. *Factors affecting exposure to intercourse*

A. Those governing the formulation and dissolution of unions in the reproductive period.

1. Age of entry into sexual unions.
2. Permanent celibacy: proportion of women never entering sexual unions.
3. Amount of reproductive period spent after or between unions.
   (*a*) When unions are broken by divorce, separation or desertion.
   (*b*) When unions are broken by death of husband.

B. Those governing the exposure to intercourse within unions.

1. Voluntary abstinence.
2. Involuntary abstinence (from impotence, illness unavoidable but temporary separations).
3. Coital frequency (excluding period of abstinence).

II. *Factors affecting exposure to conception*

A. Fecundity or infecundity, as affected by involuntary causes.

B. Use or non-use of contraception.

1. By mechanical and chemical means.
2. By other means.

C. Fecundity or infecundity, as affected by voluntary causes (sterilization, subincision, medical treatment, etc.).

III. *Factors affecting gestation and successful parturition*

A. Foetal mortality from voluntary causes.

B. Foetal mortality from involuntary causes.

Appendix IV. Selected Results of a Study of Factors Associated with Approval and Use of Family Planning in Taichung, Taiwan (Pilot Study of 241 Couples with Wife 25 to 29 Years Old)

characteristics of wife or of couple	% of couples who have practised some form of family planning	% of couples who approve of family planning unconditionally
Wife's education:		
none	18	56
some primary	20	47
primary graduate	26	79
some secondary school	60	74
secondary school graduate	71	83
Frequency of reading daily newspaper — wife:		
never	19	61
sometimes	33	92
once or twice a week	41	86
daily	58	75
Family expenditures per month (N.T.):		
less than 1000	26	64
1000–1999	34	75
2000–2999	41	67
3000 or more	37	63
Farm background — wife:		
some	31	67
none	40	73
No. of 'modern' consumer objects owned:		
less than 4	18	50
4	17	77
5	21	76
6	41	69
7	47	77
8 or 9	48	66
Type of family:		
joint	27	60
stem	27	68
nuclear	40	72

NOTES AND REFERENCES

1. Smith, T. E., The Cocos-Keeling Islands: a demographic laboratory. *Population Studies*, 14, No. 2, November 1960, pp. 94–130.
2. For example, birth rates of sixty or more are reported for several African populations in the United Nations, *Demographic Yearbook, 1961* on the basis of sample surveys.
3. *Royal Commission on Population, Report*. London: H.M.S.O., (1949), p. 24. Women recorded as married in the fertility census of 1911 and born in the period 1841–45 reported an average of 5.71 live births.
4. For example, in the United Nations, *The Mysore population study*. New York: The United Nations, 1962; and in Sovani, N. V. & Dandekar, K., *Fertility survey of Nasik, Kolaba, and Satara Districts*. Poona: Gokhale Institute of Politics and Economics, Publication No. 31, 1955.
5. Cf. Eaton, J. & Mayer, A., *Man's capacity to reproduce*. Glencoe: The Free Press, 1954, pp. 20 ff.
6. For example, Dandekar, K., *Demographic survey of six rural communities*. Poona: Gokhale Institute of Politics and Economics, 1959;

   Hatt, P. K., *Backgrounds of human fertility in Puerto Rico: a sociological survey*. Princeton: Princeton University Press, 1952;

   Hill, R., Stycos, J. M. & Back, K. W., *The family and population control: a Puerto Rican experiment in social change*. Chapel Hill: University of North Carolina Press, 1959;

   Mukherjee, S. B., *Studies on fertility rates in Calcutta*. Calcutta: Bookland Private Ltd., 1961;

   Singh, B., *Five years of family planning in the country-side*. Lucknow: J. K. Institute of Sociology and Human Relations, 1958;

   Stycos, J. M. & Back, K., *Prospects for fertility reduction*. New York: The Conservation Foundation, 1957;

   Tabah, L. & Samuel, R., Preliminary findings of a survey on fertility and attitudes toward family formation in Santiago. In Milbank Memorial Fund, *Research in family planning*. Princeton: Princeton University Press, 1962;

   United Nations. *The Mysore population study*. New York: United Nations, 1962;

   Yaukey, D., *Fertility differences in a modernizing country*. Princeton: Princeton University Press, 1961.

   A more complete annotated bibliography of such studies appears in *The sociology of human fertility: a trend report and bibliography*, Vol. 10/11, No. 2. 1961–2 in the series *Current Sociology* published by the International Sociological Association with the support of Unesco.
7. Richards, A. J. & Reining, P., Reports on fertility surveys in Buganda and Buhaya, 1952, pp. 351–404. In Lorimer, F. *et al. Culture and human fertility*, Paris: Unesco, 1954.
8. Ford, C. S., *A comparative study of human reproduction*. New Haven: Yale University Press, 1945, Yale University Publications in Anthropology, no. 32.
9. Davis, K. & Blake, J., Social structure and fertility: an analytic framework. *Economic development and cultural change*, **4**, No. 3, April 1956, pp. 211–235.
10. Coale, A. J. & Tye, C. Y., The significance of age-patterns of fertility in high fertility populations. *Milbank Memorial Fund Quarterly*, **39**, No. 4, October 1961, pp. 631–646.
11. For example, Eversley, D. E. C., Population and economic growth in England before the 'takeoff'. In *Contributions and Communications to the First International Conference of Economic History*. Stockholm, 1960, pp. 457–473; Habakkuk, H. J., The economic history of modern Britain. *J. Econom. Hist.* **18**, No. 4, December 1958, pp. 486–501;

    Krause, J. T., Some implications of recent work in historical demography. *Comp. Stud. Soc. Hist.* **1**, No. 2, January 1959, pp. 164–188.
12. Carr-Saunders, A. M., *The population problem*. Oxford: Clarendon Press, 1922. The frame of reference of this important work has influenced greatly the ideas presented in the present paper.
13. Himes, N. E., *Medical history of contraception*. Baltimore: The Williams and Wilkins Co., 1936.
14. *Op. cit.* (see note 8).
15. Devereux, G., *A study of abortion in primitive societies*. New York: Julian Press, 1955.
16. For relevant evidence see Bergues, H. *et al. La prevention des naissances dans la famille*. Paris: Presses Universitaries de France, 1960; and Lewis-Faning, E., *Report on an inquiry into family limitation and its influence on human fertility during the past fifty years*. Papers of the Royal Commission on Population, Vol. I. London: H.M.S.O. 1949.
17. Pierce, R. M. & Rowntree, G., Birth control in Britain. Part 2, *Population Studies*, **15**, No. 2, November 1961, pp. 121–160.
18. *Op. cit.* (see note 6).
19. For a general discussion of this issue see Stycos, J. M., A critique of the traditional planned parenthood approach in underdeveloped areas. In Kiser, C. V., ed., *Research in family planning*. Princeton: Princeton University Press, 1962. References to Taiwanese data in this paper are all drawn from unpublished work of the Taiwan Population Studies Center in which participating personnel include Dr. C. H. Yen, Dr. J. Y. Peng, Dr. Y. Takeshita, Mr. T. H. Sun and Mr. S. Y. Soong.
20. United Nations, *The Mysore population study*. *Op. cit.* (see note 4).

21. Lorimer, F. *et al.*, *Culture and human fertility.* Paris: Unesco, 1954.
22. *Op. cit.* (see note 9).
23. For example, in the experimental study in Singur, India described by Mathen, K. K., in 'Preliminary lessons learned from the rural population control study of Singur'. In Kiser, C. V., *op. cit.*, pp. 33–50 (see note 19).
24. The Population Problems Research Council, *Fifth public opinion survey on birth control in Japan* and *Sixth opinion survey on family planning and birth control*, Tokyo: The Mainichi Newspapers, 1959 and 1962.
25. France and Spain are among possible exceptions.
26. Glass, D. V., Population growth, fertility, and population policy. *The advancement of science*, November, 1960, pp. 1–11.
27. The African rates are based on estimates made by the Princeton African Demography Project, from Census Inquiry data. They were kindly supplied by Professor W. Brass of the University of Aberdeen. The data supplied were in the form of total fertility rates. These were converted to gross reproduction rates for this presentation on the assumption of a uniform sex-ratio at birth of 106.
28. From Sarkar, N. K., Population trends and population policy in Ceylon. *Population Studies*, 9, No. 3, March 1956, pp. 195–216.
29. Smith, T. E., *op. cit.* (see note 1).
30. Cf. Coale, A. J. & Hoover, E. M., *Population growth and economic development in low-income countries.* Princeton: Princeton University Press, 1958, p. 352.
31. Estimated by Smith, T. E., in *Population growth in Malaya.* London: Royal Institute of Royal Affairs, 1952, Ch. II.
32. From unpublished calculations of the Taiwan Population Studies Center.
33. From Roberts, G. W., Some aspects of mating and fertility in the West Indies. *Population Studies*, 8, No. 3, March 1955, pp. 199–227. Mr. Roberts shows that joint reproduction rates based on both male and female rates may be more useful than the conventional female gross reproduction rates, but only the female rates are cited here, for comparability with those of other countries.
34. From Eaton, J. & Mayer, A., *op. cit.* (see note 5) p. 40.
35. The rates for England and Wales are from reports of the Registrar General for England and Wales. All other figures in this set are from *Population Index*, April 1961, 28, No. 2.
36. From Hill, R., Stycos, J. M. & Back, K. W., *op. cit.* (see note 6) 1959, p. 72.
37. United Nations, *The Mysore population study. Op. cit.* (see note 4) p. 142.
38. Sovani, W. V. & Dandekar, K., *op. cit.* (see note 4) p. 104.
39. Stycos, J. M. & Back, K., *op. cit.* (see note 6).
40. From unpublished data collected by Taiwan Population Studies Center, associated with the Provincial Maternal and Child Health Institute, Taiwan.

*Factors Affecting Moslem Natality**

DUDLEY KIRK

This paper differs in scope and approach from others presented for this session of the Conference.[1] The author has not conducted an attitude survey in Moslem countries, but rather a study of common factors affecting the present and future level of natality in Islam as a whole. This is supplemented by a summary of the empirical studies done in specific Moslem countries, which are or will be more fully reported in separate publications by those who supervised the investigations.

Religion is often mentioned as a factor potentially affecting natality, but studies of this subject are most frequently focused on Roman Catholics because of the church's well-known doctrines concerning family planning and birth control. Most writers on the demography of the

[1] Session on Research and Evaluation, International Conference on Family Planning Programs, Geneva, August 23-27, 1965.

developing countries have stressed the absence of specific prohibitions on contraception in other major religions. They have often relegated the influence of religion on natality to rather vague effects, attributed to some religions, in engendering a fatalistic view of life unfavorable to the initiative and motivations required to adopt family planning.

In my judgment this restricted view is in error, at least as concerns the Moslem world. Empirically Islam has been a more effective barrier to the diffusion of family planning than Catholicism. The monolithic character of Islam in this regard is overlooked because of its enormous territory, its linguistic diversity, its political atomization, and the absence of a central religious hierarchy. What follows is a study of (1) the distinctive aspects of Moslem natality, (2) their possible explanation, and (3) evidences of prospective and potentially very rapid changes, including those from field studies of knowledge, attitudes, and practices relating to family planning.

Islam, or the community of Moslem peoples, includes some 500 million adherents. Its heartland is a solid bloc of Moslem settlement and nomadic occupation, extending from the Straits of Gibraltar and Dakar in the west some 5,000 miles into Chinese Sinkiang and to the borders of India in the east. In a rough way this enormous area of contiguous Moslem settlement is coterminous with the great continuous arid region of Northern Africa, Asia Minor, and Central Asia. Separated by a thousand miles of Indian territory are some forty-five million Moslems in the enclave of East Pakistan, and as many more are scattered through India itself. In Southeast Asia, and even farther separated from the Moslem heartland, is a bloc of close to 100 million Moslems in Indonesia, Malaysia, and the southern Philippines. Mohammedanism is the dominant religion in at least twenty-two countries and important in many more. The chief areas of Moslem settlement cover an area roughly equivalent to that of the North American continent, with about twice the population.

Moslem Natality

Few Moslem countries have official vital statistics complete enough to provide reliable measures of natality. But progress in measurement is being made by national and international agencies even in the absence of reliable vital statistics. Estimates of birth rates are variously derived from sample surveys in the countries concerned or indirectly from the census age distributions, usually computed by the "reverse-survival" method. Use of population models and stable age distribution theory where data are otherwise unavailable has provided another approach,[2] but this has not been used in the present study, which relies chiefly on the compilations of the United Nations. These are presented in Table 1. None of the individual figures should be regarded as highly accurate, but collectively they are thought to represent a reasonably accurate picture.

Insofar as data are available, Moslem countries range from annual birth rates in the low 40's (per thousand population) to very high rates, up to 60, estimated for certain Moslem countries of West Africa. Aside from the sub-Saharan area, Moslem natality seems to be concentrated within a rather narrow range. Among the five Arab countries of North Africa the birth rates obtained from a variety of sources are clustered from 43–50 and the computed gross reproduction rates range from 2.8 to 3.1. The Middle Eastern countries display a similar homogeneity in natality. Again the computed gross reproduction rates vary only from 2.9 in Turkey to 3.4 in Jordan. There are almost no data for the original homeland of Islam in the Arabian peninsula except for Aden and Kuwait, where the reported birth rates of 47–48 (1962) are consistent with the figures for other Arab countries.

West Pakistan appears to have a birth rate comparable to her Moslem neighbors to the west.[3] However, there is strong suggestion from field studies of continuous registration that the birth rate in East Pakistan is significantly higher,

[2] This approach has been used in the African Demography Project of the Office of Population Research, Princeton University. Cf. Lorimer, Brass, and van de Walle, "Demography," in *The African World,* ed. Robert A. Lystad (New York: Praeger, 1965).

[3] A number of studies listed in chapter 4, "Levels and Trends of Fertility in Asia," *United Nations Population Bulletin No. 7,* 1965, have found birth rates in the range of 41-50 in West Pakistan, including field surveys and analyses of both the 1951 and 1961 census data.

TABLE 1

Population, Crude Birth Rates, and Gross Reproduction Rates in Moslem Countries[a] *from United Nations Sources*[b]

Moslem Countries	Estimated Population 1963 (millions)	Natality Data			
		Basis[c]	Year	Estimated Crude Birth Rate[d]	Estimated Gross Reproduction Rate[e]
North Africa:					
Algeria	11.6	C (2)	1944–49	45	3.0
(Moslems)		B	1959–60	47–50	
Libya	1.5	C (2)	1944–49	43	3.0
Morocco	12.7	C (2)	1955–60	47	2.9
(Moslems)		B	1962	46	
Tunisia	4.5	A	1960–63	43	3.1[f]
U.A.R.	28.0	C (1)	1950–55	45	2.8
		A	1960–63	43	
Middle East:					
Afghanistan	14.9		Not available		
Iran	22.2	C (2)	1946–51	48	3.1
		B	1959	44	
		B	1963	45–48	
Iraq	6.9	C (2)	1947–52	48	3.3
Jordan	1.8	C (1)	1951–56	45	3.4
		A	1960–63	46	
Saudi Arabia	6.6		Not available		
Syria	5.3		Not available		
Turkey	30.0	C (2)	1950–55	43	2.9
Yemen	5.0		Not available		
South Asia:					
Indonesia	100.8	C (2)	1951–56	52	2.8
		B and C (2)	1962	43	
Pakistan	98.6	C (2)	1946–61	48	3.3
		B	1962	43–46[g]	
Europe:					
Albania	1.8	A	1960–62	41	3.4[f]
Subsaharan Africa:					
Mali	4.4	B	1960–61	56	3.4
Mauritania	1.0	E	1962	49	
Niger	3.1	B	1959–60	61	3.5
Senegal	3.4	B	1957	45	
		B	1960–61	43	
		B	1963	48–54[h]	
Somalia	2.3		Not available		
Sudan	12.8	B	1955–56	52 (45–54)	3.0–3.5

[a] Including only countries having large Moslem majorities and with a total population of one million or more. Other countries with probable Moslem majorities or strong Moslem pluralities include Guinée, Nigeria, Lebanon, and Malaysia. The first two apparently have very high birth rates as determined from survey and census data; the reported national birth rate in Lebanon in 1961 was 42, the Moslem rate undoubtedly being higher than the Christian; the reported birth rate of Malays (i.e., Moslems) in Malaya averaged 41 in 1960-63 with a gross reproduction rate of 2.9 in 1960.

[b] All data, unless otherwise indicated, are from *United Nations Demographic Yearbook*, 1963 and *United Nations Population Bulletin No. 7*, 1965.

[c] Bases for rates: A — official birth registration statistics; B — sample survey data; C — "reverse-survival" estimates: (1) based on relatively satisfactory census data on population by age groups; (2) based on age data of relatively poor or uncertain reliability.

[d] Annual birth rates per 1,000 population.

[e] As defined in sources given in note[b] above.

[f] 1960.

[g] From early results of *Population Growth Estimation Study*. More recent results are presented in a paper based on this study by Karol J. Krotki, "The Problem of Estimating Vital Rates in Pakistan," United Nations World Population Conference (Belgrade), August 30-September 10, 1965. They give substantially higher figures on the assumption that the sample registration alone was (perhaps 10%) incomplete. The latter give birth rates of approximately 45 for West Pakistan and 55 for East Pakistan in 1962-63.

[h] Two surveys reported by Pierre Cantrelle, "Observation démographique répétée en milieu rural au Sénégal," United Nations World Population Conference (Belgrade) August 30-September 10, 1965.

perhaps over 50.[4] A very high birth rate of 52 was determined for Indonesia from its census of 1961 but a relatively low gross reproduction rate of 2.8 was computed from the same data. The discrepancy is ascribed to distortions of the population age structure due to war and civil war that resulted in birth deficits in the 1940's and relatively small numbers of older children in 1961. A United Nations expert, posted in Indonesia, using the same data but making corrections for systematic biases in age reporting and using post-censal checks, estimated a birth rate of 43 (42 in Java and 45 in the outer islands).[5] Natality in Indonesia is clearly high but how high remains a matter for speculation. The birth rate for Moslem Malays in Malaysia is, however, believed to be accurately recorded (43.3 in 1960).

Moslem areas in Europe and the Soviet Union report somewhat lower birth rates but in all of these there are substantial non-Moslem populations that may affect the birth rates recorded for the total populations. Albania and the neighboring Moslem areas of Yugoslavia (Kosovo and Metokija) report birth rates of about 40, by contrast with 18 for Greece and an average of 22 for Yugoslavia as a whole. The five Soviet republics in which nationalities of Moslem background were a majority reported birth rates (1962) from 34 to 40 as compared with 20 for the RSFSR.[6]

There is greater variability in the natality of Moslems south of the Sahara, where the Moslem religion and way of life fuse with tropical African cultures and religions. In Zanzibar natality of Afro-Arab women is estimated by Blacker to be barely at the level of replacement, a condition which he finds only partly explained by the high incidence of sterility and venereal disease.[7] Other Moslem groups of comparatively low natality have been identified in East Africa, in the Camerouns, and elsewhere, again at least partly determined by a high incidence of sterility. On the other hand some of the highest birth rates ever recorded have been reported for Moslem (and other populations) of West Africa. The latter rates are, however, of especially dubious validity. They are obtained from sample surveys designed to record births during the preceding twelve-month period. It is believed that such surveys in Africa tend to exaggerate the crude birth rate because of inclusion of births which actually occurred prior to the reference period.[8] Nevertheless, in the absence of other evidence the presumption is that natality is variable and in some places very high among some Moslem populations of this region, though perhaps not so high as recorded in the surveys.[9]

Despite serious limitations of the data the evidence points to a rather narrow range of variability in Moslem natality, with birth rates generally in the 40's and gross reproduction rates in the range of 2.8–3.4 for the continuous bloc of Moslems living in the vast region from North Africa to Central Asia and West Pakistan. It

[4] See footnote g to Table 1.

[5] Vaino Kannisto, "Population Increase in Indonesia," 1963, quoted in *United Nations Population Bulletin No. 7,* 1965. Computed rates in this general range (i.e., 40-43 for Java, 1954-58) are also given in Hilde Wander, *Die Beziehung Bevölkerungs und Wirtschaftsentwicklung dargestellt am Beispeil Indonesiens* (Institut für Weltwirtschaft an der Universität Kiel No. 70, 1965), pp. 87 ff.

[6] USSR, *Vestnik statistiki,* No. 8, 1963, p. 92. The official birth rates in 1962 are as follows: Azerbaidzhan SSR (40), Tadzhik SSR (34), Turkman SSR (40), and Uzbek SSR (40). The Soviet Union has conducted a vigorous campaign against the practice of Mohammedanism (as against other religions) and therefore does not recognize religious classifications — only nationalities. In each of these four republics about three-fourths of the population were reported to be of traditional Moslem nationalities in the census of 1959. The birth rate in the Kirgiz SSR (about three-fifths Moslem) was 34, and in Kazak SSR (less than half Moslem) it was 33. In the RSFR much the highest birth rate (41 in 1959) was reported in Daghestan, which is predominantly Moslem. The author is indebted to Mr. Allen Hetmanek of the U.S. Library of Congress and Mr. James Brackett of the U.S. Census Bureau for making these data available.

[7] J. G. C. Blacker, "Population Growth and Differential Fertility in Zanzibar Protectorate," *Population Studies,* 15 (3): 258-66 (March, 1962).

[8] *United Nations Population Bulletin No.* 7, 1965, chap. 3, "Levels and Trends of Fertility in Africa."

[9] It may well be that Moslem and earlier tropical African values on fertility reinforce each other. In a representative sample study of attitudes concerning "the best number of children in completed families" the modal size of family recommended by the male respondents was in the range of 5-9 in coastal and central Ghana (50% of respondents in each case) but 10-14 (28%) in northern Ghana, which has strong Moslem influence. J. C. Caldwell, "Fertility Attitudes in Three Economically Contrasting Research Regions of Ghana," to be published in *Population Studies,* 1966.

appears likely that there is greater variability among the Moslems south of the Sahara, and that the Moslems of the Indo-Pakistan subcontinent, particularly in East Pakistan, have a different pattern.

For the few Moslem countries for which there is a continuous record, there is little evidence of fundamental trends in natality either up or down. Aside from temporary reductions in the birth rate attributable to wars the birth rate in Egypt has apparently remained stable since the beginning of the century.[10] Though some Moslem populations such as the Algerian have been in close contact with the West for a long time, there is little evidence of the declines in the birth rate that have swept through Western populations[11] and more recently have appeared among East Asian populations.

As a consequence Moslem populations generally show higher natality than their non-Moslem neighbors. As noted above, Moslems in Europe and the Soviet Union have very much higher natality than Christian and other non-Moslem groups. Albania and the related Moslem districts in Yugoslavia are the only high natality areas remaining on the European continent. In the Soviet Union the Moslem republics stand out as the remaining areas of high natality in that country. In the Near East the sharp discontinuity is suggested by the birth rate in Turkey, estimated at 43, as compared with 18 for Greece. All available data show that the Moslems in North Africa had far higher natality than the dominant European minorities before the countries in this region achieved independence. The Arabs have a much higher birth rate than Jews in Israel. Moslems have higher natality than indigenous Christians in Lebanon and the United Arab Republic.[12]

While conditions are very different in South and Southeast Asia, there is evidence that again Moslems show higher natality than their Hindu and Buddhist neighbors, for example, in India and in Malaysia. Historically Moslems had consistently higher rates of natural increase in pre-partition India than Hindus, strongly suggesting higher natality, since there seems to be little reason for supposing lower mortality among Moslems. This hypothesis is borne out by other measures (e.g., ratios of children to women from the censuses). More recently some survey data show higher natality for the Moslems remaining in India where other conditions, for example, residence and economic class, are held constant.[13] Others do not show such differentiation,[14] and so it would be rash to generalize about the remaining Moslem minority which lives under very diverse conditions in the different regions of the country. But there seems little doubt that natality in present-day Pakistan is higher than in India and that in the subcontinent as a whole Moslems have higher natality. Finally, in Malaysia, where Moslems are a plurality living beside an almost equally large population of Chinese origin, birth rates and reproduction rates are higher for the Moslem Malays. It should be pointed out, however, that this is a recent development; until quite recently the Chinese, largely of immigrant background, showed higher birth rates than the indigenous Malay population, partly because the Chinese had an age distribution more favorable to high birth rates. In the past few years Chinese birth rates have shown a steady downward trend, associated with a rising age at marriage and probably with the beginnings of contraceptive practice on the Western model.[15]

[10] M. A. El Badry, "Trends in the Components of Population Growth in the Arab Countries of the Middle East," Conference on Demographic and Economic Trends, New York, October 10-12, 1963.

[11] Cf. Jacques Breil, *La population en Algérie* (Paris: Imprimerie nationale, 1957), p. 110. Had we more complete information we might see the beginnings of decline in the birth rate on the Western pattern in the secular states of Turkey and Albania. In Turkey census data show lower than average ratios of children to women in the more urbanized and developed regions of European Turkey and Western Anatolia.

[12] El Badry, *op. cit.*

[13] Cf. United Nations, Department of Economic and Social Affairs, *The Mysore Population Study,* U.N. Population Studies, No. 34 (New York, 1961); J. N. Sinha, "Differential Fertility and Family Limitation in an Urban Community of Uttar Pradesh," *Population Studies,* 11:157-69 (November, 1957); J. R. Rele, "Fertility Differentials in India: Evidence from a Rural Background," *Milbank Memorial Fund Quarterly,* 41 (2):183-200 (April, 1963).

[14] Cf. V. M. Dandekar and K. Dandekar, *Survey of Fertility and Mortality in Poona District* (Poona: Kokhale Institute of Politics and Economics, Publication No. 27, 1953), pp. 63, 101.

[15] Another possible exception exists in the Philippines, where lower ratios of children to women have been re-

The above observations are demonstrable only in relation to populations adhering to one or another of the major world religions. Where Moslems live beside, or are fused with, tribal groups (e.g., in tropical Africa and in Indonesia) such consistent differentials are not observed.

Conclusions

Within the important limitations of the data it may be said that Moslem natality (1) is almost universally high, (2) shows no evidence of important trends over time, and (3) is generally higher than that of neighboring peoples of other major religions.

Such observations do not apply to any other major world religion. Roman Catholic populations range in reported birth rates (1963) from 17 in Belgium to just under 50 in Costa Rica, and from gross reproduction rates of slightly above 1.0 in several European countries to 3.6 in Costa Rica. Among populations of Eastern Orthodox tradition (now largely Communist) birth rates are almost universally low, from 16.2 (1962) in Romania to 20.2 in the RSFSR and 22.2 in White Russia. Protestant and Jewish populations also have birth rates in this general range. In the spheres of Buddhist and Confucian influence birth rates range from 17 in Japan to over 40 in Thailand and several other Buddhist Southeast Asian countries (though only in the middle 30's in Ceylon); gross reproduction rates range from that 1 in Japan to well over 2 in Thailand. The birth rate is low in Japan and falling in Taiwan, Hong Kong, Singapore, and probably Korea (present trends in Communist China are unknown). The religious group most comparable to the Moslems in natality is the Hindus, among whom natality is generally high, though not quite so high as among the Moslems of the Indo-Pakistan subcontinent.

It would seem that Moslem institutions, more than those of other world religions, favor a generally high natality. Religion and high natality are more closely correlated for Moslems than for any other major religious group. The next sections will explore possible reasons why Islam displays this uniformity.

The factors favoring high birth rates may be conveniently discussed at three levels: (1) general cultural and religious factors, (2) specific characteristics of Moslem belief and practice related to the family, and (3) mechanisms by which these determine natality.

General Factors Favoring High Birth Rates in Moslem Countries

Moslem countries are all in the category of developing nations, and all have low indices of material development. These are usually lower than those of non-Moslem neighbors. High levels of education, industrialization, and other aspects of modernization associated with declines in the birth rate have not made strong headway as yet in Moslem countries. In fact, class differentials in natality in the UAR, for example, suggest that a general rise in the level of living might at first tend to *raise* the birth rate, because of better nutrition, health, and other factors.

Islam partakes of the pro-natalist social forces that exist generally in peasant and pastoral societies. High mortality, especially of infants and children, have in the past called for unrestricted reproduction. Sons are valued for many purposes: for continuity of family line and landownership; for contribution to agricultural labor; to strengthen family numbers in village rivalry and strife; for support in old age; for religious intervention at and after death. As in other developing societies, particularly in Asia, the joint family system in Islam buffers the direct burdens of childbearing on the parents.

Moslem influence is strongly conservative. In many ways *all* religions are conservative, but it is often noted that this is especially true of Islam, in which religion and way of life are so intertwined as to be inseparable. Mohammedanism shares with other religions injunctions to marry and multiply. Children are among the richest blessing that Allah bestows — He will provide for the souls He permits to come into the world.

ported in the censuses for Moslem than for Christian women. These data are suspect and are being re-examined for possible greater underenumeration of Moslem children and special biases in age reporting for Moslems (e.g., overstatement of age of children) that might affect such measures. Private communications from Drs. Mercedes Concepción and Frank Lorimer of the Population Center, University of the Philippines.

Moslems share with other religions important fatalistic themes that might well dispose them against conscious efforts to control family size or on occasion to adopt health measures that would reduce illness and postpone death. But these ideas are characteristic of many traditional societies; the difference is the tenacity with which old beliefs and practices are maintained by Moslems and influence life today. The contribution of this general conservatism to the maintenance of pre-modern natality is diffuse, difficult to measure, but probably very important.

The persistent resistance of Moslems to change has both historical and religious origins. The last of the world religions to appear, it has a strong tradition of military conquest and cultural domination. It has had over a millennium of conflict with Christianity and therefore has a conscious resistance to modern (often identified as Christian) influences which threaten the integrity of Islam. A large part of Islam, much the greater part, has within a generation been under the domination of European countries, and many Moslems have found solace and effective resistance in the continuing practice of their faith. The religions of the Orient, for example, do not have this deep-seated historical sense of conflict with the Western (i.e., Christian and Jewish) influences. Moslem sensitivities have understandably led to a cultural wall against diffusion from Europe despite proximity, political connections, and long-standing trade and communication.

The nature of the Moslem religion also is relevant to conservative influences. Mohammedanism is often described as a religion of practice rather than doctrine. True Believers are united by their faith in simple doctrine, with nothing comparable, for example, to the Christian concept of the Trinity. Essentially, all that is required is affirmation of belief in One God, who is Allah, and in Mohammed, as the Messenger of God. More important than doctrine in Islam is conformity to religious and social practices which are so closely interwoven in Moslem life.[16] Several of these that seem most pertinent will be discussed in the next section.

Special Moslem Characteristics That Might Be Expected To Favor High Birth Rates

Three of these characteristics will be discussed briefly below: (1) marriage institutions, (2) emphasis on sexuality, and (3) subordination of women.[17]

The traditional Moslem family is strongly patrilinear and patrilocal with male dominance and responsibility specifically prescribed by the Koran. The Moslem family derives from the agnate family of Mohammed's day. Polygamy was customary and Moslem doctrine prescribes that in the event of plural marriage the husband must treat his wives equally; there has been much dispute over whether this also means that he should distribute his favors equally among them. Divorce is theoretically easy but is in fact restrained by the fact that the husband must return the dowry with the wife, sacrifice the wedding bond, or in other ways pay a substantial penalty. Religious precepts are favorable to early remarriage of the widowed and the divorced; the scriptures require only a sufficient interval (3–4 months) to determine whether or not the woman was pregnant at the time of separation and thereby establish legitimate male responsibility for offspring.

Moslem doctrine holds that pleasures of the flesh, and specifically sexual intercourse, are a God-given virtue to be enjoyed and conjugal obligation to be fulfilled. The great medieval theologian Al-Ghazzali held that Mohammed was superior to Christ in that the latter never successfully integrated family life and sexual pleasure into Christian belief. While Moham-

[16] These views of Islam are presented in standard works, including Louis Gardet, *La Cité musulmane: vie sociale et politique* (Paris: Librairie Philosophique J. Vrin, 1954); G. E. von Grunebaum, *Islam* (London: Routledge & Kegan Paul, 1961) and *Medieval Islam* (Chicago: University of Chicago Press, 1946); and, with more sociological orientation, Morroe Berger, *The Arab World Today* (New York: Doubleday, 1962), and Clifford Geertz, *The Religion of Java* (Glencoe, Ill.: Free Press, 1960).

[17] These subjects are discussed, with extensive citations to other sources, in Mahmoud Seklani, "La fecondité dans les pays arabes," *Population* (Paris), 15(5): 831-56 (October-December, 1960); Special issue of *Confluent* on "Problèmes démographiques au Maghreb," particularly articles by J. G., "L'Islam face à la prévention des naissances," and Hédi Madani, "Le control des naissances et l'Islam," No. 50, April-June, 1965; and William J. Goode, *World Revolution and Family Patterns* (New York: Free Press-Macmillan, 1963), esp. chap. 3.

medanism imposed dietary restrictions and restraints relating to art and music, there is a striking absence of the value that is placed on sexual asceticism in Christianity, in Buddhism, and in Hinduism.[18] A celibate clergy or celibate religious orders are foreign to Islam. In traditional Moslem belief the permanent state of celibacy is abnormal for men and unthinkable for able-bodied women.

The place of women in traditional Moslem society was an unusually subordinate one. In Moslem practice women were and still are commonly not permitted to enter the mosque proper or to participate directly in its religious ceremonies. They were supposed to wear the veil, and on the Indian subcontinent to observe the often unhealthful seclusion of purdah. These restrictions were not always practical or enforceable, especially among the poor, but they have had prestige and were applied most rigorously among the upper and middle classes that otherwise would have been most receptive to modern influences. While the position of women is changing rapidly in the more progressive Moslem states, earlier attitudes are reflected, for example, in the low level of education of Moslem women. Less than 10% of the women over age 15 are literate in Morocco, Iran, Iraq, Pakistan, and doubtless most of the Moslem countries for which there are no data. In each case the number of male literates is three to four times greater. Only in the Soviet Moslem republics, in Albania, and in Indonesia are more than a fourth of the women reported as literate. Male dominance within marriage is thus strengthened by the greater education of males and by the differences in age at marriage — women are characteristically married young to more mature men, usually in their twenties.[19]

Mechanisms by Which Moslem Practices May Determine Natality

These traditional family institutions and the traditional role of women affect natality through (1) proportion of the reproductive life that is spent in marital or other sexual unions and (2) within such unions the practices determining exposure to pregnancy. Statistical information is available on the first but not generally on the second. In the ten Moslem countries for which comparable data are available 70%–86% of all females aged 15–44 are married. This is a higher proportion than exists in the Far East and Southeast Asia and in almost all Western countries, which range from a low of 47% in Ireland to a high of 71% in the United States. It is apparent that Moslem women spend a larger part of their reproductive life in marriage than do their sisters in these other major regions. This is the result of the following several (in some cases contradictory) influences:

1. In accordance with Moslem practice marriage of women is well-nigh universal. In those countries for which data are available 3% or less (more often only 1%) are not married by the end of the reproductive period.

2. Age at marriage is low for women in all Moslem countries. In the ten countries for which reasonably comparable information was available from recent censuses, the proportion of females married among all females aged 15–19 ranges from 31% in the UAR to 73% in Pakistan.[20] In the latter, age at marriage approximates the early Moslem rule of marriage at puberty. The percentages were in the range 31–40 for Middle Eastern countries (Iran, Iraq, Turkey, Tunisia and the UAR) and 49% in Morocco. A figure of 57% for Kuwait confirms fragmentary evidence that age at marriage in the Arabian peninsula is lower, as it is also in West Africa (60% in Guinea). The figure for Moslem Malays is 40% and this is thought to be comparable for their ethnic cousins in Indonesia.[21] Differential age at marriage may well be a factor in the somewhat higher birth rates in Pakistan than in other Moslem countries, and in the very high birth rates apparently prevailing in West Africa.

[18] Perhaps more evident in Christianity and Buddhism than in Hinduism, where fertility has been glorified in the construction of temples, etc. Nevertheless, there is a strong theme of the value of sexual asceticism in Hinduism (e.g., in teachings of Gandhi).

[19] Data in this and the succeeding paragraphs were computed from compilations in the United Nations, *Demographic Yearbook,* recent issues.

[20] These may be compared with 1% women married in this age group in Ireland and in Japan, 3% in France, 8% in Korea, 12-13% in the Philippines and Thailand, 16% in the United States, and 70% in India.

[21] To be contrasted with the figures for the Christian Philippines and Buddhist Thailand above. T. E. Smith, "Population Characteristics of South and South-East Asia," in *Women in the New Asia,* ed. Barbara Ward (Paris: UNESCO, 1963), p. 507.

It is certainly an important element in the generally higher natality of Moslems.

3. Widowhood during the reproductive years is more common than in the West owing to higher mortality, which of course varies from country to country. This tends to reduce natality. Widowhood is generally declining with reductions in mortality.

4. As might be expected, divorce is more common in Islam than elsewhere. The reported figures, which probably understate the fact, show higher divorce rates than in the West and in the non-Moslem countries of Asia. The reported rates are not so high as to seriously jeopardize reproduction (e.g., annual rates of less than 1.5 per thousand population in Turkey, Albania, and Iraq and 2–3 in Morocco and the UAR).[22]

5. The effects of widowhood and divorce on natality are tempered in Moslem countries by institutions favoring the early remarriage of widows and divorcees. The proportions of marriages involving a widow or a divorced person are much higher than in the West (except in Albania and Turkey, which more closely follow the European pattern). Furthermore, in the United Arab Republic, for example, 8% of all Moslem grooms were (in 1955) reported as marrying an additional wife, suggesting that at least here polygamy was an appreciable factor in increasing the possibilities for women of marriage and remarriage.

6. Nevertheless polygamy is probably more a spectacular feature of Moslem institutions than a decisive factor in Moslem natality. There is inadequate evidence on its prevalence but available information suggests that some nine-tenths of Arab farmers, for example, are monogamous, and polygamy is most commonly adopted when the first wife fails to produce a child. Polygamy is more common among the Arab Bedouins and the Moslems south of the Sahara, where Moslem customs in this matter converge with earlier tribal practices. But among the more advanced Moslem countries polygamy is in disrepute and in some instances (e.g., Tunisia) has been made illegal and is presumably declining.

There is an extensive and inconclusive literature about the effects of polygamy on the total birth rate of the communities concerned.[23] One thing is clear — in Moslem societies it does promote opportunities for marriage of all females, single, widowed, and divorced. It may be recalled that the Prophet's nine wives were mostly widows. Plural marriage can be important to natality in societies where mortality is high, as it has been in Moslem countries, and where the difference in age at marriage between bride and groom (e.g., five years) is greater than in Western societies. Polygamy is certainly a pro-natalist factor in promoting marriage opportunities for women.[24]

There is only the most fragmentary evidence on the relation of Moslem institutions to practices determining the risk of pregnancy within marriage. Ritual abstinence is apparently less common among Moslems than, for instance, among Hindus, though abstinence is required during the daylight hours of Ramadan, the month of fasting. Moslem customs do not require prolonged abstinence following childbirth, and Moslem women do not so frequently return to their parents' home for confinement as, for example, do Hindus; so post-partum separation is likely to be shorter. Such factors may explain the somewhat higher birth rates of Moslems than Hindus in the Indian subcontinent despite similar patterns of early marriage, high rates of widow remarriage, and high proportions of reproductive life spent by women in marriage.[25]

In a society which emphasizes the value, even the religious merit, of sexual exuberance within marriage it might be hypothesized that the frequency of intercourse might be higher than in societies more restrained on this subject. This

[22] These may be compared with estimated United States rates of 2.12 to 2.35 for the years 1954-60, which are the highest for Western countries.

[23] Cf. United Nations, *Population Bulletin No.* 7, 1965, esp. chap. 3, "Levels and Trends of Fertility in Africa."

[24] The opposite argument rests on comparisons that show higher average numbers of children born to women in monogamous than in polygamous unions, presumably because of differences in frequency of intercourse and the greater age of polygamous men (in most cultures polygamy is a luxury, usually requiring the accumulation of capital). But such comparisons are biased by the fact that barrenness of the first wife is the most common reason for marrying another — hence polygamous unions have a disproportionate number of sterile women.

[25] Census data for India and Pakistan suggest little difference in the proportion of widows remarrying despite the Brahmin prohibition against this practice.

might be expected to contribute to a higher birth rate. There is almost no direct evidence. Very fragmentary and inconclusive data show higher frequencies of intercourse for Moslems in special studies in Lebanon and Bengal, but the populations included were small and the data are verbal responses that might reflect cultural biases as well as real differences.[26] Similar problems arise in evaluating the possible effects of polygamy (referred to above) and of the joint or extended family, which is an ideal over much of the Moslem world. In the Bengal field study reported by Nag, women living in simple or nuclear families were found to have both higher coital frequency and higher natality than women in joint families. This is ascribed to the lack of privacy and greater adherence to traditional periods of abstinence in joint households.[27] There is too little evidence on the true prevalence of the extended family, quite aside from other problems, to make any generalizations on this subject.

Aside from the above, physiological factors in Islam would generally work against the attainment of maximum fertility. Problems of epidemic disease and malnutrition, still common in the Moslem world, probably reduce the capacity to conceive and certainly the capacity to carry pregnancy full term, but this influence is not now measurable. Further, Moslem women do indulge in prolonged lactation after childbirth; this practice presumably reduces natality somewhat. These several physiological influences are not specifically Moslem; they reduce natality below physiological potentialities in most traditional societies.

In sum, the traditional Islamic way of life is culturally favorable to high natality in the absence of voluntary restriction of births within marriage. The maximum potential fertility is reduced by high mortality and widowhood and probably by adverse physiological factors such as malnutrition and disease and by certain practices such as prolonged lactation. The general effect of modernization should be to ameliorate the adverse factors and hence raise the birth rate in the absence of voluntary control of family size.

Mohammedan doctrine does not prohibit the voluntary restriction of births, though as a militant religion Islam historically put pressure on men to produce numerous children and especially sons. Nevertheless there are clear authoritative statements, for example by the highly respected medieval theologian Al-Ghazzali, that would permit the practice of birth control (i.e., coitus interruptus) under certain conditions.[28] Also important are the *fatwas* made by religious authorities in the light of modern conditions. Because Islam does not have the hierarchial structure of the Roman Catholic Church, these pronouncements do not have the authority of a papal encyclical, but they have significant influence. One of the clearest and most authoritative of these, by the Mufti of Egypt, came to the conclusion that "it is permissible for either husband or wife, by mutual consent, to take any measures to prevent semen entering the uterus, in order to prevent conception."[29] While this conclusion has not gone unchallenged, the preponderance of religious authority has not been unfavorable to birth control. On the other hand, abortion after the "quickening" of the embryo is absolutely forbidden. The existing pronouncements on family limitation did not contemplate and hence do not pass judgment on the use of radically new methods such as the oral contraceptives and intra-uterine devices.

The above describes the traditional factors affecting natality in Islam. They explain why Moslems have not adopted family planning on the European pattern despite geographical proximity and long association with Europe. This is the cultural background within which rapid changes may now be occurring in the more advanced Moslem countries, though not yet gen-

[26] David Yaukey, *Fertility Differentials in a Modernizing Country* (Princeton: Princeton University Press, 1961), p. 201; and Moni Nag, *Factors Affecting Human Fertility in Nonindustrial Societies: A Cross-Cultural Study,* Yale University Publications in Anthropology, 1962, pp. 72-73.

[27] Moni Nag, "Family Type and Fertility," World Population Conference, Belgrade, August 30-September 10, 1965.

[28] Akhter Hameed Khan, *Islamic Opinions on Contraception,* (Comilla, East Pakistan: Pakistan Academy for Village Development, 1961). Includes translations of extracts from Al-Ghazzali and Ibn Kaiyim.

[29] "A Mohammedan 'Fatwa' on Contraception," *Human Fertility,* 10(2): 45-46 (June, 1945). Includes translation of Arabic original published in the *Journal of the Egyptian Medical Association,* 20(7): 54-56 (July, 1937).

eral enough to be reflected in measurable declines in the birth rate. The next section deals with empirical studies of what Moslems *today* know, think, and do about family planning.

The Moslem World Today: Field Studies of Knowledge, Attitudes, and Practices Relating to Family Limitation

There is now a rapidly growing number of such studies of general populations in Moslem countries. The most ambitious of these is a survey of a national sample in Turkey, taken preparatory to the adoption of a government program to promote family planning in that country. There are several studies in Pakistan, which has had a government family planning program for several years. Two studies were conducted on a comparable basis in the UAR and in Lebanon. Studies are being conducted in Tunisia and in Indonesia, the first results of which were presented to this conference (as reported in chapters 43 and 47 in this volume). While these various studies were conducted under different auspices and are in some respects not comparable, they lead to certain consistent results. These are summarized below, though so brief a statement cannot hope to do justice to the individual studies involved.[30]

Such Studies Are Feasible

They can provide valuable and reliable information for general populations, as opposed to clinic or other unrepresentative groups. This is true despite initial skepticism encountered in every country concerning the feasibility of obtaining responses on such delicate subjects in a household survey.

Knowledge

Men and women in Moslem countries, as elsewhere, display ignorance about the physiology of reproduction, as, for example, the time of ovulation and the fertile period in the menstrual cycle. Knowledge of modern methods of birth control (i.e., other than abstinence or abortion) is largely confined to the small educated minority in the cities. In Turkey, perhaps the most advanced Moslem country, only 43% of the national sample said they knew of *any* method of contraception. In rural Lebanon and rural Egypt, very few respondents reported such knowledge.

Desired Family Size

All the studies show that a substantial proportion of couples in both urban and rural areas is concerned about the size of their families and do not want more children. In each of the studies where the appropriate questions were asked, a large proportion of the respondents gave as an ideal family size a smaller number of children than the actual number in completed families in their own society.[31] Women in Moslem countries apparently want fewer children than their husbands, though the difference is not large. Families with one or more sons are more interested in limiting family size than those having only daughters. Among Moslem countries, only in Turkey has the small family norm gained general acceptance, though even here only in principle, not in fact. The modal number of children desired by both men and women is 3, the average (mean) being 3.7 for men and 3.2 for women.

[30] Results of the studies are available in the following publications: "Turkey: National Survey on Population," *Studies in Family Planning,* No. 5, December, 1964 (Population Council, New York); Social Sciences Research Centre, University of the Panjab, *Knowledge of and Attitudes towards Family Planning,* Family Planning Association of Pakistan, Lahore, Pakistan; A. Majeed Khan, *Rural Pilot Family Planning Action Programme: First Annual Report, March, 1961-May, 1962,* Pakistan Academy for Rural Development, Comilla, East Pakistan; Beryl J. Roberts, David Yaukey, William Griffiths, Elizabeth W. Clark, A. B. M. Shafiullah, and Raisunnessa Huq, "Family Planning Survey in Dacca, East Pakistan," *Demography,* Vol. 2, 1965; Hanna Rizk, "Social and Psychological Factors Affecting Fertility in the United Arab Republic," *Marriage and Family Living,* 25 (1): 69-73 (February, 1963); David Yaukey, *Fertility Differences in a Modernizing Country: A Survey of Lebanese Couples* (Princeton: Princeton University Press, 1961).

[31] A compilation of responses on "desired family size" and on persons stating they do not want more children for many studies including several in Moslem countries aie presented in W. Parker Mauldin, "Fertility Studies: Knowledge, Attitude, and Practice," *Studies in Family Planning,* No. 7, pp. 1-10 (June, 1965). As the author points out, however, specific comparisons are treacherous because the responses are often to different questions, put in different ways, to different types of samples. This is particularly true of the studies made in Moslem areas; so no attempt has been made here to make numerical comparisons.

In actual fact Turkish women completing the childbearing period report an average of 6.3 pregnancies, 5.8 live births, and 4.1 living children. Only about one-fourth of the Turkish couples in their thirties, married 10–14 years, and already having three children want more children. This position is not now representative of more than the most progressive Moslem populations but probably indicates the direction in which the more advanced Moslem countries are going. A very different atmosphere of opinion exists in the more rural populations: in the UAR study, for example, one-third of the women in the younger reproductive ages thought questions on desired size of family meaningless "because God alone determines the number of children a wife might have." [32]

Practice of Family Planning

Despite widespread favorable attitudes toward the restriction of family size, the actual practice of birth control by Moslems is very limited. As stated by the author of the UAR study, "It is evident from this analysis that while more than half the wives in this study consider their families too large, yet they could not or would not limit them to the desired size." [33] Among the rural Moslem populations studied, the existing practice of contraception was negligible except in Turkey, where there was definite progression from 6% practicing in rural areas, 18% in the town, 21% in the cities, and 29% in the metropolitan areas. In the Dacca sample (an educated and urban group) the proportion ever having practiced contraception was 36% or 21% depending on whether one relies on the reports of the husbands or of the wives, and in Lahore the comparable figures are 18% and 8% for a somewhat broader urban sample. The highest figures reported for any Moslem population are those reported by Yaukey for Beirut, which is a cosmopolitan and Westernized city: for women married ten years or more, 60% of the uneducated and 83% of the educated reported some attempts at control of contraception.[34]

[32] Rizk, *op. cit.*, p. 72.

[33] *Ibid.*

[34] David Yaukey, "Some Immediate Determinants of Fertility Differences in Lebanon," *Marriage and Family Living*, 25 (1): 27-34 (February, 1963). Other data in this paragraph from sources given in note 30.

Reduction of the Birth Rate Owing to Family Planning

Where such information was obtained, the studies show smaller family size among the better educated urban couples included in the samples. In Moslem countries, as everywhere, education is highly correlated with knowledge of contraceptive methods, with favorable attitudes toward their use, and with the actual practice of family planning. As in most Western countries the educated were the first to adopt family limitation. But as yet these groups are too small to have any measurable impact on the birth rate of Moslem populations as a whole. It is possible that among the Moslem populations most exposed to European influence (in Albania, in Western Turkey, and among the Soviet Moslem Republics) the birth rate has begun to decline on the Western model and that this may soon become evident in statistical data.

Now a new factor has entered — *the intervention of governments.* The high birth rates and accelerating rates of population growth in relation to economic growth have caused concern in Moslem countries. Several of the above studies were undertaken as result of government concern about population growth and of government interest in introducing family planning programs. Moslem countries have been among the first to adopt such programs: four of these are described in papers in this volume, on national programs in Pakistan, Turkey, the UAR and Tunisia (chaps. 10, 11, 12, 13). None of these has yet been on a scale sufficient to affect the national birth rates of the countries concerned. But the results of the above studies suggest that in each of these countries, at least, there is a major reservoir of couples already motivated to adopt family planning if given the relevant information and services suited to their needs. The latter offer a major opportunity for government family planning programs if the necessary administrative services can be established. Nevertheless government programs may have to give more attention to stimulating motivation for family planning, especially among men, than would be true in other major religious groups.

General Conclusions

Conclusions relevant to family planning programs may be summarized as follows:

1. Islamic countries uniformly have high birth rates.

2. These are supported by distinctive Islamic attitudes and practices in family life rather than by political or religious doctrine.

3. The "normal" diffusion of birth control to and within Moslem countries on the European pattern has been inhibited by the cultural discontinuity between Moslem peoples and their neighbors.

4. The continuing high birth rates in Moslem countries, matched with encouraging progress in reducing deaths, now lead to rapid population growth and its especially high visibility as a handicap to economic and social progress.

5. As a result several Moslem countries have adopted measures to introduce birth control.

6. KAP and other studies show: (*a*) that a substantial number of couples in all Moslem societies studied have favorable attitudes toward family limitation and would like to practice it given suitable methods — where the question was asked (Turkey) the respondents said they favored a government birth control program; (*b*) that the actual practice of birth control is still limited to a small urban and educated minority; (*c*) that efforts to introduce birth control on a large scale encounter much more salient lack of motivation, than, for example, in Buddhist and Far Eastern countries.[35]

7. Despite these difficulties the present attitudes and programs of governments, and the availablity of more suitable contraceptive methods, augur much more rapid adoption of family planning in Moslem countries than could have been expected even a few years ago.

[35] Cf. action research experiments in Pakistan: "Pakistan: The Medical Research Project at Lulliani," and "Pakistan: The Public Health Education Research Project in Dacca," *Studies in Family Planning,* No. 4, pp. 5-9 (August, 1964) and No. 5, pp. 6-12 (December, 1964); in Indonesia, in paper by Gille and Pardoko, and in Tunisia, in paper by Morsa, chapters 43 and 47 in this volume. These may be compared with other experiments, e.g., those described in "India: The Singur Study"; "Korea: The Koyang Study"; "Ceylon: The Swedish-Ceylon Family Planning Project"; "Taiwan: The Taichung Program of Pre-Pregnancy Health," *Studies in Family Planning,* No. 1, pp. 1-4 (July, 1963); No. 2, pp. 7-9 and 9-12 (December, 1963); No. 4, p. 12 (August, 1964).

STUDY AND DISCUSSION QUESTIONS

1. Using the Davis-Blake analytical framework, examine the fertility patterns in Japan or India. Isolate variables of intercourse, conception, and gestation and parturition in the country and tell how each affects fertility.
2. Compare differential fertility in Peru and a more economically-advanced nation, using the data given by Stycos and United Nations or other sources. What similarities and differences are there in the fertility patterns of the two countries?
3. Dudley Kirk discusses norms which affect Moslem natality. In his article on family planning in underdeveloped areas, Ronald Freedman notes several variables which may contribute to high birth rates in a country. Which of these variables apply in the Islamic nations Kirk mentions? Give specific examples.
4. Look up the crude birth rate in the United States and in Ireland or Japan for 1960. Now compare the general fertility rate in the same two countries in this same year. Does this refinement of the fertility measure make a difference? Why? Which measure is better for comparison?
5. How do the three sets of factors concerning fertility (individual, group, and institutional) affect the Davis-Blake variables in fertility?
6. To show the influence of religious institutions on fertility practices, compare Roman Catholic fertility in Ireland and Mormon fertility in the United States.
7. Since future population growth patterns in the world will largely be determined by the course of fertility, discuss what trends in world population growth may be expected in the next twenty years on the basis of fertility trends given in the United Nations article.

SUGGESTED ADDITIONAL READING

Berelson, Bernard, *et al. Family Planning and Population Programs*, Chicago: University of Chicago Press, 1966.
A recent collection of articles covering the progress of family planning programs throughout the world.

United Nations. *Population Bulletin of the United Nations, No. 7.* New York: United Nations, 1965.
Surveys conditions and trends of fertility in the world in a detailed study.

Lorimer, Frank. *Culture and Human Fertility.* Paris: UNESCO, 1954.
An attempt to study social and cultural conditions affecting fertility in non-industrial societies, drawing heavily on anthropological materials.

Freedman, Ronald. "The Sociology of Human Fertility: a Trend Report and Bibliography," *Current Sociology*, X/XI (1961–62), 35–121.
Report on the status of international fertility since World War II with a theoretical orientation and topical bibliography.

CHAPTER 5

Fertility Trends and Differentials: The United States

Although the "vital revolution" has not run its course in developing nations, a transition from high birth and death rates to relatively low birth and death rates has come about in most Western societies. In this chapter, fertility trends and differentials in the United States are examined intensively in order to see how fertility has typically changed in a society that has passed through the transition. The assumption is not made that developing nations will follow this course since it is quite clear that conditions that existed in Western societies during the transition may not exist in other countries now moving through the transition. Rather, it is hoped that by looking at the mechanisms bringing about fertility changes in one country, some insights might be gained into the dynamic aspects of the demographic revolution occurring throughout the world.

Considering the relatively low levels of fertility in the United States today, it is sometimes difficult to realize that the birth rate in the country was once at the level presently found in underdeveloped countries. Yet, as the selection by Grabill, Kiser, and Whelpton shows, the birth rate in colonial America is estimated to have been about 50 to 57 per 1,000. With mortality then undergoing a decline, the American population stood in the early stages of the demographic transition. Fertility began to drop significantly in the United States at least by 1810, and the decline continued uninterruptedly, apart from small annual variations. By 1915 the birth rate was about 30, and by the period of economic depression of the 1930's it was down to 18. Then, contrary to the expectations provided by demographic transition theory, the birth rate turned significantly upward right after World War II and remained at a high level until the latter part of the 1950's when it reversed its course again and started downward. At the time of this writing, it was again approaching depression-period levels.

What accounts for these historical reversals in the birth rate of the United States? Can social science provide an explanation? An attempt at explanation must consider five broad factors: 1) changes in fecundity; 2) compositional and distributional factors; 3) the timing and spacing of births; 4) changing completed family size; and 5) trends in family planning.

Fecundity refers to the physiological capacity of women to bear children. In all societies at all points in time, some women have been sterile or relatively sterile due to some type of physical impairment or chemical imbalance. It is reasonable to assume that the extent of this condition in a society is correlated with the levels of health and mortality. In the United States, generally, there is some evidence that the female population has become somewhat more fecund over time. This increase in fecundity has no doubt contributed to the fertility increases of some groups in the population at some points in time, although it could not account for the reversals of the long-term trend in the birth rate.

Compositional factors refer to the demographic variables which describe the way the population is composed — age, sex, ethnic status and marital status, in particular. By *distributional factors* are meant the variables which describe the geographical location of the population. Chapter 8 deals wholly with population composition as an element of population analysis, and Chapter 9 with population distribution. At this point, we are interested only in examining the effect of compositional and distributional factors on the birth rate. For example, a changing age structure can have a profound effect on fertility by varying the proportion of the female population in the reproductive ages. The anticipation of a new increase in fertility in the years just ahead is partly a function of the approach to womanhood of the unusually large numbers of girls born in the late 1940's, the "baby boom" years. This is to say, in the coming years, the proportion of the female population which is in the reproductive years will increase.

The sex ratio (ratio of males per 100 females in the population) is another compositional factor of some importance to fertility in that an unbalanced sex ratio, particularly at the reproductive ages, can affect the potential for mating. In the United States, as in most societies, this would operate through the institutionalized form of mating known as marriage. Marital status is important as a compositional factor in other ways as well. The proportion of the population which eventually marries, the ages at which people marry, and the number of years couples have been married have an impact on the birth rate.

Distributional factors affect the birth rate because fertility levels vary among parts of the country and, as population shifts from one part of the country to another, the birth rate is thereby raised or lowered. The dominant distributional effect on the United States birth rate has been the urbanization of the population, reflecting in great part the rural-to-urban migration. Since typically urban values support a lower fertility level than do typically rural values, the net effect has been some depression of the birth rate.

The timing and spacing of births have come to be recognized as crucial factors in fertility changes in the United States over the past few decades. Couples seem to consider putting off having children or hastening the family-building process depending on the state of affairs in the society as well as on their own peculiar circumstances. It has been demonstrated that part of the "baby boom" after World War II reflected a "making up" of births deferred during the late depression and early war years. It is clear that some persons time the having of children so that "good times" will favor their upbringing. It is also the case that a great change over time has been taking place with regard to the spacing of children — how many years apart the children are born. The trend in the United States has been for earlier family building; that is, even where couples are having the same number of children, they are now beginning and completing childbearing sooner than in past years.

Because compositional, distributional, timing, and spacing factors do affect the birth rate, the question is often raised as to whether or not the size of completed families is changing. Are young American women eventually having more children than did their mothers and grandmothers? The answer seems to be that over the long run there has been a decrease in the *average size of completed family* in the United States; however, there has been a decline in large families and a concomitant decline in childlessness and in one-child families. Having two, three, or four children has become a characteristic feature of contemporary American fertility. And, as the article by Freedman explains, the average size of American families is consistent with the ideals and expectations of women in the United States. There is a remarkable consensus, he points out, on a moderate-size family.

The consistency of fertility ideals and behavior can be related to the increasing use and success of *family planning* techniques. In recent years, there has been a revolution in contraceptive technology, as described later in Chapter 10. The practice of contraception in the United States has become nearly universal; yet, many couples use inefficient methods and, as some studies have shown, family planning has been used mainly to control the size of completed families rather than to determine the spacing and timing of births.

As family planning becomes more widespread and more efficient, the ability of Americans to control family size and spacing of children will become more complete. Differences in fertility behavior will then be precisely a function of the ideals people hold.

In the United States, both ideals and behavior with regard to fertility vary among population subgroups. Some of the traditional differentials have been narrowing, however, while others persist or widen. As the selection by the Population Reference Bureau indicates, religious differences in both ideals and behavior are strong and, in some respects, growing larger. Catholics average more births than Protestants or Jews. Among Catholics, those who are more devout are more fertile. In general, there has been an inverse relationship between socioeconomic status and fertility; but highly-educated Catholics have relatively high fertility expectations as well as performance. Moreover, the pattern of fertility by income now takes the form of a U-shaped curve. These high-fertility levels attained by the high-status groups may reflect growing economic security among the top status class, or it may be the formation of a new value consensus about ideal family size which has not yet filtered down to the middle and lower classes.

Urban-rural and regional differences in fertility are gradually becoming smaller, while racial differentials, which once appeared to be narrowing, have widened again. The trends of white and nonwhite fertility over the past forty or fifty years have generally been parallel, although nonwhite fertility has remained higher. The past migrations of Negroes out of the rural South, where fertility rates are highest, and the overall upward social mobility of Negroes in the United States portend a narrowing of racial differentials in fertility in the years to come.

Apart from the general characteristics which differentiate groups by their fertility, there are specific cultural groups within American society whose birth rates deviate considerably from the national pattern. One such group is the Hutterites, whose fertility behavior is described by Eaton and Mayer. Their near-maximum birth rate is traceable to their religious values and accompanying style of life. Until now, they have been relatively isolated from the rest of the national society; but time will tell if culture contacts in the future will bring about change in their fertility values and ideals. Other cultural groups in American society, such as the Mormons and French Canadians, have fertility patterns which differ sharply from the national pattern.

The picture of fertility in the United States, then, is one of a relatively low but fluctuating birth rate. The birth rate, it has been observed, changes in response to a number of factors whose relative importance cannot easily be estimated. Continuing research on the values, norms, and behavior of Americans with regard to fertility should give us a better understanding of the principal forces at work in determining the level of the birth rate and the conditions under which these forces operate.

*The Fertility of American Women: The Colonial and Early Federal Periods**

Wilson H. Grabill · Clyde V. Kiser
Pascal K. Whelpton

For more than two centuries, from the time of the first permanent settlements to the early decades of the nineteenth century, the fertility of the American people ranked among the world's highest. Estimates made by both contemporary and modern authorities, utilizing a variety of techniques and data, place the annual birth rate in the Colonial and early Federal periods at 50 to 57 births per 1,000 inhabitants. The women of completed fertility are variously estimated to have borne an average of eight children. According to Miller, the high American birth rate was sometimes cited for propaganda purposes before the Revolutionary War to indicate that it was only a question of time before the American population growth would shift the British Empire's balance of power westward.[1] Benjamin Franklin made this type of forecast himself.

Contemporary Observations

The contemporary explanation for America's high fertility is illustrated by the following quotations.

In 1751, Benjamin Franklin wrote:

Tables of the proportion of Marriages to Births, of Deaths to Births, of Marriages to the number of inhabitants, &c., form'd on observations made upon the Bills of Mortality, Christenings, &c., of populous cities, will not suit countries; nor will tables form'd on observations made in full settled old countries, as *Europe*, suit new countries, as *America*.

2. For people increase in proportion to the number of marriages, and that is greater in proportion to the ease and convenience of supporting a family . . .

. . . which charges are greater in the cities, as Luxury is more common: many live single during life, and continue servants to families, journeymen to Trades, &c., hence cities do not by natural generation supply themselves with inhabitants; the deaths are more than the births.

4. In countries full settled, the case must be nearly the same; all Lands being occupied and improved to the heighth; those who cannot get land must labour for others that have it; when laborers are plenty, their wages will be low; by low wages a family is supported with difficulty; this difficulty deters many from marriage, who therefore long continue servants and single. Only as the Cities take supplies of people from the country, and thereby make a little more room in the country; Marriage is a little more encourag'd there, and the births exceed the deaths . . .

7. Hence, marriages in *America* are more general and more generally early, than in *Europe*. And if it is reckoned there, that there is but one marriage per annum among one hundred persons, perhaps we may here reckon two; and if in *Europe* they have but four Births to a marriage (many of their marriages being late) we may here reckon eight, of which one half grow up, and our marriages are made, reckoning one with another at twenty years of age our people must be at least doubled every twenty years.[2]

Thomas Jefferson in a letter to Count de Montborin, dated July 1787 said:

A century's experience has shown that we double our numbers every twenty or twenty-five years. No circumstances can be foreseen, at this moment, which will lessen our rate of multiplication for centuries to come.

The Chevalier Félix de Beaujour, a former French consular official in the United States declared in 1814:

* Reprinted with permission from Wilson H. Grabill, Clyde V. Kiser, and Pascal K. Whelpton, *The Fertility of American Women*. New York; John Wiley, 1959, pp. 5-12.

[1] John C. Miller, *Origins of the American Revolution,* Little, Brown and Company, Boston, 1943, pp. 433-435.

[2] Benjamin Franklin, "Observations Concerning The Increase of Mankind, The Peopling of Countries, &c.," *The Magazine of History, with Notes and Quotes,* Extra Number, No. 63, 1755.

Every thing in the United States favours the progress of population; the emigrations from Europe, the disasters of the European colonies, but, above all, the abundance of the means of subsistence. Marriages are there easier than in Europe, births more multiplied, and deaths relatively less frequent. It is calculated that out of sixty individuals, two are married annually, that one is born out of every twenty, and that the proportion of deaths is only one in forty. This last report, founded on careful observations, seems incredible in a country so recently cleared and naturally not healthy; but it is nonetheless true, because it accords with the number of births, which there is greater than in Europe. In the United States, more children are necessarily born than among us, because the inhabitants, in such an extent of country, finding the means of subsistence more abundant, marry at an earlier age. No human consideration there operates as a hindrance to reproduction, and the children swarm on the rich land in the same manner as do insects.[3]

Beaujour's "observations" probably were based in part on estimates made by Samuel Blodget, which are reproduced in table 1 as an example of the work done in early times.[4]

[3] Chevalier Félix de Beaujour, *Sketch of the United States of North America,* jointly published by several printing firms, London, 1814.

[4] Blodget probably made his estimates somewhat as follows: He began with data from the first two censuses of the United States (1790 and 1800) and figured the average annual percent increase in population (3 percent). This percent was then applied in a chain computation to obtain annual population estimates and annual amounts of numerical increase. From custom house and port records, Blodget secured data on "passengers arriving," and allowed for Americans returning from abroad, aliens in transit to Canada or here temporarily, etc. Subtraction of the (net) migration from annual population increase gave annual natural increase. From bills of mortality for a few communities and rural areas, Blodget estimated the national death rate to be "near 2½ percent." The estimated numbers of deaths

TABLE 1

Abstract of Samuel Blodget's Estimates of Annual Population Increase, Births, Deaths, and Net Immigration: 1790 to 1805

Year	Free persons	Slaves, increase yearly near 2 percent	Free blacks and persons of color	Annual migrations, free men and slaves	Births in each year, near 5¾ percent	Deaths in each year, near 2½ percent	Total population, including Louisiana in the year 1804	Total increase each year, near 3 percent
1790	3,232,303	697,697	59,511	3,500	...	...	3,930,000	...
1791	3,333,761	714,139	63,500	4,000	215,900	101,000	4,047,900	117,900
1792	3,438,237	731,000	67,500	5,000	220,937	103,500	4,169,337	121,337
1793	3,446,417	748,000	71,600	3,600	227,680	107,100	4,294,417	125,180
1794	3,657,189	766,000	75,700	3,500	235,382	110,200	4,423,249	128,632
1795	3,771,946	784,000	79,800	3,900	242,197	113,400	4,555,946	132,697
1796	3,890,124	802,500	84,900	4,500	249,117	117,000	4,692,624	136,678
1797	4,012,902	820,500	89,900	3,500	257,516	120,300	4,833,402	140,776
1798	4,940,404	837,000	95,000	3,800	266,202	124,000	4,978,404	145,002
1799	4,273,756	854,000	100,600	4,000	273,334	128,000	5,127,756	149,352
1800	4,404,798	876,790	105,643	3,800	282,132	132,100	5,281,588	153,823
1801	4,544,300	898,300	110,800	4,000	290,712	136,200	5,440,100	158,512
1802	4,682,313	921,000	115,900	4,500	299,113	140,400	5,603,313	163,213
1803	4,727,412	944,000	121,900	3,900	308,749	144,550	5,771,412	168,099
1804	5,000,100	999,900	126,000	9,500	810,500	149,000	6,000,000	228,588
1805	5,156,000	1,024,900	131,000	...	321,000	153,000	6,180,000	180,000

No correction has been made for errors in original table.

Source: Samuel Blodget, *Economica, A Statistical Manual for the United States of America,* Washington, 1806, p. 58

Franklin's references to Europe seem to be based on an extensive investigation of parish records in several European countries by Süssmilch, a clergyman, who was much interested in population data and in the "laws" of population growth.[5] Franklin's remarks on urban and rural differences in marriages, etc., are evidently for Europe. Blodget's later data indicate that American cities around 1800 had about two births for every death (table 2). The population of America increased by about 35 percent in most decades from 1660 to 1790 (table 3). This corresponds to a doubling of population every 23 years.

Fertility and Migration

Although Franklin and some of his contemporaries spoke of the high rate of population growth in the American Colonies, they gave relatively little attention to the role played by migration of population from abroad. Bountiful natural increase was regarded as the main source of future growth. A birth rate of about 55 and a population of about 1,207,000 in 1750 meant about 66,000 births per year at that time, compared with annual net immigration amounting to perhaps 4,000. It is likely that annual births exceeded annual net immigration shortly after the initial settlements were made in the seventeenth century and that the proportion of the population

are uniformly 2½ percent of the total population. The births seem to be a residual estimate, obtained by adding deaths to the estimated annual natural increase. The birth estimates are the only component of population growth shown to the last digit.

[5] Johann Peter Süssmilch, Die göttliche Ordnung in der Veränderungen des menschlichen Geschlechts, aus der Geburt, dem Tode und der Fortpflanzung desselben erwiesen, Berlin, 1741, and later editions. For an extended account in English, see Frederick S. Crum, "The Statistical Work of Süssmilch," *Quarterly Publications of the American Statistical Association,* Vol. VII, New Series, No. 55, September 1901.

TABLE 2

Samuel Blodget's Vital Rates for Various Localities: Circa 1805

Area	Deaths per 100 births	Area	Population per death
Portsmouth, N. H.	50	Portsmouth, N. H.	48–49
Salem, Mass.	49–51	Salem, Mass.	48–49
Boston, Mass.	49–52	Boston, Mass.	47–49
Hartford, Conn.	48–49	Philadelphia, Pa.	44–50
Philadelphia, Pa.	51–54	Baltimore, Md.	43–49
Baltimore, Md.	51–53	Washington, D. C.	48–50
Washington, D. C.	50–51	Norfolk, Va.	40–47
Norfolk, Va.	52–54	Charleston, S. C.	35–40
Charleston, S. C.	55–60	Healthiest parts of Georgia	45–50
Healthiest parts of South Carolina and Georgia	45–49	New York State	44–50
New York City	51–53	Hartford, Conn.	50–55
		Rhode Island	50–56
Average for United States	49–51	Low grounds south of 38° N. latitude	34–39
		Average for United States	39–41

Source: Samuel Blodget, *Economica, A Statistical Manual for the United States of America,* Washington, 1806, pp. 75 and 76.

TABLE 3

Estimated Population During Colonial and Continental Periods: 1610 to 1790

Year	Number	Decennial increase, percent
1790....	3,929,625	41.3
1780....	2,781,000	26.1
1770....	2,205,000	37.0
1760....	1,610,000	33.4
1750....	1,207,000	35.8
1740....	889,000	35.7
1730....	654,950	38.1
1720....	474,388	32.7
1710....	357,500	30.0
1700....	275,000	28.8
1690....	210,500	37.2
1680....	155,600	35.9
1670....	114,500	35.0
1660....	84,800	64.0
1650....	51,700	85.0
1640....	27,947	390.3
1630....	5,700	128.1
1620....	2,499	1,090.0
1610....	210	...

Source: U.S. Bureau of the Census, *A Century of Population Growth in the United States, 1790–1900*, by W. S. Rossiter, pp. 9 and 10. Data based on estimates for separate Colonies made by a number of scholars who used tax lists, militia records, Colonial censuses, etc.

that was native increased rapidly.[6] The steady rate of decennial population increase after 1660, in contrast to an irregular flow of immigration, suggests that natural increase predominated in population growth. Various Colonial censuses show a fair balance of males and females in the population, probably from natural increase, whereas seventeenth century European data on emigration to the New World indicate that males much outnumbered females. Some examples of sex ratios from Colonial censuses are shown in the accompanying table:

	Males per 100 females		*Males per 100 females*
New Hampshire:		Connecticut:	
1767..................	107.4	1774..................	93.2
1773..................	103.0		
		New York:	
Massachusetts:		1698..................	108.3
1754..................	104.5	1703..................	101.2
1764..................	90.3	1731..................	[1]136.5
		1737..................	103.8
Maine:		1771..................	106.8
1764..................	103.3		
		New Jersey:	
		1726..................	111.4
Rhode Island:		1737..................	119.0
1774..................	96.6	1745..................	102.8

[1] The high ratio in New York in 1731 reflected the presence of English soldiers and Indian braves in two towns; the ratios were much smaller in other parts of New York.

In 1790, if not at a much earlier date, the proportion of the population that was American

[6] Hypothetical computations can indicate something of the possibilities. One may assume, for illustrative purposes, (*a*) a constant flow of in-migration from year to year (the amount of immigration does not matter if one assumes an unchanging flow), (*b*) a sex ratio of 125 males per 100 females among the in-migrants, (*c*) an age distribution that places most of the immigrants within the young adult ages, (*d*) age-specific birth rates for women, of a level sufficient to yield a crude birth rate of 50 when applied to a population having an age-sex distribution similar to the one in the general population in 1800, and (*e*) mortality according to English life tables for 1838-1854.

The results of the computation indicate that within 10 years the annual number of births would be more than twice the annual number of immigrants. Within 20 years there would be more native- than European-born persons in the population. Thus, if the birth and death rates used were at all reasonable, there was a strong tendency for an early emergence of a large native population.

born was over 90 percent as determined by computation. Further evidence of the existence of a largely native population appears in the 1820 Census which counted only 53,687 "foreigners not naturalized" in the population of 9,638,453. (Over half of these "foreigners" were in the State of New York.)

Lest what has just been said lead to an under-evaluation of the very important role played by immigration, mention is made of the Beards' estimate that between 1600 and 1770 about 750,000 persons journeyed from Europe to America to seek a new way of life.[7] Others have estimated that migration to the New World prior to the Revolutionary War exceeded 2,000,000. There are several difficulties in using such data. Many of the out-migrants from Europe died enroute; others went to places such as Canada, the Caribbean, and South America. Many who came to North America found conditions not to their liking and returned to Europe. The numerous male immigrants sometimes died without progeny and in that sense proved to have been only temporary additions to the population. There were enough immigrants of the family type to account for the much larger population growth in America than in Canada or in the French and Spanish colonies.

One theory for the high fertility in Colonial times is that the women had little to say in such matters. According to Willison, it was a man's world.[8] Governor Bradford is quoted as indignantly denying a libel that women in New Plymouth had any new rights or privileges: "Touching our governemente, you are quite mistaken if you thing we admite weomen . . . to have to doe in the same, for they are excluded, as both reason and nature teacheth they should be." Willison says that more than one foreign visitor noted that the women of New England were all "pittifully Toothshaken" and apt to look much older than their years.

Fertility and Household Size

Although the women who reached the end of the childbearing ages had an average of about eight children ever born in Colonial and early Federal times, this did not necessarily mean that the average household was very large. In 1790, the average size of private households was 5.7 persons, or less than twice the size of households in 1950, 3.4 persons (table 4). In 1790, there was an average of 2.8 children (persons) under 16 years old per household, and in 1950 the average was 1.0 children of this age. The number of living children per household was thus about three times as large in 1790 as in 1950.

TABLE 4

Percent Distribution of Households, by Size: 1790, 1900, and 1950

Household size	Private households, 1790 (white and free colored)	Private households and quasi households 1900	Occupied dwelling units, 1950
Total....	100.0	100.0	100.0
1 person....	3.7	5.1	9.3
2 persons...	7.8	15.0	28.1
3 persons...	11.7	17.6	22.8
4 persons...	13.8	16.9	18.4
5 persons...	13.9	14.2	10.4
6 persons...	13.2	10.9	5.3
7 persons...	11.2	7.7	2.7
8 persons...	9.0	5.2	1.4
9 persons...	6.5	3.2	0.8
10 persons or more...	9.1	4.1	0.9
Average number of persons...	5.7	4.6	3.4

Source: U.S. Bureau of the Census, *A Century of Population Growth in the United States, 1790–1900,* by W. S. Rossiter, p. 98; *1950 Census of Housing,* Vol. I, *General Characteristics,* Part 1, U.S. Summary, p. 8.

Infant Mortality

What proportion of the high fertility in Colonial and early Federal times was offset by high mortality among the children? A very rough idea can be obtained thus: Tests indicate that a life table for England and Wales in 1838–54 may

[7] Charles A. and Mary R. Beard, *The Beards' Basic History of the United States,* Doubleday, Doran and Company, New York, 1944, p. 17.

[8] George F. Willison, *Saints and Strangers,* Reynal and Hitchcock, New York, 1945, p. 385.

fit fairly well the mortality conditions in the United States around 1800.[9] According to this table, about 78 percent of the children born in a 5-year period would live to be enumerated at the end of the period as children under 5 years old in a census, and about 66 percent of newborn infants would live to the age of 20 years. Applied to a rapidly growing population having an age-sex distribution similar to the one existing in 1800, this mortality would result in as many annual reports of deaths at ages under 20 years as at all later ages. This agrees with the little information on ages that was available in bills of mortality of the type seen by Franklin when he assumed that half of the children "grew up."

A discussion of mortality is incomplete without some mention of early American life tables such as the Wigglesworth life table for 1789 for Massachusetts and New Hampshire combined. These life tables were based on deaths alone, without adequate allowance for the age distribution of the population at risk of dying, and they underestimated the expectation of life if they included too many infant deaths in relation to adult deaths. The expectation of life at birth in the Wigglesworth table was 36 years. The earliest American life tables that take specific account of the population at risk of dying are the Kennedy life tables for Massachusetts and Maryland in 1850. The registration data used were of questionable reliability, however, and for this reason the life tables are of value mainly for checking on the applicability of the English life tables. The Massachusetts life tables yield an expectation of life at birth of 38.3 years for males and 40.5 years for females; for Maryland the corresponding figures are 41.8 for males and 44.9 for females. It is possible that the death rates really were larger in more urban Massachusetts than in less urban Maryland and thus did not necessarily reflect a more nearly complete registration in Massachusetts. Around 1850 Massachusetts was host to many thousands of immigrants who fled a serious potato famine in Ireland. These immigrants were crowded into slum areas with poor sanitation facilities.

Slaves

Early censuses obtained little detail on the characteristics of Negroes, many of whom were slaves. It may be inferred, nonetheless, that the Negroes were quite fertile. Despite high mortality and no appreciable immigration after 1790, the Negro population increased at an average rate of about 2.5 percent per year between 1790 and 1870. Fertility data for rural-farm Negro women 70 to 74 years old in the 1910 Census indicate an average of seven to eight births in a lifetime. Most of these women were slaves during a major part of their childbearing years. The early available ratios of young children to Negro women are not impressively large, probably because of the effect of heavy infant mortality and also because of a large undercount of children. Negro fertility is discussed more thoroughly in the section on trends in the nineteenth century.

Urban-Rural Differentials

The subject of urban-rural differentials in fertility is of interest but not of great numerical importance for America in the Colonial period because American cities were few and small. In 1750, the largest city in America (Boston) had only 15,731 inhabitants, Philadelphia and its suburbs had 13,400, New York had 13,300, and Newport had 6,000. As late as 1790 there were only 24 places in the United States with 2,500 inhabitants or more. Nationally, only 5 percent of the population resided in urban areas in 1790. The proportion ranged from none in a number of States to 13.1 percent in Massachusetts.

Table 5 presents a specially computed series of ratios of children under 16 to white women 16 years old and over, based on a series of early enumerations in the Colony of New York. No other Colony had as extensive a series of censuses. It may be noted from the figures in this

[9] Glover's life tables for white persons in the Original Death Registration Area in 1901 would yield a crude death rate of about 16 if applied to a population having an age-sex distribution similar to that of the white population in 1800. Obviously, this level of mortality is much too low if Blodget's estimate of about 25 for this time is correct. A similar computation, using Glover's life tables for Negroes in the District of Columbia in 1901 as an example of very high mortality, would yield a crude death rate of about 37. Interpolation between these two tables may be performed to obtain mortality rates that would yield a crude death rate of about 25. The result is a life table with an expectation of life of about 42 years for females and 39 years for males, or a table that closely resembles one for England and Wales in 1838-1854.

table that the ratio of children to women declined appreciably as New York County (City) grew, but that between 1712 and 1786 the ratio remained nearly constant in the remainder of the Colony. The population outside of New York County (City) was practically all rural. The data in table 5 indicate, therefore, that differential urban-rural fertility began in the Colonies at a very early date. It is possible, as Franklin suggests, that at least some of the difference came from relatively more unmarried adults and a later marriage age in cities than on farms.

TABLE 5

Total Number of Inhabitants and Number of Children Under 16 Years Old per 1,000 White Women 16 Years Old and Over, for New York County and the Remainder of the Colony or State of New York: 1703 to 1786

Year	New York County		Remainder of the Colony or State of New York	
	Population	Children per 1,000 women	Population	Children per 1,000 women
1786	23,614	1,278	215,283	1,998
1771	21,863	1,279	146,154	1,886
1756	13,046	1,260	83,544	2,022
1749	13,294	1,441	60,054	2,025
1746	11,717	1,426	[1]49,872	2,179
1723	7,248	1,564	33,316	1,968
1712[2]	5,841	1,743	[3]13,563	2,057
1703	4,375	1,906	16,290	2,446

[New York City, then at the southern tip of Manhattan Island, contained almost all of the population of New York County at each census]

[1] Albany County was excluded from the enumeration "because of the enemy."

[2] The returns of this census are deemed imperfect, "the people being deterred by a simple superstition, and observation that sickness followed upon the last numbering of the people."

[3] Kings and Richmond Counties are excluded because no age detail is available.

Source: Computed from data on early Colonial enumerations presented in U.S. Bureau of the Census, *A Century of Population Growth in the United States, 1790–1900,* by W. S. Rossiter.

*American Studies of Family Planning and Fertility: A Review of Major Trends and Issues**

RONALD FREEDMAN

On balance we probably know more about the fertility and family planning of the American population than about that of any other country in the world. While this accumulation of information is impressive, the gaps in knowledge are large. As Dr. Kiser has indicated our large-scale field surveys have been much more successful in measuring and describing the variations in fertility and family planning than in finding the causes of these variations. Both the GAF and Princeton Studies[1] are adding significantly to our descriptive knowledge. In addition the Princeton Study is making especially notable contributions to measurement techniques for studying various aspects of reproductive behavior. But we do not yet have many principles or theories about causal factors sufficiently well established to permit their application with assurance in other countries. This is not to minimize the great value of what has been done. The significant findings are sufficiently numerous to make my assignment of summarizing the main trends very difficult, if not presumptuous. Necessarily, I shall confine myself to a limited number of ideas and methodological developments which are central tendencies or which are especially significant, in my view.

STUDIES BASED ON OFFICIAL GOVERNMENT DATA

As in other countries, studies based on official government reports have been important in developing our knowledge of American fertility and — by inference — of family planning. Special field studies like those just reported have been unusually extensive and intensive in the United States, but they have much of their meaning in amplifying and interpreting the trends developed from official data which are more massive and regular, if limited in the variables treated.

Despite some serious limitations, there are unusually rich resources for fertility research in our decennial censuses, the interim Current Population Surveys, and the birth registration statistics. Many excellent studies are based on these data. I call attention to two of special importance: the continuing series of studies of cohort fertility by P. K. Whelpton and his colleagues[2] and *The Fertility of American Women*[3] by Grabill, Kiser, and Whelpton, which provides an admirable summary of the long-run trends as well as the early post-war developments.

For the prewar period, the studies based on official statistics have documented a series of changes roughly similar to those of other countries in the process of industrialization:

(1) There is the long-run secular decline in fertility associated with our transformation to an urban industrial nation. Deviations from this secular trend are strongly correlated with cyclical economic changes both in the cohort analyses and in a series of time series analyses — the most

* Reprinted with permission from C. V. Kiser, *Research in Family Planning*. Princeton: Princeton University Press, 1962, pp. 211-227.

[1] The references for the Princeton Study, the Indianapolis Study, and the Growth of American Families Study are found in the preceding papers by Kiser, Westoff, and Campbell. In addition, some of my comments are based on materials in *Family Growth in Metropolitan America* (Princeton: Princeton University Press, 1961), by Westoff, Potter, Sagi, and Mishler.

[2] See especially Whelpton, P. K.: *Cohort Fertility: Native White Women in the United States* (Princeton: Princeton University Press, 1954), and Whelpton, P. K., and Campbell, Arthur A.: *Fertility Tables for Birth Cohorts of American Women*. U.S. National Office of Vital Statistics, Special Reports, Vol. 51, No. 1, January 29, 1960.

[3] Grabill, Wilson H.; Kiser, Clyde V.; and Whelpton, Pascal K.: *The Fertility of American Women* (New York: John Wiley and Sons, 1958).

recent by Dudley Kirk.[4] Both the secular decline and the cyclical variations are — by inference — evidence for the spread of family limitation practices, but we have almost no historical trend data bearing directly on family planning practices.

(2) There is considerable evidence for the prewar period of a negative correlation of fertility and social status as measured by occupation, education, or income.[5] That such fertility differentials were linked with differentials in contraceptive practice is again mainly a plausible inference for the national population, although we have supporting evidence for such limited populations as that of the Indianapolis Study. There was some evidence of a positive correlation with fertility at the upper end of the status scale long before the war.

(3) The higher fertility of the rural population — and especially the farm sector — has been well documented for a long time. Recent analyses[6] have added the important conclusion that the long-run secular decline occurred simultaneously in both the rural and urban sectors and was not primarily a direct consequence of the transfer of population between the sectors. Changes in the rural sector, although undoubtedly linked to changes in the urban sector, accounted for a large part of the long-run decline. Probably changes in the rural sector were produced by its involvement in a specialized market economy centered in the city. It suggests that the farmer need not go to the city to become urbanized. In various ways the city can come to him. This may be significant for progress for the newly industrializing countries.

(4) According to the cohort fertility studies particular cohorts have responded to changing social and economic circumstances by variations in the age at marriage and the spacing of children independently of the variations in completed family size. Again, by inference, this is evidence for family planning practice. However, we have only crude general ideas about the particular historical variables producing these shifts in fertility.

In the postwar period the studies based on the official statistics have helped to define and to describe the continuing baby boom which has been more or less distinctive of the Western countries outside of Europe.

The official statistics have also documented for period rates an important contraction of almost all the standard traditional fertility differentials — by education, occupation, income, or residence.[7] They do not indicate the elimination of these differentials — only a trend for their contraction involving a reduction of the variability of family size both within and between major strata. There appears to be an emerging consensus on family size throughout the population.

We can see now from the official statistics to 1958 that the baby boom has had four major components: first, in the early stages, a making up of babies postponed in the depression; second, a shift in the timing of marriages and births to earlier stages independently of the changes in completed family size; third, a significant increase in the proportion marrying; and fourth, an apparent shift from small to moderate size for completed families among the married. There has been a remarkable decrease in childlessness to levels below what was formerly considered to be the physiological minimum for complete sterility. The increase in average family size is still almost entirely a result of more births of the first to fourth orders.[8]

[4] Kirk, Dudley and Nortman, Dorothy L.: "Business and Babies: The Influence of the Business Cycle on Birth Rates," *Proceedings of the Social Statistics Section, American Statistical Association,* December 1958, pp. 151-160. For earlier studies see: Galbraith, Virginia L., and Thomas, Dorothy S.: "Birth Rates and the Inter-war Business Cycles," *Journal of the American Statistical Association,* Vol. 36, No. 216, December 1941, pp. 465-476; and Ogburn, William F., and Thomas, Dorothy S.: "The Influence of the Business Cycle on Certain Social Conditions," *Quarterly Publications of the American Statistical Association,* Vol. 18, 1922, pp. 324-340.

[5] Grabill, Kiser, and Whelpton, *op. cit.*

[6] Okun, Bernard: "Trends in Birth Rates in the United States Since 1870." *The Johns Hopkins University Studies in Historical and Political Science,* Series LXXVI, No. 1, 1958; also Grabill, Kiser, and Whelpton, pp. 16-19.

[7] Grabill, Kiser, and Whelpton, *op. cit.*

[8] For example, the cohort reaching age 30-34 in 1958 had 710 births per thousand more than the cohort reaching this age in 1942. Ninety-two per cent of this increase resulted from more births of the first to fourth orders and 80 per cent from more births of the first to third orders. Only 8 per cent of the increase is attributable to births beyond the fourth order while 21 per cent is attributable to larger numbers of first births. A similar result is obtained by comparing the cohort reaching age 35-39 in 1958 with the cohort reaching this age in 1946

So far as we can tell at present, the demographers were right in their early insistence that the baby boom was not an indication of a return to a large family system. All of the changes are consistent with the view that the postwar American family model involves the early creation by almost all adults of their own families with at least some children, but not too many — a moderate number indicated by the range of two to four.

We must admit, I think, that in the early stages of the baby boom demographers were inclined to view the whole development as a temporary deviation from the long-run secular decline. In part, this resulted from the fact that there was little in the official statistics to signal the basic change that was occurring, until it was far advanced. Demographers, along with many other social scientists, tended to assume that fertility would return to former low levels without appreciation of the shifts in family size that were occurring. If such special field studies as Growth of American Families had been available at that time, or if we had annual national time series for expected and desired family size, such changes might be caught at an earlier point and studied in relation to other historical series.[9]

I think the failure to appreciate earlier that aspect of the baby boom which did involve larger families also resulted from a theoretical bias demographers shared with sociologists. This was the view that urbanization with its accompanying specialization and high rate of mobility inevitably would lead to a growth of secularism and rationality, to the declining influence of such traditional forces as religious faith, to a shattering of traditional family ties and other primary group influences, to a growth of individualism, and to the attachment of the individual to large, impersonal, and rational organizations. The functions of the family were seen as becoming dispersed among specialized institutions, and children were seen as an impediment to participation in the larger organizations from which the rewards of the urban society came. The dominant view among both demographers and sociologists was that as all of the population becomes closely involved in an urban society, family planning would become universal and the size of families planned would continue to decline. A logical extension of the basic premises of this model made it appear that the family would continue to decline in importance among the major institutions. Some of us still are inclined to view childbearing as a rather irrational act. The costs of bearing children are emphasized without a balancing assessment of the continuing positive functions of the family and of children in a modern society.

A continuing revision of the older view of urban society since the war gives more weight to the persistence of religious and other traditional allegiances. There is growing emphasis on the persistence and even resurgence of the family and other primary groups as the channels through which the larger bureaucratic organizations reach the individual, in large measure. Urbanization and industrialization are seen as leading to the reorganization of society in new forms rather than to inevitable disorganization and mass anomy. This basic shift in the sociological orientation toward urbanism in the United States is important in interpreting both the official statistics and the special field studies such as those just reported to us.

Before turning from the official statistics to the special field studies I want to stress an important limitation of the latter — they give us very little about marriage itself. For this we rely on the official statistics. In fact, neither the field studies nor the official statistics cover a number of the important intermediate variables which Davis and Blake[10] have outlined as standing between the structure of the society and fertility itself.

Special Studies

The special field studies have many objectives and their findings are too diverse for any succinct summary. I shall try to deal with some of their

(the latter cohort having the lowest cumulative fertility to age 35-39 recorded in the United States). These data are from Whelpton and Campbell, *op. cit.*

[9] Dr. Philip Hauser has stressed the desirability of time series studies in several earlier Milbank Round Table meetings.

[10] Davis, Kingsley, and Blake, Judith: "Social Structure and Fertility: An Analytic Framework." *Economic Development and Cultural Change,* Vol. 4, No. 3, April 1956.

leading findings only as they bear on four broad questions:

(1) Does what appears from the official statistics to be an emerging consensus on a moderate size family have support in the value system of the population? Can we use these survey data on values to anticipate the change to a new fertility pattern while it is in process?

(2) Is the widespread adoption of a moderate size family pattern supported by effective family limitation practices of a particular kind? Here we are looking for direct evidence to support the inferences about contraception from the official statistics.

(3) Given an apparent consensus on a range of two to four children, can we explain the variations within this range by reference to a combination of social and psychological variables?

(4) Can we explain the existence of the range itself? For example, why is the consensus and the performance at a higher level now than during the 30's and why is it higher here than in the European countries?

THE CONSENSUS IN VALUES

The GAF and Princeton Studies as well as others on a smaller scale[11] indicate a remarkable consensus in the American population on a moderate size family of two to four children, whether the measure of values used is desired, ideal, or expected number of children. As Dr. Westoff has indicated, 90 per cent of the two parity women in the Princeton Study desire two, three, or four children. The GAF Study covering a wider range of parities and backgrounds shows a similar consensus with respect to desires and ideals. As to the number of children actually expected the GAF Study indicates that many of the variations found are due to involuntary factors: fecundity impairments among those with fewer than two children and involuntary excess fertility for those with five or more children.

The studies also indicate that the consensus on a moderate size family exists in all the major strata of the population. If expectations and desires of the younger cohorts are realized the contraction of differences noted in the official statistics for incomplete families will apply also to completed families. It is likely that these analyses based on attitudes and values exaggerate the contraction that will occur because they fail to take into account the likelihood that over the whole childbearing period the lower social strata will be least effective in limiting family size to the desired range. This will have the effect of increasing differentially low status fertility rates late in the childbearing period. The value statements in the Princeton Study especially may underestimate eventual fertility differentials because all of its subjects are at the bottom end of the desired range. Many of them don't know yet just how ineffective their family planning will be. In any case, the Princeton Study asks about desired rather than expected number of children, and the GAF Study indicates that there is a discrepancy between what is wanted and what is expected. No doubt differentials in completed family size will be greater than the differentials in values, but there is little doubt that the value data do support the inference from current official statistics of a marked contraction in the differentials.

The extensive use of data on such attitudes as expectations, plans, or desires in the recent American studies — as well as in other countries — raises important methodological issues. Can such statements be used to predict the future fertility for incompleted cohorts? It can be argued that in a society in which the use of contraceptions is almost universal the plans and expectations of the married couples will guide their behavior more or less closely so that fertility of each cohort is predictable and the cumulation of cohort predictions will give a value for the total population. Unfortunately, the situation is more complex than this simple model suggests.

[11] Similar results for the national United States population were obtained in 1954 in an unpublished Survey Research Center Study based on 500 couples with questions only on expected and ideal family size. The Detroit Area Study has periodically collected data on family size and ideals for the Detroit Metropolitan Area. See Freedman, Ronald, and Sharp, Harry: "Correlates of Values About Ideal Family Size in the Detroit Metropolitan Area." *Population Studies,* July 1954, Vol. 8, No. 1, pp. 35-45; Freedman, Ronald; Goldberg, David; and Sharp, Harry: "Ideals About Family Size in the Detroit Metropolitan Area." Milbank Memorial Fund *Quarterly,* 1954, Vol. 33, No. 2, pp. 187-197. Goldberg, David: "The Fertility of Two Generation Urbanites." *Population Studies,* Vol. XII, No. 3, March 1959.

First, it seems unlikely that the prediction of completed family size for specific individual couples based on their desires and expectations at an early point in marriage will be very successful. The remarkable 20-year longitudinal study by Kelly and others[12] produced a rather low correlation for individuals between their desires just before marriage and their actual performance after 20 years. It may be, as the Princeton Study assumes, that greater success can be achieved in making predictions for couples who have had some experience in married life and who state their desires at a similar stage in the family life cycle. But difficulty in predicting fertility from individual value statements should not be too surprising. Even if we assume that there exists during a given generation a stable social norm about the right number of children (e.g. two-four) many variations within that range are to be expected. The large complex of forces in varied permutations for individual couples during the long childbearing period certainly will lead many couples to revise their expectations and desires upward or downward within the acceptable range. In a stable social situation we might expect such changes to balance each other in their effects on the total distribution of family size. This supposes a range of acceptable variation for each cultural epoch so that only minor sanctions are attached to variations within the range but significant sanctions do operate outside the range. For example, in the contemporary American situation this would mean that two, three, or four are all acceptable numbers of children and are not socially defined as very different, but being childless or with an only child or having a large family does carry negative consequences. A recent study by Goldberg and others[13] in Detroit indicates that in the recent economic recession a significant number of couples did change their expectations as to a family size up or down but the net change for all the couples was almost zero. Even in the 20 year Kelly Study the final average number of children closely approximated the average desires 20 years earlier.

While predictions for the distributions of cohorts or other groups probably will be more successful than predictions for individuals, it is unlikely that social norms will be so stable as to be unaffected by social and economic changes occurring in the several decades of reproductive life. How much change there is and under what circumstances are important topics for further research. The Princeton Study will shortly give us better information on the short-run stability of desires for a particular parity. The new GAF Study will test the utility of the expectation data for the entire childbearing population over a five year period. Neither can give definitive assessments of the utility of the attitudinal data. What is needed is a time series on an annual basis for the national population of expected and desired number of children. Such a series along with data on actual fertility can then be related to a variety of other series on other basic social and economic data as well as to unique historical events as they occur. Such time series will have maximum value if there are simultaneous intensive longitudinal studies to establish how net changes are produced by a balance of different kinds of individual changes. It is quite likely that we shall have to learn how to adjust or discount data on expectations or desires on the basis of what we can learn from such time series analyses as well as data on fecundity impairments and contraceptive effectiveness. In the longitudinal study of Kelly's data social and psychological factors were more accurate than the couple's stated desires in predicting individual fertility. The social scientist eventually may be able to predict a couple's fertility better than the couple can, but it is likely that the attitudes and values of the couple and the groups to which it belongs will enter the calculation.

The Use of Contraception

The Princeton and GAF Studies have demonstrated that contraception is used almost uni-

[12] Westoff, Charles F.; Mishler, Elliot G.; and Kelly, E. Lowell: "Preferences in Size of Family and Eventual Fertility Twenty Years After." *American Journal of Sociology,* Vol. LXII, No. 5, March 1957, pp. 491-497. Westoff, Charles F.; Sagi, Philip; and Kelly, E. Lowell: "Fertility Through Twenty Years of Marriage: A Study in Predictive Possibilities." *American Sociological Review,* Vol. 23, October 1958, pp. 549-556.

[13] Goldberg, David; Sharp, Harry; and Freedman, Ronald: "The Stability and Reliability of Expected Family Size Data." Milbank Memorial Fund *Quarterly,* October 1959, Vol. 37, No. 4, pp. 369-385.

versally by fecund couples in the United States to make their desires for a moderate size family a reality. Building on the Indianapolis Study these new studies give us the most comprehensive description ever available of a nation's family planning activity. This information will be relevant for many research and policy questions.

While the practice of contraception at some stages of the reproductive process is virtually universal, it is very far from a rational model of the effective use of modern contraceptives to carefully plan and space all births. The Indianapolis Study and both the recent major studies show that a rather large proportion of all pregnancies are "accidents" or otherwise unplanned. Among the large number of couples who do not begin to use contraception before their first conception, a significant number do not want their first pregnancy as soon as possible. Many use methods they consider unreliable. Far from being rational planners many do not seriously think about contraception until the pressure of a growing family brings the problem to their attention. There are even significant sectors at the bottom of the social structure in which a majority of the families can be described as very ineffective in family planning. Lee Rainwater's interesting exploratory study[14] of lower working class families has documented this very dramatically. The evidence about communication and consensus between husbands and wives also does not strongly support the image of the American family as a highly rational, effective, joint planning unit.

Despite the fact that the rational model does not fit well, the patterns of family planning followed are successful in enabling most couples to have the number of children they want. The contraceptive practice — imperfect though it may be for individuals — is successful for the society in reducing fertility far below its physiological potential. This confirms what we already know from English data: average family size can be reduced to very low levels in a large modern society with far less than the most rational use of the modern contraceptive methods.

[14] Rainwater, Lee: *And the Poor Get Children* (Chicago: Quadrangles Books, 1960).

Factors Explaining Variations in Fertility and Family Planning

While the great majority of Americans are having small or moderate size families, there remains a considerable variability within and around the range of consensus even after we have taken into account the families that are smaller or larger than desired. A central objective in American studies has been to explain this variation or at least to find its correlates. Overall, we have not been conspicuously successful — as Dr. Kiser has indicated. Only a small amount of the variance was explained in the Indianapolis Study and most of the explanation finally achieved was attributable to socio-economic status. Despite heroic efforts, the Princeton Study has not yet been able to account for the major part of the variance, although it may come closer to this objective when the data from its follow-up interviews are analyzed.

Socio-Economic Status

In the postwar studies, unlike the Indianapolis Study, correlations with socio-economic status measures are non-existent or very modest. In fact, all of the traditional differentials with respect to education, occupation, income, and rural-urban origin are destined to disappear or to contract sharply, if current desires and expectations are realized in action. The contraction of these differentials is somewhat less pronounced in the GAF Study than in the Princeton Study, because the representation of a wider range of parities and backgrounds permits the less effective fertility control of the lower status and rural sectors to widen the differentials somewhat. In the GAF Study education appears to be more important than income, occupation, or rural background. It accounts for most of the correlation between these other variables and family planning, for example. This may be an important clue to what is fundamental in the complex we call socio-economic status.

The apparent contraction of the traditional differentials is certainly a development of major importance. This is a major finding, even if it doesn't help to explain the variation remaining. While we do not have any definitive explanation for the contraction of status or rural-urban differentials there are several plausible theories:

(1) Contraceptive practice has spread through all strata of the population, thus diminishing the role of differential contraceptive practice as a basis for differential fertility. Our evidence here is mainly the present widespread use of contraception in all major population strata. The existence of greater contraceptive differentials at an earlier period is mainly an inference from the fertility patterns.

(2) There is evidence that the higher fertility of the lower status groups in the past may have been largely a function of their recent rural origin. Goldberg found this to be the case for women of completed fertility in Detroit. In the Detroit data as well as in a reanalysis of Indianapolis data [15] he found that the traditional inverse relation of status and fertility was most characteristic of the couples with a farm background and least characteristic of the couples with an urban background. Eliminating the effect of both ineffective fertility planning and farm background produced a significant — if modest — positive correlation between fertility and measures of economic status. Few Americans in the younger generation will have been reared on farms, so this rural basis for fertility differentials will cease to be important.

(3) More speculative is the theory that the change is related to the fact that class differences are becoming blurred in the United States as the working class takes on many middle class characteristics.[16] Without time for development, I only can suggest here the idea that the functions of children and of the family are becoming more similar in different major social strata. If this is true, then it is reasonable to expect a contraction of fertility differentials, since family size in the various strata should depend on the functions in those strata of children and of the family in relation to other institutions.

The Economic Factor

The specifically economic status measures deserve special attention. It has seemed plausible to many scholars that the couple's economic position should be positively rather than negatively correlated with fertility once effective contraception is widespread in all economic strata. The argument has been stated in various ways but in essence it involves the following assumptions: (1) that under conditions of a specialized urban society children play similar roles in the families at various economic levels. In particular, children cease to have a differential economic value either as laborers in family enterprises or as safeguards for old age security; (2) under these conditions children become only consumer goods; they yield direct emotional satisfactions to their parents which must compete with satisfactions derived from other consumer goods; (3) since children are expensive, couples of higher economic status can afford more children and are under less pressure to choose between children and other consumer durables. Better economic status should also permit the parents to overcome more easily some of the negative aspects of child-rearing by paying for more household help. This line of argument leads to the conclusion that economic status should be positively correlated with fertility once the disturbing effects of differential contraceptive practice and of anachronistic farm backgrounds are eliminated from the social situation.

There is another possibility suggested by Becker.[17] Higher economic status may also lead to "better quality" children rather than to a larger number of children. The parents may invest more in each child rather than having a larger number. In the purchase of automobiles economic status is more closely correlated with the price of the car purchased than with the number. A similar situation may exist with respect to children.

The empirical evidence relevant to the economic variable is rather contradictory. The Indianapolis Study did find a small positive correlation between economic status and fertility for

[15] Goldberg, David: "The Fertility of Two Generation Urbanites." *Population Studies,* Vol. 12, No. 3, March 1959, pp. 214-222; and "Another Look at the Indianapolis Fertility Data." The Milbank Memorial Fund *Quarterly,* Vol. 28, No. 1, January 1960, pp. 23-36.

[16] Mayer, Kurt: "Fertility Changes and Population Forecasts in the United States." *Social Research,* Vol. 26, No. 3, Autumn 1959, pp. 347-366.

[17] Becker, Gary: "An Economic Analysis of Fertility," a paper in *Demographic and Economic Change in Developed Countries,* A conference of the Universities-National Bureau Committee for Economic Research (Princeton: Princeton University Press, 1960), pp. 209-231.

completely planned families, and this correlation was increased when the influence of rural background was eliminated. A series of studies — the latest by Kirk — have found that period fertility rates are strongly correlated to variations of the business cycle from secular trends. These variations in fertility are mainly a result of variations in the marriage rate and of the lower order births. But such variation may simply result from changes in the timing of vital events without any necessary effect on completed fertility or long-run fertility trends. Kirk points out that the secular trend of fertility bears no significant relation to the secular trend of business conditions.

In an interesting, unpublished, and still preliminary analysis, Arthur Campbell of the Scripps Foundation constructs a weighted economic index for the whole childbearing period of each of a series of completed cohorts. He finds no consistent relation between the economic index and the completed fertility for the cohort.

Neither the Princeton Study nor GAF has found any consistent significant relation between various measures of economic status or attitudes and fertility planning. However, in both studies more refined analyses are still in process.

The finding of no correlation in the recent studies instead of the expected positive correlation may indicate simply that we have been passing through a necessary transition from the former negative correlation to a future positive correlation. It may also be that the postwar cohorts need to proceed farther into the childbearing period before differences positively associated with economic status will appear. Since most people are having at least two children now differences are more likely to develop only after all strata have passed together through the early parities and the real differentials will develop only in the later half of the childbearing period.

It is also possible, however, that there really is no significant positive relationship. While children may be consumer's goods, whether higher income will lead to consuming more of them depends on the elasticity of demands for them. A case can be made for the theory that this demand, like that for salt, is rather inelastic. Under present conditions, everybody must have at least a few children but nobody wants very many.

Wife's Labor Force Participation

One characteristic that continues to be associated with differential fertility is the wife's status as a worker. Official statistics have documented lower fertility for working wives for some time. In the Indianapolis Study the wife's work history was one of the very few variables fairly strongly correlated with planning status and fertility even when socio-economic status was controlled. In the GAF Study both fertility to date and total expected fertility decrease with the increasing length of the wife's work experience and this relationship persists when fecundity and a variety of socio-economic factors are controlled.[18] The GAF Study shows that part — but only part — of the relationship is a function of fecundity impairments. Many wives work because fecundity impairments prevent them from having many children, thus creating an opportunity for work. It is also true, however, that even when only the fecund wives are considered, a long work history for the wife is associated with lower fertility and more effective fertility planning. These results are supported in general by the Princeton Study findings, although the authors attach less importance to them than I would.

These findings are important for several reasons: (1) the proportion of working wives is increasingly steadily in the United States despite the baby boom; (2) the wife's work experience is an excellent index — but only one — of the extent to which this central family figure is seriously affected by the competing influences of non-familial institutions and activities. It seems plausible that such extra-familial activity will change the division of labor within the family and between the family and other institutions. These changes in turn are likely to have an impact on the functions of children in the family. In an analysis of the Indianapolis data Pratt and Whelton[19] found that not only the wife's work history but also a crude measure of other extra-

[18] Ridley, Jeanne Clare: "Number of Children Expected in Relation to Non-Familial Activities of the Wife." Milbank Memorial Fund *Quarterly,* July 1959, Vol. 37, No. 3, pp. 277-296.

[19] Pratt, Lois, and Whelpton, P. K.: "Attitudes Toward Restriction of Personal Freedom in Relation to Fertility Planning and Fertility." Milbank Memorial Fund *Quarterly,* Vol. 33, No. 1, January 1955, pp. 63-111.

familial involvements was associated with better family planning and lower fertility — even after allowance for the effect of socio-economic status. This probably is an especially promising area for further research. We must know more about the conditions under which wives work or engage in other extra-familial activities and how these activities affect the organization of family life and family growth.

Religious Differentials

One of the striking findings of the postwar American studies is the persistent importance of religious differentials, and in particular the higher fertility and the lesser use of appliance contraceptives by Catholics. The distinctive Catholic pattern apparently is not a result of low social or educational status or of recent urbanization. In fact it is most distinctive among the well educated urban group.

These findings are striking, because most American demographers have until recently assumed, I think, that religious differentials represented a cultural lag which would disappear with increasing education and urbanization. This was part of the erroneous view of urban life mentioned earlier — a view that urbanism would eventually and inevitably secularize all relationships and destroy the power of such traditional institutions as the Church. This view is contradicted not only by the fertility data but also by evidence on the persistence of Catholic-Protestant differences in the United States in a variety of other behavioral areas.[20] European sociologists and demographers who are more accustomed to the persistence of ethnic and religious differentials for generations under presumably secularizing urban conditions might have been less inclined than Americans to discount prematurely the influence of religious institutions. While these religious differentials are clear and marked we certainly do not yet understand their origin or meaning. In particular we need to know more on a comparative basis as to why Catholic institutions appear to affect reproductive patterns much more in some countries than in others. What is distinctive about Catholic institutions in such countries as the United States and the Netherlands, for example, as compared with other countries? The persistence of religious differences under urbanized conditions is relevant for the doubts that some have expressed that urbanization in underdeveloped areas necessarily will have only secularizing effects.

[20] Extensively documented in Lenski, Gerhard: *The Religious Factor* (Garden City, N.Y.: Doubleday, 1961).

Social Psychological Factors

The search for social-psychological and strictly psychological factors to explain variations in current fertility has not yet been successful. In retrospect, the failure of the strictly psychological variables in the Indianapolis Study to predict fertility was ascribed by critics as well as by the authors themselves to poor conceptualization or poor measurement. The Princeton Study has not yet been much more successful in this area although the authors worked with newer psychological measurements and with commendably thorough pretests and analyses.

On a more social psychological level and as a central concern, the Princeton Study has investigated very thoroughly the hypothesis that social mobility is associated with more effective family planning and lower fertility. The already reported finding of essentially no relationship has been supported in at least three other studies,[21] and there is even some evidence for the United States of a modest positive correlation of mobility with fertility rather than the hypothesized negative relationship.

In retrospect — and it is easy to second guess — I suggest that the original hypothesis of a negative correlation is linked to the erroneous view of urban society mentioned earlier. It assumes that the mobile family is one of many individualistic units which rationally restrict family commitments and costs in order to compete successfully in an impersonal and highly individualistic market. Such a model may be applicable to the transitional stage when an urban society

[21] Yellin, Seymour: "Social Mobility and Familism," Ph.D. dissertation in Sociology, Northwestern University, 1955; Brooks, Hugh E., and Henry, Franklin J.: "An Empirical Study of the Relationships of Catholic Practice and Occupational Mobility to Fertility," Milbank Memorial Fund *Quarterly,* July 1958, Vol. 36, No. 3, pp. 222-281; Boggs, Stephen T.: "Family Size and Social Mobility in a California Suburb," *Eugenics Quarterly,* December 1957, Vol. 4, No. 4, pp. 208-213.

is developing indigenous institutions and drawing large masses of immigrants from rural areas. In this situation large numbers of people are unaccustomed to urban institutions and without established precedents or rules to guide their careers. But in the contemporary American scene large numbers have been socialized as indigenous urbanites to expect social change. Change and mobility are an established part of the social structure. The large bureaucratic enterprises in which more and more people work institutionalize mobility. People learn to expect and plan for change within reasonable limits as part of the routine of life. As Boggs has suggested in interpreting his interesting study, the young urban American husband is accustomed to change and expects to be able to make the adjustment it requires while his family is growing.

As I have suggested elsewhere,[22] it is precisely in such a highly mobile and specialized urban society that the nuclear family has the unique function of serving the individual as the only continuing primary group which he can carry with him in his travels in space and society and which selects and integrates for him the specialized stimuli and services of a complex society. It may be a positive functional necessity rather than a negative cost in a society of institutionalized mobility.

Explaining Variations in the Social Norms About Reproduction

In my opinion the most significant problem for fertility research in the United States now may be why the social norm is for two to four children rather than why particular individuals prefer one instead of another number within this generally acceptable range. A similar question is why a social norm condemning contraception has been transformed to one of approval and the practice of contraception almost as a matter of course.

It appears likely that the difficulty we are having in predicting variations among individual couples in fertility may result partly from the fact that most of the variation is in a narrow range within which the significance of the differentials is not great. In any case, providing that the whole distribution is reasonably stable, which particular individuals have a somewhat larger and which a somewhat smaller number of children may be interesting but not really important for many demographic and social problems. The more significant social problem may be what changes the nature of the distribution rather than why some people are at one point rather than another on the distribution.

Such questions probably can only be answered by more general comparative and historical studies.[23] Neither American nor other demographers really have given much serious systematic study to these problems, although the quantitative data for comparative and historical studies are probably better in demography than in most other social science fields. For the United States we do have business cycle studies mentioned already. The work in cohort analysis is providing us with excellent data about the range of some of the dependent variables but we have little systematic analyses of the factors affecting the cohort variations.

For the historical and comparative questions I am raising, a single major cross-section survey may only provide some of the descriptive parameters for a single case in the analysis — a society or a stratum at a particular period in history. The independent variables may be derived from the survey but they may have to be characteristics of the society or the stratum rather than of an individual. A series of such studies in different times and places supplemented by the mounting volume of comparable international demographic statistics will be necessary to provide data for comparative analysis. This is not to deingrate the value of the individual surveys. They help us to understand a particular time and place. Probably, they are indispensable as the units in a larger sample of studies, but they are not the only source of significant data.

Certainly factors related to individual variations in a cross-section sample may also be the causes of major historical changes. But this may

[22] "Social Values About Family Size in the United States," *International Population Conference* (Vienna: 1959), pp. 173-183.

[23] Mayer, Kurt: *op. cit.* also makes a case for the importance of historical and comparative analyses.

not necessarily be the case. We very well may find that factors which are related to differences in fertility and family planning as between societies do not explain differences within the society. This may be true for income variations, for example. We still need to learn how cross-section data can best be related to historical series.

The long-run secular decline in fertility in the West and the development of family planning usually is explained as a consequence of basic changes in the functions of the family and of children in relation to new institutions and principles of social organization. This seems to me to be an eminently reasonable frame of reference if not scientifically demonstrable. I see the broad task of comparative demography as seeking the variations in the functions of the family and of children which can explain the variations in social norms and practices about family planning and fertility. I doubt that we can ever really understand the current American demographic situation except in the perspective of such a comparative and historical approach. Without the comparative frame of reference we are trying to accomplish the impossible task of generalizing from the unique case.

*"Boom Babies" Come of Age: The American Family at the Crossroads**

Population Reference Bureau

Nearly all American parents would ridicule the idea that having one additional child could contribute to a national calamity. Yet this is the situation today. Within recent years American women have averaged slightly over three children each. Were they to achieve an average of 3.5 and maintain it to the end of the century, the U. S. population would total 400 million, twice what it is today. So sudden a doubling would have dire effects on the American scene. Famine would not be a threat, of course. But the asphalt and the concrete jungles would grow relentlessly. Congestion and pollution would prevail. The psychological effects of crowding — in crime and violence — would be more prevalent than they are today. After a second generation of such growth, the population would approach the billion mark and the American dream, as we now envision it, would be on the way to becoming a nightmare.

Ten years ago, this alarming prospect seemed much more likely than it does today. The U.S. birth rate has shown a downward trend since 1957, which, if it continues, would reduce the average family by one child to about 2.5. Such a cutback would shrink the national increase by 70 million for a total of 330 million Americans by the end of the century. A further reduction to 1.5 children would slice the population to 260 million by the year 2000. This last figure would still be a substantial increase over the present 200 million total, but the rate of growth would be far more manageable.

Short range, however, there is little likelihood of a further downswing in the birth rate. If anything, the coming of age of boom babies will bring an unprecedented number of couples into parenthood, thus boosting the birth rate.

Were the fertility consensus to tilt the other way and were the four- or five-child family to become the popular ideal — fortunately, a most unlikely prospect — the United States would definitely be on the economic toboggan snowed under with burgeoning population.

The intriguing aspect of such reflections is that in the United States at the present time the level of fertility is predominantly determined by a

* Reprinted with permission from *Population Bulletin,* Vol. 24, No. 3 (August 1966), pp. 61-79.

multitude of individual decisions: some couples cannot have any children for a variety of physiological reasons; another cadre of couples overshoot their ideal by one or even two children. But the record proves that an impressive majority of couples are highly competent sharpshooters when it comes to calling the shots on how many children they want to have. If they have a problem, it is one of timing their marksmanship so that they are able to space their children more comfortably.

This record, over the past century, proves that even though befogged in ignorance of population dynamics, and shrouded in reactionary laws, the people of the United States have managed to make astonishingly wise decisions. Now in the age of increased enlightment, that excellent record of past performance will hopefully be sustained.

The fertility transition which has already taken place is truly phenomenal. In the early decades of the Republic, the number of children ever born per woman is believed to have been between 8 and 10. In compensating for ever declining death rates, the American people, with very little statistical enlightenment and no govermental nudging, cut the children-per-woman ratio from 8 to 10 to about 3 by 1920 and to just over 2 in the parlous days of the great depression.

Such a level of fertility dips toward the long-pull replacement level which necessitates that each woman average a fraction over two children. To keep population growth in balance, each woman must have one adult daughter who lives through the childbearing age.

Whatever the future brings, there are several paradoxes in the population situation in the United States at the present moment. Though the birth rate has been declining for a decade, the population continues to grow substantially. Even with a further decline in the birth rate, the population will continue to grow. Recent alarmist statements have been published warning that the United States is approaching an actual population decline. This opinion is not justified by any realistic appraisal of the present situation.

The future welfare of the United States is intimately related to population pattern. And no basic indicator of the future exists than the national birth rate, because it represents an integral part of a vast number of decisions regarding family size and made by millions of individual couples, particularly the growing numbers entering on their years of maximum fertility. The attitudes of these young marrieds toward family planning are crucial as a major determinant of social and economic growth of this nation. Unfortunately, reliable information as to what they are thinking is not easy to come by. More than 15 years ago, two major university research institutes in the population field joined forces to initiate a sophisticated and statistically adequate survey that sheds light on this important point. The study was set up under the title, "Growth of American Families"; shortened to GAF as a convenient label. The first study was initiated in 1955 and published in 1959. The June 1960 *Population Bulletin* summarized this report.

The second sampling was undertaken five years later and was only recently made available. This *Bulletin* is devoted to a summary of the findings of the second GAF study published by Princeton University Press this year under the title *Fertility and Family Planning in the United States*. The book explores the fertility performance and attitudes of young couples. Their decisions as to the size of the ideal family have far-reaching influence on the future development of the nation.

The factors on which their decisions are based are those which differentiate American couples from their neighbors, most important are religious background and educational level. Even these, the GAF authors discovered, are being masked by American mass culture and the need to conform, to fit the ideal of the normal, happy American couple.

Perhaps the most important finding of the current GAF report is that the younger married couples are definitely opting for smaller families than were those interviewed in the 1955 survey.

Looking Back

That a low birth rate can produce large population increases is less of a paradox than it seems. Since the early days of the Republic, American population has multiplied impressively despite a steady decline in the birth rate. And although this has been dubbed a "nation of immigrants," considerably less of this expansion came from immigration than is popularly imagined. More, in fact, came from the offspring of fecund American couples aided by a death rate that has decreased from 20-25 to 9 since the nation began.

In 1790, the year of the first census and a time of colonization, 90 percent of the population was native born. Even after a century of resettling the oppressed from Europe, the nation remained substantially native born. In 1890, with more than 9 million foreign born in its population, the United States was still 85.3 percent native. In 1920, before the flow was dammed by barriers to immigration, this percentage rose to 86.9, with nearly 14 million immigrants.

All the while the nation was filling with people, the birth rate was changing drastically. It is estimated to have been 55 per 1,000, or near the physiological upper limits in the beginning of the 19th century. Americans numbered over 5 million then, and were increasing at a high rate. In the years between 1810 and 1820, they netted a 2.4 million gain in population, adding another 3.2 million by 1830. This was at a time when life expectancy was around 35 and the death rate ran between 20 and 25 per 1,000.

Total growth per decade in the early years of the nation was comparable to the annual growth today when more than 4 million infants are born each year and the net gain in population runs around 2.8 million. Between 1960 and 1965 the nation grew by 14.1 million, and the birth rate fell from 23.7 per 1,000 to 19.4.

How Many Mothers?

What influences both the birth rate and the absolute number of births is the number of actual and potential mothers, and the relative size of the infant and aged groups. The slide in the birth rate has in effect been offset by a continued increase of mothers, who have reproduced in such numbers that annual births set records in most years from 1791 to 1921, when the first period of sustained decline began. This downtrend in the birth rate lasted until 1933, picked up again, though with less intensity than before, and showed small increases into the 1940's. After World War II new records were set. The crude birth rate was higher in 1947 than in any recent year, but a new record for the largest annual number of births was scored in 1957.

A comparison of 1932 with 1965 emphasizes the effects of the number and structure of the population on low birth rate. In both years, the birth rate was about the same, 19.5 and 19.4 per 1,000, respectively. Yet in 1932, the number of births was a mere 2.4 million compared with 3.8 million in 1965. The difference results from the combination of different numbers of women of childbearing age, 15-44, and their varying fertility rates. The fertility rate is the annual number of live births per 1,000 women of child-bearing agc. In 1932, the fertile group constituted 23.9 percent of the population and their fertility rate was 81.7. Hence the birth rate was 19.5 or $81.7 \times .239$. In 1965, women of comparable age were only 20 percent of the population, but their fertility rate was 96.8, making a birth rate of 19.4 or $96.8 \times .20$.

The composition of the population has changed very considerably in the past three decades. In 1935, 36 percent were under 20 and 6 percent were over 64. At present, a larger proportion are very old or very young. Half are less than 25 years old, 40 percent are under 20, and more than 9 percent are over 64. Fewer men and women are in the intermediate age groups. In absolute numbers, the age categories are as follows:

	1935		*1965*	
	(millions)	(%)	(millions)	(%)
Under 20	46.2	36.3	77.0	39.6
20 - 64	73.3	57.6	99.4	51.1
65 and over	7.8	6.1	18.2	9.3
Total U.S.	127.3	100.0	194.6	100.0

The age structure of today's population is such, that in a very few years, numbers of potential mothers will soar rapidly to a new high. Oddly enough, the number of women in the prime reproductive years, 20-29, has not changed much in the last 30 years by reason of the low fertility of the depression years. There were 11.1 million of them in this age group in 1935, and 11.0 million of these women in 1960. By 1970, this fertile group will number 15.5 million; by 1980, 20 million. At the same time all potential mothers, those aged 15-44, will grow at a moderate pace. They totaled 36 million in 1960, 39 million in 1965. By 1970, they are expected to increase 3 million more for a total of 42 million.

Taking the youngest women, 15-19 years old, as a point of comparison, the last time they approached their present roster of more than 8.4 million was in 1939. In 1947 the postwar baby boom peaked and the birth rate reached its highest point since the 1920's (26.6).

It is these boom babies who are now coming to the reproductive roost, causing an enormous increase in potential fertility and placing the nation at a demographic crossroads. The young men and women born immediately after World War II are now reaching marriageable age.

Both the number of children they have and the age at which they have them hold the key to the future population trends. If the fashion of early marriage and early motherhood is perpetuated, the fertility potential can be vastly compounded and the signs for this are already posted. In 1961, mothers averaged 21.8 years old when their first offspring arrived. In 1940, the comparable age was 23.2. In the late 50's and early 60's young mothers were having second and third children sooner than women a generation earlier. Furthermore, since the average American wife has been having her last child while still in her 20's, after giving birth to from two to four children, her period of excess pregnancy risk is longer. How she handles total fertility during this time holds the key to future population growth.

Fortunately, the fertility rate of women between 20 and 24 years of age has declined in the last few years from 257.5 per 1,000 in 1959 to 219.8 in 1964. This means that seven years ago, one quarter of these women bore children each year. Two years ago, the figure was dropped towards one fifth.

This trend may lead demographers to believe that the average size of the American family will decline still further.

Since 1957, wives over 24 have also been having fewer births than during the baby boom years. A decline occurred because many wives over 30, and some between 25 and 30, had already completed their families. In other words, they had timed births early, spaced them close together, and called a halt to fertility.

"The unusually high rates observed at the older childbearing ages (30 years of age and over) during the 1950's were due to the making up of births postponed by couples who were in the early childbearing ages during the late 1930's and the early 1940's," reported the U. S. Public Health Service in February, 1966. "Most of these couples are no longer having children. The couples who followed them are now having lower birth rates at the older childbearing ages because they tended to marry earlier and have their children sooner after marriage."

THE CRUX: CHILDREN EVER BORN

In the long run, the number of children born to each woman will be the most significant factor contributing to population increase. Most recent statistics show that the present childbearers on the average have been producing larger families than did their mothers. That previous generation composed of "depression wives," born between 1906 and 1915, bore the lowest average number of children, 2.4 to 2.5. Those born in the 1930's appear to be reaching an average of 3.1 to 3.6.

What will be the average for women born in 1940's, especially for women born during the years immediately after World War II? This is a pivotal question about which revolves much conjecture on future trends. The future direction of fertility trends greatly depends on those women now moving into the marriageable ages and beginning to reproduce. Their family aims and plans will determine the amount and rate of population growth.

Because the birth rates of young couples have been declining in the last few years, some demographers suggest that a new fashion of small families may be in the making. There is a possibility that the new vogue is one of widely-spaced births rather than small families. This could mean as high an ultimate fertility spread over a longer period.

Obviously, projecting past and current statistics into the future gives an inadequate picture of possible developments. This type of activity does not take into account the thoughts and intentions of today's young married couples regarding family planning. Nor does it measure the profound effect economic changes can have on their attitudes and intentions. An awareness of the inadequacy of this failing in statistical population projections, based on past performance and purely speculative assumption, stimulated the *Growth of American Families* (GAF) studies, two unique national surveys of attitudes and practices of American women with regard to childbearing.

They are the work of the Survey Research Center of the University of Michigan and the Scripps Foundation for Research in Population Problems, Miami University, Oxford, Ohio.

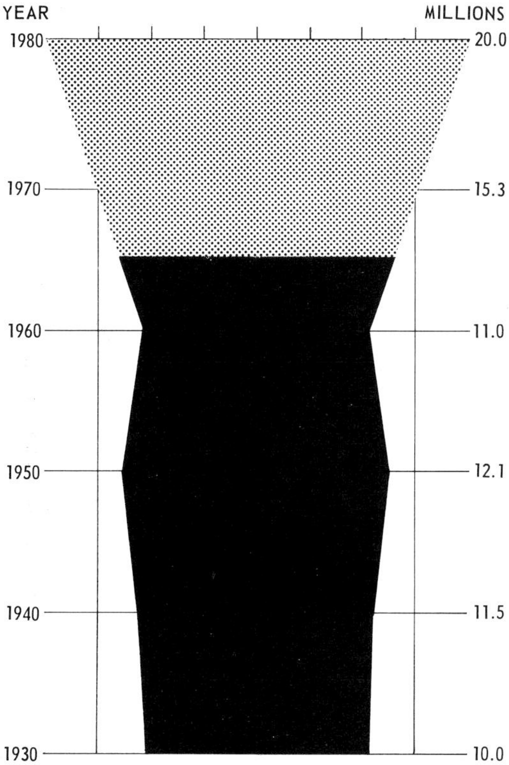

FIGURE 1

Increase in women of childbearing ages, 20–29, for 1930 to 1980.

Professors Ronald Freedman and Pascal K. Whelpton, who unfortunately did not live to see the second study completed, were the moving spirits behind the undertaking. They were assisted by Arthur A. Campbell and, in the second survey by John E. Patterson. The first was conducted in 1955 and the findings were reported in 1959 in the book *Family Planning, Sterility and Population Growth.* The second survey comprised a larger and more comprehensive sample than the first. Like the first it used an interview-in-depth technique on a probability sampling of married women 18-39 years old. The 1955 study was limited to white women; the 1960 sequel included a sampling of the nonwhite population.

A unique feature of the studies was the use of cohort analysis, a method developed by Dr. Whelpton. It was adopted by the U. S. Census Bureau in 1964 in preparing its projections. A cohort, in this study, is a group of women born in a 12-month period with January first in the center. For example, the women born between July 1, 1919, and June 30, 1920, constitute the 1920 cohort. The reproductive histories of women in each cohort are followed from the beginning to end of their child-bearing periods, with fertility treated as a cumulative process.

The advantage of the cohort system lies in forecasting. The GAF authors, in 1955, explained it this way:

> . . . By focusing attention on the childbearing of real groups of people as they live through the reproductive ages, statements can be made which are understandable in terms of the behavior of individuals and married couples. For example, one can readily comprehend what is meant by the assumptions that 95 percent of the women born in 1931–35 and living to age 45 will have married before age 45 and that the average number of births to those who marry will be 3. In contrast, it is difficult to interpret in terms of the behavior of individuals or married couples the assumptions that during 1956–65 the birth rate will remain at 24 per 1,000 (the 1955 figure) and that it will then decline to 20 per 1,000 in 1980.

The 1960 GAF sampling also included women aged 40-44 as representative survivors of those who were 35-39 years old in 1955. The later participants, however, were not the same women who were interviewed five years earlier. The newer sampling was most carefully selected, however, to assure a close matching of characteristics.

A primary objective of the 1960 survey was to determine how well wives interviewed in 1955 predicted the number of children that women the same age would have during the ensuing five years. The results were uncanny in their accuracy. In 1955, wives of fecund couples, those with normal ability to have children, expected an average of almost one birth, .90 to .93, in the next five years. In that period, comparable married women averaged precisely .92 births.

Whether such precision will hold over the long haul is yet to be determined. Not only are future GAF surveys planned, but others of a similar nature are also under way. For one, in 1962, the Population Studies Center of the University of Michigan began collecting data on the number of births in the U. S. to date and the total number of births expected, in light of information on the racial, religious, socio-economic, and demographic characteristics of married couples. Relevant questions about fertility were asked in various nationwide surveys conducted by the University's Survey Research Center. The answers will be used to update available information concerning the family-building expectations of American couples.

What is more, analyses of the American family's growth are under way at Princeton's Office of Population Research. In a 1962 Population Studies Center report based on the replies of 1,383 respondents, the results of the 1960 GAF study were generally confirmed. Certainly the high correlation between expectations and performance is a tribute to the thoroughness of the two studies. The interviews on which both GAF reports are based involved approximately 200 questions with interviews running from one to one and one half hours in length. Questions posed involved the number of children the wife had at the time of interview, the total number of children she and her husband wanted, the number she actually expected to have, and the physiological ability of the wife and the husband to have children in the future. Couples were also asked about their attitudes toward family planning, effectiveness of family planning practices, religion, level of education, husband's occupation, and whether the wife was presently working.

The 1960 study verified the prevalence of some of the 1955 practices and attitudes, and indicated changes in others. Many of the findings of the earlier survey tend to have been confirmed by other more specialized studies and by official U.S. statistics. But when all data are integrated and analyzed, what trend appears in family formation in the United States, first for the white population and then for the nonwhite?

Ideal Families Are Bigger

Most U. S. married women no longer think of the ideal average family as a foursome composed of mother, father, and two children — as they did in 1940. "An overwhelming majority of these wives (about 9 out of 10)" report the GAF authors, "said they thought two, three, or

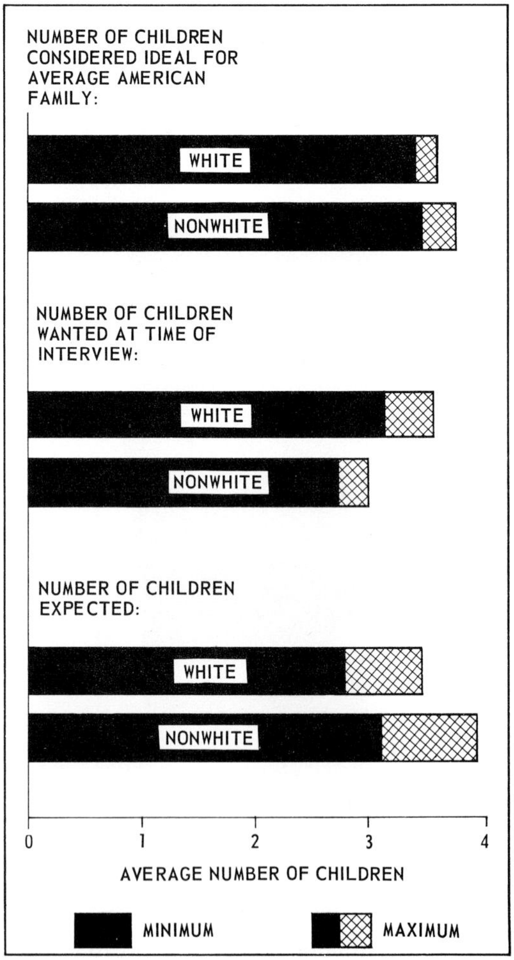

FIGURE 2

Number of children considered ideal, wanted at time of interview, and expected; for wives, by color. After 1960 GAF Report[4]

four children are ideal for the average American family, with four clearly being the most popular number." In 1941, the most popular ideal was two children; in 1945, three; and in 1955 and 1960, four.

Taking an average of minimum and maximum replies over a 19-year interval, the ideal family has increased from an average of three to an average of 3.5 children. That "half" child, if realized, could boost population to about the billion mark within a century. If families average three children, this country could expect 600 million people within a century. To maintain the population at the current size, an average of 2.1 children per woman is required.[1]

On the average, the ideal (3.5) is higher than the number desired — between 3.1 and 3.4. Desires are conditioned by income, health, ability to care for more children, size of home, and marital happiness.

If women bore the average number of children they desired (between 3.1 and 3.4), the American population in the next 100 years would climb to between 600 million and 1 billion.

In gauging expectation of family size, the report incorporated the number of children married women had at the time of their interviews with the additional births they actually anticipated. In this way, the report allows for successes and failures in family planning. Some women expect fewer children than they want because of fecundity impairments, some expect more because of unwillingness or inability to prevent unwanted conceptions, and others expect fewer or more than they themselves want because of the family size preferences of their husbands.

On the whole, the American married couple has been harmonizing its childbearing with the desired family size to a surprising degree. Expectations in 1960 came close to the ideal. Wives aged 18 to 39 who were queried in 1955 expected between 2.7 and 3.3 children. In 1960, wives in the same age bracket expected between 2.9 and 3.5 children. The average total number of expected births per woman increased from 3.0 to 3.1. Part of the increase was due to a sizeable number of wives anticipating five or six children and fewer expecting one, two, or four children.

Analysis of expectations, according to the ages of the wives, reveals an element of declining fertility. In the 1955 GAF study, the youngest wives (18-24) expected the largest families — an average of 3.2 children.

BUT — and, as noted, this is the big But to demographers — in 1960, the wives 18-24 years old expected the smallest families, 3.0. It was the wives aged 25-29 who then had the highest expectations: 3.4 births.

"This is one of our most important findings," say the 1960 GAF authors. "The lower expectations of the younger wives may forecast a reversal of the postwar trend toward larger families, and the childbearing of these wives will have an important influence on the birth rate during most of the 1960's. Wives who were 18-24 account for 43 percent of the additional births expected by all wives who were 18-39 years of age." This conservative trend of the younger wives, if it is maintained, would considerably affect the rate of future population growth.

The 1960 GAF study also signalled that the trend toward earlier childbearing may be slowing down. It found that many wives are delaying initial pregnancies. This pause may account for the 1962-1965 decline in the birth rates among wives 18-24 and 25-29. However, there is activity running counter to the trend. Offsetting it is the tendency of more wives in the same cohort to increase their expectations. This could result in a fertility higher than current expectations; still, "Unless the pattern differs substantially from wives aged 18-24 in 1955, the expectations of wives 18-24 in 1960 will remain lower," say the GAF authors. Relevant here is the fact that older wives tell the number of children they actually have while younger wives generally tell of their intentions.

Disappearance of Voluntary Childlessness

There is one component missing in this demographic picture. The childless couple has become all but extinct. Rare indeed is the married couple

[1] The assumptions made in these projections and estimates are that there will be no major wars, severe economic depressions, or other catastrophes. They assume decreasing mortality, increasing life expectancy, and minimal immigration.

who chooses to have no children. For the most part, childless couples today are frequently the consequence of one spouse suffering an impairment to the reproductive system.

Using women ever married aged 30-34 for comparison, the proportion of childlessness has dropped by two thirds from 23 percent in 1940 to 17 percent in 1950, to 10 percent in 1960, and to 7 percent in June 1964. Many of these women postponed childbearing until well after the war.

It is possible that women who were 25-29 years old in 1964 will record an even lower percent of childlessness by the end of their fertile period. In 1964, about 11 percent of women 25-29 years old and ever married had no children. This represents a drop from 30 percent of childless women in that age category in 1940.

To an extent, a woman's age when she marries and when she has her first child affects plans for family size. But then, so do religious and socio-economic background factors. Rural-urban residence, levels of education and income, occupation, and whether or not the wife works do not affect fertility to the extent that they once did. The nation has grown more uniform as a result of rapid urbanization, a sophisticated national communications system, widespread prosperity, mobility, and improved education. In short, by experiencing similar working and living conditions, Americans *en masse* have acquired like desires, hopes, and drives despite diverse backgrounds.

Religious Differences

Religion is perhaps the strongest influence affecting the number of children couples want and the question as to whether they are willing to control fertility. The average expected number of births in 1960 was 3.7 for Catholics, 2.9 for Protestants, and 2.5 for Jews. Because of increased expectations among Catholic families, the differences seem to have been widening. Thus, while average expectations for Protestants were the same in 1955 and 1960, Catholics increased their expectations from 3.4 in 1955 to 3.7 in 1960. The report on the 1960 study explained:

First, the wives who were 18–34 in 1955 and thus 23–39 in 1960 — and eligible for both studies — tended to revise their expectations upward as they grew older during 1955–1960, and this tendency may have been somewhat more pronounced for Catholics than for Protestants. Second, the Catholics who were included in the 1960 sample of 18–39-year-old wives, but were not eligible in 1955, expected to have larger families than those who were included in 1955, but were not eligible in 1960. In other words, the Catholics who entered the sample between the 1955 and 1960 studies thought they would have more children than those who left it. The Protestants who moved into the sample, on the other hand, expected *fewer* children than those who moved out of it.

Among Catholics, there is a direct relationship between expected fertility and expressed faithfulness to the Church. For example, those who receive the sacraments at least once a week expect an average of 4.4 children compared to an average of 3.2 births anticipated by those who do not receive the sacraments regularly.

Protestants differed from Catholics in that no significant relationship was found between frequency of church attendance and number of births expected.

Between Protestants and Jews, the differences in actual and expected births are fewer for urban residents with more education, income, and occupational status than for Protestants and Jews overall.

Between Protestants and Catholics, differences are larger in higher socio-economic levels than at the lower levels. It is at the upper levels that differences have grown, for Catholics with higher education and income expect more children than they did in the past — for example, they desired 3.7 in 1960 against 3.4 in 1955. Among Protestants the reverse is true. Expectations decline as education, income, and occupational status rise. Among Catholics, in contrast, the highest expectations are characteristics of the highest and the lowest socio-economic groups. This finding seems to invalidate the assumption that as Catholics become more like the rest of the population socio-economically they will copy their fertility patterns.

Education and Fertility

More than any single characteristic, education seems to determine a wife's abilities to control fertility. The young and newly-married with little schooling think they will have better fertility control than they do; hence they underestimate the size of their families. The better educated, knowing more about physiology and birth control methods do a more effective job of planning family size.

Expectations, however, do not decline consistently from grade school through college. Among Protestants they decrease as the level of education advances through the third year of high school, then remain equal for high school graduates and college graduates.

What is true for the Protestant spouse is not true for Catholics. Catholic wives with college educations expect almost as many children as wives with grade school education; Catholics with high school education have lower expectations.

This U-shaped curve of Catholic expectations tends to distort national averages.

The 1960 GAF study found that wives whose husbands were in the higher income bracket expect almost as many children as their lower income counterparts. An average of 3.1 children was expected by women whose husbands earned $10,000. Those whose husbands' incomes were under $3,000 expected an average of 3.2 children. This finding seems to challenge the adage that "the rich get richer and the poor get babies." For that matter, some demographers now predict that the time will come when the well-to-do will average more children than those in the low income brackets.

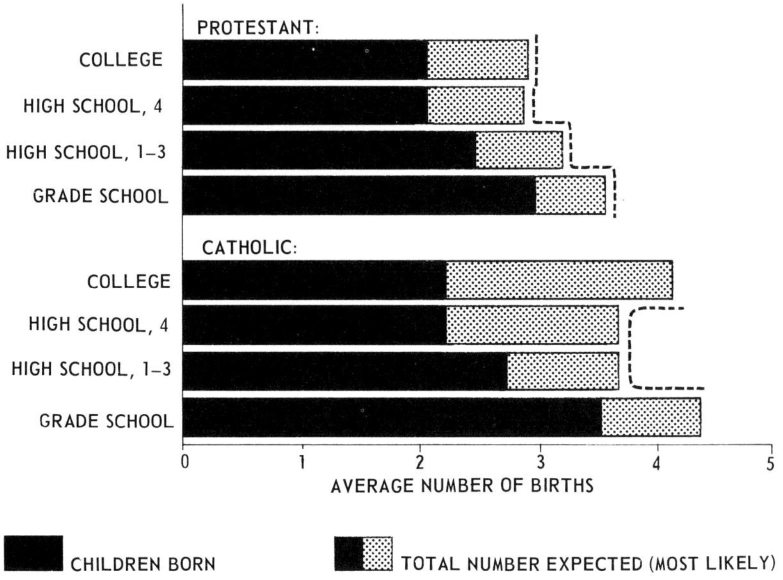

FIGURE 3

Births by 1960 and total number expected; for wives, by education and religion. After 1960 GAF Report[4]

As yet, however, procreation among low-income groups shows no sign of diminishing. At the same time, higher-income wives are bearing more children and increasing their expectations.

When the basis of comparison is family income rather than husband's income alone, there is a greater difference between upper and lower levels — average expectation is 2.8 children for a family with an income over $10,000 and 3.2 when it is under $3,000. Working wives have fewer children.

What the relationship is between the growing number of women in today's work force and the nation's fertility remains an open question.

Furthermore, an increasing number have been returning to the labor force after they have completed their families.

Fertility differences which are associated with the husband's occupation are sharper than those related to his income, but they are substantially smaller than they were before World War II. This is most true for nonfarm occupations.

Wives of husbands in blue-collar jobs anticipate 7 percent more births than wives of husbands in white-collar jobs. According to the U.S. Census Bureau, white-collar workers with moderate incomes tend to limit the size of their families because of desire for status and for a high standard of living.

In the GAF studies, the gap between farm and nonfarm occupations seemed to be shrinking. The 1960 survey found a decrease in expectations among farm wives and an increase among wives in the nonfarm group. Even so, farm population is more fertile than nonfarm population, and according to the U.S. Census Bureau, "Between 1960 and 1964, the number of children ever born per 1,000 women 15 to 44 years old, standardized for age, increased by about the same amount in the farm population as in the nonfarm population."

Notable in this connection is that the farm population continues to decrease. In 1960, 7.5 percent of the nation's people lived on farms; in 1965, the total had shrunk to 6.4 percent.

Rural-Urban and Regional Differences

One influence on the fertility rate is the size of cities and towns. Wives in cities of less than 150,000 people statistically expect more children than those in the larger metropolises.

In addition, wives in rural farm areas differ in their anticipations from wives in rural nonfarm communities. In 1960, it was found that wives who lived in rural areas but not on farms did not anticipate significantly larger families than wives who lived in cities and towns. Yet wives who had lived on farms at some time since they were first married, but were not living on farms at the time they were interviewed, expected almost as many births as wives still living on farms. However, women who left farm life before they married expected fewer births.

Since the 1930's, the rise in fertility has been sharper in the cities and towns than in the rural communities. As the rural-urban differences of the past are lessening, so too are the traditional fertility variations between regions of the country. In the old South, a high proportion of the rural, farm, and nonwhite population produced the nation's highest level of fertility. Now, along with industrialization, emigration of Negroes, integration, and civil rights movements, have come better incomes, more widespread education, and urban-type sophistication — in short, life in the South is experiencing an upheaval. According to the GAF study, this sector of the country had not only the lowest birth rate, but the lowest birth expectancy.

White wives who lived in the South — where Catholics are fewer — had borne fewer children by 1960 and expected to have smaller completed families than those who lived in the remainder of the country. The north-central region has overtaken the South as the region with both the highest fertility and the highest expectancy.

Nonwhite Fertility

The nonwhite American population in 1960 was 11.4 percent of the total. It included American Indians, Japanese, Chinese, Filipinos, Koreans, Hawaiians, Asian Indians, Eskimos, Aleuts, Malayans and Negroes, who predominated comprising 10.5 percent of the total population.

In at least three respects, fertility among nonwhites parallels trends among the white population:

(1) There is far less childlessness — only 9 percent among nonwhite women 30-34 years old in 1964 compared with 22.6 percent in 1962, or a sharp drop by more than half in two years.

(2) Families are larger: about 36 percent of nonwhite women ever married 30-34 years old in 1964 had borne five or more children; in 1962, that figure was 31 percent.

(3) Fertility seems to be declining among nonwhites under 25 years of age.

In addition, nonwhite fertility, like white, rose in the 1950's, then fell in the 1960's. However, in the 1950's, nonwhite births rose at a greater

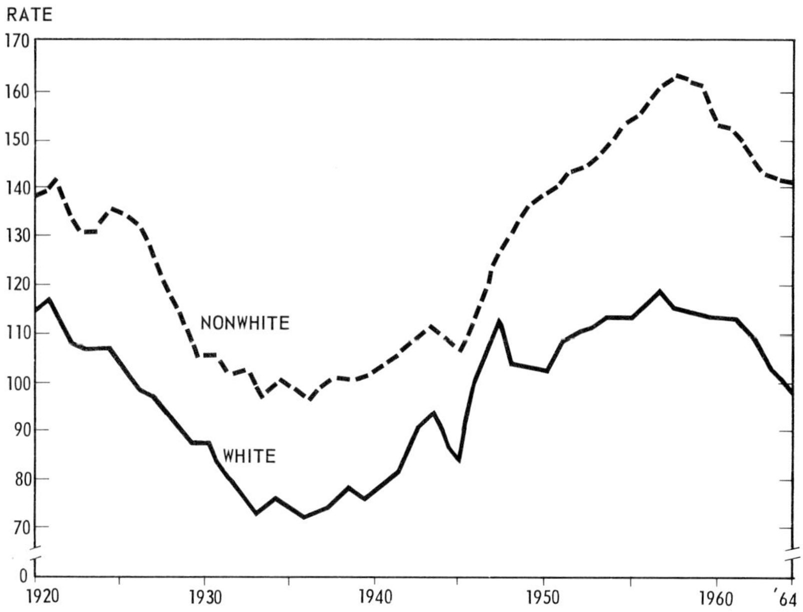

FIGURE 4

Births Per 1,000 women 15–44 years old, for white and nonwhites, United States, 1920–1964.
After 1960 GAF Report[4]

rate than among the white couples. During the ten-year period 1951-60, the crude birth rate of nonwhites ranged between 32 and 35 per 1,000, which is roughly 10 points higher than the rate for whites and marks a larger difference than at any time since the 1920's.

Significant to nonwhite fertility is the fact that since World War II, the prevalence of venereal disease has rapidly diminished among nonwhites and it is thought to be an important cause of both the increase in their birth rate and the decrease in childlessness. Overall, not only is the average fertility of nonwhites higher than whites, but also a high proportion of nonwhites have had and expect large numbers of births. In 1960, 19 percent of the nonwhite wives expected six or more births compared with only 6 percent of a group of matched whites and 7 percent of all whites.

The 1960 GAF study revealed a significant difference between whites and nonwhites. The nonwhites set the ideal number of children higher than whites, 3.6-3.8 as against 3.4-3.5 for whites. But nonwhites actually want fewer children, 2.7-3.0 compared with 3.1-3.5. Nonwhites' average expectations — 3.4-4.1 — considerably exceed their preferences. The GAF study found that nonwhite couples have a higher prevalence of excess fertility (unplanned children) than whites; 31 percent vs. 17 percent.

A group of wives was selected in order to determine the extent to which fertility differences are related to racial and socio-economic backgrounds. The white and nonwhite wives were matched in certain characteristics: duration of marriage, wife's religion, region of residence, size of place of longest residence since marriage, farm background, and husband's occupation.

In comparing white and nonwhite fertility patterns, regional factors are important. The greatest differences among whites and nonwhites are in the South.

Below the Mason-Dixon Line, in 1960, nonwhites had 50 percent more births than whites;

elsewhere in the country, the excess was merely 10 percent. In addition, fertility of Southern nonwhites on farms was more than double that of whites living on farms — an average of 4.5 children against an average of 2.1. Southern nonwhites also expected twice as many children as Southern whites — 5.9 vs. 2.9.

The GAF authors say:

> Such differentials suggest that the traditional patterns of marriage and family life that developed in the rural South during and after the period of slavery still influence nonwhite fertility perceptibly. Informal and often temporary unions between men and women beginning in adolescence, relatively ineffective sanctions against illegitimacy among the economically deprived, a genuine affection for children, and the existence of customary arrangements to provide for their care in case the mother cannot do so all contribute to high birth rates.

These trends are arrested in part by urbanization and education. The proportion of nonwhites living in cities of 50,000 or more jumped from 32 percent in 1940 to 50 percent in 1960. In that period, the proportion of nonwhites with a high school education sprang from 9 percent to 24 percent.

The sooner and further away from Southern farm life the nonwhites move and the higher the education they attain, the more their fertility resembles that of the white population. The result is a growing educated Negro middle class with relatively few children.

Summary

The American people have shown a remarkable insight into the dynamic interplay between births and deaths. In colonial times, and in the early decades of the 19th century, the fertility of the women of the United States stood very near the physiological upper limit: about 55 births per 1,000 population per year. As the attrition of early death was relaxed, the number of children born to each woman began to decline. The birth rate scaled down in about a century from its high to a low of 17 in 1933-1934, a reduction of two thirds.

So significant a change had nothing to do with governmental policies calculated to encourage a decrease in fertility. It was due to a spontaneous readjustment of family size as mortality declined and life expectation increased.

This adjustment in the level of fertility was essential to the orderly development of the economy of the United States. Real-life illustrations of what this has meant are provided by certain small religious sects which have continued a pattern of traditional fertility. The December 1961 *Bulletin* reported the experience of an old order Amish couple, Mr. and Mrs. John Miller. When he died on the eve of his 95th birthday, Miller had 410 living descendents and their number was being increased by about one a week. The Millers were married in 1888, a year when about 535,000 marriages were consummated in the United States. Had each of these couples and their descendents followed the fertility pattern of the Miller clan, the offspring of this one year's marriage cohort would have amounted to about 219 million living descendants in 1960. Had the Amish pattern been copied by all American families in the 12 years remaining until 1900, the population of the United States today would be much larger than that of China.

This footnote to demographic history illustrates how the critical interplay between births and deaths affects the social, economic, and political fate of nations. Obviously, to have "out-chinaed" China would have been in the national interest. It has been clear for some years that the 1960's will be a decade of demographic decision, for this nation and the world, in setting the pattern of future population growth.

The U.S. birth rate has oscillated considerably, since the all-time low of the mid 1930's, when for a brief period the fertility was slightly below the replacement rate. The post-war baby boom saw a level of fertility equaling that of nearly half a century earlier. This has been followed by the decline discussed in some detail in this report.

The change in prospects for population growth, which these perturbations in the birth rate suggest, are documented in the population predictions made by the U.S. Census and other demographers over the past 30 years. In the 1930's an atmosphere of gloom prevailed in the Western industrial countries because birth rates had declined so far that actual declines in population were anticipated. The consensus of U.S. demographers was that the population of the United States would level off by 1960 or 1970, at the 160 million mark. One Census Bureau release emphasized the fact that fertility was below the replacement level and that incipient population decline was imminent.

The crucial assumption underlying these projections was that the downward trend of the birth rate was irreversible, and that once down, the rate would never go back up. The demographic history of the 1940's in all of the industrial countries proved how wrong this assumption was.

As the birth rate has moved down, up, and down again, the projections of the U.S. Census Bureau have had to be constantly revised. During the 1940's and 1950's, they climbed steadily upward. For example, in 1943, when the rapid post-war increase was still in the future, government projections anticipated only 198.7 million Americans by the year 2000, a mark the population will pass by 1967. The baby boom forced a rise in population projections.

Several upward revisions were prepared in the intervening years. The high point was reached in July 1964 when the projected population in the year 2000 was bracketed as falling between 291 million for the low projection and 362 million for the high. The high projection showed a population ten years later of 438 million, a gain of 76 million.

The most recent Census projections foresee population growth by the end of the century only slightly less than that projected two years ago, ranging between 280 million and 356 million. With the extent of the decline in the birth rate problematical and with a rapid increase in the number of women in the high fertility age, 20-30, the demographic crystal ball can reveal only a cloudy view of what is in prospect. This slacking off in growth is encouraging, not only in itself, but possibly presaging a sharper decline in the growth rate.

One myth the GAF report lays to rest is that rapid U.S. population growth can be attributed to "hordes of unwanted children." This is not to say the problem of the unwanted child does not exist, but it is one increasingly confined to the fifth of our nation still quagmired in poverty. The high fertility of several million trapped in economic and educational poverty appears to be largely involuntary, a by-product of ignorance and isolation. As the war on poverty and other leavening forces bring these lagging millions into the 20th century, the tragedy of the unwanted child will eventually be resolved. There appears to be a growing consensus that the knowledge and facilities to make voluntary parenthood universal must be recognized as a basic human right.

The major component of current growth is a combination of the huge fertility potential built into our population by its present age distribution, and thc "ideal family" set at three or four children. Too many women bearing too many *wanted* babies produce the alarming rates of growth of the past decade.

Illuminating insights into the thinking that underlies decisions as to the "ideal family" were presented in a recent statement by Dr. Emily H. Mudd, the distinguished director of the Marriage Council of Philadelphia and professor of Psychiatry at the University of Pennsylvania Medical School:

Young people today feel it is their right to decide whether or not to have a baby and hence they believe it is equally their right to choose the use of contraceptives. This does not mean that they cannot be influenced, but the decision has to be theirs. Most young females and, to a lesser extent males, believe it is their inherent right to reproduce. Today's young people feel it is no one's business but their own how many children they should have and they resent anyone telling them what they should or should not do.

However, they are exposed to conflicting pressures. They recognize another inherent right: to keep up with the Joneses in the budget and in the enjoyment of the good things of the modern world. They consider material comforts essential to their way of life. Both the privileged and underprivileged realize that even though the government is moving to help them in various ways the government will not take over the family's responsibilities.

After they produce one child, they seem to feel that a child growing up alone is in a sense "underprivileged." To supply a "buddy," child number two comes along.

In this connection, once a family has proven its right and felt that it has done its duty to the child by having a second, it starts thinking seriously about the care and cost that those two will require. At this point, the couple is very apt to say "this is enough." However, in spite of all birth control procedures, there still are unplanned babies and very often it is the surprise or the unexpected that results in a three-child family.

The decision regarding the "ideal family" and the implementation of this decision is obviously a complicated matter. A consideration of growing importance in the modern world centers around the increasing cost of rearing and educating a child. In rural America only half a century ago, children became an economic asset to the family at an early age. This is no longer true in the urban, industrial environment in which an increasing majority of American families live. A recent survey by the Institute of Life Insurance estimated that the cost of rearing a child to age 18 amounted to $23,835. This applied to a family with an annual income of $6,600. With college increasingly essential, four more years of heavy expense must be added to that already impressive total.

One thing is certain: there was a time in the good old days when "cheaper by the dozen" had a plausible social and financial basis. Few couples are so favorably endowed that they can provide the emotional security and intellectual challenge required to give each child of a "cheaper by the dozen" brood the rich stimulating environment essential for individual development. And whether our concern is demographic control or family fulfillment, the end and aim should be the fullest realization of each human being's potential.

The GAF reports form the basis for hope that the historical trend toward a balanced fertility in the United States will continue. If this is to be the wave of this nation's demographic future, our grandchildren may indeed take heart. The prospects for a good life will be greatly enhanced.

Should this happy outcome be realized, our descendants may well paraphrase a celebrated Churchillian aphorism:

Never have so many been indebted to the wisdom and forbearance of so many."

(*This* Bulletin *was written from a report prepared by Goody Solomon.*)

SOURCES

1. Freedman, Ronald, Whelpton, Pascal K., and Campbell, Arthur A. *Family Planning, Sterility, and Population Growth.* New York: McGraw-Hill Book Company, Inc., 1959.
2. Institute of Life Insurance. *Family Security Feature Service.* August 1965. New York City.
3. Mudd, Emily H. Speech delivered at conference organized by the Population Reference Bureau at Hotel Roosevelt in New York City, April 14, 1966. (See Population Profile, "300 or 400 Million in 35 years? The Nation's Young Married Couples Will Decide." April 15, 1966. Population Reference Bureau.)
4. Whelpton, Pascal K., Campbell, Arthur A., and Patterson, John E. *Fertility and Family Planning in the United States.* Princeton, New Jersey: Princeton University Press, 1966.

*The Social Biology of Very High Fertility Among the Hutterites: The Demography of A Unique Population**

JOSEPH W. EATON • ALBERT J. MAYER

AN EXPERIMENT OF HISTORY

The Hutterite population has grown rapidly in a fairly stable pattern for 80 years and more, under controlled conditions almost comparable to those obtained by Raymond Pearl with *Drosophila melanogaster* in their "milk bottle universes." The entire population of 8,542 persons including their leaders were not merely passive objects of scientific scrutiny. The Hutterites collaborated actively in this undertaking. They generously furnished most of the data, made extensive searches of their colony records and responded to hundreds of written or verbal inquiries. Social scientists cannot experiment with human fertility, but historical accident has provided them here with a population which meets most of the conditions of a good ex-post-facto experiment.

What set of circumstances made this experiment possible? Among the most crucial factors may be the migration of the Hutterites to North America where good medical care became available to them. In this fortune they are not unique. In 1953 there were 172 million other Americans and Canadians on the North American half of the continent who had access to the same facilities. The Hutterites maintain a high level of fertility, virtually uninfluenced by any form of birth-control. In this also they are not unique. Many primitive populations live so. Finally, the Hutterites have a strong primary group cohesiveness and a well integrated religiously sanctioned value system, with much emphasis on mutual aid. The group guarantees each individual an equal and adequate, but austere standard of living, regardless of personal ability or fortune. The Hutterites are not unique even in this characteristic. They share these beliefs in Christian community living with many a religious order, particularly those of the Catholic Church. What is unique is the combination of the three factors. This combination makes the Hutterites appear to be "tailor-made" for a fairly well controlled study of many human problems, including the social biology of very high fertility.

BE FRUITFUL AND MULTIPLY

The Hutterites follow to the letter this biblical admonition to Noah. Women living in 1950 had on the average a probability of having 12 children if they were married during their eighteenth year and lived with their spouse through the end of their fertility period. The population was increasing at a rate of 4.1265% per year, or doubling in number in about 16 years. At this rate of growth it can be predicted that there will be 12,700 Hutterites in 1960, living in perhaps 130 colonies instead of the 93 in existence in 1950.

The rapid growth is taking place within a relatively stable pattern. This attribute facilitates a comparison of vital statistics of the group over time, since they are always based on a population which, despite its increase in numbers, remains stable in age and sex distribution. This fact greatly enhances its value as a social laboratory. Future studies, in which the members might be willing to cooperate, can be made with larger and larger numbers of subjects.

The rapid increase in population perpetually confronts the sect with the problem of maintain-

* Reprinted with permission from *Human Biology*, Vol. 25, No. 3 (September 1953), pp. 256-262.

ing its primary group structure, which may be essential for its survival as an autonomous culture. This is accomplished through the process of "swarming" as the Hutterites picturesquely refer to their custom of establishing a branch colony whenever the population gets much above 100.

Accent on Youth

There are two ways in which a population may remain predominantly youthful. In the "primitive way" individuals die prematurely; in the "Hutterite way" there is constant expansion through a very high birth rate. Although in the latter case adults live a long time, they are perpetually outnumbered by successive and increasing waves of children, most of whom survive. Over 61% of the Hutterite population in 1950 had not reached full adulthood. Such a population could not be supported easily in a highly individualistic and competitive economy, where each individual and family strives to maximize its standard of living. Through group responsibility for each member, Hutterites assure security from birth to death.

Young people are not without opportunities for satisfying their aspirations, although the Hutterite culture imposes many limitations. Many of the goals common to most young Americans are taboo to the Hutterites, including such central values as "getting ahead in the world" or a maximum utilization of new inventions designed to increase creature comforts. Hutterites recognize that their way of life is what they call "a narrow road," but they teach their young people to travel it in order to attain religious salvation. The Hutterite youth have opportunities for achieving the aspirations sanctioned by their value system. New branch colonies are established frequently. This expansion provides opportunities for persons who want to be farm department heads, managers and preachers.

Over-all Low Mortality

Hutterites are a "primitive" population in having a high fertility pattern, but are quite modern in their mortality rates. Adults tend to live longer than other American whites and Hutterite children under 15 have a slightly higher death rate. There is evidence that the sophistication of Hutterites about medical care is growing. This probably will reduce the number of juvenile deaths. Since over half of the group is composed of children under 15, a reduction in the death rate of children would increase still further the already high net-reproduction rate of the group, unless this trend is counter-balanced by birth control measures.

Men Outlive Their Wives

Unlike the situation in most other populations, Hutterite men tend to outlive their wives. This dramatic reversal of the generalization that females are the "stronger" sex with regard to longevity is probably largely a result of the very high fertility of Hutterite females. Few Hutterite women die because of pregnancy or in childbirth but it is probable that the frequent repetition of child bearing lowers their resistance to morbidity. We do not know if the relationship between fertility and mortality is linear and direct. There may be an optimum number of pregnancies which have no unfavorable effect on longevity, but beyond which such effects begin to set in. The implications need to be studied further.

Fecundity versus Poverty

The claim advanced by the nutritionist de Castro ('52) that the hungry peoples of the earth are the most fertile is certainly not borne out in the case of the Hutterites. Not only are the Hutterites amply fed but their fertility has increased since their early days in this country when their diet was often far less adequate than it is today. The steady rise in fertility coupled with an increasing standard of living completely contradicts the concept of de Castro, in so far as this group is concerned.

Fertility Decreases Slowly With Age

The population fecundity of the Hutterites has been estimated to lie within the range of 12 to 14 live births for the average woman who is exposed to pregnancy throughout her reproductive period from menarche to menopause.

The peak of fertility of the population lies at the 22nd year of life, when 7 of every 10 women who were married between 1941–1950 had a live birth. There was an average of more than three babies per woman if they were married during the 20–24 year age span. Fertility declined gradually, but not rapidly. At 39 one in three Hutterite women had a child annually. In the forty-sixth year, only one in ten women had a baby, and after that age fertility dropped very rapidly. Nevertheless, there were 86 chances per 1,000 that a woman who had lived with her husband between her forty-seventh and fifty-first year of life became a mother.

The high fertility of the Hutterite population is not due to the presence of a small number of extremely fecund couples. It is a result of a generally high level of reproductivity. No Hutterite female had more than 16 children. Nor does the birth rate reflect an unusually large "litter" size. Twins were only about as common as they are in the general population.

The Reproductive Efficiency of Human Beings

Our evidence disagrees somewhat with that of Raymond Pearl concerning pregnancy in families which do not engage in controlled parenthood practices. Despite the short life span of both the human ovum and the sperm, copulation among the Hutterites results in conception with far greater frequency than would be expected from the reports of families whose fertility patterns were studied in detail by Pearl.

The total sterility rate of Hutterites is low. The number of women who had no children at all at the conclusion of their reproductive period was only 10 out of 340 or about 3%. Both of these facts taken together seem to suggest a higher rate of reproductive efficiency among human beings than has generally been believed in the past.

Implications for Aid to Underdeveloped Countries

The Hutterite culture is not unique in its positive emphasis on fertility. In many parts of the world people believe, for religious or nationalistic reasons, that maximum reproduction is a virtue. Areas like Japan, China, India and Java are densely populated. Most of their inhabitants know nothing about planned parenthood practices. Their religious values are often opposed to such practices. The Malthusian checks of poverty, disease, and malnutrition operate in these areas to keep population growth far below the Hutterite level.

The United States government is now giving technical aid to many of these underdeveloped regions. Agricultural, industrial, and medical "missionaries" are introducing tractors, penicillin and powdered milk. Major famines and epidemics which have reduced population of these technologically backward areas, are being gradually eradicated. The Hutterites demonstrate what might happen as these people begin to live under modern sanitary conditions without practicing birth control. Death rates will decline sharply, but fertility will remain high for a fairly long period and sharp rates of growth will ensue.

Birth as a Social-Psychological Phenomenon

The birth of a baby is a biological event, influenced by genetic factors many of which are still unknown. Within these limits, the probability of birth, survival, and death is very greatly influenced by social and psychological factors. The high rate of Hutterite reproduction is facilitated by at least 5 social-psychological tendencies:

1. The culture puts much positive value on having children; any form of birth control is regarded as sinful.
2. The community and its values assure economic support to parents who have as many children as they can biologically conceive.
3. Hutterites can and are willing to pay for good medical care.
4. Only a very small proportion of the adults fails to get married.
5. There is little migration, travelling, marital separation, or divorce to separate husband from wife during the fertility period. There are few occasions when married women have no opportunity to reproduce.

Hutterite fertility is not equal to the postulated theoretical level of fecundity because some of their values and customs work against reproduction:

1. Hutterites believe that sex relations prior to marriage are very sinful. Many measures are taken to prevent their occurrence, including strict supervision of adolescents, strong indoctrination of all persons against pre-marital relations and punishment through ritual excommunication (the most severe Hutterite punishment) of any persons who do have such illicit relations.
2. Hutterites believe that no one can be married prior to being baptised. Since baptism can be administered only to mature adults, who show a satisfactory understanding of, and appreciation for the Hutterite creed, few boys and girls are baptised before they reach the age of 19 or 20.
3. Hutterites believe it is "good" for a girl not to marry "too early." The reasons given for this attitude are numerous, such as "I do not want to leave my family too soon" or "When you get married, there is so much more work for a girl." Between 1880 and 1905, the median age of marriage for 78 females was about 19.5 years. In 1950, the median age of marriage of all women then living was 22 years.
4. There are isolated instances of surgical interference with reproduction to protect a mother's health. Certain birth control practices may already be coming into use particularly among women over 35 years of age. They have not had much impact on fertility as yet, but may become a factor in future population growth. The tendency for a reduction in the frequency of sexual relations with increasing age, which has been noted in other populations, may also exist among the Hutterites. It may always have had an effect on keeping their fertility below the theoretically possible level.

The essential core of Hutterite beliefs have changed little during the past 70 years, a period during which the sect has adopted many of the technological inventions of its neighbors. Up to now, Hutterites seem to reverse the general tendency of that human reproduction to decline with the increasing diffusion of modern technology. But the pressures of the American environment are beginning to have an effect (Eaton, '52). New values which might effect fertility are competing with the old standards. Hutterite women talk on occasion about the advantages of "worldly" mothers, who can enjoy life by not being burdened by "too many children." The limitation of family size is increasingly urged by some doctors for reasons of health. These pressures are rarely sufficient to overcome the Hutterite belief that any form of birth control will lead the user to eternal damnation. The cohesiveness of the group is still strong. However, as the acceptance of these competing social values increases, Hutterite fertility is likely to decrease. The two factors are closely related. Hutterite fertility may give a positive indication of major changes in the basic values long before these changes lead to any break-up of a community.

STUDY AND DISCUSSION QUESTIONS

1. Using one or more of the factors mentioned in this chapter that affect fertility patterns, i.e., changes in fecundity, timing and spacing of births, etc., compare the United States pattern with that of an underdeveloped country. Can we expect these factors to bring about fertility changes in this underdeveloped country similar to those that have taken place in the United States?
2. Exactly how much can we expect the birth rate to change in the coming years due to the aging of girls born in the "baby boom" years? Construct an age pyramid which shows how much change we may expect.
3. Why do you suppose fertility and income are no longer completely inversely related but are now related so as to form a U-shaped curve? Have there been any stratification changes in this country that would account for such a shift?
4. Using only one of the sets of factors which may influence fertility or mortality (i.e., in-

dividual, group, or institutional), trace how the course of fertility in this country has been affected by such decisions. For example, from colonial times to the present, how have governmental decisions affected the pattern of United States fertility?

5. Compare the fertility of two cultural groups in the United States (e.g., the Hutterites and the Jews).
6. Compare the fertility ratio in the United States for a recent year with the cumulative fertility rate for the same year. Which measure tells more about current fertility? Which tells more about United States family size norms?
7. How does the "baby boom" after World War II fit into demographic transition theory? Was this rise in the birth rate enough to invalidate the theory or can it be allowed for within the transition framework?
8. The migration from the eastern United States to the western United States is regarded as one of the major migration streams in world history. How did this change in population distribution change the birth rates in these two parts of the country?

SUGGESTED ADDITIONAL READING

Freedman, Ronald, Pascal K. Whelpton, and Arthur A. Campbell. *Family Planning, Sterility and Population Growth.* New York: McGraw-Hill Publishing Company, 1959.

Whelpton, Pascal K., Arthur A. Campbell, and John E. Patterson. *Fertility and Family Planning in the United States.* Princeton: Princeton University Press, 1965.

Two volumes reporting the findings of the Growth of American Families studies, the third phase of which is being conducted by Charles F. Westoff and Norman B. Ryder.

Westoff, Charles F., Robert G. Potter, Jr., Philip C. Sagi, and Elliot G. Mishler. *Family Growth in Metropolitan America.* Princeton: Princeton University Press, 1961.

Westoff, Charles F., Robert G. Potter, Jr., and Philip C. Sagi. *The Third Child: A Study in the Prediction of Fertility.* Princeton: Princeton University Press, 1963.

Sometimes referred to as the Princeton Fertility Studies, two volumes reporting on a longitudinal study of fertility patterns in metropolitan areas of the United States.

U.S. National Center for Health Statistics. *Vital and Health Statistics.*

Series 21 is concerned with fertility statistics and analysis.

Grabill, Wilson H., Clyde V. Kiser, and Pascal K. Whelpton. *The Fertility of American Women.* New York: John Wiley and Sons, 1958.

Historical analysis of U.S. census materials on human fertility, with emphasis on data from the 1950 census.

CHAPTER 6

International Migration Patterns

Population change, as indicated earlier, comes about not only through natural increase or decrease (the balance of births and deaths) but also through the net effect of migration in and out of an area. When the area or areas being considered are nations, the terms conventionally used to denote migration affecting population size of the whole area are "immigration" (migration of outsiders into the nation) and "emigration" (migration of insiders out of the nation). Since most concerns about population size relate to the relatively permanent population of an area, it is the people who move to change their residence who are the subjects of migration research. Those who make temporary moves (such as persons on vacation trips or on short business visits away from their home areas) are not regarded as migrants. Statistics about immigration and emigration so defined usually are obtained from the records of governmental immigration and naturalization services or from censuses.

There are many ways of viewing the international migrations of people and thus many ways of classifying these migrations. The article by Petersen adopts a classification scheme that is initially based on the forces which bring about the migration. The five classes of migration so delimited include *primitive* migration (resulting from an ecological push to change the relationship between man and nature), *forced* migration (deriving from a governmental policy affecting the relationship between man and his state which leaves the migrant no alternative), *impelled* migration (also deriving from a governmental policy affecting the relationship between man and his state, but which grants the person some option as to whether or not to leave), *free* migration (based on the individual's will or aspiration, which may involve relatively small groups), and *mass* migration (in which the aspirations of large groups of people produce social momentum that generates their migration from an area). These five classes of migration are further divided according to whether the movement was designed to retain a way of life (conservative) or to bring about a new mode of life (innovating).

Any classification of migration based on the intentions of people presents difficulties for statistical analysis, since the data typically available identify at most the characteristics of the migrants and areas at origin and destination and nothing about the migrants' attitudes or aspirations. However, Petersen's classification does give us some understanding of the varying nature of international migratory movements and helps us to differentiate in a general way some of the more notable migrations in human history. More importantly, it makes us aware that the mass international migration of modern times is only one of many types of migratory movement.

Covering much the same ground as Petersen but using an historical approach, the selection by the Woytinskys provides somewhat more depth and documentation in the analysis of international migratory flows through World War II. Basic data are lacking on the migrations before the modern era, but these can be described from historical accounts. The five major currents of modern times the Woytinskys identify are emigration from Europe to North America beginning early in the seventeenth century; emigration to South America and the Caribbean since the beginning of the sixteenth century; emigration to South Africa, Australia, and Australasia in a somewhat later period; importation of slaves from Africa to the New World since the sixteenth century; and population shifts in the Far East, mainly from China and India to neighboring countries.

International migration has changed its character considerably in recent decades. The mass migrations of former years have been checked by restrictive legislation in many countries. Since World War II, movements across national boundaries have been observed in all continents. These movements differ in volume and in nature.

One significant pattern of international migration in modern times was the readjustment of European peoples following the dislocations occasioned by the war. Two general movements involving the resettlement of displaced persons were the return of German nationals living outside post-war German territory who had to return to Germany in accord with the Potsdam Agreement, and the migration back to their native countries of citizens of Poland, Czechoslovakia, and other European nations who had been uprooted from their homes during the war. The end of the war also opened up some of the channels of cross-oceanic migration. The United Kingdom and Italy were prime contributors to this overseas movement directed largely to North America and Oceania. However, it should be pointed out that European nations in recent decades have been receivers as well as senders of migrants. The United Kingdom, the Netherlands, and Germany were all areas of immigration as well as areas of emigration.

Six countries (the United States, Canada, Australia, New Zealand, South Africa, and Israel) were the main receiving countries for emigrants from northern and central Europe and, later, from southern Europe. Latin America was also a destination for southern Europeans. At the same time, there were shifts between European countries, the countries most affected being the United Kingdom, Sweden, Belgium, France, and Switzerland.

Other significant international migrations have taken place in recent years in the Americas, Asia and the Middle East, and in Africa. A dominant movement in the American continent has been the migration from Mexico and Canada to the United States. In the case of Canada there has been a countermovement from the United States as well. Also observed in recent decades have been some exchanges among South and Central American countries. Most significant among the international migrations in Asia and the Middle East have been the shifts of people between India and Pakistan, involving largely the mobility of Hindus to India and Moslems to Pakistan; the movements to Jordan, Lebanon, Syria, and the Gaza strip resulting from the partition of Palestine; the migrations of East Asian people to Japan; and the flow of Chinese population to Hong Kong. Finally, there have been the exchanges affecting Africa, namely, out-migration of Europeans from African countries gaining independence and the mobility between African nations.

The United States provides a good example of a country significantly effected by immigration; in fact, the nation's history is strongly based on the early immigrant settlements, colonization, and continued later immigration streams. As indicated in the selection by the Taeubers, large waves of immigrants to America first came in the middle of the nineteenth century, with periodic waves of larger magnitude until the peak period early in the twentieth century. Restrictive federal legislation following World War I, and maintained since, retarded the flow of immigrants and stabilized the number at a moderate level.

It is not easy to trace the factors affecting the timing and volume of international migration, but three broad sets of conditions might be subsumed under the categories of economic, demographic, and cultural and political factors. Dissatisfaction with the economic situation in one's native land and the attraction of better economic opportunities in other countries has long been recognized as a principle reason for migration. Immigration has also been related to the rate of population growth in an area. Population pressures in a country may generate emigration mainly by operating through changes in economic institutions. A low rate of population growth may generate immigration by providing available land and job opportunities. It is sometimes said that the cultural ties people have to their native land inhibit emigration. While sentiment of this kind may be a factor, it has been found that once people from an area have emigrated the communities or colonies they set up provide a haven for later immigrants who may want the economic advantages of the new nation and the security they can find in their native language, religion, and general style of life. Finally, political factors determine, to some extent, the international flows of people, both through the dislocating effects of wars and political uphcavals and through the legislation and administrative policies drawn up by national governments. While these different factors can be outlined separately, in reality they can become interrelated in action and in their effects.

International migration can have an impact on population change in a country in several ways — by adding to or subtracting from the total population, by affecting mortality or fertility conditions in both sending and receiving countries, and by changing the characteristics of the population at both origin and destination. One reason why international migration has not had a great effect on population growth or decline is that every country experiences both immigration and emigration and quite often the two movements largely offset each other. There are some notable exceptions, however. In the United States from the mid-nineteenth century to the early twentieth century, roughly one-third of the total population increase was due to net immigration. A principal reason for the population decline in Ireland has been the large net immigration which more than offset the gains of natural increase.

International migration may also affect population growth rates by relieving population pressures in the country of emigration and increasing them in the country of immigration. Migration may change mortality conditions (on the assumption that greater population densities are associated with higher death rates), and it may change fertility conditions (on the assumption that low fertility will be revived by reduced pressures from emigration). But these relationships bear further scrutiny, and the effects are likely to be small and indirect.

The movements of people across national boundaries have had the effect of changing the characteristics of the population, particularly at the point of destination. For example, as the Taeubers show, immigration is selective of persons by age, sex, language, nationality, and occupation, among other traits. This selection changes the character of the population in the receiving country by altering the social structure of the society generally and by creating and expanding ethnic colonies which tend to form in the country of destination.

A General Typology of Migration*†

William Petersen

Most studies of international migration are focused on the movement from or to one particular country, and virtually all of the other, somewhat broader works are concerned with a single historical era. Moreover, the emphasis is usually on description rather than analysis, so that the theoretical framework into which these limited data are fitted is ordinarily rather primitive. In this paper, an attempt is made to bring together into one typology some of the more significant analyses of both internal and international migration, as a step toward a general theory of migration.

The best known model for the analysis of migration is the typology constructed some years ago by Fairchild.[1] He classifies migration into *invasion,* of which the Visigoth sack of Rome is given as the best example; *conquest,* in which "the people of higher culture take the aggressive;" *colonization,* when "a well established, progressive, and physically vigorous state" settles "newly discovered or thinly settled countries;" and *immigration,* or the individually motivated, peaceful movement between well established countries "on approximately the same stage of civilization." That is to say, Fairchild uses, more or less clearly, two main criteria as his axes — the difference in level of culture and whether or not the movement was predominantly peaceful. His four types, thus, can be represented schematically as follows:

Migration from	Migration to	Peaceful Movement	Warlike Movement
Low culture	High culture		Invasion
High culture	Low culture	Colonization	Conquest
Cultures on a level		Immigration	

* Reprinted with permission from the *American Sociological Review,* Vol. 23, No. 3 (June 1958), pp. 256-266. Reprinted in William Petersen, *The Politics of Population.* Garden City, N. Y.: Doubleday and Co., 1964, Anchor Books, pp. 271-290.

† An earlier version of this paper was presented at the annual meeting of the American Sociological Society, Washington, D. C., August, 1957. It was written as a chapter of a volume on population to be published in 1959.

[1] Henry Pratt Fairchild, *Immigration: A World Movement and Its American Significance,* Rev. edition, New York: Macmillan, 1925, pp. 13 ff. In spite of the fact that it has all the faults of a pioneer effort, this classification has been adopted uncritically in several other works on the subject. See, for example, Maurice R. Davie, *World Immigration with Special Reference to the United States,* New York: Macmillan, 1949, pp. 2-3; Julius Isaac, *Economics of Migration,* London: Kegan Paul, Trench, Trubner, 1947, p. 1. The most recent and in many respects the best text in the field takes over Fairchild's four types and adds a fifth, *compulsory migration;* see Donald R. Taft and Richard Robbins, *International Migrations: The Immigrant in the Modern World,* New York: Ronald Press, 1955, pp. 19-20.

Several other discussions are decidedly better than Fairchild's, though not nearly so well known. I found two particularly stimulating — Rudolf Heberle, "Theorie der Wanderungen: Sociologische Betrachtungen," *Schmollers Jahrbuch,* LXXV:1 (1955); and Ragnar Numelin, *The Wandering Spirit: A Study of Human Migration,* London: Macmillan, 1937. See also Howard Becker, "Forms of Population Movement: Prolegomena to a Study of Mental Mobility," *Social Forces,* 9 (December, 1930), pp. 147-160 and 9 (March, 1931), pp. 351-361.

Reducing the implicit underlying structure to this schematic form has the immediate advantage of indicating its incompleteness. Two types are lacking from the classification,[2] although they are well represented in history.

Such a paradigm, moreover, suggests even more strongly than the dozen pages of text it summarizes that the two axes are not the best that could have been chosen. An attempt to distinguish between "high" and "low" cultures is an invitation to ethnocentrism, which Fairchild does not always avoid. The contrast between "progressive" England and "newly discovered" India, for example, can hardly be termed a scientific analysis of *colonization*. Similarly, Rome's *conquest* of her empire was not merely the migration of a people of higher culture: much of Rome's culture was adapted from that of conquered Greece. Nor is the distinction between "peaceful" and "warlike" always an unambiguous one. Colonization is ordinarily neither one nor the other;[3] and the Visigoths' *invasion* of Rome, Fairchild's main example of this type, was predominantly a peaceful interpenetration of the two cultures, accomplished (as Fairchild points out) over more than two centuries.[4]

This criticism of Fairchild's classification illustrates two general points: that it is useful to make explicit the logical structure of a typology, and that the criteria by which types are to be distinguished must be selected with care.

Psychological Universals

Together with most other analysts of migration, Fairchild implies that man is everywhere sedentary, remaining fixed until he is impelled to move by some force. Like most psychological universals, this one can be matched by its opposite: man migrates because of wanderlust. And like all such universals, these cannot explain differential behavior: if all men are sedentary (or migratory) "by nature," why do some migrate and some not? If a simplistic metaphor is used, it should be at least as complex as its mechanical analogue, which includes not only the concept of forces but also that of inertia.

Thus one might better say that a social group at rest, or a social group in motion (e.g., nomads), tends to remain so unless impelled to change; for with any viable pattern of life a value system is developed to support that pattern. To analyze the migration of Gypsies, for example, in terms of push and pull is entirely inadequate — no better, in fact, than to

[2] It is patent that this omission was not intentional; this is not an example of what Lazarsfeld terms "reduction" — that is, the collapsing of a formally complete typology in order to adjust it to reality. See Paul F. Lazarsfeld, "Some Remarks on the Typological Procedures in Social Science," mimeographed translation of an article that appeared originally in *Zeitschrift für Sozialforschung,* vol. VI, 1937.

[3] According to Fairchild, "while the resistance of the natives may be so weak as to make the enterprise hardly a military one, yet colonization is carried on without the consent, and against the will, of the original possessors of the land, and is, consequently, to be regarded rightly as a hostile movement. . . . [Moreover,] not infrequently the rivalry of two colonizing powers for some desirable locality may involve them in war with each other" (*op. cit.,* p. 19). In spite of this hedge, classifying *colonization* as "peaceful" is in accord with his main argument, for this is how he distinguishes it from *conquest.*

[4] On the one side, Germans were taken into the Roman army, granted land in the border regions and civil rights in the city; on the other side, after Wulfilas's translation of the Bible into Gothic, Roman culture made deep inroads among the Germans through their conversion to Christianity. The relation between the two cultures, therefore, was expressed not merely in a sharp confrontation on the field of battle, but also in the divided loyalties of marginal types. Alaric, leader of the Visigoths, was a romanized German, a former officer in the Roman army, a Christian; and Stilicho, the *de facto* emperor after Theodosius's death, was a German-Roman, a German by descent who had reached his high post through a successful army career. Alaric's purpose was not to overthrow Rome but, within the framework of the Empire, to get land and increased pensions (!) for his followers; Stilicho's purpose, similarly, was not to oust the Visigoths, whom he sought as allies against Constantinople, but to keep them under control. The interpenetration of the two cultures, that is to say, was a complex and subtle process, not too different from the present-day acculturation of immigrant groups. That Alaric put pressure on the Senate by marching his army into Italy was not the characteristic of "a rude people, on a low stage of culture," but the time-honored mode of lobbying used by Roman generals. Historical studies substantiate this account of the facts; I have used principally J. B. Bury, *The Invasion of Europe by the Barbarians,* London: Macmillan, 1928.

explain modern Western migration, as Herbert Spencer did, in terms of "the restlessness inherited from ancestral nomads." [5] If this principle of inertia is accepted as valid, then the difference between gathering and nomadic peoples, on the one hand, and agricultural and industrial peoples, on the other hand, is fundamental with respect to migration. For once a people has a permanent place of residence, the relevance of push and pull factors is presumably much greater.

Sometimes the basic problem is not why people migrate but rather why they do not. The vast majority of American Negroes, for example, remained in the South until the First World War, in spite of the Jim Crow pattern and lynch law that developed there from the 1870's on and, as a powerful pull, the many opportunities available in the West and the burgeoning northern cities.[6]

If wanderlust and what might be termed sitzlust are not useful as psychological universals, they do suggest a criterion for a significant distinction. Some persons migrate as a means of achieving the new. Let us term such migration *innovating*. Others migrate in response to a change in conditions, in order to retain what they have had; they move geographically in order to remain where they are in all other respects. Let us term such migration *conservative*. When the migrants themselves play a passive role, as in the case of African slaves being transported to the New World, the migration is termed innovating or conservative depending on how it is defined by the activating agent, in this case the slave-traders.

The fact that the familiar push-pull polarity implies a uinversal sedentary quality, however, is only one of its faults. The push factors alleged to "cause" emigration ordinarily comprise a heterogeneous array, ranging from an agricultural crisis to the spirit of adventure, from the development of shipping to overpopulation. Few attempts are made to distinguish among underlying causes, facilitative environment, precipitants, and motives.[7] In particular, if we fail to distinguish between emigrants' motives and the social causes of emigration — that is, if we do not take the emigrants' level of aspiration into account — our analysis lacks logical clarity. Economic hardship, for example, can appropriately be termed a "cause" of emigration only if there is a positive correlation between hardship, however defined, and the propensity to migrate.[8] Often the relation has been an inverse one; for example, the mass emigration from Europe in modern times developed together with a marked *rise* in the European standard of living. As has been shown by several studies, the correlation was rather with the business cycle in the receiving country,[9] and even this relation explains fluctuations in the emigration rate more than its absolute level. Nor can the class differential in the rate of emigration be ascribed simply to economic differences. The middle class lived in more comfortable circumstances, but for many a move to America would have meant also a definite material improvement. During the period of mass emigration, however, this was stereotyped as lower-class behavior, as more than a bit unpatriotic for the well-to-do. For a middle-class person to emigrate meant a break with the established social pattern; therefore in the middle class, especially marginal types like idealists or black sheep left the country, and these for relevant *personal* reasons. Once a migration has reached the stage of a social movement, however, such

[5] Herbert Spencer, *The Principles of Sociology*, 3rd edition, New York: Appleton, 1892, I, p. 566.

[6] See Gunnar Myrdal, *An American Dilemma: The Negro Problem and Modern Democracy*, New York: Harper, 1944, Chapter 8, for an extended discussion of this point. For an international example, see William Petersen, *Planned Migration*, Berkeley: University of California Press, 1955, Chapter 3, which discusses the several factors in prewar Holland that seemingly should have induced a large emigration, but did not.

[7] Cf. R. M. MacIver, *Social Causation*, Boston: Ginn, 1942.

[8] Similarly, no principled difference is usually made between what is sometimes termed "absolute overpopulation," which results in hunger and starvation, and milder degrees of "overpopulation," which reflect not physiological but cultural standards. In the first case the aspiration of emigrants can be ignored, for it is a bare physiological minimum that can be taken as universal; but in the second case it is the level of aspiration itself that defines the "overpopulation" and sets an impetus to emigrate.

[9] Harry Jerome, *Migration and Business Cycles*, New York: National Bureau of Economic Research, 1926; Dorothy Swaine Thomas, *Social and Economic Aspects of Swedish Population Movements, 1750-1933*, New York: Macmillan, 1941, Chapter 9.

personal motivations are generally of little interest.

This kind of confusion is not limited to economic factors. Religious oppression or the infringement of political liberty was often a *motive* for emigration from Europe, but before the rise of modern totalitarianism emigrants were predominantly from the European countries least marked by such stigmata. An increasing propensity to emigrate spread east and south from Northwest Europe, together with democratic institutions and religious tolerance. Again, we are faced with the anomaly that those who emigrated "because" of persecution tended to come from countries where there was less than elsewhere.

When the push-pull polarity has been refined in these two senses, by distinguishing innovating from conservative migration and by including in the analysis the migrants' level of aspiration, it can form the basis of an improved typology of migration. Five broad classes of migration, designated as primitive, forced, impelled, free, and mass, are discussed below.

Primitive Migration

The first class of migration to be defined is that resulting from an ecological push, and we shall term this *primitive* migration. Here, then, primitive migration does not denote the wandering of primitive peoples as such, but rather a movement related to man's inability to cope with natural forces. Since the reaction to a deterioration in the physical environment can be either remedial action or emigration, depending on the technology available to the people concerned, there is, however, a tendency for primitive migration in this narrower sense to be associated with primitive peoples.

Many of the treks of preindustrial folk seem, moreover, to have been conservative in the sense defined above. "There is often a tendency for [such] a migrating group to hold conservatively to the same type of environment; pastoral people, for example, attempt to remain on grasslands, where their accustomed life may be continued." [10] Such conservative migrations are set not by push and pull, but by the interplay of push and control. The route is shaped by both natural and man-made barriers: mountains, rivers, or rainfall or the lack of it; and the Great Wall of China or other, less monumental, evidences of hostility toward aliens. If they are indifferent about where they are going, men migrate as liquids flow, along the lines of least resistance. Conservative migrants seek only a place where they can resume their old way of life, and when this is possible they are content. Sometimes it is not possible, and any migration, therefore, may be associated with a fundamental change in culture.

The frequent designation for migrations of prehistoric primitives used to be "wandering of peoples," a translation from the German that, however inelegant, is nevertheless appropriate, for it denotes two of the characteristics that define it. For usually peoples as a whole migrate, not merely certain families or groups, and they leave without a definite destination, as "wander" implies in English. Let us, then, term migrations induced by ecological pressure as the *wandering of peoples*. Unintended movements over the ocean — an analogous type of primitive migration, which can be termed *marine wanderings* — have occurred more frequently than was once supposed.

> There are countless examples . . . [of] more or less accidental wanderings from island to island over oceanic expanses of water, brought about by winds and currents. The space of time and extent of these voyages seem to play a subordinate part. Journeys covering 3,000 miles are not unusual. They may last six weeks or several months. Even without provisions the natives can get along, as they fish for their food and collect rainwater to drink.[11]

Contemporary primitives also often move about in a way directly related to the low level of their material culture. A food-gathering or hunting people cannot ordinarily subsist from what is available in one vicinity; it must range over a wider area, moving either haphazardly or back and forth over its traditional territory. Such movements can be called *gathering*. The analogous type of migratory movements of cattle-owning peoples is called *nomadism*, from

[10] Roland B. Dixon, "Migrations, Primitive," *Encyclopedia of the Social Sciences*, New York: Macmillan, 1934, Vol. X, pp. 420-425.

[11] Numelin, *op. cit.*, pp. 180-181.

the Greek word meaning to graze. Gatherers and nomads together are termed *rangers.*

The way of life of rangers is to be on the move, and their culture is adapted to this state. Their home is temporary or portable; some Australian peoples have no word for "home" in their language. Their value system adjudges the specific hardships of their life to be good; the contempt that the desert Arab feels for the more comfortable city Arab is traditional. Although their ordinary movement is usually over a restricted area, bounded by either physical barriers or peoples able to defend their territories, rangers are presumably more likely to migrate over longer distances (apart from differences in the means of transportation) simply because they are already in motion. Whether any particular nomad people settles down and becomes agricultural does not depend merely on geography. Geography determines only whether such a shift in their way of life is possible — it is barely feasible on the steppe, for example; but even when physical circumstances permit a change, the social pattern of ranging may be too strong to be broken down. The Soviet program of settling the Kirghiz and other nomad peoples on collective farms, for example, succeeded because it was implemented by sufficient terror to overcome their opposition.[12] That is to say, ranging, like wandering, is typically conservative.

A primitive migration of an agrarian population takes place when there is a sharp disparity between the produce of the land and the number of people subsisting from it. This can come about either suddenly, as by drought or an attack of locusts, or by the steady Malthusian pressure of a growing population on land of limited area and fertility. Persons induced to migrate by such population pressure can seek another agricultural site, but in the modern era the more usual destination has been a town: the migration has ordinarily been innovating rather than conservative. The Irish immigrants to the United States in the decades following the Great Famine, for example, resolutely ignored the Homestead Act and other inducements to settle on the land; in overwhelming proportion, they moved to the cities and stayed there. Let us term such an innovating movement *flight from the land* (again, an inelegant but useful translation from the German).

To recapitulate, primitive migration may be divided as follows:

Primitive	Wandering	Wandering of peoples
		Marine wandering
	Ranging	Gathering
		Nomadism
	Flight from the land	

These are the types of migration set by ecological push and controls, usually geographical but sometimes social.

Forced and Impelled Migrations

If in primitive migrations the activating agent is ecological pressure, in forced migrations it is the state or some functionally equivalent social institution. It is useful to divide this class into *impelled* migration, when the migrants retain some power to decide whether or not to leave, and *forced* migration, when they do not have this power. Often the boundary between the two, the point at which the choice becomes nominal, may be difficult to set. Analytically, however, the distinction is clearcut, and historically it is often so. The difference is real, for example, between the Nazis' policy (roughly 1933–1938) of encouraging Jewish emigration by various anti-Semitic acts and laws, and the later policy (roughly 1938–45) of herding Jews into cattle-trains and transporting them to camps.

A second criterion by which we can delineate types of forced or impelled migration is its function, defined not by the migrant but by the activating agent. Persons may be induced to move simply to rid their homeland of them; such a migration, since it does not ordinarily bring about a change in the migrants' way of life, is analogous to conservative migration and can be subsumed under it. Others are induced to move in order that their labor power can be used elsewhere; and such a migration, which constitutes a shift in behavior patterns as well as in locale, is designated as innovating.

[12] For a documentation from two sources of divergent political views, see Rudolf Schlesinger, *The Nationalities Problem and Social Administration,* London: Routledge & Kegan Paul, 1956; Walter Kolarz, *The Peoples of the Soviet Far East,* New York: Praeger, 1954.

Four types are thus defined, as follows:

	Impelled	Forced
To be rid of migrants (conservative)	Flight	Displacement
To use migrants' labor (innovating)	Coolie trade	Slave trade

In all of human history, *flight* has been an important form of migration. Whenever a stronger people moves into a new territory, it may drive before it the weaker former occupants. The invasion of Europe during the early centuries of the Christian era thus was induced not only by the power vacuum resulting from the disintegration of the Roman Empire, but also by a series of successive pushes, originating from either the desiccation of the Central Asian steppes (Huntington) or the expansion of the Chinese empire still farther east (Teggart).[13]

Many more recent migrations have also been primarily a flight before invading armies.[14] In modern times, however, those induced to flee have often been specific groups among the population, rather than everyone occupying a particular territory. Political dissidents, of course, always were ousted when they became a danger to state security; but with the growth of nationalism ethnic as well as political homogeneity has been sought. The right of national self-determination proclaimed by the Treaty of Versailles included no provision for the minorities scattered through Central Europe; and in the interwar period the League of Nations negotiated a series of population transfers designed to eliminate national minorities from adjacent countries or, more usually, to legitimate expulsions already effected.[15] The separation of Pakistan from India, another example, was accompanied by one of the largest migrations in human history, in part induced by terrorist groups on both sides and in part arranged under official auspices.

It is useful to distinguish between two classes of those who have fled their homeland — *émigrés,* who regard their exile as temporary and live abroad for the day when they may return, and *refugees,* who intend to settle permanently in the new country. Under otherwise similar circumstances, the acculturation of the latter would presumably be much more rapid than that of persons still living spiritually in another country.

Frequently, even the pretense that the movement is voluntary has been lacking. As part of its European population policy, Nazi Germany exported Jews to camps and imported forced laborers from all occupied countries. The latter movement was a modern variant of the earlier slave-trade, but the largely successful attempt to kill off some millions of persons because of their supposed racial inferiority was something new in history. In the jargon of official bureaus, those that survived such forced migration have been termed "displaced persons," a designation that clearly implies their passive role. The forced movement itself is here called *displacement.*

The forced migrations under Soviet auspices have typically served two purposes, to remove a dissident or potentially dissident group from its home[16] and to furnish an unskilled labor

[13] Ellsworth Huntington, *Civilization and Climate,* New Haven: Yale University Press, 1951; Frederick Teggart, *Rome and China: A Study of Correlations in Historical Events,* Berkeley: University of California Press, 1939.

[14] See, for example, Eugene M. Kulischer, *Europe on the Move,* New York: Columbia University Press, 1948.

[15] Cf. Stephen P. Ladas, *The Exchange of Minorities: Bulgaria, Greece and Turkey,* New York: Macmillan, 1932, p. 721: "Both conventions [of Neuilly and Lausanne], and especially that of Lausanne, proved to be agreements confirming accomplished facts," and the Greek-Turkish exchange, while "voluntary in theory, became in fact to a great extent compulsory."

[16] For example, after Poland was divided between Nazi Germany and Communist Russia in 1939, the more than a million Poles deported to Asiatic Russia were chosen not merely on the basis of actual or alleged opposition to their country's invasion but more often as members of a large variety of occupational groups, which were defined as potentially oppositionist. "Regarded as 'anti-Soviet elements,' and so treated, were administrative officials, police, judges, lawyers, members of Parliament, prominent members of political parties, non-communist nonpolitical societies, clubs, and the Red Cross; civil servants not included above, retired military officers, officers in the reserve, priests, tradesmen, landowners, hotel and restaurant owners, clerks of the local Chambers of Commerce, and any class of persons engaged in trade or correspondence with foreign countries — the latter definition extending even to stamp collectors and Esperantists — were also deported. Many artisans, peasants, and laborers (both agricultural and industrial), were banished too, so that, in effect, no Polish element was spared." Edward J. Rozek, *Allied Wartime Diplomacy: A Pattern in Poland,* New York: Wiley, 1958, p. 39.

force in an inhospitable area. During the first two five-year plans, several million "kulaks" were removed en masse to the sites of cities-to-be, and the inhabitants of the five national units of the USSR abolished during the war were deported wholesale to forced-labor camps.[17] Such movements combine displacement with *slave trade,* or the forcible migration of laborers. While the overseas shipment of Africans during the mercantile age differed in some respects from the use of forced labor in an industrial economy, the two criteria that define the type are the same — the use of force and the supply of labor power.

The analogous form of impelled migration is termed *coolie trade.* This includes not only the movement of Asians to plantations, the most typical form, but also, for example, the migration of white indentured servants to the British colonies in the 18th century. Such migrants, while formally bound only for the period of a definite contract, very often are forced into indebtedness and thus to extend their period of service indefinitely.[18] But as in other cases of impelled and forced migration, even when the difference between historical instances becomes blurred, the analytical distinction is clear. Another important difference between slave and coolie migration is that many coolies eventually return to their homeland. The total emigration from India from 1834 to 1937, for example, has been estimated at slightly more than 30 million, but of these almost 24 million returned, leaving a net emigration over the century of only six million.[19]

Free Migration

In the types of migration discussed so far, the will of the migrants has been a relatively unimportant factor. A primitive migration results from the lack of means to satisfy basic physiological needs, and in forced (or impelled) migration the migrants are largely passive. We now consider the types in which the will of the migrants is the decisive element, that is, *free* migrations.

Overseas movements from Europe during the 19th century afford important illustrations of this class of migration. Because of the excellence of its formal analysis, Lindberg's monograph on emigration from Sweden[20] has been chosen as an example. Lindberg distinguishes three periods, each with a characteristic type of emigrant. During the first stage, beginning around 1840, emigrants came principally from the two university towns of Upsala and Lund; they were "men with a good cultural and social background, mostly young and of a romantic disposition" (p. 3). Since the risks in emigration were great and difficult to calculate, those who left tended to be adventurers or intellectuals motivated by their ideals, especially by their alienation from European society during a period of political reaction. The significance of this *pioneer* movement was not in its size, which was never large, but in the example it set: "It was this emigration that helped to break the ice and clear the way for the later emigration, which included quite different classes" (p. 7). These pioneers wrote letters home; their adventures in the new world were recounted in Swedish newspapers. Once settled in the new country, they helped finance the passage of their families or friends.

Imperceptibly, this first stage developed into the second, the period of *group migration* — the emigration, for example, of Pietist communities

[17] The Volga-German ASSR, the Kalmyk ASSR, the Chechen-Ingush ASSR, the Crimean ASSR, and the Karachayev Region were designated as "disloyal nationalities," and the major portion of the 2.8 million inhabitants were removed from their immemorial homeland. The million or so Tatars brought into Crimea to replace the deportees also proved to be unreliable, and in 1945 most of these were also deported to forced labor. See David J. Dallin and Boris I. Nicolaevsky, *Forced Labor in Soviet Russia,* New Haven: Yale University Press, 1947, pp. 274-277. According to a decree dated January 9, 1957, the survivors among five of the uprooted peoples are to be shipped back to their homes over the next several years. Even under this new policy however, the Volga Germans and the Tatars are presumably to be left in their Siberian exile (*New York Times,* February 12, 1957).

[18] See, for example, Victor Purcell, *The Chinese in Southeast Asia,* London: Oxford University Press, 1951, p. 345.

[19] Kingsley Davis, *The Population of India and Pakistan,* Princeton: Princeton University Press, 1951, p. 99.

[20] John S. Lindberg, *The Background of Swedish Emigration to the United States: An Economic and Sociological Study in the Dynamics of Migration,* Minneapolis: Universiy of Minnesota Press, 1930.

under the leadership of their pastor or another person of recognized authority. Even when not associated through their adherence to a dissident sect, emigrants banded together for mutual protection during the hazardous journey and against the wilderness and the often hostile Indians at its end. Again, the significance of this group migration lay not in its size but in the further impulse it gave. During the decade beginning in 1841, an average of only 400 persons left Sweden annually, and during the following decade, this average was still only 1,500.

Mass Migration

Free migration is always rather small,[21] for individuals strongly motivated to seek novelty or improvement are not commonplace. The most significant attribute of pioneers, as in other areas of life, is that they blaze trails that others follow, and sometimes the number who do so grows into a broad stream. Migration becomes a style, an established pattern, an example of collective behavior. Once it is well begun, the growth of such a movement is semi-automatic: so long as there are people to emigrate, the principal cause of emigration is prior emigration. Other circumstances operate as deterrents or incentives, but within this kind of attitudinal framework; all factors except population growth are important principally in terms of the established behavior. As we have already noted, when emigration has been set as a *social* pattern, it is no longer relevant to inquire concerning the *individual* motivations. For the individual is, in Lindberg's phrase, in an "unstable state of equilibrium," in which only a small impulse in either direction decides his course; hence the motives he ascribes to his emigration are either trivial or, more likely, the generalities that he thinks are expected.[22]

The development of migration as collective behavior is aptly illustrated by the Swedish case. During the decade 1861–70, when the average number of emigrants jumped to 9,300 per year, the transition to the third stage of *mass* emigration began. Transportation facilities improved: railroads connected the interior with the port cities, and the sailing ship began to be replaced by the much faster and safer steamer. While its relation to mass migration was important, this improvement in transportation facilities was not a cause; rather, it is "possible and even probable that emigration and the development of transportation were largely caused by the same forces" (p. 15, n. 17). Not only was the geographical distance cut down but also what Lindberg terms the social distance: as communities in the new country grew in size and importance, the shift from Sweden to America required less and less of a personal adjustment. Before the migrant left his homeland, he began his acculturation in an American-Swedish milieu, made up of New World letters, photographs, mementoes, knickknacks. There developed what the peasants called "America fever": in some districts, there was not a farm without some relatives in America, and from many all the

[21] As in general throughout this essay, the words used to designate the classes or types of migration are terms in common usage rather than neologisms. Since they are here more precisely defined than in most contexts, however, they denote a narrower range of meaning; thus free migration is not all unforced migration, for it is one of five rather than two classes.

[22] Hansen has pointed out that the migrant's motivation was likely to be pruned to suit the person asking for it. The official in the home country was told of material difficulties, but to cite these in America would confirm the natives' belief that the foreigner was a dangerous economic competitor. The village clergyman, should he attempt to dissuade a prospective migrant, was told that his sons were growing up without a future and becoming lazy and shiftless; but in America these moral motives would give point to the argument that immigrants were depraved. Hence, "the newcomer said, 'I came to the United States to enjoy the blessings of your marvelous government and laws,' [and] the native warmed to him and was likely to inquire whether there was not something he could do to assist him. Immigrants soon learned the magic charm of this confession of faith. They seized every opportunity to contrast the liberty of the New World with the despotism of the Old." Marcus Lee Hansen, *The Immigrant in American History,* Cambridge: Harvard University Press, 1940, pp. 77-78.

This is a good example of why public opinion polling can be deficient as a method of social — rather than social psychological — analysis. Each respondent queried replies in terms of his own norms, and for the whole sample these may differ considerably, depending on how heterogeneous the respondents are with respect to the subject of the poll. To sum up the Yes's and No's without taking into account the criteria that determined these replies is appropriate only when we are interested solely in the sum, as in an election.

children had emigrated. According to a government report that Lindberg quotes, children were "educated to emigrate," and he continues —

> When they finally arrived at a decision, they merely followed a tradition which made emigration the natural thing in a certain situation. In fact, after the imagination and fantasy had, so to speak, become "charged with America," a positive decision *not* to emigrate may have been necessary if difficulties arose. (pp. 56–57.)

The Swedes who migrated to Minnesota became farmers or small-town craftsmen or merchants. In a more general analysis, it is useful to distinguish two types of mass movement according to the nature of the destination — *settlement,* such as Lindberg described, and *urbanization,* or mass migration to a larger town or city. No distinction in principle is made here between internal and international migration, for the fundamentals of the rural-urban shift so characteristic of the modern era are generally the same whether or not the new city-dwellers cross a national border.

Conclusions

The typology developed in this paper is summarized in the attached table. Such a typology is a tool, and it is worth constructing only if it is useful. What is its utility?

This question may be answered against a perspective of the present undeveloped status of migration theory. Classifications of modern migrations tend to derive from the statistics that are collected, whether or not these have any relevance to theoretical questions. It is as if those interested in the *causes* of divorce studied this matter exclusively with data classified according to the *grounds* on which divorces are granted. Even the principal statistical differentiation, that between internal and international migration, is not necessarily of theoretical significance.[23] Similarly, when the species *migrant* is set off from the genus *traveler* by arbitrarily defining removal for a year or more as "permanent" migration, such a distinction clearly has little or no theoretical basis, and it is not even certain that it is the most convenient one that could be made.[24] The preferable procedure in any discipline is to establish our concepts and the logical relation among them, and to collect our statistics in terms of this conceptual framework. The principal purpose of the typology, then, is to offer, by such an ordering of conceptual types, a basis for the possible development of theory. "Since sound sociological interpretation inevitably *implies* some theoretic paradigm, it seems the better part of wisdom to bring it out into the open," first of all because such a paradigm "provides a compact parsimonious arrangement of the central concepts and their interrelations as these are utilized for description and analysis." [25]

Migration differs from fertility and mortality in that it cannot be analyzed, even at the outset, in terms of non-cultural, physiological factors, but must be differentiated with respect to relevant social conditions. This means that the most general statement that one makes concerning migration should be in the form of a typology, rather than a law.[26] While few today would follow Ravenstein's example by denoting their statements "laws," [27] most treatments of migratory selection still imply a comparable de-

[23] The movement westward across the United States, for example, included a swing northward to the western provinces of Canada at the turn of the century, and today American cities attract both Americans and Canadians. In both cases, one may interpret English-speaking North America as a single labor market, with the international border acting primarily as an added friction to free mobility. See Brinley Thomas, *Migration and Economy Growth: A Study of Great Britain and the Atlantic Economy* (National Institute of Economic and Social Research), London: Cambridge University Press, 1954, pp. 134-138.

[24] Thus in his recent study of British migration, Isaac found it useful to distinguish between those who intend to settle elsewhere permanently and what he termed "quasi-permanent" migrants or those who leave for a year or more but intend to return. See Julius Isaac, *British Post-War Migration* (National Institute of Economic and Social Research), Occasional Paper XVII, Cambridge University Press, 1954, p. 2.

[25] Robert K. Merton, *Social Theory and Social Structure,* Glencoe, Ill.: Free Press, 1949, p. 14. For an interesting article exemplifying the usefulness of such a typology, see Merton, "Intermarriage and the Social Structure: Fact and Theory," *Psychiatry,* 4 (August, 1941), pp. 361-374.

[26] This point is very effectively argued by Heberle, *op. cit.*

[27] E. G. Ravenstein, "The Laws of Migration," *Journal of the Royal Statistical Society,* XLVIII (June, 1885), pp. 167-235; LII (June, 1889), pp. 241-305.

gree of generality. Even the best discussions[28] typically neglect to point out that selection ranges along a continuum, from total migration to total non-migration, or that the predominance of females in rural-urban migration that Ravenstein noted must be contrasted with male predominance in, for example, India's urbanization. As we have seen, the familiar push-pull polarity implies a universal sedentary tendency, which has little empirical basis in either history or psychology. Analogously, the distinction between conservative and innovating migration challenges the usual notion that persons universally migrate in order to change their way of life.

Relation	Migratory Force	Class of Migration	Type of Migration: Conservative	Type of Migration: Innovating
Nature and man	Ecological push	Primitive	Wandering	Flight from the land
			Ranging	
State (or equivalent) and man	Migration policy	Forced	Displacement	Slave trade
		Impelled	Flight	Coolie trade
Man and his norms	Higher aspirations	Free	Group	Pioneer
Collective behavior	Social momentum	Mass	Settlement	Urbanization

Sometimes an analytical problem can be clarified by defining more precisely the two more or less synonymous terms that denote a confusion in concepts. For example, the question of whether the secular decline in the Western birth rate was due to a physiological deterioration or to new cultural standards was often not put clearly until *fecundity* was precisely distinguished from *fertility*. Several such pairs of terms are differentiated here. Whether a movement from the countryside to towns is *urbanization* or *flight from the land* can be a very important distinction; the discussion of Canada's immigration policy, for example, has largely centered on this point.[29] While the distinction between *urbanization* and *settlement* would seem to be so obvious that it can hardly be missed, one can say that the national-quota system of American immigration law is based in part at least on neglect of the implications of this differentiation.[30] The most useful distinction in the typology, perhaps, is that between *mass* migration and all other types, for it emphasizes the fact that the movement of Europeans to the New World during the 19th century, the migration with which we are most familiar, does not constitute the whole of the phenomenon. When this type of migration declined after the First World War, largely because of new political limitations imposed by both emigration and immigration countries, this was very often interpreted, not as a change to a different type, but as the end of significant human migration altogether.[31] A world in which hardly anyone dies in the place where he was born, however, can hardly be termed sedentary.

[28] See, for example, Dorothy Swaine Thomas (ed.), *Research Memorandum of Migration Differentials*, New York: Social Science Research Council, Bulletin 43, 1938; E. W. Hofstee, *Some Remarks on Selective Migration*, The Hague: Nijhoff, 1952.

[29] See Petersen, *op. cit.*, pp. 202 ff.

[30] The main source of immigration to the United States shifted from Northwest Europe to Southern and Eastern Europe at about the same time that the American economy underwent a fundamental transformation from an agrarian to an industrial base; consequently *some* of the observed differences between the "old" and the "new" immigration were due not to variations among European cultures, as is assumed in the law, but to the different rate of acculturation of peasants undergoing settlement or urbanization.

[31] The two best known statements of this point of view are W. D. Forsyth, *The Myth of Open Spaces*, Melbourne: Melbourne University Press, 1942, and Isaiah Bowman (ed.), *Limits of Land Settlement*, New York: Council on Foreign Relations, 1937.

*World Immigration Patterns**

W. S. Woytinsky • E. S. Woytinsky

Moving from place to place was the usual way of life of many primitive tribes, and faint traces of their wanderings are about all that is left to tell us of migration in prehistoric times. As long as climatic conditions and food supplies remained about the same, a tribe of hunters may have roamed within the same area century after century. When conditions proved more favorable as the tribe wandered in a certain direction — along a river, a valley or a seacoast — this was likely to become the route of migration.

History of Migration

Migration in the Ancient World

The beginning of agriculture cut down the mobility of primitive tribes but did not stop migration. As centuries passed and climatic conditions changed or lands became poorer or the supply of feed for cattle declined, a tribe abandoned a settlement and moved away, sometimes blazing a trail for others to follow, sometimes invading the territory of another tribe and forcing it to move. Thucydides wrote:

> The country now called Hellas had in ancient times no settled population. On the contrary, migrations were of frequent occurrence, the several tribes readily abandoning their homes under the pressure of superior numbers . . . Cultivating no more of their territory than the exigencies of life required, destitute of capital, never planting their land for they could not tell when an invader might come and take it all away . . . thinking that the necessities of daily sustenance could be supplied at one place as well as another, they cared little for their habitation, and consequently neither built large cities nor attained to any other form of greatness.[1]

Permanent settlements and cities developed in regions where the hunting and fishing were particularly good and the soil fertile, or in places that, for one reason or another, were not likely to be invaded. Sometimes an austere environment seemed to favor permanent settlement.

> The richest soils were always most subject to changes of masters [wrote Thucydides]. The goodness of the land . . . invited invasion. . . . Attica, from the poverty of its soil enjoying from a very remote period freedom from faction, never changed its inhabitants.[2]

The big and prosperous settlements naturally became centers toward which nomadic and half-nomadic people gravitated from surrounding regions.[3] Their polyglot crowds struck the imagination of men of smaller, more primitive tribes who occasionally came in contact with them. The biblical story of the confusion of tongues among the builders of a tower reaching to heaven may reflect the bewilderment of half-nomadic shepherds on their occasional trips to the swarming city of Babel.

Eventually some communities outgrew their food resources. To quote the Greek historian again:

> Victims of war or faction from the rest of Hellas took refuge with Athenians as a safe retreat; and . . . becoming naturalized, swelled the already large population of the city to such a height that Attica became at last too small to hold them, and they had to send out colonies to Ionia.[4]

Thus a center of immigration became the nucleus of a colonial empire. Colonies, independent in internal affairs but tied to the motherland by military agreements, played an important part in promoting the trade of Greece with

* Reprinted with permission from W. S. Woytinsky and E. S. Woytinsky, *World Population and Production.* New York: Twentieth Century Fund, 1953, pp. 67-83.

[1] **43,** pp. 3-4.

[2] **43,** p. 4.

[3] **45,** pp. 65 ff.

[4] **43,** p. 4.

the Orient and in helping radiate ancient civilization far beyond the limits of the Peloponnesus. Emigration predominated in ancient Greece as a whole and the Mediterranean basin is littered with traces of its colonial expansion.

Rome, in contrast, was an immigration center, both early in its history and at the peak of its glory. For centuries the influx of foreigners and the importation of slaves and war prisoners swelled the population, and after a few generations their descendants predominated in the plebian crowd of the great city. At the same time, Roman citizens of the old native stock were moving to the fringes of the Empire, Africa, Asia Minor, Syria and Mesopotamia, as military potentates, administrators and officials.

The Age of Great Migrations

The first millennium of the Christian era is often called the age of great migrations. That is how the period appeared to observers within the Roman Empire, exposed to successive waves of barbaric hordes and ready to collapse under their blows. There is no evidence, however, that shifts of population in that thousand years were greater, century by century and decade by decade, than in the following millennium. They were relatively smaller than the migrations and displacements in modern times.

As Eugene M. Kulischer has pointed out, when the era of great migrations ended and Europe was entering the so-called "sedentary" era, there was not a single German at the site of Berlin, not one Russian on the shores of the Moskva River, not one Hungarian in the locality of Budapest, and only a few Turkish slaves and mercenaries lived in what was to become Istanbul.[5] The white man had not yet set foot on the soil of the New World. When the "great migrations" seemed to be at an end, the shaping of the map of the world by migration was just beginning.

The best-known migrations in the Middle Ages — the invasion of Europe by the Mongols and the drives of the European Crusaders to the Near East — were predominantly military. A process more like the colonization in the ancient world was developing at that time on the eastern European plains, where the Slavs were moving slowly but steadily eastward and northward from their original settlements on the Dnieper.

Changing Character of Migration

In the march of time, the character of migration has changed. Before men invented wheel and raft, shifts were slow and usually restricted to small groups of people who moved short distances on foot or on the backs of animals. Later, in ancient Hellas and under the Roman Empire, migrants were carried farther by sailing ships and galleys or were drawn by horses.

Many centuries later, the compass opened the oceans to migrants from Europe. By the middle of the nineteenth century, steamships made the ocean the cheapest thoroughfare for passengers and goods, and a new era in the history of migration began. Population shifts in antiquity and the Middle Ages left a deep imprint on the composition of races, languages, religions and mores of the world, but settlement of vast areas of our planet did not begin until the newer means of transportation made possible mass migrations over long distances.

Major Currents of Migration in Modern Times

Seven major currents are evident in migrations since the beginning of the sixteenth century, five between, and two within, nations. They are (1) emigration from Europe to North America; (2) emigration to South America and the Caribbean; (3) emigration to South Africa, Australia and Australasia; (4) importation of slaves from Africa to the New World; (5) population shifts in the Far East, mainly from China and India to neighboring countries, such as Africa and Australasia; (6) intracontinental migration in North America, from the Atlantic coast westward; and (7) internal migration in Russia eastward. (See Figure 1.)

International Shifts of Population

Among the five great currents of international migration in modern times the most important have been those from Europe to the New World, beginning soon after its discovery, in the sixteenth century.

[5] **33**, p. 8.

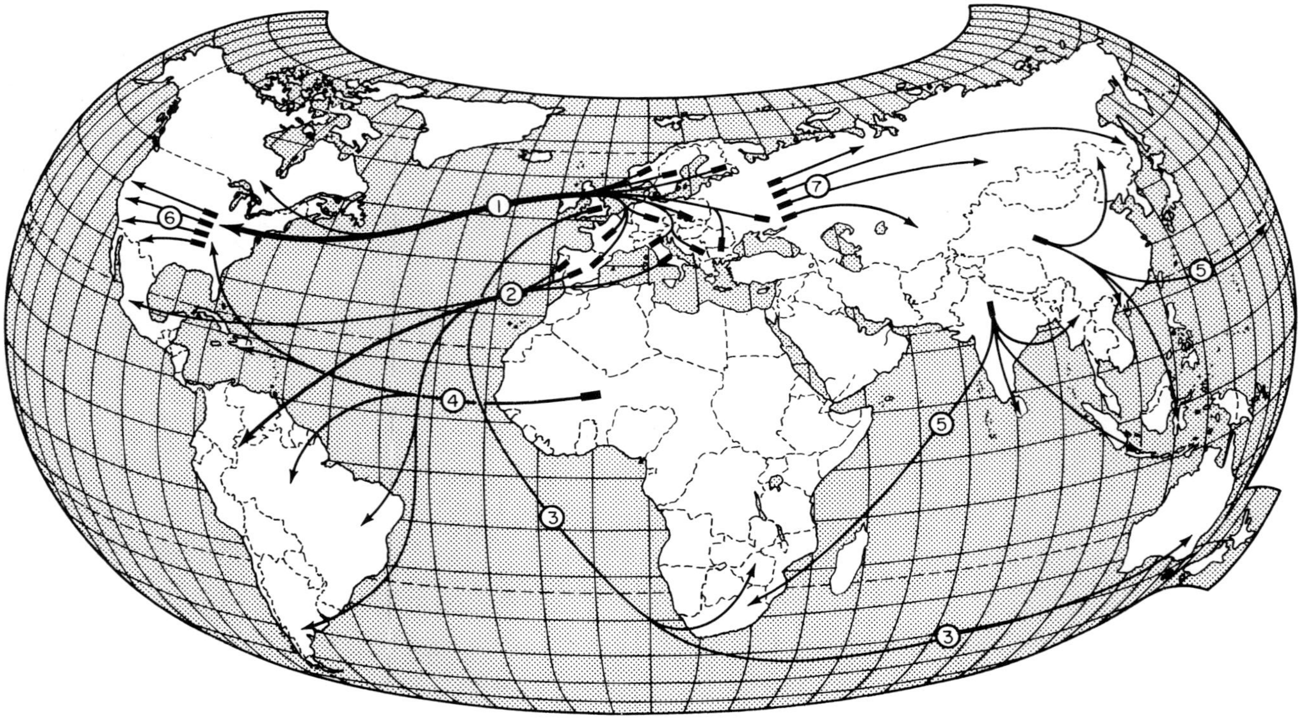

FIGURE 1

Intercontinental migration: Principal currents in modern times.

The main currents of intercontinental migration since the beginning of the sixteenth century have been: (1) from all parts of Europe to North America; (2) from Latin countries of Europe to Middle and South America; (3) from Great Britain to Africa and Australia; (4) import of slaves from Africa to America. Another current (5), partly intercontinental, partly intracontinental, has flowed from China and India. The most important internal migration has been (6) westward in the United States and (7) eastward in Russia.

At first only fringes of the Americas were known and accessible to Europe. White men first learned to know the Caribbean — the islands of Hispaniola, Cuba and Jamaica, the peninsula of Florida, the eastern coast of South America. They had only vague ideas of what lay northward and westward and until the end of the sixteenth century, men on the other side of the Atlantic continued to regard the Americas merely as new islands located somewhere between Hispaniola and India.

European migration, directed first to the Caribbean and South America, gradually fanned northward. As time went on, the flow toward North America became increasingly important, but the importance of South America as a goal of European migration increased after World War I.

From Europe to North America

Nearly 45 million persons emigrated from various parts of Europe to North America between the beginning of the seventeenth century and the outbreak of World War II. Some of them returned to their old homes, but more than 25 million settled permanently in the areas now occupied by the United States and Canada. Today they account for nearly 150 million persons of European stock in these countries.

From Europe to Central and South America

Approximately 20 million Europeans, predominantly Spaniards, Portuguese and Italians, have emigrated to Middle and South America since the beginning of the sixteenth century. Some 2 million of them returned to Europe. Of those who remained, some intermingled with native Indians and imported Negroes, so that there are now close to 50 million persons in Latin America of European or partly European origin.

From Europe to Africa and Oceania

Colonization of Africa and Oceania, primarily by the British and the Dutch, has given origin to approximately 17 million persons of European stock among the 210 million who now people those continents and their islands. Together these three streams of intercontinental migration propagated European stock and European civilization over the world.

Decimation of the aboriginal population often accompanied settlement of the New World. Apart from massacres during the conquest, native populations dwindled in America, Australia and Australasia, not primarily because of oppression by the invaders, but, rather, as a result of epidemic diseases they brought with them. Ailments endemic and relatively benign in Europe became scourges among the previously unexposed natives. Death outran the white man and emptied the land for him.[6] In good measure, occupation of the New World has been replacement of its relatively sparse native population by people of European and mixed stock.

From Africa to the Americas

This flow of intercontinental migration brought persons of African stock into regions of America settled and dominated by immigrants from Europe.

The slave trade began in the sixteenth century, reached its peak at the end of the eighteenth, and continued illegally until the middle of the nineteenth. We do not know exactly how many slaves were imported into the Americas. Carr-Saunders believes that approximately 20 million Africans were taken from their homes to be sold as slaves.[7] Some died before they reached the market, and some were shipped to Asia and Europe.

The number of Negro slaves imported into the Americas is estimated at nearly 15 million: less than a million in the sixteenth century, almost 3 million in the seventeenth, 7 million in the eighteenth, and 4 million in the nineteenth.[8] The main slave markets in the Western Hemisphere were in South America and the Caribbean. Gunnar Myrdal has estimated that less than a million Negro slaves were ever imported — directly from Africa or from the West Indies — into the United States and areas that later became part of the United States.[9]

Importation of slaves had a deep impact on the early colonial economy, played a tragic role in the split between South and North in the United States, and left the country with the

[6] **37**, p. 19.
[7] **21**, p. 48.
[8] **34**, p. 12.
[9] **34**, p. 119.

Negro problem of today. It has also had a deep influence on the racial composition of the population of the Western Hemisphere.

From China and India

Migration from China had become noticeable by the beginning of the seventeenth century. In 1718, China passed a law prohibiting emigration and ordering all Chinese residing abroad to return. After 1840, emigration from China was resumed, mainly to other Asiatic countries. In 1922 the number of Chinese residing abroad was estimated at 8.2 million — 2.3 million in Formosa, 1.8 million in Java, 1.5 million in Siam, 1.1 million in the Straits Settlements, Hong Kong, Annam and Burma, 1.0 million in the East Indies, half a million in other countries.[10] In 1948 the Chinese government issued a new estimate giving the total number of Chinese abroad as 9.5 million: 9.1 million in Asia, more than 200,000 in America, 54,000 in Europe, 64,000 in Oceania, 15,000 in Africa.[11]

Like the Chinese, most emigrants from India have settled within the confines of Asia. In 1944-45 the number of Indians abroad was estimated at more than 3.7 million: more than a million in Burma, about 750,000 in Ceylon, as many in British Malaya, some 300,000 on the island of Mauritius, 100,000 in Fiji.[12] The largest settlements of Indians outside Asia are in Trinidad and British Guiana (300,000) and in British colonies in Africa — Kenya, Tanganyika, Uganda and Zanzibar (about 100,000).

INTERNAL SHIFTS OF POPULATION

The population shifts continually within many countries, from primarily agricultural areas toward industrial centers, for example, or from densely settled to sparsely populated areas. Often these shifts have a clear geographical pattern, like the westward migration in Germany or the northward migration in Italy. Such movements are usually of only local significance, but two currents of intranational migration have played an important role in the history of mankind.

[10] **23**, p. 149; **21**, p. 57.
[11] **4**, September 1949, p. 321.
[12] **19**, pp. 921-22.

Internal Migration in the United States

In North America, migration was directed inland from the ports along the Atlantic coast. Step by step, it carried the early settlers beyond the Appalachian ridge to the Mississippi valley and beyond it, until the whole expanse between the Atlantic and Pacific was settled. Thus the colonies clustered along the seashore were transformed into a nation spanning a continent. Without intracontinental migration, the capacity of the New World to absorb immigrants would have been exhausted long ago.

Internal Migration in Russia

Internal migration in Russia, combined with the rapid growth of population and the open spaces around the original settlements, has been instrumental in developing the country from a handful of petty princedoms on the western fringe of the east European plain into one of the greatest powers in the world.

INTERCONTINENTAL MIGRATION

The composition of the successive waves of newcomers who carried European stock and ways of life to the Western Hemisphere changed as time went on. Emigration from Europe to Middle and South America was distinctly different from that to North America, and immigration to North America after the revolutionary wars was different from that in the preceding period.

IMMIGRATION INTO THE AMERICAS

BEFORE 1800

The first white men who found their way to the Western Hemisphere across the Atlantic were probably fishermen and hunters from the Scandinavian countries who stayed temporarily on Newfoundland and briefly ventured onto the mainland. They had no desire to settle and left few traces of their stay in America. A wholly different situation arose when, after Columbus' discovery of the Caribbean in 1492 and especially after Cortez' conquest of Mexico in 1521 and Pizarro's seizure of Peru in 1533, swarms of adventurers and missionaries descended on the New World and took possession of it.

Adventurers and Spoilsmen: Latin America

All the unexplored regions of South America, as well as the Caribbean, Mexico and Peru, became spoils of the Spanish crown early in the sixteenth century, and the population was added to the flocks of the Catholic Church. At that time neither Spain nor Portugal was looking for new land to colonize, for they could not spare enough men to settle it. Their aim was to get gold, rare spices and other valuable products from these lands, using as few men as possible. The conquered territory was, therefore, closed to settlers. King's subjects were admitted into crown possessions, individually or in groups, only by special permission or special order. Early Spanish-Portuguese settlers in this region represented either the king's armed forces or the Catholic Church. Civil administration was divided between the two. In addition, a few craftsmen were sent overseas to make the life of the occupation forces more comfortable.

Later, Spain and Portugal adopted the custom of rewarding noblemen for services to the crown by title to land in America. This practice was in line with customs in feudal Europe, and it is natural that the tracts of land carved out in the wilderness had to be large enough to warrant the venture of sailing over the ocean to take possession of them. The new landowners came with their families and servants, often accompanied by armed guards, carpenters, bricklayers and other craftsmen. As time went on, cathedrals and cloisters were erected, old native cities were reshaped in a mixture of Indian and Spanish patterns, and in three centuries, a huge overseas empire had been built.

The number of persons who moved from Europe to the Caribbean and South America in the early colonization period is not known. It has been estimated that by 1570, when Spain's colonial administration was fairly well established, about 100,000 Spaniards and Portuguese were ruling over an Indian population of about 10 million.

Since most of the European settlers in South and Central America were adventurer-soldiers without families, marriage with native women became usual. Thus the foundation was laid for the present national and racial composition of the local population. At the beginning of the nineteenth century, the number of persons of unmixed European blood (mainly Spainish or Portuguese) was insignificant; a considerable part of the population was mixed — predominantly Indian in blood, Spanish or Portuguese in language, and Roman Catholic in religion.

Colonists and Settlers: North America

Early immigration into North America was very different. Colonization prevailed, if not from the day when the first French, British and Dutch settlers landed, then at least from the beginning of the eighteenth century.

> New England was not settled originally because of agricultural attractions, nor did agriculture become the chief interest of the colonists. . . . Lack of sufficient areas of good soil and a climate marked by a brief growing season and little summer heat placed [New England] at a disadvantage with the colonies farther south. . . . It was to the middle colonies that the greatest number of people came who were by birth and training tillers of the soil. . . . From all Northwestern Europe, farmers poured into the [middle] colonies during the eighteenth century, settling from the Mohawk Valley to Pennsylvania and in the back country of Maryland.[13]

European settlements in North America were somewhat like the colonies in the ancient world. Apart from their search for religious and political freedom, colonists were lured by the vision of free land. Their goal was to develop self-supporting communities on virgin soil. This objective eventually brought them into conflict with the Indians after both groups had discovered that there was not enough land for all and that farming in the European style was incompatible with the way of life of tribes of hunters.

When each community had to rely on itself for survival, each newcomer was an asset as an additional worker and also as an additional fighter. Unlike the exploitation colonies in South America, the North American settlements needed more and still more men. Hence their

[13] **38**, pp. 163-65.

TABLE 1

Intercontinental Migration Before 1933 (Thousands)

Emigration (1846–1932)		Immigration (1821–1932)	
Country of Emigration	Emigrants	Country of Immigration	Immigrants
Total	53,450	Total	59,187
Europe	51,696	The Americas	53,826
British Isles[a]	18,083	United States	34,244
Sweden	1,203	Canada and Newfoundland	5,226
Norway	854	Mexico (1911–36)	226
Finland (1871–1934)	371	Cuba	857
Denmark	387	Brazil	4,431
France	519	Uruguay	713
Belgium	193	Paraguay	26
Netherlands	224	Argentina	6,405
Germany	4,889	British West Indies	1,587
Austria-Hungary[b]	5,196	Guadeloupe	42
Switzerland	332	Dutch Guiana	69
Spain	4,653		
Portugal	1,805	Non-American countries	5,361
Italy	10,092	Philippines	90
Russia (USSR) (1846–1924)	2,253	South Africa	852
Poland (1920–34)	642	Mauritius	573
		Seychelles	12
Non-European countries	1,756	Australia	2,913
British India	1,194	New Zealand	594
Japan	518	Hawaii	216
Cape Verde	30	Other islands	111
St. Helena	12		

Source: **21**, p. 49. Reprinted by permission of the Clarendon Press.
a. Includes Malta.
b. Since 1919, Austria, Hungary and Czechoslovakia.

policy of open gates for immigrants of all races, languages and faiths.

Benjamin Franklin estimated that North America held a million persons of British origin in 1751. Carr-Saunders believed that perhaps 250,000 persons left the British Isles for the New World in the seventeenth century and 1.5 million in the eighteenth,[14] figures that agree fairly well with Franklin's for the middle of the eighteenth century. The number of immigrants from Germany before 1800 is estimated at 200,000,[15] and the number from the Netherlands and France combined may have been about the same. Net immigration from Europe into America north of the Rio Grande may have totaled about 2 million by 1800.

INTERCONTINENTAL MIGRATION AFTER 1800

In the second half of the eighteenth century North America became the goal of overseas migration from Europe.[16] Each year from 10,000 to 15,000 colonists crossed the North Atlantic, while only an insignificant number journeyed to South America and the Caribbean. During the clash between the rebellious American colonies and Great Britain, European emi-

[14] **21**, p. 47.
[15] **21**, p. 47.
[16] Cf. **48**, pp. 113 ff.

gration almost ceased. It was resumed on a small scale at the beginning of the nineteenth century and skyrocketed after the end of the Napoleonic wars. In addition to the main flow toward North America, Europeans then were emigrating to South America, South Africa and Australia.

The Great Migration from Europe

In all, at least 65 million emigrants left Europe between 1820 and 1930, and 2 million between 1930 and 1950. More specifically, 16 European countries recorded some 51.7 million emigrants from 1846 to 1932. On the receiving side, American countries listed 53.8 million immigrants between 1821 and 1932, and Australia, New Zealand, South Africa and other non-American areas recorded 5.4 million.[17] (See Table 1.) Among the 67 million emigrants who crossed the ocean from 1800 to 1950, approximately 60 million were Europeans and, of these, some 40 million came to the United States.[18]

Migration statistics after 1932 are not strictly comparable with those in Table 1, because of changes in classification and in routes of intercontinental migration. Moreover, they would not be very significant for countries that were predominantly emigration countries before 1932 but in recent years have had more immigrants than emigrants, such as the United Kingdom, Germany, Belgium, Italy and Sweden.

European emigration to America declined in the 1930's during the depression in the United States and practically ceased during World War II. From 1933 to 1947 approximately 2 million emigrants left European ports and approximately 1.5 million persons returned to their motherland. The Netherlands ranked first in number of emigrants (nearly 600,000) but had an almost equal number of immigrants (about 580,000).[19] The era of great migration from Europe to the New World has ended, and we can now take stock of its results.

During the past 130 years, the United States, Canada, Argentina and Australia have admitted immigrants equivalent to about 40 per cent of the present population of each of these countries. The comparable figure for Brazil is about 10 per cent, for New Zealand 35 per cent, for the Union of South Africa 5 per cent. (See Figure 2.)

Variations in the Volume of Migration

The volume of migration has varied widely, over the past century, from decade to decade and from year to year. The principal currents of intercontinental migration varied by five-year periods as follows (annual average, in thousands):[20]

	Citizens Leaving Europe	*Aliens Entering the Americas*
1846-50	256	299
1851-55	342	397
1856-60	201	213
1861-65	223	207
1866-70	346	405
1871-75	372	410
1876-80	283	260
1881-85	686	650
1886-90	779	709
1891-95	729	650
1896-1900	602	528
1901-05	1,053	1,040
1906-10	1,389	1,482
1911-15	1,345	1,403
1916-20	431	375
1921-25	800	844
1926-30	552	726
1931-35	189	111
1936-40	148	116
1941-45	57	32

[17] The first statistical records on emigration date from 1815 (Great Britain); those on immigration, from 1820 (United States). More or less comprehensive international surveys of immigration begin with 1822; of emigration, with 1846. A detailed analysis of available statistics on international migration, with occasional estimates for missing items, has been prepared by the National Bureau of Economic Research, under the direction of Walter F. Wilcox, in cooperation with the International Labor Office and a score of international experts (47). Carr-Saunders has extended this estimate to 1932 (21). Cf. **47**, pp. 111 ff.

[18] The last figure is appreciably higher than that shown in Table 1 (34.2 million, for the period 1821-1932) because, in addition to immigrants arriving directly from Europe, the United States has admitted several million immigrants of European stock from Canada and other American countries.

[19] Intercontinental and continental migrations combined.

[20] For 1846-1924, **47**, Vol. I, pp. 168 and 230-31; for 1925-45, **3**, 1945-46, pp. 233-44; and **4**.

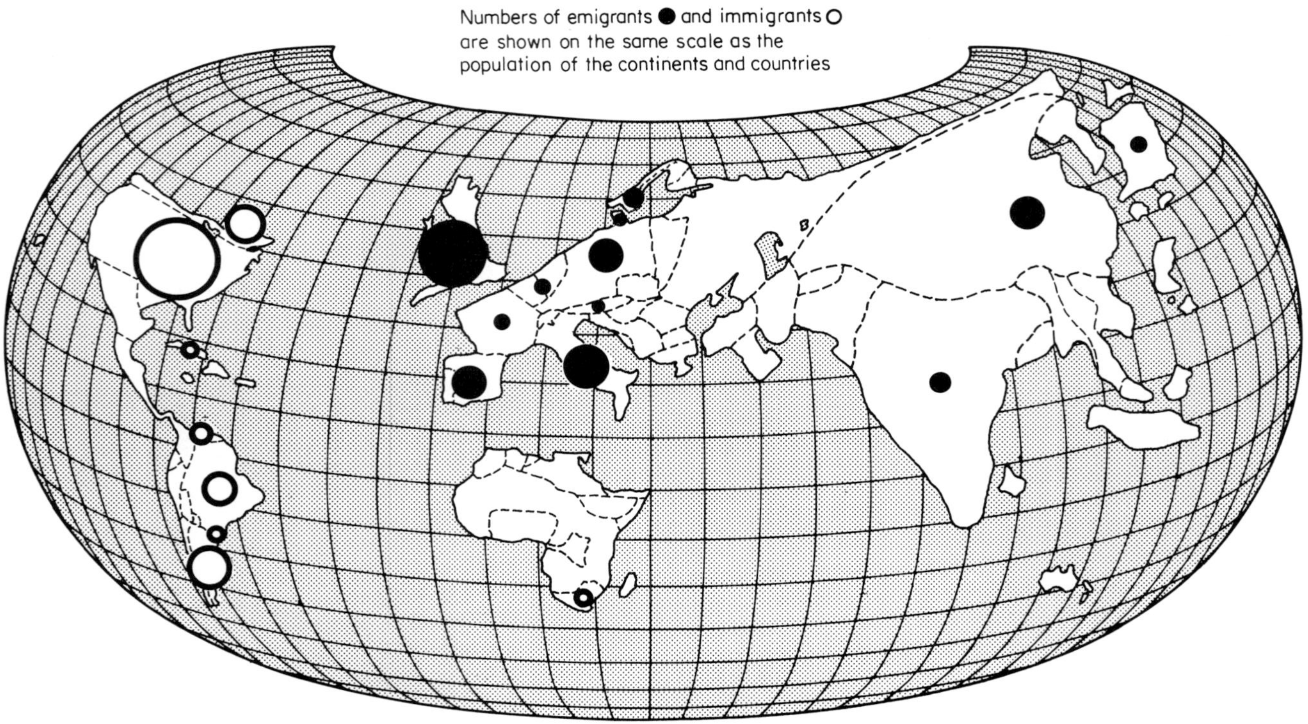
Numbers of emigrants ● and immigrants ○
are shown on the same scale as the
population of the continents and countries

FIGURE 2

Intercontinental migration: Total number of emigrants and immigrants, 1846–1945, as compared with present population of major emigration and immigration countries.

Continents and countries are shown on this map on a scale proportionate to their population about 1950, so that such thinly populated regions as Canada, Siberia, Australia and central Africa appear smaller than on conventional maps, densely populated regions of the Far East and western and central Europe larger. The numbers of migrants who have left or entered a country since the middle of the nineteenth century are shown on the same scale as the 1940 population. The circle in central Europe refers to Germany, Austria-Hungary and countries that were part of the Austro-Hungarian Empire before World War I.

The figure shows that the number of emigrants who left the British Isles from 1846 to 1945 amounted to about 40 percent of the 1940 population of that area (including Ireland). The ratio of the total number to its population in 1940 is equally high for immigrants accepted by the United States.

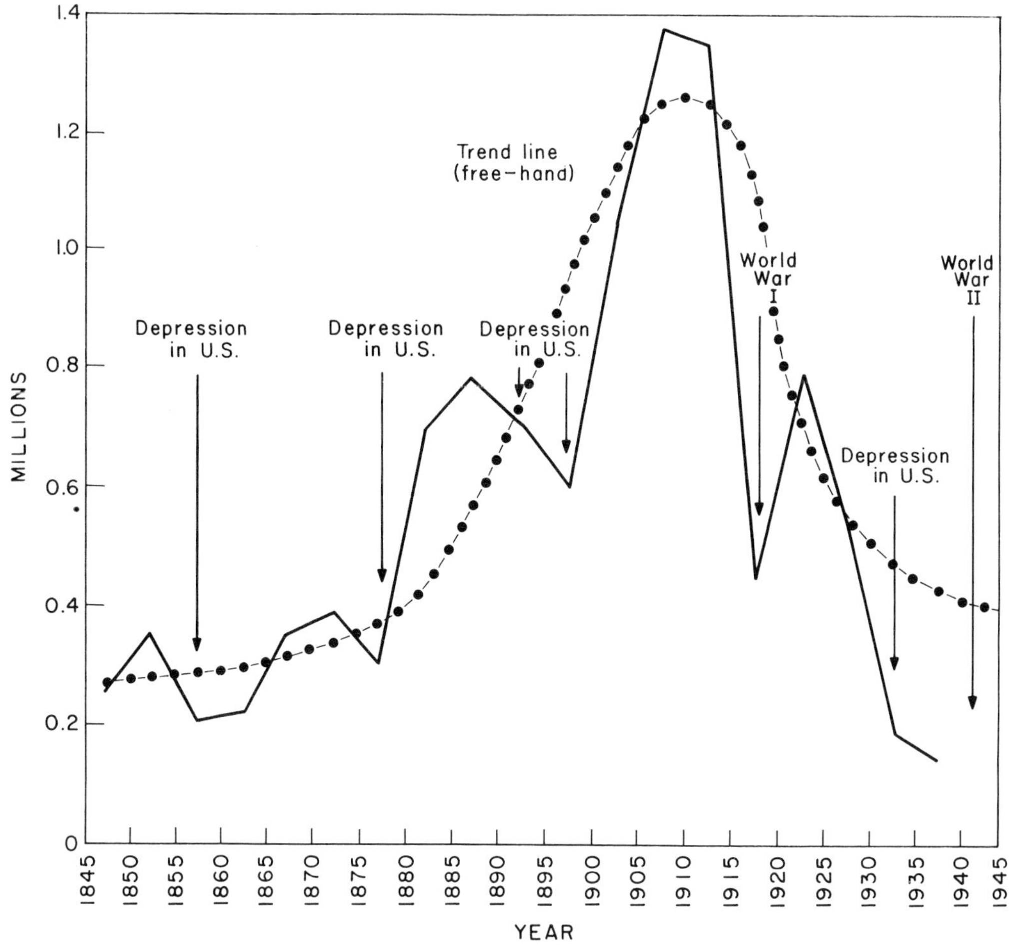

FIGURE 3

Intercontinental migration: Average annual number of emigrants from Europe in each five-year period, 1846–1945.

Emigration from Europe grew slowly until the middle of the 1870's, when steamships replaced sailing vessels, and then increased rapidly for forty years to a peak just before World War I. Temporary setbacks were due mainly to business slumps in the United States. The decline after World War I was caused by restrictive policies of the immigration countries.

Migration increased after the middle of the nineteenth century, reached a peak shortly before the outbreak of World War I, and had almost ceased by the beginning of World War II. This main movement has been overlapped by a series of shorter waves, the most significant of which were the almost complete cessation of migration in 1914-18 and the resumption immediately after World War I. (See Figure 3.)

Ups and downs in emigration in the early part of the past century resulted from economic difficulties and social turmoil in European countries. The depression in Great Britain, the potato famine in Ireland, and revolutionary upheavals in Germany were responsible for mass emigration from these countries in the 1840's. In the second half of the century, the difficult situation of farmers all over Europe, due partly to the competition of foreign grain, induced millions of farmers and farm laborers to go overseas.

The rapid increase in emigration after 1870 was due largely to progress in transportation. After the steamship replaced the sailing vessel, overseas travel became easier and less expensive. Moreover, steamship companies carried on an intensive drive to sell the golden dream of the New World to European farmers, miners and factory workers. The steep rise in immigrants coming into the United States in the last quarter of the nineteenth century was due partly to this advertising campaign and partly to the direct recruitment of European workers by agents of American industrial corporations. Shortage of labor was the main — and perhaps the only — bottleneck in the rapid economic growth of the country when it was putting the plow to the Great Plains and building railroads.

The long-range upward trend in European emigration (dotted line in Figure 3 was broken by setbacks in the late 1850's, in the 1870's and in the 1890's: world migration shrank whenever business slumped seriously in the United States. The decisive drop in the late 1920's was due largely to change in the immigration policy of the United States.

Countries of Origin and Destination

Until 1890, northwestern Europe, especially Great Britain, accounted for more than half of all intercontinental migration. After that time the flow from the Latin countries and central and eastern Europe increased steadily. (See Table 2.) In the 1870's nearly two thirds of all Euro-

TABLE 2

Intercontinental Migration: Number of Emigrants from Europe and Asia, by Country, in Each Decade, 1846–1950 (Thousands)

Country of Emigration[a]	1846–50	1851–60	1861–70	1871–80	1881–90	1891–1900	1901–10	1911–20	1921–30	1931–40	1941–50
Total	477	2,362	2,839	3,264	7,145	6,397	11,591	7,813	6,753	1,914	...
Great Britain[b]	199	1,313	1,572	1,674	2,559	1,743	2,841	2,452	1,984	252	750
Ireland	...	...	...	175	700	406	309	135	167	10	12
Sweden	2	17	122	103	327	205	224	86	107	8	19
Norway	12	36	98	85	187	95	191	62	87	6	11
Finland	...	...	...	...	26	59	159	67	73	3	24
Denmark	...	...	8	39	82	51	73	52	64	100	133[c]
France	11	27	36	66	119	51	53	32	4	5	...
Belgium	1	1	2	2	25	22	43	28	17	16	112
Netherlands	12	16	20	17	52	24	28	22	32	...	318[d]
Germany	183	622	634	626	1,342	527	274	91	721	124	...
Austria-Hungary[e]	2	31	40	111	436	724	2,342	788	357	57	24
Switzerland	...	6	15	36	85	35	37	31	50	47	21[d]
Spain	...	3	7	13	572	791	1,091	1,306	560	132	45[c]
Portugal	...	45	79	131	185	266	324	402	995	108	40
Italy	...	5	27	168	992	1,580	3,615	2,194	1,370	235	120[c]
Russia	...	...	...	58	288	481	911	420	80[f]	...	...
Poland	...	...	...	...	...	90	189	183	458	160	...
India	55	242	179	189	156	170	164	56	5	138	182
Japan	...	...	...	...	...	54	132	144	122	91	...

Sources: For 1846-1924, **47**, Vol. 1, pp. 230-31; for 1925-40, **3**, various years; for 1941-50, **1**, various years.

a. Countries are arrayed by type of emigration.

b. Includes Malta and, since 1911, North Ireland.

c. Incomplete.

d. Includes continental and temporary migration.

e. Since 1919, Austria, Hungary and Czechoslovakia.

f. Estonia and Lithuania.

TABLE 3

Intercontinental Migration: Distribution of Emigrants from Europe, by Area, in Each Decade, 1871–1930 (Per Cent)

Area	1871–80	1881–90	1891–1900	1901–10	1911–20	1921–30
Total	100.0	100.0	100.0	100.0	100.0	100.0
Northwestern Europe	65.4	51.1	37.2	30.9	35.2	35.6
Central Europe	23.4	23.4	18.0	20.9	10.9	15.8
Latin countries	9.4	21.9	36.9	39.6	46.7	41.1
Russia and Poland	1.8	3.6	8.0	8.6	7.2	7.5

Source: Derived from Table 2.

pean emigrants came from northwestern Europe; in the 1880's about half; in 1901-30, a third. The share of the Latin countries increased from less than 10 per cent in the 1870's to more than 40 per cent in the period 1911-30. (See Table 3; cf. Figure 4.)

The change was due essentially to economic and demographic trends in emigration countries — decline in birth rates and increase in industrialization in northwestern Europe, on the one hand, and pressure of growing population and distress of farmers in southeastern Europe, on the other.

The new migrants differed from the old not only in origin and language but also in occupation and educational attainment. Skilled workers

TABLE 4

Intercontinental Migration: Number of Immigrants Entering Selected Countries in Each Decade 1846–1940, and 1941–48 (Thousands)

Country of Immigration	1846–50	1851–60	1861–70	1871–80	1881–90	1891–1900	1901–10	1911–20	1921–30	1931–40	1941–48
Total[a]	1,588	3,394	3,372	3,987	7,518	6,423	14,939	11,113	8,709	1,885	...
United States[b]	1,251	2,598	2,315	2,812	5,247	3,688	8,795	5,736	4,107	528	662
Canada	246	310	290	220	359	237	1,143	1,055	992	80	338
Mexico	...	...	...	...	...	...	...	107	74	96	14
British West Indies	51	73	101	98	66	61	107	459	129	...	...
Cuba	...	6	13	...	...	...	243	367	213	10	...
Brazil	5	122	98	229	531	1,144	689	792	834	283	...
Uruguay	...	...	85	112	140	90	21	57	79	53	...
Argentina	...	67	113	261	841	648	1,764	1,205	1,311	310	...
Philippines	...	...	...	...	...	...	...	55	31	...	...
Australia	...	...	116	72	213	416	1,516	902	562	103	153
New Zealand	...	33	69	145	65	35	89	91	108	18	39
Hawaii	...	...	...	...	...	...	...	85	49	...	...
Other islands	...	...	...	...	14	15	29	22	4	26	...
Union of South Africa	...	...	...	...	...	...	...	71	101	62	83
Other territories in Africa	35	185	73	38	42	89	480	109	15	376	...

Sources: For the United States, **10**, various years, other countries: for 1846-1924, **47**, Vol. 1, pp. 236-37; for 1925-40, **3**, various years; for 1941-48, **1**, various years.

a. Because of different figures for the United States, the totals in this table differ from those shown in **47**, Vol. 1, pp. 236-37.

b. Includes immigration from Canada and Mexico.

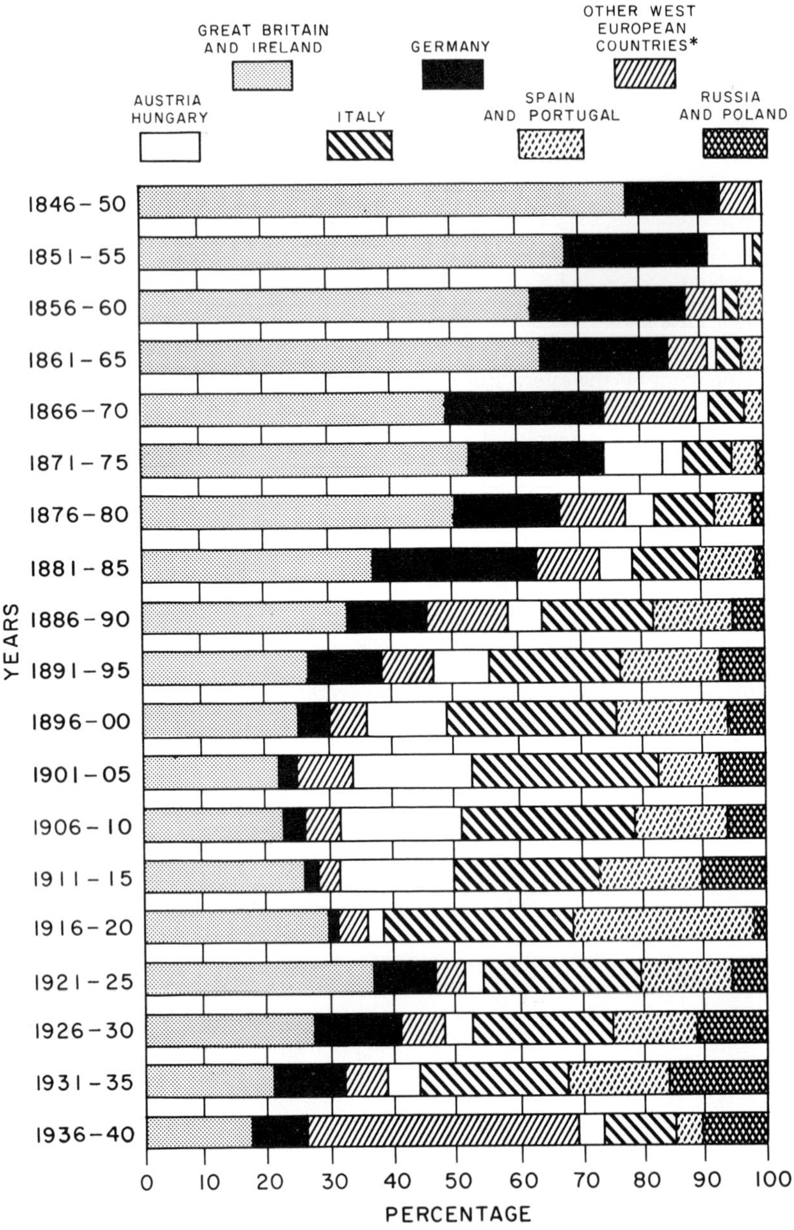

*SWEDEN, NORWAY, FINLAND, DENMARK, FRANCE, BELGIUM, NETHERLANDS, AND SWITZERLAND

FIGURE 4

Intercontinental migration: Distribution of emigrants from Europe by country of origin in each five-year period, 1846–1940.

Until the middle of the 1880's, Great Britain, including Ireland, ranked first among emigration countries, and Germany held second place. By the turn of the century the number of emigrants from Latin and Slavic countries exceeded the number from Great Britain and Germany. (Cf. Table 2.)

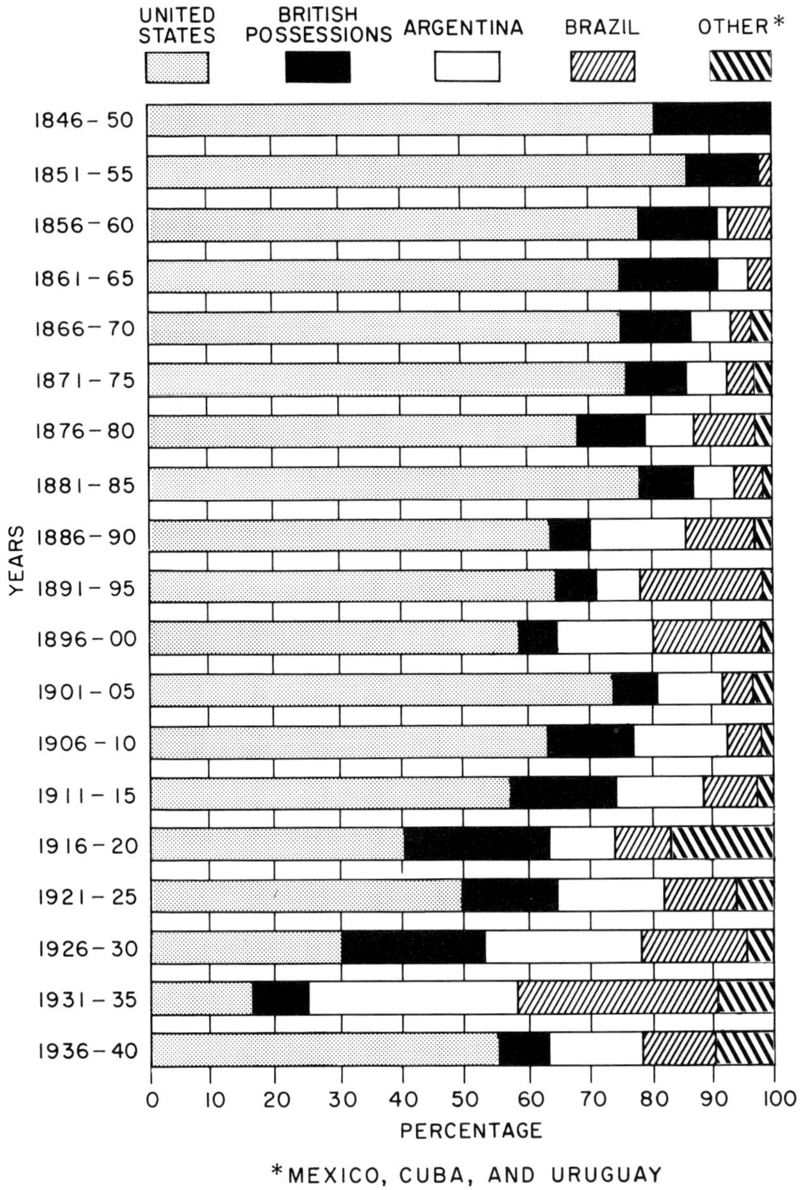

FIGURE 5

Intercontinental migration: Distribution of immigrants to the Americas by country of destination in each five-year period, 1846–1940.

Before World War I the United States absorbed more than half of all immigration from Europe into the Americas. Since the early 1920's its share has declined as a result of restrictions on immigration. (See Table 4.)

and craftsmen had predominated among emigrants from Great Britain and Germany, which were then more highly industralized than the United States. In contrast, the Latin countries — Italy, Spain and Portugal — and the Slavic provinces of Austria-Hungary sent abroad mainly landless farmers, farm laborers and unskilled workers. In this period, however, not all farmers and farm laborers came to America to till the soil. Opportunities for settlement on free land in the New World were shrinking rapidly, but this decline was more than offset by the expansion of American industry. The open frontier for many emigrants arriving in the United States lay a few blocks from New York harbor rather than on the fringes of plowland in the West. For many Europeans, crossing the Atlantic meant a shift from farm to factory.

Emigration from Spain and Portugal was directed mainly toward Argentina and Brazil. Nineteenth-century Italian emigrants went in almost equal numbers to these two countries and the United States: from 1861 to 1900 each country received about a million. From 1901 to 1921 the main goal of Italian emigration was the United States, and then the flow again turned to Latin America.[21] The United States received about 70 per cent of all intercontinental migrants during 1851-90; its share declined to 60 per cent during 1891-1910, 50 per cent during 1911-30, and 20 per cent during 1931-40. In the last decade before World War II, Brazil and Argentina became the promised land. (See Table 4; cf. Figure 5.)

REFERENCES

1. United Nations, *Demographic Yearbook*, New York.
2. ———, Conciliation Commission for Palestine, *Final Report of the United Nations Economic Survey Mission for the Middle East*, Part I, Final Report and Appendices, New York, December 1949.
3. International Labor Office, *Year Book of Labour Statistics*, Montreal.
4. ———, *International Labour Review*, Geneva.
5. ———, Preliminary Migration Conference, Geneva, April–May 1950, *Organization of Migration Movements and Obstacles to the International Mobility of Manpower*, Working Paper submitted by the Italian Government.
6. International Union for the Scientific Study of Population, "Cultural Assimilation of Immigration," supplement to *Population Studies*, Vol. III, Cambridge University Press, London, 1950.
7. Department of Commerce, Bureau of the Census, Fifteenth Census of the United States (1930), *Population*, Vol. II, 1933.
8. ———, ———, Sixteenth Census of the United States (1940), *Population*, Vol. II, 1943.
9. ———, ———, Sixteenth Census of the United States (1940), *Population, Internal Migration, 1935–1940*, 1946.
10. ———, ———, *Statistical Abstract of the United States.*
11. ———, ———, *Current Population Reports — Population Characteristics*, "Internal Migration in the United States, April 1940 to April 1947," Series P-20, No. 14, April 15, 1948.
12. ———, ———, *Interstate Migration and Other Population Changes, 1940 to 1943*, Series P-44, No. 17, August 28, 1944.
13. Department of Justice, Immigration and Naturalization Service, *Annual Reports.*
14. National Resources Committee, *The Problems of a Changing Population*, Report of the Committee on Population Problems, May 1938.
15. CHINA. National Government, *Crop Reports*, National Agricultural Research Bureau, Nanking.
16. FRANCE. Statistique Générale, *Mouvements Migratoires entre la France et l'Étranger*, by Henri Bunle, Paris, 1943.
17. Deutsches Institut für Wirtschaftsforschung, *Die Deutsche Wirtschaft. Zwei Jahre nach dem Zusammenbruch*, Berlin, 1947.
18. Länderrat des Amerikanischen Besetzungsgebiets, *Statistisches Handbuch von Deutschland, 1928–1944*, Munich, 1949.
19. INDIA. *Indian Year-Book*, a Statistical and Historical Annual of the Indian Empire, 1944–1945, Times of India Press, Bombay.
20. Bowman, Isaiah, *The Pioneer Fringe* (Special Publication No. 13), American Geographical Society, New York, 1931.
21. Carr-Saunders, Alexander M., *World Population: Past Growth and Present Trends*, Oxford University Press, London, 1936.
22. Edding, Friedrich, Hornschu, Hans-Erich, and Wander, Hilde, *Das Deutsche Flüchtlingsproblem*, Institut für Weltwirtschaft an der Universität Kiel, 1949.
23. Ferenczi, Irme, "International Migration Statistics," in *International Migrations*, Vol. I, *Statistics*, Walter F. Wilcox (Ed.), National Bureau of Economic Research, New York, 1929.
24. Forsyth, William D., *The Myth of the Open Spaces*, Melbourne University Press, Melbourne, 1942.
25. Friis, Herman R., *A Series of Population Maps of*

[21] **47**, p. 271.

the Colonies and the United States, 1625–1790 (Mimeographed Publication No. 3), American Geographical Society, New York, 1940.

26. Hutchinson, Edward P., *Current Problems of Immigration Policy*, American Enterprise Association, Washington, 1949.
27. ———, "The Present Status of Our Immigration Laws and Policy," *Milbank Memorial Fund Quarterly*, April 1947.
28. Isaac, Julius, "European Migration Potential and Prospects," *Population Studies*, March 1949.
29. Joerg, W. L. G. (Ed.), *Pioneer Settlement*, American Geographical Society, New York, 1932.
30. Kimble, George H. T., *The World's Open Spaces*, T. Nelson and Sons, New York and London, 1939.
31. Kirk, Dudley, "European Migrations: Prewar Trends and Future Prospects," *Milbank Memorial Fund Quarterly*, April 1947.
32. Kulischer, Eugene M., *The Displacement of Population in Europe*, International Labor Office, Montreal, 1943.
33. ———, *Europe on the Move: War and Population Changes, 1917–1947.* Columbia University Press, New York, 1948.
34. Myrdal, Gunnar, *An American Dilemma: The Negro Problem and Modern Democracy*, 2d edition, Harper and Brothers, New York, 1944.
35. Pelzer, Karl J., *Population and Land Utilization* (*An Economic Survey of the Pacific Area*, Part I), Institute of Pacific Relations, New York, 1942.
36. Revusky, Abraham, *Jews in Palestine*, Vanguard Press, New York, 1945.
37. Sauer, Carl O., "The Prospect of a Redistribution of Population," in *Limits of Land Settlement*, Isaiah Bowman (Ed.), Council on Foreign Relations, New York, 1937.
38. ———, "The Settlement of the Humid East," *Climate and Man* (*Yearbook of Agriculture, 1941*), U.S. Department of Agriculture, 1941.
39. Schechtman, Joseph B., *European Population Transfers, 1939–1945*, Oxford University Press, New York, 1946.
40. Sutherland, Stella U., *Population Distribution in Colonial America*, Columbia University Press, New York, 1936.
41. Thompson, Warren S., *Population Problems*, 3d edition, McGraw-Hill Book Company, New York, 1942.
42. Thornthwaite, C. Warren, and Slentz, H. I., *Internal Migration in the United States*, University of Pennsylvania Press, Philadelphia, 1934.
43. Thucydides, *The Peloponnesian War* (R. Crawley, trans.), Modern Library, New York, 1934.
44. Trewartha, Glenn T., "Climate and Settlement of the Sub-humid Land," in *Climate and Man* (*Yearbook of Agriculture, 1941*), U.S. Department of Agriculture, 1941.
45. Vidal de la Blache, J. M. C., *Principes de Géographie Humaine*, A. Colin, Paris, 1922.
46. Wander, Hilde, *The Importance of Emigration for the Solution of Population Problems in Western Europe* (Research Group for European Migration Problems, Publication No. 1), Martinus Niihoff, The Hague, 1951.
47. Wilcox, Walter F. (Ed.), *International Migrations*, Vol. I, *Statistics*, 1929; Vol. II, *Interpretations*, 1931, National Bureau of Economic Research, New York.
48. Woytinsky, Wl. (W.S.), *Die Welt in Zahlen*, Vol. I: *Die Erde — Die Bevölkerung — Der Volksreichtum*, Rudolf Mosse, Berlin, 1925.
49. Woytinsky, W. S., "Interstate Migration during the War," *State Government*, March 1946.
50. ———, "Internal Migration during the War," Special Report, Social Security Board, November 1944 (mimeographed).

*Immigration to the United States**

Conrad Taeuber • Irene B. Taeuber

In the earliest years the immigrants were few relative to the Indians beyond the perimeters of settlement, but conditions were favorable to survival and expansion. The Indians of the coastal areas were neither numerous nor organized, and the European pressures to displace them were persistent. Though resistance was sometimes fierce, the superior technologies of the Europeans were decisive. As the frontier was extended, some groups of Indians accepted peaceful coexistence with the invading strangers. Members of Indian groups merged into European society, and some intermarriages occurred. In the main, however, the Indians who survived the joint hazards of conflict, disease, and economic dislocation withdrew westward. The Secretary of War in President Washington's cabinet estimated the Indians east of the Mississippi as numbering 76,000 in 1789.[1] At that time, all of New England except the northern portion of Maine, all but the most westerly areas of New York and Pennsylvania, all of Virginia, nearly all of the Carolinas, and half of Georgia were free of hostile Indians.[2]

Although there were Spanish settlements in Florida and in the Southwest and French settlements along the water routes from the St. Lawrence to the Gulf, the major settlement of the United States was made by the descendants of the European immigrants who came directly to the East Coast. Those who made this perilous Atlantic crossing were as diverse in social and economic background and motivations as they were in culture and language. Shiploads of girls were sent "whereby the Planters' minds may be the faster tyed to Virginia by the bonds of wyves and children."[3] Since men were sparse and land plentiful, head rights in land were given to men who would procure and finance others. People wishing to come to the new world but lacking in funds committed years of indentured labor as payment for passage. Dissident sectarian groups sought religious freedom in a land remote from the princes of church and State. Armies conquered in battle were transported across the Atlantic. Families fleeing severe deprivation or famine managed somehow to get to coastal cities and across the ocean. The lowly and the disadvantaged were not the only groups who came, for the new land offered opportunities to younger sons and lesser nobility, to hard-pressed gentry, and to professional and technical people. There was the lure of fortune for investors, traders, and businessmen. Idealists found a powerful attraction in the virgin lands and the new culture beyond the seas.[4]

Not all who came to the new world found it satisfactory, and some born here migrated elsewhere. In the early days of sailing ships few crossed the Atlantic intending to return shortly, but some who survived the trip and a period of life here returned disillusioned to the country of origin in Europe. Some people moved westward or northward into areas beyond the

* Reprinted with permission from Conrad Taeuber and Irene B. Taeuber, *The Changing Population of the United States.* New York: John Wiley, 1958, pp. 48-70.

[1] U.S. Bureau of the Census, *A Century of Population Growth in the United States: 1790-1900,* by W. S. Rossiter, Government Printing Office, Washington, D.C., 1909, p. 40.

[2] The instructions of the First Census provided for the exclusion of Indians not taxed, and no Indians were reported. The data relating to Indians really go back only to 1890, when one fourth of a million Indians were returned in a total population of 60 million.

[3] Virginia Company, *Records,* Vol. 1, p. 566, cited by Marcus Lee Hansen, *The Atlantic Migration, 1607-1860,* Harvard University Press, Cambridge, 1940, p. 29.

[4] Marcus Lee Hansen, *op. cit.,* Chapter II, "The Peopling of the Colonies," and Ch. III, "The First Americanization." See also Maurice R. Davie, *World Immigration.* The Macmillan Company, New York, 1936, pp. 19-50.

limits of European occupation. There was continuing movement between the islands of the Caribbean and the mainland, between the various British colonies on the mainland, between Spanish colonies in the north and those further south. There were also losses in periods of crisis. Colonists loyal to England moved to Canada or to Latin American countries during or after the Revolution, just as later some of the people who were loyal to the Confederate cause moved to other countries in the Hemisphere. The fact that departure from the United States was noteworthy only attests the more to the lifelong nature of the migrations of most of those who came here.

The European colonization was a great movement of individuals from an old world they found undesirable for one reason or another to a new world in which there was freedom and opportunity. The African immigration was a forced movement of chattels to be sold and to live and work as slaves in an alien land. The first slaves were brought into Virginia in 1619; between this year and the termination of the legal importation of slaves in the early nineteenth century some 370,000 to 400,000 Africans were imported into this country.[5]

Some inferences as to the course of immigration and slave importations can be made from the estimates of the growth of the population in the colonial period.[6] In the first few decades of settlement, erratic fluctuations in numbers reflected the arrival of new immigrants or the decimations of populations already here. Soon, though, growth became quite regular; in the 110 years from 1660 to 1770 population increased a third or more in almost all 10-year periods. The general regularity of the decennial rates of increase after the first half century of settlement could not have occurred unless the predominant factor in growth had been natural increase rather than current immigration. To argue that net immigration was less significant than the natural increase of earlier immigrants and their descendants is not to fix the rate of that immigration or its periodicity. Whatever the rate, the total immigration in any decade or century cannot have been large in absolute terms. It was more than 180 years from the first permanent English settlement in the United States to the Census of 1790. It had taken more than half or our entire history on this continent for the continuing immigration from Europe and Africa and the natural increase of the immigrants and their descendants to build up a total population of less than 4 million people.

[5] U.S. Bureau of the Census, *op. cit.*, p. 36.

[6] Total populations, including slave and free colored. U.S. Bureau of the Census, *op. cit*, pp. 9-10.

International Migration, 1819-1955

One of the complaints voiced in the Declaration of Independence against the British King was: "he has endeavoured to prevent the population of these States; for that purpose obstructing the Laws of Naturalization of foreigners; refusing to pass others to encourage their migration hither, and raising the conditions of new Appropriations of Lands." Once the United States established itself, immigrants were welcome. In the words of President Washington, "The bosom of America is open to receive not only the Opulent and Respectable Stranger, but the oppressed and persecuted of all Nations and Religions, whom we shall wellcome to a participation of all our rights and previleges, if by decency and propriety of conduct they appear to merit the enjoyment."[7] However, the Congress rejected suggestions that land be used as family grants for immigrants, or that industrial labor be subsidized. In the early decades the United States had ". . . no encouragement to immigrants except that offered by its opportunities, and . . . no barriers except those confronting native and foreigner alike."[8]

Immigration was slight from the beginning of the Revolutionary War in 1776 to the Peace of Vienna in 1815. Thus the new Nation was given time to consolidate its political structure and social institutions before the quickening currents of immigrants created major problems of economic and cultural integration.

The counting of immigrants by the Federal

[7] George Washington, December 2, 1783, from John C. Fitzpatrick (Editor), *The Writings of George Washington, from the Original Manuscript Sources, 1745-1799*, Vol. XXVII, *June 11, 1783 to November 28, 1784*, p. 254.

[8] Marcus Lee Hansen, *op. cit.*, p. 56.

Government did not begin until the year 1819. An act of that year to regulate the transportation of people in steerage provided that the captain or master of any vessel arriving in the United States from any foreign place should deliver to the collector of customs of the district a manifest of all passengers, ". . . in which list or manifest it shall be the duty of the said master to designate, particularly, the age, sex, and occupation of said passengers, respectively, the country to which they severally belong, and that of which it is their intention to become inhabitants."[9]

Thus for 1819 and later years there are some official reports on immigrants, incomplete and inaccurate though they may be. For the years prior to 1819 there are only estimates and conjectures. Most people who have studied the history of the period and whatever local records were available believe that something less than a quarter of a million white immigrants entered the country in the 30 years from 1790 to 1819.[10]

In the 136 years from 1819 to 1955 more than 40 million aliens entered the United States. Some 34 million of the total were from Europe and so survivors of the Atlantic crossing. Many criticisms can be made of these figures, and many have been made, but the migration that is reflected here remains almost awesome in its magnitude.

The perusal of the immigration data of the nineteenth and early twentieth centuries indicates that statistics were an ever-changing byproduct of administrative functioning. The Act of 1819 provided only that masters of ships report to the collectors of customs on passengers in steerage.[11] Immigrants arriving by land or on ships docking at other than the main Atlantic and Gulf ports escaped the reckoning. It is reported that prior to 1864 ships' manifests included those who died in passage.[12] From 1819 to 1867 the lists referred to alien passengers; from 1868 to 1900 they referred to alien immigrants. After 1903, first and second class passengers were included, and people in transit were excluded. After 1906 aliens not admitted were excluded from the reports; after 1907 immigrants who entered the country a second time were not counted again. The system of land border registrations was developed in the years from 1904 to 1908. Hawaii, Puerto Rico, and Alaska were added as ports of entry in 1901, 1902, and 1904, respectively. Philippine-United States movements were internal rather than international movements between July 1, 1898, and May 1, 1934. It is quite apparent that the historic statistics of international migrations are not precise, and that the degree of the imprecision differs for types of immigrants and areas of origin. Many of the errors are compensating insofar as total numbers are concerned, however, so that the general picture across the last century and a quarter may be reasonably accurate.

The Immigrants.

In the early nineteenth century the numbers of immigrants were limited both by the nature of the transportation available for the Atlantic crossing and the limited absorptive capacity of the American economy. The situation changed sharply after the middle of the nineteenth century. The great land areas beyond the Mississippi were available for agricultural use. Rapid industrialization created major demands for unskilled labor to work in factories, build canals and roads and later railroads, and carry on many tasks not yet mechanized. At this same time conditions in Europe were becoming more favorable to movement. Means of communication were improved, and more and more people learned of the opportunities in the United States. Improved transportation within Europe facilitated movement to the coast, while steamships permitted quicker, safer, and cheaper passage across the ocean than had the sailing ships of earlier days. The critical factors in the magnitude and the timing of migrations became the economic opportunities known or believed to exist in the United States, the financial ability of the people who wished to migrate to do so, and the willingness of the United States to receive those who wished to come.

In 1820, when the ships' captains made their first reports to the collectors in the ports, they

[9] U.S. Immigration Commission, 1907-1910, *Statistical Review of Immigration, 1820-1910,* Vol. 3, p. 3.

[10] U.S. Census Office, 1860, *Population of the United States in 1860,* p. xviii. See also Marcus Lee Hansen, *op. cit.,* pp. 77-78.

[11] U.S. Immigration Commission, 1907-1910, *op. cit.,* Vol. 3, pp. 2-3.

[12] National Bureau of Economic Research, *International Migrations,* Vol. 1, *Statistics,* by Imré Ferenczi, National Bureau of Economic Research, New York, 1929, p. 374.

TABLE 1

Recorded Immigration, by Continents: 1819 to 1954

[In thousands. Data are for years ending June 30, except as noted. 1819 to 1867, figures represent alien passengers arriving in steerage; 1868 to 1891 and 1895 to 1897, immigrant aliens arriving; 1892 to 1894 and 1898 to 1954, immigrant aliens admitted; 1819 to 1868, by nationality; 1869 to 1898, by country of origin or nationality; 1899 to 1954, by country of last permanent address.]

Period	Total[1]	Europe	America	Asia	Australia and New Zealand	Pacific Islands	Africa
Total, 1819 to 1954	40,173	33,764	5,038	982	71	20	37
1819 to 1820[2]	8	8	...	...	...	...	...
1821 to 1830[2]	143	99	12	...	...	...	...
1831 to 1840[3]	599	496	33	...	...	...	...
1841 to 1850[4]	1,713	1,598	62	...	...	...	...
1851 to 1860[4]	2,598	2,453	75	41	...	...	...
1861 to 1870[5]	2,315	2,065	167	65	...	...	...
1871 to 1880	2,812	2,272	404	124	10	1	...
1881 to 1890	5,247	4,737	[6]427	68	7	6	1
1891 to 1900	3,688	3,559	[6]39	71	3	1	...
1901 to 1910	8,795	8,136	362	244	12	1	7
1911 to 1920	5,736	4,377	1,144	193	12	1	8
1921 to 1930	4,107	2,478	1,517	97	8	...	6
1931 to 1940	528	348	160	15	2	...	2
1941 to 1950	1,035	622	355	32	14	5	7
1951 to 1954	850	518	282	31	2	3	4

[1] Includes some immigrants of unspecified origins.
[2] October 1 to September 30.
[3] October 1, 1830, to December 1, 1840.
[4] Calendar years.
[5] January 1, 1861, to June 30, 1870.
[6] No reports of British, North American, or Mexican immigration, 1886 to 1893.
Source: Based on U.S. Immigration and Naturalization Service, *Annual Report . . . 1954,* table 4.

had recorded 8,385 alien passengers in steerage[13] (table 1). In 1825 the number exceeded 10,000; in 1828 it exceeded 20,000. Numbers moved rapidly upward in the thirties, the total passengers for the decade exceeding half a million. With the forties and the westward expansion and industrial growth in the United States, the great famines in Ireland, and the political difficulties on the continent, the migrant tides assumed massive proportions. Arrivals exceeded 100,000 in 1842, 200,000 in 1847, and 300,000 in 1850. The tide continued strong until 1854, when 400,000 entered. Numbers of immigrants declined with depression and the Civil War, but after the war immigrants increased until there were fears of inundation. Numbers dropped in the great depression of the 1890's but moved upward again in the first decade of the new century. In 6 of the 11 years from 1905 through 1915 there were more than a million immigrants.

Immigration was blocked by World War I, but there was every indication of a resumption of the great movements at the end of the War. However, the public concern over immigration led to drastic restrictions on immigrant admissions. These in conjunction with the economic paralysis of the great depression of the 1930's reduced immigration to its lowest level since

[13] Precisely, 1819-1820, since the immigration reports were usually for fiscal years.

TABLE 2

Immigration and Emigration of Aliens: 1907 to 1955

Year ending June 30	Number (thousands)			Emigrants per 100 immigrants	Net increment per 100 immigrants
	Immigrants	Emigrants	Net movement		
Total, 1907 to 1955...	15,070	4,766	10,305	31.6	68.4
1907 to 1910............	2,576	823	1,753	32.0	68.0
1911 to 1915............	4,460	1,445	3,015	32.4	67.6
1916 to 1920............	1,276	702	574	55.0	45.0
1921 to 1925............	2,639	697	1,942	26.4	73.6
1926 to 1930............	1,468	348	1,121	23.7	76.3
1931 to 1935............	220	324	−104	−147.1	−47.1
1936 to 1940............	308	136	172	44.1	55.9
1941 to 1945............	171	43	128	25.0	75.0
1946 to 1950............	864	114	750	13.2	86.8
1951 to 1955............	1,088	134	953	12.3	87.7

Source: Based on U.S. Immigration and Naturalization Service, *Annual Report . . . 1954,* tables I and II; *idem.* tabulation, 1955; U.S. Bureau of the Census, *Statistical Abstract of the United States, 1955,* table 102.

1831. The great era of international migration had ended, but the migrations of the years after World War II are quite substantial if measured against any international movements other than our own migrations in the years from 1850 to 1920. Annual migrations in the years from 1950 through 1955 were as large as those in the early years of the Irish famines.

In the perspective of the 165 years since the population was first counted in 1790, massive flows of immigrants appear as a transitory phase in the development of the country. If immigration is viewed in terms of its relative contributions, the strongest flows were those of the quarter century preceding the Civil War. This is true whether numbers of immigrants are related to the total population or to the existing stock of the foreign-born population.[14] In absolute terms, the trend in numbers of immigrants was upward throughout the nineteenth and early twentieth centuries, then sharply downward. Total immigrants, as variously recorded in the statistics, numbered less than a million from 1790 to 1840, almost 10 million from 1840 to 1880, 23.5 million from 1880 to 1920. By the latter date the country was maturing economically and demographically and the political climate of the United States and other countries was changing. The era in which the unskilled and the uneducated could move as they willed had passed.

Emigration and Net Migration

Numbers of immigrants would measure the direct contribution of migrants to the population only if there were neither return migrations of the foreign-born nor emigrations of citizens, Obviously both types of departures occurred, although throughout most periods of American history the emigration of citizens who were not also foreign-born has been slight. It cannot be assumed that the return migration of the foreign-born was slight, nor can it be assumed that there were uniform relations between immigration, emigration, and hence net gain by migration. The direct data on the movements of aliens, available since July 1, 1907, are summarized in table 2. Annual estimates of alien movements for the years from 1870 to 1945 are pictured in figure 1.[15]

It is commonly assumed that the departures of aliens were perhaps 10 to 15 percent as

[14] Simon Kuznets and Ernest Rubin, *Immigration and the Foreign Born,* National Bureau of Economic Research, Occasional Paper 46, New York, 1954, pp. 25-26.

[15] Annual departures estimated on the basis of data from reporting ports. Simon Kuznets and Ernest Rubin, *op. cit.,* p. 57.

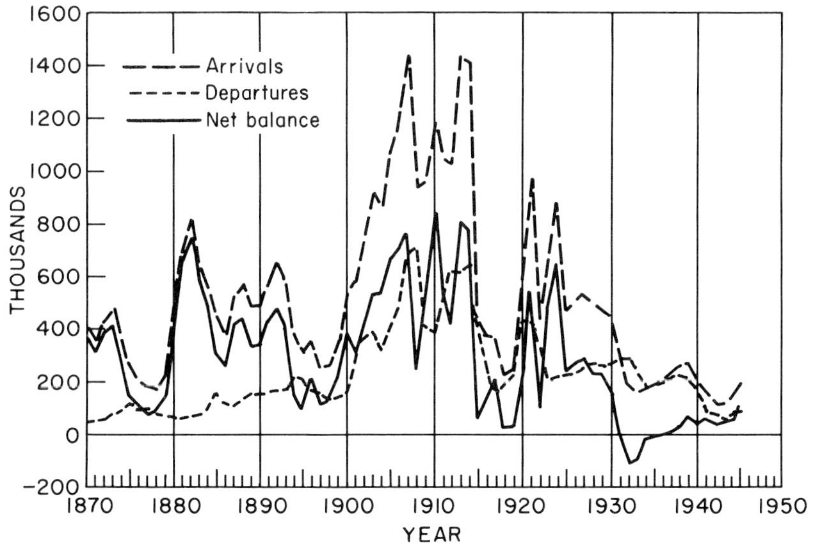

FIGURE 1*

Immigration, emigration, and net migration of alien passengers: 1870 to 1945.

* Source: Simon Kuznets and Ernest Rubin, *Immigration and the Foreign Born,* National Bureau of Economic Research, Occasional Paper 46, New York, 1954, p. 20.

numerous as alien arrivals in the decades from 1820 to 1870. The situation changed as demands for labor and easier transportation permitted major movements.[16] In the years from 1870 to 1910 the ratios of outflow to inflow for total alien migration were sharply upward, the specific figures being 24.3 percent in 1870-1880 and 44.8 percent in 1900-1910.[17] The comparable ratios for alien immigration and emigration were given in table 2 for the years from 1907 to 1955. The course of business cycles and political conditions have been decisive factors in the size of the movements in and out of the country and the type of relationship between the two. Recently, restricted immigration in a period of economic prosperity has produced rates of retention as high as those of the early nineteenth century.

Numerous factors were responsible for the increasing rates of exodus in the era of relatively free migration.[18] Ease and cheapness of transportation itself would create a closer relationship between immigrant and emigrant flows. Many of the early immigrants had gone into agriculture and so were in locations and occupations where the reactions to business conditions were less immediately acute and the response in emigration more difficult. Later immigrants were more concentrated in wage employment and so necessarily more responsive to economic difficulties. There are many arguments and some data indicating changes in the motivations of immigrants, the argument being that the immigrants of the late nineteenth and early twentieth centuries included many transients, people who would return home when sufficient funds were accumulated.

Since immigration has been related directly to cyclical and secular swings in business activity in the United States, it might be argued with considerable plausibility that emigration should be related inversely to business activity and hence to immigration.[19] If cyclical fluctuations

[16] Simon Kuznets and Ernest Rubin, *op. cit.,* pp. 22-24.

[17] *Ibid.,* p. 39.

[18] *Ibid.,* pp. 19-37.

[19] Harry Jerome, *Migration and Business Cycles,* National Bureau of Economic Research, New York, 1926, p. 256.

TABLE 3

Major Sources of Immigrants: 1819 to 1954 (*In thousands. For explanations, see table*)

Year	Great Britain	Ireland[1]	Germany	Denmark, Norway, Sweden	Austria-Hungary[2]	Russia[3]	Italy
Total, 1819 to 1954...	[4]4,460	4,635	6,501	2,405	4,209	3,344	4,819
1819 to 1820............	2	4	1	...	...	...	...
1821 to 1830............	25	51	7	...	...	...	...
1831 to 1840............	76	207	152	2	...	...	2
1841 to 1850............	267	781	435	14	...	...	2
1851 to 1860............	424	914	952	25	...	...	9
1861 to 1870............	607	436	787	126	8	3	12
1871 to 1880............	548	437	718	243	73	39	56
1881 to 1890............	807	655	1,453	656	354	213	307
1891 to 1900............	272	388	505	372	593	505	652
1901 to 1910............	526	339	341	505	2,145	1,597	2,046
1911 to 1920............	341	146	144	203	896	921	1,110
1921 to 1930............	330	221	412	198	64	62	455
1931 to 1940............	29	13	114	11	11	1	68
1941 to 1950............	132	27	226	26	28	1	57
1951 to 1954............	73	16	252	21	37	1	42

[1] Including Northern Ireland.
[2] Austro-Hungarian Empire and the Succession States.
[3] Imperial Russia to 1917; 1917—, U.S.S.R.
[4] Of whom 3,663,000 were allocated specifically to England, Scotland, or Wales.
Source: Reference, table 1.

alone are noted, this relationship tends to hold. Over the longer time, other forces blunt the anticipated inverse relation between immigration and emigration. The long-run trend was toward higher ratios of departures to arrivals, and periods of heavy inflow generated heavy outflow. As a result of these complex relations and the differences in the timing of the flows, fluctuations in net migration were greater than those in immigration or in emigration. The adaptability of the labor supply to labor demands was increased, but problems of immigrant adjustment and cultural assimilation became more difficult.

Immigration Origins, 1819-1954

From the earliest days of settlement to the present, the free migrants to the territory that is now the United States have been predominantly European in geographic and ethnic origin. Some few free colored moved in from the Caribbean in the colonial period; some Indians crossed the northern and southern frontiers. As the data of table 1 indicate, 34 of the 40 million immigrants were attributed to Europe, 5 million to the Americas, and 71,000 to Australia and New Zealand. The true figures would differ appreciably from these, since immigrant records have always been most complete for those who made ocean crossings. In the early days land movements were ignored; in recent periods much border crossing has gone unrecorded. However, the European predominance is so great that no reasonable estimates of error can alter the broad picture.

The course of the migrations of the nativity groups of Europeans reflect the economic development, the demographic expansion, and the political vicissitudes of the regions of the continent (table 3). Population pressures and population increases in European areas created a supply of people available as migrants. Land and industry that meant opportunity and em-

TABLE 4

Reported Immigration from Europe, by Major Regions: 1819 to 1954
(In thousands. For explanations, see table 1)

Year	All Europe	Regions			
		North and West	East and Central	South	Other
Total, 1819 to 1954.......	33,764	19,457	8,549	5,715	43
1819 to 1820.................	8	8	...	...	...
1821 to 1830.................	99	96	...	3	...
1831 to 1840.................	496	490	...	5	...
1841 to 1850.................	1,598	1,592	1	5	...
1851 to 1860.................	2,453	2,431	2	20	...
1861 to 1870.................	2,065	2,032	12	21	...
1871 to 1880.................	2,272	2,070	126	75	1
1881 to 1890.................	4,737	3,779	627	331	1
1891 to 1900.................	3,559	1,643	1,211	704	...
1901 to 1910.................	8,136	1,910	3,915	2,310	1
1911 to 1920.................	4,377	998	1,918	1,452	8
1921 to 1930.................	2,478	1,300	590	565	23
1931 to 1940.................	348	205	58	84	2
1941 to 1950.................	622	492	48	77	4
1951 to 1954.................	518	411	41	63	3

Source: Reference, table 1.

ployment in the United States were forces of attraction. Bringing these forces of availability and attraction together in the early days were a developing commerce that left ships empty in European harbors with money to be made from immigrants who would pay small fees for the westward passage. Timber for Ireland, cotton for England, tobacco for Germany — these were major factors in the timing of the early streams of immigrants. So were events in Europe — the failure of the potato crops in Ireland and Germany, the repeal of the British Corn Laws, and the local inequities of the years after the Peace of Vienna. Later as the steamship replaced the sailing ship and American industry needed cheap labor, the seemingly inexhaustible human resources of Europe lay in the agrarian countries to the east and south of the continent.

The British have been the continuing immigrants to the United States. In the 135 years from 1819 to 1954, 3.7 million were counted as alien passengers or immigrants — 2.8 million English, 760,000 Scottish, and 91,000 Welsh. It was the Irish who contributed most heavily in relation to the size of the home population. The 4.6 million immigrants from Ireland are actually more numerous than the combined populations of Eire and Northern Ireland in 1951. The Germans were continuing immigrants, and their numbers were greater than those for Great Britain, Ireland, or any other single country. The Scandinavian countries contributed greatly, too, particularly if the streams of immigrants are related to the small populations of the countries of origin.

The early immigrants came predominantly from western Europe. As the nineteenth century advanced, people in these areas found increasing opportunities for employment in the growing cities and the developing industry and commerce of their home countries or nearby and culturally similar countries. Although there were differences among the individual countries, the peak emigration from northern and western Europe came in the decade from 1881 to 1890. During this single decade 3.8 million immigrants from these areas of Europe entered the United States (table 4). After this the currents receded until in the last quarter century the quotas have been left partially unutilized.

By the time the immigration from northern and western Europe reached its peak in the 1880's, there were already substantial immigrant flows from countries to the east and south. In the 1880's themselves, as was shown in table 3, 354,000 immigrants entered from the Austro-Hungarian Empire, 307,000 from Italy, and 213,000 from Russia. Thus, one fifth of the total immigration of the decade came from outside the historic areas of immigrant recruitment in the north and west. The flows from the east and south of Europe increased sharply as more and more people learned of the opportunities beyond the sea and found some way to make the trek to a seaport and pay for passage across the Atlantic. In the decade from 1901 to 1910 the Austro-Hungarian Empire, Russia, and Italy furnished 5.8 million immigrants. Italy's 2.0 million exceeded the 1.9 million from all the countries of northern and western Europe combined. It is not surprising that in 1907 the Congress authorized an Immigration Commission to make ". . . full inquiry, examination, and investigation of immigration." [20]

The Immigration Commission made the chief basis of its work a study of the changed character of the immigration in the quarter century between 1882 and 1907. The premise underlying its appointment and the conclusions from its extensive studies are alike implicit in the Commission's summary statement of its investigations:[21]

> The old and the new immigration differ in many essentials. The former was, from the beginning, largely a movement of settlers who came from the most progressive sections of Europe for the purpose of making for themselves homes in the New World. They entered practically every line of activity in nearly every part of the country. Coming during a period of agricultural development, many of them entered agricultural pursuits, sometimes as independent farmers, but more often as farm laborers, who, nevertheless, as a rule soon became landowners. They formed an important part of the great movement toward the West during the last century, and as pioneers were most potent factors in the development of the territory between the Allegheny Mountains and the Pacific Coast. They mingled freely with the native Americans and were quickly assimilated . . .
>
> The new immigration has been largely a movement of unskilled laboring men who have come, in large part temporarily, from the less progressive and advanced countries of Europe in response to the call for industrial workers in the eastern and middle western States. They have almost entirely avoided agricultural pursuits, and in cities and industrial communities have congregated together in sections apart from native Americans and the older immigrants to such an extent that assimilation has been slow as compared to that of the earlier non-English speaking races . . .

While the Immigration Commission was devoting its attention primarily to the changing sources of the immigration from Europe, migration from other areas was assuming major proportions. Increasing numbers of people were crossing the land borders to the north and south, while flows had begun from the densely settled and almost inexhaustible peopled lands of Asia.

National concern over immigration and the problems of immigrants abated during the years of World War I, but it came again in more incisive form in the early years after that war as migration was resumed, and it resulted in drastic restrictions that altered the amount and the composition of the migration to the United States.[22] The Act of 1917, passed over the veto of President Wilson, doubled the head tax, increased the power of officials to exclude and deport aliens, established an Asiatic Barred Zone, and required a literacy test of all aliens aged 16 and above who sought permanent entry. As immigration quickened again after the war, there was a drive for specific quantitative limitations. An Act of May 17, 1921, provided for a quota system under which each nation should have an annual immigration allowance equal to 3 percent of the number of its foreign-born in the United States according to the Census of

[20] U.S. Immigration Commission, 1907-1910, *Abstracts of Reports of the Immigration Commission, with Conclusions and Recommendations and Views of the Minority*, Vol. 1, p. 12.

[21] *Ibid.*, Vol. 1, p. 14.

[22] Edward P. Hutchinson, "Immigration Policy since World War I," *The Annals of the American Academy of Political and Social Science*, Vol. 262, pp. 15-21 (1949).

1910.[23] A law of 1924 established interim quotas for 5 years at 2 percent of the foreign born of the nationality resident in the United States in 1890 and provided that permanent quotas should be established on the basis of the national origins of the white population of 1920.[24] Quotas were to apply primarily to the European nations, for the American nations were not subjected to quota regulation and practically all Asian and African peoples were excluded from entrance to the United States as immigrants.

The quotas promulgated in 1929 have been changed only slightly since that time.[25] Minor adjustments have been made because of political boundaries, and minimum quotas have been allocated to hitherto excluded peoples. The quota in effect in 1929 permitted 153,714 quota immigrants annually; the Immigration and Nationality Act of 1952 permitted 154,657.[26] As of 1952, almost 150,000 of the quota immigrants were allocated to Europe, 2,990 to Asia, and 1,400 to Africa.

It was the purpose of the quota system to restore immigration to the proportionate ethnic composition that characterized the white population of the United States in 1920. Complications were introduced through the priorities established for quota immigrants, the exemption of countries and individuals from the quotas, and legal provisions for borrowing from future quotas.

The quotas themselves are filled in priority orders that condition the characteristics of immigrants. The first preference goes to selected immigrants with special skills or abilities. Second to fourth preferences go respectively to parents of United States citizens, spouses and children of resident aliens, and, finally, the brothers or sisters and mature or married children of United States citizens.

The nonquota immigrants of normal periods consist primarily of natives of Western Hemisphere countries, their spouses, and their children. There are other sizable groups, however, including the alien wives, husbands, and children of United States citizens; persons who have had United States citizenship; and ministers, their spouses, and children.

Under a Presidential Directive of December 22, 1945, and the Displaced Persons Act of 1948, 387,000 displaced persons were admitted in the years from 1946 through 1953; of these, 380,000 were charged against quotas.[27] Under the Act of December 28, 1945, 120,000 alien wives, husbands, and children of members of the Armed Forces were admitted outside the quotas.[28] The Refugee Relief Act of 1953 provided for 209,000 special visas between 1953 and the end of 1956 for refugees, escapees, and German expellees and their accompanying wives and children.[29]

Modification of or exemptions from the quota provisions have been numerous. The altered places of origin and the changed characteristics of the immigrants of the last quarter century as contrasted with earlier periods are products both of the operations of the quota system and of its various modifying provisions. The results of the legal provisions and the extralegal forces of the quarter century has been an immigration somewhat different from that envisioned in the various legislative acts. The percentage comparisons by

[23] L. Paul Winings, "Development of Immigration and Naturalization Laws," U.S. Immigration and Naturalization Service, *Monthly Review,* Vol. 3, pp. 172-175 (1945).

[24] When the decision was made to base immigration quotas on the proportions of the white population deriving from the national origin groups in the country, a special study was made to determine the contributions of the various nationality groups. The estimates were tenuous, for birth and death records were even more inadequate than those on migration. The techniques and the estimates are presented in *Immigration Quotas on the Basis of National Origins,* Senate Document No. 65, 70th Congress, February, 1926. See also U.S. Bureau of the Census, *Increase in Population in the United States: 1910-1920,* by W. S. Rossiter; Warren Thompson and P. K. Whelpton, *Population Trends in the United States,* McGraw-Hill Book Company, New York, 1933, pp. 83-94.

[25] U.S. Immigration and Naturalization Service, "Immigration Restrictions in the United States," by Helen F. Eckerson and Gertrude Krichefsky, *Monthly Review,* Vol. 4, pp. 82-86 (1947).

[26] U.S. Bureau of the Census, *Statistical Abstract of the United States, 1955,* p. 94.

[27] U.S. Bureau of the Census, *Statistical Abstract of the United States, 1954,* table 112.

[28] The Act expired December 28, 1948, but further provisions were made under Public Law 51 of April 21, 1949.

[29] U.S. Immigration and Naturalization Service, *Annual Report . . . 1954,* p. 14.

areas of origin are shown in the accompanying table: [30]

Place	National origins 1920	Immigrants admitted 1929–44	1945–49
Total	100.0	100.0	100.0
All quota countries	94.4	73.7	68.0
North and West Europe	79.1	41.7	42.1
South and East Europe	15.1	29.2	26.0
Other	0.3	2.8	4.8
Nonquota countries	5.6	26.3	27.1

The pattern of the new migration is in accord with the basic principles of limitation and qualitative restriction, though the desired ethnic composition has not been secured. Immigration is sharply restricted; it includes few nonwhites and is selective of the skilled and the educated. Eventually ethnic origins may conform more closely to the stated goal of the 1920 relationships, for the naturalized citizens who could bring families in outside the quotas are an aging group. In 1930–1934, 15.6 percent of all immigrants were nonquota immigrants from South and East Europe; this percentage had dropped to 8.8 by 1945–1949. The majority of the immigrants from the Americas are Canadians and are of British or French origin, both of which countries are favored in the quotas.

Dispersion and Cumulation

Although immigrants played a direct and important role in the settlement of a number of midwestern States and in other areas, they have been concentrated in the cities, especially in the East.[31] The fact that the immigrants were themselves predominantly of European peasant origin played an important part in some of the problems of adjustments to the industrial and urban environment of the strange new country. In some cases, as Hutchinson shows, the second generation has found its way into agriculture, but only in a very limited way. An important element in the urban concentration of the immigrants lies in the timetable of their arrival. With few exceptions the immigrants from southern and eastern Europe began coming in large numbers only after the main areas in which the Homestead Act was effective had been settled. They could have become farm operators only through the expenditure of capital, which few of them had, and then generally under circumstances in which their European agricultural background would have proved of little help.[32] The productivity in agriculture was increasing, its manpower requirements declining. The expanding industrial, transportation, and service sectors of the economy needed manpower and were able to use the relatively untrained immigrants. This meant concentration in industrial centers, first along the East Coast and then inland to other areas of industrial expansion. Although this was less applicable to the immigrants who came earlier, the difference was largely a matter of degree. The immigrants who labored in construction crews to build canals and railroads and then settled near the new facilities were a minority of all immigrants. The majority of the earlier immigrants, as the latter, remained in the cities.

New York City, the primary port of entry, retained very large numbers of immigrants. In 1910, 1920, and 1930 it included more first or second generation Italians than the population of Rome, Italy. At every census between 1900 and 1940, it included more first and second generation Irish than Dublin. Its Jewish population is estimated to be greater than that of Israel.

There were a few groups of immigrants who deliberately established themselves in remote areas where they hoped to preserve their distinctive cultures. In the formative period of the United States many groups here and in Europe wished to develop ethnic enclaves. There

[30] U.S. Immigration and Naturalization Service, "Immigrants and National Origins," by Helen F. Eckerson, *Monthly Review,* Vol. 3, p. 214 (1945).

[31] Edward P. Hutchinson, *Immigrants and Their Children, 1850 to 1950,* John Wiley and Sons, New York, 1956.

[32] For the later immigrants the exceptions are found primarily in the fruit and vegetable-growing areas on the West Coast, though cultural islands with specialized agriculture are to be found in all parts of the United States.

were proposals among the Germans to establish a town or city to serve as a cultural center for the surrounding settlers; at one time there was talk of peopling an American state and adopting German as the official language.[33] In 1818, the Irish Society of New York and Philadelphia petitioned Congress for a land grant in the West to which to send the numerous charity cases in their charge. Congress refused, agreeing with the report of the special committee that it would be undesirable to concentrate alien peoples geographically. Had the grant been made, other national groups no doubt would have asked for similar treatment and there might soon have been a patchwork of foreign settlements under official sponsorship. As it was, the foreign settlements that were created resulted primarily from the natural process of the clustering of immigrants where some of their number had already established themselves. An important aspect of these settlements was that the members were free to leave when they felt that it was to their advantage to do so.

[33] Marcus Lee Hansen, *op. cit.*, pp. 131-132.

Distribution of the Foreign-born

Both the timing of immigrant movements and the concentrations of immigrant settlements differed greatly among the States.[34] Figure 2 gives the maximum percentage of foreign-born whites in the total population of each State and the year in which that maximum was reached. The industrial States of the East have had percentages of foreign-born whites above the national average at all censuses. The percentages of the foreign-born have always been small in the South.

The native population was predominant in the settlement of the territories that formed the States of Ohio, Indiana, Illinois, and Michigan. With the exception of Louisiana, none of the

[34] The number of the foreign-born who are not white has always been so small that it may be disregarded in this discussion.

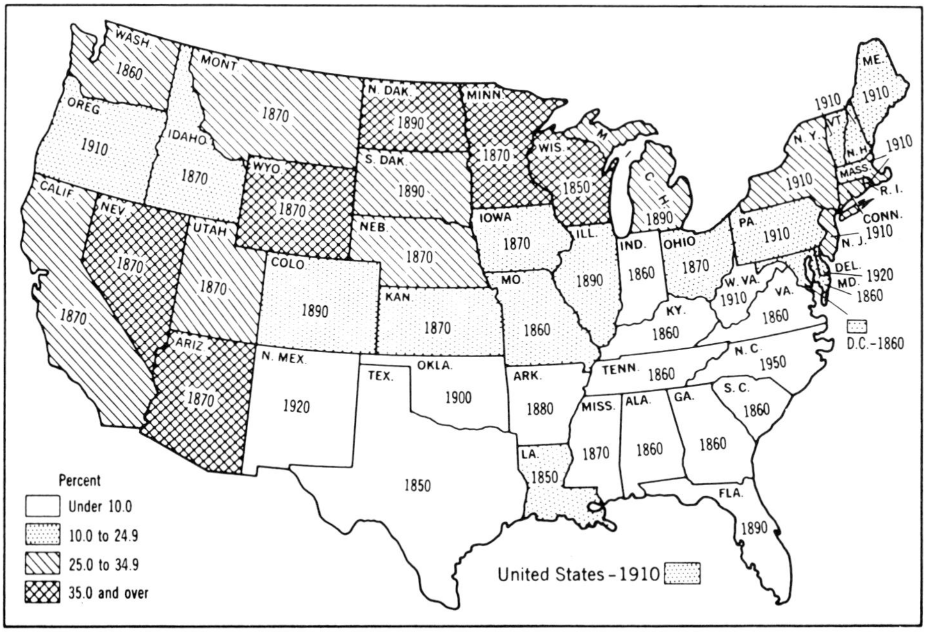

FIGURE 2*

Peak percentages of foreign-born whites in the total population and years of occurrence, by states.

* Source: U.S. Censuses of Population, 1850 to 1950.

southern States ever had enough foreign-born residents to make 10 percent of its total population. Iowa, Missouri, Kansas, and Colorado never reported more than a fourth of their total as foreign-born. In Iowa 11 percent of the total were foreign-born in 1850; this percentage increased to 17 in 1870 and declined after 1890.

Wisconsin and Minnesota were the first States in which the foreign-born accounted for a third or more of the population during the early years of the States' history. The proportion was slightly over 36 percent in Wisconsin in 1850 and reached that level in Minnesota in 1870. The later arrivals of foreign-born settlers in these States were not sufficiently numerous to keep the percentage of the foreign-born from declining steadily; by 1950 only 6 or 7 percent were foreign-born. The foreign-born also played a large role in the early development of the Dakotas.

Arizona is the only State that ever had more than half its total population foreign-born. In 1870, when that territory had fewer than 10,000 inhabitants, nearly 60 percent of the total were classified as foreign-born. Three fourths of them had been born in Mexico, however, and most of these probably were not immigrants but persons who remained when the allegiance of the area shifted from Mexico to the United States. During the next decade of rapid population growth, the percentage of the foreign-born dropped to 36, and nearly three fifths of them reported Mexico as the country of birth. Ten percent had come from China.

The year 1870 was the peak year for the percentage of the total population foreign-born for a number of the Mountain States and California. Although only Arizona exceeded 50 percent for the total population, more than half the men 21 and over in Utah, Nevada, Arizona, Idaho, and California were foreign-born in 1870.

A review of the proportion of the population reported as foreign-born at the successive censuses tells only one part of the story of the role of the foreign-born in the settlement of the country. It ignores the substantial contributions that groups and individuals made in the opening and development of the expanding area of the United States. The fact is that there was always a large contingent of native-born persons among the settlers who opened the West. Though the foreign-born were sometimes large and coherent groups, they were minorities who conformed in major ways to the standards of the native Americans. The fact that the children of the foreign-born were reported as native may initially have been merely a census procedure, but the classification soon corresponded to the facts of assimilation. The political, economic, and educational institutions, and the language which was used in contacts with the outside world were established by the dominant group of native Americans. The process of assimilation of the foreign-born and their descendants would no doubt have required much longer to complete had it not been for this circumstance.

The immigrants who went directly to the frontier made many important contributions, but they did so in large part within the pattern which had already been set by the earlier settlers. There were small isolated communities that attempted to provide a replica of the old world at the frontier. In terms of total numbers, their role was a limited one. The development of national unity did not need to contend with significant claims of another government to the political or cultural allegiance of the population of any major political area. That aspect of an immigration problem was successfully avoided.

Cumulations

Immigrant flows achieve demographic significance when they are related to the populations of the areas into which the immigrants move, and particularly to the cumulations of earlier immigrants in those areas. The censuses of the last century have counted the foreign-born; each census from 1890 through 1930 also included a query to the immigrant as to how many years he had been in this country. Tabulations for the years from 1900 through 1930 are sufficiently detailed to permit analysis of immigrant stocks, the contributions of decennial flows to those stocks, and the rates of cumulation or depletion. More than 5 million of the 13.5 million foreign-born in the country in 1910 had entered between 1901 and 1910. Proportions of recent immigrants were also great among the foreign-born enumerated in 1920 and 1930 (table 5). However, numbers of foreign-born enumerated in the censuses were substantially less than the numbers of immigrant aliens who entered the United States in the respective

TABLE 5

Year of Immigration of the Foreign-Born Population: 1900 to 1930

Census year	Total	Period of arrival			
		1900 or earlier	1901 to 1910	1911 to 1919	1920 to 1930
NUMBER (Thousands)					
Total:					
1900	10,341	10,341	...	...	...
1910	13,516	8,418	5,098	...	...
1920	13,921	6,340	4,444	3,137	...
1930	14,204	4,618	3,986	2,652	2,948
Change:					
1901 to 1910	+3,175	−1,924	+5,098	...	...
1911 to 1919	+405	−2,078	−654	+3,137	...
1920 to 1930	+283	−1,722	−458	−484	+2,948
PERCENT DISTRIBUTION					
Decade of arrival:					
1910	100.0	100.0	...	...	...
1920	100.0	62.3	37.7	...	...
1930	100.0	45.5	31.9	22.5	...
1940	100.0	32.5	28.1	18.7	20.7
PERCENT CHANGE					
Change by decades:					
1901 to 1910	+30.7	−18.6	...	...	...
1911 to 1919	+3.0	−24.7	−12.8	...	...
1920 to 1930	+2.0	−27.2	−10.3	−15.4	...

Source: Based on *1930 Census of Population,* Vol. II, *General Report—Statistics by Subjects.* Chapter 9, table 6.

decades.[35] Some of the immigrants had died before the census date, while others had left the country.

In the years from 1900 to 1930 current immigrant flows made smaller and smaller net additions to the immigrant stock. And as immigrants of earlier periods aged, rates of disappearance through death rose rapidly. The great immigrant flows of the decades from 1910 to 1930 did little more than maintain the immigrant stock at its 1910 level.

The slight increases in the numbers of foreign-born in the early decades of the century seem strangely inconsistent with the major attention devoted to the quantitative problems of immigrant absorption and the qualitative aspects of changing national origins. The reconciliation of the factual picture with the national worries lies in major part in the geographic and urban-rural distribution of the surviving immigrants of the successive time periods.[36]

Changes in the pattern of immigrant dispersion were already apparent in 1900.[37] In that year, two fifths of the immigrants had been in the

[35] See table 1.

[36] This is a further analysis of the immigrant dispersion that was considered in the previous section on the basis of the percentage of foreign-born and the years in which these percentages reached maxima.

[37] U.S. Census Office, 1900, *Population,* Part 1, pp. ccxviii-ccxix, table cvi.

United States 20 years or more, and so were "old" immigrants, while one fourth of them had been here 10 years or less, and so were "new" immigrants. The "old" immigrants, the survivors of those who had entered the country before 1880, constituted half or more of all immigrants in the East North Central States of Ohio, Indiana, and Wisconsin; in the West North Central States of Iowa, Missouri, and Kansas; in most of the southern States; and in Utah, Nevada, and California. These "old" migrants of the pre-1880 days constituted only a third of the immigrants in the industrial States of the New England and Middle Atlantic divisions. "New" immigrants, those of the decade from 1890 to 1900, were concentrated in the industrial States of the North and East. Outside the major urban and industrial areas there were only isolated instances of continuing immigrant cumulations — on the farms of North and South Dakota, in the mining areas of West Virginia, and in the lower States of the Mountain division. Immigrant increments may once have been diffused and diversified, but by the late nineteenth century they were concentrated geographically and specialized economically.

The urban and industrial character of the "new" immigrants as contrasted with the more rural and more agricultural character of the "old" are revealed in striking form in the chronology of immigrant cumulations. For all the foreign-born present in the United States in 1930, the percentage distributions by time of arrival were as shown in the accompanying table:

Time of arrival	*Urban*	*Rural nonfarm*	*Rural farm*
Total	100.0	100.0	100.0
1900 or earlier	31.1	41.9	52.5
1901–1910	29.1	27.5	26.3
1911–1914	13.8	12.3	9.8
1915–1919	4.5	3.8	2.8
1920–1924	13.2	9.2	5.4
1925–1930	8.2	5.3	3.2

This overall picture of time changes reflects the changes in the needs of the American economy rather than the altered sources of immigrant recruitment. As the earlier descriptions of the immigrant successions would indicate, percentages of the foreign-born who were the survivors of pre-1900 immigrants were greatest for those from northern and western Europe, lowest for those from southern Europe. In each immigrant group, however, the percentage of the foreign-born of 1930 who were the survivors of pre-1900 immigrants was greatest among those members of the group resident in rural-farm areas, least for those resident in urban areas.

The comparisons of the period of origin of the immigrant cumulations in the various types of areas seem to corroborate the views expressed by the Immigration Commission of 1907–1910. The immigrants in rural areas included higher proportions of those who had come many years or decades earlier, whereas urban areas included larger proportions of more recent immigrants. This is only part of the picture of selective distribution, however, since percentage comparisons of the composition of urban, rural-nonfarm, and rural-farm populations equate the various types of areas. In fact, immigrant absorption was fundamentally an urban phenomenon at all periods. In 1930, each 1,000 foreign-born whites included 804 in urban areas, 114 in rural-nonfarm areas, and 81 in rural-farm areas. Whatever the period of arrival, the absolute numbers were largest in urban areas, intermediate in rural-nonfarm areas, smallest in rural-farm areas. Moreover, this numerical predominance of the urban residents characterized all immigrant groups, whatever their place of origin and whatever their time of arrival. The influences of changing places of origin in Europe, changing economic conditions in the United States, and restrictions on immigrant admissions were reflected far more in the total numbers of immigrants admitted rather than in the areas of residence of those immigrants who entered the United States. The contributions of the immigrant, the problems of the immigrant, the assimilation of immigrants and their children to American life — these were basically phenomena of the cities and hence processes of urban life. The immigrants were a major segment of the population flows that produced the rapid urbanization of the economy and society. Cities, in turn, conditioned the ways of life of the immigrants and provided the educational and other facilities for their children.

CHARACTERISTICS

The roles of the individual immigrants after arrival and the contributions of immigrants as such to the evolution of the American population cannot be considered apart from the characteristics of the immigrants themselves. It is quite obvious that the cultures both of Europe and of the United States have changed greatly in the period of more than a century and a quarter in which immigration records of sorts have been kept. It is equally obvious that migrant streams have differed widely in origin and in composition.[38] Throughout the period of unrestricted immigration, however, the great majority of the migrants were people without acceptable economic opportunities in their own countries who came here relatively untrained and socially disadvantaged to secure jobs at the bottom of the hierarchy of urban occupations and incomes. The documentation for this broad statement will be presented first from the more abundant materials on the formal demographic characeristics of age and sex, then from the more limited materials on social and economic composition and status.

Immigrants shared the characteristics of internal migrants in that they were young, without the burdens of dependency that marriage brings or the barriers to movement inherent in a secure position in the economy of the home area. From the earliest records through the eighties of the nineteenth century two thirds of all immigrants were in the central productive ages from 15 to 39.[39] About one fifth were youth under age 15, while about one tenth were aged 40 or above. Something of a shift in age structures began with the immigration of the 1890's and continued in the years of great migration that ended with the outbreak of World War I. The proportions of productive workers increased, while the proportions of youth and older people declined. In the years from 1899 through 1914 more than four fifths of all immigrants were between the ages of 14 and 44.

The age structure of the migrants shifted again with World War I and the quota restrictions. In the 1930's and the early 1940's the proportion of aged immigrants increased, while in the last decade there have been higher proportions of youth. The age structures of recent immigrant groups have been more similar to those of the early nineteenth century than to those of the era of the great migrations.

In the long period of relatively unrestricted movement most of the immigrants were males. In some years of the third decade of the nineteenth century three fourths of all immigrants were male, but as the Atlantic crossing became simpler and immigrants increased in numbers, women constituted larger proportions of the total. With the large migrations of the late nineteenth and early twentieth centuries, the proportion of males increased again.

The processes of selection by age and sex were complex ones. Independent migrants among women were predominantly young girls, and so sex ratios were nearer equality in the younger ages but increased progressively with age.[40] The migrations of women as individuals differed greatly among the nationality groups. Whatever the variations in conditions of the passage or sources of immigrants, however, men remained predominant. The numbers of males per 1,000 females among the immigrants were 1,541 in the years from 1820 to 1860, 2,315 in the years from 1900 to 1910.[41]

The age and sex characteristics of quota migrants reflect many selective processes that are essentially non-economic in nature. Quota restrictions barred the streams of young male immigrants, but the alien wives and children of citizens were permitted to enter the country. The inflow of the female relatives of naturalized citizens was a major factor in the reduction of

[38] U.S. Immigration Commission, 1907-1910, *Statistical Review . . . 1820-1910,* pp. 5-8.

[39] U.S. Bureau of the Census, *Historical Statistics of the United States, 1789-1945,* p. 37; *Continuation to 1952 . . . ,* p. 6; U.S. Immigration and Naturalization Service, *Annual Report . . . , 1954,* table 10A.

[40] U.S. Census Office, 1860, *Population of the United States in 1860,* p. xx; U.S. Census Office, 1850, *The Seventh Census of the United States, 1850, Embracing a Statistical View of Each of the States and Territories . . . An Appendix,* p. xc.

[41] U.S. Immigration and Naturalization Service, "Relation of the Quota Law to the General Characteristics of Immigrants," by Gertrude Krichefsky, *Monthly Review,* Vol. 3, p. 269 (1946); special compilations.

the sex ratio of migrants to 776 in 1931–1940, 696 in 1941–1945, and 674 in 1946–1950. The ratio for the 5 years from 1951 through 1955 was 682. Thus the humanitarian exemption of families in the quota laws reversed one of the long-standing characteristics of immigration. Women rather than men have predominated in the immigration of the last quarter century.

The young and predominantly male immigrants of the great movements included large portions of the single and small portions of the widowed and the divorced. Under the quotas the majority of the immigrants either were or had been married. The proportionate marital status of the immigrants of selected periods from 1911 to 1955 portrays the shift that has occurred:[42]

Status	*1911–1920*	*1931–1940*	*1951–1955*
Single	61.3	48.7	47.2
Married	36.2	45.5	48.0
Widowed	2.5	5.0	3.3
Divorced	....	0.8	1.5

It is widely assumed that the immigrants were common people with little education and lowly occupations. Precise documentation of this statement is difficult. For a considerable period of time steerage passengers were counted as immigrants, while the upper social and occupational groups who travelled as first and second class passengers were ignored in the government reports. There were further and more basic difficulties in securing data on the occupational composition of immigrant groups. Out of all the uncertainties there comes a picture that is clear-cut in its most significant aspect. The immigrants of the period of the great movements were largely illiterate; they became unskilled and semiskilled workers. The immigrants of the present are at least as educated as the native population, and they include substantially larger proportions of individuals in the upper occupational groups.

The characteristics and status of immigrants at the successive time periods are reflected in the simple figures on illiteracy. As late as 1899 to 1910 more than one fourth of the immigrants reported that they could neither read nor write.[43] Illiteracy was infrequent among immigrants from the countries of North and West Europe, Germany, and Czechoslovakia, but it was widespread among those who came from other areas of the Continent. In the decade from 1946 to 1955 less than 1 percent of the immigrants aged 16 and above were illiterate.[44]

The fragmentary records of the nineteenth and twentieth centuries suggest that earlier immigrant streams may have included somewhat larger proportions of the middle and professional classes than later streams. In the years from 1820 to 1860 only 40 to 45 percent of the immigrants reported occupations.[45] "Farmers" constituted one fifth of the immigrants with occupations in 1820–1830, three tenths of those in 1830–1860. "Merchants" were one fourth the immigrants with occupations in 1820–1830, less than one seventh in 1830–1840, less than one tenth in 1850–1860. "Laborers" increased from 13.7 percent of the immigrants with occupations in 1820–1830 to 39.7 percent of those in 1850–1860. All the professions combined included 2.5 percent of the immigrants with occupations in 1820–1830, 0.4 percent in 1850–1860.

In the decade from 1901 to 1910, three fifths of all immigrants who reported occupations were unskilled laborers, while only 1.4 percent were professional or semiprofessional (table 6). In the years from 1951 to 1955 the professional and clerical workers together constituted almost 30 percent of all immigrants with occupations, while laborers constituted less than 13 percent. The imposition of quotas combined with the pressures to move from Europe created a major qualitative transformation as well as a numerical limitation of migration. Immigrants now contribute disproportionately to the upper classes in the occupational hierarchy rather than the lower, to the ranks of the skilled rather than the unskilled.

[42] *Ibid.*, p. 269, and special compilations.

[43] U.S. Immigration Commission, 1907-1910, *Statistical Review . . . 1820-1910,* pp. 84-85.

[44] References, Footnote 41. Literacy and other characteristics of immigrants are given in the *Annual Reports* of the U.S. Immigration and Naturalization Service.

[45] U.S. Census Office, 1860, *op. cit.*, p. xxii.

TABLE 6

Occupation of Immigrants: Selected Periods, 1899 to 1955

Occupation	1899 to 1955	1901 to 1920	1921 to 1930	1931 to 1940	1941 to 1945	1946 to 1950	1951 to 1955
Percent reporting occupation..........	67.1	74.3	60.8	41.9	43.3	45.7	47.8
PERCENT DISTRIBUTION							
Total..............................	100.0	100.0	100.0	100.0	100.0	100.0	100.0
Professional, semiprofessional..............	3.3	1.4	4.5	17.3	24.2	16.2	13.9
Farmers, farm managers..................	2.7	1.6	4.9	4.2	2.3	9.1	6.2
Proprietors, managers, officials, except farm............................	3.3	2.7	3.5	15.3	15.2	7.1	5.2
Clerical, sales, etc.........................	3.9	1.5	7.0	10.6	16.7	17.5	15.4
Craftsmen, foremen, operatives, etc.........	19.9	17.8	23.7	19.3	21.9	30.7	32.6
Domestic...............................	14.9	14.1	17.2	15.0	7.8	7.5	8.4
Service[1]................................	3.0	1.3	6.0	6.7	5.6	4.9	5.3
Farm laborers............................	20.0	24.5	8.5	2.9	1.1	1.6	3.8
Laborers, except farm.....................	29.0	35.1	24.7	8.6	5.2	5.3	9.1

[1] Includes protective service workers.

Source: Based on U.S. Immigration and Naturalization Service, "Relation of the Quota Law to General Characteristics of Immigrants," by Gertrude Krichefsky, *Monthly Review,* Vol. 3, p. 269 (1946); *idem, Annual Report . . . 1950,* table 10A; *idem, Annual Report . . . 1955,* table 10A.

STUDY AND DISCUSSION QUESTIONS

1. The U.S. Census gathers some data on international migration indirectly, i.e., it gathers data on certain characteristics of persons which may tell us something about their migration history. What sorts of questions might the census ask to obtain such information? Look up the history of international migration data collection in the census.
2. Petersen's typology of migration was developed on the basis of "motives" for migration. On what other characteristics of migration might a typology be based? Discuss the merits of your suggested typology in comparison with the merits of Petersen's work.
3. The two purposes of theory are to synthesize knowledge in an area and to point up needs for future research. How might Petersen's typology fit in with these purposes of migration theory?
4. Analyze one of the mass migrations discussed by the Woytinskys, considering the roles of economic, demographic, and cultural and political factors in bringing about this migration.
5. Immigration into the United States was virtually halted around 1920 with the enactment of the quota system. Look up the history of this system. How was it developed? What factors were considered? Is the present system different from the original quota system?
6. Some states have major ports of entry for receiving immigrants into the United States, e.g., Florida, New York, California, or Texas. If your state has such an entry point, find out what kinds of records are kept on these immigrants. How reliable is the data? How extensive is it?
7. A nation's governmental policy on emigration can have a great effect on how many persons leave a country. Compare the policy on emigration in the United States with the policy in Russia or East Germany.
8. Demographers often use what is known as the population equation in their analyses. This

equation is $P_2 = P_1 + B - D \pm M$, or a population at a later point in time is equal to the population at an earlier point in time, plus the births, minus the deaths, and plus or minus the net migration in the interim. Using this equation, determine the net migration in your state between 1950 and 1960.

SUGGESTED ADDITIONAL READING

Taft, Donald, and Richard Robbins. *International Migrations: The Immigrant in the Modern World.* New York: The Ronald Press, 1955.
A comprehensive study of the trends, causes, and consequences of international migration.

Kulischer, Eugene. *Europe on the Move: War and Population Changes, 1917–1947.* New York: Columbia University Press, 1948.
Measures and analyzes the dislocations and relocations occasioned by two world wars and their aftermath.

Thomas, Brinley. "International Migration," pp. 510–543 in *The Study of Population*, eds., Philip M. Hauser and Otis Dudley Duncan. Chicago: University of Chicago Press, 1959.
A general treatise which examines sources of data, methods of analysis, existing knowledge, and further research needed.

Spengler, Joseph J. "Some Economic Aspects of Immigration into the United States," *Law and Contemporary Problems*, 21:2 (Spring, 1956), pp. 236–255.
An economic perspective of the mass movements to the United States in the nineteenth and twentieth centuries.

CHAPTER 7

Internal Migration Patterns

International migration is important to demographic study because it deals with population shifts between nations. Internal migration, on the other hand, is a part of demographic study mainly because it deals with population shifts within nations. The distinction between the two types of migration analysis is based on the historical interest in factors affecting the population *size* of individual nations as opposed to the distribution and mobility of population *within* nations, and on the independent sources of data about the two types of movement.

While the term "internal migration" connotes movement within a country, demographers have further refined the term to limit its meaning to only certain types of movements. *Migrants* are typically defined as persons who change their permanent residence from one community to another or from some other large geographical unit to another. In the United States census, a migrant is one who has moved from one county to a different county. The intent is to define migrants as those who have severed connections with one area of residence and established connections in another. Given the limited number of geographical distinctions that can be made in census data, one type of geographical unit (the county, in the case of the United States) is chosen as representing the best approximation to movements that involve severance of community ties. It is obvious that this approximation is crude, at best, but it has been traditional to define migration in this way.

Local movers are persons who change their residence but who do not cross the critical boundary necessary for identification as migrants. Thus, someone who moves next door is a local mover, as is a person who moves several miles but does not cross a migration-defining geographical unit (such as a county in the United States). On the other hand, someone who moves only one street block but crosses a county line is regarded as a migrant, as is the person who shifts residence from one corner of a country to another. Actual distance moved is correlated with, but not an integral component of, the definitions. The difficulty in measuring currents and trends of migration within a country can be easily perceived. However, the dilemma is not one that is likely to be resolved in the immediate future since there are practical limits on the detail about residential mobility that can be collected through official sources.

The volume of internal migration in countries far exceeds that of international migration. It has been estimated that in Europe, in about 1930, at least seventy-five million inhabitants were living outside their native communities while only about ten million were outside their countries of birth. Internal migration rates, of course, vary from country to country. They tend to be higher in more developed countries. For example, the rate of internal migration is quite small in India compared with that in the United States. It is also true, as in the case of international migration, that streams of internal migration tend to offset one another; thus, "net" migration between two areas is often a very small proportion of "gross" migration between the two areas. Some demographers have referred to such offsetting migration patterns as "ineffective" or "inefficient" in the sense that very little numerical redistribution of the population results, but they can be seen as potentially effective in allowing individuals to adjust to new, more satisfying residential situations.

At least five types of residential mobility are emphasized by students of population: rural to urban; city to suburban; between counties (or similar areas in other countries); between states (or similar areas in other countries); and between regions. These are overlapping categories, since the first two may or may not involve crossing of county, state, or regional lines. Migration from rural to urban areas, as indicated by Kuroda, is a dominant migration pattern, especially in developing countries which are heavily rural. Rural-urban movements of people have contributed substantially to the growing urbanization of many countries in recent decades. Moreover, a considerable part of these movements has been to large cities, thereby increasing the urban density of these places and making these places dominant urban centers. In the United States, rural-urban migration has been associated with the mechanization of farms and the consequent reduced need for farm personnel, as well as with industrial development and economic opportunities generated in cities.

As urbanization grows in a country, an increasing amount of migration takes the form of exchanges between cities. People may move from one city to another to change jobs, to be closer to relatives, to go to college, or to increase their satisfactions or decrease their dissatisfactions in any number of ways. But another type of urban migration has become more prevalent. In modernized countries, as cities get larger, the population tends to spread out beyond the political boundaries of the city. A considerable amount of contemporary migration in such countries is from cities to their surrounding areas (popularly known as suburbs). In the United States, the population of large cities has stabilized while the population of areas outside the cities has increased sharply, mainly because of the "flight to the suburbs."

While the greater volume of internal migration in a country involves short-distance moves (rural-urban and city-suburban migrations generally falling into this class), longer-distance moves are fairly frequent. Moves to distant counties within a state, from state to state within a region, and from one region to another are made by many people, as indicated by Shryock in his analysis of recent migration patterns in the United States.

Although migration is characteristic of all kinds of people, it is more selective of some classes of the population than of others. For example, young adults (those at the typical ages for finishing school, getting married, and taking a job) have a higher propensity to migrate than do persons at other ages. Long-distance migration is more selective of professional and well-educated people than those in other socioeconomic categories. Shorter-distance moves are more characteristic of those in the lower socioeconomic classes. An analysis of white-nonwhite differences in migration patterns in the United States, which examines some of the selective tendencies, is provided by Hamilton in the article cited in the Suggested Additional Reading.

Demographic research on internal migration has been largely descriptive and has been concerned primarily with the measurement of migration trends and differentials among subclasses of the population. Studies comparable to the Indianapolis Study, the Growth of American Families Studies (GAF), and the Princeton Fertility Studies in the area of fertility analysis have not yet been made to identify the factors underlying migration. However, there has been some cataloguing of research findings concerning migratory behavior and some approaches to the formulation of a conceptual scheme.

In the late nineteenth century, E. G. Ravenstein set down what he regarded as "laws" of migration. Based upon analysis of census data for Great Britain, other parts of Europe, and the United States, he derived certain generalizations, among which were that:

1. The great body of migrants move only a short distance.
2. People tend to move in the direction of great centers of commerce and industry.
3. Rural residents near a city tend to move into the city and their places are taken by persons living in more remote places.
4. Each main current of migration produces a compensating countercurrent.

5. The natives of towns are less migratory than those of the rural parts of the country.
6. Females are more migratory than males.
7. Migration from rural to urban, and from urban to rural, areas generally proceeds by stages.

Dorothy Thomas, in a monograph prepared in the late 1930's, evaluated the state of existing knowledge about migration differentials by summarizing the findings of studies done throughout the world up to that time. Examining differentials by age, sex, family status, physical health, mental health, intelligence, occupation, motivation, and assimilation, she concluded that there were "almost no acceptable generalizations about the strength and direction of selective internal migration," which she attributed in part to the lack of adequate data and techniques at the time. Still, differentials by age, sex, and occupation were apparent. In a recent work, Everett Lee has attempted to provide a theoretical framework for these kinds of generalizations. The reading by Shryock documents some of the migration differentials found in the United States based on contemporary data. While there has been much elaboration of research describing the tendencies in internal migration, theoretical development has not been advanced very far by these descriptions of empirical regularities.

Another approach to the formulation of principles of migration has been the statement of relationships between the volume of migration and distance between areas. Typical of this approach have been the works of Stewart, Zipf, and Stouffer. John Q. Stewart proposed that the number of migrants into an area is a function of the number of people residing in other areas divided by the distance those areas were from the area of destination. George K. Zipf hypothesized that the number of migrants between any two communities is proportionate to the product of their populations divided by the shortest transportation distance. Samuel A. Stouffer offered what has become known as the "intervening opportunities theory," namely, that the number of persons going a given distance is directly proportional to the number of opportunities at that distance and inversely proportional to the number of intervening opportunities. All these, and other formulations of this type, have been tested empirically and given at least partial support; but their principal value has been in estimating the size of migration streams rather than in explaining why people migrate.

Bogue has identified a number of variables which appear to be of some help in understanding why people migrate. He has classified these variables under the broad headings of comparative economic opportunity, basic social and economic changes in a society, relative levels of living, mobility requirements for the routine functioning of the economy, and changes in personal status. Bogue and Hauser have also grouped attempted explanations of migration behavior into the more traditional classes of demographic, social, and economic factors, on the one hand, and the newer study of motives for migration, on the other.

Approaches which make greater use of contemporary sociological theory have been emerging in more recent years. Migration has thus been related to deprivation and cohesion within a social system, to goal orientations, to the family decision-making process, to housing satisfactions, and to the interaction between stage in the family life cycle and career development. The selection by Leslie and Richardson focuses on the last of these sets of variables.

As in the case of mortality and fertility analysis, migration analysis lends itself to an approach which recognizes the normative behavior of groups, the actions of governments and other national institutions, and the decisions made by individuals and families. Moreover, the same set of variables can be used to understand local residential mobility as well as longer-distance migration. Individuals and families are guided by the norms of the groups to which they belong in deciding the appropriateness of making a residential move; they are often influenced by societal conditions and are at times required or encouraged by governmental action to change residence; and they incorporate their own motives and preferences in reaching a decision about where they will live. Future research in migration will undoubtedly take account of these factors in attempting to arrive at more explicit and more reliable generalizations about why some people move, as well as why some do not.

*Internal Migration: An Overview of Problems and Studies**

TOSHIO KURODA

I

The internal migration of population has not only demographic, but also socio-economic implications, and its effects are certainly more serious in most of the developing countries than in the developed areas. There are many types of internal migration as is well known. But, the most important is the flow of people from rural agrarian areas to urban industrial districts because such a flow of people usually reflects the extent of socio-economic development and is also certain to cause changes in such demographic behavior as fertility and mortality, together with changes in population structure as a whole.

Urbanization has been accelerated throughout the world particularly since World War II. This, as a matter of fact, has implied a rapid rural-urban migration of people. A problem is that only limited data and information about the rural-urban migration are available at the present time.

One possible approach is to examine data and information about growth rates of urban population because they can suggest something about the general trend of rural-urban migration. In this connection, it may be said that the growth rates of population of "primate" or the greatest city in a country can be a rough indicator.

According to the available data, one cannot find any appreciable rural-urban difference of natural increase rate in many developing countries. Hence, it may be safe to assume that an increase of urban population in the developing countries is mostly attributable to migration of people to cities from rural areas.

It must be noticed that the majority of rural migrants are those young people who would eventually affect fertility levels both in the areas of their origin and also in their destinations. They have a high fertility potential, and their migration tends to reduce natality rate in rural areas and, at the same time, to increase it in urban areas, even if the present high fertility level in rural areas is to be maintained for the time being.[1]

As mentioned earlier, the increase of urban population in developing countries is mostly due to the out-migration of rural people. Characteristics implied in this phenomenon are similar to those which were experienced by Western nations. But, its background — ecological pattern, technological standard and the extent of socio-economic development — is essentially different.

II

Internal migration may be studied with respect to the following three points; first motivation, second mechanism of migration and finally socio-economic implications of migration. A number of studies have been made by sociologists and economists to find what the motivations of migration are. Their methods of approach vary, and it is very difficult to make a proper evaluation of their works. Furthermore, most of the studies are based on the specific data and information of the country studied, and also they were undertaken at different times.

Numerous factors — economic, social, cultural, demographic and even physical — and their combinations have been considered to motivate internal migration. So far, a single factor or a combination of particular factors has not been accepted universally to be the most predominant one. Generally speaking, how-

* An unpublished paper printed by permission of the author and the United Nations. Originally presented to the 1965 World Population Conference.

[1] Recent experience in Japan may give an illustration. Crude birth rates in Tokyo and Osaka, both highly urbanized prefectures, have begun to show higher rates than those of some agricultural prefectures most recently.

ever, economic factors have been emphasized by social scientists as the primary important motives of internal migration, particularly of the rural-urban migration.

The familistic system and agrarian culture in rural society have often been considered to be the factors which impede urbanward movement of people. But, a recent Indian study indicates that these social and cultural factors are "stimulants" rather than "deterrents". According to the study, the pile-up of unemployment in urban areas is a more powerful factor to obstruct exodus of rural population.[2]

There is a persistant regional disparity in economic level and employment opportunities. Such a disparity tends to become larger. Such an economic situation must be seriously considered as a motivating factor of internal migration. The rural-urban disparity in economic life tends to become larger, partly because the reproduction of population is larger in rural areas than in urban districts. The continuous increase of population has resulted in the heavy accumulation of surplus population in rural areas. The population pressure on the productivity of land is tremendous. This provides a condition to push surplus people out of rural communities to the areas of greater economic opportunities. The net result is an alleviation of population pressure in rural areas.

Only a few recent works which the author could know up to now are referred here very briefly. Tachi tested his hypothesis that the mechanism of population migration is a movement to bring about such a distribution of population as would level off the disparities in the level of living among different areas, by using post-war data of Japan.[3] His major conclusions will be summarized as follows: (1) He recognized a substantial levelling effect of population migration upon the regional distribution of income, by comparing the Lorenz' curve of hypothetical population distribution by prefecture, biggest administrative unit in Japan, against real income, with the same curve drawn of the actual population. Hypothetical population here is derived from the presumption of no inter-prefectural migration. (2) Then, he probed a good correlation between the rate of actual population increase, or the net migration-rate, of a given prefecture and its potential of population migration. Migration potential defined by him was computed from the population figures which are derived under the ultimate situation in which even distribution of population against the regional distribution of income will be attained under his hypothesis.

Finally, the author refers to the importance of regional differences of population reproduction as a motivating factor of migration.

Another prominent work has been undertaken by the Pennsylvania University Population Study group. They have analyzed relationships between population redistribution and economic growth in the United States over a long period of time, that is, the period of 80 years from 1870 to 1950.[4] The results of their studies have already been published in two volumes as far as the analysis of economic implication of population growth and redistribution is concerned. However, we understand a third volume which is expected to cover demographic links and rate of migration has not been published yet.

With regard to the so-called income theory of migration, we are also interested in the analysis of employment opportunity because it can be a factor to directly contribute to the economic potentials of migration. The employment opportunity may come from an excess of demand of labor over the supply. Therefore, it is natural to assume that the flow of people heads for the area where abundant employment opportunity exists. In such an area, wage and income levels tend to become higher. So, the index of income level can be used as indicator of employment opportunity.[5]

[2] Bogue, D. J., and Zacharia K. C., "Urbanization and Migration in India", in *India's Urban Future,* edited by Turner, R. (1962), p. 45.

[3] Tachi, M., "Regional Income Disparity and Internal Migration of Population in Japan", *Economic Development and Cultural Change,* Jan. 1964, and also "Shotoku no Chiikibunpu to Kokunai Jinkoido" (Regional Distribution of Income and Internal Migration), *Keizaigaku Kenkyu* (Studies in Economics), 1963.

[4] Kuznets, S., Millar, A. R., and Easterlin, R. A., *Population Redistribution and Economic Growth,* United States, 1870-1950 (Vol. I and Vol. II, 1960).

[5] Okazaki, Y., and Oyama, M., "Daitoshi no Shakaikeizaiteki Jinkogakuteki Kozo to sono Tokucho" (Socio-economic and Demographic Structure of Metropolitan Population, in *Daitoshijinko no Shomondai* (Metropolitan Population in Japan) edited by Tachi, M. (1962).

It may also be interesting to introduce the work done by Nishikawa and his group.[6] They have found that economic factors are dominant, though not exclusive, in internal migration of labor force, after examining inter-prefectural migration in prewar and postwar days. Their study may be summarized as follows: There is a regularity in migration, that is the volume of out-migration of labor force of each prefecture is inversely correlated with income level y_j of sending prefecture, and also the volume of in-migration of labor force is positively correlated with wage rates w_i in receiving prefecture. Furthermore, he has recognized that volume of migration value n_j^i of labor force from *j* prefecture to *i* prefecture depends upon average rates of wage rates w_j in different prefectures besides *i* prefecture, which expressed by the following equation.

$$n_j^i = f(w_j/\overline{w}_i, y_j)$$

This relation is empirically approximated to a linear semi-logarithmic equation, which he calls "Labor Application Equation".

$$\log n_j^i = c_0 + c_1(\overline{w}_j + w_i) + c_2 y_j + u$$

Here *u* is possibility variable depending upon the distribution of $N(0,6)$. He further extended this equation, taking into account various factors affecting regional migration, besides economic factors, as follows.

$$n_j = f(\overline{w}_j/w_i, y_i, \psi)$$

Kono and his group conducted a multiple regression analysis of a variety of postwar migration data in Japan to examine inter-relationship between migration and demographic and economic factors. They found that two economic factors, interprefectural difference in income level and interprefectural difference in the proportion of non-agricultural workers in the total employment, play a significant part in migration.[7]

Another type of study is macroscopic approach. Some studies have indicated the existence of strong positive correlation between economic activities and migration rates. For example, Thomas found a positive correlation between the level of economic activity and the net interstate migration rates in the United States.[8]

A similar study has been undertaken in Japan. Minami found a closer relationship between migration and economic activity, after analyzing relationships between economic trends and migration of agricultural population (since 1920) and also between economic trends and migration of general population (since 1885).[9]

III

It is generally known that the rural-urban migration is considerably selective of age and sex, that is, young males move more often. However, the sex composition of migrants becomes balanced gradually after a pattern of migration is established. The age groups, 15–19 and 20–24, are the majority of migrants. This age pattern of migrants is common to every country with different socio-economic and cultural backgrounds. A slight difference has been found when the age pattern in the United States was compared with that in Japan and India. In the United States, the migration rate comes to the peak at the age 25–29 and then declines gradually and regularly, while the tempo decline is more sharp particularly after age 30 in India and Japan.[10]

[6] Nishikawa, S., and Ohi, K., "Labor market and Regional Mobility" (relatively longer summary in English of "Obohoteishiki ni yoru Rodoshijo no Bunseki"), *Keizaigaku Nempo* (Annual Report of Economics, Keio Economic Society, No. 4, 1960), and also Nishikawa, S., "Chiikikan Rodoido ni Tsuite" (on the Regional Mobility of Labor), *Keizai Kenkyu* (The Economic Review, Jan. 1962), pp. 63-67.

[7] Kono, S., and Shio, M., *Inter-Prefectural Migration in Japan, 1956 and 1961: Migration Analysis,* Demographic Training and Research Centre, Bombay (1963).

[8] Thomas, D. S., "Age and Economic Differences in Interstate Migration", *Population Index* (Vol. 24, No. 4, October 1958), pp. 313-324.

[9] Minami, R., "Keizaihendo to Rodoryoku no Sangyokan Ryudosei" (Economic Change and Redistribution of Labor Force among Industries), *The Hitotsubashi Ronso* (The Hitotsubashi Review, Vol. 51, No. 3, 1964), pp. 73-96. - - - , "Jinkotoshishuchu no Keiko to Hendo" (Trends and Fluctuations in Urbanization in Japan), *Keizai Kenkyu* (The Economic Review, Vol. 16, No. 1, 1965, under press).

[10] Bogue and Zachariah, op. cit., p. 24. Thomas, "Age and Economic Differences . . . . ", op. cit., p. 316

Another question is social and economic characteristics of migrants. There is evidence showing that the educational level of migrants is relatively higher than that of population of their native communities. The Calcutta Industrial Region Survey indicates that the average level of education among migrants is considerably higher than the general population in the states of origin, but lower than the average level among indigenous urban residents. Available data suggest that in India the literate and educated people tend to migrate to urban areas more often than illiterate people. The travel distance in migration is also positively associated with education level of migrants.

A social-medical survey of young migrants in the post-war years conducted in Scotland also indicated that magnitudes into the city of Aberdeen showed much higher educational level than the city born population.[11]

A 10 per cent sample of the 1928 male birth cohort chosen serially in 1948–1949 was surveyed in Sweden recently to study internal migration. This study indicates that migrants increased proportionately with level of competence expressed in various ways.[12]

The Scotland survey also suggests strong occupational selectivity of migration, that is, the professional and high educated groups are most likely to move and also social background (as indicated primarily by parental occupation) strongly influences residential choices. However, it seems to be quite possible that in developing countries the migrants to cities are likely to have poorer working status and less income than indigenous urban residents, although their average educational level is higher than that of remaining people in their original communities.[13]

[11] Illsley, R, Finlayson, A., and Thompson, B., "The Motivation and Characteristics of Internal Migrants", *Milbank Memorial Fund Quarterly* (Vol. XII, No. 2 and 3).

[12] Thomas, D. S., "Internal Migration in Sweden: A Recent Study", *Population Index,* (Vol. 29, No. 2, 1963), pp. 125-129.

[13] Bogue and Zacharia, *op. cit.,* pp. 48-51.

IV

Some questions are raised in view of the intensity of rural-urban migration in the world, particularly in developing countries.

One question is concerned with the social selectivity of migration. If young rural people, able physically and mentally, move to urban areas continuously, only illiterate, unskilled and infirm people might be left in rural communities. The quantitative and qualitative imbalance of population between rural and urban areas would be a disadvantage for not only regional development but also the growth of the nation as a whole.

Another question is concerned with changes in the age composition pattern caused by heavy rural-urban migration; aging of population in rural areas, while rejuvenation of population in urban areas. Regional changes in demographic structure just mentioned above surely affects regional development, economically and socially.

As far as experiences of Western countries are concerned, no serious troubles concerning the first question did come out, but rural versus urban and agriculture versus industry seems to have contributed to the achievement of modernization by rather mutually complementing.

Some theoretical studies on the mechanism of internal migration as mentioned earlier, suggest that internal migration, especially rural-urban migration, is a movement to adjust the distribution of economic opportuntities. If this holds true, higher mobility of population might be desirable. However, the issue is not so simple.

In order to promote balanced development of regional communities, migration behavior which may accelerate the rural versus urban polarization should be deeply explored by a comprehensive project of experts in various disciplines.

A few suggestions may be given in connection with this point; necessity of putting more emphasis on micro-demographic analysis, and of making detailed surveys on the relationships between internal migration and socio-economic development. Finally, international discussion on the collection and presentation of data on internal migration would be useful.

*Mobility Within the United States**

Henry S. Shryock

Trends in Types of Mobility

The remarkable thing about the rates of various types of mobility over the 11 consecutive years for which we have annual observations is their stability. About one-fifth of the population had lived in a different house a year ago. Of these movers, about two-thirds moved only within the same county and less than one-sixth moved from one state to another. These results confirm other findings that mobility within a country is mostly short-distance mobility. If movers were simply distributed in proportion to the population at each potential destination within the country, the majority of movers would move to a noncontiguous state.

There has been no discernable trend in any of these types of mobility rates since the year 1947 to 1948. Dips in the rates for the years of economic recession, 1949 to 1950 (as well as 1948 to 1949) and 1953 to 1954, were relatively slight. The recession that began about July 1957 had no visible effect on the rate for the period from March 1957 to March 1958, but there was a slight dip in some rates in the following 12 months. The outbreak of the Korean War in the summer of 1950 stimulated the mobility of the population somewhat. Although trends in mobility rates are still not found within specific age-sex groups, there has been some evidence of an upward trend in the intracounty mobility rate for nonwhites and very slight downward trends in the nonwhite migration rate and the white intracounty mobility rate.

Differences in the data available for earlier periods limit our ability to make comparisons, especially for the shorter types of moves. Mobility probably reached a peak during World War II and in the year or two following V-J Day. The war and returning prosperity stimulated interstate migration, in particular. Military migration is characteristically long-distance migration; and, in many areas, the burgeoning of defense production soon exhausted the local pools of unemployed and other labor reserves. As compared with 1940, from 16 to 18 million civilians were living in a different county on V-J Day. Wartime moves made by members of the armed forces are obviously less likely than those made by civilians to lead to a permanent change of residence, but many "G.I.'s" made permanent changes as the result of their military experience and the new vistas that were opened for them. All the interregional streams were accelerated by the war — even those to regions usually characterized by net out-migration.

In the Great Depression of the 1930's, migration and particularly interstate migration were at a relatively low ebb. Estimates of decennial interstate migration from statistics on state of birth give peak rates for the 1850's and the 1940's, which were at least twice as high as the rate for the 1930's.

Both the Great Depression and recession of 1949 to 1950 seem to have had a more inhibiting effect upon the migration of nonwhites than upon that of whites. As economic opportunities shrink, we should expect the Negro worker to be more adversely affected than the white worker.

Relation of Residential Location to Mobility Status and to Propensity to Move

The conventional Census tables on mobility status for geographic areas and residential types show the mobility experience over a past period of the persons now living in the area. At the beginning of the period, some of the movers lived in a different area. It seems appropriate to describe a population that contains a relatively high proportion of recent in-migrants to the area as being a relatively mobile population. On the

* Reprinted with permission from Henry S. Shryock, *Population Mobility Within the United States.* Chicago: Family and Community Study Center, 1964, pp. 411-425.

other hand, it is only when we exclude in-migrants and include out-migrants that we can characterize the population of an area in terms of its propensity to move. Both mobility status and propensity to move are meaningful concepts for characterizing the population of an area . An area containing a high proportion of recent movers may be hypothesized to have certain associated characteristics and problems. Also, an area whose residents have a high propensity to move may typically have certain characteristics and problems. The two types of areas may differ markedly in these respects when the former has a high net in-migration and the latter a high net out-migration. For most areas over a one-year period, however, the two measures have very similar values for total mobility; and the proportion of resident movers in an area's population can usually be taken to indicate the propensity to move.

Geographic Areas

If the regions or geographic divisions are listed in their usual publication order, there is a persistent tendency for the mobility rate to increase as we go down the list. This pattern is also fairly persistent for specific types of mobility and for population turnover. Furthermore, this geographic pattern also tends to persist within the urban, rural-nonfarm, and rural-farm populations considered separately although the Southern farm population has higher rates of short-distance mobility than the Western farm population. It seems very likely that the high local circulation of Southern farm people is caused by the prevalence of sharecropping and other forms of tenancy. With some exceptions in the case of the nonwhite population — chiefly a matter of somewhat lower proportions of migrants in Southern divisions than in Northern divisions, the order of mobility rates found among geographic divisions was the same for the white and nonwhite populations as that previously described for the total population. When out-migration is taken into account for the period 1935 to 1940, there seems to have been only slight regional differences in the propensity of nonwhites to make interstate moves.

Not only does the West attract many migrants but also its people have a high propensity to make local, short-distance moves; and there seems to be a tendency toward an increasing out-migration rate. Within the West, Utah has relatively low mobility rates of all types. Within the Deep South, Louisiana has relatively low intracounty mobility whereas Florida contains relatively high proportions of intracounty movers and of migrants from noncontiguous states.

When we turn to counties and state economic areas, we find even more diversity among mobility rates, including considerable diversity within regions. Nonetheless, interregional variation seems to be greater than intraregional variation. No areas with very high rates are found in the Northeast, but there is a fairly wide range even within this region. The areas with very high intracounty mobility rates include many in the Cotton Belt as well as those where atomic energy plants and missile production are located. The latter type also contains large proportions of migrants, of course. High intracounty mobility rates were found in both metropolitan and nonmetropolitan counties; the metropolitan counties with highest local mobility rates were mostly in the Southern Pacific area, the Southwest, and Florida. Very low local mobility rates were observed in the Chesapeake Bay reaches, the upper Missouri Valley, and the Lake States Cutover, as well as in the Northeast. The counties with high in-migration rates typically had small populations, whereas those with the lowest rates comprised both very large metropolitan counties and small agricultural counties. Northeastern metropolitan and mining counties usually had very low migration rates for the 1949–1950 period.

Some of the variation in mobility rates is an artifact of the type of areal unit used or, as just mentioned, of population size. Intrastate migration rates, for example, tend to vary directly with the land area of states; and the rate of migration from contiguous states tends to vary inversely with the population of the given state. Nonetheless, it is apparent that even if area and population size were held constant a great deal of geographic variability in mobility rates would still remain.

Type of Residence

In the 1950 Census and subsequent annual surveys, nonmetropolitan areas were found to have higher migration rates than metropolitan areas and, in 1950, a higher short-distance mobility rate as well. (This differential was most typical of the Northeast and was not typical of the South and North Central region.) This is a surprising finding. Moreover, when we look at the urban fringe population (which may be viewed as approximating the suburban population), we find that its mobility rate has been less than that of the nonfarm population outside metropolitan areas. It is possible that, if the boundaries of urbanized areas could have been brought up to date in the 1950 Census or if the mobility questions had referred to a somewhat longer period, the population living in fringe areas would have shown the expected maximal rate. More recent evidence, however, from the March 1958 C.P.S., is that the rural-nonfarm population out beyond the 1950 urbanized areas but within 1950 standard metropolitan areas, has high mobility rates but again not so high as those of the nonfarm population outside metropolitan areas. Since the populations of both the inner and outer "suburban" zones have both been growing rapidly, it would appear that the explanation of the paradox lies in a minimal out-movement from these areas.

In the largest urbanized areas, the fringe areas have higher mobility rates than their central cities, but in the other urbanized areas rates are about the same for fringes and central cities. The literature on internal migration tends to give the impression that migrants to metropolitan areas settle first in the central cities and that the suburbs are settled chiefly by migrants from their own central cities. There may be a good deal of this kind of migration by stages, but actually the rates of in-migration from other states and of in-movement from farms are at least as high in the urban-fringe areas as in central cities. Long-distance migrants to suburbs may come characteristically from other metropolitan areas, however, and particularly from their suburbs. Professional workers and salaried members of the managerial class are probably likely to make moves of this last sort.

The largest central cities contain relatively fewer recent movers than even the farm population. The urban population as a whole has a higher mobility rate than the farm population, on the other hand. When mobility rates are plotted against size of place, we get a rough convex parabola with a peak in the middle-sized urban places. In terms of the total mobility rate for 1949–1950, movers constitute only about one-eighth of the population in urbanized areas of 3 million or more, one-fifth in cities of 10,000 or more outside urbanized areas, and one-sixth in rural areas. The nonfarm population in the "open country" has a rate just about at the peak level, also. It is the farm population and, to a lesser extent, the village population that pulls down the mobility rates in rural areas.

The farm population lags especially in its proportion of long-distance migrants whereas the urban and rural-nonfarm population have about the same rate. The state-of-birth data suggest that, until roughly a generation ago, the interstate migration rate was highest in urban areas. The intrastate migration rate is relatively low in central cities of urbanized areas, notably in the larger urbanized areas. These low rates depress that for the total urban population to a point where it is below that of the farm population.

The differentials according to size of place were greater for migration rates than for intracounty mobility rates. In the postcensal years, mobility rates are higher for all size-of-place categories, but the patterns are very similar to those of 1950.

The above generalizations about the relationships between mobility and size of place apply mainly to the white population. In the nonwhite population, there is less variability of mobility rates with size of place. The rural-nonfarm population does not have a particularly high mobility rate among nonwhites. The nonwhite farm population exhibits the high intracounty mobility characteristic of the Southern farm population; there is much overlap of these two groups, of course. In the postcensal period, the short-distance mobility rate of nonwhites has increased sharply in urbanized areas so that this part of the nonwhite population is now the most mobile. Possibly the breaking down of residential segregation in Northern cities or the overflow of Negroes into new neighborhoods there is responsible for this sharp rise in local mobility.

The estimates show that the nonfarm population does not consistently have a greater propensity for moving that the farm population, and excesses here are smaller than excesses in the proportion of resident movers because of the net movement from farms to nonfarm residences. The nonfarm population has a much greater propensity to make long-distance moves — between noncontiguous states — than the farm population. In the year 1949 to 1950, nonwhites on farms had a greater propensity to move than nonwhites living in nonfarm residences.

Population Redistribution and Streams of Migration

The major types of population redistribution are well-known because they have long been evident from differential rates of population growth, estimates of net migration by the residual method, and state-of-birth data. Study of the census and survey data on migration for specific periods tells us more about such things as fluctuations in net migration in shorter periods of time than a decade, the relationships between net and gross migration, and the changing patterns of migration streams.

Geographic Redistribution

The strong Westward movement of the American people has continued from the time when the first settlers stepped ashore on the Atlantic coast to the present time. As the frontier advanced, however, what were once areas of net in-migration have successively become areas of net out-migration. There are no signs yet that the flow into the Pacific Coast States is ceasing although we do have records of periods when the net gain was relatively small. The late 1940's was such a period for California. Furthermore, both the number of out-migrants and the rate of gross out-migration from the West seem to be picking up. The volume of migration of Negroes to the West Coast was relatively small until the 1940's when the war gave it an added impetus.

Settlement of the Great Plains was concentrated into a relatively short period of our history. The early state of birth data show net in-migration at its peak; but, by roughly the turn of the century, the rate of net out-migration from this area had become much greater than that from many areas further east. Much of this loss went to the Pacific and Mountain States. Now with some industrialization and a better man-land ratio in agriculture, net out-migration seems to be slackening.

But there is much internal migration that is not a part of the westward movement. The growing importance of easterly counterstreams has already been mentioned. There have always been many other streams, mostly over short distances but some to more distant goals. In most periods, there has been a net shift of population from South to North; much of this is associated with concomitant population concentration in urban and metropolitan areas, as manufacturing, commerce, and the service industries burgeoned and drew workers from agriculture. In recent decades older manufacturing and mining areas in the Northeast have fallen upon hard times while new industries and centers of trade have sprung up in the Southern Piedmont and along the Gulf Coast. Government employment and climatic amenities have also made magnets of the Washington area and of Florida, respectively. The South-North migration picture is becoming more complex. The basic net flow is still northward, but the tide may be turning.

The emerging tendency toward net flows into some parts of the South from other regions is mainly a matter of whites migrating down into some of the South Atlantic States and, to a lesser extent, into Texas and Louisiana. We do have the anomaly of the net in-migration for the South as a whole shown by the 1950 Census statistics. It is important to bear in mind that the indicated net migration of Southern nonwhites was just about nil in this year, and even for whites the net in-migration contituted only 0.3 percent of the South's white population. As compared with the war years and postcensal years, the annual rate of out-migration was depressed. Furthermore, the annual rate of in-migration was lower for 1949–1950 than for the 1953–1958 period, but we cannot be sure about the comparison with the war years.

The slight net in-migration into the South was essentially one of civilians and cannot be explained away as resulting from shifts of members of the armed forces. A major contributor to this net in-migration was the net gain of both whites and nonwhites by the South Atlantic from the Middle Atlantic division. For whites, the balance of this interchange was in the same direction in the 1935–1940 period; and if we had the necessary detail in our data for other periods, we might find that this situation was not at all unusual. The slight net gain of Oklahoma and Texas from California in the 1949–1950 period is a far cry from the situation back in the late 1930's when "Okies" and other Southwesterners were pouring into California. The stream of migrants from the West to the South has become more important, moreover.

Although bias in the 1950 Census data cannot be altogether ruled out as a contributing factor, additional evidence cited in the earlier chapters leads me to conclude that there may well have been a small net in-migration to the South in this particular year and possibly in other years in the late 1940's as well. After the very great displacements of population by the war, it seems plausible that even the slight economic recession may have dammed the normal prevailing channels of migration and led to considerable return migration, for example, to the Southwest from California and of Negroes to the South Atlantic States from the Northern cities up the coast. It is true that the 1935–1940 period was a depression period and that its migration fails to resemble 1949–1950 in a number of respects. The acceleration of return migration probably took place earlier in the Great Depression, however; and, in fact, the Department of Agriculture estimated net in-movement to farms for two years in the early 1930's but none in the later 1930's.

Net migration from the South has resumed, and the South had a net loss to every other region for the period 1953–1958. Nonetheless, many parts of the South are still receiving a net in-migration, particularly of whites. Decreasing differentials in fertility coupled with relatively greater growth of Southern industry and Southern resort areas should continue to play important roles in breaking up a monolithic pattern.

Two factors were very important to net migration in the 1930–1940 decade — the depression and the drought. Drought accelerated out-migration from the tier of Plain States from North Dakota down to Texas. There was a tremendous net out-migration from these states, mostly to the Pacific States. Elsewhere, however, the Depression reduced net out-migration from the more agricultural to the more industrial and urbanized states and sometimes reversed the direction of the net flow.

World War II restored much of the pattern that had prevailed before the Depression and accelerated all interregional streams. The net migrations to the Pacific States and out of the South probably reached their peak in these war years. Most of the effects were permanent. Reconversion to a peacetime economy and the recession of 1948–1950 did accelerate return migration; but, since the outbreak of the Korean War, migration has been concentrated in its normal channels with relatively few new ones assuming importance.

In the 1949–1950 period, all three streams to the West from other regions were decelerated. The normal channels of interstate migration seem to have been more dammed up for nonwhites than for whites, and there was apparently more return migration on the part of nonwhites.

On the basis of net migration for states, this brief period seems to have been one of the most atypical periods since the 1880's. In general, there has been a fair amount of association between the amount of net migration in one period and that in another. When we use shorter periods instead of decades, we find more frequent reversals in the direction of net migration, as we might expect. The most striking part of the historic picture of net migration by states is the persistently large gain by California. Florida and Oregon also had net in-migration in all the periods examined from 1880 to 1953, whereas Iowa, South Carolina, Kentucky, and Mississippi had persistent net out-migration.

The point has been made repeatedly that the 1949–1950 migration picture differed in many respects from that of the whole decade of the 1940's and notably from that of the war years. A score of state economic areas shifted from significant net in-migration for the decade to significant net out-migration for the final year, and another score experienced a marked deceleration of net in-migration. Both groups included many areas that were centers of considerable wartime activity, either of defense production or of military training. Shipbuilding centers were particularly hard hit by reconversion. The S.E.A.'s that shifted markedly in the other direction — toward net in-migration or less out-migration — were located in the South, the Southwest, the Great Plains, or the Rocky Mountains and appear to be areas to which return migration was accelerated by the recession.

The pattern of gross migration seems to be

less affected by economic and political events than does that of net migration. For example, the rank correlation was +.78 between the rates of gross interdivisional streams for the 1949–1950 and 1935–1940 periods even though net migration patterns of the two periods showed only a moderate association (tau of +.41). The size of the rates of the gross streams is sensitive to these events, of course; but there is a tendency for most streams to change their size in the same direction during a given period.

The fact that gross migration for an area tends to be much greater than its net migration has frequently been noted in the literature. In this monograph, an attempt has been made to measure this relationship and to study variations in the measure over time and space. The ratio between net and gross migration has been interpreted as one broad indicator of the effectiveness of migration in that it shows the total amount of migration that was required to effect the indicated net redistribution of population.

In these terms then, migration among regions or geographic divisions seems to be becoming less effective. Both the 1949–1950 and the 1953–1958 periods had markedly lower ratios than the 1935–1940 and the 1940–1947 periods. In the 1949–1950 period, migration was slightly more effective than in the 1953–1958 period. One of the most unidirectional migration exchanges of record was that between West North Central and the Pacific States in the late depression years; here, the net loss of the former was 85 percent of the total migration in both directions. In contrast, the net loss of the New England to the Middle Atlantic division in the 1949–1950 period was less than 1 percent of the gross interchange. As the West loses the last remnants of its frontier character and if sectional differences in economic opportunities and level of living are tending to disappear, the interregional migration may become largely a matter of milling around within the country in response to fairly specific job situations and to personal factors. On the other hand, such compensating migration should result in more exchange of customs and attitudes and may cause more social change than an equal volume of unidirectional migration.

In terms of the index used, nonwhite migration is more effective than white migration. In the 1935–1940 period, some of the interchanges of nonwhites between Southern and Northern divisions were both large and highly unidirectional. In the more recent period, they were less unidirectional. In both periods, nonwhite interdivisional migration was more concentrated into a few streams than was white interdivisional migration — partly because of greater effectiveness and partly because of the greater concentration of nonwhite population in a few divisions. Because of both social and economic factors, it is likely that the prevailing streams of Negro migration will long continue to be those out of the South. Figuratively, the large cities of the North and West still represent a New World of settlement for the Southern Negro.

Related to the fact that net migration is usually small relative to gross migration for an area is the fact that there is a positive association between rates of in- and out-migration. One might try to explain this association in terms of the old hypothesis that a stream of migration generates a counter-stream, presumably consisting in considerable part of return migrants. There is also another possible explanatory factor, however — a factor of the type earlier described as an artifact of the areal units used. For example, in the case of states, rates of in- and out-migration and of turnover all tend to vary inversely with population size.

A number of demographers have examined the relationships between the size of migrant streams, on the one hand, and such factors as population size of origin and destination, distance between areas, and direction, on the other hand. It is fairly obvious that stream size tends to vary directly with some function of population size and inversely with some function of distance, but there are other factors that also have their effect. The "preference indices" computed for this book take account of population sizes only, so that variation in the index reflects the effects of both distance and of other factors. The inhibiting effect of distance is readily apparent. For example, in interdivisional migration, the median index is 175 (75 percent above the expected volume) for 1949–50 streams between contiguous divisions and only 66 (34 percent below the expected volume) for those between noncontiguous divisions. Nonetheless, many of the streams to the Pacific division from noncontiguous divisions were considerably larger than their expected sizes. In the 1935–1940 period, the observed number of migrants from the West North Central division to the Pacific division was 10 times larger than the expected number. Both in 1940 and in 1950, the South Atlantic division had more total in-migrants from other divisions than expected and fewer out-migrants. The indices show that whites had a greater preference for lateral migration across the South than nonwhites, and also for migration between the South and West. Nonwhites, however, had a greater preference for migration between the North and the South — in both directions — and for east-west migration above the Mason-Dixon Line. Among whites, just as the volumes of streams and their counterstreams have a positive association, so also there is a positive association between the preference indices of streams and counterstreams.

Shifts in Type of Residence

Although historically the movement from farms was of considerable magnitude, nowadays it constitutes but a small part of population mobility. Only about 8 percent of all movers in the year 1949–1950 moved from a farm to a nonfarm residence whereas 80 percent moved from one nonfarm residence to another. Past migrations have depleted the farm population to the point where it can no longer provide many movers. On the other hand, an estimated 17 percent of the persons 18 years old and over living in nonfarm residences were born on a farm, according to the Current Population Survey of May 1958. Goldberg and the Freedmans have shown how their origin differentiates the farm-nonfarm movers from those who were reared in nonfarm homes. Behavior in such areas as social participation and fertility are affected.[1] Movement from farms and changing land use have reduced the farm population from 32.5 million in 1916 to 21 million in 1959, with a corresponding drop from 32 to 12 percent of the total population. Furthermore, the net movement from farms continues, although Censuses and surveys probably understate it.

Although historically females have had a considerably higher propensity for leaving farms than males, in recent years there has not been much difference between the sexes in this tendency. One new factor has been the induction of young men into the armed forces. Many of these men settle in nonfarm homes after their discharge.

Even in the recession year 1949–1950, the role of migration in shifting people from farm to nonfarm residences is evident. For example, of the 1.75 million persons reported as leaving farms in the year 1949–1950, less than half went to urban areas and of these a minority went to the largest urban areas. About 42 percent went to nonfarm residences in the open country and to hamlets. Unfortunately, the available data do not permit us to determine the proportion of movers into the combined urbanized areas from outside such areas who came from farms, but the data suggest that the farm population was a very minor direct source of the growth of these areas. Thus, it seems likely that the shift of population towards places of larger size is essentially a process of movement to places of the next largest size class rather than of considerable movement from open country to metropolis. Ravenstein described this process many years ago.

Long-distance migration was most prevalent among movers from one urban place to another and least prevalent among those from one farm to another. In terms simply of the farm-nonfarm dichotomy, movers between unlike types of residences usually spanned longer distances than those between like types.

The average (median) economic subregion had a reported net out-movement of 2 percent from its rural-farm population in the single year 1949 to 1950, and this is probably an understatement. The Agricultural Marketing Service estimated a net movement from farms amounting to 1,300,000 in this year. The highest rates of net out-movement from farms occurred in subregions containing metropolitan areas. Again, it seems unlikely that these movers went typically to the metropolises themselves; rather the pull of the metropolis on the nonfarm people in the hinterland may have created "vacuums" in the villages and small towns into which there was an exodus from farms.

Of movers from farms, a larger proportion

[1] David Goldberg. "Another Look at the Indianapolis Fertility Data," *Milbank Memorial Fund Quarterly,* 38 (1): 23-36. January 1960.

of the nonwhites than of the whites went to open-country nonfarm residences and to the central cities of urbanized areas — the extremes of the size-of-place scale. Conversely, a larger proportion of whites leaving farms went to hamlets, villages, small towns, and the fringes of urbanized areas. Longitudinal data would probably show some interesting contrasts between whites and Negroes in the extent and types of migration by stages.

Although it is estimated that in the 1940–1950 decade, there was a net flow of about 5 million persons from nonmetropolitan to metropolitan areas, there was virtually no net migration in the last year of this decade, according to the 1950 Census. Thus, this is another peculiarity of the 1949–1950 period. There may be genuine interruptions of the net flow over short periods of time, but there is no doubt about the increasing concentration of our population in metropolitan areas and the continuation of this trend past 1950. Unfortunately, one of the worst defects of the Census data on population mobility is their paucity of information on the dispersion of population *within* metropolitan areas. Largely because of difficulties of measurement, we know little of the gross movements between cities and their suburbs, in whatever manner the latter may be defined. From comparative data on population growth, however, we do know that there is a tremendous net movement out to the suburbs and that this is probably accelerating. Moreover, in a number of the large, mature metropolitan areas of the Northeast and Middle West, population size in the central city already seems to have reached its peak.

Most of the individual state economic areas with the highest rates of net out-migration in the 1949–1950 year were nonmetropolitan, whereas those with the highest rates of net in-migration were fairly evenly divided between metropolitan and nonmetropolitan. The Northeastern metropolitan S.E.A.'s tended to have relatively low *gross* rates of both in- and out-migration; in fact the S.E.A. representing the New York State part of the New York — Northeastern New Jersey Standard Metropolitan Area had the lowest turnover rate of all S.E.A.'s. The highest gross out-migration rates were characteristically from nonmetropolitan areas.

Differentials According to Personal Characteristics

The higher rates of short-distance mobility among Negroes than among whites seem to reflect (1) frequent changes of residence and of landlord by tenants and sharecroppers in Southern agriculture, and (2) frequent changes of address by Negro renters living in big cities. The greater intracounty mobility of Negroes in recent years than in the past is probably associated mainly with the latter phenomenon. The relative lack of stability in the Negro family, as indicated by the high proportion of families headed by a woman and the high proportion of children living with the mother only or with grandparents, must also be a factor in the high rate of short-distance mobility.

Despite the considerable and persistent flow of Negroes out of the Deep South, in most comparisons, nonwhites have lower migration rates than whites. The exceptions have been periods like the late stages of World War II and World War I when there was an acute labor shortage and even the disadvantaged groups (Negroes, women, the elderly, adolescents, and the physically handicapped) were being actively recruited for distant labor markets. Despite the importance of interregional migration for Negroes, the rates for nonwhites seldom approach those for whites in the case of migration between noncontiguous states. Nonwhites also lag in "middle-distance moves" such as those between counties within a state. Certainly, knowledge of opportunities at a distance and the financial ability to make the move must be less, on the average, for Negroes than for whites. Then too, although Negroes may have frequent changes of residence within the ghetto-like areas to which they tend to be confined in large cities, they have not shared very much in the recent extensive movements to the suburbs. In the big metropolitan areas, a move to a new suburban development means a move across a county line, in other words, short-distance migration.

Since the Negro population was at first highly concentrated in the plantation South, its migration history has been in large part a diffusion to the North and West. The first great exodus began in World War I. Not only greater job opportunities and more liberal welfare programs but also generally less discrimination in education, recreation, shopping, and other aspects of daily life have tended to maintain a strong flow of a relatively unidirectional nature. Presumably Negroes would return to their Southern homes mostly when forced to do so by a crisis situation such as loss of job or the sickness of nonmigrant parents. One exception has been the Negro teacher reared and educated in the North, who found a job most readily in the segregated schools of the Southern States. Increasingly, white workers have been finding economic opportunities in professional and managerial positions in the booming industries of the South and Southwest even while less skilled whites continue to leave Southern rural areas for factory jobs in Northern cities. As the result of these various currents and counter-currents, we may find that the gross migration rate from the South was often higher for whites than for nonwhites whereas the net out-migration rate was greater for nonwhites.

The persistent slight excess of the over-all mobility rate of males over that of females is the resultant of a higher migration rate for males with virtually identical rates of intracounty mobility. In fact, the sex ratio of movers tends to increase with the distance spanned. The pattern by age is more complicated, however. From 14 to 19 years, girls are considerably more mobile than boys, but from 20 to 54 years, men are more mobile than women. At the youngest and oldest ages, the sexes have about the same mobility rates.

Over the range of ages, mobility rates of each type tend to be moderately high for young children, to decrease through high-school age, to rise again very sharply to an absolute maximum in the early 20's, and then to decline gradually with age except for a slight upturn at about 65 or 70. The peak age comes earlier for females than for males and earlier for nonwhites than for whites.

A majority of adult males move to take a job or to look for work whereas the mobility of most women and children is derivative, i. e., contingent upon the mobility of the husband or father. Even among adult males, reasons not directly connected with employment, such as a change in marital status, a housing problem, or a health problem, account for many moves. These non-economic reasons are more prominent in the shorter than in the longer types of moves. We see then that mobility differentials by age and sex are closely tied in with the family cycle, as broadly defined.

After the completion of his education, the young person, particularly the boy or young man, is likely to leave home to take a job or go into the armed forces. At marriage, both the groom and bride will usually move again, often from a rooming-house to an apartment. When children arrive, the family may move to a house in the suburbs, both to obtain a housing unit with more rooms and to obtain a better neighborhood from the standpoint of playspace, schools, and congenial neighbors. In fact, both a few years before and a few years after marriage, one is likely to make a number of moves in the process of settling down in a job, a home, and a community. In middle life, however, there are strong ties to the children's school and playmates, the husband's job, and the formal and informal organizations to which the various family members belong. As the children leave home in their turn, the surviving adults may find the home less well-suited to their needs. Retirement and widowhood also tend to cause new moves. So far, however, there is not a great deal of evidence of the much-heralded return from the suburbs. The movements of older people to areas with mild climates and from farms to villages are reflected in the available statistics, however.

*Life-Cycle, Career Pattern, and the Decision to Move**†

GERALD R. LESLIE • ARTHUR H. RICHARDSON

The analysis of urban residential mobility is not new.[1] As a phenomenon involving peculiar convergence of social structure with demographic and social psychological influence, however, it is of broad theoretical significance and of considerable research interest.[2] As "urban residential mobility," we shall treat here, not upward social mobility nor urban migration rates but the process whereby families and individuals change their places of residence. Explanation will be sought in two contrasting approaches — life-cycle and career pattern — for the decision to move.

* Reprinted with permission from the *American Sociological Review,* Vol. 26, No. 6 (December 1961), pp. 894-902.

† Revised version of a paper presented at the International Conference on the Family, sponsored by the International Union of Family Organizations and the National Council on Family Relations, New York City, August, 1960.

The data presented in this paper were collected under an XR grant from the Purdue Research Foundation, Purdue University. Acknowledgment is made to James Beshers and James Norton who served as statistical consultants.

[1] Among the earlier studies are William Albig, "The Mobility of Urban Population," *Social Forces,* 11 (March, 1933), pp. 351-367; Donald O. Cowgill, "Residential Mobility of an Urban Population," Master's Thesis, Washington University, St. Louis, 1936; Charles E. Lively, "Spatial and Occupational Changes of Particular Significance to the Student of Population Mobility," *Social Forces,* 15 (March, 1937), pp. 351-355; Andrew W. Lind, *A Study of Mobility of Population in Seattle,* Seattle: The University of Washington Publications in Social Sciences, 3 (October, 1925); and Bessie A. McClenahan, *The Changing Urban Neighborhood* Los Angeles: The University of Southern California, 1929.

[2] Sidney Goldstein, *Patterns of Mobility, 1910-1950; The Norristown Study,* (Philadelphia: University of Pennsylvania Press, 1958); Arthur H. Richardson, "The Prediction of Household Mobility from an Urban Subdivision," Ph.D. Dissertation, Purdue University, 1958; and Peter H. Rossi, *Why Families Move: A Study in the Social Psychology of Urban Residential Mobility,* Glencoe, Ill.: The Free Press, 1955.

LIFE-CYCLE ANALYSIS

It is reasonably well established that residential mobility is high among young families and declines with increased age of the household head.[3] In 1950, the mobility rate was twice as high in families where the head was under 35 years of age as in those where he was from 35–44 years old and five times higher than where he had reached age 65.[4] The high mobility rates for young persons presumably reflect new marriages, families expanding with the birth of children, and moves associated with the husband's employment. Each of these factors operates with less force at older ages. Thus, viewed in terms of migration rates, residential mobility appears to be associated with the expansion stage of the family life-cycle.

A major attempt to explain individual household mobility in terms of life-cycle appeared in Rossi's, *Why Families Move.*[5] Rossi sampled four Philadelphia census tracts, selected to represent areas of high and low mobility rates and high and low socio-economic status, to: (a) illustrate the application of modern survey research to the study of residential mobility; and (b) draw generalizations concerning the social psychology of residential mobility.[6] Rossi affirmed that his study design could not serve both aims with equal efficiency and emphasized the application of survey research to the discovery of causal factors in residential mobility. However, he concluded that his "empirical generalizations are so strongly supported in the data that they

[3] Paul C. Glick, *American Families,* New York: John Wiley and Sons, Inc., 1957, p. 89. Data from 1950 Census of Population, Vol. IV, Special Reports, Part 2, Chapter A, General Characteristics of Families, Table 15.

[4] Glick, *op. cit.*

[5] *Op. cit.*

[6] *Ibid.*, p. 4.

are almost certain to hold up in subsequent researches." [7]

Rossi's analysis focussed upon mobility patterns in each of the four residential areas, upon household mobility, and upon the factors entering into the individual decisions to move. Household mobility was defined in terms of desires and plans for moving: mobile households were considered to be those who were anxious to move and who planned to do so while stable households were defined as those who expressed no inclination to move.[8] The major characteristics that were found to differentiate mobile from stable households were variables closely related to the family life-cycle. Thus, large families were more prone to move than were small ones, the younger the household head the more likely the family was to move, and renters — particularly those who desired to own — were more likely to move than were owners.[9] Mobile households also differed from stable ones in the frequency of the complaints they expressed about the dwelling and the neighborhood.[10] Two arbitrary indexes, the Mobility Potential Index (composed of age, household size and tenure preference) and the Complaints Index, were found to correlate well with mobility inclinations but not too highly with one another. The two indexes, combined, permitted approximately 75 per cent accuracy in the prediction of mobility inclinations.[11]

The decision to move was seen as a function of various "pushes" from the original dwelling and various "pulls" toward the new one.[12] About one-fourth of the moves were involuntary — the result of evictions and destructions, or accompaniments of other decisions such as to marry, to divorce, or to take a job in a distant location. Among the voluntary moves, dissatisfaction with the amount of space in the dwelling was the most important factor; then came dissatisfaction with the neighborhood and the costs associated with the present dwelling. The most important feature of the new dwelling sought was its size. When two dwellings of equal size were available, the cheaper one generally was chosen.

Rossi concluded that the major function of residential mobility is to enable families to "adjust their housing to the housing needs that are generated by the shifts in family composition that accompany life-cycle changes." [13]

Career Pattern Analysis

Several early studies showed a general association between migration and upward vertical mobility.[14] These early works failed to compare the amount of upward mobility experienced by migrants and non-migrants and were succeeded, in a sense, by Hobbs' analysis of migration in an economically depressed region. He found that the relationship held even when a control group was used.[15] However, Hobbs' conclusion that "migrants are superior to non-migrants in those characteristics necessary for socio-economic occupational success," [16] has not been systematically tested in further research. Instead the emphasis shifted toward use of residential mobility as a dependent variable.

The influence of individual career patterns, involving upward vertical mobility, upon residential mobility received attention in William H. Whyte's analysis of Park Forest, Illinois. Whyte pictured Park Forest and, by implication, other residential suburbs as the dwelling areas of young lower-echelon management officials in commerce and industry. He stressed the homogeneity of

[7] *Ibid.*

[8] The correspondence between moving inclinations and actual mobility experience was tested by returning to the 924 housholds eight months after the initial interviews to see whether the dwellings were still occupied by the original respondents. The respondents had been asked to predict their own behavior over a ten month period. Of those who definitely planned to remain in their present homes, 96 per cent did so. Eighty per cent of those definitely planning to move did so, and of those who gave themselves an even chance to move or stay, 26 per cent moved. This evidence was regarded as justifying the use of mobility intentions to stand for actual mobility behavior. *Ibid.*, pp. 105-107.

[9] *Ibid.*, pp. 68-71.

[10] *Ibid.*, pp. 80-85.

[11] *Ibid.*, p. 94.

[12] *Ibid.*, pp. 8-9.

[13] *Ibid.*, p. 9.

[14] C. J. Galpin, *Analysis of Migration of Population to and from Farms*, U.S. Department of Agriculture, Bureau of Agricultural Economics, Washington, D.C., 1927; Carle C. Zimmerman, "The Migration to Towns and Cities, II," *American Journal of Sociology*, 33 (September, 1927), pp. 237-241.

[15] Albert H. Hobbs, *Differentials in Internal Migration*, Ph.D. Dissertation, The University of Pennsylvania, 1942.

[16] *Ibid.*, p. 87.

backgrounds, present positions, and tastes of suburbanites, and the inevitability of their residential mobility with occupational advancement.[17] The idea of a distinctive suburban pattern also received support from Jaco and Belknap in their analysis of a new family form emerging in the urban fringe.[18]

Analysis of one Lafayette, Indiana, residential subdivision showed that it did not conform completely to Whyte's description. Partridge did find, in North Park, a young management group who had definite expectations of both social and geographical mobility, but she also found residential mobility not associated with occupational advancement. Some 80 per cent of North Park residents were not Whyte's upwardly mobile management group.[19] She concluded that the superficial homogeneity found among North Park residents in age, income, and life-style concealed fundamental differences in the career patterns that male residents of the area follow.

Since the data to be reported in the next section of this paper were gathered, several studies have appeared that bear upon the influence of career pattern upon residential mobility, and that offer some prospect of reconciling Whyte's and Partridge's divergent findings. Mowrer, studying Chicago suburbs, found evidence of a suburban cycle in which multiple life styles and family forms follow upon the migration of young family units of husband, wife, and one or more children to the suburbs.[20] He concluded that suburban patterns are not homogeneous but that "the cycle of suburban life is in microcosm the cycle from the rural to the urban both with respect to the family relationship and community organization." [21]

Other studies have suggested selective migration to the suburbs as a function of factors that might or might not be directly linked to occupational advancement and upward social mobility. Fava, in a study of urban and suburban residents in the New York City area, found evidence for a selective migration to the suburbs "on the basis of non-rational elements of habit, belief, feelings, and experience," and concluded that the suburbs may attract those who are willing to be neighborly.[22]

The idea of an association between life-style and suburban migration was carried further by Bell.[23] He postulated three general preference patterns for life-styles in modern society: (1) a high valuation on family living (familism); (2) upward vertical mobility (career); and (3) striving for a high standard of living in the present (consumership). He hypothesized that persons moving to the suburbs are principally those who have chosen familism over either career or consumership and presented supporting data from two interview studies in the Chicago area. Thirty-one per cent of his moves involved pure familism with no other reason being given, and familism entered into the decision to move in 83 per cent of the cases. Ten per cent of the cases were cited as pure examples of the consumership pattern, and 43 per cent gave consumership along with other reasons. Only 10 per cent had upward mobility aspirations involved in their moves, while 20 per cent said that the husband's job was in some way a factor in the move. Bell recognized that his findings might not hold for different types of suburbs and recommended study of more neighborhoods of many different types.[24]

Bell's emphasis upon the importance of familism in residential mobility and his conclusion

[17] The substance of this argument was later included in William H. Whyte, Jr., *The Organization Man,* (Garden City: Doubleday Anchor Books, 1957).

[18] E. Gartly Jaco and Ivan Belknap, "Is a New Family Form Emerging in the Urban Fringe?" *American Sociological Review,* 18 (October, 1953), pp. 551-557.

[19] Janice Partridge, "A Descriptive Analysis of the Social Characteristics of Residents of a Prefabricated Housing Subdivision," Master's Thesis, Purdue University, August, 1956. North Park residents ran the gamut of occupations found in small mid-western cities. They included young executives, small-businessmen, civil servants, whitecollar workers, and skilled and semi-skilled workers. This does not mean, of course, that Park Forest was not the homogeneous community that Whyte found it to be. It does mean that Whyte's model cannot be uncritically generalized to all residential suburbs.

[20] Ernest R. Mowrer, "The Family in Suburbia," in William A. Dobriner, editor, *The Suburban Community,* New York: G. P. Putnam's Sons, 1958, pp. 147-164.

[21] *Ibid.,* p. 163.

[22] Sylvia F. Fava, "Contrasts in Neighboring: New York City and a Suburban County," in William A. Dobriner, editor, *ibid.,* pp. 122-131.

[23] Wendell Bell, "Social Choice, Life Styles, and Suburban Residence," in William A. Dobriner, editor, *ibid.,* pp. 225-247.

[24] *Ibid.,* p. 238.

concerning the small influence of the occupational pattern are at variance with our thesis here.[25] Unfortunately, Bell's data were not available to us at the time the Vinton Homes survey was designed and we cannot present a test of the relative influence upon household mobility of life-cycle, career pattern, familism and consumership. Instead, we seek adequate explanation for residential mobility in a combination of life-cycle and career pattern variables and propose a model for use in further research.

The Vinton Homes Survey

The Vinton Homes survey applied Rossi's methodology to analysis of residential mobility in a relatively new urban subdivision. Vinton Homes is an area of 402 two and three bedroom single houses in Lafayette, Indiana. In March, 1957, the area was approximately six years old. the houses currently range in value from just over ten to twenty thousand dollars. Lafayette is a diversified industrial city of approximately 40,000 population. The Purdue University community of West Lafayette is located across the Wabash River and is a separate municipality.

A 50 per cent probability sample of the households was interviewed. The three life-cycle items comprising Rossi's Mobility Potential Index and five items reflecting the influence of the career pattern were included in the interview schedule. These eight items available for predicting residential mobility were: (a) age of household head; (b) household size; (c) tenure status;[26] (d) years of formal education completed by the household head; (e) the respondent's estimate of his social class position compared with that of his neighbors;[27] (f) the respondent's estimate of his prospects for upward social mobility;[28] (g) the respondent's attitude toward his present dwelling; and (h) the respondent's attitude toward his present neighborhood.[29]

To select items for inclusion in a predictive equation, the eight variables were intercorrelated and were also correlated with stated mobility intentions.[30] The resulting point correlations are shown in Table 1. A multiple correlation regression design was then formulated for processing through a datatron computer. The correlation of all eight variables to mobility intentions was found to be .76.

Table 2 represents the squares of the correlations of stated mobility intentions to succeeding independent variables along a path of greatest increments. The path started with X_8, social mobility expectations; then X_7, perceived class differences; then X_4, house attitude; and finally X_6, education. The selection of variables by the computer stopped there, for the addition of others would have done nothing to increase the correlation with stated mobility intentions.[31]

A predictive equation based upon these correlations was then developed.[32] For each household appropriate variable data were inserted into the equation. The values assigned to stated mobility intentions were .00 if there was no intention to move during the year and 1.00 if there was intention to move during the period. The predicted values for individual households ranged from

[25] A very recent article points out that explanations of occupational residence patterns have stressed either occupational differences in resources or in style of life. Its authors conclude that residential association is a function of similarity in rank and reflects education more directly than income. See Arnold S. Feldman and Charles Tilly, "The Interaction of Social and Physical Space," *American Sociological Review,* 25 (December, 1960), pp. 877-884.

[26] Whereas Rossi had asked whether respondents preferred to own or rent, tenure status in the Vinton Homes study referred to whether the respondents actually owned or rented.

[27] Each respondent was asked to place himself and then to place most of his neighbors into one of four classes: upper, middle, working, or lower. The ratings "above," "same as," and "below" neighbors then were used.

[28] Respondents were asked to indicate the reasons why they might move from their present dwellings. These reasons were then probed to see whether they involved any significant increases in income or other occupational advancment.

[29] Both "dwelling" and "neighborhood" attitudes were assessed by means of Likert-Type items providing five alternatives ranging from "excellent" to "unsatisfactory."

[30] Like Rossi, we used stated mobility intentions (for one year) to represent household mobility. We reinterviewed our respondents ten months after the initial contact to check the correspondence between mobility intentions and actual mobility experience. Of 47 households predicting mobility within a year, 40 actually moved within ten months. Of 154 households not planning to move, only 4 did so (Phi coefficient, .84).

[31] The Summerfield-Lubin method was used to test each succeeding increment. See A. Summerfield, and A. Lubin, "A Square Root Method of Selecting A Minimum Set of Variables in Multiple Regression," *Psychometrika,* 16 (September, 1951), pp. 271-284.

[32] $y^1 = .10\ X_4 + .06\ X_6 + .46\ X_7 + .42\ X_8$.

TABLE 1

Intercorrelations of Eight Mobility Variables and Their Correlation with Stated Mobility Intentions, 201 Households, Lafayette, Indiana

	Age	House-hold Size	Owner-ship	House Attitude	Sub-division Attitude	Education	Perceived Class Differences	Social Mobility Expecta-tions	Stated Mobility Inten-tions
Age	...	.10	.02	.07	.05	.10	.20	.18	.17
Household size	...	...	.06	.11	.08	.10	.13	.06	.02
Ownership	...	...	...	.02	.05	.01	.10	.06	.01
House-attitude	...	...	...	...	.54	.32	.34	.36	.45
Subdivision attitude	...	...	...	...	...	.30	.16	.16	.25
Education	...	...	...	...	...	...	.47	.48	.52
Perceived class differences	...	...	...	...	...	...	...	.54	.62
Social mobility expectations	...	...	...	...	...	...	...	...	.64
Stated mobility intentions	...	...	...	...	...	...	...	...	...

.22 to 2.12. The .05 level of significance was used to test the differences between the predicted and actual values. For 182 of the 201 households the differences between predicted and actual values were not significant. With a sample of this size, ten households would be expected to fall outside these limits purely by chance.

For 19 of the 201 households, the equation failed to predict the respondent's mobility intentions. In 17 of the 19, however, the equation did predict the actual mobility experience. Apparently, in this instance, the discrepancy between stated mobility intentions and actual mobility experience is considerably greater than the error in predicting mobility from the equation.

Two things stood out at this point. First a high degree of predictive accuracy had been achieved; and, second, the variables that had proved useful in making the predictions were not life-cycle variables. The correlations of age, household size, and tenure status with mobility intentions were all quite low (see Table 1), while the correlations of social mobility expectations, perceived class differences, education, and house attitude with mobility intentions were substantial.

TABLE 2

Multiple Correlations of Eight Variables to Stated Mobility Intentions Along the Path of Greatest Increments, 201 Households, Lafayette, Indiana

j	X_1	X_2	X_3	X_4	X_5	X_6	X_7	X_8
r^2yj	.0303	.0006	.0001	.2043	.0613	.2728	.3861	.4040
$R^2y.8j$	.4075	.4042	.4047	.4609	.4261	.4646	.5144	.....
$R^2y.78j$	.5148	.5172	.5174	.5466	.5282	.5392	.....	.....
$R^2y.478j$	.5472	.5502	.5492	.....	.5474	.5648	.....	.....
$R^2y.4678j$	not obtained			.....	.5648	.....	.....	.....

y = stated mobility intentions.
X_1 = age of head of household.
X_2 = household size.
X_3 = owning or renting status.
X_4 = house attitude.
X_5 = subdivision attitude.
X_6 = number of years of education.
X_7 = perceived class differences.
X_8 = social mobility expectations.

Consequently, further exploration of the link between career pattern and residential mobility was suggested.

We looked to comprehensive job history data and to data on the respondents' present occupations for clues. In some instances the data showed obvious career mobility through promotions, salary increases, and transfers extending over periods of ten or more years. Such respondents generally replied affirmatively to the question whether further upward mobility was anticipated. Other respondents had held the same position for many years and did not anticipate upward mobility. With these cases as guides all respondents were classified into potentially mobile and non-mobile groups. Though this classification occasionally resulted in persons who followed superficially similar occupations being placed in different categories, an independent ranking of the respondents verified the reliability of the procedure. Forty-seven of the 201 household heads were classified as having significant upward mobility potential. They came entirely from professional, business, and upper white-collar ranks. The 154 household heads who were classified as non-socially mobile came from the lower white-collar, skilled, and semiskilled ranks.[33]

When the residential mobility intentions of the 201 households were related to their upward social mobility potential, a striking pattern emerged. The pattern is shown in Table 3.

TABLE 3

Upward Mobility Potential and Residential Mobility Intentions Over a One Year Period, 201 Households, Lafayette, Indiana

	Upward Mobility Potential	No Upward Mobility Potential
Residential mobility intentions	44	20
No residential mobility intentions	3	144

[33] As may be apparent from the text, persons presently in the lower ranks were never classified as potentially mobile, while some upper white-collar and business people were classified as non-mobile.

Forty-four of the 47 upwardly mobile households planned to move within the year. Only 20 of the 154 non-upwardly mobile households planned to do so.[34] Of 44 households who moved during the year, 42 were judged to have done so as part of the process of upward social mobility and only two moves occurred independently of upward mobility.

These data are not completely consistent with those presented by Bell for two Chicago suburbs where he found the influence of upward mobility upon the suburban move to be almost negligible.[35] Unfortunately, Bell's data were not available to us at the time and we made no effort to assess the relative influence of familism and career patterns in our sample. The association between upward mobility and residential mobility was so striking, however, that we are inclined to believe that the samples are from different populations. We have consistently described Vinton Homes as a residential subdivision rather than a suburb because it is located within the corporate limits of a small city and may not involve the same selective migration that occurs in the commuter suburbs of larger metropolitan centers.

It seemed apparent that in Vinton Homes upward social mobility far outweighed all other considerations in producing residential mobility. While at first glance these findings might be interpreted as refutation of Rossi's conclusions concerning the importance of life-cycle variables in residential mobility, there is no necessary inconsistency between the findings of the two studies. Rossi's respondents were drawn from diverse economic circumstances and from a wide variety of living conditions.[36] Moreover, the predictive accuracy demanded for his study was not so high as in the Vinton Homes study. The

[34] When actual mobility experience over the next ten months was added to the picture, still another relationship was discovered. When households fail to predict their mobility behavior correctly, the direction of the error is a function of the household's upward mobility potential. Among upwardly mobile households the tendency is to underestimate the chances for residential mobility, whereas non-upwardly mobile respondents overestimate the opportunities for residential mobility.

[35] *Op. cit.*

[36] The fact that 25 per cent of the moves from his areas were involuntary suggests a significant number of demolitions, fires, evictions, and so on, all of which failed to appear in Vinton Homes.

Vinton Homes sample was a more homogeneous one. The operation of age as a factor in residential mobility was limited by the fact that only seven heads of household in Vinton Homes were more than 50 years old.[37] Nor was it possible for household size to operate with equal effect in Vinton since there were no one-person households in the area.[38] Vinton also is an area of home owners, with only 18 of 201 households renting their dwellings.

If the conclusions from these two studies are not necessarily inconsistent, however, one or both of their theoretical bases must be inadequate.[39] An adequate explanation of residential mobility would need to encompass the significant factors operating in a wide variety of residential circumstances. An approximation of a model for the explanation of *voluntary* residential mobility can be found in the following paradigm based upon both family life-cycle and upward social mobility.

Stage of Family Life-Cycle	Upward Mobility Potential		No Upward Mobility Potential	
	Move	Stay	Move	Stay
Expansion Stage	1	2	5	6
Non-Expansion Stage	3	4	7	8

The paradigm assumes that both the need for more living space as the family increases in size and the need to adjust housing to changes in social status are potent forces inducing families to move. The push toward residential mobility would be greatest when the two forces act in concert and least when neither is operative. The expected distribution of cases, for heterogeneous universes, in the eight cells might be summarized as follows:

Cell No. 1. There should be many more cases in cell No. 1 than in cell No. 2.

Cell No. 2. Families socially tied to an ancestral home or experiencing similar restriction upon moving would be found here. The arbitrary time period covered in the prediction would force some potential movers into this cell.

Cell No. 3. Upward social mobility alone would produce a significant number of moves. Luxury features in the new dwelling would take priority over additional space.

Cell No. 4. There should be fewer cases here than in cell No. 3. The absence of pressure for additional space would permit some households to shunt their resources into values other than housing. Conscious rejection of the ideology of status striving through material possessions should be common.

Cell No. 5. Increased household size alone would produce a significant number of moves. Additional space would take priority over luxury features.

Cell No. 6. Lack of resources would prevent a large number of households from moving even when there is a pressing need for additional space.

Cell No. 7. Cases would appear in this cell only in response to factors not included in the theoretical framework: demolitions, evictions, fires, straight job transfers, etc. These moves would be involuntary.

Cell No. 8. No significant pushes toward residential mobility. At any one time, this cell likely would contain the largest number of cases.

It would be highly desirable to test this model in a variety of urban circumstances: with probability samples drawn from small and large cities, and from metropolitan areas; and with more homogeneous samples from deteriorated areas, middle-class suburbs, and so forth. Any gross deviations from the expected distributions of cases in the various cells would require revision

[37] None of these 7 households moved or otherwise displayed significant mobility potential.

[38] Rossi distinguished one-person households, two-person households, and households with 3 or more persons.

[39] Either of the two studies may be based upon such atypical samples as to cast doubt upon the generalizability of their findings. Rossi has confidence that his data, based upon four census tracts, are not seriously so-limited. Since the Vinton sample was much more homogeneous, a follow-up study using a probability sample of Lafayette households is now being completed. Preliminary screening of the data indicates that career pattern and upward social mobility will remain as highly significant determinants of residential mobility.

of the model and the introduction of additional casual factors.[40]

The Decision to Move

Thus far we have surveyed the empirical evidence and incorporated family life-cycle and career pattern variables into a framework for the description and explanation of residential mobility. One task remaining is to consider the process whereby life-cycle and career pattern variables become translated into individual decisions to move.

The method of reason analysis, however, necessarily limits the time span over which complaints as causes operate, and draws attention away from life-cycle variables as major determinants of residential mobility.

Complaints about the present dwelling can be put into fuller perspective if they are treated as intervening variables in the development of the decision to move. Viewed thus, in terms of the Philadelphia and Lafayette studies, the independent variables become "stage of the family life-cycle" and "career pattern," and the dependent variable is "residential mobility."

Independent Variables		Intervening Variable		Dependent Variable
Stage of family life-cycle	↘	Complaints about	→	Residential mobility
Career pattern	↗	present dwelling		

Rossi sought to illuminate the development of the decision to move through the method of reason analysis.[41] The decision to move was seen as the making of a conscious choice among explicit alternatives, with the emphasis upon the household's attitudes toward the present dwelling and upon the attractions of the new dwelling.[42] His assumption was that "a household starts out with some kind of complaint, decides to move, has definite ideas about the kind of dwelling it wants, and finally, makes a choice among several dwellings according to their relative merits." [43]

It seems plausible that complaints about a dwelling are not simply a function of such objective characteristics as improper construction, inadequate storage facilities, deteriorating neighborhood, and so on, but also reflect the opportunities that a household sees to escape these conditions by moving to another dwelling. Families without significant residential mobility potential may well rationalize the same features which potentionally mobile families list as objectionable. And even the same families who find a dwelling satisfactory at one point may become dissatisfied with it as the pressure of additional household members makes it inadequate and/or as the financial means are acquired to make a move possible. That verbalized complaints about the dwelling reflect more basic underlying factors is also suggested by Rossi's finding that complaints about one feature tend to be accompanied by complaints about other features of the dwelling.[44] The verbalization of specific complaints about the present dwelling and the anticipation of more satisfactory features in the new dwelling may be the vehicle for the translation of mobility potential into mobility intentions.

It should not be implied, of course, that the general model to account for residential mobility developed in this article has adequate empirical foundation. The relevant studies to date have differed sufficiently in general purposes, in popu-

[40] The point has been made that age of household head, household size, and tenure preference do not provide an adequate index of family life-cycle. With this, the authors agree. Use of the above items provides comparability with Rossi's study, but future studies might get at family life-cycle more directly through tracing changes in family composition. Such data, coupled with data on values placed upon family living versus career striving would permit definitive test of the theoretical positions assumed by Rossi, Bell, and the present authors.

[41] Paul F. Lazarsfeld, "The Statistical Analysis of Reasons as a Research Operation," *Sociometry,* 5 (February, 1942), pp. 29-47.

[42] Rossi, *op. cit.,* pp. 123-132.

[43] *Ibid.,* p. 128. It should be pointed out that Rossi's selection of complaints as the starting point in the development of the decision to move did not imply that he assigned particular theoretical significance to this factor. Since he was interested in helping modify policy in the construction of housing units, he appropriately focussed on recent conscious factors affecting the decision to move. He did note that one can be interested in why complaints arise and then search for changes in the household or dwelling unit that made the current housing unsatisfactory (p. 212).

[44] *Ibid.,* p. 83.

lations studied, and in methodological detail to make it possible that the difference in their findings are artifacts thereof. Yet a theoretical scheme including both life-cycle and career pattern variables is in accord with the general complexity of social relationships and threatens the integrity of neither Rossi's analysis nor the present study. Further, consideration of complaints as immediate pre-condition for mobility places independent, intervening and dependent variables in the potentially most fruitful relation to one another.

STUDY AND DISCUSSION QUESTIONS

1. How do you suppose Leslie and Richardson's two factors — life cycle and career pattern — might affect international migration?
2. Discuss what features of the occupational structure and economics of an industrialized nation might tend to make the population highly mobile?
3. Internal migrations may also be analyzed in terms of economic, demographic, and cultural and political factors. Discuss the roles of these factors in explaining the Negro migration to the northern United States. Which of these factors seem most important?
4. What are some of the sociological implications of a large rural-urban migration in a developing country? What problems might such a flow create both in urban and rural areas?
5. If you were to design a study of internal migration patterns in the United States similar in scope to the GAF or Princeton studies on fertility, what kinds of data would you gather? How would you gather this data?
6. Having examined fertility, mortality, and migration now, the analysis of which of these three components seems to be most developed theoretically? Can you suggest where theoretical gaps might be filled in any of them?
7. What are the advantages and disadvantages of the Census classification of people changing residence into "local movers" and "migrants?" Can you suggest how those participating in internal migration might be better classified?
8. One way to measure the net migration of an area is to first compute the total population change in that area during a given time and then subtract the natural increase (births minus deaths) of the population during that same time. This method, called the "vital statistics" method may be applied to your state or county. Look up the total population at two points in time and the data on births and deaths in the interim in one of these areas and then, using this method, compute an estimate of that area's net migration.

SUGGESTED ADDITIONAL READING

Ravenstein, E. G. "The Laws of Migration," *Journal of the Royal Statistical Society*, XLVIII (June, 1885), 167–235, and LII (June, 1889), 241–305.
Classic articles laying down first principles of migratory behavior, many of which have been modified or elaborated in more recent years.

Thomas, Dorothy Swaine. *Research Memorandum on Migration Differentials.* New York: Social Science Research Council, 1938.
A presently outdated but useful summary of research outlining the selective aspects of migration.

Lee, Everett S. "A Theory of Migration," *Demography*, 3 (1966), 47–57.
An attempt to further systematize migration research through generation of a series of interrelated hypotheses about migration patterns.

Bogue, Donald J., Henry S. Shryock, Jr., and Siegfried A. Hoerman. *Subregional Migration in the United States, 1935–40, Vol. I, Streams of Migration.* Oxford, Ohio: Scripps Foundation, 1957.

Bogue, Donald J., and Margaret Jarman Hagood. *Subregional Migration in the United States, 1935–40, Vol. II, Differential Migration in the Corn and Cotton Belts.* Oxford, Ohio: Scripps Foundation, 1953.
Companion volumes based on a detailed analysis of special tabulations of the 1940 U.S. Census, which examine the streams of migration between areas of the country and patterns of selectivity.

Stewart, John Q. "A Measure of the Influence of Population at a Distance," *Sociometry*, V (February, 1942), 63–71.

Zipf, G. K. "The P_1P_2/D Hypothesis: On the Intercity Movement of Persons," *American Sociological Review*, XI (December, 1946), 677–685.

Stouffer, Samuel A. "Intervening Opportunities: A Theory Relating Mobility and Distance," *American Sociological Review*, V (December, 1940), 845–867.
Sources of frameworks for analyzing the relationships between volume of migration and distance between areas.

Bogue, Donald J. and Philip M. Hauser. "Population Distribution, Urbanism and Internal Migration," paper presented to the United Nations World Population Conference, Belgrade, Yugoslavia, August 30–September 10, 1965.
Includes a general survey of the definitions and methods of internal migration research and a discussion of explanations of migratory behavior.

Hamilton, C. Horace. "The Negro Leaves the South," *Demography*, 1:1 (1964), pp. 273–295.
A thorough analysis of Negro migrations from southern United States, including discussion of some of its implications.

CHAPTER 8

Population Composition

Fertility, mortality, and migration combine to determine the population growth rate of an area and the amount of population increase or decrease in the area. The status of and change in population size thus determined are critical factors in demographic analysis, but populations must be examined for other characteristics for demographic as well as sociological analysis to be more meaningful. The term "population composition" is used to refer to the basic characteristics by which a population may be divided, such as *age, sex, ethnic status* and *marital status*. In later chapters, various social and economic characteristics of people will be used for further description of how a population can be meaningfully differentiated.

In demography a familiar geometric design which identifies some elements of population composition is the age-sex pyramid. (See the article by Kiser for examples.) The pyramid is formed by plotting the relative size of each age group in the population on a chart, with age groups of males to the left of a center line and age groups of females to the right. Each age group is plotted as a bar on top of the bar for the next younger age group. Because mortality tends to diminish the size of each older age group, the structure often takes the general form of a pyramid. In this way the *age composition* of the population is revealed.

As Kiser shows, the age-sex pyramid of the United States population has changed its shape considerably since the turn of the century. If a distinction is made between the pyramids for whites and Negroes, this change over time is further accentuated. In 1900, the generally high birth rates and moderately high death rates produced a conventional pyramid with a broad base and narrow top. By 1940, substantial declines in the birth rate during the 1930's had narrowed the base of the pyramid, while the survivors of earlier birth cohorts outnumbered the younger age groups. The pyramid for 1958 shows the effects of the "baby boom" in once again broadening the base of the structure, the higher birth rate of Negroes being apparent in a comparison between the races.

What factors bring about a change in the age composition of a population? To some extent, migration across the boundaries of an area changes the age composition of that area, at least when the age distribution of the migrants differ from that of the nonmigrants. Actually, migration generally has a rather minor effect on the age patterns of populations. The effect of mortality is usually more substantial. Reductions in infant mortality, in particular, have made the population younger by permitting more infants to survive. But it has been principally variations in fertility over time that have altered an age distribution. While it is difficult to realize, the aging of populations in Western societies has not come about to any signficant extent through improvements in mortality at the older ages, but instead mainly through survival of the relatively large birth cohorts of earlier years. This phenomenon can perhaps be seen best by referring to the age pyramids in the Kiser article. By comparing the pyramids for different dates, one can observe the way in which the relatively larger older age groups in 1958 are associated with the relatively larger younger age groups in 1900, while the younger age groups in 1958 were smaller in size than in 1900.

Stockwell, in the second article in this chapter, describes some other measures of the age composition of a population and indicates how the age structure of the United States population has changed decade by decade from 1900 to 1960. Broad age categories of people, he points out, can be used to identify major phases of the life cycle. Youth, adulthood, and old age describe three broad age categories, the first and third of which are viewed as being dependent on the second for their livelihood. Recent demographic trends have led to an increased *dependency ratio* (the ratio of dependent age categories to the adult age category). In underdeveloped nations today, the extraordinarily high birth rates make for exceedingly high dependency ratios.

The *sex composition* of a population, particularly in relation to age, is vital to demographic analysis. Boys outnumber girls at birth, but from the time of birth onward mortality takes a heavier toll of the males. After the first fifteen or so years of life, females outnumber males and the advantage of females increases from that time on. The greater life expectancy of women results in a disproportionately low *sex ratio* (the ratio of males per 100 females in the population) at the older ages. The much higher number of widows than widowers is evidence of that pattern.

Sex composition has social as well as biological implications. Men and women differ with respect to amount of schooling, age at marriage, entrance into and length of labor force activity, types of occupations held, amount of income received, amount of social group activity, and numerous other social, psychological, cultural, and economic characteristics.

A third dimension of the compositional structure of the population referred to quite widely in demographic analysis is *ethnic status*. The items of demographic information which provide knowledge about ethnic status are race or color, nativity, country of origin, language, and religion. As Bogue indicates in his selection in this chapter, the problem of classifying individuals by race and color is an exceeding difficult one. Racial classifications used in censuses are designed to distinguish people on a cultural rather than a biological basis. The United States census categories, in fact, usually represent some mixture of skin color (e.g., white), biological racial stock (e.g., Negro, Indian), nationality (e.g., Korean, Chinese), and religion (e.g., Hindu). However, many demographic and social phenomena vary by these "racial" categories and thus these categories are analytically meaningful.

Individuals in the population can also be classified by *nativity status,* that is, whether they are native or foreign born. A further distinction of the native born by the native or foreign birth of their parents serves to identify the first, second, and third and later generations of the population. Many social and economic characteristics of the population vary according to the generation removed from foreign residence.

An important cultural distinction among people is made by classifying first- and second-generation individuals by their *country of origin* or the country of origin of their parents. In the United States census, this serves not only to identify the nationality distribution of the population but to differentiate the shifting currents of international migration and the population growth patterns of various ethnic groups. Even where the foreign stock from a particular country can be identified, there are ethnic distinctions within the group which are important for social analysis. *Language* and *religion* are characteristics which further separate cultural groups within countries.

A fourth dimension of the compositional structure of the population deals with *marriage.* Demographic items relevant here include marital status (married, single, widowed, separated, divorced); age at marriage; number of times married; and number of years married, widowed, or divorced.

From a demographic point of view, marriage is most important as an event that marks the beginning of the potential period of childbearing. While some childbearing takes place outside marriage, in most societies fertility is culturally prescribed only within marriage. The total number of married couples, the marriage rates at each age, and the proportions of the population in each marital status category are vital to fertility analysis. From a more general sociological point of view, marriage can be observed as an event that is a critical turning-point in the life cycle of an individual, establishing for him or her new social relationships, severing or limiting older ones, and changing life styles.

Marriage statistics are obtained both from censuses and from vital registrations. The census describes the current marital status of individuals and reveals only a limited amount of information about the past marital history of these individuals. In many areas records of marriage and divorce are collected which permit compilation at any point in time of the marriage rate of men and women. It is possible through these data to describe trends and differentials in marital patterns. The article by Rele undertakes this task with regard to age at marriage in the United States over the past few decades.

The various dimensions of basic population composition which have been discussed can be related to each other to show the essential demographic structure of the population and how it is changing. Moreover, they describe the kind of population that provides the basis of societal action.

*The Aging of Human Populations: Mechanisms of Change**

CLYDE V. KISER

The aging of individuals and the aging of populations are two distinct but interrelated problems. By definition, a living individual's chronological age increases with the passage of time. The problems in the aging of the individual are those of biological and psychological changes inherent in passage from infancy to old age. The aging of a population, in contrast, refers to the *increase of the proportion* of old people and *decrease of the proportion* of young people in the total population of an area or society. Thus the passage of time per se does not necessarily bring an aging of the population. The age distribution of a population may remain virtually unchanged for a long period. In fact, the population might even become younger, for a period at least, with the passage of time.

The age structure of a population has much to do with its form and functioning. A society with a high proportion of young people may be expected to differ in its outlook and way of life from one that has a high proportion of older members. Changes in the age composition of a society may be expected to produce adaptive changes in many areas of behavior.

In this paper we shall consider, with special reference to the United States: (1) the trends in aging of the population, (2) the mechanisms of change, (3) differentials in aging, and (4) some demographic characteristics of aged people.

TRENDS IN AGING

The number and proportion of aged persons — i.e., those 65 years of age and over — have increased continuously in this country for well over a century (Thompson and Whelpton, 1933; von Mering and Weniger, 1959). As late as 1900, however, there were only about 3.1 million people 65 years of age and over in the United States and they constituted only 4.1 percent of the total population. In 1958, according to estimates of the Bureau of the Census, there were some 15.0 million people 65 years of age and over and they

* Reprinted with permission from Clark Tibbitts and Wilma Donahue, Eds., *Social and Psychological Aspects of Aging*. New York; Columbia University Press, 1962, pp. 18-35.

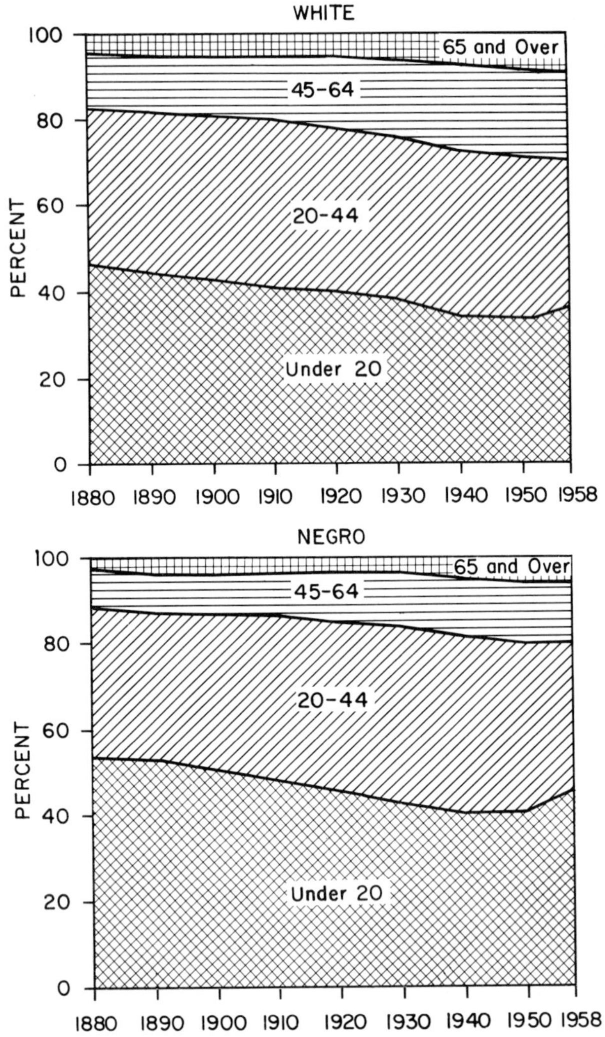

FIGURE 1

The aging of human populations: Mechanisms of change.

Composition by broad age groups of the white and Negro populations of the United States, 1880–1958. The data in the lower section for 1880, 1890, and 1958 relate to nonwhites.

comprised about 8.7 percent of the population (U.S. Bureau of the Census, 1959). The 1960 Census is expected to show that persons 65 years and over number about 15.8 million and constitute about 8.8 percent of the total population. There is a sounder basis for estimating the number of aged persons 15 to 25 years in the future than the percentage that they will form of the total population because of uncertainties as to the course of fertility. Estimates of about 21.9 million aged persons constituting 9.0 to 10.1 percent of the population have been made for the year 1975 (U.S. Department of Health, Education, and Welfare, 1960).

Trends in the age distribution of the whites and Negroes of the United States during 1880–

1958 are shown in Figure 1.[1] This chart shows the changing proportions of the population in four broad age groups: under 20; 20–44; 45–64; and 65 and over. These groups are sometimes labeled, respectively, children and youth, the younger working force, the older working force, and the aged. The proportion of persons under 20 years old declined continuously until 1950. It subsequently increased because of the increases in fertility that have been under way since 1940. In contrast, there have been continuous increases in the proportion of persons 45 years of age and over. For both whites and Negroes the proportion of persons in the younger working force, 20–44, remained fairly constant until about 1950 when the small crop of babies born during the thirties began advancing into the 20–44 bracket and being replaced in the under-20 category by the larger cohorts of the baby boom.

The nature of the recent changes induced by changing fertility may be illustrated more clearly by comparing the age pyramids for the United States for the years 1900, 1940, and 1958, shown in Figs. 2, 3, and 4. Age pyramids are simply devices for showing the age-sex distribution of a population at a given time. They may indicate absolute numbers in given age-sex categories, or, as in the present instance, they may indicate the percentage that a given age-sex group forms of the total population.

As indicated in Figure 2, the population profile for the whites in this country in 1900 was that of a virtually perfect pyramid. With advancing 5-year age groups, there were successively smaller proportions of people. The base of the pyramid is broad, reflecting high birth rates, and the top of the pyramid tapers off sharply and consistently. The age pyramid for the Negroes in 1900 was much like that of an underdeveloped country. The relatively broad base reflects the high birth rates of Negroes, who in 1900 were largely concentrated in the rural areas of the South.

The 1940 pyramid, depicted in Figure 3, shows marked erosion of the base, due to the sharp decline in fertility that had been under way during the twenties and thirties. In 1940, because of 2 decades of sharp declines in birth rates, there were fewer white people 10–14 than 15–19, fewer 5–9 than 10–14, and fewer under 5 than 5–9. To some extent this situation also prevailed for Negroes in 1940. The decrease in the proportion of children and youth rather automatically increased the proportion of persons in the other age categories because the percentages add to 100.

The 1958 age profile in Figure 4 reflects the restorative effect of the baby boom on the base of the pyramid. If we conceal the data for the whites under 20 years old, we see again the shape of the 1940 pyramid. The gash that is in the pyramid because of the low birth rates of the previous times will travel upward in the pyramid with the passage of time.

Mechanisms of Aging of Populations

Attention may now be turned to the components of population change and their effects on the age structure. If a group of young men of precisely the same age are imprisoned or put on an island for life, with no further admissions and with no departures except through death, the aging of the group will be the same as that for any surviving individual. The average age of the survivors would increase by 1 year annually until the last one died.

In a more normal society, of course, there are people of both sexes and all ages. There are annual increments through births and immigration and there are annual decrements through deaths and out-migration. Births, deaths, immigration, and out-migration are the four components of population change, and they have bearing on composition as well as size of the population. Consideration of migration may be deferred for the moment and attention will be given to the relative importance of fertility and mortality trends on the aging of human population.

Until about 10 years ago most demographers interpreted the increase in the proportion of old people in Western countries as the result of the jointly operating declines in fertility and declines in mortality. Until then it was thought that while declines in fertility were eroding the base of the population pyramid, the declines in mortality were enabling people to live longer and

[1] The data for the years 1880, 1890, and 1958 are for nonwhites instead of Negroes.

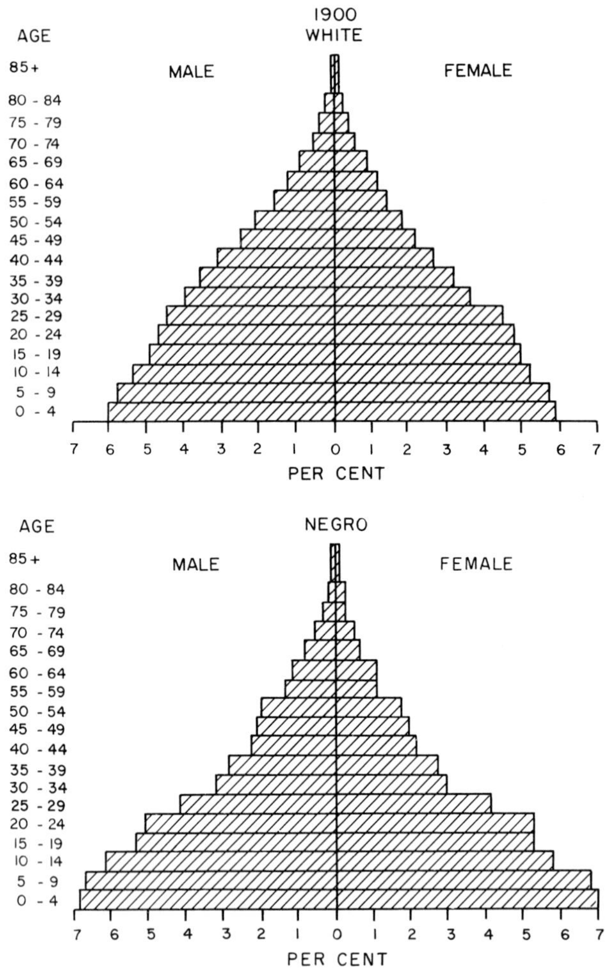

FIGURE 2

The aging of human populations; Mechanisms of change.

Age pyramids for the white and Negro populations of the United States, 1900.

hence were enhancing the proportions in the older ages. In this sense declines in fertility and mortality were often said to be working hand in hand to bring large proportions of people into the older age groups.

During the past decade, however, the researches of Valaoras (1950), Lorimer (1951), Sauvy (1954), Coale (1956*a* and *b*), Stolnitz (1956), the United Nations (1954, 1956), and others have demonstrated that *past* increases in proportion of older persons in the United States and other Western countries have been a result almost entirely of declines in the fertility rate and virtually not at all of declines in the mortality rate.

It should be emphasized that this statement refers to *past* trends and more specifically to trends up to about 1940. In the future, declines in the death rate may well emerge as the dominant factor in the further aging of the population in this country.

The *past* reductions in mortality rates have

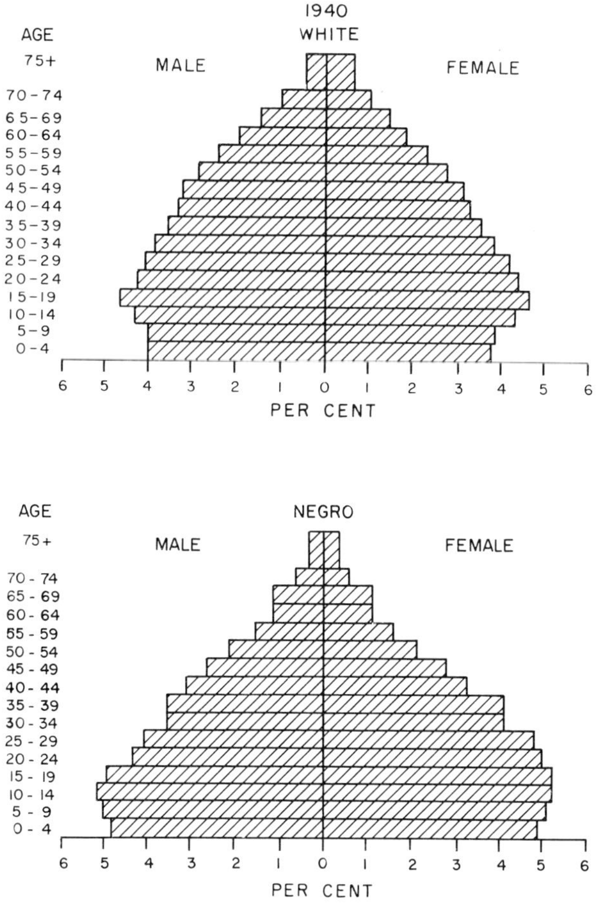

FIGURE 3

The aging of human populations: Mechanisms of change.

Age pyramids for the white and Negro populations of the United States, 1940.

been concentrated heavily at the young ages. They have been especially marked among infants and children. As a consequence, the *past* declines in mortality in this country have had much the same effect that increases in the birth rate would have. Hence, they have tended to increase the proportion of youngsters and to retard rather than to accelerate the aging of the population. Thus the declines in mortality in the past have not contributed to any appreciable increase in the proportion of older people because there has thus far been relatively little decline in the mortality rates at the older ages. If the *future* declines in mortality are concentrated largely in the older age groups, as indeed they might well be, the declines in mortality will produce an older population.

Empirical evidence of the irrelevance of *past* mortality trends to the aging of the population has been supplied by Coale who demonstrated that with the existing declines in fertility in Sweden since 1860 the age distribution in 1950 would have been virtually what it actually was in 1950, even if mortality had remained at the 1860 levels. He has also shown that with the existing declines in fertility since 1860, the age

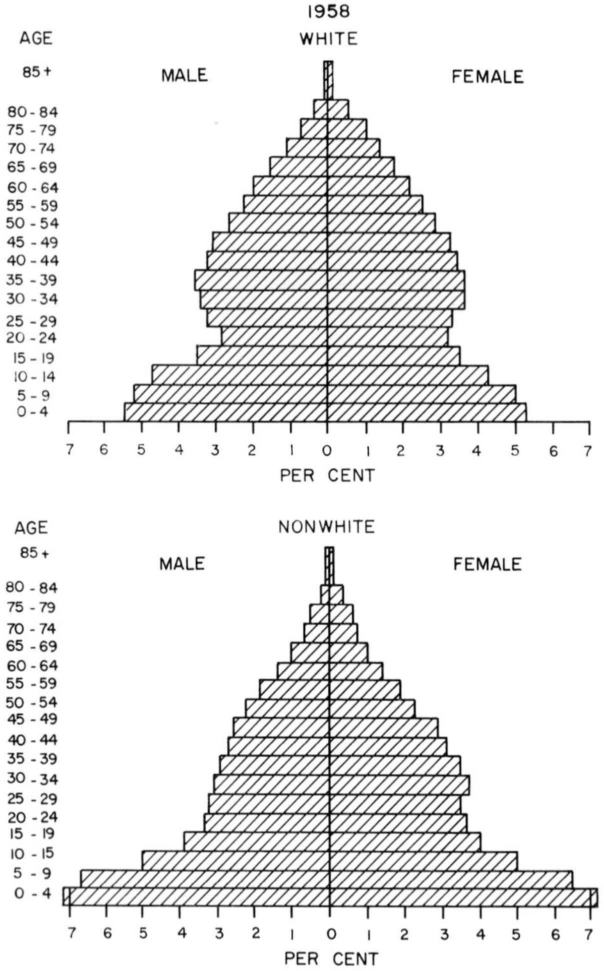

FIGURE 4

Age pyramids for the white and nonwhite populations of the United States, 1958. Estimates of population from U.S. Bureau of the Census, *Current Population Reports*, Series P-25, No. 193 (February 11, 1959).

distribution in 1950 would have been approximately the same as the actual for 1950, even if mortality had been at the 1950 level throughout the entire period of the preceding 90 years. To generalize, the life table of Sweden for 1860 with a life expectancy of about 45 years, and that for 1946–1950, with a life expectancy of about 72 years produce about the same age distributions when combined with the same fertility schedule (Coale, 1957).

In a recent report, the Population Branch of the United Nations has provided similar findings. Figure 5 shows the composition by broad age groups of model stable populations corresponding to given levels of fertility and mortality, as computed by the Population Branch (United Nations, 1956). Under similar gross reproduction rates above 1.0 the proportions of the stable population 60 years of age and over are much the same with increasing expectation of life at

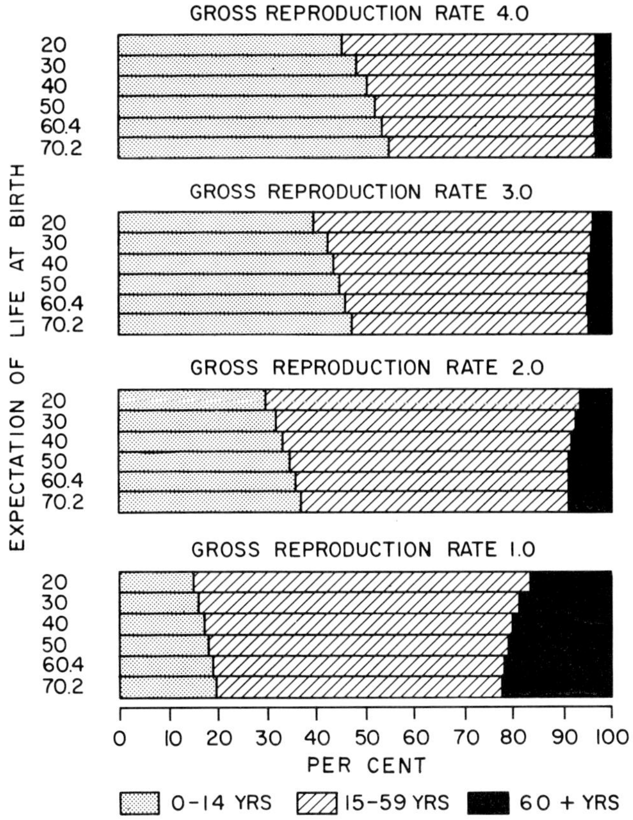

FIGURE 5

Composition by broad age groups of model stable populations corresponding to different levels of fertility and mortality. Based on "The Aging of Populations and its Economic and Social Implications," *Population Studies*, No. 26, United Nations, New York, 1956, p. 26.

birth. In fact, the proportion of people 0–14 tends to increase with rise of expectation and constancy of reproduction.

In contrast, with lowering of reproduction and constancy of mortality there are marked reductions in proportions 0–14 years old and increases in the proportion of persons 60 years old and over. This is evident by comparison of the four panels in Figure 5.

The United Nations report carefully points out that age structure is not simply a function of existing levels of expectation of life and reproduction rates. It is rather a function of the past levels of these variables. Nevertheless the data demonstrate the sharper relevance of declines in fertility than of declines in mortality to the past aging of populations.

It is also emphasized that since 1940 the increases in fertility in the United States have served to increase the proportions of people in the young age groups and to lower the median age of the population; although the proportion of people 65 years of age and over continued to increase.[2]

[2] In terms of age differentials in rates of growth, since 1940 the United States population has increased most at the two extremes, i.e., the young and the old. Thus, during 1950-1958 the estimated increase was 15 percent for the total population. It was 29 percent for those under 20, 1 percent for those 20-44, 15 percent for those 45-64, and 23 percent for those 65 and over.

The writer realizes that people in medical and health circles may be surprised to learn that declines in mortality have had very little to do with past aging of the population of modern Western countries. Some of them have tended to attribute most of the responsibility for aging to declining mortality. In this connection, much depends upon what one means by *aging* of the population. If we mean increase in expectation of life at birth, the declines in mortality rates are obviously the virtually sole factor. Declines in fertility may be indirectly involved in that the spacing of births may facilitate declines in mortality. Nevertheless, mortality rates alone form the basis from which average length of life is computed by actuarial methods.

Also, if by aging of the population we mean the increase in sheer numbers of old people, declines in mortality again constitute the responsible agency. In this connection we may also acknowledge that the growing numbers of the aged in this country and the outlook for still larger increases make the problem a massive one. When one considers costs of programs of medical care for the aged, for instance, the future trends in the number of aged are factors of major concern. It is the sheer magnitude of the expected numbers of aged persons that baffles those concerned with future problems of chronic disease and mental illness.

However, when the demographer speaks of the aging of populations he generally means the increase in the proportion of people in the older age groups. He does not mean increases in the expectation of life or increases in sheer numbers of old people.

Migration

Most of the recent studies of the relative roles of declining fertility and declining mortality on the age structure of the population have utilized closed population models or countries with relatively little immigration or emigration in order to rule out the factor of migration. This has not been based on any assumption of the unimportance of migration. It has been prompted instead by recognition of the complexity of the factor of migration and the desire to avoid this complexity in the assessment of the relative roles of fertility and mortality.

Since both international movements and internal migrations of human populations are frequently selective with respect to age, these factors often affect the age distribution of both sending and receiving areas.

With respect to international movements, the sudden stoppage of immigration to this country in the twenties means that the existing foreign-born population has aged considerably and is now concentrated largely in the older ages. In considering the effects of migration from abroad, however, we should remember that, without getting credit for it, the native children of foreign-born parents have to some extent mitigated the effects of the foreign-born on the age distribution of the United States in recent years.

Internal migration frequently has bearing on the regional and urban-rural differences in age distribution to be discussed later.

Another aspect of this question is the mobility of the aged people themselves. The aged persons in 1950 were somewhat less mobile during the preceding year than were the younger people. It will be recalled that in the 1950 Census, people were asked where they were living 12 months previous. The replies were tabulated in terms of same or different house, same or different county, and same or different state. About 90 percent of the aged males and females were classified as nonmovers as compared with 78 percent for males 20–64, and 81 percent for females of this age. Only about 5 percent of the aged as compared with 7–9 percent of the persons 20–64 reported that they had lived in a different county 1 year previous.

Differentials in Aging

Aging in Relation to Modernization

In general the proportion of population aged 65 and over tends to be directly related to degree of modernization. Data for nations as units probably would show that the proportion of aged persons in the population is directly related to the percentage of the population that is urban. It tends to be directly related to the educational attainment of the population. The percent of population 65 and over is inversely correlated with magnitude of the birth and death rates. There is good reason to believe that the inverse relation with the death rate simply reflects the relation with modernization; the causal relation stems from the declines in the birth rates. At least this has been the case in Western countries in the past, up to about 1940.

To some extent the positive relation of aging with modernization helps to explain some of the detailed correlates with aging, such as color, region, and urban-rural status. However, the detailed correlates may also reflect other factors, especially selective factors.

Color

The process of aging has advanced further among the whites than nonwhites in the United States. Thus in 1950 about 8.4 percent of the whites and 5.7 percent of the nonwhites were 65 years old and over. However, the gap between the two groups has narrowed considerably. The differential has been due to the greater lag in the decline of the birth rate among the nonwhites than among the whites.

In terms of distribution of the aged by color, in 1950 about 93 percent were white and 7 percent were nonwhite.

Nativity

Differences in age composition of the native and foreign-born reflect periods and ages of migration, historical trends in immigration policy, and differences inherent in the definitions of the terms. In the nature of the case the foreign-born population includes relatively few infants; children born in the new country are natives of it. Since the large migrations from Europe to this country were virtually stopped by the quota laws of the twenties, a heavy proportion of the foreign-born residents of this country are in the older age groups. In 1950, about 27 percent of the foreign-born whites as compared with 7 percent of the native whites were 65 years old and over. The median age was 56 for the foreign-born whites and 29 for the native whites. It is because of their relatively high proportion of older people that the foreign-born whites contributed 18 percent of the deaths in the United States in 1950 although they constituted only 7 percent of the total population. As already noted, if the offspring of the foreign-born people in this country could be allocated to their parents, a considerable part of the difference between the natives and foreign-born with respect to age structure would be eliminated.

Urban-rural Residence

The age distribution by urban-rural residence reflects differences in fertility rates in the past. It also reflects age selections in the past migrations from rural to urban areas. Thus the base of the age pyramid tends to be broader in rural than in urban areas, reflecting the higher birth rates in the rural areas. The high proportion of youngsters is especially prominent in the rural-farm areas.

The relatively high proportion of young adults in urban areas reflects the migration of youngsters to the cities. The rural-farm population is especially short on this segment of population.

In terms of distribution, the aged are somewhat less urbanized than the general population. Among 11 million whites 65 years old and over in 1950, about 64 percent were in urban areas, 22 percent in rural-nonfarm areas, and 14 percent in rural-farm areas. The nonwhite aged are more rural Among the 900,000 nonwhites 65 years old and over in 1950, 57 percent were in urban areas, 22 percent were in rural-nonfarm areas, and 22 percent were in rural-farm areas.

Regional Differences in Age Structure

Regional differences in age structure reflect regional differences in fertility and in composition of the population by color, nativity, urban-rural residence, and migration status. Thus the South ranks above average in proportions rural and nonwhite. It is an area marked by a long period of high fertility and high natural increase but also of out-migration of both whites and Negroes to other regions.

The attractiveness of certain areas with mild winters to the older people sometimes serves noticeably to inflate the proportion of older people within given states and regions. However, the influence of this factor on the proportion of older people is not as strong as one might think. In 1950 persons 65 years of age and over comprised 8.5 percent of the population in California, 8.6 percent in Florida, and 8.1 percent in the United States as a whole. California is attractive to older people but it is also attractive to the middle-aged and younger people. Some cities in Florida cater to the older people but in the state as a whole there are also many inducements for younger people.

TABLE 1

Sex Ratios (Males per 100 Females) by Age, Residence, and Color, United States, 1950[a]

Age	Total: Total	Total: White	Total: Non-white	Urban: Total	Urban: White	Urban: Non-white	Rural-nonfarm: Total	Rural-nonfarm: White	Rural-nonfarm: Non-white	Rural-farm: Total	Rural-farm: White	Rural-farm: Non-white
All ages	99	99	96	95	95	92	104	104	103	110	111	103
Under 5	104	104	101	104	104	100	104	105	101	104	105	101
5–9	104	104	100	103	103	98	104	105	100	105	106	101
10–14	104	104	101	102	102	98	105	105	103	108	109	105
15–19	100	101	95	92	93	86	108	109	102	118	121	107
20–24	95	97	86	90	91	78	104	103	109	117	122	95
25–29	95	96	90	93	94	86	99	98	108	101	103	91
30–34	96	96	88	93	94	85	101	101	103	99	100	90
35–39	96	97	90	93	94	87	104	105	102	103	105	93
40–44	99	99	96	95	95	94	107	107	104	108	109	101
45–49	100	100	98	96	96	96	107	107	103	109	110	103
50–54	100	99	102	96	96	102	105	105	102	111	112	104
55–59	101	100	107	97	96	104	103	103	107	118	118	119
60–64	101	100	105	95	95	100	102	102	101	127	127	127
65–69	94	94	93	86	86	86	98	99	89	131	132	124
70–74	91	91	101	81	81	89	100	100	101	135	134	137
75–84	85	84	99	74	73	84	100	99	109	126	125	131
85+	70	70	72	60	60	62	85	84	86	95	97	80

[a] Source: U.S. Bureau of the Census, *1950 Census of Population,* Vol. II, *Characteristics of the Population,* Part 1, "United States Summary," Washington, D.C., U.S. Government Printing Office, 1953, Table, 38, p. 1-91.

Demographic Characteristics of Aged People

Sex in Relation to Aging

Because of their greater longevity, females are conspicuously more numerous than males among the aged. In 1958, among 15 million persons 65 years old and over in the United States slightly fewer than 7 million (46 percent) were males and over 8 million (54 percent) were females. The sex ratio, i.e., the number of males per 100 females, was 84 for all persons 65 years of age and over. By specific age group, the sex ratio was about 90 at ages 65–69, 85 at ages 70–74, and 76 at ages 75 and over. Further details are given in Table 1.

By residence, the number of males per 100 females 65 years old and over in 1950 was lowest in urban areas (79), intermediate in rural-nonfarm areas (95), and highest in rural-farm areas (126). Stated differently, among the males 65 years of age and over in 1950, 60 percent were in urban areas, 23 percent were in rural-nonfarm areas, and 17 percent were in rural-farm areas. Among the females the corresponding percentages were 67, 21, and 12.

Marital Status

The high proportion of broken marriages complicates the problem of the aged. In 1950, among the persons 65 years of age and over, about two-thirds of the males and only one-third of the females reported themselves as married in the 1950 Census. About one-fourth of the males and over half of the females were widowed. Only about 8 percent of the males and females 65 years of age and over reported themselves as single and about 2 percent as divorced.

Several factors account for the higher proportion of widowhood among aged females than aged males. Wives tend to outlive husbands because they have the dual advantage of younger age at marriage and longer expectation of life. Furthermore, remarriages are more frequent among aged males than among aged females because the males tend to choose brides under age 65.

Widowhood among the aged is more pro-

TABLE 2

Percentage Distribution of Persons 65 Years Old and Over by Relationship to Head of Household, by Sex, Residence, and Color, United States, 1950[a,b]

Relation to head	White Male	White Female	Nonwhite Male	Nonwhite Female
		All residences		
Head or spouse	76	63	75	59
Parent or parent-in-law	10	21	7	22
Other relative	4	7	5	9
Other	11	9	13	10
		Urban		
Head or spouse	74	62	69	56
Parent or parent-in-law	10	21	8	23
Other relative	4	7	5	9
Other	12	11	18	12
		Rural-nonfarm		
Head or spouse	78	68	80	70
Parent or parent-in-law	8	16	6	15
Other relative	4	6	4	7
Other	11	10	10	7
		Rural-farm		
Head or spouse	80	63	83	59
Parent or parent-in-law	11	27	8	27
Other relative	5	8	5	11
Other	4	2	4	3

[a] Source: U.S. Bureau of the Census, derived from *1950 Census of Population,* Vol. II. *Characteristics of the Population,* Part 1, "United States Summary," Washington, D.C., U.S. Government Printing Office, 1953, Tables 107 and 108, pp. 1–192, 1–205.

[b] Percentages have been rounded off.

nounced among the nonwhites than among the whites. Thus among males 65 and over in 1950 the percent widowed was 24 for whites and 29 for nonwhites Among females it was 53 for whites and 66 for nonwhites. For whites and nonwhites widowhood among the aged is more pronounced in urban than in rural areas. Thus, among males 65 years of age and over, the percent widowed in 1950 was 25 in urban areas, 24 in rural-nonfarm areas, and 21 in rural-farm areas. Among the females it was 57 percent in urban areas, 52 percent in rural-nonfarm areas, and 45 percent in rural-farm areas.

Relationship to the Head of the House

Largely because of the greater prevalence of widowhood among aged females than males, the old women live in the homes of their children and other relatives to a greater extent than do their male counterparts. In 1950, about 9 percent of the aged males and 21 percent of the aged females were living with their children, i.e., they were in households in which they were reported as parents or parents-in-law of the heads of the household (Table 2). An additional 4 percent of the males and 7 percent of the females were in homes of other relatives. The remaining 11 percent of the males and 9 percent of the females were enumerated in households of nonrelatives or in institutions of various types.

As expected, within the age groups 65 and over, the proportion of males and females reported as living in their own households (head or wife of head) declines sharply with age. Among the aged people in urban areas in particular, the proportion reported as living in their own households was somewhat higher for whites than for nonwhites. This may be partly a function of the lower proportion widowed. However, the differences are not great when age and type of community are held constant.

By type of community, the proportion of aged persons living in their own households (head or wife of head of the household) was 67 percent in urban areas, and 73 percent in both rural-nonfarm and rural-farm areas. In rural-farm areas it is probably physically easier to "take in" the aged parent or relative. In urban areas and particularly in apartment houses there is less likely to be an extra room or an extra bed that the aged parent could use. Perhaps partly for this reason the proportion of oldsters living in institutions is higher in urban than in rural areas. It is recognized, of course, that nursing homes and institutions are more likely to be in urban areas. It is also recognized that it may be easier to continue housekeeping activities in small towns than in cities.

The foregoing data on marital status of the aged and their relationship to household heads probably add up to a situation of loneliness for many of the aged. Elderly men frequently undergo a change of role from economically productive citizens to inactive ones, from that of head of a family to an onlooker, from an active to an inactive role in the church and community. Women do not so frequently face the sharp transition from full-time employment to economic inactivity, but for them the problem of loneliness may loom larger because of the greater degree of widowhood. For men and women loneliness may be increased with the onset of disabilities and defects such as deafness. A substantial proportion of old people are victims of degenerative diseases like heart diseases and cancer, or succumb to mental illness. Many are in hospitals for chronic diseases and in mental institutions.

Through strengthening the provisions of social security we may mitigate some of the economic hardships faced by the aged. Through advances in the treatment of chronic illness, we may add more years to the lives of the aged. We may even find it possible to improve the mental health of the aged. Through community efforts we may help the aged in various ways. But in all these efforts we would perhaps do well to remember that the aged are human beings who want to lead useful lives and who want to be respected, recognized, and loved, perhaps especially by their own children.

Acknowledgment. The author wishes to acknowledge the invaluable assistance of Miss Vivian Small in collecting the data for this paper.

REFERENCES

Coale, A. J. 1956*a*. The effects of changes in mortality and fertility on age composition. Milbank Mem. Fund. Quart., 34: 79–114

——— 1956*b*. The effect of declines in mortality on age distribution. *In* Trends and differentials in mortality, pp. 125–32. New York: Milbank Memorial Fund.

——— 1957. How the age distribution of a human population is determined. Cold Spring Harbor Symposia on Quantitative Biology, 22: 83–89.

Lorimer, F. 1951. Dynamics of age structure in a population with initially high fertility and mortality. (Population Bulletin, No. 1.), December, 31–41. New York: United Nations.

Mering, O., von, and Weniger, F. L. 1959. Social-cultural background of the aging individual. *In* J. E. Birren (ed.), Handbook of aging and the individual, pp. 279–335. Chicago: University of Chicago Press.

Sauvy, A. 1954. Le vieillessement des populations et l'allongement de la vie. Population, 9: 675–82.

Stolnitz, G. J. 1956. Mortality declines and age distribution. Milbank Mem. Fund Quart., 34: 178–215.

Thompson, W. S., and Whelpton, P. K. 1933. Population trends in the United States. New York: McGraw Hill Book Co.

United Nations. 1954. Population Division. The cause of the aging of populations: declining mortality or declining fertility? (Population Bulletin, No. 4), December. New York: United Nations.

——— 1956. Department of Economic and Social Affairs. The aging of populations and its economic and social implications. (Population Studies, No. 26.) New York: United Nations.

U.S. Bureau of the Census. 1959. Current population reports. (Series P-25, No. 193.) Washington, D. C.: The Bureau.

U.S. Department of Health, Education, and Welfare. Social Security Administration. 1960. Health, education, and welfare trends. Washington, D. C.: Government Printing Office.

Valaoras, V. G. 1950. Patterns of aging of human populations. *In* Social and biological challenge of our aging population, pp. 67–85. New York: Columbia University Press.

Some Notes on the Changing Age Composition of the Population of the United States[*1]

EDWARD G. STOCKWELL

The distribution of its members according to age is one of the most fundamental features of any population.[2] On the one hand, almost any aspect of human behavior, from subjective attitudes and physiological capabilities to objective characteristics such as income, labor force participation, occupation, or group membership may be expected to vary with age. On the other hand, the specific needs and problems of a given society, both now and in the future, will in large part be determined by the age structure of its population. It may be said, therefore, that a knowledge of the current age structure, how it came into being, and what consequences it is likely to have for future population trends, is essential — not only as a basis for determining the present needs of a population, but also as a basis for adequate planning with regard to probable future needs

Median Age

A convenient measure for determining quickly whether a population is young or old and how its age composition has been changing is the median age. The median age of the population of the United States at each census since 1900 is presented in Table 1. Inspection of these data indicates that, prior to the most recent decade, the prevailing trend had been for the population to become older. Between 1900 and 1950, the median age in the United States increased from 22.9 to 30.2 years, or by 7.3 years (nearly one and one-half years per decade). Partly because of the reduction of foreign immigration following the adoption of federal restrictive legislation, but mostly as a result of the cumulative effects of the historical decline in fertility, the rise in the median age was most pronounced after 1920. The marked increase of 2.6 years between 1930 and 1940 reflects the particularly low birthrate of the depression decade, while the substantially smaller increase between 1940 and 1950 reflects the initial impact of the postwar fertility revival.

TABLE 1

Trends in the Median Age of the Population of the United States: 1900–1960

Year	Median age	Change over previous decade
1900	22.9	—
1910	24.1	1.2
1920	25.3	1.2
1930	26.4	1.1
1940	29.0	2.6
1950	30.2	1.2
1960	29.5	−0.7

Source: U. S. Bureau of the Census, *U. S. Census of Population: 1960,* Final Report PC (1) — 1B, *General Population Characteristics: United States Summary* (Washington, 1961), Table 47, p. 153. Unless otherwise specified, the percentages and ratios presented in the remaining tables of this article were all computed on the basis of data contained in this table.

During the most recent decade, the upward movement in the median age of the population was halted; the median age in 1960 (29.5 years) was seven-tenths of a year lower than it was 10

* Reprinted with permission from *Rural Sociology,* Vol. 29, No. 1, (March 1964), pp. 67-74.

[1] This article grew out of a more detailed study of the changing age composition of the Northeast Land Grant College Region, which was undertaken as part of Regional Research Project NE-31, "The Effects of Urban-Industrial Expansion on Northeastern Agriculture." See: Edward G. Stockwell, *Age Composition of the Northeast Region,* Storrs: Connecticut Agr. Sta., Progress Report No. 50, November, 1962.

[2] For a detailed discussion of the importance of population age composition see: Donald J. Bogue, *The Population of the United States,* Glencoe: The Free Press, 1959, pp. 92-94.

years earlier. This reversal of a trend that had been in evidence for several decades can only be explained by reference to the cessation of the long-time fertility decline during World War II, and a subsequent rise in the birthrate and its continuation at fairly high levels since then. This reversal of the downward trend in the birthrate, which has come to be referred to in popular literature as the "baby boom," has resulted in substantial increases in both the number and proportion of youth in the population, and has consequently brought about a reduction in the median age. Moreover, unless there is a sharp decline in the current moderately high birthrate, the years ahead are likely to see the median age of the population decline even more.

The Life Cycle

Although the median is a useful measure for providing a general indication of the age composition of a population, it is of limited value in more detailed analyses. The procedure usually employed when greater precision is desired is the examination of the proportion of the population falling into particular age groups. In this respect, it is useful to designate three broad age groups which may be assumed to correspond roughly to the three major phases of the life cycle: *youth* (under 15 years), *adulthood* (15 to 64 years), and *old age* (65 years and over). The composition of the nation's population according to these three stages of the life cycle is presented in Table 2. These data clearly depict the major changes that have occurred in each stage of the life cycle during the present century.

TABLE 2

Percent Distribution of the Population of the United States by Three Broad Age Groups: 1900–1960

	Percent of the population		
Year	Under 15 years	15 to 64 years	65 years and over
1900	34.4	61.5	4.1
1910	32.1	63.6	4.3
1920	31.8	63.5	4.7
1930	29.4	65.2	5.4
1940	25.1	68.1	6.8
1950	26.9	65.0	8.1
1960	31.1	59.7	9.2

Source: See Table 1.

Prior to the 1940–50 decade, a major trend was a consistent decline in the proportion of the population under 15 years of age. At the beginning of the present century, slightly more than one out of every three persons in the United States fell into this age group, but by 1940, after several decades of declining birthrates, this ratio had fallen to one in four. Since that time, the reversal of the long-time fertility decline has led to an increase in the percent of the total population represented by this youthful segment; in 1960, the number of persons under 15 years of age in the nation was once again nearly one out of three.

Concomitant with the fall in the proportion of youth during the years of fertility decline, the proportion of the population 15 to 64 years of age increased — from 61.5 percent in 1900 to 68.1 percent in 1940. Thereafter, as a consequence of the postwar baby boom and continued high levels of fertility, the percent of the population falling into these active adult ages had declined, and by 1960 it was lower than it had been at the beginning of the century. At the time of the most recent census, only 59.7 percent of the population of the United States was between the ages of 15 and 64 years.

The major difference between the 1960 population and that of 60 years ago is found in the proportion of elderly persons. In 1960, the percentage of the population 65 years of age and over was more than twice as great as it was in 1900 — 9.2 percent as opposed to only 4.1 percent at the turn of the century. In terms of absolute numbers, the change has been even more striking. In 1900, there were slightly more than three million persons age 65 and over in the United States; by 1960 this number had swelled to more than 16.5 million, representing roughly, a fivefold increase during the past 60 years.

A particularly useful measure for depicting more precisely the changes that have taken place with regard to the older segment of the population is the *index of aging,* which may be defined as the number of persons age 65 and over per 100 children under 15 years of age.[3] The

[3] William Petersen, *Population,* New York: The Macmillan Company, 1961, p. 81.

trend in this index for the United States since the beginning of the century is depicted in Table 3. Inspection of these data indicates that, prior

TABLE 3

*Indexes of Aging in the United States: 1900–1960**

Year	Index of aging	Change between census dates
1900	11.8	—
1910	13.4	1.6
1920	14.6	1.2
1930	18.4	3.8
1940	27.3	8.9
1950	30.2	2.9
1960	29.7	0.5

* Number age 65 and over per 100 under 15 years of age.

Source: See Table 1.

to the most recent decade, the aging index had tended to increase during each decennial interval, with the increase being particularly marked since 1920. In 1950, there were 30.2 persons age 65 and over per 100 under 15 years in the United States, as opposed to only 11.8 in 1900. That is, during the first half of the twentieth century the number of older persons relative to the number of children in the population nearly trebled.

Although partly due to the drying up of the immigration stream following the adoption of federal restrictive legislation, the pronounced "aging" of the population since 1900 is largely the result of the cumulative effects of the historical decline in the birthrate.[4] This is readily apparent from the fact that the greatest increases in the aging index occurred between 1930 and 1940, or during the same period that the decline in fertility was most pronounced. By the same reasoning, the much smaller increase between 1940 and 1950, and the slight rejuvenation that has taken place during the most recent decade, reflect the relatively high levels of fertility that have prevailed since the end of World War II. Moreover, should the birthrate continue at its present level, and as the smaller birth cohorts of an earlier generation reach old age, the recent reversal in the index of aging may mark the beginning of a new downward trend. If this is the case, then the nation faces the prospect of a new "younging" of the population — a situation that would require us to reorient our thinking from a tendency to emphasize the problems of an aging population, to one which encompasses the needs and problems of youth as well as those attendant upon old age.

Dependency

One of the consequences of the changing age structure of the United States population is revealed in the trend of the *dependency ratio* (i.e., the ratio of the number of persons under 15 and over 65 years of age to the number of persons in the age group 15 to 64 years, multiplied by 100). Under the assumption that all persons under 15 and over 65 are economically dependent upon the rest of the population, and the assumption that the dependency load is evenly distributed, this measure provides an indication of the average number of persons which each 100 adults is required to support.[5] According to the data presented in Table 4, the total de-

[4] At one time, it was popular to regard the fall in the death rate as the primary cause of the aging of the population. In point of fact, however, the fraction over 65 today would be larger and the average age of the population greater if mortality had not declined during the present century. Although the increase in the absolute number of older people was indeed the consequence of improvements in death control, the fact that declines in mortality were greatest among infants and young children meant that a larger proportion of births survived, and this larger proportion who remained alive actually served to retard the aging of the population. Thus, it was a decline in the number of births rather than a decline in mortality that brought about the increase in the proportion of older people in the population. By the same token, it is the higher fertility during the postwar years that has effected a slowing down, and even a reversal, of the aging process. For a fuller discussion of the causes of population aging see: "The Cause of the Ageing of Populations: Declining Mortality or Declining Fertility?" *Population Bulletin of the United Nations,* No. 4, New York: United Nations, December, 1954, pp. 30-38.

[5] The limitations inherent in these assumptions should be obvious. For example, many older people today hold full-time jobs while a sizable proportion of the population age 15 to 64 is not engaged in any economically productive activity. Therefore, this ratio cannot be regarded as a precise measure of dependency. Nevertheless, bearing its limitations in mind, the dependency ratio does represent a useful means for depicting the changing *patterns* of economic dependency over the years.

TABLE 4

Dependency Ratios in the United States: 1900–1960

Year	Dependency ratios Total	Youth	Aged
1900	62.6	56.0	6.6
1910	57.3	50.5	6.8
1920	57.5	50.2	7.3
1930	53.4	45.1	8.3
1940	46.8	36.8	10.0
1950	53.9	41.4	12.5
1960	67.6	52.1	15.5

Source: See Table 1.

pendency ratio in the United States declined during the early decades of the twentieth century: between 1900 and 1940, the number of dependents per 100 persons age 15 to 64 fell from 62.6 to 46.8, or by 25 percent. Since that time, however, there has been a marked increase in the burden of dependency, and the 1960 ratio of 67.6 dependents per 100 active persons is the highest ever attained during the present century.

The major reason that the dependency ratio, which had been getting smaller, has become so much greater during recent years lies in the expansion of the younger segment of the population. This can readily be seen by considering the total dependency ratio in terms of its component parts: *youth dependency,* the number of children under 15 per 100 persons 15 to 64 years of age; and *aged dependency,* the number age 65 and over per 100 age 15 to 64. When these figures are considered, it can be clearly seen that two factors have contributed to the recent rise in the overall dependency ratio. First, the increase is due partly to the aging of the population which was brought about as a consequence of the long-time decline in the birthrate prior to the 1940 decade. Second, and most important, the dependency ratio has risen as a result of the postwar fertility revival and the greatly increased proportion of young people in the population. In 1960, the youth dependency ratio alone was nearly as great as the total dependency ratio in 1950, and substantially above that of 1940. All in all, the expansion of the younger population has accounted for approximately three-fourths (73.6 percent) of the increase in the burden of dependency that has taken place since 1940. Clearly, the rise in the birthrate in the mid-1940's, and its continuation at relatively high levels since that time, has had a profound effect on the age structure of the population of the United States.

Some Urban–Rural Comparisons

The historical relations between urbanization, industrialization, reduced fertility, and growth through migration have created characteristic differences in the age composition of the urban and rural populations of the nation. In general, higher rural fertility, coupled with the farm-to-city movement of adults as the country underwent the transformation from a rural agrarian to an urban industrial economy, has tended to make rural populations younger than their urban counterparts. In recent years, however, there has been a trend toward a narrowing of this traditional differential (see Table 5). For example, in contrast to the general trend observed for the nation as a whole, the median age of the rural population did not decline between 1950 and 1960, but remained constant at 27.3 years. Since it did decline in urban areas, the net result has been a reduction in the urban-rural differential from 4.3 years in 1950 to 3.1 years in 1960 — a decline of 27.9 percent.

TABLE 5

Measures of the Age Composition of the Population by Urban and Rural Residence: United States, 1950 and 1960

Measures of age composition	Urban 1950	Urban 1960	Rural 1950	Rural 1960
Median age	31.6	30.4	27.3	27.3
Percent:				
Under 15	24.2	30.1	31.5	33.5
15 to 64	67.8	60.7	60.4	57.2
65 and over	8.0	9.2	8.1	9.3
Index of aging	33.4	30.6	25.9	27.9
Dependency ratios:				
Total	47.9	64.8	65.9	74.7
Youth	35.9	49.6	52.3	58.4
Aged	12.0	15.2	13.6	16.3

Source: See Table 1. The above values were derived from Census Table 46, p. 148.

Further examination of the data presented in

Table 5 reveals that this narrowing of the age gap between urban and rural areas has resulted from the differential changes characterizing these two residence groups with regard to the number and proportion of young people in the population. Between 1950 and 1960, for example, the number of people age 65 and over in urban areas increased by well over three times as much as the corresponding population in rural areas (46.9 percent, as opposed to 13.0 percent). If this were the only change to occur, the effect would have been to intensify the differences in the age composition of urban and rural areas. During the same period, however, the number of people under 15 years of age increased by 60.5 percent in urban areas but by only 5.2 percent in rural areas.[6] This substantially greater increase in young people in urban areas was more than enough to offset the gains at the older ages, and it led to a marked increase in the proportion of the total population represented by this youthful segment (from slightly less than 1 out of 4 in 1950 to nearly 1 out of 3 in 1960). In rural areas, on the other hand, where the increase at age 65 and over was more than twice as great as the increase at the younger ages, the proportion of youth remained about the same, approximately 1 out of 3 (31.5 percent in 1950 and 33.5 percent in 1960).

A number of reasons may be cited to explain the greater increases among youth in the urban areas. In the first place, there is some evidence that the postwar fertility increase has been more pronounced in urban than in rural areas.[7] It may be, for example, that the historical decline in fertility that began in urban areas is still filtering down to the rural population at a time when the urban birthrate is in the midst of a marked revival. To this possible explanation must be added the fact that the rapid suburbanization movement of recent years has largely involved the higher socio-economic groups in the society, and those persons who are left in the city (or who are migrating to the city from declining farm areas) are the same people who have traditionally had higher birthrates. Finally, it may be noted that the metropolitan growth characterizing recent decades has been accompanied by an ever-increasing expansion of the urban fringe, and each new census sees many previously rural areas becoming reclassified as urban. There was, in fact, a major change in the definition of urban and rural residence in 1960 (a change which added some 12 million persons to the urban population).[8] Such changes, which transfer younger rural dwellers to urban areas, could easily exert an influence on the age composition of these two residence groups. Whatever the causes, and regardless of the specific influence of the many different causes, the fact remains that the urban population experienced substantially greater gains at the younger ages than the rural population during the past decade, and this phenomenon has served to bring about a convergence of the historical differences in the age composition of these two residence groups.

The above noted changes with regard to the number and proportion of young people in the population are reflected in the changing patterns of aging and dependency in urban and rural areas. Here again, the changes during the past decade have been in the direction of a narrowing of the traditional differentials. On the one hand, the substantially smaller increase in youth in rural areas has meant that the rural population did not experience the reversal in the aging process that has tended to occur recently in the United States. This is clearly indicated by the fact that the index of aging, which declined for the nation as a whole and for the urban population, continued to increase in rural areas between 1950 and 1960. The net result of these changes has been a substantial reduction in the urban–rural differential: in 1950 the urban index of aging was 29.0 percent higher than that of rural areas, but by 1960 this difference had been reduced to only 9.7 percent. On the other hand, the greater increases among youth in urban areas has led to a correspondingly larger increase in urban dependency, and this again has meant a narrowing of the traditional differential: in 1950 the total dependency ratio for rural areas was 37.6 percent higher than the corresponding urban ratio, but by 1960 this figure had been

[6] See footnote to Table 5 for source of data.

[7] Bogue, *op. cit.*, p. 100.

[8] *U.S. Census of Population: 1960*. Volume I, Part A-1, *Number of Inhabitants: United States Summary,* Washington, D.C.: U.S. Bureau of the Census, 1961, pp. XIII-XV.

reduced to only 15.0 percent. Part of this increase was due to the greater urban increase in aged dependency (27.0 percent between 1950 and 1960, as compared to 20.0 percent for the rural population), but the major factor was the increase in youth dependency: between 1950 and 1960 the youth dependency ratio increased by 38.0 percent in urban areas, as compared to only 12.0 percent in rural areas. Stated somewhat differently, the largest increase between 1950 and 1960 characterized youth dependency in urban areas but aged dependency in rural areas.

To summarize briefly: although the rural population of the United States continues to be characterized by a younger average age composition than its urban counterpart, the substantially greater increases among young people in urban areas during the past decade have served to bring about a notable narrowing of the traditional urban–rural differential.

Summary and Conclusions

The major trend in the United States during recent years has been a marked increase in the number and proportion of young people in the population. This development has served to sharply curtail the historical trend toward an aging population, and it marks the emergence of a new trend toward a younger population. This phenomenon is, of course, the result of the postwar baby boom and the subsequent continuation of relatively high levels of fertility. Should this situation persist (*i.e.,* unless the future course of fertility is considerably lower than it has been at any time during the postwar era), the population of the nation will almost certainly have a younger average age composition in the immediate future than it has had in the past.

The trend toward a younger population has been much more pronounced in urban than in rural areas, and this has led to a narrowing of the traditional urban–rural age differential. Once again, if the trends of the past decade continue, the overall trend toward a younger population is likely to result in an even greater convergence of the age differences that have historically served to distinguish rural from urban populations.

*Color-Nativity-Race Composition**

DONALD J. BOGUE

Like the characteristic of age, the population characteristics of color, nativity, and race have a social significance that reaches into almost every sphere of inquiry. Innate biological differences between races and nationality groups in regard to their physical health, longevity, and mental abilities are commonly thought to be far smaller than are the observed differences. Nevertheless, the fact should not be overlooked or minimized that actual differences of considerable magnitude are known to exist in the population of the United States at the present time. The course of history and culture-building has created systems involving attitudes toward and prescriptions for the behavior of various minority groups, and the behavior of these groups with respect to each other. These culture forces, and the limiting effect they have upon living conditions and access to income and social position, probably account for a very large share of the observable differences in behavior and capacities between racial and ethnic groups. Because parentage is one of the few traits which a human being cannot change, except by subterfuge, these cultural definitions tend to prescribe class (and even caste) lines which help to determine several other demographic, economic, and social characteristics. For these reasons, the color, nativity, and race composition of a population, and the social and economic characteristics of each race and ethnic group, are matters of rather universal interest. Population statistics provide much of the factual information which is available concerning the conditions under which each group lives and the ways in which the relative positions of the groups are changing. For much of the demographic analysis in the United States, ethnic and racial origin are basic variables that must be controlled before the effect of other factors can be considered.

The Census Inquiry Concerning Color, Nativity, and Race

As a part of each decennial enumeration, the Bureau of the Census is asked to perform the difficult task of classifying the population by race, nativity, and national origin. The cultural definitions of these classifications vary throughout the nation. A scientifically accurate and completely reliable system for classifying individuals into race and ethnic types, either on a physical or a cultural basis (or a combination of both), is something that anthropologists have not yet succeeded in developing. Even when highly elaborate measurements have been made of skeletal dimensions and proportions, of facial features, and of degree of pigmentation, and when place of residence of ancestors has been determined, a completely unambiguous classification has not yet been achieved. It is easy to see that anthropologically untrained census enumerators, whose biases on and attitudes toward the subject run the same gamut as do those of the general population, cannot even hope to make a refined and completely reliable classification when such a classification has thus far proved to be impossible under laboratory conditions. Many people would be offended, sensitive, or evasive about direct questions pertaining to this subject. The enumeration of Indians, for example, may be performed rather poorly unless the enumerators are extraordinarily conscientious and obtain full cooperation of the local officials at reservations. As a consequence, the census inquiry must be limited to aspects of race (a) that cannot be hidden from the enumerators, (b) about which the census enumerator can make assumptions without serious error, and (c) about which people will be willing to furnish information.

The Bureau of the Census must take into account other considerations in making its racial and ethnic classifications. It cannot afford to enumerate and tabulate data for racial or ethnic groups that are so small as to constitute an infinitesimal fraction of the whole population. In addition, many laws and governmental programs involve racial and ethnic considerations, and have their own special definitions of the persons to whom they apply. Legislatures and courts need statistics about the number of persons who are subject to these laws, and where these persons are located. The Census must make its inquiry in such a way that these groups, defined by law or administrative practice, are matched by official counts.

For these reasons, the present census classifications of nativity and race in the United States consist of a set of categories which combine color and place of origin of ancestors; Negroes are identified as a separate race. When given in full details, the classifications are as follows:

White races
- a. Native-born
- b. Foreign-born

Nonwhite races
- a. Negro
- b. Indian
- c. Chinese
- d. Japanese
- e. Other nonwhite races
  - Filipino
  - Hindu
  - Korean
  - Other

In this chapter, the above categories (or combinations of them) will be referred to as the color-nativity-race classification. Enumerators are instructed to obtain much of the racial

TABLE 1

Color, Nativity, and Race Composition of the Population of the United States: 1790 to 1950

Year	White			Nonwhite							
	Total	Native	Foreign born	Total nonwhite	Negro		Other nonwhite races				
					Total	Slave	Total	Indian	Japanese	Chinese	All other
1950....	134,942,028	124,780,860	10,161,168	15,755,333	15,042,286	...	713,047	343,410	141,768	117,629	110,240
1940....	118,214,870	106,795,732	11,419,138	13,454,405	12,865,518	...	588,887	333,969	126,947	77,504	50,467
1930....	110,286,740	96,303,335	13,983,405	12,488,306	11,891,143	...	597,163	332,397	138,834	74,954	50,978
1920....	94,820,915	81,108,161	13,712,754	10,889,705	10,463,131	...	426,574	244,437	111,010	61,639	9,488
1910....	81,731,957	68,386,412	13,345,545	10,240,309	9,827,763	...	412,546	265,683	72,157	71,531	3,175
1900....	66,809,196	56,595,379	10,213,817	9,185,379	8,833,994	...	351,385	237,196	24,326	89,863	...
1890....	55,101,258	45,979,391	9,121,867	7,846,456	7,488,676	...	357,780	248,253	2,039	107,488	...
1880....	43,402,970	36,843,291	6,559,679	6,752,813	6,580,793	...	172,020	66,407	148	105,465	...
1870....	33,589,377	28,095,665	5,493,712	4,968,994	4,880,009	...	88,985	25,731	55	63,199	...
1860....	26,922,537	22,825,784	4,096,753	4,520,784	4,441,830	3,953,760	78,954	44,021	...	34,933	...
1850....	19,553,068	17,312,533	2,240,535	3,638,808	3,638,808	3,204,313	...	...	...	...	...
1840....	14,195,805	...	...	2,873,648	2,873,648	2,487,355	...	...	...	...	...
1830....	10,537,378	...	...	2,328,642	2,328,642	2,009,043	...	...	...	...	...
1820....	7,866,797	...	...	1,771,656	1,771,656	1,538,022	...	...	...	...	...
1810....	5,862,073	...	...	1,377,808	1,377,808	1,191,362	...	...	...	...	...
1800....	4,306,446	...	...	1,002,037	1,002,037	893,602	...	...	...	...	...
1790....	3,172,006	...	...	757,208	757,208	697,681	...	...	...	...	...

Source: U.S. Bureau of the Census, *Historical Statistics of the United States, 1789-1945,* Washington, D.C., 1949, Tables B 13-23, and B 40-47; *U.S. Census of Population: 1950,* Volume II, Part 1, Table 36.

(a) Persons of Mexican ancestry are classed as white. In 1930, Mexicans were enumerated separately; the census count was 1,422,533. In 1950, an approximation of the Mexican population was made by identifying persons of Spanish surname in the census returns for 5 states known to have a concentration of Mexican population. The census count was 2,289,550.

(b) Counts of some individual groups, enumerated separately in several censuses and included in this group was as follows: Filipinos (1950), 47,272; Filipinos (1940), 45,563; Hindu (1940), 2,405; Korean (1940), 1,711; Filipinos (1930) 45,208; Hindu (1930), 3,130; Korean (1930), 1,860.

information by observation and to ask a question when they are in doubt.[1] It is presumed that all members of the household are of the same racial grouping as is the informant, if the informant is related to the other members. Mexicans are enumerated as white (in the 1930 census publications they are included with the group "other races."). A special coding step was introduced in 1950 to permit their separate tabulation in four southwestern states as "persons of Spanish surname." Persons of mixed white and nonwhite parentage are classed according to the classification of the nonwhite parent. Persons of mixed white and Indian parentage are classed as Indians if they are living on a reservation, if they claim major Indian ancestry, or if they report being of one-fourth Indian ancestry or more. Persons of mixed Negro and Indian parentage are classified as Negro unless the Indian blood very definitely predominates or unless the individual is accepted in the community as an Indian. In 1950, for the first time, an attempt was made to identify persons of mixed white, Negro, and Indian ancestry living in certain communities in the eastern United States in a special category so that they might be included in the category "other races." Mixtures of nonwhite races are reported according to the race of the father.

The classification given above is used in making basic counts of population characteristics. The counts for the foreign-born are supplemented by tabulations according to country of birth, both for the foreign-born white and for the total foreign-born (including nonwhite). For cross-tabulating race and nativity with other population characteristics, various combinations of the basic categories are made. Sometimes a four-fold division is made: Native white, foreign-born white, Negro, and other nonwhite.

Color-Nativity-Race Composition from 1790 to 1960

The color composition of the population in 1960 is estimated to be:

	White	*Nonwhite*
Population (millions)	159.8	20.3
Percent of total	88.7	11.3
Percent change (1950 to 1960)	18.4	28.8

Table 1 reports the number of persons who were in each of the major color, nativity, and race categories at each census from 1790 to 1950. Table 2 expresses these figures as percent distributions, and Table 3 presents percent changes between censuses. In 1950, roughly 90 percent of the total population was classed as white, and 10 percent as nonwhite (see Table 2). These proportions had remained almost unchanged for thirty years. Before 1920, the nonwhite population comprised a larger proportion of the total population, as Figure 1 indicates. In 1790, Negroes were 19.3 percent of the total population, or about twice the proportion they constituted in 1950. All but a very small part of the Negro population arrived as slaves. At the time of the Civil War, about 90 percent of the Negroes still had that status. The landing of additional slaves was prohibited by law after 1808. Between the Census of 1810 and the Census of 1930, the proportion of Negroes declined. During much of this time large numbers of white immigrants were pouring in from Europe to swell the size of the white population(see statistics for foreign-born in Tables 1 to 3). Hence, the white population was growing both by natural increase and by migration, while the Negro population could grow only by natural increase. Because of high death rates the Negro population was able to grow only at a pace considerably slower than that of the white population, until recent years. This fact may be observed by comparing the rates of intercensal change, shown in Table 3, for native whites and Negroes.

The last half of the nineteenth century witnessed the immigration of Chinese populations, and during the early decades of the twentieth century there was an influx of Japanese. In 1950, each of these two oriental populations comprised 0.1 percent of the total population. American Indians comprised 0.2 percent. The census counts of the Indian, Japanese, and Chinese groups, at each census from 1860 to 1950, are shown in Table 1, and are illustrated graphically in Figure 2. Other nonwhite races com-

[1] This paragraph is paraphrased from U.S. Bureau of the Census. *U.S. Census of Population: 1950.* Vol II, *Characteristics of the Population,* Part 1, U.S. Summary, Chapter C, pp. XII-XIII.

TABLE 2

Color, Nativity, and Race Composition of the Population of the United States: 1790 to 1950

Color, nativity, and race	Year																
	1950	1940	1930	1920	1910	1900	1890	1880	1870	1860	1850	1840	1830	1820	1810	1800	1790
All races	100.0	100.0	100.0	100.0	100.0	100.0	100.0	100.0	100.0	100.0	100.0	100.0	100.0	100.0	100.0	100.0	100.0
White, total	89.5	89.8	89.8	89.7	88.9	87.9	87.5	86.5	87.1	85.6	84.3	83.2	81.9	81.6	81.0	81.1	80.7
Native	82.8	81.1	78.4	76.7	74.4	74.5	73.0	73.4	72.9	72.6	74.6	...	...	...	...	...	...
Foreign born	6.7	8.7	11.4	13.0	14.5	13.4	14.5	13.1	14.2	13.0	9.7	...	...	...	...	...	...
Nonwhite, total	10.5	10.2	10.2	10.3	11.1	12.1	12.5	13.5	12.9	14.4	15.7	16.8	18.1	18.4	19.0	18.9	19.3
Negro	10.0	9.8	9.7	9.9	10.7	11.6	11.9	13.1	12.7	14.1	15.7	16.8	18.1	18.4	19.0	18.9	19.3
Other races	0.5	0.4	0.5	0.4	0.4	0.5	0.6	0.4	0.2	0.3	...	...	...	...	...	...	...
Indian	0.2	0.3	0.3	0.2	0.3	0.3	0.4	0.1	0.1	0.1	...	...	...	...	...	...	...
Japanese	0.1	0.1	0.1	0.1	0.1	...	...	...	...	...	...	...	...	...	...	...	...
Chinese	0.1	0.1	0.1	0.1	0.1	0.1	0.2	0.2	0.2	0.1	...	...	...	...	...	...	...
All other	0.1	...	...	...	...	...	...	...	...	...	...	...	...	...	...	...	...

Source: Data for 1850 to 1950 from U.S. Census of Population: 1950, Volume II, Part 1, Table 36; data for 1790 to 1840 from W. S. Thompson and P. K. Whelpton, *Population Trends in the United States,* Table 3, p. 6

TABLE 3

Decennial Percent Change in United States Population, by Color, Nativity, and Race: 1800 to 1950

Color, nativity, and race	Rate of decennial change during decade ending in:															
	1950	1940	1930	1920	1910	1900	1890	1880	1870	1860	1850	1840	1830	1820	1810	1800
Total	14.5	7.2	16.1	14.9	21.0	20.7	25.5	30.1	22.6	35.6	35.9	32.7	33.5	33.1	36.4	35.1
White, total	14.1	7.2	16.3	16.0	22.3	21.2	27.0	29.2	24.8	37.7	37.7	34.7	33.9	34.2	36.1	35.8
Native	16.8	10.9	18.7	18.6	20.8	23.1	24.8	31.1	23.1	31.8	...	...	...	...	...	...
Foreign born	−11.0	−18.3	2.0	2.8	30.7	12.0	39.0	19.4	34.1	82.8	...	...	...	...	...	...
Nonwhite, total	17.1	7.7	14.7	6.3	11.5	17.1	16.2	35.9	9.9	24.2	...	...	...	...	...	...
Negro	16.9	8.2	13.6	6.5	11.2	18.0	13.8	34.9	9.9	22.1	26.6	23.4	31.4	28.6	37.5	32.3
Other races	21.1	−1.4	40.0	3.4	17.4	−1.8	108.0	93.3	12.7	...	...	...	...	...	...	...
Indian	2.8	0.5	36.0	−8.0	12.0	−4.5	273.8	158.1	−41.5	...	...	...	...	...	...	...
Japanese	11.7	−8.6	25.1	53.8	196.6	1093.0	1277.7	169.1	...	...	...	...	...	...	...	...
Chinese	51.8	3.4	21.6	−13.8	−20.4	−16.4	1.9	66.9	80.9	...	...	...	...	...	...	...
All other	118.4	−1.0	437.3	198.8	...	...	...	...	...	...	...	...	...	...	...	...

Source: *U.S. Census of Population: 1950,* Volume II, Table 36; data prior to 1860 from W. S. Thompson and P. K. Whelpton, *Population Trends in the United States,* Table 4.

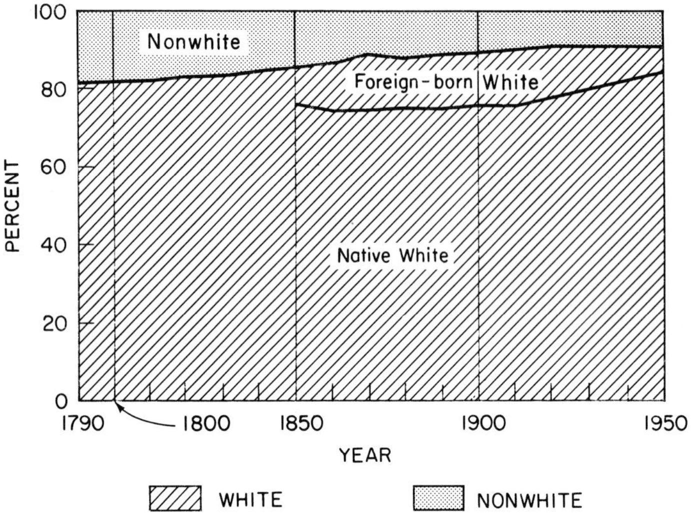

FIGURE 1

Color and nativity composition of the United States population, 1790 to 1950.

bined (Korean, Filipino, Asiatic Indian, etc.) were 0.1 percent of the total population. Thus, in 1950 there were slightly less than three-fourths of a million persons of nonwhite races other than Negro; and only about one person in 475 was classed as a member of a nonwhite race other than Negro. When statistics for the entire United States are considered, the category "nonwhite" is almost equivalent to the category "Negro," because the Negro population in 1950 was 95.5 percent of the nonwhite population. In particular regions and subregions, such as the West, which have concentrations of American Indians and Japanese populations but a comparatively small Negro population, it would not be correct to consider "nonwhite" nearly

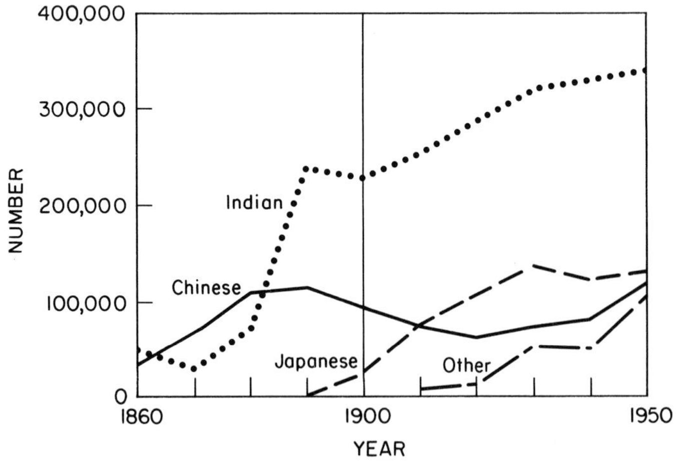

FIGURE 2

Population of the minor nonwhite races, United States, 1860 to 1950.

equivalent to Negro (see the discussion of regional distribution below).

Beginning in 1850 the white population was subclassified by nativity — that is, into native- and foreign-born. At that time, 9.7 percent of the total population consisted of foreign-born whites. During the following decades of heavy immigration, this proportion rose to a high of 14.5 percent both in 1890 and 1910. As the immigrants who arrived in the nineteenth century aged and began to die, a larger influx of immigrants would have been required to maintain the same proportion of foreign-born in the population. But restrictions upon immigration began to be imposed; they became increasingly severe during the second decade of the twentieth century. Finally, the "quota system," which has restricted immigration severely, was established in the early 1920's. As a result, the proportion of foreign-born has fallen very rapidly during the past three decades. On the one hand, the foreign-born population already residing in the nation has passed into the upper ages where death rates are high, and thus is dying out. The number of foreign-born white persons has declined rapidly from the peak of almost 14 million which was reached in 1930 to about 10 million in 1950. In 1950 the foreign-born white population was 6.7 percent of the total population; this was less than half of what it had been in 1910. If the foreign-born population remains at a constant number, while the rest of the population continues to grow, it is destined to become an even smaller proportion of the total than it was in 1950.

Table 3 provides several interesting insights concerning the decennial rates of growth of the race and nativity groups, from 1790 to 1950. First, it shows the rapid rate of growth and then the equally rapid rate of decline of the foreign-born population. Second, it shows that the Negro population grew at a slower rate than did the native white population during almost all decades prior to 1940-50. During the two decades 1940 to 1960, however, the Negro population grew slightly faster than the white. This represents a new development, which will be explained in more detail below. The growth rates of the "Other races" (sometimes called "minor nonwhite races") have been erratic. The irregularities in the statistics are due in part to the difficulties of enumerating precisely small and sometimes dispersed populations to the changing content of the group (especially the inclusion of special communities of mixed white-Indian-Negro parentage in 1950), and in part to the fact that (except for Indians) each minor nonwhite race entered the population within a span of a few years, and the growth of each has been dependent upon natural increase.

Urban-Rural Residence, by Color, Nativity, and Race

Native white populations and Negro populations, the two largest color-nativity groups, were distributed between urban and rural territories in almost identical proportions in 1950; about 62-63 percent of each was in urban areas (see Table 4). Within rural areas their distribution was less similar: proportionately more Negroes than native whites were residing on farms, and proportionately fewer Negroes were residing in rural-nonfarm areas. This difference arises, in large part, from the relative concentration of Negroes in southern agricultural areas and from the relative scarcity of Negroes in suburban areas of northern cities.

Foreign-born white populations have tended to be heavily concentrated in urban areas; in 1950, 83.5 percent were residents of urban places. Table 5 shows that this has been an outstanding characteristic of the foreign-born white population since 1870 and probably for several decades before, judging from the fact that the proportion of the foreign-born white population that was urban in 1870 was more than twice that of the native white urban population. Japanese and Chinese populations also are more urbanized than is the population at large.

The American Indian population has had an outstandingly different urban-rural distribution. More than one-half of this group was living in rural villages (primarily on reservations) in 1950, and almost one-third was living on farms. Only 16.3 percent were reported in the census as city dwellers. There is a good possibility that, when they are enumerated off the reservation, many Indians are misjudged to be Negro or white.

The 1950 distribution, described above, is only

TABLE 4

Urban-Rural Distribution of the United States Population, by Color, Nativity, and Race, 1950 and Percent-Change Difference: 1940 to 1950

Urban-rural residence	All races	White			Nonwhite						
		Total	Native	Foreign born	Total	Negro	Other races				
							Total	Indian	Japanese	Chinese	All other
PERCENT DISTRIBUTION, 1950											
U.S. total	100.0	100.0	100.0	100.0	100.0	100.0	100.0	100.0	100.0	100.0	100.0
Urban (new definition)	64.0	64.3	62.7	83.5	61.6	62.4	44.7	16.3	71.1	93.0	47.5
Rural nonfarm	20.7	21.1	21.9	11.0	17.2	16.6	30.8	52.0	10.1	5.0	18.9
Rural farm	15.3	14.6	15.4	5.4	21.2	21.0	24.5	31.6	18.9	2.0	33.6
PERCENT CHANGE, 1940–50											
U.S. total	14.5	14.1	16.8	−11.0	17.1	16.9	21.1	2.8	11.7	51.8	118.4
Urban (old definition)	19.5	17.2	22.6	−7.1	43.5	43.2	61.5	108.7	44.6	55.8	71.7
Rural nonfarm	43.2	43.4	45.3	−18.3	40.4	38.0	55.6	−6.4	−28.4	12.6	189.9
Rural farm	−23.6	−22.5	−21.8	−39.5	−29.8	−29.8	−30.2	...	...	...	...

Source: *U.S. Census of Population: 1950,* Volume II, Part 1, Table 36 and estimates prepared for this study.

TABLE 5

Percent of the Population Classed as Urban, by Color, Nativity, and Race: 1820 to 1950

Year	Total	White			Nonwhite	
		Total white	Native	Foreign born	Total nonwhite	Negro
1950 (new definition)......	64.0	64.3	62.7	83.7	61.6	62.4
1950 (old definition)......	59.0	59.0	...	...	58.8	...
1940....................	56.5	57.5	55.1	80.0	47.9	48.6
1930....................	56.2	57.6	54.5	79.2	43.2	43.7
1920....................	51.4	53.4	49.6	75.5	33.8	34.0
1910....................	45.8	48.2	43.6	71.4	27.2	27.3
1900....................	40.0	42.4	38.1	66.0	22.6	22.7
1890....................	35.1	37.5	32.9	60.7	...	19.8
1870....................	25.7	28.0	23.1	53.4	...	13.5
1850....................	15.3	...	...	...	...	7.8
1840....................	10.8	12.4	...	...	...	7.6
1820....................	7.2	7.3	...	...	...	5.9

Source: *U.S. Census of Population: 1950,* Volume II, Part 1, Tables 34 and 97; *Sixteenth Census of the United States: 1940,* Volume II, Part 1, Tables 4 and 5; Data for 1900 to 1920 from *Fourteenth Census of the United States: 1920,* Volume II, Table 23, p. 90-3. Data for years prior to 1900 from W. S. Thompson and P. K. Whelpton, *Population Trends in the United States,* Tables 13, 14, and 25 in Chapter II.

a cross-section of a rapidly changing urban-rural distribution of the various color, nativity, and race groups. The fact that Negroes were imported as slave labor for plantations dictated that they would have a more rural distribution than the white population. Since 1820, the earliest date for which data have been compiled, this difference has existed. It had almost completely disappeared by 1950. From Table 5 it may be inferred that the Negro population has been urbanizing since 1820, but that its cityward movement has proceeded at an extraordinary

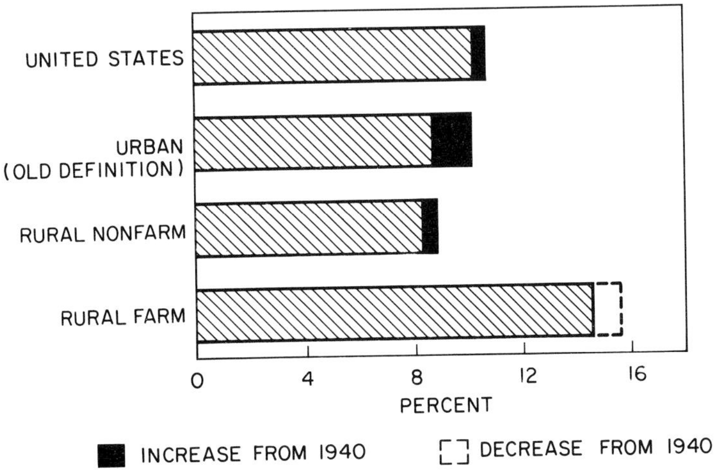

FIGURE 3

Percent of population nonwhite, by urban and rural residence, 1940 and 1950.

rapid pace since 1920, and especially during the 1940-50 decade. The large percentage changes in the nonwhite composition of urban and rural areas during the 1940-50 decade are shown in Figure 3.

From 1820 to 1910, as the urbanization movement gained momentum, the urbanization of the white population proceeded at a more rapid pace than did that of the Negro population. (Rate of urbanization is defined in terms of intercensal change in the proportion of population residing in urban places, and is obtained from Table 5 by subtracting the percent urban at the beginning of the decade from the percent urban at the end.) After the Civil War the urbanization of the Negro population began to accelerate, but not until the World War I era (1910-20 decade) was the rate of Negro urbanization able to surpass the urbanization rate of native whites. During the 1910-20 decade the point-change in the percent urban was 6.0 for native whites and 6.7 for Negroes. The boom in employment that accompanied World War I drew many thousands of Negroes from the South into northern cities. This movement continued during the 1920-30 decade. While the 1920-30 point-change in percent urban was 4.9 for native whites, it was 9.7 for Negroes. Again, during the 1930-40 decade, when urbanization was almost at a standstill for whites (point-change in percent urban was 0.6 for native whites) the point-change for Negroes was 4.9. It is clear that the depression of the 1930's slackened the pace at which Negroes were drifting urbanward faster than whites, but did not stop it.

The 1940-50 decade witnessed a greater urbanization of the Negro population than had any preceding decade. By the old urban definition, the point-change in percent urban was 10.9 for nonwhite populations and only 1.5 for the white population. (In 1950 the Census did not tabulate the urban-rural residence of Negroes by the old urban-rural definitions.) Comparing the old definition for 1940 with the new definition for 1950, the point-change was 13.8 for Negroes and 7.6 for native whites. The magnitude of this extraordinarily large urbanward migration of the nonwhite population during the 1940-50 decade may be more readily appreciated after a look at the lower section of Table 4, which presents estimated intercensal change figures.[2] Whereas the native white urban population increased by 22.6 percent (old urban-rural definitions), the Negro urban population increased by 43.2 percent, or at a rate almost twice as fast! A change of this magnitude could arise only from a large-scale migration of Negroes from rural to urban areas. This migration originated primarily from farms. Evidence of this is the fact that the Negro rural-farm population declined by 29.8 percent in the 1940-50 decade. This was a considerably larger rate of decrease than that of the native white farm population. Thus, one of the outstanding population shifts of the 1940-50 decade was the removal of many thousands of Negroes from rural-farm areas and their movement to urban places.

Although the numbers upon which the rates are based are comparatively small, it appears that the American Indian, Japanese, and Chinese populations also urbanized rapidly during the decade. The wartime removal of persons of Japanese ancestry from West Coast areas, frequently accompanied by loss of their agricultural holdings, undoubtedly accounts in part for the high rate of urbanization of this group.

CHANGE IN THE WHITE AND NONWHITE POPULATIONS: 1950 TO 1958

The following table summarizes the changes in nativity-color composition that occurred between April, 1950 and July 1, 1958.

In this table, the statistics for the white and nonwhite populations are official estimates by the Bureau of the Census, but the statistics for native-born and foreign-born whites are only the very crudest of estimates, and must be taken only as approximate indications of the changes that have taken place.

The increases of 19.5 million and 3.5 million

[2] Because of a change in the census definitions of urban populations for the 1950 census, it is impossible to compute exact rates of change, 1940-50, for subgroups of the population (such as the color-nativity-race groups being considered here) separately for urban and rural areas. By an estimating procedure . . ., these rates have been computed for this study. Since they are only estimates and not direct calculations, they must be interpreted with caution. The rates are based on the old, rather than the new, urban definitions.

Color and nativity	Population July 1, 1958 (000)	Change 1950–58 (000)	Percent change 1950–58	Percent distribution 1958
Population, total	174,064	22,932	15.2	100.0
White	154,795	19,452	14.4	88.9
Native	146,895	21,704	17.3	84.4
Foreign born	7,900	−2,252	−22.4	4.5
Nonwhite	19,269	3,480	22.0	11.1

in the white and nonwhite populations, respectively, represent growth rates of 14.4 and 22.0 percent. Thus, during the present decade the nonwhite population appears to be growing at a rate which is almost 50 percent greater than that of the white population. A part of this differential, however, is due to a very rapid decline of the foreign-born population (about 22 percent in eight years!) At the present time, the population of the nation is increased by about 300,000 immigrants per year. This is much too small a number to replace the deaths among the foreign-born, who are now at such an advanced age that they are being decimated rapidly. Consequently, there has been a net loss of more than 2¼ million foreign-born in the seven years since the last census.

When the dying out of the elderly foreign born is taken into consideration, the differential between the growth of the native white and the nonwhite population becomes much smaller. At the present time the rate of growth for nonwhites is roughly 25 to 27 percent greater than the rate for native whites. This is due, in large part, to the great improvement in the health status of the nonwhite population since 1950 and to their higher birth rates.

The percent distribution of the population by color and nativity in 1958 is shown in the right-hand column of the above table. The 1958 nonwhite population comprises 11.1 percent of the total population, instead of 10.5 percent as in 1950. This is a comparatively small change; unless it continues for several decades or becomes greatly accelerated, it betokens no great change in color composition. The most striking change has been the decline in the proportion of foreign-born whites. In 1950 they were 6.7 percent of the total population, but by 1957 only 4.5 percent. This rapid shift will continue during the next decade, with the result that by 1965 the population will be preponderantly native white and Negro. If immigration rates were to continue at about the present level, the number of foreign-born whites would level off at about 12 million, and would become a progressively smaller percentage of the population as the total number of inhabitants tended to increase.

Regional Distribution and Color-Nativity-Race Composition: 1790 to 1958

The various regions of the United States differ considerably in their color-nativity-race composition, and each color-nativity-race group has its own unique distribution among the regions. Table 6 shows the regional distribution by geographic divisions for each of the census color-nativity-race groups as they were in 1950 and in 1880. The regional distribution for the total population (the "all classes" column) may be used as a basis for determining what would be the "expected" proportion in each geographic division if all groups were distributed in the same proportions.

Foreign-born White Population

The white immigrants to the United States did not spread out evenly over the land. Instead, they concentrated heavily in the Middle Atlantic and East North Central states, and to a lesser extent in the New England and Pacific states. This tendency to concentrate in the Northeast was characteristic of their distribution both in 1880 and 1950. However, at the earlier date the West North Central Division also contained an

TABLE 6

Percent Distribution Among Geographic Divisions of Color, Nativity, and Race Classes: 1950 and 1880

Geographic division	All classes	White			Nonwhite						
		Total	Native	Foreign born	Total	Negro	Other races				
							Total	Indian	Japanese	Chinese	All other
	Census of 1950										
United States	100.0	100.0	100.0	100.0	100.0	100.0	100.0	100.0	100.0	100.0	100.0
New England	6.2	6.8	6.3	12.7	1.0	1.0	1.5	1.0	0.5	4.0	1.3
Middle Atlantic	20.0	20.9	19.5	38.5	12.2	12.5	7.1	3.6	4.7	20.6	6.7
East North Central	20.2	21.2	21.2	21.1	11.8	12.0	7.3	6.5	11.3	7.2	5.2
West North Central	9.3	10.1	10.4	5.5	3.1	2.8	8.6	15.9	1.9	1.9	1.5
South Atlantic	14.1	11.9	12.6	3.6	32.6	33.9	6.4	2.2	1.0	4.0	29.2
East South Central	7.6	6.5	7.0	0.5	17.2	17.9	1.1	1.2	0.2	1.5	1.7
West South Central	9.6	8.9	9.4	3.3	15.9	16.2	9.6	16.7	0.9	3.4	5.0
Mountain	3.4	3.6	3.7	2.3	1.5	0.4	22.9	41.4	10.0	3.2	2.6
Pacific	9.6	10.2	10.0	12.4	4.8	3.4	35.5	11.5	69.3	54.3	46.8
	Census of 1880										
United States	100.0	100.0	100.0	100.0	100.0	100.0	100.0	100.0[1]	...	100.0	...
New England	8.0	9.1	8.6	12.1	0.6	0.6	1.1	0.6	...	0.4	...
Middle Atlantic	20.9	23.7	22.5	30.8	2.8	2.9	1.4	2.9	...	1.2	...
East North Central	22.3	25.4	24.7	29.2	2.9	2.8	6.6	6.5	...	0.4	...
West North Central	12.3	13.7	13.4	15.2	3.1	3.1	3.3	18.9	...	0.4	...
South Atlantic	15.1	10.7	12.2	2.6	43.6	44.7	1.1	1.0	...	0.1	...
East South Central	11.1	8.4	9.7	1.4	28.5	29.3	1.5	1.4	...	0.1	...
West South Central	6.6	5.2	5.6	2.7	16.1	16.5	1.6	26.6	...	0.7	...
Mountain	1.3	1.4	1.3	2.2	0.6	0.1	19.3	29.0	...	13.5	...
Pacific	2.2	2.3	2.0	3.8	1.7	0.1	64.1	13.2	...	83.3	...

[1] Distribution is for 1890 instead of 1880, but 1880 totals for Indians are used in "total other races" column.

Source: *U.S. Census of Population: 1950,* Volume II, Part 1, Table 59; *Thirteenth Census of the United States: 1910,* Volume I, Table 21, p. 146 and Table 31, p. 170.

important share because of the flow of population to new land. This distribution caused the northeastern states to have a high percentage of foreign-born population (see Table 7).

In 1920, 1/4 of the population of New England was foreign-born white, and in the Middle Atlantic states a little more than 1/5 was foreign-born white. Even in 1950, more than 1/8 of the population of these two divisions was foreign-born white. The South provides a sharp contrast; less than 1/30 of the population of the southern divisions was foreign-born white.

This concentration of the foreign-born in the Northeast was fostered by the rapidly growing industrial and commercial cities which provided ready employment for immigrants arriving from Europe. The South offered much less attraction of this kind. During the period of their settlement, the West North Central states also had greater-than-average proportions of foreign-born population. With the complete settlement of the agricultural lands in this area, the inflow to the division from abroad declined. A similar cycle occurred in the Mountain Division, with a lag of two or three decades. Since a very large proportion of these pioneer and frontier immigrants arrived before the turn of the century, by 1950 they had aged and were beginning

TABLE 7

Color, Nativity, and Race Composition of the United States Population by Geographic Division: 1850 to 1950

Color, nativity, race, and year	United States total	Geographic division								
		New England	Middle Atlantic	East North Central	West North Central	South Atlantic	East South Central	West South Central	Mountain	Pacific
Percent native white										
1950	82.8	84.5	80.7	86.8	92.5	74.0	76.0	80.5	90.8	86.1
1940	81.1	81.0	78.9	86.2	91.2	71.8	73.7	78.7	89.6	84.3
1920	76.7	73.6	75.1	82.5	86.5	66.7	70.8	74.8	82.7	77.6
1900	74.5	73.2	76.3	81.9	82.5	62.2	65.6	69.0	77.2	75.3
1870	72.9	80.5	77.1	80.3	78.8	59.3	64.4	57.2	71.3	64.5
1850	74.6	87.9	80.6	86.8	78.4	58.0	65.1	51.6	94.1	77.5
Percent foreign-born white										
1950	6.7	13.8	13.0	7.1	4.0	1.7	0.5	2.3	4.7	8.7
1940	8.7	17.8	16.4	9.7	5.8	1.6	0.4	2.2	6.3	11.9
1920	13.0	25.3	22.1	15.0	10.9	2.3	0.8	4.5	13.6	18.6
1900	13.4	25.7	21.4	16.4	14.8	2.0	1.2	4.0	17.2	19.6
1870	14.2	18.7	21.2	18.2	17.4	2.9	2.3	6.3	24.4	25.6
1850	9.7	11.2	17.3	12.2	11.3	2.2	1.5	9.2	5.8	21.4
Percent Negro										
1950	10.0	1.5	6.2	5.9	3.0	24.1	23.5	16.7	1.3	3.5
1940	9.8	1.2	4.6	4.0	2.6	26.4	25.8	18.6	0.9	1.4
1920	9.9	1.1	2.7	2.4	2.2	30.9	28.4	20.1	0.9	0.9
1900	11.6	1.1	2.1	1.6	2.3	35.7	33.1	25.9	0.9	0.6
1870	12.7	0.9	1.7	1.4	3.7	37.9	33.2	36.4	0.5	0.7
1850	15.7	0.8	2.1	1.0	10.3	39.8	33.4	39.2	0.1	1.1
Percent other races										
1950	0.5	0.1	0.2	0.2	0.4	0.2	0.1	0.5	3.2	1.7
1940	0.4	0.1	0.1	0.1	0.4	0.2	...	0.5	3.2	2.3
1920	1.1	0.1	0.1	0.1	0.5	0.1	...	4.5	7.0	5.2
1900	0.5	0.1	0.1	0.1	0.4	0.1	...	1.0	4.7	4.5
1870	0.2	...	...	0.1	0.1	...	...	0.1	3.8	9.1
1850	...	...	...	...	...	...	...	...	...	...

Source: *U.S. Census of Population: 1950,* data for 1950 compiled from state reports for this study; *Sixteenth Census of the United States: 1940,* Volume II, Part 1, Table 24; Data for 1850 to 1920 from W. S. Thompson and P. K. Whelpton, *Population Trends in the United States,* Table 12, pp. 42-3.

to die off; also, native white migrants were beginning to pour in from other parts of the United States. Consequently, they had declined to a smaller-than-average proportion of the total.

Although the Pacific states contained a very small population in 1880, ¼ of their white members were foreign-born. As the division grew it continued to attract persons from abroad, and in 1950 it contained 12 percent of the nation's foreign-born white residents. From 1850 to 1950, the Pacific Division has had a higher proportion of foreign-born than the national average.

Negro Population

The Negro population is highly concentrated in the South Atlantic states; as of 1950 more than 1/3 of all Negroes resided in this area. Together, the other two divisions of the South — the East South Central and West South Central — contained another 1/3. The remaining 1/3 was distributed among the other six divisions. In spite of a large and prolonged migration to northern metropolitan areas, Negroes still have a distribution that is unlike that of the general population. The New England, Mountain, and West North Central Divisions have had very small proportions of the Negro population. Outside the South, only the Middle Atlantic and the East North Central states (which contain large manufacturing centers providing employment for in-migrating Negroes) contain sizable shares of the Negro population.

Figure 4 and Table 8 furnish the full picture of the geographic distribution and redistribution of Negroes from 1790 to 1950. The picture is one of a gradual deconcentration from the South Atlantic Division. In 1790, 88.9 percent of the Negroes were living in this division. As southern agriculture moved westward, the Negroes spread gradually into the East South Central and West South Central Divisions. Together the four northern divisions contained only 8.9 percent — which is about the same share they had a century later. The Civil War did comparatively little to move this population to the North or Far West. Only the East North Central Division appeared to gain a substantial number of Negroes between 1860 and 1870. The Negro population was growing steadily, and the North was, to be sure, absorbing its proportionate share — but little more. Between 1890 and 1900 the Middle Atlantic states began to receive a somewhat larger share of the Negro population. This gain continued in the 1900-10 decade. Then, during the decade from 1910 to 1920, the Middle Atlantic and East North Central states increased their proportions of Negroes more than they had in the previous sixty years. The economic expansion associated with World War I drew many Negroes northward. In the 1920-30 decade this movement was accelerated even more, thus almost doubling the proportionate gains of the

TABLE 8

Percent Distribution of Negroes Among Geographic Divisions: 1790 to 1950

Year	United States total	Geographic division								
		New England	Middle Atlantic	East North Central	West North Central	South Atlantic	East South Central	West South Central	Mountain	Pacific
1950	100.0	1.0	12.5	12.0	2.8	33.9	17.9	16.2	0.4	3.4
1940	100.0	0.8	9.9	8.3	2.7	36.5	21.6	18.8	0.3	1.0
1930	100.0	8.8	8.9	7.8	2.8	37.2	22.4	19.2	0.3	0.8
1920	100.0	0.8	5.7	4.9	2.7	41.3	24.1	19.7	0.3	0.5
1910	100.0	0.7	4.3	3.1	2.5	41.8	27.0	20.2	0.2	0.3
1900	100.0	0.7	3.7	2.9	2.7	42.2	28.3	19.2	0.2	0.2
1890	100.0	0.6	3.0	2.8	3.0	43.6	28.3	18.4	0.2	0.2
1880	100.0	0.6	2.9	2.8	3.1	44.7	29.3	16.5	0.1	0.1
1870	100.0	0.6	3.0	2.7	2.9	45.4	30.0	15.2	...	0.1
1860	100.0	0.6	3.0	1.4	2.7	46.3	31.4	14.5	...	0.1
1850	100.0	0.6	3.5	1.2	2.5	51.1	30.9	10.1	...	...
1840	100.0	0.8	4.2	1.0	2.1	55.6	28.9	7.5	...	...
1830	100.0	0.9	4.5	0.7	1.1	65.7	21.5	5.6	...	...
1820	100.0	1.2	5.1	0.4	0.6	71.9	16.3	4.6	...	...
1810	100.0	1.4	6.0	0.3	0.3	78.4	10.6	3.1	...	...
1800	100.0	1.9	6.4	0.1	...	85.8	5.9	...	...	...
1790	100.0	2.2	6.7	...	...	88.9	2.2	...	...	...

Source: *U.S. Census of Population: 1950,* and *Sixteenth Census of the United States: 1940;* Data for 1950 and 1940 computed from compilations of data for individual states, made for this study: *Thirteenth Census of the United States: 1910,* Volume I, Table 22, p. 154; U. S. Bureau of the Census, *Negroes in the United States, 1920-32,* Table 3, p. 5.

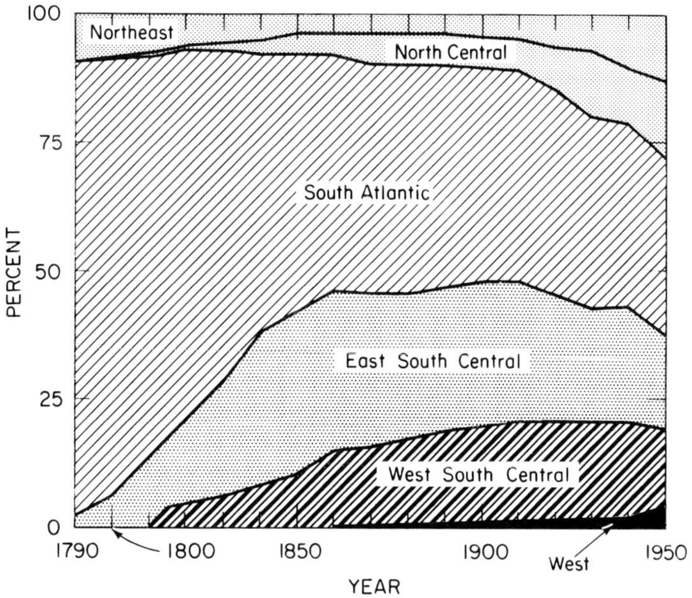

FIGURE 4

Distribution of Negroes among the geographic divisions, 1790 to 1950.

1910-20 period. Substantial but smaller gains were also made in the northeastern divisions between 1930 and 1940. Between 1940 and 1950 the northward movement of Negroes was renewed and speeded up. It effected a redistribution much greater in number than, and equal in proportion to, that of the 1920-30 decade. Simultaneously the Pacific states received a very large influx of Negroes. Thus, even though the Negro population is still heavily concentrated in the South, it shows much evidence of accomplishing a more even distribution among all the divisions.

The effect of this development upon the color-nativity-race composition of the population of each division is shown in Table 7. In the Middle Atlantic, East North Central, and Pacific states the proportion of the population that is Negro has more than doubled since 1920. By 1950 Negroes comprised about 6 percent or more of each of the two northeastern divisions, and 3.5 percent of the Pacific states. Since 1850 the proportion of the population that is Negro has declined by 40 percent in the South Atlantic states, by 30 percent in the East South Central states, and by 57 percent in the West South Central states. Even with these marked changes, in 1950 Negroes comprised 24 percent of the population of the South Atlantic and East South Central states and 17 percent of the West South Central states.

At no time has more than a very small fraction of the New England population consisted of Negroes. The Mountain states and the West North Central states likewise contain a very small Negro population. The latter division contained about the same share in 1950 as it had in 1870.

Other Nonwhite Races

During the seventy years from 1880 to 1950 the minor nonwhite races underwent a very great redistribution. In 1880 they were highly concentrated in the Pacific states (Chinese and Indians) and the Mountain states (Indians and Chinese). By 1950 the Chinese had become a little more evenly distributed among all divisions, although they were especially concentrated in the Middle Atlantic as well as the Pacific Division. Indians had become much more heavily concentrated in the Mountain Division than they had been previously, and less concentrated in the Great Plains (West South Central and West North Central). The Japanese and other minor nonwhite races did not arrive in any significant numbers until 1880.

Native White Population

The proportion of the population defined as native white has increased in those areas where the foreign-born population has decreased. It also has tended to decrease in areas where the proportion of Negroes has increased. In all divisions, the native white population was a larger proportion of the total population in 1950 than in 1940. This increase has tended to be smallest, however, in the three divisions where the proportion of Negroes increased most — the Middle Atlantic, the East North Central, and the Pacific. It tended to increase more where the proportion of Negroes declined — South Atlantic, East South Central, and West South Central states. Whereas 58 percent of the population of the South Atlantic states had been native white in 1850, in 1950 74.0 percent was native white. Similar though smaller changes have taken place in the other two divisions of the South. Undoubtedly, this change in proportions will be reflected in many other social changes in the South, just as the rapid increase in the proportion of Negroes among the population is being accompanied by rapid social change in the North.

*Trends and Differentials in the American Age at Marriage**

J. R. Rele

The age at marriage has undergone remarkable changes in the United States during the last two decades. These include the sharp decline in the age at marriage during the decade 1940–1950, a slight continuation of this trend in 1950–1960, and significant changes in the marriage patterns for subgroups of the population during both decades. Each decade was unique and distinctive in its influence on the historic trends relating to the age at marriage. Together, the two decades seem outstanding in introducing a new early marriage pattern into the changing structure of the family.

Recent Trend

First Marriage

The earliest reliable estimates of the average age at marriage in the United States are available for the year 1890, when the median age at first marriage was 26.1 years for males and 22.0 years for females (Table 1). The next 50 years saw a gradual decline in these ages to 24.4 and 21.5, respectively, in 1940, with a slight interruption of the trend during the 1930s. The decline in the age at marriage was faster among males than among females, thus reducing the interval between the median ages of husband and wife from 4.1 years in 1890 to 2.9 years in 1940. The greatest decline in the age at marriage, however, occurred for both sexes during the next decade, 1940–1950. After 1950, the marital age declined slightly,[1] but once again more

* Reprinted with permission from *Milbank Memorial Fund Quarterly,* Vol. 43, No. 2 (April 1965), pp. 219-234.

[1] This is based on the median ages at first marriage computed from the 1960 census, and is in disagreement with the Current Population Survey (CPS) data. The CPS shows no change in the median age at first marriage since 1950, though there is general agreement for earlier years. The former seems consistent with other evidences which will be considered presently. For the CPS median ages, *see U.S.* Bureau of the Census, *Current Population Reports — Population Characteristics,* Washington, D.C., Series P-20, No. 122, March 22, 1963, p. 2.

TABLE 1

*Trends in Median and Quartile Ages at First Marriage for the United States Total Population and Subgroups**

	Males				Females				Difference in Male and Female Median Ages
Census Year	Median	First Quartile Q_1	Third Quartile Q_3	Inter-quartile Range $Q_3 - Q_1$	Median	First Quartile Q_1	Third Quartile Q_3	Inter-quartile Range $Q_3 - Q_1$	
Total population									
1890	26.1				22.0				4.1
1900	25.9				21.9				4.0
1910	25.1	22.2	31.6	9.4	21.6	19.1	26.5	7.4	3.5
1920	24.5	21.5	30.3	8.8	21.2	18.8	25.9	7.1	3.3
1930	24.2	21.7	29.3	7.6	21.3	18.8	25.7	6.9	2.9
1940	24.4	21.9	29.1	7.2	21.5	19.0	25.9	6.9	2.9
1950	22.9	20.9	26.6	5.7	20.2	18.4	23.0	4.6	2.7
1960	22.3	20.4	25.8	5.4	20.0	18.4	22.4	4.0	2.3
Urban									
1940	24.7	22.2	29.4	7.2	22.2	19.6	26.9	7.3	2.5
1950	23.0	21.0	26.7	5.7	20.6	18.7	23.5	4.8	2.4
1960	22.3	20.4	25.8	5.4	20.1	18.5	22.6	4.1	2.2
Rural nonfarm									
1940	23.5	21.3	27.7	6.4	20.4	18.5	24.1	5.6	3.1
1950	22.4	20.7	25.4	4.7	19.3	17.9	21.6	3.7	3.1
1960	22.2	20.3	25.2	4.9	19.3	18.0	21.2	3.2	2.9
Rural farm									
1940	24.3	21.7	29.7	8.0	20.7	18.5	24.3	5.8	3.6
1950	23.2	21.0	27.5	6.5	19.5	18.1	22.1	4.0	3.7
1960	23.3	21.1	27.8	6.7	20.2	18.7	22.6	3.9	3.1
Nonwhites									
1940	22.9	20.7	28.3	7.6	20.2	18.1	24.6	6.5	2.7
1950	22.6	20.2	26.5	6.3	19.6	17.8	23.0	5.2	3.0
1960	22.7	20.5	27.3	6.8	20.3	18.5	23.6	5.1	2.4

*The medians and quartiles are computed from the census data on marital status by single years of age. If P is the proportion of the population who ever marry — here taken to be the proportion ever married in the age group 45 to 54 — the median age is the age at which the proportion ever married is exactly P/2. It is obtained by interpolating between the proportions ever married by single years of age.

Sources: computed from 1. U. S. Bureau of the Census, *Census of Population: 1960, Detailed Characteristics — U. S. Summary*, Final Report PC(1)-1D, Washington, D.C., 1963, pp. 424-434. 2. U. S. Bureau of the Census, *Census of Population: 1950,* Vol. II, Characteristics of the Population, Part 1: U. S. Summary, Washington, D.C., 1953, pp. 179-188. 3. U. S. Bureau of the Census, *Census of Population: 1940,* Vol. IV, Characteristics by Age, Part 1: U. S. Summary, Washington, D.C., pp. 17-20 and 22-24. Data for 1890 and 1900 are taken from: 4. U. S. Bureau of the Census, *Current Population Reports — Population Characteristics,* Series P-20, No. 122, March 22, 1963, Washington, D.C., p. 2.

for males than for females. In 1960 the male and female median ages at marriage were 22.3 and 20.0, respectively, narrowing down the difference between their average ages to 2.3 years.

These median ages are computed from the proportion of ever-married persons in the population by single years of age, available from the census. Another possible evidence is the marriage registration data based on the issuance of marriage licenses. The latter source, however, is incomplete in the United States, and the two differ slightly in the ideas they convey about the age at marriage. Whereas the median age computed from the census is largely independent of the population age distribution, the one derived from the registration data is directly affected by the changes in the age structure of the population. The registration median rests on the experience of people of all ages marrying at a given time, while the census figure depends excessively on people whose present age is close to the median age. Both measures can be affected by migration.

The registration data in the United States provide only limited information by way of trend in the age at marriage. What is available for the recent period is confined to 22 reporting states for the period 1955–1959 (Table 2). However, this confirms the decline in the age at marriage for both males and females, though the result could be influenced by the changes in the population age distribution. The 1959 registered median age at first marriage was, therefore, adjusted to conform to the 1950 population age distribution, accounting for the change in the age distribution between 1950 and 1960. For males the adjustment leaves the 1959 median age unaltered, whereas for females the 1959 adjusted median age coincides with the actual median age for 1955. Thus the decline in the registered median age from 1955 to 1959 can be explained to some extent by the changing age distribution for females, but not for males. This is consistent with our earlier finding based on the census data that the age of males at first marriage continued to decline through 1960 at a rate faster than that of females, and that the change in the marriage habits of females, as indicated by the median age, was not very substantial. The observed decline in the registered median age at marriage among females was due to the change in the age distribution of the population as a result of increased fertility in the early 1940s, which eventually raised the proportion of marriageable girls in the early ages — ages at which it is still too early for boys to marry. As the bigger hump of the postwar "baby boom" has yet to enter the marriageable ages, in itself it will soon have a tendency to lower the registered median age at first marriage for both men and women. Moreover, inherent in the growth of population is the tendency for boys and girls to be closer together in age at marriage. As the swelling numbers of each successive cohort of girls first become available for marriage, the earlier cohorts of boys are relatively smaller and hence numerically unable to respond completely. This may lead girls to find their choice among relatively younger boys. Also, female competition for marriage partners is thus enhanced, and the mere consciousness of this fact may result in earlier marriages for both sexes.

TABLE 2

Median Age at First Marriage by Sex from Registration Data for 22 Reporting States, 1955–1959

Year	Male	Female	Difference
1955–59	22.9	20.2	2.7
1955	23.2	20.4	2.8
1956	23.1	20.3	2.8
1957	22.9	20.2	2.7
1958	22.6	20.0	2.6
1959	22.6	20.0	2.6
1959 (Adj)*	22.7	20.4	2.3

* Standardized for the 1950 population age distribution, adjusting for the change in the population age distribution between 1950 and 1960. Actually the adjustment was carried out with the data on 27 reporting states, for which the number of marriages by age and sex were available (same source, p. 60), but otherwise had the same unadjusted median ages in 1959 as the 22 states to which the rest of the data belong.

Source: National Office of Vital Statistics, *Vital Statistics of the United States, 1959,* Vol. I, Section 2, Washington, D.C., p. 19.

To give some idea of the distribution of the marriage ages, Table 1 gives the first and third quartiles, which are the ages at which 25 per cent and 75 per cent, respectively, of those who ever marry are married. The shifts in the entire marriage age distributions toward earlier ages is obvious from the general declines in both quartiles for either sex. During the decade 1950–1960 the first quartile age at marriage continued to decline for males, but not for females. This again supports the previous claim of increasing popularity of young marriages among males during this later period. Strikingly enough, the tendency toward earlier marriages for both sexes is accompanied by another trend exhibited by the continuous fall in the interquartile range, which suggests concentration of marriages within a narrower range

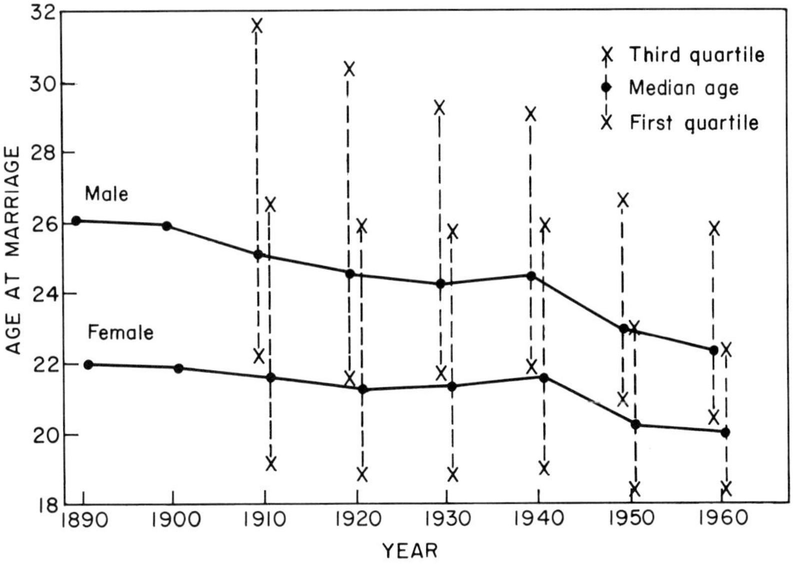

FIGURE 1

Trends in the median and quartile ages at first marriage and interquartile ranges for males and females.

of ages. In other words, the age at marriage as a cultural norm seems to be passing through the same process of standardization which has hitherto affected other aspects of the American way of life (Figure 1).

Remarriage

Remarriages constitute a substantial proportion of all marriages in the United States. According to a population survey conducted in 1953, 30 per cent of all marriages from January 1950 to April 1953 were remarriages for either party, and in 13 per cent of all marriages both parties had been married before.[2] There has been an increasing trend in the proportion of remarriages since about the time of World War I, as a result of an increased contribution of divorced men and women to remarriages.[3]

The data available on the age at remarriage are more restrictive than those for first marriages, being limited to information from marriage registration and special surveys. These are greatly affected both by the changing age distribution of eligible persons for remarriage, and by the inconsistencies in the number of reporting states. The available data suggests a trend toward increase in the age at remarriage since 1947 (Table 3). This may be due in small part to a rise in the number of third and higher remarriages. More likely, it is partly due to the changing age distribution of remarriage eligibles, as verified by standardizing the 1959 median age at remarriage for the 1950 age distribution of remarriage eligibles for 27 reporting states.[4] The observed median ages for the bride and the groom, which were 35.4 and 39.8, respectively, were reduced to 34.3 and 39.2 on standardization. Thus, in the long run, with the decreasing proportion of widowed persons among remarriage eligibles affecting their age distribution, a long-term trend toward earlier

[2] Monahan, Thomas P., Changing Nature and Instability of Remarriages, *Eugenics Quarterly,* 5, 76, June, 1958.

[3] Jacobson, Paul H., *American Marriage and Divorce,* New York, Rinehart and Company, Inc., 1959, p. 71.

[4] The data on age at remarriage by single years of age were taken from U.S. National Office of Vital Statistics, *Vital Statistics of the United States, 1959,* Washington, D.C., Vol. I, p. 60.

TABLE 3

*Median Age at Remarriage by Sex, 1947–1953 and 1955–1959**

Year	Median Age at Remarriage Groom	Bride
1947	37.1	32.0
1948	37.3	31.8
1949	39.0	32.3
1950	39.0	33.9
1951	39.5	32.9
1952	39.9	35.4
1953	41.3	33.3
1955	39.1	34.5
1956	39.4	34.9
1957	39.7	35.3
1958	39.7	35.3
1959	39.5	35.2

* The median ages for 1947-53 and 1955-59 are derived from different sources and are not comparable. The former are based on a survey covering the entire country and refer to remarriages occurring between January 1947 and June 1954. The latter are based on the registration data for 22 reporting states.

Sources: 1. National Office of Vital Statistics, *Vital Statistics — Special Reports,* Vol. 45, No. 12, Sept. 9, 1957, Washington, D.C., p. 332. 2. National Office of Vital Statistics, *Vital Statistics of the United States, 1959,* Vol. I, Section 2, Washington, D.C., p. 19.

age at remarriage may be expected. It is possible that the age at remarriage around 1947 was unduly low on account of the marriage boom and the early marriages of the 1940s, many of which ultimately proved to be unstable as revealed by a corresponding rise in the divorce rate in the immediate subsequent period.[5] The excess of these young divorced persons in the population could result in the earlier age at remarriage in the corresponding period. The increasing trend in the age at remarriage since 1947 could then only be a return to the original more stable pattern.

The remarriage rate is higher among nonwhites than among whites, and yet the age at remarriage is higher among the former (Table 4). The higher age at remarriage of nonwhites seems to be due to: 1. the greater proportion of widowed persons among the nonwhites who remarry, for widowed persons generally have a later age at remarriage than do divorced persons; and 2. the fact that the median age of husband and wife at the time of divorce is about 2.4 years higher among nonwhites than among whites.[6]

[5] Jacobson, *op. cit.,* p. 90, Table 42.

TABLE 4

*Median Age at First Marriage and Remarriage by Sex and Race, for 27 Reporting States in 1959**

Race	First Marriage Groom	Bride	Remarriage Groom	Bride
All races	22.6	20.0	39.8	35.4
White	22.5	19.9	39.3	35.1
Nonwhite	23.2	20.5	42.9	37.6
Negro	23.0	20.4	43.0	37.8
other races	25.9	22.4	39.7	32.1

* The median ages are computed from data by single years of age.

Source: National Office of Vital Statistics *Vital Statistics of the United States, 1959,* Vol. I, Section 2, Washington, D.C., p .19.

Differentials in the Age at First Marriage

The age at first marriage discussed in the earlier part of this paper refers to the national average which, of course, is subject to variation between subgroups of the population. For a better understanding of the age at marriage, including the national trends themselves, we shall deal here with regional and racial variations.

Rural-Urban Differences

The decade 1950–1960 was significant in introducing a new phase of the rural-urban differential in age at marriage, distinct for each sex (Table 1 and Figure 2). Among males, both in 1940 and 1950, there was very little difference in the age at marriage as between the urban and rural farm populations. The age was relatively earlier in the rural nonfarm areas. During the same period, urban females had a higher median age at marriage compared to the two rural subgroups which were similar in this

[6] U.S. National Office of Vital Statistics, *Vital Statistics of the United States,* 1959, Washington, D.C., Vol. I, Section 2, p. 22.

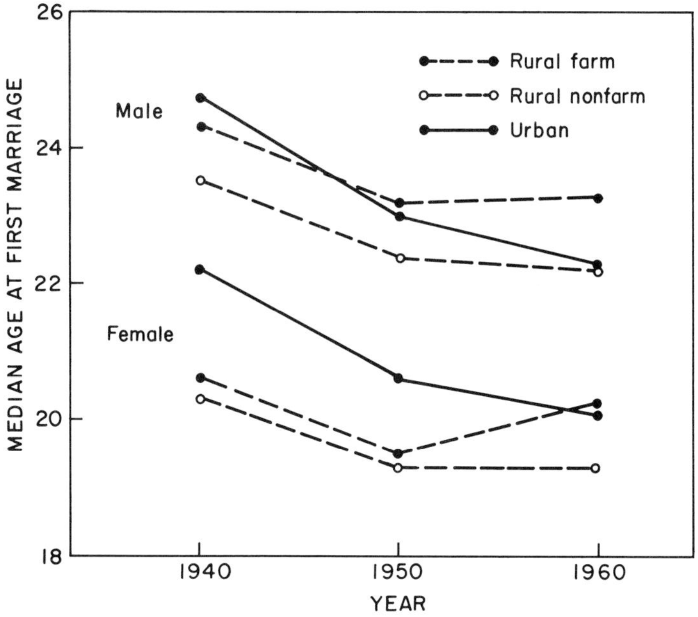

FIGURE 2

Trends and differentials in the age at marriage for each sex by type of residence.

respect. However, between 1940 and 1950, the rate of decline in the age at marriage was the fastest in the urban areas, which continued for another decade during 1950–1960. In 1960, among males, the urban age at marriage was close to that of the rural nonfarm population, which has characteristically remained the lowest. The rural farm age at marriage was relatively higher.

The discussion of rural-urban differentials in marital age during 1950–1960 is complicated by the change in the farm definition, which reduced the rural farm population 14 years old and over by about 20 per cent.[7] Since the reduction mainly added to the rural nonfarm category, it left those most characteristic of the agrarian situation. This may have contributed to the sharp rise in the age at marriage of rural farm females. However, a part of the explanation seems to lie in the inadequacy of our index, the median age at marriage computed from the proportion of single persons in the population by age, which evidently is affected by rural-urban migration. The rural farm group is particularly vulnerable in this respect because of its relatively smaller size. It is true that the economic stagnation in the rural farm sector during the earlier half of the last decade may have contributed to postponement of marriage.[8] The same could also induce migration of single persons to cities, and the two trends would have opposite effects on the median age at marriage. However, the latter half of the decade, and particularly the semi-depression of 1957–1958, was relatively harder on the urban and rural nonfarm population, and especially the new entrants into the labor market. This may have caused return migration from the young and unmarried floating popu-

[7] U.S. Bureau of the Census, *Current Population Reports — Population Characteristics,* Washington, D.C., Series P-20, No. 105, p. 3, November 2, 1960.

[8] The median total money incomes of families and unrelated individuals in households increased by 0.7 per cent in the rural farm and 23.9 per cent in urban and rural nonfarm areas during 1950-1954, whereas these percentages were 37.9 and 20.2, respectively, during 1954-1958. *Cf.* U.S. Bureau of the Census, *Current Population Reports,* Washington, D.C., Series P-60, No. 35, p. 34, Table 34, January 5, 1961.

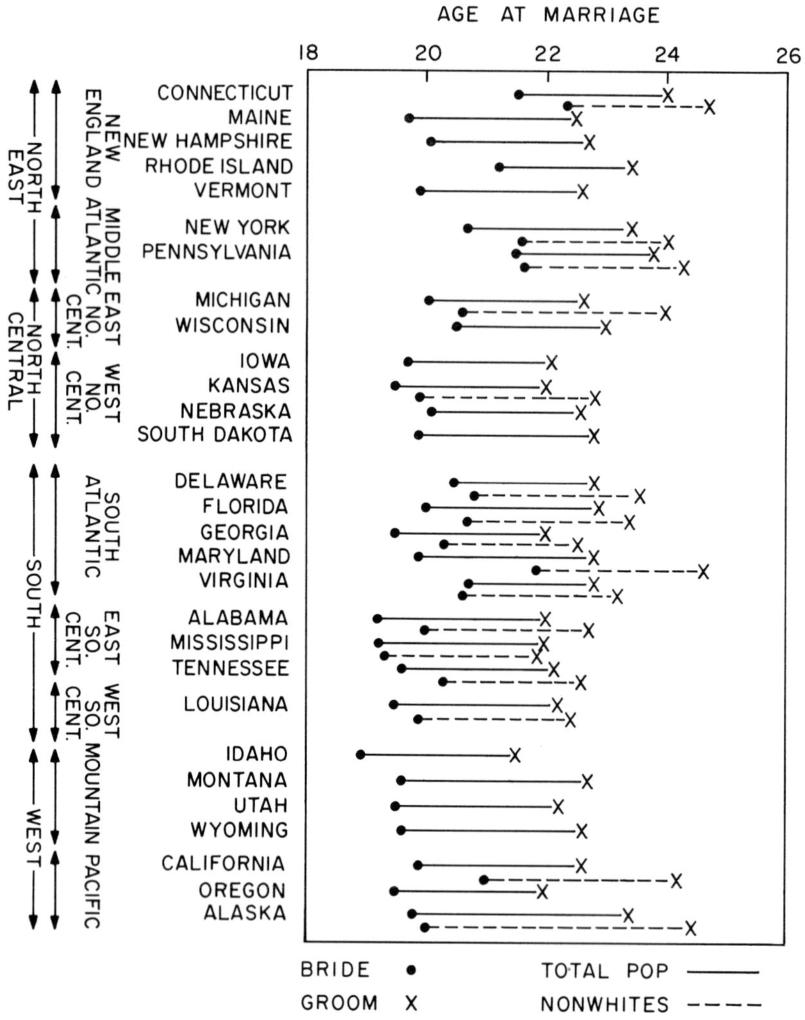

FIGURE 3

Median age at first marriage of bride and groom by geographic division for the total population as well as nonwhites.

lation in the cities, and probably arrested the migration of the new aspirants into the cities. This could account for the rise in the rural farm median age at marriage, which is conspicuous for females.

Racial Variation

Nonwhite women consistently had a median age at first marriage about one year lower than that for white women until the early 1940s, after which the difference became smaller.[9] Most of the reduction in the difference was brought about by the fall in the age at marriage among whites. In 1950, nonwhites still had a younger median age at first marriage for both males and females (Table 1), but by 1960 the situation

[9] Glick, Paul C., *American Families,* New York, U.S. Bureau of the Census, The Census Monograph Series, 1957, p. 58.

TABLE 5

Median Age at First Marriage by Sex, Color, and Geographic Division, for 29 Reporting States in 1959

Geographic Division and State	Color*	Median Age at First Marriage Groom	Bride	Geographic Division and State	Color*	Median Age at First Marriage Groom	Bride
All reporting states	T†	22.7	20.1	Georgia	T†	22.0	19.5
	W	22.7	20.1		W	21.9	19.3
	N	23.2	20.6		N	22.5	20.3
New England:				Maryland	T†	22.8	19.9
Connecticut	T†	24.0	21.5		W	22.6	19.6
	W	24.0	21.5		N	24.6	21.8
	N	24.7	22.3	Virginia	T	22.8	20.7
Maine	T	22.5	19.7		W	22.7	20.7
New Hampshire	T	22.7	20.1		N	23.2	20.6
Rhode Island	T	23.4	21.2	East South Central:			
Vermont	T	22.6	19.9	Alabama	T	22.0	19.2
Middle Atlantic:					W	21.9	18.9
New York	T	23.4	20.7		N	22.7	20.0
(excl. N.Y. City)	W	23.3	20.7	Mississippi	T	22.0	19.2
	N	24.0	21.6		W	22.0	19.1
Pennsylvania	T†	23.8	21.5		N	21.9	19.3
	W	23.8	21.5	Tennessee	T	22.1	19.6
	N	24.3	21.6		W	22.1	19.6
East North Central:					N	22.6	20.3
Michigan	T	22.6	20.0	West South Central:			
	W	22.5	20.0	Louisiana	T	22.2	19.5
	N	24.0	20.6		W	22.2	19.4
Wisconsin	T	23.0**	20.5**		N	22.4	19.9
West North Central:				Mountain:			
Iowa	T	22.1	19.7	Idaho	T	21.5	18.9
Kansas	T†	22.0	19.5	Montana	T	22.7	19.6
	W	22.0	19.5	Utah	T	22.2	19.5
	N	22.8	19.9	Wyoming	T	22.6	19.6
Nebraska	T	22.6	20.1	Pacific:			
South Dakota	T	22.8	19.9	California	T	22.6	19.9
South Atlantic:					W	22.5	19.8
Delaware	T	22.8	20.5		N	24.2	21.0
	W	22.7	20.5	Oregon	T	22.0	19.5
	N	23.6	20.9	Alaska	T†	23.4	19.8
Florida	T	22.9	20.0		W	23.0	19.7
	W	22.8	19.8		N	24.5	20.0
	N	23.4	20.7				

* T stands for total population, W for whites and N for nonwhites.
† Data include marriages for which color was not stated.
** Includes previously annulled marriages.
(The median ages are computed from data by single years of age by place of occurrence. Whites and nonwhites are shown separately for those states in which the 1950 population for nonwhite formed 10 per cent or more of the total or numbered 50,000 or more.)

Source: National Office of Vital Statistics, *Vital Statistics of the United States, 1959,* Section 2, Washington, D.C., p. 21.

was reversed. This resulted from the continued decline in the marital age of white males, whereas among females it was the rise in the nonwhite age at marriage which contributed the major change. The reversal is also observed when the survey or registration data are considered.[10] However, in this situation, the reason seems to be the fall in the age at marriage among whites for both sexes. As mentioned earlier, this interpretation is influenced by the changing age distribution of the population during this period, which has had a definite effect on the female registered age at marriage. The distinctly higher dispersion in the age at marriage of nonwhites compared to whites is striking. In 1950, it was due to a relatively higher proportion of nonwhite men and women marrying in their teens. This was no longer true in 1960, when the proportion marrying during their teens was almost identical for the two races. However, the greater variability in the age at marriage of nonwhites was maintained by the relatively higher proportion of these men and women marrying in their thirties or later.

Geographical Variation

Prominent in the geographical variation is the relatively late marriage in the northeast region as compared to the early marriage pattern of the South.[11] The pattern is repeated in 1959, when again a higher age at marriage is observed among states in the northeast region, for both sexes, and for both whites and nonwhites (Table 5 and Figure 3). Even when dealing with individual states, the analysis has to be carried out in a broader regional context, since the marriages for individual states are likely to be affected by the interstate migration for marriage. This is particularly important with the special characteristics of these migrant marriages, which seek to avoid difficulties in their own state. Among whites, the states with distinctly higher age at marriage for both males and females were Connecticut, New York (excluding New York City), Pennsylvania, and Rhode Island, all of which belong to the northeast region. Among nonwhites, in addition to the northeast, all reporting states (with the exception of Georgia) in the South Atlantic, namely, Delaware, Florida, Maryland, and Virginia, and California in the Pacific region, had a relatively higher median age at marriage. Usually, the states with a higher age at marriage of the groom were also those where the age at marriage of the bride was high. As a result, there is almost no geographical variation in the difference between bride and groom in median age at marriage. Even between the states, the difference varies within the relatively narrow range of 2.0 to 3.1 years for whites and 2.2 to 3.4 years for nonwhites. Consistent with the earlier finding, nonwhites are seen to have a higher median age at marriage in 1959 in all reporting states, excepting males in Mississippi and females in Virginia.

Conclusion

Although this paper traces the historic trends in the age at marriage in the United States, one of its main objectives is to analyze the trends after 1950 in the context of a sharp decline in the age at marriage during the decade 1940–1950.[12] For the period after 1950, data from the dual sources of census and registration provide ample evidence of continued decline in the age at marriage among males, though the magnitude of change was small compared to the earlier decade. Among females, the age at marriage computed from the census did not show any substantial change after 1950; the registration data did suggest a decline in the median age at marriage, but this was an outcome of the changing age distribution which had an increased proportion of young marriageable girls. The narrowing of the interquartile range (the span of ages within which 50 per cent of all marriages

[10] The median ages at first marriage among whites and nonwhites were, respectively, 24.2 and 23.8 for males, and 20.8 and 20.5 for females, for marriages between January 1947 and June 1954; computed from U.S. National Office of Vital Statistics, *Vital Statistics — Special Reports,* Washington, D.C., Vol. 45, No. 12, September 9, 1957, pp. 339-341. The median ages for 1959 have been presented earlier in Table 4.

[11] This can be seen from the data on the age at marriage of couples with first marriage between January 1947 and June 1954 in U.S. National Office of Vital Statistics, *Vital Statistics — Special Reports,* Washington, D.C., Vol. 45, No. 12, September 9, 1957, p. 313.

[12] Certain concomitants of these trends in the age at marriage are discussed separately in Rele, J. R., Some Correlates of the Age at Marriage in the United States, *Eugenics Quarterly,* 12, 1-6, March, 1965.

take place) over the last half century or more indicates that the age at marriage in the United States is undergoing a process of standardization whereby people tend to marry within a smaller span of ages.

Although remarriages constitute an increasing proportion of all marriages in the United States, the age of remarriage has been rising since 1947. This may seem contradictory, especially when the former fact is due to an increased contribution of divorced persons to remarriages, who generally have an earlier age at remarriage than the widowed. Standardization suggests that the rise in the age at remarriage is at least partly due to the changing age distribution of remarriage eligibles. It is possible that the age at remarriage around 1947 was unduly low because of the excess of young divorced persons in the population following the marriage boom and early marriages of the 1940s, many of which proved to be short-lived. The increase in the age at remarriage since 1947 may then be only a return to the original more stable pattern.

The trends in the age at marriage vary significantly for various subgroups of the population. As a result, the last decade saw the introduction of new intergroup patterns in the age at first marriage. Among the urban, rural farm, and rural nonfarm populations, the urban showed the fastest decline in the age at marriage for two consecutive decades from 1940–1960. Hence, by 1960 urban areas were no longer characterized by relatively late marriage, whereas the age at marriage continued to remain the lowest in rural nonfarm populations.

The decline in the age at marriage during the decade 1950–1960 was entirely due to the country's white population. Nonwhite males showed no trend, while nonwhite females showed a rise in the age at marriage. This had the effect of reversing the traditional pattern of racial differential in the age at first marriage. For the first time, around 1960, the age at marriage was lower among whites than among nonwhites, and the same pattern was repeated in almost each state. The geographic variation reveals no substantial deviation from the earlier pattern of relatively late marriage in the northeast region.

STUDY AND DISCUSSION QUESTIONS

1. Changes in age composition of a population may have many sociological implications for the society in question. If a society's population were to age greatly, for instance, what kinds of other changes or needs would you expect to arise?
2. The U.S. Census publishes a report each decennial year on the nativity and parentage of the population of this country. What kinds of information does this report contain? Construct an age-sex pyramid from a recent census on one subgroup of the population included in this report.
3. In enumerating "race" of an individual, it was mentioned that the U.S. Census tries to distinguish individuals on a cultural rather than a biological basis. How is this done? Look up the census policy in labeling persons by race. How is each race defined? What are the weaknesses of such a classification? The strengths?
4. Apply what you have learned about sex differentials in mortality to the sex composition of the population at different ages. Is this composition what we would expect given these differential patterns?
5. Age-sex pyramids may be refined somewhat by including other characteristics, e.g., race. What kinds of graphic configurations might be designed to show the several dimensions of a population's composition?
6. It has been stated that fertility, mortality, and migration combine to determine the population size of an area. How might the composition factors discussed in this chapter operate through these three components to affect population size? Discuss some ways, for example, that specific changes in population composition may cause population size to increase.
7. As in many areas of demography, the area of population composition is strong in facts and weak in theory. What kinds of questions would a theory of population composition attempt to answer? Where would such a theory begin?

SUGGESTED ADDITIONAL READING

Coale, Ansley J. "How a Population Ages or Grows Younger," in *Population: the Vital Revolution*, ed. Ronald Freedman. Garden City, New York: Anchor Books, Doubleday, 1964, 47–57.
A brief but incisive analysis of how the age distribution of a population changes and some of the consequences of these changes.

Greenberg, Joseph H. *Numerical Sex Disproportion.* Boulder, Colorado: University of Colorado Press, 1950.
Examines the association between the sex ratio of a population and other demographic and social characteristics.

Sheldon, Henry D. *The Older Population of the United States.* New York: John Wiley and Sons, 1958.
A 1950 U.S. Census Monograph dealing with the age structure of the population, particularly the older segment.

Jacobson, Paul H. *American Marriage and Divorce.* New York: Rinehart and Company, 1959.
A demographic analysis of the subject, covering trends and differentials in marriage and divorce, and related factors.

CHAPTER 9

Population Distribution

Just as information about the population of an area is incomplete without some knowledge of how the population is composed, so is information about the population limited without knowledge of how the population is distributed over the land. Consider the case of two states with equal population size, the first of which has its population fairly evenly distributed over ten major cities and twenty or thirty smaller urban places, and the second of which has three-fourths of its population concentrated in one large city. The kinds of social activity in these two states will differ considerably, their economic bases will vary sharply, and their transportation networks will be quite different. In short, a person travelling about the states would find two quite unlike areas. While areas with about equal population size ordinarily do not differ that much, they usually do differ to some extent with regard to the geographic distribution of their population. What forms population distribution takes, how populations become distributed as they are, and some of the consequences of these distributions are the subject of this chapter.

Broadly speaking, there are two types of areal units over which people are distributed on the land — political units and nonpolitical units. *Political units* include nations, states, counties, cities, towns, and smaller urban places, or equivalent types of areas in countries other than the United States. The importance of political units for the analysis of population distribution rests on the significance of legal residences and governmental functions. The population base of an economy, the population eligible to vote in an election of governmental representatives, people holding automobile licenses, the number of property owners, and the number of children attending schools are examples of demographic statistics which are keyed to political boundaries.

An examination of any country in the world will reveal that population tends to be distributed unevenly over these political areas. For example, in the United States, even within one section of the country, differences exist by states, with Rhode Island being more densely populated than Maine. Within a given state, the population varies by counties, those counties having more cities and towns usually being more populated than rural counties. Within counties there is obviously wide variation in the population of cities and towns.

Nonpolitical units include regions (combinations of states), territory classified as urban or rural on the basis of land use or population density, urbanized areas or other types of urban agglomerations (which have a city as a center and a densely-populated surrounding area), metropolitan areas (which sometimes are organized as political units with metropolitan governments but which are more often complexes of counties or other areas surrounding a city of some substantial size), and areas internal to a city such as census tracts or city blocks. The importance of nonpolitical units of analysis lies in the fact that in many types of areas people tend to concentrate without regard to political boundaries; that is, some residential locations are popular because of their natural attributes, social climates, or economic activity, and these often span political boundaries.

As countries develop economically and socially, the population and land area tends to become more and more urbanized. Cities existed in antiquity but urbanization of the type observed in the modern world, particularly in economically-advanced nations, has a rather short history. Davis, in the first reading in this chapter, traces the origin and growth of urbanization in the world. The prospects are for continued development of urbanization throughout the world, especially in countries in the early stages of industrialization. The counterpart to rapid urbanization is the decline in population of rural areas. In the second selection, Beale analyzes the trends in rural depopulation in the United States and discusses some demographic and social changes which have resulted. In a country like the United States, which has been increasing in population size for the past several decades, it is difficult to reconcile the fact that roughly half the counties are losing population. However, this anomaly can be explained by the recognition that a large proportion of the counties losing more people than they are gaining are predominantly rural counties.

Urbanization means not only the multiplication of points of population concentration and increases in size of these points of concentration but changes in the social life of the people as well. Modern urban life has undoubtedly had a strong influence on the form of the American family and it certainly has changed patterns of social interaction. To cite an example, the extent of neighboring in a farm area, a small town, a big city, and a suburb differ considerably.

With such a high and increasing proportion of the population being located in cities and their nearby territory, how people are distributed within these areas is of vital concern. Census tracts are one kind of nonpolitical unit which can be used to describe the internal structure of cities and surrounding areas. Census tracts are small, permanently established, geographical areas containing about 4000 people. Boundaries are drawn to achieve some uniformity of population characteristics, economic status, and living conditions. Schmid describes the age-sex composition of census tracts in one American city. Age-sex pyramids drawn for each tract reveal some rather distinct patterns. Given the pyramids alone, one might identify the nature of an area and the characteristics of its population. A "Skid Row" area, a college dormitory area, and a retirement village can easily be spotted this way; their age-sex profiles differ sharply.

One particular feature of urban areas is that the population is mobile not only over long periods of time but over periods as short as a day. Commuting to and from work, traveling to shop in stores, going to entertainment or athletic centers, and many other kinds of activities keep the population of an urban complex in flux during the day. Foley's article talks about this relationship between time, location, and activity. The implications for urban planning, for economic development, for transportation networks, and for civil defense, to name just a few, are readily apparent.

There are various means by which an area has its population distributed and redistributed. The distributional pattern of countries is determined initially by the location of ports of entry of immigration, areas of economic opportunity, and transportation lines, and later by the same factors in conjunction with tastes in kinds of housing and environmental conditions and availability of desired jobs, schools, and other activities. Basically, population is redistributed through migration and differential reproduction. Geographic mobility of the population in an area results in some redistribution of people but, as indicated in Chapter 7, there are streams of people moving in both directions between locations. As a result, a large volume of migration might result in very little population redistribution. Differential reproduction also contributes to changes in relative proportions of population in various places because greater natural increase in one location than another will raise the proportion of total population which resides in the location of greater increase.

The study of population distribution and redistribution has particular importance for students of society since where people live and the relative size of population in different areas are crucial to the understanding of what the needs of the society are and why the social institutions function as they do.

The Origin and Growth of Urbanization in the World*

KINGSLEY DAVIS

Urban phenomena attract sociological attention primarily for four reasons. First, such phenomena are relatively recent in human history. Compared to most other aspects of society — e.g., language, religion, stratification, or the family — cities appeared only yesterday, and urbanization, meaning that a sizable proportion of the population lives in cities, has developed only in the last few moments of man's existence. Second, urbanism represents a revolutionary change in the whole pattern of social life. Itself a product of basic economic and technological developments, it tends in turn, once it comes into being, to affect every aspect of existence. It exercises its pervasive influence not only within the urban milieu strictly defined but also in the rural hinterland. The third source of sociological interest in cities is the fact that, once established, they tend to be centers of power and influence throughout the whole society, no matter how agricultural and rural it may be. Finally, the process of urbanization is still occurring; many of the problems associated with it are unsolved; and, consequently, its future direction and potentialities are still a matter of uncertainty. This paper examines the first and last points: the origin, growth, and present rate of progress of urbanization in the world. Since good statistics on urban concentration do not exist even today for substantial parts of the world, and hardly exist for any part during most of the time since cities have been in existence, we are forced to rely on whatever credible evidence can be found and so can reach only broad conclusions concerning early periods and only approximations for recent times. Nevertheless, it can be said that our information, both statistical and non-statistical, is much better today than when Adna Weber wrote his classic treatise on comparative urbanization at the turn of the present century.[1]

THE RISE OF EARLY URBAN CENTERS

Because the archeological evidence is fragmentary, the role of cities in antiquity has often been exaggerated. Archeologists in particular are inclined to call any settlement a "city" which had a few streets and a public building or two. Yet there is surely some point in not mistaking a town for a city. Moreover, what is important is not only the appearance of a few towns or cities but also their place in the total society of which they were a part. Thus, even though in particular regions around the Mediterranean and in southern and western Asia many towns and a few cities arose prior to the Christian Era, there were severe limitations both on the size that such cities could reach and on the proportion of the total population that could live in them.

Speaking generally, one can agree with the dominant view that the diverse technological innovations constituting Neolithic culture were necessary for the existence of settled communities.[2] Yet one should not infer that these innovations, which began some 8,000–10,000 years ago, were sufficient to give rise to towns as distinct from villages. Even though the Neolithic population was more densely settled than the purely hunting or food-gathering peoples, it was nevertheless chiefly engaged in an occupation — agriculture — which requires a large amount of land per person. The Neolithic population

* Reprinted from the *American Journal of Sociology*, Vol. 60 (March 1955), pp. 429-437 by permission of The University of Chicago Press.

[1] Adna F. Weber, *The Growth of Cities in the Nineteenth Century* (New York: Columbia University Press 1899).

[2] V. Gordon Childe, *Man Makes Himself* (rev. ed.; London: Watts, 1941), chaps. v-vi; *What Happened in History* (London and New York: Penguin Books, 1946 [first printed in 1942]), chaps. iii-iv.

density was therefore not a matter of town concentration but rather a matter of tiny villages scattered over the land.

What had to be added to the Neolithic complex to make possible the first towns? Between 6000 and 4000 B.C. certain inventions — such as the ox-drawn plow and wheeled cart, the sailboat, metallurgy, irrigation, and the domestication of new plants — facilitated, when taken together, a more intensive and more productive use of the Neolithic elements themselves. When this enriched technology was utilized in certain unusual regions where climate, soil, water, and topography were most favorable (broad river valleys with alluvial soil not exhausted by successive cropping, with a dry climate that minimized soil leaching, with plenty of sunshine, and with sediment-containing water for irrigation from the river itself), the result was a sufficiently productive economy to make possible the *sine qua non* of urban existence, the concentration in one place of people who do not grow their own food.

But a productive economy, though necessary, was not sufficient: high productivity per acre does not necessarily mean high per capita productivity. Instead of producing a surplus for town dwellers, the cultivators can, theoretically at least, multiply on the land until they end up producing just enough to sustain themselves. The rise of towns and cities therefore required, in addition to highly favorable agricultural conditions, a form of social organization in which certain strata could appropriate for themselves part of the produce grown by the cultivators. Such strata — religious and governing officials, traders, and artisans — could live in towns, because their power over goods did not depend on their presence on the land as such. They could thus realize the advantages of town living, which gave them additional power over the cultivators.

The first cities, doubtless small and hard to distinguish from towns, seem to have appeared in the most favorable places sometime between 6000 and 5000 B.C. From that time on, it can be assumed that some of the inventions which made larger settlements possible were due to towns and cities themselves — viz., writing and accountancy, bronze, the beginnings of science, a solar calendar, bureaucracy. By 3000 B.C., when these innovations were all exercising an influence in Egypt, Mesopotamia, and India, there were in existence what may be called "true" cities. After that there appears to have been, for some 2,000 years, a lull during which the most important innovations, toward the end of the period, were alphabetic writing and the smelting of iron. Curiously, the cities in the regions where city life had originated eventually went into eclipse, and it was not until Greco-Roman times that new principles made possible, in new regions, a marked gain in city existence. The fact that the greatest subsequent cultural developments did not occur primarily in the regions where the first cities arose suggests that cities are not always and everywhere a stimulant of economic and social advance. Childe admits that, if anything, the first cities had a stultifying effect on cultural progress,[3] due perhaps to the unproductive insulation and excessive power of the urban elite. There is no doubt that the religio-magical traditionalism of the early cities was profound.

Why was there so little urbanization in ancient times, and why did it proceed so slowly from that point? The sites of the earliest "cities" themselves show that they were small affairs. The walls of ancient Babylon, for example, embraced an area of roughly 3.2 square miles,[4] and "Ur, with its canals, harbors, and temples, occupied some 220 acres; the walls of Erech encompass an area of just on two square miles."[5] This suggests that the famous Ur could hardly have boasted more than 5,000 inhabitants and Erech hardly more than 25,000. The mounds of Mohenjo-daro in Sind cover a square mile,[6] and Harappa in the Punjab had a walled area visible in 1853 with a perimeter of 2½ miles.[7] These were evidently "cities" of 5,000–15,000 inhabitants, yet they were the chief centers for the entire Indus region, an area nearly two-thirds the size of Texas. Less is known about the earliest Egyptian cities, for they were built with mud bricks and have long

[3] *Man Makes Himself,* p. 227.

[4] Deduced from data given in Marguerite Rutten, *Babylone* (Paris: Presses Universitaires de France, 1948), p. 34.

[5] Childe, *What Happened in History,* p. 87.

[6] Stuart Piggott, *Prehistoric India* (Harmondsworth: Penguin Books, 1950), p. 165.

[7] Childe, *What Happened in History,* p. 118.

since disappeared beneath the alluvial soil. Tell el 'Amarna, the temporary capital built much later, about 1400 B.C., perhaps held something like 40,000 people. The wall of Hotep-Sanusert, an earlier capital built about 1900 B.C. on the Fayum, measured 350 by 400 meters[8] and inclosed an area of approximately one-twentieth of a square mile. Thebes, at the height of its splendor as the capital of Egypt about 1600, was described by Greek writers as having a circumference of 14 miles. By a liberal estimate it may have contained 225,000 inhabitants.

To the questions why even the largest cities prior to 1000 B.C. were small by modern standards, why even the small ones were relatively few, and why the degree of urbanization even in the most advanced regions was very slight, the answer seems as follows: Agriculture was so cumbersome, static, and labor-intensive that it took many cultivators to support one man in the city. The ox-drawn plow, the wooden plowshare, inundation irrigation, stone hoes, sickles, and axes were instruments of production, to be sure, but clumsy ones. Not until iron came into use in Asia Minor about 1300 B.C. could general improvement in agriculture be achieved. The static character of agriculture and of the economy generally was fostered perhaps by the insulation of the religio-political officials from the practical arts and the reduction of the peasant to virtually the status of a beast of burden. The technology of transport was as labor-intensive as that of agriculture. The only means of conveying bulky goods for mass consumption was by boat, and, though sails had been invented, the sailboat was so inefficient that rowing was still necessary. The oxcart, with its solid wheels and rigidly attached axle, the pack animal, and the human burden-bearer were all short-distance means of transport, the only exception being the camel caravan. Long-distance transport was reserved largely for goods which had high value and small bulk — i.e., goods for the elite — which could not maintain a large urban population. The size of the early cities was therefore limited by the amount of food, fibers, and other bulky materials that could be obtained from the immediate hinterland by labor-intensive methods, a severe limitation which the Greek cities of a later period, small as they remained, nevertheless had to escape before they could attain their full size.

There were political limitations as well. The difficulty of communication and transport and the existence of multifarious local tribal cultures made the formation of large national units virtually impossible. The first urban-centered units were city-states, and when so-called "empires" were formed, as in Egypt, in the Sumerian region, and later in Assyria, much local autonomy was left to the subordinated areas, and the constant danger of revolt prevented the extension of the hinterlands of the cities very far or very effectively. It is symptomatic of the weakness of the early cities that they were constantly threatened and frequently conquered not only by neighboring towns but also by nonurban barbarians. Each wave of barbarians tended to rebuild the urban centers and to become agricultural and sedentary, only to be eventually overwhelmed in turn by new invaders. Other limiting factors were the lack of scientific medicine (which made urban living deadly), the fixity of the peasant on the land (which minimized rural-urban migration), the absence of large-scale manufacturing (which would have derived more advantage from urban concentration than did handicraft), the bureaucratic control of the peasantry (which stifled free trade in the hinterland), and the traditionalism and religiosity of all classes (which hampered technological and economic advance).

The limitations explain why we find, when the sites furnish adequate evidence, that the earliest cities were small affairs, usually no more than towns. Whether in the new or in the old world, even the biggest places could scarcely have exceeded 200,000 inhabitants, and the proportion of the total population living in them must have been not more than 1 or 2 per cent. From 50 to 90 farmers must have been required to support one man in a city.

Subsequent City Development

If urbanization was to escape its early limitations, it had to do so in a new region, a region more open to innovation and new conceptions. As it turned out, the region that saw a later and

[8] Pierre Montet, *La Vie quotidienne en Égypte* (Paris: Hachette, 1946), p. 16.

greater urban development was farther north, the Greco-Roman world of Europe, flourishing approximately during the period from 600 B.C. to 400 A.D. Iron tools and weapons, alphabetic writing, improved sailboats, cheap coinage, more democratic institutions, systematic colonization — all tended to increase production, stimulate trade, and expand the effective political unit. Towns and cities became more numerous, the degree of urbanization greater. A few cities reached a substantial size. Athens, at its peak in the fifth century B.C., achieved a population of between 120,000 and 180,000. Syracuse and Carthage were perhaps larger.

The full potentialities of the ancient world to support a large city were realized only with the Romans. Through their ability to conquer, organize, and govern an empire, to put the immediate Italian hinterland to fruitful cultivation, to use both force and trade to bring slaves, goods, food, and culture to the imperial capital, they were able to create in Rome (with the possible exception of Constantinople some centuries later) the largest city that was to be known in the world until the rise of London in the nineteenth century. Yet, despite the fact that Rome and Constantinople came to hold populations of several hundred thousand, they were not able to resist conquest by far less urbanized outsiders. The eclipse of cities in Europe was striking. Commerce declined to the barest minimum; each locale became isolated and virtually self-sufficient; the social system congealed into a hereditary system.[9] When finally towns and cities began to revive, they were small, as the following estimates suggest: Florence (1338), 90,000; Venice (1422), 190,000; Antwerp (sixteenth century), 200,000; London (1377), 30,000[10] Nuremberg (1450), 20,165; Frankfort (1440), 8,719.[11]

Yet it was precisely in western Europe, where cities and urbanization had reached a nadir during the Dark Ages, that the limitations that had characterized the ancient world were finally to be overcome. The cities of Mesopotamia, India, and Egypt, of Persia, Greece, and Rome, had all been tied to an economy that was primarily agricultural, where handicraft played at best a secondary role and where the city was still attempting to supplement its economic weakness with military strength, to command its sustenance rather than to buy it honestly. In western Europe, starting at the zero point, the development of cities not only reached the stage that the ancient world had achieved but kept going after that. It kept going on the basis of improvements in agriculture and transport, the opening of new lands and new trade routes, and, above all, the rise in productive activity, first in highly organized handicraft and eventually in a revolutionary new form of production — the factory run by machinery and fossil fuel. The transformation thus achieved in the nineteenth century was the true urban revolution, for it meant not only the rise of a few scattered towns and cities but the appearance of genuine urbanization, in the sense that a substantial portion of the population lived in towns and cities.

The World Trend from 1800 to 1950[12]

Urbanization has, in fact, gone ahead much faster and reached proportions far greater during the last century and a half than at any previous time in world history. The tremendous growth in world trade during this period has enabled the urban population to draw its sustenance from an ever wider area. Indeed, it can truly be said that the hinterland of today's cities is the entire world. Contemporary Britain, Holland, and Japan, for example, could not maintain their urban population solely from their own territory. The number of rural inhabitants required to maintain one urban inhabitant is still great — greater than one would imagine from the rural-urban ratio *within* each of the highly ur-

[9] Henri Pirenne, *Medieval Cities* (Princeton: Princeton University Press, 1939), pp. 84-85.

[10] Pierre Clerget, "Urbanism: A Historic, Geographic, and Economic Study," *Annual Report of the Smithsonian Institution for 1912* (Washington, D.C.: Government Printing Office, 1913), p. 656.

[11] Henri Pirenne, *Economic and Social History of Medieval Europe* (London: Routledge & Kegan Paul, 1936), p. 172.

[12] The writer acknowledges with pleasure the collaboration of Mrs. Hilda Hertz Golden in the statistical work on which this and succeeding sections are based. Such work has been done as part of a continuing program of comparative urban research in the population division of the Bureau of Applied Social Research, Columbia University.

banized countries. The reason is that much of agriculture around the world is still technologically and economically backward. Yet there can be no doubt that, whether for particuar countries or for the entire globe, the ratio of urban dwellers to those who grow their food has risen remarkably. This is shown by the fact that the proportion of people living in cities in 1950 is higher than that found in any particular country prior to modern times and many times higher than that formerly characterizing the earth as a whole.

The rapidity of urbanization in recent times can be seen by looking at the most urbanized country, England. In 1801, although London had already reached nearly the million mark (865,000), England and Wales had less than 10 per cent of their population in cities of 100,000 or more. By 1901 no less than 35 per cent of the population of England and Wales was living in cities of 100,000 or more, and 58 per cent was living in cities of 20,000 or more. By 1951 these two proportions had risen to 38.4 and 69.3 per cent, respectively.

Britain was in the van of urban development. A degree of urbanization equal to that she had attained in 1801 was not achieved by any other country until after 1850. Thereafter the British rate of urbanization began slowly to decline, whereas that of most other countries continued at a high level. By assembling available data and preparing estimates where data were lacking, we have arrived at figures on urbanization in the world as a whole, beginning with 1800, the earliest date for which anything like a reasonable estimate can be obtained. The percentage of the world's population found living in cities is as shown in Table 1. It can be seen that the proportion has tended to do a bit better than double itself each half-century and that by 1950 the world as a whole was considerably more urbanized than Britain was in 1800. As everyone knows, the earth's total population has grown at an extremely rapid rate since 1800, reaching 2.4 billion by 1950. But the urban population has grown much faster. In 1800 there were about 15.6 million people living in cities of 100,000 or more. By 1950 it was 313.7 million, more than twenty times the earlier figure. Much of this increase has obviously come from rural-urban migration, clearly the most massive migration in modern times.

In 1800 there were apparently less than 50 cities with 100,000 or more inhabitants. This was less than the number in the million class today and less than the number of 100,000-plus cities currently found in many single countries. By 1950 there were close to 900 cities of 100,000 or more people, which is more than the number of towns and cities of 5,000 or more in 1800.

As yet there is no indication of a slackening of the rate of urbanization in the world as a whole. If the present rate should continue, more than a fourth of the earth's people will be living

TABLE 1

Percentage of World's Population Living in Cities

	Cities of 20,000 or More	Cities of 100,000 or More
1800	2.4	1.7
1850	4.3	2.3
1900	9.2	5.5
1950	20.9	13.1

TABLE 2

Percentage of World's Population Living in Cities, by Regions

	In Cities of 20,000 Plus	In Cities of 100,000 Plus
World	21	13
Oceania	47	41
North America (Canada and U.S.A.)	42	29
Europe (except U.S.S.R.)	35	21
U.S.S.R.	31	18
South America	26	18
Middle America and Caribbean	21	12
Asia (except U.S.S.R.)	13	8
Africa	9	5

in cities of 100,000 or more in the year 2000, and more than half in the year 2050. For places of 20,000 or more, the proportions at the two dates would be something like 45 per cent and 90 per cent. Whether such figures prove too low or too high, they nevertheless suggest that the human species is moving rapidly in the direction of an almost exclusively urban existence. We have used the proportion of the population in cities of 20,000 and 100,000 or more as a convenient index of differences and changes in degree of urbanization. Places of less than 20,000 also fit a demographic definition of "urban." When, therefore, more than a third of the population of a country lives in cities of the 100,000 class (38.4 per cent in England and Wales in 1951), the country can be described as almost completely urbanized (81 per cent being designated as "urban" in the English case in 1951). We thus have today what can be called "urbanized societies," nations in which the great majority of inhabitants live in cities. The prospect is that, as time goes on, a greater and greater proportion of humanity will be members of such societies.

The question may be raised as to how such an extreme degree of world urbanization will prove possible. Who will grow the food and fibers necessary for the enormous urban population? The answer is that agriculture may prove to be an archaic mode of production. Already, one of the great factors giving rise to urbanization is the rather late and as yet very incomplete industrialization of agriculture. As farming becomes increasingly mechanized and rationalized, fewer people are needed on the land. On the average, the more urbanized a country, the lower is its rural density.[13] If, in addition to industrialized agriculture, food and fiber come to be increasingly produced by manufacturing processes using materials that utilize the sun's energy more efficiently than plants do, there is no technological reason why nearly all of mankind could not live in conurbations of large size.

[13] See Kingsley Davis and Hilda Hertz, "Urbanization and the Development of Pre-industrial Areas," *Economic Development and Cultural Change,* III (October, 1954), 6-26. See also the writer's paper, "Population and the Further Spread of Industrial Society," *Proceedings of the American Philosophical Society,* XCV (February, 1951), 10-13.

The Regional Pattern of Urbanization

The highest levels of urbanization are found today in northwestern Europe and in those new regions where northwest Europeans have settled and extended their industrial civilization. The figures are as shown in Table 2.[14] Oceania is the most urbanized of the world's major regions, because Australia and New Zealand are its principal components. North America is next, if it is defined as including only Canada and the United States. The regions least urbanized are those least affected by northwest European culture, namely, Asia and Africa.

The figures for world regions are less valuable for purposes of analysis than are those for individual countries. The latter show clearly that urbanization has tended to reach its highest point wherever economic productivity has been greatest — that is, where the economy is industrialized and rationalized. This explains why urbanization is so closely associated with northwest Europeans and their culture, since they were mainly responsible for the industrial revolution. Of the fifteen most urbanized countries in the world, all but one, Japan, are European in culture, and all but four derive that culture from the northwest or central part of Europe.

The rate of urbanization in the older industrial countries, however, is slowing down. During the twenty years from 1870 to 1890 Germany's proportion in large cities more than doubled; it nearly doubled again from 1890 to 1910; but from 1910 to 1940 the increase was only 36 per cent. In Sweden the gain slowed down noticeably after 1920. In England and Wales the most rapid urbanization occurred between 1811 and 1851. Contrary to popular belief, the fastest rate in the United States occurred between 1861 and 1891. Since, as we noted earlier, there has been no slowing-down of urbanization in the world as a whole, it must be that, as the more established industrial countries have slackened, the less-developed countries have exhibited a faster rate. In fact, such historical evidence as we have for underdeveloped areas seems to show that their

[14] From Kingsley Davis and Hilda Hertz, "The World Distribution of Urbanization," *Bulletin of the International Statistical Institute,* XXXIII, Part IV, 230.

rates of urbanization have been rising in recent decades. This has been the case in Egypt, where the rate is higher after 1920 than before; in India, where the fastest urbanization has occurred since 1941; in Mexico, where the speed-up began in 1921; and in Greece, where the fastest period ran from 1900 to 1930. Asia, for example, had only 22 per cent of the world's city population in 1900 but 34 per cent of it in 1950, and Africa had 1.5 per cent in 1900 but 3.2 per cent at the later date.

With respect to urbanization, then, the gap between the industrial and the preindustrial nations is beginning to diminish. The less-developed parts of the world will eventually, it seems, begin in their turn to move gradually toward a saturation point. As the degree of urbanization rises, it of course becomes impossible for the rate of gain to continue. The growth in the urban proportion is made possible by the movement of people from rural areas to the cities. As the rural population becomes a progressively smaller percentage of the total, the cities no longer can draw on a noncity population of any size. Yet in no country can it be said that the process of urbanization is yet finished. Although there have been short periods in recent times in England, the United States, and Japan when the city population increased at a slightly slower rate than the rural, these were mere interludes in the ongoing but ever slower progress of urban concentration.

The Tendency Toward Metropolitan Expansion

The continuance of urbanization in the world does not mean the persistence of something that remains the same in detail. A city of a million inhabitants today is not the sort of place that a city of the same number was in 1900 or in 1850. Moreover, with the emergence of giant cities of five to fifteen million, something new has been added. Such cities are creatures of the twentieth century. Their sheer quantitative difference means a qualitative change as well.

One of the most noticeable developments is the ever stronger tendency of cities to expand outward — a development already observed in the nineteenth century. Since 1861, the first date when the comparison can be made, the Outer Ring of Greater London has been growing more rapidly than London itself. French writers prior to 1900 pointed out the dispersive tendency,[15] as did Adna Weber in 1899.[16] There is no doubt, however, that the process of metropolitan dispersion has increased with time. This fact is shown for the United States by comparing the percentage gains in population made by the central cities with those made by their satellite areas in forty-four metropolitan districts for which Thompson could get comparable data going back to 1900. The gains are as shown in Table 3.[17]

TABLE 3

Percentage Increase in Population in 44 Metropolitan Districts in the United States, 1900–1940

	Central Cities	Rest of Districts
1900–1910	33.6	38.2
1910–20	23.4	31.3
1920–30	20.5	48.7
1930–40	4.2	13.0

The difference increases, until in 1930-40 the population outside the central city is growing more than three times as fast as that inside the central city. Furthermore, Thompson has shown that *within the metropolitan area outside the central cities* it was the "rural" parts which gained faster than the urban parts, as the percentage increases per decade shown in Table 4, indicate. Clearly, the metropolitan districts were increasingly dependent on the areas outside the central cities, and especially upon the sparsely settled parts at the periphery of these areas, for their

[15] Paul Meuriot, *Des agglomérations urbaines dans l'Europe contemporaine* (Paris: Bélin Frères, 1898), pp. 249-78. Literature on the movement of industry and people to the periphery of cities is cited, and a theoretical discussion of the subject given, in René Maunier, *L'Origine et la fonction économique des villes* (Paris: Giard & Brière, 1910), pp. 231-314.

[16] *Op. cit.*, pp. 458-75.

[17] Warren S. Thompson, *The Growth of Metropolitan Districts in the United States, 1900-1940* (Washington, D.C.: Government Printing Office, 1948), p. 5. The picture is much the same for the rest of the metropolitan districts for decades in which comparability could be established.

TABLE 4

Percentage Population Increase Outside Central Cities in 44 Metropolitan Districts

	Urban Parts	Rural Parts
1900–1910	35.9	43.2
1910–20	30.2	34.5
1920–30	40.6	68.1
1930–40	7.3	28.1

continued growth. Thompson showed that, the greater the distance from the center of the city, the faster the rate of growth.[18]

The same forces which have made extreme urbanization possible have also made metropolitan dispersion possible, and the dispersion itself has contributed to further urbanization by making large conurbations more efficient and more endurable. The outward movement of urban residences, of urban services and commercial establishments, and of light industry — all facilitated by improvements in motor transport and communications — has made it possible for huge agglomerations to keep on growing without the inconveniences of proportionate increases in density. In many ways the metropolis of three million today is an easier place to live and work in than the city of five hundred thousand yesterday. Granted that the economic advantages of urban concentration still continue and still push populations in the direction of urbanization, the effect of metropolitan dispersion is thus to minimize the disadvantages of this continued urban growth.

The new type of metropolitan expansion occurring in the highly industrial countries is not without its repercussions in less-developed lands as well. Most of the rapid urbanization now occurring in Africa and Asia, for example, is affected by direct contact with industrial nations and by a concomitant rise in consumption standards. Although private automobiles may not be available to the urban masses, bicycles and busses generally are. Hence Brazzaville and Abidjan, Takoradi and Nairobi, Jamshedpur and New Delhi, Ankara and Colombo, are not evolving in the same manner as did the cities of the eighteenth and nineteenth centuries. Their ecological pattern, their technological base, their economic activity, all reflect the twentieth century, no matter how primitive or backward their hinterlands may be. Thus the fact that their main growth is occurring in the present century is not without significance for the kind of cities they are turning out to be.

Future Trends in World Urbanization

Speculation concerning the future of urbanization is as hazardous as that concerning any other aspect of human society. Following the direction of modern trends, however, one may conclude that, with the industrial revolution, for the first time in history urbanization began to reach a stage from which there was no return. The cities of antiquity were vulnerable, and the degree of urbanization reached was so thin in many societies as to be transitory. Today virtually every part of the world is more urbanized than any region was in antiquity. Urbanization is so widespread, so much a part of industrial civilization, and gaining so rapidly, that any return to rurality, even with major catastrophes, appears unlikely. On the contrary, since every city is obsolescent to some degree — more obsolescent the older it is — the massive destruction of many would probably add eventually to the impetus of urban growth.

The fact that the rate of world urbanization has shown no slackening since 1800 suggests that we are far from the end of this process, perhaps not yet at the peak. Although the industrial countries have shown a decline in their rates, these countries, because they embrace only about a fourth of the world's population, have not dampened the world trend. The three-fourths of humanity who live in underdeveloped countries are still in the early stages of an urbanization that promises to be more rapid than that which occurred earlier in the areas of northwest European culture.

How urbanized the world will eventually become is an unanswerable question. As stated earlier, there is no apparent reason why it should not become as urbanized as the most urban countries today — with perhaps 85-90 per cent

[18] *Ibid.*, p. 9.

of the population living in cities and towns of 5,000 or more and practicing urban occupations. Our present degree of urbanization in advanced countries is still so new that we have no clear idea of how such complete world urbanization would affect human society; but the chances are that the effects would be profound.

In visualizing the nature and effects of complete urbanization in the future, however, one must guard against assuming that cities will retain their present form. The tendency to form huge metropolitan aggregates which are increasingly decentralized will undoubtedly continue but probably will not go so far as to eliminate the central business district altogether, though it may greatly weaken it. At the periphery, it may well be that the metropolis and the countryside, as the one expands and the other shrinks, will merge together, until the boundaries of one sprawling conurbation will touch those of another, with no intervening pure countryside at all. The world's population doubles itself twice in a century, becoming at the same time highly urbanized, and as new sources of energy are tapped, the possibility of centrifugal metropolitan growth is enormously enhanced. If commuting to work could be done with the speed of sound and cheaply, one would not mind living two hundred miles from work. Almost any technological advance from now on is likely to contribute more to the centrifugal than to the centripetal tendency. It may turn out that urbanization in the sense of emptying the countryside and concentrating huge numbers in little space will reverse itself — not, however, in the direction of returning people to the farm but rather in that of spreading them more evenly over the land for purposes of residence and industrial work. "Rurality" would have disappeared, leaving only a new kind of urban existence.

*Rural Depopulation in the United States: Some Demographic Consequences of Agricultural Adjustments**†

CALVIN L. BEALE

The fact that the number of farm people in the United States is steadily decreasing is no longer news. It was news fifteen — even ten — years ago, but the decline has become so prolonged, so deep and so common that it has been widely noted and accepted as a fact of life. Indeed, the Department of Agriculture itself has repeatedly emphasized in very recent years the fact that only a small proportion of all farm youth can expect to find careers as operators of adequate-sized commercial farms. Nevertheless, despite recognition of a decline in the farm segment of the population and knowledge that a similar trend characterizes other advanced nations, the existence of a widespread overall depopulation in rural areas remains a paradoxical phenomenon when one considers that the nation as a whole has been in a period of unparalleled population growth.

An annual average of 2.8 million persons has been added to our population since 1950. With two-thirds of the United States population now concentrated in a little more than 200 metropolitan centers, and with the equivalent of 85 per cent of our growth taking place in these metrocenters, it is not surprising that the bulk of demographic attention has been focused on the

* Reprinted with permission from *Demography*, Vol. 1, No. 1 (1964), pp. 264-272.

† This paper was presented at the annual meeting of the American Association for the Advancement of Science, Cleveland, December 27, 1963.

growth aspects and metropolitan character of our development. Meanwhile, back at the ranch and down on the farm, some demographic consequences of agricultural adjustments are evident which both reflect and foster a different set of problems from those of most metro areas. Whereas rural life has become increasingly similar to urban life in many respects — such as material possessions, educational levels, and life styles — the demographic situation of many rural areas has never been more divergent from that of the cities or metro areas than it is today.

It is not the principal purpose of this paper to discuss the factors producing rural population change but rather to delineate broadly the scope of depopulation resulting from loss in rural areas and to point to some of the structural changes brought about in the residual population.

Migration from the Farm

In considering the process of agricultural adjustment as it affects population, it is well for perspective's sake to note that the trend from the land to the cities is not new.

> During the last quarter of a century farm machinery, inventive genius, and new discoveries . . . have made it possible for one man to produce four times as much of many farm products as formerly. If a greater percent of the farm boys did not find some other occupation . . . it is evident that there would not be employment for all . . . .
>
> [They see] . . . that three-fourths of the labor formerly required for harvesting . . . crops annually (is) being performed in the cities . . . [that is in] the construction of binders, mowers, harvesting machines, thrashers. . . ."
>
> The exodus from the farm was inevitable and justified. . . .[1]

These excerpts are not from a speech made yesterday by a rural sociologist. They are taken from an address by the Director of the Cornell Agricultural Experiment Station in 1896. What is new today is the rate of the agricultural exodus and its widespread nature.

[1] I. P. Roberts, "The Exodus from the Farm," *Proceedings of the Tenth Annual Convention of the Association of American Agricultural Colleges and Experiment Stations* (Washington, 1897), pp. 80-82.

Depopulation resulting from agricultural changes has taken place in some part of the nation at practically every stage of our national history, although the total farm population did not reach its peak of 32,530,000 persons until 1916. Under the migration-inhibiting conditions of the Depression Era, the farm population remained as high as 30,547,000 in 1940, with some areas still gaining farm people.[2]

In this situation the effect of World War II was electrifying. Five million people of labor force age alone left the farms in four years (April 1940 to April 1944), the great majority for civilian work rather than for military service.[3] The policy of federal encouragement of subsistence farming ceased and agriculture began an accelerated progress toward use of advanced techniques and specialized production for the commercial market. Since the war the number of farms has declined everywhere except in a few newly irrigated localities. The 30,547,000 farm population of 1940 has become the 13,367,000 of 1963.[4] Not all this loss has involved migration. Some of it has resulted from reclassification of places as nonfarm when operations ceased or definitions changed. But the great majority of the decline does represent outmovement. It is estimated that net migration (and reclassification) from farms amounted to about 11,390,000 persons in the 1940's and 10,130,000 in the 1950's. Inasmuch as the base farm population was lower in the 1950's than in the 1940's, maintenance of nearly the same absolute level of net loss in the 1950's required a higher rate of migration than in the 1940's. The average annual net migration from farms is estimated at 4.4 percent in the 1940's and 5.5 percent in the 1950's. In the three years since 1960, the rate appears to have risen to 6.3 per 100 an-

[2] Except as otherwise stated, all farm population and migration figures cited are taken from Vera J. Banks, Calvin L. Beale, and Gladys K. Bowles *Farm Population —Estimates for 1910-62* (Economic Research Service, October, 1963).

[3] *Net Movement away from Farms in the United States, by Age and Sex: 1940 to 1944* (Series Census-BAE No. 4, Bureau of the Census and Bureau of Agricultural Economics, June, 1945).

[4] Figure for 1963 from *Estimates of the Farm Population of the United States: April 1963* (Series Census-ERS (P-27), No. 34, Bureau of the Census and Economic Research Service, March, 1964).

nually.[5] The current rate is fully as high as that prevailing during the peak of outmovement in World War II.

The factors permitting such a reduction in farm people are numerous and reasonably well known. Mechanization, improved seeds, better breeds and animal nutrition, good management, and advances in fertilizer, pest control, and weed control have all combined to raise productivity and reduce manpower. In addition, the generally high operating level of the nonfarm economy, the ease of physical access to the cities, and the dominant stylistic position of metropolitan life have attracted people away from farming areas. Some federal agricultural programs such as acreage restrictions and conservation reserves (the "soil bank") also have tended to reduce manpower needs in agriculture.

In addition to agricultural outmigration, other factors lowered the level of rural population, such as the decline in coal mining employment and the reclassification of territory from rural to urban through suburbanization, annexation, or census definitional changes.

[5] Rate for 1960-63 period from forthcoming release of the Economic Research Service.

Rural Population Change

Total U.S. rural population remained almost stationary between 1950 and 1960, dropping from 54,479,000 to 54,054,000, as gains nearly offset losses. The gains, however, tended to be larger per county and more concentrated than the losses. Thus, more than five-eighths of all counties lost rural population as a substantial redistribution took place.

Rural population change in the 1950's by state economic areas is shown on the accompanying map (Fig. 1). Heavy rural loss (more than 10 percent) characterized the interior coastal plain of the Lower South from Georgia through Texas. This was also true of contiguous areas of the Great Plains, especially from Texas to

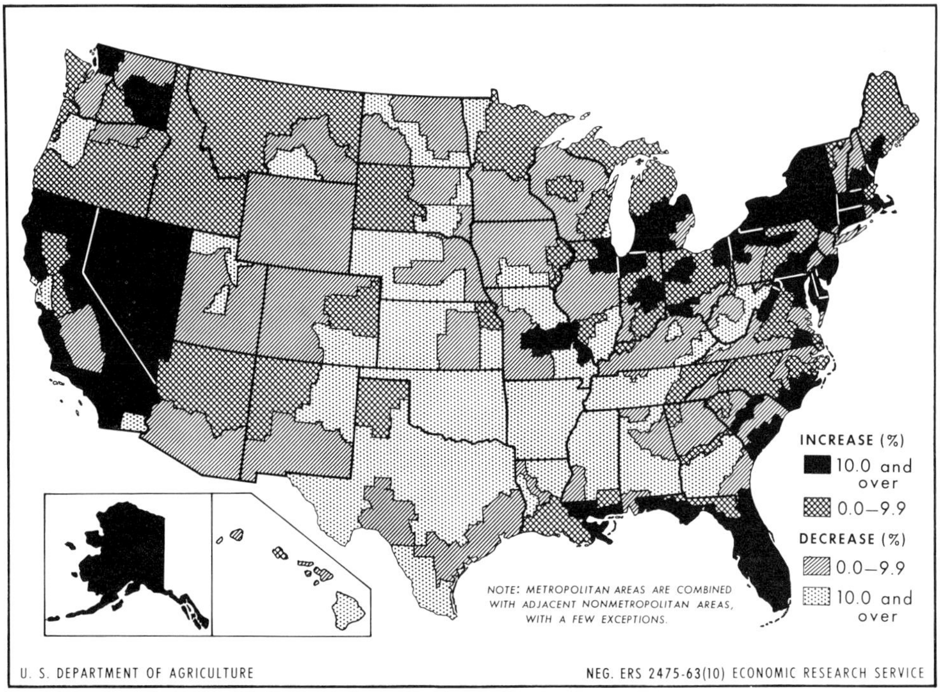

Rural population change from 1950 to 1960 by state economic areas.

Nebraska. Other prominent zones of heavy loss were sections of the Allegheny Plateau (particularly the coal fields), much of the Ozark and other upland country of Arkansas, Oklahoma, and Missouri, and marginal Corn Belt areas of Iowa and Missouri. For the most part these areas are bordered by others that had rural losses of up to 10 percent.

At the other extreme are areas of sizable rural increase (10 percent gain or more), which often grew from net migration as well as from natural increase. These were noticeable in Florida, California, and Nevada, as might be anticipated from the boom character of those states. They were also widespread in the hinterlands of the large industrial centers of the Lower Great Lakes and the Atlantic Seaboard. For the most part areas of growing rural population have had large farm population losses, but agriculture has not been the principal rural activity in them and gains of rural nonfarm people have more than offset farm losses. Many of the areas of recent rural population growth in the Northeast and the East North Central States earlier passed through a period of mild rural population losses based on agricultural changes. The revival of rural growth here is associated with factors seldom related to the traditional rural primary industries of farming, mining, and lumbering. Zelinsky has aptly referred to this population as the "neorural society." [6]

County Changes in Total Population

In all, 1,532 counties or a little less than half of the nation's total of 3,081 dropped in total population during the 1950's. Of the 1,060 counties that were entirely rural three-fourths declined, of the 1,355 that were primarily rural one-half declined, and of the 662 that were primarily urban only one-sixth declined (see Table 1). Thus, the overwhelming majority of instances of total population loss stemmed from events in the rural population. And the rural economy of most of the declining counties was dominated by agriculture.

A major effect of widespread population declines in the midst of national population growth has been to increase the variation in size and density among counties — the basic political geographical units of the nation. This is a demographic exception to general reduction of group differences within the United States population — such as in education, income, and fertility — which I believe it fair to say has been widely considered a dominant trend of our generation.

[6] See Wilbur Zelinsky, "Changes in the Geographic Patterns of Rural Population in the United States 1950-1960," *Geographical Review* LII, No. 4 (October, 1962), 523. This study, with the monumental amount of work that it reflects, is basic to any investigation of rural population trends in the United States.

TABLE 1

Population Growth Trend of Counties in the United States, 1950–60, by Whether Predominantly Urban or Rural in Residence of Population in 1950

Residence type	Number of counties (a)			Percent losing
	Total	Gaining	Losing	
Total............	3,081	1,549	1,532	49.7
Urban.............	662	556	106	16.0
Rural..............	2,419	993	1,426	58.9
Partly urban.......	1,358	701	657	48.4
Entirely rural......	1,061	292	769	72.5

(a) Independent cities consolidated with counties in Virginia, Alaskan Election Districts combined to 1950 Judicial Division boundaries. County with no change treated as gaining.

Source: Bureau of the Census, 1960 Census of Population, Volume I.

The fact that many more counties have lost population during a period of high national growth (the 1950's) than did so during the period of lowest national growth (the 1930's) is reasonably well known, at least among demographers. What may have escaped notice, however, is the circumstance that in each of the last four decades the proportion of losing counties that have been heavy losers has grown (see Table 2). For example, in the 1920's, little more than a fourth of the declining counties fell in population by more than 10 percent. But by the 1950's the proportion of losers in this class exceeded one-half. Concurrently, the proportion of gaining counties that have had sizable rates of gain has grown since the 1930's and the proportion with only modest gains has been reduced. Therefore, at the same period when more counties are faced with problems associated with rapid population growth than heretofore in this century, more counties than ever before are also confronted with the dilemmas posed by rapid loss.

The effect of this pattern of change on the distribution of counties by size can be seen in Table 3. Since 1940 the number of counties in the modal class — from 10,000 to 50,000 inhabitants — has diminished, while the number at both extremes — more than 50,000 people or less than 10,000 — has increased. Conceptions of traditional levels of rural settlement density have to be altered. There are Corn Belt parts of Missouri and Iowa today that have only 15 persons per square mile, including all townspeople, whereas at one time densities of less than 25 or 30 per square mile were unheard of. And the density is still falling. The same changes are true of old Cotton Belt counties in Georgia. In varied areas of Arkansas and Oklahoma, county densities have been reduced to 10 per square mile where once they were 20 or 25. In the Plains, areas which may once have aspired to an over-all density of 10 are now lucky to have 5 per square mile.

Age Selectivity of Migration

Migration other than enforced transfers rarely is nonselective by age, and the movement from farms is no exception. Although some estab-

TABLE 2

Distribution of Counties in the United States by Population Change, 1950–60, 1940–50, and 1930–40

Population change	Number of counties			
	1950–60 (a)	1940–50	1930–40 (b)	1920–30 (b)
Total	3,114	3,111	3,089	(c)
Gain:				
10 percent or more	957	888	929	(c)
0–10 percent	621	702	1,196	(c)
Loss:				
0–10 percent	754	811	650	934
10 percent or more	782	710	314	324
Distribution of losing counties by amount of loss				
0–10 percent	49.1	53.3	67.4	74.2
10 percent or more	50.9	46.7	32.6	25.8

(a) 1960 Election Districts of Alaska consolidated to Judical Divisions for 1950-60 comparison.
(b) Independent cities of Virginia consolidated with counties of origin in 1930-40 and 1920-30.
(c) Not computed.
Source: Bureau of the Census, 1930, 1940, 1950, and 1960 Censuses of Population, Volume I for each year.

TABLE 3

Number of Counties in the United States, Classified by Population Size, 1940–60

(Includes county equivalents such as independent cities, Louisiana parishes, Alaska election districts and judicial divisions)

Population size of county	1960		1950		1940	
	Number	Percent of total	Number	Percent of total	Number	Percent of total
Total..........	3,134	100.0	3,112	100.0	3,109	100.0
100,000 or more....	303	9.7	242	7.8	187	6.0
50,000–100,000....	293	9.3	259	8.3	258	8.3
25,000– 50,000....	589	18.8	651	20.9	680	21.9
10,000– 25,000....	1,094	34.9	1,182	38.0	1,265	40.7
5,000– 10,000....	561	17.9	516	16.6	475	15.3
Under 5,000......	294	9.4	262	8.4	244	7.8

Source: Bureau of the Census, 1950 and 1960 Censuses of Population, Volume I for each year.

lished young or middle-aged farmers have sold out and moved away in the past decade, most of the reduction in farm population is taking place now through the heavy outmovement of young people who have decided not to enter agriculture. Thus, as many older farmers die or retire, their manpower is not replaced, although their land may be absorbed by another farm. Gladys K. Bowles has estimated that of all net migrants from the farm in the 1950's, at least 60 percent was less than 20 years old or reached age 20 some time during the decade.[7] By contrast, it can be shown that decade outmigration rates for middle-aged groups seldom exceed 10 percent even in rapidly declining counties.

The existence of a significant amount of migration from an area usually stimulates questions about the social and economic selectivity of the migrants. One demographic aspect of rural migration that is often overlooked when the question of selectivity is raised is the fact that in areas where the total rural population has declined by as little as 5 to 10 percent in a decade, the net outmigration of young adults is typically more than 50 percent in the decade. There were about 1,500 counties in the United States in 1960 where this was true.[8] To the extent that the term "selectivity" is generally employed to connote the characteristics of a minority coming from a mass, it is the nonmigrants at prime labor force ages 25 to 45 or 50 in the counties just mentioned who are in effect the "selected" minority. The majority of the original population that grew up in such rural areas has gone. The pertinent research question in such cases would seem to be "Who has remained?" rather than "Who has left?"

The Emergence of Natural Decrease

As a result of the prolonged and increasingly high net outmigration of young rural adults in many counties, a condition has now been reached in a number of areas in which births occurring to the depleted population of childbearing age are exceeded by the number of deaths taking place in the numerically larger older population. In other words, sections of the nation are experiencing a natural decrease in the midst of the more widely heralded population explosion.

This is not the first time such cases have occurred. During the Depression of the 1930's

[7] "Net Migration from the Farm Population, 1950-1960" (paper presented to 1961 annual meeting of the Population Association of America).

[8] Estimated by the author.

some counties showed a natural decrease. This fact attracted little attention however, apparently being mentioned first by Harold Dorn in a brief note in 1939, when the Depression Era with its accompanying low fertility was nearing its close.[9]

A total of 143 different counties showed an excess of deaths in either 1937 or 1938. A majority of these had a conventional net reproduction rate for the white population of less than 1,000 for the period 1935–40, indicating the dominant role that low age-specific fertility played in producing the natural decrease. Some of the counties were farming counties in the Midwest or small rural mining counties in the mountain West, but many were in the industrial Northeast, where every state was represented, or in California.[10]

In recent years, the practically unnoticed occurrence of natural decrease has been almost entirely rural and heavily agricultural. In contrast to the 1930's, it has without exception occurred in counties where the level of fertility of women of childbearing age is more than adequate for generational replacement. The excess of deaths has occurred solely because of the distorted age structure, the cohorts from which most deaths occur being large compared with the migration-depleted childbearing groups.

The extent to which the current pattern is new may be judged from the fact that all except one of the 98 counties showing a natural decrease in some year from 1955 to 1961 had a natural *increase* in 1950. With the revival of the birth rate during and immediately after World War II, the Depression-born instances of natural decrease had disappeared almost entirely.

Two principal concentrations of naturally declining counties now have emerged. One is in the southern fringe of the Corn Belt, in southern Iowa, northern and western Missouri, and eastern Kansas. In most of these counties population started to drop from outmigration as early as 1890 or 1900, but farms today are still too small or marginally productive to maintain even the reduced level of population, and industrial alternatives have not developed. In addition, age-specific fertility, although adequate for replacement, has long been about the lowest of any farming region.

The second clustering of counties with an excess of deaths is in Texas and part of Oklahoma. Several economic subregions are involved, but with very few exceptions the counties have in common the heritage of a former commitment to cotton under rather marginal climatic and competitive conditions. For a generation they have been subject to a drastic reorganization of land use into more extensive forms (grazing and forestry) and to a flight of people to cities or to the West.

Other types of counties represented elsewhere are small relict Western mining counties, dating from the gold and silver rushes of the last century, and a few widely scattered resort and retirement counties. Whereas counties of the latter type have a distorted age structure, they usually differ from all other types by being areas of inmigration of older people rather than outmigration of young persons.

Perhaps just as meaningful in a discussion of natural decrease is a notation of the predominantly rural areas that have *not* experienced the phenomenon. The condition is entirely absent from the northern half of the Great Plains. This seems in part to derive from the higher than average fertility of the population in this region. The relative recency of farming settlement in the northwestern plains may be a second factor, for it contributes to a younger population and fewer deaths.

The southeastern states, too, are conspicuous for the absence of natural decrease, except for two retirement counties. The essential reason is fertility, which has always been high enough to keep the age structure young despite heavy outmigration. The general picture does conceal the fact, however, that in the Lower South the demographic structure of rural population is usually radically different between whites and Negroes. Both groups have moved out in large numbers. The median age of the white rural

[9] "The Natural Decrease of Population in Certain American Communities," *Journal of the American Statistical Association,* XXXIV, No. 205 (March 1939), 106-9. The fact that births were not tabulated by county of residence (as well as county of occurrence) until the 1937 data year may have concealed the trend from notice.

[10] Some instances of natural decrease in the 1930's may have been spurious, reflecting the poorer birth registration completeness of that period. These seem to have been few, however, for most of the natural decrease cases occurred in areas with the best registration systems.

population has risen, and in some counties white deaths have come to exceed births (17 counties in 1961). In the Negro population, however, an increased fertility since 1950 and a pattern of higher outmigration at middle ages than is true for white have been instrumental in producing more births than deaths. Thus where Negroes are a significant element in the population, an over-all natural decrease has not occurred and is not likely to occur in the foreseeable future.

Should employment opportunities stabilize in counties having a natural decrease, the more normal relationship of births and deaths would reassert itself as the outmigration of the young was considerably reduced or halted. In many areas natural decrease or the near approach of such a condition is most likely to be a temporary stage during the transition of rural sections to forms of agriculture or other land use that directly support fewer people than were present in the past. Temporary may mean a generation, however. The phenomenon of natural decrease has been dwelt on here at some length because it is so counter to cherished American themes of youth, growth, and progress. The very existence of depopulation through migration that is so severe it begets further loss by natural decline epitomizes the magnitude and rapidity of present day change in rural society. But, the basic problems and prospects of the natural decrease counties are little different from those of hundreds of other essentially rural areas that are groping for antidotes to the demographic and other consequences of agricultural adjustment.

Future Considerations

With respect to the future, one point that can be made with certainty is that in the United States as a whole the bulk of the demographic adjustment stemming from agricultural changes has now taken place, for the farm population has already declined by more than one-half. The rate of change from a reduced base can remain high for another decade or two, however. This seems probable from the fact that there are still hundreds of thousands of small-sized farms in the hands of late middle-aged or elderly operators, who have some years of activity remaining before retirement or death.[11] Under foreseeable trends few of these operators are likely to migrate at their stage of life, but in the future most of their farms are likely to be absorbed by other farmers through lease or purchase, or in many upland areas even removed from agriculture altogether and returned to woodland.[12] In addition, the advance of labor-reducing equipment and techniques continues apace. For example, technical advances are permitting the replacement of most cotton and peanut tenants with smaller numbers of wage workers, and threaten in the coming decade to reduce the still heavy inputs of tenant and family manpower used in tobacco culture.[13]

The forms of agricultural change are usually not as radical in the northern states as in the South, but the trend toward larger and fewer farms continues without slackening, both in the dairy belts and in the grain and livestock country. In addition, mining employment in the rural coal fields is expected to drift lower.

Modifying factors of a growth nature for presently depopulating areas are (1) the spreading peripheries of metropolitan centers, which bring more rural districts into urban commuting distance, and (2) the decision of the federal government since 1961 to promote the nonagricultural development of rural areas through such instruments as the Area Redevelopment Act.

The nation has never been free of the social costs of space associated with low settlement densities. They have always been present in the Great Plains and the Mountain West. But, when the combination of a small total population in the county or other local government unit with (in many areas) a low density is aggravated by a

[11] In 1959 there were about 500,000 farmers aged 55 years and over who sold less than $2,500 worth of farm products and had little or no off-farm work or other sources of income.

[12] The proportion of all farm real estate purposes in the United States in which the land was bought for farm enlargement, rather than use as a single farm, rose from 26 percent in 1950-54 to 46 percent in 1962. See *Farm Real Estate Market Developments* (Economic Research Service, Department of Agriculture, December 1962), p. 9.

[13] The proportion of the United States cotton crop harvested by machine increased from 34 percent in 1958 to 70 percent in 1962, and the proportion of the peanut crop combined rather than stacked rose from 20 percent in 1950 to 76 percent in 1959. (Data from Economic Research Service, Department of Agriculture.)

steady downward trend of population and is extended over much greater areas of the nation, the problems arising in almost every field of social and economic life become severe and perplexing.[14]

The demography and sociology of decline are not attractive subjects for most researchers.[15] The power and the glory and the action are in megalopolis. But if 70 percent of the United States population is urban, 99 percent of the land area is rural, and the need for additional attention to the demography of depopulating rural areas and for the insights that such research can provide seems to be rising.

[14] Good recent discussions of some of these problems include: Clarence J. Hein, "Rural Local Government in Sparsely Populated Areas," *Journal of Farm Economics,* XLII, No. 4 (November 1960), 827-41; Frederick D. Stocker, "Local Government Costs and Services under Conditions of Sparse Population" (speech at Western Farm Economic Association, July 1963); Luther G. Tweeten and Odell L. Walker, "Estimating Socio-Economic Effects of a Declining Farm Population in a Sparse Area" (paper prepared for Workshop on Regional Development Analysis, Stillwater, Oklahoma, May 1963); Ward W. Bauder, *The Impact of Population Change on Rural Community Life: The Economic System* (Iowa State University of Science and Technology, October 1963), 52 pp.

[15] Lowenthal and Comitas note that neither the term "depopulation" nor any of its equivalents is listed in the Index to the extensive survey of the field of demography by Philip M. Hauser and Otis Dudley Duncan, *The Study of Population: An Inventory and Appraisal* (Chicago, 1959; 864 pp). See David Lowenthal and Lambros Comitas, "Emigration and Depopulation: Some Neglected Aspects of Population Geography," *Geographical Review,* III, No. 2 (April 1962), 195-210.

*Age and Sex Composition of Urban Subareas**

CALVIN F. SCHMID

SEX AND AGE COMPOSITION OF CERTAIN TYPICAL CENSUS TRACTS

In order to obtain a more detailed and comprehensive picture of the age and sex structure of the population in various parts of the city, certain tracts were selected for special analysis. These tracts represent typical ecological areas found in most large American cities. In this group of nine census tracts selected for special study are the central business district, a major apartment and rooming house area, Skid Road and two other transitional areas in the central segment of the city, a public housing project, a Negro family area, an outlying business and industrial area, and a peripheral middle-class residential section.

In order to facilitate more reliable comparisons of the sex and age structure of the nine census tracts, the age and sex configuration for the city as a whole has been superimposed in dashed lines on each of the nine pyramids in the figure.

It will be observed that the pyramid for Tract M1, which embraces most of the central business district, is markedly asymmetrical, indicating a pronounced excess of males (85.3 per cent), and a very small proportion of children (0.4 per cent under 5 or 1.4 per cent under 15 years of age). The proportion of the population in the upper age groups is considerably higher in the central business district than in the city as a whole (22.0 per cent of the population in the central business district are 65 years and over, as compared to 12.0 for the entire city). In addition, the Negro

* Reprinted with major adaptations and 1960 census data from Calvin F. Schmid, *Social Trends in Seattle,* Seattle, University of Washington Press, 1944, pp. 93-97. Used by permission.

AGE AND SEX DIFFERENTIALS
SELECTED CENSUS TRACTS, SEATTLE: 1960*

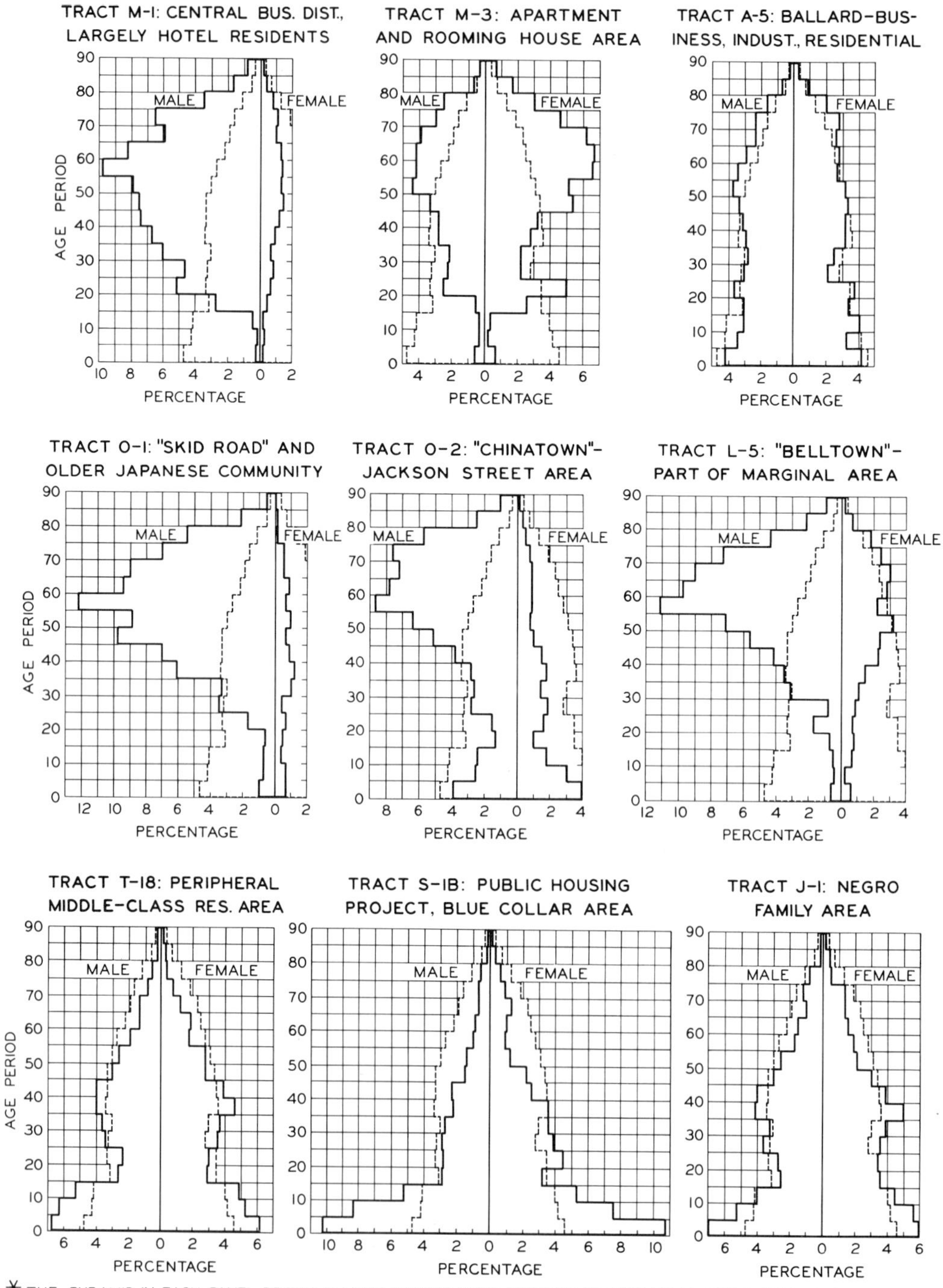

* THE PYRAMID IN EACH PANEL DRAWN IN LIGHT DASHED LINES REPRESENTS THE TOTAL POPULATION OF SEATTLE.

(0.1 per cent as compared to 4.8 per cent for the entire city), as well as other non-white population (1.8 per cent for the central business district and 3.5 per cent for the city as a whole), is relatively small. The educational level of the population in the central business district is relatively low (median grade for the population 25 years old and over is 9.0, as compared to 12.2 for the entire city; 3.8 per cent are college graduates, in comparison to 12.4 for the city as a whole). In the central business district, the proportion of male laborers is high (20.2 per cent) as is the proportion of unemployed males (32.9 per cent).

Tract M3 is representative of a centrally located rooming-house and apartment-house area, characterized by a high proportion of females (59.3 per cent) and a small proportion of children (2.4 per cent of the population is under 15 years of age, as compared to 25.9 per cent for the city as a whole). Also, there is a pronounced excess of people in the older age brackets (26.7 per cent are 65 and over, in comparison to 12.0 per cent for the entire city). The socio-economic status of the population is relatively high in terms of educational level and occupation. Only 31.9 per cent of the population 14 years of age and over are married, as compared to 62.6 per cent for the city as a whole. The incidence of separation, divorce, and widowhood is very high.

Tract A5 represents the main business district of Ballard, one of the more important outlying industrial sections of Seattle. A relatively high proportion of both native and foreign-born Scandinavians live in this area. It will be observed from the figures that there is a marked coincidence between the age and sex structures of Tract A5 and of the entire city. In Tract A5, 49.2 per cent of the population is male, as compared to 48.9 per cent for the city as a whole. The age group under 15 years comprises 22.0 per cent of the population in A5 and 25.9 per cent for the entire city. The corresponding percentages for the population 65 years and over are 15.8 and 12.0.

Also included in the figure are three tracts — O1, O2, and L5 — which represent transitional areas contiguous to the central business district. O1 is mainly a "hobohemia" colloquially referred to as "Skid Road"; O2 includes Chinatown and smaller clusterings of Filipinos, Negroes, and Japanese; and L5 is inhabited largely by an unstable proletarian white population. In all three tracts there is a heavy preponderance of the male sex, with 88.8 per cent in O1, 75.6 per cent in O2, and 72.5 per cent in L5. The proportion of children under 15 years of age in these three tracts is small, with 4.3 per cent, 17.6 per cent, and 3.0 per cent, respectively; while on the other hand, the proportion of the population 65 years of age and over is comparatively large, with 25.4 per cent in O1, 26.6 per cent in O2, and 31.6 per cent in L5. It will be recalled that for the city as a whole, 25.9 per cent of the population is under 15 years of age and 12.0 per cent 65 years and over. These three tracts are also characterized by a declining population, a high proportion of foreign-born, a high proportion of separated, divorced, and widowed, low educational level, low occupational status, and a large proportion of unemployed.

Tract T18 represents a relatively new, growing, middle-class residential area toward the northern periphery of the city. The great majority of the homes (84.7 per cent) are owner-occupied. There is a relatively high proportion of children (34.4 per cent under 15, as compared to 25.9 per cent for the city as a whole) and a low proportion of older people (5.9 per cent in comparison to 12.0 per cent for the entire city). There is only one Negro and 25 other non-white in this tract. The proportion of the population 14 years of age and over that is married is relatively high (77.5), the incidence of separation, divorce, and widowhood is low (3.9 per cent); and the proportion of foreign-born is small (5.8 per cent). The educational level of the population, as well as occupational status, conforms very closely to that for the city as a whole.

The most distinctive characteristic of the age and sex structure of the population in Tract Slb is the extraordinarily large proportion of children; 47.5 per cent of those living in this tract are under 15 years of age. Also, the proportion of adults in the childbearing age group is high. The educational and occupational level of this group is noticeably below that of the city as a whole.

The most highly concentrated Negro population in Seattle is found in Tract J1; 84.3 per cent are Negro, 4.3 other non-white, and 11.4

white. The percentage of males (48.3) is very close to that for the city as a whole (48.9). The proportion of children in this tract is above the city average (32.3 per cent under 15 years of age, as compared to 25.9 per cent for the entire city) and the proportion of older people below the city average (7.1 per cent 65 years of age and over, in comparison to 12.0 for the city as a whole). Home-ownership, as indicated by the percentage of owner-occupied housing units (55.6 per cent), is slightly above the city average (53.3 per cent). The median value of owner-occupied housing units in Tract J1 is $9,800, as compared to $13,500 for the entire city. The educational and occupational level of the population in this tract is below the city average and the incidence of separation and divorce, above the city average.

*Urban Daytime Population: A Field for Demographic-Ecological Analysis**†

DONALD L. FOLEY

In large American cities there is a marked discrepancy between the spatial distributions of resident population and daytime population. Viewed dynamically, this involves daily movement from place of residence to various other locations and return. The most typical form of such movement is embraced in the term commuting, referring to the daily trip to and from work, presumably from a residence sufficiently distant so that some form of transportation other than walking is involved.

Three main questions will be treated in this paper: (1) What salient features of urban ecological structure contribute to extensive differences between daytime and nighttime population distributions? (2) What key characteristics of daytime population movement and distribution can we identify, as relating to large American cities? (3) What are the status and prospects of daytime population study as a subfield of demography and ecology?

URBAN ECOLOGICAL STRUCTURE AND DAYTIME POPULATION

The phenomenon of daytime population has an ecological basis, for it is the fact that large numbers of residents have different *spatial* locations during the day than they have at night that concerns us. But we must not assume that we "explain" daytime population by describing the American city's ecological patterning. We must go beyond the ecological to identify contributing historical, economic, and technological factors.

Two main points deserve stress: (1) In the contemporary large American city a mosaic of functional areas has evolved seemingly as an inevitable counterpart of the broader fact of economic specialization. Ecologists term this process segregation. So long as a city is characterized by specialization and, specifically, by segregation, we can expect that communication and movement among these divergent functional areas will be necessary if that city is to function

* Reprinted with permission from *Social Forces,* Vol. 32, No. 4 (May 1954), pp. 323-328.

† Paper read at the annual meeting of the Population Association of America, May 2-3, 1953, Cincinnati and Oxford, Ohio. The author gratefully acknowledges reading of the manuscript and comments by Hilda Hertz, Walter Martin, Chester Rapkin and Natalie Rogoff. Conrad Taeuber kindly suggested some rephrasing with respect to the Bureau of the Census' daytime population estimates prepared for the Federal Civil Defense Administration.

as an integrated community. As Hawley has stated:

> . . . from a spatial standpoint, the community may be defined as comprising that area the resident population of which is interrelated and integrated with reference to its daily requirements, whether contacts be direct or indirect.[1]

The development of efficient communication devices, particularly the telephone and postal service, has made it possible for much daily activity to be handled without movement of persons. Nevertheless, as will be further documented below, a vast amount of daily travel *is* necessary. In Liepmann's words, based mainly on British experience but also applicable to our cities:

> The functioning of modern conurbations, with dormitories and work places divorced, is absolutely dependent upon an elaborate system of transport services. What has happened is that the technical possibility of carrying masses of people considerable distances to and from work has been utilised, and more or less lengthy journeys have become the routine of millions of workers. . . .[2]

Summarizing, then, we have stressed the general and very fundamental fact that our movement of persons in the course of carrying out day-to-day activities provides a dynamic mechanism by which the city's various functional areas are linked. Up to this point, however, we have not indicated anything about the ecological patterning of functional areas as this bears on the daily movement of persons.

(2) A major characteristic of American city ecological structure is that for a variety of reasons centrally located daytime destinations tend to remain fairly strong, while residential areas have for several decades been undergoing considerable dispersal. The full impact of this fact on daytime population will be discussed in the next section of this paper. At this point it seems appropriate to discuss the combination of technological and other factors that have contributed to this centralization of work and other nonresidential functional areas and to the dispersal of residential areas.

The early American factories were generally developed in multi-storied buildings and surrounded by densely packed workers' residences. The particular manner in which steam or water power could be applied to industrial operations and the absence of good transportation discouraged dispersion. Early cities also tended to develop a centrally located commercial district which could conveniently serve the compactly developed community.

In each of our older cities, we have inherited such a densely built-up and functionally important central area, the heart of which we typically term the downtown or central business district. This contains the large department stores, other specialized stores, a welter of offices, and various services and amusements. This district tends to shade off into loft-building types of functions: warehousing and light manufacturing.[3] There may also be other industrial uses but these are by no means restricted to the central area.[4] The surrounding areas that once contained workers' homes have by now typically deteriorated into slums. They have been invaded for various nonresidential uses: parking lots, small repair firms, warehousing, etc.

With the advent of improved transportation, coupled with our particular history of successive waves of immigrants who tended to locate in close-in slum areas, it became possible and socially "desirable" for those who could to move farther out to "better" residential areas. With the exception of certain high- and medium-rent apartment districts in our largest cities, the strong and general trend was toward the development of a veritable sprawl of outlying middle and upper-class residential districts. The newest post-World War II developments have,

[1] Amos H. Hawley, *Human Ecology: A Theory of Community Structure* (New York: Ronald Press, 1950), p. 257.

[2] Kate K. Liepmann, *The Journal to Work: Its Significance for Industrial and Community Life* (New York: Oxford University Press, 1944), p. 81.

[3] See Chester Rapkin, An Approach to the Study of the Movement of Persons and Goods in Urban Areas (unpublished doctoral dissertation, Columbia University, 1953), especially chap. 6; Robert B. Mitchell and Chester Rapkin, Traffic and Urban Land Use (forthcoming volume); Richard U. Ratcliffe, *Urban Land Economics* (New York: McGraw-Hill, 1949), chap. 13; and Gerald W. Breese, *The Daytime Population of the Central Business District of Chicago* (Chicago: University of Chicago Press, 1949), especially chap 3.

[4] Edgar M. Hoover, *The Location of Economic Activity* (New York: McGraw-Hill, 1948), p. 128.

of course, pushed far-out suburban "colonies" to new extremes. Some close-in newer apartments have been erected and more may be in store with continued urban redevelopment, but essentially the trend has been for central residential densities to drop off while central daytime destinations — for employment, shopping, business errands or professional visits — continue in strength.

Manufacturing plants have in recent years been undergoing very considerable dispersal. In the long run, this outward movement of industry may well revolutionize our cities. But as of the present, two facts need airing: (1) This industrial dispersal is usually not so well coordinated with the development of new satellite communities that we can expect to find most employees of these new plants being accommodated in immediately adjacent communities. Thus, while the direction of homework movements is being shifted, long trips are by no means eliminated. (2) For a variety of reasons there is still tremendous inertia in industrial location, involving the fact that many well-established, centrally located firms have huge investments in their present plants so that they continue to cling to them. There is evidence, for example, that the net impact of World War II military production, with prime contracts being channelled as they were through the large established firms, was to strengthen the existing pattern. Only currently does the dispersion policy that the federal government has been encouraging for defense reasons seem to be adequately implemented.

It is much more conceivable that suburban residents in the future may be able to shop nearby than to work nearby. The carefully planned outlying shopping center — with one or more branch department stores as a nucleus, with adequate parking and with convenient shopping hours — has been coming into its own during the past few years. However, there seem to be marked differentials in the extent to which outlying residents do in fact use facilities in their own districts rather than traveling to more distant facilities, particularly those in or near the central business district.[5]

[5] Donald L. Foley, *Neighbors or Urbanites? The Study of a Rochester Residential District* (Rochester: Department of Sociology, University of Rochester, 1952).

Key Characteristics of Daytime Population Movement and Distribution

Our next task will be to present something of a profile describing the general character of this travel and the resulting daytime distribution of population for large American cities.

Here we are obviously attempting to cut through the maze of individual trips made in any one city during the course of a day. We shall use Mitchell's and Rapkin's concept, "movement system," which Rapkin defines as

> . . . an analytical classification of individual movements within the total structure of movement. It consists of a large group of individual movements which occur within a particular period of time, but which are not necessarily concurrent . . . systems of movement are specified in such fashion that they relate functionally to organized patterns of social and economic activity.[6]

Two main movement systems are suggested:[7] (1) Movement of persons classified by "purpose" of trip, such as utilized in origin-destination surveys now being conducted in the U. S.: work, shopping, medical-dental care, etc. (2) Movement of persons cross-classified by the general functional areas in which each trip has its origin and destination (hence by such areas as industrial, central business district, residential, etc.). These two movement systems represent alternate ways of classifying total daily trips within a city.

Let us summarize some of what is known about weekday trips, classified by purpose.[8]

(1) The most important single type of trip is the "journey to work." Roughly two out of every five trips from home are to work. Since these trips tend to be concentrated during morning and afternoon peak hours they are a major factor in causing heavy rush hour traffic. (As will

[6] Rapkin, *op. cit.,* p. 81.

[7] Rapkin himself utilizes the second system. He feels that the first system, re purpose, should only be added at a future time "when the conception of trip purpose is further clarified"; *ibid,* p. 82. We use the first system in order to take advantage of origin-destination survey findings, but thereby restrict this usage to the particular definitions of "purposes" that are used in such surveys.

[8] Based on averages from recent origin-destination surveys (Minneapolis-St. Paul, 1950; Portland, Oregon, 1946; Salt Lake City, 1946; Tacoma, 1947; Harrisburg, 1946; Racine, 1951; and Johnstown, Pennsylvania, 1949).

be noted below, the more traditional European concern has been for this work trip only; the British, for example, have defined daytime population as workers at their "work places.")

(2) The next most prevalent trip is for "social-recreational" purposes, accounting for about one-fourth of all trips (as defined for origin-destination survey purposes). During work days, this is typically an evening trip.

(3) "Shopping" and "business" trips are next in importance. Shopping tends to be most prevalent in the afternoon. Thus, the weekday business district density is greatest in the afternoon, and the late-afternoon trips home from the downtown districts directly contribute to the 5:00 p.m. transportation congestion.

The trip to work warrants the closest examination:

(1) Generally, the larger the city, the longer the trip to work.[9] In cities under 100,000 the bulk of these trips take no more than half an hour. For New York City, on the other hand, a pre-war survey of Manhattan workers showed that two out of three spent at least 40 minutes each way.[10]

(2) According to Carroll, the central district is "generally the greatest single point of employment concentration." [11] Since such a large portion of all employment is centrally located, the farther one lives from the central part of the city, the longer is the average trip to work. A recent Chicago study, for example, found that for a housing project 1.5 miles from the city center, the average distance to work was 1.6 miles; but for a project 16.5 miles from the center, this average increased to 8.6 miles.[12]

(3) Trips to work in the central district are typically longer than trips to work in off-center industrial districts, for any given city.[13] Lower income groups tend to live closer to work, and are more likely to use automobiles.[14]

(4) Carroll has hypothesized that "each worker seeks to minimize distance from home to work . . ." [15] Ranyak, by way of exploring Carroll's research and striving for a more inclusive theory, has suggested this modification: "People tend to minimize their journey to work, maximize their employment benefits and maximize their residential amenities." [16]

Now let us turn to the second movement system: trips cross-classified by general functional areas of origin and destination. During each weekday there is an exodus from residential areas and an inflow into industrial and commercial areas. The question is: how great are the exodus and the inflow? We shall present certain relevant empirical findings.

The broadest view has been provided by recent special tabulations of origin-destination traffic survey data carried out by a research group at the University of North Carolina.[17] Their findings are summarized as Table 1. For the five cities studied, they found that by early afternoon only about three out of every four residents remain in residential areas. During most of the regular working hours, about 13 percent of all residents are to be found in the city's industrial areas. During the early afternoon a peak of about 16 percent of the residents are in commercial areas. (Which portion is in the central business district and which portion is in outlying shopping districts is not reported.) Streets claim nearly one in ten residents during the late afternoon rush hour and early evening.

[9] J. Douglas Carroll, Jr., Home-Work Relationships of Industrial Employees: An Investigation of Relationships of Living and Working Places for Industrial Employees with Attention to Implications for Industrial Siting and City Planning (unpublished doctoral dissertation, Harvard University, 1950), pp. 34, 40; hereafter referred to as Home-Work Relationships of Industrial Employees.

[10] Homer Hoyt and L. Durward Badgley, *The Housing Demand of Workers in Manhattan* (New York, 1939), Table 5, p. 29.

[11] J. Douglas Carroll, Jr., "The Relation of Homes to Work Places and the Spatial Pattern of Cities," *Social Forces,* 30 (March 1952), p. 280.

[12] Robert F. Whiting, "Home-to-Work Relationships of Workers Living in Public Housing Projects in Chicago," *Land Economics,* 28 (August 1952), p. 287.

[13] J. Douglas Carroll, Jr., "The Relation of Homes to Work Places and the Spatial Pattern of Cities," *loc. cit.,* pp. 277-279.

[14] J. Douglas Carroll, Jr., Home-Work Relationships of Industrial Employees, chap. 6.

[15] *Ibid.,* p. 160.

[16] John A. Ranyak, A Theoretical Approach to the Journey to Work (unpublished bachelor's thesis, Massachusetts Institute of Technology, 1952), pp. 11-12.

[17] Institute for Research in Social Science, University of North Carolina, Industrial Areas Study, *Population Distribution — Spatial and Temporal: A Study of Daytime-Nighttime Differentials in the Proportionate Distribution of the Total Population of Selected Urban Areas* (September 1952).

TABLE 1

*Mean Percent of Resident Population Present in Functional Areas, Selected Hours, Five U.S. Cities**

Hour of day	Total study area	Commercial areas	Industrial areas	Residential areas	Streets**
3:00 a.m.	101	4	7	89	1
6:00 a.m.	101	3	7	89	2
9:00 a.m.	102	9	16	73	3
12:00 noon	102	13	16	68	4
3:00 p.m.	102	13	16	66	6
6:00 p.m.	101	5	9	78	9
9:00 p.m.	101	5	9	76	9
12:00 midnight	101	3	8	85	5

* These cities with date of survey and population of study area in thousands were:

Philadelphia-Camden	(1947-2,479)
Minneapolis-St. Paul	(1949- 919)
Grand Rapids	(1947- 221)
Flint	(1950- 206)
Erie	(1948- 135)

** Peak "Street" percentages occurred at 8:00 a.m., with 6 percent, and at 5:00 p.m., with 10 percent, as computed for each hour on the hour.

Source: Adapted from Institute for Research in Social Science, University of North Carolina, *Population Distribution — Spatial and Temporal* (September 1952, Table 5, p. 76. Figures may not add to totals because of rounding and the omission of a "miscellaneous" category.

We also know that on each weekday there is an overwhelming tendency for population to move in toward the central areas (whether business or industrial) during the morning with a reverse flow back to the outlying residential areas late in the afternoon.

Some general evidence for this inward daily flow, is shown in Table 2, providing an interpretive summary of recent population estimates prepared by the U. S. Bureau of the Census for the Federal Civil Defense Administration. Neither the Bureau of the Census nor the F. C. D. A., of course, assumes responsibility for the use or interpretation made of these data. From the 120 U.S. cities included in the project, the five largest cities were selected for which the concentric rings used for estimating purposes appeared to have been centered within their respective central business districts. The daytime population estimates are intended to represent "expected normal maximum" figures in the sense of maximums that might usually be expected to occur under normal daytime conditions. Therefore the over-all estimates may be some what high for the purposes intended here. It should be further noted that "these estimates can only be considered very rough," because several of the "more important assumptions, while appearing not unreasonable, have been made with little actual supporting evidence." Nevertheless, a general trend is certainly clear. While on the average only 4 percent of the population in these cities resides in a zone approximating a radius of one mile from the central business district, the estimated daytime equivalent amounts to 30 percent. Similarly within a radius of two miles resident population amounts to about 15 percent of the city total, but estimated daytime population equals half of the city's resident population. And within a radius of four miles, the resident population totals less than half of the city population, while estimated daytime population slightly exceeds three-fourths of the city's resident population.

TABLE 2

Estimated Normal Maximum Day Population in Relation to Resident Population, by Concentric Zones from City Center; Means for Five of the Largest U.S. Cities, 1950

Concentric Zones*	Percent of Total Resident Population		Cumulative Percent of Total Resident Population		Ratio of Daytime to Resident Population**
	Resident	Daytime	Resident	Daytime	
Zone 1............	1.4	11.0	1.4	11.0	23.84
Zone 2............	2.9	19.4	4.3	30.4	7.41
Zone 3............	5.1	11.0	9.4	41.4	2.33
Zone 4............	5.6	7.5	15.0	48.9	1.53
Zone 5............	7.1	7.9	22.1	56.8	1.15
Zone 6............	7.6	6.8	29.7	63.6	.93
Zone 7............	7.3	6.8	37.0	70.4	.95
Zone 8............	8.9	8.1	45.9	78.5	.94
Total Zones 1–8...	45.8	78.5			1.77
Remainder of City	54.2	45.7			.82
City Total.....	100.0	124.2			1.24

* Zones are groups of census tracts intended to approximate the populations of concentric half-mile rings and extending out to a distance of four miles or city limits, whichever is closer.

** Each ratio is the unweighted mean of the respective city ratios. It differs from the ratio that would have been obtained by dividing each second-column figure in this table by the corresponding first-column figure.

Source: Computed from U.S. Bureau of the Census special reports.

Clearly, these figures illustrate the definite tendency for daytime population to show concentration within the metropolitan area.

A recent study of travel to the various commercial centers within the Washington, D. C. metropolitan area compared trips to the core area of the central business district with trips to 16 outlying shopping centers. It is possible that the central business district is less important in Washington than it is in other large American cities because of Washington's unique economic base. Yet slightly over three-fifths of the total trips were to the core area. Of all trips to commercial districts for "work," 77 percent of the destinations were in the core area. Shopping and recreational trips, on the other hand, were about evenly split between the core area and the outlying centers (as a group).[18]

In a recent study of daytime population entering and accumulating in central business districts of large American cities, it was found that for every 100 metropolitan residents, between 40 and 50 persons enter the business district during each weekday, about 20–25 have destinations there, and from 8–13 are there in the afternoon at the time of maximum accumulation. Since this study has been reported in some detail elsewhere,[19] we shall indicate only two or three main conclusions at this time. In general, the larger the city, the lower are these ratios, presumably indicating that in the large cities daily facility uses are more likely to be handled by outlying centers. Insofar as admittedly scanty data permit, these ratios seem to be holding up over time, with post-World War II ratios comparing favorably with those in the late 1920's. This writer is also inclined to support Carroll's contention that the central business

[18] Gordon B. Sharpe, "Travel to Commercial Centers of the Washington, D. C. Metropolitan Area" (Washington: Highway Transport Research Branch, Bureau of Public Roads, January 1953), mimeographed; see especially Table 1.

[19] Donald L. Foley, "The Daily Movement of Population Into Central Business Districts," *American Sociological Review,* 17 (October 1952), pp. 538-543.

district has relatively less drawing power when a city has strongly dispersed industrial employment. Detroit is a case in point.

Daytime Population as a Subfield for Study

The interest that some social scientists are currently showing in daily trips from home to various activities is by no means new. Since summaries by Liepmann and Breese of the earlier European studies are available in published form, we shall limit our remarks to a few comments about the major emphases of the earlier work.[20]

The bulk of the earlier research in this area was conducted in Great Britain, Germany, and France in the 30-year period up to the outbreak of World War II. In these and other European nations, government statistical agencies were typically called into service, either at the national or municipal levels. The focus was characteristically confined to the relation of workplace to residence, with the flow that in our country we label "commuting" termed *Pendelwanderung* or *migrations alternantes*. Industrial conurbations and the largest metropolitan areas were particularly investigated. For example, the Leipzig area,[21] Paris,[22] and London,[23] were selected. In some of the studies, such as those for Hamburg, the city was districted much as we would introduce census tracts, and cross-tabulations by district of residence and district of work place were made.

European studies since World War II have not been adequately summarized, although Iklé's doctoral dissertation includes a valuable annotated bibliography.[24] Menzler has reported an estimate of London's daytime population based on the London Travel Survey of 1949.[25] According to this report, over 700,000 persons daily enter the central commercial area, swelling the resident population of 170,000 to about 878,000. Caplow's interesting discussion of city structure in France contains references to recent studies and the brief observation that:

> The degree of centralization in France . . . is always less marked than would be expected in an American community of comparable size. . . . Schaeffer and Chaumbart de Lauwe are able to demonstrate the absence of any single point of concentration in Paris, and the absence as well of the radical daily movement of population which characterizes Chicago. Instead there is a sort of general spiral movement, inwardly directed, but without convergence to a central point, and the volume of this spiral movement appears to be diminishing. . . . The separation of home from workplace is far less complete in France than in the United States.[26]

Watson has recently reported on some aspects of commuting in New Zealand.[27]

Realistically viewed, there has been no great burst of American activity in this field during recent years. At a theoretical, social science level there has been but a handful of contributors, so far as we are aware. The work by these persons has in general already been referred to during this presentation: Breese, Carroll, Mitchell, Ranyak, and Rapkin.[28] A limited amount of work has been carried out by city or regional planning agencies.[29] The report by F. Stuart Chapin, Jr.,

[20] Kate K. Liepmann, *op. cit.*, especially pp. 111-130; Gerald W. Breese, *op. cit.*, pp. 6-13.

[21] Statisches Reichsamt, "Die Pendelwanderung im Mitteldeutschen Industriegebiet," *Vierteljahrshefte zur Statistik des Deutschen Reichs*, Heft 1, 40 (Jg. 1931), pp. 132-148.

[22] Henri Bunle, "Migrations alternantes des professionels dans la région parisienne," *Bulletin de la Statistique Générale de France*, Tome 21 (1932), pp. 585-612.

[23] Census of England and Wales, 1921, *General Report*, Part XII, "Workplaces," especially Tables 90 and 91.

[24] Fred Charles Iklé, The Impact of War Upon the Spacing of Urban Population (unpublished doctoral dissertation, University of Chicago, 1950).

[25] F. A. A. Menzler, "An Estimate of the Day-time Population of London," *Journal of the Town Planning Institute*, 38 (March 1952), pp. 116-120.

[26] Theodore Caplow, "Urban Structure in France," *American Sociological Review*, 17 (October 1952), pp. 545-549.

[27] John E. Watson, "Travelling Time to Work: Some Notes from the New Zealand Census of 1945," *Social Forces*, 30 (March 1952), pp. 283-292.

[28] Since this was written, our attention has been directed to the valuable series of research reports prepared by Otis Dudley Duncan and his group at the University of Chicago, 1951-1953, under contract with the Human Resources Research Institute, Maxwell Air Force Base. Report Numbers 5, 11, 13, 17, and 20 are particularly relevant.

[29] See, for example: Seattle City Planning Commission, "Daytime and Night-time Population Distribution in Metropolitan Seattle: April, 1950" (September 17, 1951), mimeographed; New York Regional Plan Association, "Persons and Vehicles Entering Manhattan South of

and others in the Department of City and Regional Planning, University of North Carolina, should be seen by those interested in this field.[30] The American Society of Planning Officials recently published a report entitled *The Journey to Work*.[31]

The greatest promise of empirical data comes from the highway research field, as carried out by traffic engineers. A bibliography by Barkley lists origin-destination surveys that have been conducted.[32] Two recent papers by Sharpe [33] and Hitchcock[34] provide good examples of traffic survey analyses.

What of the future prospects for daytime population study? We might break this down into the two requisite phases between which there must be effective collaboration: theoretical formulation and data collection.

The crying need is for imaginative conceptualization. The problem here has an interdisciplinary setting, for it can be approached by land economists, geographers, sociologists, and students of transportation. To be maximally useful such theoretical work should be essentially dynamic in its orientation so as to handle population movement and functional interrelationships. The theoretical formulation by Mitchell and Rapkin, to be forthcoming in monograph form, may well be an important steppingstone.[35]

But for the field of daytime population to prosper, there must be organized and, probably, *official* resources at the data collecting phase. A most logical next step would be some additional Census assistance. In some cases, even one or two additional questions to relate place of residence with workplace or facilities would provide a vast new sphere in which cross-tabulations could be run. Information on travel time, mode, and cost might be considered, although these are secondary to the main need for cross-tabulating the origin and destination of daily trips. There is also considerable room for collaborating with traffic engineers who now conduct large-scale sampling surveys of trip movements. Dr. Carroll has recently become the director of a new origin-destination survey of Detroit; we hope that he will be able to contribute additional research approaches to the present origin-destination survey design.

From both practical and theoretical viewpoints, it would seem essential to expand the work on daytime population. Consider for example this quotation from a memorandum prepared in 1951 by Henry Cohen, Director of Research for the New York City Planning Commission:

> The continuing congestion of transit facilities, the seriously aggravated traffic situation, and the exaggerated separation of residential areas from work areas, are excessive drains on the economy of the city and the well-being of the population.
>
> It has been estimated that in transit alone, New Yorkers consume some 500,000 to 600,000 man-days of employable time each day. The estimated costs of the waste and loss due to traffic congestion are fantastic. The strain on the individual is virtually inestimable.[36]

The memorandum goes on to propose as a major research project:

> To study the experience of workers in getting to and from establishments in different parts of the City; to analyze the transit and land use problems involved in reducing travel time to work for a large proportion of the City's inhabitants; to review the measures that may be taken to reduce travel time to work; to help reduce congestion in downtown areas by exploring alternative locations of employment establishments.[37]

To our knowledge this particular research project has not been approved, but here certainly is a blunt statement of need.

In conclusion, analyses in the population field already cover a wide range. Demographers have

61st Street, 1924-1948," *Regional Plan Bulletin*, 74 (October 1949); and Port of New York Authority, "Supplement to Regional Plan Association Bulletin No. 74" (December 1949), mimeographed.

[30] Institute for Research in Social Science, University of North Carolina, Industrial Areas Study, *op. cit.*

[31] American Society of Planning Officials, *The Journey to Work: Relation Between Employment and Residence*, Planning Advisory Service Information Report No. 26 (May 1951).

[32] Robert Emmanuel Barkley, *Origin-Destination Surveys and Traffic Volume Studies* (Washington: Highway Research Board, December 1951).

[33] Gordon B. Sharpe, *op. cit.*

[34] S. T. Hitchcock, "Influence of Population, Sales, and Employment on Parking" (Washington: Highway Transport Research Branch, Bureau of Public Roads, January 1953), mimeographed.

[35] Mitchell and Rapkin, *op cit.*

[36] New York City Planning Commission, Draft of a Travel to Work Memo (January 17, 1951), unpublished.

[37] *Ibid.*

generally displayed a willingness to search broadly for those factors that have a bearing on or are in turn affected by population size and composition and their changes. At least some of us are of the opinion that urban daytime population is a phenomenon of our times that could stand concerted descriptive and analytical research. We have the hopeful idea that the development of conceptual approaches and operational measures for bringing the nature of daytime population movement and distribution out into the open should considerably further our understanding of the city as a dynamic socio-economic complex.

STUDY AND DISCUSSION QUESTIONS

1. Census tract reports by the U.S. Census provide much valuable information on the characteristics of persons living in various parts of America's large cities. What kinds of information are included in these reports? Look for information on how the tracts were originally drawn.
2. Locate the latest census tract report for the metropolitan area in which you reside or the one nearest you. Within the report, locate a tracted area with which you are personally familiar. What is the median age of persons living in this tract? How many nonwhites are in the tract? What proportion of families in the tract have incomes over $5000? How do these compare with other tracted areas in the same and other parts of the metropolitan area?
3. It has been stated that people first distribute themselves on the land around the major ports of immigration. Where have these ports been in American history? Can you cite major developments in transportation lines in America that have been responsible for rather substantial redistributions of the population?
4. What are the sociological implications for the American family of the development of urbanization? How are interpersonal relationships within the family affected?
5. Can you think of specific examples of non-political units in this country that have become popular areas of settlement because of natural attributes, social climates, or economic activity? Which of these qualities does each area you name possess?
6. If you were to design the optimum or best distribution of the population in the United States today, what kinds of criteria would you consider? How would you distribute the population, taking into account these criteria?

SUGGESTED ADDITIONAL READING

Bogue, Donald J., and Calvin L. Beale. *Economic Areas of the United States.* New York: The Free Press of Glencoe, 1961.
Describes the method of delimiting state economic areas, and analyzes population and social and economic conditions in these areas in the United States.

Hauser, Philip M., and Leo F. Schnore, eds. *The Study of Urbanization.* New York: John Wiley and Sons, 1965.
A review of the major frameworks for research on urbanization and discussion of some methodological approaches.

Gibbs, Jack P., ed. *Urban Research Methods.* Princeton: D. Van Nostrand Company, Inc., 1961.
Sets forth scientific problems concerning cities and urbanization, and describes methods especially suited for their investigation.

Duncan, Otis Dudley, *et al. Metropolis and Region.* Baltimore: The Johns Hopkins Press, 1960.
Information on, and analysis of, the metropolitan structure of the United States, with emphasis on the links between population, geographic, and economic factors.

Taeuber, Karl E., and Alma F. Taeuber. *Negroes in Cities.* Chicago: Aldine Publishing Company, 1965.
A study of residential segregation and racial changes in neighborhoods of American cities.

Duncan, Otis Dudley, and Albert J. Reiss, Jr. *Social Characteristics of Urban and Rural Communities, 1950.* New York: John Wiley & Sons, 1956.
This monograph, one of the U.S. 1950 Census series, describes the demographic, economic, and social characteristics of types of places along the urban-rural continuum and relates these characteristics to various kinds of functional specialization.

Turner, Roy, ed. *India's Urban Future.* Berkeley and Los Angeles: University of California Press, 1962.
An analysis of urbanization in one of the world's developing nations.

PART II

Interrelations Between Population and Areas of Social Life

Part I dealt with the elements of population analysis. The aim was to expose the reader to the theoretical and empirical analyses conducted by demographers and others specializing in population research, with particular emphasis on the basic components of population change. Part II is concerned with the relation of population, its components and traits, to selected areas of social life. Areas of social life that are examined include the family, systems of social stratification, education, religion, the economy, and the polity.

Population and these areas of social life are viewed as being in mutual interaction. Each chapter in this part of the book examines a separate area of social life in this way, first, studying how the variables associated with the area may affect population statuses and changes, and second, studying the way in which population factors help shape the particular social area and the behavior of individuals within it. To some extent, the first of these foci overlaps with orientations found in the first part of the book; the second is more distinctive. However, the importance of this part of the volume lies in the analysis of *interaction* between the variables, with overlaps reinforcing some of the fundamental points made in the book.

Obviously, only a selected number of areas of social life are covered here. One could extend the list of areas to include other aspects of society. Some economy of effort was required, however, to restrict the length of this part of the volume, and those areas of social life were selected which sociologists usually regard as basic to the maintenance of a society, that is, those areas involving patterns of behavior that meet basic social needs.

This discussion of the interrelationships between population and society will enable the reader to see how intricately the facets of demographic development are interwoven with the elements of society and how important an understanding of population changes are to a full appreciation of the dynamics of social and cultural change. It is only this kind of understanding that can lead individuals and governments to plan intelligently for the kind of society in which they wish to live.

CHAPTER 10

Population and the Family

The family, as a social group, plays an important role in demographic analysis, and demographic factors are critical variables with regard to family formation, composition, change, and dissolution. Generally speaking, each of the basic components of population change — fertility, mortality, and migration — involve decisions to be made by the family as a unit or by certain segments of the family. These decisions may take the form of choosing (a) whether or not to bear a child (a fertility decision), (b) the extent and types of health practices to adopt (a mortality-postponing decision), and (c) whether or not to relocate one's residence (a migration decision). Patterns of births, deaths, migration, and population composition and distribution are all related to the place of the family in the society. These will be discussed more fully below.

There are a number of ways in which the family unit is an important social unit in fertility behavior. The major fertility decision to be made by the family is whether or not to bear a child. Family members, individually and collectively, have certain values concerning childbearing as well as particular family-size ideals; patterns of communication among the members influence these ideals and define the strategies that will be used to achieve the fertility goals being set. Then, continued interaction among the family members, or the lack of it, will help determine the success with which these goals are reached. Of course, not all behavior directed toward fertility goals is rational; however, we are assuming that most fertility-related behavior involves an awareness of the possibility of planning and controlling fertility and that this awareness is becoming more and more characteristic of the human race as time goes on.

The selection by Stycos in this chapter focuses on husband-wife interaction within the family as it relates to the childbearing process in Puerto Rico. Husbands and wives may differ in their family-size ideals and, even when their ideals are the same, lack of communication between the partners may inhibit efficient planning of the number of children the couple will have.

As Stycos and others point out, the key to the whole question of fertility control has been the extent of family planning within a population and the efficiency of this planning. Family planning may take many forms, including abstention from sexual intercourse, withdrawal during intercourse, surgery to make one or both partners to a marriage incapable of contributing to childbearing, and abortion or the termination of a pregnancy before the fetus is capable of survival; but the principal means of family planning today are mechanical or chemical contraceptive methods. The article by Tietze surveys the history of contraceptive methods and show that some forms of contraception were used at all stages of history but the particular kinds of contraception used have changed with time. The oral contraceptive pill and the IUD (intra-uterine device) are the methods which today offer the best hope of successful planning by those who want to regulate their family size and the spacing of their offspring. But the revolution in contraceptive technology suggests that new methods may be developed in the near future which are even more efficient than those now being used.

The importance of the family with regard to mortality may not be as obvious as its importance with regard to fertility. The family is the principal social group which provides for the protection, care, and nourishment of the bodies of the family members. The kinds of health practices adopted in the home, the extent to which the family avails itself of medical services and drugs, provisions for safety against accidents, and the nature of the diet provided are examples of ways in which the family can have an effect on the probability of life and death of individuals.

As the selection from Shyrock's monograph indicates, the family is also an important factor in migration. Many moves that individuals make are moves made along with other family members or moves to join a family member who has moved to another location in advance. Some changes in residence result from the breakdown or dissolution of family units or from other changes occurring within the family, such as the splitting of married couples and the relocation of one or both of them, the separation of young couples from parental residences to set up a home of their own, the establishment of a new residence by the survivors of a family in which a death has occurred, and the acquisition of a new home by a family which has grown beyond the size their previous residence could comfortably accommodate.

The article by Glick, Heer, and Beresford turns attention from the effect of family factors on population change to the effect of population dynamics on family formation, composition, and dissolution, with particular reference to stages of the family life cycle. The authors show that demographic developments bring about changes in the family in various ways, for example, in the number of families and in average family size, in the probability that married couples will jointly survive the family-building process, in the average ages of husbands and wives at the various stages of the family-building process, and in the composition of different types of families. The family structure in a society at any point in time is, therefore, partly determined by the course of population events in earlier years.

*Husband-Wife Communication and Fertility**

J. Mayone Stycos

Communication of Family Ideals

Although in general both husbands and wives have small-family ideals, lack of communication between the sexes often obstructs the awareness of a common ideal. That is, the general lack of communication, which we have described as typical of many lower-class families, and the specific lack of communication on sexual matters often result in the peculiar situation where both adults want few children but neither is aware that the other feels this way.[1]

Thus, when women were asked how many children their husbands wanted, nine showed a complete lack of knowledge of their husbands' ideals, saying, "He never says anything about that" or, "He has never talked with me about

* Reprinted with permission from J. Mayone Stycos, *Family and Fertility in Puerto Rico*. New York: Columbia University Press, 1955, pp. 166-180.

[1] Fifteen percent of the married women in Hatt's sample said they did not know how many children their husbands wanted. The percentage was considerably higher among the older couples. Hatt, *op cit.*, Table 276, p. 325.

that."[2] A check on the husband's interviews shows that all but one of the nine husbands wanted the same number of children as their wives or fewer children.

Of those women who ventured an estimate of their husbands' family-size ideals, over half estimated incorrectly, as judged by their husbands' own stated ideals. Table 1 shows the extent to which wives are aware of the ideal number desired by their husbands.

For those families for which information is available for both sexes, only 21 wives attributed the same ideal number of children to their husbands as the husbands themselves gave the interviewer. Roughly five out of every ten wives who ventured an opinion did not correctly reflect the husbands' opinions. This figure is particularly striking when we consider that the median and modal ideal number of children is three for *both* sexes. Thus, even by chance, a woman would be likely to guess correctly for her spouse.

[2] Whelpton and Kiser, in their study of urban, largely middle-class families describe a case which illustrates the problem: "Although there were two children in this family the husband and wife had never talked about the number of children they desired. During recent years, the wife had come to think that the husband did not want a third child, hence that they would not have another even though she herself wanted it. The husband, on his part, had formed a similar opinion. As a result of being interviewed, however, the couple talked over some of the questions that had been asked, and discovered that each was mistaken as to the other's attitude. When last seen they were planning to have a third child" (P. Whelpton, and C. Kiser, "Developing the Schedules, and Choosing the Type of Couples and the Area to Be Studied," in *Social and Psychological Factors Affecting Fertility,* New York, Milbank Memorial Fund, 1950, p. 152).

TABLE 1

Awareness on Part of Wife of Husband's Ideal Number of Children

Wife Thinks	Husband Actually Wants		
Husband Wants	Same as Wife	More than Wife	Less than Wife
Same as she	17	3	1
More than she	11	3	2
Less than she	6	1	1
Number of families	(34)	(7)	(4)

More men have the same ideals as their wives than the latter realize. A total of seventeen men have the same ideals as their wives, whereas their wives believe that the ideals vary. Thus it may be concluded that whereas both sexes prefer small families, these preferences may not become sufficiently verbalized within the family to allow for concerted action. Table 2 shows that lack of correct knowledge of the husband's ideal family size has some relation to a general lack of communication between the spouses.

While lack of information on one or the other of the indices[3] makes the number of cases awkwardly few, those cases tend in the expected direction. Only in the high communication group does a large proportion of the women appear to

[3] See Appendix C for details on the communication index construction.

TABLE 2

Degree of General Communication between Spouses, by Wife's Awareness of Husband's Ideal Family Size

	High Communication (percent)	Medium Communication (percent)	Low Communication (percent)
Wife guesses correctly	69	23	31
Wife guesses incorrectly	25	45	63
Wife does not know	6	32	6
	100	100	100
Number of families	(16)	(22)	(16)

be accurately aware of their husbands' fertility ideals. The largest proportion of incorrect evaluations was given by women in the least-communication families, although, if the "Don't Know's" are considered, those with medium communication have even larger discrepancies. If this statistic reflects reality, it would suggest that effective communication on ideal family size occurs *only* when general communication is quite high between the married couple of the lower class.

Conflicting Fertility Ideals

Despite the fact that the bulk of the evidence suggests an interest in small families, there are present a number of contrary beliefs more characteristic of large-family mentalities. That such can exist side by side with modern ideals concerning the small family may be an evidence of cultural lag, or it may represent genuine ambivalence. The present research cannot determine which of these alternatives seems more prominent, but the considerable indications of large-family mentality will be presented. These may be subsumed under three broad categories: (1) the hope that children will be of assistance in one's old age; (2) the belief in immediate impregnation following marriage; (3) the tendency on the part of males to identify a large family with *machismo*.

Children and Old Age

When respondents were asked why they held X to be the ideal number of children, only 34 out of 143 men and women answered in terms of the advantages of children. However, when asked the more leading question, "What are the advantages of a large family?" about half of the males and a quarter of the females mentioned unqualified advantages.

Thus, while the small family may be said to be a general ideal, a good proportion also think there are advantages to large families.[4] That such exist may well cause a certain amount of ambivalence with respect to family-size ideals. What are the advantages of the large family as seen by lower-class respondents?

The principal advantage appears to be a hope that children will help in one's old age. Of the 34 respondents who think in terms of the advantages of children when giving an ideal number of children for a family, half cited help in old age as their reason. When Hatt's respondents were asked why they did not choose a lower number for their ideal family size, about half of the 13,000 gave this same reason.[5]

In the present survey, however, there is a good deal of contrary evidence on this score. There are, first of all, respondents who deny that children help their parents in the latter's old age.

> Sons don't help their parents. . . . I have seen so many cases in which the father has worked hard supporting his sons, and later on, when they were men, they helped nobody. (B5M)

> The son is rare who helps his parents. (H9F)

Some can see certain advantages but feel that these are outweighed by the disadvantage of having to struggle to support a large family. The physical and economic pains of bringing them up are not worth the dubious prospect of security in one's old age.

> All of them can help to support the family. (Then why do you prefer a small family?) Because my earnings are not enough to support them. (A8M)

> Some say it is more profitable to have a lot of children because in the future they will help, but the wife is the one who has to give birth to them, exposing herself to death, so she doesn't like it. (H19F)

A frequently held attitude was that one's real obligation is to his wife and children. To help

[4] There is some evidence that feelings of small-family-mindedness do not resemble those more typical of the United States. Most of the reasons given by the sample for preferring a small family are in terms of the *children* rather than in terms of the parents. The health, rearing, and education of the children are seen to be jeopardized in the large family more frequently than are the interests, health, and goals of the parents. (In response to the question, "What do you think are the main reasons why couples do not have more children?" 20 percent of a cross section of Americans said,, "Interference with one's freedom." H. Cantril and M. Strunk, *Public Opinion 1935-1946* (Princeton: Princeton University Press, 1951), p. 43. Possibly the ideals in Puerto Rico are in transition. midway between the large-family-mindedness of truly underdeveloped areas and the more hedonistic and individualistic small-family-mindedness of modern society. This hypothesis is also lent credence by the fact that, of the 42 women who were asked whether they would want more children "if they had money," 17 replied in the affirmative.

[5] Hatt, *op. cit.,* Table 42, p. 59.

one's parents as well is commendable and noble if money is available, but it is a luxury which many respondents do not really expect.

If he is a good son, he helps his parents, but he is not obliged to do it, because he belongs to his wife and sons. (Y5F)

If he is a good son he always remembers his parents, but not because it's his duty. After he gets married, his obligation is to his wife and children. (H19F)

The logical conclusion to the foregoing reasoning was well stated by one respondent.

If they are going to help, few will help as well as many, so it is preferable to have few. (H7F)

But despite such arguments we are still left with a not inconsiderable number of respondents who are looking forward to help in old age. One might conclude that social change has been such as to make many lower-class individuals dubious about economic help on the part of their children. Landlessness, minimum-age laws for working, and the popularity of formal education make the son's contribution minimal and of short duration. Increasing physical mobility, the breakdown of extended family obligations, and the increasing isolation of the nuclear family make subsequent help less likely than in the past. Yet some parents still hope that children are an investment which pays good dividends when these are needed most. Such parents may not cherish such hopes for long in Puerto Rico's rapidly industrializing economy, but the fact that many still do suggests that family-size ideals, while predominantly in the direction of the small family, are not unequivocally so.

The Desire for a Rapid First Pregnancy

Most Puerto Ricans, despite small-family ideals, want to start their families immediately. Slightly over half of Hatt's sample wanted their first child "as soon as possible" after marriage, and another third wanted it between the first and second years of marriage. Hatt concluded that "the importance of beginning a family soon, then, is a value rather more generally accepted throughout the society than are any principles with regard to either the size of the family or the acceptability of planning the family."[6] In our own sample, 49 percent of the males and 36 percent of the females felt that the ideal time for the first birth was "as soon as possible."

Let us consider the reasons for desiring an immediate pregnancy. The reason most frequently stated by the wives, and one of the more frequent for the husbands, is the argument, frequently heard in our own society, that one should get childbearing and child rearing over as quickly as possible. There is, first of all, the belief, voiced by nine women, that the "sooner you start the sooner you finish." Wanting to get child rearing over with quickly may lead many women to behavior which has the opposite effect, for the sooner they start, the more children ultimately will be born, barring contraception.

The second reason for believing in an early start is that "you see them grow up sooner." This kind of reason, stated by eight women and six men, means that the parents will still be young when the children are grown. The advantage to this, as seen by the respondents, are several. Most of the men and some of the women in this group wanted to put the children on their feet before the death of their parents. While still young and in the labor force, the parents can assist their growing children. This attitude may stem partly from a low life-expectancy outlook. (Life expectancy in 1940 was only forty-five years for all of Puerto Rico.) It probably also takes into account the difficulties which the aged have in continuing to support themselves, not to mention their children.

For the males particularly, however, other reasons are equally important. One of these is that a marriage without children is not really a marriage, and that the sooner one can establish himself as a *padre de familia,* the sooner does his prestige go up — that is, the sooner does he become a real adult.[7]

[6] Hatt, *op. cit.,* p. 185.

[7] "[Because] working people here do not regard a marriage as truly consummated before the birth of the first child, consensually married couples will seek to have a child . . . within a year of their union" S. Mintz, "Cañamelar: The Contemporary Culture of a Rural Puerto Rican Proletariat," unpublished Ph.D. dissertation, Columbia University, 1951, Chap. VI, p. 21.

Closely related to this is the already-mentioned hypothesis that men tend to be uncertain about their virility. One way of proving virility is to be a *conquistadorde mujeres;* but, since impregnation of other women is tabued, the man will either not father children of these illicit partners or not take credit for them. Consequently, he still has to prove his virility in the sense of being able to procreate.

I was anxious to have my first child to see if I was sterile or not, because one has to avoid children with other women before marriage. (B4M)

The sooner the male can prove this, the sooner his anxiety is relieved and the sooner is he accepted into the male adult world. Of the 39 men who answered "Immediately" to the question as to the ideal time after marriage to have the first child, 8 gave the reason, "To show that the man is not sterile." In answer to the question, "Is a man anxious to have his first child?" all but five males replied in the affirmative. When asked why, no less than 31 of the 63 men replied, "In order to prove that one is a man," or "To show that one is not sterile." Some of these responses are illustrated below.

That business of being married and having no children looks bad. One likes to have them to prove he is not *machorro* (barren). (Z7M)

. . . a man feels more virile when he knows he can make a child. (Z3M)

A man is anxious to have his son early to prove his *hombría* (manliness). . . . I mean that he wants his first child in order to prove that he can make sons, that he is not barren. (A11M)

One of the interesting aspects of this anxiety is that much of its motive power comes from the adult male community. A number of men expressed the fear of being laughed at and ridiculed by their fellows if they did not have a child. Perhaps there is a tendency to assume that a man is not a man unless proven to be one. From the safety of their offspring, fathers build up their own sense of virility by mocking those who have not yet been proven. Note in the quotations below how strong the community pressure appears to be.

If one is not *un hombre completo*, he can't live in town. The people talk about him (What do they say?) Well, that he is not a real man because he doesn't have children. . . . When I had my children, I felt happy. (Why?) Because I knew that I could have children, that I am not sterile. (Y8M)

One wants to have a child so that people don't talk about him. (How is that?) Yes, man, if you don't have children, people say that you're sterile and make fun of you. That's why when I had my first child I was all happy inside. (Y4M)

. . . that proves if one is sterile or not, and if you are sterile you are worthless in the public eye. (What do you mean?) If a man is not *completo* here, he would be the laughing stock of everyone around here, and that is very painful for a man. (X8M)

We have seen that women are not especially concerned about proving their fertility, but many of them recognize that such is not the case with men. Several women expressed disdain that the man should feel this way, one woman phrasing it particularly effectively.

Men want children soon. They say they are an entertainment and they go crazy for the first-born; but it is really that they want to be sure they can have children. (A13F)

In one case, a young man uses his children to convince his fellows that he is a man.

My husband's brother, who is sixteen, got married and has a child, and his wife is now pregnant again. When he fights with other men, people tell him he is not a man, he is only sixteen. He tells them, "Well, I have children, I am *un hombre completo*." (C6F)

There is a final factor encouraging the early inception of fertility which merits some discussion. This is the suspicion of infidelity with which each sex tends to regard the other. The first manifestation of this is the fear that a late pregnancy may be interpreted by the male as a sign of infidelity. As one woman put it, "If she gets pregnant too late, the man may say that she is pregnant of another man and not of him." While this is a logical consequence of the infidelity phobias on the part of the male, it is infrequently mentioned. The more usual attitude on the part of both sexes, but particularly of the male, is that children tie down the spouse and make it much more difficult for her to desert.[8]

He told me the more kids I have, the more tied to him I was . . . that with so many kids I could not abandon him to go with another man or return to my family. (TRC)

[Men want children soon] so as to have their women tied to the home. (C6F)

In one case this was carried out quite methodically. The story was told independently by both husband and wife. The husband told the interviewer that he wanted no children at all.

(Then why did you have a child?) Because I got angry with my wife. Her mother took her to town and got her work as a servant. Later she came back to me full of love, and I forgave her, so she stopped working. I had that child so that she couldn't go away any more. Having a child, she was bound to stay. (B5M)

One woman opined that men wanted children soon so that they could secure their wives in the home while they themselves were able to seek other conquests.

When they have children and like to go out alone, they can do it, because they know that their wives are obliged to stay at home while they go after other women. (H23F)

With some women suspicion has the contrary effect, however. They are so uncertain that their marriages will last that they want pregnancy *delayed,* so that separation will be easier if they do not get along. The majority of women in our sample wanted a delayed pregnancy (although not put off for long), and one of the most frequent reasons given for this was "to see if the marriage will turn out all right" — an expression clearly manifesting the misgivings with which many women face marriage.[9]

The Large Family and *Machismo*

As we have already suggested, women are not greatly concerned with proving their fecundity, but the situation is quite different with men. When asked whether men in general wanted to have many or few children, 20 out of the 51 mothers who answered said that men wanted many, or that men didn't care how many they had. As seen by the women, the principal reason for this was that the men only "make" the children, the women must bear and rear them.

The kind of man who likes to have many children is the sort who says that it's the women who bear the children and raise them. The man doesn't have to care for them. That's why he doesn't object to having many. (H12F)

They don't care because they only care about making them. They don't have troubles with them. They like making a lot of them. (X7F)

I say to my husband, "When you don't expect it, you are going to have two or three more kids." And he says, "When did you ever see a man giving birth to child? It is your concern." And I say, "But you make them." (Z6F)

If it is the husband who "makes" the children, we would expect more anxiety on his part about this function, and indeed this is true. We have already discussed the sterility fears which encourage the male to produce a rapid first birth, but there may be other forces which en-

[8] Carried to its extreme, suspicion becomes hostility, and impregnation may even be used as an instrument of revenge or hostility on the part of the male. One unhappily married woman, for example, says that the only thing her husband can do to her now is to get her pregnant again; but that she is "being shrewd and not letting him touch me." In another case, a woman told of a man who impregnated his wife out of pure malice. They had agreed to use condoms, but the male tricked her by tearing them before having intercourse. Her subsequent comment might suggest that the practice may not be unique: "That's why the nurses always advise us to examine the condoms very carefully, because some men make tiny holes in them, just to get the wife pregnant. I am always very careful of that." (B8F)

[9] An even more frequently given reason for delayed pregnancy may indicate new conceptions of husband-wife relations. Twenty-nine women said they preferred a delayed pregnancy because they wanted more freedom and more opportunity to enjoy their honeymoons and subsequent husband-wife relationships. This would suggest both a growing sense of independence on the part of the women and the beginning of a tendency toward marriages resembling the companionate type.

courage him to keep producing. One of these is *machismo*.[10] Women realize this male motivation and contrast males with themselves in this regard.

Some women feel sad not having any children, but that is because they like children and not because they don't want to be called *machorras*. (And what about the husbands?) Men care more about having them; they want to know that they can have them. (X8F)

Men feel bad if they are called *machorros*. Mine likes it when another baby is coming, for he feels more *macho* if he has many. . . . He feels more of a man having many. (X3F)

Many husbands like them because there is more happiness having children. I believe sometimes they like to have children in order to prove that they are *machos*. (Z4F)

Although many men said that at least one child was needed to prove one's virility, few of them said explicitly that many were needed for this reason. A large family helps the ego in other ways, however. There are very few ways in which a lower-class male can gain prestige in a community, for he has neither the economic nor the educational capital to improve himself.[11] Completely frustrated in the economic sphere, it is all a man can do to obtain enough food to allow himself and his family to exist.[12] It is virtually impossible to purchase articles of the conspicuous-consumption variety which might gain him prestige among his peers. Children become a major showpiece. The folk saying, that "Children are the capital of the poor," may no longer reflect economic reality, but it may still reflect the function of children as evidences of conspicuous consumption. Many men, when they said that a large family gives a man prestige, appeared to mean the prestige of being able to *support* such a large family rather that that of being able to *produce* one.

It is my opinion that in order to be an *hombre completo* a man should have a wife and children, and that these should be well fed and have clothes to wear and the necessary things to live well. (Y4M)

A large family helps to prove the *hombría* of a man. (How?) Because it takes a real man to maintain and educate a large family. (B4M)

Thus, despite his lowly status and inability to advance in life, a man can prove that he is a real man after all, by showing his ability to support a large family. The female has no such motivation. Economically derived prestige is not normally a part of the feminine world. She is not expected to provide sustenance for the children. The good mother is she who takes care of the goods, including children, which are provided by the husband. Moreover, since the male "makes the children," it is the male more than the female who fears sterility. Thus, *the burden of proof both in economic and sexual sense lies with the male.*

There are several other reasons encouraging the male to high fertility, but these need only be mentioned. There are men who say that the more children one has, the surer one is of the wife's fidelity and of her inability to abandon her husband. This has already been explored in the discussion of immediate pregnancy. There

[10] This point would not appear to merit the importance it was given in the original design, where it was supposed that the need to prove one's *machismo* drove men to have large families. This does drive some men to have at least one child, but not necessarily to have many. Several men said that one or two children were enough to demonstrate that one is not sterile. The weight of the emphasis here is on *sterility* rather than on general virility or the ability to produce a large number of sons.

[11] The extraordinary amount of internal and external migration which occurs on the part of the lower class is one of the manifestations of the desire to improve one's self. Although the individual is unable to do so in the home environment, recent developments have made it possible for him to "leave the scene" and seek prestige by achievements outside the community. For an excellent account of internal migration, see R. Parke, "Internal Migration in Puerto Rico" (unpublished Master's essay, Columbia University, 1952).

[12] "Sixty-two percent [of the population] have less than the amount needed to buy a minimum adequate diet [$140 per year]" L. J. Roberts and R. L. Stefani, *Patterns of Living in Puerto Rican Families,* (Río Piedras, University of Puerto Rico, 1949, p. 13). Standards of living, however, have improved substantially in the past decade. Whereas the median annual income of wage earners' families was $360 in 1941, it rose to $919 by 1952, a 68-percent increase in real income. Puerto Rico Department of Labor, Preliminary Release No. 1, August 1953.

are also a fair number of men who hold that children give stability and responsibility to the male — "something to fight for." Perhaps this attitude mitigates the sense of hopelessness about the economic world. There is really no point in trying, since only luck can produce fortune.[13] But if one has children, one has to strive — at least to the point of providing them with food and clothing. This much can be done, and it gives the male a sense of purpose and responsibility which he otherwise would not have.

One minor factor in encouraging fertility is the requirement that the husband should have at least one male offspring. This is probably universally true of patriarchal societies, where a male is required to carry on the family line. In the lower-class society of Puerto Rico, however, the relative absence of clans, the relative isolation of the nuclear family, and the lack of land or possessions for inheritance might be expected to weaken the emphasis on the continuation of the family line. More detailed study is needed before reaching any conclusions on this point, but there is considerable evidence from the interview materials suggesting that *other* factors play a role in the desire for a male son.

One of these has already been mentioned. Since the male is the symbol of virility, male offspring are one indication of one's *machismo*. More accurately, at least one male heir is a *sine qua non* of manliness, and the producer of girls is seen as laughable. With all the predispositions toward anxiety concerning his *hombría* which we have described, the married male is particularly concerned lest he fall into the luckless group of fathers known as *chancleteros*. Moreover, since the man is seen as the "maker" of children, the production of too many *chancletas* reflects upon him.

We men want the other men to see that we can have male sons. (What about the women?) The women, too, so they can't gossip about us, saying that we make only *chancletas*. (A5M)

[13] See Padilla's discussion of gambling in the lower class: "Nocora: An Agrarian Reform Sugar Community in Puerto Rico" (unpublished Ph.D. dissertation, Columbia University, 1951), Chap. VII, pp. 10-16. The legal and illegal lottery is of immense popularity in the lower class, for it is practically the only way in which a lower-class man can amass capital in his own community.

I wanted a male son . . . so as to know I was a *macho*. (A *macho?*) Yes, to show that I am not like the men that only have females. (B5M)

Other men desire male offspring narcissistically. No women gave such reasons for desiring girls. Perhaps their own self-images are too unfavorable to allow such explicit narcissistic preferences.

I hope for boys because I like the males better, *like I am* . . . for my own self love and pride. (Y8M)

The father prefers boys, so they will *grow up like him*. So that they learn his occupation, play an instrument like him, go out and have a good time like him, and *so that they will be machos like him*. (Y4F)

I would have liked to have had my first child later, but my husband wanted a son soon. He said he was eager *to see whom he* [*the child*] *resembled*. (B1F)

Such desires could affect fertility by encouraging a rapid succession of births until at least one male offspring occurs. At each *chancleta*, a man's anxiety about his virility and his need for narcissistic fulfillment might encourage him to "keep trying" until a male son dissipates his fears.[14] How frequently this occurs we do not know. That it does occur, however, we can conclude from the statements below.

Out there lives a man who has five daughters and doesn't want to have his wife operated on until they have a son — so she goes on having children. (Z1F)

He didn't want to avoid children because he wanted a son. After the third girl he decided to have no more, but only because I begged him so much that I convinced him. . . . He said he wouldn't let me be sterilized until I had a boy. (H4F)

This attitude, of course, also leads to various difficulties in marital relations. There is no way of ascertaining how many lower-class women have been abandoned for this reason, but several statements from female respondents would suggest that this, too, occurs.

[14] One son may not be enough. High-mortality-mindedness in the lower class may lead a man to require more than one for the sake of security. See Chap. I, note 30.

When I had a still birth on the first one, he told me he was going to abandon me. Soon after I became pregnant again and had a boy, and he was glad. (C2F)

[He threatened to leave me], but after we had the male son he behaved better. (Why would that be?) He said that he would stay living with the woman who gave him a son. (H1F)

[After the first one was born a girl] he used to say that if he didn't get a boy this time he would leave me, as he didn't want any more women. (A12F)

History of Contraceptive Methods[*1]

CHRISTOPHER TIETZE

WHILE the origin of contraception antedates the dawn of history, it would appear that efforts to control fertility were relatively infrequent or ineffectual throughout most of man's long history. Since death rates were generally high in premodern societies, the population could survive only if high birth rates were encouraged and maintained by custom, law, and religion.

TRADITIONAL METHODS

Mentioned in the Old Testament (Genesis 38) and reported by anthropologists from many parts of the world (Nag 1962), the oldest contraceptive procedure known to man is believed to be coitus interruptus or withdrawal of the penis prior to ejaculation. In the western and northern Europe of the middle ages and early modern times, where relatively late marriages coexisted with close and frequent contacts between unmarried adults and with a strong condemnation of pregnancy out of wedlock, coitus interruptus appears to have been the principal method by which premarital conception was avoided (Ryder 1959). It is referred to in the *Zimmerische Chronik* (Barack 1881), written in Swabia about 1465, and in the *Vie des dames galantes* by the Seigneur de Brantôme (De Bourdelles 1841), who died in 1614, to mention only two early sources. At a later time, coitus interruptus came to be used by a large proportion of married couples. It appears certain that it was the most widely used method of contraception during the first 100 or 150 years of the decline of the birth rate in the western world, which began in France toward the end of the eighteenth century and elsewhere in the nineteenth century (Bergues et al. 1969, Kirk 1959).

Coitus interruptus has been condemned by the medical profession as an unreliable method and as damaging to health. This unfavorable opinion is, however, not supported by available evidence. Many couples continue to practice for years, not only successfully, but without apparent ill effects and with adequate sexual satisfaction for both partners.

Sponges and tampons of various kinds, placed in the vagina for purposes of contraception, are mentioned in the Tosephta, a Hebrew document edited about 230 A.D. (Himes 1963). More recently, the sponge was recommended by Francis Place in his famous, or according to certain contemporaries infamous, handbills, which were distributed in London and the North of England in 1823. Doubtless such occlusive devices have been used for a long time throughout the world, mainly among the poor and uneducated as improvised household contraceptives.

Douches with plain water, vinegar, and various products advertised under the name of "feminine hygiene" have also long been used for purposes of family limitation. The bidet made its first appearance in France early in the eighteenth cen-

* Reprinted with permission from *The Journal of Sex Research,* Vol. 1, No. 2 (July 1965), pp. 69-85.

[1] This article is the revised version of a paper presented at the International College of Surgeons Hall of Fame, Chicago, on January 12, 1965.

tury. The douche was the principal contraceptive method recommended by Dr. Charles Knowlton (1833), one of the earliest American writers on the subject, and remained a widely used method until World War II (Westoff et al. 1953). Since then, its popularity has declined markedly, at least in the United States (Freedman et al. 1959).

The condom made its first recorded appearance in the sixteenth century as a cover for the penis during intercourse, recommended as a prophylactic against veneral infection by the Italian anatomist, Fallopio (Himes 1963). This cover was made of linen and, therefore, probably not an effective contraceptive. Condoms made from the intestines of sheep and other animals first appeared in the eighteenth century. This innovation has been attributed to an Englishman named Cundum, sometimes — but erroneously — identified as a physician at the court of Charles II (Bernstein 1940).

Use of the condom on a large scale became possible after the vulcanization of rubber was invented by Goodyear and Hancock in the 1840's. Since that time, so-called "skin" condoms have gradually been replaced by cheaper and more convenient rubber sheaths which can be mass-produced on intricate machines operating around the clock. In recent years, however, the manufacture of skin condoms has been revived in the United States, catering to the affluent society.

Prior to 1938, a large proportion of the condoms sold in the United States was inferior in quality. In that year, supervision was instituted by the Food and Drug Administration, including spot checking of shipments in interstate commerce, confiscation of substandard lots, and periodic factory inspections. As a result of government supervision, the quality of condoms in the United States has greatly improved. In 1960, it was estimated that about 997 out of every 1,000 rubber condoms were free from defects demonstrable by a water leakage test (Tiezte 1960). Since condoms subjected to this test are destroyed in the process, it can be used by the manufacturer or the supervising agency on a sample basis only. However, all condoms sold in the United States are electronically tested for holes prior to packaging, a procedure which does not damage the rubber.

The condom offers protection not only against pregnancy, but also against venereal disease. Without special instruction and elaborate preparation, it can be used in almost any situation where coitus is possible. The evidence immediately after intercourse of an intact contraceptive barrier affords a gratifying assurance to many users. Because of these advantages and because of the success of the method in their own experience, the condom is often preferred by couples to whom other effective methods are also known and available. Sales of condoms in the United States were estimated a few years ago at more than 600 million units annually.

The vaginal diaphragm was invented by Wilhelm P. J. Mensinga (1882a, b), a German physician, sometime before 1882, and is still in use with relatively minor modifications. Prior to the recent introduction of oral contraceptives, the diaphragm, prescribed in combination with jelly or cream, was the contraceptive device most often recommended by physicians in private practice and in birth control clinics throughout the United States (Calderone 1963, Lafitte 1962) as well as in Europe. Because the method requires a pelvic examination by a physician or other trained health worker, such as a midwife or nurse, it is not suitable for general use in countries where medical personnel and medical facilities, such as hospitals and clinics, are not available in sufficient numbers. The diaphragm must be inserted either daily as a bedtime routine or before each intercourse. In either case, the method makes great demands on persistent and purposeful behavior, and is easily abandoned if adequate motivation is lacking or if neurotic mechanisms intervene (Lehfeldt 1959).

Some failures of the diaphragm have been reported even by women who used the device at each sexual exposure without taking any chances. A recent investigation by V. E. Johnson and W. H. Masters (1962), using the technique of artificial coitus, has thrown new light on these reports. Thirty subjects were observed in three coital positions (supine, female-superior, and knee-chest); a fourth series involved repeated coitus in individually selected combinations of positions.

The authors were able to demonstrate that the expansion of the inner two-thirds of the vaginal barrel during sexual excitement may permit the dislocation of a well-fitted diaphragm and expose the cervix to insemination. This event occurred primarily in parous women during a sequence of repeated coitus or in the female-superior position.

Chemical contraceptives consist of a compound able to immobilize sperm on contact and a vehicle for its introduction and distribution within the vagina. The spermicide represents a small fraction of the total material. The vehicle, which may also act as a mechanical barrier, is usually a semisolid or solid capable of being liquefied or dissolved in the vagina.

Various creams and jellies and, more recently, foams with highly spermacidal action, intended for use without a diaphragm, have been developed by the pharmaceutical industry. Injection into the vagina is accomplished, prior to intercourse, by means of an applicator, and no waiting period is required (Tyler 1964).

Spermicides are also used in vaginal suppositories and tablets. The former employ, as a vehicle, cocoa butter or other substances, which remain solid at room temperatures in temperate climates but melt quickly after insertion (Gamble 1964). Vaginal tablets are designed to crumble and dissolve on contact with moisture. Most brands release carbon dioxide to produce a dense foam, which is thought to serve as a mechanical barrier as well as a means of distributing the spermicidal agent. The tablet is inserted prior to intercourse and a waiting period of a few minutes is recommended. It has been shown, however, that the amount of vaginal fluid present does not always suffice to cause disintegration of the tablet (Dingle 1964).

A satisfactory contraceptive tablet must be sufficiently stable to resist deterioration, even in a hot and humid climate, and at the same time, be capable of dissolving rapidly and completely. Because vaginal tablets can be manufactured easily and cheaply and because no pelvic examination, fitting, or apparatus is needed, they have been considered eminently suitable for programs of population control in the economically underdeveloped regions of the world. However, the results of clinical and field trials have not been encouraging and it does not appear likely that this method will prove sufficiently acceptable and effective to be of great value in reducing the rate of population growth.

Spermicidal Tests

A great deal of effort has been devoted to the development of tests by which the spermicidal effectiveness of chemical contraceptives can be evaluated in vitro. All tests currently used are based on the complete immobilization of spermatozoa in samples of human semen of good quality. A majority of investigators in this field favors a type of test involving the mixing of semen and contraceptive, with or without a diluent. Spermicidal action is assessed in terms of the maximum ratio, by volume, of semen to contraceptive at which all spermatozoa are immobilized within a given time, usually 20 seconds (MacLeod et al. 1961, Int. Planned Par. 1964).

Several investigators, notably C. J. Gamble (1953), have rejected the principle of mixing semen and a contraceptive on the grounds that it is an inadequate reproduction of conditions in the vagina. Instead, they have recommended a type of test in which measured amounts of semen and of undiluted contraceptive are placed in contact without any mixing procedure. Ingredients of the spermicidal material are permitted to diffuse into the semen and the spermicidal action is assessed in terms of the time required to achieve complete immobilization of spermatozoa. Unfortunately, the ranking of contraceptive products by "diffusion tests" appears to be quite unrelated to their ranking according to "mixing tests."

The technique of artificial coitus under direct observation was also used by Johnson and Masters in an investigation of chemical contraceptives: The test involved seven representative preparations: two jellies, two creams, a foam, a foaming vaginal tablet, and a suppository. Observations were made on 30 volunteers, admittedly a small sample. Each subject read the instructions accompanying the product under investigation and inserted the material according to her interpretation of these instructions. After the material was introduced into the vagina, the subject engaged in artificial coital activity through a complete cycle of sexual response. At orgasm a previously examined seminal specimen was injected into the vagina, simulating ejaculation. Artificial coitus was repeated twice, 1 hour and

5–8 hours after the original injection of semen, without insertion of additional contraceptive material. At each occasion, six specimens were obtained at intervals ranging from 1–5 seconds to 5 minutes after insemination.

The authors found complete immobilization of sperm in all specimens obtained after the first and second insemination with the foam and with one cream and only slightly less satisfactory results with one of the jellies. It is a curious fact that the cream with the high intravaginal rating was also the most spermicidal according to three mixing tests, but relatively poor according to Gamble's diffusion test; while the most spermicidal jelly in the intravaginal study rated highest on the diffusion test and low on each of the three tests involving mixing of semen and contraceptive. The lowest ratings on the intravaginal test were obtained for the suppository and the vaginal tablet. Neither product was able to immobilize all sperm in all specimens obtained after the first insemination, and both failed in about two-thirds of all specimens obtained after the second insemination, and in almost all specimens drawn after the third insemination (Johnson & Masters 1963).

Rhythm Method

One of the oldest methods of contraception, which has been given a valid scientific foundation during the past three decades, is the rhythm method, also referred to as the safe period method and as perodic continence. The notion is very old that the human female cannot conceive during part of the menstrual cycle. However, the early ideas of what constituted the sterile period were often the direct opposite of what we now know to be correct. Following earlier writers of the Hippocratic period (5th century, B.C.), the Greek gynecologist Soranos (98–138 A.D.) recommended as a contraceptive measure abstinence from coitus during the days directly before and after menstruation (Guttmacher 1953). The same or similar advice was given by Aëtios of Amida (Himes 1963) in the sixth century and by Capellmann (1883) as late as 1883. One is not surprised to learn that these prescriptions resulted in frequent failures and it is small wonder that the entire concept of cyclic sterility fell into disrepute.

The modern form of the rhythm method was developed independently in the early 1930's by Ogino (1932) in Japan and Knaus (1933) in Austria, and is based on the fact that the ovum is released from the ovary about two weeks prior to the onset of the next menstrual flow. According to Ogino, the first fertile day is determined by subtracting 18 from the number of days in the shortest menstrual cycle observed during the preceding year, and the last fertile day, by subtracting 11 days from the longest cycle. If, for example, the observed cycles ranged from 26 days to 29 days, the fertile period would extend from the eighth day (26 minus 18) to the eighteenth day (29 minus 11) of the current cycle. The greater the difference between the shortest and longest menstrual cycle, the longer must be the period of abstinence, but even moderate irregularity of menstruation requires avoidance of sexual relations during a major portion of each cycle. Knaus recommends a period of abstention which is shorter by 3 days than that prescribed by Ogino.

The period of abstinence may be reduced by the use of a basal body temperature chart. It has long been known that body temperatures, measured with a rectal or oral thermometer each morning before arising, are higher during the later portion of the menstrual cycle than during the earlier portion. However, since the rise in temperature on the order of 0.4° C. occurs one or two days after ovulation when conception is no longer possible, a temperature chart can be used to determine when coital relations can be resumed but not to predict the day of ovulation.

Rhythm is the only method of fertility control, other than complete abstinence, currently sanctioned by the Roman Catholic Church. In the 1950's about one-half of the Catholic couples in the United States who practiced contraception in any form, limited themselves to the rhythm method; the other half used methods considered illicit by their church (Freedman et al. 1959).

The contraceptive effectiveness of the rhythm method has been the subject of much controversy. Correctly taught, correctly understood, and consistently practiced, the method may be quite effective, especially if women with grossly irregular cycles are excluded (Tietze & Potter 1962). However, successful practice requires considerable self-control, plus strong religious conviction and an equally strong desire to control fertility. Self-taught rhythm, haphazardly practiced, is a very ineffectual method of contraception and deserves its facetious designation, "Vatican roulette."

Oral Contraception

Oral contraception has long been an attractive solution to the problem of fertility control. Ancient manuscripts are replete with prescriptions for potions and other oral medications, without any rationale apparent to the modern reader. In the late 1950's the dream became a reality. The most important early work in this field was done in the United States, where the names of Gregory Pincus (1958), John Rock (1956), and other pioneers are associated with the development of "the pill" (Tyler & Olson 1959).

The compounds most intensively investigated have been the 19-nor steroids, especially norethynodrel and norethindrone. These compounds are related to the endogenous hormones, progesterone and testosterone. Given in appropriate dosages combined with an estrogen, they suppress ovulation. Two additional factors are thought to contribute to the contraceptive effect: (1) the consistency of the cervical mucus is maintained in its non-ovulatory impenetrable state, and (2) the endometrium is made unsuitable for implantation since the full secretory pattern is not reached.

Since 1956, several oral contraceptives have been extensively tested in the United States, Puerto Rico (Satterthwaite 1964) and Mexico (Rice-Wray 1963), and elsewhere. They have established themselves not only as extremely effective if taken according to prescription but also as highly acceptable to most users, including many women in the lower socio-economic strata who had been unsuccessful with other contraceptives (Frank & Tietze 1965).

Some of the women taking oral contraceptives have reported nausea and other side effects which they have attributed to the drug. In some instances, these complaints are undoubtedly psychosomatic in origin and unrelated to the medication. If the drug is stopped, the side effects disappear promptly; if it is continued, they tend to taper off within a few months. No permanent or serious side effects were noted in any of the clinical trials. Laboratory studies in some instances have revealed deviations from normal values. The significance of these changes cannot yet be evaluated. Women who discontinued the medication conceived promptly unless they resorted to other types of contraception.

In 1960, the Food and Drug Administration approved the sale of a norethynodrel-menstranol combination, on prescription, under the trade name Enovid, for purposes of contraception. In 1961 and 1962, after this product had been marketed on a large scale, a number of cases of thrombophlebitis, resulting in several deaths from pulmonary embolism, were reported among women who had taken Enovid. These reports, coinciding with the thalidomide disaster, attracted considerable attention in the daily papers with repercussions in the stock market.

In early 1963, the Food and Drug Administration convened an ad hoc advisory committee of nine experts, under the chairmanship of Dr. I. S. Wright of New York, to evaluate a possible etiologic relation of thromboembolic conditions with the use of Enovid as a contraceptive. After careful study of all available data, the committee concluded that the incidence of fatal thromboembolism was not significantly higher among users of oral contraceptives than among non-pregnant women of reproductive age. The committee recommended, however, that large-scale studies be continued and this recommendation is being carried out. So far, no unfavorable findings have been reported (Wright 1963).

Since 1962, the Food and Drug Administration has approved the sale, on prescription, of several oral contraceptive products. Each of these combines a progestin component with a considerably smaller amount of an estrogen. It has been possible, as experience has accumulated, to reduce the amount of progestin without loss of effectiveness and with a marked reduction in side effects. As a result, the retail price of oral contraceptive in the United States has dropped from about \$10 to between \$2.10 and \$2.25 per cycle (Consumers Union 1964). Abroad, the drugs are generally cheaper and it is reported that at least in one country, where oral contraceptives are imported and distributed by the government, competition between manufacturers has reduced the price to about $0.50 per month.

By mid-1964, that is, eight years after Pincus started his first field study in Puerto Rico and four years after the first commercial product became available, the number of women in the United States taking oral contraceptives had grown to an estimated 3.5 million. This figure represents about one-fourth of all couples currently practicing birth control in any form. At present no comprehensive information is available on the distribution of these users by region, age, income level, and other characteristics, nor is it known to what extent they are new contraceptors or have previously used other methods. It is expected, however, that a nationwide survey later this year will furnish much needed information.

Intra-Uterine Contraception

While research in oral contraceptives is continuing all over the world, another method has become the focus of attention of those who are primarily interested in the demographic and public health aspects of birth control, rather than in its application by the individual couple. I am referring to the intra-uterine contraceptive devices or IUCD which have been my particular concern over the past two years.

Once more it can be said that the idea has been around for some time. Various types of intra-uterine, or more accurately intracervical, devices were used in the nineteenth century. Among the better known were those in the shape of collar buttons or wishbones. All had their defenders, but the majority of gynecologists rejected them as abortefacients and because their use was associated, at least in untrained hands, with inflammatory conditions of the pelvic organs which in those days were difficult to treat and, not infrequently, fatal.

Early in the twentieth century, a German physician, R. Richter (1909) of Waldenburg, described and recommended the insertion of two or three strands of silkworm gut into the uterine cavity. This contribution remained almost unnoticed. Twenty years later, Ernst Gräfenberg (1928, 1930) of Berlin reported on his experience with silkworm gut rolled into rings. A further modification, a pliable coil of silver wire, became widely known as the Gräfenberg ring. After a brief flurry of popularity, opposition to the new device again developed rapidly and universally among gynecologists, the majority of whom had never had any experience with it, but judged it in terms of what they had been taught about its forerunners. In fact, the reaction was so severe that, with a single exception (Halton et al. 1948), no reports on IUCD appeared anywhere in the medical literature of western countries between 1934 and 1959. Textbooks of gynecology, if they discussed contraception at all, mentioned the Gräfenberg ring only to condemn it.

In 1959, two papers on intra-uterine devices appeared in two widely separated countries. The highly respected *American Journal of Obstetrics and Gynecology* published a report by W. Oppenheimer (1959) of Israel; the other paper was by A. Ishihama (1959) of Japan. Intra-uterine contraception had been used on a modest scale in Japan since 1934, when T. Ota described his modification of the Gräfenberg ring, consisting of an outer coil with a small, hollow, lentil-shape capsule suspended in the center from three radial springs. This device, known as the Ota ring, is still used in Japan, with a flat disk substituted for the hollow capsule. Both Oppenheimer and Ishihama reported low pregnancy rates and the absence of any serious side effects.

In 1962, H. Hall and M. Stone (1962) of New York City published a paper on their experience with a replica of the Gräfenberg ring made of coiled stainless steel wire. Hall had been a close associate of Gräfenberg for a number of years. Hall and Stone, like their Israeli and Japanese colleagues, also reported low pregnancy rates and no serious side effects.

In the meantime (1960), L. C. Margulies (1962, 1964) of Mt. Sinai Hospital in New York City, who had been experimenting for some time with a variety of shapes and plastic materials, designed his spiral of linear polyethylene. At about the same time, J. Lippes (1965) of the University of Buffalo School of Medicine started to use plastic Ota rings from which he had removed the central disk. His experience with the Ota ring led him to develop a new device of polyethylene in the shape of a double S, now known as the loop. A third type of plastic IUCD, developed by C. Birnberg (1964) of New York City, consists of two triangles, one slightly larger than the other, joined at the apexes, and resembling a bow. Independently of the work done in the United States, J. Zipper (1962) in Santiago, Chile, developed his own device, made from about 2 meters of nylon thread, hand-rolled into a ring with a diameter of 25 mm.

Unlike the Gräfenberg silver ring, which required periodic removal, the new plastic IUCD, as well as the stainless steel ring, can remain in the uterus indefinitely. The flexibility of the plastic devices used in the United States also permits a simple insertion technique, first developed by Margulies, by which they are stretched full length within a narrow plastic tube and resume their original shape upon extrusion from the inserter into the uterine cavity.

The IUCD of Margulies, Lippes, and Zipper are equipped with an appendage or "tail" which extends through the cervical canal into the vagina. The tail of the spiral is a polyethylene stem with seven small beads, which are cut off so that only one is allowed to emerge from the cervical os. A thin double thread is attached to the loop, while the appendage of Zipper's ring is a part of the nylon thread constituting the device itself. These tails make it easy to remove the IUCD and make it possible for the user, as well as the physician, to determine whether it is in place. Birnberg's plastic bow and the stainless steel ring, neither of which has an appendage, must be removed with an instrument, and require probing or x-ray to determine their presence.

In the Spring of 1962, the First International Conference on Intra-Uterine Contraception was held in New York City under the auspices of the Population Council (Tietze & Lewit 1962). The consensus of the 40 or so attending physicians, who came from 11 countries in all parts of the world, as to the effectiveness, acceptability, and safety of the IUCD was so encouraging that a number of new clinical and laboratory studies were initiated. The great majority of these studies has received financial support from the Population Council, which has made grants in this field totaling about two million dollars. When the Second International Conference on Intra-Uterine Contraception was held in New York City in October, 1964, again under the auspices of the Population Council, interest in and experience with this method of contraception had become so widespread that attendance exceeded 500, including physicians, biologists, social scientists, administrators, and others from more than 40 countries (Segal & Southam 1964).

In mid-1963, a cooperative statistical program for the evaluation of clinical data was inaugurated by the Population Council as a part of its broad investigation of intra-uterine contraception. Responsibility for this program has been assigned to the National Committee on Maternal Health, which, up to the present time, has accumulated individual case records of almost 25,000 women, submitted by 41 participating institutions and investigators in private practice, and covering approximately 245,000 woman-months of use.

In order to present data of maximum comparability and relevance on the four most intensively studied devices currently considered appropriate for parous women (spiral, loop, bow, and steel ring), Table 1 is restricted to experience following first insertions performed in hospitals and extramural clinics in the United States, including Puerto Rico. All reinsertions and all investigators in private practice or in foreign countries have been excluded (Tietze 1965).

All rates shown here refer to events during the first year after insertion and are computed per 100 cases, using a life table procedure. In interpreting the pregnancy rates, it should be remembered that they were obtained in a clinical research program under which most patients are seen by the investigators at shorter intervals than would be feasible either in private practice or in a public health setting. These frequent visits favor early detection of expulsions not noticed by wearer. It can be shown, however, that even without any routine check-ups whatsoever, pregnancy rates would not be more than about twice the levels actually observed.

Expulsions include complete expulsions into or from the vagina and partial expulsions requiring removal from the cervix. Two sets of expulsion rates are shown — one excludes and

TABLE 1

Numbers of First Insertions of Four Intra-Uterine Devices and Cumulative Rates of Pregnancies, Expulsions, Removals, and Pelvic Inflammatory Disease during First Year per 100 Cases

	Spiral	Loop	Bow	Ring
Number of insertions	2,654	5,326	2,085	1,157
Rate per 100 cases:				
Pregnancies	1.8 ± 0.4	2.4 ± 0.3	5.7 ± 2.1	7.5 ± 1.4
Expulsions				
Low estimate	21.8 ± 0.9	9.3 ± 0.5	1.1 ± 0.2	15.8 ± 1.4
High estimate	22.5 ± 1.0	9.9 ± 0.5	2.4 ± 0.4	18.2 ± 1.5
Removals				
Medical reasons	22.4 ± 1.0	13.7 ± 0.6	9.1 ± 1.5	9.3 ± 1.4
Personal reasons	3.3 ± 0.5	1.9 ± 0.3	2.0 ± 1.1	0.9 ± 0.4
Pelvic inflammatory disease	3.9 ± 0.5	1.7 ± 0.2	2.2 ± 0.4	3.2 ± 0.8

the other includes all expulsions followed by pregnancy. Because of the difficulty of determining the presence or absence of a tailless device, it is likely that for the Birnberg bow and the steel ring the lower estimate of the expulsion rate is too low and the higher one, too high.

The medical reasons for removal range from medical necessity, as perceived by the investigator, to complaints interpreted as related to the IUCD by the patient or her family physician. They also include preexisting and intercurrent conditions requiring treatment, but clearly unrelated to the use of the device. The most frequently reported reasons were bleeding (including spotting) and pain (including cramps, backache, and other kinds of discomfort). These two reasons, frequently reported together, accounted for about seven out of ten removals on medical grounds. Removals for medical reasons also include a small number of cases of discomfort to the male partner, attributed to the transcervical appendage of an IUCD, and all instances of pregnancy at insertion.

The personal reasons for removal include all those considered relevant to the acceptability of intra-uterine contraception: fear of injury or cancer, lack of confidence, objections by husband or family physician (without a specific complaint), religious scruples, and a small group of removals at the patient's request without further explanation.

Devices were also removed because a pregnancy was desired, protection was no longer needed, or the patient departed from the locality of the study. Other removals were incidental to research procedures, such as endometrial biopsy, or the replacement of a device by another type or size considered more effective. Since none of these reasons is relevant to the acceptability of intra-uterine contraception, the removals assigned to them are not included in the computation of removal rates.

The rates shown for pelvic inflammatory disease (PID) are based on a total of 193 cases. Of these, 46 were designated by the investigators as severe, 115 as mild, and 32 as doubtful. In more than one-half of these cases the IUCD was allowed to remain in situ while the infection was treated with antibiotics. Information is not available on the incidence of PID among women not wearing intra-uterine devices in the populations from which the patients were drawn.

One of the most important aspects of the IUCD which remains to be clarified is their mode of action. At the Second International Conference on Intra-Uterine Contraception it was brought out that the devices apparently do not interfere with ovulation, nor with the entry of sperm into the fallopian tubes. Their normal modus operandi is certainly not interference with the implanted embryo. All we can say at the moment is that the point of impact is somewhere between fertilization and implantation, both included.

The importance of the IUCD lies in the fact that they represent the only known fully reversible method of fertility control, requiring only the decision to have the device inserted, rather than the sustained motivation of one or both sexual partners. Intelligent and well-adjusted couples of the "private patient" type must not expect a higher degree of protection against pregnancy from the IUCD than they can achieve by the consistent use of traditional contraceptives, such as the condom or the diaphragm, and they will certainly be less well protected by the IUCD than by the orals. However, the choice of a contraceptive method is a matter for individual decision and each couple must assess the advantages and disadvantages in terms of its own needs.

The situation is quite different in populations not accustomed to the contraceptive way of life, whether they reside in an Indian village or in an American slum. In this type of population one would expect in the course of a year 20 to 40 conceptions per 100 couples using traditional methods, but only 2 or 3 with the more successful types of IUCD. This is an enormous difference in personal as well as demographic terms and justifies the hope that a real breakthrough in the population problem is now within man's reach.

BIBLIOGRAPHY

Barack, K. A. (ed.). *Zimmerische Chronik*, 2nd ed. Freiburg i.B. & Tübingen: Mohr, 1881–82, vol. 4, p. 10.

Bergues, H., Hélin, E., Henry L., Riquet, M., Sauvy, A., and Sutter, J. *La prévention des naissances dans la famille: ses origines dans les temps modernes.* Paris: Presses universitaires de France, 1960, p. 382.

Bernstein, E. L. "Who was Condom?," *Human Fertility, 5:* 172–175 and 186, Dec. 1940.

Birnberg, C. H., and Burnhill, M. S. "A new intrauterine contraceptive device," *American Journal of Obstetrics and Gynecology, 89:* 137–138, 1 May 1964.

Calderone, M. S. "Impact of new methods on practice in 73 Planned Parenthood Centers," *Seventh International Conference on Planned Parenthood*, 169–174, 1963.

Capellmann, C. F. N. *Fakultative Sterilität ohne Verletzung der Sittengesetze.* Aachen: Barth, 1883.

Consumers Union. "Progress in family planning," *Consumer Reports, 29:* 400–403, Aug. 1964.

de Bourdelles, P. *Vie de dames galantes par le seigneur de Brantôme. Paris:* Garnier, 1841, p. 36.

Dingle, J. T. "Vaginal foam tablets," *Manual of Contraceptive Practice* (M. S. Calderone, ed.), 190–195. Baltimore: Williams & Wilkins, 1964.

Frank, R., and Tietze, C. "Acceptance of an oral contraceptive program in a large metropolitan area," *American Journal of Obstetrics and Gynecology*, in press.

Freedman, R., Whelpton, P. K., and Campbell, A.A. *Family Planning, Sterility, and Population Growth.* New York: McGraw Hill, 1959, p. 176.

Gamble, C. J. "An improved test of spermicidal activity without dilution or mixing," *Journal of the American Medical Association, 152:* 1037–1041, 11 July 1953.

Gamble, C. J. "Suppositories," *Manual of Contraceptive Practice* (M. S. Calderone, ed.), 199–200. Baltimore: Williams & Wilkins, 1964.

Gräfenberg, E. "Silk als Antikonzipiens," *Geburtenregelung: Vorträge und Verhandlungen des Ärztekursus vom 28–30. Dezember 1928* (K. Bendix, ed.). 50–64. Berlin: Selbstverlag.

Gräfenberg, E. "An intrauterine contraceptive method," *Seventh International Birth Control Conference*, 33–47, 1930.

Guttmacher, A. F. "Early attitudes toward infertility," *Fertility and Sterility, 4:* 250–262, July–Aug. 1953.

Hall, H. H., and Stone, M. L. "Observations on the use of the intrauterine pessary, with special reference to the Grafenberg ring," *American Journal of Obstetrics and Gynecology, 83:* 683–688, 1 Mar. 1962.

Halton, M., Dickinson, R. L., and Tietze, C. "Contraception with an intrauterine silk coil," *Human Fertility, 13:* 10–13, Mar. 1948.

Himes, N. E. *Medical History of Contraception.* New York: Gamut Press, 1963, pp. 72–75, 94–96, 188–190.

International Planned Parenthood Federation. *Medical Handbook. Part I: Contraception*, 2nd ed. London, 1964, pp. 69–77.

Ishihama, A. "Clinical studies on intrauterine rings, especially the present state of contraception in Japan and the experiences in the use of intrauterine rings," *Yokohama Medical Bulletin, 10:* 89–105, Apr. 1959.

Johnson, V. E., and Masters, W. H. "Intravaginal contraceptive study: anatomy," *Western Journal of Surgery, Obstetrics and Gynecology, 70:* 202–207, July–Aug. 1962.

Johnson, V. E., and Masters, W. H. "Intravaginal contraceptive study: physiology," *Western Journal of Surgery, Obstetrics and Gynecology, 71:* 144–153, May–June, 1963.

Kirk, D. "Possible lessons from historical experience for family planning programmes in Asia," *Sixth International Conference on Planned Parenthood*, 63–67, 1959.

Knaus, H. "Die periodische Frucht- und Unfruchtbarkeit des Weibes," *Zentralblatt fur Gynäkologie, 57:* 1393–1408, 17 June 1933.

Knowlton, C. *The Fruits of Philosophy.* Boston: Kneeland, 1833.

Lafitte, F. "The users of birth control clinics," *Population Studies, 16:* 12–30, July 1962.

Lehfeldt, H. "Willful exposure to unwanted pregnancy (WEUP): psychological explanation for patient failures in contraception," *American Journal of Obstetrics and Gynecology, 78:* 661–665, Sept. 1959.

Lippes, J. "A study of intra-uterine contraception: development of a plastic loop," *Intra-Uterine Contraceptive Devices* (C. Tietze, S. Lewit, eds.), 69–75. Amsterdam: Excerpta Medica International Congress Series #54, 1962.

Lippes, J. "Contraception with intrauterine plastic loops," *American Journal of Obstetrics and Gynecology*, in press.

MacLeod, J., Sobrero, A. J., and Inglis, W. "In vitro assessment of commercial contraceptive jellies and creams," *Journal of the American Medical Association, 176:* 427–431, 6 May 1961.

Margulies, L. C. "Permanent reversible contraception with an intra-uterine plastic spiral (perma-spiral)," *Intra-Uterine Contraceptive Devices* (C. Tietze, S. Lewit, eds.), 61–68. Amsterdam: Excerpta Medica International Congress Series #54, 1962.

Margulies, L. C. "Intrauterine contraception: a new approach," *Obstetrics and Gynecology, 24:* 515–520, Oct. 1964.

Mensinga, W. P. J. (pseudonym C. Hasse). *Ueber facultative Sterilität beleuchtet vom prophylactischen und hygienischen Standpunkte für practische Aerzte.* Neuwied & Leipzig: Heuser, 1882a.

Mensinga, W. P. J. *Das Pessarium Occlusivum und dessen Application.* Neuwied & Leipzig: Heuser, 1882b.

Nag, M. *Factors Affecting Human Fertility in Nonindustrial Societies: A Cross-Cultural Study. New Haven:* Yale University Publications in Anthropology #66, 1962, p. 130.

Ogino, K. "Über den Konzeptionstermin des Weibes und seine Anwendung in der Praxis," *Zentralblatt für Gynäkologie, 56:* 721–732, 1932.

Oppenheimer, W. "Prevention of pregnancy by the Graefenberg ring method," *American Journal of Obstetrics and Gynecology, 78:* 446–454, Aug. 1959.

Pincus, G., Rock, J., Garcia, C-R., Rice-Wray, E., Paniagua, M., and Rodriguez, I. "Fertility control with oral medication," *American Journal of Obstetrics and Gynecology, 75:* 1333–1346, June 1958.

Rice-Wray, E. "Oral contraception in Latin America," *Seventh International Conference on Planned Parenthood*, 358–368, 1963.

Richter, R. "Ein Mittel zur Verhütung der Konzeption." *Deutsche medizinische Wochenschrift, 35:* 1525–1527, 2 Sept. 1909.

Rock, J., Pincus, G., and Garcia, C-R. "Effects of certain 19-nor steroids on the normal human menstrual cycle," *Science, 124:* 891–893, 2 Nov. 1956.

Ryder, N. B. "Fertility," *The Study of Population* (P. M. Hauser, O. D. Duncan, eds.), 400–436. Chicago: University of Chicago Press, 1959.

Satterthwaite, A. P. "A comparative study of low dosage oral contraceptives," *Applied Therapeutics, 6:* 410–418, May 1964.

Segal, S. J., and Southam, A. L. (eds.). *Intra-Uterine Contraception. Proceedings of the Second International Conference, New York City, 2–3 Oct., 1964.* Amsterdam: Excerpta Medica International Congress Series #86.

Tietze, C. *The Condom as a Contraceptive.* New York: National Committee on Maternal Health, 1960, p. 17.

Tietze, C., and Lewit, S. (eds.), *Intra-Uterine Contraceptive Devices. Proceedings of the Conference, New York City, 30 Apr.–1 May, 1962.* Amsterdam: Excerpta Medica International Congress Series #54, pp. 154.

Tietze, C., and Potter, R. G. "Statistical evaluation of the rhythm method," *American Journal of Obstetrics and Gynecology, 84:* 692–698, 1 Sept. 1962.

Tietze, C. *Fifth Progress Report of the Cooperative Statistical Program for the Evaluation of Intra-Uterine Contraceptive Devices.* New York: National Committee on Maternal Health, 1965.

Tyler, E. T., and Olson, H. J. "Fertility promoting and inhibiting effects of new steroid hormonal substances," *Journal of the American Medical Association, 169:* 1843–1854, 18 Apr. 1959.

Tyler, E. T. "Jels, creams, and aerosol foams," *Manual of Contraceptive Practice* (M. S. Calderone, ed.), 187–190. Baltimore: Williams & Wilkins, 1964.

Tyler, E. T. "Current status of oral contraception," *Journal of the American Medical Association, 187:* 562–565, 22 Feb. 1964.

Westoff, C. F., Herrera, L. F., and Whelpton, P. K. "The use, effectiveness, and acceptability of methods of fertility control," *Milbank Memorial Fund Quarterly, 31:* 291–357, July 1953.

Wright, I. S. (chm.). "FDA report on Enovid: Ad Hoc Advisory Committee for the evaluation of a possible etiologic relation with thromboembolic conditions," *Journal of the American Medical Association, 182:* 140, 7 Sept. 1963.

Zipper, J. A., and Sanhueza, H. D. "Clinical experience with the use of a flexible nylon ring (Gräfenberg ring) as a contraceptive technique," *Intra-Uterine Contraceptive Devices* (C. Tietze, S. Lewit, eds.), 57–59. Amsterdam: Excerpta Medica International Congress Series #54, 1962.

*The Family as a Factor in Migration**

Henry S. Shryock

An illustrative list of reasons for moving was given previously. Some are economic and some are personal or social. It seems likely that many decisions are based on consideration of both economic and noneconomic factors and that what is known about the present residence is compared with what is known about one or more addresses or areas of potential residence. The relative importance of the various reasons must vary according to type of move (farm to farm, city to suburb, one city to another, etc.), distance spanned, and geographic stream. The data that have been analyzed thus far in this book provide only a few suggestions; they do not quantify the importance of various reasons even in the simplest conceptual terms.

Comparative net migrations for various geographic areas and residence types tend to be consistent with the frequently-made generalization that migration is from areas of lower consumer income and lower levels of living to those where these are higher. Some of the rapidly industrializing areas in the South and Southwest are now attracting migrants from other regions. The often nearly equal size of counterstreams suggest that much migration cannot be explained by over-all economic differentials among areas. These counterstreams may arise from a variety of causes: (1) return migration by workers who failed to improve their lot or who had personal reasons bringing them home; (2) the existence of "subuniverses" of economic opportunity, which differ according to industry, occupation, race, sex, age, and so on; (3) noneconomic reasons; (4) imperfect knowledge of relative opportunities in two areas. I recall a hitchhiking trip during the Depression on which I met two different groups of young textile workers — one headed from New England to North Carolina, the other in the opposite direction. Neither group had job prospects at their destination, but both felt that conditions were bound to be better there.

The international literature on urbanization and the rural exodus is replete with references to greater cultural advantages in the cities, greater opportunities for education, bright lights and excitement, anomie and escape from primary-group ties. The migration of Negroes out of the South has obviously been stimulated by prospects of more social freedom as well as of greater economic opportunities. Migration to such areas as Southern California, Arizona, the Gulf Coast, Florida, and other pleasant and healthful areas is motivated in large part by climatic factors and the accessibility of the seashore, lakes, and mountains.[1] Most of the men moving to such areas are of working age, and possibly many have been willing to forego some of their earning potential for the sake of these noneconomic attractions.

Several major studies have been made on an ecological basis relating net and gross migration and the characteristics of migrants to the economic characteristics of areas and to changing economic conditions over time.[2] These deal with some of the causes of migration but contain no

* Reprinted with permission from Henry S. Shryock, *Population Mobility Within the United States.* Chicago: Community and Family Study Center, 1964, pp. 403-409 and 411-425.

[1] Ullman, Edward L. "Amenities as a Factor in Regional Growth," *Geographical Review,* 44(1):119-132, January 1954.

[2] Notably: Carter Goodrich, *et al. Migration and Economic Opportunity,* Philadelphia: University of Pennsylvania Press, 1936.

C. E. Lively and Conrad Taeuber. *Rural Migration in the United States,* Works Progress Administration, Research Monograph XIX, Washington, Government Printing Office, 1939.

Hope T. Eldridge, et al. *Population Redistribution and Economic Growth, United States: 1870-1950.* Volume III, Philadelphia, American Philosophical Society. (Forthcoming) direct material on the motivation of individual migrants. There are also a few studies that have used interviews in which the movers themselves have been asked about their reasons for moving.[3] These have typically dealt with fairly specific groups or streams: Negro migrants from St. Helena Island (S. C.) to Harlem, movers within the Philadelphia metropolitan area or the Milwaukee metropolitan area, out-migration of high school graduates from a rural Mississippi community, families in the transient relief program of the Federal Emergency Relief Administration.

In the Current Population Survey of October 1946, the Bureau of the Census collected the first, and until 1963 the only, data on reasons for migration given by a national sample of migrants. Intracounty movers were not included. The period covering the 14 months from V-J Day (14 August 1945) was one of very high migration, as already implied. Only the last move as a civilian was counted, but, even so, many of the moves were made by veterans in the process of settling down. A check list was used in asking for reasons, but there was an opportunity to give other reasons.

In analyzing the reasons given, it is necessary to make a fundamental distinction between two types of migrants — those persons who made the basic decisions either for themselves alone or for their families as well as those whose migration was merely derivative from a decision made by the head of the family. We may refer to these two classes as "primary" and "secondary" migrants, respectively. In the latter type, I have also included persons who migrated to join the head of the family, often a man still in the armed forces or recently discharged from the armed forces. This last was a reason volunteered by respondents; it was not listed on the schedule.

From Table 1 it may seem that more than half of the migrants were of the secondary type. For only about 4 percent of the children under 14 was a primary reason given (for example, one connected with their schooling). Among adult males, however, more than 9 out of 10 were primary migrants. The proportion of primary migrants among females rose to 36 percent in the age group 14 to 24, fell to 23 in the age group 25 to 44, and then rose again to 43 percent in later life. This profile must reflect the typical transition of females through four stages of family status: (1) dependency on the father, (2) independence in the period between leaving school and marriage, (3) dependency on the husband, or at least having a residence in a general area that is selected on the basis of his economic interests, and (4) widowhood, with increased independence of choice. That form of secondary migration that involved joining the head of the family — rather than moving with him — was somewhat more typical of interstate than of intrastate migration; otherwise, differences in broad type of reason were slight as between interstate and intrastate migrants.

If we confine our attention to the "primary" migrants, the importance of economic reasons becomes very evident (Table 2). In particular, 40 percent of all primary migrants moved to take a job and 12 percent to look for work, making a total of about half. "Taking a job" includes obtaining a new job before moving as well as having one's old job transferred to a new location. The "other reasons" undoubtedly included such work-associated causes as losing one's job and retirement. "To take a job" accounts for its maximal proportion of migration in the prime working years from 25 to 44. "To look for work" is a little more important, relatively, in the younger ages when there are presumably fewer family ties to impede a person from migrating without an advance commitment of a job in the destination community. Within each broad age group, job-connected reasons account for a much larger proportion of migration among males than among females. Among males, looking for work accounted for

[3] For example: Clyde V. Kiser. *Sea Island to City: A Study of St. Helena Islanders in Harlem and Other Urban Centers.* New York: Columbia University Studies in History, Economics and Public Law No. 368, 1932.

Peter H. Rossi. *Why Families Move: A Study in the Social Psychology of Urban Residential Mobility,* Glencoe, Illinois: The Free Press, 1955.

Harald A. Pedersen and Willis Joe Robertson. "Migration of High School Graduates from a Mississippi Community," *Mississippi Quarterly,* November 1954: 7-10.

John N. Webb and Malcolm Brown. *Migrant Families,* Works Progress Administration, Research Monograph XVIII, Washington, Government Printing Office, 1938.

TABLE 1

Percent Distribution by Type of Reason for Last Civilian Move of Migrants in the Civilian Noninstitutional Population, by Veteran Status, Type of Last Civilian Move, Age, and Sex, for the United States: August 1945 to October 1946

(Percent not shown where base is less than 100,000; the sum of the reasons reported (10,805,000) was slightly greater than the total number of migrants since some migrants reported more than one reason for their last civilian move, but it is assumed here that persons did not give both a primary and a secondary reason)

Sex: veteran status, and reason for last civilian move	Total*	Age				Type of move	
		Under 14 years	14 to 24 years	25 to 44 years	45 years and over	Within a State	Between States
Total migrants (000's).......	10,717	3,126	2,354	3,801	1,437	5,532	5,016
Primary reason...........	43.7	3.9	49.3	60.5	69.1	43.3	41.4
To join head of family....	5.0	6.0	6.6	5.1	0.3	2.3	7.4
Moved with head.........	52.3	90.1	44.1	34.4	30.6	54.4	51.2
Male migrants (000's).......	5,022	1,554	867	1,889	713	2,655	2,300
Primary reason...........	64.2	4.6	71.6	98.3	95.5	63.4	65.2
To join head of family....	2.2	6.8	0.3	...	...	1.0	3.0
Moved with head.........	33.6	88.6	28.1	1.7	4.5	35.6	31.8
Veteran (000's)...........	1,501	...	463	1,004	35	768	732
Primary reason.........	96.6	...	93.5	97.9	...	96.0	97.3
To join head of family..	...	...	...	...	...	...	...
Moved with head.......	3.4	...	6.5	2.1	...	4.0	2.7
Nonveteran (000's).......	3,521	1,554	404	885	679	1,887	1,568
Primary reason.........	50.5	4.6	46.3	98.6	95.3	50.1	50.2
To join head of family..	3.1	6.8	0.7	...	...	1.4	4.4
Moved with head.......	46.4	88.6	53.0	1.4	4.7	48.5	45.4
Female migrants (000's).....	5,695	1,572	1,487	1,912	724	2,877	2,715
Primary reason...........	23.6	3.3	36.2	23.2	43.0	24.6	21.2
To join head of family....	7.6	5.2	10.3	10.1	0.6	3.6	11.2
Moved with head.........	68.8	91.5	53.5	66.7	56.4	71.8	67.6

* Including 170,000 movers from outside continental United States, not shown separately.
Source: P-20, No. 4, Table 2.

a notably larger proportion of interstate than of intrastate migration whereas the corresponding difference for taking a job was slight. This association between long-distance migration and looking for work suggests that this reason represents a fairly large number of migrants who could be described either as "adventurous" or as "improvident," depending on one's point of view.

"Housing problems" were probably a relatively more important reason for migration in the period of critical shortage following World War II than they would be today. About one-seventh of all primary migrants gave this reason. As we should expect, housing problems accounted for a much larger share of intrastate than of interstate migration and certainly must have been a very important factor in intra-county mobility. The relative importance of this factor tended to increase with age, but the increase was sharpest in the transition from youth

TABLE 2

Percent Distribution by Reason for Last Civilian Move of Primary Migrants in the Civilian Noninstitutional Population, by Veteran Status. Type of Last Civilian Move, Age, and Sex, for the United States: August 1945 to October 1946

(Percent not shown where base is less than 100,000. The cases tallied are actually reasons given, but the number of these is only slightly above the number of migrants)

Sex, veteran status, and reason for last civilian move	Age					Type of move	
	Total*	Under 14 years	14 to 24 years	25 to 44 years	45 years and over	Within a State	Between States
Total primary migrants (000's)..	4,661	152	1,183	2,321	1,005	2,423	2,126
To take a job..............	40.2	0.7	29.4	51.7	32.4	40.7	41.5
To look for work...........	11.7	...	15.0	12.9	7.1	8.3	15.6
Housing problems...........	14.7	4.6	9.6	16.1	18.8	20.4	8.8
Change in marital status......	10.1	...	23.2	7.2	3.2	9.9	9.8
Health.....................	2.9	1.3	0.8	2.1	7.4	1.6	4.4
Other reasons..............	20.4	93.4	22.1	10.0	31.1	19.1	19.9
Male primary migrants (000's)...	3,277	86	634	1,869	689	1,698	1,531
To take a job..............	49.9	...	38.8	59.3	40.5	49.3	51.9
To look for work...........	13.2	...	18.0	13.4	9.6	8.5	17.6
Housing problems...........	15.0	...	10.4	15.6	19.3	22.0	7.8
Change in marital status......	3.5	...	10.6	2.4	0.3	4.0	2.7
Health.....................	2.7	...	0.8	1.7	7.8	1.4	4.3
Other reasons..............	15.7	...	21.5	7.7	22.5	14.8	15.7
Veteran (000's).............	1,462	...	437	989	34	739	723
To take a job............	53.8	...	40.3	60.6	...	51.0	56.7
To look for work..........	13.5	...	16.2	12.2	...	10.3	16.7
Housing problems.........	14.8	...	11.7	16.6	...	22.2	7.5
Change in marital status....	5.9	...	11.4	3.6	...	6.8	5.0
Health...................	1.0	...	0.2	0.8	...	0.5	1.4
Other reasons............	11.0	...	20.1	6.2	...	9.2	12.7
Nonveteran (000's)..........	1,816	86	196	880	653	962	809
To take a job............	46.6	...	35.7	57.8	40.9	47.8	47.6
To look for work..........	12.9	...	21.9	14.8	9.2	7.3	18.3
Housing problems.........	15.2	...	7.7	14.4	20.1	21.9	8.0
Change in marital status....	1.5	...	8.7	1.0	0.3	1.9	0.6
Health...................	4.1	...	1.5	2.6	7.5	2.0	7.0
Other reasons............	19.6	...	24.5	9.3	22.1	19.1	18.4
Female primary migrants (000's)	1,382	65	549	452	317	724	598
To take a job..............	17.5	...	18.6	20.6	14.8	20.4	14.9
To look for work...........	8.4	...	11.5	10.8	1.6	7.6	10.4
Housing problems...........	13.7	...	8.6	18.4	17.7	16.7	11.5
Change in marital status......	26.0	...	37.9	26.8	9.5	23.8	28.1
Health.....................	3.1	...	0.7	3.8	6.6	2.2	4.5
Other reasons..............	31.3	...	22.8	19.7	49.8	29.3	30.6

* Including 110,000 movers from outside continental United States, not shown separately.
Source: P-20, No. 4, Table 2.

to the ages in which married couples are establishing themselves in their own homes.

At each age, "change in marital status" was a more important reason for females than for males. Of women and girl migrants in the age groups 14 to 24 years, about three out of eight gave this reason. Among women we do not find the expected inverse association with distance spanned, but marriages in this period of demobilization were probably associated with an unusual amount of interstate migration. Certainly a change in marital status accounted for a much larger proportion of local moves, but such moves were not covered by this survey. The rather low proportions of older people giving this reason and the high proportion giving other reasons suggest that respondents tended to interpret "change in marital status" too narrowly — that is, as referring to marriage but not to widowhood and divorce. About half of female migrants 45 years old and over gave reasons other than those specified on the schedule.

The importance of health as a factor tended to increase with age but did not exceed 8 percent in any of the groups shown in the table. The fact that this reason figured more prominently in interstate than in intrastate migration suggests that what was typically sought was a change of climate rather than avoidance of some unfavorable aspect of the specific local environment.

The foregoing analysis is in terms of the proportion of migrants in a specified population subgroup who gave the indicated reason for their migration. As we already know, the subgroups have different migration rates from all causes combined. An example will bring out the point. Among nonveteran males who were primary migrants, housing problems were the reason given by 20 percent of those 45 years old and over and 14 percent of those 25 to 44 years old. In the male nonveteran population 45 years old and over, however, 0.7 percent migrated because of housing problems as compared with 1.0 percent of the corresponding population in the younger age group.

This discussion of reasons has been confined to migrants since intracounty movers were not covered by the survey. Job factors undoubtedly figured less prominently in these local moves whereas housing and changes of marital status figured more prominently. Studies by Rossi, Dewey, Martin, and others suggest that local mobility is closely associated with the family cycle. The newly-married couple usually start out in their own quarters although in some cases there is a period of living "doubled up" with relatives. Thus, there is usually a move for both partners, either at the time of marriage or shortly thereafter. The periods of increasing family income and increasing family size overlap to a considerable degree, and these factors typically lead to a move to more commodious quarters. In our predominantly metropolitan society, this move will frequently be from a down-town apartment to a detached house in the suburbs. The quality of the local schools, as well as other aspects of the local environment, is given considerable weight when choosing a new home. By the time the children are of high-school age, the family members have many strong ties with their community and the husband is firmly established in a job where his seniority and retirement rights are very important to him. At this stage of the family cycle, the forces making for residential stability are much stronger than those for mobility. When the size of the family shrinks as children leave home to take jobs or to marry or as the older members die, there should be more reasons for moving again. The home may be too large for the needs of the remaining members, the family income may be less, and it may be physically very difficult for the old couple, or the widow, to keep up the place. At this stage, we should expect some moves back into smaller quarters, to "double up" with married children, or to enter an institution.

The effects of this typical family life cycle upon mobility can indeed be traced to some extent from our cross-sectional data for persons classified by age, sex, marital status, and family status. There is only a fairly small rise in mobility among the elderly, however. Either the plausible reasons just given for their moving have had but slight impact; or there is, at the same time, a partially offsetting reduction of the other reasons for moving. The association with marriage is more apparent. Annual statistics compiled by the National Vital Statistics Division on marriages by age of bride permit some rough estimates of the importance of this factor for women. Let us assume that all women who marry change their address. Then by dividing the number of brides of a given age by the total number of women of the same age who were movers (as reported in the April 1957 C. P. S.), estimates are obtained of the proportion of these movers who moved at the time of marriage. The results are as follows: 18 to 19, about one-half; 20 to 21, about one-third; 22 to 24, about one-fifth; and 25 to 29, about one-tenth. Thus, it seems likely that a large proportion of all moves, and especially of local moves, in young adulthood are the result of marriage and that the importance of this factor declines sharply with age. The corresponding proportions for men are probably a little lower, and the peak influence comes a few years later.

*Family Formation and Family Composition: Trends and Prospects**†

PAUL C. GLICK • DAVID M. HEER
JOHN C. BERESFORD

THE average married couple lives together about 40 years. Innumerable factors contribute to the entry of the bride and groom into marriage and to their continuation of the marriage. These factors include the cultural conditioning which the prospective bride and groom acquired as they grew up, the type of economic and political conditions they experienced, the prevailing attitudes of young people about when to marry and whether to remain married, and the unique factors pertaining to their own personal characteristics and environment. Complex though these forces may be, a million and a half decisions to marry are made — and carried out — each year.

Likewise, four million babies are born each year, four hundred thousand divorces are granted annually, and seven hundred fifty thousand marriages are terminated per year by the death of the husband or wife. All of these vital events bring about changes in the structure of the family. Moreover, additions to, or subtractions from, the family because of marriage, entry into college away from home, taking a job in another city, admission to or discharge from an institution — all of these reasons for moving imply changes in family structure. During the 40 years of married life, however, these rhythmic patterns tend to occur in a fairly predictable manner for the population as a whole. A description of changes in these patterns in the United States since 1940 and some indications of further changes between now and 1980 are discussed in the present paper.[1]

The source material for this analysis was obtained from past censuses and from the Census

* Revision of a paper presented at the annual meetings of the American Association for the Advancement of Science in Chicago, December 29, 1959, and reprinted here with the permission of the authors.

† The opinions expressed are those of the authors and and not necessarily those of the Bureau of Census.

[1] Related reports and articles include: Donald J. Bogue, *Applications of Demography: The Population Situation in the U.S. in 1975,* Scripps Foundation for Research in Population Problems (Miami University) and Population Research and Training Center (University of Chicago), 1957; William Hodgkinson, Jr., "A Method of Projecting the Number of Households in Small Areas," proceedings of Social Statistics Section, American Statistical Association, annual meeting in Chicago, December 27-30, 1958; Dudley Kirk, "The Influence of Business Cycles on Marriage and Birth Rates," and Frank W. Notestein, "Mortality, Fertility, the Size-Age Distribution and the Growth Rate," in National Bureau of Economic Research, *Demographic and Economic Change in Developed Countries,* Princeton: Princeton University Press, 1960, pp. 241 to 284; and Alfred Tella, "The Economic Cycle in Marriages," *Business Record,* November 1960, pp. 20-22 and 25.

Bureau's Current Population Survey. For the last several years, the Current Population Survey has been based on an area probability sample of approximately 35,000 households. Figures from the survey are available annually since the mid-1940's. The sample data are subject to sampling variability, but this factor is generally of minor concern where trends over a span of several years are being studied, as is the case here.

The projections presented here stem largely from an earlier report on projections published by the Bureau of the Census.[2] The main object of that report was to make available the Bureau's most recent projections of the numbers of households and families in the United States up to 1980. For the present paper, the authors projected the average annual number of first marriages for each five-year period from 1960 to 1980. These marriage figures are consistent with marital status projections that were used in preparing the projections of households and families. To simplify the presentation, only the highest and lowest of the four series of projections initially prepared will be discussed. The highest is designated Series A and the lowest, Series D. Series D is based on the assumption that there will be a continuation until 1980 of the same proportions by marital status (by age and sex) as in 1957, and that within each marital status category (by age and sex) the proportion who are household or family heads will likewise remain as in 1957. In Series D, therefore, the figures for future dates reflect only the influence of anticipated changes in the number of persons classified by age and sex. Series A likewise reflects these demographic changes. Moreover, Series A assumes that the proportion (by age and sex) who have ever married will, in general, continue to rise, as it did between 1950 and 1957, and that, within each subgroup by age, sex, and marital status, the average annual increase from 1950 to 1957 in the proportion of persons who were heads of households or families will continue to 1965; one-half this average annual change is assumed for the period 1965 to 1975, and one-fourth is assumed for the period 1975 to 1980. Series A and D are based on different population projections (Series II and III, respectively),[3] but there are no differences in the results from this source for adults until the 1970's and then the differences are minor; the effect on the projected number of children in families is more important.

The Bureau of the Census takes no official position as to whether future family changes will come closer to the Series A or to the Series D projections. However, the weight of evidence seems to the authors to be on the side of the Series A projections, provided the economy continues to prosper. Series D assumes an abrupt halt in the trends toward a larger proportion married and toward a dispersal of family units into separate living quarters, whereas Series A assumes a continuation of these trends, with a gradual slackening after 1965. The Series D projections provide a convenient criterion, however, against which to compare the more probable projections in Series A.

Family Formation

The probable emergence of a new upward trend in family formation in the near future is revealed by the results in Figure 1 and Tables 1 and 2. Thus, the trend in the estimated number of first marriages reflects the record numbers of marriages in the 1940's, the reduced number of young persons reaching the age of marriage in the 1950's because of low birth rates in the 1930's, and the greatly increased number who will be entering marriage in the 1960's and 1970's because of high birth rates in the 1940's and 1950's. (About three-fourths of the marriages since 1940 have been first marriages.)

Even if the generally upward trend in the age-specific proportion ever married should cease immediately — as the data for Series D imply — the projected number of first marriages during the latter part of the 1970's will exceed that of the mid-1950's by about 60 percent. Under the more favorable conditions implied in Series A, the number in the late 1970's will

[2] David M. Heer and Paul C. Glick, "Illustrative Projections of the Number of Households and Families: 1960 to 1980," *Current Population Reports,* Series P-20, No. 90. December 29, 1958. This report contains a fuller statement of the methodology for preparing the projections that are given here.

[3] Meyer Zitter and Jacob S. Siegel, "Illustrative Projections of the Population of the United States, by Age and Sex, 1960 to 1980," *Current Population Reports,* Series P-25, No. 187, November 10, 1958.

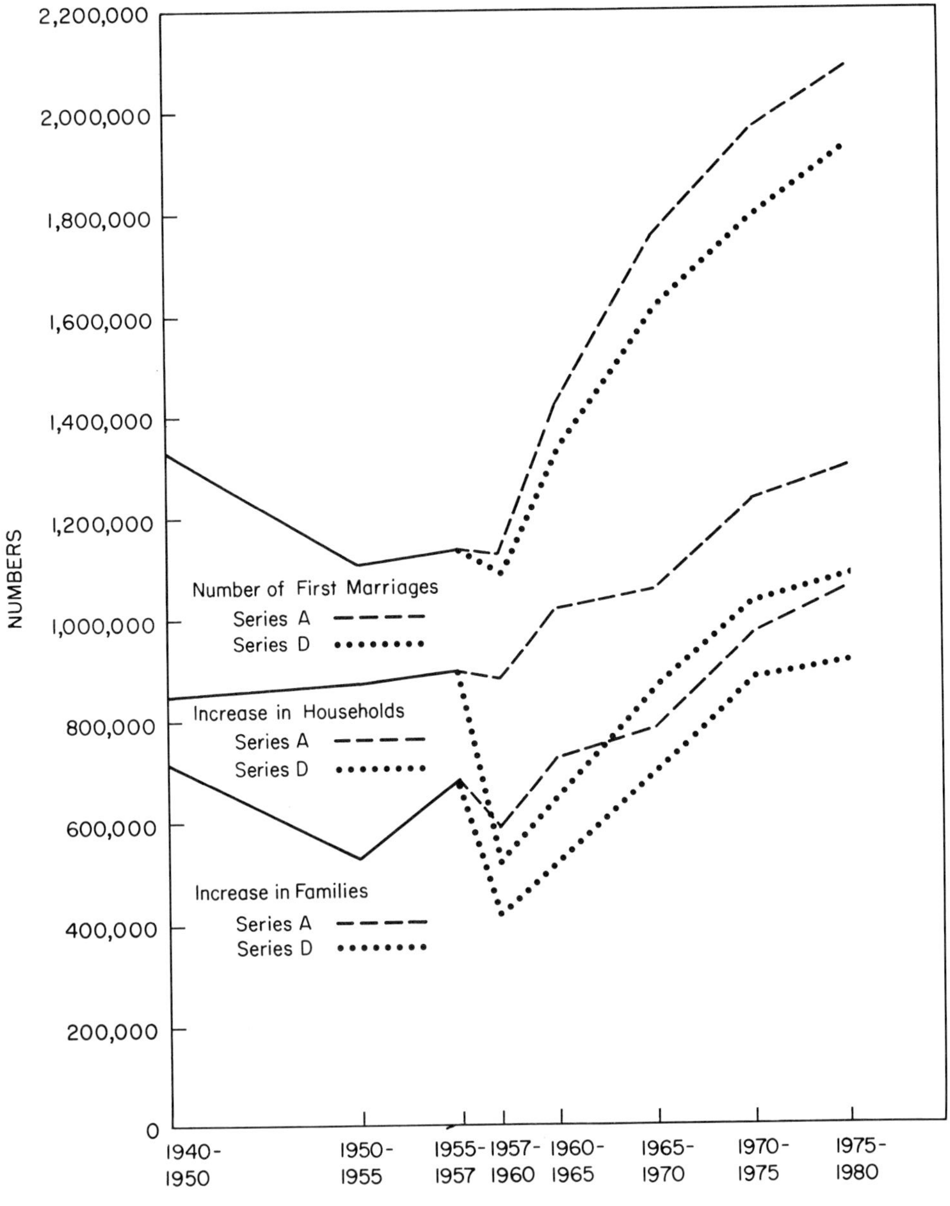

FIGURE 1

Average annual number of first marriages and average annual increase in numbers of households and families, 1940 to 1957, and projections, 1957 to 1980.

TABLE 1

Number of Household Heads and Potential Household Heads, for the United States, 1940 to 1957, and Projections, 1960 to 1980 (numbers in thousands)

Date and series	Household heads			Potential household heads*	
	Total	Family heads	Primary individuals	Number	Per household
1940	34,949	31,491	3,458	26,995	.77
1950	43,554	38,838	4,716	22,577	.52
1955	47,788	41,713	6,075	20,629	.43
1957	49,543	43,210	6,333	19,838	.40
1960: Series A	52,425	45,103	7,322	19,500	.37
Series D	51,350	44,476	6,874	20,913	.41
1965: Series A	57,517	48,648	8,869	20,100	.35
Series D	54,565	47,097	7,468	23,769	.44
1970: Series A	62,933	52,748	10,185	21,850	.35
Series D	58,814	50,651	8,163	27,122	.46
1975: Series A	69,318	57,669	11,649	23,279	.34
Series D	63,900	54,980	8,920	30,333	.47
1980: Series A	76,006	63,096	12,910	24,614	.32
Series D	69,382	59,644	9,738	32,747	.47

* Persons 18 years old and over other than household heads, married women with husband present, inmates of institutions, and Armed Forces living in military barracks.

Source: David M. Heer and Paul C. Glick, "Illustrative Projections of the Number of Households and Families: 1960 to 1980," U.S. Bureau of the Census, *Current Population Reports,* Series P-20, No. 90, December 29, 1958; also, other reports in Series P-20.

exceed that in the mid-1950's by about 80 percent. By way of contrast, the corresponding growth in the total population over this approximately 25-year span is likely to be only 48 to 57 percent. A comparison of these key figures shows the effects of differences in growth rates for the various age groups, and demonstrates the fallibility of using projections of total population to estimate future demand for consumer items that are more or less peculiar to specific segments of the population — in this case, to newly wedded couples.

The net growth in the number of families for all dates is smaller than the number of first marriages.[4] Net changes in the number of families result from numerous types of additions and subtractions, some of which are difficult

[4] The term "families" here means a group of two or more persons related by blood, marriage, or adoption who live together; generally a family, in this sense, is a married couple with or without children or one parent with children, but occasionally it comprises two related married couples, a bachelor and his spinster sister, or some other combination of relatives.

TABLE 2

Average Annual Number of First Marriages and Average Annual Increase in Numbers of Families and Households, for the United States, 1940 to 1957, and Projections, 1957 to 1980 (numbers in thousands)

Period and series	Average annual number of first marriages	Average annual increase in—	
		Number of families	Number of households
1940–50	1,331	711*	850*
1950–55	1,095	542*	872*
1955–57	1,137	690*	903*
1957–60: Series A	1,126	596*	865*
Series D	1,024	426*	539*
1960–65: Series A	1,331	690	1,018
Series D	1,241	529	643
1965–70: Series A	1,619	819	1,083
Series D	1,514	719	850
1970–75: Series A	1,845	987	1,277
Series D	1,719	873	1,017
1975–80: Series A	2,015	1,087	1,338
Series D	1,839	939	1,096

* 1950 based on average of 1949-51, 1955 on average of 1954-56, and 1957 on average of 1956-58.

Source: U.S. Bureau of the Census, *Current Population Reports,* Series P-20, Nos. 90 and 94; and unpublished data.

or impossible to isolate and measure separately with available data. One of the chief types of additions, however, is first marriages and one of the chief types of subtractions is deaths of married persons.

The trend of the increase in the number of households since 1940 can be explained partly by the trend in marriages and family formation, and partly by the trend in the doubling-up of married couples and other family groups.[5] Be-

[5] A household, as defined by the U.S. Bureau of the Census from 1940 to 1959 — and as used in this paper — is the entire group of persons (regardless of their relationship to each other) who occupy one dwelling unit. A dwelling unit is defined as separate living quarters occupied by, or intended for occupancy by, one family or person living alone; such quarters generally have either (1) separate cooking equipment or (2) two or more rooms and a separate entrance to the outside or to a common hall. In 1960, the census definition of a household is in terms of occupants of a housing unit, rather than a dwelling unit. Housing units differ from dwelling units mainly in that separate living quarters consisting of one room with direct access but without cooking equipment always qualify as a housing unit in 1960 but qualified as a dwelling unit in 1950 only when located in a regular apartment house or when the room was the only living quarters in the structure. The effect of the change in definitions is to increase by several hundred thousand the number of

tween 1947, when doubling reached a peak, and the middle 1950's, an unprecedented dispersal of these extra family units into separate households took place. Accordingly, during the period, household formation was at a high level, while the number of marriages dropped sharply. Evidently the economic prosperity of the 1950's and the greater abundance of housing permitted millions of persons, particularly widows, to maintain their own homes rather than live with their children or others. Such conditions resulted in an amazing 56-percent growth between 1950 and 1959 in the number of individuals with homes of their own but no relatives present, as contrasted with a mere 13-percent growth in the number of families with separate homes.

If demographic factors alone determine the course of events between now and 1980, the rate of growth in number of families during this period will be about the same as that of households. According to Series D, these conditions would lead to a rate of net household increase in the late 1970's only about 20 percent above that in the middle 1950's. On the other hand, the more optimistic conditions portrayed in Series A would lead to a rate of household formation 50 percent higher; as noted above, Series A implies a continuation of the recent tendency for family groups to sub-divide into more separate households.

From the latter half of the 1960's onward, the full force of the postwar elevation of the birth rate will manifest itself in the form of higher numbers of first marriages and higher rates of family and household growth, regardless of whether Series D or Series A comes closer to reality. However, the demographic changes set in motion by the increase in the birth rate will have been largely exhausted by 1980. Barring a major shift in nondemographic factors, there should be relative stability during the early 1980's in the annual number of first marriages and in the annual increase in the numbers of households and families.

---

small (usually one-person) households, mostly in congested areas where many persons have light-housekeeping quarters. The figures on households in this paper relate to the conterminous United States, that is, they cover the 48 States and the District of Columbia and exclude Alaska and Hawaii.

In concluding the discussion of household and family formation, it may be noted that there is always a large number of persons who might have been heads of households but who are not. These persons consist mainly of young and old adults who live in with relatives. In 1940, there were 27 million of these persons 18 years old and over. The corresponding figure in 1958 was 20 million, and that for a given future date may range widely, depending upon the extent to which past trends toward subdivision of family groups continues. Population growth alone (as in Series D) would increase the number to 33 million by 1980, whereas a rate of further subdivision which tends to increase but taper off asymptotically (as in Series A) might cut that figure by one-fourth, to about 25 million. It is quite possible that shifts in mode of living will speed this process to an extent even beyond that implied in the Series A projections; in that event, 25 million would prove too high an estimate of potential heads of households for 1980.

Family Composition

New families generally grow from a regrouping of persons in pre-established families. The ages at which young persons decide to marry and leave home, or simply to leave home without marrying, depends upon the benefits from staying or leaving and the ability to support oneself or a family. Likewise, among older persons, the decision to live in with the younger generation or not depends on numerous social and economic considerations. It is much more feasible, however, to describe the changes in family formation and family composition than to say with confidence what the causal factors have been.

Changes in family composition can be profitably analyzed in terms of the trend in average size of family. This trend is shown in the first column of Table 3. If this table had extended farther back in time, it would have shown a systematic downward tendency from about 5.7 persons per family in 1790 to 4.6 persons in 1900 and 3.5 persons in 1950. During the early 1950's, the average size of family reversed the historic downtrend. Both the lower and higher projections show a gradual upward movement in the average size of family to 1965, followed

TABLE 3

Components of Average Family Size, for the United States, 1940 to 1957, and Projections, 1960 to 1980

Date and series	Average size of family	Head of family	Wife of head	Other family members, by age: Under 14	14 to 17	18 to 24	25 and over
1940	3.76	1.00	.84	.95	.29	.32	.36
1950	3.54	1.00	.87	.97	.20	.22	.28
1955	3.60	1.00	.87	1.09	.21	.17	.26
1957	3.61	1.00	.87	1.12	.22	.17	.23
1960: Series A	3.66	1.00	.87	1.18	.24	.16	.21
Series D	3.70	1.00	.87	1.18	.24	.17	.24
1965: Series A	3.69	1.00	.87	1.18	.28	.18	.18
Series D	3.76	1.00	.87	1.16	.29	.20	.24
1970: Series A	3.72	1.00	.88	1.19	.29	.20	.16
Series D	3.76	1.00	.87	1.12	.30	.23	.24
1975: Series A	3.74	1.00	.88	1.22	.28	.20	.16
Series D	3.75	1.00	.87	1.11	.28	.24	.25
1980: Series A	3.78	1.00	.88	1.27	.28	.19	.16
Series D	3.76	1.00	.87	1.14	.26	.23	.26

Source: Paul C. Glick, *American Families*, New York, John Wiley and Sons, Inc., 1957, p. 33; U.S. Bureau of the Census, *Current Population Reports*, Series P-20, Nos. 62, 81, and 90; and unpublished data. Reprinted by permission.

by no further change, according to the lower projection, or a slight increase, according to the higher projection. Thus, by 1980, both levels show an average size of family of about 3.8 persons, or five to ten percent more than the low point reached in the early 1950's.

The manner in which the changes in family size since 1940 have taken place, and by which the prospective changes to 1980 may take place, is clarified through an examination of the changing components of family size. As Table 3 shows, the head, by definition, constitutes one member of the family at all dates. Moreover, a virtually constant seven-eighths of the families also contain a wife of the head. The variable components in family size, therefore, are the children and the adults other than the head or his wife who are sharing the family's living quarters.

Sharp contrasts in the relative magnitudes of these variable components are quite apparent over the sweep of years. Note first the figures for 1940, at the end of the depression during which family formation had ebbed. At that time, for every 100 families there were about 124 children under 18 years of age and about 68 members who were 18 years old and over other than the head and wife. Thus, in 1940, children of "dependent age" outnumbered "adult relatives" (including adult children) by a ratio of nearly 2 to 1. By 1950, the ratio of children to adult relatives had risen to 2½ to 1. By 1980, it may be 3 or 4 to 1. The underlying numbers imply an *increase* of about 15 to 25 percent in the number of *young* dependents per family between 1940 and 1980 but a *decrease* of about 30 to 50 percent in the number of *adult* relatives per family.

The fact that the number of young dependents in the average home shows such a modest change in spite of the tidal wave of births after World War II can be explained in large part by the fact that so many of those were first or second births to newly married couples and, hence, were distributed among many small families, rather than being high order births in families that were already established.

Another aspect of the changing pattern of household composition is presented in Table 4. This table shows the proportion of married couples who maintain a household and the proportion who share the homes of relatives or of nonrelatives. In substance, it shows the increasing tendency for couples to live apart from others. From a crest of nine percent doubling up in 1947, the proportion has dwindled to three percent and either may rise slightly as a larger proportion of couples become concentrated in the ages at which persons usually marry (as indicated by Series D), or may go down still further if conditions foster the de-

TABLE 4

Married Couples by Type, for the United States, 1940 to 1957, and Projections, 1960 to 1980 (numbers in thousands)

Date and series	All married couples	Percent—			
		Total	With own household	Living with relatives	Living with nonrelatives
1940................	28,517	100.0	93.2	5.4	1.4
1950................	36,091	100.0	94.4	4.6	1.0
1955................	37,570	100.0	96.5	3.1	0.4
1957................	38,940	100.0	96.8	2.8	0.4
1960: Series A.......	40,263	100.0	97.7	2.0	0.3
Series D.......	39,922	100.0	96.8	2.8	0.4
1965: Series A.......	42,989	100.0	98.9	1.0	0.1
Series D.......	42,260	100.0	96.7	2.9	0.4
1970: Series A.......	46,729	100.0	99.0	0.9	0.1
Series D.......	45,559	100.0	96.5	3.1	0.4
1975: Series A.......	51,239	100.0	99.0	0.9	0.1
Series D.......	49,563	100.0	96.3	3.3	0.4
1980: Series A.......	56,216	100.0	99.0	0.9	0.1
Series D.......	53,800	100.0	96.3	3.3	0.4

Source: U.S. Bureau of the Census, *Current Population Reports,* Series P-20, Nos. 90 and 94; and unpublished data.

parture of an even higher proportion of young couples from their parental homes than at present, and also if conditions foster the maintenance of separate homes by a higher proportion of old couples (as indicated by Series A). There will, of course, always be some couples who marry before they are financially independent and others who choose to live in with relatives in order to care for them or be cared for.

One of the consequences of the downward trend in doubling has been in increasing homogeneity in the structure of households. More and more nuclear family groups are residing apart from relatives. Couples evidently are using their increased annual incomes partly, at least, for the greater measure of privacy and domestic comfort which comes from living in a home of their own.

The Life Cycle of the Family

Changes in the family formation and family composition have far-reaching effects on the life cycle of the hypothetical "average family." This cycle may be considered as beginning with marriage and extending through childbearing, marriage of the children, and eventual dissolution by death of the husband or wife. Trends and prospects in this facet of family life are summarized in Table 5.

The downward trend in age at marriage has lowered the median age of men at first marriage by close to four years since 1890, half of which has occurred since 1940. Meantime, the median age at first marriage for women has gone down two years, with most of the decline occurring during the 1940's. Currently, these figures stand at about 22.3 years for men and 20.2 years for women. These declining ages at first marriage reflect in part the greater excess of males in the prime years for marriage around the turn of the century when heavy immigration brought more men than women into the country. In recent years, economic and social factors have probably been the most important factors affecting age at marriage. To a greater extent than in previous decades, young adults today can marry at an early age with confidence that the husband — and the wife, if she wishes — will have continuous future employment which will be sufficiently remunerative to support a family.

Despite the earlier ages at marriage, the divorce rate has declined since 1950. Meanwhile, a continuing decline in death rates has extended the period of joint survival of husbands and wives. Hence, the average person below mid-

TABLE 5

Median Age of Husband and Wife at Selected Stages of the Life Cycle of the Family, for the United States: 1890 to 1980

Stage	1890	1940	1950	1960	1980
MEDIAN AGE OF WIFE AT—					
First marriage	22.0	21.5	20.1	20.2	19.5–20.4
Birth of last child	31.9	27.1	26.1	25.8	27–28
Marriage of last child	55.3	50.0	47.6	47.1	48–49
Death of husband	53.3	60.9	61.4	63.6	65–66
MEDIAN AGE OF HUSBAND AT—					
First marriage	26.1	24.3	22.8	22.3	22–23
Birth of last child	36.0	29.9	28.8	27.9	29–30
Marriage of last child	59.4	52.8	50.3	49.2	51–52
Death of wife	57.4	63.6	64.1	65.7	68–69

Source: The figures in this table for 1890, 1940, and 1950 were previously published in Paul C. Glick, "The Life Cycle of the Family," *Marriage and Family Living,* Vol. XVII, No. 1, February 1955, Table 1. Those for 1960 and 1980 have not been previously published; they were estimated by methods similar to those used for earlier dates. See footnote 6.

dle age today has lived more of his years in the married state than his counterpart ten years ago.

During the last decade, the median age at first marriage in the country as a whole has changed very little. For men, the median has evidently gone down about half a year since 1950, but for women there has been no significant change. Increases during the current decade in the proportion married among relatively young persons have been virtually balanced by increases among older persons. Projections of the median age at marriage have been made on the basis of assumptions implying various amounts of deviation from recent trends in the proportion who have ever married. These projections point to practically the same median age at first marriage in future years, up to 1980, as at present. This fact reflects an underlying hypothesis that future changes, if any, in the proportion who have ever married will continue to be widely distributed along the age scale rather than concentrated above or below the current median age at first marriage.

An unusual marriage phenomenon is evidently taking place at the present and may recur in exaggerated form around the middle of the 1960's. This situation arises because there is generally a gap of two to three years between the ages of the husband and wife at first marriage. The birth rate went up during the latter part of the 1930's and the early part of the 1940's, and the children born in that period of rising birth rates are now in the principal ages for entering their first marriage. This means that each year is now bringing more 18-year-old women than 21-year-old men into the "marriage market." The effect is a tendency toward an excess of marriageable women and a deficit of marriageable men. The opinion has been expressed that the small drop in median age at first marriage for men since 1950 may have resulted from this "squeeze" on marriageable men. If this situation had not arisen, the median age at first marriage of women might have continued its historic decline. But the mild "marriage squeeze" of today may be followed by a more pronounced one in the mid-1960's, when the tidal wave of postwar babies passes into the marriageable ages.

Until the recent resurgence of the birth rate, earlier marriage and the bearing of fewer children tended to bring the birth of the last child at an earlier average age than formerly. As a consequence, the median age by which childbearing was completed fell about six years between 1890 and 1950.[6] Though the birth rate has risen during the 1950's, the average age at first marriage and the average age of mother at birth of first child are still below the corresponding ages for earlier cohorts; furthermore, the proportion of high order births remains small in comparison with that of one or two generations ago. The net effect of these and other factors (such as changing patterns of child-spacing) appears tentatively to have been a virtually unchanged average age of mother at birth of last child during the 1950's. Projections for the next two decades show that the marriage age may not change significantly and that the average number of children per ever-married woman in her late forties may rise from the current two and one-half children to about three (2.8 to 3.2) children by 1980. If these projections are supported by future events, the average woman will be a year or two older at the end of childbearing in 1980 than her counterpart is today. The projected mother of 1980 will still be in her late twenties when she has her last child — some four or five years younger than her great grandmother in 1890 at the corresponding stage of the family life cycle.

The upswing in the birth rate during the last two decades is affecting family structure in numerous ways, one of which is that more families are having two or three children and fewer are having none or one. Thus, fully 20 percent of the women in 1950 who had ever been married and who had just reached the end of their child-bearing period were still childless, and another

[6] The median age of mother at birth of her last child as shown in Table 4 is probably too young by a year or two for all dates, according to data from cohorts of women collected in August 1959 by the Bureau of the Census. The results of this new survey were received too late to be incorporated into the present paper before the deadline. However, they confirm the results of other studies, notably those for Japan published by Louis Henry, "Intervalles entre Naissances" (Intervals between Births), *Population,* Vol. 9, No. 4, October-December 1954, pp. 759-61, which show that the interval between the last two children is substantially greater, on the average, than that between other children, regardless of the eventual number of births.

20 percent had borne one child and no more. By contrast, only about 10 percent of the married women who are now 30 to 34 years old are childless and only 15 percent have borne one child. The projections used in this paper are consistent with the continuance of the corresponding proportions until 1980. The current data imply that women now nearing the end of the reproductive ages are sharing much more widely in the bearing and rearing of children than the corresponding women ten years ago. The fact remains, however, that this sharing is not as wide as it was for some more distant generations.

At the present time, the most popular numbers of children, judging from the childbearing of ever-married women now 35 to 39 years old, are two children, three children, and one child, in that order; these numbers of children account for about two-thirds of all women in this age range. Only a decade ago, the corresponding rank orders of popularity were two, one, and no children. Although these facts do not imply a growing homogeneity in the ages of parents at childbearing or in the number of children they eventually will have, they do reflect a significant expansion in the average number of young dependents per family during the 1950's.

Earlier marriages and earlier childbearing have had the effect of compressing more of the period of childbearing into the years before the age of 40 and fewer into the 40's and 50's. Thus, more of the responsibility for nurturing, educating, and otherwise bringing up young people has been shifted to the years preceding middle age. In turn, more middle and later years of life are being freed from direct supervision and care of one's children, though continuing material assistance to married sons and daughters has no doubt become a more widely accepted practice. Women now have a wider range of choice in the way they spend their middle years of life, though the rising cost of living and increasing recognition of the need for giving their children a college education is rapidly convincing many to spend these years at gainful employment. Per capita income figures suggest that families with the head and wife between 45 and 64 years old are about twice as able to assume such added responsibilities as families at the height of childbearing.

Today the average parent can expect to see his last child marry before he (the parent) is 50 years old. Two generations ago, mothers were closer to 55 and fathers to 60 when this event occurred, if they lived that long. Projections which are being used here imply that persons will reach the corresponding phase of their life cycle one to three years later in 1980 than at present, but still six to nine years sooner than their ancestors in 1890.

Nearly all young couples establish a household when they marry. Only about one-half million couples with the wife under 30 years old do not maintain their own household today. This is only about one-third as large as the number of marriages that occur in a year's time.

With the death of one spouse or the other, the typical family as a nuclear unit comes to an end. On the basis of the present level of mortality rates and present ages at first marriage, a married couple can expect to survive jointly for about 43 years after marriage. This figure contrasts sharply with the corresponding figure for the average married couple in 1890, when there was a 50–50 chance that the couple would survive jointly for only about 31 years. Turning to the future, projections point toward a period of about 45 to 47 years of joint survival of marriage partners by 1980. The lower figure is based on the assumption that the number of years of joint survival will increase between now and 1980 only half as much as it has since 1940; the higher figure is based on the assumption that the amount of increase in the next 20 years will be the same as that in the last 20 years.

These figures imply that the average married couple today can expect to have about 15 or 16 years to themselves after their last child marries and before the husband or wife dies. By 1980, this period may be lengthened to about 17 years. These facts, in turn, signify that from now on into the near future, the average married couple will be having close to one-third of their years of married life to live after their last child leaves home. By contrast, less than half of the married couples living under mortality, fertility, and marriage conditions of 1890 could have expected to survive jointly until their last child had married.

This tremendous change in the later years

of married life has had a revolutionizing effect on the structure and function of families as they approached dissolution. The change has been of importance especially for women, who now have a far longer period of time after their last child is in school, during which to perform their roles as wife, mother, joint breadwinner, club woman, and/or community servant.[7]

The foregoing discussion disregards the fact that some families are dissolved by divorce long before one or the other spouse dies. Currently, about one marriage out of every four or five ends in divorce. This inference rests on the following observations: During the last decade, between one-fourth and one-fifth of the persons entering marriage had been previously married. About two-thirds of those remarrying had been previously divorced. However, roughly one-third of the divorced women and one-fourth of the divorced men never remarry. If account is taken of the years of married life that are lost between the time of divorce or widowhood and eventual remarriage — or lost because of failure to remarry — the average length of married life would be about 40 years rather than 43 years, as cited above.

Summary and Conclusions

This paper has shown that there were record numbers of first marriages and of new households during the 1940's, followed by lower levels of first marriages but continued high levels of new households during much of the 1950's. It has also pointed to the prospects for gradually increasing numbers of first marriages, and for either a larger or smaller annual number of new households until the middle 1960's, depending on whether past tendencies for subdivision into more and smaller households continues. After the mid-1960's, the numbers of first marriages and new households should be moving up more sharply, as the aftereffects of the high marriage and birth rates of the 1940's and 1950's reach their full impact.

These high marriage rates and the rapid decline in the doubling rate for married couples which accompanied the improvement in the housing situation during the last decade were, no doubt, key factors in the continued historic decline of the average family size to 1950, despite the resurgence of the birth rate after World War II. By now, however, the average size of family — in terms of the number of related persons living together — has risen. From 1940 to the present, children have constituted a generally increasing proportion of the family members, other than the head and wife, and adult relatives have constituted a declining proportion. Regardless of which of the two projections is used, the projected changes seem likely to have the net effect of showing a further increase between now and 1980 in the average size of family.

Changes in family formation and composition have left their mark on the life cycle of the family. The pattern of earlier marriage and the declining number of children among women of completed fertility have sharply reduced the average age of the mother at the birth of her last child. Since 1890, this age has dropped six years. If age at first marriage remains fairly constant and the average number of children per ever-married woman in her late forties rises ten to thirty percent, as projected, the average woman at the end of childbearing in 1980 will be a year or two older than the corresponding woman of today. In turn, by 1980, one to three years may be added to the mother's age at the marriage of her last child and to her age at eventual dissolution of the marriage by death of the husband or wife. Thus, the span of married life is now close to 40 years — if one allows for the fact that some marriages end in divorce or widowhood. This span may rise two or three years in the next two decades, on the assumption that continued improvements are made in survival rates.

[7] For a discussion of the length of widowhood or widowerhood, see Robert J. Myers, "Statistical Measures in the Marital Life Cycles of Men and Women," in the proceedings of the *International Population Conference, Vienna 1959* (edited by Louis Henry and Wilhelm Winkler), Vienna, Im Selbstverlag, 1959, pp. 229-233.

STUDY AND DISCUSSION QUESTIONS

1. Refer back to the Davis-Blake article on variables affecting fertility in Chapter 4. How might family decisions regarding each of these variables affect both family structure and population change?
2. Chapter 2 discusses the model of the demographic transition as a way of viewing population change in industrializing nations. How might a family's decision to use or not to use contraceptive devices affect the pattern of the transition? At what point in the transition would this decision be most crucial?
3. Look up the history of westward migration in the United States. In its early phases, was this primarily a migration of families or of individuals? How might family decisions have affected the nature of this migration?
4. Some writers have expressed the idea that the sex differential in mortality (See Chapter 3) may be due, in part, to an erroneous conception on the part of the American male that he is inherently physically superior to women. Such an attitude, it is postulated, may lead men to ignore or neglect their own health care. What other traditional social norms or roles within the family could have an appreciable affect on mortality or morbidity?
5. What historical examples can you think of to illustrate the changes in population composition that may affect the family? (e.g., selective character of immigration into the United States.)
6. A death in the family may be followed by migration or a change of residence by the survivors of that family. Name several ways that morbidity could affect migration within the family framework.
7. The American family is primarily a nuclear unit, that is, parents and offspring. In other societies, however, stem families or extended families (those which include more distant relatives) may exist. Discuss how variations in family types may affect the patterns of fertility, mortality, and migration in the society.
8. In its early enumerations, the U.S. Census used families and not individuals as the basis for counting. Look up the history of this practice and the reason for the change. What kinds of information does the census collect by family units now?

SUGGESTED ADDITIONAL READING

Nimkoff, M. F., ed. *Comparative Family Systems.* Boston: Houghton Mifflin Company, 1965.
A cross-national analysis of family systems throughout the world that identifies changes in family types and organization and relates these to varying functions of the family.

Blake, Judith. *Family Structure in Jamaica: The Social Context of Reproduction.* Glencoe: The Free Press, 1961.
An intensive analysis of the relation between marriage and family patterns to fertility in a Caribbean country.

Glick, Paul C. *American Families.* New York: John Wiley & Sons, 1957.
Another of the 1950 U.S. Census monographs, this one concerned with marriage and family trends and relationships, and factors associated with them.

Kiser, Clyde V., ed. *Research in Family Planning.* Princeton: Princeton University Press, 1962.
An international appraisal and analysis of fertility and family planning programs.

Rainwater, Lee. *Family Design: Marital Sexuality, Family Size, and Contraception.* Chicago: Aldine Publishing Company, 1965.
A study of factors associated with birth control, focusing on lower-class families.

CHAPTER 11

Population and Social Stratification

Sociologists have come to regard social stratification of a society as vitally important to an appreciation of how the society is structured and how it undergoes change. *Social stratification* refers to the division of a society, community, or other social group into strata or an hierarchy of levels to which persons are assigned on the basis of certain valued attributes which they have. Many attributes are used in reckoning an individual's place in the stratification system. Often an individual will be located at about the same point in the hierarchy no matter what attributes are used, but frequently his assignment to a stratum will vary depending on which attributes are considered. In this chapter, occupation, income, and education, the variables most often used by social scientists in studying social stratification, are the attributes of individuals principally used in relating population factors to social stratification. The terms "social class" and "socioeconomic status" are used here synonomously in referring to stratification along occupation, income, and education lines, or some combination of these.

There are interrelationships between population and social stratification, as in the case of population and other areas of social life. Mortality, fertility, and migration vary by social class within the population. In turn, demographic factors may affect the social class structure in a society at a particular point in time as well as the extent and nature of social mobility in the society. These relationships are discussed in somewhat greater detail in the following paragraphs.

Earlier chapters on the basic components of population change referred to social class as one characteristic by which these vital demographic processes are differentiated. In general, mortality is inversely related to social class, the upper social strata having lower age-specific death rates and greater life expectancy. However, it was pointed out that these differentials seem to be narrowing in most societies as styles of life and exposure to the risks of death become more similar for the different classes. Moreover, for some causes of death the traditional inverse relationship is not observed; deaths due to some types of heart disease and those associated with ailments of the digestive organs are relatively greater among the upper social strata. Stresses related to status maintenance and social mobility and the diets typical of the upper classes may have something to do with these mortality patterns for specific causes of death.

Socioeconomic differentials in fertility have also been observed by demographers, but a traditional inverse relationship here is seen to be changing in societies where high proportions of families are planned. Contemporary fertility studies have shown that there is a direct relationship between social class and fertility among couples who use methods of contraception to control the size of their families; thus, as family planning becomes more widespread, we might expect further changes in the association between social class and fertility. Reversals in the traditional inverse relationship in recent decades in Western societies provide evidence of this.

Variations in the propensity to migrate among social strata have also been documented in numerous studies. However, the relationship between social class and migration is dependent on distance traveled. People in the higher social strata are more likely to move long distances, whereas those in the lower strata are more apt to be local movers. These facts are consistent with the knowledge that the more specialized occupations pursued by persons in the middle and upper classes are more widely dispersed in location than those positions held by lower-class persons. Thus, job changes for these higher-strata persons will often necessitate a move of some distance. Lower-class workers, on the other hand, can usually find employment in the same occupation a relatively short distance from their current residence. The tentative nature of many lower-class jobs requires reemployment, hence, frequent residential relocation.

The system of social stratification found in a society is partly dependent on demographic factors. Higher fertility among the lower classes, all other things being equal, will have the effect of broadening the base of the stratification pyramid. Higher mortality among the same classes, on the other hand, will compensate for much of the higher fertility. The social class selectivity of migration into and out of an area will determine the effect of net migration on the class structure. Goldstein and Mayer report on a study which evaluated the relative impact of migration on the socioeconomic structure of cities and suburbs in one United States metropolitan area.

Aspects of population composition and distribution are also relevant factors in the determination of the social class structure. In the second selection, Nam and Powers examine the association of age, race, and type of residential location with socioeconomic status and with status consistency of individuals. *Status consistency* refers to the extent of agreement between a person's rankings on different status hierarchies. In their analysis, occupation, education, and income make up the three hierarchies. Their findings show that socioeconomic status and patterns of status consistency vary among population groups significantly.

Stratification systems in societies are altered with the passage of time, and individuals in the society are subject to *social mobility* (changes in status over time). Schnore's article presents a broad perspective of the connections between population and social mobility, emphasizing the contribution demography can make to the study of social mobility. An analysis of sources of social mobility indicates that, among the four basic sources of mobility (technological change with its impact on the occupational structure, immigration with its selective tendencies, differential reproduction with its effect on the relative natural increase of the various classes, and individual initiative and competition), the two demographic sources, immigration and differential reproduction, have contributed substantially during the past several decades to social mobility in America.

*The Impact of Migration on the Socio-Economic Structure of Cities and Suburbs**†

SIDNEY GOLDSTEIN • KURT B. MAYER††

The rapid growth of metropolitan areas in the United States involves an increasing differentiation of the socioeconomic structure of their urban and suburban components. The role of migration in producing this differentiation has been the subject of considerable speculation. The availability in the 1960 census of a comprehensive body of migration data for metropolitan areas permits detailed analysis of the size and selective character of the opposing streams of movement between central cities and suburban rings and their relative importance in producing more or less homogeneity in the various parts of the metropolitan area. A recent investigation of the nation's twelve largest Standard Metropolitan Statistical Areas (SMSA's) tests the thesis that the increasing differential in the socioeconomic status of large cities and their suburban rings results from an influx of low-status migrants to cities and an outflow of high-status persons from cities to suburbs.[1] The findings show this assumption to be oversimplified and the relations between migration and changing socioeconomic level as more complex. On the whole, the analysis found

> migrants to be similar to each other, regardless of destination. Since nonmigrants in the city are of lower status than nonmigrants in the ring, the addition of similar relative volumes of in-migrants to city and ring would raise the average status level of the city relative to that of the ring. Out-migration, on the other hand, tends to remove from the cities persons of distinctly higher status than those remaining behind, while the rings lose migrants whose status is only slightly higher. Out-migration by itself tends to widen the status gap between cities and rings. . . . In recent decades, cities have been contributing more high-status migrants than they receive to the flow of population within and between metropolitan areas while suburban rings have been receiving more high-status migrants than they lose. The inter- and intra-metropolitan circulation of persons of higher levels of educational attainment and occupational status has the net effect of diminishing the socioeconomic level of the population in central cities and augmenting the socioeconomic level of suburban populations.[2]

As the authors recognize, these findings apply only to the twelve largest metropolitan areas and continued study of other areas is necessary to explore the generality of the findings.

Such an opportunity arose as part of a larger study of the impact of metropolitanization in Providence-Pawtucket, a medium-sized metropolitan area. Special tabulations were obtained for each census tract indicating the migration status of the population cross-tabulated by such variables as age, sex, education, occupation, and income. In the 1960 Census, migration status was measured by comparison between place of residence reported for April 1, 1955, and place of residence in April, 1960. Based on residence at these two dates all persons five years and over in 1960 were classified into one of seven migra-

* Reprinted with permission from *Sociology and Social Research*, Vol. 50, No. 1 (1965), pp. 5-23.

† This is a revised version of a paper presented at the annual meeting of the American Sociological Association, Chicago, Illinois, August 30-September 2, 1965. This investigation is supported by a grant from the National Science Foundation, G-16009.

†† Dr. Goldstein is Professor of Sociology and Chairman of the Department of Sociology and Anthropology, and Dr. Mayer is Professor of Sociology, Brown University, Providence, Rhode Island.

[1] Karl E. and Alma F. Taeuber, "White Migration and Socio-Economic Differences between Cities and Suburbs," *American Sociological Review*, 29 (October, 1964), 718-29.

[2] *Ibid.*, 728.

tion categories: (1) Those living in the same house at both dates, i.e. nonmovers. (2) Those living in the two central cities of the metropolitan area in 1955. Within this group, persons still living in the central cities in 1960 constituted the intraurban movers; those living in the suburban towns by 1960 constituted the city to suburb movers. (3) Those whose residence in 1955 was in the ring of the SMSA. Such persons, whose residence in 1960 was in the central cities, constituted the suburb to city migrants; those living in the suburban towns represented intrasuburban movers. (4) Persons resident outside the SMSA, but in Rhode Island, in 1955. (5) Those resident outside Rhode Island in 1955. (6) Those abroad in 1955. (7) Those who moved between 1955 and 1960 but whose 1955 residence was unknown. (This group constituted only 2.2 per cent of the entire population.) Whereas the Taeubers' analysis was restricted to whites, the data of this study include nonwhites. Because of the relatively small number of nonwhites in the Providence-Pawtucket metropolitan area, only 2.0 per cent of the total, race is not a major variable.

Using the census tract as a unit of analysis enables more refined combinations of types of residence, particularly with reference to the suburban area. In this analysis, the tracts have been combined into three categories: (1) the central cities of Providence and Pawtucket; (2) the satellite industrial cities, Central Falls and Woonsocket, which lie in the ring of the metropolitan area; and (3) the immediate suburbs, consisting of all the census tracts in those Rhode Island towns and cities exclusive of the industrial satellites that form the inner part of the SMSA. On the basis of time and distance transportation studies, the towns and cities classified as immediate suburbs were within approximately 20 minutes' commuting time of the central cities. Such classification contrasts with the more usual practice of designating as suburban all parts of metropolitan areas outside the central cities proper although the peripheral part often includes highly urbanized satellite cities and miscellaneous congeries of real suburbs, semirural, and rural areas. To measure the selectivity of population exchange between city and suburbs it is highly desirable to refine the classification of the metropolitan ring.[3]

These data by individual census tracts for the two central cities, the satellite industrial cities, and the suburban communities permit classification and combination of the small area data by socioeconomic status. The socioeconomic status of the different census tracts was measured through use of the Shevky and Bell Index of Social Rank.[4] This index is a simple arithmetic mean of the standardized scores of education and occupation.[5] For purposes of the analysis, the 58 tracts of the two central cities, the 18 tracts of the satellite industrial cities, and the 62 tracts of the immediate suburbs[6] were

[3] Cf. Jeffrey Hadden, "Suburbs: Concept or Hodge-Podge?" Paper presented at 59th Annual Meeting, American Sociological Association, Montreal, Canada, August 31-September 3, 1964.

[4] Eshref Shevky and Wendell Bell, *Social Area Analysis,* (Stanford: Stanford University Press, 1955), 54-58.

[5] The scores composing this index were standardized to a range of 0-100 for Providence in 1960. For the census tracts outside Providence, it is possible to achieve a standard score of less than zero or greater than 100, since their ranking is relative to those of Providence. Although both the theoretical rationale and the empirical validity of social area analysis has been questioned [see, Amos Hawley and Otis Dudley Duncan, "Social Area Analysis: A Critical Appraisal," *Land Economics,* 33 (November, 1957), 337-45], the general applicability of Shevky's indexes has been confirmed by Calvin Schmid and Associates in a series of articles: See Calvin F. Schmid, "Generalizations Concerning the Ecology of the American City," *American Sociological Review,* 15 (April, 1950) 264-81; Maurice D. Van Arsdol, Jr., Santo Camilleri, and Calvin F. Schmid, "The Generality of Urban Social Area Indexes," *American Sociological Review,* 23 (June, 1958), 277-84; Calvin F. Schmid, Earle H. MacCannell, and Maurice D. Van Arsdol, Jr., "The Ecology of the American City; Further Comparison and Validation of Generalizations," *American Sociological Review,* 23 (August, 1958), 392-401. Providence was included in each of these three ecological studies. Moreover, the index has provided the basis for two further investigations of the relation between social rank and population change in Providence. See Kurt Mayer and Sidney Goldstein, "Interrelationships between Social and Demographic Processes in an American City," *Transactions of the International Population Conference, Vienna,* 1959 (International Union for the Scientific Study of Population, 1959), 92-105; and Sidney Goldstein and Kurt Mayer, "Population Decline and the Social and Demographic Structure of an American City," *American Sociological Review,* 29 (February, 1964), 48-54.

[6] Two tracts in Providence were eliminated from the analysis because they contain sizeable numbers of college students. One tract in the suburbs, containing the state's institutional population, was also excluded.

grouped into five status categories, I-V, in descending order based on a division of the index scores into quintiles. Analysis of the migration streams in terms of status levels permits determination of the ways in which movement to the suburbs and cities differs according to the status level of the place of destination. Moreover, a comparison of areas of similar status in cities and suburbs should indicate whether the type of migrants attracted to comparable socio-economic levels varies among the central cities, the satellite cities and the suburbs.

The Providence-Pawtucket Metropolitan Area is one of the oldest settlements in the United States. The area has already experienced the type of economic and demographic development through which many other areas are still passing. Suburbanization began in the late 19th century and deconcentration of population has continued to the present. The city of Providence itself was among the first large cities in the United States to lose population and has continued to do so at an accelerated pace. The census statistics showing the changing distribution of population between 1950 and 1960 indicate the relatively high rates of population decline of the central cities and to a somewhat lesser extent of the satellite cities and the contrasting rapid growth of the suburbs (see Table 1). As a result, a sharp redistribution of population within the area has occurred, with the central cities' share of the total declining from over half to only 44 per cent and the suburban segment's share rising from 36 per cent in 1950 to 46 per cent by 1960. In 1960 the suburbs actually contained more population than did the two central cities. Because the similar experience of the satellite cities more closely resembles that of the central cities, treating them apart from the suburban part of the ring in which they are ordinarily included in census tabulations is justified.

The availability of birth and death statistics for small areas for the entire decade permits use of the vital statistics method for estimating the net migration gain or loss characterizing the three residential areas during this period. The data show quite clearly that migration is

TABLE 1

Population Distribution, Rate of Change, and Components of Change, 1950–1960 for Urban and Suburban Segments of Providence-Pawtucket Metropolitan Area

a. Number and Distribution

Area of Residence	Population		Percentage Distribution by Area	
	1950	1960	1950	1960
Central Cities	330,110	288,499	52.6	44.2
Satellite Cities	73,761	66,938	11.7	10.3
Immediate Suburbs	224,481	297,262	35.7	45.5
Total	628,352	652,699	100.0	100.0

b. Components of Change 1950–1960

	Natural Increase	Rate of Natural Increase*	Net Migration	Rate of Net Migration*	Net Change 1950–1960	Per cent Change 1950–1960
Central Cities	28,913	8.8	−70,524	−21.4	−41,611	−12.6
Satellite Cities	8,333	11.3	−15,156	−20.5	−6,823	−9.2
Immediate Suburbs	32,552	14.5	40,229	17.9	72,781	32.4
Total	69,798	11.1	−45,451	−7.2	24,347	3.9

* Based on 1950 Population.

the most important factor in the redistribution patterns noted. For the two central cities the net out-migration of over 70,000 exceeded by 2.5 times the gain resulting from natural increase and accounted therefore for the sharp drop in population. Migration played a similar role in the decline of the satellite cities. In the suburbs the rate of natural increase was much higher than in the central cities; yet migration contributed the greater part of the population increase.

As the net migration data clearly indicate, not all of the movement from either the central cities or the satellites was to the suburbs. The excess of 45,000 out-migrants for the total area involves movement both to the outlying areas of the state and out of the state. During the same period Rhode Island as a whole experienced a net out-migration of 25,500 persons. But, since measures of net migration do not permit identification of the actual streams of population movement, one must turn for further insights to the 1960 census statistics in which migration was measured directly by comparison with residence in 1955.

General Mobility Rates

The overall level of mobility characterizing the three residential categories showed remarkable similarity.[7] The proportion of persons classified as nonmovers varied only between 58 and 60 per cent, and those changing residence within the United States during these five years accounted for between 38 and 41 per cent of the total population in each area. Although the percentage of persons classified as mobile is similar, the areas vary with respect to 1955 place of residence of the movers. In the central cities, the great majority of mobile persons changed residence only within the cities themselves and a small minority moved in from the balance of the SMSA[8] and from outside Rhode Island. For the satellite cities, over 80 per cent of the mobile persons originated in the ring of the metropolitan area. Since this includes the satellite cities themselves, quite probably, as in the case of the central cities, most of this movement involved intraurban mobility. Of the 38 per cent of the suburban residents who were mobile almost one third had moved to the suburbs from the two central cities and about 15 per cent came from outside the state. Over half of the mobile persons in the suburbs had moved within the ring, of the metropolitan area, including some persons who left the satellite industrial cities for the suburbs. This movement amounted to 55,000 persons, indicating that the greater part of it consisted of intrasuburban mobility. In the suburbs, as in the cities themselves, most mobility consists of changing residence within the same type of residential category. Although intra-area mobility is the most prevalent type in both cities and suburbs, the lower level of such mobility in the suburbs reflects the higher rate of homeownership. Homeowners are known to be less mobile than renters.[9]

There are sharp differentials among the various status levels within residential areas as well as between similar status levels in different areas. (See Table 2). Within the central cities, the major status differential distinguishes the lowest status level from the four higher ones. Considerably more of the 1960 residents of status area V were movers, and of these a high proportion had either lived in the balance of the SMSA or were unable to report their exact residence in 1955. The larger proportion moving in from the ring most likely represent migrants from the industrial satellite cities rather than persons moving from suburbs. Reflecting the correlation between mobility and homeownership, the proportion moving within the central cities varies inversely with socioeconomic status. On the other hand, there is a tendency for more of the movers to the higher status areas to come from outside of Rhode Island, but this differential is large only for the highest status area.

[7] In comparing the mobility status of current residents, it must be recognized that no account is taken of persons who moved out of the respective areas. Had the out-migrants from cities and suburbs been included, the mobility rates would differ sharply.

[8] The tabulation of place of residence in 1955 does not permit separation of the industrial satellite cities from the balance of the SMSA.

[9] Lillian Cohen, "Family Charactersitics of Home Owners," *American Journal of Sociology,* 55 (May, 1950), 565-71.

TABLE 2

Percentage Distribution of Population, 5 Years Old and Over, by Migration Status, According to Socio-Economic Status of Area of Residence

	Number	Per cent			Place of Residence 1955					
Socio-Economic Status of Area of Residence, 1960	Total Population 5 Years Old and Over		Same House (Non Movers)	Total Movers	Central City	Balance of SMSA	Elsewhere in Rhode Island	Outside Rhode Island	Abroad in 1955	Moved 1955 Residence Unknown
Central Cities										
I	10,777	100.0	56.4	39.6	22.9	5.5	0.5	10.7	1.6	2.4
II	26,706	100.0	60.4	36.8	28.0	3.7	0.1	4.9	0.6	2.2
III	104,564	100.0	59.7	37.4	29.1	4.8	0.3	3.2	0.6	2.3
IV	103,311	100.0	56.9	39.7	32.1	4.6	0.2	2.8	1.1	2.4
V	1,616	100.0	42.3	47.0	32.7	10.5	—	3.9	1.1	9.5
Total	246,974	100.0	58.3	38.5	30.0	4.7	0.2	3.6	0.8	2.4
Satellite Cities										
I	—	—	—	—	—	—	—	—	—	—
II	—	—	—	—	—	—	—	—	—	—
III	7,053	100.0	63.1	36.1	0.9	31.7	—	3.6	0.4	0.4
IV	27,718	100.0	56.8	41.6	3.8	34.5	0.1	3.2	0.5	1.0
V	25,292	100.0	57.7	40.8	2.2	36.2	0.1	2.3	0.5	1.0
Total	60,063	100.0	58.0	40.6	2.8	34.9	0.1	2.8	0.5	0.9
Immediate Suburbs										
I	16,081	100.0	51.2	47.0	11.5	24.1	0.4	11.1	1.0	0.7
II	91,438	100.0	58.7	39.3	14.0	18.7	0.5	6.1	0.5	1.4
III	81,737	100.0	60.7	37.5	9.5	23.3	0.4	4.3	0.5	1.2
IV	67,099	100.0	64.2	33.3	9.9	21.0	0.3	2.2	0.6	1.8
V	3,696	100.0	71.6	27.1	0.4	25.7	—	1.0	0.6	0.8
Total	260,051	100.0	60.5	37.5	11.2	21.1	0.4	4.8	0.6	1.4

For the satellite cities, comparison by status level is restricted because all of the census tracts are concentrated in the three lower status levels. Within this narrow range, the differences in the proportion of nonmovers and movers and in the distribution of movers by place of residence in 1955 are not particularly striking.

The most clearcut status differentials characterize the suburbs. The proportion of nonmovers increases consistently from 51 per cent of those in status level I to 72 per cent of those in status level V. This inverse relation between stability and socioeconomic status reflects two factors: (1) The new suburban developments surround older mill villages and rural slums, which form pockets of low status persons. Their higher rate of stability in part reflects the greater tendency of suburbanites in general to be homeowners, even at the lowest status level. This differential rate of homeownership contributes to the much higher stability in the low status suburban area compared to the low status city area. (2) It is the high status suburban areas which attract the in-migrants to the suburbs (See Table 3). For example, 50 per cent of the persons moving to the suburbs from the central cities and 60 per cent of those coming from outside the state took up residence in the two highest status levels of the suburbs. By contrast, of those moving to the central city from the balance of the metropolitan area, only 14 per cent moved into the two highest level residential categories, and of those moving in from outside the state only 28 per cent did so. The very high concentration of recent migrants in these high status areas reduces the proportion of nonmovers in those areas. Compared to the low status areas, there is a much higher proportion of movers in the high status areas whose former residence was either in the central cities or outside Rhode Island. (See Table 2.) Among those classified as intrasuburban migrants, the status differentials are much less sharp and in no way patterned. Finally, the data point to the much greater attractiveness of the high status suburbs than of the low status suburbs for migrants from outside the state. In status category I, of all movers, equal proportions came from the central cities and from outside Rhode Island. With decreasing status level, this distribution increasingly favored the central city, except in status category V where the movement from both places was minimal.

The foregoing analysis has shown important differences in the overall volume of movement into and out of the various sectors of the metropolitan area. The effects of migration do not result merely from numbers but also depend upon the characteristics of the migrants. To test the selectivity of movement, three socioeconomic variables are examined: occupation, education, and income. Occupational selectivity is measured by per cent of white collar workers, education by per cent of persons with one or more years of college education, and income by per cent of persons 14 years old or over with income of $6,000 or more. These data will be used (1) to ascertain whether the mobility patterns for those living in the suburbs as a whole differ from those in the two categories of urban centers, and (2) to ascertain whether a selective process operates in movement to or from comparable status levels. In using the data on occupation, education, and income to measure the selectivity of migration for specific status levels it must be recognized that the status levels themselves are delineated on the basis of education and occupation. The characteristics of the nonmovers in the respective status levels, and within limits, of the movers to and from specific status levels will therefore reflect the characteristics of the population of the area. Despite this limitation, these data are valuable for comparing the characteristics of the different streams of migration to a particular status level and also for comparison of the streams of movement to similar status levels of the different residential areas.

Occupational Selectivity

The central cities, satellite cities, and suburbs differ in the occupational composition of their population. Reflecting their industrial character, only 27 per cent of the employed labor force living in the satellite cities are white collar workers compared to 36 per cent in the central cities and 43 per cent in the suburbs. The occupational status differentials between cities and suburbs are substantial. (See Table 4.) Moreover, the very sharp difference between the satellite cities located in the ring of the metro-

TABLE 3

Percentage Distribution of Population, 5 Years Old and Over, by Socio-Economic Status of Area of Residence, According to Migration Status

		Place of Residence 1955							
Central Cities Socio-Economic Status of Area of Residence, 1960	Total Population 5 Years Old and Over	Same House (Non-Movers)	Total Movers	Central City	Balance of SMSA	Elsewhere in Rhode Island	Outside Rhode Island	Abroad in 1955	Moved 1955 Residence Unknown
I	4.4	4.2	4.5	3.3	5.1	10.5	13.1	8.2	8.2
II	10.8	11.2	10.3	10.1	8.6	6.4	15.1	7.9	7.9
III	42.3	43.3	41.2	41.1	43.5	49.5	38.3	30.2	30.2
IV	41.8	40.8	43.2	44.7	41.4	33.5	32.8	52.8	52.8
V	0.7	0.5	0.8	0.7	1.4	—	0.7	0.8	0.8
Total Per cent	100.0	100.0	100.0	100.0	100.0	100.0	100.0	100.0	100.0
Total Number	246,974	144,061	95,028	74,114	11,591	543	8,780	2,076	5,809
Satellite Cities									
I	—	—	—	—	—	—	—	—	—
II	—	—	—	—	—	—	—	—	—
III	11.7	12.7	10.4	3.7	10.7	—	14.7	8.5	4.7
IV	46.1	45.3	47.3	63.4	45.7	*	51.1	50.5	50.1
V	42.1	41.9	42.3	32.8	43.6	*	34.1	41.0	45.2
Total Per cent	100.0	100.0	100.0	100.0	100.0	*	100.0	100.0	100.0
Total Number	60,063	34,807	24,410	1,660	20,971	—	1,711	293	553
Immediate Suburbs									
I	6.2	5.2	7.6	6.3	7.0	6.5	14.3	14.3	3.3
II	35.2	34.1	36.9	44.0	31.0	45.1	45.2	45.2	35.2
III	31.4	31.5	31.4	26.8	34.6	28.1	28.4	28.4	26.8
IV	25.8	27.4	23.0	22.8	25.6	20.3	11.7	11.7	34.0
V	1.4	1.7	1.0	0.1	1.7	—	0.3	0.3	0.7
Total Per cent	100.0	100.0	100.0	100.0	100.0	100.0	100.0	100.0	100.0
Total Number	260,051	157,300	97,579	29,087	54,996	1,048	12,448	1,539	3,633

* No percentage computed; base is under 100 persons.

TABLE 4

Per Cent of White Collar Employees Among Total Population, Non-Movers, and Movers, by Socio-Economic Status of Area of Residence

Socio-Economic Status of Area of Residence, 1960	Total Employed Population	Non-Movers	Place of Residence 1955: Central Cities	Balance of SMSA	Rest of Rhode Island	Outside Rhode Island
Central Cities						
I	71.1	73.1	72.0	81.0	61.3	77.4
II	57.8	61.2	52.5	51.8	63.2	77.4
III	36.7	38.7	33.2	39.3	37.1	48.7
IV	26.9	29.2	23.3	28.2	47.7	41.7
V	15.4	18.5	17.0	17.6	—	12.1
Total	36.4	38.7	32.4	37.4	45.2	54.5
Satellite Cities						
I	—	—	—	—	—	—
II	—	—	—	—	—	—
III	47.4	49.2	*	44.1	—	53.1
IV	26.5	27.9	26.7	23.9	*	38.4
V	21.4	22.8	17.0	18.4	48.1	40.5
Total	26.8	28.4	24.7	23.8	48.5	41.6
Immediate Suburbs						
I	72.0	69.0	69.9	77.2	81.5	84.7
II	52.3	51.1	54.7	52.4	57.8	72.6
III	39.9	39.5	43.5	38.8	44.3	59.1
IV	29.2	29.8	30.5	27.9	45.9	41.6
V	20.3	15.5	*	32.0	—	*
Total	42.8	41.6	47.0	37.8	52.5	66.3

* Fewer than 25 cases in base population.

politan area and the suburbs emphasizes the desirability of separating these two residential categories.

Since a majority of the total population in each of the three residential categories consists of nonmovers, the occupational composition of the nonmovers closely parallels that of the total population. Differentials become obvious, however, in the various migration categories. Of those who had moved between 1955 and 1960 and who were living in the central cities in 1960, only 32 per cent of the intracentral city movers were white collar workers. This percentage increased as the distance of place of origin of the migrants increased. Of those moving into the central cities from outside the state over half were white collar workers.

The only streams containing more white collar workers than the resident population of the central cities are those from outside the metropolitan area and these contributed less than 5 per cent of the total 1960 population. The movers from the balance of SMSA, which included both the movers from the suburbs and from the satellite cities, did not differ from the nonmovers and the total population. The lower concentration of white collar workers among the intracity movers no doubt stems from the higher rate of homeownership of the white collar segments of the population. The migration streams to the satellite cities exhibit a fairly similar pattern.

For the suburbs too, the intra-area movement (encompassed in the balance of the SMSA category) has the lowest proportion of white collar workers. Again, the proportion of white collar migrants varies directly with the distance of their place of origin, rising from 47 per cent of those moving to the suburbs from the central cities to 66 per cent of those coming from outside the state. The considerably larger movement from the central cities to the suburbs than in reverse, combined with the much higher concentration of white collar workers in the exodus to the suburbs has the net result of lowering the overall occupational status of the cities and raising that of the suburbs. Moreover, the larger number of migrants to the suburbs than to the cities from the balance of the state and from outside the state and the higher concentration of white collar workers in the suburban streams reinforces this trend.

Consistent with the use of occupation as one of the variables for classifying the socioeconomic status of census tracts, the proportion of white collar workers in each migration category varies directly with the socioeconomic level of the tract. The more significant comparison is therefore among comparable status levels of the different areas and among the different migration categories of the same status level. In general, the former comparison suggests minimal variation among the different areas. For example, the proportion of nonmovers who are white collar workers is 69 per cent in the highest status level of the suburbs and 73 per cent in the central cities; and, with some exceptions, equally small differences characterize both the other status levels of nonmovers and the various status levels of the other migration categories. Therefore, whatever variations characterize the cities and suburbs as a whole in their selection of migrants result from the greater concentration of the migrants to suburbs in the higher status census tracts. Suburbs attract a higher proportion of white collar workers because of both the larger number of migrants going to the suburbs than to the cities and the greater attractiveness of the suburban high status areas to white collar migrants. This accounts for the widening overall status disparity between the cities and the suburbs.

Educational Selectivity

Since education and occupation are related, the pattern of residential and migration differentials according to education parallels that of occupation. Only 6 per cent of the population 25 years and over living in the satellite cities had any college education, compared to 10 per cent of those in the central cities and 16 per cent of those in the suburbs. Each of the migration categories had the same pattern of residential differentials. The selective role of migration in affecting the educational composition of the population resident in cities and suburbs is evidenced by the statistics shown in Table 5. Of those moving to the suburbs from the central cities 17 per cent had some college education, compared to only 11 per cent of those moving into the cities from the ring. The effect of this difference is accentuated by the much larger volume of the movement to the suburbs than to the cities and by the higher concentration of college educated persons in the movement to the suburbs from the rest of the state and from areas outside of the state.

Within each area the operation of a selection process is also clearly evident. For example, in the central cities the proportion of college educated persons increases from only 8 per cent of the intracity movers to almost one-third of those moving in from outside the state; in the suburbs the proportion increases from 15 per cent of those whose previous residence was in the ring to 43 per cent of those moving in from outside the state. Among those moving to the satellite industrial cities from both the central cities and the ring the proportion of college educated is very low. Although the number of persons moving to these cities from distant places is very small, a higher proportion of the more distant migrants are college educated.

Again, with several exceptions, the level of college education among migrants and nonmovers in comparable status levels of the central cities and the suburbs bears a close resemblance to each other. It is therefore the greater con-

TABLE 5

Per Cent of Persons with One Year or More of College Education Among Total Population, Non-Movers, and Movers, by Socio-Economic Status of Area of Residence

Socio-Economic Status of Area of Residence, 1960	Total Population 25 Years Old and Over	Non-Movers	Place of Residence 1955			
			Central Cities	Balance of SMSA	Rest of Rhode Island	Outside Rhode Island
Central Cities						
I	44.4	43.7	39.7	46.8	61.5	62.8
II	20.7	20.4	16.8	22.3	53.3	47.6
III	9.2	9.1	7.4	4.6	9.2	25.2
IV	5.3	5.2	4.1	5.3	19.8	18.5
V	2.4	1.5	1.0	7.5	—	18.4
Total	10.5	10.3	8.1	11.4	22.1	31.4
Satellite Cities						
I	—	—	—	—	—	—
II	—	—	—	—	—	—
III	16.5	16.6	21.0	13.5	—	41.1
IV	5.5	5.4	3.7	4.4	0.0	19.5
V	4.1	4.1	3.4	2.7	*	15.8
Total	6.3	6.3	4.5	4.4	26.5	21.8
Immediate Suburbs						
I	39.7	36.9	33.0	39.6	62.5	60.6
II	21.1	18.3	20.5	21.2	26.5	46.6
III	12.9	11.6	13.9	11.9	21.8	36.2
IV	6.3	5.7	7.9	6.0	16.4	19.8
V	3.8	3.5	*	4.6	—	*
Total	15.6	13.5	16.8	15.2	26.2	42.9

* Fewer than 25 cases in base population.

centration of college educated persons among migrants to the high status characteristics of the total suburban migrants and the total central city migrants. In short, the same status levels of both suburbs and cities attract persons of similar educational level, but the suburban areas attract more of them.

INCOME SELECTIVITY

Income represents the third socioeconomic variable examined here and the only one not included in the Index of Social Rank. Yet to the extent that income is correlated with occupation and education one would expect to find similar differentials. This is generally true, but the degree of difference varies considerably, as is evident in the income composition of the total population living in each area. Only 4 per cent of those in the satellite cities, but 7 per cent of the central city residents and 13 per cent of the suburbanites, had incomes of $6,000 and over. Among both the nonmovers and the within-area movers, the differences were of the same magnitude. They were somewhat higher in the exchange between the central cities and the suburbs; 14 per cent of those who moved to the suburbs from the central cities but only 7 per cent who moved from the ring to the central cities belong to the high-income category.

As with education and occupation, this selective movement is reinforced by the differentials among those moving from the rest of the state and outside areas. It is most evident in the latter stream; only 8 per cent of those moving to the central cities compared to 21 per cent of those going to the suburbs from outside the state had incomes of $6,000 and over. For all migration groups the proportion of high income persons among those moving to the satellite cities is well below that of the movers to the suburbs and to the central cities.

As Table 6 shows, the pattern of income selectivity differs from that of occupation and education in one major respect. For both the central cities and the suburbs the proportion of persons who were white collar workers or who were college educated increased with the distance of the origin of the move. The proportion in the high income bracket showed a less consistent pattern of variation. For the central cities the proportion of in-migrants in the high income bracket from outside the metropolitan area was distinctly higher than for those originating within the metropolitan area but the percentage was somewhat higher among those from other areas within rather than outside the state. For the suburbs there was very little difference among those whose move originated either within the metropolitan area or in the rest of the state, but among those moving in from outside the state a significantly higher proportion were in the high-income category.

TABLE 6

Per Cent of Persons with Income of $6,000 and Over in 1959 Among Total Population, Non-Movers, and Movers by Socio-Economic Status of Area of Residence

			Place of Residence 1955			
Socio-Economic Status of Area of Residence, 1960	Total Persons with Income in 1959	Non-Movers	Central Cities	Balance of SMSA	Rest of Rhode Island	Outside Rhode Island
Central Cities						
I	22.5	24.6	21.4	21.0	22.7	16.4
II	13.0	13.7	11.7	11.7	11.4	15.5
III	6.8	7.3	5.5	7.1	11.3	7.8
IV	3.6	4.1	2.6	3.1	2.7	2.8
V	2.3	2.0	2.8	2.9	—	5.1
Total	6.8	7.5	5.4	6.6	9.7	8.4
Satellite Cities						
I	—	—	—	—	—	—
II	—	—	—	—	—	—
III	9.5	10.4	0.0	7.2	—	15.4
IV	4.0	4.5	2.0	3.0	0.0	3.0
V	3.4	4.0	1.9	2.7	12.9	1.4
Total	4.4	5.1	1.9	3.3	6.8	4.4
Immediate Suburbs						
I	24.2	21.6	24.9	27.1	21.9	31.4
II	16.3	15.6	16.1	16.0	16.8	24.0
III	11.3	11.1	12.8	10.5	9.6	17.1
IV	7.2	7.0	8.1	6.8	7.7	9.7
V	3.0	2.3	*	4.2	—	*
Total	12.6	11.9	13.9	12.3	12.6	21.2

* Fewer than 25 cases in base population.

This differential also manifests itself in the data for specific status levels of the suburbs. For example, in all but the lowest status level of the suburbs the proportion of high-income persons among migrants is highest among those moving in from outside the state, whereas the differences are much less pronounced among the other migration streams. Moreover, the similarities among comparable status levels of suburbs and central cities are generally greater for the nonmovers and for the three migration categories involving movement from within the state than for the migrants from outside the state. For example, between 21 and 23 per cent of the within-state migrants to high status tracts of the central cities had incomes of $6,000 and over compared to only 16 per cent of those from outside the state; for the same status level of the suburbs, the respective percentages were between 22 and 27 per cent for within-state migrants but 31 per cent for in-migrants from outside the state. The similarity for the nonmovers and the within-state movers does not hold as strongly for the low status levels. In general, the suburbs are more selective of persons with high incomes, even at these low levels. One might speculate that even in the low status tracts of suburbs the added cost of commuting and the higher rate of homeownership result in a higher income type of migrant than for comparable low status areas of the central cities.

Discussion and Summary

The conclusion that migration contributes to the increasing differentiation of cities from their suburbs in socioeconomic status is supported by this analysis. First, the findings emphasize the much larger numerical flow of persons to the suburbs than to the cities and, more specifically, large net gain for the suburbs in their exchange with the cities. Numbers alone do not account for the differential impact of migration on the socioeconomic structures of the respective areas: The migrants, compared to the nonmovers, tend to be more heavily concentrated in the higher socioeconomic groups, as measured by occupation, education, and income. This differs, however, depending on the particular origin of the migrants. More important, the selectivity in favor of the higher socioeconomic groups is stronger in the movement to the suburbs than to the cities. This in itself would be sufficient to produce differentials between cities and suburbs. Coupled with the much larger movement to the suburbs than to the cities, the selective factor accentuates the differentials. For example, of the migrants to the central cities 20 per cent or 2,500 had some college education. Of those moving to the suburbs 24 per cent had some college education, but these college educated migrants numbered 6,400 persons. Since the total population of the central cities and the suburbs was approximately equal both in total numbers and in the number of persons 25 years old and over (for whom education data are available), the fact that the number of college educated migrants is two-and-a-half times as great for the suburbs as for the cities indicates the differential impact of migration. The same pattern holds with respect to occupation and income.

But in-migration is only one part of the migration process; the other aspect is the number and composition of the population leaving the respective areas. Unfortunately, the census tabulations do not permit comprehensive evaluation of the out-migrants for the small areas considered here. Comparison can be made, however, of those migrants who move within the area encompassed by this study. Of particular relevance is the exchange between the central cities and the suburbs. The socioeconomic status of the city to suburb migrants was considerably higher than that of the movement from the balance of the metropolitan area to the cities, particularly with respect to income. This differential pattern takes on added significance in view of the variation in numbers involved in the various migration streams. For example, 3,100 of the migrants moving from the central cities to the suburbs had some college education but only 800 of those moving into the central cities from the balance of the SMSA had at least one year of college education.

Our data confirm the Tauebers' conclusions that migrants into both the central cities and the suburbs resemble each other more closely than they do the nonmigrants in the respective areas. Yet our data also point to a consistently higher concentration of migrants of high socioeconomic status among those moving to the suburbs than among those moving to the cities. For an older and somewhat smaller metropolitan area, such as Providence-Pawtucket, the movement into cities and suburbs is not as similar as the Taeubers found for the 12 large metropolitan areas. Despite this difference, the net result of migration is in the same direction, that is, a widening in the status gap between cities and suburbs. But if the Providence data are typical of comparable areas, the process may be even sharper than the Taeuber statistics suggest. Possibly the difference stems from the attempt in this analysis to delineate the suburbs more clearly by giving separate treatment to satellite cities. Since such cities contain a disproportionate number of low status areas and attract a disproportionate number of low status migrants, a lowering results in the proportion of high-status persons moving to the ring part of the metropolitan area as a whole. This in turn suggests that the widespread notion that "truly suburban" areas attract higher status migrants than cities is correct but that this is masked by the inadequate delineation of suburbs in census statistics. Moreover, our findings of differences in migration selectivity for low status and high status tracts in both the cities and suburban areas suggest that the overall differences noted for the suburbs versus the cities are in large measure a function of the greater concentration of high status areas in the suburbs and, in turn, the greater attractiveness of those areas to migrants.

*Variations in Socioeconomic Structure by Race, Residence, and the Life Cycle**†

CHARLES B. NAM • MARY G. POWERS

The literature on social stratification in the U.S. does not clearly specify the relation between population characteristics and socioeconomic variables; yet this relationship is relevant to research in a wide range of areas in social science and therefore deserves more critical examination than it has hitherto received. In this study, census data were used to examine race, residence, and age in relation to two dimensions of the stratification system, namely the distribution of socioeconomic status (SES) and the pattern of status consistency.

* Reprinted with permission from *American Sociological Review,* Vol. 30, No. 1 (February 1965), pp. 97-103.

† Revision of a paper presented at the annual meeting of the Southern Sociological Society in Asheville, North Carolina, April, 1964. The views expressed by the authors are not necessarily those of the Bureau of the Census.

DATA AND METHODS

The data on which this analysis was based were derived from tabulations of the national 0.1 per cent sample enumerated in the 1960 Census of Population.[1] These data provide a description of the U.S. population which is statistically highly reliable.

Two socioeconomic measures were developed in connection with the 1960 Census program, and recodes for them were entered on a 5 per cent sample of census records, from which the 0.1 per cent sample was drawn. The socioeconomic status score is a multiple-item measure derived by averaging scores for the component

[1] Data from this sample are available on computer tapes or punch cards and already have been sold by the Census Bureau to a large number of organizations, mostly universities, for research purposes.

items of occupation, education, and family income. The status consistency measure indicates whether the components of the multiple-item score are at about the same or different levels and, if at different levels, the pattern of their inconsistency. These indexes were derived for chief income recipients in families, and assigned to other family members, and for nonfamily members.[2]

Scores were assigned to the categories of the component items as follows: (1) The scores for education were obtained by computing a cumulative percentage distribution of the education of chief income recipients in families as of 1959. The score assigned to each category of education was the midpoint of the cumulative percentage interval for the category. (For example, persons who had completed five or more years of college were distributed between the 96th and 100th percentiles. A score of 98 was thus assigned to persons who had completed five or more years of college.) (2) The scores for family income were obtained in a similar manner. (3) The scores for detailed occupations were based on the most recently available data, those for males 14 years old and over in the experienced civilian labor force as of 1950.[3] The detailed occupations were scored according to the combined average levels of education and income for the given occupation. Thus, the score obtained is an average score for the occupation and it contributes an independent effect to the total socioeconomic score, which also includes the individual's *own* educational and income levels. Using the number of workers in each occupation, a cumulative percentage distribution was obtained. The score for a given occupation was then determined by taking the midpoint of the cumulative percentage interval for that occupation.

The socioeconomic status score is a simple average of occupation, education, and family income scores for the chief income recipient. The scores for each component item are distributed so that about 10 per cent of the universe falls in each tenth of the distribution of the item. The socioeconomic status scores are, however, distributed so that larger percentages of persons are in the central part of the distribution and smaller percentages are at the extremes.

The status consistency category was also determined from the occupation, education and family income scores. Thirteen categories were derived as follows:[4]

Status consistency category	Characteristics
1	All three components consistent
2	Occupation and education consistent; income high
3	Occupation and education consistent; income low
4	Occupation and income consistent; education high
5	Occupation and income consistent; education low
6	Education and income consistent; occupation high
7	Education and income consistent; occupation low
8	All inconsistent; occupation highest, income lowest
9	All inconsistent; occupation highest, education lowest
10	All inconsistent; education highest, occupation lowest
11	All inconsistent; education highest, income lowest
12	All inconsistent; income highest, occupation lowest
13	All inconsistent; income highest, education lowest

[2] For a fuller statement of the methodology, as well as scores for the component items and other background information see U.S. Bureau of the Census, *Methodology and Scores of Socioeconomic Status.* Working Paper No. 15, Washington, D.C., 1963.

[3] The Pearsonian correlation coefficient between the 1950 scores and scores based on 1960 data, which recently became available is .96. For a few specific occupations, however, the discrepancy in scores between the two dates was substantial.

[4] "Consistency" means a difference of 20 points or less between the scores designated. A score designated as inconsistent (e.g., education in categories 4 and 5) is more than 20 points higher (or lower) than at least one of the other two scores, but the latter (e.g., occupation and income in categories 4 and 5) are no more than 20 points apart. For those classified as Category 1, the difference between lowest and highest scores does not exceed 20 points. For those classified as having all three scores inconsistent (Categories 8-13), the difference between the highest and the middle, and the difference between the middle and the lowest scores, both exceeded 20 points.

The socioeconomic measures used here were designed for comparative analysis and have limited absolute meaning. They may be most useful for comparing different areas or population subgroups, or for using socioeconomic status as a control in studying other relationships. Other approaches may be more useful for other purposes.

SOCIOECONOMIC PATTERNS

Socioeconomic Status

The SES distribution of family heads by race and residence is depicted in Figure 1. Since the distribution for all family heads combined is essentially normal, with a slight skewness toward the lower levels, group differences in socioeconomic status can be viewed graphically in terms of departures from a normal distribution.

For both white and nonwhite family heads, a more favorable socioeconomic distribution was found in the central cities and urban fringes of these cities than outside urbanized areas (that is, in rural areas and small towns and cities).[5] Concentration in the lowest third of the SES range was especially marked among nonwhite family heads residing outside urbanized areas, but the proportion of nonwhite family heads in the highest SES level was also larger outside than inside urbanized areas. Although there is virtually no nonwhite middle class in these areas, a small nonwhite elite does exist, probably consisting of professional and business people serving the nonwhite population, especially in segregated communities.

Other data, not shown in the figure, reveal that persons in urban places outside urbanized areas, like those in central cities, had status distributions much like the total population. In contrast, the status disadvantages of the rural population, particularly the rural-farm population, were striking. Whereas 39 per cent of urban fringe residents had SES scores of 70 or higher, only 6 per cent of the rural-farm population had such high scores. Only 8 per cent of persons in the urban fringe had scores below 30, compared with 49 per cent of the farm population, and half of the nonwhites on farms had scores below 10. The distribution of whites in farm areas was similar to that of nonwhites in central cities.[6]

Status Consistency

A great many articles on status consistency or congruency have appeared recently in the sociological literature.[7] It has been suggested, for example, that persons whose statuses are inconsistent, that is, who rank differently on different status hierarchies, tend to be more subject to abnormalities of personal and social behavior than persons with consistent statuses. If this is so, then it is important to know how status consistency varies among subgroups of the population. Table 1 shows patterns of status consistency for white and nonwhite family heads 35 to 54 years old in various residence areas. By limiting the data to family heads of prime working ages, we have minimized the influence of the irregular status pattern displayed by many younger and older family heads. Consistent and inconsistent types, grouped by extent of inconsistency, are shown within broad cate-

[5] An urbanized area contains at least one city of 50,000 inhabitants or more (1960) and is surrounded by closely settled incorporated places and unincorporated areas that meet certain criteria of population density or land use. An urbanized area may be thought of as divided into the central city, or cities, and the remainder of the area, or the urban fringe. Complete definitions of the urban and rural residence categories used in the 1960 Census are in Bureau of the Census, *General Social and Economic Characteristics, United States Summary,* PC (1)-IC, Washington, D.C., 1960.

[6] The other data referred to in this paragraph were for the total population rather than for family heads, but the socioeconomic distributions for these two universes are very similar.

[7] Examples are: Werner S. Landecker, "Class Stratification" and "Stratification in the Urban Society" in Ronald Freedman, *et al.* (eds.), *Principles of Sociology,* New York: Henry Holt, 1952, pp. 228-239 and 449-463, and "Class Crystallization and Its Urban Patterns," *Social Research,* 27 (Autumn, 1960), pp. 308-320; Gerhard F. Lenski, "Status Crystallization: A Non-Vertical Dimension of Social Status," *American Sociological Review,* 19 (August, 1954), pp. 405-413, and "Social Participation and Status Crystallization," *American Sociological Review,* 21 (August, 1956), pp. 458-464; Elton F. Jackson, "Status Consistency and Symptoms of Stress," *American Sociological Review,* 27 (August, 1962), pp. 469-480; and Leonard Broom, "Social Differentiation and Stratification," in Robert K. Merton, Leonard Broom, and Leonard S. Cottrell, Jr. (eds.), *Sociology Today,* New York: Basic Books, 1959, pp. 429-441.

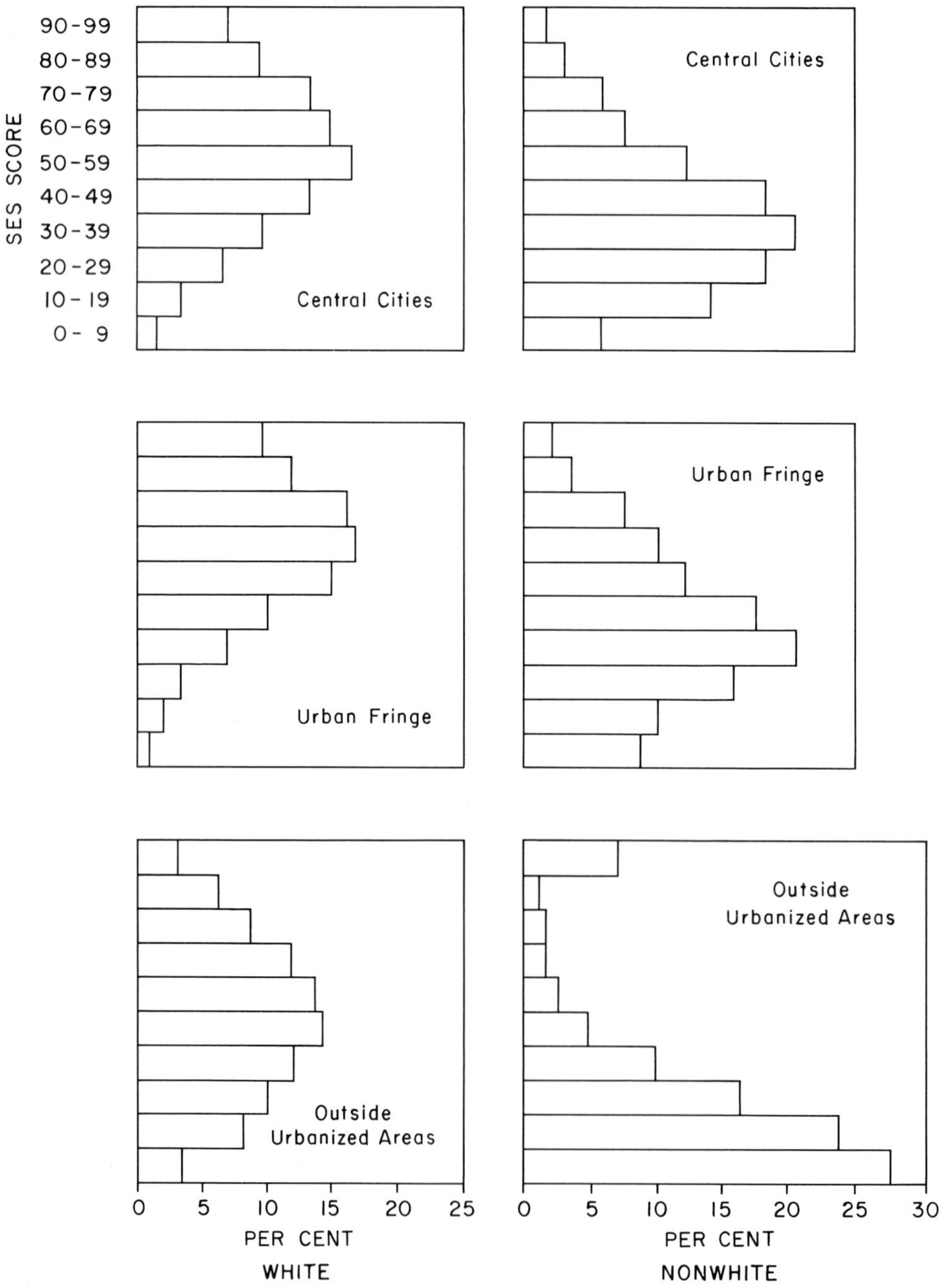

FIGURE 1

Socioeconomic status of family heads by race and residence: 1960.

TABLE 1

Status Consistency of Family Heads Ages 35 to 54, by Race, Residence, and Socioeconomic Status: 1960 (in percentages)[a]

Socioeconomic status and consistency type	White family heads: Central cities	Urban fringe	Outside urbanized areas	Nonwhite family heads: Central cities	Urban fringe	Outside urbanized areas
All SES scores	(5,575)	(4,733)	(8,493)	(1,096)	(187)	(704)
	100	100	100	100	100	100
All statuses consistent	28	31	28	26	25	46
One status inconsistent	62	59	63	63	65	50
All statuses inconsistent	11	10	9	11	11	4
SES scores 80 to 99 (high)	(1,118)	(1,289)	(1,040)	(47)	(10)	(9)
	100	100	100	100	100	100
All statuses consistent	64	64	61	68	70	22
One status inconsistent	36	36	39	32	30	78
All statuses inconsistent[b]	..	..	..	..	..	..
SES scores 50 to 79	(2,834)	(2,551)	(3,474)	(271)	(49)	(52)
	100	100	100	100	100	100
All statuses consistent	19	21	21	19	16	10
One status inconsistent	68	67	68	70	74	83
All statuses inconsistent	13	12	11	11	10	8
SES scores 20 to 49	(1,476)	(847)	(3,225)	(600)	(100)	(260)
	100	100	100	100	100	100
All statuses consistent	12	11	14	15	13	11
One status inconsistent	72	72	75	70	72	79
All statuses inconsistent	16	17	11	15	15	10
SES scores of 0 to 19 (low)	(147)	(46)	(754)	(178)	(28)	(383)
	100	100	100	100	100	100
All statuses consistent	61	57	73	61	64	76
One status inconsistent	39	44	27	39	36	25
All statuses inconsistent[b]	..	..	..	..	..	..

[a] Number of sample cases is shown in parentheses.

[b] The criterion for consistency (see footnote 4) makes it impossible for persons with extreme SES status scores to have all statuses inconsistent.

gories of SES to indicate the general status levels at which the consistency patterns occur. Since the patterns obtained are, in part, a function of the procedures used, greater emphasis should be placed on using these data for comparative analysis than on determining absolute levels of SES and consistency in different groups.[8]

The proportion of persons with consistent statuses was greatest at the lowest and highest

[8] The method used to measure status consistency results in about 30 per cent of all family heads having consistent statuses. The definition of consistency used here is similar to that used by Lenski, *op. cit.*, but differs in the variables used (does not include ethnicity) and in the criterion for establishing consistency.

SES levels in every group, and inconsistency was characteristic of the middle socioeconomic ranges. Variations in consistency distributions among racial and residence groups were generally small, but there were some notable deviations from the general pattern.

Among family heads with status scores of 80 or higher, the percentage with consistent statuses was slightly higher for nonwhites than for whites in urbanized areas but much lower for nonwhites than whites outside urbanized areas. These differences may be partly a function of the dissimilarity of SES distributions by race even within the top status range and of the small, and hence statistically less reliable, sample of nonwhites at this socioeconomic level.

Nonwhite family heads with SES scores of 50 to 79 who did not live in large cities were somewhat less likely than whites to have consistent statuses. Detailed data by consistency type reveal that unequal opportunities for nonwhites to achieve jobs and income commensurate with their education characterized all areas but particularly areas outside central cities. For family heads with scores of 20 to 49, broad consistency patterns among color and residence groups were more similar than in the upper part of the middle SES range, but the economic disadvantage of nonwhites could still be observed.[9] Among family heads at the lowest status levels, consistency differentials by color were moderate but those by residence were sharply drawn.

By combining SES and consistency data, we can learn more about particular status groups in our society. For example, abject poverty is not based on low income alone. Individuals who also rank low on occupation and education lack the potential for mobility. Three-fourths of the family heads 35 to 54 years old with SES scores under 20 who were living outside urbanized areas, ranked low in all three status hierarchies, compared with three-fifths of those in urbanized areas (Table 1). Among all nonwhite family heads outside urbanized areas, 41 per cent had consistently low statuses, compared to 10 per cent of nonwhites in urbanized areas, 7 per cent of whites outside urbanized areas, and 1 per cent of whites in urbanized areas. Data for the farm population indicate that about 20 per cent of white family heads and about 60 per cent of nonwhite family heads had consistently low statuses.

Families in an impoverished condition, as indexed by low status in all three hierarchies, numbered three and one-half million in 1960; one million of these were nonwhite. Other census data indicate that the total number of families with incomes of less than $3,000 was about nine and one-half million, of whom two million were nonwhite. Thus, about one-third of the white families who would be regarded as poor on the basis of income alone were also of low education and occupational status, whereas this proportion was one-half for nonwhites.

Status, consistency, and the life cycle.

Variations in socioeconomic level throughout the life cycle can be described in terms of age. Family heads under 25 years of age had a fairly normal SES distribution with a concentration at the center. At ages 25 to 34, the distribution shifted toward the higher status levels, so that the modal status was in the 50-59 score range. Family heads 35 to 44 years old had still a higher average SES level and a much more platykurtic distribution than the younger groups. Among family heads 45 to 54, the average socioeconomic level was lower and the distribution again approached normality with a slight bias toward high scores. (Our tabulations do not indicate the specific age at which the decline begins.) The reversal continued among those 55 to 64 years old, with the modal status in the 40-49 range. Status levels among the oldest family heads, those 65 and over, were extremely low, with the modal score in the 10-19 range.

The attainment of peak status in education, occupation, and income occurs at different times in the life span of the average individual. Ordinarily, one's formal education is completed at an early age, at least before age 35; the type of occupation in which a person settles may have been entered at an early age but usually is not clearly determined until formal education has been completed; and peak earnings are usually not achieved, nor is family income at its highest, until some years of employment have passed.

[9] The frequencies in specific inconsistency categories generally were small, but the data show that the chief difference between whites and nonwhites was that, more often than whites, the nonwhites' income was discrepantly low or their education discrepantly high.

Of course, subgroups of the population vary in the timing of these events. For these reasons, the point in the life cycle at which persons are evaluated decidedly affects their socioeconomic position.

The diagrams in Figure 2 describe status levels and consistency patterns for family heads in six consecutive age groups.[10] The eleven possible categories of inconsistency have been grouped differently here than they were in Table 1, where the distinction was based on the number of inconsistent status components. In Figure 2, inconsistency is defined in terms of the expected education-occupation-income sequence of attained statuses.[11] Type 1 inconsistency includes categories 3, 4, and 11; Type 2 inconsistency encompasses categories 6, 7, 8, and 10; and Type 3 inconsistency includes categories 2, 5, 9, and 12.

"Type 1 inconsistency" patterns could conceivably stem from a time lag in the attainment of peak statuses. Thus, occupation and income are at lower levels than education, as is often the case for recent college graduates. In "Type 2 inconsistency," none of the statuses is more than one step out of line from the sequential pattern. For example, occupation may be higher than education, which is higher than income, for such persons as self-appointed ministers and preachers. Finally, "Type 3 inconsistency" includes patterns in which a status is two steps out of line. For instance, education may be lower than income, which in turn is lower than occupation, as for older retail store proprietors.

Since Type 1 inconsistency includes persons in the process of attaining their peak statuses, it was, of course, inversely related to age. This type of inconsistency is typical of family heads under 35 years old, most of whom have completed their education but are still gaining in economic status. Because Type 1 inconsistency is normal for persons under 35, they are not likely to view such a situation as unfavorable but, for older persons with similar status inconsistencies, the situation is less normal and less likely to be temporary. Consequently, behavior patterns associated with different types of status inconsistency can be expected to vary with age.

Type 2 inconsistency showed no pronounced change with age, although it did tend to be higher in the 20-49 SES score range. Type 3 inconsistency, at each status level, increased with age until age 65, at which point it began to decline. The trend in this abnormal type of inconsistency is partly a function of historical changes in the societal level of education and occupation. The index used to measure inconsistency was based on standards for a population covering all adult ages; middle-aged and older family heads tend to have less education and, to some extent, lower occupational status, than the younger ones, but their income is higher. The better earning capacity of persons in the middle years, resulting from tenure, job experience, and other income-producing factors, makes the tendency toward status inconsistency all the stronger. For many aged family heads, income drops to a level more commensurate with their education, thus producing less Type 3 inconsistency in the 65-and-over group.

Discussion

Several implications for research in social stratification can be drawn from the foregoing analysis: (1) The characteristic socioeconomic differences between whites and nonwhites and between rural and urban residents should be carefully considered — and controlled where appropriate and feasible — in any study of the relation between socioeconomic status and other variables. (2) Age affects the distribution of socioeconomic status because shifts in status patterns occur as persons pass through the life cycle; hence, analysis involving status variables should take account of the ages of persons in the sample. (3) The introduction of a measure of status consistency into socioeconomic analysis helps to identify more precisely certain status groups in the society, for example, the "hard-core poor," whose education and occupational

[10] Limitations in the extent of tabulation possible at the time the data were obtained precluded obtaining separate data for white and nonwhite family heads. Note that these data by age are based on cross-sectional data containing a mixture of life-cycle effects and inter-cohort differentials.

[11] Otis Dudley Duncan applies this normal sequence in an explanation of the relation between education and income in "Occupational Components of Educational Differences in Income," *Journal of the American Statistical Association,* 56 (December, 1961), pp. 783-792.

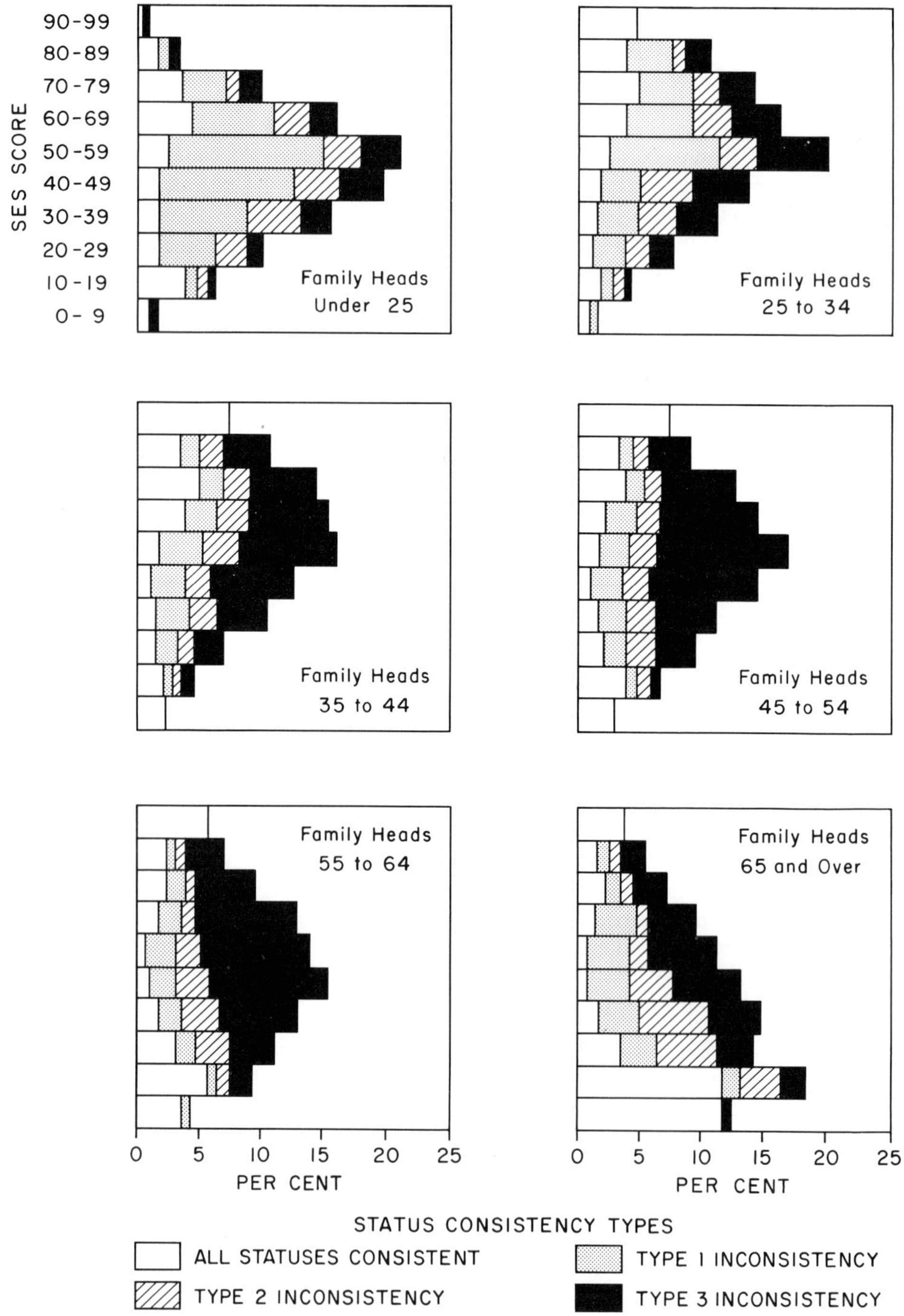

FIGURE 2

Socioeconomic status and status consistency of family heads, by age: 1960.

status is as low as their income. Other status groups that can be identified in the same way include elites (consistently high statuses) and the "normal" middle class (consistently medium SES levels). (4) Analyses of status inconsistency should distinguish specific types of inconsistency, which may have different behavioral consequences.[12] For example, when status inconsistency is a function of the normal time lag in attaining certain statuses, it may produce little mental stress, whereas greater stress may result from status inconsistency stemming from more permanent disadvantage in some statuses.

The demographic approach to the study of social stratification is promising because population variables are so intimately related to status variables.[13] Further research along the lines of the present study should lead to significant contributions to our knowledge of social structure in the United States.[14]

[12] Jackson, *op. cit.*, found these distinctions useful in differentiating status correlates of stress.

[13] For a general discussion of this point of view, see Leo F. Schnore, "Social Mobility in Demographic Perspective," *American Sociological Review*, 26 (June, 1961), pp. 407-423.

[14] The authors and Professor Basil Zimmer, of Brown University, have begun work on a more elaborate study of the socioeconomic structure using the measures cited in this article, and based on a larger sample of the 1960 Census. Among the research foci are the ecology of stratification; family life cycle changes in status patterns; the interrelations of socioeconomic level, status consistency, and level of living; and the effect of variations in measurement techniques on the interpretation of status variables. The analysis contemplated will not begin to exhaust the possible research in this area.

*Social Mobility in Demographic Perspective**†

LEO F. SCHNORE

THE SCOPE OF DEMOGRAPHY

Although its place in demographic analysis is not fully appreciated, the topic of social mobility can be easily shown to lie within the province of demography when the field is realistically defined. All that is required is an awareness of the demographer's interest in population composition. The concept of "population composition" refers to any view of an aggregate that recognizes differences within it. In theory, the criteria and cutting points employed and the categories utilized could cover an unlimited range of quantitive and qualitative characteristics amenable to being distinguished and counted; the fact that they do not do so is a matter of convention.[1]

Failure to recognize the place of social mobility in the field is not surprising, for demography has presented definitional difficulties since the term was coined in 1855.[2] In fact, it appears that there is no clear-cut conception of demography as a discipline with distinguishable boundaries until the present century. One widely quoted definition was set out by Wolfe in 1931, wherein demography was described as, "The

* Reprinted with permission from *American Sociological Review*, Vol. 26, No. 3 (June 1961), pp. 407-423.

† Prepared for the Workshop on Methodology and Systems Formulation, Social Systems Research Institute, University of Wisconsin.

[1] See Joseph J. Spengler and Otis Dudley Duncan, editors, *Demographic Analysis*, Glencoe: Free Press, 1956, p. 439; George Lundberg, *Foundations of Sociology*, New York: Macmillan, 1939, pp. 459-460; and Kingsley Davis, *Human Society*, New York: Macmillan, 1949, p. 552.

[2] Achille Guillard, *Élements de statistique humaine; ou démographie comparée*, Paris: Gullaumin et cie., 1855.

numerical analysis of the state and movement of human population inclusive of census enumeration and registration of vital processes."[3] This definition has the virtue of specifying the basic sources of demographic data, but its broad reference to the "state and movement" of population is unnecessarily ambiguous. As we shall see, only certain aspects of the "state" of a population come under demographic purview, while the "movements" to which demographers attend — social as well as physical — are quite readily specified.

Sources of Data

The "state" of a population is ordinarily ascertained by means of a *census* — an enumeration, whether complete or partial (via sampling), of the number and characteristics of a given population at a given point in time. The cross-sectional element in this definition is critical; a census offers a snapshot, or an essentially static portrait of a population. However, only three facets are of demographic interest: (1) size, (2) spatial distribution, and (3) composition. This last aspect — the "make-up" of a population — represents the subdivision of a population into significant biological, social or economic categories.

In sharp contrast with the census stands the *registration* system, designed to record and compile the incidence of certain events at or near the time of their occurrence. Note that "events" and not persons are the units employed; more important, recording occurs more or less continuously, rather than at arbitrary points in time, so that the census "snapshot" may be augmented by a "moving picture" of closely spaced observations. Now "registration," as a system of data collection, is not to be confused with "vital statistics," which typically include only births, adoptions, marriages, separations, annulments, divorces, and deaths.[4] Other events that are amenable to registration are migration and various types of mobility. Movements between modern nation-states, or "international migrations," are commonly registered. In contrast, "internal migration," or change of residence within a country, is less frequently a subject of registration. Registration is also logically applicable to other types of mobility, in the sense of movements in the social system, or status changes. For example, occupational changes may be recorded in a registration system; they are analogous to changes in marital status, and may be registered just like marriages and divorces, albeit at great expense.[5]

In any event, the two major sources of demographic data — census and registration systems — must be seen as complementary devices, and they are particularly informative when their products are combined. The mutual relevance of the two types of demographic data is readily appreciated as soon as it is recognized that the "movements" of population that are of interest to demographers include all those events that bring about alterations in a population's size, distribution, or composition.[6]

The Demographic Equation

The demographer is obviously interested in such phenomena as fertility and mortality, the "vital processes" by means of which the size of the world's population is determined. Here is also the basis of the demographer's concern with migration or physical movement through space. Even in the absence of significant variations in fertility and mortality, substantial changes in distribution, and in the size of local populations, can be readily effected by migratory movements.

[3] A. B. Wolfe, "Demography," *Encyclopaedia of the Social Sciences,* New York: Macmillan & Co., 1931, 5, pp. 85-86.

[4] Although sometimes discussed as the means of entering or leaving a particular population, closer examination reveals that vital statistics refer to ways of entering or leaving a given family. This fact is undoubtedly related to the legal basis of these data collection systems.

[5] A census may provide surrogate data on mobility. See Donald J. Bogue, "The Quantitative Study of Social Dynamics and Social Change," *American Journal of Sociology,* 57 (May, 1952), pp. 565-568; Bogue describes "mobility statistics" as census data referring to a "change in some status during an arbitrarily selected interval of time," and "tenure statistics," wherein "each person is asked when he entered his present status."

[6] For more detailed accounts, see George W. Barclay, *Techniques of Population Analysis,* New York: John Wiley and Sons, 1958; Mortimer Spiegelman, *Introduction to Demography,* Chicago: The Society of Actuaries, 1955; Peter R. Cox, *Demography,* Cambridge: At the University Press, 1950; Hugh H. Wolfenden, *Population Statistics and Their Compilation,* Chicago: University of Chicago Press, 1954, rev. ed.

Recognition of the fundamental role of the vital processes (fertility and mortality) in producing changes in population size has given rise to definitions of the field phrased solely in terms of vital statistics.[7] This emphasis has survived in more recent definitions, although migration is typically added. As an example, consider Davis's delineation of the province of demography:

"The primary tasks of demography are (1) to ascertain the number of people in a given area, (2) to determine what change — what growth or decline — this number represents; (3) to explain the change, and (4) to estimate on this basis the future trend. In explaining a change in numbers the populationist begins with three variables: births, deaths, and migration. He subtracts the deaths from the births to get 'natural increase' and he subtracts the emigrants from the immigrants to get 'net migration' . . . It is clear that any factor influencing the number of people must operate through one or more of the variables mentioned. *In no other way can a population be changed.* For this reason we may call the four variables [fertility, mortality, immigration, and emigration] 'the primary demographic processes.' They represent the core of population analysis."[8]

More recently, Davis has identified these four variables as "strictly demographic realm [containing] the first-order variables — those through which, and only through which, any other factor can influence population change."[9] While it is an adequate representation of demographic interest in population size and distribution, we shall see that this view contains a serious deficiency as a characterization of demography as it has actually developed in the course of the past century. What it fails to include is an explicit recognition of the demographer's interest in population *composition,* and his complimentary concern with *social mobility.*

Compositional change occurs in the absence of vital events, and in the absence of any migratory movement whatsoever. Consider a population composed of persons in various marital statuses. The marital composition of the population in any short time interval can obviously be altered without any births, deaths, or migrations if a substantial number of persons marry or secure a divorce, i.e., change their marital status. Although not ordinarily so labelled, these movements are forms of "social mobility" in the generic sense that we want to develop here.

Another, more complicated example will serve to show that many compositional changes are the effects of variations in fertility, mortality, migration, *and* social mobility operating in combination. Consider the problem of the changing "social class" composition of a purely hypothetical nation. In this imaginary country, *fertility* is inversely related to social class — i.e., the higher classes exhibit significantly lower fertility. Similarly, *mortality* and social class are negatively associated, so that substantially higher death rates occur in the lowest strata. Let us suppose, however, that the net effect of these tendencies favors the lower classes, whose fertility rates are high enough to compensate for their higher mortality rates, so that their rates of natural increase consistently remain above replacement requirements. Let us further assume that the higher strata are reproducing themselves at levels so low that even their low mortality rates cannot prevent net deficits from being sustained year after year. With respect to *migration* into and out of this hypothetical country, moreover, let us imagine that immigrants typically arrive with occupational skills that fit them for unskilled and menial labor; immigrants thus tend to enter the national class structure at the bottom. At the same time, emigration from the country — much smaller in volume — is not occupationally selective, so that neither upper nor lower strata lose disproportionate numbers from their ranks.

Now the combined effect of all these class-contingent demographic processes, operating over a period of time, would yield a class structure exhibiting a progressively greater bulge at the bottom, accompanied by a radical shrinkage at the top. The lower strata, constantly replenished by the numbers represented by the "gap" between the vital rates, and further swollen by net immigration, would expand rapidly. At the

[7] See, for example, George Chandler Whipple, *Vital Statistics,* New York: John Wiley and Sons, 1919, p. 1.

[8] *Op. cit.,* pp. 551-552; italics added.

[9] Kingsley Davis, "The Demographic Consequences of Changes in Productive Technology: An Essay on the Problem of Measurement," in *Social, Economic and Technological Change,* Paris: UNESCO, 1958, p. 197.

same time, the upper strata would be suffering the numerical decimation of an unfavorable balance between the vital rates, and — unable to depend upon immigration to compensate for the "natural" deficits — would exhibit absolute losses.

Up to this point we have considered only certain simple relations between social class, vital rates, and migration. What of the implications of this situation for class composition and social mobility? Let us suppose that a series of censuses over the period of observation disclosed no noticeable change in class composition, as indexed by the proportions in various occupations. Despite the implications of immobility or class equilibrium suggested by these data, we would actually have to infer considerable net upward *social mobility*. In other words, substantial numbers of persons would have to experience occupational changes — either intergenerationally or in individual career terms — from lower to higher positions, in order to preserve the same over-all class composition. This is because the remaining demographic variables are behaving in such fashion as to yield surpluses at the bottom and deficits at the top. If the successive censuses revealed changes in class composition representing an occupational "up-grading" of the entire population, by means of expansions at the top and contractions at the base, then even more net upward mobility would have to be inferred. Note that we specify "net" upward mobility, in recognition of the fact that changes may occur in either direction as far as individuals are concerned.

We may summarize the foregoing argument in more abstract terms. If one is exclusively interested in changes in population size and/or distribution in a given time interval, then the four "first-order variables" specified by Davis are sufficient for demographic analysis. As he has pointed out,

"If 'r' is the rate of growth, then the following equation holds:

$$r = (b - d) + (i - e)$$

where 'b' is the birth rate, 'd' the death rate, 'i' the immigration rate, and 'e' the emigration rate for a given period. If the population in question is that of the whole world, migration drops out of the picture, leaving only natural increase."[10]

By strictly analogous reasoning, changes in population distribution can be disaggregated or separated into their demographic components, and appropriate weights can be assigned to the responsible processes according to their actual contributions.

If one is concerned with changes in composition, however, the "demographic equation" must be modified accordingly, in order to take account of the possible role of social mobility. Thus for the changes in the size of a particular occupational stratum or marital status category, the proper expression would read:

$$(B-D)+(I-E)+(X-Y)$$

where "B," "D," "I," and "E" refer to the *absolute* numbers of births, deaths, immigrants and emigrants respectively, and where "X" signifies movement into, and "Y" denotes movement out of, the stratum or category.

Thus social mobility is a subject of vital interest to demographers. The concern may be direct and for its own sake, as in the analysis of accessions to and departures from the labor force. More frequently, certain kinds of mobility are of interest for the bearing they may have upon vital rates, as exemplified by the concern shown by students of fertility over the marriage rate, which reflects the relative frequency of one kind of change in status. Demographers frequently analyze changes in composition into their "components," as portrayed in the expression given immediately above. Whatever the motivation behind the work, however, and whatever the practical or theoretical ends that are served, the study of various kinds of social mobility is an important part of the demographer's stock in trade.

Defining the Field

The most serviceable definition of demography — one that is neither unmanageably broad nor unduly restrictive, and one that gives due attention to the actual activities of professional demographers — has recently appeared in a formulation by Hauser and Duncan:

[10] *Ibid.*, p. 197.

"Demography is the study of the size, territorial distribution, and composition of population, changes therein, and the components of such changes, which may be identified as natality, mortality, territorial movement (migration), and social mobility (change of status)." [11]

These writers distinguish rather sharply between "demography" and what they choose to call "population studies," reserving the former term for the more technical and descriptive aspects of demographic inquiry. Under the rubric of "population studies" they refer to any analysis, undertaken from any of a wide variety of disciplinary viewpoints, that focusses upon demographic phenomena as either independent or dependent variables. This distinction gives formal recognition to the many points of contact between demography and a host of scientific specialties, both biological and social, and these links deserve a few brief remarks.

It should be obvious that demography is not the exclusive property of any one discipline. Demographic study is informed by any body of theory or research that bears upon the questions of human birth, death, and movement, whether through social or physical space. Many subfields of biology thus qualify as conducting "population studies," although there is some disposition among social scientists to pre-empt the field, as when Davis asserts that "whenever the demographer pushes his inquiry to the point of asking why the demographic processes behave as they do, he enters the social field." [12] Moreover, it is futile to try to link demography to any one of the special social sciences. The fact that most demographers in the United States are trained as sociologists is as fortuitous as that most representatives of the profession in Europe are trained as economists, actuaries, public health statisticians, or anthropologists.[13] Nevertheless, we will attempt to show that demography has immediate relevance for sociology, in that (1) a *compositional* view of population inevitably provides a proximate description of *social structure,* and (2) a demographic treatment of *changes in status* yields invaluable data on *social mobility.* Nothing that is said here should suggest that similar arguments could not be made for the special relevance of demography for (say) economics or geography.[14] The author writes as a sociologist, and as one especially concerned with macroscopic aspects of social structure and social mobility as major foci of that discipline. In general, he subscribes to the view that

"Demography may be considered as a service discipline to the other branches of social science. Its data and findings are basic to every other social science because of their immediate descriptive value and, what is even more important, because of their use in suggesting problems for research in other disciplines."[15]

These preliminary remarks should serve to establish the relevance of social mobility for demography. Our next task is to focus more closely upon mobility, to distinguish subtypes of mobility, and to specify the manner in which they are treated demographically.

Types of Mobility and Their Measurement

Up to this point, we have been content to speak of mobility as change in status. Satisfactory as this may be for preliminary purposes, closer analysis must begin by classifying statuses, and then proceed to subdivide them according to the manner in which they may be altered. As it happens, our initial distinction derives, not from demography, but from the literature of anthropology and sociology. It is the widely recognized distinction between *"as-*

[11] Philip M. Hauser and Otis Dudley Duncan, "Overview and Conclusions," in Hauser and Duncan, editors, *The Study of Population,* Chicago: University of Chicago Press, 1959, p. 2.

[12] Davis, *Human Society, op. cit.,* p. 552.

[13] David V. Glass, editor, *The University Teaching of Social Sciences: Demography,* Paris: UNESCO, 1957.

[14] See Glenn T. Trewartha, "A Case for Population Geography," *Annals of the Association of American Geographers,* 43 (June, 1953), pp. 71-97, and the essays concerned with the various disciplines in Hauser and Duncan, *op. cit.,* Part IV.

[15] Amos H. Hawley, *Human Ecology: A Theory of Community Structure,* New York: Ronald Press, 1950, p. 70. See also, Philip M. Hauser, "Demography in Relation to Sociology," *American Journal of Sociology,* 65 (September, 1959), pp. 169-173.

cribed" and *"achieved"* statuses usually credited to Linton.[16]

Ascribed Statuses

Commonly cited examples of universally "ascribed" statuses are age, sex, and certain kinship statuses; these share a non-volitional quality, in that no amount of effort on the part of the individual can alter them. An equally apt example is one's place of birth; although one may lie about it, one's birthplace cannot be changed. By contrast, "achieved" statuses are more clearly subject to change, and as the term itself suggests, effort and volition frequently have a role. In addition, one's educational or marital status, his occupation, and his place of residence are not immutably fixed. Even if they cannot be changed at will (since the norms of many societies treat them in ways as fully deterministic as those governing age and sex) they have the common quality of *potential* for change. The basis of the distinction, however, does not turn upon the presence or absence of a capacity for change *per se;* we shall see that at least one ascribed status changes automatically, and that the forms of change taken by various achieved statuses do not reduce to a single type. Nor does the distinction rest, at bottom, upon the capacity for volition to be exercised. As it turns out, this dimension of status — ascription versus achievement — hinges upon whether or not the status can be determined at birth.[17]

As concrete examples, let us consider the universally "ascribed" statuses first. These include age, sex, place of birth, and kinship within the family of orientation.[18] Among these, age stands out distinctly as a changeable status; while all of the others are immutable, one's age is constantly changing from the instant of birth, for aging is a biological fact to be reckoned with continuously. Equally vital for our purposes is the fact that this change has the quality of irreversibility. Trivial as it may seem at first blush, the fact that one's age changes in only one direction turns out to be of critical significance conceptually and in terms of measurement.[19]

Achieved Statuses

Upon superficial examination, it may seem that "achieved" statuses are simply those that are changeable, since it is difficult to conceive of any that are absolutely resistant to change.[20] Why then utilize the ascribed-achieved dichotomy at all? We shall deal with this issue below; it is more profitable, for the moment, to consider some concrete instances of changeable statuses that fall under the "achieved" rubric. Among the important achieved statuses that are commonly recognized are the following: education, occupation, income, religion, marital status, and kinship in the family of procreation. Each of these could serve as the subject for detailed discussion, but two or three of them merit special attention.

First of all, when educational status is defined in terms of school years completed (as in

[16] Ralph Linton, *The Study of Man,* New York: Appleton-Century-Crofts, Inc., 1936, p. 115.

[17] The fact that they can be ascertained at birth may tempt one to call them "biological" characteristics, but the inclusion of kinship and birthplace as important subtypes stretches the meaning of the term to a point of diminishing utility. Moreover, age and sex are socially defined statuses in every society.

[18] This type of family refers to the kin group into which one is born; it is to be contrasted with the "family of procreation," created when one marries. Adoption into another family of orientation is possible, of course, and it has actually served as an avenue of social mobility in some societies; the existence of the practice makes for a certain degree of ambiguity in classification.

[19] Viewed more broadly, "age" can be conceived in a manner that makes it reversible: one begins life in a state of dependence, moves to a stage of relative independence, and then ages into dependency with respect to a wide range of social responsibilities. The status of "citizen" is also an interesting one, typologically speaking. Determined at birth, at least in the United States, it can be legally lost and regained, as by inmates of certain custodial institutions; in this sense it is changeable and reversible, albeit technically ascribed. The status is also open to achievement, by naturalization. We are ignoring here those cases of changes in sex that occur from time to time. For a distinction between "population structure" (referring to "unalterable characteristics") and "population composition" (referring to "changeable features") see John V. Grauman, "Population Estimates and Projections," in Hauser and Duncan, *op. cit.,* pp. 565-569.

[20] Perhaps "veteran" is one such status; it is clearly not reversible. This example, by the way, should be enlightening to those who persist in attaching particular significance to the exercise of will in "achieved" statuses, for volition may or may not operate.

our census system), it has a more or less unique quality. One may add to, but never subtract from, the number of years of attendance.[21] Another interesting case illustrates the importance of the definitions of the categories employed. If one is concerned with marital status, one is likely to work with a set of categories similar to those used in the United States census, viz., single, married, separated, divorced, and widowed. If so, some of the statuses are clearly reversible, in the sense that a person can be divorced or widowed and he may subsequently remarry, at which time he reassumes a status previously held. For some purposes, however, demographers find it profitable to work with only a crude dichotomy: "never-married" (single) and "ever-married" (including the currently married, separated, divorced, and widowed). In this case, the only possible status change is irreversible.

The other achieved statuses are chiefly marked by the fact of reversibility. Adherents of a particular religion may enter and leave, they may join another church or sect, rejoin their original faith, or forswear allegiance to any religious group. Similarly, an individual may move through a whole series of occupations, from time to time reassuming a position that had been previously abandoned. Finally, one can alter his place of residence, with the obvious option of returning to a place previously occupied. Although we prefer to discuss changes in place of residence as "migration," it is important to recognize the fundamental parallel between such changes and those that may ensue between other statuses; they are cognate processes, and offer a number of interesting problems when they are jointly considered.[22]

Status Changes

It remains only to identify the traditional interest of sociologists in "social mobility" in these terms. This task will be facilitated, however, if we summarize the foregoing discussion in graphic form. Figure 1 encompasses all of the concrete cases discussed above; note that the "unchangeable-reversible" cells are empty by definition, since reversal is a form of change. It is undoubtedly the irreversible and unchangeable quality of most ascribed statuses, together with the changeable and reversible character of most achieved statuses, that have tempted most writers to emphasize the matter of volition. Our analysis, however, has demonstrated that this is not the crucial basis of distinction; rather, it is the extent to which a status is amenable to assignment at birth.

Sociological interest in statuses has taken a number of directions. Perhaps the most popular approach starts from the image of the individual as simultaneously occupying a number of statuses, each of which constitutes a membership in some group or social category. This line of thought leads naturally to a statistical consideration of the co-occupancy of statuses, as in the work of Lenski, Gibbs and Martin,[23] or (more frequently) into a non-statistical analysis of the compatibility of statuses. Concern with "role conflicts" and "marginality" are typical problems here. Both of these approaches may derive from a simple cross-sectional consideration of statuses held at a given point in time. But still another direction of sociological effort begins with the observation that individuals pass through a series of statuses in sequence during the course of a lifetime. Thus some writers are concerned with modal sequences and with the appropriateness of one status for its probable *sequelae* (e.g., youth for adulthood).[24] Allied concepts that have grown out of this area of discussion include "anticipatory socialization" and "resocialization," and the general interest is longitudinal or developmental, with the individual career at issue.

[21] If educational status is defined in terms of simple literacy, the possibility of forgetting acquired skills of reading and writing would make this a potentially "reversible" attribute.

[22] One example will serve. Residence rules (e.g., matrilocal, patrilocal, neolocal) require migration of one or both spouses at the time of change in marital status.

[23] Gerhard Lenski, "Status Crystallization: A Non-Vertical Dimension of Social Status," *American Sociological Review,* 19 (August, 1954), pp. 405-413; Jack P. Gibbs and Walter T. Martin, "A Theory of Status Integration and Its Relationship to Suicide," *American Sociological Review,* 23 (April, 1958), pp. 140-147.

[24] See, for example, Talcott Parsons, "Age and Sex in the Social Structure of the United States," *American Sociological Review,* 7 (October, 1942), pp. 604-616.

All of these theoretical and empirical efforts bear the common stamp of an individualistic emphasis, although degrees of status crystallization or integration can be properly regarded as variable properties of populations in certain applications. Quite different facets of the problem come into view, however, if we assume another posture and consider status from the standpoint of social structure in the large. As Gutman has observed, "Many population characteristics about which information is collected in census tabulations are relevant also to the analysis of social structure." [25] Social structure, in other words, is amenable to study in terms of population composition. The United States has recommended the following items for inclusion in all censuses: sex, age, marital status, place of birth, citizenship, mother tongue, educational characteristics, fertility data, economic characteristics, household data (including the relationship of the individual to the head of the household), and urban and rural place of residence.[26] Such data would comprise a rich mine, indeed, for the student of comparative social structure, for they include all of the specific statuses discussed above, and census cross-tabulations permit an elaborate description of a society's gross morphology. Unfortunately, very few countries compile and publish data on all of these subjects, and the amount of cross-tabular detail is even more limited. Truly comparative structural analysis of more than a small and biased sample of countries will have to await the implementation of these recommendations by nations and territories outside the Western sphere. This fact notwithstanding, it is important to take note of the potential for structural analysis that resides in a compositional view of population.

[25] Robert Gutman, "In Defense of Population Theory," *American Sociological Review,* 25 (June, 1960), p. 328.

[26] United Nations, *Population Census Methods,* New York: United Nations, 1949.

Sociological Views

Our final task in this section is to locate the traditional interest of sociologists in "social mobility" within the framework that we have developed here. Sociological effort has been focussed almost exclusively upon the cluster of statuses in the lower left-hand corner of Figure 1, or more explicitly, on the "reversible achieved" statuses. Not all of these, however, have been the subject of scrutiny in terms of

	Type of Status Change			
	CHANGEABLE		UNCHANGEABLE	
Type of Status	REVERSIBLE	IRREVERSIBLE	REVERSIBLE	IRREVERSIBLE
ASCRIBED	"Citizen"	Age		Sex Place of birth Kinship in family of orientation "Race"
ACHIEVED	Occupation Income Religion Marital status Place of residence Kinship in family of procreation	Education		"Veteran"

FIGURE 1
Types of Status Change, with Examples

mobility. Studies of changes in marital status are ordinarily taken up in the context of family studies. Changes in place of residence and religion have been somewhat slighted in the mobility literature in favor of emphasis upon occupation, income and education, and "social mobility," in the sociological lexicon, has primary reference to changes in these statuses.[27]

Now these three statuses — education, occupation, and income — have seemingly come into analytical prominence because of two facts: (1) social mobility, as a subject of sociological inquiry, has been absorbed into a more general content area, i.e., "stratification;" (2) much of the theoretical and empirical literature in this latter area treats statuses unidimensionally. It ranks them along a single scale, e.g., in accordance with the differential evaluation accorded various statuses. These three statuses have the common feature of being more or less readily ranked; for contrast, one need only think of marital statuses, the "ranking" of which is difficult. Of all the achieved statuses listed in Figure 1, only educational, income, or occupational movements can be meaningfully labelled as "upward" or "downward." Indeed, two of them (income and education) are almost intrinsically quantitative, and can be easily represented as relatively unambiguous scales. It might also be added that a whole host of studies have shown the utility of these variables in predicting a wide variety of behavior of sociological interest — including consumer decisions, voting performance, fertility preferences, and life styles in general. Our intention is not to deny or minimize the value of these inquiries. Rather, it is to point to the rather narrow canvas upon which mobility has been portrayed, and to point to some possible advantages that might derive from a generic conception of "social mobility."

To take only one example, sociologists concerned with mobility are in the habit of dealing only with occupational movements *between* broadly defined strata, ignoring movements *within* the stratum. (Such movements have come to be labelled shifts within a "situs" by a few writers.)[28] There is also a tendency to regard only changes across a particular occupational line — such as those between manual and non-manual jobs — as "true" mobility. Although sometimes dictated by the small number of cases under analysis, and by the demand for imposing comparability upon data derived from different sources, such procedures harbor grave methodological hazards if one is setting out to assess the total amount of occupational mobility in a system wherein the strata consist of assemblages of occupations. Finally, there is the vexing problem of the disposition of agricultural occupations, which do not fit nicely into the usual ranking schemes; what constitutes "upward" versus "downward" mobility is sometimes difficult to determine in rural to urban shifts. Some of these problems are clarified by the adoption of a demographic perspective. Toward this end, we will turn to a review of some demographic contributions to the study of social mobility, viewed in the larger sense to which we have alluded.

Demographic Contributions to the Study of Social Mobility

Demographers, of course, are likely to work with all of the variables enumerated in Figure 1, at least in simple combination. For the most part, however, their empirical efforts have been confined to cross-sectional examinations of cooccupancy patterns among the various statuses. Thus differences between various age grades in education, occupation, income, marital status,

[27] The related topics of "race" and ethnic membership constitute difficult problems of conceptualization and measurement, and they have been practically ignored in this presentation. At first glance, they are obviously ascribed, unchangeable, and irreversible. Such a classification, however, reckons without such phenomena as "race passing" and "assimilation," and evades a whole series of problems arising out of "race mixtures" — problems which render the subject somewhat resistant to systematic treatment. Moreover, an entire racial group may experience upward or downward mobility. The space required to deal with these complex issues can be better devoted to other matters.

[28] See Émile Benoit-Smullyan, "Status, Status Types, Status Inter-relations," *American Sociological Review,* 9 (April, 1944), pp. 151-161; Paul K. Hatt, "Occupations and Social Stratification," *American Journal of Sociology,* 45 (May, 1950), pp. 533-543; Richard T. Morris and Raymond J. Murphy, "The Situs Dimension in Occupational Structure," *American Sociological Review,* 24 (April, 1959), pp. 231-239.

place of residence, etc., are rather well known for countries possessing modern census systems. Still, it must be recognized that these materials do not furnish *direct* evidence concerning mobility between statuses. The cross-sectional emphasis stems from the fact that censuses are typically far more inclusive, with respect to the list of statuses treated, than are registration systems.[29]

Items that are widely registered include the following: births, adoptions, marriages, separations, annulments, divorces, and deaths. Certain countries maintaining "continuous registration" systems add data on changes in place of residence; these record-linkage systems, however, are expensive to maintain, and they tend to be rather fragile, in the sense that they are easily subject to error.[30] Direct demographic evidence is thus effectively confined to changes in marital and familial statuses. Marriage and divorce statistics are especially favored by demographers because of the fundamental bearing of nuptiality upon fertility. These materials are probably of limited interest to most sociologists concerned with social mobility.

There are other changes in status that have not been adequately treated in demographic terms. One of these concerns religious affiliation. In the United States, this item is not even enumerated in the decennial census, and though religion is recorded in some state vital registration systems, actual changes in religious affiliation are not registered as such. Still, this topic is of considerable interest from the standpoint of mobility, when it is regarded in prestige terms. Moore has observed that "Protestant religious denominations in the United States have differential prestige, at least at the community level, and there is some indication of changes in affiliation with career success," and he goes on to suggest the desirability of measuring the more general relation "between income-and-occupational mobility and changes in number and types of associational memberships." [31]

As we have indicated, sociologists evince considerable interest in the relationship between education and social mobility. Although relatively little demographic effort has gone into this subject in the United States, it is perhaps significant that the most intensive investigation thus far conducted in a Western country was carried out under the general direction of a demographer, and that it makes effective use of a variety of demographic techniques.[32] As in the case of religion, this represents another instance in which American demography has not contributed its full potential to the study of mobility.

American demographers, like their sociological counterparts, have been much more concerned with occupational mobility. They have become increasingly involved in various types of "labor force analysis," and this is one area in which occupational mobility is approached more or less directly. Combining data from censuses, sample surveys, and a variety of statistical sources, a large amount of information has been assembled on such matters as rates of entry into and separation from the work force; labor force participation rates by sex, age, and other characteristics; migration and labor mobility; and the length of working life. [33] A number of contact points between this work and various specialities within sociology — including social stratification and social mobility — are concisely enumerated in an essay by Philip M. Hauser on "The Labor Force as a Field of Interest for the Sociologist." [34]

The demographic analysis of social mobility is typically focussed on the relationship between mobility and the "traditional" demographic variables, particularly migration and fertility. The

[29] See the recommendations listed in United Nations, *Principles for a Vital Statistics System,* New York: United Nations, 1953, and the review of actual registration practices summarized in United Nations, *Handbook of Vital Statistics,* New York: United Nations, 1955, pp. 114-119.

[30] Such systems are described in some detail by Dorothy S. Thomas in Appendix C, National Resources Committee, *Problems of a Changing Population,* Washington: U.S. Government Printing Office, 1938.

[31] Wilbert E. Moore, "Measurement of Organizational and Institutional Implications of Changes in Productive Technology," in *Social, Economic and Technological Change, op. cit.*, p. 245.

[32] David V. Glass, editor, *Social Mobility in Britain,* London: Routledge and Kegan Paul, 1954.

[33] The best general introduction to this area is still A. J. Jaffe and Charles D. Stewart, *Manpower Resources and Utilization,* New York: John Wiley and Sons, 1951.

[34] *American Sociological Review,* 16 (August, 1951), pp. 530-538.

literature on rural-urban migration contains a wealth of indirect evidence on occupational mobility, since this shift in place of residence typically involves occupational changes from agricultural to non-agricultural pursuits; selectivity of migration, or the characteristics of movers versus non-movers, has been frequently studied. However, more direct inquiries into the relationship between migration and occupational mobility have been conducted by Goldstein, Bogue, and Freedman and Hawley.[35] Each of these studies, although conducted by a professional demographer, made use of data from other than the traditional demographic sources (nationwide censuses and registration systems). Goldstein employed data from a series of city directories, Bogue used quarterly reports from the Bureau of Old Age and Survivors Insurance for two states, and Freedman and Hawley utilized materials from a special state census of unemployment in which complete work histories were collected. (The latter data are not gathered in the typical census.) It is also important to note that all of these studies conceive mobility in career terms, i.e., as taking place within the individual's own working life, rather than inter-generationally. Both of these features — "non-demographic" data and a career definition of mobility — also characterize another recent demographic study of mobility, that by Jaffe and Carleton, in which the results of a six-city sample survey are utilized.[36]

Demographers have also displayed some interest in mobility in the course of studying fertility. In the empirical work that has been accomplished, mobility has ordinarily entered the analysis as an independent variable, both inter-generational and career measures have been employed, and income changes as well as occupational shifts have sometimes been considered.[37] These sources are perhaps of less direct interest to sociologists concerned with mobility because they offer little in the way of an explanation of the phenomenon, rich as they are in suggesting some behavioral consequences of mobility.

Of greater general interest to the sociologist is the demographic perspective on social mobility provided in Elbridge Sibley's well-known essay, "Some Demographic Clues to Stratification." Sibley succeeded in integrating differential fertility, immigration, and technological progress, considered as factors contributing to a long-term

[35] Sidney Goldstein, "Migration and Occupational Mobility in Norristown, Pennsylvania," *American Sociological Review,* 20 (August, 1955), pp. 402-408; Donald J. Brogue, *An Exploratory Study of Migration and Labor Mobility Using Social Security Data,* Oxford, Ohio: Scripps Foundation for Research in Population Problems, 1950; Ronald Freedman and Amos H. Hawley, "Migration and Occupational Mobility in the Depression," *American Journal of Sociology,* 55 (September, 1945), pp. 170-177.

[36] A. J. Jaffe and R. O. Carleton, *Occupational Mobility in the United States, 1930-1960,* New York: King's Crown Press, 1954. Strictly speaking, a "career" definition of mobility is the only one that conforms to the demographic model elaborated above, in that it yields (together with data on migration, mortality, and fertility) a complete accounting for compositional change in a population. An inter-generational approach to mobility, although somewhat more convenient from the standpoint of data collection, provides only an indirect and incomplete accounting. Comparison of an individual's occupation with that of his father, for example, is roughly analogous to a comparison of population distribution at two points in time. Net shifts can be approximately inferred but there are numerous gaps, including the omission of losses through mortality. Methodological pitfalls include the difficulty of specifying one occupation for the father, when he may have actually held many in the course of his career. (See Richard Centers, "Occupational Mobility of Urban Occupational Strata," *American Sociological Review,* 12 (April, 1948), pp. 197-203). A third type of mobility measurement — relating occupations of newly married men to those of their wives, or to those of the fathers of the spouse — has even more severe methodological restrictions, and is without a direct demographic analogue. Some studies of assortative mating and homogamy have used demographic techniques, but not the "demographic equation." Inter-generational and intermarriage measures of mobility are discussed in Ruth Schonle Cavan, *The American Family,* New York: Thomas Y. Crowell Co., 1953, pp. 226-233. For other problems of measurement, see Melvin M. Tumin and Arnold S. Feldman, "Theory and Measurement of Occupational Mobility," *American Sociological Review,* 22 (June, 1957), pp. 281-288.

[37] For general statements, see Jerzy Berent, "Fertility and Social Mobility," *Population Studies,* 5 (March, 1952), pp. 244-260; Charles F. Westoff, "The Changing Focus of Differential Fertility Research: The Social Mobility Hypothesis," *Milbank Memorial Fund Quarterly,* 32 (January, 1954), pp. 69-103; and Ruth Riemer and Clyde V. Kiser, "Economic Tension and Social Mobility in Relation to Fertility Planning and Size of Planned Family," *ibid.,* 32 (April, 1954), pp. 167-231. Both of these latter reports are from the Indianapolis Study.

net upward mobility in the United States, and offered a cogent discussion of the potential role of education in continuing the process. He concluded that, "Together, immigration and differential fertility have contributed more than technological progress to the upward movement of individuals in America." [38] Although he made no effort to demonstrate this thesis statistically, his discussion remains one of the most lucid analyses of the ways in which the demographic processes bear upon each other, and the ways in which they combine to effect changes in population composition.

Freedman and Freedman have more recently been able to show that rural-to-urban migrants in the United States tend to be found near the bottom of the urban class structure, when their status is measured by income, education, and occupation.[39] Though this may result from excessive downward mobility on the part of migrants (since the survey materials do not identify the point of entrance), the Freedmans infer that rural-urban migrants tend to enter the urban class structure at the bottom. Building upon this basic finding, Goldberg has recently argued that this disproportionate representation of rural migrants in the lower urban strata accounts for the usually observed inverse relationship between social class and fertility in urban populations. Goldberg finds insignificant differences in the fertility of "two-generation urbanites" in the various class levels. The usual inverse pattern is observed only in the farm-reared segment of the urban population. The relevance of his argument at this point should be clear: if the farm-reared typically enter the urban class structure at or near the bottom, it is apparently the upwardly mobile farm-reared migrants who limit their child-bearing most severely.[40] An additional possibility worthy of investigation is that many of the traits and behaviors found to be related to social class standing in urban areas (a) are products of the heavier representation of rural migrants in the lower strata, and/or (b) result from selective upward mobility of farm-reared elements in the urban class structure. In any event, Goldberg's work represents another instance of a demographer working simultaneously with three broad variables — fertility, migration, and mobility. It is out of such detailed investigations that the empirical dimensions of social mobility will be filled in with greater precision.

All of the foregoing studies exemplify ways in which demographic techniques and a demographic perspective throw light upon a subject that is rarely viewed as lying within the province of the discipline. With his repertoire of sophisticated techniques, the demographer seems particularly well qualified to aid the sociologist in the tasks of measuring the volume, direction, and characteristics of the mobile portion of the population. By virtue of his awareness of certain methodological dangers, such as those attending the use of inter-generational measures of mobility, the demographer is also able to provide warning against incomplete treatment of the subject. (Since the demographer employs the concept of a closed system in working with the demographic equation, he is inclined to be sensitive to various "leaks" that characterize sample survey data, as illustrated in our earlier discussion of intergenerational mobility in footnote 36.) The fact that more demographic research on mobility has not been accomplished to date can probably be attributed to the absence of systematic registration of most status changes. The increasing use of sample survey materials by

[38] *American Sociological Review,* 7 (June, 1942), pp. 322-330.

[39] Ronald and Deborah Freedman, "Farm-Reared Elements in the Nonfarm Population," *Rural Sociology,* 21 (March, 1956), pp. 50-61. This study was based on data from a national sample survey; unfortunately, native and foreign-born migrants were not distinguished in the analysis. Similar findings from a survey of a single city are reported in Seymour Martin Lipset, "Social Mobility and Urbanization," *Rural Sociology,* 20 (September-December, 1955), pp. 220-228. See also Howard W. Beers and Catherine Heflin, "The Urban Status of Rural Migrants," *Social Forces,* 23 (October, 1944), pp. 32-37.

[40] David Goldberg, "The Fertility of Two-Generation Urbanites," *Population Studies,* 12 (March, 1959), pp. 214-222. Goldberg questions the relevance of mobility in explaining differentials in fertility, and presents data showing no systematic variation among various (intergenerational) mobility categories. See also David Goldberg, "Another Look at the Indianapolis Fertility Data," *Milbank Memorial Fund Quarterly,* 38 (January, 1960), pp. 23-36. For an earlier study, see Clyde V. Kiser, "Birth Rates Among Rural Migrants to Cities," *Milbank Memorial Fund Quarterly,* 26 (October, 1938), pp. 369-381.

demographers should fill in these lacunae in the traditional sources of demographic data, and they can learn a great deal from those sociologists who have already acquired the methodological sophistication required for handling these materials. Equally important, however, is an awareness on the part of both sociologists and demographers that the latter are well equipped, both technically and conceptually, to tackle the problem of social mobility.

Contributions of Sociologists to the Demographic Analysis of Mobility

With its tradition of descriptive research, it might be thought that the greatest single deficiency characterizing the treatment of social mobility in demography is in regard to conceptualization. Indeed, demographers have been criticized as being inclined to describe without explaining, and as if they were at least averse to theory-building if not actually debilitated by a trained incapacity to theorize.[41] This view represents a gross over-simplification, although students of population have no cause for complacency; their methodological assurance and the somewhat restricted scope of their specialty should have permitted the construction of far more elegant theory than is currently available. In actual fact, however, demographers have much to learn from sociological students of mobility in matters other than concept manipulation at the verbal level.

First of all, there are a number of empirical investigations by non-demographers that merit attention on methodological grounds.[42] The most familiar study is probably the one by Rogoff, in which data from marriage license applications in a single county in Indiana were employed in order to assess the amount, direction and character of occupational mobility in two different time periods.[43] Aside from the substantive results, the main interest of this study lies in Rogoff's effort to distinguish between "individual mobility," as it is ordinarily conceived in intergenerational terms, and "structurally-induced mobility." The latter type of mobility derives from alterations in the occupational structure wrought by technological and organizational changes; different time periods may thus offer different probabilities of mobility for the individuals concerned. By means of an ingenious variant on familiar contingency methods, Rogoff attempted to control structurally-induced mobility and to observe changes in individual mobility. She was unable, of course, to separate the latter from the mobility resulting from differential fertility and mortality, as well as from other sources, but the possible application of her general method to other areas of demographic interest has yet to be attempted; it appears to be

[41] See Rupert B. Vance, "Is Theory for Demographers?" *Social Forces,* 31 (October, 1952), pp. 9-13; George A. Hillery, Jr., "Toward a Conceptualization of Demography," *Social Forces,* 37 (October, 1958), pp. 45-51; and Leighton van Nort, "On Values in Population Theory," *Milbank Memorial Fund Quarterly,* 38 (October, 1960), pp. 387-395. For effective contradictions of this view, see Kingsley Davis, "The Sociology of Demographic Behavior," in Robert K. Merton, *et al.*, editors, *Sociology Today,* New York: Basic Books, 1959, pp. 309-333, and Robert Gutman, *op. cit.* If general sociology offers a more elegant "middle-range" theory than the stable population model developed by A. J. Lotka, the author is unaware of it. Even the theory of demographic transition fares well in comparison with many sociological efforts.

[42] Our identification of "non-demographers" is according to apparent major interest and affiliation with professional societies. Actually, no sharp boundary can or should be drawn; it is the problem, the technique, and the conceptual perspective that counts. Some relevant efforts, however, seem to escape the attention of sociologists and demographers by reason of title or place of publication, so that this rough classification may be useful to the reader. We cannot possibly review all of the relevant sociological contributions here. Useful bibliographies are to be found in Kurt B. Mayer, *Class and Society,* Garden City: Doubleday and Co., 1955; and Raymond W. Mack, Linton Freeman, and Seymour Yellin, *Social Mobility: Thirty Years of Research and Theory,* Syracuse: Syracuse University Press, 1957. A rich literature from other countries has been ignored; see, for example, Theodore Geiger, "Mobilité Sociale dans les sociétés européennes de notre temps," in *Problèmes de population,* Strasbourg: Center Universitaire de Hautes Études Européennes, 1951, pp. 123-134.

[43] Natalie Rogoff, *Recent Trends in Occupational Mobility,* Glencoe: Free Press, 1953. A useful summary of the main facts for the nation, together with a discussion of their implications for social mobility may be found in Albert J. Reiss, Jr., "Change in the Occupational Structure of the United States, 1910 to 1950," in Paul K. Hatt and Albert J. Reiss, Jr., editors, *Cities and Society,* Glencoe: Free Press, 1957, pp. 424-431.

appropriate to the study of rural-urban migration in periods and in areas (e.g., nations) characterized by different distributions of population according to size of place.

In a similar vein, Kahl's work on the sources of social mobility merits close attention by demographers.[44] First of all, Kahl distinguished "technological mobility" (roughly synonymous with the "structurally-induced mobility" discussed above) from "immigration mobility" and "reproductive mobility," with the latter types referring to the differential demographic behavior of the various social strata. By comparing occupational distributions in the United States in 1920 and 1950, by employing estimates of the occupational distribution of net immigration in the same period, and by the use of occupational net reproduction rates, Kahl attempted to estimate the amount of occupational mobility attributable to these sources. Drawing upon data from a national sample survey, in order to estimate total inter-generational mobility, he then proceeded to subtract the foregoing "component" estimates from this total, and thus to derive the amount of "individual" mobility. Although necessarily rough and inexact, Kahl's effort deserves attention, if only as an attempt to give statistical substance to Sibley's discussion.

Another study that stems from a sociological concern with stratification and mobility is the recent comparative study by Seymour Martin Lipset and Reinhard Bendix.[45] Although it has been properly heralded as the first general theoretical treatment of the subject since Sorokin's classic appeared some thirty years earlier,[46] the major interest in the work attaches to the data presented. Most of these derive from two sources: (1) a study of career mobility in a sample of Oakland, California workers; (2) a large number of sample surveys from various nations, dealing mainly with inter-generational mobility. There are few innovations in the career-mobility materials, and the analysis of the international data is marred by several minor technical deficiencies caused by the nature of the data. For one thing, attention is focused upon the inter-generational crossing of the "manual-nonmanual" line, despite evidence that such a dichotomous treatment obscures the total volume of mobility; indirect evidence to this effect, in fact, is to be found in the authors' own Oakland data. Secondly, the study fails satisfactorily to resolve the problem of rural-to-urban occupational mobility, the significance of which varies from country to country, depending upon levels of urbanization. Despite these methodological defects, the volume warrants close attention by reason of the sheer scope of its comparative coverage, which is certainly the most ambitious to be found in the literature.

Lest it be inferred from earlier remarks that demographers have little to learn from sociologists in the way of theoretical insights, attention must be called to the analysis of social mobility by Sorokin, mentioned above. After thirty-odd years, this volume remains the most rewarding general treatment of the topic in the sociological literature, and it deserves perusal by any demographer who undertakes work in the area. Examination of the Lipset-Bendix volume also yields large dividends. Yet there are gaps in the sociologists' discussion of the topic, and some of them are surprising in view of the discipline's presumed interest in explaining variations in mobility at the macroscopic level. By and large, a great deal of attention has been devoted to such matters as motivations for mobility, the emotional consequences of mobility, the stresses and strains that impinge upon the mobile person, and the individual behavioral correlates of mobility. Few sociologists appear to have grappled with the broad issue of *the determinants of variations in mobility at the societal level.* Sorokin, Sibley, Kahl, Lipset and Bendix are certainly prominent exceptions, but there have been only occasional efforts by other sociologists.

The Determinants of Mobility

One little-known discussion of the sources of mobility that deserves some attention has been offered by Havighurst. The major portion of this paper is devoted to an effort at comparing mobility in the United States, England, Australia,

[44] Joseph A. Kahl, *The American Class Structure,* New York: Rinehart & Co., 1957. Chapter IX.

[45] *Social Mobility in Industrial Society,* Berkeley: University of California Press, 1959.

[46] Pitirim Sorokin, *Social Mobility,* New York: Harper and Brothers, 1927; republished as *Social and Cultural Mobility,* Glencoe: Free Press, 1960.

and Brazil by reference to sample survey data; unfortunately, some of the methodological difficulties that characterize the Lipset-Bendix comparative materials are even more in evidence here. In the course of his discussion, however, Havighurst attempts to identify the conditions that make for net upward mobility in a society. First, although he neglects class-selective migration, Havighurst correctly identifies a demographic factor by pointing to the role of differential reproduction; in this respect, his analysis is similar to that of Sibley and Kahl. Havighurst goes on, however, to specify in detail another general condition — the one variously identified as "structurally-induced mobility" by Rogoff, and as "technological mobility" by Sibley and Kahl. In Havighurst's words, this condition is

> "*A shift in occupational distribution so as to increase the proportion of middle and higher status occupational positions.* This could result from:
>
> "a. Change in technology of production which increases the proportion of more technical and highly-skilled jobs. For instance, automation does this.
>
> "b. Change in type of industry from those with many unskilled jobs to those with more jobs requiring technical training. The change from agriculture to manufacturing industry usually does this; and so does a change from farming with human labor to farming with machinery.
>
> "c. Introduction of new industries which require a high proportion of technically-trained and well-paid workers.
>
> "d. Increase of industrial productivity with resultant increase in wages and salaries, which allows people to spend more of their income on services provided by professional people, thus increasing the proportion of such people.
>
> "e. Free or easy access to valuable natural resources, such as good land, gold, diamonds, oil, uranium. This creates people with wealth who take the status positions of owners of wealth." [47]

The principal merit of this brief discussion is that it attempts to move beyond the simple recognition of the possibility of changes in occupational structure — changes that may affect the individual's chances for moving within that structure — to a specification of some sources of structural change *per se.* Although the list he presents is probably not exhaustive, and though it is clearly not made up of mutually exclusive "factors," it serves as a starting point for further analysis.

An Ecological Approach

The sources of change in occupational structure enumerated by Havighurst appear to be amenable to reformulation in terms of the "ecological complex," a heuristic device that seems particularly appropriate to this problem.[48] From the ecological standpoint, mobility may be treated as a demographic variable, with sources of change in that variable to be sought in four general areas, i.e., among other demographic, organizational, technological, and environmental factors. Let us specify social mobility as the *explanandum,* or dependent variable, in an analysis that takes the nation-state as the unit of observation. The independent variables may then be said to include the following:

A. *Other demographic factors:*
   1. Differential replacement, according to social strata, brought about by differential fertility and mortality;
   2. Class-selective net immigration.

B. *Technological factors:*
   1. Innovations in the technology of production (see Havighurst's item "a");
   2. Innovations in the technology of distribution, and especially in transportation and communication, that yield changes analogous to B-1 above, or to C-4, C-5, or D-3 below.

C. *Organizational factors:*
   1. Change in type of industry (see Havighurst's item "b");
   2. Introduction of new industries (see Havighurst's item "c");

[47] Robert J. Havighurst, "Education and Social Mobility in Four Countries," *Human Development Bulletin,* University of Chicago, Committee on Human Development, 1958, pp. 35-36; italics added.

[48] For brief discussions and analytical uses of the ecological complex, see Otis Dudley Duncan, "Population Distribution and Community Structure," *Cold Spring Harbor Symposia on Quantitative Biology,* 22 (1957), pp. 357-371; Leo F. Schnore, "Social Morphology and Human Ecology," *American Journal of Sociology,* 63 (May, 1958), pp. 620-634; Otis Dudley Duncan, "Human Ecology and Population Studies," in Hauser and Duncan, *op. cit.,* pp. 678-716; and Otis Dudley Duncan and Leo F. Schnore, "Cultural, Behavioral, and Ecological Perspectives in the Study of Social Organization," *American Journal of Sociology,* 65 (September, 1959), pp. 132-146.

3. Increases in the size of firms, in order to realize "internal economies," which tend to increase employment in white-collar jobs;
4. A redistribution of wealth resulting from increased productivity, leading to increased demand for certain services (see Havighurst's item "d");
5. A redistribution of wealth by political means, involving either a more or less equitable allocation among the various strata, leading to changes in demand for certain services;
6. A re-organization of external relationships with other nation-states, leading to the creation or expansion of certain occupations (e.g., those in trade and military activities).

D. *Environmental changes:*
1. Bringing new elements of the physical environment under control by technological changes, leading to new industries (see C-2 above) or redistribution of wealth (see C-4 above);
2. Bringing new natural resources into use by discovery or conquest, leading to results similar to those suggested in D-1 above;
3. Bringing new natural resources into use via organizational changes (see C-6 above) or by increased ease of distribution (see B-2 above).
4. The exhaustion of non-replaceable resources, by depletion, erosion, dessication, etc.

Although this scheme undoubtedly remains incomplete, it suggests a new direction for research and analysis that would push our understanding of the sources of social mobility beyond its present point. For one thing, this ecological treatment — based upon an extension and reorientation of Havighurst's reasoning — suggests that we should not be content to point to changes in occupational structure as a prime source of mobility; rather, we should be encouraged to press our analysis one step further, in the direction of a consideration of the *sources* of alterations in occupational structure *per se*. Secondly, this brief effort should indicate how complex and ramified a question is posed when we consider the sources of upward mobility; it should be evident that we cannot be satisfied to point to "industrialization" and leave it at that. Finally, this discussion should serve to demonstrate the potential utility of viewing social mobility from a demographic perspective. Although the adoption of an ecological framework — or any other analytical scheme — obliges the analyst to work with other variables as well, nothing appears to be lost and much might be gained when mobility is treated as a demographic variable.

Summary and Implications

This paper has attempted to show the relevance of a demographic approach to the study of social mobility. Starting with a brief consideration of demography's actual scope, we have tried to show that certain salient aspects of the subject are within the province of demography, and that, in fact, it is a frequent subject for demographic study. Working with a typology of statuses and status changes, we then proceeded to review some demographic contributions to the study of mobility in the large, and as it is more narrowly conceived by sociologists. Reversing the procedure, we then reviewed a number of works by sociologists that recommend themselves to demographers on either methodological or conceptual grounds. In conclusion, we sketched an ecological approach to the problem, in order to illustrate the mutual relevance of a demographic conception of mobility and at least one sociological point of view.

In general, there appear to be three potential contributions — theoretical, technical, and empirical — that would serve to facilitate interchange between sociology and demography in the study of social mobility:

(1) Conceptually, it appears that there is much to be gained from a rigorous exploration of the formal analogies between migration and mobility. It is commonplace that territorial movement and movement through "social space" possess more than a few commonalities, but the potential utility of such a theoretical undertaking appears to be substantial. First of all, the sociologist studying mobility and the demographer studying migration share an obvious interest in the volume and direction of these movements, as well as in the characteristics of movers versus non-movers. Starting with the conceptual apparatus currently employed in migration analysis, it seems that certain concepts and hypotheses recommend themselves for use in the study of mobility; among them are the following: the concepts of migratory pushes, pulls, and opportunities; the intervening-opportunities hypothesis; the concept of migratory backflow, or return migration; the con-

cept of selective migration; the problem of the exhaustion of "pools" of potential migrants; and the distinction between "migration" and "residential mobility." [49]

(2) Technically, the major task confronting both sociologists and demographers is the creation of better classificatory systems. Comparatively speaking, the problem of metrics seems to be a minor one in the case of income and education. Hierarchical classification of occupations, however, constitutes an extremely difficult issue. Representatives of both disciplines in this country are prone to use either the census classification developed by Edwards or a modification of the Hatt-North scale, although recognizing the severe limitations of both schemes.[50] Among other difficulties, the lack of an adequate taxonomy has prevented intensive demographic research into occupational and class differentials in mortality in the United States;[51] this deficiency renders equivocal some of the findings on differential fertility. With respect to mobility, the problem is clear: the very volume of mobility observed is partially dependent upon the number of strata distinguished in the analysis. A reclassification of occupations might proceed along the lines taken by Edwards in his effort to validate his original scheme, i.e., by exploring the educational and income levels achieved by the various occupations, but employing age controls and more up-to-date techniques.[52] Ideally, such a reclassification would take account of census practices in other countries, so that comparative analyses would be facilitated.

(3) Empirically, the great need is for further comparative study. We should not be satisfied with the type of material reviewed by Lipset and Bendix, suggestive as it is, but we should exploit other existing sources of data. One such source is represented by census statistics on occupation. Comparisons of successive censuses in a number of countries, and the computation of simple coefficients of redistribution,[53] would serve to test the major conclusions of the Hollingshead and Lipset-Bendix reviews: that rates of social mobility are substantially the same in all industrialized nations. The ecological approach to mobility sketched here also contained the implicit

[49] See Otis Dudley Duncan, "Human Ecology and Population Studies," *op. cit.*, pp. 699-700. Migration is defined as *inter*-community movement, residential mobility as *intra*-community movement; the mobility analogue of the latter may be movement within a "situs." (See the previous references in Footnote 28.) An interesting taxonomic treatment of migration that has no counterpart in the mobility literature is to be found in William Petersen, "A General Typology of Migration," *American Sociological Review*, 23 (June, 1958), pp. 256-266. One might even seek the mobility analogues of such recurrent physical movements as commuting, for the latter involves temporary shifts in status, i.e., between familial or domestic and occupational roles. See Talcott Parsons, "The Principal Structures of Community," in his *Structure and Process in Modern Societies*, Glencoe: Free Press, 1960, pp. 250-279; and Leo F. Schnore, "Transportation Systems, Socioeconomic Systems, and the Individual," in *Proceedings*, Conference on Transportation Research, National Academy of Sciences, August, 1960 (in press).

[50] See Alba M. Edwards, *A Social-Economic Grouping of the Gainful Workers in the United States*, Washington: U.S. Government Printing Office, 1938; Paul K. Hatt and Cecil C. North, "Jobs and Occupations: A Popular Evaluation," *Opinion News*, 9 (September 1, 1947), pp. 3-13.

[51] See Iwao M. Moriyama and L. Guralnick, "Occupational and Social Class Differentials in Mortality," in *Trends and Differentials in Mortality*, New York: Milbank Memorial Fund, 1956, pp. 61-73.

[52] See Alba M. Edwards, *Comparative Occupation Statistics for the United States, 1870-1940*, Washington: U.S. Government Printing Office, 1943. For a modern approach, see Otis Dudley Duncan, "A Socio-economic Index for All Occupations" (unpublished paper), and his working paper on "The Study of Social Change" (Committee on Social Trends, Social Science Research Council, hectographed, 1958).

[53] The coefficient is equal to the sum of the plus or minus percentage-point differences between two distributions, when the data are arrayed according to the same categories. The latter stipulation renders comparison between countries difficult in some instances, but exploratory work with a number of censuses suggests that the problem is not insurmountable. For an illustrative use of the coefficient of redistribution, see Edgar M. Hoover, "The Interstate Redistribution of Population, 1850-1940," *Journal of Economic History*, 1 (May, 1941), pp. 199-205. Since this procedure ignores differential reproduction and immigration, the results yield inexact estimates of total mobility, but precise assessments of the net shifts. The use of Kahl's method would be preferable, but the requisite data are not at hand for most countries. A large-scale study under the direction of Simon Kuznets and Dorothy S. Thomas has already yielded a rich body of historical statistics on the redistribution of the labor force, manufacturing activity, and residential population; see *Population Redistribution and Economic Growth, United States, 1870-1950*, Volumes I and II, Philadelphia: American Philosophical Society, 1957 and 1960.

hypothesis that societal rates of mobility are linked to levels of economic development and urbanization. If these census-based tests tended to confirm these hypotheses, we would be enabled to pursue more extensive comparative investigations, utilizing data for many nations in which sample survey studies of mobility *per se* have yet to be conducted; all that would be required would be two or three successive censuses. Demographers profess pride in the comparative heritage of their discipline, while American sociologists are frequently accused of an ethnocentric preoccupation with their own culture. Be that as it may, the cross-cultural study of social mobility offers still another logical contact point between the interests of demographers and sociologists.

STUDY AND DISCUSSION QUESTIONS

1. Differential net reproduction among social classes creates an opportunity for upward mobility in the society. How does this operate? Is this factor more or less influential in producing mobility today as compared with twenty years ago? Why?
2. Look up how distributions by cause of death vary by social class. What are the most common causes of death in the lower classes? In the upper classes? Can you give reasons for these patterns?
3. What kinds of data are collected in the census that can be used as measures of social class? What kinds of data of this type are included on vital statistics certificates? What additional items of information might be collected in these sources to obtain a more complete description of the social class composition of the population?
4. It has been stated that upper-class and middle-class persons often pursue specialized jobs which may necessitate long-distance moves from time to time. What sorts of jobs in the United States are included here? Why should they necessitate long-distance moves?
5. It has been noted by many authors that societies based on "caste" organization instead of class organization are often very slow, or nearly impossible, to industrialize. What requirements of industrialization would make this so? How might a caste system affect a nation's migration patterns?
6. Look up the composition of the immigrant population to the United States from the mid-1800's to the early 1900's. How might the various characteristics which these immigrants possessed have affected the social mobility of the population at that time? What effects did it then have on the social stratification picture in the United States?
7. Authors often refer to such characteristics as age, sex, marital status, and race or ethnic status as "basic demographic variables." What part do these variables play in the social stratification system of the United States?

SUGGESTED ADDITIONAL READING

Lasswell, Thomas E. *Class and Stratum.* Boston: Houghton Mifflin Company, 1965.
An introduction to the general area of social stratification.

Kahl, Joseph A. *The American Class Structure.* New York: Rinehart & Company, 1957.
An insightful analysis of social stratification in the United States, which includes a demographic perspective.

Reiss, Albert J., Jr. *Occupations and Social Status.* New York: The Free Press of Glencoe, 1961.
A general treatise on occupational prestige, chapters VI and VII of which trace the development and properties of a socioeconomic index of census occupation categories prepared by Otis Dudley Duncan.

U.S. Bureau of the Census. *Methodology and Scores of Socioeconomic Status.* Working Paper No. 15. Washington: U.S. Government Printing Office, 1963.
Description of techniques used in classifying all persons enumerated in the 1960 U.S. Census according to a multiple-item index of socioeconomic status and a measure of status consistency.

Miller, S. M. "Comparative Social Mobility," *Current Sociology*, IX (1960), 1–89.
A trend report and bibliography on the title topic which covers the material available from a number of different societies.

Wrong, Dennis H. *Population and Society*, 2d. ed. New York: Random House, 1961.
A short introduction to the study of population which includes discussion of class differentials in the basic components of population change.

CHAPTER 12

Population and Education

Another area of social life with which population factors interact is education. By *education* we mean the various ways in which an individual systematically acquires knowledge about the world around him. Included in this definition is formal training in organized schools, colleges, and in specialized programs such as adult education through which instruction is received on a regular basis. Omitted from this definition would be the more casual type of learning individuals acquire, that is, the gradual accumulation of knowledge during everyday observation of people, things, and processes around them, as well as instruction received for recreational purposes.

The effect of education on population is seen most clearly in the relation of education to fertility. One might think of education as operating in two ways to influence fertility. First, it affects the level of living and life style of an individual. These help to shape the norms about fertility behavior he will adopt and may determine the means to uphold these norms available to him. Second, through the extent and nature of instruction received, education operates to provide an individual with the knowledge he needs to regulate his fertility behavior. The article by Dinkel provides evidence of the inverse relation between educational level and fertility and examines the relative education of husbands and wives as factors affecting fertility.

Education is also related to mortality through the two principal avenues mentioned above. On the one hand, the level of living and life style associated with a given amount of education identifies the social milieu within which individuals regulate their health care. Different norms concerning actions that have mortality implications are adopted depending on one's educational level. On the other hand, knowledge the individual has gained about ways to avoid death will improve his life chances, and persons with high levels of education will usually have greater knowledge about these means of mortality postponement than will persons with little education.

Migration rates also vary among persons in different educational categories. Research has shown that long-distance migrations within the United States are selective of the better educated, regardless of the direction or actual distance of movement. Shorter-distance migrants, many of whom are rural-to-urban migrants, are drawn from both the upper and lower educational categories. Here we note that education and general socioeconomic status are highly related and that this relation may help explain the relation of education to migration. At the same time, knowledge about opportunities to improve one's residential location is more often available to better-educated than to poorer-educated persons; this would also seem to have an effect on migration selectivity by education.

Demographic factors are instrumental in the educational development of a country. Both in terms of current educational effort (as indicated by measures of school *enrollment* of young persons) and educational attainment (as indicated by measures of *literacy* and *years of schooling completed*), educational conditions are affected by population changes in a society. Surveying the historical trends in American education documented in census reports, Folger and Nam separate total increase in the numbers enrolled in school over the past several decades into that part which is due to population increase and that part which is due to higher proportions of children and youth at each age enrolling in, and continuing on in, school. The relative effects of these two factors is observed to have changed with time, as population conditions and educational opportunities have changed. The effects of population compositional and distributional factors on enrollment are also seen in differential enrollment rates by age, sex, color, and urban-rural residence. Compulsory school attendance laws, socioeconomic status, and norms concerning the education of boys and girls are probably relevant explanatory variables.

Long-term trends in literacy and years of schooling completed by the population are also observed to be a function of demographic processes interrelated with educational change. Many older persons who generally had poorer educational opportunities and, consequently, relatively low educational levels, leave the population through death, and many infants are born into the population whose educational opportunities are vastly superior to those of their parents and grandparents. The net effect is an improvement in the education level of the population. A high birth rate combined with strong educational opportunities will have a beneficial effect on the educational level of the population; a high birth rate combined with lack of educational opportunities will not lead to a higher educational level. The latter situation obtains in many developing nations.

Migration may affect the educational status of a population in a couple of ways. Immigration and emigration may be selective enough to change the educational composition of the national population. Selective internal migration may result in a redistribution of the population with given educational levels or in a shift in the educational composition of the population in areas within the country. In a recent paper Price analyzes the effect of outmigration of nonwhite males from the southern United States prior to 1960 on the educational distribution of nonwhites remaining in the region. He demonstrates that the substantial out-migration of better-educated persons had a depressing effect on the educational level of the residual population, even though in-migration compensated to some extent for the loss of better-educated persons.

Much can be learned about the educational characteristics of a population from census data; but one major difficulty in studying educational trends in this way is that census figures refer only to schooling obtained in regular schools and colleges leading to a degree; they do not include other kinds of regular training which may contribute substantially to an individual's state of knowledge. While it is difficult to collect reliable statistics on many factors affecting educational achievement, it is likely that such factors as the types of education received and the schools at which people were educated will become important with time as larger and larger proportions of the population attain high levels of education.

Educational attainment is often confused with native ability. While the two are positively associated, the association is far from perfect. Motivations to become formally educated and achieve high status in life, availability of economic means to continue in school, genetic endowment, and personality factors are variables which might intervene to make educational status and ability different. However, ability has been used as a measure of population quality, and not only has the ability distribution of large segments of the population been measured (through standard intelligence tests) but some analysts have related ability to family size and social class in order to demonstrate that the intelligence of the population is declining. In the last article in this chapter, Duncan examines these studies and casts doubt on their findings. While better-designed studies are needed to conclude definitively what the effects of differential fertility might be on the intelligence distribution of the population, social scientists are increasingly becoming aware of the need, as Duncan suggests, of defining population quality in terms of the educational, occupational, and other social skills which people possess, as well as in terms of their potential ability.

*Education and Fertility in the United States**

ROBERT M. DINKEL

Relating family size to the characteristics of both husband and wife has become a common practice in fertility studies during the past twenty years in the United States, giving expression to the obvious fact that not only are two persons involved in the interaction that leads to the birth of a child, but also to the equally obvious fact that these two people often differ quite widely in their backgrounds, attitudes, ideals, values, and other personality traits.[1] Noting such differences between the spouses, researchers have, as you might expect, raised the question of whose interests usually predominate or are compromised in decisions regarding the number of children that the couple will give birth to and rear.

The data of this study are from a five per cent sample of the 1960 census of the United States. The population studied is that of the white ever married women 35 years old and over or white women 35 to 54 years old married and husband present. There were in the United States in 1960 about 34½ million women in the first group and about 9½ million in the second group.

The following hypotheses have been used to organize the data: (1) the more years of school completed by the wife the fewer the number of children ever born to the couple and (2) the number of years of school completed by the wife is more strongly associated with the number of children ever born to the couple than is the number of years of school completed by the husband.

The purpose of the first hypothesis is to establish the nature of the relation between education and fertility as a useful preliminary to the investigation of the relative influence of the education of the husband and wife when jointly considered.

The second hypothesis attempts to clarify the nature of the relation between education and fertility by asserting that when the education of the spouses differs the education of the wife exerts the greater influence upon the size of their completed family. The assumption here is that the role of the wife is the principal determinant of the number of children in the family and that her role is dependent upon how many years of school she completed.

Women of little education are assumed to be more familistic in their values than women of higher education. It is thought that the wife with few years schooling will be concerned with rearing a relatively large family regardless of the education of her husband since with such schooling she probably would find an adequate expression of her interests and function in life only within the family. If she attains, on the other hand, a relatively high education, it is our belief that she will have acquired values that would be satisfied adequately only through a larger measure of community or outside interests that compete with the demands of child rearing and thus tend to reduce the number of children desired. She likely will seek the satisfaction of such nonfamily interests whether her husband has had a similar schooling or has been more limited in his educational attainment.

FINDINGS

The data for the United States given in Table 1 show that the more years of schooling that the

* Unpublished paper presented to the 1965 World Population Conference. Used by permission of the author and the United Nations.

[1] See, e.g., Kiser, Clyde V., "Trends and Differentials in Fertility by Education of the Woman" in Grabill, Wilson H., Kiser, Clyde V. and Whelpton, Pascal K., *The Fertility of American Women,* John Wiley and Sons, New York (1958), pp. 231-238; Freedman, Ronald, Whelpton, Pascal K. and Campbell, Arthur A., *Family Planning and Population Growth,* McGraw-Hill Book Co., Inc., New York (1959), pp. 112-122 and 288-295; and Westoff, Charles F., Potter, Robert G. Jr., Sagi, Philip C. and Mishler, Elliot G., *Family Growth in Metropolitan America,* Princeton University Press, Princeton, New Jersey (1961), pp. 215-220.

woman had completed the lower was her fertility; that is, the relation between education and size of family is negative or inverse. The comparison of age and educational subgroups in this table has been facilitated by conversion of number of children ever born per 1,000 women into index figures or ratios. The fertility of women who had completed 12 years of school has been taken arbitrarily as the base figure of 100 in each age class.

Using the appropriate base group in all of our comparisons, we find that women who had completed less than eight years of schooling had substantially lower fertility, that women who had from eight to 11 years of schooling had moderately lower fertility; and that women who had from 13 to 16 years had approximately the same fertility with one major exception as the women who had finished 12 years of schooling. Only when women had finished 17 or more years of school do we find that their fertility was consistently and appreciably lower than that of the women of the base group.

It can be seen from the data of Table 1, furthermore, that during the historical period covered by the child-bearing years of the women included in our sample there took place a substantial reduction in the fertility differentials noted above.

Our second table brings us to the heart of the problem posed for this paper; that is, to the relative influence upon fertility of the education of the husband and the education of the wife. We can see from the data of Table 2 the direction and extent of variation in the number of children ever born as the number of years of school completed by the other spouse changes. It is not entirely clear from the data of this table, however, whether the greater variation is according to the education of the husband or to the education of the wife. To clarify this relation, we have regrouped the data to bring together complementary pairs. This regrouping is done in Table 3.

Complementary pairs are subgroups so chosen that the difference in years of schooling of the spouses in one subgroup is exactly reversed in the other. For example, consider the subgroup in which the wife had eight years of schooling and the husband had twelve. It would be paired and compared in Table 3 with the subgroup in which the wife had twelve years of schooling and the husband had eight.

With a six-fold breakdown of years of schooling in a cross classification of the education of wife by that of husband, there are 36 subgroups or cells of the table in which to show the fertility of the couple. In six of these cells the education of the spouses is the same and these cells are discarded in our analysis. The other 30 cells can be grouped into 15 pairs of the kind described above as complementary.

The method used in determining whose education is more strongly associated with the fertility of the couple might best be shown by illustration. There are for women 45 to 54 years of age 2,186 children in the subgroup in which the wife had less than eight years of schooling and the husband had 16 or more years. There are 1,507 children in the other member of the complementary pair; that is, in the subgroup in which the

TABLE 1

Number of Children Ever Born Per 1,000 White Ever Married Women by Education and Age of Woman, for the United States: 1960 (Fertility of Women with 4 Years High School—100)

	Years of Schooling Completed by Woman								
Age of Woman	None	1–4	5–7	8	9–11	12	13–15	16	17 or More
35–39	169	157	133	118	110	100	100	100	85
40–44	190	169	139	122	112	100	100	100	87
45–49	205	189	150	129	116	100	98	94	82
50–Over	224	210	171	145	121	100	95	86	70

Source: *United States Census of Population: 1960. Women by Number of Children Ever Born,* U.S. Department of Commerce, Bureau of the Census. Washington: Government Printing Office, 1964, p. 100.

TABLE 2

Number of Children Ever Born Per 1,000 White Women 35 to 54 Years Old Married and Husband Present by Years of School Completed by Husband and Wife and by Age of Woman, for the United States: 1960

Education of Wife—Years	Wives 35 to 44 Years Old, Education of Husband—Years: Less 8	8	9–11	12	13–15	16 & Over	Wives 45 to 54 Years Old, Education of Husband—Years: Less 8	8	9–11	12	13–15	16 & Over
Less 8	3717	3217	2927	2647	2420	2447	3479	2987	2703	2294	2306	2186
8	3219	2910	2711	2529	2550	2290	2975	2618	2349	2169	2138	1894
9–11	2911	2805	2590	2530	2457	2362	2672	2458	2228	2066	1932	1858
12	2532	2542	2417	2386	2354	2409	2193	2148	2002	1900	1834	1862
13–15	2317	2492	2291	2388	2381	2572	2045	2076	1887	1846	1852	1973
16 and Over	1853	1964	2000	2175	2275	2461	1507	1455	1449	1543	1697	1922

Source: *United States Census of Population: 1960. Women by Number of Children Ever Born,* U.S. Department of Commerce, Bureau of the Census. Washington: Government Printing Office, 1964, p. 109.

wife had 16 or more years of schooling and the husband had less than eight years. Since the greater number of children occurs with the relatively low education of the wife and the smaller number with the relatively high educational status of this spouse and since fertility is correlated negatively with years of schooling, we conclude that in this instance the size of family was more influenced by the wife's than by the husband's education.

Using this method for the analysis of the data of Table 3, we find that the education of the wife was more strongly associated with number of children ever born in 13 of the 15 pairs for women 45 to 54 years of age and in 11 of the 15 pairs for women 35 to 44 years of age. Four of the six exceptions to this relation of fertility to joint education of the spouses are of small size. The other two that are of moderate size occur in the situation in which the wife had eight years and the husband had nine to eleven years of schooling.

The size of the difference in the fertility of complementary pairs indicates the cases in which the difference in the education of the spouses appears highly significant. In five of the 15 pairs for each age group, we find that the size of the difference is comparatively large. These five complementary pairs are made up of subgroups in which one of the spouses had 16 or more years of schooling and the other spouse had less education. Apparently these differences are large, because the fertility of the couple was relatively low when the wife had 16 or more years of schooling and the husband had a smaller number.

There are two plausible explanations of this fact that come readily to mind. The first is that there is a difference in the age of marriage of the wife in the complementary pairs. No doubt, the college graduate wife who marries a man of less education does so on the average at a later age than the wife with a grade-school or high-school education who marries a man with a college degree. The second explanation is that the woman who has 16 or more years of schooling participates in community and other outside activities to a much greater extent than the woman who does not obtain more than a high-school education. In other words, the college woman has many other interests than child bearing and rearing competing for her time than has the woman with an elementary or high-school education.

Conclusion

The two hypotheses of this study have been supported by the data and so far as this study goes can be accepted. The first hypothesis asserted an inverse or negative relation between education of wife and her completed fertility. The second hypothesis stated that education of wife has a stronger association with fertility than education of the husband.

TABLE 3

Number of Children Ever Born by Education of Husband and Wife and Differences between Complementary Pairs of Educational Subgroups According to Age of the Woman

Years of Education		Number of Children Ever Born					
		Woman 35–44		Woman 45–54		Differences between Complementary pairs	
		Education					
One Spouse	Other Spouse	Wife Less	Husb. Less	Wife Less	Husb. Less	Woman 35–44	Woman 45–54
Under 8	16 & Over	2447	1853	2186	1507	594	679
8	"	2290	1964	1894	1455	326	439
9–11	"	2362	2000	1858	1449	362	409
12	"	2409	2175	1862	1543	234	319
13–15	"	2572	2275	1973	1697	297	276
Under 8	13–15	2420	2317	2306	2045	103	261
8	"	2550	2492	2138	2076	58	62
9–11	"	2457	2291	1932	1887	166	45
12	"	2354	2388	1834	1846	−34	−12
Under 8	12	2647	2532	2294	2193	115	101
8	"	2529	2542	2169	2148	−13	21
9–11	"	2530	2417	2066	2002	113	64
Under 8	9–11	2927	2911	2703	2672	16	31
8	"	2711	2805	2349	2458	−94	−109
Under 8	8	3217	3219	2987	2975	−2	12

Source: Table 2.

*Educational Trends from Census Data**†

John K. Folger • Charles B. Nam

I. Introduction

Statistics on education were collected in a decennial census as far back as 1840. The U.S. Office of Education, the primary federal agency for the collection and dissemination of education data, was not organized until 1867, and its statistical series date back only to 1870. There is, in fact, very little overlap in the statistical information which has come from the two sources since 1870. The Office of Education data have been assembled from reports of state and local school systems and institutions of higher learning, and they relate to counts of children and youth in school, and to information on graduates, instructional staff, curricula, school district organization, educational receipts and expenditures, property, and other aspects of the school systems.

An inquiry on school enrollment has been part of each U.S. decennial census of population

* Reprinted with permission from *Demography,* Vol. 1, No. 1 (1964), pp. 247-257.

† This article is based on research performed for a forthcoming monograph, *Education of the American Population.*

from 1840 to 1960, and a question on illiteracy was included in the census of 1840 to 1930, after which it was replaced by one on years of school completed. The unique contributions of the census data have been the description of characteristics of those enrolled, such as age, race, and residence, and an accounting of the educational status of the general population, including those not in school as well as those attending.

From census data alone, one may trace educational trends in the United States for a period of 120 years. The analysis in the present paper is restricted to census data for the period from 1910 to 1960, primarily because the desired data are either not available from earlier censuses, are not comparable with later data, or are of such questionable quality as to limit their usefulness.

The matters of comparability and quality are also of importance for the time period discussed and have particular relevance to an analysis of trends. The following analysis, therefore, incorporates some evaluation of the data and indicates the effect of inaccuracies in the statistics on the interpretation of trends.

II. Trends in School Enrollment

The census is providing increasingly detailed information for the analysis of enrollment growth. Part of this increase in information is related to the explosive growth of enrollment since 1950 and the consequent heightened interest in this kind of information.

Enrollment of persons 5 to 19 years old grew 23.6 million between 1910 and 1960 — from about 17.5 million to 41.1 million persons (see Table 1). Considerably more than half of this growth, or 13 out of 23.6 million, occurred between 1950 and 1960. About two-thirds of the growth in enrollment in the last 10 years has been due to growth in the population of school age, while for the period from 1910 to 1950, a little less than half the enrollment growth was due to population increase.

It is difficult to estimate how much of the total increase in enrollment reported in the census may be due to improved coverage and reduced errors of reporting, collecting, and tabulating the census. There are two sources of data for the assessment of census enrollment statistics; one is the Post Enumeration Surveys of 1950 and 1960 and the other is comparison of census data with other enrollment reports, principally those of the Office of Education.

By comparison with the Office of Education, census figures reveal more enrollment growth in the 1910–60 period. During this period, the census reported a 23.6 million growth in enrollment, the Office of Education a 19.5 million increase, or about four million less. The census appears to be closer to the "true" increase, since the Office of Education figures contained many duplicates for the earlier period, and elimination of duplicates in recent years would have the effect of understanding the "true" growth.

TABLE 1

Components of Growth in School Enrollment from 1910 to 1960, for the Population 5 to 19 Years Old, by Age, for the United States (Numbers in thousands)

Age	Total gain in enrollment 1910 to 1960	Percent of growth		
		Total	Due to population growth	Due to increased enrollment rates
Total..........	23,659	100	55	45
5 and 6 years.......	3,566	100	36	64
7 to 13 years.......	13,178	100	78	22
14 to 15 years......	2,547	100	58	42
16 and 17 years.....	3,049	100	29	71
18 and 19 years.....	1,320	100	16	84

Comparisons between census and Office of Education data on "grade in which enrolled" indicate that there was substantial net over-reporting of grade in which enrolled in the census of 1940. If the Office of Education is taken as "standard," net census over-reporting of grade enrolled in 1940 was about two-thirds of a grade. The over-reporting was reduced in 1950 to .2 of a grade, probably largely due to improved census question wording, and estimates for 1960 indicate a further reduction to less than .1 of a grade.

A fairly similar estimate of the magnitude of misreporting grade in which enrolled is provided by the 1960 Content Evaluation Study, which indicated 2.0 per cent gross over-reporting of grade enrolled and 0.6 per cent under-reporting for a net error of 1.4 per cent.

By all these comparisons, it appears that the quality of census data on enrollment in 1960 is good. It also appears that the accuracy of reporting grade in which enrolled has improved considerably in the last two decades. The effect of this improved accuracy in reporting grade is to understate the magnitude of the very substantial decline in grade retardation which has taken place.

III. Trends in Grade Retardation

The history of census enrollment statistics parallels that of many other population characteristics in that more information and tabulations are available for recent years. In 1910, information was provided on enrollment by single years of age, by sex, and by ethnic background. Enrollment by rural-urban residence was added in 1920. In 1940, a big step forward came with enrollment by grade or level cross-tabulated by age. This made possible the age-grade table, which adds to enrollment analysis in much the same way that the introduction of statistics on birth parity adds to fertility analysis.

Unfortunately, the census data on grade in which enrolled have been a by-product of the data on educational attainment (that is, the reply to the enrollment question has been combined with the reply to the question on highest grade attended). Improvement in the question wording in 1950 and 1960 makes the 1940 figures noncomparable for the analysis of grade retardation and the study of the age-grade table. It is now possible, however, to compare grade retardation and acceleration between 1950 and 1960 and to identify the rather substantial decline that has occurred in grade retardation.[1]

Between 1950 and 1960, grade retardation in the pre-college years was reduced by nearly half (see Table 2). In 1950, about 16 per cent of 10-year-olds was retarded one or more grades; by 1960, only 8 per cent was retarded. In 1950, over a fourth (26 per cent) of 15-year-olds was retarded; by 1960, only 15 per cent of this age group was retarded. By contrast, the per cent of accelerated students in 1960 was about the same as that in 1950; in both years it varied from 4 to 6 per cent.

In 1950, retardation of the rural population approached 40 per cent at age 15; by 1960, it had been reduced to half that percentage, i.e., to less than 20 per cent. Yet retardation in school is still about twice as prevalent in rural farm areas as in urban areas. The difference between rural and urban schools in amount of grade retardation is declining as both approach the norm of regular progression through the grades; the concept of "social promotion" is approaching social reality.

It seems unlikely that grade retardation can be reduced much below 5 to 10 per cent in the American school system; we are already near this point in the urban areas. Future declines in grade retardation will largely be confined to youths in rural areas and to nonwhites, for whom retardation is still substantial.

IV. The Analysis of Enrollment Differentials

Enrollment rates vary markedly with age. In 1960, about 64 per cent of 5- and 6-year-olds were enrolled in school, about 98 per cent of 7- to 13-year-olds, 98 per cent of 14- and 15-year-olds, 81 per cent of those 16 to 17, and only 42 per cent of those aged 18 and 19. Since 1910, enrollment rates at school ages 7 to 15 have risen less than 20 per cent, while those for the younger

[1] We define two years as "normal" for each grade. Thus, both six- and seven-year-olds in the first grade at the time of the census are considered normal. Seven- and eight-year-olds in the second grade are normal, and similarly for other grades.

TABLE 2

Percent of Enrolled Persons 8 to 17 Years Old Retarded in School by Age, for the United States, 1950 and 1960

Age	1960			1950		
	Retarded[a]			Retarded[a]		
	Total	One year	More than one year	Total	One year	More than one year
8 years......	4.0	4.0	...	6.6	6.6	...
9 years......	6.5	5.7	0.8	11.2	9.1	2.1
10 years.....	8.2	6.7	1.5	15.7	11.5	4.2
11 years.....	9.2	7.1	2.1	18.1	12.0	6.1
12 years.....	10.5	7.6	2.9	21.5	12.7	8.8
13 years.....	11.6	8.1	3.5	23.6	13.2	10.4
14 years.....	13.9	9.2	4.7	25.0	13.5	11.5
15 years.....	15.3	9.3	6.0	26.3	13.6	12.7
16 years.....	15.2	8.8	6.4	24.7	11.9	12.8
17 years.....	14.9	8.2	6.7	21.9	11.1	10.8

(a) School retardation is defined in terms of enrollment in school in a grade below the modal grades for a given age.

(5- and 6-year-olds) and older (16- to 19-year-olds) ages have approximately doubled. For the older ages, most of the enrollment growth since 1910 reflects increases in enrollment rates, while for the 7- to 15-year-olds most of the change reflects population growth.

For the younger ages, the sex differential in enrollment rates is very small but consistently favors the females at ages up to 14 or 15. This has been true since 1910. At ages above 17, there is a much higher percentage of males than of females enrolled in school. For age 19, enrollment rates for males in 1960 were about 30 per cent higher than for females. For ages 20 to 24, rates for males were more than double those for females.

The sex differential in enrollment rates at ages above 17 has been increasing since 1940. One might conclude from these figures that college enrollment of men has been going up more rapidly than that of women; yet, actually, the percentage of men among those in college in 1960 was about the same as in 1910 (66 per cent), and the per cent of undergraduates who are men has actually declined slightly.[2] The main explanation of the more rapid increase of enrollment rates for males at the older ages is in the decline in grade retardation and the consequent decline in the proportion of students over 17 enrolled in high school where the sex distribution is approximately equal. In 1910, it can be estimated that about 72 per cent of the enrollment of persons over 18 was below college level, while in 1960 comparable census figures for the population 18 to 24 years old indicate that only 36 per cent of those over 18 who were enrolled was below the college level.

At the college level, nonwhite students have a pattern of enrollment quite different from the white students. Whereas about 65 per cent of white college students are male, only about 53 per cent of nonwhite college students are male

[2] U.S. Office of Education, *Biennial Survey of Education,* 1956-58, chap. iv, sec. 1, Table 2, and *Total Enrollment,* 1959-60 (OE-54205), Table 1.

(Table 3). The higher ratio of nonwhite female to male college students undoubtedly reflects the kind of occupational opportunities open to nonwhite with advanced education.

Census data do not reveal a uniform superiority of the city over the rural areas in enrollment rates. At the younger ages (5 to 15), urban enrollment rates have been higher than rural since 1920, when data were first available in comparable form, and the differentials between urban and rural rates have declined markedly since 1940. At the high school and early college ages (16 to 19), rural enrollment rates were actually higher in 1930; urban were higher in 1940 and the differential in favor of the urban areas widened until 1950, only to decrease in the last decade. Part of the change between 1940 and 1950 may have been a function of the change in the residence definition of college students.

What these figures reveal is the sharper break between school and work in the urban environment. Presumably, in the city, youths stay in school full time until they take a full-time job, and then they leave school. There is more grade retardation in rural areas, and high school graduation comes later, on the average, in rural areas. Rural youths tend to stay in school to high school graduation, even though they are more often over-age for the grade in which they are enrolled.

Even if the entire differential in enrollment rates of youths 7 to 19 years old were eliminated by raising the rural rates to the urban level, total enrollment in the United States would only be increased about 300,000 or less than eight-tenths of one per cent.

The census records steady progress in reducing enrollment differentials between whites and nonwhites at ages 5–19 during the past half-century. Reductions in the differential have been most pronounced at the younger ages. At ages 5 and 6, a differential that amounted to 14 percentage points in 1910 has been reduced to only 3 percentage points; at ages 7 to 13, a differential of over 20 percentage points has been reduced to only 2 percentage points. At the older ages, the differential has not been reduced very much. At ages above 19 the differential (for college attendance) may be widening.

Another way of expressing the gap is to indicate that if the differential were entirely eliminated, nonwhite enrollment would be increased by only about 200,000. This is only four per cent of nonwhite enrollment and less than one-half of one per cent of the total enrollment in the nation.

Elimination of sex, color, and residence enrollment rate differentials would have only a small effect on the total enrollment in the United States — adding less than one million students to a total enrollment of over 40 million in the 5 to 19 age range. The development of kindergartens as a universal feature of the American educational scene might add as many as 800,000 more children to the rolls yearly. The other place where enrollment rates can rise is at the college level. Will we have junior colleges available

TABLE 3

College Enrollment by Color, Sex, and Year in Which Enrolled for the United States, 1960 (Numbers in thousands)

Year of college in which enrolled	White			Nonwhite		
	Total	Male	Female	Total	Male	Female
Total...........	2,743	1,777	966	192	101	91
1st to 4th years......	2,376	1,469	907	169	85	84
5th year or higher . . .	367	308	59	23	16	7
Total...........	100.0	64.8	35.2	100.0	52.9	47.1
1st to 4th years......	100.0	61.8	38.2	100.0	50.5	49.5
5th year or higher....	100.0	83.9	16.1	100.0	70.1	29.9

throughout the country? The social definition of who should attend college is still in transition, as are the enrollment rates for the older ages. With these exceptions, the future of enrollment will be determined almost entirely by the future changes in the size of the population of school age.

V. Trends in Educational Attainment

The 1960 census was only the third census in which data on years of school completed by the population had been collected. It is possible, however, by retrojecting the data for age cohorts, to obtain reasonable estimates of the educational status of the population as far back as 1910 (that is, the educational distribution of those 50 to 59 in 1940 was assumed to be the same as for those 40 to 49 in 1930, those 30 to 39 in 1920, and so forth).

As Table 4 shows, the trend in educational attainment has been continually upward, with most indicators pointing to the greatest improvement in the educational level during the past few decades. To be more exact the decline in the percentage of the population with low educational levels was greatest in the 1920's and 1930's, whereas the increase in the percentage of the population with a high school or college education was generally greatest in the later decades. This may reflect the fact that in a country with a belief in universal education and compulsory school attendance laws, the effort to give everyone a minimum acceptable level of schooling has taken priority over the effort to expand advanced education, at least until very recently.

Comparison of the statistics for 1910 and 1960 reveals an enormous rate of educational progress over half a century. If one looks at the adult population as a whole (that is, those 25 years old and over), the educational stock of the country is seen to have risen sharply — from 24 out of 100 without as many as five years of school in 1910 to 8 out of 100 in 1960; from 14 out of 100 attaining a complete high school education in 1910 to 41 out of 100 in 1960; and from the average adult in 1910 having received an elementary school certificate to his counterpart in 1960 having attained a partial high school education.

The increased output of the school systems during the 1910–60 period is inadequately indicated by these data for all adults, since the educational distribution of the adult population changes only to the extent that better-educated young persons attain adulthood and less well-educated adults, mainly older persons, leave the population through death. Educational progress may be measured on a more current basis by studying the data for those 25 to 29 years old at each date, persons who at the time were recent products of their schools. In 1910, one out of five had failed to complete the fifth year of school; in 1960, only one out of 36 had failed to do so. In 1910, 2 out of 10 were high school graduates, whereas in 1960 there were 6 out of 10; and while the average young adult in 1910 was an elementary school graduate, in 1960 he was a high school graduate. In half a century, this nation had achieved an educational objective that no country had before achieved — and few, if any, are likely to achieve in the near future.

Table 5 provides data to answer the question, "Have educational differentials by color been narrowing?" For the adult population as a whole, there was a smaller difference in the medians for whites and nonwhites in 1960 than in 1940. On further examination of the data, this narrowing of the differential in the median is seen to result exclusively from a greater reduction for nonwhites in the per cent with low levels of education. In fact, there were slightly greater percentage increases for white than nonwhite adults in the attainment of a high school diploma or college degree.

Here again, it may be more meaningful to look at the data for young adults whose educational statuses represent recent educational developments and to view a longer period of time. One striking finding is that, between 1920 and 1940, educational differentials by color for young people in this country were actually widening by most indicators. Expanding differentials were particularly pronounced at the high school and college level but were also observed in terms of average educational levels. Between 1940 and 1960, however, the situation changed dramatically. On both an absolute and a relative basis, young nonwhites had made greater gains than young whites. To illustrate, the percentage of high school graduates increased between 1940 and 1960 from 41 to 64 per cent (or 23 percentage points) for whites and from 12 to 39 per

TABLE 4

Educational Attainment of Persons 25 Years Old and Over, and 25 to 29 Years Old, by Sex: Censuses of 1960, 1950, and 1940 Estimates for 1930, 1920, and 1910

(Data for 1960 and 1950 include Alaska and Hawaii, not included in earlier years. Estimates for 1930, 1920, and 1910, based on retrojection or reported 1940 census data on education by age and sex.)

Age and Year	Both sexes				Male				Female			
	Median school years completed	Percent with—			Median school years completed	Percent with—			Median school years completed	Percent with—		
		Less than 5 years of school	High school 4 years or beyond	College 4 or more years		Less than 5 years of school	High school 4 years or beyond	College 4 or more years		Less than 5 years of school	High school 4 years or beyond	College 4 or more years
25 years and over												
Census: 1960..........	10.5	8.3	41.1	7.7	10.3	9.4	39.5	9.7	10.7	7.4	42.5	5.8
1950..........	9.3	11.1	34.3	6.2	9.0	12.2	32.6	7.3	9.6	10.0	36.0	5.2
1940..........	8.6	13.7	24.5	4.6	8.6	15.1	22.7	5.5	8.7	12.4	26.3	3.8
Estimate: 1930........	8.4	17.5	19.1	3.9	8.3	19.1	17.5	4.6	8.5	15.9	20.7	3.1
1920........	8.2	22.0	16.4	3.3	8.2	23.0	14.5	3.9	8.3	19.1	17.1	2.4
1910........	8.1	23.8	13.5	2.7	8.1	25.9	12.4	3.4	8.2	21.6	14.6	1.9
25 to 29 years old												
Census: 1960..........	12.3	2.8	60.7	11.1	12.3	3.4	59.7	14.4	12.3	2.2	61.7	7.8
1950..........	12.1	4.7	52.8	7.7	12.0	5.4	50.6	9.6	12.1	4.0	55.0	5.9
1940..........	10.3	5.9	38.1	5.9	10.1	6.9	36.0	6.9	10.5	5.0	40.1	4.9
Estimate: 1930........	8.8	9.7	26.9	5.5	8.7	10.6	24.6	6.5	8.9	8.9	29.1	4.5
1920........	8.5	15.6	20.7	4.1	8.4	16.7	19.2	4.9	8.5	14.6	22.1	3.4
1910........	8.3	19.3	17.0	3.4	8.2	21.2	15.7	4.1	8.4	17.3	18.5	2.6

TABLE 5

Educational Attainment of Persons 25 Years Old and Over, for 1960 and 1940, and 25 to 29 Years Old, for 1960, 1940, and 1920, by Color and Sex

(Data for 1960 include Alaska and Hawaii, excluded from data for 1940 and 1920)

Age, color, and year	Both sexes				Male				Female			
	Median school years completed	Percent with—			Median school years completed	Percent with—			Median school years completed	Percent with—		
		Less than 5 years of school	High school 4 years or beyond	College 4 or more years		Less than 5 years of school	High school 4 years or beyond	College 4 or more years		Less than 5 years of school	High school 4 years or beyond	College 4 or more years
25 years and over												
White: 1960	10.8	6.7	43.2	8.1	10.6	7.4	41.6	10.3	11.0	6.0	44.7	6.0
1940	8.7	10.9	26.1	4.9	8.7	12.0	24.2	5.9	8.8	9.8	28.1	4.0
Nonwhite: 1960	8.2	23.5	21.8	3.5	7.9	27.7	20.0	3.5	8.5	19.7	23.1	3.6
1940	5.8	41.8	7.7	1.3	5.4	46.2	6.9	1.4	6.1	37.5	8.4	1.2
25 to 29 years old												
White: 1960	12.3	2.2	63.7	11.8	12.4	2.6	62.7	15.6	12.3	1.8	64.8	8.1
1940	10.7	3.4	41.2	6.4	10.5	3.9	38.9	7.5	10.9	2.9	43.4	5.3
1920[a]	8.5	12.9	22.0	4.5	8.5	13.7	20.5	5.3	8.6	12.0	23.5	3.6
Nonwhite: 1960	10.8	7.2	38.6	5.4	10.5	9.6	36.2	5.3	11.1	5.1	40.6	5.4
1940	7.0	27.0	12.3	1.6	6.5	33.3	10.6	1.5	7.5	21.5	13.8	1.7
1920[a]	5.4	44.6	6.3	1.2	5.2	48.2	5.9	1.4	5.7	40.9	6.8	1.1

[a] Based on reports for persons 45 to 49 years old in 1940, who would have been 25 to 29 years old in 1920.

cent (or 27 percentage points) for nonwhites. While the per cent for whites was half again as high in 1960, for nonwhites it had tripled. Nonwhites in 1960 thus had about reached the level of whites in 1940. It probably will not, however, take young nonwhite adults another twenty years to reach the levels of whites in 1960.

The trends just described are based on reported census data for the past three decades and estimates for earlier years based on the reported data. What, we might ask, is the "true" trend? How would the data appear if we were able to adjust them for errors of reporting and other biases? Analysis of evaluation material does not give us precise estimates of the "true" figures but it does enable us to say in which direction and to what extent the reported figures are in error.[3]

The most important facts which emerge from this analysis are: (1) In both 1950 and 1960, there were considerable gross overstatement and gross understatement of years of schooling. Because there was somewhat more overstatement than understatement, the result was a small, but significant, amount of net overreporting. (2) Gross misreporting was lower in 1960 than in 1950 but net misreporting (for all grades combined) was generally the same at both dates. With regard to high school and college graduation, net overreporting was somewhat less in 1960 than in 1950. (3) Net overreporting at the high school and college level in 1950 tended to be relatively greater at the older than at the younger ages. (4) For given age cohorts, the 1940 data tended to be distributed more like the 1960 than the 1950 data. Thus, while there was net overreporting at all three dates, it was greatest in 1950 and generally of about the same order in 1940 and 1960.

What are the implications of these findings for the interpretation of trends? First, the "true" levels of education at all dates are probably slightly lower than they appear in Table I. Second, the improvement in years of schooling between 1910 and 1960 was probably slightly greater than is indicated in the table. Third, the 1950 figures are out of line with the 1940 and 1960 figures to the extent that improvement between 1940 and 1950 is overstated and between 1950 and 1960 is understated.

No consideration has been given in this paper to measurement of educational attainment in terms of units other than years of schooling or to measurement of the trend in quality of education received. A number of persons in recent years, notably some economists, have examined attainment trends in terms of days of school received, largely because the length of the school year, on the national average, has changed so dramatically over the past fifty or sixty years. We believe that, at present, there is no information to indicate what the effect of the change in length of the school year on educational attainment is, when the latter is thought of in terms of the amount of fundamental knowledge acquired through the formal school systems. Likewise, historical information is lacking which would permit adjustments of trend data for changes in educational quality. Moreover, variations in the quality of education received have probably been almost as great among areas and subgroups of the population at one point in time as for the United States as a whole over a long period of time.

Table 6 is designed to show how improvement in education has spread to all parts of the country.[4] Substantial gains between 1940 and 1960 in the per cent of the population with a completed high school education were recorded in every state, and at least some increase in this percentage was observed for every county in the United States. Because of changes in urban and rural and farm and non-farm definitions, it is not possible to measure accurately the changes in educational attainment for these areas, but, because of selective migration patterns, farm areas in the country as a whole have shown much less improvement in the educational stock of their people than have non-farm areas.

[3] Three types of evaluation material were analyzed: First, the Post-Enumeration Survey results for 1950 and 1960 for the population 25 and over, which show the attainment distribution as reported in the census cross-classified by the attainment distribution as reported in the survey, were studied. Second, some unpublished 1950 Post-Enumeration Survey data on educational attainment by age were evaluated. Finally, census data on education for age cohorts over the three censuses, 1940, 1950, and 1960, were compared.

[4] A table comparable to Table 6, but referring to counties, may be obtained by writing to the senior author.

TABLE 6

Percent of the Population 25 Years Old and Over and 25 to 29 Years Old Who Have Completed High School 4 Years or Beyond, by State, 1940 and 1960

Division and State	Percentage				Rank*			
	25 and over		25 to 29		25 and over		25 to 29	
	1940	1960	1940	1960	1940	1960	1940	1960
NEW ENGLAND:								
Maine	28.8	43.3	44.2	58.2	15	20	18.5	32
New Hampshire	26.8	42.9	41.6	62.8	18	21	22	24
Vermont	27.9	42.8	42.8	60.4	17	22	20	31
Massachusetts	31.0	47.0	48.5	68.5	9	13	12	11
Rhode Island	21.1	35.0	32.4	56.0	38.5	39	36	37
Connecticut	25.1	43.9	38.1	66.0	22	17.5	28	17
MIDDLE ATLANTIC:								
New York	23.4	40.8	38.3	63.3	31	29	27	22
New Jersey	23.0	40.7	34.9	63.9	32	30	33	18
Pennsylvania	21.2	38.1	35.0	63.5	37	36	32	19.5
EAST NORTH CENTRAL:								
Ohio	25.7	42.0	45.2	61.2	20	25	16	28
Indiana	24.8	41.8	46.2	60.7	24	26	15	30
Illinois	24.3	40.4	40.9	63.5	28	32	24	19.5
Michigan	24.7	40.9	41.0	62.1	25.5	28	23	26
Wisconsin	22.4	41.6	41.7	69.3	34	27	21	8
WEST NORTH CENTRAL:								
Minnesota	25.1	43.9	44.2	72.3	22	17.5	18.5	3
Iowa	28.9	46.3	52.1	72.1	13.5	14	7	4
Missouri	22.2	36.6	36.8	61.4	35	38	30	27
North Dakota	22.5	38.9	38.4	63.2	33	35	26	23
South Dakota	25.1	47.7	44.7	66.3	22	24	17	15.5
Nebraska	28.9	27.7	51.6	73.2	13.5	12	10	1.5
Kansas	28.5	48.2	51.7	71.1	16	9	9	5
SOUTH ATLANTIC:								
Delaware	23.9	43.4	36.5	62.4	29	19	31	25
Maryland	21.1	40.0	32.2	56.4	38.5	33	37	34
Dist. of Columbia	41.2	47.8	53.2	61.1	1	10.5	6	29
Virginia	21.6	37.9	28.7	52.7	36	37	40	39
West Virginia	17.8	30.5	28.9	51.1	43	43	39	40
North Carolina	19.0	32.3	25.2	48.3	40	40.5	43.5	43.5
South Carolina	18.4	30.4	22.5	43.2	41	45	45	49
Georgia	17.4	31.9	21.9	47.6	45	42	47	46
Florida	26.6	42.6	30.5	56.1	19	23	38	35.5
EAST SOUTH CENTRAL:								
Kentucky	15.7	27.6	25.2	44.2	48	49	43.5	47.5
Tennessee	18.1	30.4	25.4	47.7	42	45	42	45
Alabama	15.9	30.4	21.3	48.5	47	45	49	42
Mississippi	16.2	29.8	21.6	44.2	46	47	48	47.5
WEST SOUTH CENTRAL:								
Arkansas	15.1	28.9	22.1	48.3	49	48	46	43.5
Louisiana	17.6	32.3	25.6	49.8	44	40.5	41	41
Oklahoma	24.5	40.5	39.4	63.4	27	31	25	21
Texas	24.7	39.6	34.3	56.1	25.5	34	34	35.5
MOUNTAIN:								
Montana	29.4	47.8	48.2	67.3	11.5	10.5	14	12
Idaho	30.5	48.6	49.7	66.3	10	7	11	15.5
Wyoming	32.9	52.1	51.9	69.2	7	3	8	9
Colorado	32.1	52.0	48.3	69.4	8	4	13	7
New Mexico	23.8	45.4	34.0	57.1	30	16	35	33
Arizona	29.4	45.7	37.9	55.5	11.5	15	29	38
Utah	37.0	55.8	58.6	73.2	3	1	1	1.5
Nevada	35.6	53.3	55.0	66.4	4	2	4	14
PACIFIC:								
Washington	33.6	51.5	56.3	70.5	5	5.5	2	6
Oregon	33.1	48.4	54.3	69.1	6	8	5	10
California	37.3	51.5	55.6	66.6	2	5.5	3	13
Alaska	26.6	54.7	NA	61.8	...	...	...	...
Hawaii	20.5	46.1	NA	71.6	...	...	...	...

* Ranks do not include Alaska and Hawaii since 1940 and 1960 data are not strictly comparable

*Is the Intelligence of the General Population Declining?**†

OTIS DUDLEY DUNCAN

In his recently published book, *Human Fertility: The Modern Dilemma,* Robert C. Cook calls our attention to an alarming situation:[1]

> Competent scholars . . . are agreed that today's differential birth rate makes a decline in intelligence inevitable.
>
> (The 1949 report of the Royal Commission on Population) concluded that the average intelligence quotient of the British people was declining about 2 points every generation. The same pattern exists in the United States, where the experts consider a similar decline to be a "moral certainty." If this trend continues for less than a century, England and America will be well on the way to becoming nations of near half-wits.

Mr. Cook is a competent geneticist and the editor of the *Journal of Heredity.* His book appears with the endorsement of the well-known biologist, Julian Huxley. His statements on this question are buttressed by references to an extensive literature built up by outstanding psychologists and biological scientists. Perhaps it behooves us, as sociologists, to take account of the "gene erosion" which Mr. Cook believes is taking place, and to look into the prospect of the "destruction of modern technological culture" which he fears this loss of ability will entail.

How have "competent scholars" — to use Mr. Cook's phrase — reached this agreement on the "moral certainty" of a decline in intelligence? Two principal types of evidence have been relied on: first, differential fertility according to socio-economic status; second, the inverse correlation of family size and intelligence.

The first mentioned line of argument comes about through the coincidence of two important scientific developments, both of which can be roughly dated from the beginning of this century. On the one hand, since 1900, demographers have been busy building up a body of unequivocal evidence to show that, broadly speaking, in the Western world fertility is inversely related to socio-economic status; that is, the social groups at the top of the stratification pyramid are relatively infertile, whereas those at the base have disproportionately large families. Concurrently psychologists have been devising and perfecting tests of intelligence and applying them freely in an effort to measure the extent of group differences. Almost uniformly they find a *direct* correlation between social status and IQ. Taking them at face value, the juxtaposition of these two relationships naturally leads to fears that the dull are outbreeding the gifted in our population. A classic interpretation of this kind is to be found in the 1934 treatise of Lorimer and Osborn, *Dynamics of Population.*[2] These investigators proceed essentially as follows: Taking a set of typical results giving IQ distributions by occupational classes, they compute two weighted means. The first set of weights is based on the number of births occurring by occupational class in a current generation; the second set on the number of births projected for the succeeding generation, assuming the persistence of the observed fertility differential by occupation. The difference between the first and second calculations is approximately one IQ point, which is taken by the authors as an estimate of the expected decline in the average intelligence, attributable to differential occupational fertility, over a period of one generation.

The second, and more direct, approach to the problem has been to correlate the measured intelligence of children with the size of the families from which they come. A large number of

* Reprinted with permission from *American Sociological Review,* Vol. 17, No. 4 (August 1952), pp. 401-407.

† Paper delivered at a meeting of the Society for Social Research, Chicago, June 9, 1951.

[1] Robert C. Cook, *Human Fertility: The Modern Dilemma,* New York: William Sloane Associates, 1951, p. 261 and p. 6.

[2] Frank Lorimer and Frederick Osborn, *Dynamics of Population,* New York: The Macmillan Co., 1934, Ch. VIII.

studies, using a variety of test instruments applied to quite diverse samples, have shown almost without exception a small, but unquestionably significant, negative correlation between number of sibs and intelligence scores of school-age children, with typical coefficients running around −.2 to −.3. Recent mammoth testing projects in Scotland [3] and France [4] have established this relationship as securely as any generalization in the field of differential psychology. With data of this kind it is easy to estimate a figure for the generation decline in average IQ. Suppose tests have been administered to a sample of children all of the same age, say eleven years. The procedure followed embodies the two assumptions that the tested child's IQ may be taken as an estimate of that of the mid-parent, and also as an estimate of the average IQ of his untested siblings. The subjects are classified by family size, that is, the size of the sibships from which they are drawn. A mean IQ is calculated for children in each family size class — only children, two-child families, and so on. With these submeans — which generally show a regular pattern of decrease with increasing family size — one may compute two weighted grand means. The first grand mean, taken to represent the average IQ of the parental generation uses as weights the number of subjects in the family size class. The second grand mean takes as weights the number of subjects in a family size class multiplied by the size of family. This second grand mean is, then, regarded as the estimated average intelligence of the entire offspring generation. Given the inverse correlation of intelligence and family size, the second mean is necessarily lower than the first; and the difference is taken to be the measure of decline in average IQ over a generation.[5] Typical estimates of this decline range from two to four IQ points.

[3] Scottish Mental Survey Committee, *The Trend of Scottish Intelligence,* London: University of London Press, 1949.

[4] Institut National D'Etudes Demographiques, *Le Niveau Intellectuel des Enfants d'Age Scolaire,* Cahier No. 13, 1950.

[5] For the most explicit statement of this method of estimating the decline, and its justification, see Betty M. Giles-Bernardelli, "The Decline of Intelligence in New Zealand," *Population Studies,* IV (September, 1950), pp. 200-208.

It may be noted in passing that the inverse relation between family size and intelligence that appears when a single age group is tested cannot be successfully explained as an artifact produced by a putative correlation between intelligence and order of birth. No such correlation has yet been established. Various studies give conflicting results, and some even suggest an increase in intelligence with birth order.

To the argument that intelligence tests cannot measure a pure hereditary capacity, psychologists have replied that, although environment may account for part of the variance in IQ, heredity must account for at least 50 percent and probably more of the variance. And even if the estimated decline in IQ were reduced as much as one-half, there would still remain a grave problem of population quality. It may be noted, too, that the negative correlation between IQ and family size is found *within* broad occupation groups, as well as in samples heterogeneous with respect to occupational class.

Despite the unquestioned cogency of the evidence for a negative correlation between fertility and measured intelligence, and in the face of the strong arguments which can be advanced against some of the more obvious objections raised against the thesis, the position taken here is that the hypothesis of declining intelligence need not be accepted — though, admittedly, the problem is one which calls for further research. The arguments against this hypothesis are summarized below, under five heads.

In the first place, the "experts" are by no means as unanimous on the question as they appear in the quotation from Cook. In his plea, Cook has — perhaps out of overenthusiasm for the dire prospect which he envisions — been guilty of some misinterpretation of his sources. The Royal Commission did *not* conclude in its 1949 report "that the average intelligence quotient . . . was declining about 2 points every generation." Rather, its actual conclusion verbatim, is as follows:[6]

[6] *Royal Commission on Population,* Report, Cmd. 7695, London: H. M. Stationery Office, 1949, p. 156. Cook does quote this passage, but only after leaving the impression that the Commission had reached a much more definite conclusion, and in a context which lays emphasis on the last two sentences rather than the first.

We are not in a position to evaluate the expert evidence we have received to the effect that there is inherent in the differential birth rate a tendency towards lowering the average level of intelligence of the nation. This evidence . . . raises very serious issues. There is an urgent need for further research. . . .

One good reason for the Commission's hesitation in making a clear-cut finding is that the statements in evidence they received were conflicting. Strong statements in favor of the hypothesis were made by psychologists Thomson, Burt, and Fraser-Roberts, and supported by the eminent statistician and geneticist, R. A. Fisher. But a most emphatic dissent was registered by the likewise eminent geneticist, J. B. S. Haldane, writing as follows:[7]

I am now in complete disagreement with (Professor Thomson's) conclusion as to the effect of differential fertility. . . . The existing data give no reason to suppose that the level of innate intellectual capacity in our population is falling.

Here again Mr. Cook has been careless in compiling his account of expert opinion, for he overlooks this statement of Haldane's most recent views, and depends on a second-hand quotation from Burt:[8]

Burt points out that even a geneticist who sometimes takes an extremely environmentalist position, J. B. S. Haldane, also concludes that the decline in intelligence in England is "one or two points per generation in the mean I.Q. of the country."

Outside the ranks of experts available to the Royal Commission the thesis of declining intelligence has perhaps been urged most vehemently by the psychologist Raymond Cattell,[9] while quite firm disagreement has been expressed by L. S. Penrose,[10] a foremost authority on the biology and genetics of mental deficiency. Another prominent geneticist who is unimpressed with the case for the hypothesis is Lancelot Hogben.[11] The point of these citations is not to establish anything one way or another by the method of appeal to authority. But in considering a problem area where they lack the technical skills required — those of human genetics and mental testing — sociologists should be aware of the extent to which those presumably most competent are disagreed among themselves.

A second set of objections to the hypothesis of declining intelligence arises from a consideration of questions which have been raised as to the appropriateness of the fundamental research tool involved — the intelligence test. In 1938, Walter S. Neff, after a thorough review of the literature, found reason to reject the entire body of evidence on socio-economic differentials in innate ability. Supporting his position with citation of a number of studies which showed important environmental effects on IQ, he argued that[12]

. . . the inequality of social and economic opportunity renders suspect one of the major assumptions basic to the construction of the tests; namely that knowledge and information are a direct function of native ability, and that the former may be used to measure the latter . . . these tests cannot be used for measuring the capacity of different social levels within our own society.

This theme has been elaborated more recently by Davis, Havighurst and co-workers.[13] These investigators propose the concept of a "culture-fair" intelligence test. They claim actually to have devised such a test, one which measures intelligence validly but which does not elicit the mean differences between socio-economic groups ordinarily found with conventional tests.

[7] *Papers of the Royal Commission on Population,* Vol. V, London: H. M. Stationery Office, 1950, pp. 43-44.

[8] Cook, *op. cit.,* p. 268.

[9] R. B. Cattell, "Is National Intelligence Declining?" *Eugenics Review,* 28 (1936), pp. 181-203.

——, *The Fight for our National Intelligence,* London: P. S. King, 1937.

[10] L. S. Penrose, "Genetical Influences on the Intelligence Level of the Population," *The British Journal of Psychology, General Section,* XL (March, 1950), pp. 128-136.

——, "The Supposed Threat of Declining Intelligence," *American Journal of Mental Deficiency,* 53 (July, 1948), pp. 114-118.

[11] Lancelot Hogben, *Genetic Principles in Medicine and Social Science,* London: Williams & Norgate, 1931, p. 194.

——, (Ed.) *Political Arithmetic,* New York: Macmillan, 1938, pp. 331-333.

[12] Walter S. Neff, "Socio-Economic Status and Intelligence: A Critical Survey," *Psychological Bulletin,* 35 (December, 1938), pp. 727-757.

[13] Ernest A. Haggard, "Influence of Culture Background on Test Performance," paper presented to the Invitational Conference on Testing Problems, New York, October, 1949.

Should these positions be sustained, there would, of course, no longer be grounds for fearing a decline in intelligence solely on the basis of socio-economic differentials in fertility. However, the negative correlation of intelligence and family size within socio-economic groups might remain. It will be most interesting to see what light the new mental tests will throw on this issue.

Another pertinent question about the conventional mental test is its presumption of a general intellectual factor or capacity. In the whole discussion of declining intelligence, little reference has been made to the contention of some schools of factor analysis that mental ability may be classified into several orthogonal or independent factors. One wonders what correlations each of these factors in turn would show with family size. Presumably not all would necessarily be negative. However, the present situation in factor theory is one of much dispute. Quite recent developments in the statistical theory reported by Guttman [14] appear to give new support to the notion of a general intellectual factor. Certainly the issue should not be prejudged.

While dealing with the major props of the theory of declining intelligence, it might also be pointed out that traditional notions concerning differential fertility itself may stand in need of some revision on the basis of recent findings. Whelpton and colleagues have reported that although the usual inverse relation between fertility and socio-economic status is found in the Indianapolis survey, when separate study is made of those couples who plan the number and spacing of their children, family size is found to increase directly with income.[15] May this not adumbrate the future diminution, if not disappearance, of socio-economic differentials of the usual sort?

A third weakness in the reasoning supporting the theory of declining intelligence is the dearth of knowledge concerning the actual genetic mechanism involved in the transmission of intellectual capacity. We have to deal in terms of a hypothetical construct twice removed from direct observation. From an operational standpoint, measured intelligence is an *ability* elicited as a function of a particular standardized social situation. By hypothesis, behind this ability lies an organically structured *capacity* which is jointly determinative of observable ability, along with environmental stimuli and constraints. By further hypothesis, the organic structure which carries potential ability, or capacity, is subject to *genetic* determination according to definite but unknown laws of heredity. It is a long leap of logic — if not of imagination — from observed ability to genetic determination, in the absence of secure empirical anchorage points for these constructs and their interrelations.[16]

In a more positive vein, it has been argued by Penrose[17] that the well known correlations in intelligence between mates and relatives and the negative relationship between IQ and family size are entirely compatible with a genetic equilibrium in which the average level of intelligence remains quite constant. Penrose has actually constructed statistical models of such populations in equilibrium which have a certain plausibility, except for the admitted oversimplification as to the mode of inheritance of intelligence. Clearly, though, more complex assumptions could also well yield the same outcome. The key to Penrose's reconciliation of apparently dysgenic fertility with genetic equilibrium is the assumption of the quasi-lethal nature of extremely low intelligence. This assumption squares with the high death rates and relative sterility of imbeciles and idiots — a fact somewhat neglected by the theorists of declining intelligence.

Fourth on the list of qualifications entered against this theory, and of probably greater consequence than any mentioned yet, is the unacceptability of certain seeming corollaries. Psychologists generally believe that intelligence is positively related to other "desirable" traits — vitality, personability, beauty, etc. But if our IQ genes are "eroding," must we also suppose that dysgenic trends are lowering our capacity for health, reducing the proportion of the physically attractive, and generally debilitating the human organism? Such a conclusion is not generally drawn, but seems to be logically implied.

[14] Louis Guttman, "A New Theory of Factor Analysis," address at the University of Wisconsin, April, 1951.

[15] See Frontispiece, *Population Index,* 13 (July, 1947).

[16] For an excellent elaboration of this viewpoint, see Julian L. Woodward, "The Field of Population Quality," *Social Forces,* 17 (May, 1939), pp. 468-477.

[17] *Op cit.*

Consider longevity. There is much evidence for the existence of hereditary dispositions to long or short life spans. And longevity as a biometric character has striking analogues to intelligence in that it is a continuous variable, is probably determined by many genes, and is expressed only through a screen of strong and varied environmental influences. We find the same sort of socio-economic differential fertility with respect to longevity that has been observed in the case of intelligence. Indeed the illustrative computation in Table 1B, modelled after that of Lorimer and Osborn for intelligence, would lead to the expectation that from a genetic standpoint longevity is declining at the rate of one year per generation. (Some simplifying, but not misleading, assumptions are introduced in Table 1; the table is only illustrative.) We know, of course, that length of life has been and is increasing remarkably in the modern period.

TABLE 1

Occupational Class	Median IQ of Children	Percent of Total Births	Reproduction Rate
	(1)	(2)	(3)
Professional	116	3	.76
Business-Clerical	107	18	.85
Skilled	98	15	1.06
Semi-skilled	95	14	1.03
Farmer	91	31	1.32
Unskilled	88	19	1.17

Mean, weighted by column (2) = 95.7
Mean, weighted by product of columns (2) and (3) = 94.6
(Source of data: Lorimer and Osborn, *Dynamics of Population,* Fig. 41, and Appendix Q.)

TABLE 1B

Economic Level	Life Expectancy*	Relative Fertility
I (High)	67.1	.61
II	63.3	.82
III	61.4	.92
IV	58.0	1.12
V (Low)	54.5	1.44

Unweighted mean = 60.9
Weighted mean = 59.6

* (Life expectancies for females in Chicago, 1930, from an unpublished study by Albert J. Mayer.)

Or consider Boas' data on the stature of school children in relation to family size, roughly reproduced in Table 2B, along with typical results from an intelligence test survey, Table 2A. On the same logic as was used in producing the specter of a "nation of near half-wits" one could evoke the image of a nation of near-dwarfs (though the rate of deterioration implied would perhaps be slower). Again, the actual trend is the reverse, if anything.

TABLE 2

	A	B
Number of Children in Family	Deviation of Average Mental Test Score from Grand Mean[1]	Deviation of Average Height from Grand Mean of Sample[2]
1	6.0	.21 (cm.)
2	5.5	.10
3	1.7	.05
4	−2.5	0.00
5	−6.6	−.05
6	−9.9	−.06
7	−10.9	−.14
8+	−14.7	−.13

[1] Institut National d'Etudes Demographiques, *Le Niveau Intellectuel des Enfants d'Age Scolaire,* Cahier No. 13, 1950.

[2] Franz Boas, *Race, Language and Culture,* New York, 1940, p. 63, fig. 3.

The final and most telling blow to the theory of intellectual deterioration is the fact that, not only does no direct evidence exist to confirm the existence of such a trend, but what direct evidence there is shows the opposite movement toward a *rise* in the average level of measured intelligence! The extent to which scientific partisanship can govern response to evidence is nowhere better illustrated than in the temerity of one author who entitles her paper "The Decline of Intelligence in New Zealand" only to confess in passing that her sample scored considerably higher on the IQ test than did the earlier standardization sample taken in the same community.

The three large projects which thus far have been specifically designed to measure the trend of intelligence report the same finding that no decline can be detected, and that, if anything, a rise has taken place. Cattell, who some years ago predicted a decline of one IQ point per decade, reports a positive difference of more than one point in favor of the 1949 group of 10 year olds in Leicester and Devonshire, compared to the previously tested 1936 group.[18]

Collating results from retesting programs in a number of English school districts, Emmett finds that over an average elapsed period of 9.4 years boys' IQ's have changed at the rate of −.09 points per year, girls' at the rate of +.09 points.[19] It is noteworthy that this investigator feels able to rule out the possibility of incentive and test-sophistication effects as working in the direction of an increase.

The most ambitious resurvey is that of the Scottish Mental Survey Committee [20] which tested the entire year-group of 11-year olds in Scotland in 1947 for comparison with a similar study done in 1932. Some 70,000 subjects were involved. Although this study reiterates the familiar inverse relationship between intelligence and family size, the 1947 mean test score is found to be (the equivalent of) about two IQ points higher than the 1932 mean. The investigators consider carefully a number of possible explanations for this unexpected result. Of the various reasons for refusing to credit it at face value, the most appealing to them seems to be the supposition of an increase in test-sophistication.

No evidence of such an increase is offered, nor is any effort made to adduce instances of bona fide test-sophistication effects of this magnitude in comparably heterogeneous populations. In effect, the erstwhile "genetic determinist" has suddenly, but lamely, turned to a grossly environmental explanation of a paradox in his results. The critic will surely ask, if environment is capable of explaining so much at this juncture, might not the explanation of the original, apparently dysgenic, relationship have some non-genetic explanation? Certainly, if the improved nutrition of the children is to be advanced as an explanation of their improved test scores, one would like to see some consideration given the possibility that the lower test scores of children from large families are due to their relative nutritional disadvantage compared to children from small families.

Other examples of seeming inconsistency between cross-sectional and longitudinal relationships may be found in the social science literature. Calendar year net reproduction rates for the 1930's showed the United States reproducing below the replacement level, whereas subsequent computations of generation rates have shown that no cohort of women as yet has failed to replace itself. Although cross-sectionally fertility is inverse to income, the birth rate rises with general prosperity.

This paper holds the hypothesis of declining intelligence to be untenable — and the "modern dilemma" in that respect to be most unfortunately misstated. But the assent which sociologists will presumably give to this conclusion does not deny the need for a heroic resolution of the seeming paradox as between apparently dysgenic forces and observed improvements in measured intelligence. Two suggestions are offered as to lines of research which might lead toward clarification. The supposition is that the paradox may inhere (a) in some as yet poorly understood aspect of the relationship between measured intelligence and family size, or (b) in some selective mechanism yet to be discerned. Along the first line, attention might be given the possibility that the inverse correlation of IQ and family size is not just a simple matter of more intelligent parents limiting their families more frequently than duller parents. It might well be that the phenomenon is in part a reflection of differential rates of mental maturation in families of different sizes. Or, in line with the previously mentioned proposal of "culture-fair" intelligence tests, one might suppose that family size is associated with relatively "microscopic" differences in cultural milieux, sufficient to account for some of the observed differences.

As for selection, it is painfully obvious on review of the literature under discussion that there exists not a single well-designed study to get at the association between intelligence and family size from the standpoint of the *parents'* measured intelligence. All the evidence is in terms of children's IQ's as correlated with num-

[18] Raymond B. Cattell, "The Fate of National Intelligence: Test of a Thirteen-Year Prediction," *Eugenics Review*, 42 (October, 1950), pp. 136-148.

[19] W. G. Emmett, "The Trend of Intelligence in Certain Districts of England," *Population Studies*, III (March, 1950), pp. 324-337.

[20] *Op cit.*

ber of siblings. To remedy this, ideally a cohort of children would be followed from the earliest age at which reliable IQ scores can be determined to the end of the childbearing period, in an effort to discover intelligence differentials in survival, marriage, dissolution of marriage, and fertility. Even a segment of or an approximation to this ideal design would be most welcome in the present state of ignorance. It would contribute far more than would further demonstrations of fertility differentials by intelligence levels, or even efforts to measure IQ trends.

Of course, the sociologist may well share the concern for population quality of the psychologist and the geneticist, but yet feel that the more important problems at the present time lie in the known wastage of available ability, rather than in the hypothetical loss of potential ability. In any case, the concern is well placed, and the research task is challenging.

STUDY AND DISCUSSION QUESTIONS

1. Examine a census report to see what detailed definition is used by the U.S. Census Bureau in gathering data on educational attainment of the population? What kinds of training can you think of that are not included in this definition? Can you suggest ways of improving the definition?
2. Look up the median number of school years completed for the United States population 25 years of age and over, by sex, in 1940, 1950, and 1960. How did your state compare with the country as a whole in 1960? Did males or females have a higher median? What trends over time can you observe?
3. Consult the United Nations Demographic Yearbook to see how educational levels compare for different countries of the world. What demographic factors might be associated with these differences?
4. It has been noted that education may provide the individual with knowledge about means for regulating fertility and mortality. What kinds of courses in the formal educational system of the United States may perform this function? What other forms of education perform this function?
5. If you were given the task of planning sufficient educational facilities for one of the developing nations of the world for the next fifty years, what kinds of demographic variables would you look at in order to plan efficiently?
6. There are some areas in the United States that have extremely high proportions of highly educated people, and areas in which the educational attainment of the population is extremely low. What factors may account for these groupings? Give specific examples of each case.
7. During the early 1900's, some concern arose over the educational level of immigrants coming into the United States. What was the educational background of these immigrants? Do you think it was sufficiently different from that of the United States population at the time to greatly affect the overall educational composition of the country?
8. Discuss the importance of education as it relates to the propensity to migrate. What aspects of education would be most important in this respect?

SUGGESTED ADDITIONAL READING

Folger, John K., and Charles B. Nam. *Education of the American Population.* Washington: U.S. Government Printing Office, 1967.

A 1960 U.S. Census monograph dealing with trends and relationships in education of the population of the United States.

Bernert, Eleanor H. *America's Children.* New York: John Wiley & Sons, 1958.

A 1950 U.S. Census monograph which includes discussion of school enrollment trends and factors related to them.

United Nations Educational, Scientific and Cultural Organization. *World Illiteracy at Mid-Century.* Paris: UNESCO, 1957.

An international review of illiteracy trends and factors associated with illiteracy.

Osborn, Frederick H. *Preface to Eugenics.* New York: Harper and Brothers, 1951.
Summarizes scientific evidence related to heredity as a factor affecting the quality of populations, including the effects of selective factors on the intelligence distribution of the population.

Price, Daniel O. "The Effects of Migration on Educational Achievements of Negroes in Various Areas of the United States," paper presented to the 1965 World Population Conference, Belgrade, Yugoslavia.
Shows the effects of educational selectivity of migration on the educational structure in sending and receiving areas.

CHAPTER 13

Population and Religion

Religion is among the institutions of society which affect, and are affected by, population conditions. Considering the basic components of population change — fertility, mortality, and migration — it is the first of these with which religion is most strongly associated. However, religious factors are also involved in determining rates of mortality and migration. Viewing the effect of population factors on religion, on the other hand, one can see how changing demographic structure can result in alterations in the religious composition of a population. These topics are discussed more fully in the remainder of this chapter.

Several aspects of religion have demographic implications. *Religion,* in its broadest sense, refers to a system of attitudes, beliefs, and practices which individuals share in groups. These attitudes, beliefs, and practices usually are concerned with the service and worship of the supernatural but, in some instances, are associated with devotion to a set of values rather than to some being or aspect of nature. Religion thus implies a particular orientation toward life and death and a particular feeling about how an individual should relate himself to other persons in a society. Different religious groups vary in their expressions of these views of society and the life hereafter, so that one's religious affiliation is a relevant factor in understanding individual decisions affecting fertility, mortality, and migration.

In Chapter 4, Davis and Blake outlined a framework for analyzing the fertility process which recognizes various steps or stages at which individual and group actions affect the course of fertility. Thus, factors associated with exposure to intercourse, factors affecting exposure to conception, and factors affecting gestation and successful parturition are all related to the fertility process. All these factors are influenced by beliefs people hold, some of which they derive from the religions they observe. Glick has noted the strong effect of religion in the United States in determining the selection of marriage partners and levels of fertility. Although the data presented by Glick do not provide any deep understanding of the reasons why religion is associated with marriage and fertility patterns, they do serve to identify the religious groups whose marriage and fertility rates deviate from the national level. (See Suggested Additional Reading.)

In a detailed examination of the fertility of the Jewish population in the United States, Rosenthal draws upon both indirect and direct information relating religion to fertility. He concludes that Jews have lower family-size ideals and lower actual fertility than do other religious groups in American society, in part because of their typical urban residence and high socioeconomic position and, in part, because of their greater stress on upward social mobility. Therefore, it may not be religious doctrine per se which influences Jewish fertility as much as the firm belief of most Jews in the values of social success and opportunity according to ability. These conclusions are consistent with those of Kirk (in Chapter 4), in which he suggests that high Moslem fertility is probably related less to items of religious faith than to typical Islamic ways of life.

Religious doctrine has, however, had an important influence on fertility practices. In the third selection, Campbell traces the history of the position of Christian churches on birth control and demonstrates that world events and changing culture have led church officials to modify religious doctrine concerning the regulation of fertility behavior. To some extent, the churches have shaped their pronouncements about birth control and family life according to the dominant attitudes of constituents. Where religious doctrine conflicts with secular beliefs of people the doctrine is often not upheld, as evidenced by the widespread use of methods of contraception not approved by the Church by Catholic couples in the United States and other parts of the world. Church officials have been taking these practices into account in determining church policy.

Religion probably has less effect on mortality than on fertility in most cultures. Continuation of life is a universal value among religions, although some means of postponing death are avoided by certain religious groups. For example, Christian Scientists shun many medical services and drugs, and Pentecostal sects advocate healing through faith in Christ. Religion can affect migration through the movement of whole religious groups because of religious persecution or the desire for greater religious freedom, and through the movement of individuals and families who wish to locate their residences closer to those who maintain the same faith. Such religious groups as the Pilgrims, Waldensians, and Hutterites migrated to the United States because of the need for greater religious freedom. The establishment of the state of Israel attracted many Jews from all parts of the world to the new nation. Within the United States, many religious groups have become dispersed over time as their earlier ethnic enclaves have been disintegrated by urban renewal and residential invasion by other groups. One consideration by members of these groups in selecting a new area in which to live has been the availability of places of worship for their faith.

The reading by Bogue describes the religious composition of the population of the United States and the demographic, social, and economic characteristics of the several religious groups. The data are obtained from public and private survey sources, since questions on religion have never been asked in a United States census. However, this information is gathered in a majority of national censuses around the world. The information available to us from these sample surveys in the United States is only for the nation as a whole. Knowledge about how demographic factors are related to the religious composition of the population in particular areas of the country must await changed attitudes about the appropriateness of a question on religion in a census.

Changes in the population size of a religious group will depend on several factors, among which are (1) the birth rate among members of the group, (2) the death rate among members, (3) net migration of adherents to the faith, (4) additions to the religious group through baptism or conversion, and (5) losses from the group through conversion or withdrawal. Thus, the population of a religious group changes both through the basic components of population change and through changes in religious identification. While some statistics on these phenomena are collected by church sources and through private surveys, more complete understanding of the association of demographic changes and religion in the United States will be lacking until a question on religion is included in the national census.

*Jewish Fertility in the United States**

ERICH ROSENTHAL

Births, deaths and migrations are the basic factors of every human society. During the 19th century the population growth of the United States was influenced by immigration as well as by the surplus of births over deaths, but since the cessation of mass migration in the early 1920's the balance of births over deaths has been the dominant force in the growth of the American people.[1] The Jewish group in the United States has fully shared in this change and for nearly 40 years now has not been able to rely on immigration as a prime source of growth. It is the purpose of this report to examine the natural growth of the Jewish population of the United States in recent years.

A number of recent nationwide sample surveys make it possible to analyze the current fertility pattern of the Jewish population, to compare it with patterns of other groups, and to examine some of the factors responsible for the specific fertility of the Jewish population. Earlier descriptions and analyses of the natural growth of the Jewish population, while useful and valuable, were deficient in three respects: they were confined to local communities; they were not designed for the measurement of natural growth and only rarely analyzed it, and they lacked comparability with non-Jewish groups.

CURRENT JEWISH FERTILITY PATTERN

Nature of the Data

Our description of the current fertility pattern of the Jewish population is based on the results of a nationwide sample survey by the U.S. Bureau of the Census in March 1957 of 35,000 households. Some of the statistical data concerning the religious composition of the American people were published by the bureau under the title, "Religion Reported by the Civilian Population of the United States: March 1957."[2] Since survey results are seriously affected by the way questions are worded and by the nature of the inquiry, it should be emphasized that the Census Bureau's question was "What is your religion?" and that answers were voluntary. (Only 1 per cent of the sample population refused to reply.) The question was designed to elicit a respondent's religious preference or background, rather than church or synagogue membership and attendance, or religious belief. Because Jewish self-identification and identification by others is not based solely on religious adherence to Judaism, but also refers to culture, ancestry, and family background as well, we may reasonably assume that the Census Bureau's question was answered in Jewish terms even by persons not religious in any precise sense.

The Census Bureau's question did not differ from the one customarily used by Jewish communal agencies. It therefore came as no surprise that the sample census confirmed the Jewish population in the United States to be close to 5 million, a figure which had been arrived at independently through a variety of private surveys.[3]

Age Distribution

"What is your religion?" was asked only of

* Reprinted from *The American Jewish Yearbook,* 62: 3-27, 1961 by permission of The American Jewish Committee and the Jewish Publication Society of America.

[1] In 1896 Francis A. Walker argued that during a certain period of the 19th century mass immigration contributed nothing to population growth because the gains from immigration were offset by the lowering of fertility of the native population which the process of immigration had induced. Wilson H. Grabill *et al., The Fertility of American Women* (New York, 1958), pp. 103-105.

[2] U. S. Bureau of the Census, *Current Population Reports,* Series P-20, No. 79, Washington, D. C., February 2, 1958.

[3] Erich Rosenthal, "Five Million American Jews," *Commentary,* December 1958, p. 500 and Alvin Chenkin, "Jewish Population in the United States, 1958," AJYB, 1959 (Vol. 60), pp 3-12.

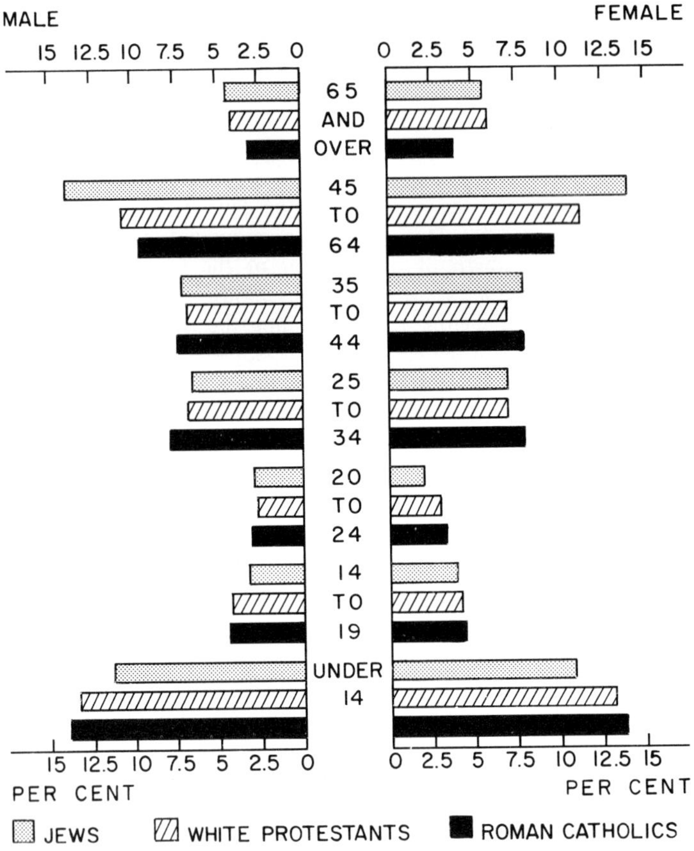

FIGURE 1

Age and sex distribution of the Jewish, White Protestant, and Roman Catholic civilian populations, March 1957.

persons 14 years old and over, "because some religious groups regard baptized infants as members and others count only persons who have 'joined' at about 12 to 14 years of age or older. This difference would undoubtedly affect the replies for persons under 14."[4] However, the sample survey did enumerate the population under 14 years of age, and a tabulation of this child population by religion of parents was presented. It was thus possible to obtain a complete picture of the age composition of the various religious groups. What was published about the children did not include data on sex, so this writer arbitrarily assigned one-half of the children to either sex. In Table 1 and Figure 1 the age composition of the Jewish population has been compared with that of the white Protestant population. Because a separate tabulation for nonwhite Roman Catholics was not available, the Roman Catholic figure includes 774,000 nonwhites.

This tabulation reveals that the Jews in the United States did not participate in the postwar "baby boom" as much as the Roman Catholics and Protestants. Children under 14 years of age constituted 27.7 per cent of Roman Catholics and 26.7 per cent of white Protestants, but

[4] Paul C. Glick, "Intermarriage and Fertility Patterns Among Persons in Major Religious Groups," *Eugenics Quarterly*, March 1960, p. 31.

TABLE 1

Age and Sex Distribution of the Jewish, White Protestant, and Roman Catholic Civilian Populations, March 1957

	Total No.	Total %	Male No.	Male %	Female No.	Female %
JEWS						
All ages	4,975,000	100.0	2,414,500	48.5	2,560,500	51.5
65 and over	503,000	10.1	230,000	4.6	273,000	5.5
45–64	1,393,000	28.0	698,000	14.0	695,000	14.0
35–44	729,000	14.6	337,000	6.8	392,000	7.9
25–34	660,000	13.3	309,000	6.2	351,000	7.1
20–24	233,000	4.7	127,000	2.6	106,000	2.1
14–19	350,000	7.0	160,000	3.2	190,000	3.8
Under 14[a]	1,107,000	22.2	553,500	11.1	553,500	11.1
WHITE PROTESTANTS						
All ages	93,460,000	100.0	44,812,500	47.9	48,647,500	52.1
65 and over	9,341,000	10.0	4,124,000	4.4	5,217,000	5.6
45–64	20,181,000	21.6	9,611,000	10.3	10,570,000	11.3
35–44	12,899,000	13.8	6,237,000	6.7	6,662,000	7.1
25–34	12,916,000	13.8	6,211,000	6.6	6,705,000	7.2
20–24	5,288,000	5.7	2,325,000	2.5	2,963,000	3.2
14–19	7,850,000	8.4	3,812,000	4.1	4,038,000	4.3
Under 14[a]	24,985,000	26.7	12,492,500	13.3	12,492,500	13.4
ROMAN CATHOLICS[b]						
All ages	42,426,000	100.0	20,635,500	48.6	21,790,500	51.4
65 and over	3,059,000	7.2	1,408,000	3.3	1,651,000	3.9
45–64	8,266,000	19.5	4,042,000	9.5	4,224,000	10.0
35–44	6,407,000	15.1	3,118,000	7.3	3,289,000	7.8
25–34	6,555,000	15.5	3,163,000	7.5	3,392,000	8.0
20–24	2,675,000	6.3	1,209,000	2.8	1,466,000	3.5
14–19	3,707,000	8.7	1,817,000	4.3	1,890,000	4.4
Under 14[a]	11,757,000	27.7	5,878,500	13.9	5,878,500	13.8

Source: *Current Population Reports,* Series P-20, No. 79, February 2, 1958, p. 7, Table 7, p. 8, Table 7.

[a] Children under 14 years old from religiously mixed families are omitted. Children are here assumed to be evenly divided between boys and girls.

[b] Including 774,000 nonwhites.

only 22.2 per cent of Jews. Thus, in the 14 years between 1943 and 1957 Jewish fertility was 80.1 and 83.1 per cent of Catholic and Protestant fertility, respectively.

The child population in Table 1 includes only children living in households where the parents adhered to a common religion. However, the sample survey indicated that there were about 4 million additional children from religiously mixed marriages. The writer has arbitrarily allocated such children to the religion of their mothers and added them to the child populations of the appropriate religious groups in order to determine whether this addition effectively changes the relationship between the fertility pattern of the Jewish population and that of each of the other two groups. From Table 2 and Figure 2 it appears that with inclusion of children from mixed marriages, there is a possibility that the fertility of the Jewish population was as little

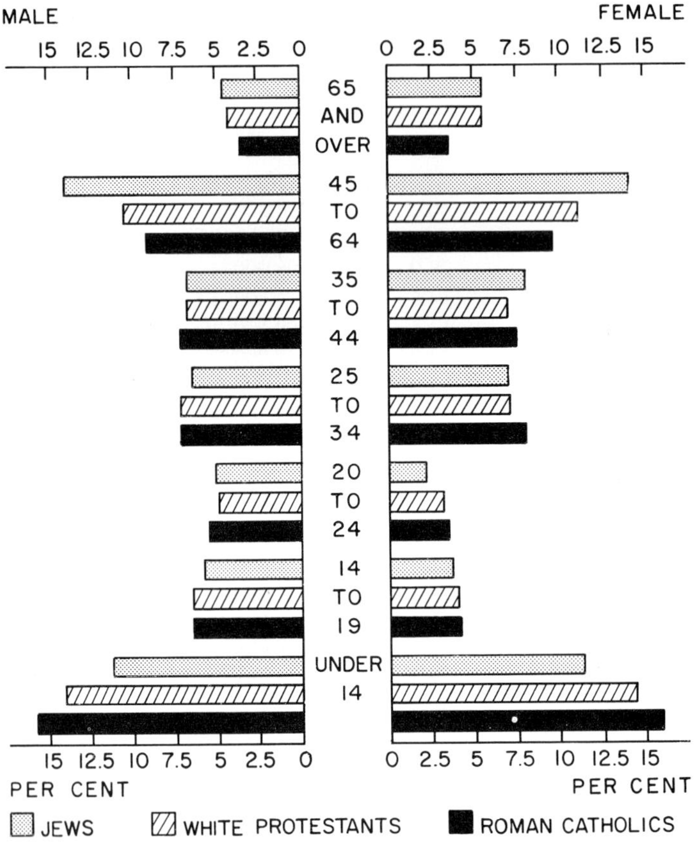

FIGURE 2

Age and sex distribution of the Jewish, White Protestant, and Roman Catholic civilian populations, March 1957 (including children of mixed marriages).

as 73.6 per cent of the Roman Catholic and 79.5 per cent of the white Protestant fertilities between 1943 and 1957.

While there is no other study available which compares the age distribution of the three religious groups for the country as a whole, a 1952 sample survey of New York City, by the Health Insurance Plan of Greater New York (HIP), found that in New York youths under 15 years of age constituted 23 per cent of the Jewish, 22.2 per cent of the white Protestant, and 27.4 per cent of the white Catholic populations.[5] Comparing these figures with those in Table 2, we see that the proportions of youth in the Jewish population of New York City and of the country as a whole are nearly identical, and of those in the Catholic population very similar. That the proportion of white Protestant youth is somewhat smaller in New York City than in the country as a whole is probably due to the greater degree of suburbanization of white Protestants in 1952.

[5] Neva R. Deardorff, "The Religio-Cultural Background of New York City's Population," *The Milbank Memorial Fund Quarterly,* April 1955, p. 159.

Fertility Differences by Religion

The difference in relative sizes of youth populations is the first indication that each group has a distinctive fertility pattern. Further and more direct evidence is provided in Table 3, which relates fertility — measured by the number of

TABLE 2

Age and Sex Distribution of the Jewish, White Protestant, and Roman Catholic Civilian Populations, March 1957 (Including Children of Mixed Marriages)

	Total	%	Male No.	Male %	Female No.	Female %
JEWS						
All ages	4,994,000	100.0	2,424,000	48.5	2,570,000	51.4
65 and over	503,000	10.1	230,000	4.6	273,000	5.5
45–64	1,393,000	27.9	698,000	14.0	695,000	13.9
35–44	729,000	14.6	337,000	6.7	392,000	7.8
25–34	660,000	13.2	309,000	6.2	351,000	7.0
20–24	233,000	4.7	127,000	2.5	106,000	2.1
14–19	350,000	7.0	160,000	3.2	190,000	3.8
Under 14[a]	1,126,000[b]	22.5	563,000	11.3	563,000	11.3
WHITE PROTESTANTS						
All ages	95,448,000	100.0	45,806,500	48.0	49,641,500	52.0
65 and over	9,341,000	9.8	4,124,000	4.3	5,217,000	5.5
45–64	20,181,000	21.1	9,611,000	10.1	10,570,000	11.0
35–44	12,899,000	13.5	6,237,000	6.5	6,662,000	7.0
25–34	12,916,000	13.5	6,211,000	6.5	6,705,000	7.0
20–24	5,288,000	5.5	2,325,000	2.4	2,963,000	3.1
14–19	7,850,000	8.2	3,812,000	4.0	4,038,000	4.2
Under 14[a]	26,973,000[c]	28.3	13,486,500	14.1	13,486,500	14.1
ROMAN CATHOLICS[d]						
All ages	44,185,000	100.0	21,515,000	48.7	22,670,000	51.3
65 and over	3,059,000	6.9	1,408,000	3.2	1,651,000	3.7
45–64	8,266,000	18.7	4,042,000	9.1	4,224,000	9.6
35–44	6,407,000	14.5	3,118,000	7.1	3,289,000	7.4
25–34	6,555,000	14.8	3,163,000	7.1	3,392,000	7.7
20–24	2,675,000	6.0	1,209,000	2.7	1,466,000	3.3
14–19	3,707,000	8.4	1,817,000	4.1	1,890,000	4.3
Under 14[a]	13,516,000[e]	30.6	6,758,000	15.3	6,758,000	15.3

Source: *Current Population Reports,* Series P-20, No. 79, February 2, 1958, p. 7, Table 4, p. 8, Table 7.

[a] The population under 14 years was assumed to be evenly divided between males and females.

[b] Including 19,000 children from religiously mixed marriages where the wife was Jewish.

[c] Including 1,988,000 children from religiously mixed marriages where the wife was Protestant.

[d] Including 774,000 nonwhites.

[e] Including 1,759,000 children from religiously mixed marriages where the wife was Roman Catholic.

children ever born per 1,000 women ever married — with a religious affiliation. The evidence is that the differential between the fertility of the Jewish population and that of the other major denominations was not limited to the 14 years before 1957 but extends much farther back. For the childbearing age (15 to 44) the fertility of Jewish wives was 78.8 per cent of that of (white and nonwhite) Protestant wives and 76.6 per cent of that of (white and nonwhite) Roman Catholic wives. The age group beyond the childbearing age (45 years and over) showed a similar pattern: the fertility of Jewish wives was 80.6 and 72.6 per cent, respectively, of those of Protestant and Roman Catholic wives. Of the two sets of data the set for the completed fertility period (45 years old and over) is the more significant, since the differences recorded for the women still of an age to bear children were influenced by differences in

TABLE 3

Cumulative Fertility Rate (Unstandardized) of Major Religious Groups (Number of Children Ever Born per 1,000 Women Ever Married), March 1957

Age of Women	Protestants[a]	Roman Catholics[a]	Jews	Excess[b]			
				P over J		C over J	
				No.	%	No.	%
15–44	2,220	2,282	1,749	471	21.2	533	23.4
45 and over	2,753	3,056	2,218	535	19.4	838	27.4

Source: *Statistical Abstract of the United States, 1958,* p. 41, Table 40.
[a] All races.
[b] P = Protestant rate; J = Jewish rate; C = Catholic rate.

age at marriage, child spacing, and similar factors. The most significant fact revealed by Table 3 is that the fertility of the Jewish women has lagged behind for two generations.

The table also reveals that fertility patterns are not permanent, but are subject to change over time. Comparing the Jewish with the Protestant group, we see that the difference in incomplete or current fertility was greater (21.2 per cent) than in completed fertility (19.4 per cent). The opposite relationship holds true in a comparison of the Jewish with the Roman Catholic group, where the difference in current fertility was smaller (23.4 per cent) than in completed fertility (27.4 per cent).

Further, there are considerable variations of fertility patterns within each group at a given point in time, as shown in Table 4. Among Protestants, Baptists are the most fertile group. Their current and completed fertilities are 6 and 11 per cent, respectively, higher than the average for the country as a whole. Lutherans and Presbyterians are the least fertile Protestant groups recorded. The completed fertility of the Presbyterians is 1 per cent below that of the Jews. The above-average fertility of the Baptists has been attributed to two factors: the first, that about one-third of the Baptists are Negroes, whose fertility is considerably higher than that of whites, and the second, that a large number of white Baptists are rural. By contrast, the low fertility of the Presbyterians has been at-

TABLE 4

Cumulative Fertility Rate (Number of Children Ever Born per 1,000 Women Ever Married), by Religion Reported, March 1957

Religion	Age		Ratio to Total	
	15 to 44	45 and Over	15 to 44	45 and Over
Total	2,218	2,798	1.00	1.00
Jewish	1,749	2,218	.79	.79
Roman Catholic	2,282	3,056	1.03	1.09
Protestant	2,220	2,753	1.00	.98
Baptist	2,359	3,275	1.06	1.11
Lutheran	2,013	2,382	.91	.85
Methodist	2,155	2,638	.97	.94
Presbyterian	2,001	2,188	.90	.78
Other Protestant	2,237	2,702	1.01	.97
Other, none, and not reported	2,069	2,674	.93	.96

Source: *Statistical Abstract of the United States, 1958,* p. 41, Table 40.

tributed to urban residence, combined with a high level of education, occupation, and income.[6]

That the Jewish fertility rate is shared or approached by one or two Protestant denominations is a first indication that there may be nothing "inherently Jewish" about it.

The relatively low level of Jewish fertility in the United States has been observed before, though in a fragmentary manner. Goldberg's findings were limited to the fertility of married women who reported Yiddish as their mother tongue in the 1940 census.[7] More recently for 13 communities surveyed between 1947 and 1950, Seligman found that in each the fertility of the Jewish population was lower than that of the total white population.[8]

Social Determinants

It has been known for a long time that different social groups have different fertilities. Size of community (degree of urbanization), home ownership, education, occupation, and income have been found to be key factors. The evidence indicates that racial, ethnic, and religious factors are of secondary importance. Within any religious, ethnic, or racial group there is considerable variation in fertility, depending upon place of residence, home ownership, education, occupation, and income. Conversely, members of different religious groups who are alike in residence, education, occupation, and income display a virtually identical pattern of fertility. The latter forces must therefore be regarded as the basic determinants of variations in fertility.[9]

Residence

Urban-rural difference in fertility is among the oldest and best known of demographic phenomena. The main reasons for the difference are most likely to be found in the greater financial cost and physical difficulty of raising children in an urban environment.[10] In the United States urban fertility seems to have been two-thirds of rural fertility as early as 1810. By 1940 urban fertility had dropped to 56 per cent of the rural rate, but it rose to 71 per cent in 1950.[11]

"Urban" refers to places with a population of only 2,500 as well as to cities with more than a million. Within the urban category, the larger

[6] Donald J. Bogue, *The Population of the United States* (Glencoe, Ill., 1959), pp. 696-97.

[7] For a detailed analysis of these data and a summary of findings from Jewish community studies conducted in the thirties see Nathan Goldberg, "Jewish Population in America," *Jewish Review* (published by the Jewish Teacher's Seminary and People's University, New York), December 1948, pp. 30-55.

[8] Ben B. Seligman, "Some Aspects of Jewish Demography," in Marshall Sklare, ed., *The Jews* (Glencoe, Ill., 1958), p. 67.

[9] P. K. Whelpton and C. V. Kiser, *Social and Psychological Factors Affecting Fertility* (New York, 1945), Vol. I, *passim.*

[10] Wilson H. Grabill *et al., op. cit.,* p. 83.

[11] *Ibid.,* pp. 16-17.

TABLE 5

Urban-Rural Residence of Persons 14 Years Old and Over, by Religion Reported for the Civilian Population, March 1957

Residence	Total Population (%)	White Protestants (%)	Roman Catholics (%)	Jews (%)
United States	100.0	100.0	100.0	100.0
Total Urban	63.9	55.2	78.8	96.1
Urbanized areas of 250,000 or more	36.6	24.5	53.9	87.4
Other urban	27.3	30.7	24.9	8.7
Rural nonfarm	24.4	30.1	15.8	3.6
Rural farm	11.7	14.7	5.4	0.2

Source: *Current Population Reports,* Series P-20, No. 79, February 2, 1958, p. 7, Table 3.

the size of a community, the lower the fertility. This inverse relationship was last observed for the United States in the 1950 population census, which found that the fertility ratio in cities with more than three million inhabitants was only 85 per cent of that in cities with fewer than 250,000.[12]

In these respects, the most outstanding characteristic of the Jewish population and the one that distinguishes it most from the other major religious groups is its heavy concentration in cities. Table 5 reveals that in 1957, 96.1 per cent of the Jews resided in cities, as compared with 78.8 per cent of the Roman Catholics and 55.2 per cent of the white Protestants. Furthermore, Jews are concentrated in the larger cities, 87.4 per cent living in "urbanized areas" of 250,000 or more persons, as compared with 53.9 per cent of the Roman Catholics and 24.5 per cent of the white Protestants.[13] Even this fails to indicate fully the degree of Jewish ur-

[12] *Ibid.*, p. 89.

[13] "Urbanized area" has been defined as follows: "Each urbanized area contains at least one city with 50,000 inhabitants or more in 1940 or according to a special census taken since 1940. Each urbanized area also includes the surrounding closely settled incorporated places and unincorporated areas that comprise its urban fringe. The boundaries of these fringe areas were established to conform as nearly as possible to the actual boundaries of thickly settled territory, usually characterized by a closely spaced street pattern" (*1950 Census of Population:* Vol. IV, *Special Reports,* Part 5, Chapter A, "Characteristics by Size of Place," p. 6).

TABLE 6

Rank of Urbanized Areas According to Population, 1950, and Estimated Jewish Population, 1958

Rank	Area	Total Population, 1950 Number[a]	Estimated Jewish Population 1958: No.[b]	Estimated Jewish Population 1958: Cumulative Ratio to Total (%)
1	New York-Northeastern New Jersey	12,296,117	2,600,000[c]	52.3
2	Chicago	4,920,816	282,000[d]	57.9
3	Los Angeles	3,996,946	390,000[d]	65.8
4	Philadelphia	2,922,470	330,500[d]	72.4
5	Detroit	2,659,398	75,000	73.9
6	Boston	2,233,448	150,000	76.9
7	San Francisco-Oakland	2,022,078	55,000	78.0
8	Pittsburgh	1,532,953	47,000	79.0
9	St. Louis	1,400,058	57,500	80.1
10	Cleveland	1,383,581	88,000	81.9
11	Washington	1,287,333	80,900[d]	83.5
12	Baltimore	1,161,852	80,000	85.1
13	Minneapolis	985,101	20,000	85.5
14	Milwaukee	829,495	30,000	86.1
15	Cincinnati	813,292	25,000	86.6

[a] *1950 Census of Population:* Vol. II, *Characteristics of the Population,* Part I, "United States Summary," pp. 1-29.

[b] AJYB 1959 (Vol. 60), pp. 13-17. The figures refer to the population in central cities (i.e., exclusive of suburbs) unless otherwise indicated.

[c] Refers to the New York Metropolitan Area and is taken from Henry Cohn, *Jewish Population Trends in New York City, 1940-1970* (New York: Federation of Jewish Philanthropies, 1956).

[d] Refers to the metropolitan area.

banization. Further analysis, as in Table 6, leads to the conclusion that at least 86.6 per cent of all Jews in the United States actually reside in urbanized areas with 750,000 or more inhabitants. This conclusion is supported by independent surveys by the National Opinion Research Center, in 1953 and 1955, which found that 84 per cent of the Jews of the United States live in "standard metropolitan areas" with a population of a million or more.[14] What is more,

[14] Bogue, *op. cit.*, pp. 699-700. Standard metropolitan areas are larger than urbanized areas. In general, urbanized areas represent the thickly settled core of standard metropolitan areas (*1950 Census of Population:* Vol. II, *Characteristics of the Population,* Part 1, "United States Summary," p. 28).

TABLE 7

Cumulative Fertility Rate (Number of Children Ever Born Per 1,000 Women Ever Married) by Type of Community, Years of School Completed, and Labor-force Status Compared with Number of Children Ever Born Per 1,000 Jewish Women Ever Married, March 1957

Characteristic	Unstandardized Cumulative Fertility Rate[a]		Ratio	
	15 to 44	45 and Over	15 to 44	45 and Over
A. Type of community				
Total	2,218	2,798	1.00	1.00
Rural farm	3,009	3,910	1.35	1.40
Rural nonfarm	2,356	3,069	1.06	1.10
Urban	2,035	2,514	.92	.90
Urban white	2,007	2,494	.90	.89
Jews (urban and rural)	1,749	2,218	.79	.79
B. Type of urban community				
Total urban	2,035	2,514	1.00	1.00
In urbanized areas	1,990	2,386	.98	.95
Areas of 250,000 to 1,000,000	1,993	2,410	.98	.96
Areas of 1,000,000 to 3,000,000	1,981	2,367	.97	.94
Areas of 3,000,000 or more	1,877	2,228	.92	.89
Jews (urban and rural)	1,749	2,218	.86	.88
C. Years of school completed				
Total urban	2,035	2,514	1.00	1.00
High school: 1 to 3 years	2,164	2,280	1.06	.91
4 years	1,857	1,923	.91	.76
College: 1 to 3 years	1,748	1,865	.86	.74
4 years or more	1,746	1,498	.86	.60
D. Labor-force status (married, husbands present)				
Urban	2,057	2,375	1.00	1.00
Wife in labor force	1,580	1,950	.77	.82
Wife not in labor force	2,291	2,544	1.11	1.07

Source: *Current Population Reports,* Series P-20, No. 84, August 8, 1958.

[a] Most returns of the 1957 sample survey were standardized for age in order to reduce "the effect of intergroup differences in the distribution by age." (For details see source above, pp. 5, 6.) Since returns for the Jewish population were not large enough to permit standardization, the unstandarized rates were used here.

52.3 per cent reside in the largest urban agglomeration, the New York area, and 65.8 per cent live in urbanized areas with more than three million residents (Table 6).

Other things being equal, one should reasonably expect that the fertility of the Jewish population as a whole would be closer to that prevailing among all whites in large cities than to any other. This expectation is borne out. Part A of Table 7 shows that Jewish fertility is, indeed, closer to the urban white than to the other three fertilities. While the current Jewish rate is 11 points lower and the completed rate 10 points lower than the respective urban white rates, they are both 21 points below those of the nation as a whole.

Part B of Table 7 shows that with increasing intensity of urbanization the fertility rate declines progressively, but that the current Jewish fertility is 6 points below the rate that prevails in even the most intensively urbanized areas. Since about half of the Jews of the United States live in the New York area, which in 1950 had a population of over 12 million, and two-thirds live in urbanized areas of 3 million and more, one can justify the conclusion that residence is the most significant factor in the low Jewish fertility. Other factors are examined below.

Educational Attainment of Women

The relationship of women's education to fertility is twofold: while prolonged education depresses women's fertility very considerably, the gains in fertility since 1940 have been most pronounced among women of the highest educational attainment. As shown in Table 8, the fertility of women college graduates was only about half of the fertility of all American women. This was true for the United States as a whole in 1940, 1950, and probably in 1957.[15] It will also be seen from Table 8, however, that the fertility of urban college graduates rose from 52 per cent of the fertility of all urban white women in 1940 to 61 per cent in 1950,[16] and

[15] The returns from the 1957 sample survey were tabulated in a slightly different manner, thus preventing a strict comparison ("Fertility of the Population: March 1957," *Current Population Reports,* Series P-20, No. 84, August 8, 1958, Table 4, p. 10).

[16] For the gains in cumulative fertility between 1940 and 1950 among college graduates 20 to 39 years old, see Grabill *et al., op. cit.,* pp. 194-200.

TABLE 8

Standardized Number of Children Ever Born Per 1,000 White Women Ever Married 15 to 49 Years Old, by Years of School Completed, Total Population Compared with Urban, 1940 and 1950

Years of School Completed	Nationwide No.	Nationwide Ratio	Urban No.	Urban Ratio
1940				
None or elementary	2,521	1.00	2,042	1.00
High school, 1–3 years	1,925	.76	1,648	.81
High school, 4 years	1,460	.58	1,304	.64
College, 1–3 years	1,365	.54	1,225	.60
College, 4 and more years	1,145	.45	1,064	.52
1950				
None or elementary	2,421	1.00	2,065	1.00
High school, 1–3 years	1,948	.80	1,774	.86
High school, 4 years	1,569	.65	1,461	.71
College, 1–3 years	1,479	.61	1,385	.67
College, 4 and more years	1,296	.53	1,262	.61

Source: W. H. Grabill, *et al., The Fertility of American Women* (New York, 1958), p. 201.

from Part C of Table 7 that the gain continued in 1957 for women of childbearing age. While for women past the childbearing age (45 and over) the inverse relationship between fertility and education was as clear in 1957 as in 1950 and 1940, for women of childbearing age (15 to 44) the inverse relationship became blurred.

Table 7 shows that the cumulative fertility rate of urban women 15 to 44 years old with four years or more of college was 1,746, while the rate for all Jewish women of that age was 1,749. The similarity calls for an examination of the educational attainment of Jewish women.

Table 9 shows that in 1950, 6 per cent of the total population — including both sexes and all races — had had 4 years of college or had also had graduate education. By 1957 the proportion had risen to 7.5 per cent. The percentage of women achieving this educational level rose from 5 per cent in 1950 to 5.7 per cent in 1957.

TABLE 9

Persons 25 Years Old and Over with Four or More Years of College, 1950 and 1957

	Per Cent	
	1950	1957
Total	6.0	7.5
White	6.4	No. Inf.
Nonwhite	2.2	2.8
White female	No. Inf.	6.0
Marital status (All races)		
Female	5.0	5.7
Single	13.3	16.2
Married	4.5	5.2
Widowed	2.7	3.4 (Widowed and Divorced)
Divorced	5.0	

Source: *1950 Population Census: Special Reports: Education,* p. 13, Table B, and *Current Population Reports,* Series P-20, No. 77, March 1957, p. 3, Table C.

Table 10, showing the percentage of such women in each of six cities where the Jewish population is concentrated, shows that between large cities the intensity of urbanization does not significantly affect the length of school attendance for women. In Philadelphia, the fourth largest city in the United States, only 3.3 per cent of white women 25 years old and over were college graduates, while in San Francisco, the seventh largest city, 7.4 per cent were college graduates.

TABLE 10

White Women 25 Years Old and Over with Four Years of College, in Selected Cities, 1950

	Per Cent	
City	City	SMA[a]
Philadelphia	3.3	4.7
Chicago	4.4	5.3
New York City	5.2	5.8
Los Angeles	7.1	7.2
San Francisco	7.4	8.6
Washington, D. C.	11.7	12.5

Source: *1950 Census of Population:* Vol. II, *Characteristics of the Population,* p. 116, Table 65.

[a] Standard Metropolitan Area.

Although there have been no specific studies of the educational achievement of Jewish women, two recent surveys, one of Washington, D. C. and the other of San Francisco, have provided some material, summarized in Table 11, on the basis of which a tentative conclusion may be essayed:[17] that the ratio of Jewish women who

TABLE 11

Women with Four or More Years of College, Washington, D. C., and San Francisco

	Washington, D. C. Standard Metropolitan Area	
Age	% Jews 1956	% Total White 1950
25 and over	22.9	12.5
25–44	30.1	14.4
45 and over	11.5	8.7
	San Francisco	
Age	% Jews 1959	% Total White 1950
30–44	15.6	8.6

[17] Stanley K. Bigman, *The Jewish Population of Greater Washington in 1956* (Washington: Jewish Community Council, May 1957), pp. 18-19, Tables 2-1 and 2-2, and Fred Massarik, *The Jewish Population of San Francisco, Marin County and the Peninsula, 1959* (San Francisco: Jewish Welfare Federation, November 1959), p. 99, Table 58.

have graduated from college is almost double that of the total white female population. Washington may be unrepresentative, because the large proportion of women college graduates there could be due to the peculiarity of job opportunities in the capital, but the roughly 2-to-1 ratio of Jewish to all white women college graduates obtains in San Francisco as well. The conclusion seems justified that the educational level of Jewish women of childbearing age is comparatively high, and does have a significant effect upon their fertility.

Husband's Occupation

That occupational groups differ considerably in their reproductivity is a fact which has aroused considerable curiosity and anxiety.[18] White-collar workers have fewer children than manual workers and rural residents. (This differential was observed for rural farm, rural nonfarm, and urban areas in 1940 and 1950.)[19] Table 12 shows that the wives of white-collar workers of childbearing age have up to 20 per cent fewer children than the national average, while such women past the childbearing age have had up to 30 per cent fewer children than the national average.

The relatively low fertility of the white-collar groups is a social determinant of great weight in the specific fertility pattern of the Jewish population. Next to urban residence, the second most distinctive sociological attribute of American Jews is their concentration in the white-collar occupations. Community surveys in the late 30's indicated that an average of 76.8 per cent of Jews in the labor force were professional workers, managers, officials and proprietors, and clerical and sales workers.[20] Similar surveys in the late 1940's showed that 84.2 per cent were so employed.[21] Data from national surveys now show that the heavy concentration of Jews in white-collar occupations holds true for the country as a whole. It will be seen from Table 13 that between 1953 and 1955, 78.2 per cent of Jewish heads of households were employed in

[18] Grabill *et al., op. cit.,* p. 113.
[19] *Ibid.,* p. 130.

[20] Sophia M. Robison, ed., *Jewish Population Studies* (New York, 1943), p. 189.
[21] Seligman, *loc. cit.,* pp. 76-77.

TABLE 12

Number of Children Ever Born Per 1,000 Women 15 Years Old and Over, Married and Husband Present, by Age of Woman and Major Occupation Group of Employed Civilian Husband, March 1957.

	Age of Wife			
	Unstandardized		Ratio	
Major Occupation Group of Husband	15 to 44	45 and Over	15 to 44	45 and Over
Total with employed civilian husband	2,343	2,708	1.00	1.00
Professional, technical, and kindred workers	1,996	1,908	.85	.70
Farmers and farm managers	3,149	4,029	1.34	1.49
Managers, officials, and proprietors, excluding farmers	2,209	2,273	.94	.84
Clerical and kindred workers	1,884	2,270	.80	.84
Sales workers	2,056	2,090	.88	.77
Craftsmen, foremen, and kindred workers	2,333	2,564	1.00	.95
Operatives and kindred workers	2,422	2,791	1.03	1.03
Service workers, including private household	2,277	2,701	.97	1.00
Farm laborers and foremen	3,729	—	1.59	—
Laborers, excluding farmers and miners	2,649	3,337	1.13	1.23

Source: "Fertility of the Population: March 1957," *Current Population Reports,* Series P-20, No. 84, August 8, 1958, p. 11, Table 5.

TABLE 13

Occupational Distribution of Household Heads, by Religious Affiliation, 1953–55

Occupation of Head of Household	All Religions %	Jewish %	Protestant %	Roman Catholic %
Total	100.0	100.0	100.0	100.0
Professional, technical, and kindred workers	10.0	17.6	9.5	9.6
Farmers and farm managers	10.8	1.3	12.9	5.4
Managers, officials, and proprietors, excluding farmers	12.6	36.0	11.8	11.4
Clerical and kindred workers	6.4	9.6	6.3	7.6
Sales workers	4.8	15.0	4.5	4.6
Craftsmen, foremen, and kindred workers	19.4	7.2	19.2	21.6
Operatives and kindred workers	20.3	12.0	19.7	23.8
Service workers, including private households	7.6	—	7.4	8.6
Farm laborers	2.0	—	1.6	3.0
Laborers, excluding farmers and miners	6.1	1.3	7.0	4.6

Source: Bogue, *op. cit.*, p. 703.

the four categories comprising the white-collar group, with a concentration of "managers, officials, proprietors" and "sales workers." In each of these categories the proportion of Jews was about three times that of the national average. Again the conclusion must be drawn that the occupational distribution of American Jews depresses their fertility. The 12 per cent of Jewish household heads who were manual workers ("operatives and kindred workers") might be expected to show greater fertility, but they do not. They are most likely to reside in New York, according to a finding that 28 per cent of the Jewish labor force of that city are skilled and unskilled workers.[22] A recent survey of the ninth grade of a Brooklyn, N.Y., junior high school found that there was virtually no difference between Jewish manual and white-collar workers in the size of the family. The average number of children for the white-collar worker was 2.28, that for manual workers 2.32.[23] Admittedly limited, the study allows the inference that for the Jewish population of New York City, occupation does not affect fertility differentials.

[22] Seligman, "The Jewish Population of New York City," in Sklare, ed., *The Jews,* p. 102.

[23] Erwin S. Solomon, "Social Characteristics and Fertility," *Eugenics Quarterly,* June 1956, p. 101.

This startling propensity of Jewish manual workers to behave like white-collar people in the distinctive and crucial respect of fertility can at least be reconciled with, if not fully explained by, Glazer's conclusion that Jews in the United States have tended to have middle-class values — sobriety, foresight, etc. — even when earning a living as manual workers.[24]

Husband's Income and Family Income

The collection of income data by the Bureau of the Census was started on a limited basis in connection with the 1940 census. Since then, many sample surveys as well as the 1950 census not only have built up a continuous record of the income of Americans but have also made it possible to relate size of income to a number of social and physical characteristics. The 1950 census returns were analyzed in a monograph by Herman P. Miller, who found that incomes tend to increase with size of city, length of education, proximity to the apex of professional status, and increasing age up to 54 years. Nearly all of these factors help explain the relatively high income of the Jewish population.[25]

[24] Nathan Glazer, "Social Characteristics of American Jews, 1654-1954," AJYB 1955 (Vol. 56), pp. 30 ff.

[25] Herman P. Miller, *Income of the American People* (New York, 1955), p. 39, Table 14; p. 67, Table 30, and p. 54, Table 24.

As a result of the concentration of the Jewish labor force in white-collar fields in the largest urban centers, the median family income of Jewish households is higher than that of the combined membership of Protestant denominations and of Roman Catholics. The Bureau of the Census does not publish income data for the various religious denominations, but sample surveys by the National Opinion Research Center in 1953 and 1955 found that the median family income of Jewish households was $5,954, that of Protestant households $3,933, and that of Roman Catholic households $4,340.[26]

Bogue concludes that "income differentials between religions tend to disappear and become simply differentials between occupations."[27]

If income is such a close correlate of occupation, one should expect an inverse relationship between income and fertility. Most empirical studies have found this to be so, except for the highest-income group, which has a higher level of fertility. The pattern is that of a "J-shaped relation of fertility with economic status."[28]

The excess of total family income over husband's income is most likely to come from the wife's earnings, at the cost of limiting her fertility. Part D of Table 7 shows that urban, married women in the labor force, 15 to 44, have only 69 per cent as many children as women of their age not in the labor force, and women 45 and over only 77 per cent.

Table 14 shows that the one exception to the inverse relationship between family income and fertility is in the highest income — $7,000 and over — for women 45 and older. The inverse relationship between husband's income and fertility holds true for all income groups for women

[26] Bogue, *op. cit.*, p. 706.
[27] *Ibid.*

[28] Wilson H. Grabill, "The Fertility of the United States Population," in Bogue, *op. cit.*, p. 311. For a critical evaluation of current theories regarding the relationship of income to fertility see pp. 311-14, *ibid.*

TABLE 14

Number of Children Ever Born Per 1,000 Women 15 Years Old and Over, Married and Husband Present, by Age of Woman, Husband's Income, and Total Family Income, March 1957.

Husband's Income in Previous Calendar Year	Unstandardized 15 to 44	Unstandardized 45 and Over	Ratio 15 to 44	Ratio 45 and Over
Total	2,350	2,866	1.00	1.00
Under $1,000	2,857	3,829	1.22	1.34
$1,000 to $1,999	2,671	3,414	1.14	1.19
$2,000 to $2,999	2,330	3,044	.99	1.06
$3,000 to $3,999	2,267	2,794	.96	.97
$4,000 to $4,999	2,232	2,403	.95	.84
$5,000 to $6,999	2,306	2,300	.98	.80
$7,000 and over	2,384	2,134	1.01	.74
Family Income in Previous Calendar Year				
Total	2,271	2,785	1.00	1.00
Under $1,000	2,689	3,549	1.18	1.27
$1,000 to $1,999	2,674	3,356	1.18	1.20
$2,000 to $2,999	2,431	2,950	1.07	1.06
$3,000 to $3,999	2,345	2,882	1.03	1.03
$4,000 to $4,999	2,308	2,475	1.02	.89
$5,000 to $6,999	2,217	2,414	.98	.87
$7,000 and over	2,073	2,480	.91	.89

Source: *Current Population Reports,* Series P-20, No. 84, August 8, 1958, p. 12, Table 6.

past the childbearing age. However, for women of childbearing age the inverse relationship holds true only for incomes up to $5,000, after which fertility rises. Nevertheless, a comparison of the 1957 data of Table 14 with a similar set of data gathered in 1952 shows, during the 5-year interval, "a strong pattern of relatively more children among people with little income than among people with more income."[29] Since the Jews are concentrated in white-collar occupations, which typically bring greater financial rewards, the conclusion must be drawn that the income factor contributes its share toward depressing the level of Jewish fertility.

Jewishness as a Determinant of Fertility

Our step-by-step analysis of the data would make it appear that the religio-cultural complex called Jewishness is not, as has been often theorized, a major factor in the Jewish fertility rate.

Goldberg has repeatedly advanced the thesis that the low level of fertility among the Jews in the United States is due to their status as a minority group.[30] He maintains that because of discriminatory practices, Jews require more education, training, and experience than non-Jews to achieve comparable positions. According to Goldberg, minority status affects Jewish fertility in two ways: it defers marriage, and it keeps children dependent on their parents for a longer period of time because of the need for more intensive preparation for adult careers.

To the extent that differences in fertility levels have here been explained by differences in rural-urban distribution, in the educational attainment of women, and in husbands' occupation and income, Goldberg's thesis is unsupported. Bogue asserts:

> The meager data available gives little evidence either that any religious group is extraordinarily favored, or that there is severe discrimination (independent of any other factors) against any religious group because of its beliefs — with respect to broad categories of occupational attainment. Although the religious groups differ substantially with respect to occupational composition, in general the members of each religion seem to be located just about as high on the occupational ladder as the level of their educational attainment would lead one to expect.[31]

For Bogue it is clear that education and occupation are "much more potent factors than religious preference in determining the income level of households." [32]

Though the low level of Jewish fertility, accordingly, seems unrelated to discrimination, it may be related to rapid upward social movement. American Jews have successfully tested the promise of an open, democratic society. Glazer found that the "rise in the social and economic position of the Jews has been extremely rapid, far surpassing that which can be shown for any other immigrant group, and indeed surpassing, for the same period, changes in the socio-economic position of long-settled groups." [33] There is some evidence available that the class composition of the Jewish population had approached that of Episcopalians, Congregationalists, and Presbyterians 10 years ago and even earlier. Twenty-two per cent of the Jews were in the upper class, 32 per cent in the middle class, and 46 per cent in the lower, while the corresponding figures for the Presbyterians were 22, 40, and 38 per cent.[34]

A relationship between low fertility and rapid social mobility has been postulated in the theory of social capillarity, according to which a family must be small if it is to rise in the social scale.[35] The Princeton Fertility Study is the first to reveal empirically the operation of social capillarity in the Jewish case, finding that a major factor governing the fertility behavior of the

[29] *Current Population Reports,* Series P-20, No. 84, August 1958, p. 3.

[30] For the most recent and most accessible formulation of this thesis see Nathan Goldberg, "The Jewish Population in the United States," in *The Jewish People Past and Present* (New York, 1948), pp. 28-29.

[31] Bogue, *op. cit.*, p. 704.

[32] *Ibid.*, pp. 707, 708.

[33] Glazer, "Social Characteristics of American Jews, 1654-1954," *loc. cit.*, p. 29.

[34] Liston Pope, "Religion and the Class Structure," *Annals of the American Academy of Political and Social Science,* March 1948, p. 86.

[35] Charles F. Westoff, "The Changing Focus of Differential Fertility Research: The Social Mobility Hypothesis, "*The Milbank Memorial Fund Quarterly,* January 1953, pp. 24-38; reprinted in Joseph J. Spengler and Otis Dudley Duncan, eds., *Population Theory and Policy: Selected Readings* (Glencoe, 1956), pp. 400-09.

Jewish couples in the sample survey was "a perceived incompatibility between sending children to college and having large families."[36] Low fertility, therefore, has been an important means for rising in the social and economic scale for Jews. Another means has been moving to desirable residential areas.[37]

Jewish Fertility in Canada and Great Britain

Low fertility is not limited to the Jews of the United States. The fertility of Canadian Jews is considerably lower than that of the Canadian population as a whole. While the fertility rate of all married women 15 to 49 years old was 168.7 per 1,000 in 1951, the corresponding Jewish rate was only 114.2, or 67.6 per cent as high; in the same year the average size of the Jewish family was 3.2, compared with 3.7 for all Canadian families. The average Jewish family "was the smallest of any among the eight largest groups in Canada."[38] The low fertility of the Jews in Canada is not recent. As early as 1926 the Jewish birth rate was only 70 per cent of that of the total population.[39] A detailed study of the fertility patterns and trends among Jews of Canada between 1931 and 1941 found that the Jewish concentration in urban centers and in white-collar occupations contributed to low fertility.[40]

In Great Britain official statistics do not include data on religious preference or origin, and the demographer must therefore rely on local community surveys and nongovernmental sample surveys. Analysis of the available studies indicates that the Jewish birth rate has lagged considerably behind. The estimated Jewish birth rate for the period 1945-49 was 11.6 per thousand, compared with 16.8 for the total population in the same period.[41]

Family Limitation: Attitudes and Practices

The significance of the 1957 sample survey of the U. S. Bureau of the Census for Jewish demography is matched by two recent studies of attitudes toward family planning. The first, the Growth of American Families (GAF) study, was by Ronald Freedman of the Survey Research Center of the University of Michigan and P. K. Whelpton and A. A. Campbell of the Scripps Foundation for Research in Population Problems.[42] The second, the Princeton Fertility Study (PFS), was conducted by the Office of Population Research, Princeton.[43] Some of the findings of the Princeton Fertility Study cited below were taken from a published paper by Charles F. Westoff and an unpublished paper by Robert G. Potter, Jr.[44]

The GAF study found that Jewish couples "expect significantly fewer children (2.4) than either Catholics (3.4) or Protestants (2.9)." In the 12 largest cities included in the GAF sample, Jews and Protestants expected the same average number of births (2.3). The authors therefore attribute the low fertility expectation of the Jewish families primarily to their concentration in large cities.[45] Their low expectations are realized because, as the Princeton study found, consensus about the number of children wanted was greatest among Jewish couples.[46]

[36] Charles F. Westoff, "The Social-psychological Structure of Fertility," *Proceedings, International Population Conference* (Vienna, 1959), p. 363.

[37] Erich Rosenthal, "Acculturation Without Assimilation? The Jewish Community of Chicago, Illinois," *American Journal of Sociology,* November 1960, pp. 275-88.

[38] Louis Rosenberg, "The Demography of the Jewish Community in Canada," *Jewish Journal of Sociology,* December 1959, p. 227.

[39] *Ibid.,* p. 226.

[40] Mortimer Spiegelman, "The Reproductivity of Jews in Canada, 1940-1942," *Population Studies,* December 1950, pp. 299-313.

[41] Hannah Neustatter, "Demographic and Other Statistical Aspects of Anglo-Jewry," in Maurice Freedman, *ed., A Minority in Britain* (London, 1955), p. 82.

[42] Ronald Freedman, Pascal K. Whelpton, and Arthur A. Campbell, *Family Planning, Sterility, and Population Growth* (New York, 1959).

[43] Charles S. Westoff, Robert G. Potter, Jr., Philip C. Sagi, and Elliott G. Mishler, *Family Growth in Metropolitan America* (Princeton 1961).

[44] Charles F. Westoff, "Religion and Fertility in Metropolitan America," in *Proceedings of . . . Milbank Memorial Fund: Thirty Years of Research in Human Fertility Retrospect and Prospect* (New York, 1959), pp. 117-34, and Robert G. Potter, Jr., "Fertility: A Multi-dimensional Analysis," paper presented at the April 1960 meeting of the Eastern Sociological Society.

[45] Freedman *et al., op. cit.,* p. 287.

[46] Potter, *loc. cit.,* p. 9.

The GAF study found that Jewish wives were most favorably inclined toward family limitation — 88 per cent expressing unqualified approval, compared with 33 per cent for Catholic and 72 per cent for Protestant wives.[47] A smaller study suggests that comparable differences in attitude exist before marriage, as well. In a group of 222 unmarried women undergraduates between 18 and 23 it was found that 85 per cent of the Jewish women "would consider the use of contraceptives," 58 per cent of the Protestants, and 18 per cent of the Catholics.[48]

Accordingly, the GAF study found that Jews practiced contraception more than the other two groups.[49] Both the GAF and the Princeton studies found that Jewish couples were much more likely to begin contraception at the time of marriage.[50] Of the variety of birth-control techniques available, Jews used the most effective ones.[51] As a consequence, "Jews are much more likely than others to have Completely Planned Fertility."[52] This was complemented by the Princeton finding that "the Jewish rate of contraceptive failure is less than half that of the other religious groups,"[53] confirming that Jews are the most successful in family planning.[54]

Earlier studies had led to similar conclusions. A survey of family planning by patients in urban hospitals east of the Mississippi in the early 30's found a higher proportion of Jews than of others using contraceptive devices,[55] and according to the records of a birth-control clinic in New York City around 1930, a higher proportion of Jewish couples planned pregnancies, used more effective birth-control methods, and used them earlier than couples of other religions.[56]

When Roman Catholic, Protestant, and Jewish couples were recently matched for urban residence, husband's education and income, and wife's education, it was found that similarity of background factors produced a considerable degree of similarity in the fertility behavior of Protestants and Jews. However, this matching procedure failed to diminish the original differences between the Catholics and the other two groups.[57]

FUTURE JEWISH FERTILITY

In view of the low Jewish fertility rate the question must be raised whether past and current fertility levels are high enough to maintain the size of the Jewish population.

Natural Growth

About 20 years ago the net reproduction rate was held to be the best device for measuring the growth of a population, but this measure, which treats current fertility and mortality as constants, has since been found inadequate for societies where birth rates are subject to rapid change.[58] The absence of a specific mortality rate and the effects of intermarriage and of conversions from and to Judaism further complicate estimating a replacement rate for the Jewish population. Bogue's opinion that American Jews "are scarcely reproducing themselves"[59] is supported by a calculation of replacement quotas by the Census Bureau in connection with the 1957 sample survey, which found that on the basis of current fertility and mortality levels, replacement of the white population required 2,130 live births per 1,000 women, single as

[47] Freedman *et al., op. cit.,* p. 161.

[48] Victor A. Christopherson and James Walters, "Responses of Protestants, Catholics, and Jews Concerning Marriage and Family Life," *Sociology and Social Research,* Sept.-Oct. 1958, p. 21.

[49] Freedman *et al., op. cit.,* p. 104.

[50] *Ibid.,* p. 110, and Potter, *loc. cit.,* p. 5.

[51] Freedman *et al., op. cit.,* pp. 178-80.

[52] *Ibid.,* pp. 112-13. Completely Planned Fertility has been defined as follows: "The couple used contraception regularly and conceived only when they stopped it for that purpose," p. 78.

[53] Potter, *loc. cit.,* p. 6.

[54] Westoff, *loc. cit.,* p. 123.

[55] Raymond Pearl, *Natural History of Population* (New York, 1939), p. 241.

[56] Regine K. Stix and Frank W. Notestein. *Controlled Fertility* (Baltimore, 1940), p. 29.

[57] Ronald Freedman, P. K. Whelpton, and John W. Smit, "Socio-economic Factors in Fertility Behavior Differences Among Protestants, Catholics, and Jews," *Population Index,* July 1960, p. 206.

[58] George J. Stolnitz and Norman B. Ryder, "Recent Discussion of the Net Reproduction Rate," in J. J. Spengler and O. D. Duncan, ed., *Demographic Analysis* (Glencoe, 1956), pp. 147-61.

[59] Bogue, *op. cit.,* pp. 696-97.

well as married.[60] While the fertility rate of 1,749 per 1,000 ever-married Jewish women of child-bearing age is considerably lower, the hypothetical and static nature of that measure of replacement should be kept in mind.

It appears quite likely that in the future, Jewish fertility in the United States will continue to be influenced primarily by urban residence and concentration in the white-collar occupations, but will be modified by three new factors: the move to the suburbs, satisfaction of the status drive, and new goals of completely planned fertility.

Suburban Residence

The depressive effect of urban residence upon Jewish fertility can be attributed to tenancy (rather than home ownership) and living in the central city. Fragmentary data indicate that Jews in the large urban centers lived in rental multiple-dwelling units rather than in homes of their own until the end of World War II.[61] There are two well-known drawbacks to rearing large families in either walk-up or elevator apartments. One is the considerable physical difficulty of caring for children on levels other than the ground floor.[62] The other is the preference of landlords for tenants with few or no children.[63] The author is aware of only one study where the differential effect of home tenure upon fertility was measured. A survey of Indianapolis in 1941 found "that fertility rates are consistently higher for owners than for renters when rental value of the home is held constant."[64]

Suburbs, on the other hand, have been very hospitable to small children and to large families. An analysis of the 1950 population census found that "as compared with the central-city population, the suburban population has a substantial excess of persons aged 0 to 4 and 5 to 13."[65] Since the Jewish population ever since the end of World War II has been moving into city neighborhoods bordering on suburbs as well as into suburbs proper, and is continuing to do so, it is likely to adopt the higher fertility pattern prevalent there.[66]

Social Status

We have seen that the ambition to rise in the social and economic scale was fulfilled in a relatively brief time, but was probably accomplished at the cost of considerable restriction of fertility. Now that many Jews have achieved this goal or can be confident of moving toward it without encountering major obstacles, it is conceivable that Jewish fertility will rise. Independently of religious or ethnic factors, in Philadelphia it has been found that people who have achieved their class position themselves have fewer children, on the average, than people who have inherited their position.[67]

Completely Planned Families

That Jews show a more positive attitude toward birth control than other groups and use birth-control methods more effectively could lead to the conclusion that fertility planning

[60] Bureau of the Census, "Fertility of the Population: March 1957," *Current Population Reports*, Series P-20, No. 84, August 1958, p. 4.

[61] In Chicago, for example, only about 15 per cent of the Jewish population lived in "owner-occupied dwelling units in 1940: Otis D. Duncan and Stanley Lieberson, "Ethnic Segregation and Assimilation," *American Journal of Sociology*, 1959, p. 371. In Chicago, neighborhoods "which had the highest Jewish density had the highest proportion of multiple-dwelling units, while conversely, neighborhoods with the lowest Jewish density had the smallest proportion of such units": Eric Rosenthal, "The Jewish Population of Chicago," in Simon Rawidowicz, ed., *The Chicago Pinkas* (Chicago, 1952), p. 86.

[62] It may be that before the end of World War II parked and moving cars did not so congest residential streets as to be a major deterrent to apartment-house living.

[63] A formal study of landlords' discrimination against families with children does not seem to exist.

[64] P. K. Whelpton and C. V. Kiser, *Social and Psychological Factors Affecting Fertility* (New York, 1945), Vol. I, p. 18.

[65] Otis D. Duncan and Albert J. Reiss, Jr., *Social Characteristics of Urban and Rural Communities, 1950,* (New York, 1956), p. 120.

[66] For the suburban migration of the Jews of Chicago see Esther Beckenstein, *Report on Jewish Population of Metropolitan Chicago* (Chicago: Jewish Federation of Philanthropies, May 1959); for New York see Henry Cohn, *Jewish Population Trends in New York City, 1940-1970* (New York: Federation of Jewish Philanthropies, January 1956) and C. Morris Horowitz and Lawrence J. Kaplan, *The Estimated Jewish Population of the New York Area* (New York: Federation of Jewish Philanthropies, 1959).

[67] Westoff, "Changing Focus of Differential Fertility . . . ," *loc. cit.*, p. 407.

itself contributes to the low Jewish fertility in the United States. The following evidence shows that that conclusion may not be warranted.

As we have seen, most studies reveal an inverse relationship between income and fertility, which does not appear to hold for the highest income group. The Indianapolis Study — easily the most significant research project in demography in recent decades, and the first to succeed in sorting out couples by the degree of family planning they had exercised — found that for those couples who had planned their fertility most completely, in numbers and spacing of children, there was a direct rather than an inverse relationship between fertility and socioeconomic status: couples of higher socioeconomic status had a higher fertility than couples of lower status.[68]

Any prediction about the future fertility behavior of the Jewish population must take into account the GAF and Princeton findings that Jews tend markedly toward completely planned fertility. If our assumption of a direct relationship between rapid upward mobility and fertility restriction in the past is correct, it is possible that with further gains in social and economic status the Jewish fertility level will rise. Freedman and his associates found that in response to the question of how many births could be expected for their families to be completed, Jewish couples gave an average number of 2.4. When asked how many children they would have if they could start life over again, Jewish couples gave an average of 3.1. This is also the number of children Jewish couples consider ideal for Americans.[69]

[68] Whelpton and Kiser *op. cit.*, Vol. II, p. 394.

[69] Ronald Freedman, P. K. Whelpton, and John W. Smit, "Socio-economic Factors in Religious Differentials in Fertility," *American Sociological Review*, August 1961, Table 1, p. 610.

*Birth Control and the Christian Churches**

FLANN CAMPBELL

The attitude of the Christian Churches towards population policies and movements is a subject of growing social and political importance throughout the world. The Churches' concern at current demographic trends is shown by a series of solemn pronouncements from Rome, Lambeth, Geneva and other guiding centres of the Christian faith; while scientists, eugenists and social planners — who in the past may not generally have felt called upon to intervene in doctrinal disputes about the nature of sex and sin — increasingly find themselves involved in debates about marriage principles and family planning practices which raise issues as much theological as sociological. At international population conferences there are frequent clashes of opinion between delegates of different religious (or agnostic) views which cut across national and professional boundaries and which discuss matters that formerly might have been considered to lie outside the scope of demography. The work of the World Health Organization, for example, has been seriously hampered in some fields because of failure by members to agree as to the desirability of certain methods of family limitation. In the U.S.A. birth control, which a generation ago no respectable politician would have dared mention, was raised as a sensational issue in the presidential election campaign.

During such a period, when the area of public controversy widens and the problems raised become more acute because of new chemical and biological discoveries, it will be useful to out-

* Reprinted with permission from *Population Studies*, Vol. 14, No. 2 (November 1960), pp. 131-147.

line the history of the Christian Churches' teachings on contraception.

For centuries the Christian doctrine regarding deliberate family limitation was clear-cut and unambiguous. The primary (some Fathers of the Church claimed the *only*) aim of sexual intercourse in marriage was the procreation of children. Secondary aims such as mutual help between husband and wife or the alleviation of concupiscence were much less important in the marriage relationship. Any artificial interference with the natural processes of coitus and conception was contrary to the laws of God, and must be condemned as gravely sinful. St. Augustine of Hippo wrote: "Sexual intercourse even with a lawful wife is unlawful and shameful, if the offspring of children is prevented. This is what Onan, the son of Juda, did, and on that account God put him to death." For priests or laymen to query these eternal and immutable laws as laid down by St. Augustine in the fourth century, and elaborated by St. Thomas Aquinas in the thirteenth century, was not merely presumptuous but possibly heretical. Even the coming of the Reformation and all it represented in the way of challenge to the dogmas of the mediæval Catholic Church had no apparent influence on Christian doctrine concerning birth control. Protestant divines were as much in agreement on this point as they were in disagreement about others. During the nineteenth century, in spite of the warnings of Malthus, and the reforming zeal of Place, Knowlton, Bradlaugh, Besant and others, the policy of the Churches — with very rare exceptions — was publicly to say as little as possible about such a disagreeable subject, and privately, if any warning was needed, to repeat the traditional condemnation by the Church.

In striking contrast to the centuries of relatively inflexible dogma reinforced by a policy of secrecy and silence, the last fifty years have been remarkable for an almost complete reversal of traditional doctrine on birth control by the Protestant Churches, and serious modifications by the Roman Catholic Church. Simultaneously, there has been an outpouring of literature on the whole subject of marriage in all its aspects — medical, social and spiritual. Once the floodgates of discussion were open the Church authorities realised that they must try and direct the dangerous waters of controversy into clerically-approved channels.

The volume of this published work, particularly during the last two or three decades, is impressive, as is also the skilful way in which presentation of doctrine is adapted to audiences of widely differing levels of culture and environment. This is especially true of Roman Catholic publications which range from serious, scholarly works designed for the clergy and theologians down to popular works written for the mass of the Roman Catholic population. At the highest level there are the Papal Encyclicals such as the celebrated Encyclical *Casti Conubii* issued by Pope Pius XI in 1930. These documents are addressed to the faithful all over the world, are translated into numerous languages, and contain the definitive teachings of the Church on a variety of subjects related to married life. They are binding on all members of the Church.

Roman Catholic priests are supplied with manuals of pastoral theology giving detailed instructions how to deal in the confessional with sexual as well as other problems.[1] Medical textbooks are also available in both Britain and the U.S.A. in which most aspects of sexual and obstetrical practice are discussed from the Roman Catholic viewpoint. Some of these are written for doctors and midwives rather than priests or laymen, and to non-Roman Catholics the curious mixture of theology and gynæcology may appear somewhat gruesome — not to say comic!

For the less educated but none the less faithful masses of the population there are nowadays many cheap and simply written booklets and pamphlets usually available at the Church door or nearby religious bookshop. Even in the Republic of Ireland, where a strict literary censorship operates and where the Roman Catholic hierarchy are almost Manichæan in their hostility towards discussion about sex, it is now possible to buy for a few shillings a booklet giving the most precise details how to avoid conception after coitus by means of the "safe period."

[1] These manuals are normally written in English (or other vernacular) but those sections which deal with the more physical aspects of sexual behaviour are usually written in Latin.

Some of these popular writings may seem naive, over-censorious, or even absurdly puritanical in theme, but their continued publication (and some pamphlets run into dozens of editions) suggest that the hierarchy regard them as serving a useful purpose, and their readers welcome them as guides to behaviour.

The Anglican and Nonconformist literature on the subject is less abundant, and appears to be written more for the "middle-brow" Protestant minister or layman than for the theologian on the one hand or the semi-literate masses on the other. The appearance of *The Family in Contemporary Society*[2] shortly before the last Lambeth Conference was a landmark in the history of Church of England publications about marriage, for several reasons. The volume is a remarkable document — well-written, refreshingly free from moralising and censoriousness, sharply aware of modern world demographic problems, and having among its authors a group of distinguished social scientists. The most recent and comprehensive statement of the Protestant position is contained in *The Population Explosion and Christian Responsibility* written by the American demographer and churchman, Dr. Richard M. Fagley, on behalf of the World Council of Churches.[3]

The first public support by a Christian minister in Britain of the view that other means of family limitation, apart from continence or the use of the "safe period," might be justifiable under certain circumstances came shortly after the Bradlaugh-Besant trial. Preaching at the South Place Chapel, London, in 1878, the prominent American radical clergyman, Moncure Conway, denounced the police persecution of the publishers of birth control literature, and afterwards expressed sympathy with some of the aims of the Malthusian League.[4] Seven years later the Christian Socialist parson, Stewart Headlam, speaking at a meeting of the Junior Clergy Society in London at which a paper was read on "Marriage and Neo-Malthusianism" said he could find nothing anti-Christian "in the use of the checks recommended by Mrs. Besant."[5]

However, the advanced liberal views of Conway and Headlam were not by any means representative of prevailing Christian opinion during this period, and it was among the Nonconformist Churches that a more broadly-based movement developed in favour of birth control. This was hardly surprising in view of the more liberal theology of these Churches, their greater emphasis on freedom of individual conscience, and also their wider representation among the lower middle classes among whom there was the strongest economic pressure to limit the size of families.

In 1893 a Nonconformist weekly journal, *The Christian World* published a letter from a Methodist minister's wife which expressed many of the anxieties so typical of the harrassed and economically struggling professional family of that time — too many children and too little money, physical exhaustion resulting from too frequent childbearing, lack of opportunity for outside interests or recreation, endless household chores, the selfishness of husbands. Immediately there was a flood of letters to the editor sympathising with the minister's wife, and asking what could be done to help those many Godly and long-suffering wives ("hundreds of thousands of them," according to one correspondent) bearing similar burdens.

The reply of *The Christian World* was guarded and cautious (due to the "delicacy of the subject") but was none the less forthright. "The conditions are assuredly wrong which bring one member of the marriage partnership into a bondage so cruel," said the editor. "There was a time when any idea of voluntary limitation was regarded by pious people as interfering with Providence. We are beyond that now and have become capable of recognising that Providence works through the commonsense of individual brains. We limit population just as much by deferring marriage for prudential motives as by any action that may be taken after it. . . . It would obviously be impossible for us to enter into the details of such a topic, but this much

[2] *The Family in Contemporary Society* (S.P.C.K., 1958).

[3] *The Population Explosion and Christian Responsibility* by Richard M. Fagley. (Oxford University Press, New York, 1960.)

[4] *Liberty and Morality*: A Discourse given at the South Place Chapel, Finsbury by Moncure D. Conway, M. A. (Freethought Publishing Co., 1878.)

[5] *The Malthusian*. June, 1885.

may, at least be said, that, apart from certain methods of limitation, the morality of which is gravely questioned by many, there are certain easily understood physiological laws of the subject the failure to know and to observe which is inexcusable on the part either of men or women in these circumstances."[6]

Twenty years later, the Rev. W. F. Lofthouse, a spokesman of the Methodist Church, giving evidence at the National Birth Rate Commission,[7] said that the Protestant Churches had been too reticent, both publicly and privately, in expressing their views about contraception. Cross-examined as to the attitude of the Free Church Council on the subject, he thought that as there were so many economic, social and medical issues involved, Church ministers could not be expected to lay down the law on so "difficult and delicate" a matter as family limitation. Asked if in his opinion, where moral restraint was not possible, he would allow mechanical means of contraception, he replied unequivocally "Yes."

The contemporary Nonconformist attitude broadly speaking is that so long as the aims of birth control are not merely selfishness or unrestricted sensuality, and the techniques used are not unhealthy or æsthetically objectionable, then the methods themselves are not important. The decision should be a matter for the individual conscience.[8]

The Church of England was slower to face the challenge presented by new social conditions — particularly the growing demand for women's emancipation — and was more reluctant to change its traditional doctrine about sex, marriage and the family. There was, for example, no mention at all of contraception during the Lambeth Conferences of 1867 and 1897, and the first official Anglican statement on the subject did not appear until 1908 when the Lambeth Conference produced a long report on what was described as "Restriction of Population." Regret was expressed at the decline of the birth rate among English-speaking peoples, especially the upper and middle classes, and it was suggested that many physical and mental diseases might be a direct consequence of the use of contraceptives.[9] The bishops,[10] having denounced birth control as "preventive abortion," recommended that all contraceptive appliances and drugs be prohibited by law and their advocates prosecuted.

The theme that sexual pleasure, even in marriage, was sinful if indulged in for its own sake, and that large families were to be preferred to material comforts, was again emphasised in a memorandum presented to the National Birth Rate Commission which first met in October, 1913, in London.[11] Chastity in married people "may be exceedingly hard but it is entirely consistent with health," said this report. Christian men and women "must bear the Cross and keep themselves in purity and temperance." Women "should not shrink from the heavy burthens which marriage may entail for them . . ." Large families were "admirable schools of vigorous, dutiful and unselfish character" and husbands and wives must avoid a "love of pleasure and comfort, and a standard of expenditure on dress, furniture or holidays higher than the family means reasonably allow." The bishop of Southwark gave it as his own personal opinion that sexual intercourse was only justified if the pro-

[6] *The Christian World.* Editorial entitled "A Marriage Problem". June 15, 1893.

[7] *Report of the National Birth Rate Commission.* Evidence of the Rev. W. F. Lofthouse, pp. 374-380. (Chapman & Hall, 1916.)

[8] *Man and Wife Together* by Kenneth G. Greet. (Epworth Press, 1958.)

[9] "Mental and moral vigour may become impaired, and the question has been asked whether the increase of insanity may not be closely connected with the habits of restriction". *The Six Lambeth Conferences* 1867-1920, p. 401 by Lord Davidson of Lambeth, Archbishop of Canterbury, 1903-28 (S.P.C.K., 1929.)

[10] The fact that many of the laity and clergy differed from their bishops on this point is evident from the report given to the National Birth Rate Commission a few years later. "In the absence of any recognised authoritative teaching, there are wide differences of opinion among the Anglican clergy on this subject (of birth control)", said this Report. "The objections formerly felt by almost all of them to family limitation have grown decidely weaker since the beginning of the century; but their condemnation of mechanical and chemical devices is still almost unanimous. Among conscientious and high-minded laymen and women in the Anglican Church there are many who openly justify the use of preventives, and this attitude has become far more common during the last few years". *Report of the National Birth Rate Commission,* pp. 64-65 (Chapman & Hall, 1916).

[11] *Report of the National Birth Rate Commission,* pp. 383-387 (Chapman & Hall, 1916).

creation of children was intended (otherwise it was "mere gratification"), and that continence might have to be practised even if it meant the break up of the marriage.[12]

At the next Lambeth Conference, despite the shattering impact of the first World War upon accepted patterns of social behaviour, and the emergence of a much more tolerant attitude towards family planning in many communities, the episcopal language was almost as vehement and condemnation equally strong. The bishops by this time were thoroughly alarmed at what they considered to be the spread of sexual immorality (which they believed to be partly fostered by easier methods of birth control) and the freer way in which sex was generally discussed.

"The temptations of sexual sin are probably the most universal in the world," stated one Conference report,[13] while Resolution 68, which was adopted without opposition, declared unequivocally:

The Conference, while declining to lay down rules which will meet the needs of every abnormal case, regards with grave concern the spread of theories and practices hostile to the family. We utter an emphatic warning against the use of unnatural means for the avoidance of conception, together with the grave dangers — physical, moral and religious — thereby incurred, and against the evils with which the extension of such use threatens the race. In opposition to the teaching, which under the name of science and religion, encourages married people in the deliberate cultivation of sexual union as an end in itself, we steadfastly uphold what must always be regarded as the governing considerations of Christian marriage. One is the primary purpose for which marriage exists, namely the continuation of the race through the gift and heritage of children; the other is the paramount importance in married life of deliberate and thoughtful self-control.

By 1930, however, a significant shift had occurred in the Church's attitude, and there had emerged a strong group of Anglicans, at first a minority, but before many years had elapsed a majority, with a more liberal viewpoint on the subject. The Lambeth Conference of that year produced a long report entitled "Marriage and Sex" which again warned about the dangers of sexual license and fornication but admitted that sexual desire had its own value and importance in the Christian home and must be recognised as a "God-given factor."[14] On this occasion the Conference was deeply divided on the permissibility of birth control, and after much debate the following resolution was carried by 193 to 67 votes:

Where there is a clearly felt moral obligation to limit or avoid parenthood, the method must be decided on Christian principles. The primary and obvious method is complete abstinence from intercourse (as far as may be necessary) in a life of discipline and self-control lived in the power of the Holy Spirit. Nevertheless, in those cases where there is such a clearly felt moral obligation to limit or avoid parenthood, and where there is a morally sound reason for avoiding complete abstinence, the Conference agrees that other methods may be used, provided that this is done in the light of the same Christian principles. The Conference records its strong condemnation of the use of any methods of conception control from motives of selfishness, luxury, or mere convenience.

Further to emphasize the cleavage of opinion among Anglicans, this Conference was soon followed by the publication of *Marriage and Birth Control* which collected in one volume the conflicting points of view on contraception. The Bishop of St. Albans persisted in the traditional viewpoint that contraception was intrinsically sinful and contrary to God's law. He admitted that sexual abstinence might be difficult and even cause neurosis, but it was, as he expressed it, the "heroic way." "I have a strong instinctive feeling that the whole thing (birth control) is repellent, degrading and wrong," he concluded.[15]

[12] *Report of the National Birth Rate Commission*, pp. 436-450. Evidence of the Bishop of Southwark.

[13] *The Six Lambeth Conferences*, 1867-1920, p. 107 by Lord Davidson of Lambeth, Archbishop of Canterbury, 1903-28. (S. P. C. K., 1929.)

[14] "Sex is a God-given factor in the life of mankind, and its functions are therefore essentially noble and creative . . . a new day has dawned, in which sex and sex matters are emerging from the mists of suspicion and even shame, in which for centuries they have been enveloped into the clear atmosphere of candour, honesty and truth". Resolution from the 1930 Lambeth Conference, *Marriage and Birth Control*, p. 10 by Rt. Rev. A. A. David, Bishop of Liverpool and Rt. Rev. M. B. Furse, Bishop of St. Albans (James Nisbet, c. 1930).

[15] *Marriage and Birth Control*, p. 27 by the Rt. Rev. A. A. David and the Rt. Rev. M. B. Furse (James Nisbet, c. 1930).

The Bishop of Liverpool believed that previously the bishops' minds were too much set upon the dangers and evils of sex, and that the sex-impulse was instituted by God not merely for ensuring the continuance of the human race, but also for fostering the mutual love of husband and wife.[16] Abstinence from sex relations within marriage would be a severe strain, possibly with harmful results. He criticised the viewpoint of the minority at the Conference, which included some "bishops without experience of married life" who implied that sexual intercourse even in marriage was a regrettable necessity, and stressed new social developments such as the emancipation of women, advances in medicine and psychology, and the threat of overpopulation (though he did not sharply emphasise the latter point).

Thus for nearly thirty years — the 1948 Lambeth Conference did not discuss the topic — the Anglican layman was presented with two alternative viewpoints, and he (or she) could choose between them according to conscience.

The Lambeth Conference of 1958 which was attended by 310 bishops from 46 countries, was held in an atmosphere very different from that prevailing during previous conferences. The traditionalists were by this time thoroughly routed, and no delegate spoke in complete condemnation of birth control. On this occasion, instead of repeated warnings about the possible dangers of unbridled sexuality, there was far more emphasis on the broader social aspects of family life. A remarkable feature of the conference and the reports which followed it was the concentration upon social and economic trends, housing, factory conditions, urbanisation, and living standards in different countries. At all stages of debate there was refreshing evidence that the Church authorities were by now fully aware of current demographic trends in Christian and non-Christian countries alike. On this occasion, at least, it was a case of the bishops quoting more from the blue books and less from the Bible.

Finally, the following resolution[17] was passed without a single dissentient:

The Conference believes that the responsibility for deciding upon the number and frequency of children has been laid by God upon the conscience of parents everywhere; that this planning, in such ways as are mutually acceptable to husband and wife in Christian conscience, is a right and important factor in Christian family life and should be the result of positive choice before God. Such responsible parenthood built on obedience to all the duties of marriage, requires a wise stewardship of the resources and abilities of the family as well as a thoughtful consideration of the varying population needs and problems of society and the claims of future generations.

Since then there has been growing interest among all the Protestant denominations in the problems of marriage, parenthood and population culminating in a meeting of a study group of the World Council of Churches[18] at Oxford in April, 1959, and followed by the publication of *The Population Explosion and Christian Responsibility* a year later.

The development of the Roman Catholic Church's doctrine on contraception provides an even more striking example of the way in which a dogmatic theology may be forced to respond to changed social, scientific and medical circumstances.

Traditionally, the Vatican's teachings on this point had always been quite explicit — not even acute poverty, overcrowding, serious ill health, the possibility, of bringing diseased children into the world or immediate danger to the wife through pregnancy could be accepted as excuses for artificial means of birth control.[19] If husband and wife for any reason whatsoever wished to avoid having children (and the Church's strongly held view was that children were the supreme blessing of a happy marriage) then the only alternative was the strictest sexual continence.

[16] The words of the marriage ceremony in the Revised Prayer Book had recently been altered to include this second aspect of marriage.

[17] *The Lambeth Conference,* 1958, p. 57 (S.P.C.K., 1958).

[18] The report of this group was published in the *Ecumenical Review,* Geneva, October 1959. Dr. Fagley points out in his book that during the last ten years the following churches have issued statements which are in broad agreement with the Lambeth thesis on family planning: the Church of Sweden, the Presbyterian Church of Ireland, the Calvinist Church of Holland, United Lutheran Church of America, Methodist Church of the U.S.A., Reformed Church of France, Lutheran Church of Finland, Baptist Union of Denmark, and the United Presbyterian Church of the U.S.A.

[19] " . . . if God sends another mouth to fill, he will find means to fill it". *Birth Control and Ethics,* p. 53 by Henry J. Davis (Burns Oates & Washbourne, 1927).

If such abstention from normal married relations proved difficult, then God's grace would help the suffering people. This simple, easily understood and unchanging doctrine of the Church had been accepted throughout the ages and was expected to be obeyed by the faithful in all lands and among all societies in which the Church had members.

Generally, during the latter half of the nineteenth century there was little need — except possibly in France where the birth rate had fallen substantially — for the Church to become involved in public controversy about birth control. Roman Catholic husbands and wives might not always be as strict in their marriage practices (especially about *coitus interruptus*) as their priests would have liked, but there was little serious questioning of the basic principles of the Church's teachings on this point. The danger of contamination by freethinkers or Protestants was also not nearly so serious as it became later.

Nevertheless, by the outbreak of the first World War the problem had grown acute enough in Britain for the Catholic hierarchy to feel it necessary to restate and amplify their views. The Rev. Monsignor Brown, Vicar-General of the Diocese of Southwark, gave to the National Birth Rate Commission a lengthy exposition of his Church's attitude towards family limitation, concluding with the usual warning against the "grave sin of Onanism."[20]

During the 1920's the situation from the Church's point of view rapidly deteriorated — propaganda in favour of contraception became more widespread, birth control clinics were opened in several countries, the danger of Catholics being led astray became more obvious — and the Pope found it advisable in 1930 to issue a special encyclical on the duties and responsibilities of Christian marriage.[21] This celebrated encyclical was a lengthy document covering a wide range of related subjects such as divorce, abortion, euthanasia, and sterilisation, but its main theme was on the question of birth control, and on this point the Pope's words were forceful and unambiguous. Artificial contraception was "shameful and intrinsically immoral," "criminal abuse," "an unspeakable crime," and so forth. The sharpness of the language and the detailed manner in which the Pope developed his arguments were clearly meant as a solemn warning to actual or potential backsliders in the Church; and before long all the resources of the Vatican, from the proudest Cardinal to the humblest parish priest, and drawing in Catholic physicians, lay workers and publicists, were mobilized in the campaign. In those countries where Roman Catholics were in a majority, the hierarchy made every effort to ensure that legislation already in force prohibiting the sale of contraceptives (e.g. France, Italy and Belgium) should be continued, or new legislation introduced (as in the Irish Free State). For this policy they usually had the enthusiastic support of the pro-natalist groups (including some non-Catholics) which wanted larger populations for nationalistic or militarist reasons.[22]

In countries such as the U.S.A. or Britain, where Roman Catholics are in a minority, they advised that all possible pressure should be brought to bear upon the faithful to prevent them from following the example of their non-Catholic fellow citizens.[23]

However, the important — and from the long-term point of view, revolutionary — development in Church doctrine during this period was not that the Pope reaffirmed a viewpoint which was already well known, but the new medical discoveries relating to the alleged "safe period" in the ovulation cycle of women. The fact that there are certain times of the month when women appear less likely to conceive after normal coitus had long been suspected, but the physiological reasons for it were obscure. It was commonly suspected that conception in women

[20] *Report of the National Birth Rate Commission.* Evidence of the Right Rev. W. F. Brown, Vicar-General of the Diocese of Southwark, pp. 392-393 (Chapman & Hall, 1916). For the Church's attitude towards the use of the "safe period", see later pages.

[21] *Encyclical Letter on Christian Marriage* (Casti Conubii) by Pope Pius XI (new translation by Canon G. D. Smith, Catholic Truth Society, 1951).

[22] For account of the pro-natalist movement see *Population Policies and Movements in Europe* by D. V. Glass, (O.U.P., 1940).

[23] For an account of a particularly violent campaign against the suggested opening of birth control clinics in Massachusetts (a state with many inhabitants of Irish or Italian descent) during 1942 and 1947 see *Freedom and Catholic Power* by Paul Blanshard (Secker & Warburg, 1951).

was most likely to occur during or near menstruation.[24] Many biologists and gynæcologists denied the existence of a "safe period" altogether,[25] and as late as 1924 such an eminent authority as Dr. Marie Stopes could write. ". . . the ordinary working-class healthy woman has no safe period at all."[26]

[24] "It used to be thought that ovulation coincided with menstruation, and according to this erroneous view, it was believed that the woman would conceive most readily just before or just after the period". *Reports of the Biological and Medical Committee,* P. 42. Vol. IV. Papers of the Royal Commission on Population. (H.-M.S.O. 1950).

The American demographers Freedman, Whelpton and Campbell quote the following query about the "safe period" addressed by some French Roman Catholics to the Sacred Penitentiary in Rome in 1880. "In the judgment of learned physicians and physiologists, women for the most part are not permanently able to conceive, but only periodically able, that is, from the time at which the menstrual flow begins to the fourth day after it has ceased; in the rest of the month they are usually sterile. They assert that this theory has been verified in 94 per cent of the women observed.

Having learned of this, Doctor L. thought that a remedy might therein be found to prevent many serious sins, by persuading spouses who turn to onanism from fear of conception, to abstain from relations at that time at which conception is possible, and to have relations in the proper way at the time at which conception does not usually take place . . . . Doctor L. has asked of the Sacred Penitentiary: (1) Whether spouses can so act without mortal or venial sin; (2) Whether a confessor may urge this way of acting on a wife who detests the onanism of her husband but is unable to correct it, or on either spouse who wishes to avoid too many children; (3) Whether the danger of a reduction in the number of offspring must be provided against or whether this must be considered of secondary importance to the profit realised from avoidance of sin and peace of conscience".

In reply the Sacred Penitentiary stated: "Spouses using marriage in the aforesaid way should not be disturbed, and a confessor may suggest, but cautiously, the opinion under discussion to those spouses whom he has vainly tried by another method to lead away from the detestable crime of Onan". The same reply had been given to a similar question addressed by the Bishop of Amiens to Rome in 1853. *Family Planning, Sterility and Population Growth.* Appendix A, p. 416. By Ronald Freedman, Pascal K. Whelpton and Arthur A. Campbell. (McGraw Hill. New York. 1959).

[25] "Up till about 1930 it was generally believed that women could conceive at any time during the menstrual cycle. This theory remains a cardinal point in the classical theory of the physiology of human reproduction", p. 67 *The Rhythm of Sterility and Fertility in Women* by Leo J. Latz (Latz Foundation, Chicago, 1939).

[26] *Contraception,* p. 89, by Marie Carmichael Stopes (Health Promotions Ltd., 1924).

It was the publication in 1930 of the results of two independently conducted research investigations by the distinguished Japanese gynæcologist, Dr. K. Ogino, and Prof. H. Knaus of the University of Prague, that gave scientific validity to the "safe-period" theory. Ogino concluded that ovulation in women takes place 12-16 days before menstruation, and that the ovum only survived (if not fertilised) for 3-12 hours.[27] The male spermatozoa, in his opinion, might live for up to three days after coitus. Knaus suggested that ovulation takes place 14-16 days before menstruation, that the ovum survived "only a few hours after it leaves the Graafian follicle," and that the male spermatozoa might live for two days.[28]

If these theories are true — and most informed medical opinion now supports them[29] — then it necessarily followed that for only a comparatively short time during the monthly cycle would it be possible for the normal woman to conceive. Sexual intercourse outside this period would inevitably be sterile. The difficulty, of course, was how to calculate accurately the fertile and infertile phases.[30]

[27] *Conception Period of Women* by Dr. Kyusaka Ogino (translated into English, Medical Arts Publishing Co., Harrisburg, U.S.A. 1934). Dr. Ogino's work was published in Japan several years earlier, and in Germany in 1930 — the same year as the publication of Dr. Knaus's work.

[28] *The Rhythm of Sterility and Fertility in Women,* p. 24 by Leo J. Latz (Latz Foundation, Chicago, 1939).

[29] "Evidence has now accumulated to show that ovulation takes place, as a general rule, 13-15 days before the onset of menstruation, and that the fertile phase lies therefore in mid-cycle. It is thought that the ovum remains fertilisable for only about one day after ovulation, and that sperms retain their powers of fertilising an ovum for not more than three days." *Reports of the Biological and Medical Committee,* p. 42, vol. IV, Papers of the Royal Commission on Population (H.M. S.O., 1950).

[30] It is well known that the menstrual cycle may be affected by a large number of factors such as pregnancy, miscarriage, illness, emotional disturbances, etc. Moreover, if the "safe period" method is to be used regularly with any hope of success the woman concerned must record her menstrual flows systematically, be given competent medical advice, and have an unusual capacity for self-control in her sexual relationships. In view of this, how safe is the "safe period"? Roman Catholic physicians claim a high degree of reliability if the proper precautions are taken, but non-Catholics generally regard it as a relatively ineffective method of birth control. For example, Dr. C. P. Blacker expresses grave doubts as to its efficacy when tried among

The increasing number of Roman Catholic theologians who were becoming keenly aware of the conflict between what was described as the "irresistible pressure of society in favour of contraception" and the "immovable condemnation of the Church"[31] warmly welcomed the discoveries of Ogino and Knaus. The use of the "safe period," as has already been pointed out, had been approved as early as the mid-nineteenth century in France, and Monsignor Brown, a spokesman of the English hierarchy, giving evidence to the National Birth Rate Commission during the first World War, stated: "Where all other deterrents fail, married couples may be allowed to limit intercourse to the intermenstrual period, sometimes called *tempus agenesos*."[32] It was the work of Ogino and Knaus, however, which provided a more scientific basis for the theory, while it was the American gynæcologist, Latz, who popularized the new ideas in his book *The Rhythm*[33] which sold over 200,000 copies (mostly in the U.S.A.) between 1932 and 1939.

Nevertheless, though Latz's book was given semi-official approval by American ecclesiastics, the more conservative[34] elements in the Church, steeped in the old traditions about sex and birth control, persisted in their distaste for the whole subject, and only a few years ago a priest writing in a widely-circulated marriage manual (containing the *Imprimatur* of the Vicar-General) made this very plain when replying to a question about the right of husband and wife to limit their family if they had a small income, poor health, and were living in overcrowded conditions. "The right thing is to live a normal married life," he wrote. "Leave the number of children to God. He is the Creator. We do not dictate a number to him . . . no priest and no pope give a calendar chart to couples to follow. . . . Rhythm frequently leads to denying one another, birth prevention, drunkenness and divorce."[35]

On the other hand, Keenan and Ryan in their officially-approved and widely circulated book, *Marriage: A Medical and Sacramental Study*[36] say that the temporary use of the "safe period" would be justified in cases of minor illness or disease, after a recent pregnancy, too great frequency of pregnancies, economic difficulties, or for fostering mutual concord between husband and wife who agree over intercourse but not over a fresh pregnancy in the near future. The persistent use of the "safe period" would be justified only in cases in which there was grave danger to the mother from a further pregnancy, the impossibility of supporting or educating further children, incurable hereditary disease, or the prevention of perversion if this were likely in one partner because the other refused the use of the infertile period.

But the final word, as always in the Roman Catholic Church, rests with the Pope, and the most recent statements from the Vatican make it quite clear that the "safe period" method may be quite legitimately used to limit the number of children in marriage.

Speaking in 1951, Pope Pius XII said:[37]

> . . . the Church knows how to consider with sympathy and understanding the real difficulties of the married state in our day. Therefore, in our late

a backward and largely uneducated population (*Eugenics Review*, July, 1955 and October, 1955. "The Rhythm Method: Two Indian Experiments.")

[31] *Family Limitation*, p. 9, by John Ryan, with a Foreword by Alan Keenan, O.F.M. (Sheed & Ward, 1957).

[32] *Report of the National Birth Rate Commission*, p. 393. Evidence of the Right Rev. W. F. Brown, Vicar-General of the Diocese of Southwark (Chapman & Hall, 1916).

[33] *The Rhythm of Sterility and Fertility in Women*, by Leo J. Latz (6th edition, Latz Foundation, Chicago, 1939) has a Foreword by the Jesuist Father Joseph Reiner, and is described as being published with "ecclesiastical approbation".

[34] In a Church so dogmatic in theology and monolithic in organisation as the Roman Catholic, it is probably unwise to contrast too sharply the differences between "conservative" and "liberal", "traditionalist" or "modernist" viewpoints. Nevertheless, on questions of sexual relationships and birth control there would appear to be marked differences of approach by various groups within the Church. Dr. Richard Fagley examines this problem in some detail in his book, distinguishing between what he describes as the "profertility" and "responsible parenthood" factors among Roman Catholics. He claims that the former group has tended to re-establish its ascendancy during recent years. (*The Population Explosion and Christian Responsibility*, pp. 184-7, by Richard M. Fagley, O.U.P., New York 1960.)

[35] *The Catholic Book of Marriage*, pp. 84, 94, 96 by the Rev. P. C. M. Kelly (Longmans, 1952).

[36] *Marriage: A Medical and Sacramental Study* by Alan Keenan, O.F.M., and John Ryan (Sheed and Ward, 1955). This book has the *Imprimatur* of the Archbishop of Boston.

[37] "Morality in Marriage, A pronouncement by Pius XII". Original text in Italian, *Acta Apostolica Sedis*. Dec. 20th, 1951.

allocution on conjugal morality, we affirmed the legitimacy and, at the same time, the limits — in truth very wide — of a regulation of offspring, which, unlike so-called "birth control", is compatible with the law of God. One may even hope (but in this matter the Church naturally leaves the judgment to medical science) that science will succeed in providing this licit method with a sufficiently secure basis, and the most recent information seems to confirm such a hope.

The Pope was speaking before the recent experiments with an oral contraceptive pill, and it is possible that ultimately this method may provide the "sufficiently secure basis" to which the Pope referred. If the chemists produce a pill which can, without harmful side effects, regulate the ovulatory cycle with a high degree of accuracy then the theologians may have to reconsider their views about what are "artificial" and what are "natural" methods of family limitation. The complicated charts and elaborate calculations which must be used at present by the good Catholic wife who wishes to estimate her "safe period" with any hope of success are in many ways more artificial than conventional mechanical methods of birth control, and the Church authorities have already shown in the case of Ogino-Knaus that they would welcome new scientific methods which would make for greater accuracy and effectiveness. In this aspect, as in so many other aspects of the problem, the progress of science continually presents the theologians with new difficulties.[38]

The Christian Churches, with their varying historical backgrounds, doctrines, and forms of organisation, reacted, as we have seen, in different ways and with different degrees of urgency to the challenge presented by the spread of birth control throughout the world, but the external forces which compelled them to modify their traditional dogma have been broadly similar — namely, the rapid increase in population in certain territories, the advances in medical science, and the failure of the Churches to enforce discipline among their own flocks.

The Churches can no longer ignore the fact that world population is increasing at the rate of fifty millions a year, and that — if present trends continue — in the year 2000 there may be twice as many people on the earth as there are to-day. Even the most unworldly bishop or cloistered cardinal can hardly fail to appreciate the significance in terms of food supply, living standards, race relations and political conflict, of the extraordinarily rapid multiplication of the peoples of China, India, Japan, South-East Asia, Brazil, Egypt and Central America. One of the most striking sections of *The Family in Contemporary Society* is the contribution of the Anglican bishops of India who show a very keen awareness of the demographic problems of that country. Dr. Richard Fagley as an official spokesman for the World Council of Churches devotes over one-third of his book *The Population Explosion and Christian Responsibility* to the broader economic and technological aspects of population growth. Roman Catholic demographers, both clerical and lay, are also becoming increasingly concerned at the need for a social programme which will be practical and realistic as well as in conformity with traditional philosophy in a period of rapid population expansion. Such authorities as Gibbons and Burch in the U.S.A., Lestapis in France, Zeegers in Holland, and Fogarty in Britain have written with sympathy and understanding of the threatened population crisis in those regions of the world already suffering from poor nutrition, lack of capital and low labour productivity.[39] In 1957 the journal *Social Compass* published by the Catholic Institute of Social Research in Geneva offered a prize of $5,000 for an essay on the population problems of under-developed

[38] Problems of greater complexity may arise for all the Christian Churches as chemists and biologists produce ever more refined methods of contraception. At what precise moment, for example, does conception occur — at the moment when the egg is fertilised or when nidation in the wall of the womb takes place? The distinction between contraception and abortion may present theologians with as much difficulty during the second half of the twentieth century as the debate over the questions when the soul entered the body did in mediæval Europe.

[39] *Population and World Resources,* a statement by Prof. M. P. Fogarty presented to the International Union of Social Studies, 1953.

La Limitation des Naissances by S. de Lestapis, S.J. (Spes, Paris, 1959).

Over-Population — Is Birth Control the Answer? by the Rev. Arthur MacCormack (Catholic Truth Society, 1960).

countries. The Church's spokesmen do not all agree as to what is the best social policy to adopt (it is perhaps significant that so far the judges in the essay contest have not announced the award of the $5,000 prize), but there is a general consensus of opinion that the more intensive cultivation of the earth's surface would produce a much larger food supply.[40] Colin Clark, the Oxford economist, states in a recent article, for example, that the agricultural resources of the world would suffice for ten times the present world population.[41] It is doubtful whether other Catholic experts would support such a claim.

The second powerful reason for the evolution of religious doctrine is the immense progress in medical science and psychology since the beginning of the century. Sixty years ago gynæcology was in a fairly primitive state and comparatively little was known about reliable birth control techniques. The physiology of the human male and female reproductive systems was understood only in general terms, and there was no exact knowledge about the length of life of the human sperm and ova. Such contraceptives as were available were generally crude, unreliable, expensive and difficult to obtain, and regular birth control (apart from *coitus interruptus*) was the practice of only a relatively small minority, mostly from the upper and middle classes. Marie Stopes and Margaret Sanger were schoolgirls, while Havelock Ellis was an obscure figure on the edge of respectable medicine and being harried by the police. Freud's revolutionary discoveries about the nature of human sexuality were still being treated, outside a small group of devotees, with contempt or ridicule. In these circumstances it was not surprising that the Church authorities should either ignore, or else condemn outright, any suggestion of birth control.

But in modern industrial communities (at least among those where Protestants predominate) with a better educated and less subservient population, with cheap manuals of sexual technique available in many book stores and condoms sold in most chemist's shops, a simple policy of silence or disapproval is not enough. Social realities must be faced, arguments met and answered, new formulæ invented. Can we imagine, for example, Cardinal Manning debating birth control before a nation-wide audience as the Roman Catholic Bishop of Salford did on a television programme in 1959?

A related aspect of this problem is the way in which the Christian Churches generally have faced up to the whole problem of sex in the modern world. Nowadays probably only a minority of obscurantist and puritanical clergymen (as in Spain or Ireland) still regard the sexual instinct as "nasty" and debased, and there is much wider appreciation by all Churches that there may be secondary (some claim equal) aims in marriage apart from the procreation of children.[42] "Sex is a God-given factor in the life of mankind, and its functions are therefore essentially noble and creative", says a report of the 1930 Lambeth Conference.[43] "Sexual intercourse (in marriage) . . . is lawful, honourable, morally good and may be meritorious", writes the Jesuit Father Davis.[44]

Freud may still be an unpleasant word for some theologians (in all the extensive Roman Catholic literature read by the present writer on sex, birth control and the family, Freud's name was hardly ever mentioned) but there can be no doubt that his influence on certain aspects of religious teaching has been considerable. What could be more steeped in Freudianism, for example, than the following extract from a book on Christian marriage by the Jesuit Father J. Leycester King?

[40] Catholics agree with Communists in this respect!

[41] "Over-Population — Is Birth Control the Answer?" by Colin Clark. (Review article in *Family Planning,* April, 1960.)

[42] Both the Protestant and Roman Catholic Churches show remarkably similar develoments in doctrine in this respect. Traditionally, the view was that sexual pleasure within marriage was somewhat sinful (even if venially so) and that the sole aim of marriage was begetting children. The more recent view is that "mutual help" (a wide phrase covering a multitude of ways in which husbands and wives may help and please each other) is also an essential part of the marriage contract. The newest Roman Catholic manuals on marriage insist that a happy and mutually satisfying sexual relationship may be an important factor in keeping husbands and wives together and thus preventing divorce.

[43] *Marriage and Birth Control,* p. 10, by the Rt. Rev. A. A. David and the Rt. Rev. M. B. Furse (James Nisbet, c. 1930).

[44] *Moral and Pastoral Theology,* vol. IV, p. 243, by Rev. Henry Davis, S.J. (Sheed & Ward, 1948).

Sex and its implications are indeed of all-pervading importance and significance to society and the individual human personality, and failure to recognise this can only lead to error and disaster. Sex is not, as it were, a separable aspect of human nature, rather is it the case that sex is in some way relevant to every aspect of human nature, and that scarcely any single facet of man's complexity can be adequately understood without it.[45]

The third important factor encouraging a new approach to the problem by Church authorities is the gradual realisation by those most closely in touch with the realities of family life, and not merely living a cloistered life with their exegesis of the Bible[46] and texts of the Fathers of the Church, that social and environmental pressures were proving stronger than episcopal edicts so far as contraception is concerned. "The birth control movement has established itself with little regard for ecclesiastical pronouncement", admit the authors of *The Family in Contemporary Society,*[47] while Father Alan Keenan, O.F.M., in his Preface to a widely circulated booklet on family limitation, speaks of a "crisis" in the Church because "the Church condemns birth control and some Catholics use contraceptives".[48] In the U.S.A. the Jesuit Father Reiner speaks of the "heresy" of contraception having made "terrifying advances" which bring "danger of disruption" to the Roman Catholic Church.[49]

The extent to which this "heresy" has spread naturally depends upon the strictness of the particular Church's rules, the powers — clerical or lay — which the Church may have to enforce its edicts, and the kind of society in which the Church operates. Thus, among the Protestant communities of Britain, U.S.A. or northern Europe the problem may only be an issue for a devout minority, and even for them the doctrine may be so loose or vague as to allow wide individual interpretation, whereas in Spain, Italy or the Republic of Ireland the combined influence of Church and state may be very powerful indeed.[50] Clearly also, the problem would be very different in, say, a simple village community in Portugal as compared with an urbanised cosmopolitan population in New York or London.[51]

That there is good reason for the authorities of the Roman Catholic Church to be alarmed may be seen in the evidence — direct and indirect — from widely differing communities.

In three southern European countries the birth rate declined as follows during the last thirty years:

Birth rate in Italy, Spain and Portugal

Year	Italy	Spain	Portugal
1920–4	30.1	30.0	33.0
1930–4	24.5	27.5	29.3
1956	18.1	20.7	22.9

In the Republic of Ireland the higher professional classes are restricting their families much more than the working classes, as may be seen in the following table:

[45] *Two in One Flesh: An Introduction to Sex and Marriage,* p. XIII., by the Rev. E. C. Messenger. (Sands, 1948).

[46] For example, the debate whether Onan was punished for "spilling his seed upon the ground" or for failing to obey the levirate law of the Old Testament Jews.

[47] *The Family in Contemporary Society,* p. 13 (S.P.C.K., 1958).

[48] *Family Limitation,* p. 8, by John Ryan, M.B., B.S., F.R.C.S., F.I.C.S. with a Preface by Alan Keenan, O.F.M. (Sheed & Ward, 1957).

[49] *The Rhythm of Sterility and Fertility in Women* by Leo J. Latz (Latz Foundation, Chicago, 1939). Preface by Joseph Reiner, S.J.

[50] Not only, as previously explained, may the sale of contraceptives be forbidden by law, but local priests will try to ensure that their warnings are not being ignored by, for example, discreet enquiries to young married couples, if childless, why they are not beginning a family.

[51] Roman Catholic priests are particularly concerned at the danger of contamination of their flocks in mixed Protestant-Catholic communities. For example, Father Keenan in his Foreword to *Family Limitation* points out that Roman Catholics in Britain and the U.S.A. are only a minority of the population living in a society built largely on principles contrary to what they believe. "But they must breath its air," he says, "share its life, seek its rewards, accept its responsibilities, endure its social pressures and accept its outlook. As sharers in this society, they are relentlessly moulded by its mass media of communication. Like other citizens, they have the same wish to conform to the group, to be good Englishmen or good Americans, never deviants as far as they can be from accepted social practice". *Family Limitation,* p. 6, by John Ryan, M.B., B.S., F.R.C.S., F.I.C.S., foreward by Alan Keenan, O.F.M.

Number of children born per 100 married women (aged 20–34 at marriage) in the Republic of Ireland, 1946[52]

Social group (non-agricultural)	Number
Higher professional ..	286
Lower professional ..	358
Employers and managers ..	343
Skilled wage earners ..	401
General labourers ..	434

This evidence, of course, is only indirect — it might be that in these countries or among certain occupations the birth rate varies for other reasons apart from birth control — but there is more direct proof that Roman Catholics are practising contraception in increasing numbers. For example, in Britain the official *Report on Family Limitation*[53] estimates the following percentages of Roman Catholics as using contraceptive devices:

Date of marriage	Percentage of Roman Catholic women in sample using birth control methods
1900–9	0
1910–9	21
1925–9	32
1935–9	46
1940 and later	39

Dr. Eustace Chesser in his survey of the marital relationships of English women found that 47% of his sample of married Roman Catholic women used birth control, and that 39% of single Roman Catholic women thought they should use it.[54] Slater and Woodside in their study of urban working-class marriage concluded: ". . . the evidence in nearly every case suggests that where contraception is concerned, the Roman Catholic Church, at least in an urban area, is fighting a losing battle".[55]

In the U.S.A. in the 1930's Himes found that about one quarter of the patients in birth control clinics in Baltimore, Cleveland, and Newark were Roman Catholics, though the latter only comprised between one-third and one-half the population of those cities.[56] Latz quotes figures to show that between 1921–28 in New York and Chicago birth control clinics 36% of the users were Roman Catholics. ". . . We Catholics are furnishing more than our quota of clients", he laments.[57] More recently, an investigation of the contraceptive practices of a representative cross-section of white married women aged 18–39 years showed that even among those Catholic wives who were regular churchgoers 26% were using birth control methods condemned as gravely sinful by their Church.[58]

In view of these figures it is not surprising that the prominent American Roman Catholic publicist, Father John A. O'Brien,[59] could write: ". . . a large proportion, if not the great majority (of Catholics) are probably practising birth control already, salving their conscience with the plea that the Catholic law as understood by them is morally impossible of observance", or that Father Andrew Beck[60] (now Roman Catholic Bishop of Salford) can say: ". . . among Catholics, though in a lesser degree than among non-Catholics, there has been a marked decline in fertility, and there seems little doubt that in one form or another family limitation is being adopted as a policy".

[52] *Report of the Commission on Emigration and Other Population Problems.* 1948-54, p. 96 (Stationery Office, Dublin).

In Britain the Royal Commission on Population, *Report,* para. 72 (H.M.S.O., 1949) comments: " . . . Roman Catholics of different occupational groups seem to differ in average family size in very much the same way as non-Catholics".

[53] *Papers of the Royal Commission on Population,* vol. I, p. 81 (H.M.S.O., 1949).

[54] *The Sexual, Marital and Family Relationships of the English Women* by Dr. Eustace Chesser, Joan, Maizels, Leonard Jones and Brian Emmet (Hutchinson, 1956).

[55] *Patterns of Marriage: A Study of Marriage Relationships in the Urban Working Classes,* p. 210, by Eliot Slater and Moya Woodside (Cassell, 1951).

[56] *Medical History of Contraception,* by Norman E. Himes, p. 415 (Allen & Unwin, 1936).

[57] *The Rhythm of Sterility and Fertility in Women,* by Leo J. Latz, p. 149 (Latz Foundation, Chicago, 1939).

[58] *Family Planning, Sterility and Population Growth,* p. 174 by Ronald Freedman, Pascal K. Whelpton and Arthur A. Campbell (McGraw Hill, New York, 1959).

[59] *Homiletic and Pastoral Review,* May, 1933. "Birth Control and Catholic Leakage", by John A. O'Brien.

[60] *The Family and the Future,* p. 37 by Andrew Beck (Catholic Social Guild, Oxford, 1948).

In the past the Christian Churches have faced other crises brought about by the progress of science, but in some ways the problems which then arose proved simpler for the theologians to handle because they concerned (at least to begin with) the theory rather than the practical application of scientific discovery, and they involved the beliefs of an educated minority rather than those of the majority of the population. Presumably, the average man in the street of sixteenth-century Italy did not worry over-much whether the sun went round the earth or *vice versa,* and most people in nineteenth-century England did not lose much sleep over the argument whether they were descended from apes or angles. These were points for experts to debate, and they certainly did not involve, except for a few individuals, grave and immediate issues of ethics and mortality. Eventually, the Christian Churches — with the exception of the fundamentalists — came to terms with such "heretics" as Galileo and Darwin; and the new astronomy and the new evolution are now encompassed in the wide folds of modern Christian theology.

But when scientific discovery touches intimately the lives of ordinary families, and when everyday standards of human conduct and behaviour are involved then the dilemma from the Churches' point of view is much more acute. Particularly is this true of any discussion of sexual mortality, surrounded as the subject is with so much emotion, hedged in with so many traditional beliefs, and laden historically with such a burden of anxiety and guilt. In the strange borderland where sex and metaphysics meet, it is not surprising to find that sociologists and theologians often disagree — they must travel a good deal further before they meet on common ground.

*Religious Composition of the Population of the United States**

DONALD J. BOGUE

N.O.R.C. MATERIALS ON RELIGION: NUMBER AND DISTRIBUTION

The special tabulation of materials from the National Opinion Research Center used the results of two nationwide sample surveys — study 335, conducted in the summer of 1953, and study 367, conducted in the summer of 1955. Jacob J. Feldman, Senior Study Director, was the principal designer, the supervisor of coding, and the analyst for both these surveys. In each case there was a sample of approximately 2,500 households. In both surveys a question was asked concerning the religious preference of the respondent (and, presumably, of the entire household), who was also questioned as to the standard population characteristics of the household head.[1] Hence, by retabulating the data from these surveys it was possible to obtain information concerning the spatial distribution and the population characteristics of household heads, according to their religious preference.[2]

* Reprinted with permission of The Free Press from *The Population of the United States* by Donald J. Bogue.

[1] These questions were answered in a straightforward and matter-of-fact way in each survey. It is the experience of NORC that such questions are among the easier items on its interviews attempt to obtain information.

[2] These tabulations were made separately for each survey, and the desired analytical tables were prepared independently from each survey's results. These duplicate tables were then compared, item by item. In most cases the twin tables were simply averaged to obtain the most accurate possible unbiased estimate; for a few cells in most of the tables, however, the results of one survey

The NORC statistics given for Protestants and Roman Catholics, as total groups, have only small sampling variances. However, the statistics for individual Protestant denominations are subject to a larger sampling error. And the data for the three small groups — "Jewish," "No Religion," and "Other Religion" — are subject to very large sampling errors, since the data for each of these groups are based on less than 75 households in each survey. However, as modern sampling theory asserts, and as has been demonstrated empirically hundred of times, probability samples of this size are capable of yielding much valuable information about particular homogeneous groups, so the results concerning these three smallest groups should not be disregarded entirely.

The close correpondence between the results of the NORC surveys and the Cenus Bureau's survey of March, 1957, may be observed from the following comparison of religious composition as reported by each survey:

Religion	NORC surveys	Census Bureau survey	Difference (NORC minus Census)
Total	100.0	100.0	. . .
Protestant	71.5	66.2	5.3
Baptist	22.0	19.7	2.3
Methodist	17.4	14.0	3.4
Presbyterian	6.7	5.6	1.1
Lutheran	7.6	7.1	1.1
Episcopal	2.8	(n.a.)	−2.1
Other Protestant	14.9	19.8	
Roman Catholic	21.1	25.7	−4.6
Jewish	3.0	3.2	−0.2
Other	1.4	1.3	0.1
No religion	2.8	2.7	0.1
Religion not reported	. . .	0.9	−0.9

Considering that the NORC data refer to *household heads* (most of whom are male, and heavily concentrated at ages above 35 years), whereas the Census data refer to all *persons* aged 14 and over, much of the overcount of Protestants and undercount of Catholics in the NORC sample, in comparison with the Census data, may be attributed to differences in the age composition of the two samples. Also, the training of NORC interviewers, who are taught to probe until their questions are answered fully, may have meant that a considerable number of persons who belong to small offshoots of the Baptist and Methodist denominations (see Table 23-2*) were correctly allocated to those denominations rather than grouped with "Other Protestant." Also, minor differences in coding instructions could create small differences in the final distribution.

Region of Residence of Household Heads (Table 1)

A comparison of Table 1 (NORC) and Table 23-3* (Census), with respect to regional distribution of household heads by religious affiliation, shows very similar proportions for the major religious groups in the two surveys. However, Table 1 provides additional valuable information by showing the regional distribution of the individual Protestant denominations. Nearly two-thirds of all *Baptists* are concentrated in the South, and one-half of those living outside the South are found in the North Central states (to which southerners have been migrating). Baptists are a minority religious group outside these two regions, but within these two regions they are quite numerous. *Methodists* and *Presbyterians* tend to be more widely distributed among all regions; however, a slightly above-average share of Methodists live in the South, and the Presbyterians have a similar concentration in the Northeast and North Central regions. The membership of the *Episcopal* religion is quite concentrated in the Northeast and the West, although there is a substantial share in every region.

were arbitrarily accepted in preference to those of the other survey — if one survey had a substantial number of cases with which to make the particular calculation and the other survey, as a result of sampling fluctuations, had almost none. Although this procedure yields results that are internally consistent in almost every way, and which agree remarkably well with the much larger sample taken by the Bureau of the Census in its March, 1957 survey, it must be kept in mind that the possibility of large sampling errors exists, especially for some of the more detailed cross-tabulations. These NORC data are submitted as tentative evidence, until statistics based upon larger samples of the population are available.

*Tables 23-2 and -3 are not included in this selection.

TABLE 1

Region of Residence of Household Heads, by Religious Affiliation

Religion	All	Region			
		North-east	North-central	South	West
Total	100.0	25.4	28.8	31.2	14.6
Protestant total	100.0	17.6	29.2	40.0	13.2
Baptist	100.0	8.3	15.6	69.4	6.7
Methodist	100.0	20.1	32.6	35.2	12.2
Presbyterian	100.0	30.1	32.0	21.6	16.4
Episcopal	100.0	37.2	15.6	26.4	21.0
Lutheran	100.0	24.0	54.4	6.6	15.0
Other Protestant	100.0	15.0	33.5	29.6	21.8
Roman Catholic	100.0	46.0	29.8	7.7	16.6
Jewish	100.0	61.2	11.4	9.4	18.0
Other	100.0	34.2	34.4	6.0	25.4
No religion	100.0	20.8	30.6	22.6	26.0

Source: Special tabulations of survey data from National Opinion Research Center, Jacob J. Feldman, Senior Study Director.

TABLE 2

Type of County of Residence of Household Head by Religious Affiliation

Religion	Total	Metropolitan areas		Nonmetropolitan areas	
		Large — 1 million or more inhabitants	Small — less than 1 million inhabitants	Largest town in county 10,000 or more	Largest town in county less than 10,000
Total	100.0	30.4	28.2	19.2	22.2
Protestant total	100.0	22.8	28.8	21.6	26.8
Baptist	100.0	15.6	31.7	22.8	30.0
Methodist	100.0	21.6	29.0	19.0	30.4
Presbyterian	100.0	29.9	32.8	16.0	21.2
Episcopal	100.0	52.7	25.0	8.8	13.6
Lutheran	100.0	30.1	21.8	29.6	18.5
Other Protestant	100.0	22.4	26.0	22.4	29.0
Roman Catholic	100.0	45.3	28.4	14.7	11.6
Jewish	100.0	84.0	14.8	1.2	...
Other	100.0	55.8	28.1	8.4	7.7
No religion	100.0	38.2	26.4	19.4	16.0

Source: Special tabulations from National Opinion Research Center, Jacob J. Feldman, Senior Study Director.

Lutherans, by contrast, are almost nonexistent in the South; they are heavily concentrated in the North Central states, which have large populations of German descent.

To summarize: All religious groups for which data are available, except three, tend to be rather widely distributed among the regions, and to show only a moderate degree of concentration. Four generalizations that may be made concerning the distribution of religious groups are:

Baptists are concentrated in the South, and are very scarce in the Northeast and the West.
Lutherans are concentrated in the Midwest, and are very scarce in the South.
Jews are concentrated in the Northeast, and are very scarce in the South.
Roman Catholics are concentrated in the Northeast, and are very scarce in the South.

Religious Affiliation and Metropolitan and Nonmetropolitan Residence

In Table 2 the household heads of each religious affiliation are classified according to residence inside or outside a standard metropolitan area (S.M.A.). Those living inside standard metropolitan areas are further dichotomized, according to whether the S.M.A. in which they live had more or less than 1 million inhabitants at the 1950 census. Nonmetropolitan areas are also dichotomized, according to whether the largest city in the county contained more or fewer than 10,000 inhabitants in 1950. Approximately one fourth of the NORC sample of households falls into each of these four categories. Three religious groups stand out as having exceptionally high concentrations of their membership in metropolitan areas: Jewish, Episcopal, and Roman Catholic. Whereas roughly one-half of the total sample of households falls in the S.M.A.'s, 98 percent of Jewish, 78 percent of Episcopal, and 74 percent of Roman Catholic household heads lived in an S.M.A. Moreover, all three of these groups were much more heavily concentrated in the very largest S.M.A.'s than they were in the smaller ones; 23 percent of the household heads in the total sample lived in S.M.A.'s having a population of one million or more, but 84 percent of Jewish, 53 percent of Episcopal, and 45 percent of Roman Catholic household heads live in these largest places. Also, persons reporting "other religion" and "no religion" are highly concentrated in places with one million or more inhabitants.

Baptists, as one would suspect from their regional distribution, have a substantial concentration in the nonmetropolitan areas and the small S.M.A.'s. Methodists have a similar tendency to be concentrated in these areas. Presbyterians tend to be slightly metropolitanized, but a substantial share of their membership also lives in nonmetropolitan areas.

Religious Affiliation and Degree of Industrialization of Community of Residence

Table 3 classifies household heads by religion, and also according to the degree of industrialization of the country in which they reside. (Industrialization is measured in terms of the percentage of employed persons who were working in mining or manufacturing industries at the time of the 1950 census.) The outstanding fact brought out by this table is that Roman Catholics comprise a disproportionately large share of the population in the most heavily industrialized areas, whereas the other highly urbanized and metropolitanized populations — the Jewish and the Episcopal — tend to be distributed in the counties that are moderately, but not extremely, industrialized. Methodists and Presbyterians tend to be concentrated toward each of the two extremes; disproportionately large shares of these groups are found both in the more-industrialized and in the less-industrialized counties.

Religious Preference and Educational Attainment (N.O.R.C. Materials)

Two religious groups stand out above all others as well-educated: those with Jewish and those with Episcopal religious preference. A third group, the Presbyterian, had attained an educational level considerably above the average. More than one-fifth of the members of each of these groups were college graduates (Table 4), and only a comparatively small percent had less than 8 years of schooling. More than 60 percent of the household heads in each of these groups were high school graduates, whereas among the gen-

TABLE 3

Degree of Industrialization of County of Residence, by Religious Affiliation

Religion	All county residence	Percentage of employed labor force in county of residence who are employed in mining or manufacturing industries							
		44.3 percent or more	37.2 to 42.8 percent	31.9 to 37.1 percent	27.3 to 31.9 percent	23.5 to 27.0 percent	18.0 to 23.3 percent	11.1 to 17.8 percent	Less than 11.1 percent
Total........	100.0	13.0	12.4	12.5	11.7	12.3	12.8	11.7	13.7
Protestant........	100.0	12.2	11.9	10.8	12.0	11.0	14.0	12.4	15.5
Baptist.........	100.0	6.8	11.7	15.4	12.1	10.4	17.7	14.4	11.5
Methodist......	100.0	12.0	10.2	10.4	16.8	8.7	11.5	10.2	20.2
Presbyterian....	100.0	13.3	14.5	6.6	8.4	12.7	17.5	15.1	12.0
Episcopal......	100.0	12.2	12.2	12.2	9.5	20.3	14.9	12.2	6.8
Lutheran.......	100.0	18.8	11.6	8.2	13.5	11.6	3.9	14.0	18.4
Other Protestant	100.0	15.3	13.1	8.7	8.7	11.6	15.2	11.0	16.5
Roman Catholic..	100.0	15.9	14.9	15.5	10.0	14.9	8.3	11.4	9.2
Jewish...........	100.0	10.1	6.1	31.3	20.2	22.2	8.1	...	2.0
Other............	100.0	20.8	14.6	4.2	6.2	14.6	22.9	8.3	8.3
No religion.......	100.0	8.8	11.2	12.5	7.5	13.8	15.0	11.2	20.0

Source: Special tabulations of survey materials from National Opinion Research Center, Jacob J. Feldman, Senior Study Director.

eral population only 40 percent had this much schooling.

Among the white population, Protestant household heads showed a slightly higher level of education than Roman Catholic: Proportionately fewer Protestants had less than a grammar school education, and proportionately more Protestants had a college education, than was the case among Catholics (Table 4). This difference may be due in part to the fact that among the Roman Catholics there were many elderly and less-educated immigrants.

Baptists reported a much lower level of educational attainment than any other denomination or religious group. Almost one-fifth of the white Baptists had less than 7 years of schooling, whereas only about one-eighth of the Protestant population as a whole had this small an amount of education. Although 42 percent of Protestants had graduated from high school or attended college, only 31 percent of Baptists had attained this level.

Lutherans and Presbyterians were noteworthy for having a great concentration of their household heads near the average level of education; this group contained comparatively few very poorly-educated persons, as well as somewhat below-average percentage of college-trained persons.

The various religious groups could be ranked as follows with respect to their average level of educational attainment:

Episcopal
Jewish
Presbyterian
Methodist
Other Protestant
Lutheran
No Religion
Roman Catholic
Baptist

Undoubtedly, the "Other Protestant" category hides some denominations which, if tabulated

TABLE 4

Educational Composition of Household Heads, by Religious Affiliation 1955 to 1956

Religious preference	Total	Education: Highest grade of school completed						
		Elementary School			High School		College	
		0–4 years	5–6 years	7–8 years	1–3 years	4 years	1–3 years	4 or more
Total..................	100.0	8.9	7.8	24.0	20.2	21.1	9.6	8.4
Protestant Total..........	100.0	8.8	7.8	24.2	20.6	20.8	9.8	8.2
Baptist................	100.0	16.9	11.6	26.0	20.4	14.8	6.1	4.2
Methodist.............	100.0	5.3	6.2	20.9	21.5	26.0	11.6	8.6
Presbyterian...........	100.0	3.2	3.2	17.6	23.6	24.6	14.9	13.0
Episcopal..............	100.0	2.0	4.2	16.4	10.3	23.2	21.2	22.6
Lutheran..............	100.0	5.4	5.2	29.3	22.4	22.4	8.5	7.0
Other Protestant.......	100.0	6.7	8.7	27.0	18.5	20.5	9.2	9.4
Roman Catholic..........	100.0	8.0	7.4	25.8	20.6	22.4	8.9	6.8
Jewish..................	100.0	8.3	4.2	13.4	13.2	27.8	10.9	22.3
Other...................	100.0	23.4	13.6	11.0	11.0	22.4	5.7	12.8
No religion..............	100.0	10.7	8.7	23.4	20.4	16.9	8.8	11.0

Source: Special tabulations of survey materials from National Opinion Research Center, Jacob J. Feldman, Senior Study Director.

separately, using samples large enough to be reliable, would rank near the top with the Episcopal and Jewish groups. Unitarians, for example, might well out-rank both. Such groups as Christian Scientist and Congregationalist might rank near, or even above, the Presbyterian and Methodist groups.

Table 5, which shows separately the educational attainment of white and nonwhite persons in each religious group, shows that the average level of educational attainment is much lower among nonwhite household heads where the head is a Baptist than where he is a member of some other denomination. This suggests that as Negroes obtain more education and move out of the rural South, they or their children tend to change their religious preference.

Religious Preference and Occupational Composition (N.O.R.C. Materials)

Quite a large amount of diversity exists among the various religious groups with respect to occupational composition of household heads (see Table 6). Three religions stand out distinctively as having large percentages of their groups in "white-collar employment: the Episcopal, the Jewish, and the Presbyterian. Of these three, the Episcopal group contains the largest percentage of professional and technical persons, while the Jewish group has substantial proportions in managerial and proprietary jobs. At the other extreme are three religions with above-average proportions of "blue-collar" workers: Baptists, Methodists, and Lutherans. All three of these last-named groups contain substantial numbers of farmers, craftsman, operatives, and unskilled workers.

Except for a comparative scarcity of farmers, and a compensating small excess of factory workers and service workers, Roman Catholics and Protestants tend to have quite similar occupational compositions. In the past, there has been a tendency to think of Catholics as being considerably lower in socio-economic status than Protestants. A close examination of Table 6

TABLE 5

Educational Attainment of Household Head, by Color and Religious Affiliation

Religious preference	Total	Education: Highest grade of school completed						
		Elementary school			High school		College	
		0–4 years	5–6 years	7–8 years	1–3 years	4 years	1–3 years	4 or more years
White, Total..........	100.0	6.8	6.6	24.2	20.5	22.4	10.3	9.1
Protestant total..........	100.0	6.0	6.1	24.6	21.0	22.4	10.8	9.1
Baptist...............	100.0	10.4	8.4	28.3	22.1	17.7	7.6	5.4
Methodist.............	100.0	4.3	5.2	21.0	21.8	26.5	12.2	9.0
Presbyterian...........	100.0	3.2	3.2	17.4	23.6	24.7	15.1	12.8
Episcopal.............	100.0	2.1	2.9	17.1	8.8	22.5	23.1	23.5
Lutheran..............	100.0	5.4	5.1	29.2	21.8	22.5	8.5	7.5
Other Protestant.......	100.0	6.1	7.1	26.9	19.0	21.4	9.8	9.8
Roman Catholic.........	100.0	7.5	7.6	25.8	20.8	22.5	9.0	6.8
Jewish..................	100.0	8.3	4.2	13.4	13.2	28.2	10.8	21.8
Other....................	100.0	25.2	13.4	12.4	9.8	21.2	3.7	14.2
No religion.............	100.0	11.0	9.5	23.6	19.1	16.3	9.5	11.0
Nonwhite...............	100.0	27.1	18.0	21.4	17.5	10.7	3.4	2.1
Baptist...............	100.0	32.0	18.4	21.6	16.4	7.8	2.8	1.2
Other.................	100.0	18.6	17.6	20.6	18.9	16.4	4.3	3.6

Source: Special tabulations of survey data from National Opinion Research Center, Jacob J. Feldman, Senior Study Director.

will show that in the Catholic group the proportion of household heads who are professional, proprietary, and clerical workers is about as large as it is among Protestants. The major difference is that such Protestant religions as Baptist, Methodist, and Lutheran contain a large proportion of farmers; Catholics have an excess of urban working-class persons, which compensates for the scarcity of Catholic farmers.

To what extent are the occupational differences noted above due to religious affiliation, and to what extent are they due simply to the fact, noted in the preceding section, that some religious groups have had more education than others? For example, are Baptist household heads concentrated in the blue-collar occupational group because they are Baptists, or because a preference for the Baptist religion is more common among socio-economic groups whose members have not had an opportunity to complete as many years of schooling as the rest of the population? A completely valid answer to this question would require much more detailed data than are available at the present time; it would require a simultaneous cross-tabulation of religious affiliation by single years of schooling, by occupation (using a fairly detailed breakdown), by color, by sex, and by age. The sample of data available at the present time is much too small to permit a full control even of education as a

TABLE 6

Occupational Composition of Household Heads, by Religious Affiliation

Religious affiliation	Total	Occupation—percent distribution: Prop. prof. tech.	Farm oper. or mgrs.	Mgrs. off. prop.	Clerical workers	Sales wkrs.	Crafts-men	Oper-atives	Serv-ice wkrs.	Farm labor-ers	Labor-ers, non-farm
Total	100.0	10.0	10.8	12.6	6.4	4.8	19.4	20.3	7.6	2.0	6.1
Protestant total	100.0	9.5	12.9	11.8	6.3	4.5	19.2	19.7	7.4	1.6	7.0
Baptist	100.0	6.0	13.3	7.6	4.1	3.0	18.2	25.3	10.0	2.4	10.0
Methodist	100.0	10.2	15.7	13.2	7.5	4.8	19.2	16.6	5.6	1.4	5.5
Presbyterian	100.0	15.3	8.0	16.1	8.2	10.6	16.7	15.8	4.8	1.2	3.6
Episcopal	199.9	19.6	1.5	20.4	11.0	5.4	16.7	9.6	10.7	. . .	5.3
Lutheran	100.0	8.0	15.6	15.4	5.4	4.4	24.0	15.1	6.2	0.6	5.2
Other Protestant	100.0	10.4	11.6	10.2	7.0	3.4	19.9	21.6	6.8	2.4	6.8
Roman Catholic	100.0	9.6	5.4	11.4	7.6	4.6	21.6	23.8	8.6	3.0	4.6
Jewish	100.0	17.6	1.3	36.0	9.6	15.0	7.2	12.0	. . .	. . .	1.3
Other	100.0	17.7	4.6	15.2	2.2	3.0	18.0	16.9	14.4	1.2	6.8
No religion	100.0	11.7	13.0	13.0	0.8	4.2	20.2	19.6	10.8	3.7	3.0

Source: Special tabulations of survey data from National Opinion Research Center, Jacob J. Feldman, Senior Study Director.

general factor in explaining the broad occupational groups.[3] Table 7 shows the median years of schooling completed by the members of each religious group who are in each of the broad occupational categories. These data permit only a few tentative statements. It seems that *educational attainment is a much more powerful factor in determining occupation than is religious preference.* Support for this conclusion is provided in Table 6, which shows that household heads employed in a particular occupation have generally reached the same educational level, irrespective of their religious preference. Some variations, however, are too large to be explained on the basis of sampling error, and are not easily accounted for except by attributing them to variations within the occupational groups. These variations probably arise from the fact that the Census fails to count postgraduate college training separately. For example, a person with an A.B. degree and a person with an M.D. or Ph.D. degree are both simply classed as having had "4 years or more of college." The fact that professional persons, except Baptists and Roman Catholics, have an average educational attainment of four years of college does not necessarily mean that these two religious groups have a "special pipeline" that allows their members to reach the nation's upper socio-economic levels without bothering to complete the amount of schooling that is generally considered a prerequisite. Instead, it probably means that a high proportion of Jewish, Episcopal, and Presbyterian professionals are physicians, college professors, or lawyers, while an unusually high percentage of Baptist and Catholic professionals may be artists, entertainers, photographers, or employed in

[3] This is especially true for the Jewish, the "Other Religion" and the "No Religion" groups, where the number of cases in the sample is extremely small.

other occupations which are classified by the Census as "professional" but which require much less schooling. Similarly, household heads who are Roman Catholic, Baptist, or Lutheran appear to have reached a status enabling them to be classified as proprietors, managers, or officials with the aid of less formal education than was obtained by the members of other religious groups who are classified as proprietors, managers or officials. It is quite possible that Episcopal, Jewish, and Presbyterian household heads, again because of higher educational achievement, hold very responsible positions in banks, manufacturing concerns, or as self-employed proprietors in wholesale and retail establishments, and that a higher proportion of Baptist, Catholic, and Lutheran workers with less education may be employed as railroad conductors, postmasters, or managers, or may be owners of small neighborhood grocery stores, restaurants, or filling stations — jobs which the Census also classifies as managerial or proprietary.[4]

From the materials in Table 7, one might expect to obtain the answer to a different kind of question: "Are the members of any religious group discriminated against, in their efforts to find employment, simply because of their particular religious preference?" One might conclude that they are if, in any religious group, the

[4] Also, the use of median education, which does not show the full education distribution for each combination of occupation and religion, is a very crude approach to this problem, but is made necessary by lack of a larger sample.

TABLE 7

Median Years of School Completed by Household Heads, by Occupation and Religious Affiliation: 1955

Religious affiliation	Median years of school completed by occupation										
	Total	Prop. prof. tech.	Farm oper. or mgrs.	Mgrs. off. prop.	Clerical workers	Sales wkrs.	Crafts-men	Oper-atives	Serv-ice wkrs.	Farm labor-ers	Labor-ers, non-farm
Total	9.5	16+	7.4	11.2	11.5	11.4	9.0	7.9	7.4	6.2	6.7
Protestant											
Total	9.5	16+	7.6	11.2	11.5	11.6	9.0	8.0	7.3	6.9	6.7
Baptist	7.8	15.0	6.4	10.5	11.0	11.0	8.2	7.2	7.0	5.1	6.0
Methodist	10.7	16+	8.1	11.4	11.7	11.6	9.6	9.4	7.8	8.0	7.0
Presbyterian	11.0	16+	9.5	11.4	11.9	12.0	9.8	8.8	7.5	7.5	8.2
Episcopal	11.8	16+	13.5	12.5	12.2	13.5	11.6	8.8	9.5	...	7.2
Lutheran	9.6	16+	7.4	10.8	10.6	11.4	8.7	9.2	7.0	7.0	7.5
Other Protestant	9.3	16+	8.2	10.0	11.8	11.6	9.0	7.6	7.1	6.6	7.0
Roman Catholic	9.4	14.6	7.0	10.7	11.3	11.0	9.2	8.0	8.2	5.4	6.5
Jewish	11.4	16+	...	11.4	11.6	9.2	8.2	8.6	...	...	9.2
Other	8.8	12.8	5.0	8.5	...	...	7.2	5.5	2.0	5.0	...
No religion	9.2	16+	7.2	11.0	12.0	12.5	8.8	8.0	7.4	6.7	5.3

Note: Each median is based upon comparatively few cases. The over-all pattern of differences between entire rows or entire columns may be considered as general evidence. Individual cells should not be accepted as precise estimates.

Source: Special tabulations of survey data from National Opinion Research Center, Jacob J. Feldman, Senior Study Director.

household heads have jobs that are low in the socio-economic scale and levels of educational attainment that are extraordinarily high. An examination of Table 7 shows that three groups seem to fit this pattern: the Presbyterian, the Methodist, and the Episcopal.[5] If the data are accepted as valid, one would be forced to conclude that the Episcopal group is more severely discriminated against than any other. Common-sense reflection suggests that such is not the case; if there is discrimination of the type defined above, it should show up among the Baptists, a group having a very large Negro population. Probably nothing more is involved than the fact that Episcopalians, Presbyterians, and Methodists place a stronger emphasis on educational achievement than many other religious groups do, and, hence, that their members tend to attain above-average educational levels irrespective of the occupational levels at which they may eventually work.

[5] However, it will be shown in the next section that there are proportionately few Episcopalians and Presbyterians with low socio-economic status.

To summarize: The meager data available gives little evidence either that any religious group is extraordinarily favored, or that there is severe discrimination (independent of any other factors) against any religious group because of its beliefs — with respect to broad categories of occupational attainment. Although the religious groups differ substantially with respect to occupational composition, in general the members of each religion seem to be located just about as high on the occupational ladder as the level of their educational attainment would lead one to expect.

Religious Preference and Income (N.O.R.C. Materials)

There is a high concentration of poverty among the Baptist population, while being in the upper income brackets is closely related to a preference for the Episcopal or Jewish religion (see Table 8). Methodists, Presbyterians, and Roman Catholics tend to be concentrated in the

TABLE 8

Income Distribution of Household Heads by Religious Affiliation

Religious affiliation	Total	Income							
		Less than $1,000	$1,000 to $1,999	$2,000 to $2,999	$3,000 to $3,999	$4,000 to $4,999	$5,000 to $7,499	$7,500 to $9,999	$10,000 and over
Total	100.0	7.3	10.0	13.8	17.4	17.7	21.3	7.0	5.6
Protestant total	100.0	8.2	11.0	14.6	17.6	17.4	19.8	6.4	5.2
Baptist	100.0	12.6	15.2	19.0	17.8	15.2	13.8	4.0	2.1
Methodist	100.0	7.0	9.6	11.3	18.2	16.6	24.0	7.5	5.9
Presbyterian	100.0	2.4	8.5	9.2	18.0	20.8	23.5	9.0	8.7
Episcopal	100.0	6.4	8.4	10.9	11.2	15.8	23.6	9.7	14.1
Lutheran	100.0	3.6	8.1	13.2	19.4	19.2	23.0	8.2	5.2
Other Protestant	100.0	8.4	9.6	15.7	16.2	20.2	18.6	6.2	5.2
Roman Catholic	100.0	5.0	7.2	11.7	18.4	19.6	25.0	8.4	4.6
Jewish	100.0	1.3	7.3	6.2	11.6	11.8	31.5	11.4	18.9
Other	100.0	2.2	16.4	17.4	16.2	15.1	22.1	7.2	3.4
No religion	100.0	10.2	7.2	13.0	12.2	19.7	18.4	7.6	11.6

Source: Special tabulations from National Opinion Research Center, Jacob J. Feldman, Senior Study Director.

upper middle income brackets, while Lutherans and other Protestants seem to be in the lower-middle grades. Persons who claim no religion tend to be distributed more or less evenly throughout all income levels. This means that, in comparison with the general population, disproportionately large numbers of people who have no religious preference are located at the extremely high and the extremely low income levels. If one were to rank and classify the leading religions according to "high income," "median income," and "low income" these groups would be listed as follows:

Religion

High income
- Jewish
- Episcopal
- Presbyterian

Median income
- Catholic
- Lutheran
- No religion
- Methodist

Low income
- Baptist
- Small Protestant sects

How much of this income difference between religious groups is due to the differences in occupational composition that are described above? Here again, an answer to this question requires a multiple-variable cross-tabulation, which the sample of NORC data was too small to support. Since the measure of income employed here is family income, such items as the number of earners in the family, the occupational and educational level of the secondary earners, etc., could also affect the comparisons. Even such aspects of family structure and composition as age of head and family reaction to poverty (some groups support elderly low-income parents in their own households, while other groups may allow them to live apart) may affect these data to a marked degree. As a very rough substitute for completely adequate evidence, Table 9 reports the median family income for each occupational group, subdivided according to religious preference. Except in the case of the Baptists, most of the income differentials between religions, mentioned above, tend to disappear and become simply income differentials between occupations.

When comparisons are made for all categories in the occupational scale, household heads whose religious preference is Roman Catholic tend to receive higher incomes than those who are Protestant. For example, the family incomes of Catholic craft workers tend to be higher than the family incomes of Protestant craft workers, and so on for most occupational groups. Since Catholics have a lower educational level than Protestants, one might expect that some factor specifically associated with religion as such would explain this situation. However, the facts that most farmers have small cash incomes, and that most farmers are Protestants, probably constitute one of the major reasons for this differential. Also, because they have more children, there may be more earners in Catholic families (working children as well as working mothers) than in Protestant families.

Jewish and Episcopal household heads who are employed as professional, proprietary, or managerial workers tend to have higher median incomes than the members of other religious groups employed in these same broad occupational categories. This is probably due to the kind of internal variation between occupations within each of the broad occupational categories that was described and illustrated in connection with educational attainment. Thus, *occupation is a much more potent factor than religious preference in determining the income level of household heads.*

How completely do inter-faith differences with respect in educational attainment explain the differences in income between religious groups? Table 10, which reports the median income of each educational group, for each religion, provides very rough data with which to examine this question. This table shows that the differences in income between religious groups are greatly reduced when the factor of education is introduced. A general, over-all difference does seem to remain, however. Roman Catholic household heads tend to have higher incomes, for a given amount of schooling completed, than Protestant household heads. Similarly, Jewish household heads tend to receive larger incomes than Catholic household heads for a given amount of schooling completed. The difference between the Ro-

TABLE 9

Median Incomes of Heads of Households by Occupation and Religious Affiliation

Religious affiliation	Total	Median income by occupation									
		Prof. and tech.	Farm oper. or mgrs.	Mgrs. off. prop.	Cleri-cal wkrs.	Sales wkrs.	Crafts-men	Oper-atives	Serv-ice wkrs.	Farm labor-ers	Labor-ers, non-farm
Total	4,094	5,876	2,838	5,936	4,032	4,882	4,462	3,762	2,610	1,779	2,852
Protestant total	3,933	5,457	2,703	5,570	3,960	4,893	4,418	3,656	2,399	1,726	2,659
Baptist	3,174	4,529	1,639	4,116	4,111	4,250	4,056	3,310	1,868	1,798	2,311
Methodist	4,235	5,586	3,134	5,992	3,901	4,929	4,756	4,018	2,155	2,000	3,326
Presbyterian	4,586	5,794	4,479	6,405	4,958	5,178	3,916	4,106	3,750	2,000	2,666
Episcopal	5,000	6,156	...	7,208	5,500	4,750	5,250	3,146	3,375	...	2,000
Lutheran	4,278	5,858	2,854	5,802	4,333	6,372	4,662	3,800	2,375	...	2,834
Other Protestant	4,008	5,458	2,708	5,188	3,778	3,916	4,574	3,613	2,842	2,250	2,598
Roman Catholic	4,340	6,334	4,250	6,281	4,118	5,688	4,636	3,964	3,562	1,792	3,450
Jewish	5,954	7,333	...	6,294	4,775	4,300	5,000	3,792	...	...	...
Other	3,875	...	4,000	5,334	...	...	4,000	3,625	2,542	...	...
No religion	4,320	10,000+	3,250	6,010	...	4,125	4,250	3,854	2,125	2,000	...

Note: Each median is based upon comparatively few cases. The over-all pattern of differences between entire rows or entire columns may be considered as general evidence. Individual cells should not be accepted as precise estimates.

Source: Special tabulations of survey data from National Opinion Research Center, Jacob J. Feldman, Senior Study Director.

man Catholic and the Protestant groups are of about the same magnitude as those between the Catholic and the Jewish. Within the Protestant group, the Episcopalians, Presbyterians, and Methodists who had had college educations received higher incomes than the Baptists. All of these differences may be due to differences in age of head, number and type of secondary earners, family structure, and occupation — as well as to cultural factors associated with religious affiliation. Clarification of this point must await the availability of data.

It should not be concluded hastily that any of the socio-economic differences shown here are due directly to religious membership as such. The kind of occupational use to which a given amount of educational attainment is put has a great deal to do with the amount of income received. People with college degrees who choose law, medicine, or business administration as a career (as a high proportion of Jewish and Episcopal members do), and who have spent 5 to 8 years in college, will almost certainly receive much larger incomes than other college graduates who have spent 4 years in college and have chosen to teach elementary school or to hold other kinds of low-paying jobs as professionals or officials. Moreover, persons who live in large metropolitan areas (as a high proportion of Jews and Episcopalians do) receive higher incomes for a given occupation than workers living in other places. To summarize: *education is a much more potent factor than religious preference in determining the income level of households,* and even observed differences between religious groups, when amount of education is controlled, may be due to "intervening variables" other than religious affiliation.

TABLE 10

Median Income of Heads of Households, by Educational Attainment and Religious Affiliation

Religious affiliation	Total	Elementary school			High school		College	
		0–4 years	5–6 years	7–8 years	1–3 years	4 years	1–3 years	4 or more years
Total	4,012	1,932	2,560	3,320	4,050	4,644	5,134	6,500
Protestant total	3,850	1,710	2,360	3,096	3,946	4,588	4,935	5,900
Baptist	3,032	1,629	2,312	2,839	3,670	4,034	4,128	4,614
Methodist	4,077	2,688	2,208	3,088	4,019	4,670	5,260	6,245
Presbyterian	4,494	2,250	3,125	3,500	4,282	4,682	5,625	6,000
Episcopal	4,750	...	...	3,250	3,375	5,475	4,584	7,062
Lutheran	4,230	1,688	3,300	3,526	4,103	4,759	5,458	6,584
Other Protestant	3,916	1,734	2,274	3,242	4,036	4,628	4,538	5,416
Roman Catholic	4,354	2,710	3,219	3,992	4,368	4,612	5,644	6,789
Jewish	5,956	2,916	...	4,334	5,500	5,472	6,050	8,500
Other	3,822	2,292	2,500	3,500	4,875	3,875	4,000	6,667
No religion	4,184	2,666	2,125	3,300	3,708	6,000	4,875	8,638

Note: Each median is based upon comparatively few cases. The over-all pattern of differences between entire rows or entire columns may be considered as general evidence. Individual cells should not be accepted as precise estimates.

Source: Special tabulations of survey data from National Opinion Research Center, Jacob J. Feldman, Senior Study Director.

Summary and Conclusion

The various religious groups differ greatly from each other in their distribution among regions, metropolitan and nonmetropolitan areas, and with respect to the size of places in which they live. They also differ as to age of the family head, ethnic composition, propensity to intermarry, and educational, occupational, and income levels. However, these differences are not due solely to religious affiliation as such. For example, it has been demonstrated in this chapter that occupational differences and educational differences each "explain" a large part of the income difference between religious groups. (Data were not available with which to measure how much of the total income differences between religious groups would be explained by both occupation and education considered simultaneously, but these factors probably would explain by far the larger part of these differences, if detailed occupation and education categories were used in the analysis.) There is comparatively little evidence that any particular group is receiving favored social or economic treatment simply on the basis of its religious affiliation. Neither is there much evidence to support a conclusion that any major religious group is being persecuted or disadvantaged in an economic sense solely because of its beliefs. Nevertheless, there is evidence that some economic and other differences between religious groups would still be found to persist, independent of other variables.

It would be very wrong to assert that because religious affiliation does not always have a strong effect, independent of all other variables, it is not an important variable for demographic and sociological analysis. This chapter has made it abundantly clear that unique "clusters of traits" are associated with each of the various religious groups. The hypothesis that these clusters are part of a tradition or culture which is transmitted from one generation to another is plausible, and is worthy of test and study. For example, in order to explain the results of this chapter it is almost mandatory to develop the hypothesis that members of the Episcopal, Jewish, and Presbyterian religions place a very high value on obtaining as much education as possible, that they strive to gain employment in the professional, managerial, or proprietary occupations, and that they attempt to save from current income so they can invest and increase their future income. This complex of traits or ambitions may lead to later marriage, fewer children, metropolitan residence, greater willingness to migrate, the accumulation of above-average amounts of wealth, and many other demographic and social phenomena reflecting values that our society deems praiseworthy. On the other hand, if we are familiar with the population composition of particular denominations, it helps us to understand the position these groups take with respect to particular social and economic issues. For this reason, and because religion *sometimes* is an important explanatory factor even when it is considered independently of other variables (as in the case of fertility analysis), much scientific and public good could be accomplished if religion were added as an item on the decennial census.

The analysis presented in this chapter concerning the interrelationships between religious affiliation and other population variables has had to be based on incomplete and inadequate data. These materials have enabled the analysis to demonstrate only that some highly meaningful relationships exist; as data with which to measure the magnitude of these relationships, however, they have permitted only approximate conclusions. There was not enough data to permit exploration of the reasons behind the existence of these relationships, and how they varied with changes in other circumstances. Further research must await more adequate information. It is to be hoped that the Bureau of the Census will give a high priority to this item in 1970, as penance for the policy forced on it in 1960.

STUDY AND DISCUSSION QUESTIONS

1. Review the article on the Hutterites in Chapter 5. How do the religious beliefs of this group affect their fertility, mortality, and migration?
2. Can you think of any religious groups in the United States which are devoted to a set of values rather than to a supernatural being or aspect of nature? How might their religious views affect fertility, mortality and migration?
3. The Roman Catholic Church provides a good example of the way in which fertility values of a religious group may affect that group's position in the world. Look up the history of this church's stand on issues affecting fertility. To what extent do the practices of Roman Catholic parishioners relating to fertility conform to those specified by the church?
4. Look up some data on interfaith marriages. Which groups cross religious lines most often? Which least often? Can you give reasons for the differences?
5. If the U.S. census does not contain data on religious affiliation of the population, what other sources might contain such data? How much detail can you find on the characteristics of various church members?
6. During the period before the 1960 Census of the United States, information on the religious composition of the population was collected in a government survey. Try to determine what data were published. What uses can be made of these data?
7. Compare the fertility and mortality rates of Jews in Israel with Jews in the United States. Are there differences? Why or why not?
8. Think back to what you have learned about the demographic transition. How might the Protestant Reformation and the doctrines of its leaders have affected the transition in Western Europe?

SUGGESTED ADDITIONAL READING

Pyle, Lee, ed. *The Pill and Birth Regulation.* Baltimore: Helicon Press, 1964.
Catholic debate, including statements, articles, and letters from the Pope, bishops, priests, and married and unmarried laity.

Fagley, Richard. *Population Explosion and Christian Responsibility.* New York: Oxford University Press, 1960.
A theological view of population problems and their solutions from certain religious perspectives.

Davis, Kingsley. *The Population of India and Pakistan.* Princeton: Princeton University Press, 1951.
Includes consideration of the effect of religious factors on population development and analyzes the religious structure of the population of the two countries.

Landis, Benson Y. "A Guide to the Literature on Statistics of Religious Affiliation with References to Related Social Studies," *Journal of the American Statistical Association*, 54 (June, 1959), 335–357.
A survey of the sources and kinds of data available, with some reference to international experience.

Foster, Charles R. *A Question on Religion.* ICP Case Series: Number 66. University, Alabama: University of Alabama Press, 1961.
A study by a political scientist of factors leading to a bureaucratic decision, in this case the decision not to include a question on religion in the 1960 Census.

Petersen, William. "Religious Statistics in the United States," *Journal for the Scientific Study of Religion*, 1 (Spring, 1962), 165–178.
Analysis of public and official attitudes toward collecting data on religion through government sources, from a sociological point of view.

Glick, Paul C. "Intermarriage and Fertility Patterns Among Persons in Major Religious Groups," *Eugenics Quarterly*, 7:1 (March, 1960), pp. 31–38.
An informative analysis of the religious factor as it relates to some of the basic components of population change in the United States.

CHAPTER 14

Population and the Economy

The interrelationships between economic and demographic factors are crucial to an understanding of both economic development and population change. Viewing the situation in most countries of Asia, Africa, and Latin America, we see these nations faced with the dilemma that low economic productivity handicaps them in their efforts to control population growth and continued high population growth limits their ability to improve the state of the economy. How to break this "vicious cycle" is a problem. It is not only in underdeveloped regions of the world, however, that economic factors interact with demographic variables; in developed regions, too, this interaction can be observed. How economic and population variables are generally related is the concern of this chapter.

Focusing attention first on the effects of economic factors on population change, one can see how the economic status of a country, both in terms of the relative prosperity and economic growth potential of the nation as a whole and the relative level of living of individuals and families within it, can influence patterns of fertility, mortality, and migration. The current concern about rapid population increase and economic insufficiency in underdeveloped parts of the world has been based on doubts about the ability of nations to increase their rates of economic growth, capital investment, industrial development, and technological change to the point where a sound economic base for population control and an adequate level of living for the population of the country can be achieved.

An appreciation of the problems involved can be attained by tracing the course of the demographic transition in underdeveloped nations and considering the forces which have brought these nations to their present stage. These countries were characterized for many years by high rates of both fertility and mortality so that their populations were fairly stable in size. As mortality began to decline, developed nations which had already achieved low mortality levels began to assist the underdeveloped nations in further reducing their death rates by contributing aid in the form of money, drugs, disinfectants, other goods, and advice about means to combat filth and disease. At the same time that death rates were being brought down precipitously in these countries, birth rates remained high. As a consequence, the "population explosion" we have observed in these nations was brought about.

In view of rapid population increases, economic development within these countries and economic aid from countries outside have been serving merely to maintain, rather than improve, the existing level of living which in many underdeveloped nations is barely above that required for survival. Recognition of the need to bring fertility and mortality more into balance in order to achieve greater stability in population growth, and to raise the level of living, has led increasing numbers of these nations to take actions to reduce the birth rate. Among these actions are the development of national family-planning programs and stimulation of the economy through the acceptance of outside economic aid and through the more efficient use of natural resources, manpower, and economic planning within the country. Whether the "vicious cycle" can be broken through these means remains to be seen.

The prospects of relieving population pressures in countries with high rates of population growth through migration of large numbers to other parts of the world have been diminished by the restrictive immigration policies of some nations and the decline in available arable land for settlement. The "Malthusian solution" of rising mortality rates remains a possibility, as evidenced by famines which have already occurred in some of these nations.

In the developed nations, where the demographic transition has already occurred, the cyclical nature of economic activity affords better explanation of variations in population factors. The business cycle has been related by some analysts to fluctuations in marriage rates which, in turn, have influenced birth rates. Poor economic conditions, as in the depression period, are associated with depressed fertility rates, whereas favorable economic conditions, as in the post-World War II period, are associated with increased fertility. The causal mechanisms are not firmly established, but some studies have shown that individual decisions about fertility are influenced by the prospects for continued economic progress as well as the current economic position of the nation and the relative welfare of the individual himself.

The association between economic conditions and migration in a developed economy are perhaps clearer than fertility and economic relationships. For example, the "Okies" in the United States moved west when farming in southwestern United States did not offer the means for continued survival, and Negroes moved out of the South to achieve better jobs and higher income. There is continuing mobility of persons in the United States and other countries as they adjust to the changing job market situation.

Population growth or decline can be a vital force in shaping the economic institutions of a society. Population increase will lead to a greater demand for housing, for products of business and industry, and for the creation of schools and other service industries. The changing compositional and distributional aspects of population also have an impact on the economy. In the first reading in this chapter, Spengler examines the economic effects of a changing age composition of a population and shows how the age distribution may affect the composition and productivity of the labor force.

Not only age, but sex, race, residence, and other compositional elements of the population affect the trends and make-up of the labor force, as indicated by Cook and Fisher. These authors examine labor force changes in the United States broadly in terms of adaptation of manpower supply to economic needs. The paradox of pockets of unemployment and poverty in a country of abundance, they point out, is a function of rapid demographic and technological changes which have altered the occupational structure and have created imbalances in the economy that may be overcome as further social adjustments take place.

Changes in fertility and mortality, and their resulting impact on family and economic institutions, have altered patterns of working life, as noted by Garfinkle in his article. As life expectancy increased in the United States over the decades, remaining years of working life for the average man also increased; the slowdown in mortality reductions coupled with earlier retirement from work in some fields of endeavor have led to a slight decline in years of working life in recent periods. Continued improvements in life expectancy will increase the amount of time spent in retirement, and any shortening of workweeks and workdays will increase the amount of leisure time available to persons in productive ages. Demographic changes and consequent economic changes will thus bring about modifications and innovations in other areas of social life.

That population conditions partly determine the state of the economy, not only in the size and composition of the labor force and distribution of income, but in the nature of economic development as well, is brought out clearly in the concluding article by Whitney. Population elements, he points out, influence the probability of the development of atomic power in a particular nation or region. His discussion might be extended to the relationship between population and war and population and the exploration of space. In each case, the effect of population factors may be indirect and intertwined with other social effects, but it can be identified.

*The Economic Effects of Changes in Age Composition**

JOSEPH J. SPENGLER

The economic consequences of a change in age composition may be grouped under four principal heads: (a) those which affect the *ratio* of workers to the total population; (b) those which affect the net output per continuously employed worker; (c) those which temporarily interrupt the continuity of a worker's employment; and (d) those which affect either the manner in which the working population is distributed among occupations, or the fullness of employment.

Upon these four groups of effects depend virtually all changes in per capita income properly imputable to changes in the age composition of a population. There remain additional economic consequences of a change in age composition, but these have to do with the adjusting of an economy to changes in age composition and not with the income-affecting consequences of such changes.

In Section I the basic theory underlying the analysis in this paper is outlined. Effects (a)–(d) are treated in Sections II–V. In Section VI incidental matters are treated.

I. THE BASIC THEORY

Three circumstances operating separately or in combination may produce a change in the age composition of the population of a national state or one of its subdivisions. (1) An increase in the expectation of life at birth will operate *ceteris paribus* to augment the relative number of persons in the higher age groups; a decrease will reduce the relative number. (2) A decrease in the gross reproduction rate will operate *ceteris paribus* to reduce the relative number of persons in the lower age groups until the age composition of the population has become adjusted to this lower rate; an increase will augment the relative number. (3) Migration will operate *ceteris paribus* to modify the age composition of a population if the age composition of the migrating population differs, in *net* terms, from the initial age composition of the population subject to the influence of migration.

In this paper we examine certain of the economic consequences which tend to accompany an increase in the relative number of persons in the higher age groups and a decrease in the relative number in the lower age groups. For it is principally this kind of change in age composition that has been produced and is being produced in the populations of the United States and of individual American states by past and/or prospective increases in life expectancy and decreases in gross reproduction. The influence of migration upon age composition, together with its economic consequences, will not be separately considered; for while the influences of prospec-

* Reprinted with permission from New York State Joint Legislative Committee on Problems of the Aging, *Birthdays Don't Count.* Albany, New York, 1948. Legislative Document No. 61, pp. 102-122.

tive migration upon age composition may differ from that of changes in mortality and natality, the analysis of these influences does not differ.

The economic effects of a given change in the age composition of a population originate in such changes in the *relative* numerical importance of economically significant attributes and attitudes as are produced by this change in age composition.

Let us suppose a population with individuals in every year of life from under-one to *n*. Let *n*, for the sake of concreteness, be assigned a value of 105. Let A denote the per cent of the total population in any particular yearly age group. Let the subscript *0*, denote the single year age group under one year of age; *1*, the single year age group lying between the 366th and the 730th days of life inclusive; and so on. Then, given that $n = 105$, the age composition of a population may be represented as follows:

$$
\begin{array}{c} A_0 \\ A_1 \\ \cdots\cdot \\ \cdots\cdot \\ A_{105} \end{array}
$$

Should sex composition also be required, the subscripts *m* and *f* may be used to denote male and female, respectively: e.g., A_1 becomes A_{m1} and A_{f1}.

A change in age composition modifies the *relative* numerical importance of those economically significant attributes and attitudes which vary, in each individual, with his age. This variation may be continuous from year to year, or it may be discontinuous, being manifest only in certain years. Let *a* denote such an attribute or attitude. Its value will vary with age, increasing to a maximum at some age, and thereafter declining. This variation may be expressed in index number terms, with an index of 100 assigned to the maximum value reached at some age, say 40, and with corresponding index numbers assigned to the values associated with other years. Since there are supposedly 105 single years of life the subscripts *0* to *105* may be used to denote the age of the possessor of the attribute or attitude and, therefore, its known index value. The numerical importance of *a* in a population may then be represented as follows:

$$
\begin{array}{c} A_0a_0 \\ A_1a_1 \\ \cdots\cdots \\ \cdots\cdots \\ A_{105}a_{105} \end{array}
$$

The aggregate value S_a in index terms of *a* for the population as a whole then is $\Sigma A_0a_0 + A_1a_1 + \ldots\ldots + A_{105}a_{105}$. The numerical importance of each other attribute or attitude *b, c, d,* etc., may be represented in like manner. It is evident that, if there is an increase in those *A* values with which high *a* values are associated, the aggregate value s_a for the population will increase; if these same *A* values diminish, aggregate value s_a will diminish. Like changes in the *A* values will produce like changes in the aggregate values s_b, s_c, s_d . . . . . , s_z.

Not all economic attributes and attitudes *a, b,* . . . . . , *z* are of equal economic significance. If all were of equal economic significance and independent one of another, their aggregate numerical importance *s* in index value terms might be represented as follows, as of any given time, for each yearly age group:

$$
\begin{array}{l}
S_0 = A_0\ (a_0 + b_0 + \ldots\ldots\ldots\ldots + z_0) \\
S_1 = A_1\ (a_1 + b_1 + \ldots\ldots\ldots\ldots + z_1) \\
\ldots\ldots\ldots\ldots\ldots\ldots\ldots\ldots\ldots\ldots \\
\ldots\ldots\ldots\ldots\ldots\ldots\ldots\ldots\ldots\ldots \\
S_{105} = A_{105}\ (a_{105} + b_{105} + \ldots\ldots + z_{105})
\end{array}
$$

The aggregate for the whole population then becomes the sum of the values for the individual years

$$
\sum_{S_0}^{S_{105}} s.
$$

Since attributes and attitudes *a, b,* . . . ., *z* are not of equal economic significance, a corrective coefficient *C* designed to reduce the index value for each attribute or attitude to comparable index terms must be introduced. Let this corrective coefficient be assigned a value of 1 for the most important attribute or attitude (say *a*) and appropriate lesser values for less important attributes or attitudes. Then the preceding summary statement may be rewritten as follows:

$$S_0 = A_0(a_0C_a + b_0C_b + \ldots. + z_0C_z)$$
$$S_1 = A_1(a_1C_a + b_1C_b + \ldots. + z_1C_z)$$
$$\ldots\ldots\ldots\ldots\ldots\ldots\ldots\ldots\ldots\ldots$$
$$\ldots\ldots\ldots\ldots\ldots\ldots\ldots\ldots\ldots\ldots$$
$$S_{105} = A_{105}(a_{105}C_a + b_{105}C_b + \ldots + z_{105}C_z)$$

The aggregate for the whole population is, of course, $\sum_{S_0}^{S_{105}} s$.

The importance, absolute and relative, of an economically significant attribute or attitude is not constant but variable through time, being dependent upon what may be called the structure *S* of an economy. That is, $C_a = f(S)$ $C_b = f(S)$, etc.; or, generally, $C = f(S)$. If only one time period is under consideration, or if *S* continues essentially unchanged between the two time periods being compared, the value of *S* may be ignored. If, however, the change in age composition between two periods has been accompanied by a change in *S*, the latter change must be taken into account; for the net economic effect of the change in age composition is then conditioned by the change in *S*.

It has been implicitly assumed that attributes and attitudes *a, b, ... z* are conditioned by age alone. Actually, however, each attribute or attitude is function of both age and the cultural or institutional arrangements *I* in effect in the economy. Thus, if *y* denotes the age of the possessor of an attribute *a,* the value of this attribute $v_a = f(y, I)$. Accordingly, given the age of the possessor of attribute *a,* its value is governed by *I;* and the effect of a change in the age composition of a population is conditioned by the institutional arrangements *I* in effect. Moreover, if *I* changes at the same time that the age composition changes, the economic effect of the change in age composition as such may be accentuated or partly offset by the change in *I*.

If all the economic attributes and attitudes conditioned by age are independent of one another, their aggregate numerical importance *s* in index value terms may be represented as follows, as of any given time, for each yearly age group:

$$S_0 = A_0(a_0C_a + b_0C_b + \ldots. + z_0C_z)SI$$
$$S_1 = A_1(a_1C_a + b_1C_b + \ldots. + z_1C_z)SI$$
$$\ldots\ldots\ldots\ldots\ldots\ldots\ldots\ldots\ldots\ldots$$
$$\ldots\ldots\ldots\ldots\ldots\ldots\ldots\ldots\ldots\ldots$$
$$S_{105} = A_{105}(a_{105}C_a + b_{105}C_b + \ldots. + z_{105}C_z)SI$$

The aggregate for the whole population composing the economy is $\sum_{S_0}^{S_{105}} s$. If the age composition of the population changes between two time periods, while both the structure *S* of the economy and its institutional arrangements *I* continue unchanged, the change in *s* will be the result solely of changes in the values of $A_0, A_1, \ldots, A_{105}$. If, however, *S* and/or *I* undergo modification simultaneously with the change in age composition, the change in $\sum_{S_0}^{S_{105}} s$ may be accentuated or reduced.

II. The Worker: Population Ratio

The *relative* number of workers in a population varies with its age composition. This variation is due in part to the fact that persons below and above certain ages are not members of a nation's labor force, that is, of that group of persons who either are employed or are seeking work. Thus in 1940, when the median age of the American population was 29 years, 71 and 58.8 per cent, respectively, of this population were in age groups 15–69 and 20–64; in the year 2000, when the median age will approximate 37.4, these two percentages will approximate 72 and 61, respectively.[1] These figures

[1] For purposes of discussion in this essay use is made of the population forecast based on the assumption of medium fertility and mortality and no net immigration after July 1, 1945. See Special Report of the Bureau of the Census, Series P-46, No. 7, September 15, 1946. Other forecasts will become available in 1948 upon the publication, by the Bureau of the Census, of *Forecasts of the Population of the United States, 1945-1975.* See also John D. Durand's *The Labor Force in the United States,* 1890-1960 (Social Science Research Council, New York, 1948), which appeared after this study was completed.

suggest that for each 100 inhabitants there may be slightly more workers in the future than at present.

This supposition must be slightly modified, however; for circumstances associated with variations in age affect the relative number of persons in the age group 15–75 who are qualified to be members of the labor force of a state or nation. In this section and the following section only data relating to males will be used for purposes of demonstration. This restriction is permissible since males comprise about three-fourths of the labor force, since findings for males hold in substance for females, and since many of the circumstances affecting the actual occupational status of females are not connected with age.

Relevant data for all males are given in Table 1. In 1930 gainful employment was at a maximum in the age group 25–44 (col. 2). In 1940 membership in the labor force was at a maximum in the age group 25–44; it was lower in higher age groups, decreasing at an increasing rate with the height of the age group (col. 3). Should the percentages reported in column 3 persist, the percentage of all males in the labor force will increase somewhat (under 1 per cent by 1960; about 5 per cent by 2000) in consequence of the change in age composition.

Since membership in the labor force does not imply actual employment, account must be taken of such variations in employment as are associated with age. In column 4 of Table 1 there is reported by age group the percentage of the labor force employed otherwise than on public emergency work, March 24–30, 1940; it is only slightly lower in the higher age groups than in the peak range, 25–44. On line 2 of Table 2 the relative number of males "seeking work" in this same week is given by age. The

TABLE 1

*Per Cent of Males, Gainfully Employed in 1930 or in Labor Force in 1940, and Median Earnings of Males in 1939, by Age**

Age Group	Per Cent of Males in Age Group Reported as		Per cent of labor force employed (excluding public emergency work) in 1940[b]	Median Earnings of Males Employed for 12 Months, in 1939[c]		Index to Productivity[d]
	Gainfully employed, 1930[a]	In labor force, 1940[b]		Absolute	Relative	
15–19.......	[48.0]	[40.0]	[68.9]	[$512]	[33]	14
20–24.......	89.9	88.0	79.7	913	58	53
25–34.......	97.3	95.2	87.4	1324	83	81
35–44.......	97.7	94.7	88.4	1572	100	95
45–54.......	96.4	92.1	86.9	1590	101	92
55–59.......	93.0	87.8	84.9	1484	94	83
60–64.......	86.8	78.9	84.6	1398	88	70
65–74.......	68.4	50.8	89.3	1238	78	40
Over 74.....	32.3	17.8	95.4	....	...	..
All ages.....	76.2	79.0	85.2	1354	85	67

* Figure in brackets are estimates.

[a] Fifteenth Census: 1930, V, p. 115.

[b] Sixteenth Census: 1940, III, *The Labor Force. Occupation, Industry, Employment and Income,* p. 19. The per cent (e.g., 9.6 in last line) not accounted for are reported as "seeking work."

[c] *Ibid., Wage or Salary Income in 1939,* p. 106. The figure for the 65-74 group is based upon that reported for the group over 64.

[d] Obtained by rounding or slightly adjusting percentages in cols. 3 and 6 and multiplying col. 3 by col. 6.

percentage falls from a maximum in age group 15–19 to a minimum in group 35–44, then rises gradually to a secondary peak in the 60–64 group, thereafter declining slightly.[2] In Table 2 (last line) are given the fractions by which the median earnings for *all* male members of the labor force, irrespective of months worked in 1939, fell below the median earnings of the continuously employed (i.e., 12 months) males.[3] This fraction, at a maximum in the 15–19 group, falls to a minimum in the 35–44 group, thereafter rising gradually to a secondary peak in the 65–74 group. While this fraction is dominated by the earnings-depressing effect of unemployment, it should also reflect the similar effect of accidents and sickness; yet only in the 65–74 group is there possibly evidence that the latter effect is relatively significant.[4]

[2] According to the National Health Survey in 1935-36 the per cent of urban male workers who were unemployed, were, by age: 15-24, 37.4; 25-44, 17.2; 45-64, 22.3; 65 and over, 31; all ages, 22.6. Unemployment varied with age in much the same manner among both white and colored male workers, but unemployment rates were much higher among the latter (see Population Series, Bulletin No. D, pp. 6-7).

[3] For urban male members of the labor force the corresponding fractions were: 15-19, 48; 20-24, 23; 45-64 and "all ages," 17; 35-44, 14; 25-34, 12.

[4] The Spearman rank correlation coefficient between the unemployment and wage data on the last two lines of Table 2 is 0.923 with a probable error of 0.127. The 65-74 group ranks 5 in per cent seeking work and 3 in depression of earnings below full-time level.

The data presented in this section indicate that the prospective changes in age composition will not increase the relative number of nonworkers in the population, and may even slightly increase the relative number of workers; for the increase in the relative number of older nonworkers will be offset by the decrease in the relative number of younger nonworkers. It is not likely, moreover, that prospective changes in age composition will tend to reduce the percentage of the labor force that is regularly employed.

It is not likely, therefore, that the worker: population ratio will be adversely affected by prospective changes in age composition.

III. Age and Output Per Continuously Employed Worker

Information respecting the functional relation between age and output per continuously employed worker, while less complete than precise analysis requires,[5] indicates that a worker's output usually is influenced by his age and tends to fall as he moves into higher age groups. This

[5] As a rule variations in output per employed worker must be inferred from variations in his earnings; and these may be used to measure the influence of age upon productivity only when: (a) the worker's behavior rates (i.e., speed, energy output, etc.) are governed primarily by himself; (b) earnings accurately reflect performance; and (c) it is possible to isolate variations in earnings attributable to variations in hours worked.

TABLE 2

Unemployment and Earnings in Male Labor Force, 1939–40

Age Groups	15–19	20–24	25–34	35–44	45–54	55–59	60–64	65–74	All
Per cent seeking work[a]	23	14.4	8	6.8	7.7	9.5	9.7	8.2	9.6
1— (wage of all ÷ wage of 12 month workers)[b]	.48	.28	.18	.16	.18	.20	.22	.23	.22

[a] See note (b) under Table 1.

[b] Computed from pp. 99,106 of census report cited in note (c) under Table 1.

tendency has its origin principally in psychophysiological concomitants of aging.

It is almost impossible to determine the role of age in industrial output. However, on the basis of our physiologic knowledge, it seems probable that work output may diminish in older workers.[6]

Old age weakens most abilities, especially those requiring energy and speed, but the drop from age 50 to age 75 is probably only 1 or 2 per cent per year.[7]

This tendency may also be attributable in some part to an increase in the worker's inclination to restrict output as he advances in age.[8]

The functional relation between output and age varies with occupation; for the physiological and psychological responses of workers vary with age, while the physiological and psychological requirements of occupations differ. Thus, the effectiveness of a boxer is usually at a peak in his twenties, whilst that of a craftsman or of a professional man may remain at or near the peak even in his fifties. In general the more the product of a man's occupational behavior involves experience, wisdom, and judgment, the less marked will be the tendency of this product to decline in consequence of age-induced physiological and psychological deterioration. Furthermore, in so far as older workers, in comparison with younger workers, tend to perform more evenly and to turn out relatively fewer spoiled or substandard products, they will enjoy a comparative advantage in occupations in which evenness of performance and maintenance of quality is important.[9]

Because the functional relation between age and output varies with occupation, the overall effect of an increase in the age composition of a population will be conditioned by its occupational composition. Such an increase is much more likely to have an adverse effect upon aggregate output in an economy dominated by occupations resembling boxing in its demands upon the practitioner than in an economy dominated by crafts and professions. For the sake of simplicity it will here be assumed that the occupational composition is stable through time. In fact, the changes in occupational composition that are taking place appear to be increasing the relative importance of those forms of behavior which are more resistant to age-induced deterioration.

Output appears to vary less with the age of a representative individual than from individual to individual of stipulated age.[10] For a given individual's productivity is conditioned by his Biological Age in greater measure than by his Chronologic Age which is but one of the several determinants of an individual's Biologic Age. The productivity of a given individual will usually exceed, or fall short of, the average productivity of his age and occupational group, if his Vitality Index exceeds or falls short of that representative of his group.[11] An individual's Vitality Index is conditioned by his Biologic Age which is governed in part by genetic and other conditions

[6] Dr. N. W. Shock, "Older People and Their Potentialities for Gainful Employment," *Journal of Gerontology,* II, 1947, p. 98.

[7] E. L. Thorndike, *Human Nature and the Social Order,* The Macmillan Company, New York, 1940, p. 55. Various aspects of gerontology are treated in E. V. Cowdry, ed., *Problems of Ageing,* Williams and Wilkins, Baltimore, 2d ed., 1942. On social aspects of ageing and bibliography relating thereto see E. W. Burgess et al, *Social Adjustment in Old Age,* a preliminary mimeographed research planning report sponsored by the Social Science Research Council, New York, 1946.

[8] G. F. Bloom and N. Belfer state that "the inclination to restrict output and the age of the union worker are closely correlated." See "Unionism and Real Labor Income, *Southern Economic Journal,* XIV, 1948, p. 293. Dr. Frank T. de Vyner informs the writer that it is his observation from experience that older workers are less likely than younger workers to restrict output.

[9] W. R. Miles, "Psychological Aspects of Ageing," in Cowdry, *op. cit.* See also R. A. McFarland, "The Older Worker in Industry," *Harvard Business Review,* XXI, 1943, pp. 505-520; H. C. Lehman, "The Most Proficent Years at Sports and Games," *Research Quarterly, American Association of Health and Physical Education,* IX, 1938, pp. 3-19; and C. Tibbitts and O. Pollak in Burgess et al, *op. cit.,* pp. 83-85.

[10] Miles, *op. cit.*

[11] Vitality Index = V.I. = 100 [1 ÷ (Biologic Age ÷ Chronologic Age)]. This index which is analogous to Intelligent Quotient, is suggested by Dr. Harry Benjamin's distinction between Chronologic Age, measured in years, and Biologic Age, measured in terms of an individual's health and biologic state. See "Biologic Versus Chronologic Age," *Journal of Gerontology,* II, 1947, pp. 217-228. The term "usually" is used in the text above because an individual's productivity depends not only upon his Biologic Age but also upon other circumstances.

not susceptible of modification, and in part by conditions which are susceptible of some modification through education and improvements in managerial, medical and psychological approaches to problems associated with ageing. These modifying circumstances will operate also in other ways to increase the productivity of individuals of given age, and on the balance to diminish interindividual differences in productivity. Presumably, therefore, although interindividual differences in the functional relation between age and output cannot be eliminated, they can be made less pronounced than at present.[12]

The productivity, or the earnings, of continuously employed workers rise to a maximum, remain there for some years, and then decline. Among male agricultural workers productivity is supposedly at the peak in the 18–44 age group, and thereafter declines.[13] Among railway employees there appears to be a tendency, not completely continuous, for efficiency to decline slightly after the early forties.[14] A careful study, based upon the production records of 249 male weavers, spinners, and nonferrous-metal workers, reveals that output per worker per full-time week was at the maximum in the age group 25–55, about 5 per cent below the maximum in the age group 55–64, about 10–15 per cent below the maximum in the age group 65–74, and about 10 per cent below in the age group 15–24.[15] A study of professional incomes in 1941 reveals the following rough maximum earnings age ranges: veterinarians, 35–39; dentists and osteopaths, 35–49; physicians, 35–54; lawyers, 45–59.[16] It is not wide of the truth to say, in general, that the earnings of the vast majority (i.e., over 90 per cent) of continuously employed workers rise to a maximum in the thirties and remain there for 15–25 years; and that the earnings of the high-income minority reach a peak in the forties or early fifties and remain at this level for a shorter period.[17]

Absolute and relative median earnings data presented in columns 5–6 of Table 1 for continuously[18] employed males in 1939 indicate that the productivity of such workers is at a maximum

[12] According to Shock (*op. cit.,* p. 100), effective utilization of older workers presupposes "(1) careful and complete job analysis, (2) development of individual tests to assess the physiological age of various organ systems, (3) development of individual tests for performance capacity, and (4) education of the community to realize the necessity for utilizing the work capacities present in older people."

[13] In the State of Washington male workers in 1943 were considered by farmers to have the following work capacity, expressed in terms of an able-bodied man: 10-14, one third; 15-17, three-fourths; 18-44, one; 45-64, nine-tenths; 65 and older, three-fifths. See Carl F. Reuss, "Effect of Age and Sex on Productive Capacity at Farm Work," State College of Washington Agricultural Experiment Station, V Circular No. 13, July, 1943, p. 2.

[14] Dan H. Mater, "A Statistical Study of the Effect of Seniority Upon Employee Efficiency," *Journal of Business* XIV, April, 1941, p. 195. This study is continued in *ibid.,* October, 1941, pp. 384 ff. as "Effects of Seniority Upon the Welfare of the Employee, the Employer and Society."

[15] D. L. Palmer and J. A. Brownell, "Influence of Age on Employment Opportunities," *Monthly Labor Review,* XLVIII, 1939, pp. 765-780, Tables 6-7. In pre-1939 Germany and Czechoslovakia earnings reached a peak in the early and middle forties; at age 60 they were about 12 per cent below the maximum (*ibid.,* p. 265). Several American studies cited by McFarland (*op. cit.,* p. 515) show little or no decline in productivity with advancing years. A study conducted by the Erwin Cotton Mills Company, Dr. Frank T. de Vyner informs the writer, suggested no inverse relationship between age of worker and output of worker.

[16] E. F. Denison, "Incomes in Selected Professions," *Survey of Current Business,* XXIV, 1944, p. 16. Unlike the previous study, this inquiry is based upon reported actual earnings, and not upon the earnings that would have been realized had each professional worker been continously employed in 1941. For the influence of the number of years in practice upon professional income see M. Friedman and S. Kuznets, *Income from Independent Professional Practice,* National Bureau of Economic Research, New York, 1945, pp. 237 ff.

[17] Data presented by Dublin and Lotka and Leven suggest this pattern. See L. I. Dublin and A. J. Lotka, *The Money Value of Man,* The Ronald Press Company, New York, rev. ed., 1946, pp. 65, 182; M. Leven, *The Income Structure of the United States,* The Brookings Institution, Washington, 1938, pp. 51-52, 156. See also Table I and note 19 below.

[18] Males who are reported as having worked 12 months in 1939 are here described as continuously employed even though some may have been absent from work at times because of sickness, accidents, etc. The figures in Table I relate to *all* males in the labor force. While the earnings of *urban* continuously employed males were slightly higher than earnings of all continuously employed males, the relative values, by age group, were almost identical for both groups; substantially the same holds for *all* males and *urban* males, irrespective of months worked.

in the age group 35–54 and thereafter declines about one point per year. In column 7 of Table 1 there is presented an index of productivity[19] based upon columns 3 and 6. If the productivity index value for each age group is multiplied by the percentage of the male population in the corresponding age group and the products are summated for any year, a comparative measure of output per capita is obtained. If the sum obtained for 1940 is assigned a relative value of 100, the comparative values for 1960, 1980, and 2000 approximate 101, 106, and 107. In short, if the age composition of the American population changes in the future along the lines noted above, and other conditions remain substantially unchanged, *output per capita,* together with the capacity of the population to satisfy its wants, will increase somewhat. While the future age composition may not develop quite along the lines here supposed, it is unlikely that it will develop in such wise as to bring about a decline in *output per capita.*

IV. Age and Continuity, or Regularity of Employment

The annual output of a member of the labor force may tend to fall as he advances in age if (a), though he be regularly employed, his being on the job declines because of an increasing proneness to accidents, sickness or absenteeism, and uneconomic job-changing; or if (b), when he is out of work, the ease with which he can find employment diminishes. The evidence indicates that, on the whole, the worker's being on the job is not greatly affected by his age; and that the difficulties which the older worker encounters in finding employment have their origin chiefly in misinformation respecting his capacities and in institutional arrangements which may readily be corrected. The circumstances falling under (a) and (b), respectively, will be treated in order.

(a) Respecting proneness to accident and their cost, the evidence suggests that at worst the older worker is not significantly more expensive than the younger worker. First, the annual number of days of disability per worker imputable to accidents is less than one, with accidents accounting for slightly less than one-tenth of the days lost by persons aged 15–64.[20] Second, although the data respecting the incidence of accident by age do not all yield the same conclusion regarding incidence, they do indicate that incidence does not increase significantly with age. Among male workers both all occupational injuries and injuries disabling for a week or more increased slightly with age.[21] Other studies indicate that

[19] This index differs appreciably only from the one suggested by the Palmer-Brownell study (see note 15 above) which implies that, since productivity per worker varies little with age, a change in age composition will exercise little influence upon average per worker output. See Dublin and Lotka, *op. cit.,* p. 182, and W. S. Woytinski's estimate of taxable wages per worker by age in *Earnings and Social Security in the United States,* Social Science Research Council, Washington, 1943, pp. 100, 127.

[20] In 1935-36 accidents caused 9.8 and 7.9 per cent, respectively, of the days of disability per year suffered by persons aged 15-64 and by persons of all ages. The days of disability per person per year attributed, respectively, to accident and to all causes, were, by age: 15-24, 0.51 and 5.1; 35-64, 0.88 and 9.9; over 64, 0.97 and 35.1. Among the members of families on relief the corresponding rates were higher than in the population as a whole: 15-24, 0.65 and 8; 25-64, 1.49 and 20.7; over 64, 2.49 and 58. Accidental injuries, disabling for one week or more, per 1,000 urban males, by age, were: 15-24, 20.9; 25-44, 22.7; 45-64, 27; over 64, 30.4. This class of accidents was not so important, however, constituting only 27.4 per cent of all accidents; only 22.5 per cent of this class of accidents were occupational in origin, the disability thereby caused per person being only 0.19 day. See The National Health Survey: 1935-36, Sickness and Medical Care Series, Bulletin 3, pp. 1-5, Bulletin 9, pp. 2, 8, 12, Washington, 1938.

[21] The number of male workers per 100 found disabled (on the day of inquiry) by all illnesses and injuries including and excluding occupational injuries, respectively, were, by age: 15-24, 1.33 and 1.16; 25-34, 1.54 and 1.34; 35-44, 2.05 and 1.81; 45-54, 2.63 and 2.37; 55-64, 3.48 and 3.18. Among manual workers the rates were slightly higher than among nonmanual workers, and the occupational rates — measured by the difference between two rates referred to — rose slightly more than among nonmanual workers. See D. E. Hailman, "The Prevalence of Disabling Illness Among Male and Female Workers and Housewives," United States Public Health Bulletin No. 260, 1941, pp. 9, 14. The annual frequency of industrial injuries lasting 7-365 days per 1,000 male workers and the number of days of disability per worker per year caused thereby, are respectively, by age: 16-24, 11.6 and 0.52; 25-34, 11.2 and 0.50; 35-44, 11.9 and 0.63; 45-54, 12.1 and 0.68; 55-64, 13.0 and 0.77. The rates are higher among manual than among nonmanual workers. See Joan Klebba, "Industrial Injuries Among the Urban Population," United States Public Health Reports, LVI, 1941, pp. 2380, 2385. Both studies are based upon the National Health Survey, 1935-36.

for some groups of workers the injuries sustained by older workers are more severe and, for this reason and because the rapidity of the healing process slows down with age, disable them longer than the injuries of younger workers disable the latter, but that the frequency of accidents is lower among older workers.[22]

Data relating to age and illness among workers indicate that the incidence and the adverse effects of illness increase with age, but not enough to justify discrimination against older workers. Moreover, as Dr. Shock observes, "most problems of sickness or absenteeism among older workers can be solved by adequate programs of medical care." [23] Some studies indicate that older workers fall sick less frequently than younger workers, but remain sick longer per case of illness.[24] A study of railroad employees indicates that the number of days of disability per employee per year attributable to sickness and nonindustrial accidents causing eight or more calendar days of disability rises with age.[25] The incidence of chronic diseases, which, when it does not permanently disable a worker, reduces his attendance at work, rises with age.[26] In 1935–36 the annual number of days of disability per person attributable to diseases and impairments (other than accidents) rose from 4.59 in the 15–24 age group through 9.02 in the 25–64 group to 33.13 in the over 64 group.[27] Rates among persons on relief, while higher, were nearly of the same pattern as those prevailing in the nonrelief population. While disability rates among workers are lower than disability rates in the unselected population as a whole, disability rates among employed workers rise with age.[28] Labor turnover is more frequent among younger than among older workers, length of employment tending to increase with age, and occupational mobility being greater among workers under 35 than among those who are older.[29] This greater mobility is economically desirable in so far as it serves to maintain a proper balance among occupations, or to enable individual workers to find jobs in which their respective aptitudes are at a maximum comparative advantage. Beyond this mobility is economically disadvantageous, for it increases the overall cost of training employees, sometimes diminishes the work output of the job-changing workers, and usually operates directly and indirectly to increase the volume of temporary unemployment.

Since the data relating to incidence of illness, accidents, and labor turnover do not indicate the older worker to be generally inferior to the younger worker, albeit he may be inferior in some occupations, objections to the employment of older workers on grounds of supposedly greater proneness to accidents, illness, and absenteeism are based upon misinformation and therefore are discriminatory. Consideration of the available evidence will dispell these objections.

(b) Employers may object to employment of older workers on the ground that their addition to the payroll will augment the cost of compensation and/or group insurance, or that of pension plans in effect. These objections may

[22] M. D. Kossoris, "Relation of Age to Industrial Injuries," *Monthly Labor Review,* LI, 1940, pp. 789-804; D. K. Brundage, "A Ten Year Record of Absences from Work on Account of Sickness and Accident," *Public Health Reports,* XLII, 1927, pp. 529-550; and McFarland's summary of relevant studies, *op. cit.,* pp. 515-18.

[23] *Op. cit.,* p. 100.

[24] McFarland, *op. cit.,* p. 518; Brundage, *op. cit.*

[25] Days of disability per employee per year by age are: under 25, 4.3; 25-34, 6.9; 35-44, 9.8; 45-54, 14.2; 55-64, 27.9; 65 and over, 39.1. See W. M. Gafafer, "Frequency of Sickness and Nonindustrial Accidents Causing Disability Lasting 8 Calendar Days or Longer Among 60,000 White Male Railroad Employees, 1930-34, Inclusive," U. S. Public Health Reports, LIII, 1938, p. 561; also "Disabling Sickness Among Industrial Workers with Particular Reference to Time Changes in Duration," *American Journal of Public Health,* XXXI, 1941, pp. 443-51. Cp. Klebba, *op. cit.,* note 21, above.

[26] National Health Survey, Sickness and Medical Care Series, Bulletin No. 6, pp. 8-9; also D. E. Hailman, "Health Status of Adults in the Productive Ages," U. S. Public Health Reports, LVI, 1941, pp. 2071-87.

[27] Computed from National Health Survey, Sickness and Medical Care Series, Bulletin No. 9, pp. 2, 8. According to an earlier study, the frequency of illness that caused the loss of one or more days from usual activities was lower in the 40-64 than in the 25-39 age group. It suggests also that the incidence of time-costing illness does not become relatively high until in the sixties. See S. D. Collins, "The Incidence and Causes of Illness at Specific Ages," *Milbank Memorial Fund Quarterly,* XIII, 1935, pp. 330-34.

[28] The number disabled by illness per 1,000 employed male workers, by age in 1935-36, is: 15-24, 11.7; 25-44; 15.5; 45-64, 23.8; 65 and over, 47.2 The rates among the unemployed were much higher, and rose with age. See National Health Survey, Sickness and Medical Care Series, Bulletin No. 7, pp. 3-5. Cp. also the rates from Hailman, given in note 21 above.

[29] McFarland, *op. cit.,* p. 515.

be founded upon a misunderstanding of the facts.[30] When these objections are founded upon fact, they can be overcome in several ways. Premiums and/or claims may be adjusted to the age status of the older worker in such wise that the expense entailed by his employment is not appreciably in excess of the average or mode per worker. Or equalization funds covering a large number of representative firms and industries may be established under private or under governmental auspices. Member firms would pay into these funds on the basis of the number of covered workers on their payrolls and would be reimbursed by the funds for payments made in excess of average premiums, etc., on behalf of older workers. Either of these arrangements, or a combination thereof, will free any particular firm of such increases in expense as are entailed by the employment of older workers and the consequent necessity of paying higher insurance, compensation, and related rates.

Employers sometimes object to employing older workers on the ground that they must be paid higher wages (or salaries) than younger workers. The principle underlying this objection is valid in an economy such as ours in which remuneration supposedly is based upon productivity. This objection does not hold under pure competition when, irrespective of a worker's age, his wage equals in value his *net* product; nor does it hold, even though competition is not pure and the worker is paid less than the market value of his *net* product, so long as the absolute rate of exploitation per worker is independent of his age and/or the employer's aggregate exploitation return is not reduced by the hiring of older workers. This objection will hold, of course, if neither the former nor the latter condition is met; but then it can be removed either by introducing pure competition respecting the payment of labor, or by establishing appropriate rates of worker exploitation.[31]

[30] The grounds of discrimination against older workers are summarised and scrutinized in the *Final Report* of the New York Joint Legislative Committee on Discrimination in Employment of the Middle Aged, Legislative Document No. 80, Albany, 1940.

[31] If an employer is compelled to pay workers at rates exceeding their respective net products, he will endeavor to minimize this exploitation of himself and his choice of older, or younger, workers will be governed accordingly.

The preceding argument holds whether the employer sells his product under conditions of pure or of imperfect competition. In view of what has been said it is evident that a wage or salary structure can always be so adjusted as to place older and younger workers on a par respecting their comparative desirability as employees. As a rule, therefore, the age of a worker is not sufficient, by itself, to affect his employability appreciably.

V. Occupational Balance and the Level of Employment

In this section consideration is given to the functional relation between age composition, on the one hand, and both (1) occupational balance and (2) the level of employment, on the other.

(1) Aggregate and per capita income are conditioned by the manner in which the working population is distributed among occupations and industries. In general, so long as workers (who are willing to transfer) could produce and earn more in other occupations than in the ones in which they are engaged, the transfer of such workers from the occupations where they earn less to the occupations where they can earn more will increase their real income and that of the economy as a whole. The optimum distribution of workers among occupations and, therefore, the ideal occupational balance, have been attained when it is no longer possible for workers, though they be free to change occupations if they wish, to improve their situations by changing occupation or place of work.

An increase in the relative number of older workers such as is in prospect may operate in one or several of three ways to make more difficult the maintenance of an optimum distribution of workers among occupations and places of employment: (a) by reducing the relative number of young workers entering the laboring force for the first time; (b) by acting, in conjunction with a deceleration of population growth or a decrease in population, to slow down the adjustment of the distribution of workers among occupations to the structure of the general demand for labor; and (c) by affecting apprenticeship, seniority, and related rules respecting conditions of employment in such manner as to restrict access to relatively attractive occupations and to reduce productivity-increasing mobility of labor between occupations and places of employment. Of course, if the wage structure is permitted to reflect the *relative* scarcity or abundance of labor in particular occupations or places of employment, circumstances (a), (b), and (c) are not likely to occasion much difficulty.[32]

(a) Although the relative number of young workers entering the labor force will diminish somewhat, this diminution will not by itself greatly intensify the task of properly distributing workers among occupations. Changes in the ratio of the number of persons aged 20–24 to that of persons aged 25–69 may be used to measure changes in the relative number of young workers just entering the labor force. This ratio, 0.167 in 1940, will fall to something like 0.132, 0.119, and 0.116, respectively, by 1960, 1980, and 2000. That is, the number of entrants per 100 persons in the labor force will fall from about 3.3 in 1940 to slightly under 2.4 after 1980.[33] This number, if kept out of relatively contracting occupations and directed into relatively expanding occupations, should suffice to preserve the desired occupational distribution, since a considerable fraction of those under 30 and already in the labor force are able and willing to change employment if such change is actually or potentially advantageous.

(b) But suppose that the increase in the *relative* number of older workers is accompanied by a fall in the schedule of demand for labor in particular occupations. This decrease in absolute demand might be caused either by a decline in the size of the total population, or by a decline in per capita consumption of the particular kind of labor[34] in question. Such a decrease in the demand for a particular kind of labor need not occasion particularized unemployment, even though the demand for the labor in question is inelastic.[35] For the forces of mortality and retirement alone rapidly deplete the number of workers attached to an occupation, and their influence is reenforced by the withdrawal of mobile workers in the younger age groups. Suppose the age composition of the workers attached to an occupation is the same as that of the (1945) white female life table population lying between 15 and 64, workers entering the occupation at 15 and leaving at 65. If no recruits are added to this occupation, mortality and retirement will reduce its membership about two per cent per year — 10.7 per cent in five years and 21.3 in ten years. A projection based upon English mortality and fertility in the early 1930's indicates that the rate at which mortality and retirement reduce the number of workers attached to an occupation is about three times that at which a total population decreases when the rate of decrease becomes stable at 1 per cent per year. Transfer out of an occupation of those in the mobile age groups will raise appreciably above 2–3 per cent the annual rate at which an occupational group diminishes.[36]

In a population whose size is declining, whose age composition is not stable, and whose average age is rising, one would expect the demand for labor serving the needs of youth to decline appreciably. The demand for elementary school teachers is a case in point. Suppose this demand

[32] In England in 1938-45 the response of workers to changes in the wage structure indicated a high degree of labor mobility. See J. L. Nicholson, "Earnings, Hours, and Mobility of Labor," *Bulletin* of the Oxford University Institute of Statistics, VIII, May, 1946, pp. 156-57, 160, 163.

[33] Accordingly to the Census of 1940 only 1.5 per cent of the number in the labor force were reported as seeking work for the first time.

[34] Aggregate demand at any particular price is the product of two variables, that is, of individual demand multiplied by the number of individuals in the population. Accordingly, aggregate demand will decline if population declines with per capita demand remaining constant, or if per capita demand declines with population remaining constant, or, in general, when a decline in one of the two variables is not offset by an increase in the other. A decrease in population, or a decrease in the rate of population growth, therefore may be accompanied by a decline in absolute demand for given kinds of labor.

[35] The demand for any particular kind of labor usually is inelastic, since the outlay for such labor usually constitutes a small fraction of the cost of the finished goods or service into whose composition it enters.

[36] Of the (1945) white female life table population lying between 15 and 64, 21.3 per cent were in the age group 15-24. In the stable English population referred to above, those aged 15-24 constitute 18.3 per cent of the male population aged 15-64 at a time when the total male population is declining 1 per cent per year. See Joseph J. Spengler, "Population Movements, Employment, and Income," *Southern Economic Journal,* V, 1938, Table II, and study by E. Charles, there referred to.

to be directly proportional to the number of children of elementary school age and therefore to decline at the same rate as the number of children. Even then mortality and retirement will reduce the number of teachers over 1.5 times as fast as the need for teachers declines.[37] It may be concluded that, in general, a decline in the relative number of workers in the lower age groups will not operate directly to make much more difficult the maintenance of a desired occupational balance even though the total population should decline in number.

(c) Occupational imbalance may be intensified if the increase in the relative number of older workers is accompanied by changes in apprenticeship, seniority and related rules which reduce interoccupational mobility or make more difficult the entry of young workers into attractive occupations. The motive for such changes would be the desire of older workers to make their situations more secure against cyclical and other declines in the demand for their services and against efforts of employers to substitute (for whatever reason) younger for older workers.

As the relative number of older workers increases they will probably seek to strengthen seniority and related rules in their favor, for the number of older workers presumably will increase more rapidly than the number of "choice" jobs. Not all jobs are equally attractive. The aspiration to hold a choice job probably tends within limits to increase with age. Relatively more older than younger workers hold choice jobs.[38] Suppose that in 1940 30 per cent of all jobs were "choice," and that one-half of these jobs were held by workers over 44. Then "choice" jobs would be held by 50 in each 100 workers over 44, and by 21 in each 100 below 45. By 1980, however, given the then age composition and the supposition that 30 per cent of the jobs remain "choice," there can be only 43 "choice" jobs for each 100 workers over 44 provided that the 1940 rate of 21 per 100 holds for workers under 45; and there can be only 18.8 for younger workers if the 1940 rate of 50 per 100 holds for older workers. Whence there may be a conflict in interest between younger and older workers, and the latter may seek to guard their situations by strengthening seniority and related rules.

The tendency of older workers to resort to strengthened seniority rules may be eased somewhat provided that approximately full employment persists and that hourly productivity and earnings are not adversely affected by advancing age, or that the relative number of choice jobs increases.

If apprenticeship, seniority, and related rules are diffused and strengthened for the purpose of guarding and improving the relative status of older workers, the adverse effects of these rules will be intensified, an ideal occupational balance will not be realizable, and eventually a conflict will be precipitated between the older beneficiaries and the younger victims of these rules. The apprenticeship rules will restrict the access of younger workers to relatively expanding and economically attractive occupations and reduce the mobility of workers between occupations and jobs. Seniority and related rules substitute for efficiency-generation competition and reward according to merit a system of status which makes an individual's success and progress depend almost entirely upon his growing older.[39] These rules make for inefficiency and incorrect job allocation;[40] for increased resistance to technological change and welfare-favoring price and wage policies; and probably for an intensification of casual and related forms of unemployment. In general these rules, unless carefully circumscribed, make for the diminution of output per worker and income per capita.[41] It is socially desirable, therefore, that present appren-

[37] See Joseph J. Spengler, "Population Trends and the Future Demand for Teachers," *Social Forces,* XIX, 1941, Table III.

[38] Joseph J. Spengler, "Some Effects of Changes in the Age Composition of the Labor Force," *Southern Economic Journal,* VIII, 1941, pp. 166-67.

[39] See Mater, *op. cit.,* pp. 413-18.

[40] *Ibid.,* pp. 176, 196, 201, 402, 408.

[41] On the effects of apprenticeship, seniority, and related rules, see Mater, *op. cit.;* S. H. Slichter, *Union Policies and Industrial Management,* Brookings Institution, Washington, 1941, chaps. 2, 4-5; Frederick H. Harbison, "Seniority in Mass-Production Industries," *Journal of Political Economy,* XLVIII, 1940, pp. 851-64, and Reports No. 17 (*The Seniority Principle in Union-Management Relations,* 1939) and No. 63 (*Seniority Policies and Procedures as Developed Through Collective Bargaining,* 1941) of the Industrial Relations Section of Princeton University.

ticeship, seniority, and related rules be modified when they reduce mobility and access to occupations appreciably; and it is essential that legal or other precautions be taken lest, under the impact of an increasing number of older workers, these rules be changed in a manner detrimental to the general welfare.

Careful consideration of rules such as those respecting seniority implies a distinction between the correct pricing of labor and the provision of enough income to satisfy needs. Improperly conceived seniority rules tend to over-price the labor of older workers and at the same time force their employment; they thus violate the principle of correct pricing and disadvantage younger workers and/or consumers. When the principle of payment of individual workers according to need is introduced, it can be properly introduced only in the form of a family wage system which takes due account of the principle of correct pricing. In any event the principle of needs cannot be used to bolster a set of seniority rules favoring older workers, for the average number of consumption units per male family head falls steadily after he passes the 39th year; at age 60 his need is what it was at age 25.[42]

(2) The economic condition of the older worker is dependent in marked degree upon the fullness of employment. When employment is nearly full, most older workers who are really capable of working can find employment. In 1942–46, for example, when unemployment averaged only 2.9 per cent of the civilian labor force and never exceeded 4.7 per cent, the situation of the older worker improved greatly. The male population 55 and over was supplying 870,000 workers in excess of "normal" in 1945.[43] In 1942–45 the number of recipients of old-age assistance declined 218,000 whereas, given prewar conditions, it would have increased about 150,000.[44] This decrease was attributable in part to the fact that aged workers receiving assistance — something like half of whom were involuntarily unemployed — could find remunerative employment. When, on the contrary, employment becomes less than full, older workers along with other workers lose jobs, and older workers lose them at a higher rate when there is prejudice against older workers. Moreover, having lost their jobs, older workers have more trouble than younger workers recovering them. In a considerable measure, therefore, the real solution of the older worker's employment problem is to be found in the maintenance of approximately full employment.

The existence of full employment makes it much easier for the older workers to adjust to technological changes which displace workers and render acquired skills obsolete. Retraining, adult education, and related programs are essential.[45] But such programs are not adequate in themselves. There must always be present the opportunity for effective demand for such rehabilitated labor to be generated and sustained with ease.

Full employment presupposes among other things that the annual outlay in the form of consumption and investment (a large part of which is independent of the current rate of consumption and therefore autonomous) is sufficient to provide employment for a very large fraction (say 94–95 per cent) of the labor force. As a rule this means, since investment usually is the prime mover, that employment is full only when the rate of investment is adequate. Private investment and, in some measure, public investment tend to be high when creative and innovating entrepreneurs are relatively numerous, and the rate of invention and technological change is high. In some degree younger entrepreneurs probably are more disposed than older entrepreneurs to innovate, invest, and stimulate investment. Innovation is less likely, therefore, when corporations and partnerships include an insufficient number of younger policy makers. This insufficiency is more likely to arise in a population of the age composition of 30–40 years from now than in one of the present age

[42] The number of consumption units per male family head at certain years of age is: 20-21, 1.05; 25-26, 2.06; 30-31, 3.05; 39-40, 3.75; 44-45, 3.42; 50-51, 2.71; 60-61, 2.04. Figures for all years have been computed by Dublin and Lotka, *op. cit.*, p. 175.

[43] H. Wool, "Recent Trends in the Labor Force," *Monthly Labor Review*, LXV, 1947, Table 2, p. 641, also p. 638. The number of workers 65 years of age and over was nearly one-fourth above "normal."

[44] *Monthly Labor Review*, LXII, 1936, p. 388.

[45] Ewan Clague, "Employment Problems of the Older Worker," *Monthly Labor Review*, LXV, 1947, pp. 662-63.

composition; and it will tend to be accentuated if the control of economic affairs, already highly concentrated; is centered in even fewer hands than at present. This insufficiency can be guarded against, however, through the establishment of an appropriate rule of thumb. It might be provided, for example, that of a corporation's board of directors, one-third must be under 45, one-third 45–60, and not over one-third above 60.

It has been said that, because of the changes in age composition in prospect, the ratio of "consuming units" to "producing units" in the population will decrease slightly,[46] and that, consequently, the tendency to unemployment will increase unless the anticipated decline in the propensity to consume is offset by an increase in the propensity to invest. This argument is open to doubt and not borne out by data on the propensity to consume in medium and low income families. Consumption does vary somewhat with age. Yet an increase in the income of medium and low income groups — and this includes the vast majority — tends to be accompanied by a corresponding relative increase in consumption. It is not likely, therefore, that the anticipated small decrease in the ratio of "consuming" to "producing" units will have a significant effect upon the level of employment.

If the analysis presented in this section is valid, it may be concluded that prospective changes in age composition may make somewhat more difficult the maintenance of full employment and proper occupational balance. Yet, since these difficulties are easily surmounted, there is no need to view the change in age composition with apprehension.

VI. Miscellaneous Effects

The prospective changes in age composition will also be accompanied by miscellaneous effects, of which the following are examples. The prolongation of life beyond the retirement age of 65 makes it necessary for the individual to make income provision for a larger number of unproductive years after retirement. In 1945 the expectation of life at age 65 for white males was 12.4 years; it may increase to something like 14.75.[47] Accordingly, should the latter expectation figure replace the former, about 15 per cent more money must be accumulated to buy a given annual annuity income.[48]

A change in age composition affects the structure of the demand for goods and services, for the disposition to use some goods and services varies with age. For example, if changing age composition is the only factor influencing demand between 1940 and 1960, the consumption of goods and services designed primarily for persons under 15 will drop about 2 points while that of goods and services used chiefly by persons over 64 will increase about 2.5 points. These changes in the structure of demand should occasion no difficulties, however. For the age structure changes slowly and in a quite predictable manner, and data can be amassed on the extent to which the consumption of classes of goods and services is affected by the age factor. Moreover, since the number of persons attached to an occupation will usually be reduced at least as rapidly by mortality and retirement as the demand for their services is reduced by secular forces, unemployment attributable to the overcrowding of an occupation by age changes will be rare; and if it does arise, it can be eliminated through the removal of younger mobile workers from the over-crowded to other relatively undermanned occupations.

It is frequently said that the structure of values is undergoing a fundamental modification, with emphasis upon economic change and progress giving way in considerable measure to emphasis upon what is somewhat incorrectly supposed to be economic security and stability.[49] Those mak-

[46] For such an estimate see W. S. Thompson and P. K. Whelpton, *Population Trends in the United States*, New York, 1933, p. 169.

[47] Based on hypothetical life table in Dublin and Lotka, *op. cit.*, p. 130. Expectation of life at age 65 in the 1937 standard annuity male table is 14.4.

[48] A 3 per cent interest rate is assumed.

[49] For example, O. H. Taylor suggests that the present age is groping its way "to some new arrangement of its ruling hierarchy of ultimate, human ends or values, in which . . . economic progress will no longer as decisively outrank security in the sense of a good measure of stability of valued patterns of life, as it did in the nineteenth century." See "Economic Theory and the Age We Live In," *Review of Economic Statistics*, XXIX, 1947, p. 105. See also K. Polanyi, *The Great Transition*, Rinehart & Company, New York, 1944.

ing this observation usually fail to distinguish between insecurity which makes for happiness and progress and insecurity which is wholly or predominantly bad in effect,[50] or to indicate whether there is increased demand for both good and bad security. The change in age composition may accentuate this modification of value structure, but it cannot be said to have been one of its major causes. For the system of values held by a people is determined by many factors of which age composition is merely one, and probably not even an important one.

In Brief

1. In Section I the theoretical basis of the relationship between age composition and collective economic behavior is stated.
2. In Section II it is shown that the relative number of workers in the population is not likely to decline because of prospective changes in age composition.
3. In Section III it is shown that although in many occupations output per worker does tend to fall in the later years of the representative worker's productive life, prospective changes in age composition will not make for a decline in output and income per inhabitant.
4. In Section IV it is shown that although proneness to accident and sickness increases with age, this increase is not highly significant and is offset in part by a diminution in labor turnover.
5. In Section IV it is also shown that discrimination against the older worker may be corrected through the diffusion of correct information respecting his capacities and use, and through the modification of those institutional arrangements which are unwarrantedly disadvantageous to older workers.
6. In Section V it is shown: (a) that the change in age composition need not make more difficult the maintenance of an optimum distribution of workers among occupations; (b) that precautions must be taken lest apprenticeship, seniority, and related rules established under collective bargaining become prejudicial, in any economy in which the relative number of older workers is increasing, to the true interests of younger workers and to the general welfare.
7. In Section V it is also shown that if something like full employment can be maintained, prospective changes in age composition will have little or no adverse effect upon the economic situation of the older worker.
8. In Section VI miscellaneous effects of the prospective change in age composition are considered, and it is shown, among other things, that these effects are not or need not be adverse with respect to the situation of the older worker.
9. Should the current desire at the close of the sixtieth year come to be realized by most workers, the aggregate output of goods and services will be appreciably reduced. Two decades hence the order of magnitude of this reduction will be ten per cent.
10. It is shown in general, in this report, that, while the increase in the relative number of older workers will precipitate certain new problems or aggravate certain old problems, it is easy to cope with this new situation, and its advent is no cause for apprehension.

[50] On this distinction see J. M. Clark, *Social Control of Business,* 2d ed., McGraw-Hill Book Company, New York, 1939, pp. 61-62

The U.S. Labor Force: 1950-1960: "Islands of Obsolete Capacity and Unwanted Skills" *

ROBERT C. COOK • TADD FISHER

The characteristic ability of the labor force to adapt to change — despite initial resistance at times — has been the mainspring of the United States' economic progress. It made possible the remarkably successful shift from an agrarian to an industrial economy, the miracles of mass production, and the highest standard of living in the world.

But the exigencies of World War II hastened the development of certain technological innovations which accelerated change unbelievably. By mid-century the bewildered human race had spent several uneasy years in the atomic age and stood on the threshold of the space age. Only 15 years (1942–1957) separated the advent of these awesome eras which brought more changes, occurring more swiftly and in greater magnitude, than man had ever experienced.

Cold-war pressure heightened the order of change as the U.S.S.R. and the U. S. began vying for leadership in science, technology, and production. Scientists utilized the limitless resources of light, sound, and electricity in novel ways. They sped the development of computers (introduced commercially in 1951) which accomplished in seconds what men could not do in days — and indeed some things they could not do at all.

As the basic human resource of the U.S., the American labor force was on the front lines of the technological revolution. In this advance position many workers were finding that their historic ability to adapt was being strained severely.

During the 1950's, machines of unprecedented accuracy and speed significantly transformed production and work patterns. A cybernated productive system created new industries, revolutionized others, and sent still others into decline. It also began to make obsolete the skills of a growing number of workers in mines, on farms, on assembly lines, and on construction projects. Brawn was losing its value in a nation whose muscle work, for the most part, was being done by machines. A seller's market was opening for workers who could offer exceptional skills and brain power.

TRENDS IN REVIEW:

EMPLOYMENT

Between 1950 and 1960, employment opportunities grew most rapidly for those providing professional, technical, clerical, and personal services. The U. S. and Canada became the only nations in the world having more people engaged in supplying services than in producing goods. In 1956, for the first time in U. S. history, white-collar workers (professional, office, and sales) outnumbered blue-collar workers (semiskilled and unskilled).

The number of employed professional and technical workers increased by 47 percent; more than any other occupational group. But operatives, the largest group of workers, increased by only 6.4 percent. Of the various operative jobs listed in the 1963 *Manpower Report of the President,* more than half lost workers during the decade. Employment for unskilled industrial laborers decreased by 10 percent, and for agricultural workers, by 40 percent. It was significant that, despite the continuation of a long-term reduction in farm workers, mechanization largely made it possible for agricultural productivity to outstrip that of any other sector of the economy.

In general, the economy was characterized by soaring productivity and rising over-all employ-

* Reprinted by permission from *Population Bulletin,* Vol. 20, No. 3 (May 1964), pp. 57-87.

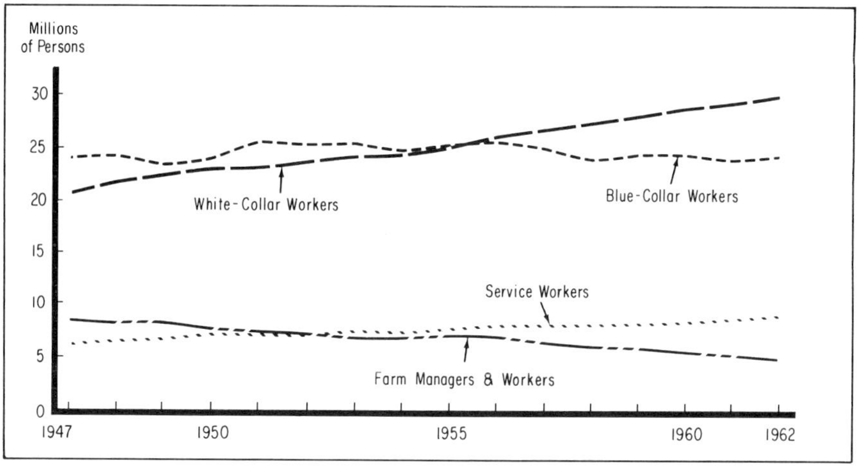

FIGURE 1

Employment by type of occupation, 1947–62.

Technological change largely has been responsible for the steady decline in agricultural employment and for the fact that white-collar workers now exceed blue-collar workers. *Modified from 1963 Manpower Report of the President.*

ment, but seriously declining employment opportunities in many industries. In manufacturing, for instance, total employment was at a peak of 17.6 million workers in 1953. By 1960, 700,000 non-production jobs had been added, but 1.5 million production jobs had disappeared. The result: with a net loss of 800,000 employees, output increased 17 percent — and the plants were using only 75 percent of capacity.

Simultaneously, many industries experienced severe shortages of qualified workers. Part-time employment rose much faster than full-time, and unemployment became a chronic condition — and still is — in the world's richest, most productive nation.

Although it was not always possible to say to what extent changes of this kind were due to technology alone, they kindled a national debate revolving around one ambiguous word — "automation." Attention focused on several troublesome questions:

Were job opportunities being reduced, or were they merely shifting?

Was increasing unemployment due to expanding technology or actually to technological lag?

Why were Japan and several of the Western European nations surpassing the U. S. in their rates of economic growth and technological development, while maintaining much lower rates of unemployment?

It remains as difficult to answer these questions satisfactorily as to define automation or to usefully measure its effects. But putting aside the arguments of pro and con extremists, several realities must be acknowledged. Automation in one form or another has existed for centuries. Increasingly sophisticated technology has been the catalyst for material progress in the U. S. and must continue to be if this country is to retain its position of world leadership and if Americans are to maintain their high standard of living. In the past, constantly expanding technology always has spawned problems which burdened the labor force, and eventually the burden has been lifted so that the benefits of progress could be enjoyed.

But the most disturbing reality is that scarcely any solutions effective in the past are applicable in the present. During the 1950's, the problems were compounded by the phenomenal acceleration and complexity of technological advancement, in combination with equally swift and complex socio-economic and demographic transitions. And the impact of a growing machine culture cannot be considered apart from trends which both affect and are caused by people themselves — although this relationship too often has been ignored.

TRENDS IN REVIEW: SOCIO-ECONOMIC

People were very busy in the 1950's initiating new trends, continuing some that had been growing on the statisticians' charts for some time, and reversing others. Most important, the postwar baby boom had sent the population sky-rocketing to a new high in 10-year growth — 28 million.

The proclivity for family life on the part of most Americans made industry hum to supply their needs. On the other hand, near chaos resulted in many communities when they were forced to accommodate a tidal wave of school-age children. Concerned national leaders began to wonder how to provide future college facilities for this crop of youngsters and how, later, to make room for them in the labor force.

The under-14 age group accounted for more than half the decade increase in population growth. The number of young adults (20–34) declined by 1.7 million, hence there were fewer young people than usual in the labor force. Older workers chalked up the largest increases in the labor force — and a surprisingly large number were women. In fact, women accounted for three-fifths of the total labor force growth during the decade. And between 1940 and 1957, the proportion of working women with small children nearly tripled.

Americans in the 1950's carried on a long tradition of farm to city migration, often contributing to urban unemployment problems and causing dwindling prosperity in rural areas that could not afford to lose population. In 1820, when the employed labor force numbered less than 3 million, 72 percent of its members worked on farms. In exactly 100 years, the reverse had become true. By 1920, there were 42.4 million employed people in the labor force, but 73 percent were engaged in non-agricultural work. In 1960, more than 93 percent of the 64.6 million employed members of the labor force were in non-agricultural work.

The plight of nonwhite workers became more apparent than ever when the battle for civil rights began in earnest following the Supreme Court's school desegregation decree in 1954. Although nonwhites constituted only 11.2 percent of the U. S. population in 1960 and only 10.6 percent of the labor force, their rate of unemployment (8.5 percent) was about twice that of white workers (4.6 percent). This sorry truth was due to widespread discrimination, as well as to the nonwhites' general lack of education and skills — deficiencies which kept most of them in types of employment most often adversely affected by recessions and technological change.

Between 1950 and 1960, the gross national product rose by some $122 billion. But at the decade's end, approximately 22 percent of the nation's productive capacity was lying idle, and the record of the wealthiest country in the world was sullied with the most unfortunate statistic of them all — 7 million families and unattached individuals had personal incomes of less than $2,000.

As unemployment became a persistent economic ill, a search for cures revealed, among other things, a woefully antiquated system for educating and training Americans to make the most of today's employment opportunities. Obviously, not everyone can or wants to attend college. These who do not seek a diploma should have a reasonable expectation of acquiring vocational and technical training pertinent to the times. In the 1950's, the answer to their expectations was often thoroughly unrealistic. For instance, although farm employment fell by nearly 3 million between 1950 and 1960, 28 percent of vocation education funds were still being devoted to training in agriculture.

From our vantage point in 1964, we are better able to recognize a condition prevalent in the 1950's that exacerbated the often unique problems faced by American wage earners: technologically the U. S. was casting the mold of things to come in the 21st Century; socially and economically it often showed signs of not having advanced beyond the horse and buggy days. Today, pressure generated by the consequences of this imbalance is spurring reform measures which, hopefully, will help more workers to find a more rewarding niche in the 20th Century.

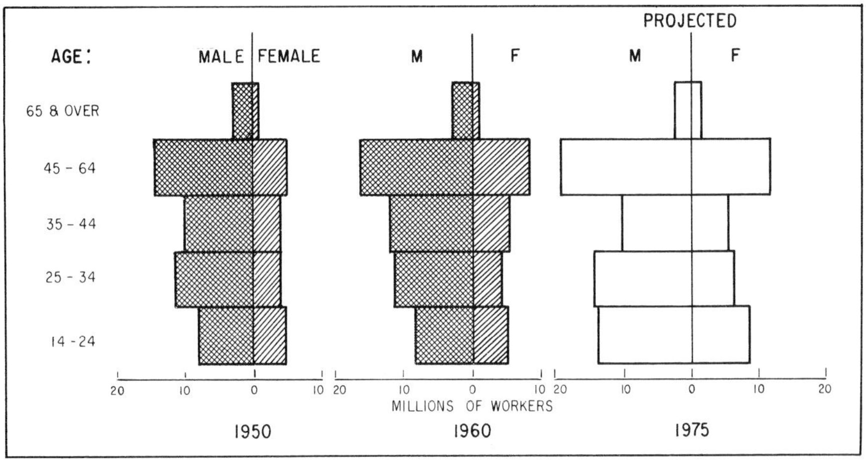

FIGURE 2

Changes in total labor force, 1950–75.

There has been a striking increase in workers, 45–64, particularly among women. By 1975, when the labor force will number 93 million, this group will be even larger and may offer serious competition to the growing number of young workers.[20]

Detailed summaries prepared by the electronic wizards of the Bureau of the Census and the Department of Labor make it possible to study the trends of the past with an eye to the present and future of American manpower. The following is a report on 1950–60 social and demographic trends, in relation to the industrial metamorphosis, which shows their influence on the labor force now and in the future.

The Infants' Influence on the Labor Force

Between 1950 and 1960, the U. S. population increased by 18.7 percent, from 152.3 million to 180.7 million. This addition of 28 million people marked the largest growth in absolute numbers of any single decade in the nation's history.

Portent for the labor force lay in both the size and the unevenness of this growth. Two age groups within the total population — those under 14 and those 65 and over — showed the largest increases, each expanding by more than one-third. People of working age, currently defined as those between 14 and 65, increased only slightly (10 percent) by comparison. Hence, labor force growth, although substantial, did not quite keep pace with total population growth. During the 1950's, the labor force increased by 13 percent, from 65 million to 73 million.

The postwar baby boom, which reached its peak in 1947, had given the U. S. its 1950–60 bumper crop of juveniles. The extended upper end of the age scale showed the influences of steadily declining mortality rates and a period of high birth rates and heavy immigration during the late 19th Century. But low fertility during the depression years caused an actual decline in the number of people between 20 and 35 during the 1950's.

These unequal rates of population growth were reflected in the age composition of the labor force and will be a serious matter to contend with throughout the present decade. Although the median age of the population as a whole fell slightly between 1950 and 1960, reversing a century-long trend, the labor force was growing older.

Of the 8 million more workers in the labor force in the 1950's, nearly two-thirds were 45 or over; less than one-twentieth were between 14 and 25. This was so because of the population "hollow" in the young adult age groups and the rising participation rates of middle-aged women.

During the 1960's, the expected labor force increase of 12.6 million will be one-third larger than in the previous decade. Nearly one-half of this increase will be among inexperienced workers between 14 and 25. Workers 45 and over will account for more than two-fifths of the increase, workers in the prime 25–44 age group for only one-tenth.

It is estimated that a more favorable age balance will not be achieved until 1970–75. At that time, the baby boom youngsters of the 1940's will be men and women in their late 20's and early 30's and will increase the number of workers in that age group. Retirements and declining participation rates (the proportion of the working age population in the labor force), particularly for men, are expected to reduce the number of older workers. In the meantime, during the current decade, a total of some 26 million young workers will be stampeding the labor market seeking their places in the sun. Never before has this country faced such a challenge.

Make Way for the Ladies

If youngsters have been piling up notable statistics in relation to the labor force, the ladies have not been far behind. Following a long-established trend, women continued to seek and to find places for themselves in this "man's world." Nearly three-fifths of the 1950–60 labor force growth occurred among women, although they constituted less than one-third of all workers. Women 45 and over accounted for 58 percent of the growth.

Prior to 1940, the male labor force had grown steadily, always with annual average increases greater than those of the female labor force. Then between 1940 and 1950, so many women entered the wartime labor force that increases for the sexes were almost equal. In the following five years, the rate of increment for women began to grow larger than that for men. These were years during which mobilization of peacetime armed forces had drained many men from the civilian labor force and taken them to overseas posts. At the same time, many women who had planned to work only for the duration of the war, found breadwinning to their liking and decided to remain on the job.

As a result, during the 1950's, the female labor force expanded by 4.8 million, in contrast to the male labor force increase of only 3.5 million.

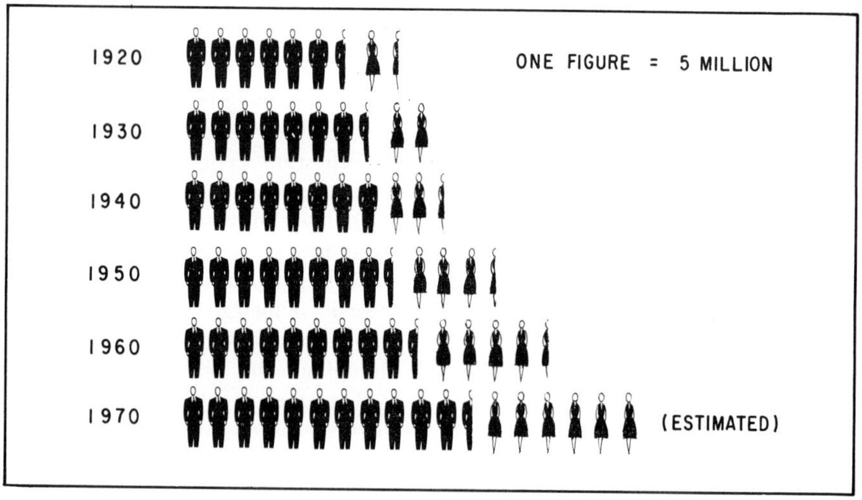

FIGURE 3

Every third worker is now a woman.

In 1920, when the "working girl" was only beginning to gain acceptance, one-fifth of all workers were women. Today women constitute about one-third of the labor force.[22]

Most of the distaff-side expansion was due to a tremendous influx of married women. By 1960, more than half of the female labor force were working wives. One-fifth were widowed or divorced. The number of single women in the labor force actually declined by 220,000.

Aside from the fact that spinsters were vanishing from the American scene, various factors were prompting married women to combine homemaking and paid employment. For one thing, there was need for them in the economy, which, however troublesome at times, was expanding during the 1950's — as was family size and the desire for an ever higher standard of living. This was the decade when critical attention riveted on the "status seekers" of this "affluent society." If adults wanted two cars and split-level, picture-window houses, children wanted — everything, and these juvenile consumers who were not producers had become, as a group multi-billion dollar spenders. With home and community getting to be as competitive as the market place, two pay checks were imperative in many families.

Technological improvements may have been causing dismay on the assembly line, but married women welcomed the household variety of automation which freed them from tasks at home so that they could become wage earners. Abatement of criticism toward married women who work also sped them forward in their dual roles.

On the other hand, sheer economic necessity forced numbers of wives and mothers to go to work — to help put their husbands through college, to augment a husband's inadequate income, to insure education or medical care for children, to support aged dependents, or to provide for children in fatherless homes.

In 1960, there were 23.5 million husband-wife families with children under 18 years of age. In 6.2 million of these families both husband and wife were in the labor force. Some 3 million mothers with children under six were employed outside the home. Large numbers of working wives and mothers sought part-time work in order to spend as much time as possible at home. This was not always a successful arrangement, either for the economy or for many children who needed the full-time attention of their mothers.

While the labor force participation rate for women was rising from 33 percent to 37 percent during the 1950's, that for men was declining from 84 percent to 81 percent. But this decrease had a bright side because it resulted mainly from declining participation of boys in the 14–19 age group (7 percentage points) and men 65 and over (13 percentage points). Evidence showed that more younger men were pursuing their educations for longer periods of time, thus delaying their entry into the labor force until they were better prepared. Older men, who survive in such great numbers today, were able to leave employment earlier because of Social Security and the extension of private retirement plans.

Racial Differences in Employment

Between 1950 and 1960, differences in the labor force status of white and nonwhite people emphasized enduring discriminatory practices in employment and education. Although judiciary and legislative actions pertaining to civil rights did much to advance the cause of racial minorities, long-standing prejudices did not give way easily to such pressures.

In 1960, nonwhites made up about 11.2 percent of the population. The majority, 10.6 percent (19 million), were Negroes.

Historically, Negroes have had consistently higher birth and death rates than whites. However, by 1960, the Negro death rate had been reduced almost to the white level. Consequently, from 1950 to 1960, there was a greater rate of population increase for Negroes (27 percent) than for whites (18 percent).

Throughout the decade, labor force participation rates for white and nonwhite men were very nearly equal, as in 1960 when the rate was 79 percent for nonwhites and 81 percent for whites. On the other hand, the average rate for nonwhite women was generally 10 percentage points higher — or more — than that for white women. In 1960, 46 percent of nonwhite females were in the labor force, but only 36 percent of white females. Differences within the various age groups were even more pronounced.

During the past 22 years, Negroes have managed to raise their occupational levels appreciably faster than whites — understandably, since they started with so much less. But lack of training, combined with the prejudicial attitudes of the white community, continues to force a disproportionate number of Negroes into unskilled work. Because unskilled workers are the most expendable during economic crises or wherever machines displace men, Negro unemployment rates are usually double those of white workers. Nonwhites have also had to resort to part-time work more often than whites and the competition for such work is very great.

Negro males were especially beset with problems in finding employment during the 1950's. Largely under-educated and bereft of saleable skills, they also faced a wall of discrimination erected by labor unions and employers. Frequently, the women of their households had to assume the burden of earning the family's living, totally or in part. It was — and is — easier for nonwhite women to find work in private households and other semiskilled occupations than it is for nonwhite men.

Although Negro citizens constitute a minority, they have major problems in obtaining an education and work and in raising their levels of living. Fortunately, progress is being made, particularly in education. According to the *Manpower Report of the President,* issued in March 1963:

> The persistent differences between white and nonwhite workers in educational attainment have . . . been dramatically reduced in recent years. In the past decade, the proportion of nonwhite workers with at least a high school education nearly doubled, rising from 17 to 32 percent. The corresponding increase for white workers was much less rapid — from 46 to 57 percent. At the same time, the proportion of nonwhite workers who had completed 8 years of school or less fell from 65 to 45 percent.

Education, more than anything else, is needed to establish a sound economic position for Negroes. For one thing, they have been migrating in large numbers to urban areas where their lack of knowledge and skills often has placed them in especially vulnerable positions — or no positions at all! At the turn of the century, approximately 90 percent of them lived in the rural South. In 1960, only 60 percent remained in the South, and more than half of these had abandoned the farms for the towns and cities. About 38 percent were living in urban areas in the North and West.

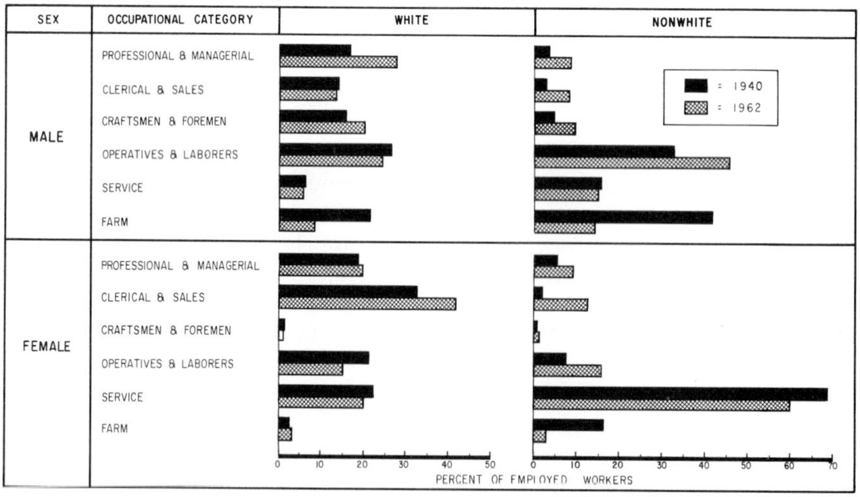

FIGURE 4

Shifting employment opportunities, 1940–1962.

Between 1940 and 1962, both white and nonwhite men gained in occupational status, but particularly the latter. During the same period, nonwhite women continued to be concentrated in service work, mainly in private households, but they also acquired many more clerical and sales jobs.[30]

Continuing Exodus From Farms

This latter-day movement of Negroes to the city became part of a nationwide trend that has been going on for years. Between 1950 and 1960, the shift of total population from farms was substantial, and agricultural workers declined from 7.4 million to 5.3 million.

When the U.S. was a young frontier nation, its agrarian economy rested on the muscle power of men and beasts and on the cooperative endeavors within each family unit. Food, housing, and clothing were provided on a do-it-yourself basis. In 1790, nearly everyone lived "down on the farm" or in villages; less than one person in 10 lives on a farm today.

With the advent of the industrial revolution, machines (and the higher pay which could be earned by operating them) lured men away to the factory and, conversely, began to do more and more of the work on the farm. In 1800, a man had to toil for 373 hours to produce 100 bushels of wheat. In 1950, the same amount was produced by only 28 man-hours. By 1960, the required man-hours had been reduced to 11.

This declining need for agricultural labor has been the cause of heavy farm to city migration, which has eliminated some problems but caused others. It certainly contributed to the growth of the nonfarm economy by supplying workers when and where they were needed to relieve acute labor shortages. Migration also helped many farm people to free themselves from the bondage of exceedingly hard work which brought insufficient financial rewards.

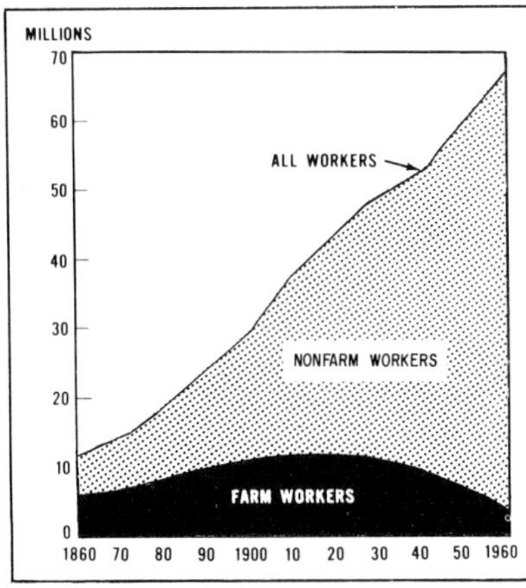

FIGURE 5

Farm and nonfarm workers, 1860–1960.

The employed labor force, which numbered about 10 million in 1860, increased seven-fold by 1960. During the same period, farm workers declined from more than half of all employed workers to less than one-tenth. *1964 Manpower Report of the President.*

But outmigration often has had socio-economic repercussions in rural communities where losses of population seriously affect schools, churches, and businesses. And, in the metropolitan areas they invade, the migrants frequently lack the education and skills necessary for successful assimilation into the urban economy.

The problem in the future is that workers must continue to be siphoned off the farms. Since their educational achievement is so far below that of urban workers, the kind of work available to them or the retraining they could absorb is very limited.

Farming Becomes "Agribusiness"

Those who remain on the farm must arm themselves with complex knowledge that would have bewildered their grandfathers. Farming has become a science which leans heavily on a multitude of other sciences, and, today the farmer's best help is mechanical rather than human. Seeds, a plow, and an almanac no longer suffice.

Helen Henley, farm editor of the *Christian Science Monitor,* recently described the demanding nature of modern farming:

> The modern farm is an efficient, tightly organized business operation which requires considerable capital. Around $50,000 is said to represent the value of the average farm today and this sum does not include equipment or livestock.
>
> The man who runs such a farm . . . must understand cost-price relationships, accounting, unit efficiency, machinery maintenance, conservation, animal husbandry, . . . market demands and marketing methods, consumer preferences — not to mention the application of chemicals to growing crops and the general utilization of new technological processes.

Ideally, then, the farmer must possess the abilities which a corporation president assembles by choosing well-equipped assistants. Only very large farming operations can afford full-time assistants; and such assistants, like the boss himself, must combine several abilities and serve varied functions.

. . . Tomorrow's farmer, it is certain, will have all the odds against him if he has neglected to acquire the basic education necessary for literacy, plus such special training as his chosen type of farming demands.

Discussing the emergence of "agribusiness," Miss Henley pointed out that "40 percent of the nation's 'private' jobs are estimated to be related to agriculture." Thus, she says, farm youths who must seek careers in the nonfarm economy can prepare themselves — *if capable* — for a multitude of jobs in industry which are closely allied to agriculture — genetics, agronomy, chemistry, biology, geology, forestry, veterinary medicine, agricultural engineering, etc.

In short, they must seek advanced education or training which will fit them to offer the type of specialized services in demand today. What happened during the 1950's made this a clear mandate for workers in every field. Employment opportunities grew most rapidly for people providing professional, technical, clerical, and personal services. This trend will continue.

The White Collar Is "In"

Labor Department surveys show that total employment for the 1950–60 decade rose by 14 percent. But the real story of employment growth lay in its component parts. The number of employed white-collar workers and service workers each increased by about 26 percent. Blue-collar workers, on the other hand, nudged up by not quite 6 percent. The number of employed farm workers dropped precipitously by 41 percent. During this same period, the *proportion* of employed persons engaged in white-collar and service occupations rose, but it fell for both blue-collar and farm workers.

And who was doing what within these broad groups of workers? For one thing, a larger proportion (55 percent) of employed women were doing white-collar work than were the men (37 percent). This was also true in the service occupations, where the proportions were 25 and 7 percent. However, 46 percent of the men came under the blue-collar classification, as compared to only 16 percent of the women. Farm work claimed about 10 percent of the men and 5 percent of the women.

These variations are not too surprising considering the types of activity to which men and women are drawn by necessity or choice. Large numbers of women are found in clerical and sales work and many give services such as hairdressing, practical nursing, waiting tables, charring, etc. Blue-collar occupations, however, largely demand either muscular strength or skills which are of particular interest to men.

After age 25, the proportion of women in white-collar occupations in 1960 decreased steadily, but for men it remained at around 40 percent. Proportionately, both men and women in older age groups were found in larger numbers in service and farm work. Men over 25 declined in relative numbers in blue-collar occupations; for women, the proportions increased to age 45, and then began to fall off.

Emphasis on science and technology during the 1950's started employers on a competitive marathon of bidding for the talents of technicians, scientists, mathematicians, engineers, etc. For example, the census revealed that in 1950 there were approximately 12,000 employed electrical and electronic technicians. By 1960, this group, although still small, had expanded to more than 91,000 — an increase of 679 percent!

The ranks of employed mathematicians increased by 345 percent, rising from less than 2,000 to more than 7,000. Phenomenal increases like these helped to boost total employment of professional and technical workers (who constituted only 11 percent of the employed labor force in 1960) up 47 percent — the biggest jump for any of the major occupational classifications.

Figure 6 shows how employment changed in other broad occupational groupings. Excessive gains and losses, similar to those occurring in the professional and technical category, also greatly affected the employment totals for these other groups. Operatives, the largest occupational group, are a good example.

These semiskilled blue-collar workers — truck drivers, machine operators, factory assembly workers, etc. — represented about 19 percent of all employed workers in 1960, but their numbers

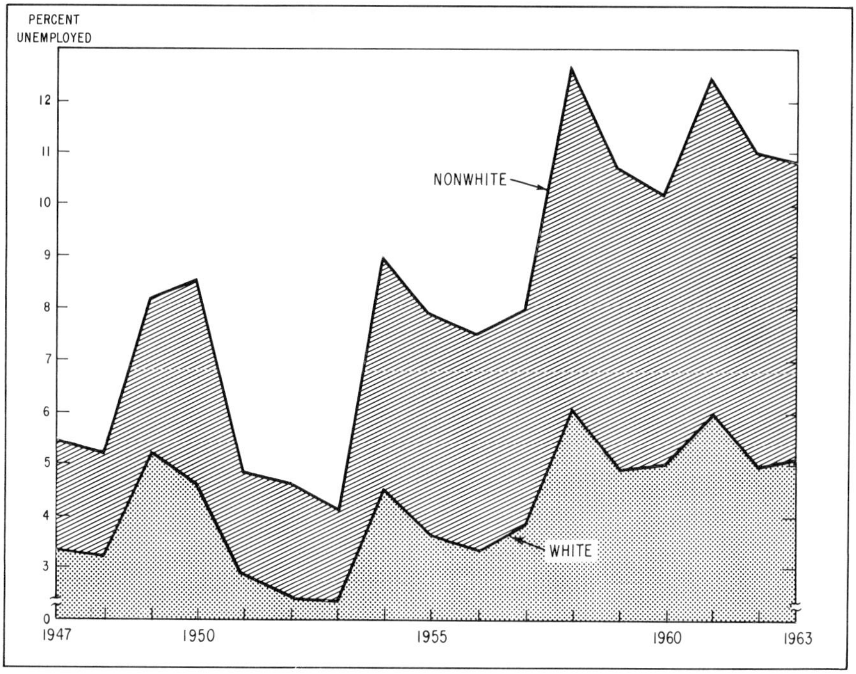

FIGURE 6

Shifting employment patterns, 1950–60.

During the 1950's, employment of professional and technical workers rose 47 percent; that for agricultural workers declined by more than 40 percent. Between these extremes, employment changes in various occupational categories indicated the increasing demand for skilled workers and the dwindling need for the unskilled. *1963 Manpower Report of the President.*

increased by only 6.4 percent. This was because gains made by some operative workers were offset by heavy losses among others. Coal mining operatives, for instance, decreased by about 68 percent. Among printing trade operators, the loss was 26 percent. These losses are symptomatic of changes in industries undergoing varied and revolutionary developments.

One of the best places to seek a job during the entire postwar period was in government, where civilian employment grew more rapidly than in any sector of private industry. Between 1950 and 1960, 2.5 million people were added to Federal state, and local payrolls, bringing the total to 8.5 million.

For further study of 1950–60 employment fluctuations in specific jobs, the reader may find it useful to consult the lengthy table on this subject which appears in the 1963 *Manpower Report of the President.*

Unemployment — "Number One Domestic Concern"

When the plus and minus sides of the employment ledger for the 1950–60 decade were totalled, it was obvious that too many workers were on the minus side. Seasonal fluctuations and current events, as well as technological change, had kept the over-all rate of unemployment rising and falling.

In 1950, 3.1 million people were unemployed — 5 percent of the labor force. As the Korean "police action" grew into full-scale war, the number of unemployed dropped steadily, reaching 1.6 million in 1953, its lowest point for the

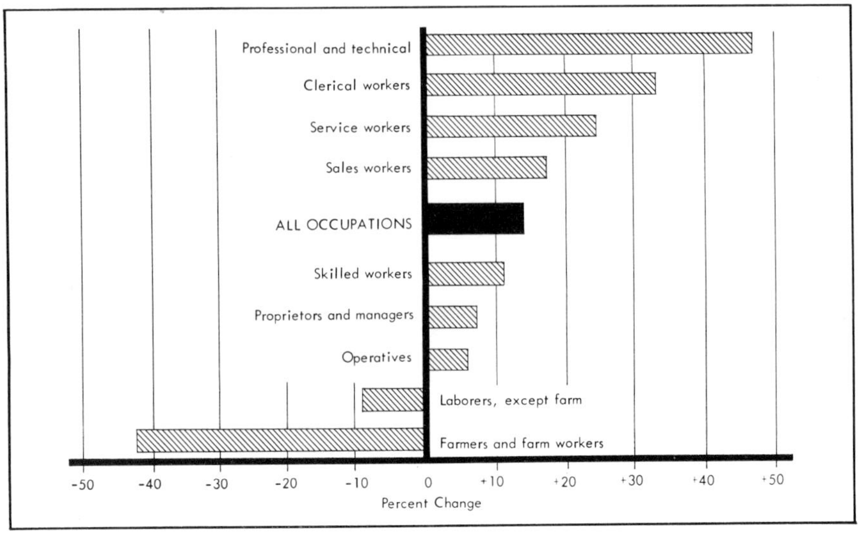

FIGURE 7

Unemployment rates for white and nonwhite workers, 1947–63.

Nonwhite workers, who are found largely in unskilled or semiskilled occupations, are usually the first to suffer job loss during economic setbacks. In general, their rates of unemployment are about double those for white workers. *1964 Manpower Report of the President.*

decade. The high point came during a period of recession in 1958 when 4.7 million workers, or 6.8 percent of the labor force, were unemployed.

In 1960, the unemployment rate, 5.6 percent, remained disturbingly high. A comparison of eight highly industrialized nations [1] made by the Department of Labor revealed that only Canada had a higher unemployment rate than the U. S. Chronic unemployment continues to plague this country despite a tremendous productive capacity and an ever-increasing supply of consumers. The late President John F. Kennedy, recognizing the threats implicit in automation, galloping population growth, lagging economic growth, and the dwindling need for unskilled labor, named unemployment "the number one domestic concern."

The variety, dimensions, and pace of change were particularly devastating to the employment outlook of younger and older workers, the uneducated, and those who were disadvantaged or discriminated against.

[1] Federal Republic of Germany, Japan, Sweden, France, Great Britain, Italy, U.S.A., and Canada.

In 1958, when the national rate of unemployment was nearly 7 percent, the rate for 18- and 19-year-old males was close to 18 percent; for females in the same age group, it was 12.9 percent. Men and women between 20 and 25 had rates of 12.7 and 8.9 percent, respectively. Older male workers suffered not so much from a high rate of unemployment as from difficulties in finding work once they had lost it due to rapid industrial change.

The High Cost of Discrimination

The status of nonwhite workers emerges most clearly in unemployment statistics. Always, and in every age group, they have been handicapped by more and longer unemployment than white workers. Nonwhite teenagers, both male and female, suffer from joblessness more than any other segment of the population. According to the 1964 *Manpower Report:*

The social implications of Negro unemployment can be fully appreciated only in the context of its concentration in large urban centers, and specifically in the Negro areas of those cities to which Negro workers from the South have flocked in the hope of improving their economic status. For example, 41 percent of Negro men in one census tract in Detroit, wholly populated by Negroes, were jobless in 1960; in certain census tracts in Chicago, Los Angeles, and Baltimore — where 90 percent or more of the inhabitants were Negro — the rates ranged from 24 percent to 36 percent. If youth unemployment is as much above the over-all average in these neighborhoods as in the Nation generally, the situation is indeed charged with social dynamite.

Two years ago, the Council of Economic Advisors sought to determine the economic loss resulting from racial discrimination in U.S. employment. Commenting on this in his book, *Rich Man, Poor Man,* Herman P. Miller, of the Bureau of the Census, said:

This study showed that if the education and training of the Negro population were fully utilized by the elimination of racial barriers in employment, our national product might rise by as much as 2½ percent each year. In 1961, this would have increased our income as a nation by $13 billion. These wasted skills amounted to one-fourth of the total that was spent for national defense in that year. The monetary loss in national income is, of course, only a small part of the total social burden of discrimination. When the costs of higher crime rates, poor health, urban decay, and many other problems that stem directly or indirectly from discrimination are added, the amount becomes astronomical.

THE BECLOUDED GNP

During the postwar years, the gross national product (i.e the total value of final goods and services produced during a given year) grew impressively from $282.3 billion in 1947 to $439.9 billion in 1960 (constant dollars). But this growth had many ramifications which must be considered in order to bring it into realistic perspective.

It varied widely and was more rapid during the early postwar years than in the late 1950's. The average annual growth rate of the GNP between

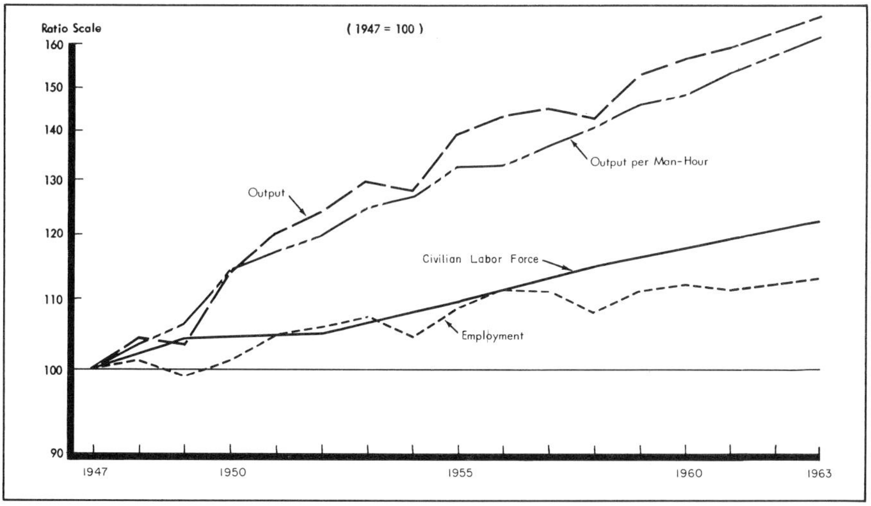

FIGURE 8

Parade of the indices.

Taking 1947 as the base, output (the total production of the U.S. economy) and output per man-hour have increased by about one-half. The labor force has grown by one-fifth, but employment by only one-tenth. The widening gap between these indices symbolizes the U.S. manpower and employment predicament. *Modified from 1964 Manpower Report of the President.*

1947 and 1957 was nearly 4 percent. Between 1957 and 1962, it slowed down to only 2.9 percent. There was an accompanying drop in job growth in the nonfarm private economy, from 700,000 more jobs a year between 1947 and 1957 to only 175,000 between 1957 and 1962.

The 1963 *Manpower Report of the President* states:

> Aided by the rise in output per man-hour [productivity], the country achieved an impressive gain in output (as measured by gross private product in constant dollars) amounting to about three-fifths (59 percent) between 1947 and 1961. Over the same 14-year period, employment rose only 11 percent. And man-hours rose even less — by a little more than 3 percent — because of the drop in average annual hours of work per employee which was a concurrent development. Thus, well over four-fifths of the increase in aggregate output from 1947 onward can be explained by increases in output per man-hour, leaving only a small fraction of the rise attributable to man-hours worked.

Agricultural productivity is a striking example. Rising by 135 percent between 1947 and 1961, it outstripped any other sector of the economy — although agriculture had lost nearly two-fifths of its workers.

In regard to heavy industry, the AFL-CIO has pointed out that:

> For motor vehicles, in 1960 the industry produced over one-half million more passenger cars and about the same number of trucks and buses as in 1953. But this was accomplished by 172,000 fewer production workers. And, despite the increased output, the industry, according to McGraw-Hill, was working at only 80 percent of its 1960 potential.

Under-utilization of manpower characterized the late 1950's and is a problem that has spilled over into the 1960's. Today, it is being accentuated by the more rapid rate of labor force growth resulting from the postwar babies coming of working age.

Part-time employment increased markedly during the 1950's, both that which is voluntary (persons not desiring full-time work) and that which is involuntary (reduction from work for economic reasons).

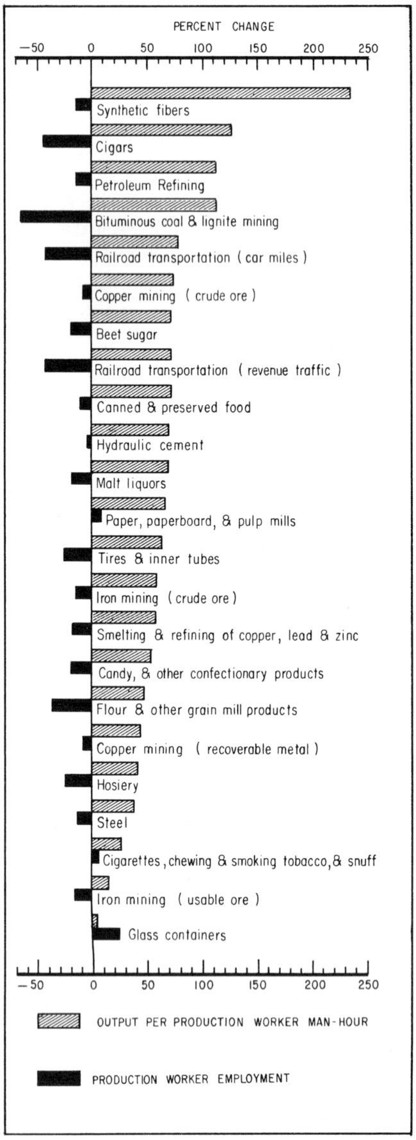

FIGURE 9

Increasing production-declining employment.

In 23 industries showing increasing production between 1947–1960, 20 showed an actual decline in employment; only 3 showed slight increases in employment. *Modified from 1963 Manpower Report of the President.*

Employment for all part-time workers rose by 62 percent between 1949 and 1962, from not quite 7 million to over 11 million. In 1962, 20 percent (2.3 million) of these workers were on part-time for economic reasons. Full-time employment increased by only 20 percent during the same period.

Why this growth in part-time work?

The economy needed workers in many areas, and the most available were married women who had to divide their time between the office and the family hearth. It also suggested that employers were more willing to be flexible in their scheduling, thus giving more work to more people.

But the Department of Labor warns that "the part-time employment increase reflected in higher figures of [total] employment may be giving an impression of greater utilization of our manpower resources than is actually warranted." Since 1957, full-time employment has shown relatively little growth, *except in government.* At the same time, the U.S. has been suffering from serious manpower shortages in essential occupations, but the gap can only be filled by well-educated, highly trained people — of whom there is a dearth for industry's needs.

These are some of the inescapable facts behind the currently much-discussed need for a speed-up in economic growth. The recent past has left us today with a tangled mass of economic troubles. The population, the labor force, and productivity are increasing, but *production,* while considerable, has not increased enough since 1957 to keep job opportunities growing as fast as the number of job seekers. And since demand does not equal actual output, let alone the hoped for potential that would result if unemployment dropped to the "desired" (interim) 4 percent level, excessive unemployment continues.

The theory is that if we produce more, we can employ more workers, and that if we tempt people to consume what is being produced, all will be well. There are those — concerned about the impact of cybernation — who do not agree. Their viewpoint is discussed later in this *Bulletin.*

Lessons To Be Learned From Abroad

Strangely enough, American economists are studying the records of other nations — who once looked to the U.S. for guidance — to discover how they are managing so well when we are not. The following rather defensive passage appeared in the 1964 *Economic Report of the President:*

> Our own recent economic history assures us of the economy's ability to adapt to rapid change. Additional assurance . . . is found in the experience of other countries whose systems and values are similar to our own. During the past decade, the Western European economy has undergone staggering structural changes. France and Belgium have adjusted to the decline of important mining areas, Germany to the inflow of millions of refugees from the East, and Italy to the problem of absorbing migrants into urban occupations. And all of Western Europe has adjusted to the replacement of obsolete capital, and of productive methods often unchanged for a century or more with machinery and methods geared to the most advanced technology in the world. The advance of productivity has been revolutionary. During the 1950's, output per manufacturing worker increased 2¼ times as fast in Germany as in the United States, 3 times as fast in France, and 4 times as fast in Italy. In their adjustment to these changes the Europeans, though they may have other advantages, did not have the advantage of a labor force nearly as well-educated, as well trained, as mobile, or as flexible as ours.

The report goes on to state that Europeans, nonetheless, had considerably lower rates of unemployment than ours in 1960 — 1.0 percent in Germany, 1.9 percent in France, and 4.3 percent in Italy. (The latter has since been reduced.)

The given explanation:

> The major explanation for such low employment rates in economies undergoing such profound transitions lies in the maintenance of a very high level of demand. During the 1950's the average annual growth rate in France was 4 percent, in Italy, 6 percent, and in Germany, over 7 percent — and both Italy and France have had even higher rates so far in the 1960's. This experience demonstrates beyond any doubt that, under the stimulus of adequate demand, and with the aid of active labor market policies, modern economics are sufficiently resilient to absorb poorly educated workers, to adapt to skill shortages, and to adjust to rapid technological change in a manner which maintains extremely low unemployment rates. This European experience — which in broad outline has been matched in Japan — reassures us that, once high

and growing demand presses our capacity, we too will adapt to rapid change and maintain our economic health.

The trouble is that economic health does not equal social welfare. In 1962, President Kennedy had discussed the "growing pains" of economic progress. He had acknowledged the need for an adequate level of demand as a *precondition* to alleviating the pains. He referred to "the creation of islands of obsolete capacity and unwanted skills" as the most pressing social problem resulting from technological change.

In his 1963 *Manpower Report,* the late President stressed the importance of education as a fundamental to the solution of labor force and economic growth problems:

> Manpower policy looks not only to the short run, but to the future in terms of generations. The lead time for the production of many professional skills must be thought of in terms of a decade or more. Things we do or fail to do this year will, for example, significantly affect — in some ways irrevocably — the supply of physicians in the 1980's.
>
> . . . it has been calculated by one authority that for the period 1929 to 1957 the improved education of the work force accounted for more than one-fifth of the increase in real national product. This was a larger share than that provided for by the increase in capital investment. Education combined with the advance of knowledge accounted altogether for about two-fifths of national growth during this period.

EDUCATION = $$

Real incomes are higher in the U.S. than anywhere in the world, but Herman Miller has pointed out that "a myth has been created . . . that incomes are gradually becoming more evenly distributed." Statistics show, Dr. Miller said, that "the share of income received by lower income groups has not changed for twenty years." The gap in incomes between whites and nonwhites actually began to widen in 1957.

In 1960, the median income for white families was $5,835; for nonwhite families it was only $3,233. Although income for the latter had increased by more than $1,000 since 1947, nearly one-third of nonwhite families had incomes of less than $2,000 in 1960, as opposed to only one-tenth of white families. Thirty-seven percent of the white families had incomes of $7,000 or more, and only 14 percent of the nonwhite families.

The 1960 Census showed that nearly 10 million families had incomes of less than $3,000. It is not a simple task to define who is poor and who is not, but the recent emphasis on eliminating "pockets of poverty" indicates that the government is making the attempt — and finding that, by any definition, too many Americans are poor.

It has been well-documented that education is closely related to a person's employment status and income. Well-educated workers generally tend to have lower rates of unemployment (Figure 10) and higher incomes. But in some cases this is not always so. Between 1958 and 1961, education had less effect upon rising income for women than for men, and less for white women than for nonwhite women.

The results of a 1959 Labor Department study showed that half of the labor force had at least a high school education. Twenty years ago, the same proportion had completed little more than the first year of high school. Only 6 percent had completed college in 1940; in 1959, 10 percent had completed college. The proportion of men completing college has been greater than that of women, probably due to rising incomes and to the large number of veterans who took advantage of the GI Bill.

Nonwhite workers between 25 and 30, who have completed high school and who have had one year of college or more, tripled in number since 1940. As with white workers, more men, proportionately, receive a college education than women.

Nonetheless, educational attainment for nonwhites is far below that of whites. The 1960 Census revealed that nearly 5 percent of the nonwhites suffered the handicap of having no schooling at all, compared with less than 2 percent of the whites. The proportion of whites who had completed high school was nearly twice as great as that of the nonwhites and more than twice as great for those who had completed college.

Perhaps this is partly because of a social sys-

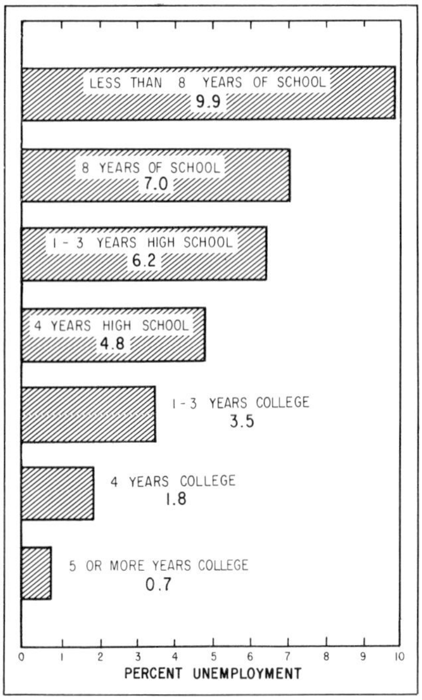

FIGURE 10

The relationship of education to unemployment.

In the civilian labor force, the highest unemployment rates are found among workers with the least education. Advancing technology is spurring the demand for well-educated, highly trained workers. *Modified from Vocational Education and Federal Policy.*

tem which gives rewards for educational attainment on the basis of the color of one's skin. Dr. Miller has observed:

> . . . nonwhites (largely Negroes) who have completed four years of college, *can expect to earn only as much in a lifetime as whites who have not gone beyond the eighth grade.* And this applies not only to the South, but to the North as well. No wonder nonwhites show so little enthusiasm for schooling. Indeed, it is surprising that so many have continued with their education until the average nonwhite man in his twenties is now only about one and a half years behind the white in years of schooling.

As the demand for unskilled laborers decreased during the 1950's, the trend for lower-income workers to make the largest gains in income reversed itself. Professional and skilled workers took the lead in income gains.

As we embark on an era in which there very well might be a demand for more "chiefs" than "Indians," the educational requirements for workers will mount. Complex equipment and industrial methods call for the custodianship of workers who are able to comprehend them.

It is imperative for young people to prepare now for their place in the world of work of tomorrow. And it is equally imperative for educators to assess and to improve the quality of an educational system marred by the sorry statistics concerning dropouts. The scope of the problem is apparent when one realizes that of the 700,000 youths who were no longer in school in 1962, half had less than a high school education.

U.S. workers, as a group, may be better educated than those in other countries, but are enough of them educated sufficiently to insure their own and the nation's security? The 1962 *Economic Report of the President* reported:

> Of each 1,000 pupils who entered the fifth grade in 1952, 900 entered high school in 1956, 600 graduated from high school in 1960, and 300 entered college in the fall of 1960. Thus 40 percent of the original 1,000 students did not graduate from high school and half of those graduating from high school did not enter college.

Workers on the Move

Next to education, perhaps the best asset a worker can have is willingness to move to a new location when, by doing so, he can improve his employment status. Americans have always been known for their astonishing mobility. According to the Bureau of the Census, of the 159 million Americans five years old and over in 1960, 75 million (about 10 percent annually) had changed residence since 1955. Of these, more than 14 million had moved to a different state. Another 14 million were residing in a different county of the same state.

In general, population shifts have been toward areas of the country which are experiencing an economic boom. Between 1950 and 1960,

Florida and the Western states attracted more "movers" than any other sections of the country. They also had rapid growth in industry and recreational facilities. Florida, New Jersey, Colorado, and Delaware all had a net gain from migration double that of the previous decade.

Decreasing industrial production characterized many of the states losing more population than they gained. New England and the North Central region had particularly severe losses. So did the South, where outmigration of non-white residents has persisted for several decades. The South also lost more white residents than it gained.

Pennsylvania, which is pocked by depressed areas resulting from the decline in the coal mining industry, had the largest outflow — 475,000 more people left the state than entered it in the 1950's. West Virginia's net loss was almost double that of the 1940's. Here, too, coal mining was a factor.

During the 1950's employment growth rates were highest in the Mountain, Pacific, and South Atlantic regions, and lowest in the Northeast and Central regions. In five of the Central states which depend mainly upon farming, the number of employed workers actually decreased. Except for these states, only West Virginia and the District of Columbia had fewer workers in 1960 than in 1950.

While Americans as a whole are inclined to move in search of greener pastures, there remain many who are reluctant or unable to be so adventurous. Regrettably, the inert ones often reside in depressed areas (comprising almost one-half of the nation's land area) where a livelihood is hard to come by. Nonetheless, they either cannot or will not move to more prosperous regions. Thus they help to promote the high rate of U.S. unemployment.

Some workers — coal miners, for instance — often have worked at the same job, requiring specialized skills, all of their lives. If their industry declines, relocates, or introduces technology which makes their skills obsolete, they may lack the money, motivation, or ability to learn new skills and to seek other employment in an unfamiliar place. This problem is particularly acute for older workers.

During the 1950's, the young moved more frequently than the old, and they also changed jobs more often as a consequence of inexperience and the desire to find work that satisfied them economically and personally. More men, especially those between 20 and 25, changed jobs than women.

If the labor force has been mobile in the past, its members are being urged to be even more so and to become ever more flexible in adapting to new circumstances. About the only thing they can be sure of is that there will be a swift round of new circumstances. The changing tides in the affairs of men have gathered too much momentum to be halted, unless by the possible nuclear holocaust which haunts all our lives. Old answers simply do not fit the new questions confronting the labor force.

What of the Future?

Continued Change

Undeniably, it is time for us to put as much thought into how to *adjust* to change as to how to *create* change in the first place. Bernard Muller-Thym, Visiting Professor of Industrial Management, Massachusetts Institute of Technology, discussing our transformed society, said that man is experiencing "an order of change which is completely different from anything which our ancestors knew, unless we go back 10,000 years, when they invented property, when they invented ownership, when they invented work, and mechanics based on the wheel, and bureaucracy."

He indicted our lagging comprehension of the new family of machines and of their inevitable effect on our lives — an effect for the better, *if we employ the necessary vision:*

> We do not have any concept of how to adjust. Fringe benefits, unemployment insurance, shorter hours, are just stop-gap measures. Retraining of workers — a farce. Of course, there will be training and education, but they will be of a different kind. We will not have to spend as much time at education because the knowledge will not be organized according to the subject matter, and we will not proceed linearly from one course to another. Then we can learn much more rapidly.

Fortunately, some of our political and industrial leaders are beginning to recognize the implications of cybernation for what they are, and to discuss them more constructively and less emotionally. Consequently, they also are absorbing the chief lesson imbedded in the experiences of the 1950's: willingness to work did not and will not suffice; one must be *capable* in the 20th-Century meaning of the word. This demand imposes equal responsibility on workers, employers, and labor and political leaders to accomplish the greatest change of all — the transformation of their own attitudes.

More People

The population is expected to increase to 194 million by 1965, 210 million by 1970, and 226 million by 1975. The increase of some 30 million in the present decade will not greatly exceed that of the 1950's, but growth in specific age groups will differ. The 25–44 age group — containing many of the nation's most vigorous and proficient workers — will grow hardly at all, and will represent only 23 percent of the total population in 1970, compared to 26 percent in 1960. Those under 14 and those 45 to 65 will continue to form about the same proportion of the population (30 percent and 20 percent, respectively), although their total numbers will grow by about 7.3 million for the under-14 group and 5.6 million for the 45-64 group.

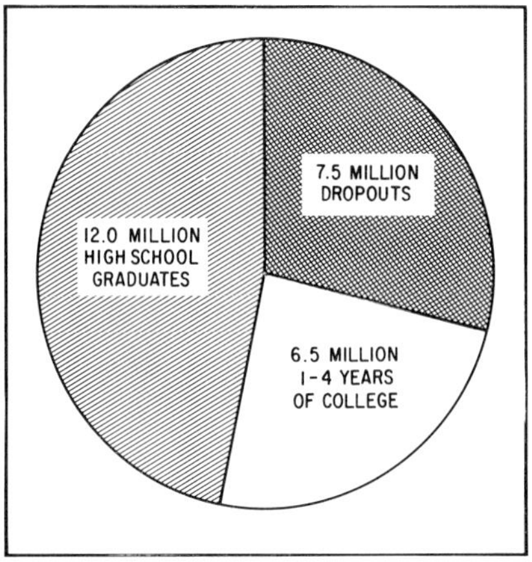

FIGURE 11

Education of new young workers in the 1960's.

Some 26 million young people will enter the labor force during the 1960's. About one-quarter will have had from one to four years of college. Nearly one-half will have graduated from high school, and about one-third will fall into the handicapped dropout category. *1964 Manpower Report of the President.*

More Workers

Between 1960-75, the labor force will experience unparalleled growth, rising by 20 million to a total of 93 million. One can scarcely quarrel with this projection because it is based on statistics concerning people who have already been born.

An addition of 6 million young workers between 14 and 25 is expected in the present decade, as compared to less than one-half million in the 1950's. Never before has the country faced the prospect of educating, training, and giving employment to so many youths.

The need for farmers, farm laborers, and the unskilled will continue to decrease. The demand for professional workers, technicians, and certain highly skilled laborers will continue to expand. Only an educated labor force can meet this demand; and only the educated and adequately trained will readily find employment.

Need to Reform Educational Practices

At present, our educational system is not keeping pace with changing employment patterns. There is an insufficient number of qualified teachers for institutions of higher learning and, in many areas, high school students continue to drop out at an alarming degree.

Probably 70 percent of the 26 million new young workers will have at least a high school diploma, but 30 percent (7.5 million) will not. Particularly in urban areas, this ill-prepared minority threatens communities with staggering sociological problems. The pity is that a large proportion of dropouts have an average or higher I.Q. and are constitutionally qualified to participate in the economy.

College enrollments may increase by as much as 3.4 million by 1970, to a total of 7 million. But scores of young men and women will have neither the funds nor the ability to pursue a college education. Some, but not enough, will profit from recent attempts to expand and improve vocational education opportunities. Others, lacking the necessary native endowment, will find there is no room for them in this culture-in-transition, with its growing disorder and complexities. *Harper's* editor, John Fischer, in a brave editorial tussle with the "stupidity problem," remarked:

> . . . the chief characteristic of The Over-developed Society (if that is the right label) will be a permanent surplus of some kinds of workers, together with a permanent shortage of others. For the assortment of jobs which need to be done is simply out of kilter with the natural distribution of brains.

He suggests that

> . . . we'll have to face up to the fact that all men are *not* created equal, except in the limited political sense which Jefferson had in mind when he drafted the Declaration of Independence. Until we do that, it will be impossible for our public officials to find useful work for the 20-plus percent of the population with below-normal intelligence, or to train them for jobs they are capable of handling. And it will remain almost equally hard to make the best use of our limited supply of high IQs.

Growth and Unemployment

The year 1963 pleasantly upset predictions by producing record rises in output and employment. But unemployment remained the country's chief social and economic problem; for the sixth consecutive year, it averaged over 5.5 percent. Thirteen percent of U.S. factory capacity was idle.

President Johnson, in his January 1964 economic message to Congress stated, "We need about two million new jobs each year to offset the labor-saving effects of rising output per worker." He proposed the establishment of a high-level commission "to determine how we can best gain the benefits of automation while minimizing its human costs."

Americans are earning and spending more than ever. Yet, despite a GNP of $600 billion at the end of 1963, the President noted that "men, machines, and materials that lie idle today could readily add about $30 billion" to the GNP.

Sore Spots and Federal Poultices

So far in the 1960's, a start — of sorts — has been made to eradicate forms of social stagnation that close off too many Americans from contributing to and benefiting from dramatic technological change. Private and governmental agencies alike are probing the nation's sore spots. Studies of every variety are disclosing areas of need.

For instance, the country was shocked to learn that one-half of the draftees called for duty by Selective Service in 1962 were unfit either mentally or physically. The Department of Defense estimates that approximately one-third of *all* young men, including volunteers and draftees, would be rejected, if examined.

These alarming facts were presented in a recent report, *One-Third of a Nation,* prepared at the request of President Kennedy by a Cabinet-level task force. Probably no single document of its kind has more clearly delineated festering social and economic conditions which, if allowed to continue, would negate many of the hoped for benefits of technology.

These young men represent a cross-section of the nation. Incapable of serving in the armed forces, they are not likely to find employers hospitable to them either. When 2,500 of the mental rejectees were interviewed in 1963, the results took the form of an illuminating socio-economic profile.

Three out of four of the mental rejectees had grown up in urban areas. Almost half had come from families with six or more children, and poverty was characteristic. About one-fifth of their fathers — and fathers-in-law with whom they were living — were not working. One-fourth of their parents who were employed held unskilled jobs. Half of the rejectees' fathers had never completed grade school.

The average mental rejectee had gone only part way through high school; 80 percent were school dropouts and 9 percent had court records. Their unemployment rate was 28 percent. Of those who were employed, 75 percent worked in unskilled, semiskilled, and service jobs. They averaged $56 a week in earnings.

The tragedy is that these youths did not choose arbitrarily to fall into such a dreary way of life. In many cases, they were ensnared by inherited poverty and its quicksands of despair. After being examined, four out of five of them expressed willingness to accept help in acquiring basic education or training. On July 1, 1964, the government will initiate a program by which it hopes to salvage some of these young men.

This is one of too few signs that the U.S. Government, which spent some $40 billion on scientific-industrial reasearch and development during the 1950's, is beginning to realize the need to open its purse to perfect the performance of men as well as missiles.

The Federal State Employment Service has been directed to become more active in placement activities. Since 1961, it has increased nonfarm job placements by almost 25 percent. The vocational retraining program of the Department of Labor and the Area Redevelopment Administration has helped numbers of displaced workers, particularly those in depressed areas. In 1964, about 148,000 workers will receive training or retraining in diverse skills; next year this program will aid 288,000 workers.

In 1962, Congress passed the Manpower Development and Training Act, designed to provide funds for vocational training for jobs that are known to exist. As first conceived, it would have served only about 400,000 people and it held no provisions for many who most needed such assistance. Last year, it was broadened to include future training for 85,000 unemployed youths and for 60,000 persons lacking basic literacy.

The 1963 Vocational Education Act — long overdue — will broaden and redirect existing programs, placing new emphasis on training for business and office occupations. It also provides for residential vocational schools.

The proposed Youth Employment Act would offer work opportunities in conservation camps and local communities to 60,000 young people this year and to more than 100,000 in 1965.

The President's Committee on Equal Employment Opportunities has made progress in reducing discriminatory hiring practices, and an amendment to the Manpower Act authorizes experiments to aid mobility of unemployed workers. A "war on poverty" is being waged to liberate some 35 million Americans from substandard living levels.

These are only a few of the remedial measures that have been instituted. Many others are being proposed, discussed, and considered. Unfortunately, none is adequate to the enormous task of reconciling the needs of American manpower with the demands of technological progress.

Machines or Men?

The U.S. manpower situation is paradoxical in the extreme. Despite steady growth in the GNP — the traditional barometer by which the U.S. economic climate is measured — there remain "pockets of poverty" large enough to inspire an all-out drive to eradicate them. With unprecedented productivity, employment *and* unemployment are high. A declining unemployment rate rests on a great many "if's."

In 1963, the Subcommittee on Employment and Manpower, with Senator Joseph Clark of Pennsylvania as chairman, conducted extensive hearings on the "nation's manpower revolution." A review of the report on the hearings does not disclose a clear pattern for legislation which might resolve some of the prevailing perplexities. Senator Clark said that he wondered if "change, not only in the field of cybernation, but in terms of population growth, perhaps in a good many other areas of human life, has not suddenly begun to shift into an almost geometric progresssion of speed and we are just not prepared to cope with it all." He found the implications of cybernation "enough to frighten us to death." [2]

In essence, the conventional policy regarding manpower is based on the Biblical aphorism "Seek and ye shall find." The assumption is that anyone who really desires a job will be able to find work that will provide him with the wherewithal to live — even to make down payments on a variety of modern "necessities," such as automobiles, dish washers, TV sets, etc. Historically, this "seek ye" formula goes back to the philosophy of an unmanipulated laissez-faire economy. Actually, it is sustained today under an economy which, in most varied ways, is "managed."

The policy makers argue that if GNP growth keeps up with, or leaps ahead of, population and labor force growth — and if demand can be made to equal supply, economic security can be guaranteed.

But there is a growing school of thought which contends that conventional policy approaches absurdity in this time of rapid change in production techniques. Those who advance this point

[2] The final report and recommendations of this Subcommittee were published in April 1964. The Subcommittee found that "the scientific and technological revolution has shaken our social and cultural foundations to the roots." Its perplexity is perhaps reflected in the number and variety of its recommendations.

of view maintain that the problem no longer is one of balancing production and demand but of how to distribute more equitably the abundance we already have.

They represent only a small sector of economic thought. Speaking for them, Robert Theobald, economic consultant and author, maintains that "machines will take over most of the repetitive mental and physical tasks within the foreseeable future." Commenting on the current situation, he noted:

It is already clear . . . that the rate of productivity increase has risen with the onset of cybernation, that an industrial system postulated on scarcity has been unable to distribute the abundant goods and services available from a cybernated productive system, that surplus capacity and unemployment have therefore continued at excessive levels over the last six years, that the underlying cause of excessive unemployment is the fact that the skill levels of machines are rising more rapidly than the educational achievements of human beings and that as a consequence of all these trends a permanent poverty-stricken class is emerging in the midst of potential abundance.

Men of his persuasion believe that the Federal programs mentioned previously are mere palliatives because they are based on an unrealistic appraisal of present and future needs; that they offer limited training to a limited number of people for types of work that are vanishing. They further believe that white- and blue-collar workers alike are vulnerable to the machine take-over.

These convictions were presented to the President in March 1964 in a memorandum prepared by the Ad Hoc Committee on the Triple Revolution. The 26 signers included economists, labor leaders, historians, and publishers who warned that we are enmeshed in three closely related revolutions — cybernation, weaponry, and human rights. The Committee made one of the most controversial proposals of the day:

Wealth produced by machines rather than men is still wealth. We urge, therefore, that society, through its appropriate legal and governmental institutions, undertake an unqualified commitment to provide every individual and every family with an adequate income as a matter of right.

In another portion of the memorandum the Committee declared:

With public policy and research concentrated on people rather than processes we believe that many creative activities and interests commonly thought of as non-economic will absorb the time and the commitment of many of those no longer needed to produce goods and services. Society as a whole must encourage new modes of constructive, rewarding and ennobling activity. Principal among these are activities such as teaching and learning that relate people to people rather than people to things.

The weight of tradition and authority is certainly on the side of those who maintain that the present maldistribution of U.S. abundance is no more than a cyclical phase in a steadily upward trend. Secretary of Labor W. Willard Wirtz, for one, promptly denounced the memorandum. But the Committee has provocatively shocked us into considering whether the cybernation revolution and our current economic policies are compatible.

Limitations of both space and wisdom prevent an appraisal of the two sides of the great debate which is opening. However, it is interesting to note that Secretary Wirtz has conceded that "machines now have, in general, a high school education," and that they are "in the most real sense, responsible for putting uneducated people out of work."

Something momentous is happening. The implications for further social, economic, and political change are tremendous.

With the air thick with economic principles and abstractions such as the GNP, there is danger that *the* essential element in the discussion will be lost sight of, namely people. The GNPP — the *gross national people potential* — is, in the last analysis, the most important factor. Today, some kinds of people are in grievously short supply. Other kinds of people — and in increasing numbers — are to all intents and purposes out of the labor market.

If the conventional view is correct, and all that need be done is to manipulate a cyclical deviation back onto the track of an onward and upward trend, then reopening the CCC camps and retraining a few hundred thousand dropouts and displacees may be all that is needed.

If this diagnosis is wrong and if cybernation is indeed revolutionizing modern society, then the emergence of the "new social mind" Henry Adams saw as necessary 60 years ago is overdue. This mind will have to think in terms of people as the masters — and of power and machines as servants. The other way around does not project a future pleasant to contemplate.

SOURCES

Books

1. Bancroft, Gertrude. *The American Labor Force: Its Growth and Changing Composition.* N. Y.: John Wiley & Sons, Inc., 1958.
2. Miller, H. P. *Rich Man, Poor Man.* N. Y.: Thomas Y. Crowell Co., 1964.
3. Muller-Thym, Bernard, "Cultural and Social Changes," *The Changing American Population,* American Assembly, Englewood Cliffs, N. J.: Prentice-Hall, 1962.
4. Nat'l. Bureau of Economic Research. *Demographic and Economic Change in Developed Countries.* Princeton: Princeton Univ. Press, 1960.
5. Weiner, Norbert. *Cybernetics: Or Control and Communication in the Animal and the Machine.* N. Y.: John Wiley & Sons, Inc., 1948.

Newspapers and Periodicals

6. *Christian Science Monitor.* Nov. 2, 1963.

7-8. *Washington Post-Times Herald.* Jan. 8, 1964, and Jan. 24, 1964.

9. Fischer, J. "The Stupidity Problem," *Harper's* Magazine. Sept. 1962.
10. Spiegelman, Mortimer. "The Changing Demographic Spectrum and Its Implications for Health," *Eugenics Quarterly*, Vol. 10, No. 4. Dec. 1963.

Other

11-12. *Population Bulletin*, May 1963, "The American Farmer." Feb. 1964, "U.S. Population Growth."

13. The Ad Hoc Committee on the Triple Revolution. *The Triple Revolution.* Memorandum to the President, March 22, 1964.
14. AFL-CIO. *Automation's Unkept Promise.* Publ. No. 47. Washington, D. C., June 1962.
15. Kennedy, Senator John F. Speech before the Economic Club of Chicago. Oct. 9, 1957.
16. Levitan, Sar. A. *Vocational Education and Federal Policy.* W. E. Upjohn Institute for Employment Research, Kalamazoo, Mich., May 1963.
17. Wirtz, W. Willard. Address: Univ. of Michigan, Dec. 19, 1963.

U. S. Government

18-19. *Economic Report of the President.* Jan. 1962 and Jan. 1964.

20-21. *Manpower Report of the President and a Report on Manpower Requirements, Resources, Utilization, and Training.* 1963 and 1964.

22. *American Women.* President's Commission on the Status of women. 1963.
23. *One-Third of a Nation: A Report on Young Men Found Unqualified for Military Service.* President's Task Force on Manpower Conservation. Jan. 1, 1964.

Bureau of the Census

24. *Current Population Reports.* Series P-25, No. 279. Feb. 4, 1964.
25. *Historical Statistics of the United States.* 1960.
26. *Statistical Abstract of the United States.* 1960.

27-29. *United States Census of Population, 1960.* Final Report, PC(1)-1B, PC(1)-1C, PC(1)-1D.

Department of Labor

30. *The Economic Situation of Negroes in the United States.* (Rev. 1962)
31. Hathaway, Dale E. "Migration from Farms and Its Meaning," *Monthly Labor Review*, Feb. 1960.
32. Johnston, Denis F. "Educational Attainment of Workers, March 1962," *Monthly Labor Review*, May 1963.
33. Katz, Arnold. "Educational Attainment of workers, 1959," *Monthly Labor Review*, Feb. 1960.
34. Manor, S. P. "Geographic Changes in U.S. Employment from 1950 to 1960," *Monthly Labor Review*, Jan. 1963.
35. Rutzick, Max and Sol Swerdloff, "The Occupational Structure of U.S. Employment, 1940–60," *Monthly Labor Review*, Nov. 1962.

U. S. Senate

36. Committee on Labor and Public Welfare. *Hearings Relating to the Training and Utilization of the Manpower Resources of the Nation.* Part 1, 88th Congress, 1st S., May 1963.

*The Length of Working Life for Males, 1900-60**

STUART H. GARFINKLE

During the decade of the 1950's, the length of working life — a key indicator of economic and social development — reversed its long-term rise. Work life expectancy for men declined by one-half year between 1950 and 1960. This decline is associated with a longer training period prior to entering upon a work career and a drop in the age of retirement, both of which are hallmarks of modern industrial society.[1] During past periods the effects on the length of working life of the longer training period and earlier retirement had been offset by large increases in life expectancy, and work life expectancy had continued to increase. Between 1900 and 1950 life expectancy for a male child increased 18 years, from 48 to 66 years. Work life expectancy also rose but only by 10 years — from 32 to 42 years.

As we approach the Biblical threescore and ten years, however, gains in life expectancy become harder to achieve and life expectancy for males rose only 1 year between 1950 and 1960. This small increase in life expectancy combined with accelerated trends towards longer schooling and earlier retirement have resulted in the striking decline in work life expectancy.

One of the circumstances most directly associated with the decline in the age of retirement has been the continued liberalization of social security benefits and coverage. The tendency to retire between the 64th and 65th year of age — the youngest age at which full benefits become available for men — was about three times as high in 1960 as it was in 1950. Between 1950 and 1960, the number of retired aged workers receiving benefits increased from 1.8 million to 8.1 million and the average monthly benefit rose from 44 to 74 dollars. The continued development of private pension systems — some of which include compulsory retirement provisions, the decline in the relative importance of nonagricultural self-employment, in farm employment, and the difficulties faced by older workers in searching for new jobs all contributed to the early retirement pattern.

The implications of the decline in the length of working life are extremely complex. First, the decision to retire from the labor force is becoming more a matter of choice as social security and other retirement benefits increase in scope and amount. Second, the working abilities and experience of the older retired persons are not utilized. Third, the wishes and needs of older persons for more adequate income as well as the desire for recognition often go unheeded when they cannot find satisfactory employment. Fourth, the trend toward earlier retirement seems to be more or less irreversible as does the growth of the population 65 years of age and over. Thus, the economic, social, and political effects of these considerations will become substantially greater in the years ahead.

Obviously, the issues raised by the trend toward a shorter working life cannot be readily resolved or summarily dismissed. The American work force is expected to increase dramatically in the next several years as record numbers of young people reach labor force ages. Providing useful employment for young and old who wish to work will continue to be one of our major manpower problems. The following article on tables of working life for men provides some basic perspectives on major labor market de-

* Reprinted from *Manpower Report,* No. 8, U.S. Department of Labor, July 1963.

[1] *Demographic Aspects of Manpower — Sex and Age Patterns of Participation in Economic Activities,* United Nations, New York, 1962. See also *Journal of Health and Human Behavior,* Volume III, No. 2, "Mortality Rates and Participation in Sustenance Activities: An Ecological Analysis, Summer 1962."

velopments for men. It is intended to provide a background for the study of training and retraining needs in our modern industrial society.

The Length of Working Life for Males, 1960

Under 1960 conditions a male worker at age 20 could expect to live almost 50 years and to work almost 43 years (table A). During his remaining 43 years of working life, many changes in the economic climate and in industrial processes are certain to occur. Viewing in retrospect changes that have occurred in our industrial structure in the past 40 years enables one to appreciate the almost overwhelming task of providing our workers with the kinds of training and retraining that will help them to meet new developments. During the last 40 years, the proportion of our labor force in farming has dropped from about 30 percent to less than 10 percent. Manufacturing employment has risen to a peak and begun to decline as a percent of total employment. Mining, an industry that provided employment for over a million persons, has declined and today employs less than 700,000 workers. The tempo of change may accelerate in the next 40 years. The flexibility that must be provided for our young workers is thus one of our major problems.

The need for a continuous retraining program is also evident from the extent of life-time job changing. A recent study of job mobility prepared by the Bureau of Labor Statistics showed the number of job changes that were made in 1961 by men in each age group. If it is assumed that the 1961 age patterns of job changing remain constant during the next 40 or so years, it can be estimated from the 1960 table of working life that a 20-year-old man will make more than 6 job changes (defined as a change of employer) during his remaining working life. Even at age 40, he can still be expected to make more than 2 job changes. These, of course, are averages, as some men will probably work at one job all their lives while others will make many more than the average number of job changes.

The table of working life for 1960 enables us to set in perspective many other changes in work life patterns and provides guidelines in many policy areas. The table shows, in addition to the length of working life, measures of the rate of entry into the labor force and the rate of separation from the labor force due to death and to retirement.

The tables are based upon a technique for measuring life expectancy which has been used for many years as a means of measuring social and economic progress and as an aid in the estimation of life insurance premiums. The table of working life starts with a group of 100,000 male babies, and follows them through life until the age when the last person has died. The 1960 tables show at age 14, the age when labor force measurement begins by definition, that 95,452 of the original group are still alive. Death rates between age 14 and age 40 are rather low and at age 40, 91,330 of the original group are still alive. The next 20 years of a man's life are much more hazardous, however, and only 72,624 are expected to be alive to age 60. After age 60 the death rates rise even more rapidly and by age 80, only 23,308 are still alive. It is nevertheless remarkable that in this country almost a quarter of all male babies can be expected to live until they are 80 years old.

Patterns of Working Life, 1960

The table of working life differs from an ordinary life table in that it reflects not only the effects of death on a group of 100,000 males born alive, but also the effects of labor market activities. For example, at age 14, some 15 percent of the male population are working or looking for work. This proportion rises very rapidly after age 14, particularly at those ages when young men are graduating from or otherwise leaving school. Between ages 16 and 17, for instance, 15 percent of the population begin a work career and between ages 17 and 18 about 18 percent begin a work career. The rates of labor force entry drop off very rapidly after the late teens, and after age 30 there are very few men who begin a work career.

The early years of a work career are very different from the prime working years. During 1960, for example, 40 percent of the 18- to 19-year-old young men who did any work during the

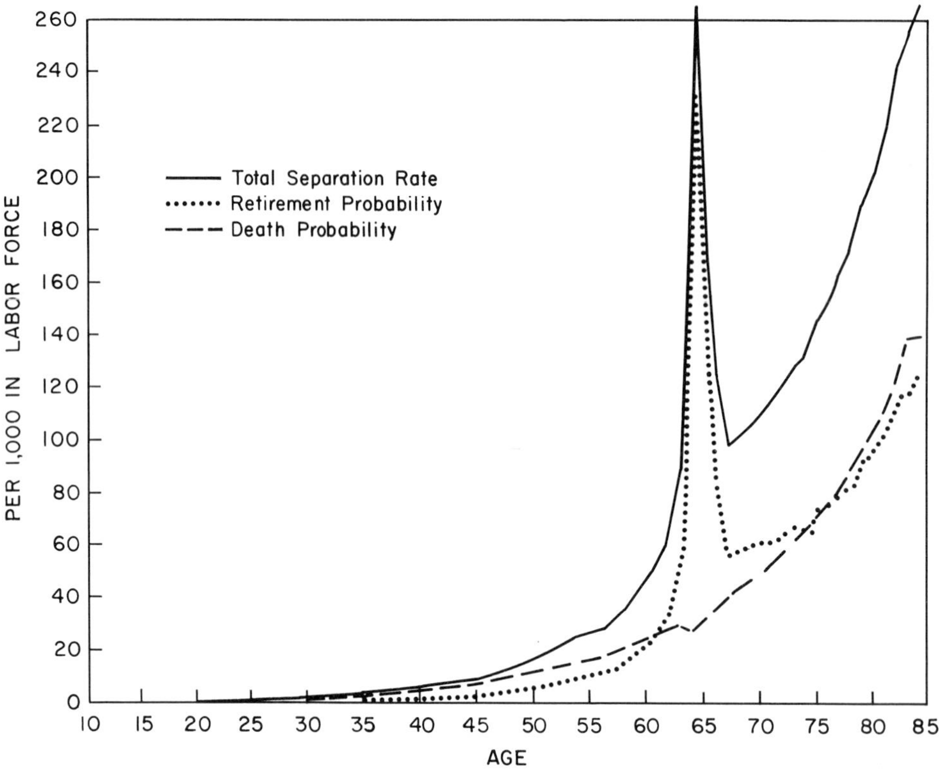

CHART 1

Annual rates of labor force separation due to death and retirement, males: 1960 rate (or probability).

year worked primarily at part-time jobs and only 30 percent worked more than 49 weeks.[2] With advancing age, work patterns changed considerably and, for example, among men 25–34 years old, only 4 percent worked part-time and 75 percent worked more than 49 weeks during 1960.

Labor force participation for men reaches a peak in the early 30's and remains relatively stable at a level of over 95 percent until age 50, although declining very slightly between ages 35 and 50. After age 50 the incidence of disabling conditions, the difficulties of finding work among unemployed workers who have lost jobs, and other circumstances result in more rapid separations from the labor force. The 1960 patterns of labor force participation show that between ages 50 and 60 the labor force rate declined from 95 to 85 percent; and between ages 60 and 65, it declined from 85 to 56 percent.

The labor force activity of men in their late 60's is somewhat similar to that of young men beginning a work career. Almost one-half of the men 65–69 years old who worked at all during the year worked less than 50 weeks.

One of the sharpest changes that takes place in the work lives of men occurs between the ages of 64 and 65, the age at which social security benefits become available without penalty and the age at which many private pension plans provide for compulsory retirement. Almost a fourth of the men in the labor force at age 64

[2] *Work Experience of the Population in 1960,* Special Labor Force Report No. 19 (U. S. Department of Labor, Bureau of Labor Statistics).

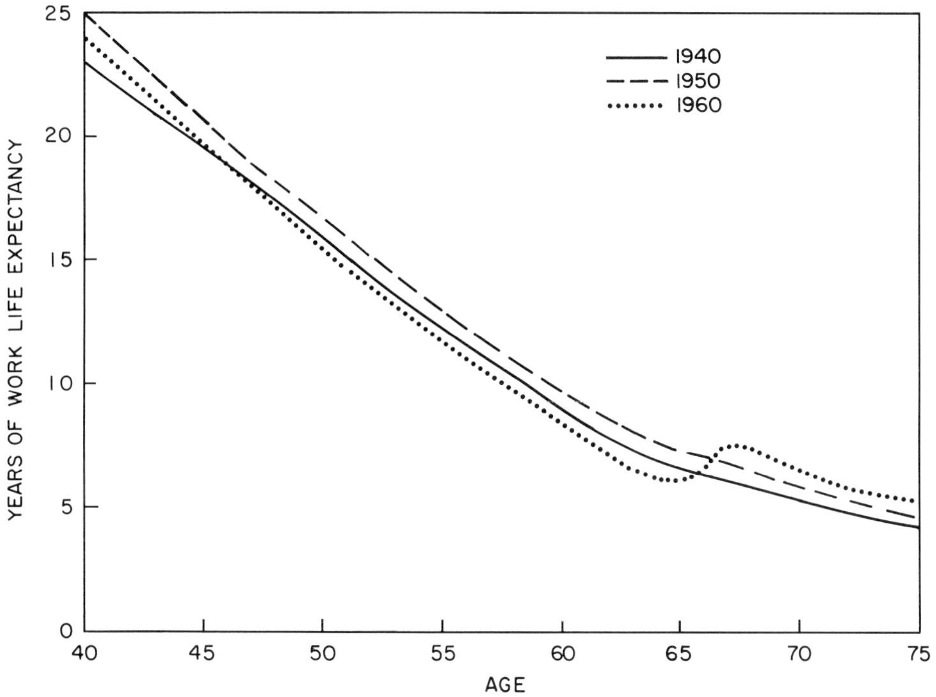

CHART 2

Work life expectancy for men 40–75 years of age, 1940, 1950, 1960.

retire by the time they are 65 years of age (chart 1). Retirement continues to be a more important reason than death for separation from the labor force for several years after age 65, although the tendency to retire declines very sharply after age 65. The rise in the retirement rate at age 65 does not show fully the extent of the reduction in labor force activity at this age. The proportion of employed men who work on part-time schedules increases from 14 to 21 percent between ages 64 and 65. Thus, the labor input of those who remain employed after age 65 is sharply reduced in part as a result of the availability of social security benefits to those over 65 whose earnings do not exceed specified amounts.

The Length of Working Life, 1960

As mentioned earlier, men at age 20 can expect to live an additional 50 years and to work 43 years, leaving about 7 years outside the labor force. These figures are averages. They include the man who leaves the labor force at age 20 because of death; the man who leaves the labor force because of disability but who lives for many years beyond age 20; and they also include the 20-year-old who will continue to work virtually until he dies. Even among persons 85 years old and over, about 8 percent appear to perform some labor force activities.

At age 40 life expectancy has declined to 31 years and work life expectancy to 24 with 7 years still expected in retirement. Even at age 60, men can expect to live an additional 15.8 years, on the average, and to work an additional 8½ years. Because of the very rapid rate of retirement between the 64th and 65th year of age, those remaining in the labor force at age 65 actually have a longer work life expectancy than did those in the labor force at age 64 (chart 2). This, of course, does not mean that a 65-year-old male worker will work longer than a 64-year-old worker, but simply that the work life expectancy is longer for those who continue to work beyond age 65.

Changes in the Length and Patterns of Working Life, 1900–60

A male baby born in 1960 is entering a much more complex world than if he had been born in 1900. The increase in life expectancy at birth from 48 years in 1900 to 67 years by 1960 is one reflection of the differences between the two periods. Most of the improvements in mortality conditions which have resulted in the longer life expectancy have occurred in the younger ages. Under 1960 mortality patterns more than 95 out of 100 male babies will reach age 20, compared with only 76 under 1900 conditions (table 1).

TABLE 1

Number Living Out of 100,000 Male Babies Born Alive, at Selected Ages: 1900, 1940, 1950, and 1960

Age	1900[1]	1940	1950	1960
15	78,037	92,508	95,366	96,071
20	76,376	91,617	94,695	95,472
40	64,954	85,246	90,207	91,502
60	46,452	65,142	71,246	73,502
80	12,266	18,995	23,237	24,639

[1] White males in 11 original death registration States of 1900.

Note: Data on life expectancy in this paper are from the National Vital Statistics Division of the U.S. Department of Health, Education and Welfare.

Perhaps it is in some part because of this circumstance that education and training have been given much greater emphasis in recent years. Even aside from personal attitudes, this country can feel reassured that education for the young is a good investment since virtually all reach adult ages and use their training in some way. Not only are more babies living to age 20, but the chances of living longer after age 20 have also improved. A 20-year-old man could expect to live another 42 years under 1900 mortality conditions compared with 49½ years in 1960 (table 2).

Recent trends, however, indicate that the improvements in life expectancy seem to be leveling off, although perhaps temporarily. Between 1950 and 1960 the number of 100,000 male babies expected to reach their 20th birthday increased from 95,366 to 96,071 and life expectancy for a 20-year-old man increased very slightly from 48.9 to 49.6. There was virtually no change in life expectancy for a 60-year-old man, indicating that little recent progress has been made in the reduction of death rates at the older ages.

TABLE 2

Average Remaining Lifetime for Males, at Selected Ages, 1900, 1940, 1950, and 1960

Age	1900[1]	1940	1950	1960
0	48.2	61.2	65.5	66.6
20	42.2	46.8	48.9	49.6
40	27.7	29.5	30.8	31.2
60	14.4	15.1	15.7	15.8
80	5.1	5.5	5.9	6.0

[1] White males in 11 original death registration States of 1900.

Work Life Potential

These long-range and short-range changes have many important effects on working life patterns. One of the most notable changes is the increase in the total number of man-years that a male baby can be expected to spend in the labor force. About 9 additional man-years of work have been added since 1900 (table 3). Virtually all of the change has been due to the longer life expectancy as more men live through the prime years of labor force activity. Since the propensity to work or seek work has declined at both ends of the age range, work life expectancy would have been reduced if life expectancy had remained unchanged.

TABLE 3

Life and Work Life Expectancy at Birth for Men, 1900, 1940, 1950, and 1960 (Number of years)

Year	Life expectancy	Work life expectancy	Outside labor force
1900	48.2[1]	32.1	16.1
1940	61.2	38.3	22.9
1950	65.5	41.9	23.6
1960	66.6	41.4	25.2

[1] White males in 11 original death registration States of 1900.

The meaning of this 9-year increase in work life expectancy becomes increasingly important to our manpower training and retraining programs if the figures are examined in greater detail. Under 1900 conditions about two-thirds of a man's life would be spent in the labor force. Although this figure had dropped to about 62 percent by 1960, the investment in training our young workers today yields a much higher return in terms of productive years of work because of the overall increase in work life expectancy.

The Length of Working Life 1900–60

Work life expectancy for a 20-year-old man rose from 39 years in 1900 to 43 years by 1960 largely as a result of longer life expectancy (chart 3 and table 4). Retirement as it is known today

TABLE 4

Average Number of Remaining Years of Life in Labor Force and in Retirement for Males 1900, 1940, 1950, and 1960

Age and year	Average number of years remaining		
	Life expectancy	Work life expectancy	In retirement
Age 20			
1900	42.2[1]	39.4	2.8
1940	46.8	41.3	5.5
1950	48.9	43.1	5.8
1960	49.6	42.6	7.0
Age 60			
1900	14.3[1]	11.5	2.8
1940	15.1	9.2	5.9
1950	15.7	9.8	5.9
1960	15.8	8.5	7.3

[1] For white males in 11 original death registration States of 1900.

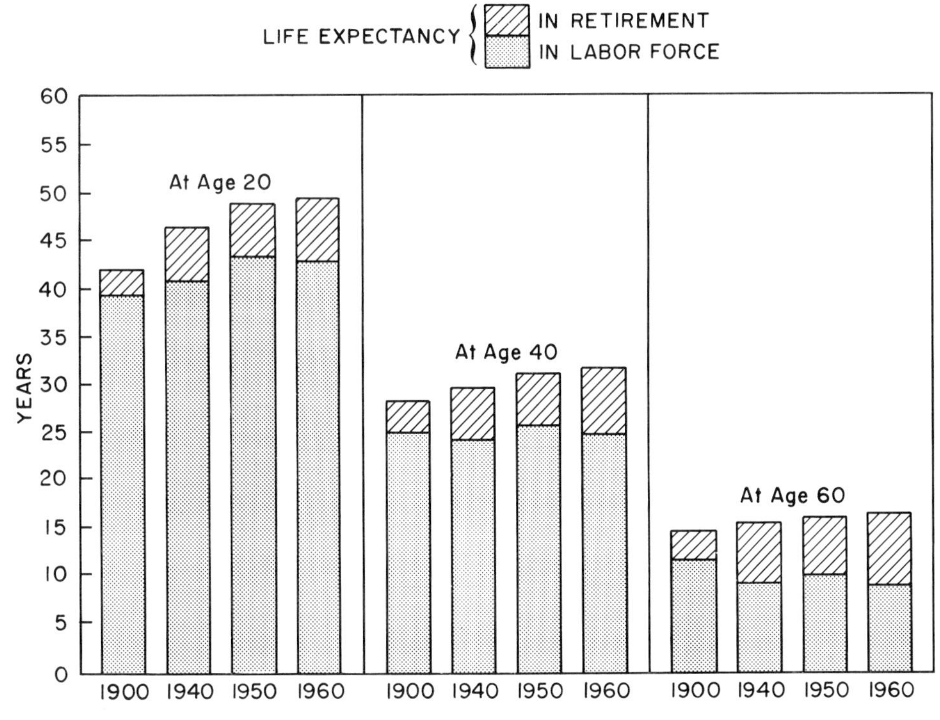

CHART 3

Average number of remaining years of life in labor force and in retirement, total males: 1900, 1940, 1950, and 1960.

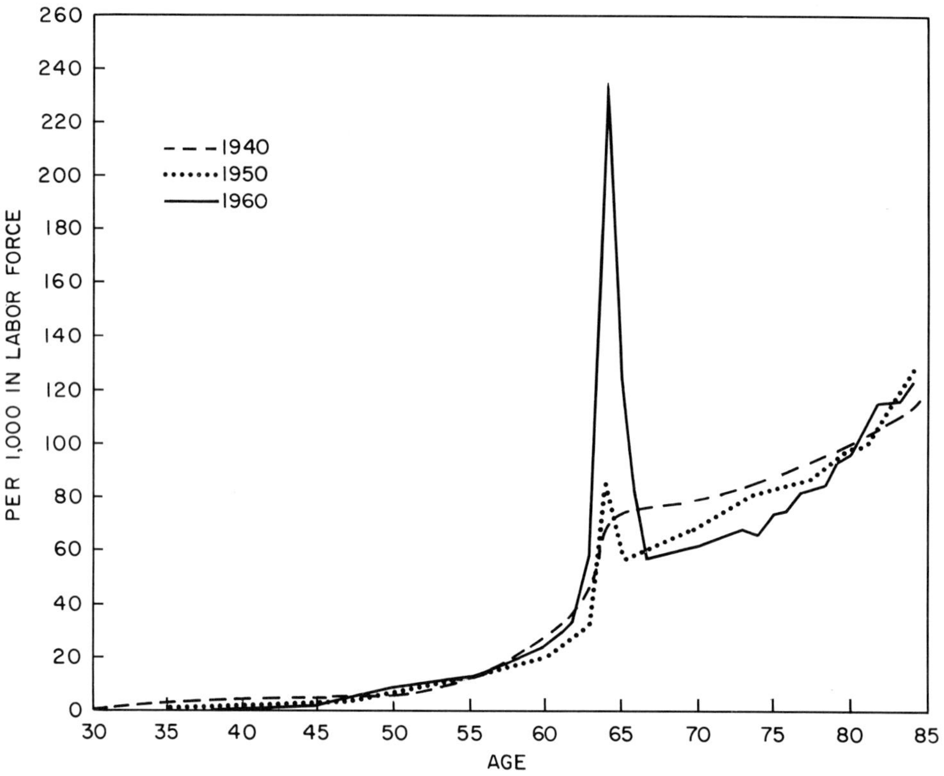

CHART 4

Annual rates of labor force separation due to retirement, males: 1940, 1950, and 1960.

was relatively uncommon in 1900 and the difference between life expectancy and work life expectancy was a scant 3 years. The longer range effects of the decline in opportunities for self-employment in agricultural as well as nonagricultural industries, and the effects of discrimination against older workers in layoff and hiring practices, are evident from 1900 and 1940 working life patterns. Life expectancy rose moderately — by almost a year — for 60-year-old men but work life expectancy declined by over 2 years. Between 1940 and 1950 both life expectancy and work life expectancy increased by about one-half year as improved employment opportunities encouraged many older workers to remain at work. Between 1950 and 1960 a surprisingly rapid increase in retirement rates for older men more than offset a moderate increase in life expectancy, and work life expectancy for 20-year-old men declined one-half year — from 43.1 to 42.6. Moreover, at age 60 the decrease in work life expectancy between 1950 and 1960 was 1.3 years, more than twice the decrease at age 20. Thus, the decrease in work life expectancy resulting from the increased rates of retirement between 1950 and 1960 was exaggerated at the older ages by the lack of improvement in life expectancy.

Changes in Labor Force Entry Rates, 1900–60

In 1900 when about 40 percent of our work force was employed on farms, the average young man entered the work force at about age 15. By 1940 the age of entry had risen to age 17 or 18, partially as a result of the depressed economic situation as well as longer schooling and other legal restraints on the employment of young people. The basic pattern of labor force entry was not strikingly different in 1940 and 1950 although the accession rates were somewhat lower in 1950 at ages 20, 21, and 22. This decline is associated with the increases in school enrollment rates for young men which have the effect of delaying entry into the work force. The general pattern of labor force entries in 1960, however, was also similar to that for 1940 and 1950 as labor force entries were concentrated among 16-, 17-, and 18-year-olds. Moderate increases did occur between 1950 and 1960 in entry rates among men 19 and over as labor force entry for these men had apparently been delayed. (See tables B and C.)

Changes in Separation Rates, 1940–60

Perhaps the most dramatic development in the work life patterns of older men is the rise in the retirement rate between ages 64 and 65 which in large part reflects the development of retirement programs under social security and private pensions plans. In 1940, 70 out of 1,000 men 64 years of age left the labor force by the time they became a year older; by 1950 this figure had risen to 83, and in 1960 the retirement rate for this group rose to 234 per thousand — a rate almost 3 times as high as in 1950. Even at age 65, the retirement rate in 1960 was over twice as high as in 1950 (chart 4).

This almost astonishing change makes it necessary to give careful attention to the kinds of jobs at which older men continue to work after reaching the age when so many retire. Data from the 1960 Census of Population on occupations of men over 65 years of age provided a source of information on this matter. Data were available for 162 separate occupation groups.[3] In 14 occupational groups more than 10 percent of the workers were over 65, and the workers in these particular groups tended to fall into the following categories: the self-employed, service workers, and professionals.

The conspicuously oldest occupational group of all was that of tailors and furriers, of whom 27 percent were more than 65 years old (table 5). In second place is found the category of independent shoemakers and repairers, of whom 19.2 percent were older than 65. Both of these occupational groups represent skilled trades which are traditionally practiced by immigrants and to which younger American workers may not be commonly attracted. Barbers represent a similar type of occupation, with 13.4 percent over 65.

TABLE 5

Occupations in which More Than 10 Percent of All Employed Males Were Aged 65 or Over

Occupation	Percent aged 65 or over
Tailors and furriers	26.9
Shoemakers and repairers, except factory	19.2
Elevator operators	15.9
Real estate agents and brokers	15.3
Private household workers	14.7
Farmers and farm managers	14.0
Guards and watchmen	13.7
Barbers	13.4
Officials and inspectors, State and local administration	13.2
Janitors and porters	12.4
Blacksmiths, forgemen, and hammermen	12.2
Locomotive engineers	11.9
Dentists	11.2
Lawyers and judges	10.5
Self-employed managers, wholesale trade	10.0
Self-employed managers, other industries n.e.c.	10.0

Source: *United States Census of Population, 1960: Detailed Characteristics, U. S. Summary.*

Other occupation groups with high proportions of self-employed older workers were real estate agents and brokers, of whom 15.3 percent were 65 and older; farmers and farm managers, with 14 percent 65 and over; and self-employed nonfarm managers with 10 percent in this upper age group. Dentists, lawyers and judges also were found to include a high proportion of older workers — 11 percent and 10 percent, respectively. Pharmacists, clergymen, architects, and physicians and surgeons were all found to have

[3] *United States Census of Population, 1960: Detailed Characteristics, U.S. Summary.*

TABLE A

Table of Working Life: Males, 1960

Year of age (1)	Number living of 100,000 born alive			Accessions to the labor force (per 1,000 in population)	Separations from the labor force (per 1,000 in labor force)			Average number of remaining years of:	
	In population	In labor force			Due to all causes	Due to death	Due to retirement	Life	Labor force participation
		Number	Percent of population						
	(2)	(3)	(4)	(5)	(6)	(7)	(8)	(9)	(10)
x	L_x	Lw_x	w_x	1000 A_x	1000 Q_x^s	1000 Q_x^d	1000 Q_x^r	$\mathring{e}_x$	$\mathring{e}w_x$
	(In years of age)			(Between years of age)				(At beginning of year of age)	
14	96,102	14,800	15.4	52.0	.9	.9	—	55.2	48.3
15	96,020	19,780	20.6	119.9	1.1	1.1	—	54.2	47.3
16	95,918	31,269	32.6	143.8	1.2	1.2	—	53.3	46.3
17	95,800	45,026	47.0	177.8	1.4	1.4	—	52.3	45.4
18	95,666	61,992	64.8	116.8	1.5	1.5	—	51.4	44.4
19	95,523	73,075	76.5	63.9	1.5	1.6	—	50.5	43.5
20	95,374	79,065	82.9	33.9	1.7	1.7	—	49.6	42.6
21	95,211	82,167	86.3	26.0	1.8	1.8	—	48.6	41.6
22	95,039	84,490	88.9	18.9	1.8	1.8	—	47.7	40.7
23	94,865	86,137	90.8	14.0	1.8	1.8	—	46.8	39.8
24	94,692	87,306	92.2	11.0	1.8	1.8	—	45.9	38.9
25	94,526	88,193	93.3	9.0	1.8	1.8	—	45.0	37.9
26	94,360	88,887	94.2	8.0	1.7	1.7	—	44.1	37.0
27	94,197	89,487	95.0	7.0	1.7	1.7	—	43.1	36.1
28	94,033	89,990	95.7	5.9	1.7	1.7	—	42.2	35.1
29	93,869	90,396	96.3	5.0	1.8	1.8	—	41.3	34.2
30	93,697	90,699	96.8	2.0	1.9	1.9	—	40.4	33.2
31	93,522	90,716	97.0	1.0	1.9	1.9	—	39.4	32.3
32	93,341	90,634	97.1	1.0	2.0	2.0	—	38.5	31.4
33	93,151	90,543	97.2	1.0	2.2	2.2	—	37.6	30.4
34	92,948	90,438	97.3	—	3.4	2.4	1.0	36.7	29.5
35	92,728	90,132	97.2	—	3.6	2.5	1.1	35.7	28.6
36	92,493	89,811	97.1	—	3.8	2.8	1.0	34.8	27.7
37	92,238	89,471	97.0	—	4.0	3.0	1.0	33.9	26.8
38	91,960	89,109	96.9	—	4.3	3.3	1.0	33.0	25.9
39	91,659	88,726	96.8	—	4.7	3.6	1.1	32.1	25.0
40	91,326	88,312	96.7	—	5.0	4.0	1.0	31.2	24.1
41	90,964	87,871	96.6	—	5.4	4.4	1.0	30.3	23.2
42	90,568	87,398	96.5	—	5.9	4.8	1.1	29.5	22.3
43	90,131	86,886	96.4	—	6.3	5.3	1.0	28.6	21.4
44	89,654	86,337	96.3	—	7.1	6.1	1.0	27.7	20.6

45	89,106	85,720	96.2	—	7.5	6.4	1.1	26.9	19.7
46	88,534	85,081	96.1	—	9.2	7.1	2.1	26.0	18.8
47	87,904	84,300	95.9	—	10.0	7.9	2.1	25.2	18.0
48	87,206	83,456	95.7	—	12.0	8.9	3.1	24.4	17.2
49	86,428	82,452	95.4	—	13.8	9.6	4.2	23.6	16.4
50	85,596	81,316	95.0	—	16.4	11.2	5.2	22.8	15.6
51	84,637	79,982	94.5	—	18.6	12.4	6.2	22.1	14.8
52	83,591	78,492	93.9	—	20.8	13.4	7.4	21.3	14.0
53	82,468	76,860	93.2	—	22.8	14.3	8.5	20.6	13.3
54	82,283	75,105	92.4	—	25.1	15.4	9.7	19.9	12.6
55	80,020	73,218	91.5	—	27.0	16.2	10.8	19.2	11.9
56	78,717	71,239	90.5	—	28.3	17.3	11.0	18.5	11.2
57	77,344	69,223	89.5	—	32.1	18.8	13.3	17.8	10.5
58	75,881	67,003	88.3	—	35.2	20.6	14.6	17.1	9.8
59	74,306	64,646	87.0	—	41.1	22.9	18.2	16.4	9.1
60	72,588	61,990	85.4	—	47.8	24.7	23.1	15.8	8.5
61	70,774	59,026	83.4	—	54.0	26.8	27.2	15.2	7.8
62	68,849	55,837	81.1	—	61.8	29.0	32.8	14.6	7.2
63	66,820	52,387	78.4	—	87.3	30.8	56.5	14.0	6.7
64	64,699	47,813	73.9	—	263.7	29.6	234.1	13.4	6.1
65	62,533	35,206	56.3	—	170.1	34.1	136.0	12.8	6.3
66	60,246	29,219	48.5	—	122.5	37.6	84.9	12.3	7.0
67	57,879	25,640	44.3	—	98.4	41.0	57.4	11.8	7.1
68	55,438	23,118	41.7	—	102.6	44.1	58.5	11.2	7.0
69	52,923	20,746	39.2	—	106.4	46.8	59.6	10.7	6.7
70	50,374	18,538	36.8	—	111.7	50.8	60.9	10.2	6.4
71	47,733	16,468	34.5	—	116.5	54.6	61.9	9.8	6.1
72	45,046	14,550	32.3	—	121.5	58.5	63.0	9.3	5.9
73	42,325	12,782	30.2	—	129.7	62.5	67.2	8.8	5.6
74	39,586	11,124	28.1	—	133.6	68.5	65.1	8.4	5.3
75	36,785	9,638	26.2	—	145.2	71.7	73.5	8.0	5.1
76	34,047	8,239	24.2	—	152.3	77.1	75.2	7.5	4.8
77	31,320	6,984	22.3	—	164.1	82.8	81.3	7.1	4.6
78	28,617	5,838	20.4	—	173.3	89.4	83.9	6.7	4.3
79	25,946	4,826	18.6	—	190.8	99.6	91.2	6.3	4.1
80	23,245	3,905	16.8	—	200.8	105.5	95.3	6.0	3.9
81	20,669	3,121	15.1	—	220.4	115.0	105.4	5.6	3.7
82	18,159	2,433	13.4	—	243.3	125.6	117.7	5.3	3.6
83	15,734	1,841	11.7	—	256.9	139.1	117.8	5.0	3.6
84	13,408	1,368	10.2	—	265.4	140.4	125.0	4.7	3.6
85 years & over	55,525	4,386	7.9	—	—	—	—	4.5	3.6

TABLE B

Table of Working Life: Males, 1950

Year of age	Number living of 100,000 born alive: In population	In labor force: Number	In labor force: Percent of population	Accessions to the labor force (per 1,000 in population)	Separations from the labor force (per 1,000 in labor force): Due to all causes	Due to death	Due to retirement	Average number of remaining years of: Life	Labor force participation
(1)	(2)	(3)	(4)	(5)	(6)	(7)	(8)	(9)	(10)
x	L_x	Lw_x	w_x	1000 A_x	1000 Q_x^s	1000 Q_x^d	1000 Q_x^r	$\mathring{e}_x$	$\mathring{e}w_x$
	(In years of age)			(Between years of age)				(At beginning of year of age)	
14	95,411	19,273	20.2	59.9	1.0	1.0	—	54.5	48.7
15	95,313	24,972	26.2	108.9	1.2	1.2	—	53.6	47.8
16	95,198	35,318	37.1	136.8	1.4	1.4	—	52.6	46.8
17	95,069	48,295	50.8	193.7	1.5	1.5	—	51.7	45.9
18	94,928	66,639	70.2	125.8	1.6	1.6	—	50.8	45.0
19	94,774	78,473	82.8	22.9	1.7	1.7	—	49.8	44.0
20	94,610	80,513	85.1	20.9	1.8	1.8	—	48.9	43.1
21	94,436	82,348	87.2	18.9	1.9	1.9	—	48.0	42.2
22	94,255	83,981	89.1	17.0	2.0	2.0	—	47.1	41.3
23	94,070	85,416	90.8	15.0	2.0	2.0	—	46.2	40.3
24	93,884	86,655	92.3	13.0	2.0	2.0	—	45.3	39.4
25	93,699	87,702	93.6	11.0	2.0	2.0	—	44.4	38.5
26	93,516	88,560	94.7	9.0	2.0	2.0	—	43.4	37.6
27	93,332	89,225	95.6	7.0	2.0	2.0	—	42.5	36.6
28	93,148	89,702	96.3	5.0	2.1	2.1	—	41.6	35.7
29	92,957	89,982	96.8	2.0	2.1	2.1	—	40.7	34.8
30	92,762	89,979	97.0	1.0	2.2	2.2	—	39.8	33.9
31	92,558	89,874	97.1	—	2.3	2.3	—	38.9	32.9
32	92,347	89,669	97.1	—	2.5	2.4	.1	38.0	32.0
33	92,121	89,449	97.1	—	3.6	2.6	1.0	37.0	31.1
34	91,883	89,127	97.0	—	3.8	2.8	1.0	36.1	30.2
35	91,628	88,788	96.9	—	4.0	3.0	1.0	35.2	29.3
36	91,355	88,432	96.8	—	4.3	3.2	1.1	34.3	28.4
37	91,059	88,054	96.7	—	4.6	3.5	1.1	33.4	27.5
38	90,738	87,653	96.6	—	4.9	3.8	1.1	32.6	26.6
39	90,389	87,225	96.5	—	5.2	4.2	1.0	31.7	25.8
40	90,009	86,769	96.4	—	5.7	4.6	1.1	30.8	24.9
41	89,593	86,278	96.3	—	6.1	5.1	1.0	29.9	24.0
42	89,140	85,753	96.2	—	6.6	5.6	1.0	29.1	23.2
43	88,644	85,187	96.1	—	7.1	6.1	1.0	28.2	22.3
44	88,102	84,578	96.0	—	7.7	6.7	1.0	27.4	21.4

45	87,511	83,928	95.9	—	9.5	7.3	2.2	26.6	20.6
46	86,868	83,133	95.7	—	10.2	8.1	2.1	25.7	19.3
47	86,167	82,289	95.5	—	10.9	8.8	2.1	24.9	19.0
48	85,408	81,394	95.3	—	12.8	9.6	3.2	24.1	18.2
49	84,585	80,356	95.0	—	14.7	10.5	4.2	23.4	17.4
50	83,697	79,177	94.6	—	15.6	11.4	4.2	22.6	16.6
51	82,739	77,940	94.2	—	17.7	12.5	5.2	21.8	15.9
52	81,708	76,560	93.7	—	19.9	13.6	6.3	21.1	15.1
53	80,596	75,035	93.1	—	22.2	14.7	7.5	20.4	14.4
54	79,400	73,366	92.4	—	24.7	16.1	8.6	19.6	13.7
55	78,117	71,555	91.6	—	27.2	17.5	9.7	19.0	13.0
56	76,744	69,607	90.7	—	28.8	19.0	9.8	18.3	12.3
57	75,280	67,601	89.7	—	31.5	20.5	11.0	17.6	11.7
58	73,728	65,470	88.6	—	34.4	22.2	12.2	17.0	11.0
59	72,087	63,220	87.4	—	43.9	23.7	20.2	16.3	10.4
60	70,363	60,442	85.9	—	46.2	25.5	20.7	15.7	9.8
61	68,551	57,651	84.1	—	51.9	27.4	24.5	15.1	9.2
62	66,655	54,657	82.0	—	58.1	29.3	28.8	14.5	8.7
63	64,674	51,480	79.6	—	65.9	31.2	34.7	13.9	8.2
64	62,615	48,088	76.8	—	115.9	32.7	83.2	13.3	7.7
65	60,479	42,517	70.3	—	92.7	35.5	57.2	12.7	7.4
66	58,270	38,575	66.2	—	97.3	38.0	59.3	12.2	7.2
67	55,984	34,822	62.2	—	102.3	40.9	61.4	11.6	6.9
68	53,619	31,260	58.3	—	107.6	44.0	63.6	11.1	6.6
69	51,185	27,896	54.5	—	113.5	47.3	66.2	10.6	6.3
70	48,683	24,731	50.8	—	119.7	50.8	68.9	10.1	6.0
71	46,122	21,770	47.2	—	126.7	54.8	71.9	9.6	5.7
72	43,503	19,011	43.7	—	134.4	59.1	75.3	9.2	5.5
73	40,832	16,455	40.3	—	142.8	63.8	79.0	8.7	5.2
74	38,121	14,105	37.0	—	149.6	68.9	80.7	8.2	5.0
75	35,383	11,995	33.9	—	156.6	74.4	82.2	7.8	4.7
76	32,637	10,117	31.0	—	163.7	80.4	83.3	7.4	4.5
77	29,899	8,461	28.3	—	170.8	86.7	84.1	7.0	4.3
78	27,193	7,016	25.8	—	181.4	92.6	88.8	6.6	4.1
79	24,544	5,743	23.4	—	192.6	99.8	92.8	6.3	3.8
80	21,974	4,637	21.1	—	205.3	107.2	98.1	5.9	3.6
81	19,498	3,685	18.9	—	214.4	115.3	99.1	5.6	3.4
82	17,132	2,895	16.9	—	233.9	124.0	109.9	5.3	3.1
83	14,884	2,218	14.9	—	251.6	133.6	118.0	5.0	2.9
84	12,771	1,660	13.0	—	271.1	143.9	127.2	4.7	2.7
85 years & over	51,827	3,554	6.9	—	—	—	—	4.4	2.5

TABLE C

Table of Working Life: Males, 1940

Year of age	Number living of 100,000 born alive			Accessions to the labor force (per 1,000 in population)	Separations from the labor force (per 1,000 in labor force)			Average number of remaining years of:	
	In population	In labor force			Due to all causes	Due to death	Due to retirement	Life	Labor force participation
		Number	Percent of population						
(1)	(2)	(3)	(4)	(5)	(6)	(7)	(8)	(9)	(10)
x	L_x	Lw_x	w_x	1000 A_x	1000 Q_x^s	1000 Q_x^d	1000 Q_x^r	$\mathring{e}_x$	$\mathring{e}w_x$
	(In years of age)			(Between years of age)				(At beginning of year of age)	
14	92,115	5,610	6.1	60.7	1.6	1.6	—	52.2	46.6
15	91,968	11,192	12.2	108.5	1.7	1.7	—	51.3	45.7
16	91,812	21,152	23.0	158.8	1.9	1.9	—	50.4	44.8
17	91,638	35,692	38.9	181.4	2.1	2.1	—	49.5	43.8
18	91,446	52,240	57.1	147.7	2.3	2.3	—	48.6	42.9
19	91,236	65,626	71.9	86.5	2.5	2.5	—	47.7	42.0
20	91,088	73,354	80.6	49.7	2.6	2.6	—	46.8	41.1
21	90,771	77,686	85.6	35.4	2.7	2.7	—	45.9	40.2
22	90,526	80,690	89.1	24.1	2.8	2.8	—	45.0	39.3
23	90,273	82,646	91.6	15.7	2.9	2.9	—	44.1	38.4
24	90,011	83,824	93.1	9.0	3.0	3.0	—	43.3	37.6
25	89,741	84,383	94.0	6.5	3.1	3.1	—	42.4	36.7
26	89,463	84,705	94.7	4.4	3.2	3.2	—	41.5	35.8
27	89,177	84,828	95.1	2.7	3.3	3.3	—	40.6	34.9
28	88,883	84,789	95.4	1.6	3.4	3.4	—	39.8	34.0
29	88,581	84,643	95.6	.7	3.5	3.5	—	38.9	33.1
30	88,271	84,409	95.6	.3	3.6	3.6	—	38.0	32.2
31	87,953	84,132	95.7	—	3.8	3.8	—	37.2	31.3
32	87,619	83,812	95.7	—	4.3	4.0	.3	36.3	30.5
33	87,269	83,452	95.6	—	4.7	4.2	.5	35.5	29.6
34	86,902	83,060	95.6	—	5.1	4.4	.7	34.6	28.7
35	86,520	82,636	95.5	—	5.6	4.6	1.0	33.7	27.8
36	86,122	82,173	95.4	—	6.2	4.9	1.3	32.9	27.0
37	85,700	81,664	95.3	—	6.8	5.2	1.6	32.0	26.1
38	85,254	81,109	95.1	—	7.5	5.6	1.9	31.2	25.3
39	84,777	80,501	95.0	—	8.1	6.0	2.1	30.4	24.5
40	84,268	79,849	94.8	—	8.6	6.4	2.2	29.5	23.7
41	83,729	79,162	94.5	—	9.1	6.8	2.3	28.7	22.9
42	83,160	78,442	94.3	—	9.7	7.3	2.4	27.9	22.1
43	82,553	77,681	94.1	—	10.5	7.9	2.6	27.1	21.3
44	81,901	76,865	93.9	—	11.3	8.5	2.8	26.3	20.5

45	81,205	75,996	93.6	—	12.2	9.2	3.0	25.5	19.7
46	80,458	75,069	93.3	—	13.2	9.9	3.3	24.8	18.9
47	79,661	74,078	93.0	—	14.2	10.7	3.5	24.0	18.2
48	78,809	73,026	92.7	—	15.3	11.6	3.7	23.2	17.4
49	77,895	71,909	92.3	—	16.5	12.5	4.0	22.5	16.7
50	76,921	70,723	91.9	—	17.7	13.5	4.2	21.8	15.9
51	75,883	69,471	91.6	—	19.1	14.5	4.6	21.0	15.2
52	74,783	68,144	91.1	—	20.7	15.6	5.1	20.3	14.5
53	73,616	66,733	90.7	—	22.6	16.8	5.8	19.6	13.8
54	72,379	65,225	90.1	—	24.6	17.9	6.7	18.9	13.1
55	71,076	63,620	89.5	—	27.0	19.2	7.8	18.3	12.4
56	69,704	61,902	88.8	—	29.8	20.6	9.2	17.6	11.7
57	68,261	60,057	88.0	—	33.4	22.0	11.4	17.0	11.0
58	66,752	58,051	87.0	—	38.3	23.4	14.9	16.3	10.3
59	65,177	55,828	85.7	—	46.8	25.0	21.8	15.7	9.7
60	63,528	53,215	83.8	—	51.6	26.9	24.7	15.1	9.1
61	61,800	50,469	81.7	—	58.6	28.9	29.7	14.5	8.6
62	59,989	47,512	79.2	—	68.2	30.9	37.3	13.9	8.0
63	58,099	44,272	76.2	—	80.6	33.1	47.5	13.3	7.5
64	56,129	40,704	72.5	—	105.1	35.2	69.9	12.7	7.1
65	54,080	36,426	67.4	—	111.8	37.8	74.0	12.2	6.8
66	51,955	32,354	62.3	—	115.9	40.7	75.2	11.6	6.5
67	49,757	28,604	57.5	—	119.8	43.8	76.0	11.1	6.3
68	47,493	25,177	53.0	—	123.9	47.0	76.9	10.6	6.1
69	45,171	22,058	48.8	—	128.8	50.3	78.5	10.1	5.8
70	42,804	19,217	44.9	—	133.5	54.2	79.3	9.6	5.6
71	40,390	16,652	41.2	—	138.8	58.1	80.7	9.1	5.4
72	37,946	14,341	37.8	—	144.7	62.5	82.2	8.6	5.2
73	35,472	12,266	34.6	—	151.3	67.5	83.8	8.2	4.9
74	32,971	10,410	31.6	—	158.7	73.3	85.4	7.7	4.7
75	30,445	8,758	28.8	—	166.9	79.8	87.1	7.3	4.5
76	27,906	7,296	26.1	—	175.9	86.9	89.0	6.9	4.3
77	25,369	6,013	23.7	—	185.7	94.6	91.1	6.5	4.1
78	22,855	4,896	21.4	—	196.3	102.8	93.5	6.1	3.8
79	20,391	3,935	19.3	—	207.7	111.4	96.3	5.8	3.6
80	18,005	3,118	17.3	—	219.9	120.4	99.5	5.5	3.5
81	15,724	2,432	15.5	—	232.9	129.8	103.1	5.2	3.3
82	13,571	1,866	13.7	—	246.7	139.7	107.0	4.9	3.1
83	11,568	1,406	12.2	—	261.3	149.9	111.4	4.6	2.9
84	9,732	1,039	10.7	—	276.7	160.3	116.4	4.3	2.7
85 years & over	36,276	2,304	6.4	—	—	—	—	4.1	2.6

only slightly less than 10 percent older than 65 years.

In the service occupations, 16 percent of elevator operators, 14 percent of the private household workers, 14 percent of guards and watchmen, and 12 percent of janitors and porters had passed the 65-year mark. It is reasonable to assume that many of the workers in these service jobs had not always worked in these jobs since they are not a significant source of employment for men in the prime working ages. Thus it would seem that these occupations provide opportunities for displaced or unemployed workers who desire to remain in the labor market.

Some Interrelations of Population and Atomic Power*†

VINCENT HEATH WHITNEY

I

A critical analysis of the social and economic consequences of nuclear development demands some understanding of fields which are professionally far removed from the areas of competence of the social scientist. Terms, concepts, and problems closely related to mathematics, physics, chemistry, engineering, and metallurgy must be comprehended and their interrelations seen.

Perhaps this is why atomic energy has received relatively little attention from sociologists and economists. Certainly it is not because the area is inappropriate for social science research as becomes clear when, for example, atomic power is viewed as a case of technological innovation with consequences for the entire social and economic system.

Atomic power is one of three principal areas of present nuclear development. The other two, which are not of concern in this paper, are the atomic and hydrogen bomb and the use of radioisotopes in medical, scientific, industrial, and agricultural research and practice. The basic technical problem of atomic power is that of the production of heat through nuclear fission and the transfer of that heat to power by mechanical means.[1] The basic economic problem of atomic power is that of producing and distributing such power at strategic sites at a cost which is competitive with that of power produced from conventional sources. The basic sociological problem of atomic power is how to overcome cultural resistances to its effective use for the promotion of collective national or regional values; or possibly, from the point of view of areas other than that in which the production of atomic power is sought, how to change social organization, and in so doing, social values, so that new goals are substituted for traditional ones. The latter is inherent in programs of assistance to areas which are economically underdeveloped.

These are problems which are meaningful and familiar to social scientists and demographers. They have already been studied in terms of many types of innovation. If atomic power is viewed as another — if unique — instance of innovation, then principles which have been derived from the study of the acceptability or non-acceptability of prior inventions, and of the consequences of their introduction into particular types of social organization, will have validity in

* Reprinted with permission from *American Sociological Review,* Vol. 21, No. 3 (June 1956), pp. 273-279.

† A paper with this title, and embodying some of these materials, was presented by the author to the annual meeting of the Population Association of America held at Oxford, Ohio, in May 1953.

[1] There are distinct hopes that such heat may in the future be utilized *directly* as a source of power, but such a development lies in the future.

assaying the significance of atomic power utilization for economic development, for societal change, or for demographic change.

At this early stage we can hardly foresee all the direct effects of the introduction of atomic power, let alone the probably more far-reaching indirect effects. We can, however, disregard the over-optimistic view that atomic power will soon be universally available at low cost simply because potentially enormous quantities of power are theoretically derivable from handfuls of fissionable material easily transported anywhere. We can also challenge the glib assumption that atomic power will thus lead to universal economic development and that the pronounced differences in social and economic indices among nations will either disappear or be sharply reduced. Similarly, there is no basis for assuming that atomic power will result in any early and major shift of either industrial plants or population. The assumptions, frequently made, that these kinds of things will occur exclude consideration of the uniformities in historical resistance to technological change as well as the specific general and local resistances which seem to be associated with the development of atomic power. They ignore the important fact that in many underdeveloped areas of the world there are first-rate, cheap and accessible alternative sources of power, such as water and coal, which have never been developed because of lack of markets, lack of capital, lack of entrepreneurs, and lack of interest. To believe that the introduction of a new power source — even if it were free, which atomic power would not be — would revolutionize social organization and demographic experience is hardly realistic. It cannot be overemphasized that the *availability* and the *use* of an invention are not synonymous. Mere access to atomic power in a technical sense does not spell any specific consequences for demographic organization.[2]

[2] The dogmatic statements in this section are supported in detail in other writings by the author. See particularly, Walter Isard and Vincent Whitney, *Atomic Power: An Economic and Social Analysis,* New York: The Blakiston Co., 1952, chs. 2, 8; Vincent Whitney, "Resistance to Innovation: The Case of Atomic Power," *American Journal of Sociology,* 56 (November, 1950), pp. 247-254; and Walter Isard and Vincent Whitney, "Pattern for America," *The Nation,* 180 (June 18, 1955), pp. 542-548.

II

With this abbreviated background, we can now examine some of the ways in which population elements influence the probability of the development of atomic power in a particular nation or region. As in the case of the relation between population and war, the role of the population factor is largely indirect. Population is only one of the influential components in a system of factors which will ultimately determine whether atomic power plants are built and operated. Other factors will include the existence or absence of alternative power resources and their relative cost; the availability or nonavailability of agricultural and mineral resources suitable as a base for general economic development; the cultural organization, especially as this influences the efficiency of the utilization of human and non-human resources; and the political and economic organization, in particular as these serve to foster or to hinder atomic development.

Population then plays a limiting or permissive role in economic development based on the establishment of atomic power plants. Our first task is to identify the population situations which are favorable or unfavorable to such development. Employing the analytically useful, if hardly realistic, dictum of "other things being equal," we can conclude that atomic power presently has the best chance of appearing and expanding in areas (1) where population growth is still rapid but (2) where the demographic revolution is well under way; (3) where the total population is sufficiently great, and contains local agglomerations of high enough density, to provide a market for the relatively large output of an atomic power plant of optimum size; (4) where migration is an established aspect of social organization; and (5) where the ratio between population and available developed resources is productive of a high or rising standard of living.

These categories obviously are not discrete. Nor will they in themselves allow us to select the specific nations where atomic power development seems most probable, for in seeking such concrete identification we can hardly ignore the political, economic, and social considerations which are excluded in the *ceteris paribus* phrase. Nevertheless, they suggest at once that atomic power is most likely to develop first in the industrialized or industrializing countries, least likely to develop in what are ordinarily characterized as the economically backward areas of the earth. This is not meant to imply that certain population conditions will *cause* the establishment of atomic power plants but only to indicate that specific demographic patterns, along with other related factors in social organization, are likely to limit or to exclude such growth, or conversely to render it feasible.

Let us look briefly at the world's underdeveloped areas. In reality every one is unique, but there is space here only to differentiate among them in broadest terms.

Some of these areas, such as British Guiana,[3] Brazil, and other parts of South America, Africa, and the Middle East are underpopulated in the sense that they are areas in which numbers are too small to achieve optimum levels of living at the attained stage of technological development.[4] Unless such areas possess unusually lavish natural food resources, the ordinarily stringent labor force will tend to be employed full time in eking out a subsistence living. If atomic power — or any other factor — initiates a nucleus of industrial activity, the required labor force may be expected to come initially from labor withdrawn from agriculture. The immediate consequence of such a redistribution of the labor force may be a decline in domestic food supplies. This does not overlook the possibilities of increasing agricultural output in the short run through such relatively low-cost devices as improved seed, stock, and methods, and over a longer period through more thoroughgoing agricultural mechanization. It simply emphasizes the fact that such compensating gains in farm production will not be immediate. There is a real possibility then that initially the total food supply will decline.

Such decline may lead directly to an increase in mortality. Or an increased death rate may be avoided by importing food. Such food will ordinarily be relatively expensive. Consequently, it will induce higher labor costs.

In either case, the spiral of economic development may be halted before a level is reached where the initial handicaps of underpopulation and consequent high food and labor costs are overcome. The critical ratio will be that of industrial to agricultural productivity. If the former can be maintained at a rate in excess of the latter, the restricting effect of any food deficit can be overcome. This will ordinarily require external markets since domestic demand will presumably be low at the start.

In actuality, it seems less probable that atomic power will spark the development of underpopulated agrarian economies than that such development, based on conventional power sources, may succeed in some to the point where markets for an atomic power plant exist. Two factors, at least, are favorable to a solution of the handicaps suggested above. One is the presence of some degree of underemployment or disguised unemployment in the relatively inefficient agricultural sectors of these underdeveloped areas. Properly organized, this additional labor can serve to minimize or eliminate food deficits. The other is the relatively sparse initial population base, which may allow time for fertility to be controlled before increasing numbers press on available resources. A sparsely settled area with adequate natural resources may in fact find a growing population a prime determinant of successful economic development.[5]

The greater number of underdeveloped areas, however, are overpopulated agricultural regions, where a subsistence economy masks a great deal of disguised unemployment, and where demographic rates are by-and-large uncontrolled. For all such areas, existing demographic trends act as one major deterrent to economic development. The picture has by now been painted in a sufficient number of versions to establish its validity. We need only repeat that in such countries what increases in productivity are achieved tend in large part to be diverted to support increases in population without comparable increases in levels of living.

[3] Irene Taeuber, "British Guiana: Some Demographic Aspects of Economic Development," *Population Index*, 18 (January, 1952), pp. 3-19.

[4] Overpopulation and underpopulation are recognized as complex states involving psychological as well as economic factors. See *Peaceful Change: Procedures, Population, Raw Materials, Colonies*, Paris: International Institute of Intellectual Cooperation, League of Nations, 1938, pp. 120-138.

[5] I have drawn here on critical comments kindly made by George Stolnitz of Princeton University. Dr. Stolnitz is, of course, in no way responsible for the form of the statements above.

Underdeveloped areas where numbers are pressing constantly on available resources consistently display subsistence economies and low standards of living, however these are measured. For such areas capital accumulation, whether for atomic power plants or for other more probable immediate goals, is an extremely difficult problem, and one which may well be insurmountable for the majority, which do not receive what limited subsidization may be made available by the United States or possibly by Russia or by an international organization. Moreover, initial capital investment may well fail to serve as the base for a continuing industrial spiral in such countries unless it is on a scale sufficient to modify the whole economy in relatively short order, and to affect social organization as well by paralleling the expected drop in the death rate with at least an equally sharp and early drop in the birth rate.

For example, India's plans for a general rise in levels of living seem futile unless they include effective controls over population growth. Indeed, India recognizes this, and has sought advice through the United Nations.[6] Yet, despite vigorous leadership, the abject poverty of the country, the illiteracy, the rural isolation, the past record of economic and political instability, the religious strife, the barriers of caste, in short the great popular wall of indifference all combine to produce a real uncertainty that the problem will be solved.

Initially, overpopulated underdeveloped areas are not likely to have either the capital or the kinds of industry for atomic power plants. Even if such areas embark on economic development under the stimulus of subsidized atomic power, the expected decline in birth rates may lag so far behind falling death rates that additional productivity will simply be diverted to supporting more people at no higher level of living. If this occurs, it will not be possible to maintain the industrialization impulse for any extended period. With birth rates uncontrolled, death rates may be expected to rise again until the two are once more in balance. In such a context atomic power would be as meaningless as were iron ore and coal resources to aboriginal peoples.

In short, it is apparent that atomic power can lead to increases in productivity in specific industries in underdeveloped areas if there is sufficient capital and sufficient motivation to utilize it. But even if this problematic situation prevails, it does not follow that the utilization of atomic power will itself lead to increases of high magnitude. Since the chances are real that the industrialization spiral will be halted by any one of a dozen major factors, conclusions that atomic power alone will transform such areas into industrialized regions with markedly higher standards of living seem unduly optimistic.

Certainly, the demographic characteristics of overpopulated and underdeveloped areas constitute one of the major obstacles to economic development in general and to the use of atomic power in particular. They are sufficiently important so that no discussion of industrialization and of rationalization of agriculture in such areas can be meaningful without their deliberate consideration. Their significance lies, of course, not only in their potentialities for population growth at a rate in excess of any achievable rate of technological growth, but also in the multiplicity of demographic, social, psychological, and historical factors which are connected in a complex and often indirect way with this basic population pattern.

One example is the spatial character of such economies, which will be strongly influenced by the presence of a broad agricultural stratum, with the distribution of population reflecting the food production orientation of the area. Along with other factors in the social organization, this implies an immobility on the part of the labor force which limits both the distribution and kind of domestic industry. This is because such industry will ordinarily be related to food processing or to the exploitation of local agricultural or mineral resources. While cheap power is necessary to any ultimate industrialization in such a situation, and while atomic power is theoretically well suited to induce a separation

[6] Abraham Stone, "Fertility Problems in India," *Fertility and Sterility,* 4 (May-June, 1953), pp. 210-217. See also the summary of an address by Carl C. Taylor, "India: 360 Million People Plan Their Development" given before the annual meeting of the Population Association of America, Princeton, New Jersey, April, 1955, and appearing in *Population Index,* 21 (July, 1955), pp. 169-170.

of industry from the primary agricultural stratum, pragmatically it may well be too costly and insufficiently well suited to the type of industry initially developing with its limited market.

Furthermore, there is the fundamental problem in such areas of labor supply in qualitative terms, and possibly in quantitative terms as well, since there may be general non-acceptance of industrial employment or, at best, inefficiencies in individual response which are rooted in the social organization.[7] Inefficiencies of this type can make even low money wages too high in terms of real wages to permit competitive operation or even to be justified in the name of economic nationalism.

On the other hand, the controlled population situation in the industrialized or industrializing nations is promising for the utilization of atomic power. In simplest terms, this is because a roughly favorable ratio of population to available resources can be maintained where the major part of the increased productivity associated with technological expansion is not constantly appropriated to the support of a larger population. In such countries, the capital accumulation necessary for atomic power development is already present or conceivably can be created. Obviously, factors inclining to the use of atomic power must again outweigh those which resist it. But, in general, widespread utilization of atomic power seems most probable in the next few decades not in countries like India and Mexico but in "westernized" nations like Great Britain, the United States, and Russia, which have or can get capital, entrepreneurship, trained labor, and adequate market for plants of optimum size, and so on, and in which the demographic pattern is not a hindrance to development.

Even here, as already suggested, some types of population pattern will constitute more favorable inclining factors than others, though none will be determining. A fairly rapid rate of growth, for example, is favorable to the active use of atomic power. We have seen historically that the exploitation of a new innovation tends to be most intensive in such a setting.[8] This is partly because the risk involved in adapting industry to new processes and in expending sizeable amounts of capital for plant and equipment is diminished where population growth creates steadily increasing demand. Psychologically, too, growth seems associated with optimism and a greater willingness to experiment. Again, where population growth is rapid, the mobility of labor is fostered, and this in turn implies easier exploitation of a competing new technique. In these terms, Russia and the United States appear most likely of all industrialized nations to utilize atomic power commercially in the near future. Other factors, notably the decreasing quantity and increasing cost of fossil fuel sources, suggest early and widespread utilization of atomic power in Great Britain. In primarily commercial agricultural countries like Denmark and Australia, there are insufficient markets for extensive quantities of new power.

Space limitations have prevented more than a partial and suggestive statement here. They have precluded both adequate presentation of supporting evidence and attention to such important considerations as nationalism and international political tensions as stimuli to atomic power utilization. In other words, population factors cannot be given more than their share of stress. Nevertheless, in underdeveloped areas generally the population pattern is a major unfavorable factor in the utilization of atomic power which does not appear in industrial nations of sizeable population. In the former, the patterns of population growth, if not adjusted, may well negate every attempt to increase levels of living even if subsidized atomic power is introduced as an impulse to industrialization. The actual utilization of atomic power in specific cases depends obviously on a host of interrelated factors both directly and only remotely related to the basic demographic equation, as for example, population composition and resultant labor-force participation variables on the one hand and the motivational system of a people on another. Population factors are relevant components in a matrix of intercorrelated social, economic, cultural, and psychological variables, the mutual relationships

[7] Cf. Wilbert E. Moore, *Industrialization and Labor: Social Aspects of Economic Development,* Ithaca: Cornell University Press, 1951.

[8] S. Lilley, *Men, Machines and History,* London: Cobbett Press, 1948, ch. 11.

of which frequently can only be implied rather analyzed in any cause-effect schema.

III

In what space remains I want to comment briefly on some implications of any utilization of atomic power for alterations in population patterns. These few remarks are shaped by the ultimate premise that atomic power will prove a useful addition to existing power sources but that it is unlikely by itself to revolutionize plant location, industrial techniques, economic organization, or any people's way of life.

Theoretically, atomic power plants for industrial use can be built in South Dakota, Madagascar, or the North Pole. In fact, there are no technological barriers to such undertakings. But the possible is quite different from the probable, and the probability of such a development is, in my estimation, zero. Such plants would be functionless without operatives and without a market to serve. Unless only small, portable atomic units were involved, an agglomeration of basic industry would almost necessarily be required, and there is nothing in location theory to suggest that these and similar areas are potential points of industrial attraction. Of course, nuclear energy can be employed for such specialized tasks as breaking down icebergs or desalting brackish water,[9] but there are possibly more acceptable alternative methods. At any event, such specialized installations would not ordinarily alter existing population distribution beyond introducing a small band of technicians at isolated spots. Except possibly in connection with irrigation, atomic power in itself has no potentialities for transferring waste regions into garden spots.[10] It will not, for example, change the character of the soil nor alter distance relationships.

While specific exceptions are conceivable, atomic power is also unlikely to change subsistence agricultural economies into industrialized ones; and certainly it will never do so by its mere technical availability. The comments above on underdeveloped areas need not be repeated here. They indicate that atomic power is likely to provoke no fundamental change in the economic and social organization of the great majority of such areas. To the extent that this is true, it will produce no changes in population patterns. It is only fair to say, however, that among the restricted number of such areas which might in the next few decades secure the necessary capital domestically or through subsidization to initiate economic development based on atomic power, or to extend industrialization which is already under way, some may possibly achieve a continuing development spiral of substantial enough proportions to affect the total societal organization. If this happens, and it must happen both rapidly and radically, presumably altered value systems will lead to the kind of demographic revolution which has already occurred in western nations. Of course, to assert that these areas will follow the same pattern is to assert an article of faith, not a proposition of fact, and I have strong personal reservations. Nevertheless, if population is not controlled ultimately, a reversion to high-waste patterns is mandatory beginning at the point where the rate of technical development no longer exceeds the rate of population growth. Successful industrialization and concomitant population control would presumably result in a redistribution of population, with focal points of heavy density around industrial agglomerations. This, in turn, implies increased population mobility, and so on. When all the *ifs* are overcome, such population changes may occur. Pragmatically, it is doubtful that atomic power spells marked population changes for the great majority of underdeveloped areas.

Then, will those nations which have undergone some substantial degree of urban-industrial growth find atomic power altering present population patterns? In my judgment, they will not to any degree. In Russia, where the immediate potentialities for the use of atomic power are relatively great, such power may be an important stimulus to more rapid industrialization than would otherwise occur, provided a shortage of capital is overcome. Again, we may assume if we wish that this would mean an earlier approach to a stable population. Since Russia's present energy resources tend to be concentrated geographically and in areas which are distant

[9] Amos de Shalit, "Irrigating the Negev," *The Nation*, 180 (June 18, 1955), pp. 531-532.

[10] Russia has hinted at gigantic blasting operations shifting land and water contours. If actually carried out, such operations could lead to drastic changes in climate and land use.

from the major points of population density, the use of atomic power may foster some alteration of population distribution by attracting industry and population to areas where resources can be aggressively developed. Still, other factors, such as an attempt to remove industrial production from attack, may be more important in effecting such redistribution.

One of the notable characteristics of American industry is the relative fixity of its locational pattern. The list of important industrial counties of the United States has shown little change over many decades. These counties, concentrated in the northeast industrial strip from Boston to Baltimore and along the deep-water rim of the Great Lakes, represent the most likely locations for atomic power plants since they are the centers of demand for power and, in fact, about the only locations in which atomic power plants of optimum size can presently find sufficient demand for their product. It seems probable that any use of atomic power will therefore simply heighten the concentration of population in these leading industrial areas. Presumably, it will also further the dispersion of population within such local concentrations. In other words, it will perpetuate existing tendencies.

Studies of the probable consequences of atomic power on the location of specific industries [11] such as iron and steel, cement, aluminum, and so on suggest that the chances of any major relocation of plants because of atomic power are small. Conceivably, changes of a limited sort might occur in the power-conscious electroprocess industries, but these would primarily be the result of expansion beyond the limits of available cheap hydropower. The mobile glass industry may relocate at the market, but if it does, this will probably occur because of construction of natural gas pipelines rather than because of atomic power.

Even if the depletion of conventional energy reserves occurs at some future time, or if these resources increase in cost or decrease in quality, industrial mobility will not be greatly enhanced. Substitute atomic power will be attracted principally to existing areas of demand. These are areas which already support important industrial complexes because of their suitability as plant sites for other reasons, such as access to market or the quality of local transport or labor. In short, any kind of equalization of population through industrial relocation based on atomic power is improbable in developed countries like the United States and Great Britain.

Changes in industrial products and processes through the use of atomic power may be expected. Some of these will undoubtedly be truly revolutionary in their consequences for producers and consumers. For instance, irradiation of plastics may permit their substitution for copper and metals in many industrial and household uses, including construction. But such new processes and products are not likely to alter our conclusions about industrial location and population distribution.

Possibly military considerations may lead to to the development of non-economic industrial sites using atomic power, such as the Arco, Idaho, area. If so, the same military considerations will probably dictate dispersion of plants and population within this limited area. Such development is dubious in itself, and, at any rate, would be of little significance for total population distribution. Furthermore, none of these developments seems to suggest any changes in demographic characteristics, even though they can contribute to increases in productivity.

The potentialities of atomic power are very great in many fields. The presently unknown indirect consequences may well be far-reaching. But in most parts of the world where atomic power is actually utilized on a sizeable scale, its demographic consequences are apt to be principally an intensification of the traits already characteristic of westernized nations, especially a fostering of further population concentration and consequently of low wastage patterns of fertility and mortality.

[11] Walter Isard and Vincent Whitney, "Atomic Power and the Location of Industry," *Harvard Business Review*, 28 (March, 1950), 45-54; Sam H. Schurr and Jacob Marschak (directors), *Economic Aspects of Atomic Power*, Princeton: Princeton University Press, 1950, chs. 3-10.

STUDY AND DISCUSSION QUESTIONS

1. The earliest societies of man survived in a hunting and gathering type of economy. Where subsistence depends on these two activities, what would be the ideal composition of the population? That is, what age structure, sex ratio, and marital composition would best facilitate hunting and gathering?
2. It has been noted that fertility fluctuates as a function of economic periods of prosperity or depression. Make a graph showing the crude birth rate in the United States since 1900. What economic factors can you associate with these patterns?
3. How would an aging population with many more females than males compare with a young population having an abundance of males in affecting the composition of the labor force of a nation? What kinds of jobs would suffer from a shortage of workers in each type of population?
4. What kinds of data does the U.S. Census Bureau collect on the labor force of this country? Who is included in the census definition of the labor force? What changes, if any, would you recommend in the definition?
5. In comparing the types of economy in the United States and the Soviet Union, what effect would varying population growth rates and changing population composition and distribution have on the efficient functioning of the economies?
6. It has been noted that the pattern of industrialization which is occurring in developing nations today is vastly different from what occurred in the United States and Western Europe in their early period of industrialization. Discuss the relationship of population factors to industrialization in developing countries as compared with the relationship that existed in the United States and Western Europe.
7. Why is a mobile population important to an industrial economy? Cite instances in American history when movement of population apparently occurred in response to a need of the nation's economy.

SUGGESTED ADDITIONAL READING

Coale, Ansley J., and Edgar M. Hoover. *Population Growth and Economic Development in Low-Income Countries.* Princeton: Princeton University Press, 1958.
Classic study by two economists, one also a demographer, on the relation between economic and demographic factors in India and Mexico, in particular.

National Bureau of Economic Research. *Demographic and Economic Change in Developed Countries.* Princeton: Princeton University Press, 1960.
Includes papers presented at a conference on the topic, including an application of economic theory to the analysis of fertility by Gary Becker and an analysis of the influence of business cycles on marriage and birth rates by Dudley Kirk.

Bancroft, Gertrude. *The American Labor Force: Its Growth and Changing Composition.* New York: John Wiley & Sons, 1958.

Long, Clarence. *The Labor Force Under Changing Income and Unemployment.* Princeton: Princeton University Press, 1958.

Wolfbein, Seymour L. *Employment and Unemployment in the United States: A Study of the American Labor Force.* Chicago: Science Research Associates, 1964.

Lebergott, Stanley. *Manpower in Economic Growth: the American Record Since 1800.* New York: McGraw-Hill Book Company, 1964.
The above four are treatments of labor force patterns in the United States, with emphasis on historical trends.

Woytinsky, Wladimir S., and Emma S. Woytinsky. *World Population and Production.* New York: The Twentieth Century Fund, 1953.
An encyclopedic volume concerning international social and economic trends and relationships, with particular attention to agriculture, energy and mining, manufactures, and living standards.

Jaffe, A. J., and Charles D. Stewart. *Manpower Resources and Utilization: Principles of Working Force Analysis.* New York: John Wiley & Sons, 1951.
Examination of the labor force, with special attention to problems of measurement and analysis.

Miller, Herman P. *Income Distribution in the United States.* Washington: U.S. Government Printing Office, 1966.
The first of the 1960 U.S. Census monographs, which analyzes the changing income distribution over time and variations in income among different population groups.

CHAPTER 15

Population and the Polity

Much demographic change has been brought about through the intentional acts of the polity, that is, governments and other political organizations. Policies affecting population which are adopted by the polity are usually directed through law but they may be an outcome of the noninstitutionalized power relationships which exist between different groups. Conversely, the demographic structure of a society and changes in the size and composition of the population may have consequences for the political structure and power relationships within the society as well as for the balance of power between that society and other societies. This final chapter examines these several relationships.

The control of population by the polity takes place through policies designed to regulate one or more of the basic components of population change — fertility, mortality, and migration. Some policies may be directed toward changing the status of the basic components; others may be directed toward maintaining these statuses. Policies designed to change a population component in one direction at one point in time may be reformulated at another time to change it in the other direction, as revised goals of the polity suggest a new attitude about population growth or decline.

The role of governments in affecting mortality conditions is well documented. Improvements in sanitation, medicine, disease control, and knowledge about public health, although contributed to some extent by private agencies, have come about mainly through government action. Control of contagious diseases, eradication of pests, investigation of the causes of chronic ailments, and experimentation with possible cures, are examples of mortality-reducing actions requiring a massive allocation of resources which is usually produced by governments. It is difficult to think of a national vaccination program administered by private groups that has been successful. Governments possess the organization and the machinery for getting the job done and they can resort to law both to communicate the policy and to enforce it. However, not all policies lead to mortality reductions; some actions of the policy result in mortality increases. Notable examples of these are genocide, the mass killing of a particular group of people in a society, such as the Jews in Nazi Germany, and capital punishment, the execution of persons believed to have committed unforgivable crimes against the society.

Government actions have been instrumental in affecting the movement of people. Policies designed to restrict or encourage immigration and emigration have been common in most parts of the world. The forced movement of peoples from one part of a country to another has been recorded in history (see article by Petersen in Chapter 6). Decisions made by local governments affecting land uses, such as urban renewal and highway expansion, have resulted in the residential mobility of people.

National policies related to fertility have endorsed various goals. Some of these policies are intended to support higher fertility, others to reduce fertility. Attempts to reduce fertility are more novel, as Dorothy Nortman points out in the first reading in this chapter, since nations had held to a belief of strength in numbers for centuries and the dysfunctional aspects of continued population growth had not yet become apparent. As Tien shows, policies affecting fertility may be manipulated by a government to raise fertility at one point in time and reduce it at another, as in the case of mainland China. Political ideology and population control in that country have been tightly intertwined and regulations concerning birth control have been intruments of national policies. In general, policies regarding fertility can take many forms, running from lowering minimum age at marriage, providing family subsidies, and making honorific awards for childbearing, on the pronatalist side, to legalizing abortion, spreading birth control knowledge and materials, and encouraging and facilitating the employment of women, on the antinatalist side.

Population factors may have an important effect on political processes and the political structure of nations and communities. In a representative form of government, the demographic composition of an electoral district will have an impact on who gets into office and whether or not he remains there. Elements of the population composition of an area, such as the increasing proportion of Negroes in large American cities and the high proportion of aged persons in places known for their health and retirement benefits, may determine the kind of candidates who run for office and help shape the political promises and actions of the candidates and office-holders. Campbell and colleagues analyze the association between residential mobility and electoral behavior. Migration, they point out, serves not only to redistribute the population of a particular political persuasion but also to put the mobile persons in a new milieu in which their political beliefs may be reshaped.

Numbers of people, their location, and their characteristics can also affect other institutions of society by modification of power relationships among groups. The movement of some militant Negro organizations in the United States, which is designed to acquire more informal and formal power to improve the status of Negroes, is drawing its strength, in part, from the great numbers of Negroes in the South and urban North, where the changes to be effected are most desired. Proposals by some states to increase expenditures for education have been defeated by voters, many of whom are in a stage of the family life cycle when educational benefits seem less rewarding than before. Young people, who form an increasing proportion of the United States population, are demanding a greater voice in the educational and military decisions that will affect them.

Finally, as discussed by Davis in the last article, the population size and composition of countries is one determinant of their ability to wage war, maintain a national defense, and influence international decisions. Numbers of people alone is an important factor, but of vital importance too is the demographic, social, and economic makeup of these people. The course of population developments in various parts of the world will affect the balance of political power in the international sphere, and the world's future will undoubtedly be greatly influenced by the actions individuals and governments take to control the population situation.

*Population Policies in Developing Countries and Related International Attitudes**

Dorothy Nortman†

The rate at which a population grows is affected by the laws and regulations it adopts to govern many areas of its affairs. For purposes of the present discussion, however, population policy is viewed as a conscious attempt to influence population size by altering the rate of population growth. In particular we are concerned with the development in many emerging countries of policies directed at reducing the rate of population growth in an effort to maximize the rate of economic development. This idea of *reducing* population growth is novel, for modern economic growth in the presently developed nations was accompanied in almost all cases by a sustained and substantial increase in population (Kuznets, 1959). Moreover, because per capita product also increased, often impressively, population growth came to be viewed not only as good for a nation, but even as indispensable for continued economic progress, power, and prestige.

This is not to say that in the course of their development the Western nations did not experience population pressures. The great waves of European emigration testify to such pressures. However, they stemmed from social, religious, ethnic, and adventurous stimuli as well as from purely economic considerations. For the most part, the Western nations observed a laissez-faire policy toward their population growth. When concern was expressed, it was over rates regarded as too low, generally considerably less than one per cent per year. Thus, after more than a century of slowly declining birth rates, French anxiety over a net reproduction rate that by the 1930's was below the level of population replacement culminated in 1939 in a "Code de la Famille" that provided "economic aid to the family, protection of maternity and infancy, the suppression of abortion, the encouragement of marriage and parenthood, and the restriction of the traffic in contraceptive devices and birth control propaganda" (Eldridge, 1954, p. 10). To implement its conclusion that "a replacement size of family is desirable in Great Britain at the present time," the United Kingdom Royal Commission on Population proposed a series of family welfare measures in 1944 (Eldridge, 1954, pp. 12, 13). Other European nations adopted similar health, family, and welfare measures to bolster their sagging rates of population growth; and the pre-war pronatalist policies promoted by Germany and Italy (and Japan, the only developed Asian nation) during their totalitarian regimes are well known.

Population policies specifically intended to *reduce* rates of growth are a post World War II phenomenon. To achieve this end, three choices are theoretically possible: external migration, a decline in the birth rate, or a deliberate increase in the death rate. To discuss why the first is not generally considered a feasible solution would take us beyond the scope of this paper. Suffice it to say that the magnitude of the problem of rapid population growth renders emigration an unrealistic solution. Of the two remaining alternatives, a deliberate increase in the death rate is universally unthinkable. Nations faced with too rapid rates of population growth therefore have only one choice — to reduce birth rates. How to do this is the population problem of today's developing countries.

In the Western nations voluntary action alone

* Reprinted with permission from *Eugenics Quarterly*, Vol. 11, No. 1 (March 1964), pp. 11-29.

† I want to express my appreciation to the staff of the Population Council to whom I am indebted for much of the information contained in this article.

on the part of thousands of individual couples, often in the face of organized opposition from church and state, proved sufficient to effect a long slow decline in the birth rate that followed in the wake of slowly declining death rates. In today's developing nations, death rates are coming down too rapidly for concomitant changes in attitudes and ways of living that impel people to modify long-standing conjugal habits, family relations, and traditional pride in many children. With birth rates at traditional levels — generally 40 to 55 — per thousand population, and death rates plunging to current Western levels of 9 or 10 per thousand, the countries of Asia, Africa, and Latin America are growing at 2 to 3.5 per cent per year; that is, 2 to 4 times more rapidly than Europe in its comparable period of development. On the threshold of modernizing their economies, the developing nations are finding these rates incompatible with the growing aspiration of their people for an adequate level of living.

With the impeding of economic development plans by high rates of population increase, more and more governments of developing countries are expressing concern over their population problems. This concern now ranges from explicit national policies to promote widespread contraceptive practice to what may be considered an emerging interest in population matters. Between the two extremes are countries permitting or involved in some way in the distribution of contraceptive information and supplies and another group whose national governments either support or at least permit experimental, pilot family planning programs which may or may not eventually lead to the adoption of a national policy. A review of the specific countries that fall within this classification follows:

Countries with National Population Policies

India

With a population of some 460 million people, India, the second largest country in the world, has taken the lead in providing central government support of a National Family Planning Programme. Precise estimates of birth and death rates are lacking, but the intercensal growth rate of 2 per cent between 1951 and 1961 plus other considerations suggest that India's population is currently growing by 2.2 to 2.5 per cent per year, rates at which numbers double in 31 to 27 years, respectively.

India's national population policy dates from 1951 when the Panel of Health Programmes of the Planning Commission appointed a committee to report on population growth and family planning (Mauldin, 1960, p. 14). According to Lt. Col. B. L. Raina, present Director of Family Planning, "After independence, it became obvious that family planning was not only necessary on the basis of humanitarian concern for individuals, but was also of the most fundamental importance to the plans for over all economic development of India" (Raina, 1963, p. 3). The current Development Plan regards the Family Planning Programme as "at the very centre of planned development." (Raina, 1963, p. 45). Although expenditures have been considerably below allocations, the estimated expenditure during the single year 1962–1963 — 259.34 lakhs of rupees ($5.4 million U. S.) — exceeded the total spent during the whole five years of the Second Plan [1] (Raina, 1963, p. 45).

Under the National Family Planning Programme, by January 1963 some 25,000 medical and social workers had been trained in regular and short-term courses, and 6774 rural and 1667 urban family planning service centers had been opened. Thus far the family planning clinics have been the main channel for distribution of supplies to the people (Raina, 1963, p. 22). However, since the clinical approach concentrates on individual contact between doctor and patient and "most people do not, and need not, use the clinic as a regular contraceptive supply source" (Raina, 1963, p. 22), future plans envisage a public health and community distribution system whereby simple supplies will be available within easy geographic distance, "without questions being asked, and without other psychological barriers such as inconvenient time of day, having

[1] Allocations for family planning have been stepped up from 65 lakhs of rupees (about $1.4 million) in the First Five Year Plan (1951-56) to 497 lakhs of rupees ($10.5 million) in the Second Five Year Plan (1956-61) to 2697.57 lakhs of rupees ($56 million) for the Third Five Year Plan, 1961-66 (Raina, 1963, p. 5).

to wait, or lack of privacy" (Raina, 1963, p. 34). At present contraceptive supplies imported by the Government of India are despatched from regional to district medical stores and thence distributed to peripheral clinic units. State health authorities may also purchase supplies on the open market. The most serious bottlenecks are at the point of peripheral distribution.

Emphasis on method has been shifting from rhythm in the early 1950's to foam tablets after the Ramanagram-Lodi Colony Study — in which the field work was performed during 1952–54 (Mauldin, 1960, p. 17) — and more recently to condoms and foam tablets. A school of thought exists in India that regards sterilization of appropriate persons — that is, those of suitable age with an adequate number of living children — as the solution to India's population problems.[2] According to Lt. Col. Raina, "voluntary sterilization far exceeded the expectation" (Raina, 1963, p. 11). Free facilities are available on a fairly wide scale, in hospitals and maternity and health centers in the States and Centrally administered areas. The State of Maharashtra has initiated sterilization camps and some States provide financial compensation of from 10 to 30 rupees per sterilization in addition to free transportation and time off from work. Female sterilization has also been well received. For example, in Bombay City it is estimated that five per cent of all deliveries are followed by voluntary sterilization. The reported number of sterilizations through February 1963 is 334,000, almost $\frac{2}{3}$ on males (Raina, 1963, p. 11). The number of unreported sterilizations has not been officially estimated.

Among the many research projects under way, the Singur program in West Bengal has produced the most encouraging results. Births per 1000 population fell from 45.2 in 1956 to 36.9 in 1961, compared with 45.0 and 42.9 respectively in the control area. (Population Council, July 1963, p. 4). Experts and Government officials realize, however, that it may well be some years before the National Planning Programme of India makes its impact on the national birth rate. The reasons are suggested by the difficulties of launching and implementing a program among masses of illiterate and rural people involving changes in their most intimate and personal relations and attitudes. According to Col. Raina:

> The accomplishments, for a programme having no simple precedents to follow . . . have been many. These include the setting up a basic organizational structure at Central, State, and, in some places, at District levels. A large number of centres for training personnel have been rapidly organized. The overall programme is in balance, it is based on firm scientific research, is well developed in medical aspects, and is now in a position to extend the educational and supply wings (Raina, 1963, p. 45).

The target of the Family Planning Programme is ambitious; namely, to reduce India's current birth rate of about 40 to 25 per 1000 population by 1973 (Raina, 1963, p. 32). Parallel with the official health structure from the National Health Ministry to the State Planning Boards down through the block levels, the programme calls for voluntary educational workers or advisory groups at different levels. Community educational work, to produce the group support necessary for successful contraceptive practice, is recognized as a basic, integral aspect of population policy. Other vital functions include statistical evaluation of the impact of the program on the birth rate, administrative coordination, training of personnel, and research projects to determine the means by which goals may be most readily achieved (Raina, 1963, p. 38).

Pakistan

At the Asian Population Conference in New Delhi this past December, it was reported that for the Third Five Year Development Plan, 1965–70, the Planning Commission was using 2.6 per cent as the current annual growth rate of Pakistan's 97 million people. This contrasts sharply with the 1.4 per cent assumed for the First Five Year Plan, 1955–60, a figure adopted, in the words of Mr. Said Hasan, former Ambassador to the U.N. and now Vice-Chairman of the Planning Commission, "to keep despair away. We are all convinced that population is growing faster than that" (Qureshi, 1959, p. vii). Population projections in the Second Five Year Plan

[2] Its chief spokesman is R. A. Gopalaswami, former Registrar-General, until recently Adviser and Programme Administrator of the Madras State Family Planning Board.

implied a 1.7 per cent average annual increase between 1960 and 1965.

Pakistan's population policy to reduce the national birth rate may be said to date from 1960, but serious interest was displayed in February 1958 when the Director General of Health convened a special meeting to discuss plans submitted by the Family Planning Association and 500,000 rupees were authorized for family planning (Mauldin, 1963, p. 66). By September 1959, Brigadier M. Sharif, then Director General of the Health Ministry stated:

In view of the rapid rate of population increase which may become very alarming, Pakistan's Second Five-Year Plan has strongly advocated a policy of family planning and has made adequate provision for a family planning programme. (Qureshi, 1959, p. 351).

The program is administered by a Director of Family Planning under the Director General of the Ministry of Health. Two family planning officers — one in the East and one in West Pakistan — are responsible for implementation and execution. Brigadier M. Sharif described the design of the program at a conference in New York in 1960 as follows (Kiser, 1962, p. 145).[3]

1. Through a health approach, to provide a family planning service from all existing medical centers.
2. To teach the virtues of family planning through simple written or spoken words, pictures, etc., and through the example of successful experience.
3. To provide mobile teams of jeep-vans furnished with audio-visual equipment, first in urban areas and moving progressively into rural areas, for education and motivation.
4. To concentrate, at least initially, on the simplest methods, all contraceptive supplies to be provided free in rural areas, at a token charge in urban centers; with gradual introduction of male sterilization as motivation increases.
5. To establish training and research centers and provide intensive training for medical and paramedical personnel, as well as village and community workers.
6. By means of an action-cum-study and research program in selected areas, to collect vital statistics and ascertain acceptability and success of the program.

[3] The Second Five Year Plan, 1960-65, allocated rupees 30.5 million (a little over $6 million), for family planning expenditures out of a total health budget of rupees 400 million.

Existing hospitals, dispensaries, and maternal and child health centers are expected to add family planning advice and supplies to their services. For rural areas, where 85 per cent of the people live, village workers are to share responsibility for family planning with the rural health centers. An interesting study currently in progress is that of the intrauterine plastic coil, launched by the National Research Institute of Family Planning in Karachi in October 1962. Three important action research programs are now under way which may show favorable results in a year or two.

As in India, success measured by a decline in the national birth rate is not to be expected in a short period of time. Experts consider that some of the requirements are an administrative structure under the direction of full-time, high-status health personnel, an effective public information program, removal of import restrictions on contraceptives, and family planning training in the medical centers.

Korea

The Revolutionary Government of the Republic of Korea came into being on May 16, 1961, prior to which time there had been no family planning program. After discussion by the Supreme Council for National Reconstruction of the necessity to control population to achieve economic goals, the Ministry of Health and Social Affairs proposed a Family Planning Policy which the Council approved in November 1961. A month later the Health Ministry removed the ban on the importation and home production of contraceptive supplies (Rep. of Korea, Oct. 1963).

The target of the Family Planning Program[4] is to reduce the annual rate of natural increase of Korea's 27 million people from an estimated 3 per cent in 1963 to 2.5 per cent by 1966 and to 1.82 per cent by 1971. According to the Health Ministry, to achieve this goal requires the prevention of about 1.5 million births in a ten-year period.[5] The Economic Planning Board

[4] The National Budget provided 42 million won for family planning in 1962, 83 million ($664,000 U.S.) in 1963 (Rep. of Korea, Dec. 1963).

[5] Examination of the data suggests that this figure is predicated on prevailing mortality rates, a further reasonable decline in which would necessitate the prevention of 2 million rather than 1.5 million births in the next ten years.

estimates that by 1980 implementation of the Population Policy will result in a growth rate of 1.16 per cent per annum compared with 3.15 per cent under a laissez-faire situation and will produce a per capita income 36 per cent above a laissez-faire level (Rep. of Korea, Sept. 1963).

The Korean Government is pursuing its family planning program with vigor. In addition, Korea is favored by relatively high literacy and school attendance for that part of the world as well as increasing urbanization. To implement the program, the Prime Minister has instructed the Economic Planning Board to establish a "Population Policy Council" as an advisory organ. He requested the Ministry of Justice to consider whether to enact a Eugenic Protection Law (similar to Japan's) which would permit abortion for economic as well as hereditary considerations. The Defense Ministry was requested to establish a plan whereby doctors in the armed services will educate the soldiers in contraceptive techniques. Research and training projects, as well as improvement in vital statistics, are also considered basic by the Health Ministry although it has yet to implement these aspects into its Family Planning Program.

The major research undertaking to date is a pilot project under the direction of the Yonsei University Medical College Department of Preventive Medicine and Public Health, in a rural area of about 9000 population, 13 miles north of Seoul. The objective is to assess the possibility of reducing the birth rate through family planning education and services. Preliminary results indicate 35.8 pregnancies per 100 women years for the group accepting the services compared with about 56–58 for noncontraceptors in the area. A full report is due in February 1964 (Population Council, Dec. 1963, p. 8).

Countries with Limited Involvement in Family Planning

Although the countries in this group do not have a national policy to reduce rates of population growth, most of them have encouraged private efforts to promote family planning, offering some combination of financial assistance, medical facilities, services, and supplies. Private efforts stem mainly from family planning associations motivated by concern for individual family welfare, not the need to reduce national rates of population growth. The increasing identification of the two, however, has led these governments to support the activities of the Family Planning Association, even though no ministry or planning commission has announced an official policy to lower the birth rate.

Malaysia

Singapore's Family Planning Association is one of the most successful in the world. In 1960 the Government promoted a family planning campaign, the success of which taxed all of the Association's facilities. In his Foreword to the 1962 Annual Report of the Association, Singapore Prime Minister Lee Kuan Yew stated:

> Every year as we draw up our budget we are faced with a terrifying increase on education and health services, the need for more jobs, the need for more homes, all because our rate of population expansion is about 4% per annum. . . . All those entrusted with the business of government in any of the countries in Asia are acutely aware of the enormous problems of economic imbalance and impoverishment as a result of rapid growth in population. (Singapore, 1962, p. 3).

The favorable climate of opinion toward the practice of birth control has undoubtedly been an important factor in the notable decline in Singapore's crude birth rate, from 45.4 in 1952 to 34.5 in 1962.[6] (UN, Oct. 1963). In addition to support of the Family Planning Association, the Government offers contraceptive advice and supplies in its hospitals and clinics. Singapore was host to the Seventh International Conference on Planned Parenthood on February 10, 1963, at which Prime Minister Yew delivered the opening address.

Although Malaya has no official policy for moderating fertility, it does support the family planning clinics run by the Family Planning Association. With the formation of three new Associations in 1962, every State in the Federation now has an Association. The President of the Federated Associations stated recently, "the aim is to train every doctor, nurse and midwife

[6] The latter suggests a 3 per cent rate of natural increase, with immigration adding perhaps another 1 per cent to yield the 4 per cent growth rate mentioned by the Prime Minister.

in Malaya in family planning methods and to incorporate family planning into the Government Rural Health Development programme" (Singapore, 1962, p. 29).

Hong Kong

As in the case of Singapore, the mode of living has created a public sentiment that favors family planning. The Government's contribution to the Association during the fiscal year ending March 31, 1963, was $42,000 (U.S.), about 70 per cent of the Association's total income (Family Planning, 1962–63).

By Asian standards, Hong Kong's crude birth rate is low, 32 for 1962, but its economic and social problems are strained by the influx of refugees from mainland China. The Family Planning Association is seeking more clinic facilities and greater financial assistance from the Government.

Ceylon

The Ceylon Government accepted the offer of the Swedish Government to undertake a pilot project to study the implementation of family planning in Ceylon. The Project began in 1959 in two areas, one rural, one suburban, and has since been extended to two additional areas.[7] Preliminary results in one of the village areas suggest a sharp drop in the birth rate, from 31.2 per 1000 population in 1959 at the start of the project, to 21.9 in 1962. The village is considered somewhat atypical, however, in that its rate was already about 20 per cent below that for Ceylon at the start of the program (Pop. Council, Dec. 1963, p. 11). The present agreement between the two Governments terminates in 1965, after which it is problematical whether the Ceylon Government will continue the program.

Other Government activities include financial support of the Family Planning Association which derived more than half its income from the Government in the fiscal year 1961–62, and the use of Government hospitals and clinics for contraceptive advice and supplies. As in other countries, the clinics are poorly attended and are not a suitable medium for a mass promotional effort.

[7] Its 1963-64 budget is estimated at 770,000 Swedish Kronen (about U.S. $145,000).

Puerto Rico

Puerto Rico's 2.5 million people are growing at the high rate of 2.5 per cent per year despite a birth rate (31.4 in 1962) that is low for underdeveloped nations. To what extent the relatively low birth rate results from migration of young couples and husbands to the United States or economic ties with the mainland that somehow are conducive to contraceptive practice, is not clear. Whatever the reason, Government attempts at family planning in Puerto Rico are unprecedented for Latin America and much older than in Asian countries. The earliest action was the establishment of clinics in 1935 by the Puerto Rico Emergency Relief Administration (Duke, 1960, p. 563). While the Government encountered public apathy, Catholic opposition, and disfavor from Washington, under pro-birth-control administrators, "population control as a policy was advocated by local officials" (Duke, 1960, p. 565). The result is that Puerto Rico surpasses most countries of the world in government facilities dispensing birth control information and supplies. (Kiser, 1962, p. 310). Nevertheless, the clinics are not popular, they receive little publicity, and it cannot be said that family planning has become a governmental policy or is a positive part of the culture (Duke, 1960, p. 565).

Because of the limitations of the clinics in reaching the mass of the people, the Family Planning Association of Puerto Rico has designed a unique program "to bring contraception to the people." Since 1958 volunteers chosen for their good name in the community have been distributing a vaginal foam contraceptive free of charge to potential users willing to accept a bottle. A survey of 253 women in the program indicated that 60 per cent were practicing some form of contraception compared with 47 per cent prior to enrollment.

Barbados

With a density of some 1400 persons per square mile, Barbados' 232,000 people constitute one of the world's most densely populated agricultural economies. In recognition of this situation, the Legislative Council and House of Assembly appointed a Joint Committee to make recommendations. Its report, published in 1954, stated:

After most careful and exhaustive consideration, the Committee is satisfied that a system of Family Planning under the aegis of the Government is a solution that offers some hope. . . . It is recommended that Family Planning Clinics should be set up and be operated directly by the Department of Medical Services and with the assistance of other Departments. (UN Technical, 1957, pp. 2, 3).

The clinics are private organizations run by the Family Planning Association with a grant from the Government of about $20,000 (Barbadian). The President of the Association has recently proposed that the Minister of Education undertake to teach "senior" children the responsibilities of family life "including knowledge of family planning" (Family Planning, 1960).

Countries with Experimental or Pilot Projects

The implementation of a formal policy of population control requires detailed knowledge of prevailing mores, modes of living, marriage patterns, attitudes toward family planning, literacy levels, and other social, economic, and demographic characteristics of the population. Will the people accept birth control? If so, what methods are most likely to be accepted? What are the effective means of communication? What are the best channels of supply?

With the growing concern over rapid rates of population increase, these questions are interesting governments in experimental or pilot projects in advance of any formal decision to adopt or declare a national policy on population. This is not to say that official expressions of concern over high growth rates are lacking. The economic development plans of developing countries usually emphasize the difficulties posed by rapid population increase. The point is that the countries in this group are in an exploratory stage. Governmental advocacy of family planning is a new and novel concept, not to be hastily declared, but to be preceded by careful scientific study and investigation.

Taiwan

Taiwan's statement prepared for the Asian Population Conference held in New Delhi last December sums up the attitude discussed below:

Although our cultural, social and political background does not at the moment permit the government to formulate and declare a clear population policy, yet the government is deeply concerned with the problem. The actions on the improvement in population registration and studies on population are all in line with government policy. The setting up of Family Planning Association by social organizations, represents the awareness of the importance of population problems by social leaders and the general public.

The action program undertaken by the Maternal and Child Health Institute of the Provincial Government in February 1963 to implement prepregnancy health and family planning is probably one of the most extensive and elaborate social science experiments ever carried out in a natural setting (Berelson, 1963). The scene of the program is Taichung city with a population of about 300,000 people.[8] According to the program's technical advisor, the findings indicate that "such a program can implement family planning economically" and "so far as the central question is concerned, about the implementation of family planning in such a society, the important answer is: it can be done."

The birth rate in Taiwan as a whole has been falling, from a level of 45.3 per 1000 population as recently as 1955 to 37.4 in 1962 (U. N., *Statistical,* 1962). In other respects, too, Taiwan is different from the rest of Asia. Outside of Japan, it is perhaps the most economically developed area of its size, and in Taichung City, the program's survey found that 90 per cent of the men and 70 per cent of the women over age 11 were literate, at least in an elementary way.

Official interest in population matters can be gauged not only from the action program but also from the fact that in 1961 the Provincial Government established the Taiwan Population Studies Center for social-demographic research and action on a practical basis. The Provincial Department of Health is now providing contraceptive information as part of its prepregnancy health program.

[8] Details are described in the July 1963 publication of the Population Council, *Studies in Family Planning.*

Tunisia

Tunisia has initiated an experimental family planning program. The central purpose of the study is to experiment with different ways of implementing family planning to determine the most effective and efficient means of establishing the program on a broader basis. If the results are successful, the Tunisian Government hopes and expects to incorporate family planning services as part of the regular services of the Ministry of Health (Pop. Council, Dec. 1963, p. 3, 4).

The program began with a mission of Tunisian representatives in the latter part of 1963 to the United States and certain Asian countries to observe family planning activities and consult with technical experts. Following this, a seminar was held in Tunis in January 1964 for training on modern contraceptive methods and involvement of the medical community, leaders of women's movements, and others who logically have a stake in the enterprise. Experts estimate it will take about two years for results to develop that can be assessed for a broadly based program.

Turkey

Turkey's First Five Year Development Plan 1963–1967 proposes to adopt a population policy "to slow down the rate of population growth (now estimated at about 3 per cent per year), as well as the ratio of child population to active population" (Turkish Rep., 1963). The goal is a 10 per cent decline in fertility every five years for the next 15 years. The Plan advocates:

a. Repeal of laws that prohibit spreading contraceptive information and importing and selling supplies;
b. Education of public health personnel in population planning;
c. Provision of free information and where necessary, supplies;
d. Use of existing facilities for mass education;
e. Home production and import of contraceptives at low prices. (Ibid).

Turkey's assets are its homogeneity in nationality and language, suggesting a more rapid cultural diffusion once family planning practice begins to take hold. Also, it is in a more favorable economic position compared with other underdeveloped nations. Its per capita income is one of the highest in the Middle East, and it is not currently dependent upon outside sources of food supply to feed its population. Nevertheless, "In a country such as Turkey, where the giving of birth control information has been illegal, it is evident that education in the essentials is needed by nearly every category of worker" (Pop. Council, Dec., 1963, p. 5).

United Arab Republic

A statement on population incorporated in a major official document gave encouragement to family planning efforts in the United Arab Republic. President Nasser declared in the May 1962 draft of the Charter:

> Population increase constitutes the most dangerous obstacle that faces the Egyptian people in their drive towards raising the standard of production in their country in an effective and efficient way. . . . Attempts at family planning . . . deserve the most sincere efforts supported by modern scientific methods . . . (UAR, 1962).

The family planning movement dates from 1955 when the National Population Commission, (which had been formed in 1953), opened four planned parenthood clinics. Typically, the clinics were poorly attended, the total number of visits not exceeding 6000 per year, a third of whom came for sterility treatment. The next major development was a conference in May 1962 sponsored by the Egyptian Medical Association on Social and Medical Aspects of Family Planning, attended by the Vice President of the United Arab Republic and the Minister for Public Health. Both spoke of the importance attached by the Government to family planning (Rizk, 1963).

The Egyptian Association for Population Studies, whose budget includes a 50,000 pound (Egyptian) grant from the Government, has recommended that a national program of population planning be adopted and implemented. About 100 centers are scheduled to be set up during the year to give premarital examinations and advice on planned parenthood.

Countries with Emerging Interest in Population Matters

To limit this group to two countries is obviously to draw an arbitrary line between what is the natural interest of all nations in the size of their populations and what may be regarded as an emerging interest in determining that size for the future. Among Latin American countries Chile seems to be most conscious of the difficulties created by population growth. Thailand also differs from countries not otherwise specified in that it is taking a conscious look at the implication of its population growth.

Chile

Motivated by concern over the high abortion rate, estimated at 35 to 40 per cent of pregnancies, the Health Services of the Government are now providing birth control services in some hospitals and clinics (New York Times, Oct. 1963). They have also created a National Committee for Family Protection to consider problems of action and policy in this sphere. Inasmuch as 90 per cent of Chile's eight million people are Roman Catholic, these developments have aroused considerable interest. However, it should be stressed that these actions are regarded as health measures and not a national policy to regulate the rate of population growth.

Thailand

Thailand's 28 million people have a proud history free from colonial rule. In fact, it was in recognition of this heritage that in 1939 the official name of the country was changed from Siam to Thailand, "land of the free." At the same time, however, Western manners and dress were encouraged (Hall, 1955).

Today discussion of the problems posed by rapid population growth is at the Cabinet level. As an outgrowth of a Population Seminar held in March 1963, the National Research Council submitted a national population program to the Prime Minister. Although it is too early to say how far this will be implemented, the Prime Minister has already endorsed a family planning pilot project. Other proposals are to improve the collection of vital data, to study and ascertain the attitudes of people toward family planning, and to train medical and paramedical personnel in family planning techniques.

Thus far we have discussed existing or emerging attention to population problems in some 14 developing countries. Their population rates of growth range from about 2 to 3.5 per cent per year, rates at which numbers double in 35 to 20 years respectively. With a combined population exceeding 700 million, this group of countries constitutes one-third of the more than 2 billion people who inhabit the underdeveloped areas of the world.

Communist China

Another third of the underdeveloped world lives in Communist China, which, according to to recent newspaper accounts, is trying to reduce fertility by encouraging later age at marriage and reviving its birth control campaign. In an interview last January with the writer Edgar Snow, Premier Chou En-Lai is quoted as saying: "with improved living conditions over the past two years our rate of increase again rose to 2.5 per cent! Therefore our emphasis on planned parenthood is entirely positive; planned parenthood, where there is increased production of goods and services, is conducive to raising the people's standard of living" (New York Times, February 3, 1964).

China's intensive birth control campaign first undertaken in the mid 1950's caused considerable speculation in the Western World because of traditional Marxist opposition to Malthusian concepts. Premier Chou En-lai declared to the Eighth National Party Congress in 1956:

> To protect women and children and bring up and educate our younger generation in a way conducive to the health and prosperity of the nation, we agree that a due measure of birth control is desirable. Health departments should, in cooperation with other institutions concerned, carry out intelligent propaganda and adopt effective measures toward this end. (Aird, 1962).

Still the Health Department hesitated to act in this matter. Then, in February 1957, Mao Tse-tung was reported to have said: "Steps must be taken to keep our population for a long time at a stable level, say, of 600,000,000. A wide campaign of explanation and proper help must be undertaken to achieve this aim" (Tien, 1963, p. 276). In March, an editorial in the *People's Daily* criticized the Health Department for failing to meet this urgent need of the masses. Immediately thereafter, until June 1958, the birth control campaign was put into high gear (Mauldin, Milbank, 1960).

By 1958 the political winds had begun to shift. China was engaged on her Great Leap Forward and the birth control campaign slowed to a standstill. It is not clear why or whether the two were regarded as incompatible. Western scholars have speculated that perhaps the Great Leap forward "pointed to a quick transition from an agricultural and backward nation to an industrialized and advanced state, implying the automatic emergence of the practice of fertility control at no extra cost" (Tien, 1963, p. 228). Other possibilities were the prospect of a bumper harvest, the expediency of abandoning a difficult campaign that at best would not produce results for years or the re-emergence of traditional theorists within the Party circles.

In any event, although the birth control campaign was halted in 1958, contraceptive devices were not banned, were generally available in the cities, and "although during the 1959–61 period almost no mention apparently was made in the press of abortion and sterilization, as far we know these operations were not made illegal and were available to those who requested them" (Orleans, 1962).

Recent developments suggest a resumption of the birth control campaign. In January 1962 the State Council revised import duties to permit contraceptive supplies to enter China duty free. At the end of the year the *People's Daily* began to print advertisements to promote the sale of publications in which birth control is advocated (Tien, 1963, p. 290). More recently the Government has been advocating later age at marriage. These are not unexpected developments. A growth rate in the past two years of 2.5 per cent as stated by Premier Chou means a net addition to the population of about 17.5 million people a year, an increase the Government is not likely to ignore, Marxist anti-Malthusianism notwithstanding.

Other Countries

Another country deserving discussion is Indonesia, not for any policy in the sense under review, but because it is a nation of 100 million people. Population density varies widely, from intensely populated Java with one of the highest densities in the world, to the sparsely settled outer islands. Government interest to date has been in resettlement projects to effect a more equitable distribution of the population. Statements by the Indonesian delegates to the Asian Population Conference in December 1963 emphasize that resettlement is the government policy on population, but it was pointed out that the population is permitted to practice, and private organizations may disseminate contraceptive information. The Family Planning Association, formed in 1957, includes many influential persons.

The Indonesian Council for Sciences is interested in research and testing and since 1960 has collected demographic and economic data from several sample surveys. A more intensive survey including experimental introduction of birth control is the Tjermee Family Life Study in East Java (Balfour).

As an economically developed nation with a low birth rate, Japan does not belong in a discussion of underdeveloped countries. It is included for two reasons: (1) it is an Asian country; (2) it achieved within an unprecedented short period a reduction in fertility that many of the countries discussed would like to emulate.

Japan is credited with a permissive population policy that resulted in a dramatic reduction in births, from a post-war high of 34 per 1000 population in 1947 to 17 in 1957. As far as official statement is concerned, the essence of Japan's policy is the Eugenic Protection Law passed in 1948 to replace the National Eugenic Law. The main feature of the new law was to permit induced abortion for economic reasons as well as for physical considerations to protect the mother's health. The liberal interpretation of economic difficulty and the designation of doctors to perform the abortion at low cost in order to drive out black market operations appeared to give official sanction to a practice to which Japanese women were resorting in increasing numbers. The point is that industrial and literate Japan, caught in the throes of economic collapse after the War, was highly motivated to limit family size. The Government's major concern was to guard against unsafe abortion and to try to replace abortion by contraception. Thus there are important differences, but Japan is of much interest to the rest of Asia because of likenesses in moral values, customs and religion.

Conspicuous by their omission from this listing of underdeveloped nations are two vast areas: Africa south of the Sahara and most of

Latin America. In the former, nations are in the throes of political birth, with various factions vying for position and the powers that be involved in formulating administrative machinery to run the everyday affairs of government. These countries are too new to deal with any but current, pressing problems.

Latin America has the fastest growing population of any continent, over 2.7 per cent per year. As part of the New World, its history until now has been as an area of immigration, not one experiencing population pressure. High birth rates are only partially explained by the prevalence of Catholicism. Like Spain, Portugal, and Italy, Europeanized Argentina and Uruguay have low birth rates, while their Northern neighbors, whose peoples are varying mixtures of European, Amerindian, and Negro backgrounds, have high birth rates. Although contraception is neither encouraged nor widely practiced, the extensive resort to induced abortion is recognized as a problem.

International Action and Attitudes

Repercussions to the population developments in the emerging countries are resounding around the world. By 1963 birth control, a subject hitherto discussed in hushed tones, had become a topic of open debate in the great forums of legislative bodies and the mass media of world news and opinion. The argument still centers on the necessity, desirability, or morality of adopting measures to reduce world fertility. On the other hand, responsible opinion now generally concedes that increasing growth rates, ranging at present from 2 to almost 4 per cent per year in the developing nations of the world compared to an average of 1.2 per cent in the technically advanced countries, are incompatible with political stability and efforts to eradicate poverty.

United Nations

Population matters reached the floor of the United Nations General Assembly for the first time in December 1962. The discussion and debate culminated in the passage by 69 to 0 with 27 abstentions, of Resolution 1838 (XVII), *Population Growth and Economic Development* at the 1197th plenary meeting of the Seventeenth Session on December 18, 1962. The Resolution requests the Secretary-General

> to conduct an inquiry among the Governments of States Members of the United Nations and members of the specialized agencies concerning the particular problems confronting them as a result of the reciprocal action of economic development and population changes,

and recommends that

> the Economic and Social Council, in cooperation with the specialized agencies, the regional economic commissions and the Population Commission . . . should intensify its studies and research on the interrelationship of population growth and economic and social development, with particular reference to the needs of the developing countries for investment in health and educational facilities within the framework of their general development programmes.

The interesting aspects of the debate concerned the clause that the United Nations "give technical assistance, as requested by Governments, for national projects and programmes dealing with the problems of population." Technical assistance was generally interpreted to incorporate family planning. The clause was rejected by a vote of 34 in favor, 34 against and 32 abstentions. The United States, which voted for the final resolution, voted against the technical assistance clause on the ground that "operative paragraph 6 does not add or subtract from the authority which the United Nations already possesses as a result of resolutions of the General Assembly and of the Economic and Social Council concerning the granting of technical assistance upon request to Member States. In our view, the paragraph is therefore superfluous" (U. N. Gen. Assemb., 18 Dec. 1962).

To carry out the Assembly's Resolution, an "outline of inquiry on problems resulting from reciprocal action of economic development and population changes" was sent to all member states of the United Nations in June 1963. The results will provide the basis for a comprehensive analysis of existing population knowledge, problems and policies.

The complexity of the subject as well as the attitude of various nations toward the question of world population control are discernible in the statements of their United Nations representatives during the course of the discussion on the Assembly Resolution. With this in mind, some brief excerpts from the paraphrased statements of the Provisional Summary Record of the December 1962 Meetings are quoted (U. N. Gen. Assemb. 7–17 Dec. 1962):

Sweden (Mrs. Lindstrom): If the coming generations in Asia, Africa and South America were to attain a level of living comparable with that of the other regions, much more economic and technical assistance would have to be given to the less developed countries, and Sweden was fully conscious of its share of the responsibility. . . . It was a matter not of choosing between a more energetic food policy and a wise population policy, but of applying both.

United States (Mr. Gardner): In his Government's opinion, progress could not be measured merely in terms of increases in gross national product, for the object of economic development was the welfare and dignity of the individual human being. The United Nations must therefore concern itself with population trends. . . .

United Kingdom (Mr. Unwin): The whole question was as yet too little explored, and the United Nations had its part to play in promoting and assisting the preparation of studies and statistics in that sphere. The draft resolution seemed likely to strengthen that role of the Organization.

France (Mr. Viaud): The draft resolution envisaged the planning of population expansion under State control, but birth control could be effective only when it was the result of a free choice by individuals. . . . Another danger of that policy was that it might lead to an aging of the population.

Ireland (Mr. Cullen): Study of the population problem should . . . not divert attention from the fundamental causes of poverty and the real possibilities of progress in economic development. . . . As to technical assistance in dealing with population problems, his delegation felt entitled to stand by its principles and not to supply technical assistance under a programme of assistance in artificial birth control.

Italy (Mr. Zadotti): So far as his delegation was concerned, it would categorically oppose any attempt to use technical assistance . . . for the purpose of initiating a birth control policy without stating explicitly how or where that policy would be applied.

Union of Soviet Socialist Republics (Mr. Arkadyev): The socialist method of production offered a solution to the problem. . . . The Soviet Union and the other socialist countries drew up their plans so as to meet the needs of their growing populations by increased production. . . . Those methods should be used to cope with the problem of population growth. It was wrong to concentrate on a policy of family reduction.

Ukrainian Soviet Socialist Republic (Mr. Kochubei): The theories of Malthus and their modern variants had been used as a pretext to distract attention from the abject poverty of the underdeveloped countries. The economic backwardness of those countries could not be explained away by such theories; it was the result of colonialist domination and exploitation.

Romania (Mr. Dimbu): The draft resolution . . . was based on the theory that mankind was faced with the dangers of the insurmountable gap between "limited" production capabilities and "uncontrolled" population growth. That theory had been disproved by history itself.

Yugoslavia (Mr. Čvorovič): His delegation would support any proposal which recommended the provision of technical assistance for family planning in close relationship with economic development. Each dollar spent on family planning should be matched by a much larger counterpart investment in economic progress.

Argentina (Mr. Bernardo): Argentina had always opposed the idea of using the United Nations to disseminate any artificial system of birth control . . . there were two possible attitudes to the relationship between population growth and economic development: a static attitude, of limiting the population, and a dynamic attitude, of increasing resources. . . . The United Nations, moreover, had no authority to take a decision with regard to birth control.

Ghana (Mr. Nylander): The rate of population increase in Africa was 2.2 percent *per annum*. It was clear that a number of African countries would face the danger of a population explosion sooner than they had expected. . . . His delegation noted with interest that the population problem was now a matter of concern to the Roman Catholic Church. That being the case, it should be possible for the Committee to adopt draft resolution A/C.2/L.657 without giving offence to anyone. His delegation had therefore decided not only to vote for the draft resolution but also to become a sponsor.

Tunisia (Mr. Ayari): To say that nothing could be done about population growth was to take a fatalistic attitude; the sponsors, on the contrary, felt that population growth was a variable which could be acted upon like any other economic factor.

Syria (Mr. Tomeh): Population growth might have a stimulating effect on economic development in the countries of Western Europe, but the question was whether the solutions found by those countries were applicable in the same degree to the underdeveloped countries.

Lebanon (Mr. Hakim): The present draft resolution made the implicit assumption that a lower rate of population growth would be a better condition for economic development; his delegation disagreed with that view. . . . His delegation also disagreed that the United Nations should provide technical assistance for family planning.

United Arab Republic (Mr. El-Banna): Some countries — the United Arab Republic for instance — had been successful in increasing their volume of production. . . . But the pressure of population impeded their development plans. They must tackle the problem immediately and should be helped by the United Nations, upon request, to draw up family planning programmes.

India (Mr. Anjaria): Although the aggregate national income of India had increased according to plan, the *per capita* income had not risen at a corresponding rate because of the steady expansion in the population. Family planning must be viewed in the wider context of general education.

Pakistan (Mr. Karim): His country faced an alarming growth in population and had to fight desperately for its economic development . . . His delegation was happy that the United Nations was at last discussing the part it could play insofar as the problem affected economic development.

In addition to a consideration of population matters in connection with its usual work, the United Nations sponsors from time to time regional and world conferences on population. The last World Conference was held in Rome in 1954; the next one is to be held in Belgrade in 1965. References to the last regional conference, the Asian Population Conference, have been made elsewhere in this paper, but its overall highlights are worth noting.

Asian Population Conference, New Delhi, December 10–20, 1963

The Conference, at which about half the world's population was represented, was notable in two important respects. One, it was the first international conference on population that included representatives of governments, who alone were entitled to vote, as well as individual experts. Second, its delegates voiced strong support for U. N. aid on population matters. The major accomplishment of the conference was agreement on organizing workshops on different aspects of action programs.

During the course of the Conference, no governmental or nongovernmental representative expressed opposition to family planning. In the field of policy only one country, Iran, stated that it "does not believe in birth control." No country raised any objection to family planning programs such as those in India, Korea, and Pakistan. As for the Catholic position, the statement prepared by Francis C. Madigan, S. J., Ph.D., Director, Research Institute for Mindanao Culture, Xavier University, Philippines, read: "I believe — although some might disagree with me — that the Church would not object to a family-centered program for responsible parenthood in which Catholic couples as well as other would be encouraged to limit the number of their children. . . ." No Catholic present voiced any objection to governmental programs provided "limitation methods proposed by government at least include such methods as Catholics — and others — could use without offense to their consciences, and that these latter methods be made as fully available as any other. . . ."

It should be noted that among the more than 2 billion people in the underdeveloped areas, the Buddhist, Hindu and Moslem religions predominate. In these religions interpretations are conveyed to the people by numerous priests and scholars, the force of the ruling depending upon the personal following of its conveyor. Their religious attitudes toward family planning are therefore better sought in custom and tradition than in doctrine.

Among Hindus, several religious practices and values may reduce fertility considerably. These include the ban on the remarriage of widows, the custom for women to deliver their children in their childhood homes, long lactation periods, periodic abstinence from sexual relations during certain religious holidays, and so on. The intent of these practices may or may not be related to fertility, but the general concensus among Hindus is that their religion is free of any doctrine that would proscribe the practice of contraception. This is probably even more true of Buddhist society, which is secular and pragmatic and among whom religion appears to be a much less pervasive factor than among Hindus (Kirk).

Moslems characteristically have higher fertility than other religious groups. The institutions of polygamy, easy divorce, the inferior status of women, and the relatively few customs and taboos relating to sexual abstinence and the interval between births, may be factors. In 1937 a group of university professors in Egypt interested in family planning sought a Fatwa — that is a point of interpretation of Islamic Law — regarding contraceptive practice. The Fatwa declared that under certain conditions birth control was permissible with the consent of both partners (Rizk, 1963). In general, experience in the pilot and experimental projects has confirmed the general view that, outside of Latin America, religious doctrine in the underdeveloped countries is not opposed to modern techniques of contraception.

Conclusion

Recent developments relating to the current high rate of world population growth suggest a deepening appreciation of the effect of high fertility on efforts to raise living standards. Hampered in their economic development by their rapidly increasing populations, a growing number of developing countries have adopted or are considering the feasibility of adopting rational policies of population control. The problems of motivation, communication, and suitable family planning techniques are such that even with intense effort, a rapid decline in fertility is not likely. A world population of at least six billion in the year 2000 seems inevitable. The question is whether that figure is reached with reduced birth rates, reduced dependency loads and reduced poverty, or with spreading misery and an upturn in death rates.

Hope lies in the fact that latent among all people — in Asia, Africa, and Latin America, as well as in the Western world — is the desire to limit births to the numbers that can be adequately cared for and raised. Public opinion polls in various parts of the world indicate that large proportions of all people have some concept of an ideal number of children. Not all know that they can restrict their births to this ideal, but there is sufficient evidence to indicate that people in the emerging countries can acquire and apply the necessary knowledge.

REFERENCES

Aird, John S., 1962. Population Policy in Mainland China. *Population Studies* (London). 16 (1): 42. (July).

Balfour, M. C. Asian Representative of The Population Council, New York.

Berelson, Bernard, Vice-President of The Population Council, 1963. Speech delivered November 11, 1963, p. 1 (mimeo.).

Duke University School of Law, 1960. *Law and Contemporary Problems: Population Control*, 25 (3). (Summer).

Eldridge, Hope T., 1954. *Population Policies: A Survey of Recent Developments.* International Union for the Scientific Study of Population.

Family Planning Association of Barbados, 1960. *Annual Report 1st April 1959 to 31st March 1960:* 2. (6 May).

Family Planning Association of Hong Kong, 1963. *12th Annual Report, 1962–63:* 32–33.

Hall, D. G. E., 1955. *A History of South-East Asia.* St. Martin's Press, Inc., New York, p. 681.

Kirk, Dudley, Director of Demographic Division, The Population Council, New York.

Kiser, Clyde V. (Ed.), 1962. *Research in Family Planning.* Papers presented at a conference sponsored jointly by The Milbank Memorial Fund and The Population Council, October 13–19, 1960. Princeton University Press, Princeton, New Jersey.

Kuznets, Simon, 1959. *Six Lectures on Economic Growth.* Free Press, Glencoe, Ill., p. 14.

Mauldin, W. Parker, 1960. The Population of India: Policy, Action and Research. *Economic Digest* (Karachi). 3 (2). (Summer).

———, 1960. Fertility Control in Communist Countries. *Population Trends in Eastern Europe, The USSR and Mainland China.* Milbank Memorial Fund, N. Y., p. 199.

———, 1963. Population and Population Policy in Pakistan. *Marriage and Family Living*, Journal of the National Council on Family Relations, 25 (1): 66. (Feb.).

The New York Times, October 8, 1963; February 3, 1964.

Orleans, Leo A., 1962. A New Birth Control Campaign? *The China Quarterly* (London, W. 1): 209. (Oct.–Dec. 1962).

The Population Council, 1963. *Studies in Family Planning*, no. 1, New York. (July).

The Population Council, 1963. *Studies in Family Planning*, no. 2, New York. (Dec.).

Qureshi, M. L., ed., 1959. *Population Growth and Economic Development, Summary Report of a Seminar.* Institute of Development Economics, Karachi. (September 8–13, 1959).

Raina, Lieut, Col. B. L., 1963. *Family Planning Pro-*

gramme Report for 1962–63. New Delhi (mimeo.). (April).

Republic of Korea, Ministry of Health and Social Affairs, 1963. *Population and Family Planning in Korea*, p. 1, 2 (mimeo.). (Oct.).

Republic of Korea, Economic Planning Board, Bureau of Statistics, 1963. *Statement of the Republic of Korea for the Asian Population Conference*, New Delhi, p. 53–58. (Dec.).

Republic of Korea, Economic Planning Board, 1963. *An Extract from Family Planning Encouragement Plan*, p. 4, 6. (Sept. 10).

Rizk, Hanna, 1963. Population Growth and its Effect on Economic and Social Goals in the United Arab Republic. *Population Review* (Indian Institute for Population Studies, Madras), 7 (1): 55. (Jan.).

Singapore Family Planning Association. 1962. *13th Annual Report, 1962.*

Tien, H. Yuan, 1963. Birth Control in Mainland China: Ideology and Politics. *Milbank Memorial Fund Quarterly*, 41 (3). (July).

Turkish Republic, Prime Ministry, State Planning Organization, 1963. *First Five Year Development Plan 1963–67*, Ankara, p. 69.

United Arab Republic, Information Department, 1962. *The Charter.* Draft presented by President Gamal Abdel Nasser on 21st May, 1962, p. 53.

United Nations, Dept of Economic and Social Affairs, Statistical Office, 1962. *Demographic Yearbook*, Table 14.

United Nations, Dept. of Economic and Social Affairs, Statistical Office, 1963. *Statistical Papers, Population and Vital Statistics Report*, Series A., 15 (4). (1 Oct.).

United Nations General Assembly, 7–17 Dec. 1962. *Provisional Summary Record*, Seventeenth Session, Second Committee, Meetings held December 7–17, 1962.

———, 18 Dec. 1962. *Provisional Verbatim Record of the Eleven Hundred and Ninety-Seventh Plenary Meeting*, 18 December 1962, A/PV. 1197, p. 61.

United Nations Technical Assistance Programme, 1957. *The Family Planning Service in Barbados.* Prepared for the Government of Barbados by Dr. C. Tietze, TAA/BAR/2, 3 July 1957, p. 2.

*Population Movement and Political Behavior**

Angus Campbell • Philip E. Converse
Warren E. Miller • Donald E. Stokes

The movement of peoples is a fascinating theme in American history. The commonplace fact of large scale migration to the West was transformed by Frederick Jackson Turner into a provocative thesis on the development of our modern culture.[1] More recently, and somewhat more narrowly, professional students of politics have turned to basic social and economic characteristics of the population for explanation of new developments in national politics. Arthur Holcombe made evident the extent to which urbanization replaced regional politics with the now familiar phenomena of the rural-urban conflict.[2] Of still more recent vintage are the arguments advanced by such observers as Louis Harris and Samuel Lubell.[3] Their understanding of political cleavage in mid-twentieth century rested in part on the perceptive realization that movement away from the central city and into the burgeoning suburbs had serious political implications beyond the mere redistribution of political partisans.

The winning of the West, the growth of the city, and the rise of suburbia have contemporary as well as historical interest for us in

* Reprinted with permission from Angus Campbell, Philip E. Converse, Warren E. Miller, and Donald E. Stokes, *The American Voter,* abridged version. New York: John Wiley, 1960, pp. 231-249.

[1] Frederick J. Turner, *The Frontier in American History* (Henry Holt and Co., New York, 1921).

[2] Arthur N. Holcombe, *The New Party Politics* (W. W. Norton and Co., New York, 1933).

[3] Louis Harris, *Is There a Republican Majority?* (Harper and Brothers, New York, 1954). Samuel Lubell, *The Future of American Politics* (Harper and Brothers, New York, 1952), and particularly *The Revolt of the Moderates* (Harper and Brothers, New York, 1956).

our present analysis. More than half of the present residents of our large cities grew up in other and smaller cities. Almost 40 per cent of the people who grew up in large cities have now moved to smaller cities, into the suburbs, or to a home in the country. At least one of every two members of the electorate of the 1950's had moved far enough from the home in which he grew up to be living in a place of different population size.[4] Four out of ten native White Americans have moved from one state to another since growing up, and three out of every twenty have moved from one of four major geographic regions to another. As of the 1950's almost half the voters in the Far West had grown up in the South or in the East and had moved west in their adult years.[5]

These gross views of population movement do not capture any change of residence within the same town or city, nor do they reflect intrastate movement which does not also involve a shift in population size of place of residence. Even without including such less dramatic movement in a description of change in residence, almost 60 per cent of the adult population can still be described as "movers."

At least three kinds of political effects may be identified as possible concomitants of population movement. The first is the aggregate change in political composition of areas that "movers" leave and into which they move. Another kind of political effect associated with change of residence occurs when the individuals who move undergo political change. Such changes may be categorized under two distinct headings. In one situation a common factor or set of factors puts into motion both the residential change and the political change. For example, a person's financial success may lead to changes in a wide range of behaviors and values, social and political. The second way in which individual change is related to a change in residence involves the hypothesis that political change is the later result of moving and of the social changes that moving implies. A change of residence, for whatever reason, places a person in a new environment and in responding to the new environment he undergoes political change. Thus in the classic contemporary example, the working man moves to the suburbs as a Democrat, but there associates with Republicans and with greater or lesser speed takes on Republican characteristics.

All three kinds of political change that can be associated with population movements and changes in residence are potentially important, in part because of the local base on which American politics rests. There have been major redistributions of members of the electorate that are important because they result in a shift in the balance of power both among and within political units. Changes in personal political predispositions are also in evidence in the national electorate. In our discussion we shall not always be able to distinguish empirically between political effects that are concomitants of change in residence and those political effects that are caused by the act of moving. Whatever their respective importance, their combined importance may be considerable and we shall review something of the net result.

Our discussion of population movement centers on two aspects of individual moving: (1) interstate movement, which will be analyzed largely in terms of regional population movements, and (2) movement from place to place that results in a change in the population size of one's place of residence. The time dimension embraced by our definition of a change in residence includes two points in each person's life history, the period in which "he was growing up" and "now" (1952 or 1956). The occurrence of moving is further pinpointed by some analyses of how long each person has lived in the community of present residence.[6]

[4] Here and later in the chapter we mean to distinguish three categories for the size of place of residence: (1) metropolitan centers; (2) suburbs, smaller cities, and large towns; and (3) rural villages, open country residences, and farms. The categories are so defined that a change in the population size of one's place of residence cannot be the result of national changes in urbanization but occurs only by a personal change in residence as a result of geographical movement *and* the crossing of a boundary between places of different population size.

[5] U.S. Bureau of the Census, Series P-25, #198 (1959). In this chapter as well as elsewhere throughout the book we utilize the Bureau of the Census definitions of regional boundaries separating Northeast, South, Midwest, and Far West.

[6] We will distinguish people who may have moved to their present home in the postwar period (having lived in the community ten years or less) from those who must have moved in earlier (because they have lived there for more than ten years). Between the time a per-

Interregional Migration

The broadest class of political change — redistribution of the population with or without accompanying individual changes — will be discussed in terms of regional populations. The end result of all the moving to and fro that has gone on in the past half century or more finds about one out of every seven persons living in a region other than that in which he grew up. The proportion of native born in regional populations varies as shown in Table 1.

TABLE 1

Regional Distribution of "Native Born"

	Present Residence				
	North-east	South	Mid-west	Far West	Total
Grew up in region	92%	92%	89%	52%	86%
Grew up in another region	8	8	11	48	14
	100%	100%	100%	100%	100%

Who are the movers? As a single gross category they are men who tend to be somewhat better educated and who have considerably better jobs and higher incomes than the natives of the regions they leave. As this syndrome of characteristics strongly suggests, for some of these people, geographical mobility is associated with upward social mobility — professional and business men on the make and on the move, leaving home territory for greener pastures. To go beyond such generalities we must examine some of the larger categories of movers.[7] We shall examine three major groups: (1) people who have moved to the Far West, (2) those who have moved to the South, and (3) the remainder, those who have moved from the South or from a northern region into either the Midwest or the Northeast.

The West and How It Grew

Half of all the people who have moved to a region other than that in which they grew up have moved to the Far West. There, in turn, they constitute almost half of the total population of that region. They constitute a prime example of a massive redistribution of the population, and they provide us with a considerable potential for observing important political implications in population movements.

Our analysis allows us to identify two streams of westward migration, one from the South and the other from the North. Northerners who have moved West are relatively well educated (28 per cent have attended college) and they tend to hold white-collar jobs. They show a slight Democratic majority in their party affiliations and they vote with about the same diligence as their former neighbors in the Midwest and Northeast. There are at least two interesting points of political difference, however, between the movers and those they left behind. The movers' affinity for the Republicans nearly equals that of the other Northerners, but it does not depend on any pro-Republican advantage resulting from changes of party identification. This stands in contrast to the quite visible pro-Republican change reported by the natives of their home regions. The implication is, of course, that at sometime past these movers were markedly *more* pro-Republican than their former associates, who have since caught up with them. The second difference lies in their presidential votes of 1952 and 1956. The movers gave Mr. Eisenhower almost 75 per cent of their votes in these two elections — significantly more than the Republican proportion cast by those they left behind.

It is evident that this Northern migration to the West has meant the introduction of a relatively heavily Republican population into a region dominated by sentiments that were much more pro-Democratic. There is little evidence, however, that the incoming Republicans have been converted or softened in their Republican-

son "was growing up" and "now" he may have lived in a dozen other states and in places of a dozen different sizes. This we do not know. We do know (1) where he grew up—by city size and by state, (2) where he now lives, and (3) how long he has lived there.

[7] Even though almost 30 per cent of all Negroes have moved to a new home in a new region, they are too few in absolute numbers in our sample data to analyze within these categories. Consequently, Negroes have been excluded from the general investigation of regional movement and will be considered separately at the end of the discussion. Unless specifically noted, the following discussion pertains only to native-born Whites.

ism. Instead, their contribution to Western politics would seem to be more that of minimizing political differences between the Far West and the other Northern regions. They constitute a third of the Western population, and without them the Democrats hypothetically would outnumber the Republicans by more than two to one in the eleven Western States.

The second stream of Western migration, that from the South, constitutes about 14 per cent of the total Western population. (Northern migrants contribute 34 per cent of the total.) Both groups of Western immigrants are considerably older than any other group of movers or nonmovers we shall examine. Despite the age of the Southern migrants, their educational attainments are about the same as those of the Southern nonmover. However, they are somewhat lower than the average for the North, and markedly below the educational background of other migrants to the West. Although the income level of the Southern migrants is equivalent to that of the Northern migrants (and above that of the native South), their average occupational status is very low — lower than that of the South generally and much lower than that of their fellow migrants.

If these former Southerners now differ somewhat in socio-economic terms from the people still living in the South, they have retained a major part of the Southern pattern of political behavior. Their voting rate is low — only two-thirds voted in 1952 and 1956 — and the vote that is cast is very strongly Democratic. Where native Southerners reported an average vote of some 56 per cent for Mr. Stevenson in 1952 and 1956, the Southerners in the West reported that 60 per cent of their votes had been cast for him — a truly remarkable record in those years of Mr. Eisenhower's dominance. Although they followed the national pattern in reporting a diminution of Democratic Party identification over the years, they still ranked only slightly behind the South in their continuing Democratic allegiances.

Thus, in their political behavior the former Southerners provide a marked contrast to the other newcomers to the West in the extremity of their Democratic predispositions. Moreover, as with the Northern migrants to the West, four out of five party identifiers among the Southern migrants report no change in party identification, and their reported Democratic partisanship does not depart substantially from that of the Southerners who had not ventured from home.

In short, the movement of an extremely Democratic group into a *relatively* more Republican environment appears to have resulted in virtually no individual change or dilution of Democratic allegiances. The North-to-West movement brought a relatively Republican group into a relatively more pro-Democratic region, where they remained as Republicans and, in like manner, showed little sign of political acculturation. Both movements contribute a significant portion of the political complexion of the Far West. Both must be described primarily as a redistribution of partisans and participants. The absence of the Northern emigrant would leave Western politics nearly as strongly Democratic as the politics of the Solid South. Their presence, however, gives the West an electorate that is to some extent an amalgam of North and South. With party identification as the vehicle for transmission of hereditary loyalties, it is not surprising to find transplanted partisans confounding some of the traditions of nonpartisanship once so strong in the coastal states.

Movement to the South

Northerners moving to the South are the second major category we shall discuss. Though a relatively small group, less than 2 per cent of the total White population and slightly less than 10 per cent of the Southern Whites, they are worth describing because of their possible strategic contribution to American politics. These migrants are also of interest because they are, in fact, quite different from the usual description of the Yankee who has gone South. In the first place they are not merely Northerners who have retired and moved to the sunny climes. They boast a very high current average income — certainly not merely the annuities of pensioners from the North — and two of every five are presently engaged in a professional or business career. A third have attended college and nine out of ten have at least some high school education.

As one might expect, their political predispositions do not strongly favor the Democratic Party — they divide about equally between Democratic and Republican allegiance — and their reports of changing party identification do not indicate they are succumbing to the appeals of Southern Democracy. In 1952 and 1956 they resembled Northern migrants to the Far West as they cast over two-thirds of their votes for Mr. Eisenhower. However, their contribution to the Republican effort in the South was limited not only by their restricted numbers but also by a modest rate of voting — only 68 per cent voted, despite socio-economic characteristics that would suggest a much higher rate.

These migrants would seem to possess considerable potential to influence Southern politics. Above all other groups in our population analysis they feel themselves to be politically effective. They also appear to possess an unusually well-organized set of political attitudes, showing more partisan consistency in their appraisal of national political objects than does any other group. Finally, they show little sign of being changed themselves by the environment around them. They report a change in party identification no more frequently than does the rest of the nation, and the changes they do report follow the national mode *away from the Democratic Party,* not to it.

The Invasion of the North

The third and last stream of regional population movement which we shall consider is composed of persons moving into the Midwest or Northeast. As with the case of the Far West, this immigration has two distinct parts, one from the South and the other consisting of movement within the North itself. The two parts are polar opposites on almost every social, economic, and political dimension we have considered. The Southern White migrants, a minuscule 4 per cent of the Northern population, are young (40 per cent under 35), poorly educated (40 per cent have not gone beyond grade school), and tend to hold low status jobs (60 per cent are blue collar). Nevertheless, their sense of personal political effectiveness compares favorably with all but one or two of our groups, and their level of participation apparently reflects their Northern environment. Their turnout rate is well above that of the other Southerners we have examined — 72 per cent voted in 1952 and 1956. They predictably reflect their Southern origin in the Democratic nature of their party identifications and in their vote for President.

On the other hand, the Northerners who have moved from one Northern region to another are not particularly young. This group, constituting slightly more than 2 per cent of the Northern population, is well educated; over half of them are business and professional people, and they report an extremely high average family income. As fits the stereotype of people with such social social and economic characteristics they are heavily pro-Republican in their political sentiments: only 25 per cent call themselves Democrats, whereas 52 per cent identify themselves with the Republican Party. A share of this Republican predominance is apparently of relatively recent origin; some 18 per cent describe themselves as *former* Democrats, whereas only 7 per cent report they have left the Republican ranks. The members of this category of movers are highly motivated as citizens and manifest their sense of great political effectiveness: 89 per cent voted for President in 1952 and 1956. They voted three to one for Eisenhower.

The two groups that compose the Northern immigration are of interest because of the extreme differences between them. They do not, however, give us any new insights into the impact of moving on the politics of the movers. And, contrary to the situation in the Far West, these migrants comprise such a small portion of the electorates they join as to accomplish little in the way of an immediate reshaping of the regional politics in their new homes.

Negro Migration from the South

A quite different impact on local, regional, and national politics has resulted from the migration of Southern Negroes. We may first note that the attention given to the growing Negro vote in the North reflects the visibility and strategic location of that vote rather than its size alone. Even though the proportion of Negroes who have moved from one region to another is double the proportion of Whites who have changed regions (29 per cent of all Negroes against 13 per cent for all Whites), Negroes still constitute but one-fifth of all such movement. In absolute numbers the Negroes who have moved North are almost equalled by the Northern Whites who have moved South.

The social and economic characteristics of the migrant Negro provide an insightful commentary on the contemporary nature of the American dilemma. Compared to Southern Negroes who *have not* left the region, the immigrants now in the North are of about the same age, but they have received more years of formal education. They do not on the average hold higher status jobs, but their average income is much higher. Some 35 per cent report a family income of over $4000, whereas only 6 per cent of the Southern Negroes give a similar report. In both the North and the South the nonfarming Negro is a blue-collar worker in more than seven out of ten cases; he is a white-collar man in only one out of ten. The better education of the Northern Negro is thus likely to be associated with a much higher income, but not necessarily with a substantially higher occupational status.

In 1952 and 1956 three out of every four Southern Negroes who claimed a partisan allegiance described themselves as Democrats rather than as Republicans. And those who did vote voted just as heavily for the Democratic candidate as did the Southern White. Moreover, the *ratio* of Democratic to Republican Party identification was just as high among Southern Negroes as among Negro migrants to the North. Nevertheless, some contrast with the Negro who had moved North was still evident. Negroes in the South divided their votes for President in the two elections about equally between the two parties; Negroes who had left the South were much more strongly Democratic, giving over three-fourths of their votes to Stevenson. The sharpest contrast was provided, of course, in the extent of participation. Only one in six Southern Negroes reported a vote in 1952 and 1956, whereas four in six immigrants in the North reported voting. The greater political involvement of Northern Negroes was also evident on a number of attitudinal dimensions such as sense of personal political effectiveness and range of attention to national political events and objects.

The contrasts and similarities between movers and nonmovers among Southern-born Negroes become quite understandable when viewed in relation to the characteristics of Negroes who have lived all of their lives in the North. When the three groups of Negroes are compared, it is apparent that the natives of the two regions represent social, economic, and political extremes. The emigrants to the North occupy a position suggestive of partial but not complete transition from one subculture to the other.

Our inspection of four categories of travelers has provided evidence relating population movement to individual political change. Three of the four categories contain very few individuals who have changed to conform to their new environment. Northerners moving West and South and White Southerners moving West have retained or accentuated the distinctions that set them apart from their new neighbors. Only Southern Negroes moving North have showed any tendency to shed some of their traditional attitudes and thereby become more like their new associates and less like those who remained behind.

Urbanization, Suburbanization, and Political Change

In this era of urbanization it may come as something of a surprise to note that some 21 per cent of the total population has moved away from larger towns and cities to smaller ones than those in which the movers grew up.[8] At the same time, three out of five persons who have moved to a residence in a different population density category have moved into more densely populated centers.

Social Mobility and Political Change

The voters who have deserted the metropolitan centers in favor of suburbia have drawn much comment from the political commentators and analysts. One favorite theme has held that this change in residence is an indicator of upward social mobility and has been accompanied by a

[8] We shall not treat suburban areas here as a special population category. There are several reasons for this omission of special treatment of the suburbs. First, when we proceed with a comparison of persons who were brought up in metropolitan central city areas but have now moved to less densely populated places, we cannot discern any substantial empirical differences between the subgroupings that are identified in our data. Second, the nature of our data does not allow us to investigate the many smaller categories subsumed under the single heading, "suburb." We can only describe as one group the residents of the heterogeneous category of places that share the general character of being suburban areas.

change in politics that has seen Democrats turned into Republicans. We shall not attempt to verify or deny this thesis as it applies to particular suburbs or even to the categories of suburbs in which this phenomenon has been reported. We will, however, move directly to a confrontation of the hypothesis that upward social mobility, outward geographical mobility away from the metropolitan center, and a turn away from Democracy to Republicanism are interrelated. It may be noted in passing that this analysis is a story with a more general moral as its conclusion. It illustrates how more appropriate data may affirm the accuracy of observations based on less appropriate data while at the same time disclosing a basic fallacy in the conclusions drawn from those observations.[9]

Many of the emigrants from big city living occupy the top rung of the social and economic ladder. They tend to be well-educated members of well-to-do families of professional people and businessmen. They are more often than not Republicans, and they reflected this in their voting in 1956. A full analysis of the problem, however, does not support the simple thesis that upward social mobility has led to a Republican surge among these ex-city dwellers. The first data to indicate a flaw in the theory concern the widespread occurrence of social mobility. Whether defined by occupational status or subjective social class affiliation, and whether described in terms of intergenerational movement or by the intragenerational mobility of the individual, upward social mobility is shared in identical measure among all of the relevant population groupings. Mobility cuts uniformly across all population categories except those involving persons who grew up on farms. The upward social mobility of the former urbanites is fully matched by that of the folk they left behind, as well as by all other groups of nonrural origin. Thus, even before turning our attention to questions of stability and change in political partisanship, it is apparent that any *differences* among the population groups in their movements away from the Democrats or to the Republican fold cannot be explained by differences in the incidence of upward social mobility.

The second relevant datum in this analysis concerns change in political partisanship. Our most direct indicator of this is the citizen's report of change in his own sense of partisan identification. Although the picture of change in party identification is not as uniform across all groups as was the pattern of intragenerational occupational mobility, it is so uniform as to undercut decisively the hypothesis that we are testing. Former metropolitan residents have indeed moved away from the Democrats and toward Republicans in their party loyalties. A total net shift of 16 percentage points in their partisan division has been recorded in this group. There is, however, a 12-point shift in the same direction on the part of lifelong metropolitan residents. A Democratic to Republican switch by 2 per cent of the former metropolitan dwellers, or an Independent to Republican movement by 4 per cent, would account for all of the difference we observe between the two groups. This scarcely can be taken as evidence that the trend toward Republicanism is significantly greater on the part of the émigrés from the big city.

The further implication that upward social mobility is, in general, *not* associated with changes in party identification away from the Democratic Party may be tested directly. As Table 2 indicates, even among the people who

TABLE 2

Relation of Reported Changes in Own Occupational Status to Changes in Self-Identification with Parties, 1956

	Occupational Mobility	
	Down	Up
Changes in party identification		
From Republican to Democratic	28%	24%
From Republican to Independent	8	12
From Democratic to Independent	32	29
From Democratic to Republican	32	35
	100%	100%
Number of cases	47	121

[9] All of the following data and the discussion they support refer only to native-born Northern Whites. Non-Whites and Southern residents deserve similar attention, but the available data are not adequate to do more than indicate the necessity for dealing separately with the three groups.

report both a change in partisanship and a change in their own occupational status there is no suggestion of a relationship between the two kinds of change.[10]

If the validity of these data is granted, the logic of the argument follows quite readily. The hypothesis is that upward social mobility among émigrés from the metropolis has been accompanied by conversion to Republicanism. The implication has been that movement *out* from the city is associated with upward social mobility, whereas retention of a central city address means either downward mobility or at least an absence of change in social status. It appears, to the contrary, that upward social mobility has been experienced every bit as often by the nonmovers as by those who have traded convenience for space, and it is associated equally in both groups with pro-Republican changes in political partisanship. Moreover, the absence of a really unique change in political allegiance among ex-urbanites further indicates that movement out of the metropolitan centers cannot stand as the factor responsible for changes in partisan loyalties that cut across nonmovers as well.

We may speculate that the visibility of suburban politics has been responsible for explanations of political behavior that now must be qualified. The mushrooming colonies of former big-city dwellers are indeed properly described as containing a great many Republicans, many former Democrats, and many upwardly mobile residents. What has been missed are the similar movements away from the Democratic Party and upward on the social scale that have gone on, quite independently, in the less visible homes of the old central-city areas as well. Moreover, without actual knowledge about the political histories of the former urbanites, the extent of their traditional Republicanism could not be determined. With our reports of their own past behavior at the polls we can now establish that much of their Republican sentiment is of extremely long duration, if not a matter of a family heritage. The combination of a tradition of Republican sympathy and an "average" rate of defection on the part of the minority Democrats adds up, of course, to the formidable Republican strength that many of these communities brought to the political wars in the 1950's.

The Metropolitan Electorate — Past and Present

Two population groupings stand out as particularly interesting: one comprised of persons who grew up in a major city but have since moved to smaller cities or towns or to homes in the country, the other consisting of persons who were raised in rural hamlets or on farms and who have now become central-city residents of a major metropolis. These two groups stand at the polar extremes among the array of population groupings with regard to almost every social and economic characteristic. The urban emigrants enjoy the highest occupational status, boast the most substantial family incomes, and are individually the most likely to have received a college education. At the other extreme the immigrants from the country are not well equipped in terms of formal education (only one out of two has gone beyond grade school) and a generally low occupational status is reflected in the low proportion whose families had incomes in excess of $6000 in 1956.

On each count, the native of the metropolis stands roughly midway between the extremes, sharing his position with former residents of towns and cities. But when we turn to a study of the clearly political variables, this order among sometime metropolitan residents changes rather drastically.

Emigrants from the metropolis and migrants to it are arrayed in almost identical fashions on the party identification continuum. Despite great differences in their social origins, the former big-city dwellers and the onetime country folk are remarkably similar in the nature of their underlying partisan allegiances. Furthermore, members of both groups present a remembered history of almost unalloyed support for Republican presidential candidates. Their behavior in 1956

[10] Similarly, when we compare the occupational status of our respondents with that of their parents we find very little evidence that upward or downward changes in status from one generation to the next are associated with shifts toward the Republican or Democratic Party. Upward mobile people are slightly more likely to have shifted from Democratic to Republican identification than those people whose status has moved downward, but both types of status-changers are much more likely to have moved toward the Republican Party than away from it. Their changes in status appear to have very little relationship to their changes in partisanship.

proved no exception: only two groupings gave Mr. Eisenhower more support than did the former metropolitan dwellers, and one of those was the immigrants from the rural areas. The latter group — although socially and economically the most disadvantaged of the three components of the metropolitan electorate — gave Mr. Eisenhower almost four out of every five votes they cast.

On the other hand the lifelong inhabitants of the metropolitan centers constitute a sturdy core of Northern Democratic support. In 1956 they provided the strongest resistance to the Eisenhower sweep of the North. And even this was not commensurate with their predominant partisan loyalties, for they are even more heavily Democratic in their division of party allegiances than the other two groups are Republican in theirs.

There are, nevertheless, some expected political manifestations of the social and economic characteristics of the three groups. These appear in the area of political participation. The one-time rural residents had the poorest record of turnout in 1956. The former members of the metropolitan electorate shared honors with the neighbors they left behind in demonstrating their civic virtue. The low turnout of former farmers reflects the agrarian political heritage described earlier. It is also consistent with their presently relatively low sense of political efficacy. At the same time, the migrant from metropolitan living was supported in his participation by a sense of efficacy commensurate with his objectively demonstrated ability to attain the higher goals among those valued by our society.

Residential Mobility among Democrats and Republicans

Probably because they are *less* visible, people who have moved *into* the metropolitan centers have not been the object of extended scrutiny or comment. Nevertheless they are in some ways as unique as the urban-to-rural mover — and in their greater numbers (60 per cent greater than the number of outward movers) they constitute a category of considerable political importance. Before turning to a closer examination of these new members of the metropolitan electorate, we may draw attention to an interesting consequence of their Republican affiliation that we have already observed. When viewed in conjunction with the staunch Republicanism of the big-city émigré they complete a picture of a preponderantly Republican circulation through the metropolitan center.

One corollary of the exodus of Republicans from the metropolitan centers lies in the heavy Democratic preponderance among the metropolitan residents who do not move. If a third of the emigrants are Democrats, over half of the metropolitan-bred nonmovers are Democrats. The striking extent of partisan differential in this movement out from the metropolitan center is highlighted by the discovery that 71 per cent of the Democrats raised in a metropolitan center still live there or in another similar central-city area, whereas only 46 per cent of the metropolitan-bred Republicans have resisted the movement away from these central cities.

The net result of the two streams of movement, in and out of the major metropolitan centers, apparently has been to leave the partisan balance within the metropolitan center almost unchanged. The Republican-dominated in-migration has almost exactly offset the out-migration. Among all persons who grew up in the metropolis, the division in party identification is 47 per cent Democrats, 25 per cent Independents, and 28 per cent Republicans; among the present residents of the same cities the division is 49 per cent Democrats, 24 per cent Independents, and 27 per cent Republicans. But here the balancing-out ends. Among Democrats who are sometime residents of a metropolitan center, 47 per cent are lifelong residents; among sometime metropolitan Republicans, only 28 per cent have spent their lives in a metropolitan home.

The definitive explanation of the greater residential stability of Democrats or the greater mobility of Republicans is not at hand. There are, however, two lines of speculation that may be suggested. In the first place, the Republican character of the movement into the metropolis seems quite reasonable. After all, the in-migrants come from farms, villages, towns, and smaller cities. The preponderance of Republican sentiment in these places is well documented in voting statistics.

To the extent that this argument is persuasive, the explanation of party differences among big-city emigrants is made more difficult. Despite a sometime Democratic-Republican division of 47-28 in the metropolitan electorate, the emigrants divide 33–37 in favor of Republican identifications. This situation occurs because, as we have noted, 53 per cent of the sometime metropolitan Republicans have moved out, whereas only 29 per cent of their Democratic counterparts have left for less crowded surroundings. But why the difference between 53 per cent and 29 per cent?[11]

The data pertaining to intergenerational occupational mobility suggest a promising line of speculation and future inquiry. Among persons whose occupational status is lower than that of their father's there are no party differences in the frequency of movement away from the big city. But among persons who have achieved upward mobility and have exceeded their father's occupational status, the differences are striking indeed. Among Democrats the proportion of nonmovers is 76 per cent (N = 62); among Republicans the same proportion is only 37 per cent (N = 40). Moreover, comparing the upward mobile with the downward, upward mobility *increases* the proportion of nonmoving Democrats, from 66 per cent to 76 per cent. Upward mobility among Republicans decreases nonmoving or, stated positively, increases the frequency of movement out. Where only 37 per cent of the downward mobile Republicans move out, a full 63 per cent of the upward mobile follow the trail to suburbia, exurbia, and beyond.[12]

In the absence of needed data we can only speculate about the meaning of these discrepancies in partisan response to intergenerational mobility. It seems likely that fairly basic differences in social values are involved. It may be that the Republicans, despite their own metropolitan origins, are more often linked through enduring family ties to ancestral beginnings in small cities, towns, and on farms. The urban Democrat, on the other hand, may be the child of a thoroughly urban culture. Whether the metropolis of his family line once was Warsaw or Rome or Dublin, or Boston, Baltimore, or New York, he may accept more often the way of life of the metropolitan center.

Changing Electorates

The greater residential mobility of Republicans, in the setting of metropolitan politics, is in itself of considerable interest. But the implications are even more intriguing when we recall the greatly different social and economic characteristics of people who move into and out of the metropolitan centers. In aggregate group characteristics these two groups are similar politically but dissimilar on the other dimensions. It remains for us to discover the extent to which the dissimilarities are particularly true of the Republicans (or the Democrats) in each group or the extent to which they cut across all political comparisons that we might make.

We are, of course, interested in the social and economic comparisons because they will indicate the extent to which the "circulation" of partisans out of and into the city changes the clientele to which each party must appeal. Let us consider education as the first social characteristic of interest and let us first compare movers with nonmovers. People who have moved *out* of the central city are better educated than those who stayed behind. The extent to which this is true is reflected by the following measure of *differences in education level* within each partisan group:

Emigrants compared to nonmovers among:

Democrats	+18 →	(18% more with college education among emigrants, or 18% more with grade school education among life-long residents)
Independents	+28	
Republicans	+32	

People who have moved *into* the central city also differ from those already there, but they do so by virtue of being *less* well educated. The differences within each of these groups of partisans are:

[11] The difference does not appear to be a function of financial ability to move. Indeed, there is a tendency for the difference to be accentuated among higher income families where freedom to move is least limited by such factors.

[12] Intragenerational mobility does not appear to be at all related to change of residence for Republicans, although it is related to Democratic movement. Among Independents, both intergenerational and intragenerational mobility are sharply related to changes in residence. In all instances upward mobility is associated with movement away from the metropolitan center.

Immigrants compared to nonmovers among:

Democrats	−5
Independents	−11
Republicans	−30

If outgoing Democrats were *better* educated than nonmovers by a mean difference of +18, and if incoming Democrats were *less well* educated than nonmovers to the extent of a difference of −5, the net difference between those moving in and those moving out is −23. For Independents, the difference in educational level is somewhat greater, expressed by a difference score of −39. For Republicans, the difference amounts to −62. The comparable data pertaining to incomes are as follows:

Emigrants compared to nonmovers on family income:

Democrats	+6 →	(6% more with income over $6000 *or* 6% fewer with incomes under $6000)
Independents	+31	
Republicans	+9	

Immigrants compared to nonmovers:

Democrats	−28
Independents	−20
Republicans	−58

Net difference between movers, immigrants compared to emigrants:

Democrats	−34
Independents	−51
Republicans	−67

As far as the background variables of education and income are concerned, the differences between incoming and outgoing citizens are greatest among Republicans and least among Democrats. The same is true with regard to the occupation of those citizens in the labor force. The following data refer to differences in proportions of white-collar jobs in each pair of groups.

Emigrants compared to nonmovers:

Democrats	−5 →	(5% fewer in white-collar jobs among emigrants than among nonmovers)
Independents	+30	
Republicans	+25	

Immigrants compared to nonmovers:

Democrats	−15
Independents	+10
Republicans	−10

Net difference between movers, immigrants compared to emigrants:

Democrats	−10
Independents	−20
Republicans	−35

Much the same picture is presented by data pertaining to the citizen's subjective social class position. There is virtually no difference between incoming and outgoing Democrats; the former include only 5 per cent fewer middle class people. Incoming Independents include 26 per cent fewer middle class persons than do Independents who have moved from the metropolis; the comparable difference among Republicans is 23 per cent fewer among immigrants than among emigrants.

Some of the consequences of the parade into and out of the metropolis are by now apparent. The movement involves Republicans more often than Democrats, and the social and economic differences between the pairs of Republicans are far more extreme than are those for comparable Democratic groups. It is fair to conclude that the nature of metropolitan Republicanism has changed rather dramatically during the recent decades. For example, instead of a onetime Republican metropolitan electorate composed of 35 per cent with some college education and only 18 per cent with no more than grade school behind them, metropolitan Republicans now have only 19 per cent with some college and a full 37 per cent with no more than grade school education. For Democrats the change has been from 11 per cent college and 20 per cent grade school to 11 per cent college and 27 per cent grade school. Among Republicans the change in occupational composition has been from 48 per cent white-collar to 29 per cent white-collar; among Democrats the change has been a much smaller decline, from 36 per cent to 32 per cent.

For politician and analyst alike the influx of relatively low status Republicans in metropolitan politics suggests fascinating potentials for political change. Most Democrats who have moved into the metropolitan center from elsewhere have been living in their present homes since before the Second World War.[13] Most of the incoming Republicans moved to their present residences after the war. Even assuming that these Republican newcomers may be unable to achieve complete insulation from the politics of their new neighbors, social integration (and the subsequent acceptance of community norms) appears to be a very slow process. It is a matter of critical significance for metropolitan politics, however, whether these Democratic influences may in time make themselves felt. It would seem we have discovered in these new members of metropolitan Republicanism an acid test for the durability of party identification.

The last point to be made concerns the phenomenon of status polarization in politics. Viewed in terms of status polarization, the newcomers to metropolitan politics constitute a major unpolarized segment of the electorate. The Republican newcomers are not of sufficiently low status to reverse the direction of status polarization when placed next to the new Democrats. They are, instead, merely similar—so similar as to contribute a depressing effect on the level of polarization within the total metropolitan electorate. Moreover, the changing of polarization within the metropolitan centers has been furthered by the nature of the movement *away* from the cities. Among the former metropolitan residents polarization is considerably more pronounced than among the nonmovers and, of course, much more accentuated than among the unpolarized newcomers. The three groups of sometime metropolitan dwellers thus display three distinctly different levels of polarization, ranging from high polarization among emigrants to no polarization among immigrants. Another consequence of population flow around the metropolitan center is thus observed in the reduction of polarization within the metropolitan electorate. The reduction has taken place, however, without necessary reference to class ideology, economic stress, or any of the other elements that were identified earlier in the analytic delineation of the components of polarization. The redistribution of political partisans has again been of major importance, even in the absence of individual political change.

[13] The reader is reminded that this analysis excludes Negroes.

*Birth Control in Mainland China: Ideology and Politics**†

H. YUAN TIEN

The epic campaign to promote birth control in Mainland China several years ago aroused wide interest, and its ebb and flow has been chronicled in the press and other publications the world over. Such terms as "unexpected," "sudden," "spasmodic" and the like have often been used to describe the beginning and the ending of this official attempt at mass contraceptive education. The notion that the campaign was sudden and abrupt owes much to the unavoidable reliance on Chinese newspapers and periodicals for information about developments in Mainland China since 1949. In order to extract information from these sources it is necessary to read between the lines which, in itself, is not easy. But, when items from these sources are pursued apart from the over-all situation, the chance for errors is accordingly greater, especially with respect to the chronology of specific events (such as the birth control campaign), the circumstances which gave rise to them, and their connections with other developments.

It is maintained here that the beginning of the birth control campaign was not as abrupt as has been generally believed, nor was its subsequent abatement. It is further maintained that the latter development was not attributable to a desire to disguise the imminent failure of the birth control program, which was said to have occurred because the government could neither supply the necessary paraphernalia for effective contraception, nor convince the people to apply them.

The problem of supply and persuasion, in any birth control program in the Chinese situation, does not indeed present very real difficulties. In the recent attempt in 1957–8, the resistance among rural peasants appears to have been substantial, and a great majority of them were not even reached during the campaign. But, why then could not the effort have been limited to urban areas only, where the reception was relatively favorable and where the amount of supplies required would be much smaller than for the whole nation? No nation gives up so easily and completely unless there is a lack of deep conviction from the start, or a change in thinking and policy.[1]

Accordingly, the present paper has two aims, one of which is to rectify some of the inaccuracies as regards the inception and evolution of the birth control campaign. The other is to suggest a more plausible explanation for its subsequent deflation. Briefly stated, the paper takes into account both the ideological setting and the political milieu in which the whole episode transpired. While ideology is a pervasive force in Communist China, population policies are also politics, and are necessarily and intimately tied to individuals who participate in this oldest form of human drama. A policy and its proponents invariably succeed or fail together on the open stage, particularly when high stakes are involved. At times, moreover, drastic actions may be taken to eliminate both the policy and those closely identified with it, even if there are objective imperatives for the continuation of the policy itself. Such actions are only the more easily resorted to when the ideological definition of the situation takes precedence over a realistic assessment of existing circumstances.

THE INNOCUOUS BEGINNING

Events in the birth control campaign in China can be conveniently divided into four phases. A speech by Shao Li-tzu on September 18, 1954, at

* Reprinted with permission from *Milbank Memorial Fund Quarterly,* Vol. 41, No. 3 (July 1963), pp. 269-290.

† This study was supported by a grant from the Social Science Research Council.

[1] Cf. Cheng, Chu-yuan: The Changing Pattern of Rural Communes in Communist China, *Asian Survey,* November, 1961, 1(9): 3-9.

the First National People's Congress, has been generally, and erroneously, taken to be the beginning of the first phase of the birth control campaign. Shao was a deputy to the Congress and also had held high positions in the previous regime.

The inception of the campaign to promote birth control was much more innocuous than this widely publicized speech of 1954. In an editorial in the *People's Daily* more than two years later, in March, 1957, it was disclosed that the State Council (the highest administrative organ in China) had in August, 1953, quietly instructed the Ministry of Health to help the masses to control reproduction and also had approved the Ministry's revised regulations governing contraception and induced abortion.[2] The original regulations, therefore, must have already existed for some time, and the actual work to revise them must also have begun before that date. The other significant point here is this: the introduction of birth control programs was not, as has also been generally assumed, simply a reaction to the consequences, real and imagined, of the fact that the 1953 population of Mainland China was nearly 600 million; the action by the State Council in 1953 preceded the 1954 announcement of the census results by some ten months.

To be sure, the census "confirmation" of the size of the large and growing population undoubtedly furnished a great deal of support to the person or persons who apparently had already made some small headway in introducing a *de facto* change in the official view regarding fertility control. Who were they? Available information suggests that Shao Li-tzu was one of them, or indeed could have been alone in this endeavor. He was then a member of the State Council, serving apparently in a non-Communist capacity. But there were other non-Party members on the Council at that time, six of whom were later purged when the so-called rightists were accused of using the birth control issue to advance their own political ambitions.[3]

While Shao Li-tzu certainly played an important role in the birth control campaign, the timing of his open advocacy of its necessity in September, 1954, seems to have been accidental as the National People's Congress then met for the first time and provided an opportunity which did not previously exist. The significance of his speech lies in the fact that it anticipated much of what was said subsequently in the birth control campaign. Shao introduced the subject in language which, in harmony with official views, discredited Malthus and argued for birth control in terms of the welfare of mothers and children during the transition to socialism.[4]

The Slow Acquiescence

Shao's speech therefore probably should be regarded as the beginning of the second phase of the birth control campaign. Whether Shao spoke out on his own or was the spokesman for himself and others, similarly inclined on the birth control issue, seems immaterial. In either case, the seed of the birth control campaign was, from the point of view of the Party, of an "alien" variety. And its germination was very slow in the then ideologically unfavorable soil; the article in *People's Daily* (November 1, 1954) which discussed the result of the 1953 Census, played up the theme "Six Hundred Million People — A Great Strength for Socialist Construction." Note also the long interval of over two years between the first steps taken in August, 1953 and the appearance in October, 1955, in the Party's chief journal for ideological indoctrination, of the first major article defining and accepting the need for birth control.[5]

In all probability, the leadership of the Party was not then prepared for an all-out acceptance of birth control, even if it did tacitly allow the adoption of the 1953 measure by the State Council. At best, it was probably a marriage of convenience rather than true love. Nonetheless, some steps were taken to cultivate the ground for possible further developments: "following the symposium on the problem of birth control called by Comrade Liu Shao-chi on December 27, 1954, the Second Bureau of the State Council designated the responsible officials of the

[2] *People's Daily* (Hereafter *JMJP*), March 5, 1957.

[3] See *People's Handbook* for 1953.

[4] *See* Communist China—The Population Problem, *Current Notes on International Affairs,* Department of External Affairs, Canberra, Australia, November, 1958, 29(11): 713-26.

[5] Yang, Ssu-ying: On Malthusianism, *Hsueh Hsi* (*Study*), October 2, 1955, (10): 24-5.

government departments concerned to form study groups on the question of contraception, (and) put forth a number of methods to promote birth control."[6] The Central Committee of the Chinese Communist Party, which, in fact, is the highest policy-maker in China, followed with instructions in March, 1955: "under the present historical circumstances and in the interest of the nation, family, and the new generation, our Party seconds appropriately planned births."[7]

But the climate remained unfavorable as far as any concrete measures to implement the policy were concerned. At the Second Plenary Session of thc Chinese People's Political Consultative Conference in February, 1956, Chen Po-ta, a highly-placed theoretician of the Party, proclaimed, "There is no sign of overpopulation in China, . . . (and) China can provide room for at least another 600 million people."[8] It was also reiterated that "under the leadership of the Communist Party, as long as there are people, any miracle known to men can be accomplished."[9]

This unfavorable climate was later recalled by Ma Yin-chu (who was to become the most vocal advocate of birth control in 1957–59): "in 1955 . . . I drafted a speech concerning the population question (New Population Theory), . . . and planned to deliver it at the 1955 session of the National People's Congress. Before doing so, I submitted it to the Chekiang subcommittee for discussion. At the meeting of the subcommittee, all but a minority of the members either refrained from expressing any opinions, or disagreed with my views. There were people who asserted that my statements were the same as Malthus'. There were also people who maintained that, though my phraseology differed from that of Malthus, the essence of my thought was of the same persuasion. Although their opinions were not acceptable to me, I felt that they were given in goodwill. On my own initiative, I therefore withdrew the draft of the speech and waited quietly for the time to ripen enough for its presentation to the whole Congress."[10] It was not until March 31, 1957, that Ma made the contents of the speech known to the public.[11]

Another salient indication of the unfavorable climate lies in the more or less completely silent treatment accorded to birth control in the pages of the *People's Daily*. From August, 1953, when the State Council first took action, to the end of 1956, only a handful of items on the subject were given space, none of which was of any consequence. Apart from a few short articles in *New China's Women* and *China Youth* (both of which have a nation-wide circulation),[12] news about birth control appeared mostly, and infrequently, in newspapers in major provincial capitals and in Peking and Shanghai.[13]

The appearance of these articles seems to have emanated from the almost single-handed and persistent efforts of Shao Li-tzu, who repeatedly raised the issue at both the 1955 and 1956 sessions of the National People's Congress. He urged in 1956 the acceleration of birth control propaganda and the relaxation of restrictions on the use of birth prevention techniques, particularly sterilization. Instead of limiting either vasectomy or salpingectomy to couples with six or more children, he recommended that sterilization be permitted after the birth of three or four children if both the husband and wife give the consent for one of them to undergo the operation.[14] About a year later, the Ministry of

[6] *JMJP*, March 5, 1957.

[7] See Wu, Ching-chao: A New Treatise on the Problem of China's Population, *Hsin Chien She* (*New Construction*), March 3, 1957, (3): 8.

[8] *New China News Agency* (Hereafter *NCNA*), February, 2, 1956.

[9] Chao, Ching: A Critique of Recent Reactionary Population Theories in China, *New Construction,* December 3, 1955, (5): 26-32. This thesis was first stated by Mao Tse-tung in 1949. *See* SELECTED WORKS OF MAO TSE-TUNG, Vol. IV. Peking, Foreign Languages Press, 1961, p. 454.

[10] Ma, Yin-chu: New Population Theory, THE COMPLETE REPORT. First National People's Congress, 4th session, Peking, 1957, pp. 297-317. A revised version of this speech later appeared in *New Construction,* November 7, 1959, (11): 52-53.

[11] *Kuang-ming Jih-pao* (Peking), April 4, 1957. It has been erroneously reported that Ma first publicized his "Population Theory" at the National People's Congress on July 3, 1957.

[12] See *China Youth,* February 16, 1955, (4): 39-40; and *New China's Women,* April 28, 1955, (4): 27, and May 28, 1955, (5): 28.

[13] This is based on the author's examination and classification of over 500 news items on birth control which appeared in Chinese newspapers in the course of the birth control campaign.

[14] The recommendation was contained in Shao's speech in THE COMPLETE REPORT. The First National People's Congress, 3rd Session, Peking, 1956, pp. 372-75.

Health announced that sterilization would be allowed without reference to family size.[15]

Meantime, in his report to the Eighth National Congress of the Communist Party of China on September 16, 1956, Premier Chou En-lai declared: "To protect women and children and bring up and educate our younger generation in a way conducive to the health and prosperity of the nation, we agree that a due measure of birth control is desirable." [16] However, Li Teh-chuan, the Minister of Health, devoted only two sentences to birth control in her report to the 1956 People's Congress and placed it far behind such other pressing issues as the control of plague, malaria, and schistosomiasis and the establishment of health clinics at the local level.[17]

Thus, a real improvement in the over-all situation had yet to evolve and it did so in February, 1957, when Mao Tse-tung is reported to have said the number of births each year was indicative of:

> great progress made in medical service and the general rise in living standards, especially in the countryside; and of the faith people have in the future. But this figure must also be of great concern to us all. . . . The increase in grain harvest for the last two years has been 10,000,000 tons a year. This is barely sufficient to cover the needs of our growing population. . . . It is estimated that at present 40 percent of our youth have not been placed in primary schools. Steps must therefore be taken to keep our population for a long time at a stable level, say, of 600,000,000. A wide campaign of explanation and proper help must be undertaken to achieve this aim.[18]

The above quotation appears to have been one of the portions of a speech which Mao delivered at a meeting of the Supreme State Council, but which was later deleted. The revised version of this speech was published in June, 1957, under the well-known title "On the Correct Handling of Contradictions among the People." The reason for the deletion is unknown, but may have been due to its Malthusian overtone and to a lack of unanimity in the Party leadership on birth control. Be that as it may, the pronouncement represented an acquiescence, however reluctantly arrived at, to the need for birth control.

The Auspicious Moment

Meeting less than two weeks after Mao's speech, no fewer than twenty-five deputies to the Third Session of the Second National People's Political Consultative Conference, spoke out on birth control early in March, 1957. Li Teh-chuan, the Health Minister, delivered her longest and most informative speech in public in favor of contraception. All these speeches were carried in full in the *People's Daily,* even though one of them contained the most specific and undiluted remarks echoing Malthus: "if this year the number of babies should be 23,310,000, . . . then each year thereafter the population would be larger, and the total number of children born would be still larger. It would be just as astonishing as the rate of accumulation of high compound interest on loans. The proverb 'Two in the first generation means a thousand in ten generations' (1, 2, 4, 8, 16, 32, 64, 128, 256, 512, 1024) is therefore not without foundation." [19]

The moment was indeed auspicious and ripe for birth control. Yet, as Chuang Hui-nan expressed it, the need for birth control was no longer confined to the original arguments of Shao Li-tzu, who emphasized its necessity exclusively in terms of the welfare of mothers and children. This line of reasoning proved, perhaps, expedient, but acceptable as evidenced in the decision to institute intensive fertility control programs in 1957.

Throughout the ages people everywhere have been called upon (implicitly or otherwise) by

[15] *JMJP,* May 23, 1957.

[16] Chou, En-lai: Report on the Proposals for the Second Five-Year Plan for Development of the National Economy. Peking, Foreign Languages Press, 1956, p. 99.

[17] Li, Teh-chuan: The Complete Report. The First National People's Congress, 3rd Session, 1956, pp. 143-150.

[18] As quoted *in* Communist China — The Population Problem, *op. cit.,* p. 717.

[19] Chuang, Hui-man: *JMJP,* March 17, 1957. Subsequently, in 1958, Ching was accused of being a "bourgeois expert" and of resisting the leadership of the party. *See* The Journal of Chinese Medicine, October 10, 1958, 10.

society to be fruitful or to desist, as the case may be. "Population control" may be used to denote this regulation of population numbers in the interest of the society as a whole. Yet, in the modern era, the number and timing of pregnancies increasingly reflect the desire and decision of individual parents. In other words, "fertility control" refers to the regulation of childbearing in accordance with personal circumstances and inclination. This distinction is important; and, as a case in point, fertility control gained support and momentum in the West only when it was wedded to a line of appeal ". . . which insisted that over-large families were a cause of poverty, that restraint of late marriage was an overheavy burden to lay upon people at large, and that some artificial check might regulate the size of families to economic bounds and enable the conception of children to be checked." Cast in these utilitarian terms and known as neo-Malthusianism, this appeal fell a step short of recognizing Malthus' natural checks to population.[20]

Thus, the invocation of the Malthusian threat, however disguised in the writings of Ch'en Ta, Wu Ching-chao, Fei Hsiao-tung and others[21] during this third phase of the birth control movement, transformed the need for fertility control into a question of "population control." Almost no effort is required to demonstrate empirically the advantages of controlled fertility in terms of the immediate well-being of individual families; whereas, Malthus' principle of population has never been factually validated. Nor is it free from inconsistencies and ambiguities.[22] Nor, of course, have the counter-arguments of the Communists been verified by concrete examples. In the name of intellectual freedom and academic discussion, a staunch defence should and can be made on behalf of Ch'en, Wu, Fei and others who, intentionally or otherwise, resurrected the controversy centered on Malthus. But that would be far beyond the present scope.

In the name of a viable program designed to promote "fertility control," might it not be a reasonable conclusion that Ch'en, Wu, and others had unnecessarily broached the subject? The aurora of the short day of the Hundred Flowers may well have tempted them to traverse this so obviously forbidden zone, and apparently caused them to disregard the auguries of yesteryears: in December, 1955, there appeared in *New Construction* a lengthy article in which Ch'en, Wu and others were vociferously assaulted for their pre-1949 "reactionary" population views.[23] This partisan attack developed, indeed, from faiths rather than facts about economics and society and, for that very reason, probably should not have been lightly dismissed. In terms of "population control," the official arguments were indirect, and indirection should have seemed perferable to inaction.

But, the "indiscretion" of non-Communist demographers and others were not limited to discussing the need for population control in Malthusian terms. In one instance, Chen Po-ta's thesis that China could in twelve years' time absorb another 600,000,000 people was declared to be "rather too optimistic." And the attack on Wang Ya-nan, the President of Amoy University and one of the most ardent anti-Malthusian partisans in Communist China, could not have been more forceful and forthright: "Wang can be regarded as the representative of the blindly optimistic school. His great book *Marxist Population Theory and China's Population Problems,* is nothing but an exercise in the rigid transposition of dogmas and cannot have any relevance for China's existing circumstances. Therefore, his population theory has fallen behind the times and cannot solve any problems."[24]

Wang's personal indignation must have been considerable, for he had been suspicious even of the motives of Shao Li-tzu, whose views proved acceptable. In the preface of his own book, Wang declared,

[20] Micklewright, F. H. Amphlett: The Rise and Decline of English Neo-Malthusianism, *Population Studies,* July, 1961, 15(1): 32-51.

[21] See Wu, Ching-chao: *op. cit.;* Ta, Ch'en, Deferred Marriage, Birth Control, and Population Problems of New China, *New Construction,* May, 1957, (5): 1-16; and Fei, Hsiao-tung: What Is Meant by Demographic Research? *New Construction,* April, 1957, (4): 5-6.

[22] *See* Davis, Kingsley: Malthus and the Theory of Population, *in* Paul F. Lazarsfeld and Morris Rosenberg, eds.: THE LANGUAGE OF SOCIAL RESEARCH: A READER IN THE METHODOLOGY OF SOCIAL RESEARCH. Glencoe, The Fress Press, 1955, pp. 540-553.

[23] Chao, Ching: *op. cit.*

[24] Chen, Chang-hen: *Wen Hui Pao* (Shanghai), May 3 and 4, 1957.

As regards the current birth control propaganda, . . . it is very possible for people to consider the question of contraception and the population problems together, and even to look upon supporters of birth control as the supporters of the Malthusian population theory. . . . Childbearing, especially when it is too frequent and too close, is rather troublesome for the mother in any society. At the same time, it will be difficult to take good care of the children already born. This is why there are no restrictions against the use of various methods of fertility control (by those who have too many children or who have had them too closely together) in the Soviet Union where unemployment has been completely eliminated and where labor shortage is often felt. I hope this is the precise motive which led Mr. Shao Li-tzu to promote birth control. . . . If this is really true, and if we are able to view this question from the point of view of Marxism, we shall then not have to fear that, in the course of the current birth control campaign, the widespread thought remnants of Malthusianism would be able to resurrect themselves in a borrowed body.[25]

Ch'en Ta, Wu Ching-chao, Fei Hsiao-tung and others evidently misjudged the situation, even though they had no quarrel with the argument that childbearing, if unregulated, is troublesome for the mother in *any* society. What divided them and Wang Ya-nan and his optimistic school lies in their respective extrapolations, into both the immediate and distant future, of post-1949 trends in industrial and agricultural developments in *this* society, — the People's Republic of China. The dialogue ran like this:

WU CHING-CHAO: The employment of an additional 1.5 million workers each year is not a small number according to the experience of other countries. . . . In 1900, there were 28.3 million job-holders in the United States, and in 1956, there were 68.8 million. During these 56 years, the increase amounted to a total of 40.5 million, or an annual average of 0.7 million. . . . At the beginning of her First 5-year Plan, a total of 10.8 million persons were employed in the Soviet Union, but by 1955, 48.4 million were employed. The total gain of 37.6 million job-holders in 27 years meant an annual average of only 1.4 million. In our own country, the increase in the number of employed persons reached an annual average of 1.1 million during the period of the First 5-year Plan (1953–1957). . . . The Second 5-year Plan (1958–1962) calls for an increase of an additional 6 to 7 million persons, . . . (or) at most, an annual average of 1.4 million. . . . But, if our rate of natural increase were still to be 20 per 1000, then in 1967 (the end of the Third 5-year Plan) there will possibly be more than 6 million people who will demand new jobs each year![26]

WANG YA-NAN: Because [the socialist system] absorbs and mobilizes a great many more people in production, and because it can stimulate all those joining in production to exhibit selfless enthusiasm and to activate all hidden potentials, (it) can speedily increase the social wealth. . . . Having witnessed the high tide in agricultural cooperation in August, 1955, the attainment of the increases in agricultural production as envisaged in the First 5-year Plan for the expansion of our national economy has become a very conservative goal. According to the National Program for Agricultural Development, 1956–1967, agricultural production will be very greatly increased on the basis of cooperativized agriculture. . . . After the (1955) high tide in agricultural cooperativization, only about three years will be needed to bring to full maturity a new form of the socialist revolution. The elimination of unemployment and the total utilization of surplus manpower obviously need not wait until the Second and Third 5-year Plans.[27]

The gap between these estimations of future trends could not have been wider by any standards. Thus, by raising the larger question of "population control" which, in any case, can only be solved in terms of individual "fertility control," Ch'en, Wu, and others appear to have hastened, as it were, the transplanting of young seedlings before they could take root. And they also transferred the issue into a different context wherein opinions rather than facts are likely to be decisive.

THE ACRIMONIOUS REPERCUSSION

It began with the "exposure" of Chang Nai-chi, Lo Lung-chi, Chang Pai-chun, Huang Shao-hung, Wang K'un-lun, and T'an Pin-shan who were accused of being anti-Party, anti-people, anti-socialist, and anti-democratic dictator-

[25] Wang, Ya-nan: *Marxist Population Theory and China's Population Problems.* Peking, Science Publishing Co., 1956, p. 2.

[26] Wu, Ching-chao: *op. cit.*, p. 6.

[27] Wang, Ya-nan: *op. cit.*, pp. 41-2.

ship, and of harboring political ambitions. All six were members of the State Council when it first acted on birth control revisions in 1953, and belonged to either the China Democratic League or some other minority political parties. Chang Po-chun and Lo Lung-chi were the leaders of this so-called "Chang-Lo Alliance." They and Chang Nai-chi consequently were removed from their ministerial posts in the Departments of Communication, Forest Industry, and Food, respectively.[28]

While the ideological conviction of Wang Ya-nan, and those whom he typified, is unequivocal, their suspicion of Shao Li-tzu is also not without foundation; for, as Taeuber noted in passing, Shao is "a late convert from the old regime." [29] Notwithstanding this suspicion, Shao was not purged from the government along with the other rightists. In fact, he joined in the attack on them.[30] In answering the call to go after the rightists, Shao Li-tzu may well have acted either to salvage, or forestall the turning tide against birth control as a national policy. There were already clear signs of its retrenchment.

As previously noted, in March, 1957, Li Teh-chuan delivered her most vigorous speech in favor of birth control; at the July, 1957 session of the National People's Congress, however, Li was even more curt than she was at the 1956 People's Congress covering birth control in only one sentence in her report.[31] Shao seems to have been successful at that juncture as reports and articles on birth control continued to appear in newspapers even after the removal of the rightists, and might well have carried the campaign further had Ma Yin-chu also yielded to the same pressures which brought about the retreat of the rightists. Ma Yin-chu was not affiliated with any political party or clique, and until he was relieved of his post as the President of Peking University on March 26, 1960, he was increasingly more aggressive in spite of all official "persuasions" to induce a change in his population and economic views.[32] His refusal to yield may have been the last straw that decided the final outcome of the previous attempt at mass education in contraception. Nevertheless, it does not seem tenable that Ma Yin-chu could have been connected with the first wave of reactions against birth control in the spring of 1957. In his speech calling for a clear line to separate the rightists from others, Shao Li-tzu even expressed his basic agreement with Ma's "New Population Theory." [33] Wu Ching-chao, Ch'en Ta, and Fei Hsiao-tung were, among others, the rightists under attack.

A member of the China Democratic League, Fei Hsiao-tung was, according to his own "admission of crimes," involved in various activities in which the Chang-Lo Alliance had an interest.[34] Of particular significance was the "conspiracy" to restore "bourgeois" sociology in 1957 which, according to the official account, was a joint effort of Fei, Ch'en Ta, Wu Ching-chao, and others.[35] Wu Ching-chao is also a member of the Democratic League.

The abolition of sociology departments and sociology courses took place in China in 1952, when a re-organization of the curriculum of institutions of higher learning was made. In January, 1957, Wu published in *New Construction* an article "Does Sociology Still Have a Place in New China?" Fei followed with a statement in a Shanghai paper, *Wen Hui Pao,* on February 20, and also formally requested a change in the official attitude towards sociology at a conference on propaganda activities called by the Central Committee of the Chinese Communist Party (March 24). On April 10, *New Construction* organized a symposium on sociology, which was chaired by Fei. Less than two weeks later (April 23), Fei, Wu, and six others were elected at a meeting of the Department of Philosophy

[28] See *People's Handbook* for 1956 and 1957.

[29] *See* Taeuber, Irene B.: Population Policies in Communist China, POPULATION INDEX, October 1956, 22(4): 261-274.

[30] Shao Li-tzu's speech delivered before the First National People's Congress, 4th Session, Peking, 1957. *See* THE COMPLETE REPORT [of the conference], pp. 880-881.

[31] See Li's speech, *ibid.*, pp. 749-755.

[32] See Ma, Yin-chu: My Philosophy and Economic Theory, *New Construction,* November, 1959, (11): 51-55; *and* To Repeat My Request, *New Construction,* January, 1960, (1): 5-7.

[33] Shao, Li-tzu: *op. cit.*

[34] Fei, Hsiao-tung: *in* THE COMPLETE REPORT. First National People's Congress, 4th Session, Peking, 1957, pp. 1334-1340.

[35] For a fuller account of this episode, see the author's letter to the editor, *American Sociological Review,* June, 1962, 27 (3): 413.

and Social Sciences of the Academy of Sciences, to form an "organization subcommittee." Its functions were, at the suitable opportunity, to assist in establishing (within the Department) a committee of research in "social problems."

Simultaneously, Ch'en, Wu, and others were also engaged in a number of other activities; in a petition to the National Committee of the Chinese People's Political Consultative Conference (March 7), they urged the establishment of a population research organization and the reintroduction of courses in demography at the university level. In an interview published in *Wen Hui Pao* on April 16, Ch'en reiterated his view about the restoration of sociology. In May, Ch'en and others wrote a letter to the Ministry of Higher Education, voicing their opposition to the previous elimination of sociology departments. And, there was a "private" meeting in June, which was attended by Ch'en, Fei, Wu and others and was held at Ch'en's home. It was alleged that the name of the research committee on social problems was changed, without proper authorization to "Sociology Work Committee," and Ch'en was elected the committee chairman. The resolutions of that meeting included 1) a systematic recruitment of those academic colleagues trained in "bourgeois" sociology, 2) the reestablishment of the Chinese Sociological Society, 3) the restoration of sociology departments in universities, firstly, in Peking and Shanghai and then Canton and Chengtu, and 4) the tentative appointment of Wu Ching-chao as the director of a sociological research center at the People's University in Peking.

The "conspiracy" proved a complete failure as was the attempt of Wu, Fei, and Ch'en to expand the need for fertility control into a question of population control. Apart from the flood of criticism of the state of affairs during the Hundred Flowers and the allegation that the Chang-Lo Alliance sought to advance the status of minority political parties to be at parity with that of the Communist Party, Fei, Wu, Ch'en and others were also accused of using the huge population of China to prove that ". . . the transformation of China into a socialist country is impossible; it is like the building of palaces on a sand beach, a totally wasteful effort." [36] Thus, it seems that the issue of birth control was implicated in a situation where ideology, politics, and personalities were poignantly entangled and where the climate of opinions once again became hostile to a factual appreciation of population trends.

[36] Li, P'u: Do Not Allow the Rightists to Use the Population Question to Advance their Political Conspiracy, *JMJP*, October 4, 1957.

The Accelerated Solution

But, solutions must still be found to escape the demographic dilemma in which China finds herself, irrespective of the party in power. How could her existing millions be effectively (the meaningful criteria here must be related to the over-all Chinese situation rather than to Western standards of efficiency) and usefully accommodated? As Mao Tse-tung has often been quoted by writers in Communist China since 1957 to have said, "China has a population of 600 million people. This must never be forgotten," it does not seem merely a coincidence that the Great Leap Forward and the People's Commune followed closely the deflation of the birth control campaign.

Both the Great Leap Forward and People's Commune appear to have been in the making for some time before they were extensively publicized as formal national policies. Directives calling for some de-centralization of industrial and commercial enterprises were issued by the State Council as early as November, 1957. In December of the same year, a National Economic Planning Conference approved the draft of the 1958 economic plan, which already embodied the Leap Forward theme — that is, to catch up to or surpass Britain within 15 years or so in the output of steel and other major industrial products. The idea itself must therefore have been under consideration prior to that conference, though it was not until May, 1958, that the Second Session of the Eighth National Congress of the Chinese Communist Party, "guided by Mao Tse-tung's thinking, . . . formulated the general line of going all out, aiming high and achieving greater, faster, better and more economic results in building socialism." [37]

In his report on the proposals for the Second 5-year Plan at the Eighth National Congress on

[37] Tan, Chen-lin: Strive for the Fulfillment, Ahead of Schedule, of the National Programme for Agricultural Development in NATIONAL PROGRAMME FOR AGRICULTURAL DEVELOPMENT, *1956-1967*. Peking, Foreign Languages Press, 1960, pp. 31-2.

September 16, 1956, Chou En-lai also referred to a discussion then under way: ". . . some hold that we should establish more large enterprises and few small or medium enterprises. . . . Some other people, however, think we should set up more small and medium enterprises and few large enterprises, because to set up the former requires less time and the investments yield a quicker return. We think that neither is true in all cases. . . . In order that the enterprises may be built in a more rational way, we may, whenever this is necessary and feasible, establish a large enterprise stage by stage. As regards small and medium enterprises, wherever resources are plentiful and other conditions are available, we may draw up a comprehensive plan to pave the way for future development. Further, when planning the co-ordination of small and medium enterprises with large ones, we should first utilize the existing small and medium enterprises and handicrafts under state ownership or joint state-private ownership so as to exploit their productive potentialities." [38]

It must be stressed that, even if the intensive campaign of 1957 had been continued, the effect of its possible success would not have become evident until, at least, some fifteen or twenty years later. That means that birth control is a long term investment. Judging from Chou En-lai's presentation, the establishment of the People's Commune and the Great Leap Forward, particularly the mushrooming of backyard industries, seem to have been the simultaneous implementation of the two divergent views regarding industrial development. They also assumed significance in the demographic context. The belief was that the people's communes could fully mobilize and make rational use of rural manpower, and that "the countryside is like a vast expanse of the sea in which the labor force is swallowed up." [39]

Since 1949, though briefly entertaining the idea of a short-term need for fertility control, the Party leadership has also consistently maintained a fairly sanguine outlook on the long-term demographic prospects. Typical of this line of reasoning is the following:

the population of various nations can be grouped into three categories: 1) Colonial, semi-colonial countries, or countries whose productive power is low, or whose development is at the early stage of capitalism. Fertility and mortality are both high, but the rate of natural increase is small. Countries included in this group are Old China, India and Egypt before independence, Chile, Imperial Russia before the Revolution, England, France, and Germany in the 19th century; 2) Countries which have a relatively high productive capacity, or which have already reached the last stage of capitalistic expansion. Even though mortality has declined, fertility has decreased even further; therefore, the rate of natural increase is also not very high. England, France, West Germany, the United States of America, Australia, and New Zealand belong to this second group; and 3) The third group includes all socialist countries. Apart from the U.S.S.R., the other socialist nations are still in the early stages of socialist construction. In these nations, the rate of natural increase tends to go up because of the improved standard of living, a rapid decline in the death rate, and little changed fertility. And, in response to further advancement in socialist construction and a still higher standard of living, the practice of late marriage and birth control will emerge. There will be a gradual drop in the birth rate, but the speed of the decline in the death rate (which has already approached the minimum) will also slow down. A reduction in the rate of natural increase will, in turn, become evident. In short, in the course of socialist construction, population numbers will proceed, step by step, from an initial rapid increase to a stable growth.[40]

This politically-flavored population typology and prophecy serves to emphasize and outline the framework within which the question of population growth was viewed in some influential quarters in Communist China. If (as seems to be the case) the Great Leap Forward and the People's Commune were to be vehicles for economic development as well as solutions to the short-term population question in terms of labor-intensive projects,[41] questions associated with rapid population growth in the long run were postulated out of existence as the Party and government confidently pushed the plans for accelerated industrialization: economic development and its concomitant social transformation

[38] Chou, En-lai: *op. cit.,* pp. 69-70.

[39] As quoted *in* Orleans, Leo: Problems of Manpower Absorption in Rural China, *China Quarterly,* July-September, 1961, (7): 58.

[40] Chang, Pai-kun et al.: A Socialist Theory of Population and China's Population Problem, *Economic Research,* August 17, 1957, (4): 36-63.

[41] *E. g.,* irrigation schemes.

would, in due course, stimulate the practice of fertility control and, as a consequence, a reduction in the rate of natural increase.

Thus, aside from internal politics and political developments of which the birth control debate was a part, the financial and ideological costs also may have seemed too large and unnecessary. All indications, so it appeared, pointed to a quick transition from an agricultural and backward nation to an industrialized and advanced state, implying the automatic emergence of the practice of fertility control, as it were, at no extra cost. Up to the end of 1957, both the rate and volume of economic development were impressive, and agricultural forecasts to the end of the Third 5-year Plan (1967) had not been shattered by the march of events since 1958.

A Quiet Resumption

Nevertheless, even though the vigorous birth control campaign in Communist China was gradually brought to a standstill, the population problem itself has not been entirely or permanently dismissed. The door has been left ajar to allow the admission of fertility control as a national policy: "whether the stable growth in population (a by-product of socialist construction) will be at a relatively high or low level is related to whether or not the Party and government encourage fertility. In this connection, we know that, in the socialist countries, if the Party and government do not adopt a pronatal policy, the birth rate will decline and become stablized at a comparatively low level or that, if the Party and government follow a policy designed to curb population numbers the birth rate then will decrease and become stable at a still lower level." [42]

As late as in March, 1959, draft regulations of one people's commune contained provisions for birth control instructions.[43] And in the bitter aftermath of the Great Leap Forward, the National People's Congress again met after an interval of two years: among the ten tasks set for the adjustment of the national economy is one (the 4th) which reads: "To reduce the urban population and the number of workers and functionaries to an appropriate extent by persuading, first of all, those workers and functionaries who had come from the rural areas to return to rural productive work and strengthen the agricultural front." [44] Of course, even if this policy should be successfully implemented, it would not resolve the question of population numbers.

But, it has also been reliably reported that, from March 8 to April 10, 1962, an exhibition of planned parenthood was held in Canton, and over 10,000 visitors saw the display of charts, models and specimens during the first two weeks.[45] A few months earlier in January, the State Council approved a revised schedule of important duties to allow the importation of contraceptive appliances and drugs into China duty-free.[46] And, since early April, 1962, a series of articles has appeared in the *People's Daily* and other newspapers, arguing that "it is not good to get married and give birth to a child too early." [47]

Of still greater significance, *People's Daily* has recently (since November, 1962) printed advertisements to promote the sale of publications in which birth control is advocated. Descriptions of various conventional contraceptives now available in retail stores in China also appeared in Ta Kung Pao (Peking). In four of the six recent issues of *China's Women* since December, 1962, planned parenthood was promoted. Along with postponement of marriage and diaphragms, condoms, and jelly, sterilization (vasectomy and salpingectomy) has been strongly recommended in recent months.[48] No mention, however, was

[42] Chang, Pai-kun: *op. cit.*, p. 43.

[43] See *Jen-min Pao-chien* (People's Health Protection) March, 1959, (3): 276-77.

[44] Press Communique of the 3rd Session of the Second National People's Congress of China, *NCNA*, April 16, 1962.

[45] *Yang-cheng Wan-pao* (*Canton Evening*), March 25, 1962.

[46] *Ta Kung Pao* (Hong Kong), January 16, 1962.

[47] *JMJP*, April 4, 1962; *Chung-kuo Ch'ing-nien Pao* (*China Youth Daily*, Peking), April 12, and May 10, 1962; and *Kung-jen Jih-pao* (*Daily Worker*, Peking), May 4, 1962. For a fuller account of these developments, see Tien, H. Y.: Population Control: Recent Developments in Mainland China, *Asian Survey*, July, 1962, 11 (5): 12-16.

[48] *Ta Kung Pao* (Peking), April 22, 1963, and *China's Women*, December 1, 1962, (12); February 1, 1963, (2); April 1, 1963, (4); and May 1, 1963, (5).

made of abortion as a suitable means of fertility control.[49]

[49] For a discussion of the prospects for using abortion as the principal means of population control in China, *see* Tien, H. Y.: Induced Abortion and Population Control in Mainland China, *Marriage and Family Living,* February, 1963, 25 (1): 35-43.

A resumption of birth control activities clearly is under way. But, in view of the enormity and complexity and delicacy of the question of population control in China, it also seems clear that the road to success in fertility control in China will be neither smooth nor short.

*Population and Power in the Free World**

KINGSLEY DAVIS

During World War II and the succeeding decade, the struggle between the Communist and the free countries has become not only more intense but also more equal. The Communist bloc has apparently accomplished the feat of progressively expanding its territory without losing (at least yet) the solidarity of its member states.** The free world, on the other hand, lacking the principles of unity that hold together the Communist group, has achieved much less solidarity. Its member states have little to unify them other than their common fear of Communist expansion.

Necessarily, the cleavage between Communist and non-Communist peoples has its roots in the past, as does the relative strength or weakness of each side. One fact to bear in mind is this: the present struggle, recent and in many ways unique, has grown out of the much older conflicts and imbalances inherent in the origin and spread of the Industrial Revolution. Communism, which received its initial philosophical formulation in the industrial nations, has paradoxically had its subsequent applications in predominantly agrarian states. It has learned to produce an energetic and simple solution of major problems in the development of backward areas — problems which the pre-Communist world was not able to solve — and to institute drastic reforms by force when it gets control. As yet the free world, no matter how superior its long-run influence, has worked out no solution of comparable directness and clarity, or at least none that it can agree on. It is handicapped thus in its appeal to backward areas.[1]

The historical roots of the present conflict have not, however, arisen simply out of the interplay between industrial and non-industrial people. They have also sprung from a closely related interaction between the West, on the one hand, and the rest of the world on the other. It is significant that Communist and non-Communist blocs alike include both Western and Eastern, as well as industrial and agrarian, countries. Indeed, each political philosophy represents a competing way of handling relationships among these four overlapping classes of nations. Any analysis of population and political power in the free world, therefore, must necessarily take into account the complex ways in which the interdependencies of the Western and non-Western dichotomy cut across those of the industrial and nonindustrial hiatus. It is in their different ways

** [*Editor's Note:* This was written before developments in Hungary and Poland during 1956-57.]

[1] See Morris Watnick, "The Appeal of Communism to the Underdeveloped Peoples," in *Progress of Underdeveloped Areas,* Bert F. Hoselitz, ed., (Chicago: University of Chicago Press, 1952), pp. 151-72.

of handling these interdependencies that Communism and the free world seek to win the cold war.

The Changing Character of European Influence

For roughly three hundred years, from around 1600 to 1914, a dominant feature of the world was the fact that two aspects of European influence — the growth and spread of European peoples, and the growth and spread of European culture — were both rising together. Gaining momentum with the Industrial Revolution, reaching their combined pinnacle in the nineteenth and early twentieth centuries, these two processes flowed along together because they were intimately related. The Europeans were evolving a culture which gave them an increasing capacity to multiply at home and to migrate abroad; and this multiplication and dispersion, in turn, enabled them to make still further advances in their culture. When the entire Western hemisphere and Australia and New Zealand colonized, the territory settled predominantly by European stock and characterized by European culture was approximately ten times in 1850 what it had been in 1600. By 1950 the number of people of European ancestry had risen to approximately eight times what it had been three hundred years earlier — that is, to almost a third of the world's population from perhaps 18 per cent at the earlier date.

Since 1914, however, it has become increasingly apparent that the two aspects of European influence need not go together, that they are in fact tending to pursue separate paths. European peoples are no longer settling new areas by mass migration as they once did, and their rate of population growth in the areas already settled is no longer, on the whole, so strikingly ahead of that of the rest of the world. Indeed, the more economically advanced of the European peoples have slowed down in their growth, particularly in northwest Europe. Although certain areas of European culture — notably those of Latin America, Canada, and the Soviet Union — are still growing rapidly, the total picture is one of rough parity with the rest of the world in population growth.

Yet the diffusion of certain aspects of European culture, as distinct from European people, has been accelerated. Peoples who are not European in race, whose cultural roots are far different from those of Europeans, who are in some cases anti-European in sentiment, are absorbing the instrumentalities of urban-industrial civilization at a rapid rate. These instrumentalities embracing technology, economic organization, and political forms are in fact so universal that they are no longer considered European. They are regarded simply as the well-known means by which any nation, whatever its background, can enhance its national power and level of living.

This tendency of European cultural diffusion to outlast European demographic expansion was already foreshadowed in the nineteenth century — most strikingly in the economic and military achievements of Japan, but also in the progress of dependent areas, such as India and Malaya, where few Europeans were settled. Since World War I the tendency has been accelerated. Curiously, one factor leading to this result has been the rapid liquidation of colonialism and the rise of nationalism among non-European peoples. Since most of the colonies were controlled by European nations, their demise would appear to signal a decline of European influence, and in a sense this was true; but the fact is that the rise of nationalism among non-European peoples has stepped up the acquisition of technology from the West.

The transformation of colonies into nations occurred on a large scale; it involved some 600 million persons. It also occurred quickly. By 1950 only about 8 per cent of the world's population lived in officially dependent areas; in 1913 the figure was around 30 per cent. This emergence of new non-European nations was both a consequence and a stimulant of Western contact. The modern idea of a nation-state is itself a Western idea, and both the goals and the propaganda techniques employed in the independence movements are predominantly Western. Once created, the new nations have been forced to find ways of maintaining their independence and their integrity as nations in a highly competitive world. They have been forced, in short, to try to acquire the same essential techniques that have given power to Western nations. Hence they have shown, on the one side, a strong desire to borrow industrial and economic instrumentalities, and on the other side, an equally strong desire to reject domination by the West and to reject those elements of Western culture which offend their traditional values. Their acquisition of Western ways has not therefore implied a solidarity with Western peoples. Whereas the extension of European culture by the emigration of Europeans overseas added to the political hegemony of the West, the new diffusion of European technology to independent non-European nations has had the opposite effect.

Into this delicately balanced and changing relationship between the West, led by the industrial nations, and the non-West, struggling to establish itself, came the split between communism and non-communism. This split appeared within the Western world, but it gained its international scope largely from the fact that the two sides have offered radically different solutions of East-West relationships. The Communists have said, in effect, that nothing short of swift revolution will accomplish the economic and political goals of the newly emerging non-Western nations. They have offered the techniques and leadership for carrying out such revolutions, and have not hesitated to use external force to help along the process. The price, of course, is the loss of democratic freedom as the free world understands it; but the gain in power is undeniable. Characteristically, the gain in power is not so much that of the individual nation as that of the entire bloc; for the Communists have solved at least temporarily the problem of international solidarity within their ranks. They have accomplished this, perhaps more apparently than actually, by using force and propaganda to diffuse their rigid ideology downward, by linking the different national dictatorships through party control, and, above all, by the overwhelming balance of power held by the Soviet Union itself. The result is evidently a new and more systematic imperialism than has ever been achieved before.

The free world, in contrast, has continued to rely on more informal and voluntary means of maintaining unity among the European and non-European peoples within its orbit. Resting its appeal on the dissolution of colonialism and the creation of a free community of sovereign states, it has attempted to give its underdeveloped members the instrumentalities they need through technical assistance and economic aid, and has offered them protection through voluntary alliances.

An important phase of the struggle between communism and the free world is thus the effort of each side to draw in the weaker and more unstable nations. The Communists have found it possible to bring into their camp certain peoples of the East, partly because of their geographical proximity to the Soviet Union and partly because of chaotic internal conditions and opposition to past treatment by free Western powers.

Though the ultimate outcome of the struggle is not clear, it does appear that the non-Western nations outside the Communist camp are succeeding in acquiring the instrumentalities of the West. Though progress may appear slow, painful, and spotty, it is nevertheless, when we are able to measure it, often more rapid than it was at a similar stage in the now developed countries. Rapid urbanization, the rise of literacy, the spread of mass communication, the decline of mortality, the growth of trade and industry — all indicate a process of fundamental change. This massive transformation cannot be expected in all cases to result quickly in higher levels of living, nor does it guarantee future loyalty to the free world. It does, however, set the stage for further changes and disturbances and for a possible shift of power in the direction of non-Western countries.

Demographically, the progress of the non-Western free nations is showing itself in population growth. Between 1935 and 1952 the average annual rate of increase in eighteen of these countries was 1.3 per cent; that in forty-three countries in the free Western category was 1.2 per cent. In the future the rate of population increase may shift still more in favor of the non-Western countries.

Indicative of changing circumstances is the growing voice of non-Europeans in international affairs. The desire of white South Africans, for example, to get help from the West in their effort to dominate the African majority and the Indian minority, is doomed to disappointment. The Christian nations, even if they were not restrained by principle (which they certainly are), could not afford to encourage South African racialism. The population of countries holding membership in the United Nations is two-thirds non-European. In the British Commonwealth itself, often taken as a bulwark of Western unity, the non-Europeans constitute 85 per cent of the population; and in the Empire the population is overwhelmingly colored.[2] Even within the areas of European culture, racial diversity bars any unanimity of racial attitudes. The diplomacy of the free Western powers must inevitably in the struggle with communism be directed toward keeping the allegiance of the non-Western nations.

Population Size and National Power

In appraising the political power of the free world, we shall do well to keep the Western and non-Western parts in mind, not because of any implied conflict between them but because of the possibly greater vulnerability to communism of the non-Western nations.

If we had a perfect measure of power, it would take into account the degree of solidarity among the states joined together in a common struggle; but at best we have only imperfect measures of the strength of individual nations, let alone groups of nations. Probably the best single index of a nation's power is its total income. This in turn is a function of its population size and its productive efficiency. Since these two elements vary independently, a nation may have a high national income primarily because it has a huge number of citizens or primarily because it is highly productive. Thus, of the twenty nations with the highest national incomes, some rank low in per capita income. India, for example, ranked fifth in total income in 1949, but fifty-fifth in per capita income. Similarly, Italy was ninth in national income but twenty-ninth in per capita income.[3] These are nations whose high position is gained through bigger-than-average population rather than through high productivity.

The reasons why population size is a major determinant of national power seem clear. First, the magnitude of the total population is the principal factor in the size of the labor force, and it is impossible to substitute completely other factors of production for labor. In fact, as an economy develops the price of labor increases because its level of living rises, so that, from a cost standpoint, the share of labor in production remains high. In the United States in 1951, for example, the payments of salaries and wages in manufacturing establishments amounted to 55 per cent of the value added by manufacture. Second, given the adequacy of resources, the larger the population integrated in one economic system, the greater the potential advantages of scale to be gained from mass production and mass distribution. Third, since military personnel is drawn most heavily from restricted age groups, a large population is necessary to furnish a sizable army and to sustain losses in fighting strength. Fourth, the consolidation of a victory in war often requires a sizable occupation force, which cannot be supplied if the population is small.

With these considerations in mind, let us look at the total population of eighty-one countries in 1950 (see Table 1). Seventy of these, constituting the free world, had a total of 1,450 million inhabitants, as against approximately 800 million in the eleven countries under Communist control. Within the free world, the 46 Western countries had a combined population of 648 million, while the 24 others — the non-Western free countries — had a population of 800 million. Approximately 57 per cent of the free world was therefore non-Western in culture; even counting all of Russia as "Western," something like 65 per cent of the Communist world was non-Western. Both camps, in effect, contain only a minority of Westerners, and the balance of the Communist

[2] L. M. Thompson, *Democracy in Multi-Racial Societies* (Johannesburg: South African Institute of Race Relations, 1949), No. 18, New Africa Pamphlet; Edgar H. Brookes, *South Africa in a Changing World* (Cape Town: Oxford University Press, 1953), pp. 32-34. The latter demonstrates effectively the lonely and hopeless position of white South Africa in a world where power is shifting in the direction of non-European peoples.

[3] See the writer's paper, "Demographic Foundations of National Power," in *Freedom and Control in Modern Society,* Morroe Berger, *et al.*, eds., (New York: Van Nostrand, 1954), pp. 208-209. The figures on national income, except where otherwise noted, are taken from the United Nations, *National and Per Capita Incomes, Seventy Countries, 1949* (New York: 1950). It is realized that the estimates of national income are in many cases merely rough approximations, particularly for peasant countries in which a large part of production is not market-oriented. See, for example, the discussion in Simon Kuznets, *Economic Change* (New York: Norton, 1953), Chapters 6-8. Nevertheless, the figures correlate reasonably well with independent data on social and economic development and therefore may be accepted as approximations, especially as relative rather than absolute differences.

TABLE 1

Some Demographic Features of 81 Countries, by Culture and Political Allegiance, 1950[1]

	Number of Countries	Population (000's) Total	Average	Median	Area (000's Km.^{2}) Total	Average	Persons per Km.^{2}
Free							
European	46	647,804	14,083	5,144	51,316	1,116	12.6
Non-European	24	801,902	33,413	16,656	17,319	722	46.3
Total	70	1,449,706	20,710	7,488	68,635	981	21.1
Communist							
European	8	279,697	34,962	14,220	23,287	2,911	12.0
Non-European	3	510,185*	170,062		11,449	3,816	44.6
Total	11	789,882	71,807	12,340	34,736	3,158	22.7
Grand Total	*81*	*2,239,588*	*27,649*	*9,350*	*103,371*	*1,276*	*21.7*

[1] Except in the case of the population of China, the figures from which this table is computed are taken from the *United Nations Demographic Yearbook.*

* The population of Communist China in 1950 is assumed to be 500 million. This is larger than the 456 million given by the *United Nations Demographic Yearbook,* 1953, for the year 1951, but smaller than the figure of 583 million purportedly found by the communists in their census of 1953. With reference to the Chinese census, see United States Census Bureau, "The Population of Communist China: 1953," International Population Reports, Series P-90, No. 6 (March 4, 1955).

world in particular is shifting to the East, as the addition of Vietminh in 1954 indicates.

From the figures just given, it is plain that the average Communist country is larger than the average free country — 72 million inhabitants as against 21 million. This is because two of the world's largest countries, China and Russia, dominate this small bloc of nations. Within the free world, the non-European countries have bigger populations than the Western ones. In fact, in 1950 the average population of non-Western free countries was thirty-three million; that of the Western free nations fourteen million. Since, if other things are equal, advantage lies in having a large population concentrated within one political unit rather than divided up into several units, the greater average size of Communist countries represents a demographic advantage over the free world, and the greater average size of non-Western countries represents a similar advantage over the Western ones. One would think that the West, which invented the modern nation-state and developed mass production and mass communication, would have achieved larger political aggregates; but the truth is that the Asians and other non-Europeans have, at least temporarily and with the help of Western powers, managed to combine more people into single national states than have the Westerners.[4] The preponderance of non-Western people in both the Communist and free camps will probably increase, since their rate of population growth has already achieved parity with that of the West. Moreover, we have ignored colonial areas, which are mainly non-European in culture and have rapidly growing populations. Among the Western nations it is generally those that are still relatively underdeveloped that exhibit the fastest numerical increase. The demographic picture in Mexico, for example, resembles India's more than the United States'; yet we have grouped Mexico among the Western peoples. It seems, then, that insofar as power results from sheer numbers, the importance of non-Western

[4] Of course, we are making the untrue assumption that the population of each state is effectively integrated as a nation. The extent to which this is or is not the case is a function of the efficiency of political and social organization. For the moment, however, our attention is focused on sheer population, recognizing that in fact it is an important but by no means the sole factor in national power.

and less developed areas will increase, and that these will continue to be the main prizes in the cold war between communism and anti-communism.

Demographic Factors Affecting Efficiency

There are, however, several demographic factors other than sheer population size which, by their influence on economic and social efficiency affect national power. Among these are the following: (1) the relation of population to resources; (2) the state of mortality and morbidity; (3) the level of fertility; (4) the age structure; (5) the rate of internal migration; (6) the degree of urbanization.

The greatest differences in these factors occur between industrial and nonindustrial countries, not between Communist and non-Communist countries. This fact must be borne in mind as we discuss the international significance of each of these factors.

(1) Population and Resources. When other things are equal, a large population represents a source of power; but when other things are not equal it may represent a source of weakness. Examining the physical territory of our eighty-one countries, we find that the seventy free nations occupy an area nearly twice as large as that occupied by the eleven Communist countries — sixty-nine million square kilometers as against thirty-five million.[5] Since their combined population is also nearly twice as large, the over-all average density comes out about the same. It is 21.1 persons per square kilometer for the free nations; 22.7 for the Communist nations. If the lands of each were equally valuable there would be no particular advantage on either side. Unfortunately, no certainty exists as to the relative resources of the two areas taken as a whole. There is, however, no reason whatever to think that the resources of the Communist area are greater, square mile for square mile, than those of the free world. Thus the free world still enjoys a tremendous potential advantage. With a population and a territory twice as large as that of the Communist world, the free countries, if they stuck together, could greatly excel in power. Furthermore, in none of the calculations given above are the dependent territories (colonies, trust territories, etc,) included. These, as of 1950, embraced about 8 per cent of the world's total population and 23 per cent of the world's inhabitable area. Since the dependent areas are wholly controlled by countries of the free world, they add considerably to the free world's advantage in potential power.

Within the free world, as Table 1 shows, the preponderance of territory is to be found in the Western parts. The forty-six Western nations in our tabulation have three times the total land area that the twenty-four non-Western nations have. In population, as we have seen, the opposite is true; the free Western nations have less than half the number of people represented by the free *non*-Western nations. It follows from these two facts that the average population density in the non-Western nations is much greater than the density in the Western nations — in fact, it is about four times as great.

Curiously, much the same situation is true of the Communist nations. The European nations behind the Iron Curtain (including all of the Soviet Union) contain two-thirds the territory but only half the population of the whole Communist world. The density in the non-Western parts of the Communist realm, like that in similar parts of the free world, is roughly four times what it is in the Western parts.

The inequality in population density between Western and non-Western nations would represent no disadvantage for non-Western peoples if (a) the resources per unit of land were correspondingly greater; if (b) the efficiency with which resources are utilized were greater; or if (c) the population size of all countries were below the optimum for the maximum utilization of resources in the given stage of technology. Actually, it appears that none of these conditions is true. The land that lies in the non-Western countries is, if anything, less rich in soil and minerals than that which lies in the Western countries, particularly in the free world. The efficiency with which resources are utilized in the non-Westerner lands is known to be much lower. Furthermore, in the free world and probably in the Communist world too, the availability of utilized resources is limited for the local popu-

[5] Indochina, and some small or relatively unknown countries have been excluded from the calculations, as have all the colonies.

lation, because the industrial nations control the exploitation to a marked degree. Finally, some countries, particularly those in Asia, appear to have so many and such rapid growth rates that, given the existing state of the arts, they find it more difficult than it would otherwise be to reach a more advanced stage of exploitation. It appears therefore that the greater population density of non-Western areas represents for them a real disadvantage.

Whether or not a nation has too many people is independent of the absolute size of its population. Some small countries appear to be overpopulated, some big ones not. Moreover, the difficulty of overpopulation is obviously not confined to non-Western countries alone. There are several in the Western category — *e.g.,* Italy, Greece, Mexico, El Salvador — which would probably be more powerful if they had fewer people. Yet it happens that the non-Western nations as a whole are more afflicted with redundant populations than the Western nations, as the cases of India, Pakistan, Egypt, Lybia, Japan, China, and Indonesia illustrate.[6] The disadvantage for the non-Western countries is indeed great, and it is also fundamental and relatively permanent. It will not disappear overnight.

If a nation finds its population too dense and growing too rapidly for efficiency, it has two alternatives. It can elect to reduce the rate of population growth, or it can attempt to find ways of continually increasing the national income so as to take care of the increased population. These are obviously not mutually exclusive possibilities. No nation today would pursue the first policy and ignore the second. Virtually all nations, except perhaps a "hermit kingdom" or two, are committed to the goal of economic development. The strange thing, however, is that most nations, even those which plainly have too many people, actually do pursue the second policy and ignore the first, and there are many individuals who refuse to consider the first an alternative at all.

If we ask why nations generally shy away from a policy of checking population growth, the answer is not simple. Doubtless governments fear to offend the sentiments of their people, and officials often share the popular sentiments. But we find that even in countries controlled by dictatorships, where state policy is a matter of hard-boiled power politics, no attempt is made to lessen the rate of population growth, even when such growth is obviously detrimental economically. China* is a case in point, as are also Portugal, Poland, Haiti, and El Salvador. To reach a fuller explanation, therefore, one must realize that a policy of limiting population growth jettisons an important source of national power —namely, the military and industrial value of a greater population when other things are improved. Consequently, it is only nations with a strong and liberal sense of the importance of the level of living, an attitude which plays down the primacy of sheer national power, that are likely to adopt a policy limiting population that is real enough to be effective. Thus there is the possibility that in the highly competitive international world, no nation, however overpopulated it may be or may regard itself as being, is going to carry through such a policy. Perhaps an anti-natalist policy is least likely precisely in new, insecure, and emotionally nationalistic nations that have arisen out of the ashes of colonialism in the non-Western regions. It is noteworthy that India has authorized such a policy, that Japan seems hospitable to the idea of fostering birth control, and that Egypt is considering possible measures;[7] but as yet no successful implementation of a national anti-natalist policy is on record. It seems more likely that most nations — and this includes liberal Western countries —will adopt exclusively the economic policy of more wealth, more territory and more trade to feed ever more peo-

[6] The topic of overpopulation as a detriment to national power is treated more fully in Davis, *op. cit.,* pp. 221-24. See also United Nations *Determinants and Consequences of Population Trends* (New York: 1953), Chapters 13-15.

* [*Editor's Note:* China has changed her policy since this was written.]

[7] For a brief survey of policies concerning fertility control, see Hope T. Eldridge, *Population Policies* (Washington: International Union for the Scientific Study of Population, 1954), Chapter 4. On India see also *Proceedings* of the Third International Conference on Planned Parenthood (Bombay: Family Planning Association of India, 1953), pp. 56-86; Ministry of Health, *Proceedings* of the First Meeting of the Family Planning and Programmes Committee (Delhi: Government of India Press, 1954). On several underdeveloped countries, see Milbank Memorial Fund, *Interrelations of Demographic, Economic, and Social Problems in Selected Underdeveloped Areas* (New York: Milbank Fund, 1954).

ple. This, in its expansionist form, is the familiar *Lebensraum* policy made famous by pre-war Japan, Italy, and Germany. It has the advantage of appealing to a very deep and elementary sense of justice (people must have enough room to "live and breathe" in). It also tends to lead to warfare, which, if there are too many people, is an honorable and apparently inadvertent way of reducing their number. In an atomic age, the acquisition of territory by warfare is not as attractive a venture as it used to be, but the idea that economic development can be endlessly spurred on is sufficiently strong to cause most governments to forego measures aimed at checking population growth by limiting fertility.

(2) *The Role of Mortality and Morbidity.* Most of the demographic disadvantages of non-Western countries, whether Communist or not, arise from the fact that, on the average, they are more underdeveloped than the Western countries. This can be seen, for example, in the mortality figures. Although the data do not permit average mortality rates to be computed for all non-Western countries, we do know that in underdeveloped countries generally, and hence in most non-Western countries, death rates are still relatively high. It is true that the rates have been declining remarkably in recent years, and in some cases spectacularly; but they are still high enough in most non-Western areas to exact a considerable penalty. The chief waste lies in the death of people before they have a chance to repay the cost of birth and rearing by economic production. In Australia, according to life tables for the period 1946–48, the percentage of males surviving to age twenty was 95, in Egypt for the period 1936–38 it was 57, and in India for 1941–50 it was 58 (see Table 2). When 20 to 40 per cent of the males are dead before they reach age twenty, it is not only their productive life that is lost, but also the effort and expense of bearing them and rearing them to that age. In this respect, while some of the non-Western countries are better off than some Western ones (e.g., Japan or Ceylon as compared to El Salvador), on the whole the advantage still lies with the West.

Where a high death rate is found, there is a high rate of ill health as well. Accordingly, Western countries, with their low mortality, have on the average a smaller proportion of their labor force or their soldiers incapacitated and enervated by sickness; a lesser proportion of their territory left idle because of health hazards (malaria, sleeping sickness); and a smaller proportion of their population dependent.

TABLE 2

*Percentage of Males Surviving to Age 20 According to Life Tables: Selected Countries**

	Period Covered	Percentage of Males Surviving
Sweden	1946–50	95.4
United States	1949–51	94.7
Australia	1946–48	94.6
France	1950–51	92.6
Japan	1953	90.7
Argentina	1947	86.2
Portugal	1949–52	82.2
Ceylon	1952	82.1
El Salvador	1949–51	76.2
Mexico	1940	64.0
India	1941–50	58.0
Egypt	1936–38	57.4

* Taken from United Nations, *Demographic Yearbook,* 1953 and 1954.

(3) *The Level of Fertility.* Though there is resistance to admitting the fact, a high birth rate has many disadvantages. It tends to remove women from the labor force, restrict the activities of those who do enter the labor force, and increase the vulnerability of women to disease and death. If mortality is very high, then a nation must necessarily bear these costs; but if mortality has been reduced, as it has been in most underdeveloped countries, the persistence of high fertility incurs not only these costs needlessly but also adds others as well. Notably, it increases the dependency ratio in the population, puts extra obstacles in the way of adequate education and vocational training, brings too rapid a population growth, and reduces internal migration.

Since the non-Western nations are on the average less developed than the Western, they suffer more from the disadvantages of high birth rates. Indeed, it is probable that in South Asia and the Near East, though not perhaps so much in large parts of Africa, birth rates today are higher than they were in Europe in the Middle Ages.

(*4*) *The Age Structure.* The age structure of the industrial nations, due largely to previous rapid declines in fertility, has been heavily weighted in the productive ages. These are also the ages most exposed to the risk of conception and relatively little exposed to the risk of death. Consequently, the actual number of births in relation to the total population is higher than it would otherwise be, and the number of deaths lower. The industrial nations have thus had a maximum birth rate in relation to the actual reproductive effort put forth, and have had a minimum death rate in relation to the medical effort expended. This situation has contributed substantially to economic efficiency. Not only has there been a larger proportion of persons in the active ages and therefore available for the labor force, but there has been a rather safe natural increase incurred at the least cost.

The advantages of the industrial nations in this respect, however, will not last forever. The end product of the trend is an aging population. Unless means are found to keep the old vigorous as well as alive, the possibility is frighteningly real that the economy will be weakened with costly security schemes or progress stultified by allowing authority to gravitate to the old but incompetent. It should be noted that the influence of age is different in different kinds of activity. In highly capitalized warfare as well as in any other kind, military efficiency requires the use of the young in large numbers. Old age sets in, for military purposes, at age thirty-five or forty. In rapidly developing fields of science, old age also sets in early. The penalties of an aging population may therefore be greater than the mere nonparticipation of the aged in the labor would imply. In the near future it appears that the industrial societies of the West may reap more disadvantages than advantages from their age structure unless both biological and sociological measures are taken to prevent this result.

(*5*) *The Rate of Internal Migration.* The movement of people in peasant countries tends to be much less than that of people in industrial countries. Such movement, when it occurs, is often a cause as well as a consequence of economic development. The new activities associated with economic growth are seldom located where the old activities were, and they involve concentrations of workers in particular spots to a much greater degree than was possible with agriculture. Hence economic development requires a massive internal movement of people, often made all the greater by the fact that the new industrial jobs are for the most part regarded as temporary. The fixity of people in underdeveloped countries, particularly in those of non-Western culture, is partly a result of rigid social stratification, close kinship organization, regional cultural and linguistic barriers, and sharply defined age and sex roles. Western culture, even before the Industrial Revolution, was free from some, though not all, of these barriers — a fact which was perhaps one of the conditions giving rise to rapid Western development. Today in most non-Western countries the rate of internal mobility may be rising, but it is still far less than in the average Western country.[8] The barriers appear to be greater in the non-Arabic than the other parts of Asia, and perhaps least in Negro Africa. In any case, the Western countries seem to enjoy an economic advantage in this respect.

(*6*) *The Degree of Urbanization.* The industrialization of agriculture and the growth of manufacturing bring a shift of the population from the countryside to the city, because the city, for many reasons, is the most economical location for most productive and distributive functions which involve land as merely a site and do not require close proximity to raw materials. A country that is not yet heavily urbanized must still go through the process and bear the costs of urbanization; an urbanized nation has already met the costs and reaped the advantages. The industrialized countries are approaching what

[8] In India in 1931 only 3.6 per cent of the population was recorded as living outside the province of birth; in the United States in 1940 no less than 22.5 per cent were living outside the state of birth. K. Davis, *Population of India and Pakistan* (Princeton: Princeton University Press, 1951), pp. 107-108. One of the remarkable things about India was the fact that there was no evidence of an increase in internal mobility between 1891 and 1931.

appears to be the saturation point in urbanization — some 70 per cent of the population living in cities of 20,000 or more. Their further economic development can assume the advantages of urban location. Asia (outside the U.S.S.R.) has only 13 per cent of its people located in such places, and Africa even less — 9 per cent. In this respect the Western nations, and again the more industrialized ones, appear to have an advantage, at least economically. Whether in the future urbanization will prove an unmixed military blessing is a hard question, but one that should not go unmentioned.

Some Political Implications

Cross-cutting the political division between Communist and free countries, as we have seen, is a cultural division between the West (more heavily industrial) and the non-West (more heavily agrarian). This cultural division forms one of the main lines of competition and conflict between the Communist and the free world, because the struggle has developed increasingly into an effort to win the underdeveloped areas, particularly those of non-Western culture. What has been said here concerns certain of the demographic causes and conditions of this effort. On the one hand, it can be seen that the prize is great; nearly 60 per cent of the population of the eighty-one nations with which we have been dealing is contained in the twenty-seven non-Western countries. The potential manpower at stake, not to mention the natural resources, is therefore enormous. On the other hand, these countries have not realized the potential power latent in their huge populations. They are "at stake" in the struggle between communism and non-communism because they are underdeveloped and plagued with social and economic problems. Prominent among their problems are the demographic factors contributing to inefficiency — redundant populations, high death and sickness rates, extremely high birth rates, immobility, and high agrarian density. These and other problems make them relatively impotent and also extremely "ripe" for change, with communism and anti-communism offering alternative solutions.

Although the "West" embraces heterogeneous countries, some rich and some poor like the "non-West," the greater average inefficiency of the latter can be seen in the fact that in 1949 the mean per capita income for the people in twenty-one non-Western countries was $47.00 and $639 in forty-four Western countries.[9] Although the methods of calculating these estimates may exaggerate the differences, it is clear that a pronounced inequality exists. The preponderance of the Western nations on the side of efficiency is still so great that it overbalances their disadvantage on the side of sheer population. This can be seen in the fact that in 1949 the total national income of the 44 Western nations was estimated at 379 billion dollars, whereas that of the 21 non-Western nations for which data were available was estimated at 59 billion. In 1952 the two figures were approximately 500 billion to 75 billion. By this measure, then, the locus of power within the free world, and doubtless in the Communist world as well, definitely resides in the West.

The West's advantage comes from the fact that it invented the Industrial Revolution and then continued to reap advantages from it. But, as industrialization spreads to non-Western peoples, this advantage will not necessarily last. As we have seen, the weight of sheer numbers may increasingly favor the non-Western countries in both the Communist and the free worlds. For this advantage, some of them (the already over-populated countries) may have to pay a penalty — the depressing effect of dense population on the level of living; but if economic advance moves ahead of population growth, the power of these countries can be expected to grow prodigiously. Furthermore, some of the current demographic advantages of the West may turn into liabilities, e.g., the population may become so burdened with the aged that the crude death rate will rise, ill health increase, and the replacement of military losses become more difficult. Under certain conditions, the concentration of people in metropolitan areas may prove a handicap. In addition, certain non-demographic factors may tend in time to lower productivity in the older industrial nations. It may be that a hardening of

[9] These are averages weighted by the total population in each country. The unweighted averages (each country counting as an equal unit) are $62.00 and $357 respectively. Computed from United Nations, *National and Per Capital Incomes, Seventy Countries, 1949* (New York: 1950), Table 1.

the sociological arteries, only dimly seen today in such things as the quest for individual security at the expense of national strength, will set in. Assuming that the non-Western nations eventually move through the demographic transition, they will enjoy some, though not necessarily all, of the demographic advantages the West has enjoyed. If they also acquire more of the technological and social instrumentalities of the West, their superior numbers should count for much more than they do now. The struggle between the Communist and the free camps is not therefore merely a struggle for the non-Western areas as they are at present. It is a struggle for areas with great potentialities for international power.

Since the struggle may break out at any time into major warfare, it is impossible to deal with the demographic future without reckoning on the possibility of conflict. In this regard, although the future role of atomic and hydrogen weapons is not clear, it stands to reason that such weapons, *if used in a major war,* will prove far more destructive of human life than have the weapons of the past. It has to be remembered that the death rate is unrestricted at its upper limit. While the birth rate can scarcely rise above 65 per thousand per year, the death rate can, with the proper lethal instruments, approach 1,000 in a given area. It is therefore unsafe to assume that the world's population, or that of any particular region, will go on doubling every sixty to seventy years until we have untold billions. Indeed, it is strange to believe that the ingenuity and science necessary to make such population growth possible and will not also be used in the relatively simple direction of controlling fertility. If men with all their science and technology are so irrational as not to control their fertility, they cannot be expected to be so wise as to use all of their increased capacities only for productive purposes. They may well use these capacities for destructive purposes as well.

The demographic effects of nuclear weapons, if used on a large scale, are impossible to forecast under prevailing conditions of rapid advance and secrecy. It can be assumed, however, that since nuclear bombs are expensive to make and to deliver, they would probably be used on those centers where industry and hence population is highly concentrated. Since the more industrialized the nation, the more concentrated the population, the weapons would probably do more damage to the populations of the industrial nations than to those of the underdeveloped countries. With the greater concentration of capital equipment in industrial nations, destruction on the economic side would also be greater than in underdeveloped areas. The latter areas, even though their total capital is far less, would have a lesser proportion of it destroyed. In short, the population and the production of underdeveloped areas are more spread out, more dependent on the land, less dependent on equipment. Such areas would not only be less subject to attack with nuclear bombs but, possibly, would be better able to survive. On the other hand, of course, such regions would be less capable of retaliating.

If nuclear warfare should occur on a world scale, it might end by increasing in a short time both the relative demographic and the relative technological advantages of the underdeveloped and hence the non-Western peoples.

If it be granted that the demographic problems of the underdeveloped countries, especially in the areas of non-Western culture, make these nations more vulnerable to communism, the question arises: what population policies can the free world pursue? It would appear that an appropriate policy would be the control of birth rates, the lowering of death rates, the provision of technical assistance and economic aid, and the formation of military alliances. Such a combination of policies, if carried through effectively, would strengthen the free world in its constant fight against encroachment.

On the purely demographic side, however, there is little agreement on goals and certainly none on instrumentalities. The philosophy of population in overpopulated Holland bears no resemblance to that in overpopulated India. The official reticence in the United States seems not to be matched in Japan or Egypt. It is too much to expect that a concerted policy will somehow emerge as if by magic in the free world. The dominant force in this community of nations is still nationalism. Such being the case, the population policies are likely to be those of individual countries, each pursuing its course separately according to its notion of its own interest. Some free nations, bearing in mind the prospect of frightful mortality, may elect to put their faith in numbers, making a higher level of living a goal subsidiary to the sheer weight of manpower. Others may aim at economic efficiency in part through demographic moderation. If the free nations go their own individual way and fail to unite on a population policy, it means that they are giving up one possible means of strengthening their cause. The only compensation is that the Iron Curtain countries, in their search for ways of winning and keeping the backward areas, seem equally bent on ignoring the problem of population.

STUDY AND DISCUSSION QUESTIONS

1. What are the official policies of the Soviet Union concerning fertility, mortality, and migration? How do these differ from policies in the United States?
2. Look up the history of birth control policy in various Latin-American countries. How have these policies reflected the nations' political structure?
3. Certain agencies of the United Nations are concerned with the study of population conditions in nations around the world. Which are these agencies? Cite some examples of their work in this area.
4. Does the United States government have policies affecting fertility, mortality, or migration in this country? What evidences of a current or past policy stand on each can you cite? Distinguish between policies which directly affect the population components and those which indirectly affect them.
5. Can you cite some areas of your state which are noted politically as strongholds of a certain political group? Think of other areas in your state where the political composition of the population is vastly different. How might the outcome of the next election be affected by migration between or into these areas?
6. What are the regulations and practices concerning migration into and out of Communist countries? How are these different from United States regulations and practices in this regard?
7. Can you think of instances when religious views and views of the polity have been in conflict on population issues? Cite examples. What were the outcomes of these conflicts?

SUGGESTED ADDITIONAL READING

Hauser, Philip M., ed. *Population and World Politics.* Glencoe: The Free Press, 1958.
In addition to the Davis article reprinted in this chapter, includes several other articles relating population and the polity.

Organski, Katherine, and A. F. K. Organski. *Population and World Power.* New York: Alfred A. Knopf, 1961.
Explores population as one of the great determinants of power among nations.

Lubell, Samuel. *The Future of American Politics.* New York: Harper and Brothers, 1951.
Discusses social forces operating in the United States that have influenced the outcome of elections, including population changes.

Eldridge, Hope T. *Population Policies: A Survey of Recent Developments.* Washington: International Union for the Scientific Study of Population, 1954.
A somewhat outdated but still useful survey of policies affecting population development in 75 countries after World War II.

APPENDIX A. *Correlation of Chapters in This Book with Those in Standard Textbooks on Population.*

Chapter in This Book	*Landis & Hatt*	*Phelps & Henderson*	*Petersen*	*Smith*	*Thomlinson*	*Thompson & Lewis*
1	1, 3, appendix	20	1, 3, appendix	1, 2	1, 3	1, 9
2	2	1, 2, 3, 5, 6, 19	1, 2, 11, 17	21	2, 4, 14, 17, 21, 22	2, 3, 14, 15, 16, 17
3	6, 7, 10	10, 16	10, 13, 19	15, 16, 17	5, 6, 7	12, 13
4	—	—	18	11, 12, 13, 14	9	10, 11
5	8, 9, 11, 12, 13, 14	5, 11	9, 18	11, 12, 13, 14	8, 10	9, 10, 11
6	22, 23	1, 7, 9, 19	5, 6, 20	5, 18	12	18
7	20, 21	4, 5, 8, 10	7, 20	4, 19, 20	11	18
8	4, 5, 15	5, 6, 7, 8, 9, 10, 17, 18, 19	4, 6	5, 6, 7, 8	19, 20	4. 5, 6, 8, 17
9	16, 17, 18, 19	4, 5, 6, 7, 8	8	3, 4, 5	13, 14, 22	6, 18
10	4, 9	4, 5, 8, 10, 11, 12	9, 13, 15	—	10	—
11	14	—	—	—	20	—
12	—	13	—	10	20	—
13	—	14	—	—	—	—
14	—	4, 8, 10, 15, 19	12, 13, 14, 16	9	15, 20	7
15	25, 26	21	15, 16	—	16, 17, 18	19, 20, 21

Sources:

Landis, Paul H., and Paul K. Hatt. *Population Problems; a Cultural Interpretation*, 2nd ed. New York: American Book Company, 1954.

Phelps, Harold A., and David Henderson. *Population in Its Human Aspects*. New York: Appleton-Century-Crofts, 1958.

Petersen, William. *Population*. New York: The Macmillan Company, 1961.

Smith, T. Lynn. *Fundamentals of Population Study*. Chicago: J. B. Lippincott Company, 1960.

Thomlinson, Ralph. *Population Dynamics*. New York: Random House, 1965.

Thompson, Warren S., and David T. Lewis. *Population Problems*, 5th ed. New York: McGraw-Hill Book Company, 1965.

NAME INDEX

SUBJECT INDEX

ABCDEFGHIJ- H -76543210/6987